Financial Aid for Research and Creative Activities Abroad 2002-2004

ESSENTIAL FINANCIAL AID DIRECTORIES PUBLISHED BY REFERENCE SERVICE PRESS

College Student's Guide to Merit and Other No-Need Funding, 2002-2004
More than 1,200 funding opportunities for currently-enrolled or returning college students are described in this highly-praised directory. 450 pages. ISBN 1-58841-041-2. $32, plus $5 shipping.

Directory of Financial Aids for Women, 2001-2003
Nearly 1,600 funding programs set aside for women are described in this biennial directory, which *School Library Journal* calls "the cream of the crop." 552 pages. ISBN 1-58841-000-5. $45, plus $5 shipping.

Financial Aid for African Americans, 2001-2003
More than 1,400 scholarships, fellowships, loans, grants, and internships open to African Americans are described in this award-winning directory. 508 pages. ISBN 1-58841-001-3. $37.50, plus $5 shipping.

Financial Aid for Asian Americans, 2001-2003
This is the source to use if you are looking for financial aid for Asian Americans; nearly 1,000 funding opportunities are described. 336 pages. ISBN 1-58841-002-1. $35, plus $5 shipping.

Financial Aid for Hispanic Americans, 2001-2003
Nearly 1,300 funding programs open to Americans of Mexican, Puerto Rican, Central American, or other Latin American heritage are described here. 472 pages. ISBN 1-58841-003-X. $37.50, plus $5 shipping.

Financial Aid for Native Americans, 2001-2003
Detailed information is provided on 1,500 funding opportunities open to American Indians, Native Alaskans, and Native Pacific Islanders. 546 pages. ISBN 1-58841-004-8. $37.50, plus $5 shipping.

Financial Aid for Research and Creative Activities Abroad, 2002-2004
Described here are 1,200 funding programs (scholarships, fellowships, grants, etc.) available to support research, professional, or creative activities abroad. 432 pages. ISBN 1-58841-062-5. $45, plus $5 shipping.

Financial Aid for Study and Training Abroad, 2001-2003
This directory, which *Children's Bookwatch* calls "invaluable," describes more than 1,100 financial aid opportunities available to support study abroad. 398 pages. ISBN 1-58841-031-5. $39.50, plus $5 shipping.

Financial Aid for the Disabled and Their Families, 2002-2004
Named one of the "Best Reference Books of the Year" by *Library Journal*, this directory describes in detail more than 1,100 funding opportunities. 484 pages. ISBN 1-58841-042-0. $40, plus $5 shipping.

Financial Aid for Veterans, Military Personnel, and Their Dependents, 2002-2004
According to *Reference Book Review*, this directory (with its 1,150 entries) is "the most comprehensive guide available on the subject." 392 pages. ISBN 1-58841-043-9. $40, plus $5 shipping.

High School Senior's Guide to Merit and Other No-Need Funding, 2002-2004
Here's your guide to 1,100 funding programs that *never* look at income level when making awards to college-bound high school seniors. 400 pages. ISBN 1-58841-044-7. $29.95, plus $5 shipping.

Money for Graduate Students in the Biological & Health Sciences, 2001-2003
Described here are nearly 1,100 funding opportunities set aside just for students interested in working on a graduate degree in the biological or health sciences. 332 pages. ISBN 1-58841-038-2. $42.50, plus $5 shipping.

Money for Graduate Students in the Humanities, 2001-2003
Use this directory to identify nearly 1,000 funding opportunities available to support graduate study, training, research, and creative activities in the humanities. 320 pages. ISBN 1-58841-008-0. $40, plus $5 shipping.

Money for Graduate Students in the Physical & Earth Sciences, 2001-2003
More than 800 funding opportunities for graduate students in the physical and earth sciences are described in detail in this directory. 262 pages. ISBN 1-58841-039-0. $35, plus $5 shipping.

Money for Graduate Students in the Social & Behavioral Sciences, 2001-2003
If you are looking for funding to support graduate work in the social/behavioral sciences, this is the directory to use (1,100 funding programs are described). 332 pages. ISBN 1-58841-010-2. $42.50, plus $5 shipping.

Financial Aid for Research and Creative Activities Abroad 2002-2004

Gail Ann Schlachter
R. David Weber

A List of Scholarships, Fellowships, Loans, Grants, Awards, and Internships for Research and Creative Activities Abroad; An Annotated Bibliography of Financial Aid Resources; and a Set of Four Indexes: Organization, Geographic, Subject, and Deadline.

Reference Service Press
El Dorado Hills, California
2002

© 2002 Gail Ann Schlachter

All rights reserved. No part of this publication may be reproduced, stored in a retrieval system, or transmitted, in any form or by any means, electronic, mechanical, photocopying, recording, or otherwise, except for the inclusion of brief quotations in a review, without the prior permission in writing from the publisher. Violation of copyright laws is a federal crime, punishable by fine and/or imprisonment (*Title 17, United States Code, Section 104*).

ISBN 1-58841-062-5
ISSN 1072-530X

10 9 8 7 6 5 4 3 2 1

Reference Service Press (RSP) began in 1977 with a single financial aid publication *(Directory of Financial Aids for Women)* and now specializes in the development of financial aid resources in multiple formats, including books, large print books, disks, CD-ROMs, print-on-demand reports, eBooks, and online sources. Long recognized as a leader in the field, RSP has been called, by the *Simba Report on Directory Publishing,* "a true success in the world of independent directory publishers." Kaplan Educational Centers hailed RSP as "the leading authority on scholarships."

Reference Service Press
El Dorado Hills Business Park
5000 Windplay Drive, Suite 4
El Dorado Hills, CA 95762-9600
    (916) 939-9620
    Fax: (916) 939-9626
    E-mail: findaid@aol.com
Visit our web site: www.rspfunding.com

Manufactured in the United States of America

Contents

Introduction ix

    Background ix
    Scope of the Directory ix
    Extent of Updating in This Edition x
    Arrangement of the Directory x
    Sample Entry xi
    How to Use the Directory xiii
    Plans to Update the Directory xiv
    Other Related Publications xiv
    Acknowledgements xiv
    Currency Conversion Table xv
    About the Authors xvi

Financial Aid Programs for Research and Creative Activities Abroad 1

    Any Foreign Country 3
    Asia 75
    Canada/Arctic Region 129
    Europe/Scandinavia/British Isles 155
    Latin America/Caribbean 309
    Middle East/Africa 339
    Oceania 377

Annotated Bibliography of Financial Aid Resources 393

    General Directories 395
    Subject-Specific Directories 396
    Directories Aimed at Special Groups 398
    Directories Listing Awards 399
    Internship Directories 399
    Nothing over $5.50 400

Indexes 403

    Sponsoring Organization Index 403
    Geographic Index 411
    Subject Index 417
    Calendar Index 431

Introduction

BACKGROUND

The dramatic developments taking place in Europe, Latin America, the Middle East and the former Soviet Union have filled our newspapers, demanded our attention, and underscored again that America operates in a global village. More than ever, it is important for Americans to learn—from first-hand investigations—about the traditions and cultures of other countries. But, while the benefits of individual international involvement are substantial, so are the costs. That's why it is vital that Americans who are interested in research, creative, professional, and other related activities abroad learn about the numerous financial aid opportunities available.

Each year, hundreds of public and private agencies and organizations in the United States and other countries set aside billions of dollars to underwrite the considerable expenses associated with going abroad. But how can fundseekers find out about these opportunities? General financial aid directories offer little assistance. Only a small portion of the available programs are ever described there, and these are difficult to spot. For example, readers would have to scan through thousands of entries in the comprehensive *Directory of Research Grants* to uncover the several hundred programs described there that support research conducted by Americans abroad; programs for this purpose are neither highlighted in the text nor specifically identified in the table of contents or the indexes. Specialized directories, too, have been of limited utility. They tend to be either outdated (e.g., *Fellowships in International Affairs: A Guide to Opportunities in the United States and Abroad* was last published by Lynne Rienner in 1994) or restricted in scope (e.g., *Fulbright and Related Grants for Graduate Study and Research Abroad* identifies only programs offered through the Fulbright program). For current and comprehensive coverage of the full range of financial aid opportunities available to support research, professional, creative, or related activities outside the United States, there is only one source to use: *Financial Aid for Research and Creative Activities Abroad*.

SCOPE OF THE DIRECTORY

The 2002-2004 edition of *Financial Aid for Research and Creative Activities Abroad* provides current and comprehensive information, in a single volume, on the nearly 1,200 funding opportunities open to Americans interested in research, creative, professional, or related activities abroad. The directory will help Americans (and the librarians and counselors who serve them) tap into the billions of dollars available for research, lectureships, exchange programs, work assignments, conference attendance, and creative projects abroad. The listings cover every major subject area, are tenable in practically every country and region of the world (from the Aegean Islands to Zimbabwe), are sponsored by more than 500 different private and public agencies and organizations, and are open to all segments of the population—from high school students through postdoctorates and professionals.

In addition to its comprehensive coverage, *Financial Aid for Research and Creative Activities Abroad* offers several other unique features. Covered here are hundreds of funding opportunities not listed in any other source. Unlike other funding directories, which generally follow a straight alphabetical arrangement, this one groups entries by area of the world where the funds may be used (any foreign country, Asia, Canada/Arctic region, Europe, Latin America/Caribbean, Middle East/Africa, and Oceania), thus facilitating a user's search for appropriate programs. The same convenience is offered in all appropriate indexes—sponsoring organization, subject, and deadline date—where entries are subdivided by geographic location. Another convenient feature is the currency conversion table, which makes it possible for readers to approximate the value of awards offered in foreign currencies with which they are unfamiliar. Finally, everything about the directory has been designed to make the search for funding as easy as possible. You can identify programs not only by geographic location, but also by title, sponsoring organization, specific subject, and even deadline date (so fundseekers working within specific time constraints can locate programs by filing date). Plus, you'll find all the information you need to decide if a program is a match for you: purpose, eligibility requirements, financial data, duration, special features, limitations, number awarded, and application date. You even get fax numbers, toll-free numbers, e-mail addresses, and web site locations (when available), along with complete contact information, to make your requests for applications proceed smoothly.

Previous editions of this landmark work, along with its companion volume, *Financial Aid for Study and Training Abroad,* have been highly praised. *Choice* "highly recommended" both titles, because of the "valuable information" they provide "on a variety of financial aid programs available for going abroad." The Council on International Educational Exchange's *Update* called the titles "user-friendly," because they excel on "the access and readability test." *Small Press* pointed out that the works provide an "excellent representation of leads in an area that will certainly grow in the future." Perhaps *Reference and User Services Quarterly* summed up the critical assessment best: "Money seekers used to slogging through endless listings of programs for which they do not qualify will find the books' arrangement...and succinct statement of eligibility a relief, and any library with a clientele seeking financial aid for study or research will find them invaluable."

THE EXTENT OF UPDATING IN THE 2002-2004 EDITION

The 2002-2004 edition of *Financial Aid for Research and Creative Activities Abroad* completely revises and updates the earlier biennial edition. Programs that have ceased operations have been dropped. Profiles of continuing programs have been rewritten to reflect activities in 2002 through 2004; nearly 90 percent of these programs reported substantive changes in their locations, requirements (particularly application deadline), or benefits since the last edition of the directory. In addition, hundreds of new entries have been added to the program section of the directory. The resulting listing identifies more than 1,200 scholarships, fellowships, loans, grants, internships, and general financial aid directories of interest to individuals wishing to pursue research or creative activities abroad.

ARRANGEMENT OF THE DIRECTORY

The directory is divided into three separate sections: a descriptive list of financial aid programs established to support research and creative activities abroad; an annotated bibliography of directories listing general financial aid programs; and a set of four indexes.

Financial Aid Programs Designed to Support Research and Creative Activities Abroad. The first section of the directory describes nearly 1,200 financial aid programs available to support research, conference attendance, teaching assignments, lectureships, exchange programs, writing, artistic endeavors, or other creative projects abroad. The programs are sponsored by more than 500 government agencies, professional organizations, foundations, educational associations, corporations, research centers, libraries, and other public and private agencies. They are open to applicants at any level (high school through professional and postdoctoral) and cover all areas of the sciences, social sciences, and humanities.

Entries in this section are grouped by geographic region, to facilitate the reader's search for funding that will support research or creative activities abroad.

Any Foreign Country: Described here are 222 funding programs that may be used in any country in the world by American students (high school through doctoral), professionals, and postdoctorates. While these programs have no tenability limitations, they may be restricted in other ways (e.g., by subject, type of recipient, type of activity).

Asia: Described here are 151 funding programs open to American students (high school through doctoral), professionals, and postdoctorates that support research or creative activities in Asia, including Bangladesh, Cambodia, India, Japan, Mongolia, Myanmar, Nepal, People's Republic of China, Singapore, South Korea, Thailand, and many other countries in that region of the world.

INTRODUCTION

SAMPLE ENTRY

(1) **[74]**

(2) **GCA AWARDS IN TROPICAL BOTANY**

(3) Garden Club of America
Attn: Scholarship Committee
14 East 60th Street
New York, NY 10022-1006
(212) 753-8287   Fax: (212) 753-0134
E-mail: scholarship@gcamerica.org
Web site: www.gcamerica.org

(4) **Purpose** To enable American Ph.D. candidates in botany to undertake independent field work in the tropics.

(5) **Eligibility** Eligible to apply are graduate students who anticipate completing the requirements for a Ph.D. in botany within 2 years and are enrolled in a U.S. university. They must be proposing to undertake field work in tropical countries in either tropical plant systematics or tropical forest ecology. Appropriate foreign language competency may be required.

(6) **Financial data** The stipend is $5,500.

(7) **Duration** These are 1-time awards.

(8) **Special features** This program was established in 1983 in cooperation with the World Wildlife Fund, 1250 24th Street, N.W., Washington, DC 20037-1175; (202) 778-9608; Fax: (202) 861-8324, E-mail: susan.ward@wwfus.org.

(9) **Limitations** Requests for applications must be accompanied by a self-addressed stamped envelope.

(10) **Number awarded** 2 each year.

(11) **Deadline** December of each year.

DEFINITION

(1) **Entry number:** Consecutive number assigned to the references and used to index the entry.

(2) **Program title:** Title of scholarship, fellowship, loan, grant, award, or internship.

(3) **Sponsoring organization:** Name, address, telephone number, toll-free number, fax number, e-mail address, and web site (when information was supplied) for organization sponsoring the program.

(4) **Purpose:** Objectives of program and/or sponsoring institution.

(5) **Eligibility:** Qualifications required of applicants.

(6) **Financial data:** Financial details of the program, including fixed sum, average amount, or range of funds offered, expenses for which funds may and may not be applied, and cash-related benefits supplied (e.g., room and board). For the approximate value of awards stated in foreign currency, see the currency conversion table on page xv.

(7) **Duration:** Period for which support is provided; renewal prospects.

(8) **Special features:** Any unusual (generally nonmonetary) benefits associated with the program.

(9) **Limitations:** Any unusual restrictions or requirements associated with the program.

(10) **Number awarded:** Total number of recipients each year or other specified period.

(11) **Deadline:** The month by which applications must be submitted.

Canada/Arctic Region: Described here are 75 funding programs open to American students (high school through doctoral), professionals, and postdoctorates that support research or creative activities in Canada, Greenland, and the Arctic region.

Europe/Scandinavia/British Isles: Described here are 493 funding programs open to American students (high school through doctoral), professionals, and postdoctorates that support research or creative activities in eastern and western Europe, Scandinavia, and the British Isles.

Latin America/Caribbean: Described here are 79 funding programs open to American students (high school through doctoral), professionals, and postdoctorates that support research or creative activities in Central America, South America, and the Caribbean.

Middle East/Africa: Described here are 107 funding programs open to American students (high school through doctoral), professionals, and postdoctorates that support research or creative activities in the Middle East and Africa.

Oceania: Described here are 48 funding programs open to American students (high school through doctoral), professionals, and postdoctorates that support research or creative activities in Antarctica, Australia, New Zealand, and the various Pacific Island nations.

Within each of these chapters, entries appear alphabetically by program title. Since a few of the programs fund research or creative activities in more than one region, these are listed in all relevant chapters. For example, the Middle East, North Africa, South Asia Regional Research Program, administered by the Council for International Exchange of Scholars, focuses on more than one geographic region, so the program is described in both the Asia *and* Middle East/Africa chapters.

Each program entry has been designed to provide a concise profile that includes information (when available) on program title, sponsoring organization address and telephone number (including toll-free and fax numbers) e-mail addresses, web sites, purpose, eligibility, financial data, duration, special features, limitations, number of awards, and application deadline. (Refer to the sample on page xi). To assist readers who are unfamiliar with the currency of a particular country, a currency conversion table is provided on page xv. Use this table to approximate the value of awards described in foreign currency.

The information reported for each of the programs in this section was supplied in response to requests for information distributed through April, 2002. While the listing is intended to cover as comprehensively as possible programs supporting activities abroad, some sponsoring organizations did not respond to the research inquiry and, consequently, are not included in this edition of the directory.

The focus of this directory is on financial aid programs that are portable, intended for Americans (or nationals of a number of countries, including the United States), and designed specifically to support research or creative activities abroad. Excluded from this listing are:

Awards intended to support activities within the United States that only incidentally might be used abroad. See the Annotated Bibliography in this directory for publications that list and describe these domestic programs.

Awards for which American citizens or permanent residents would be ineligible (e.g., programs open to applicants from developing countries; programs open to nationals of the European Union).

Awards established to support work *on* topics related to international affairs or international locations rather than research or other activities *in* those geographic areas.

Awards under $1,000. Only the biggest and best funding opportunities are covered here. If a program awards less than $1,000, it is not included.

Annotated Bibliography of Financial Aid Resources. While the directory provides the only comprehensive and current listing of financial aid programs designed to support research and creative activities abroad, there are numerous other publications that describe the thousands of resources available for use in the United States (and may, incidentally, support activities abroad). The second section of the directory provides an annotated list of dozens of key directories published at least once during the past four years that describe these domestic programs. The directories are listed by coverage: general directories, subject-specific directories, directories aimed at specific groups, directories listing awards, internship directories, and bargain resources (nothing over $5.50). Each entry contains 1) an annotation specifying scope, arrangement, publication history, and special features of the listing; 2) price; 3) order information; and 4) publisher's web site. If a more comprehensive listing of available directories is required, the reader is directed to the evaluative guide published biennially by Reference Service Press: *How to Find Out about Financial Aid and Funding: A Guide to Print, Electronic, and Online Resources Listing Scholarships, Fellowships, Loans, Grants, Awards, and Internships.*

Indexes. The directory's four indexes facilitate the search for appropriate financial aid opportunities. Sponsoring Organization, Geographic, Subject, and Calendar Indexes follow a word-by-word alphabetical arrangement and refer the user to the appropriate entry by number.

Sponsoring Organization Index. This index provides an alphabetical listing of the more than 500 organizations sponsoring the financial aid programs described in the directory. To help users select only those programs that match their geographic interests, each entry number is preceded by an alphabetical code that identifies regional tenability: Asia, Canada/Arctic Region, Europe, Latin America/Caribbean, Middle East/Africa, Oceania, or any foreign country.

Geographic Index. This index enables the reader to identify funding available to support research or creative activities in specific geographic locations. Nearly 150 countries and regions are listed here.

Subject Index. This index allows the reader to identify by subject the financial aid programs available to support research and creative activities abroad. To facilitate access, the more than 300 subject terms in the index are subdivided by geographic focus. In addition, extensive "see" and "see also" references aid in the search for appropriate funding programs.

Calendar Index. To assist fundseekers who often must work within specific time constraints, the Calendar Index identifies financial aid programs by filing date. The Calendar is arranged by regional tenability (e.g., Asia, Oceania, any foreign country) and divided by month during which the deadline falls. The information included in the Calendar Index is current as of 2002. Filing dates can and quite often do vary over time; consequently, this index should be used only as a guide for deadlines beyond 2004. It is important to note that not all sponsoring organizations supplied information on application deadline, so some of the programs described in the directory are not listed here.

HOW TO USE THE DIRECTORY

To Locate a Particular Financial Aid Program. If you know the name of a particular financial aid program *and* where its funding can be used (e.g., Middle East/Africa, Europe, Latin America/Caribbean), then go directly to the appropriate chapter in the first section of the directory, where you will find the program profiles arranged alphabetically by title.

To Locate Programs Sponsored by a Particular Organization. The Sponsoring Organization Index makes it easy to determine groups that provide financial assistance for activities abroad or to identify specific financial aid programs offered by a particular organization. Each entry number in the index is coded to identify regional tenability, thus enabling users to identify appropriate entries.

To Locate Programs Supporting Activities in a Specific Geographic Location. The first section of the directory groups funding opportunities by region (e.g., Asia, Europe, Oceania), so you can browse through the entries listed in the area of the world that interests you (as well as the entries described in the Any Foreign Country chapter). But, if you want to target programs that support research or creative activities in a specific country, turn first to the Geographic Index. You'll find nearly 150 geographic locations listed there. Remember: in addition to checking the specific countries of interest to you in the Geographic Index, be sure to check the listings under "Foreign countries," since programs identified there can be used in any location outside the United States.

To Locate Financial Aid Programs in a Particular Subject Area. Turn to the Subject Index first if you are interested in identifying financial aid programs that support research and other related activities in a particular subject area. To ease your search, the geographic focus (e.g., Asia, Latin America/Caribbean, any foreign country) is clearly indicated in the more than 300 subject listings. Extensive cross-references are provided. Since a large number of programs are not restricted by subject, be sure to check the references listed under the "General programs" heading in the Subject Index, in addition to the specific terms that directly relate to your interest areas.

To Locate Financial Aid Programs by Deadline Date. If you are working with specific time constraints and want to weed out the financial aid programs whose filing dates you won't be able to meet, turn first to the Calendar Index and check the program references listed under the appropriate geographic area and specific month. Keep in mind that not all sponsoring organizations supplied deadline information, so not all programs are listed in this section. To identify every relevant financial aid program, regardless of filing dates, read through all the entries in each of the chapters (Asia, Middle East/Africa, Any Foreign Country, etc.) that apply.

To Locate Financial Aid Programs That Support Activities in the United States. Only programs focusing on research, creative, or related activities abroad are listed in this publication. However, there are thousands of other programs that are available to support such activities in the United States (and may, incidentally, support activities abroad). To identify those domestic programs, use the publications described in the second section of the directory, talk to your local librarian, check with your financial aid office on campus, or use a computerized grant search service.

PLANS TO UPDATE THE DIRECTORY

This volume, covering 2002-2004, is the fifth edition of *Financial Aid for Research and Creative Activities Abroad*. The next edition will cover 2004-2006 and will be released in early 2004.

OTHER RELATED PUBLICATIONS

In addition to *Financial Aid for Research and Creative Activities Abroad*, Reference Service Press publishes several other titles dealing with fundseeking, including the companion volume *Financial Aid for Study and Training Abroad* and the award-winning *Directory of Financial Aids for Women* and *Financial Aid for the Disabled and Their Families*. Since each of these titles focuses on a separate population group, there is little duplication in the listings. In fact, fewer than ten percent of the programs described in *Financial Aid for Research and Creative Activities Abroad* can be found in the other Reference Service Press directories. For more information on the financial aid titles published by Reference Service Press, you can 1) write to Reference Service Press' Marketing Department at 5000 Windplay Drive, Suite 4, El Dorado Hills, CA 95762-9600; 2) call us at (916) 939-9620; 3) fax us at (916) 939-9626; 4) send us an e-mail message at findaid@aol.com; or 5) visit our web site: http://www.rspfunding.com.

ACKNOWLEDGEMENTS

A debt of gratitude is owed all the organizations that contributed information to this edition of *Financial Aid for Research and Creative Activities Abroad*. Their generous cooperation has helped to make the publication a current and comprehensive survey of funding programs.

CURRENCY CONVERSION TABLE

This table identifies the currency used in key countries covered in *Financial Aid for Research and Creative Activities Abroad.* For each of these countries, the name of the currency, the abbreviation used in the directory, and the U.S. dollar equivalent are provided. The values presented here are current as of April 30, 2002 and were taken from data printed that day in the *Wall Street Journal.* Remember, foreign exchange rates can and do fluctuate daily. Use this table only as a guide to the approximate value of the support offered in currency with which you are unfamiliar.

Country	Name of Currency	Abbreviation (if used)	$1.00 (U.S.) =
Argentina	Peso		2.91
Australia	Dollar	$A	1.86
Austria	*See* European Union		
Bahrain	Dinar		0.38
Belgium	*See* European Union		
Brazil	Real		2.36
Britain	Pound		0.69
Canada	Dollar	$C	1.56
Chile	Peso		647.65
Colombia	Peso		2273.75
Czech Republic	Koruna		33.88
Denmark	Krone		8.23
Ecuador	U.S. Dollar		1.00
European Union	Euro		1.11
Finland	*See* European Union		
France	*See* European Union		
Germany	*See* European Union		
Greece	*See* European Union		
Hong Kong	Dollar		7.80
Hungary	Forint		269.01
India	Rupee		48.96
Indonesia	Rupiah		9325.00
Ireland	*See* European Union		
Israel	Shekel		4.89
Italy	*See* European Union		
Japan	Yen		128.02
Jordan	Dinar		0.71
Kuwait	Dinar		0.31
Lebanon	Pound		1514.00
Malaysia	Ringgit		3.80
Malta	Lira		0.45
Mexico	Peso		9.37
Netherlands	*See* European Union		
New Zealand	Dollar	$NZ	2.23
Norway	Krone	NOK	8.39
Pakistan	Rupee		59.98
People's Republic of China	Renminbi		8.28
Peru	New Sol		3.44
Philippines	Peso		50.68
Poland	Zloty		3.98
Portugal	*See* European Union		
Russia	Ruble		31.22
Saudi Arabia	Riyal		3.75
Singapore	Dollar		1.81
Slovak Republic	Koruna		46.67
South Africa	Rand		10.56
South Korea	Won		1288.60
Spain	*See* European Union		
Sweden	Krona	SEK	10.21
Switzerland	Franc	SF	1.62
Taiwan	Dollar	$NT	34.68
Thailand	Baht		43.23
Turkey	Lira		1340500.00
United Arab Republic	Dirham		3.67
Uruguay	Peso		16.48
Venezuela	Bolivar		843.50

ABOUT THE AUTHORS

Dr. Gail Schlachter has worked for nearly three decades as a library administrator, a library educator, and an administrator of library-related publishing companies. Among the reference books to her credit are the biennially-issued *Directory of Financial Aids for Women* and two award-winning bibliographic guides: *Minorities and Women: A Guide to Reference Literature in the Social Sciences* (which was chosen as an "Outstanding Reference Book of the Year" by *Choice*) and *Reference Sources in Library and Information Services* (which won the first Knowledge Industry Publications "Award for Library Literature"). She is the former editor of *Reference and User Services Quarterly,* was the reference book review editor of *RQ* for 10 years, and is a past president of the American Library Association's Reference and User Services Association. In recognition of her outstanding contributions to reference service, Dr. Schlachter has been awarded both the prestigious Isadore Gilbert Mudge Citation and the Louis Shores/Oryx Press Award.

Dr. R. David Weber teaches at East Los Angeles, where he has been named "Teacher of the Year" every year since 1991. He has written a number of critically-acclaimed reference works, including *Dissertations in Urban History* and the three-volume *Energy Information Guide.* With Gail Schlachter, he is the author of Reference Service Press' *Financial Aid for the Disabled and Their Families,* which was selected by *Library Journal* as one of the "best reference books of the year," and the companion volume to *Financial Aid for Research and Creative Activities Abroad:* the 2001-2003 edition of *Financial Aid for Study and Training Abroad.*

Financial Aid Programs for Research and Creative Activities Abroad

- *Any Foreign Country*
- *Asia*
- *Canada/Arctic Region*
- *Europe/Scandinavia/British Isles*
- *Latin America/Caribbean*
- *Middle East/Africa*
- *Oceania*

Any Foreign Country

Described here are 222 scholarships, fellowships, loans, grants, and/or internships designed to support high school students, undergraduates, graduate students, professionals, and postdoctorates interested in conducting research or participating in creative activities in any country outside the United States. After checking here, be sure to look through 1) the other chapters that represent your specific geographic focus (Asia, Canada/Arctic Region, Europe/Scandinavia/British Isles, Latin America/Caribbean, Middle East/Africa, or Oceania) and 2) the Geographic Index, to identify programs that match your specific geographic focus.

[1]
AAG GENERAL RESEARCH GRANTS

Association of American Geographers
Attn: Executive Assistant
1710 16th Street, N.W.
Washington, DC 20009-3198
(202) 234-1450   Fax: (202) 234-2744
E-mail: ekhater@aag.org
Web site: www.aag.org

Purpose To provide funding to members of the Association of American Geographers who are interested in conducting geographical research.

Eligibility Scholars who have been members of the association for at least 2 years may apply for funding if they are interested in conducting geographical research or field work in any country (preference is given to projects that deal with important gaps in geography). Awards are not presented for master's or doctoral dissertation research.

Financial data Up to $1,000. Funds are for direct research expenses only (not for overhead).

Duration Up to 1 year.

Special features Research may be conducted anywhere in the world.

Deadline December of each year.

[2]
AIDS INTERNATIONAL TRAINING AND RESEARCH PROGRAM (AITRP)

Fogarty International Center
Attn: Division of International Training and Research
31 Center Drive, Room B2C39
Bethesda, MD 20892-2220
(301) 496-2516   Fax: (301) 402-2056
E-mail: kb16r@cu.nih.gov
Web site: www.nih.gov/fic/programs/aitrp/aitrp.html

Purpose To support collaborative research and training for U.S. and foreign scientists who wish to expand their capabilities in the epidemiology, diagnosis, prevention and treatment of HIV infection, AIDS, and tuberculosis.

Eligibility This program supports the following activities: 1) training in biomedical and behavioral HIV/AIDS-related prevention and related tuberculosis research disciplines (as well as data management and analysis in support of that research), with classes conducted at a U.S. institution but field research in the trainee's home country, that leads to an M.S. or Ph.D. degree for individuals with previous field research experience; 2) similar training that leads to an M.S. degree for individuals without previous field research experience; 3) postdoctoral research experiences for foreign health scientists in the U.S. and for U.S. health scientists overseas; 4) training conducted in the U.S. in laboratory procedures and research techniques in support of specific HIV/AIDS prevention research, for individuals with M.S. and Ph.D. degrees; 5) in-country, practical and applied training targeted to specific needs in support of HIV/AIDS prevention research for professionals, technicians, and allied health professionals; 6) advanced research training for current and/or former trainees, including reentry grants to enable them to continue this advanced training in their home country and to participate in in-country prevention research projects; 7) support to enable U.S. faculty to be involved in advanced research training activities conducted in-country; and 8) support to enable new and minority U.S. health science students (including medical students and residents) to receive overseas health research experiences in collaboration with foreign trainees upon return to their home countries. Applications to participate in this program are submitted directly to the program director at the participating U.S. university.

Financial data The maximum stipend for foreign trainees while undergoing training in the United States, for foreign trainees while conducting in-country dissertation research or in-country advanced research training, and for foreign and U.S. postdoctoral researchers is $45,000 per year. Salary for U.S. faculty involved in advanced research training activities conducted in-country and for the program director is capped at 25 percent of their current annual salary (not including fringe benefits). Support is also provided for tuition, travel, and training-related expenses. Grant totals may be up to $500,000 per year for competing renewals (or $625,000 if a tuberculosis supplement is included) or up to $300,000 per year for new starts.

Duration Each type of activity has different duration provisions: 1) training for individuals with previous field experience ranges from 2 to 4 years; 2) training for individuals without previous field experience extends up to 2 years; 3) postdoctoral research experiences, including U.S. health scientists overseas, are generally of 2 years' duration; 4) training in laboratory procedures and research techniques ranges from 3 to 6 months; 5) in-country training extends up to 3 weeks; 6) advanced research training ranges from 1 to 2 years; 7) support for U.S. faculty to be involved in advanced research training activities may vary in length; 8) support for new and minority U.S. health science students to receive overseas health research experiences ranges from 3 to 12 months.

Special features For a list of universities currently participating in this program, along with the name and address of the program director and the countries with which that university is cooperating, contact the Fogarty International Center.

[3]
ALASKA STATE COUNCIL ON THE ARTS CAREER OPPORTUNITY GRANTS

Alaska State Council on the Arts
411 West Fourth Avenue, Suite 1E
Anchorage, AK 99501-2343
(907) 269-6610   (888) 278-7424
Fax: (907) 269-6601   TTY: (800) 770-8973
E-mail: info@aksca.org
Web site: www.edu.state.ak.us/asca

Purpose To enable Alaskan artists to travel to events that will enhance their artistic skills or professional standing.

Eligibility Visual artists, writers, composers, choreographers, media artists, traditional Native artists, performing artists, and other artists who are residents of Alaska involved in the creation of new works may apply. Full-time students are not eligible. Grants may be used to travel to in-state, regional, national, or international conferences, workshops, and seminars, or to travel to undertake projects directly related to the grantees' artistic careers.

Financial data Grants are awarded for up to two-thirds of travel costs by coach-class airfare or state mileage rates, whichever is less, up to a maximum of $1,000. Tuition, workshop fees, meals, lodging, and in-town surface transportation are not covered.

Limitations Full-time students are not eligible, and grants will not be awarded to an artist in consecutive years.

Number awarded Varies each year. Grants are awarded on a first-come, first-served basis.

Deadline Applications may be submitted at any time, but they must be received by the first of the month prior to the requested departure date. Work must be completed within 6 months of official notification; the project must begin and end within the same state fiscal year (July 1 to June 30).

[4]
ALICIA PATTERSON FOUNDATION FELLOWSHIP PROGRAM

Alicia Patterson Foundation
1730 Pennsylvania Avenue, N.W., Suite 850
Washington, DC 20006
(202) 393-5995   Fax: (301) 951-8512
E-mail: exec.director@aliciapatterson.org
Web site: www.aliciapatterson.org

Purpose To provide support to journalists, photographers, and editors for a year of travel and inquiry into significant issues.

Eligibility This program is open to U.S. citizens who are full-time print journalists and non-U.S. citizens who work full time for U.S. print publications, either in the United States or abroad. Applicants must define a major project to which they wish to devote a year researching, traveling (in the United States or abroad), and writing articles. As part of the selection process, they must submit a 3-page description of how they propose to use the fellowship and why, a brief summary of the 4 articles they will be required to write, samples of their work, 4 letters of recommendation, a professional autobiography, and a detailed budget of projected fellowship costs (travel, books, short-term housing, etc.) and personal maintenance (an estimate of living expenses for the fellow and family).

Financial data The fellowship provides a $35,000 stipend.

Duration 1 year.

Special features The articles written by fellows on their chosen topics are published in the *APF Reporter,* a quarterly magazine published by the foundation.

Limitations Fellows must take a leave of absence from their employers for the duration of the program.

Number awarded Varies each year; recently, 9 of these fellowships were awarded.

Deadline September of each year.

[5]
AMERICAN ASSOCIATION OF UNIVERSITY WOMEN DISSERTATION FELLOWSHIPS

American Association of University Women
Attn: AAUW Educational Foundation
2201 North Dodge Street
P.O. Box 4030
Iowa City, IA 52243-4030
(319) 337-1716   Fax: (319) 337-1204
E-mail: aauw@act.org
Web site: www.aauw.org

Purpose To provide financial assistance to women in the final year of writing their dissertation.

Eligibility Applicants must be citizens of the United States or hold permanent resident status and must intend to pursue their professional careers in the United States. They should have successfully completed all required course work for their doctorate, passed all preliminary examinations, and received written acceptance of their prospectus. Applicants may pursue research in any field except engineering (the association offers Engineering Dissertation Fellowships as a separate program).

Financial data The stipend is $20,000.

Duration 1 year, beginning in July. Recipients may reapply for a second award.

Special features There are no restrictions on the applicant's age or research location.

Limitations It is expected that the fellowship will be used for the final year of doctoral work and that the degree will be received at the end of the fellowship year. The fellowship is not intended to fund extended field research. The recipient should be prepared to devote full time to the dissertation during the fellowship year.

Number awarded 51 each year.

Deadline November of each year.

[6]
AMERICAN ASSOCIATION OF UNIVERSITY WOMEN POSTDOCTORAL RESEARCH LEAVE FELLOWSHIPS

American Association of University Women
Attn: AAUW Educational Foundation
2201 North Dodge Street
P.O. Box 4030
Iowa City, IA 52243-4030
(319) 337-1716   Fax: (319) 337-1204
E-mail: aauw@act.org
Web site: www.aauw.org

Purpose To enable American women scholars who have achieved distinction or promise of distinction in their fields of scholarly work to engage in additional research.

Eligibility Women of outstanding scholarly achievement who are working on postdoctoral research in any field and are U.S. citizens or permanent residents are eligible to apply; 1 award is set aside specifically for an underrepresented minority woman. Applicants must have earned the doctorate by the time the application is submitted. Selection is based on scholarly excellence, teaching experience, and active commitment to helping women and girls through service in community, profession, or field of research.

Financial data The stipend is $30,000.
Duration 1 year, beginning in July.
Special features There are no restrictions on the applicant's age or research location.
Limitations Postdoctoral fellowships normally will not be awarded to women who have received the doctorate within the past 3 years or for revision of the dissertation. Recipients are expected to spend the fellowship year in full-time research. The award may be not be used to cover the costs of research equipment, research assistants, publication, travel to professional meetings or seminars, tuition for additional course work, or repayment of loans or other personal obligations. Applications should be made 1 year in advance of the academic year for which funding is sought.
Number awarded 20 each year in 3 fields: the arts and humanities, the social sciences, and the natural sciences. In each field, 1 is allocated to an underrepresented minority woman.
Deadline November of each year.

[7]
AMERICAN CANCER SOCIETY INTERNATIONAL FELLOWSHIPS FOR BEGINNING INVESTIGATORS

International Union against Cancer
3 rue du Conseil-Général
CH-1205 Geneva
Switzerland
41 22 809 1840   Fax: 41 22 809 1810
E-mail: fellows@uicc.org
Web site: www.uicc.org

Purpose To enable cancer investigators who are in the early stages of their careers to carry out basic or clinical research projects in any country.
Eligibility Eligible candidates should hold assistant professorships or similar positions at their home institutes and have at least 2 years of postdoctoral experience after obtaining their M.D. or Ph.D. degrees or equivalents. They must be proposing to conduct research abroad in the areas of epidemiology, prevention, causation, detection, diagnosis, treatment, or psycho-oncology. Applicants must have adequate language fluency so they can communicate effectively at their host institution. Applications that are geared to the development of specific cancer control measures in developing and central and east European countries are particularly encouraged. Awards are conditional on the return of the fellow to the home institute at the end of the fellowship and on the availability of appropriate facilities and resources to meet the newly acquired skills.
Financial data Awards are approximately $35,000, covering stipend and travel for the fellow only.
Duration 12 months; no extensions are permitted.
Special features These fellowships are funded by the American Cancer Society and administered by the International Union against Cancer (Union Internationale Contre le Cancer—UICC).
Number awarded 8 to 10 each year.
Deadline September of each year.

[8]
AMERICAN CANCER SOCIETY POSTDOCTORAL FELLOWSHIPS

American Cancer Society
Attn: Extramural Grants Department
1599 Clifton Road, N.E.
Atlanta, GA 30329-4251
(404) 329-7558   (800) ACS-2345
Fax: (404) 321-4669   E-mail: grants@cancer.org
Web site: www.cancer.org

Purpose To train young investigators who are interested in an independent career in cancer research.
Eligibility Applicants must have completed all the requirements for a doctoral degree prior to the activation date of the fellowship but may not have completed 5 or more years of postdoctoral fellowship work. The training may be conducted in not-for-profit institutions within the United States or, if the training objectives can best be attained there, in other countries. A plan of training (didactic, teaching, research, etc.) must be formulated and agreed upon by the mentor and the applicant and described in detail in the application. Applicants must be U.S. citizens or permanent residents.
Financial data The stipend is $35,000 for the first year, $37,000 for the second year, and $40,000 for the third year. In addition, an annual institutional allowance of $2,000 is awarded to the laboratory where the fellow is working for tuition, supplies, equipment, travel to scientific meetings, or other expenses for which the institution may wish to reimburse the fellow. Funds are available for the cost of travel from the applicant's present institution to the training institution and, if training takes place overseas, for return travel to the United States; funds are not provided for travel by dependents.
Duration Up to 3 years, depending on previous postdoctoral fellowship experience.
Special features Each year, several fellows are selected to receive special 3-year fellowships with an increased stipend of $138,000. Also included in this program are the Ronald Levy Postdoctoral Research Fellowships of $50,000 per year, established in 2001 with funding from IDEC Pharmaceuticals Corporation and Genentech, Inc.
Number awarded Varies each year.
Deadline March or October of each year.

[9]
AMERICAN HEART ASSOCIATION ESTABLISHED INVESTIGATOR GRANT

American Heart Association
Attn: Division of Research Administration
7272 Greenville Avenue
Dallas, TX 75231-4596
(214) 706-1457   Fax: (214) 706-1341
E-mail: ncrp@heart.org
Web site: www.americanheart.org

Purpose To provide research funding to clinician-scientists who have recently acquired independent status as cardiovascular investigators.
Eligibility Applicants must be U.S. citizens or permanent residents who hold an M.D., Ph.D., D.O., or equivalent degree at the time of application. They must be full-time members of a department or unit within an academic or research institution,

usually with the rank of assistant professor; customarily, they should be 4 to 9 years past their first faculty appointment. The proposed research project must have received no previous financial support from other granting agencies. For research to be conducted outside the United States, the applicant must be a U.S. citizen. At least 6 percent of all funds for this program is set aside for awards to underrepresented minority scientists.

Financial data The annual award of $75,000 includes salary, fringe benefits, 10 percent indirect costs, and project costs (up to $35,000 for salary and at least $40,000 for project support).

Duration 4 years; nonrenewable.

Deadline June of each year.

Number awarded 50 each year.

[10]
AMERICAN HEART ASSOCIATION GRANT-IN-AID

American Heart Association
Attn: Division of Research Administration
7272 Greenville Avenue
Dallas, TX 75231-4596
(214) 706-1457   Fax: (214) 706-1341
E-mail: ncrp@heart.org
Web site: www.americanheart.org

Purpose To encourage development of well-defined research proposals by independent beginning investigators and by established investigators pursuing new areas of research broadly related to cardiovascular function and disease, stroke, basic science, clinical, or public health problems.

Eligibility Proposals may be submitted by junior independent investigators or established investigators pursuing new areas of research. Applicants must have earned a doctoral degree (M.D., Ph.D., D.O., or equivalent), be on the staff of nonprofit institutions, and be U.S. citizens, permanent residents, or foreign nationals holding H1, H1B, O1, TC, TN, or J1 immigrant status (only U.S. citizens may apply to conduct research outside the United States). The proposed research must be clearly distinct from ongoing research activities. At least 6 percent of all funds for this program is set aside for awards to underrepresented minority scientists.

Financial data The annual award of $71,500 includes salary, fringe benefits, 10 percent indirect costs, and project costs. Up to $32,500 per year may be requested for principal investigator salary and fringe benefits.

Duration Up to 3 years.

Number awarded 100 each year.

Deadline June of each year.

[11]
AMERICAN HEART ASSOCIATION SCIENTIST DEVELOPMENT GRANT

American Heart Association
Attn: Division of Research Administration
7272 Greenville Avenue
Dallas, TX 75231-4596
(214) 706-1457   Fax: (214) 706-1341
E-mail: ncrp@heart.org
Web site: www.americanheart.org

Purpose To assist promising beginning scientists to develop independent research programs by supporting a program that bridges the gap between completion of research training and readiness to apply for funding as an independent investigator.

Eligibility Applicants must be citizens or permanent residents of the United States who hold an M.D., Ph.D., D.O., or equivalent degree and who are in the final year of a postdoctoral research fellowship or in the initial 4 years of their first faculty appointment. They cannot hold or have held any other national award. Applications for research to be conducted outside the United States are limited to U.S. citizens. At least 6 percent of all funds for this program is set aside for awards to underrepresented minority scientists.

Financial data The award includes $65,000 annually for salary, fringe benefits, 10 percent indirect costs, and project costs (including up to $30,000 for salary and at least $35,000 for project support).

Duration 4 years; nonrenewable.

Number awarded 70 each year.

Deadline June of each year.

[12]
AMERICAN HEART ASSOCIATION–BUGHER FOUNDATION AWARD FOR THE INVESTIGATION OF STROKE

American Heart Association
Attn: Division of Research Administration
7272 Greenville Avenue
Dallas, TX 75231-4596
(214) 706-1457   Fax: (214) 706-1341
E-mail: ncrp@heart.org
Web site: www.americanheart.org

Purpose To provide funding to investigators interested in conducting research on the development of better stroke preventive measures and better stroke interventions.

Eligibility This program is open to citizens or permanent residents of the United States who hold an M.D., Ph.D., D.O., or equivalent degree and who are full-time faculty/staff members at any rank pursuing independent research. Applications for research to be conducted outside the United States are limited to U.S. citizens. The proposed research must relate to an aspect of brain vascular function, including but not limited to regulation of cerebral blood vessels, endothelial mechanisms in cerebral vessels, molecular biology of cerebral vessels, male/female differences in cerebral blood vessel function, racial differences in the function of cerebral blood vessels, mechanisms of ischemic injury involving cerebral blood vessels, blood brain barrier function, interaction of stroke risk factors with cerebral blood vessels, and molecular genetics of disorders of cerebral blood vessels.

Financial data Grants up to $100,000 per year, including up to 10 percent for indirect costs, are available. Up to $35,000 per year may be requested for principal investigator salary and fringe benefits.
Duration 4 years.
Number awarded Varies each year.
Deadline June of each year.

[13] AMERICAN PHILOSOPHICAL SOCIETY SABBATICAL FELLOWSHIPS

American Philosophical Society
Attn: Committee on Research
104 South Fifth Street
Philadelphia, PA 19106-3387
(215) 440-3429   Fax: (215) 440-3436
E-mail: eroach@amphilsoc.org
Web site: www.amphilsoc.org

Purpose To provide funding to mid-career faculty who wish to conduct research in the humanities or social sciences during a sabbatical year.
Eligibility This program is open to mid-career faculty at universities and 4-year colleges in the United States who have been granted a sabbatical/research year but for whom financial support from the parent institution is available only for the first half of the year. Applicants must not have had a financially supported leave during the past 3 years. They should have received their doctorate at least 5 but no more than 25 years prior to applying. They may be proposing to conduct research in the humanities or social sciences at any location, although the American Philosophical Society encourages candidates to use the resources of its library.
Financial data The stipend is $40,000.
Duration 1 academic year.
Number awarded Varies each year.
Deadline October of each year.

[14] AMY LOWELL POETRY TRAVELLING SCHOLARSHIP

Amy Lowell Poetry Travelling Scholarship Trust
c/o Choate, Hall & Stewart
Exchange Place
53 State Street
Boston, MA 02109-2891
(617) 248-5000   Fax: (617) 248-4000

Purpose To provide funding to American poets who are interested in spending a year abroad.
Eligibility Applicants must be U.S. citizens, published poets, and interested in spending a year outside of North America. They must submit samples of their poetry, consisting of either 1) a printed volume plus up to 20 typed pages of their most recent work or 2) 40 typed pages.
Financial data Up to $32,000 per year.
Duration 1 year; may be renewed for 1 additional year if the recipient submits 3 poems to the selection committee that it considers of sufficient merit to warrant renewal.

Limitations The year abroad must be structured to offer opportunities to advance the recipient's poetry.
Number awarded 1 each year.
Deadline October of each year.

[15] AMY LUTZ RECHEL AWARD

Association for Women in Science
1200 New York Avenue, N.W., Suite 650
Washington, DC 20005
(202) 326-8940   (800) 886-AWIS
Fax: (202) 326-8960   E-mail: awis@awis.org
Web site: www.awis.org

Purpose To provide financial assistance to women interested in working on a doctoral degree in plant biology.
Eligibility This program is open to women graduate students in the field of plant biology. Winners traditionally have been at the dissertation level of their graduate work. Foreign students must be enrolled in a U.S. institution of higher education, but U.S. citizens may study or conduct research in the United States or abroad.
Financial data The stipend is $1,000. Funds may be used for tuition, books, housing, research, equipment, etc.
Duration 1 year.
Number awarded 1 each year.
Deadline January of each year.

[16] ANDREW W. MELLON FELLOWSHIPS AT THE NATIONAL GALLERY OF ART

National Gallery of Art
Attn: Center for Advanced Study in the Visual Arts
Sixth Street and Constitution Avenue, N.W.
Washington, DC 20565
(202) 842-6482   Fax: (202) 842-6733
TDD: (202) 842-6176   E-mail: advstudy@nga.gov
Web site: www.nga.gov/resources/casvapre.htm

Purpose To provide financial assistance to doctoral candidates interested in conducting research here and abroad on the history, theory, and criticism of art, architecture, and urbanism.
Eligibility Applicants must have completed their residence requirements, course work for the Ph.D., and general or preliminary examinations before the date of application. In addition, they must know 2 foreign languages related to the topic of the dissertation and be U.S. citizens or enrolled in an American university. They must be interested in conducting research (here and abroad) on the history, theory, and criticism of art, architecture, and urbanism (in fields other than Western art). Application for this fellowship must be made through the chair of the student's graduate department of art history or other appropriate department; the chair should act as a sponsor for the applicant. Departments must limit their nominations to 1 candidate. Finalists are invited to Washington during February for interviews.
Financial data The stipend is $16,000 per year.
Duration 2 years: 1 year abroad conducting research and 1 year in residence at the National Gallery of Art's Center for

Advanced Study in the Visual Arts in Washington, D.C. to complete the dissertation. The fellowship begins in September and is not renewable.
Number awarded 1 each year.
Deadline November of each year.

[17]
ANNE S. CHATHAM FELLOWSHIP IN MEDICINAL BOTANY

Missouri Botanical Garden
Attn: Dr. James S. Miller
P.O. Box 299
St. Louis, MO 63166-0299
(314) 577-9503   Fax: (314) 577-9465
E-mail: miller@mobot.org
Web site: www.mobot.org

Purpose To provide financial assistance to Ph.D. candidates and Ph.D.s interested in conducting research in medicinal botany in the United States or abroad.
Eligibility This program is open to students currently enrolled in Ph.D. programs at recognized universities and postdoctorates who received their Ph.D. within the last 5 years. Applicants must be interested in conducting research on the medicinal use of plants. They must submit a description of their proposed research, budget, current curriculum vitae, and documentation that appropriate permits, research clearances, and permissions from governmental agencies have been obtained for foreign research.
Financial data The stipend is $4,000. Funds may be used to cover direct costs associated with travel, field studies, or laboratory research but cannot be used for indirect costs or institutional overhead.
Duration 1 year.
Special features The Missouri Botanical Garden administers this program, established in 1997 as part of the scholarship program of the Garden Club of America. Information is also available from its Scholarship Committee, 14 East 60th Street, New York, NY 10022-1006, (212) 753-8287, Fax: (212) 753-0134, E-mail: scholarship@gcamerica.org.
Number awarded 1 each year.
Deadline January of each year.

[18]
ANNE U. WHITE FUND

Association of American Geographers
Attn: Executive Assistant
1710 16th Street, N.W.
Washington, DC 20009-3198
(202) 234-1450   Fax: (202) 234-2744
E-mail: ekhater@aag.org
Web site: www.aag.org

Purpose To provide financial assistance for field research in geography to couples who are members of the Association of American Geographers.
Eligibility Eligible to apply are scholars who have been members of the association for at least 2 years and desire to conduct field research anywhere in the world jointly with their spouses. Awards are granted to proposals with the greatest prospect of obtaining subsequent support from private foundations or federal agencies and that address questions of major import to geography.
Financial data The amount of the awards depends on the nature of the proposal and the availability of funds.
Limitations Within 12 months of receiving a grant, recipients must document expenses charged to the grant and summarize the results of the field research.
Deadline December of each year.

[19]
APLASTIC ANEMIA FOUNDATION OF AMERICA NEW RESEARCHER AWARDS

Aplastic Anemia Foundation of America, Inc.
P.O. Box 613
Annapolis, MD 21404-0613
(410) 867-0242   (800) 747-2820
Fax: (410) 867-0240   E-mail: aafacenter@aol.com
Web site: www.aplastic.org

Purpose To provide funding to new investigators interested in conducting research (in the United States or abroad) related to aplastic anemia, myelodysplastic syndromes, and other bone marrow failure diseases.
Eligibility Applicants must have an M.D., Ph.D., or equivalent degree and must conduct their proposed research (in aplastic anemia, myelodysplastic syndromes, and other bone marrow failure diseases) under a sponsor who holds a formal appointment at a sponsoring institution. There are no nationality restrictions, and the work may be carried out in the United States or abroad. However, the research must not be carried out at a private sector for-profit laboratory.
Financial data The grant is $30,000 per year. Payment is made quarterly. An institutional overhead of $3,000 is the maximum allowable.
Duration 2 years.
Limitations Recipients are required to submit a final written report at the close of the award period. Recipients must cite support from the foundation in all published work relating to research conducted during the award.
Number awarded Several each year.
Deadline November of each year.

[20]
ARTHRITIS FOUNDATION POSTDOCTORAL FELLOWSHIPS

Arthritis Foundation
Attn: Research Department
1330 West Peachtree Street
Atlanta, GA 30309
(404) 965-7636   Fax: (404) 872-9559
E-mail: adeleon@arthritis.org
Web site: www.arthritis.org

Purpose To encourage qualified physicians and scientists to embark on careers in areas broadly related to arthritis and rheumatic diseases by providing financial support for the early years of their training.
Eligibility Applicants must have an M.D., Ph.D., or equivalent doctoral degree; M.D.s are not eligible after 6 years of labora-

tory training (or 7 years of a clinical training program that includes 1 year in the laboratory) and Ph.D.s are not eligible after 4 years of postdoctoral laboratory experience. Individuals at or above the assistant professor level, or those who have tenured positions, are ineligible to apply. Research must be pursued in a field broadly related to the rheumatic diseases under the supervision of a qualified supervisor, who must present the research proposal jointly with the applicant. Foreign citizens may be funded only if their training is conducted at a U.S. institution, but U.S. citizens may be funded to go abroad. Preference is given to applicants who propose work on projects with demonstrable relationship to arthritis or who, with their mentor, have established a real working relationship with a clinical academic rheumatology or musculoskeletal unit. Selection is based on the project's relevance to arthritis; the applicant's background, training, evidence of productivity, and potential for a career in arthritis research; the scientific merit of the proposed research project; and the environment in which the program will be conducted.

Financial data The stipend is $35,000 per year. The sponsoring institution receives an award of $500 to be used for health insurance, supplies, travel to scientific meetings, publication costs, etc. Indirect costs are not allowed. If the fellow wishes to conduct training abroad, no provisions are made for travel except in that institutional allowance.

Duration 2 years; may be renewed for 1 additional year.

Special features Research may be conducted abroad if the foundation considers it in the best interest of the candidate's career development. Investigators are expected to devote 90 percent of their professional time to laboratory research, clinical investigation, field studies, or training.

Deadline August of each year.

[21]
ARTHUR PATCH MCKINLAY SCHOLARSHIPS

American Classical League
Attn: Scholarships
Miami University
Oxford, OH 45056
(513) 529-7741 Fax: (513) 529-7742
E-mail: info@aclclassics.org
Web site: www.aclclassics.org

Purpose To provide financial support for a program of summer study or research (in any country) to members of the American Classical League (ACL).

Eligibility Applicants must have been members of the league for at least 3 years (plus the current academic year) and must wish to participate in a summer program (campus-centered study, tour or study abroad, or research in any country). Alternate proposals may be submitted as long as they involve structured study or research. The program is intended for teachers who have taught classics at the elementary or secondary school level during the current academic year; college and university faculty are not eligible.

Financial data The stipend ranges from $250 to $1,500.

Duration Summer months.

Special features Awards are also available to teachers who wish to attend the ACL institute and workshops for the first time; those awards cover institute expenses (registration, room, and board) and help defray the cost of transportation.

Number awarded Several each year.

Deadline January of each year.

[22]
ASSOCIATION FOR WOMEN IN SCIENCE GRADUATE SCHOLARSHIPS

Association for Women in Science
1200 New York Avenue, N.W., Suite 650
Washington, DC 20005
(202) 326-8940 (800) 886-AWIS
Fax: (202) 326-8960 E-mail: awis@awis.org
Web site: www.awis.org

Purpose To provide financial aid to predoctoral women students interested in pursuing careers in science.

Eligibility Women graduate students in any life, physical, behavioral, or social science or engineering program leading to a Ph.D. may apply. Winners traditionally have been at the dissertation stage of their graduate work. Foreign students must be enrolled in a U.S. institution of higher education, but U.S. citizens may study in the United States or abroad.

Financial data The stipends are $1,000. Citations of merit range from $250 to $500. Funds may be used for any aspect of education, including tuition, books, housing, research, equipment, etc.

Duration 1 year.

Number awarded 1 to 6 each year.

Deadline January of each year.

[23]
ASTRAZENECA TRANSLATIONAL CANCER RESEARCH FELLOWSHIPS

International Union against Cancer
3 rue du Conseil-Général
CH-1205 Geneva
Switzerland
41 22 809 1840 Fax: 41 22 809 1810
E-mail: fellows@uicc.org
Web site: www.uicc.org

Purpose To fund cancer investigators from any country who are interested in conducting cancer research in bridging areas that connect cellular and molecular biologists to patients in the clinic or populations in the field.

Eligibility This program is open to 1) basic scientists interested in conducting research involving clinical or population science, and 2) clinicians and epidemiologists interested in basic science research. Applicants may be from any country, proposing to conduct research at a cancer center in another country. They must submit, in collaboration with the proposed host institution, a scientific research plan that demonstrates how they are focused on a bridging area between basic and clinical research and how they approach the problem with a novel strategy. The proposal should elaborate on how the partnership between the host and the candidate will take full advantage of the unique facilities, resources, and materials available in their respective countries and how basic and clinical research in both will benefit. Selection is based on the innovativeness of the approach to translation; the project's scientific excellence; the professional background, experience,

and potential of the candidate; and the commitment of an enduring collaboration between the home and host institutes.
Financial data The stipend is $55,000.
Duration 12 months.
Special features This program, funded by AstraZeneca (UK), began in 2001.
Number awarded 1 each year.
Deadline November of each year.

[24]
BARBARA CRASE BURSARY
Australian Federation of University Women-South Australia
   Inc. Trust Fund
Attn: Fellowships Trustee
GPO Box 634
Adelaide, SA 5001
Australia
61 8 8401 7124
E-mail: gferrara@scomhbr3.telstra.com.au
Web site: adminwww.flinders.edu.au/WomensInfo/AFUW.htm

Purpose To provide funding to students pursuing a graduate research degree at a university in South Australia who are interested in conducting research anywhere in the world.
Eligibility This program is open to men and women of any nationality studying at a university in South Australia. They should have completed at least 1 year of study on a master's or Ph.D. degree. Students who are in full-time paid employment or on fully-paid study leave are not eligible to apply. Selection is based primarily on academic merit, but financial need, the purpose for which the bursary will be used, and extracurricular activities are also considered.
Financial data The stipend is $A2,500, to be used for equipment, field trips, research expenses, thesis publication costs, and dependent care expenses.
Duration Up to 1 year.
Special features This fellowship may be held concurrently with other awards. Research may be conducted outside Australia as long as it is part of a program for a degree at the university in South Australia where the applicant is enrolled.
Number awarded At least 1 each year.
Deadline February of each year.

[25]
BENJAMIN H. KEAN TRAVELING FELLOWSHIP IN TROPICAL MEDICINE
American Society of Tropical Medicine and Hygiene
60 Revere Drive, Suite 500
Northbrook, IL 60062
(847) 480-9592   Fax: (847) 480-9282
E-mail: astmh@astmh.org
Web site: www.astmh.org

Purpose To provide funding for travel to the tropics to medical students interested in obtaining research or clinical experiences in tropical medicine.
Eligibility This program is open to full-time currently-enrolled students, residents, and fellows at North American medical schools who are interested in pursuing clinical or research experiences in the tropics. Selection is based on academic record, recommendations, quality of the research proposal, and interest in pursuing a career in tropical medicine or international health. Preference is given to applicants sponsored by a member of the American Society of Tropical Medicine and Hygiene.
Financial data The fellowship pays for round-trip airfare and up to $700 toward living expenses.
Duration Up to 1 year.
Special features This program was established in 1997. It is jointly sponsored by the American Committee on Clinical Tropical Medicine and Traveler's Health and the American Society of Tropical Medicine and Hygiene.
Number awarded 4 each year.
Deadline April of each year.

[26]
BHP STUDENT RESEARCH GRANTS
Society of Economic Geologists Foundation
Attn: SEG Grants Program
7811 Schaffer Parkway
Littleton, CO 80127
(720) 981-7882   Fax: (720) 981-7874
E-mail: seg@segweb.org
Web site: www.segweb.org

Purpose To provide funding to graduate students from any country who wish to conduct geological research anywhere in the world.
Eligibility This program is open to graduate students from anywhere in the world who are conducting master's or doctoral thesis research (including field or laboratory, instrumental or non-instrumental, qualitative or quantitative studies). Preference is given to applicants who demonstrate how the proposed research may resolve significant issues concerning mineral deposits and plan to conduct research outside the United States. Special consideration is given to applications from students with limited access to other sources of research support.
Financial data Stipends range from $500 to $1,000. Funds may be used for travel expenses, living costs in the field, expendable supplies, field expenses, and other expenses directly necessary for the research; they are not intended for purchase of ordinary field equipment, living costs of assistants or families of the grantees, attendance at professional meetings, preparation of theses, or reimbursement for work already accomplished.
Special features Funding for these grants is provided by BHP Minerals.
Number awarded Varies each year; recently, 14 of these grants were awarded.
Deadline January of each year.

[27]
BIBLIOGRAPHICAL SOCIETY GRANTS

Bibliographical Society
c/o The Honorary Secretary, David Pearson
The Wellcome Library
183 Euston Road
London NW1 2BE
England
Web site: www.users.zetnet.co.uk/djshaw/bibsoc/grants.htm

Purpose To provide funding to scholars from any country interested in conducting bibliographical research.

Eligibility This program is open to scholars interested in conducting research in any country on such topics as book history, textual transmission, publishing, printing, book ownership, and book collecting. Applicants may be of any age or nationality and need not be members of the Bibliographical Society. Major awards provide support for both immediate research needs (e.g., microfilms or traveling expenses) and long-term support (e.g., prolonged visits to libraries and archives). Minor awards provide support for specific purposes, such as the costs of travel or of microfilming.

Financial data Major grants up to 2,000 pounds are available. Minor grants range from 50 to 200 pounds.

Duration Both short-term and long-term support is provided.

Special features Further information is also available from Dr. Maureen Bell, Birmingham University, School of English, Edgbaston, Birmingham B15 2TT, England, E-mail: M.Bell@bham.ac.uk. The Antiquarian Booksellers' Association supports 1 of the major grants.

Number awarded Approximately 10 major and a limited number of minor grants are awarded each year.

Deadline November of each year.

[28]
BOGLE/PRATT INTERNATIONAL LIBRARY TRAVEL AWARD

American Library Association
Attn: International Relations Office
50 East Huron Street
Chicago, IL 60611-2795
(312) 280-3201   (800) 545-2433, ext. 3201
Fax: (312) 944-3897   TDD: (312) 944-7298
E-mail: abrinkme@ala.org
Web site: www.ala.org

Purpose To enable members of the American Library Association (ALA) to travel to an international conference for the first time.

Eligibility Applicants must be members of the ALA who are interested in career-related international activities and can show that their institution is committed to international relations. The conference must be an international conference, but it may be held in the United States or abroad. Selection is based on a 200-word essay on the applicant's interest in the conference, its expected value to the library profession and to the applicant's career, and the need for the travel funds.

Financial data The travel grant is $1,000.

Special features Previously, these grants were made from the Sarah C. N. Bogle Memorial Fund, created in recognition of Sarah Comly Norris Bogle, a former assistant secretary of the ALA who died in 1932. Interest from the fund was used to send promising foreign students to library conferences, but in 1982 the ALA executive board directed that the interest from the fund be used for its current purpose. Now, this program is sponsored by the fund and the Pratt Institute School of Information and Library Science.

Number awarded 1 each year, but only if a suitable candidate applies.

Deadline December of each year.

[29]
BP CONSERVATION PROGRAM

BirdLife International
Attn: Programme Manager, BP Conservation Programme
Wellbrook Court
Girton Road
Cambridge CB3 0NA
England
44 1223 277318   Fax: 44 1223 277200
E-mail: bp-conservation-programme@birdlife.org.uk
Web site: www.bp.com/conservation

Purpose To provide funding to students interested in conducting international conservation field investigations.

Eligibility This program is open to teams from all countries. The majority of the project team should consist of undergraduate and graduate students in full- or part-time status. Experienced teams, with many expeditions behind them, are not eligible. In addition, the program does not support the salaries of professional academics or researchers. Applicants must propose a conservation project of international importance. It should preferably be derived from the priorities identified by international conservation organizations. The project must involve local people and must have clearance from the host government. International project teams are preferred, but teams of entirely 1 nationality planning to work within their own country are still eligible. Applications must clearly show 1) the conservation benefits to species and/or habitats; 2) the involvement of local counterparts; 3) host country acceptance either from the government, nongovernment organizations, or universities; and 4) that the majority of project team members are undergraduate or graduate students in full- or part-time education. Selection is based on conservation priority (20 points), appropriateness of project (15 points), local cooperation (10 points), team (5 points), methods (10 points), budget (10 points), and feasibility (10 points). Winning proposals are ranked as gold, silver, or bronze.

Financial data The gold award is 7,000 pounds, silver awards are 5,000 pounds, and bronze awards are 3,000 pounds. Follow-up awards for the best projects of the previous year range from 10,000 to 20,000 pounds.

Duration 1 year; follow-up awards provide funding for 1 additional year.

Special features BirdLife International established this program in 1985 and Fauna & Flora International (then the Fauna & Flora Preservation Society) joined in 1988. Since 1990, additional funding and support has been provided by BP Amoco plc.

Number awarded Up to 18 each year. Total funding available each year is 125,000 pounds.

Deadline October of each year.

[30]
CANADIAN FEDERATION OF UNIVERSITY WOMEN A. VIBERT DOUGLAS INTERNATIONAL FELLOWSHIP

International Federation of University Women
8 rue de l'Ancien-Port
CH-1201 Geneva
Switzerland
41 22 731 2380   Fax: 41 22 738 0440
E-mail: info@ifuw.org
Web site: www.ifuw.org

Purpose To encourage advanced scholarship by enabling university women to undertake a program of study or original research in another country.

Eligibility An applicant must be a member of 1 of the 67 national federations or associations affiliated with the International Federation of University Women (IFUW) or, if she resides in a country that does not yet have an IFUW affiliate, an independent member of the IFUW. She must have completed at least 1 year of graduate study and should propose to continue her study or research in a country other than where she received her education or in which she usually resides.

Financial data The stipend is $C8,000.

Duration Stipends are intended to cover at least 8 months of work and should be used within 9 months from the date of the award.

Special features This program is sponsored by the Canadian Federation of University Women. Americans should submit their applications to the American Association of University Women (AAUW), 1111 16th Street, N.W., Washington, DC 20036-4873, (202) 785-7700, (800) 821-4364.

Limitations Fellowships are not awarded for the first year of a doctoral program.

Number awarded 1 each even-numbered year.

Deadline Applications, whether submitted through a national affiliate (such as the AAUW) or by an independent member, must reach IFUW headquarters before the end of October in odd-numbered years. National affiliates set earlier deadlines; for the AAUW, this is the end of September.

[31]
CANCER RESEARCH FUND POSTDOCTORAL RESEARCH FELLOWSHIPS FOR BASIC AND PHYSICIAN SCIENTISTS

Cancer Research Fund of the Damon Runyon-Walter Winchell Foundation
Attn: Assistant to the Director of Fellowship Program
675 Third Avenue, 25th Floor
New York, NY 10017
(212) 697-9550   Fax: (212) 697-4950
E-mail: fellowship@cancerresearchfund.org
Web site: www.cancerresearchfund.org

Purpose To provide funding to promising young investigators interested in pursuing careers in cancer research.

Eligibility Applicants must have received an M.D., Ph.D., D.D.S., D.V.M., or equivalent degree prior to the application deadline. Candidates applying to work in foreign-based or U.S. government laboratories may be awarded a fellowship if they are considered to be especially meritorious or if the program represents an unusual opportunity for postdoctoral research. The proposed investigation must be conducted at a university, hospital, or research institution under the guidance of a sponsor actively engaged in the planning, execution, and supervision of the proposed research, which must be relevant to the study of cancer and the search for cancer causes, mechanisms, therapies, and prevention. Foreign candidates may only apply to do their research in the United States. Selection is based on the quality of the candidate's research proposal (importance of the problem, originality of approach, appropriateness of techniques, and clarity of presentation); the qualifications, experience, and productivity of both the candidate and the candidate's sponsor; the quality of the training provided by the research environment in which the proposed research is to be conducted, and its potential for broadening and strengthening the candidate's ability to conduct substantive research.

Financial data Fellows who have completed their degrees within 1 year prior to application receive level 1 funding of $35,000 for the first year, $40,500 for the second year, and $44,000 for the third year. The stipend for level 2 awardees, those who have completed their residencies or clinical fellowship training within 3 years before application, is $55,000 for the first year, $56,000 for the second year, and $57,000 for the third year. In addition, an annual expense allowance of $2,000 is awarded to the laboratory where the fellow is working for educational and scientific expenses (but not for institutional overhead).

Duration Up to 3 years.

Limitations No more than 2 fellows will be funded to work with the same sponsor at any given time. Postdoctoral activities in the same institution where the fellow received the doctoral degree is discouraged.

Number awarded Varies each year; recently 12 of these fellowships were awarded.

Deadline March, August, or December of each year.

[32]
CAREER ADVANCEMENT AWARDS FOR MINORITY SCIENTISTS AND ENGINEERS

National Science Foundation
Directorate for Education and Human Resources
Attn: Senior Staff Associate for Cross Directorate Programs
4201 Wilson Boulevard, Room 805
Arlington, VA 22230
(703) 292-8600   TDD: (703) 292-5090
Web site: www.nsf.gov

Purpose To enable minority researchers whose science/engineering careers are still evolving (or who are changing research direction, or who have had a significant research career interruption) to progress in their research activities.

Eligibility The applicant should have had some prior experience as a principal investigator or research project leader, hold a faculty or research-related position at a U.S. institution, be an underrepresented minority (Native American, African American, Hispanic, Native Alaskan, or Native Pacific Islander), and be a U.S. citizen or national. Normally, candidates should be

at least 5 years beyond any postdoctoral appointment and applying for funding to: 1) help acquire expertise in new areas to enhance research capability; 2) support the development of innovative research methods in collaboration with investigators at the applicant's home institution or at another appropriate institution (including 1 in a foreign country); 3) assist the conduct of exploratory or pilot work to determine the feasibility of a new line of inquiry; or 4) make it possible for those who have had a significant career interruption to acquire updating for reentry into their respective fields.
Financial data Awards of up to $50,000 are available; an additional amount of up to $10,000 may be requested for equipment. Funds are provided for salary, professional travel, consultant fees, research assistants, and other research-related expenses.
Duration 1 year; these are 1-time, nonrenewable awards.
Special features This program is offered through the various disciplinary divisions of the National Science Foundation (NSF); for the telephone numbers of the participating divisions, contact the address above.
Limitations These awards are not substitutes for regular research grants, and they are not intended to provide start-up funds to establish a laboratory.
Deadline Each of the participating NSF disciplinary divisions sets its own deadline.

[33]
CATHY CANDLER BURSARY
Australian Federation of University Women-South Australia Inc. Trust Fund
Attn: Fellowships Trustee
GPO Box 634
Adelaide, SA 5001
Australia
61 8 8401 7124
E-mail: gferrara@scomhbr3.telstra.com.au
Web site: adminwww.flinders.edu.au/WomensInfo/AFUW.htm

Purpose To assist students pursuing a graduate research degree at a university in South Australia who are interested in conducting research in any country.
Eligibility This program is open to men and women of any nationality studying at a university in South Australia. They should have completed at least 1 year of work on a master's or Ph.D. degree. Students who are in full-time paid employment or on fully-paid study leave are not eligible to apply. Selection is based primarily on academic merit, but financial need, the purpose for which the bursary will be used, and extracurricular activities are also considered.
Financial data The stipend is $A2,500, to be used for equipment, field trips, research expenses, thesis publication costs, and dependent care expenses.
Duration Up to 1 year.
Special features This fellowship may be held concurrently with other awards. Research may be conducted outside Australia as long as it is part of a program for a degree at the university in South Australia where the applicant is enrolled.
Number awarded At least 1 each year.
Deadline February of each year.

[34]
CDE GRANTS TO INDIVIDUALS
International Mathematical Union
Commission on Development and Exchanges
c/o Herb Clemens, Secretary/Treasurer
University of Utah
Department of Mathematics
155 South 1400 East, JWB 233
Salt Lake City, UT 84112-0090
(801) 581-5275   Fax: (801) 581-4148
E-mail: clemens@math.utah.edu
Web site: www.math.utah.edu/CDE

Purpose To provide funding to mathematicians who are interested in traveling to countries other than their own.
Eligibility Eligible to apply are mathematicians from any country who are interested in conducting research in another country. Candidates must hold a Ph.D. degree and be working in the core of mathematics. Applicants from developed countries must go to a university or research center in a developing country to qualify for support. Grants are not provided for training visits or travel to attend conferences.
Financial data Travel expenses are partially covered.
Duration At least 1 month.
Special features These grants are provided by the Commission on Development and Exchanges (CDE) of the International Mathematical Union.
Number awarded Varies each year.
Deadline Applications may be submitted at any time, but they must be received at least 6 months prior to the proposed travel.

[35]
CENTER FOR FIELD RESEARCH GRANTS
Center for Field Research
3 Clock Tower Place, Suite 100
P.O. Box 75
Maynard, MA 01754-0075
(978) 461-0081   (800) 776-0188
Fax: (978) 461-2332   E-mail: cfr@earthwatch.org
Web site: www.earthwatch.org

Purpose To support field research by scientists and humanists working to investigate and/or preserve our physical, biological, and cultural heritage.
Eligibility Research proposals in the sciences and humanities are accepted from advanced postdoctoral principal investigators of any nationality, as long as the research design integrates non-specialist volunteers into the field research agenda. Applicants intending to conduct research in foreign countries must include host-country nationals in their research staffs.
Financial data Grants are awarded on a per capita basis, determined by multiplying the per capita grant by the number of volunteers on the project. Per capita grants range from $250 to $1,200 and average $900; since typical projects employ 5 to 10 volunteers each on 3 to 6 sequential teams, the total project grants range from $7,000 to $130,000 and average $25,000. Grants cover all expenses for food, accommodations, and in-field transportation for the research team (principal investigator, research staff, and volunteers); principal investigator travel to and from the field; leased or rented field equipment; insurance; support of staff and visiting scientists; and

support for associates from the host country. Funds are not normally provided for capital equipment, principal investigator salaries, university overhead or indirect costs, or preparation of results for publication. Volunteers donate time, services, and skills to the research endeavor in the field and pay their own travel expenses to and from the research site.

Duration 1 to 3 years.

Special features Funding for these grants is provided by Earthwatch, established in 1971 to support the efforts of scholars to preserve the world's endangered habitats and species, to explore the vast heritage of its peoples, and to promote world health and international cooperation. The Center for Field Research reviews all applications for grants and refers those it recommends to Earthwatch for funding. Earthwatch also recruits and screens volunteers; in the past, 20 percent of these have been students, 20 percent educators, and 60 percent nonacademic professionals.

Limitations Dissertation and undergraduate researchers are not currently eligible; however, inclusion of graduate students as staff is encouraged.

Number awarded Approximately 155 each year.

Deadline Applications may be submitted at any time but no later than 1 year before the project start date.

[36]
CHARLES A. RYSKAMP FELLOWSHIPS

American Council of Learned Societies
Attn: Office of Fellowships and Grants
228 East 45th Street
New York, NY 10017-3398
(212) 697-1505   Fax: (212) 949-8058
E-mail: grants@acls.org
Web site: www.acls.org/rysguide.htm

Purpose To provide financial assistance to advanced assistant professors in all disciplines of the humanities and the humanities-related social sciences.

Eligibility This program is open to tenure-track faculty members at the assistant professor level who have successfully completed their institution's review for reappointment (or equivalent) but have not yet been reviewed for tenure. Applicants must be employed at institutions in the United States and must remain so for the duration of the fellowship. Appropriate fields of specialization include, but are not limited to, anthropology, archaeology, art history, economics, geography, history, languages and literatures, law, linguistics, musicology, philosophy, political science, psychology, religion, and sociology. Proposals in those fields of the social sciences are eligible only if they employ predominantly humanistic approaches (e.g., economic history, law and literature, political philosophy). Proposals in interdisciplinary and cross-disciplinary studies are welcome, as are proposals focused on any geographic region or on any cultural or linguistic group. Applicants are encouraged to spend substantial periods of their leaves in residential interdisciplinary centers, research libraries, or other scholarly archives in the United States or abroad. Applications are particularly invited from women and members of minority groups.

Financial data Fellows receive a stipend of $60,000, a fund of $2,500 for research and travel, and an additional 2/9 of the stipend ($13,333) for 1 summer's support, if justified by a persuasive case.

Duration 1 academic year (9 months) plus an additional summer's research (2 months) if justified.

Special features This program, first available for the 2002-03 academic year, is supported by funding from the Andrew W. Mellon Foundation.

Number awarded Up to 15 each year.

Deadline October of each year.

[37]
CHESTER DALE FELLOWSHIP

National Gallery of Art
Attn: Center for Advanced Study in the Visual Arts
Sixth Street and Constitution Avenue, N.W.
Washington, DC 20565
(202) 842-6482   Fax: (202) 842-6733
TDD: (202) 842-6176   E-mail: advstudy@nga.gov
Web site: www.nga.gov/resources/casvapre.htm

Purpose To provide financial assistance to doctoral candidates interested in conducting research in the United States or abroad on the history, theory, and criticism of Western art, architecture, and urbanism.

Eligibility Applicants be interested in conducting dissertation research, in the United States or abroad, on the history, theory, and criticism of Western art, architecture, and urbanism. They must have completed their residence requirements and course work for the Ph.D. and general or preliminary examinations before the date of application. In addition, they must know 2 foreign languages related to the topic of their dissertation and be U.S. citizens or enrolled in an American university. Application for this fellowship must be made through the chair of the student's graduate department of art history or other appropriate department; the chair should act as a sponsor for the applicant. Departments must limit their nominations to 1 candidate. Finalists are invited to Washington during February for interviews.

Financial data The stipend is $16,000 per year.

Duration 1 year. The fellowship begins in September and is not renewable.

Special features There are no residency requirements at the National Gallery of Art, although the fellow may be based at the center if desired.

Number awarded 2 each year.

Deadline November of each year.

[38]
CHRETIEN INTERNATIONAL RESEARCH GRANTS

American Astronomical Society
Attn: Chrétien International Research Grant Committee
2000 Florida Avenue, N.W., Suite 400
Washington, DC 20009-1231
(202) 328-2010   Fax: (202) 234-2560
E-mail: aas@aas.org
Web site: www.aas.org

Purpose To provide financial assistance for long-term visits that develop close working relationships among astronomers in various countries.

Eligibility The awards are open to astronomers throughout the world; applications are accepted from individuals or groups. Award decisions, made by an international committee of astronomers, are based on quality of research, importance of the proposed research to international astronomy, ability of the applicant to carry out the research, and the budget estimates. Graduate students are not eligible to apply.

Financial data Up to $20,000 is available annually for travel costs, salary, publication expenses, and small pieces of research equipment. If appropriate, recipients may be accompanied by their families.

Duration Long-term visits are encouraged.

Special features The grants, first awarded in 1982, are named in honor of the memory of Henri Chrétien, French Professor of Optics and co-originator of the Ritchey-Chrétien telescope design.

Number awarded 1 or more each year.

Deadline March of each year.

[39]
CINTAS FELLOWSHIPS PROGRAM

Institute of International Education
Attn: Student Programs Division
809 United Nations Plaza
New York, NY 10017-3580
(212) 984-5565   Fax: (212) 984-5574
E-mail: cintas@iie.org
Web site: www.iie.org/fulbright/cintas

Purpose To enable creative artists of Cuban birth or lineage to pursue their artistic endeavors anywhere outside of Cuba.

Eligibility Eligible are creative artists of Cuban citizenship or lineage living outside of Cuba who desire to pursue their artistic activities in the United States or other countries. Applications are accepted, in successive years, in the fields of literature, visual arts, music composition, and architecture. Only professionals who have completed their training may apply.

Financial data Grants are $10,000.

Duration 1 year.

Special features These fellowships are funded by the Cintas Foundation, established in memory of Oscar B. Cintas, former Cuban Ambassador to the United States.

Limitations Fellowships are not awarded for academic study, research, or writing; performing artists are not eligible.

Number awarded Up to 10 each year.

Deadline April of each year.

[40]
CLARK FRAZIER MEMORIAL SMALL GRANTS

Center for the Study of Tropical Birds, Inc.
218 Conway Drive
San Antonio, TX 78209-1716
E-mail: cstbinc1@aol.com
Web site: www.cstbinc.org

Purpose To provide funding to scholars interested in conducting research related to tropical birds.

Eligibility This program is open to researchers interested in studies of birds in tropical areas.

Financial data The amount of the grant depends on the nature of the proposal and the availability of funds.

Number awarded Varies each year; recently, 2 of these grants were awarded.

[41]
CLIMATE AND GLOBAL CHANGE PROGRAM GRANTS

National Oceanic and Atmospheric Administration
Attn: Office of Global Programs
1100 Wayne Avenue, Suite 1210
Silver Spring, MD 20910-5603
(301) 427-2089, ext. 107   Fax: (301) 427-2222
E-mail: irma.duPree@noaa.gov
Web site: www.ogp.noaa.gov

Purpose To provide funding for national and international research intended to improve our ability to observe, understand, predict, and respond to changes in the global environment.

Eligibility This program is open to researchers at U.S. universities, nonprofit organizations, for-profit organizations, state and local governments, and Indian tribes; non-academic proposers should seek collaboration with academic institutions. Applicants must be proposing research intended to provide reliable predictions of climate change and associated regional implications on time scales ranging from seasons to a century or more. Program elements include research on aerosols, atmospheric chemistry, climate observation, climate and societal interactions, climate change data and detection, climate dynamics and experimental prediction, climate variability and predictability, global carbon cycle, and paleoclimatology.

Financial data The amounts of the awards depend on the nature of the proposal and the availability of funds.

Duration Up to 3 years.

Number awarded Varies each year.

Deadline Letters of intent must be received by June of each year. Full proposals are due in August.

[42]
COLIN L. POWELL MINORITY POSTDOCTORAL FELLOWSHIP IN TROPICAL DISEASE RESEARCH

National Foundation for Infectious Diseases
Attn: Grants Manager
4733 Bethesda Avenue, Suite 750
Bethesda, MD 20814-5278
(301) 656-0003   Fax: (301) 907-0878
E-mail: info@nfid.org
Web site: www.nfid.org

Purpose To provide funding to minority researchers who wish to become specialists and researchers in the field of tropical diseases.

Eligibility This program is open to members of minority groups underrepresented in the biomedical sciences who hold a doctorate from a recognized university and are citizens or permanent residents of the United States (or the spouse of a U.S. citizen or permanent resident). Applicants must have arranged with an American or foreign laboratory where they can conduct their research. The laboratory should be supervised by a recognized leader in tropical disease research qualified to oversee the work of the fellow. Researchers who have received a fellowship, research grant, or traineeship in excess of the amount of this award from the federal government or another foundation are ineligible.

Financial data The grant is $30,000, of which $3,000 may be used for travel and supplies (at the discretion of the fellow).

Duration 1 year.

Special features This program is sponsored by the National Foundation for Infectious Diseases and GlaxoSmithKline.

Number awarded 1 each year.

Deadline January of each year.

[43] CONSTANCE M. MCCULLOUGH AWARD

International Reading Association
Attn: Professional Development Division
800 Barksdale Road
P.O. Box 8139
Newark, DE 19714-8139
(302) 731-1600, ext. 281   Fax: (302) 731-1057
E-mail: gcasey@reading.org
Web site: www.reading.org

Purpose To provide funding for research or professional development (particularly outside the United States) to members of the International Reading Association.

Eligibility This program is open to members of the International Reading Association who are looking for funding to support 1) research on reading-related problems or 2) participation in professional development activities in countries outside North America.

Financial data The grant is $5,000.

Duration 1 year.

Number awarded 1 each year.

Deadline September of each year.

[44] CSA TRAVEL RESEARCH GRANT

Costume Society of America
55 Edgewater Drive
P.O. Box 73
Earleville, MD 21919
(410) 275-1619   (800) CSA-9447
Fax: (410) 275-8936
E-mail: national.office@costumesocietyamerica.com
Web site: www.costumesocietyamerica.com

Purpose To provide members of the Costume Society of America (CSA) with funding for travel to collections for research purposes.

Eligibility This program is open to non-students who have been members of the society for at least 2 years. Applicants must be proposing to travel to a library, archive, museum, or other collection or site in any country to conduct research related to any aspect of costume (history, theater, fashion, design, etc.). The program is not limited to academic study nor to those with academic affiliation.

Financial data The award is $1,000.

Duration Up to 1 year.

Number awarded 1 each year.

Deadline August of each year.

[45] DEBORAH J. NORDEN FUND

Architectural League of New York
Attn: Deborah J. Norden Fund
457 Madison Avenue
New York, NY 10022
(212) 753-1722   E-mail: genevro@mindspring.com
Web site: www.archleague.org

Purpose To provide architecture students and recent graduates with an opportunity to travel and study abroad.

Eligibility This program is open to students and recent graduates in the field of architecture, architectural history, and urban studies. Applicants must be interested in pursuing an independent project abroad. Support is not provided for tuition or for participation in an organized program, such as a university's summer abroad program. Applicants must submit 1) a description of their proposed project that includes its objectives and how it will assist their intellectual and creative development; 2) a resume; 3) a project schedule; 4) a budget for travel and other project costs; and 5) 2 letters of recommendation.

Financial data Grants up to $5,000 are available.

Special features This program was established in 1995.

Number awarded 1 or more each year.

Deadline April of each year.

[46] DEMOCRACY FELLOWS PROGRAM

World Learning
Attn: Democracy Fellows Program
1015 15th Street, N.W., Suite 750
Washington, DC 20005-2605
(202) 408-5427, ext. 310   Fax: (202) 408-5397
E-mail: dfp.info@worldlearning.org
Web site: www.worldlearning.org

Purpose To provide an opportunity for mid-career professionals to engage in practical field work related to international democracy and governance.

Eligibility This program is open to junior and mid-level professionals who hold a J.D. or master's degree. Applicants must have at least 10 years of work experience; an interest or experience in democracy, political science, law, government, international relations, or other social science relevant to advancing democratic institutions abroad; and, for some assignments, foreign language fluency. They must be qualified to engage in activities designed to help promote and strengthen the evolution of democratic practices and institutions in transitional or emerging democracies; those activities may include providing policy analysis or advice, developing program methodologies and evaluation indicators, or providing technical comment on plans or activities of the host government. U.S. citizenship is required.

Financial data Stipends range from $30,000 to $50,000 per year, depending upon prior earnings, education, and experience. Awards also include travel to and from the fellowship, accident and health insurance, program travel to carry out the fellow's work activities, and other allowances that depend upon the nature and location of the fellowship. No allowances are provided for dependents or others who accompany a fellow.

Duration 1 year; in exceptional cases, the fellowships may be extended for 1 additional year.
Special features This program is funded by the U.S. Agency for International Development (USAID). Fellows work with overseas USAID field missions or offices in Washington, D.C.
Limitations Fellowships are not intended for recipients to pursue teaching or scholarly research.
Number awarded Approximately 15 each year.
Deadline Applications may be submitted at any time.

[47]
DENA EPSTEIN AWARD FOR ARCHIVAL AND LIBRARY RESEARCH IN AMERICAN MUSIC

Music Library Association
6707 Old Dominion Drive, Suite 315
McLean, VA 22101
(703) 556-8780   Fax: (703) 556-9301
E-mail: acadsvc@aol.com
Web site: www.musiclibraryassoc.org

Purpose To provide financial support to researchers interested in working on any aspect of American music.
Eligibility This program provides support for research in archives or libraries internationally on any aspect of American music. There are no restrictions on age, nationality, profession, or institutional affiliation. Applicants must submit a brief research proposal, a curriculum vitae, and 3 letters of support from librarians and/or scholars knowledgeable about American music.
Financial data Grants up to $2,050 are available.
Special features This program was established in 1995. Further information is also available from Joan O'Connor, Music and Media Services Librarian, Trinity College, Austin Arts Center, 300 Summit Street, Hartford, CT 06106-3100, E-mail: joan.oconnor@trincoll.edu.
Number awarded 1 or 2 each year.
Deadline July of each year.

[48]
DEVELOPMENTAL GRANTS FOR COLLABORATIVE INTERNATIONAL PROJECTS

National Institute on Alcohol Abuse and Alcoholism
Attn: Office of Collaborative Research
6000 Executive Boulevard
Bethesda, MD 20892-7003
(301) 443-1269   Fax: (301) 443-7043
E-mail: fc12b@nih.gov
Web site: www.niaaa.nih.gov

Purpose To provide funding to U.S. scientists interested in conducting research related to alcohol and alcoholism in collaboration with colleagues in foreign countries.
Eligibility This program is open to investigators at domestic nonprofit and for-profit, public and private institutions, such as universities, colleges, hospitals, laboratories, units of state and local government, and eligible agencies of the federal government. The U.S. scientist must apply as principal investigator with a colleague or colleagues from foreign laboratories or research sites. The foreign collaborator(s) must hold a position at a public or private nonprofit institution that will allow adequate time and provide appropriate facilities to conduct the proposed research. Proposals must be for basic and applied research on biochemical, physiological, genetic, and behavioral mechanisms leading to pathological drinking behavior; mechanisms of alcohol-induced organ damage, including fetal injury; and clinical, behavioral, and epidemiological approaches to more effective diagnosis, prevention, and treatment of alcoholism, alcohol abuse, and alcohol-related problems. Research that addresses epidemiological, behavioral, and biomedical research in alcohol abuse and infectious disease with a specific focus on the global epidemic of HIV infection are also welcomed. At least part of the project must be performed at the foreign collaborator's research site. Racial/ethnic minority individuals, women, and persons with disabilities are encouraged to apply as principal investigators.
Financial data Grants normally range from $50,000 to $75,000 in direct costs per year, but awards up to $100,000 per year may be considered in exceptional cases. Funds may be included to purchase supplies for the foreign collaborator's laboratory and to support travel for both the U.S. and foreign collaborators, as justified by the needs of the proposed research.
Duration Normally 2 years; a third year may be approved in exceptional cases.
Number awarded Varies each year.

[49]
DIANE H. RUSSELL AWARD

Association for Women in Science
1200 New York Avenue, N.W., Suite 650
Washington, DC 20005
(202) 326-8940   (800) 886-AWIS
Fax: (202) 326-8960   E-mail: awis@awis.org
Web site: www.serve.com/awis

Purpose To provide financial assistance to women interested in working on a doctoral degree in biochemistry or pharmacology.
Eligibility This program is open to women graduate students in the fields of biochemistry or pharmacology. Winners traditionally have been at the dissertation level of their graduate work. Foreign students must be enrolled in a U.S. institution of higher education, but U.S. citizens may be studying in the United States or abroad.
Financial data The stipend is $1,000. Funds may be used for tuition, books, housing, research, equipment, etc.
Duration 1 year.
Number awarded 1 each year.
Deadline January of each year.

FINANCIAL AID PROGRAMS

[50]
DISSERTATION FELLOWSHIPS IN EAST EUROPEAN STUDIES

American Council of Learned Societies
Attn: Office of Fellowships and Grants
228 East 45th Street
New York, NY 10017-3398
(212) 697-1505   Fax: (212) 949-8058
E-mail: grants@acls.org
Web site: www.acls.org/eeguide.htm

Purpose To provide funding to doctoral candidates interested in conducting dissertation research, anywhere in the world, in the social sciences and humanities relating to eastern Europe.

Eligibility Applicants must be U.S. citizens or permanent residents who have completed all requirements for the doctorate except the dissertation. Their field of study must be in the social sciences or humanities relating to Albania, Bulgaria, the Czech Republic, Estonia, Hungary, Latvia, Lithuania, Poland, Romania, Slovakia, or the successor states of Yugoslavia. Comparative projects are also welcomed. The fellowships are to be used for work outside east Europe, although short visits to the area may be proposed as part of a coherent program primarily based elsewhere. Selection is based on the scholarly potential of the applicant, the quality and scholarly importance of the proposed work, and its importance to the development of scholarship on east Europe. Applications are particularly invited from women and members of minority groups.

Financial data Up to $15,000 is provided as a stipend. Recipients' home universities are required (consistent with their policies and regulations) to provide or to waive normal academic year tuition payments or to provide alternative cost-sharing support.

Duration 1 year.

Special features This program is sponsored jointly by the American Council of Learned Societies, (ACLS) and the Social Science Research Council, funded by the U.S. Department of State under the Research and Training for Eastern Europe and the Independent States of the Former Soviet Union Act of 1983 (Title VIII) but administered by ACLS.

Number awarded Approximately 10 to 12 each year.

Deadline October of each year.

[51]
DISSERTATION FELLOWSHIPS ON CONFLICT, PEACE AND SOCIAL TRANSFORMATIONS

Social Science Research Council
810 Seventh Avenue
New York, NY 10019
(212) 377-2700   Fax: (212) 377-2727
E-mail: gsc@ssrc.org
Web site: www.ssrc.org

Purpose To provide financial assistance to doctoral students interested in conducting research anywhere in the world on the causes and conditions of international conflict and insecurity.

Eligibility This program is open to full-time graduate students in accredited Ph.D. programs who have completed all doctoral requirements except the dissertation. Applicants must speak, read, and write English at a level that allows for intellectual exchange between fellows. Proposals must include a period of 12 months of work experience in a non-governmental, international, or multilateral organization directly involved in peace, international cooperation, or security issues. The hosting organization must be based outside the applicant's country of residence. The other 12 months of the fellowship must be spent doing research on a topic directly related to or informed by that experience; the research can be part of the applicant's work towards completion of the dissertation. Topics of interest include, but are not limited to, the human security implications of human rights; inequality; religious, national, and ethnic revivalism; military affairs; weapons proliferation and arms control; peace-keeping and peace-building; the spread of disease; ecosystem degradation; international migration; international crime; trafficking in humans; food supplies; and global finance and trade. There are no citizenship, nationality, or residence requirements for this program. Women and residents of developing countries are encouraged to apply.

Financial data The amount of the grant depends on need, to a maximum of $19,000 per year. In addition, each fellow has a budget for research and institutional expenses.

Duration 2 years.

Number awarded Varies each year.

Deadline November of each year.

[52]
DOROTHY LEET GRANTS

International Federation of University Women
8 rue de l'Ancien-Port
CH-1201 Geneva
Switzerland
41 22 731 2380   Fax: 41 22 738 0440
E-mail: info@ifuw.org
Web site: www.ifuw.org

Purpose To assist women graduates interested in pursuing a program of additional study or research in another country.

Eligibility Applicants must be members of 1 of the 67 national federations or associations affiliated with the International Federation of University Women (IFUW) or, if a resident of a country that does not yet have an IFUW affiliate, independent members of the IFUW. They must intend to obtain specialized training essential to their research and further study and to carry out independent research, including completion of a piece of research already begun. Preference is given to candidates from countries with a comparatively low per capita income or to women who wish to work as experts in those countries or whose research is of value to those countries.

Financial data The stipend is 3,000 to 6,000 Swiss francs, depending on the recipient's need.

Duration At least 2 to 3 months.

Special features In the United States, the IFUW affiliate is the American Association of University Women (AAUW), 1111 16th Street, N.W., Washington, DC 20036-4873, (202) 785-7700, (800) 821-4364.

Number awarded Varies each year; recently, the IFUW awarded a total of 18 grants through this program and the Winifred Cullis Grants program.

Deadline Applications, whether submitted through a national affiliate (such as the AAUW) or by an independent member, must reach IFUW headquarters before the end of October in odd-numbered years. National affiliates set earlier deadlines; for the AAUW, this is the end of September.

[53] DUMBARTON OAKS PROJECT GRANTS

Dumbarton Oaks
Attn: Office of the Director
1703 32nd Street, N.W.
Washington, DC 20007-2961
(202) 339-6410   Fax: (202) 339-6419
E-mail: DumbartonOaks@doaks.org
Web site: www.doaks.org

Purpose To provide funding for scholarly projects in Byzantine studies, pre-Columbian studies, or landscape architecture.

Eligibility Scholars in Byzantine studies (including related aspects of late Roman, early Christian, western medieval, Slavic, and Near Eastern studies), pre-Columbian studies (of Mexico, Central America, and Andean South America), and studies in landscape architecture (including architectural, art historical, botanical, horticultural, cultural, economic, social, and agrarian) may apply for these grants. Support is generally for archaeological research, as well as for the recovery, recording, and analysis of materials that would otherwise be lost. Selection is based on the ability and preparation of the principal project personnel (including knowledge of the requisite languages), and interest and value of the project to the specific field of study.

Financial data Grants normally range from $3,000 to $10,000.

Duration 1 year, beginning in July.

Limitations Project awards are not offered purely for the purpose of travel, nor for work associated with a degree, for library or archive research, for catalogs, or for conservation and restoration *per se*.

Deadline October of each year.

[54] DYSAUTONOMIA FOUNDATION RESEARCH GRANTS

Dysautonomia Foundation, Inc.
Attn: Executive Director
633 Third Avenue, 12th Floor
New York, NY 10017-6706
(212) 949-6644   Fax: (212) 682-7625
E-mail: Dys212@aol.com
Web site: www.familiadysautonomia.org

Purpose To provide funding for research on dysautonomia.

Eligibility Eligible to apply are postdoctoral researchers from any country. They must be interested in conducting research on the treatment or cure for familial dysautonomia. The research may be conducted at a medical or teaching institution in any country.

Financial data The award ranges from $10,000 to $20,000 per year. Up to 10 percent may be allowed for indirect costs.

Duration 1 year; may be renewed.

Number awarded Varies; generally, at least 10 each year.

Deadline March of each year.

[55] ECOLOGY OF INFECTIOUS DISEASES INITIATIVE

Fogarty International Center
Attn: Division of International Training and Research
31 Center Drive, Room B2C39
Bethesda, MD 20892-2220
(301) 496-1653   Fax: (301) 402-2056
E-mail: jr141x@nih.gov
Web site: www.nih.gov/fic

Purpose To provide funding to U.S. scientists interested in conducting research on the underlying ecological and biological mechanisms that govern relationships between human-induced environmental changes and the emergence and transmission of infectious diseases.

Eligibility This program is open to investigators at domestic and foreign for-profit and nonprofit organizations, both public and private, such as universities, colleges, hospitals, laboratories, units of state and local governments, and eligible agencies of the federal government. Racial/ethnic minority individuals, women, and persons with disabilities are encouraged to apply as principal investigators. Applicants are also encouraged to establish collaborations with scientists at foreign institutions, especially for research projects proposed for execution in a developing country. Proposals must be for interdisciplinary research on the ecology of infectious diseases in the context of anthropogenic environmental changes, such as biodiversity loss, habitat transformation, environmental contamination, climate change, and other influences.

Financial data Grants provide up to $350,000 per year.

Duration Up to 5 years.

Special features This program, established in 2000, is jointly administered by Directorate for Biological Sciences of the National Science Foundation (NSF) and 3 components of the National Institutes of Health (NIH): the Fogarty International Center, the National Institute of Environmental Health Sciences, and the National Institute of General Medical Sciences. Additional support is provided by the U.S. Geological Survey.

Number awarded 6 to 8 each year.

Deadline Letters of intent must be submitted by March of each year; complete applications are due in May.

[56] EILEEN J. GARRETT SCHOLARSHIP FOR PARAPSYCHOLOGICAL RESEARCH

Parapsychology Foundation, Inc.
Attn: Executive Director
228 East 71st Street
New York, NY 10021
(212) 628-1550   Fax: (212) 628-1559
E-mail: lcoly@onepine.com
Web site: parapsychology.org

Purpose To provide financial assistance to undergraduate or graduate students interested in studying or conducting research in parapsychology.

Eligibility Any student attending an accredited college or university in or outside the United States who plans to pursue parapsychological studies or research is eligible to apply for support. Funding is restricted to study, research, and experimentation in the field of parapsychology; it is not for general study nor is it for those with merely a general interest in the

subject matter. Applicants must demonstrate a previous academic interest in parapsychology by including, with the application form, a sample of writings on the subject. Letters of reference are also required from 3 individuals who are familiar with the applicant's work and/or studies in parapsychology.
Financial data The stipend is $3,000.
Duration 1 year.
Number awarded 1 each year.
Deadline July of each year.

[57]
EXPLORATION FUND GRANTS

Explorers Club
46 East 70th Street
New York, NY 10021
(212) 628-8383   Fax: (212) 288-4449
E-mail: kbrush@explorers.org
Web site: www.explorers.org

Purpose To provide funding for expeditions in the United States or abroad.
Eligibility College graduates, graduate students, and researchers who are interested in conducting scientific explorations that correspond to the club's stated objectives ("to broaden our knowledge of the universe") are eligible to apply. Selection is based on the scientific and practical merit of the proposal, the competence of the investigator, and the appropriateness of the budget.
Financial data Grants up to $1,200 are available.
Limitations The fund will not support simple travel to remote areas. Recipients must submit a report of the results of their expedition.
Deadline January of each year.

[58]
FIGHT FOR SIGHT GRANTS-IN-AID

Fight for Sight, Inc.
381 Park Avenue South, Suite 809
New York, NY 10016
(212) 679-6060   Fax: (212) 679-4466
Web site: www.fightforsight.com

Purpose To assist young professionals who have limited funding for research in ophthalmology, vision, and related sciences.
Eligibility Eligible are young professionals in ophthalmology, vision, or related sciences who wish to conduct pilot research projects but have limited research funding. Applications from U.S. or Canadian citizens for research in foreign countries will be considered if the proposed investigation cannot be carried out as effectively in the United States or Canada.
Financial data Grants range from $1,000 to $12,000 and are intended to cover the costs of personnel (excluding the applicant), equipment, and supplies for a specific research project.
Duration 1 year; may be renewed.
Special features Fight for Sight is the research division of Prevent Blindness America, formerly the National Society to Prevent Blindness.

Limitations Applications are generally not considered from residents, postdoctoral fellows, or senior investigators with significant research support.
Number awarded Approximately 15 each year.
Deadline February of each year.

[59]
FORD ENVIRONMENTAL JOURNALISM FELLOWSHIP

International Center for Journalists
1616 H Street, N.W., Third Floor
Washington, DC 20006
(202) 737-3700   Fax: (202) 737-0530
E-mail: editor@icfj.org
Web site: www.icfj.org

Purpose To enable journalists from the United States to report on environmental issues in foreign countries.
Eligibility This program is open to U.S. environmental journalists and journalism educators who can demonstrate experience in environmental journalism, ability to work under difficult conditions, training and overseas experience, a spirit of adventure, and a willingness to share their expertise with others. Applicants may select a country from where they are interested in reporting on environmental matters, although preference is given to countries or regions in the developing world or in new democracies.
Financial data Fellowships provide payment of travel, housing, health insurance, and a stipend for living expenses. No allowances are made for the costs of a traveling companion or spouse.
Duration Up to 3 months.
Special features This program was established in 1999 with funding from the Ford Motor Company. While on assignment, fellows divide their time between reporting and writing about the environment and training local journalists to do so. They work closely with local hosts, usually a media association or university. Training is conducted through workshops, seminars, and lectures at local universities. Fellows may consult with newspapers and broadcasting companies to boost environmental coverage or act as a mentor to reporters. Fellows also cover environmental issues for their newspaper or broadcast station. Articles may be filed regularly while on assignment or published after the fellowship.
Number awarded 2 each year.
Deadline November of each year.

[60]
FORD FOUNDATION POSTDOCTORAL FELLOWSHIPS FOR MINORITIES

National Research Council
Attn: Fellowship Office
2101 Constitution Avenue, N.W.
Washington, DC 20418
(202) 334-2860   Fax: (202) 334-3419
E-mail: infofell@nas.edu
Web site: www4.national-academies.org/pga/fo.nsf

Purpose To help members of minority groups already engaged in college or university teaching to develop as scholars in their respective fields and to acquire the professional associations that will make them more effective and productive when they resume academic employment.

Eligibility Applicants must be U.S. citizens or nationals by the application deadline date; be members of 1 of the following ethnic minority groups: Black/African Americans, Mexican Americans/Chicanos, Native Pacific Islanders (Micronesians or Polynesians), Puerto Ricans, Alaskan Natives (Eskimo or Aleut), or Native American Indians; and have earned within the preceding 7 years a Ph.D. or Sc.D. degree in 1 of the eligible fields (behavioral and social sciences, humanities, education, engineering, mathematics, physical sciences, life sciences, and interdisciplinary programs). Awards are not made to candidates in professional fields, including medicine, law, social work, library science, public health, and nursing, nor in areas related to business administration, management, fine arts, performing arts, speech pathology, audiology, health sciences, home economics, personnel and guidance, physical education, and educational administration and leadership. Applicants who wish to affiliate with institutions outside the United States must provide evidence of the particular benefits that would accrue from affiliation with a foreign center. Selection is based on achievement and ability as evidenced by academic records and quality of proposed plan of study or research.

Financial data The stipend is $35,000; in addition, fellows receive a travel and relocation allowance up to $3,000. Most institutions receive a $2,000 cost-of-research allowance to provide partial support for the fellow's study and research program. The allowance is prorated for tenure less than 12 months. Finally, each fellow's employing institution is given a $2,500 grant-in-aid for the fellow's use once the fellowship tenure is completed. The employing institution is expected to match the grant. These funds are designated to be used for the fellow's research expenditures.

Duration Up to 12 months. This fellowship is tenable at any appropriate nonprofit institution, including a research university, government laboratory, privately-sponsored nonprofit institute, or center for advanced study (such as the Woodrow Wilson Center for Scholars, the Institute for Advanced Study, the Center for Advanced Study in the Behavioral Sciences, the Newberry Library, or the University of Wisconsin's Institute for Research on Poverty), as long as it is not the recipient's own institution.

Limitations Fellows may not accept another major fellowship while they are being supported by this program.

Number awarded Varies; approximately 30 each year.

Deadline January of each year.

[61]
FRANK HUNTINGTON BEEBE FELLOWSHIPS

Frank Huntington Beebe Fund for Musicians
Attn: Secretary
290 Huntington Avenue
Boston, MA 02115
(617) 585-1267   Fax: (617) 585-1270

Purpose To provide financial support to American musicians who wish to pursue advanced study or performance abroad.

Eligibility Applicants must be gifted musicians who have developed a well-planned project that will enhance their work in music. Enrollment in a European school or university is not required unless such study is an essential part of the project. Applicants may not have previously studied abroad for an extended period.

Financial data Grants are approximately $12,000, to cover round-trip transportation, room and board, and other expenses.

Duration 8 to 12 months.

Special features The Frank Huntington Beebe Fund for Musicians was established in 1932 under the terms of the will of Frank Huntington Beebe, a Boston philanthropist interested in music.

Number awarded 3 or 4 each year.

Deadline December of each year.

[62]
FRANK M. CHAPMAN MEMORIAL GRANTS

American Museum of Natural History
Attn: Office of Grants and Fellowships
Central Park West at 79th Street
New York, NY 10024-5192
(212) 769-5495   E-mail: bynum@amnh.org
Web site: www.amnh.org

Purpose To provide funding for research on ornithology from a broad and international point of view.

Eligibility Although no formal educational restrictions for application exist, grants are principally intended to cover research expenses of advanced predoctoral candidates and postdoctoral researchers. Applicants may propose to conduct ornithological research anywhere in the world.

Financial data Awards range from $200 to $2,000 and average $1,400.

Duration Grants are intended for short-term research only.

Number awarded Approximately 200 grants from this and other funds are awarded by the museum each year.

Deadline January of each year.

[63]
FRANKLIN RESEARCH GRANTS

American Philosophical Society
Attn: Committee on Research
104 South Fifth Street
Philadelphia, PA 19106-3387
(215) 440-3429   Fax: (215) 440-3436
E-mail: eroach@amphilsoc.org
Web site: www.amphilsoc.org

Purpose To provide funding for scholarly research in all areas of knowledge except those in which support by government or corporate enterprise is more appropriate and regularly available.

Eligibility The society encourages research by younger and less well-established scholars, but applicants must have held a doctorate for at least a year. In certain cases, the committee on research may accept an application from a person with equivalent scholarly preparation and achievement, but never for predoctoral study or research. Applications may be made by residents of the United States, by American citizens on the staffs of foreign institutions, and by foreign nationals whose research can only be carried out in the United States. Proposals are not accepted for journalistic or other writing for a general readership; the preparation of textbooks, casebooks, anthologies, or other teaching aids; or the work of creative and performing artists.

Financial data Funding is offered in multiples of $1,000, to a maximum of $6,000 per year. Grants are provided for: living costs while away from home (lodging, meals, and local transportation), up to a maximum of $65 per day; microfilms, photocopies, and photographs, to shorten the stay away from home or make the work more efficient and accurate; consumable supplies not normally available at the applicant's institution; and necessary foreign and domestic travel at the lowest charter or economy rate, or 25 cents per mile for use of the grantee's own car. Funding is not provided for conference support, scholarships, financial aid for study, work already done, costs of publication, salary replacement during a leave of absence, living expenses at current place of residence, consultant fees, typing or other secretarial services, office supplies, the purchase of permanent equipment, research assistants, or overhead or indirect costs to an institution.

Duration Up to 2 years.

Number awarded Approximately 200 each year.

Deadline September of each year.

[64]
FREDSON BOWERS AWARD

Bibliographical Society
c/o The Honorary Secretary, David Pearson
The Wellcome Library
183 Euston Road
London NW1 2BE
England
Web site:
www.users.zetnet.co.uk/djshaw/bibsoc/grants.htm

Purpose To provide funding to scholars from any country interested in conducting bibliographical research.

Eligibility This program is open to scholars interested in conducting research in any country on such topics as book history, textual transmission, publishing, printing, book ownership, and book collecting. Applicants may be of any age or nationality and need not be members of the Bibliographical Society.

Financial data The grant is $1,500.

Duration This is a 1-time grant.

Special features Further information is also available from Dr. Maureen Bell, Birmingham University, School of English, Edgbaston, Birmingham B15 2TT, England, E-mail: M.Bell@bham.ac.uk. Support for this program is provided by the Bibliographical Society of America.

Number awarded 1 each year.

Deadline November of each year.

[65]
FRITZ E. DREIFUSS INTERNATIONAL TRAVEL PROGRAM

Epilepsy Foundation
Attn: Department of Research and Professional Education
4351 Garden City Drive
Landover, MD 20785-7223
(301) 459-3700   (800) EFA-1000
Fax: (301) 577-2684   TDD: (800) 332-2070
E-mail: grants@efa.org
Web site:
www.epilepsyfoundation.org/research/grants.html

Purpose To promote the exchange of medical and scientific information and expertise on epilepsy between the United States and other countries.

Eligibility This program is open to health care professionals dealing with patients with epilepsy, including, but not limited to, physicians, nurses, technologists and other allied health professionals, and psychosocial and behavioral practitioners. Applicants must be interested in participating in an exchange program with professionals from another country. The host and visitor should design an individual program that emphasizes sharing of expertise and training in clinical care or research of the epilepsies. At least 1 party in the exchange must be from the United States.

Financial data The foundation covers the visiting professor's transportation and incidental expenses. The host institution assumes the responsibility for paying the living and subsistence costs of the visiting professor.

Duration 3 to 6 weeks.

Special features The program is supported in part by Elan Pharmaceuticals Corporation, Inc.

Number awarded Varies each year.

Deadline Applications may be submitted at any time, but they must be received at least 3 months prior to the proposed dates of travel.

[66]
FULBRIGHT FULL GRANTS

Institute of International Education
Attn: Student Programs Division
809 United Nations Plaza
New York, NY 10017-3580
(212) 984-5330   Fax: (212) 984-5325
Web site: www.iie.org/fulbright

Purpose To provide financial assistance to American graduate students and others for study or research in foreign countries.

Eligibility Applicants must be U.S. citizens who hold a B.A. degree or equivalent before the beginning date of the grant. The majority of grants are reserved for advanced graduate students conducting research for the Ph.D. dissertation, but other graduate students, graduating seniors, and candidates who wish to further their careers in the creative and performing arts may also apply for many of the countries. Proficiency in the written and spoken language of the host country is required. Other qualifications being equal, preference is given to veterans, to applicants who have received the majority of their high school and undergraduate education at academic institutions in the United States, and to candidates who have not resided or studied in the country to which they are applying for more than 6 months. Awards may not be used to obtain a medical degree, but candidates who already hold an M.D. or equivalent degree may apply if they wish to continue medical or hospital training or to obtain additional practical clinical experience abroad. Those ineligible to apply include anyone who has already held a Fulbright Grant administered by IIE, employees and immediate family members of any agency involved in administering the educational and cultural exchange programs of the Department of State, full-time permanent employees of the Department of State (and their immediate family members) for a year following the termination of their employment, and persons who hold Ph.D. degrees (although they are eligible for Fulbright Lecturing and/or Research Awards administered through the Council for International Exchange of Scholars).

Financial data These grants provide round-trip transportation, language or orientation courses (where appropriate), tuition, books, maintenance sufficient to meet the normal living costs of a single person in the host country, and limited health and accident insurance. No transportation, insurance, or in most cases, maintenance are provided for dependents. Grants are payable in local currency or U.S. dollars, depending on the country of assignment.

Duration Generally, 1 academic year; very advanced pre-doctoral candidates and candidates in the creative and performing arts may submit requests for grants of not less than 6 months.

Special features This program, created in 1946 and funded by the U.S. Department of State, is administered by the Institute of International Education (IIE). Students who are currently enrolled in the United States are to apply through the Fulbright program adviser on their campus; at-large applicants (those not currently enrolled) may obtain applications and information directly from the IIE.

Number awarded Varies each year; recently, the total number of regional awards offered to students by IIE (including both Fulbright and others), was 50 for countries in Sub-Saharan Africa, 100 for countries in the Western Hemisphere, 15 for countries in the Near East, north Africa, and south Asia, and 15 in the Pacific area. Another 773 individual countries awards were provided.

Deadline October of each year.

[67]
FULBRIGHT JUNIOR LECTURING/RESEARCH AWARDS

Council for International Exchange of Scholars
3007 Tilden Street, N.W., Suite 5L
Washington, DC 20008-3009
(202) 686-7877   Fax: (202) 362-3442
E-mail: scholars@cies.iie.org
Web site: www.iie.org/cies

Purpose To provide financial aid to Americans in the early stage of their academic careers who wish to engage in research or lecturing activities in countries around the world.

Eligibility This program is open to U.S. citizens who are recent Ph.D.s or otherwise early in their academic careers. For some fields, a doctorate is not required. Applicants must have relevant college or university teaching experience and appropriate foreign language proficiency. They must be interested in conducting research or lecturing abroad. Persons who have lived abroad for 5 or more consecutive years in the 6-year period preceding the time of application are ineligible.

Financial data Most awards provide a base stipend of $2,400 per month for lecturing or $1,700 per month for research, a monthly maintenance allowance based on local costs of living for grantee and accompanying dependents, and international travel for the grantee and up to 2 accompanying dependents for grants of 4 months or more. Special circumstances in particular countries may alter that standard formula.

Duration 3 to 12 months.

Special features This is a Fulbright scholar program, sponsored by the Bureau of Educational and Cultural Affairs of the U.S. Department of State and administered by the Council for International Exchange of Scholars.

Number awarded Approximately 30 each year.

Deadline July of each year.

[68]
FULBRIGHT LECTURING AWARDS

Council for International Exchange of Scholars
3007 Tilden Street, N.W. Suite 5L
Washington, DC 20008-3009
(202) 686-7877   Fax: (202) 362-3442
E-mail: scholars@cies.iie.org
Web site: www.iie.org/cies

Purpose To provide funding to American scholars so they can lecture in countries around the world.

Eligibility Applicants must be U.S. citizens who possess a doctorate at the time of application and have postdoctoral college or university teaching experience at the level and in the field of the lectureship sought. For some of these Fulbright programs, proficiency in a foreign language is required; generally, awards to Central and South America require fluency in Spanish and those to francophone Africa require French. In most other countries, however, the language of instruction is English. Persons who have lived abroad for 5 or more consecutive years in the 6-year period preceding the time of application are ineligible.

Financial data Most awards provide a base stipend of $2,600 per month for faculty at the associate or full professor rank or professional equivalent or $2,400 for faculty at or below the assistant professor rank or professional equivalent, a monthly maintenance allowance based on local costs of living for grantee and accompanying dependents, and international travel for the grantee and up to 2 accompanying dependents for grants of 4 months or more. Special circumstances in particular countries may alter that standard formula.

Duration 3 to 12 months; usually for a semester or academic year.

Special features This is a Fulbright scholar program, sponsored by the Bureau of Educational and Cultural Affairs of the U.S. Department of State and administered by the Council for International Exchange of Scholars.

Number awarded Approximately 700 each year.

Deadline July of each year.

[69]
FULBRIGHT LECTURING/RESEARCH AWARDS

Council for International Exchange of Scholars
3007 Tilden Street, N.W., Suite 5L
Washington, DC 20008-3009
(202) 686-7877 Fax: (202) 362-3442
E-mail: scholars@cies.iie.org
Web site: www.iie.org/cies

Purpose To provide financial aid to American scholars so they can combine research and lecturing activities in countries around the world.

Eligibility Applicants must be U.S. citizens who possess a doctorate or the equivalent at the time of application and post-doctoral college or university teaching experience at the level and in the field of the award sought. They must be interested in combining research and lecturing activities abroad. A sufficient command of the host country language to be able to work well with primary research materials is required. Persons who have lived abroad for 5 or more consecutive years in the 6-year period preceding the time of application are ineligible.

Financial data Most awards provide a base stipend of $2,600 per month for faculty at the associate or full professor rank or professional equivalent or $2,400 for faculty at or below the assistant professor rank or professional equivalent, a monthly maintenance allowance based on local costs of living for grantee and accompanying dependents, and international travel for the grantee and up to 2 accompanying dependents for grants of 4 months or more. Special circumstances in particular countries may alter that standard formula.

Duration 3 to 12 months.

Special features This is a Fulbright scholar program, sponsored by the Bureau of Educational and Cultural Affairs of the U.S. Department of State and administered by the Council for International Exchange of Scholars.

Number awarded Of the approximately 300 research and 700 lecturing awards offered each year, a certain number allow the grantee to combine research with a lighter teaching load.

Deadline July of each year.

[70]
FULBRIGHT RESEARCH AWARDS

Council for International Exchange of Scholars
3007 Tilden Street, N.W., Suite 5L
Washington, DC 20008-3009
(202) 686-7877 Fax: (202) 362-3442
E-mail: scholars@cies.iie.org
Web site: www.iie.org/cies

Purpose To provide funding to American scholars so they can conduct research in countries around the world.

Eligibility Applicants must be U.S. citizens who possess a doctorate or the equivalent at the time of application. They must be interested in conducting research abroad. A sufficient command of the host country language to be able to work well with primary research materials is required. Persons who have lived abroad for 5 or more consecutive years in the 6-year period preceding the time of application are ineligible.

Financial data Most awards provide a monthly stipend of $1,700, a monthly maintenance allowance based on local costs of living for grantee and accompanying dependents, and international travel for the grantee and up to 2 accompanying dependents for grants of 4 months or more. Special circumstances in particular countries may alter that standard formula.

Duration 3 to 12 months.

Special features This is a Fulbright scholar program, sponsored by the Bureau of Educational and Cultural Affairs of the U.S. Department of State and administered by the Council for International Exchange of Scholars.

Number awarded Approximately 300 each year.

Deadline July of each year.

[71]
FULBRIGHT-HAYS DOCTORAL DISSERTATION RESEARCH ABROAD PROGRAM

Department of Education
Office of Postsecondary Education
Attn: International Education and Graduate Programs Service
1990 K Street, N.W.
Washington, DC 20006-8500
(202) 502-7700 Fax: (202) 502-7860
E-mail: karla_verbryckblock@ed.gov
Web site: www.ed.gov

Purpose To provide funding to doctoral students interested in conducting research abroad in modern foreign languages and area studies.

Eligibility Students eligible to apply for this funding must 1) be a U.S. citizen, national, or permanent resident; 2) be a graduate student at a U.S. institution of higher education and admitted to candidacy in a doctoral program in modern foreign languages and area studies at that institution; 3) be planning a teaching career in the United States upon graduation; and 4) possess adequate skills in the language(s) necessary to carry out the dissertation project. Applications are accepted only for research projects that focus on Africa, east Asia, southeast Asia and the Pacific, south Asia, the Near East, east central Europe and Eurasia, or the Western Hemisphere; applications that propose projects focused on western Europe are not currently funded. Area studies refers to a program of comprehensive study of the aspects of a society or societies, including the study of their geography, history, culture, economy, politics, international relations, and languages. Applications must be submitted by the student's institution on behalf of the student.

Financial data Monthly maintenance allowances are based on the cost of living in foreign locations and range from $297 to $2,889. An allowance for the first dependent is 40 percent of the fellow's stipend, and the allowance for each additional dependent is 20 percent of the fellow's stipend. The program also provides travel expenses (including excess baggage), an allowance for research-related expenses overseas, and health and accident insurance. The estimated value of the awards recently ranged from $10,000 to $70,000 and averaged $27,315.

Duration 6 to 12 months.

Special features This program is authorized by the Mutual Educational and Cultural Exchange (Fulbright-Hays) Act of 1961 and is administered by the International Education and Graduate Programs Service of the U.S. Department of Education.

Number awarded Varies each year; recently, 115 fellowships were available from this program.
Deadline October of each year.

[72]
FULBRIGHT-HAYS FACULTY RESEARCH ABROAD PROGRAM

Department of Education
Office of Postsecondary Education
Attn: International Education and Graduate Programs
 Service
1990 K Street, N.W.
Washington, DC 20006-8500
(202) 502-7700   Fax: (202) 502-7859
E-mail: eliza_washington@ed.gov
Web site: www.ed.gov

Purpose To offer individual faculty members an opportunity to go abroad to research or study modern foreign languages and area studies.
Eligibility Eligible to receive funding through this program are U.S. citizens or permanent residents who are employed by an institution of higher education, have been teaching for at least 2 years, and have a research proposal that cannot be conducted in the United States (research for a Ph.D. dissertation is not permitted). Applications will be accepted only if they involve projects that focus on Africa, east Asia, southeast Asia and the Pacific, south Asia, the Near East, east central Europe and Eurasia, or the Western Hemisphere; applications that propose projects focused on western Europe are not currently funded. Area studies refers to a program of comprehensive study of the aspects of a society or societies, including the study of their geography, history, culture, economy, politics, international relations, and languages. Applications must be submitted by institutions on behalf of faculty members.
Financial data Monthly maintenance allowances are based on the cost of living in foreign locations and range from $297 to $2,889. An allowance for the first dependent is 40 percent of the fellow's stipend, and allowances for each additional dependent are 20 percent of the fellow's stipend. The program also provides travel expenses (including excess baggage), an allowance for research-related expenses overseas, and health and accident insurance. The estimated value of the awards recently ranged from $20,000 to $75,000 and averaged $49,885.
Duration From 3 to 12 months.
Special features This program is authorized by the Mutual Educational and Cultural Exchange (Fulbright-Hays) Act of 1961 and is administered by the International Education and Graduate Programs Service of the U.S. Department of Education.
Number awarded Varies each year; recently, 27 fellowships were available from this program.
Deadline October of each year.

[73]
FUND FOR U.S. ARTISTS AT INTERNATIONAL FESTIVALS AND EXHIBITIONS

Arts International
251 Park Avenue South
New York, NY 10010-7302
(212) 674-9744   Fax: (212) 674-9092
E-mail: thefund@artsinternational.org
Web site: www.artsinternational.org

Purpose To support performing and visual artists invited to international festivals abroad.
Eligibility This program is open to citizens or permanent residents of the United States who are performing artists (including traditional performing artists) working at a professional level. Applicants must be interested in participating in an arts festival that takes place outside the United States, is international in scope with representation from at least 2 countries outside the host country or has a U.S. theme with representation from at least 3 U.S. performing artists or groups, has a non-U.S. based organization as the primary sponsor or organizer, is open to the general public, and reaches a wide public audience. It may be a single-discipline, 1-time, or first-time festival. Support is not given to 1) festivals that consist primarily of workshops, training, or conference sessions or events that are part of a performing arts series; 2) appearances at events in which artists are self selected, have no established venue, and receive no artistic fee other than percentage of box office; 3) events in which artists must pay a participation, registration, or tuition fee or which are basically academic in nature; 4) amateur groups or groups composed of participants from instructions programs, such as glee clubs, bands, or performing arts ensembles of academic institutions; 5) composers, except those who are performing their own work; 6) conductors; or 7) events that consist solely of the reading of text at literary festivals. Selection is based on artistic excellence and record of professional activity, significance of the applicant's presence at the festival as it relates to the artist's professional development, significance of the festival internationally and/or in its own context, and evidence of reasonable financial support from the festival in relation to the local economic situation. Special consideration is given to applicants invited to festivals in areas of the world where U.S. work is not frequently seen, such as Africa, Asia, and Latin America.
Financial data Grants to individual artists usually range from $1,000 to $15,000 and do not exceed $25,000. Funds may be used for travel, per diem, international communications, shipping, and artists fees related to participation in the festival.
Special features Arts International, which currently operates this program, was founded in 1981 by Nancy Hanks, former chair of the National Endowment for the Arts. In 1987 it became part of the Institute of International Education but in 1999 it became an independent organization with funding from the Ford and Rockefeller Foundations.
Number awarded Varies each year.
Deadline January, April, or August of each year.

FINANCIAL AID PROGRAMS

[74]
GCA AWARDS IN TROPICAL BOTANY
Garden Club of America
Attn: Scholarship Committee
14 East 60th Street
New York, NY 10022-1006
(212) 753-8287   Fax: (212) 753-0134
E-mail: scholarship@gcamerica.org
Web site: www.gcamerica.org

Purpose To enable American Ph.D. candidates in botany to undertake independent field work in the tropics.

Eligibility Eligible to apply are graduate students who anticipate completing the requirements for a Ph.D. in botany within 2 years and are enrolled in a U.S. university. They must be proposing to undertake field work in tropical countries in either tropical plant systematics or tropical forest ecology. Appropriate foreign language competency may be required.

Financial data The stipend is $5,500.

Duration These are 1-time awards.

Special features This program was established in 1983 in cooperation with the World Wildlife Fund, 1250 24th Street, N.W., Washington, DC 20037-1175; (202) 778-9608; Fax: (202) 861-8324, E-mail: susan.ward@wwfus.org.

Limitations Requests for applications must be accompanied by a self-addressed stamped envelope.

Number awarded 2 each year.

Deadline December of each year.

[75]
HAROLD LANCOUR SCHOLARSHIP FOR FOREIGN STUDY
Beta Phi Mu
c/o Florida State University
School of Information Studies
Tallahassee, FL 32306-2100
(850) 644-3907   Fax: (850) 644-6253
E-mail: Beta_Phi_Mu@lis.fsu.edu
Web site: www.beta-phi-mu.org/scholarship.html

Purpose To provide financial assistance for international activities to librarians or library science students.

Eligibility Eligible to apply are librarians and graduate students in library science who seek funding for 1) surveys of foreign libraries or library programs; 2) attendance at a foreign library school program for a short period of time; or 3) library research in a foreign country. Selection is based on the plan of study or research and the usefulness of the study or research to the applicant and to the profession.

Financial data The award is $1,000.

Duration 1 year.

Special features Beta Phi Mu is the International Library and Information Science Honor Society.

Limitations Requests for applications must be accompanied by a self-addressed stamped envelope.

Number awarded 1 each year.

Deadline March of each year.

[76]
HARPER-WOOD STUDENTSHIP FOR ENGLISH POETRY AND LITERATURE
University of Cambridge
St. John's College
Attn: The Master
St. John's Street
Cambridge CB2 1TP
England
44 1223 338635   Fax: 44 1223 338707
E-mail: Enquiries@joh.cam.ac.uk
Web site: www.joh.cam.ac.uk

Purpose To provide financial assistance to graduates of universities in the United States, Great Britain, Ireland, or the Commonwealth for graduate study or research (in English poetry or literature) in a foreign country.

Eligibility This program is open to graduates of universities in the United States, Great Britain, Ireland, and the Commonwealth who are younger than 30 years of age. Applicants must be interested in producing original literary work while engaging in a course of study or research in English poetry or literature. Their program of study or research does not need to be conducted while attached to a university or other institution. All or part of it must be spent in a foreign country of their choice.

Financial data The amount of the studentship varies, depending upon the recipient's qualifications and financial circumstances, up to 6,800 pounds.

Duration 1 year, beginning in October; nonrenewable.

Special features The fellowship is tenable in any foreign country.

Deadline May of each year.

[77]
HARRY FRANK GUGGENHEIM FOUNDATION DISSERTATION FELLOWSHIP
Harry Frank Guggenheim Foundation
527 Madison Avenue, 15th Floor
New York, NY 10022-4304
(212) 644-4907   Fax: (212) 644-5110
Web site: www.hfg.org

Purpose To provide financial support to graduate students who wish to conduct doctoral dissertation research in any country on the causes and consequences of dominance, aggression, and violence.

Eligibility Graduate students from any country are eligible to apply if they are in the final stages of writing a doctoral dissertation in any of the natural or social sciences or the humanities that can increase understanding and amelioration of the problems of violence, aggression, and dominance in the modern world. The foundation is especially interested in research that concerns violence, aggression, and dominance in relation to social change, the socialization of children, intergroup conflict, interstate warfare, crime, family relationships, and investigations of the control of aggression and violence. Research with no useful relevance to understanding and attempting to cope with problems of human violence and aggression is not supported, nor are proposals to investigate urgent social problems where the foundation is not convinced that useful, sound research can be done. The fellowship is tenable anywhere in the world.

Financial data The grant is $15,000.
Duration 1 year.
Limitations Applications should be submitted only if the applicant and advisor can assure the foundation that the dissertation will be finished during the award year.
Number awarded Approximately 10 each year.
Deadline January of each year.

[78]
HARRY FRANK GUGGENHEIM FOUNDATION GRANTS FOR RESEARCH

Harry Frank Guggenheim Foundation
527 Madison Avenue, 15th Floor
New York, NY 10022-4304
(212) 644-4907 Fax: (212) 644-5110
Web site: www.hfg.org

Purpose To provide funding to scholars from any country who wish to conduct postdoctoral research on the causes and consequences of dominance, aggression, and violence.
Eligibility Eligible are scholars in any of the natural or social sciences or humanities who propose research projects dealing with the causes and consequences of dominance, aggression, and violence. Research may be conducted anywhere in the world by postdoctorates and other scholars from any country. The foundation is especially interested in research that concerns violence, aggression, and dominance in relation to social change, the socialization of children, intergroup conflict, interstate warfare, crime, family relationships, and investigations of the control of aggression and violence. Research with no useful relevance to understanding and attempting to cope with problems of human violence and aggression is not supported, nor are proposals to investigate urgent social problems where the foundation is not convinced that useful, sound research can be done.
Financial data Grants, which range from $15,000 to $35,000 per year, may be used to cover salaries, employee benefits, research assistantships, computer time, supplies and equipment, field work, essential secretarial and technical help, and other items necessary to the successful completion of a project.
Duration 1 year; may be renewed for 1 additional year.
Limitations Funds are not provided for overhead costs of institutions, travel to professional meetings, self-education, elaborate fixed equipment, or support while completing the requirements for advanced degrees.
Number awarded Approximately 50 each year.
Deadline July of each year.

[79]
HARVARD TRAVELLERS CLUB GRANTS

Harvard Travellers Club Permanent Fund
c/o George P. Bates
21 University Road
P.O. Box H
Canton, MA 02021-0190
(781) 821-0400 Fax: (781) 828-4254

Purpose To provide financial support for research and/or exploration projects that involve travel as part of the project.
Eligibility Normally, recipients are graduate students, but applications are also accepted from undergraduates and faculty members. Funds may be used anywhere in the world in any scientific discipline, but only for travel expenses that involve research and/or exploration. Assistance is not provided to applicants who want to spend time studying in a foreign city.
Financial data The amounts of the grants vary from $500 to $1,000.
Number awarded 3 each year.
Deadline March of each year.

[80]
HEISER PROGRAM POSTDOCTORAL RESEARCH FELLOWSHIPS

Heiser Program for Research in Leprosy and Tuberculosis
450 East 63rd Street
New York, NY 10021-7928
(212) 751-6233

Purpose To provide financial support to young biomedical scientists in beginning postdoctoral training for research in leprosy and/or tuberculosis.
Eligibility Applicants should hold an M.D., Ph.D., or equivalent degree and be interested in obtaining research training directly related to the study of leprosy and/or tuberculosis at an institution (anywhere in the world) other than that at which they obtained their degree. No citizenship or age limitations are imposed, but candidates should be at an early stage of postdoctoral research training.
Financial data The award includes a stipend of $25,000 to $28,000 per year (depending on such factors as number of dependents, previous postdoctoral experience, and cost of living in the training location), economy airfare to the training location for the fellow and family, a training allowance of $2,000 to the training laboratory, and up to $1,500 per year toward health insurance.
Duration 1 year; may be renewed for 1 additional year.
Special features The Heiser Program was established by a bequest from Dr. Victor George Heiser, a physician who devoted his life to the study and treatment of tropical diseases. Originally the program focused on training for research on leprosy, but it was expanded to include tuberculosis in 1992.
Limitations Funds may not be used to treat patients but only to train to find a cure or preventative for leprosy or tuberculosis.
Number awarded Varies each year.
Deadline January of each year.

[81]
HEISER PROGRAM RESEARCH GRANTS

Heiser Program for Research in Leprosy and Tuberculosis
450 East 63rd Street
New York, NY 10021-7928
(212) 751-6233

Purpose To promote collaborative research on leprosy by established scholars from any country.
Eligibility Applicants should be established investigators in leprosy who wish to carry out specific research objectives at distant or foreign institutions that have experience in leprosy research and productive interactions with leprosy field workers.

The proposed research should emphasize 1) innovative laboratory and operational research-based approaches for the diagnosis of cases of leprosy, particularly paucibacillary leprosy undetectable by current methods; 2) methods to reach and identify all existing and potential leprosy patients to allow their treatment; or 3) innovative research-based approaches for the detection of silent neuritis, other disabilities, and evidence of relapse and drug resistance. No citizenship requirements are imposed.

Financial data Grants are awarded up to $30,000 per year, of which no more than 10 percent may be used for institutional overhead and none for clinical trials or salaries of senior personnel.

Duration 2 years.

Special features The Heiser Program was established by a bequest from Dr. Victor George Heiser, a physician who devoted his life to the study and treatment of tropical diseases. Originally the program focused on research on leprosy, but expanded to include tuberculosis in 1992.

Number awarded Varies each year.

Deadline January of each year.

[82]
HELEN GLADSTONE WILLIAMS SCHOLARSHIPS

English-Speaking Union-Washington Branch
The Washington Club, Fourth Floor
15 Dupont Circle, N.W.
Washington, DC 20036
(202) 234-4602   Fax: (202) 234-4639
E-mail: esuwdc@erols.com
Web site: www.esu-dc.org

Purpose To provide funding to residents of the metropolitan Washington area who are interested in conducting research or other projects in an English-speaking country.

Eligibility This program is open to permanent residents of the Washington, D.C. metropolitan area who have at least a bachelor's degree. Applicants must be interested in conducting a project, either independently or in conjunction with an accredited institution, in an English-speaking country other than the United States.

Financial data The grant ranges from $3,000 to $5,000.

Number awarded 1 or more each year.

Deadline March of each year.

[83]
HELEN HAY WHITNEY FOUNDATION POSTDOCTORAL RESEARCH FELLOWSHIPS

Helen Hay Whitney Foundation
Attn: Administrative Director
450 East 63rd Street
New York, NY 10021-7928
(212) 751-8228   Fax: (212) 688-6794
Web site: www.hhwf.org

Purpose To support early postdoctoral research training in all the basic biomedical sciences.

Eligibility Candidates living in North America who hold an M.D., Ph.D., or equivalent and are seeking beginning postdoctoral training in basic biomedical research are eligible to apply.

The foundation does not accept applications from persons who are abroad. While U.S. citizenship is not required, only citizens may train abroad; noncitizens are supported for training only in the United States. Applications from established scientists or advanced fellows will not be considered, because the fellowships are for early postdoctoral training only. Applicants who have already had 1 year of postdoctoral laboratory training at the time of application will usually not be considered. Applicants may not request tenure in the same laboratory in which they already received extensive predoctoral or postdoctoral training; the aim of the fellowship is to broaden postdoctoral training and experience.

Financial data Fellows receive $33,000 for the first year, $35,000 for the second year, and $37,000 for the third year. In addition, the foundation provides funds for travel to the fellowship location for both the fellow and family. No payment is made for the transportation of household goods. An annual allowance of $2,000 is given to the fellow's laboratory to help defray research expenses.

Duration 3 years.

Special features The fellow may supplement the stipend awarded (but may not accept another fellowship from a different source during the same time).

Limitations The foundation does not usually make more than 1 award in any 1 year for training with a given supervisor and will not support more than 2 fellows per laboratory at any time. It is expected that the fellowship training will take place in an academic setting. The selection of a commercial or industrial laboratory for the training experience will not be approved. Non-research activities (such as teaching) must not occupy more than 10 percent of the fellow's time.

Deadline August of each year.

[84]
HELLY HANSEN ADVENTURE GRANT

American Alpine Club
710 Tenth Street, Suite 100
Golden, CO 80401
(303) 384-0110   Fax: (303) 384-0111
E-mail: Getinfo@americanalpineclub.org
Web site: www.americanalpineclub.org

Purpose To provide funding to American mountain climbing expeditions that rely on human power.

Eligibility This program is open to small, non-guided, non-commercial, non-research based expeditions of American climbers. Applicants must be 1) planning primarily human-powered approaches (i.e., skis, canoe/kayak, bicycle, circumnavigation, mountain traverses) to achieve their objectives; 2) planning to duplicate seldom-repeated historic routes; and 3) proposing either new routes on peaks or routes through mountain ranges. Groups may not exceed 6 individuals. Expeditions may be in any country.

Financial data Grants are $2,500. Recipients are also presented with Helly Hansen garments.

Duration Expeditions must begin within 8 months of the award date.

Limitations An expedition report must be submitted to the sponsor within 1 month of returning for use in *The American Alpine News*.

Number awarded 3 each year.

Deadline January of each year.

[85]
HICKOK-RADFORD FUND GRANTS
Society of Economic Geologists Foundation
Attn: SEG Grants Program
7811 Schaffer Parkway
Littleton, CO 80127
(720) 981-7882   Fax: (720) 981-7874
E-mail: seg@segweb.org
Web site: www.segweb.org

Purpose To provide funding to graduate students and recent graduates in geology who wish to conduct research in Alaska, British Columbia, or other northern regions.

Eligibility This program is open to 1) graduate students conducting master's or doctoral thesis research and 2) postgraduates who have completed either a bachelor's or advanced degree in geology or a related earth science within 2 years prior to applying. Applicants must be proposing to conduct field research in economic geology, especially its application in the exploration for metallic mineral deposits. The research may be conducted anywhere in the world with challenging terrain, but preference is given to projects in Alaska, British Columbia, or other regions located north of latitude 60 degrees north. Preference is also given to projects that can demonstrate an affiliation with private industry, either through direct co-sponsorship or other indications of interest or support. Applicants may be from any country.

Financial data Stipends range from $500 to $3,000. Funds may be used for travel expenses, living costs in the field, expendable supplies, field expenses, and other expenses directly necessary for the research; they are not intended for purchase of ordinary field equipment, living costs of assistants or families of the grantees, attendance at professional meetings, preparation of theses, or reimbursement for work already accomplished.

Number awarded Varies each year; recently, 3 of these grants were awarded.

Deadline January of each year.

[86]
HIV-AIDS AND RELATED ILLNESSES RESEARCH COLLABORATION AWARD
Fogarty International Center
Attn: Division of International Training and Research
31 Center Drive, Room B2C39
Bethesda, MD 20892-2220
(301) 496-1653   Fax: (301) 402-0779
E-mail: FIRCA@nih.gov
Web site: www.nih.gov/fic/programs/aidsfirc.html

Purpose To provide assistance for U.S. investigators with current funding from the National Institutes of Health (NIH) to conduct research related to AIDS at foreign sites in collaboration with foreign scientists.

Eligibility Applications may be submitted by U.S. nonprofit organizations, public and private, such as universities, colleges, hospitals, laboratories, units of state and local governments, and eligible agencies of the federal government on behalf of principal investigators. The proposed U.S. principal investigator must be the principal investigator of an AIDS or AIDS-related research grant project funded by the institutes. Racial/ethnic minority individuals, women, and persons with disabilities are encouraged to apply as principal investigators. The foreign collaborator must hold a position at an institution in a foreign country that will allow him or her adequate time and provide appropriate facilities to conduct the proposed research. Most countries are eligible for participation in this program; applications for purchase of equipment as part of the grant are limited to research in the developing countries of Africa, Asia, (except Japan, Singapore, South Korea, and Taiwan), central and eastern Europe, Russia and the Independent States of the former Soviet Union, Latin America and the non-U.S. Caribbean, the Middle East, and the Pacific Ocean Islands (except Australia and New Zealand). The application must demonstrate that the award will enhance the scientific contributions of both the U.S. and foreign scientist and will enhance or expand the contribution of the institutes-sponsored research project.

Financial data Grants up to $32,000 per year are available. Funds may be used for supplies at the foreign institution, expenses incurred at the U.S. institution to support the collaboration, and research-related travel and subsistence expenses for both the U.S. and foreign investigators. For collaborations in developing countries as defined above, requests for purchase of equipment (including computers and fax machines) are considered; up to $5,000 may be allocated as a stipend for the foreign collaborator and up to $2,000 may be allocated for the foreign collaborator to attend an AIDS-related scientific conference. Travel funds may be requested up to 20 percent of the total direct costs (up to $6,400) for the U.S. principal investigator, the foreign collaborator, and/or their colleagues or students for visits to each other's laboratory or research site, if such visits are directly related to the subject of the collaborative research.

Duration Up to 3 years.

Special features This program is the counterpart to the Fogarty International Research Collaboration Award (FIRCA) program for non-AIDS related research. It is also designated as AIDS-FIRCA.

Deadline April, August, or December of each year.

[87]
HUGH EXTON MCKINSTRY FUND GRANTS
Society of Economic Geologists Foundation
Attn: SEG Grants Program
7811 Schaffer Parkway
Littleton, CO 80127
(720) 981-7882   Fax: (720) 981-7874
E-mail: seg@segweb.org
Web site: www.segweb.org

Purpose To provide funding to graduate students and recent graduates in geology who wish to conduct research anywhere in the world.

Eligibility This program is open to graduate students from anywhere in the world who are conducting master's or doctoral thesis research, faculty, and geologists on study leave from their employment. Applicants must be proposing to conduct research that is beneficial to the science of economic geology, especially as applied to field situations. The research may be conducted in any country.

Financial data Stipends range from $600 to $2,000. Funds may be used for travel expenses, living costs in the field, expendable supplies, field expenses, and other expenses directly necessary for the research; they are not intended for purchase of ordinary field equipment, living costs of assistants or families of the grantees, attendance at professional meetings, preparation of theses, or reimbursement for work already accomplished.
Number awarded Varies each year; recently, 26 of these grants were awarded.
Deadline January of each year.

[88]
HYLAND R. JOHNS GRANT PROGRAM

International Society of Arboriculture
Attn: Research Trust
P.O. Box 3129
Champaign, IL 61826-3129
(217) 355-9411   Fax: (217) 355-9516
E-mail: isa@isa-arbor.com
Web site: www.isa-arbor.com

Purpose To provide funding for research in arboriculture.
Eligibility This program is open to scholars in agricultural plant pathology, agricultural plant physiology, entomology, forestry, horticulture, and soil sciences. Applicants must be proposing to conduct research (anywhere in the world) on the biology, management, and care of trees and their relation to environmental, social, and economic benefits. The proposed research must be useful to practicing arborists.
Financial data Awards depend on the number of successful applications, availability of funds, and value of the proposal to the arboricultural industry; grants range from $5,000 to $20,000.
Special features This program was established in 1995.
Number awarded Varies each year.
Deadline April of each year.

[89]
IARC POSTDOCTORAL FELLOWSHIPS FOR CANCER RESEARCH

International Agency for Research on Cancer
150 cours Albert-Thomas
69372 Lyon 08
France
33 4 72 73 84 48   Fax: 33 4 72 73 80 80
E-mail: fel@iarc.fr
Web site: www.iarc.fr

Purpose To stimulate research in environmental carcinogenesis by providing financial aid to junior scientists for research training in some country other than their own.
Eligibility These fellowships are intended for junior scientists with postdoctoral experience who are actively engaged in research in medical or allied sciences and who wish to pursue a career in cancer research; the fields of research may include biostatistics, epidemiology, environmental and viral carcinogenesis, cell biology, cell genetics, molecular biology, and mechanisms of carcinogenesis. Applications are accepted from any country. Fellowships are tenable in any suitable institution in any country abroad. Applicants must have an adequate knowledge of English or the language of their host country. Applications cannot normally be accepted from people already holding fellowships to study abroad.
Financial data Stipends vary, depending on the cost of living in the country where the fellowship is pursued; the amount awarded is intended to cover the cost of room, board, and incidental expenses. A travel allowance equivalent to economy-class airfare is provided for the fellow and for 1 dependent who accompanies the fellow for at least 8 months; the annual family allowance is $400 for a spouse and $450 for each dependent child.
Duration 1 year.
Special features The International Agency for Research on Cancer is an agency of the World Health Organization. This program, which began in 1966, is partially supported by the Italian Association for Research on Cancer.
Limitations Fellows are expected to return to a post in their home country.
Number awarded Varies each year; recently, 11 of these fellowships were awarded. Since the program began, more than 450 fellows have received support.
Deadline December of each year.

[90]
IAS VISITING FELLOWSHIP AWARD

International Atherosclerosis Society
Attn: Executive Director, Fellowships, Finance, and Legal Affairs
6565 Fannin Street, M.S. A-601
Houston, TX 77030
(713) 797-0401   Fax: (713) 796-8853
E-mail: ias@bcm.tmc.edu
Web site: www.athero.org

Purpose To enable members of a constituent society of the International Atherosclerosis Society (IAS) to travel abroad to learn new research techniques.
Eligibility This program is open to members of a constituent society of the IAS who hold an M.D./Ph.D. or equivalent degree and wish to improve their skills and knowledge in the field of cardiovascular disease, learn new research techniques in the field of cardiovascular disease, and/or implement new techniques or initiate new programs in atherosclerosis and cardiovascular disease. Applicants may be from any country, proposing to travel to a country other than their own.
Financial data The stipend is $5,000, consisting of $2,000 for travel and $1,000 per month for housing.
Duration 3 months.
Number awarded Varies each year; recently, 4 of these fellowships were awarded.
Deadline December of each year.

[91]
IAU EXCHANGE OF ASTRONOMERS TRAVEL GRANTS

International Astronomical Union
c/o Richard M. West, Commission 38
ESO
Karl-Schwarzschild-Strasse 2
D-85748 Garching Muenchen
Germany
49 89 320 06 276   Fax: 49 89 320 2362
E-mail: rwest@eso.org
Web site: www.eso.org/iaucom38

Purpose To provide financial aid to astronomers from any country who are interested in traveling to institutions abroad.

Eligibility This program is open to faculty/staff members, postdoctoral fellows, and graduate students at any recognized educational/research institution or observatory in any country. Applicants must have an excellent record of research and must have made permanent and professional commitments to astronomy.

Financial data The grant covers round-trip economy airfare between the home and host institutions. Some grants may be awarded on the basis of one-way fare, as in a case of graduate students applying for funds to go abroad to begin graduate study at an institution where they have been formally accepted. Applicants must indicate the source of subsistence funds available to them during their visit.

Duration At least 3 months.

Limitations These grants provide only for travel. The funds may not be used to attend symposia, summer schools, conferences, or society meetings, nor solely for the purpose of obtaining observational data.

Number awarded Varies each year.

[92]
ICTP VISITING SCHOLAR/CONSULTANT PROGRAM

Abdus Salam International Centre for Theoretical Physics
Attn: Office of External Activities
Via Beirut, 6
P.O. Box 586
I-34014 Trieste
Italy
39 040 224 0323   Fax: 39 040 224 0443
E-mail: sci_info@ictp.trieste.it
Web site: www.ictp.trieste.it

Purpose To provide funding to enable physicists and mathematicians to visit institutes or research groups in a Third World country.

Eligibility Proposals must be submitted by a Third World institute that is interested in inviting a visiting scientist to provide expert advice on enhancing existing activities or initiating a new research program. The visiting scientist, who may be from any country, is expected to deliver a series of topical lectures and seminars and to interact with the hosting scientists to ensure a long-term scientific collaboration. The department should contact and negotiate the details with the visiting scientist before the application is submitted. Applications for 1-time visits are not accepted.

Financial data The amount provided does not exceed $2,500 for each visit. That funding is normally expected to cover the travel costs of the visitor, while the institution is expected to cover local expenses and make local arrangements. It is assumed that the visitors will receive their usual salary from their home institution.

Duration The visiting scientist should make a commitment for 2 or 3 visits of about 1 month each over a period of 3 years.

Special features The ICTP is jointly sponsored by the International Atomic Energy Agency (IAEA), the United Nations Educational, Scientific and Cultural Organization (UNESCO), and the government of Italy.

Limitations The majority of the fellows are from Africa, Asia, and Europe.

Number awarded Approximately 200 each year.

Deadline Applications may be submitted at any time.

[93]
IDA SMEDLEY MACLEAN INTERNATIONAL FELLOWSHIP

International Federation of University Women
8 rue de l'Ancien-Port
CH-1201 Geneva
Switzerland
41 22 731 2380   Fax: 41 22 738 0440
E-mail: info@ifuw.org
Web site: www.ifuw.org

Purpose To enable women graduates to undertake research or study in a country other than their own.

Eligibility An applicant must be a member of 1 of the 67 national federations or associations affiliated with the International Federation of University Women (in the United States, this is the American Association of University Women) and must be involved in a research or study program. If the woman lives in a country with no IFUW affiliate, she must be an independent IFUW member. She must have completed at least 1 year of graduate work.

Financial data The award is 8,000 to 10,000 Swiss francs.

Duration Stipends are intended to cover at least 8 months of work.

Special features The award is tenable in a country other than that in which the recipient was educated or habitually resides. Americans should submit their applications to the American Association of University Women (AAUW), 1111 16th Street, N.W., Washington, DC 20036-4873, (202) 785-7700, (800) 821-4364.

Number awarded 1 to 2 each even-numbered year.

Deadline Applications, whether submitted through a national affiliate (such as the AAUW) or by an independent member, must reach IFUW headquarters before the end of October in odd-numbered years. National affiliates set earlier deadlines; for the AAUW, this is the end of September.

[94]
INTERNATIONAL CANCER TECHNOLOGY TRANSFER (ICRETT) FELLOWSHIPS

International Union against Cancer
3 rue du Conseil-Général
CH-1205 Geneva
Switzerland
41 22 809 1840 Fax: 41 22 809 1810
E-mail: fellows@uicc.org
Web site: www.uicc.org

Purpose To allow cancer investigators from any country to travel to an appropriate foreign institution to exchange information on new or improved techniques or to compile research results in the basic, clinical, or behavioral areas of cancer research.

Eligibility Eligible to apply are scientifically qualified investigators from any country who are actively engaged at the early stages of their careers in cancer research on the staff of a research laboratory, institution, teaching hospital, university, or similar establishment. Applicants must have adequate language fluency so they can communicate effectively at their host institution. Cancer investigators should be in the early stages in their careers, but clinicians should be well established in their oncology practice.

Financial data The average stipend is $3,000 per month, plus airfare; no living cost or travel cost funding is made for dependents.

Duration 1 to 3 months.

Special features This project is funded jointly by the Office of International Affairs of the National Cancer Institute of the United States and by certain member organizations of the International Union against Cancer.

Limitations These fellowships may not be granted to prolong or run consecutively with other fellowships, even those administered by other agencies, nor can they be granted to applicants already at the specified host institution. They cannot be used for the purpose of just visiting institutions, for participating in congresses or conferences, for attending meetings or lectures, or for purely clinical training.

Number awarded About 120 awards are made each year.

Deadline Applications may be submitted at any time.

[95]
INTERNATIONAL DISSERTATION FIELD RESEARCH FELLOWSHIPS

Social Science Research Council
810 Seventh Avenue
New York, NY 10019
(212) 377-2700 Fax: (212) 377-2727
E-mail: idrf@ssrc.org
Web site: www.ssrc.org

Purpose To provide financial support to doctoral candidates in the social sciences and humanities interested in conducting dissertation field research in any area or region of the world.

Eligibility This program is open to full-time graduate students, regardless of citizenship, who are enrolled in U.S. institutions and have completed all Ph.D. requirements except the field work component in the social sciences and humanities. Applicants may propose field research in all areas or regions of the world, as well as research that is comparative, cross-regional, and/or cross-cultural. Proposals that identify the United States as a case for comparative inquiry are welcome, but proposals that require no field research outside the United States are not eligible. There are no restrictions on theme or historical time-frame. Selection is based on the probability that the proposed research can inform debates that go beyond the specific topic and place chosen for study; applications should exhibit a grounding in the methods and theories of a particular discipline, but must also be of demonstrable cross-disciplinary interest. The research design of proposals should be realistic in scope, clearly formulated, and responsive to theoretical and methodological concerns. Applicants should provide evidence that they have the training and skill needed to undertake the proposed field research, including evidence of a degree of language fluency adequate to complete the project. Minorities and women are particularly encouraged to apply.

Financial data Grants provide support for research in the field plus travel expenses, normally up to $18,000.

Duration 9 to 12 months; candidates may propose less than 9 months of field work, but no award is given for less than 6 months.

Special features This program is funded by the Andrew W. Mellon Foundation and jointly administered by the Social Science Research Council and the American Council of Learned Societies.

Number awarded Up to 50 each year.

Deadline November of each year.

[96]
INTERNATIONAL RESEARCH FELLOWSHIP PROGRAM

National Science Foundation
Directorate for Social, Behavioral, and Economic Sciences
Attn: Division of International Programs
4201 Wilson Boulevard
Arlington, VA 22230
(703) 292-7225 TDD: (703) 292-5090
E-mail: sparris@nsf.gov
Web site: www.nsf.gov/sbe/int/start.htm

Purpose To enable American scientists and engineers in the early stages of their careers to establish relationships with foreign science and engineering communities.

Eligibility Applicants must be U.S. citizens or permanent residents who have earned a doctoral degree within 6 years before the date of application, or have equivalent experience beyond the master's degree, or expect to receive a doctoral degree by the award date. They must propose a program of research in a foreign institution of higher education, industrial research institute or laboratory, government research institute or laboratory, or nonprofit research organization. Women, minorities, and persons with disabilities are strongly encouraged to apply. Selection is based on the intellectual merit of the proposed activity; the broader impacts of the proposed activity (including the extent to which it integrates research and education and integrates diversity into the sponsor's programs, projects, and activities); prospective benefits to the applicant, the scientific discipline, and the United States; qualifications of the proposed host and host institution; qualifications of the applicant, including applicant's potential for continued growth;

merit of the proposed international collaboration; and expected mutual benefit to be derived from the contribution of the scientists and engineers in each country.

Financial data The average award size is $60,000. That includes round-trip economy airfare for recipient and accompanying dependents; $2,500 per year relocation allowance; an excess baggage allowance of up to $300 per person; an allowance of up to $3,000 for return professional visits to the United States; an allowance for in-country travel abroad; a living allowance of $500 to $4,500 per month for the recipient and $150 per month for accompanying dependents; partial support for language training prior to departure; health insurance at a fixed rate of $150 per month for the awardee and $50 per month per dependent; support for materials, supplies, and equipment, if justified by the proposal; and field expenses, if justified by the proposal. The supporting institution receives an allowance of up to 10 percent of the award amount for the foreign portion.

Duration 3 to 24 months.

Number awarded 20 to 30 each year. Approximately $1 million is available for this program each year.

Deadline September of each year.

[97]
INTERNATIONAL TOBACCO AND HEALTH RESEARCH AND CAPACITY BUILDING PROGRAM

Fogarty International Center
Attn: Division of International Training and Research
31 Center Drive, Room B2C39
Bethesda, MD 20892-2220
(301) 496-2516   Fax: (301) 402-0779
E-mail: jb248g@nih.gov
Web site: www.nih.gov/fic

Purpose To provide funding to investigators in the United States and other high-income nations pursuing research programs on tobacco control who are interested in collaborative research with scientists and institutions in low- and middle-income nations where tobacco consumption is a current or anticipated public health urgency.

Eligibility This program is intended to generate useful scientific information and promote collaboration between investigators and institutions in the United States or other high-income nations and low- and middle-income nations with shared interests in reducing the consequences of tobacco consumption. Proposals may reflect new or ongoing activities and may demonstrate a collaboration between a principal investigator (PI) from the United States or other high-income nation and a co-investigator from a low- or middle-income nation. If the PI is from a low- or middle-income nation, the proposal must be developed jointly by the PI and a U.S. or other high-income nation investigator. Research findings must be relevant to the collaborating low- and middle-income nation. Applicants must be investigators at for-profit and nonprofit organizations, both public and private, such as universities, colleges, hospitals, laboratories, units of state and local governments, and eligible agencies of the federal government. Racial/ethnic minority individuals in the United States, women, and persons with disabilities are encouraged to apply as principal investigators.

Financial data Grants provide up to $400,000 per year.

Duration Up to 5 years.

Special features This program is co-sponsored by the World Health Organization's Tobacco Free Initiative and 6 components of the National Institutes of Health (NIH): the Fogarty International Center, the National Institute of Child Health and Human Development, the National Institute of Mental Health, the National Institute of Nursing Research, the National Institute on Drug Abuse, and the National Cancer Institute. In addition to research, this program also provides support for capacity and infrastructure strengthening in low- and middle-income nations; those activities may include support for research training of faculty, institutional strengthening in tobacco control research, research training opportunities for investigators, and advancement of tobacco control-related training for investigators and health professionals.

Number awarded 6 to 8 each year.

Deadline Letters of intent must be submitted by early September of each year; complete applications are due in late October.

[98]
INVESTIGATOR AWARD PROGRAM IN GENERAL IMMUNOLOGY AND CANCER IMMUNOLOGY

Cancer Research Institute
Attn: Grants Administrator
681 Fifth Avenue
New York, NY 10022-4209
(212) 688-7515   (800) 99-CANCER
Fax: (212) 832-9376 E-mail: grants@cancerresearch.org
Web site: www.cancerresearch.org/investigator.html

Purpose To fund research directed at furthering the development of immunological approaches to the diagnosis, treatment, and prevention of cancer.

Eligibility Candidates must hold a doctorate, be in their first or second year as an assistant professor or at an equivalent rank (or expect to be appointed to such a position by the award activation date), and work in the field of fundamental immunology or tumor immunology. The Cancer Research Institute has no citizenship restrictions, and research supported by the award may be conducted anywhere in the United States or abroad.

Financial data Each award is $50,000 per year and may be used at the recipient's discretion for salary, technical assistance, supplies, or capital equipment.

Duration 4 years.

Limitations The awards may not be used to support research at private-sector, for-profit laboratories.

Number awarded Varies each year; recently, 6 new awards were granted.

Deadline February of each year.

[99]
ITTLESON FELLOWSHIP

National Gallery of Art
Attn: Center for Advanced Study in the Visual Arts
Sixth Street and Constitution Avenue, N.W.
Washington, DC 20565
(202) 842-6482 Fax: (202) 842-6733
TDD: (202) 842-6176 E-mail: advstudy@nga.gov
Web site: www.nga.gov/resources/casvapre.htm

Purpose To provide financial assistance to doctoral candidates interested in conducting research abroad on the visual arts.

Eligibility Applicants must have completed their residence requirements and course work for the Ph.D. and general or preliminary examinations before the date of application. In addition, they must know 2 foreign languages related to the topic of their dissertation, be U.S. citizens or enrolled in an American university, and be interested in conducting research abroad on the history, theory, and criticism of art, architecture, and urbanism (in fields other than Western art). Application for this fellowship must be made through the chair of the student's graduate department of art history or other appropriate department; the chair should act as a sponsor for the applicant. Departments must limit their nominations to 1 candidate. Finalists are invited to Washington during February for interviews.

Financial data The stipend is $16,000 per year.

Duration 2 years: 1 year abroad conducting research and 1 year in residence at the National Gallery of Art's Center for Advanced Study in the Visual Arts in Washington, D.C. to complete the dissertation. The fellowship begins in September and is not renewable.

Number awarded 1 each year.

Deadline November of each year.

[100]
J. PAUL GETTY POSTDOCTORAL FELLOWSHIPS IN THE HISTORY OF ART AND THE HUMANITIES

Getty Grant Program
1200 Getty Center Drive, Suite 800
Los Angeles, CA 90049-1685
(310) 440-7320 Fax: (310) 440-7703
Web site: www.getty.edu

Purpose To provide financial assistance to outstanding young scholars who are interested in conducting research (anywhere in the world) on the history of art or the humanities.

Eligibility Eligible to apply are individuals from any country who have received their doctorate (or the equivalent qualification in countries outside the United States) during the preceding 6 years. Candidates in related fields of the humanities may also be considered if they can demonstrate that their proposed work will make a substantial and original contribution to the history of art. The program especially seeks to encourage proposals that explore connections among the humanistic disciplines. Selection is based on an evaluation of the candidates' past research and writing; an assessment of their potential to develop into outstanding scholars, teachers, curators, or critics; and the quality of the proposal.

Financial data The stipend is $30,000 per year.

Duration 12 months; may not be renewed.

Special features These fellowships provide the opportunity for individuals of all nationalities to pursue original research and writing free from the obligations of teaching or other professional responsibilities at the early stages of their careers. The awards are completely portable; fellows may pursue their research wherever necessary to complete the proposed project.

Limitations Fellows who choose to affiliate with a university or independent research center are responsible for making their own arrangements with the host institution. Discussions with the prospective host should be initiated before the fellowship application is submitted. Postdoctoral fellows may not accept other awards or grants during the fellowship period, nor may they undertake any form of employment during the tenure of the award. Proposals may not include residency at the Getty Center for the History of Art and the Humanities or at the J. Paul Getty Museum.

Number awarded Up to 15 each year.

Deadline October of each year.

[101]
J. PAUL GETTY SENIOR RESEARCH GRANTS

Getty Grant Program
1200 Getty Center Drive, Suite 800
Los Angeles, CA 90049-1685
(310) 440-7320 Fax: (310) 440-7703
Web site: www.getty.edu

Purpose To support the research work (anywhere in the world) of scholars in the humanities at the mid-career and senior levels.

Eligibility Applications are accepted from teams of scholars working collaboratively on a single project; the team may consist of 2 or more art historians and 1 or more scholars from other fields in the humanities. Selection is based on the quality of a proposal and its originality, the potential contribution of the proposed project to the field of art history, an evaluation of the team members' past achievements and contribution to their field(s), and the feasibility of the research plan.

Financial data The amount awarded varies, depending upon the scope of the proposed project, but usually does not exceed $50,000 per individual.

Duration From 1 to 3 years, depending upon the purpose of the project.

Limitations Proposals may not include residency at the J. Paul Getty Center for the History of Art and the Humanities or at the J. Paul Getty Museum.

Deadline October of each year.

[102]
JANE COFFIN CHILDS MEMORIAL FUND FOR MEDICAL RESEARCH FELLOWSHIPS

Jane Coffin Childs Memorial Fund for Medical Research
Attn: Administrative Director
333 Cedar Street
P.O. Box 3333
New Haven, CT 06510
(203) 785-4612   Fax: (203) 785-3301
E-mail: info@jccfund.org
Web site: www.jccfund.org

Purpose To provide financial assistance to full-time postdoctoral cancer researchers in the United States or abroad.

Eligibility Applicants must hold the M.D. or Ph.D. degree but should have no more than 1 year of postdoctoral experience. Citizens of any country may apply, but foreign nationals may study in the United States only. U.S. recipients may use their fellowship in a foreign country or in the United States. The proposed work should be in the medical and related sciences bearing on cancer, although applications are also accepted in the field of structural biology with an emphasis on supramolecular structure and cryoelectron microscopy.

Financial data The basic stipend is $37,000 for the first year, $39,000 for the second year, and $41,000 for the third year. There is no dependency allowance for a spouse, but $750 is allotted for each dependent child. A $1,500 research allowance is provided to the laboratory sponsoring the fellow. In addition, a travel award is made to fellows and their families for travel to the sponsoring laboratory. Under certain circumstances, return travel for fellows is also provided.

Duration 3 years.

Special features The fund was established in 1937.

Deadline January of each year.

[103]
JAPAN ADVANCED RESEARCH GRANTS

Social Science Research Council
810 Seventh Avenue
New York, NY 10019
(212) 377-2700   Fax: (212) 377-2727
E-mail: japan@ssrc.org
Web site: www.ssrc.org

Purpose To provide financial assistance for advanced research, in any country, on Japan in all areas of the social sciences and humanities.

Eligibility Eligible to apply are scholars who are U.S. citizens (or have been resident in the United States for at least 3 consecutive years) and have either a Ph.D. or equivalent research or analytical experience. The program encourages innovative research in the social sciences that is comparative and contemporary in nature, and has long-range applied policy implications, or that engages Japan in wide regional and global debates. Special attention is given to Japan specialists who are interested in broadening their skills and expertise through additional training or comparative work in an additional geographic area. Minorities and women are particularly encouraged to apply.

Financial data The maximum award is $25,000.

Duration 2 months to 1 year.

Special features Depending on the nature of the proposed project, the research may be carried out in Japan, the United States, and/or other countries. Scholars may apply for support to conduct research in collaboration with Japanese scholars who have other support. Funding for this program is provided by the Japan-United States Friendship Commission.

Limitations These grants are not for training and candidates for academic degrees are not eligible. If travel is planned, applicants must try to arrange for affiliation with an American or foreign university or research institute.

Number awarded Varies each year.

Deadline November of each year.

[104]
JEROME FOUNDATION TRAVEL AND STUDY GRANTS

Jerome Foundation
Attn: Travel and Study Grant Program
125 Park Square Court
400 Sibley Street
St. Paul, MN 55101-1928
(651) 224-9431   (800) 995-3766
Fax: (651) 224-3439   E-mail: info@jeromefdn.org
Web site: www.jeromefdn.org

Purpose To provide funds for artists in Minnesota who wish to travel in the United States or abroad.

Eligibility This program is open to professional artists (or arts administrators in the nonprofit sector) who have lived in Minnesota for at least a year; the Twin Cities program is for current residents of Anoka, Carver, Dakota, Hennepin, Ramsey, Scott, and Washington counties; the Greater Minnesota program is for current residents of other counties in the state. Applicants must desire to travel (in the United States or abroad) for professional development, including artist-to-artist communication on aesthetic issues, the experience of seeing artistic work outside of Minnesota, time for reflection and independent study, development of collaborations, and development of work in other locations. Grants are provided for dance, music, literature, theater, media arts, and visual arts. Students in full-time degree programs are not eligible.

Financial data Up to $1,000 for short trips or up to $5,000 for longer trips.

Duration Short trips are 3 to 6 days; longer trips are 1 week or longer. Normally, international travel must be for a minimum of 4 weeks to qualify for the maximum grant of $5,000.

Special features The Twin Cities program is supported by the Dayton Hudson Foundation, the General Mills Foundation, and the Jerome Foundation. Funding for the Greater Minnesota program is provided by the Jerome Foundation.

Number awarded Varies each year; a total of $150,000 is available for the Twin Cities program and $40,000 for the Greater Minnesota program.

Deadline March of each year.

[105]
J.K. LILLY GLOBAL SOCIAL SERVICE AWARD
American Association of Diabetes Educators
Attn: Awards Program
100 West Monroe Street, Suite 400
Chicago, IL 60603-1901
(312) 424-2426   Fax: (312) 424-2427
E-mail: jfinney@aadenet.org
Web site: www.aadenet.org/Grants_Awards_Scholar/lilly.html

Purpose To provide funding to members of the American Association of Diabetes Educators (AADE) interested in developing a program to improve diabetes education and care for disadvantaged and/or underserved populations in a foreign country.

Eligibility This program is open to AADE members interested in developing a program to improve diabetes education and care for disadvantaged and/or underserved populations in a foreign country. The proposal must identify a specific problem and describe the current practice. The project must focus on developing diabetes education programs, improving diabetes education as it is practiced, or developing professional education programs. Applicants must identify the rationale behind their proposal, describe the specific aims and how they will address the problems identified, describe the population to be served and the methods for proposed work, and identify the proposed benefit or significance of the project to the field of diabetes education and to the population with which they plan to implement the project.

Financial data The grant is $25,000.

Duration Projects must be completed within 2 years.

Special features Funding for this program is provided by Eli Lilly and Company.

Number awarded 2 each year.

Deadline September of each year.

[106]
JOHN DINKELOO FELLOWSHIP COMPETITION
Van Alen Institute
30 West 22nd Street
New York, NY 10010
(212) 924-7000   Fax: (212) 366-5836
E-mail: vanalen@vanalen.org
Web site: www.vanalen.org

Purpose To provide financial assistance to architectural students and architects who wish to study and/or travel abroad, in Italy and in other countries.

Eligibility The competition is open to U.S. citizens who received their first professional degree in architecture during the preceding 4 and a half years. An application must be accompanied by a portfolio illustrating the candidate's work and a brief description of the proposed project, which must involve travel and a stay in Rome. Any submission not conforming with the presentation requirements listed on the application form will not be considered for the award.

Financial data Each fellowship is $5,000, of which $3,500 is for 4 months of travel and $1,500 is applied to 2 months' room and board at the American Academy in Rome. Any additional expenses must be covered by the recipient.

Duration 6 months: 4 months of travel and 2 months at the American Academy in Rome.

Special features This award is jointly sponsored by the Van Alen Institute (formerly the National Institute for Architectural Education), the John Dinkeloo Bequests, and the American Academy in Rome.

Number awarded The competition is held only in certain years; in those years, 1 fellow is selected.

Deadline February of the years in which the competition is held.

[107]
JOHN E. REXINE SUMMER STUDY GRANT
Classical Association of the Empire State
P.O. Box 12722
Albany, NY 12212
Web site: wwww.syr.edu/~dhmills/caes/grant.htm

Purpose To provide financial assistance to teachers of Latin or Greek who are members of the Classical Association of the Empire State and interested in furthering their study of the classics in the United States or abroad.

Eligibility This program is open to full-time Latin and/or Greek teachers who are members of the association and interested in furthering their study of the classics. Applicants may propose study programs at a college or university, a study tour abroad, or research. Other proposals, projects, or independent work (with evidence of the study, research, or writing involved) are also considered.

Financial data Up to $1,000 is awarded.

Duration Summer months.

Limitations The recipient's school must attest to the teacher's employment for the year following the award.

Number awarded 1 each year.

Deadline March of each year.

[108]
JOHN J. CLARKSON FELLOWSHIP
International Association for Dental Research
Attn: Administrative Coordinator
1619 Duke Street
Alexandria, VA 22314-3406
(703) 548-0066   Fax: (703) 548-1883
E-mail: research@iadr.com
Web site: www.iadr.com

Purpose To provide funding to members of the International Association for Dental Research (IADR) for projects on public dental health to be conducted at an institution and/or country other than their own.

Eligibility This program is open to members of the association who wish to conduct research at a facility outside their institution and/or country. The subject of the proposed research must be public dental health in its broadest context, including health services research, epidemiology, prevention, diagnostics, and health promotion. Applicants must hold a degree in dentistry or in a scientific discipline (dental, master's, or Ph.D.).

Financial data Grants up to $20,000 are available.

Duration Up to 6 months.

Number awarded 1 each year.
Deadline January of each year.

[109]
JOHN MILLER MUSSER MEMORIAL FOREST & SOCIETY FELLOWSHIPS

Institute of Current World Affairs, Inc.
Attn: Program Administrator
Wheelock House
4 West Wheelock Street
Hanover, NH 03755
(603) 643-5548   Fax: (603) 643-9599
E-mail: icwa@valley.net
Web site: www.icwa.org

Purpose To provide overseas research opportunities in forestry or forest-related areas.
Eligibility Individuals who have earned a graduate degree (master's degree or Ph.D.) in forestry or a forest-related specialty are eligible to apply if they are interested in going abroad to broaden their understanding of the relationship of forest-resource problems to humans (including policymakers, environmentalists, peasants, scientists, and forest-product industrialists). Generally, applicants must be under the age of 36 and have good command of written and spoken English.
Financial data The institute provides full support for the fellows and their families.
Duration At least 2 years.
Special features The fellowship is tenable in any country the recipient chooses.
Limitations Fellows are expected to have finished their formal education; fellowships are not awarded to support work toward academic degrees, to write books, or to undertake specific studies or research projects. Fellows are required to submit monthly reports.
Deadline This fellowship is offered from time to time.

[110]
JOHN SIMON GUGGENHEIM FELLOWSHIPS TO ASSIST RESEARCH AND ARTISTIC CREATION

John Simon Guggenheim Memorial Foundation
90 Park Avenue
New York, NY 10016
(212) 687-4470   Fax: (212) 697-3248
E-mail: fellowships@gf.org
Web site: www.gf.org

Purpose To provide funding to advanced professionals who wish to pursue research and artistic activities.
Eligibility Fellowships are awarded through 2 annual competitions: 1) for citizens and permanent residents of the United States and Canada and 2) for citizens and permanent residents of Latin America and the Caribbean. The program is open to persons who have already demonstrated exceptional capacity for productive scholarship or exceptional creative ability in the arts. Writers, scholars, and scientists should have a significant record of publication; artists, playwrights, filmmakers, photographers, composers, and other creative artists should have a significant record of exhibition or performance of their work. The foundation consults with distinguished scholars and artists regarding the accomplishments and promise of the applicants. Performing artists (people who interpret work created by others) are not eligible. Students and recent graduates are also ineligible. Scholars and writers (including playwrights) should submit a list of publications with exact titles, names of publishers, and dates and places of publication. Artists should include a chronological list of shows, citing dates and places, and a list of collections in which their work is represented. Composers should submit a chronological list of their compositions, citing titles and dates, and a list of their published compositions. Film and video makers should include a chronological list of their works, citing titles and dates of completion. In addition, applicants in the arts should submit examples of their work (although applicants in science and scholarship do not need to do so): painters, sculptors, and graphic artists should submit up to 18 35mm slides of recent works; poets, playwrights, screenwriters, and writers of fiction should submit examples of published writing; composers may submit records, compact discs, tapes, and scores of up to 3 full-length works; photographers should submit up to 20 prints; filmmakers should submit up to 3 films; video artists should submit up to 3 tapes; choreographers should submit videotapes of works choreographed.
Financial data The amounts of the grants are adjusted to meet the needs of the fellows. The average annual award for U.S. and Canadian scholars recently was $34,884; the average for Latin American and Caribbean scholars was $32,000.
Duration From 6 months to 1 year; may not be renewed.
Special features Funded research or artistic activities may be pursued in the United States or abroad.
Number awarded Varies each year; recently, the Foundation awarded 179 U.S. and Canadian fellowships and 34 Latin American and Caribbean fellowships.
Deadline September of each year for U.S. and Canadian applicants; November of each year for Latin American and Caribbean applicants.

[111]
JOHN Z. DULING GRANT PROGRAM

International Society of Arboriculture
Attn: Research Trust
P.O. Box 3129
Champaign, IL 61826-3129
(217) 355-9411   Fax: (217) 355-9516
E-mail: isa@isa-arbor.com
Web site: www.isa-arbor.com

Purpose To provide seed money for research in arboriculture.
Eligibility This program is open to scholars in agricultural plant pathology, agricultural plant physiology, entomology, forestry, horticulture, and soil sciences. Applicants must be proposing to conduct research anywhere in the world on the biology, management, and care of trees and their relation to environmental, social, and economic benefits. The proposed research must be useful to practicing arborists.
Financial data Awards depend on the value of the proposal to the needs of the arboricultural industry; the maximum is $5,000. No overhead funds are provided.
Special features This program was established in 1975.
Number awarded Varies; usually 5 to 10 grants each year.
Deadline October of each year.

FINANCIAL AID PROGRAMS

[112]
JONATHAN LINDBERGH BROWN GRANT

Charles A. and Anne Morrow Lindbergh Foundation
Attn: Grants Administrator
2150 Third Avenue, Suite 310
Anoka, MN 55303-2200
(612) 576-1596   Fax: (612) 576-1664
E-mail: lindbergh@isd.net
Web site: www.lindberghfoundation.org

Purpose To provide financing for a research project that seeks to redress imbalance between an individual and his or her environment.
Eligibility Citizens of all countries are eligible to apply, and research may be conducted anywhere in the world. Candidates need not be affiliated with an academic or nonprofit institution; the grant is to an individual, not to an institution. This grant is given to a project to support adaptive technology or biomedical research that seeks to redress imbalance between individuals and their environment.
Financial data Grants are provided up to $10,580, a symbolic amount equal to the cost of the "Spirit of St. Louis."
Duration Up to 1 year.
Special features The Charles A. Lindbergh Fund was established in 1977 as a nonprofit organization to honor the memory of Charles A. Lindbergh. Its emphasis on balance between technological progress and the environment reflects his interests and convictions. In 1994, the fund adopted its current name to reflect the partnership between the Lindberghs.
Limitations Support is not provided for tuition, scholarships, fellowships, or related travel.
Number awarded 1 each year, if a suitable application is received.
Deadline June of each year.

[113]
KERMIT E. OSSERMAN/HILBERT SOSIN/BLANCHE MCCLURE POST-DOCTORAL FELLOWSHIPS

Myasthenia Gravis Foundation of America, Inc.
Attn: Medical/Scientific Advisory Board
5841 Cedar Lake Road, Suite 204
Minneapolis, MN 55416
(952) 545-9438   (800) 541-5454
Fax: (952) 545-6073
E-mail: myastheniagravis@msn.com
Web site: www.myasthenia.org

Purpose To support postdoctoral clinical or basic research related to Myasthenia Gravis.
Eligibility This program is open to postdoctorates who are U.S. citizens, permanent residents, or foreign nationals. Applicants must have been accepted to work in the laboratory of an established investigator at an institution in the United States or abroad. They must be proposing to conduct clinical or basic research pertinent to Myasthenia Gravis or related neuromuscular disorders.
Financial data The maximum grant is $50,000.
Duration 12 months.
Number awarded 1 or more each year.
Deadline September of each year.

[114]
KNIGHT INTERNATIONAL PRESS FELLOWSHIP PROGRAM

International Center for Journalists
1616 H Street, N.W., Third Floor
Washington, DC 20006
(202) 737-3700   Fax: (202) 737-0530
E-mail: knight@icfj.org
Web site: www.icfj.org

Purpose To enable news media professionals from the United States to provide practical journalistic, management, business, and technical assistance to news organizations throughout the world.
Eligibility This program seeks news media professionals with training and consulting expertise in such areas as reporting, writing, editing, publication design, pre-press production, computer and other technologies, circulation, advertising, marketing and promotion, business management, and pressroom operations. They must be willing to work with a news organization in a foreign country. Selection is based on needs of the selected country, expertise in a media discipline, personal and professional achievement in an area of journalism, spirit of adventure, and enthusiasm for the mission.
Financial data Fellows receive transportation, living expenses, and an honorarium of $100 per day.
Duration From 2 to 9 months.
Special features Prior to going abroad, fellows participate in a comprehensive orientation session in the Washington, D.C. area conducted by the International Center for Journalists. Assignments overseas include teaching, training of trainers, and consulting. Fellows are based at training centers, universities, or news organizations. Funding for this program, established in 1993, is provided by the John S. and James L. Knight Foundation of Miami, Florida.
Limitations Participants must write a summary report of their experiences at the end of the program.
Number awarded Up to 22 each year.
Deadline January or July of each year.

[115]
KRESS TRAVEL FELLOWSHIPS

Samuel H. Kress Foundation
174 East 80th Street
New York, NY 10021
(212) 861-4993   Fax: (212) 628-3146
Web site: www.shkf.org

Purpose To provide funds for travel to American graduate students who need to complete their doctoral dissertations in art history away from their university.
Eligibility Candidates must be nominated by their department. Their doctoral dissertation research must relate to art history and they must need to travel elsewhere in the United States or abroad to conduct the research necessary to complete their dissertation. They must be U.S. citizens or students at U.S. institutions.
Financial data The amount awarded ranges, depending upon the location of the research site, from $1,000 to $5,000; funds are to be used to cover transportation costs but are not intended to support prolonged periods of primary research.

Number awarded 15 to 20 each year.
Deadline November of each year.

[116]
KURT WEILL FOUNDATION DISSERTATION FELLOWSHIPS

Kurt Weill Foundation for Music, Inc.
Attn: Associate Director for Program Administration and Business Affairs
7 East 20th Street
New York, NY 10003-1106
(212) 505-5240   Fax: (212) 353-9663
E-mail: cweber@kwf.org
Web site: www.kwf.org

Purpose To provide funding for dissertation research related to the music of Kurt Weill.
Eligibility This program is open to Ph.D. candidates who have completed all degree requirements except the dissertation. Applicants must be proposing to conduct research in music history and musicology, with an emphasis on the work of Kurt Weill. There are no restrictions on the location where the research may be conducted.
Financial data Awards are designed to cover research expenses only.
Duration 1 year.
Number awarded Varies each year.
Deadline October of each year.

[117]
KURT WEILL FOUNDATION RESEARCH AND TRAVEL GRANTS

Kurt Weill Foundation for Music, Inc.
Attn: Associate Director for Program Administration and Business Affairs
7 East 20th Street
New York, NY 10003-1106
(212) 505-5240   Fax: (212) 353-9663
E-mail: cweber@kwf.org
Web site: www.kwf.org

Purpose To provide funding for travel and research related to the music of Kurt Weill.
Eligibility This program is open to scholars planning to conduct research on Kurt Weill's work and performances and/or Lotte Lenya. There are no restrictions on the location where the research may be conducted.
Financial data Awards are designed to cover research and travel expenses.
Duration 1 year.
Number awarded Varies each year.
Deadline October of each year.

[118]
LA PIETRA DISSERTATION TRAVEL FELLOWSHIP IN TRANSNATIONAL HISTORY

Organization of American Historians
Attn: Award and Prize Committee Coordinator
112 North Bryan Street
Bloomington, IN 47408-4199
(812) 855-7311   Fax: (812) 855-0696
E-mail: oah@oah.org
Web site: www.oah.org

Purpose To provide financial assistance to doctoral candidates in U.S. history whose dissertation deals with aspects that extend beyond U.S. borders.
Eligibility This program is open to graduate students currently enrolled in a U.S. or foreign graduate program. Applicants must be working on a dissertation in U.S. history that deals with issues that extend beyond U.S. borders. They must be interested in international travel to collections vital to research on their dissertation.
Financial data The grant is $1,250.
Duration Grants are awarded annually.
Special features This program was established in 2001.
Number awarded 1 each year.
Deadline November of each year.

[119]
LADY ALLEN OF HURTWOOD GRANTS

Lady Allen of Hurtwood Memorial Trust
Attn: Secretary
21 Aspull Common
Leigh
Lances WN7 3PB
England
44 1942 674895

Purpose To provide financial assistance to professionals who wish to travel abroad to promote the welfare of children (particularly of deprived or disabled children).
Eligibility This program is open to professionals from any country who are interested in child care and have appropriate qualifications or experience. Applicants must be proposing to complete a scheduled project and be able to offer full details of how the award will help them gain specific knowledge and experience that will enhance the quality of their work with young children and their families. The project may be located anywhere in the world. Preference is given to those who work with disabled and disadvantaged children.
Financial data The amount awarded for travel varies but generally ranges from 500 to 1,000 pounds. Funds may not be used for academic course fees, attendance at specific conferences, school trips, building and equipping facilities, or supporting individual children.
Duration Up to 1 year.
Special features Information is also available from the Secretary to the Trust, Mrs. Caroline Richards, 89 Thurleigh Road, London SW12 8TY, England.
Limitations A final report is required and must be submitted within 6 months of completing the travel.
Number awarded 1 or 2 each year.
Deadline January of each year.

[120]
LADY TATA MEMORIAL TRUST INTERNATIONAL AWARDS

Lady Tata Memorial Trust
Attn: Professor D. Catovsky
The Royal Marsden Hospital
Department of Haematology & Cytogenetics
Fulham Road
London SW3 6JJ
England
44 20 7352 8171   Fax: 44 20 7351 6420
Web site: www.icr.ac.uk/haemcyto/tata/index.html

Purpose To providing funding to predoctoral and postdoctoral scholars interested in conducting research on leukemia.

Eligibility This program is open to scientists from any country who are interested in conducting research on the leukemogenic viruses or the epidemiology, pathogenesis, and immunology or leukemia. Preference is given to proposals for multilaboratory collaboration.

Financial data Stipends range from 15,000 to 20,000 pounds per year.

Duration 1 year; may be renewed for up to 2 additional years if progress reports are promising.

Special features Research may be conducted in any country.

Deadline February of each year.

[121]
LALOR FOUNDATION RESEARCH GRANTS

Lalor Foundation
180 Dudley Road
Newton Centre, MA 02459
E-mail: secretary@lalorfound.org
Web site: www.lalorfound.org

Purpose To provide funding for research related to mammalian reproductive physiology.

Eligibility This program is open to postdoctorates who wish to conduct research in mammalian reproductive physiology and biochemistry yielding improved methods of contraception, termination of pregnancy, and/or sterilization. Applicants must be nominated by tax-exempt institutions in the United States or equivalent institutions in foreign countries. Nominees may be citizens of any country but must have training and experience at least equal to the Ph.D. or M.D. level. People who have held the doctoral degree for less than 5 years are preferred.

Financial data Grants range up to $28,000 per year. These funds may be used to cover fellowship stipends, institution overhead, and laboratory and miscellaneous expenses. Less money is awarded for projects requiring less than 1 year.

Duration 1 year or less.

Number awarded Approximately 25 each year. Since its founding, the foundation has granted fellowships to 534 U.S. citizens and 463 to citizens of other nations. Included in those totals are 268 fellowships to foreign scientists for work in the United States, 40 to U.S. scientists for work abroad, and 176 to foreign scientists for work in their own country or countries other than the United States.

Deadline January of each year.

[122]
LEAKEY FOUNDATION GENERAL RESEARCH GRANTS

L.S.B. Leakey Foundation
Presidio Building 1002A, O'Reilly Avenue
P.O. Box 29346
San Francisco, CA 94129-0346
(415) 561-4646   Fax: (415) 561-4647
E-mail: grants@leakeyfoundation.org
Web site: www.leakeyfoundation.org

Purpose To support research into human origins, behavior, and survival.

Eligibility Advanced predoctoral students and postdoctoral researchers are encouraged to apply. Priority is normally given to the exploratory phase of promising new projects. There are no citizenship requirements. When research is to be undertaken abroad, evidence must be submitted that permission from the appropriate government agencies has been secured or sought.

Financial data Grants normally range from $3,000 to $12,000 for graduate students and up to $20,000 for postdoctoral scholars and senior scientists.

Duration Up to 1 year.

Special features Recent priorities have included research into the environments, archaeology, and human paleontology of the Miocene, Pliocene, and Pleistocene; behavior, morphology, and ecology of the great apes and other primate species; and the behavioral ecology of contemporary hunter-gatherers. Other areas of study related to human evolution have been funded occasionally.

Deadline August or January of each year.

[123]
LEE G. LUNA FOREIGN TRAVEL SCHOLARSHIP AWARD

National Society for Histotechnology
4201 Northview Drive, Suite 502
Bowie, MD 20716-1073
(301) 262-6221   Fax: (301) 262-9188
E-mail: histo@nsh.org
Web site: www.nsh.org/membership/awardscholar.html

Purpose To provide financial assistance to members of the National Society for Histotechnology who are interested in traveling abroad.

Eligibility This program is open to members of the society (must have been active members for at least 2 years) who are planning to go abroad to study, conduct research, or attend a conference. The applicant/nominee must submit official correspondence to/from the foreign facility, institution, laboratory, or convention chair, stating agreement with and purpose for the visit.

Financial data The grant is $3,000. Funds must be used to pay for the costs of traveling abroad for study, research, or conference attendance.

Duration The award is granted annually.

Special features Funds for this program are provided by Surgipath Medical Industries, Inc. of Richmond, Illinois.

Limitations Recipients must submit an article suitable for publication, describing the trip and experience/knowledge gained.
Number awarded 1 each year.

[124]
LERNER-GRAY GRANTS FOR MARINE RESEARCH
American Museum of Natural History
Attn: Office of Grants and Fellowships
Central Park West at 79th Street
New York, NY 10024-5192
(212) 769-5495   E-mail: bynum@amnh.org
Web site: www.amnh.org

Purpose To fund projects in marine zoology with an emphasis on systematics, evolution, ecology, and field-oriented behavior.
Eligibility Although no formal educational requirements for application exist, grants are principally intended to cover the research expenses of advanced predoctoral candidates and postdoctoral researchers. The fund does not support botanical research; it does support research in both neontology and paleontology.
Financial data Most awards range from $200 to $2,000 and average $1,400.
Duration 1 year.
Special features An applicant is usually allowed a maximum of 2 awards in successive years. Research may be conducted abroad or in the United States.
Number awarded Approximately 200 grants from this and other funds are awarded by the museum each year.
Deadline March of each year.

[125]
LIBBIE N. HYMAN MEMORIAL SCHOLARSHIP
Society for Integrative and Comparative Biology
1313 Dolley Madison Boulevard, Suite 402
McLean, VA 22101
(703) 790-1745   (800) 955-1236
Fax: (703) 790-2672   E-mail: sicb@BurkInc.com
Web site: www.sicb.org

Purpose To provide financial assistance to students interested in taking courses or conducting research at a biological field station anywhere in the world.
Eligibility This program is open to advanced undergraduates and first- and second-year graduate students. Applicants must be interested in taking courses or pursuing research on invertebrates at a marine, freshwater, or terrestrial field station anywhere in the world.
Financial data Awards are approximately $1,000.
Special features Information is also available from Michael LaBarbera, University of Chicago, Department of Organismal Biology and Anatomy, Chicago, IL 60637, Fax: (773) 834-3028, E-mail: mlabarbe@midway.uchicago.edu.
Number awarded 1 each year.
Deadline March of each year.

[126]
LIFE SCIENCES RESEARCH FOUNDATION POSTDOCTORAL FELLOWSHIPS
Life Sciences Research Foundation
c/o Lewis Thomas Laboratory
Princeton University
Washington Road
Princeton, NJ 08544
(609) 258-3551   E-mail: sdirenzo@molbio.princeton.edu
Web site: www.lsrf.org

Purpose To provide financial support for postdoctoral research anywhere in the world in the biological sciences.
Eligibility Applicants must be graduates of medical schools or graduate schools in the biological sciences who hold M.D. or Ph.D. degrees. All U.S. citizens are eligible to apply with no geographic restrictions on the laboratory of their choice; foreign applicants are eligible for placement only in U.S. laboratories. Preference is given to applicants who wish to change their field of research by bringing new ideas and methods from 1 area of biology to another. Fields of study cover the spectrum of the life sciences: biochemistry; cell, developmental, molecular, plant, structural, organismic population, and evolutionary biology; endocrinology; immunology; microbiology; neurobiology; physiology; and virology.
Financial data The fellowship of $40,000 per year covers salary, research expenses, medical insurance, fringe benefits, and travel to and from meetings. The salary portion is $30,000 for the first year, $33,000 for the second year, and $36,000 for the third year. Fellows can elect to leave up to $5,000 in escrow each year with the foundation; this money will revert to them in the form of a grant if they assume a position in a nonprofit institution in the United States at the end of their fellowship.
Duration 3 years.
Limitations Research must be conducted at nonprofit institutions, and grants may not be used to support research that has any patent commitment or other kind of agreement with a commercial profit-making company.
Number awarded Currently, the foundation has 20 sponsors, each of which supports 1 or more fellows.
Deadline September of each year.

[127]
LINDBERGH GRANTS PROGRAM
Charles A. and Anne Morrow Lindbergh Foundation
Attn: Grants Administrator
2150 Third Avenue, Suite 310
Anoka, MN 55303-2200
(612) 576-1596   Fax: (612) 576-1664
E-mail: lindbergh@isd.net
Web site: www.lindberghfoundation.org

Purpose To provide financial support for research projects that promote a balance between technological growth and preservation of the human and natural environment.
Eligibility Citizens of all countries are eligible to apply, and research may be conducted anywhere in the world. Candidates need not be affiliated with an academic or nonprofit institution; the grants are to individuals, not to institutions. Grants are provided for the following categories of research: agriculture; aviation/aerospace; conservation of natural resources, including animals, plants, water, and general conservation (land, air,

energy); education, including humanities, the arts, and intercultural communication; exploration; health, including biomedical research, health and population sciences, and adaptive technology; and waste minimization and management. Regardless of the category, the key to selection is the applicant's statement of how the project will achieve a better balance between technological growth and preservation of our human and natural environment.

Financial data Grants are provided up to $10,580, a symbolic amount equal to the cost of the "Spirit of St. Louis."

Duration Up to 1 year.

Special features The Charles A. Lindbergh Fund was established in 1977 as a nonprofit organization to honor the memory of Charles A. Lindbergh. Its emphasis on balance between technological progress and the environment reflects his interests and convictions. In 1994, the Fund adopted its current name to reflect the partnership between the Lindberghs.

Limitations Support is not provided for tuition, scholarships, fellowships, or related travel.

Number awarded Up to 10 each year.

Deadline June of each year.

[128]
LUISE MEYER-SCHUTZMEISTER AWARD

Association for Women in Science
1200 New York Avenue, N.W., Suite 650
Washington, DC 20005
(202) 326-8940   (800) 886-AWIS
Fax: (202) 326-8960   E-mail: awis@awis.org
Web site: www.awis.org

Purpose To provide financial aid to predoctoral women students interested in pursuing careers in physics.

Eligibility Women graduate students in physics may apply. Winners traditionally have been at the dissertation stage of their graduate work. Foreign students must be enrolled in a U.S. institution of higher education, but U.S. citizens may stay in the United States or go abroad.

Financial data The stipend is $1,000. Funds can be used for any aspect of education, including tuition, books, housing, research expenses, equipment, etc.

Duration 1 year.

Number awarded 1 each year.

Deadline January of each year.

[129]
LYMAN SPITZER CLIMBING GRANTS PROGRAM

American Alpine Club
710 Tenth Street, Suite 100
Golden, CO 80401
(303) 384-0110   Fax: (303) 384-0111
E-mail: Getinfo@americanalpineclub.org
Web site: www.americanalpineclub.org

Purpose To provide funding to American mountain climbing expeditions that are interested in especially challenging climbs.

Eligibility This program is open to climbing expeditions of small, lightweight teams attempting bold first ascents or difficult repeats of the most challenging routes in the world's great mountain ranges. Selection is based on the overall nature of the proposed climbing objective, the style in which the team plans to climb, and the overall experience level of the team. Preference is given to teams using a minimum of fixed ropes, camps, personnel, and equipment and to those with the highest ethical standards. Commercial, professional, and cause-related expeditions are not eligible. The grant applicant must be a U.S. citizen, although team members may be foreign citizens. All participants must be at least 18 years of age.

Financial data Grants each year total over $25,000; individual grants average $2,500.

Number awarded 3 to 8 each year.

Deadline February of each year.

[130]
M. DARIA HAUST AWARD

International Atherosclerosis Society
Attn: Executive Director, Fellowships, Finance, and Legal Affairs
6565 Fannin Street, M.S. A-601
Houston, TX 77030
(713) 797-0401   Fax: (713) 796-8853
E-mail: ias@bcm.tmc.edu
Web site: www.athero.org

Purpose To enable young members of a constituent society of the International Atherosclerosis Society (IAS) to travel abroad to learn new research techniques.

Eligibility This program is open to members of a constituent society of the IAS who hold a M.D./Ph.D. or equivalent degree and wish to improve their skills and knowledge in the field of cardiovascular disease, learn new research techniques in the field of cardiovascular disease, and/or implement new techniques or initiate new programs in atherosclerosis and cardiovascular disease. Applicants may be from any country, proposing to travel to a country other than their own. They must be 35 years of age or younger.

Financial data The stipend is $8,000, which includes $2,000 for travel and $1,000 per month for housing.

Duration 6 months.

Number awarded 1 or more each year.

Deadline December of each year.

[131]
MARCIA TUTTLE INTERNATIONAL GRANT

North American Serials Interest Group
c/o Claire Dygert
American University
Serials and Electronic Resources Librarian
4400 Massachusetts Avenue, N.W.
Washington, DC 20016
(202) 885-3203   Fax: (202) 885-3226
E-mail: cdygert@american.edu
Web site: www.nasig.org

Purpose To provide financial assistance to members of the North American Serials Interest Group (NASIG) interested in overseas activities.

Eligibility This program is open to NASIG members who are interested in such overseas activities as research, collaborative projects, job exchanges, and presentation of papers at conferences. Applicants must have at least 5 years' professional experience in the serials information chain. The proposed project must deal with an aspect of serials and include foreign travel. Foreign language skills should be adequate to project needs.

Financial data The grant is $1,000.

Duration 1 year.

Limitations Recipients are expected to submit a final project report to the NASIG board.

Number awarded 1 or more each year.

Deadline April or October of each year.

[132]
MARY DAVIS FELLOWSHIP

National Gallery of Art
Attn: Center for Advanced Study in the Visual Arts
Sixth Street and Constitution Avenue, N.W.
Washington, DC 20565
(202) 842-6482   Fax: (202) 842-6733
TDD: (202) 842-6176   E-mail: advstudy@nga.gov
Web site: www.nga.gov/resources/casvapre.htm

Purpose To provide financial assistance to doctoral candidates interested in conducting research here and abroad on the history, theory, and criticism of Western art, architecture, and urbanism.

Eligibility Applicants must have completed their residence requirements and course work for the Ph.D. as well as general or preliminary examinations before the date of application. In addition, they must know 2 foreign languages related to the topic of the dissertation and be U.S. citizens or enrolled in an American university. Application for this fellowship must be made through the chair of the student's graduate department of art history or other appropriate department; the chair should act as a sponsor for the applicant. Departments must limit their nominations to 1 candidate. Finalists are invited to Washington during February for interviews.

Financial data The stipend is $16,000 per year.

Duration 2 years: 1 year abroad conducting research for the dissertation and 1 year in residence at the National Gallery of Art's Center for Advanced Study in the Visual Arts in Washington, D.C. The fellowship begins in September and is not renewable.

Special features Fellows spend the year in residence at the National Gallery of Art, completing the dissertation and devoting half time to gallery research projects designed to complement the subject of the dissertation and to provide curatorial experience. Fellows may apply for a postdoctoral curatorial fellowship if the dissertation has been accepted by June of the second fellowship year.

Number awarded 1 each year.

Deadline November of each year.

[133]
MATHEMATICAL SCIENCES POSTDOCTORAL RESEARCH FELLOWSHIPS

National Science Foundation
Directorate for Mathematical and Physical Sciences
Attn: Division of Mathematical Sciences
4201 Wilson Boulevard, Room 1025
Arlington, VA 22230
(703) 292-4862   TDD: (703) 292-5090
E-mail: msprf@nsf.gov
Web site: www.nsf.gov/mps.general.htm

Purpose To provide financial assistance for postdoctoral research training in mathematics.

Eligibility To become fellows, candidates must 1) be U.S. citizens, nationals, or permanent residents; 2) have earned a Ph.D. in a mathematical science or have had equivalent research training and experience; 3) have held the Ph.D. for no more than 2 years; and 4) have not previously held any other postdoctoral fellowship from the National Science Foundation (NSF). They must be proposing to conduct a program of postdoctoral research training at an appropriate nonprofit U.S. institution, including government laboratories, national laboratories, and privately sponsored nonprofit institutes, as well as institutions of higher education. Occasionally, research may be conducted at a foreign institution. A senior scientist at the institution must indicate availability for consultation and agreement to work with the fellow. Women, underrepresented minorities, and persons with disabilities are strongly encouraged to apply.

Financial data The total award is $108,000, consisting of 3 components: 1) a monthly stipend of $4,000 for full-time support or $2,000 for half-time support, paid directly to the fellow; 2) a research allowance of $7,500, also paid directly to the fellow; and 3) an institutional allowance of $4,500, paid to the host institution for fringe benefits (including health insurance payments for the fellow) and expenses incurred in support of the fellow, such as space, equipment, and general purpose supplies.

Duration The program provides ongoing support for 2 9-month academic years and 6 summer months, for a total of 24 months of support, within a 48-month period. Fellows have 2 options for the academic years' stipend: 1) full-time support for any 18 academic-year months in a 3-year period, in intervals not shorter than 3 consecutive months, or 2) a combination of full-time and half-time support over a period of 3 academic years, usually 1 academic year full-time and 2 academic years half-time. Not more than 2 summer months' support may be received in any calendar year.

Special features Under certain circumstances, it may be desirable for portions of the work to be done at foreign institutions. Approval to do so must be obtained in advance from both the sponsoring senior scientist and the NSF. Information is also available from the American Mathematical Society, 210 Charles Street, P.O. Box 6248, Providence, RI 02940, (401) 455-4105, Fax: (401) 455-4004, E-mail: nsfpostdocs@ams.org.

Number awarded 30 to 35 each year.

Deadline October of each year.

[134]
MAYME AND HERBERT FRANK EDUCATIONAL FUND

Association to Unite the Democracies
502 H Street, S.W.
Washington, DC 20024-2726
(202) 544-5150   (800) AT-UNITE
Fax: (202) 544-3742   E-mail: AtUnite@aol.com
Web site: www.iaud.org

Purpose To support the study of or research on federalism and international integration at the graduate school level in the United States or abroad.

Eligibility These grants are open to graduate students who are looking for funding to complete 1 or more of the following requirements: a thesis or dissertation relating to international integration and federalism; course work that places major weight on international integration and federalism; or an independent project relating to international integration and federalism. This work may be conducted in the United States or abroad.

Financial data Awards, which generally range from $500 to $2,000, are sent to the student's academic institution to be used to pay for tuition and/or fees.

Duration Up to 1 year.

Number awarded Varies; generally, 3 or more each year.

Deadline March of each year for the fall term; September of each year for the spring term.

[135]
MCDONNELL-PEW PROGRAM IN COGNITIVE NEUROSCIENCE INVESTIGATOR-INITIATED GRANTS

James S. McDonnell Foundation
Attn: Program Associate
1034 South Brentwood Boulevard, Suite 1850
St. Louis, MO 63117
(314) 721-1532   Fax: (314) 721-7421
E-mail: susan@jsmf.org
Web site: www.jsmf.org

Purpose To provide seed funds for collaborative research in cognitive neuroscience.

Eligibility This program supports research on cognitive neuroscience that is multidisciplinary, drawing on developments in clinical and basic neuroscience, computer science, psychology, linguistics, and philosophy. Research based on descriptions of psychological functions that do not address underlying brain mechanisms or neurosciences are not supported. Preference is given to innovative, interdisciplinary research that is unlikely to be funded from traditional sources. The program particularly encourages research on higher cognitive functions, including high-order vision, language, planning, and problem solving. Proposed research may be conducted in the United States or abroad. Individual investigators at institutions with McDonnell-Pew Center grants who are already receiving support from a McDonnell-Pew Center grant are not eligible to apply. Researchers at institutions that have a McDonnell-Pew grant but who do not receive any support from the grant may apply. There are no U.S. citizenship restrictions or requirements.

Financial data Up to $50,000 per year. Indirect costs are included in this figure and cannot exceed 10 percent of total salaries plus fringe benefits. Funds may not be used to support dissertation research, workshops, conferences, or travel for the purposes of attending meetings.

Duration Up to 3 years; nonrenewable.

Special features This program is a collaborative effort established in 1990 by the James S. McDonnell Foundation (St. Louis, Missouri) and the Pew Charitable Trusts (Philadelphia, Pennsylvania). Since its inception, the program has awarded more than $38 million to institutional centers and individual investigators. Funded research may be conducted in the United States or abroad.

Number awarded Up to 25 each year.

Deadline February of each year.

[136]
MELBOURNE R. CARRIKER STUDENT RESEARCH GRANT

National Shellfisheries Association, Inc.
c/o Rick De Voe, Chair, Awards Committee
South Carolina Sea Grant Consortium
287 Meeting Street
Charleston, SC 29401
(803) 727-2078   Fax: (803) 727-2080
E-mail: devoemr@musc.edu
Web site: www.shelfish.org

Purpose To provide funding to graduate students for shellfisheries research.

Eligibility Applicants must be a member of the National Shellfisheries Association and currently working on a M.S. or Ph.D. at a recognized degree-granting institution anywhere in the world. They must need funding to conduct shellfisheries research.

Financial data The grant is $1,000. Funds may be used to purchase supplies and equipment, but not for computers or travel.

Duration 1 year; nonrenewable.

Limitations Applications may be not be submitted by fax.

Number awarded 1 each year.

Deadline September of each year.

[137]
MICHAEL P. METCALF MEMORIAL SCHOLARSHIP

Rhode Island Foundation
Attn: Special Funds Office
One Union Station
Providence, RI 02903
(401) 274-4564   Fax: (401) 331-8085
E-mail: libbym@rifoundation.org
Web site: www.rifoundation.org

Purpose To provide financial assistance to college students in Rhode Island for nontraditional, enrichment experiences.

Eligibility This program is open to college sophomores and juniors who are legal residents of Rhode Island. They may apply for grants to subsidize experiences intended to broaden their perspective and enhance their personal growth. These may include, but are not limited to, travel in this country and abroad and a variety of internship and public service programs. Traditional programs and those that are a regular part of the applicant's curriculum (e.g., junior year abroad, departmentally-sponsored summer research program) are not funded. Grants may not be used to purchase equipment. Applicants must show financial need. Criteria for evaluating applications include: clarity and thoughtfulness of application, creativity and motivation of proposed project, evidence of self direction and initiative, and financial need.

Financial data Stipends range from $2,000 to $5,000.
Duration These are 1-time awards.
Special features This award was established to honor the memory of Michael P. Metcalf, publisher of the *Providence Journal*.
Number awarded 2 to 4 each year.
Deadline January of each year.

[138]
MICHAEL VENTRIS MEMORIAL AWARD FOR MYCENAEAN STUDIES

University of London
Attn: Institute of Classical Studies
Senate House
Malet Street
London WC1E 7HU
England
44 20 7862 8700   Fax: 44 20 7862 8722
Web site: www.sas.ac.uk/icls/institute/ventris.htm

Purpose To provide financial assistance to pre- and post-doctoral scholars interested in conducting research on Mycenaean civilization and architecture.
Eligibility Postgraduate students or young scholars who have completed a doctorate within the past 5 years in the field of Mycenaean civilization or related subjects may apply for these grants to support a specific project. The award is open to applicants from any country, and the research may be conducted in any country.
Financial data Up to 1,500 pounds.
Special features The Michael Ventris Memorial Fund was founded in 1957 to promote the study of Mycenaean Civilization and study of architecture.
Limitations The awards are not intended to support a continuing program of investigation but only specific research projects.
Number awarded 1 each year.
Deadline February of each year.

[139]
MINORITY ACADEMIC INSTITUTIONS FELLOWSHIPS FOR GRADUATE ENVIRONMENTAL STUDY

Environmental Protection Agency
Attn: National Center for Environmental Research and Quality Assurance
401 M Street, S.W.
Washington, DC 20460
(800) 490-9194
Web site: www.epa.gov/ncerqa

Purpose To provide financial assistance to graduate students in minority academic institutions (MAIs) who are interested in majoring and conducting research in fields related to the environment.
Eligibility Applicants for this program must be U.S. citizens or permanent residents who are enrolled or accepted for enrollment in a master's or doctoral program in an academic discipline related to environmental management, including physical, biological, and social sciences and engineering. As part of their graduate degree program, applicants may conduct research outside the United States, but they must attend an MAI in this country, defined as Historically Black Colleges and Universities (HBCUs), Hispanic Serving Institutions (HSIs), and Tribal Colleges (TCs).
Financial data The maximum award is $34,000 per year, including a stipend of $17,000, an allowance of $5,000 for authorized expenses (including any foreign travel to conduct research), and up to $12,000 for tuition and fees.
Duration Up to 2 years for master's degree students; up to 3 years for doctoral students.
Special features These fellowships were formerly known as Culturally Diverse Academic Institutions Fellowships for Graduate Environmental Study.
Number awarded Approximately 25 each year.
Deadline November of each year.

[140]
MINORITY DISSERTATION RESEARCH GRANTS IN AGING

National Institute on Aging
Attn: Office of Extramural Affairs
7201 Wisconsin Avenue, Room 2C-218
Bethesda, MD 20892-9205
(301) 496-9322   Fax: (301) 402-2945
E-mail: rb42h@nih.gov
Web site: www.nih.gov/nia

Purpose To provide financial assistance to minority doctoral students who wish to conduct research on aging.
Eligibility This program is open to minority graduate students enrolled in an accredited doctoral program in the biomedical, social, or behavioral sciences. The National Institute on Aging (NIA) defines underrepresented minorities as African Americans, Hispanics, Native Americans, Alaskan Natives, and Pacific Islanders. Applicants must have completed all requirements for the doctoral degree except the dissertation and have had their dissertation proposal approved. Their research must deal with some aspect of aging. Grants are administered by the applicant's institution, which must be

within the United States, although the performance site may be foreign or domestic.

Financial data Direct costs may not exceed $30,000 in total or $25,000 in any 1 year. The institution may receive up to 8 percent of direct costs as facilities and administrative costs in any 1 year. Salary for the investigator, included in direct costs, may not exceed $12,000 for 12 months.

Duration Up to 2 years.

Number awarded 5 or 6 each year.

Deadline March or November of each year.

[141]
MINORITY POSTDOCTORAL RESEARCH FELLOWSHIPS

National Science Foundation
Directorate for Biological Sciences
Attn: Division of Biological Infrastructure
4201 Wilson Boulevard, Room 615
Arlington, VA 22230
(703) 292-8470   TDD: (703) 292-5090
E-mail: ckimsey@nsf.gov
Web site: www.nsf.gov/bio

Purpose To provide financial assistance for postdoctoral research training to minority scientists in the biological, social, economic, and behavioral sciences.

Eligibility Eligible to apply are underrepresented minorities (African Americans, Hispanics, Native Pacific Islanders, and Native Americans) who are American citizens or permanent residents and will complete their doctorate within a year or have completed it within the previous 4 years but have not completed more than 2 years of postdoctoral support. They must be proposing research training that falls within the program areas of the National Science Foundation (NSF) Directorate for Biological Sciences or the Directorate for Social, Behavioral, and Economic Sciences to be conducted at any appropriate nonprofit U.S. or foreign institution (government laboratory, institution of higher education, national laboratory, or public or private research institute), but not at the same institution where the doctorate was obtained.

Financial data The program provides a stipend of $36,000 per year, an institutional allowance of $5,000 for partial reimbursement of indirect research costs (space, equipment, general purpose supplies, and fringe benefits), and a special allowance of $9,000 for direct research costs (scientific supplies, research-related travel, publication expenses, and other research-related costs).

Duration 2 years; applicants who propose to spend their 2-year tenure at a foreign institution may apply for a third year of support at an appropriate U.S. institution.

Special features Information on the programs from the Directorate for Social, Behavioral, and Economic Sciences is available at (703) 292-8763, E-mail: jperhoni@nsf.gov.

Number awarded Approximately 14 each year.

Deadline November of each year.

[142]
MPS DISTINGUISHED INTERNATIONAL POSTDOCTORAL RESEARCH FELLOWSHIPS

National Science Foundation
Directorate for Mathematical and Physical Sciences
Attn: Division of Mathematical Sciences
4201 Wilson Boulevard, Room 1025
Arlington, VA 22230
(703) 292-8104   TDD: (703) 292-5090
E-mail: lwalling@nsf.gov
Web site: www.nsf.gov/mps.general.htm

Purpose To provide funding to recent doctoral recipients in mathematical and physical sciences (MPS) who are interested in conducting research abroad.

Eligibility This program is open to U.S. citizens, nationals, and permanent residents who completed a Ph.D. in a mathematical or physical science during the previous year. Applicants must be interested in establishing international collaborations in their field by conducting research at a foreign institution of higher education; industrial research institution or laboratory; government research institute, laboratory, or center; or nonprofit research organization. Women, underrepresented minorities, and persons with disabilities are strongly encouraged to apply.

Financial data Grants up to $100,000 per year are available. Funding is provided to cover round-trip airfare to the foreign site and for other research-related travel, up to $300 for excess baggage, a living allowance of up to $4,500 per month, dependent allowances of up to $150 per month, health insurance at $50 per month for awardee and each dependent, airfare for return visits to the United States (if justified by the proposal), in-country travel (if justified by the proposal), materials and supplies (if justified by the proposal), language training (if justified by the proposal), other travel required to carry out the research project, and other research-related costs. Proposals submitted through the applicant's home institution may request up to $5,000 for institutional administrative costs.

Duration Up to 24 months.

Special features Awardees are expected to work full time on their research projects. Information is also available from the Division of Chemistry, (703) 292-4948, E-mail: jstevens@nsf.gov; Division of Astronomical Sciences, (703) 292-4895, E-mail: efriel@nsf.gov; Division of Materials Research, (703) 292-4916, E-mail: lhaworth@nsf.gov; and Division of Physics, (703) 292-7378, E-mail: jwlightb@nsf.gov.

Limitations Support is not provided for teaching, writing textbooks, preparation of prior results for publication, or similar activities.

Number awarded Up to 20 each year.

Deadline October of each year.

[143]
MYRNA F. BERNATH RESEARCH FELLOWSHIPS

Society for Historians of American Foreign Relations
National Office
c/o Department of History
Wright State University
Dayton, OH 45435
(937) 873-3110
Web site: www.ohiou.edu/~shafr/shafr.htm

Purpose To provide funding to women who wish to conduct research on foreign relations.

Eligibility This program is open to American women who wish to conduct historically-based research abroad or to women from other countries who wish to conduct research in the United States. The proposed study should focus on U.S. foreign relations, transnational history, international history, peace studies, cultural interchange, or defense or strategic studies. Preference is given to applications from graduate students and recent Ph.D.s.

Financial data The grant is $2,500.

Duration These awards are presented biennially.

Special features Further information is available from Katherine Sibley, St. Joseph's University, Department of History, 5600 City Avenue, Philadelphia, PA 19131.

Number awarded 2 each odd-numbered year.

Deadline November of each even-numbered year.

[144]
NASA GRADUATE STUDENT RESEARCHERS PROGRAM

National Aeronautics and Space Administration
Attn: Office of Human Resources and Education
Code FE
Headquarters Room 4D45
Washington, DC 20546-0001
(202) 358-1524   Fax: (202) 358-3048
E-mail: gsrp@hq.nasa.gov
Web site: university.gsfc.nasa.gov/GSRP/GSRP.html

Purpose To support graduate research in aeronautics, space science, space applications, and space technology.

Eligibility Full-time students enrolled or planning to enroll in an accredited graduate program at a U.S. college or university are eligible for these awards. They must be citizens of the United States, sponsored by a faculty advisor or department chair, and interested in conducting research in space sciences at their home university, individual field centers of the National Aeronautics and Space Administration (NASA), the Jet Propulsion Laboratory, or abroad (if essential to the research project). Selection is based on academic qualifications, quality of the proposed research and its relevance to NASA's program, the student's proposed utilization of center research facilities (except for NASA headquarters), and ability of the student to accomplish the defined research. Students from traditionally underrepresented groups (African Americans, Native Americans, Alaskan Natives, Mexican Americans, Puerto Ricans, Native Pacific Islanders, women, and persons with disabilities) are strongly urged to apply.

Financial data In addition to a $16,000 student stipend, an allowance of $6,000 ($3,000 for the student and $3,000 for the university) may be requested to cover tuition costs or to provide a per diem and travel allowance for the student and faculty advisor.

Duration 1 year; may be renewed for up to 2 additional years.

Special features This program was established in 1980. Awards for NASA Headquarters are sponsored by the Office of Space Science (OSS), the Office of Life and Microgravity Sciences and Applications (OLMSA), and the Office of Earth Science (OES). The areas of interest include structure/evolution of the universe, origins/planetary systems, solar system exploration, sun-earth connection, information systems, microgravity science and applications, life sciences, and earth sciences. Fellows selected by NASA Headquarters conduct research at their respective universities. Other awards are distributed through NASA field centers, each of which has its own research agenda and facilities. These centers include Ames Research Center (Moffett Field, California), Hugh L. Dryden Flight Research Facility (Edwards, California), Goddard Space Flight Center (Greenbelt, Maryland), Jet Propulsion Laboratory (Pasadena, California), Lyndon B. Johnson Space Center (Houston, Texas), John F. Kennedy Space Center (Cape Canaveral, Florida), Langley Research Center (Hampton, Virginia), Lewis Research Center (Cleveland, Ohio), George C. Marshall Space Flight Center (Huntsville, Alabama), and John C. Stennis Space Center (Stennis Space Center, Mississippi). Fellows spend some period of time in residence at the center, taking advantage of the unique research facilities of the installation and working with center personnel. Travel outside the United States is allowed if it is essential to the research effort and charged to a grant.

Number awarded 90 new awards each year; approximately 40 of the awards are administered through NASA Headquarters and the remainder are distributed through NASA's field centers. To date, more than 1,200 students have been supported under this program.

Deadline January of each year.

[145]
NATIONAL CANCER INSTITUTE SHORT-TERM SCIENTIST EXCHANGE PROGRAM

National Cancer Institute
Attn: Office of International Affairs
6130 Executive Boulevard, Suite 100
Bethesda, MD 20892-7301
(301) 496-4761   Fax: (301) 496-3954
E-mail: nc6@cu.nih.gov
Web site: www.nci.nih.gov

Purpose To support collaborative activities between established U.S. and foreign scientists engaged in cancer research through the National Cancer Institute (NCI).

Eligibility Within the United States, principal investigators on research projects supported by the institute in either the intramural or extramural research programs may apply to travel to a foreign site as an exchangee or to serve as the sponsor of a foreign scientist to come to this country. Potential American exchangees must have a minimum of 3 years of postdoctoral experience in cancer research, must have an invitation from a qualified foreign sponsor, and must include a statement from the director of their institution verifying that they have a permanent position and will continue to receive full salary during the scientific exchange. Foreign sponsors must be established scientists recognized in the international peer reviewed literature. Candidates to be exchangees from foreign countries must be proficient in spoken and written English; preference is given to applicants from developing countries.

Financial data For American scientists, the United States pays transportation costs to and from the host country, and the host country pays all in-country expenses. For foreign visitors to the United States, a foreign source pays for the airfare and this program provides (through a contractor) a non-taxable subsistence allowance of the monthly equivalent of $25,000 per year. Cost sharing of the subsistence allowance by the sponsoring American laboratory is required.

Duration 1 week to 6 months.

Deadline Applications may be submitted at any time.

[146]
NATIONAL GEOGRAPHIC SOCIETY GRANTS FOR FIELD-BASED SCIENTIFIC RESEARCH

National Geographic Society
Attn: Committee for Research and Exploration
1145 17th Street, N.W.
Washington, DC 20036-4688
(202) 862-5200   Fax: (202) 862-5270
Web site: www.nationalgeographic.com

Purpose To support scientific research and exploration worldwide by providing grants for basic, original field research.

Eligibility Investigators may be citizens of any country who hold an advanced degree (Ph.D. or equivalent) and affiliation with institutions of higher learning or other scientific or educational organizations or museums. Independent researchers and Ph.D. candidates may also apply, but they are less likely to receive a grant. Normally, applicants should have published at least 3 articles in peer-reviewed scientific journals. The proposed research must have both a geographical dimension and relevance to other fields, including anthropology, archaeology, astronomy, biology, botany, geography, geology, oceanography, paleontology, zoology, or multi-disciplinary efforts of an environmental nature. Proposals must be for field research, not for laboratory work or archival research. Applicants planning work in foreign countries should include at least 1 local collaborator as part of their research team.

Financial data Grants range from $15,000 to $20,000 per year. Funds must be used for transportation, supplies, and daily subsistence; payment of overhead, indirect expenses, fringe benefits, or salaries is not allowed.

Number awarded Varies each year; recently, 241 grants were authorized.

Deadline Pre-proposals may be submitted at any time.

[147]
NATIONAL INSTITUTES OF HEALTH INDIVIDUAL RESEARCH PROJECT GRANTS

National Institutes of Health
Division of Extramural Outreach and Information
  Resources
Attn: GrantsInfo
6701 Rockledge Drive, Suite 6095
Bethesda, MD 20892-7910
(301) 435-0714   Fax: (301) 480-8443
E-mail: GrantsInfo@nih.gov
Web site: www.nih.gov

Purpose To support biomedical and behavioral research that will improve human health in areas of interest to the National Institutes of Health (NIH).

Eligibility Investigators at nonprofit and for-profit public and private organizations, such as universities, colleges, hospitals, laboratories, units of state and local governments, and eligible agencies of the federal government may apply for these research grants. Applications are accepted for health-related research and development in all areas within the scope of the institutes' mission and by all component institutes and centers. Specific subjects of research are announced periodically either as Program Announcements (PAs) for ongoing research or as Requests for Applications (RFAs) for specific 1-time research projects. Usually, the research is to be conducted within the United States, but research projects conducted at foreign sites may be proposed if they meet the following conditions: 1) have specific relevance to the institutes and have the potential for significantly advancing the health sciences in the United States; 2) present special opportunities for further research through the use of unusual talents, resources, populations, or environmental conditions; and 3) have a rating that falls within the normally established payline. For all projects, racial/ethnic minority individuals, women, and persons with disabilities are particularly encouraged to apply as principal investigators.

Financial data The level of funding depends on the scope of the proposed research. Funds may be used for supplies, equipment, personnel, and travel. Foreign institutions do not receive support for administrative costs associated with the research.

Duration 1 year or longer.

Special features These grants are offered by 21 of NIH's component institutes. The most meritorious first-time recipients of these awards who are new investigators (with no more than five years of research experience since completion of postdoctoral training) are also nominated to receive Presidential Early Career Awards for Scientists and Engineers.

Deadline January, May, or September of each year.

[148]
NATIONAL RESEARCH SERVICE AWARD SENIOR FELLOWSHIPS

National Institutes of Health
Division of Extramural Outreach and Information Resources
Attn: GrantsInfo
6701 Rockledge Drive, Suite 6095
Bethesda, MD 20892-7910
(301) 435-0714   Fax: (301) 480-8443
E-mail: GrantsInfo@nih.gov
Web site: www.nih.gov

Purpose To provide mentored research training for experienced scientists who wish to make major changes in the direction of their research careers.

Eligibility Applications for this program may be submitted on behalf of the candidates by a sponsoring institution, which may be private (profit or nonprofit) or public, including a federal laboratory. Individuals requesting foreign-site training must justify the particular suitability of the foreign site, based on the nature of the facilities and/or training opportunity, rather than a domestic institution. Only in cases where there are clear scientific advantages will foreign training be supported. Candidates must have received a Ph.D., D.D.S., D.M.D., or equivalent degree from an accredited domestic or foreign institution and must have had at least 7 subsequent years of relevant research experience. Applications from minorities and women are particularly encouraged.

Financial data Salaries are determined individually, based on the salary or remuneration which the individual would have received from the home institution, but may not exceed $41,268 per year. Institutional allowances for tuition, fees, individual health insurance, research supplies, equipment, travel to scientific meetings, and related items are up to $4,000 for fellows at nonfederal, nonprofit, and foreign sponsoring institutions and $3,000 for fellows at for-profit institutions or federal laboratories. The initial 12 months of postdoctoral support carries a service payback requirement, which can be fulfilled by continued training under the award or by engaging in other health-related research training, health-related research, or health-related teaching. Fellows who fail to fulfill the payback requirement of 1 month of acceptable service for each month of the initial 12 months of support received must repay all funds received with interest.

Duration 5 years; nonrenewable.

Special features This program is offered by 8 components of the National Institutes of Health: the National Institute on Aging, the National Institute on Alcohol Abuse and Alcoholism, the National Institute of Allergy and Infectious Diseases, the National Institute of Arthritis and Musculoskeletal and Skin Diseases, the National Cancer Institute, the National Institute of Child Health and Human Development, the National Institute on Deafness and Other Communication Disorders, and the National Institute of Dental and Craniofacial Research.

Number awarded Varies each year.

Deadline April, August, or December of each year.

[149]
NATIONAL RESEARCH SERVICE AWARDS FOR INDIVIDUAL POSTDOCTORAL FELLOWS

National Institutes of Health
Division of Extramural Outreach and Information Resources
Attn: GrantsInfo
6701 Rockledge Drive, Suite 6095
Bethesda, MD 20892-7910
(301) 435-0714   Fax: (301) 480-8443
E-mail: GrantsInfo@nih.gov
Web site: www.nih.gov

Purpose To provide funding for postdoctoral biomedical or behavioral research training.

Eligibility Applicants must 1) be U.S. citizens or permanent residents; 2) have received a Ph.D., M.D., D.O., D.D.S., D.V.M., or equivalent doctoral degree from an accredited domestic or foreign institution; 3) be interested in conducting biomedical or behavioral research; and 4) have arranged for appointment to an appropriate institution and acceptance by a sponsor who will supervise the training and research experience. The institution may be private (nonprofit or for-profit) or public, including a federal laboratory. If a foreign institution is selected as the research training site, applicants must explain the reasons for the choice. Applications are especially encouraged from women, minorities, individuals with disabilities, and clinicians who wish to become researchers.

Financial data The award provides an annual stipend based on the number of years of postdoctoral experience, ranging from $26,256 for less than 1 year to $41,268 for 7 or more years. For fellows sponsored by domestic nonfederal institutions, the stipend is paid through the sponsoring institution; for fellows sponsored by federal or foreign institutions, the monthly stipend is paid directly to the fellow. Institutions also receive an allowance to help defray such awardee expenses as self-only health insurance, research supplies, equipment, travel to scientific meetings, and related items; the allowance is $4,000 per 12-month period for fellows at nonfederal, nonprofit, and foreign institutions and $3,000 per 12-month period at federal laboratories and for-profit institutions. In addition, tuition and fees are reimbursed at a rate of 100 percent up to $2,000 and 60 percent for costs above $2,000. Awards for training at a foreign site include economy or coach round-trip airfare for the fellow only; no allowance is provided for dependents. The initial 12 months of National Research Service Award postdoctoral support carries a service payback requirement, which can be fulfilled by continued training under the award or by engaging in other health-related research training, health-related research, or health-related teaching. Fellows who fail to fulfill the payback requirement of 1 month of acceptable service for each month of the initial 12 months of support received must repay all funds received with interest.

Duration Up to 3 years.

Special features This award is offered by all funding Institutes and Centers of the National Institutes of Health (NIH) as part of the National Research Service Award (NRSA) program, originally established in 1974.

Number awarded Varies each year; recently, 793 awards were made through this program.

Deadline April, August, or December of each year.

[150]
NATIONAL SCIENCE FOUNDATION COOPERATIVE RESEARCH PROJECTS

National Science Foundation
Directorate for Social, Behavioral, and Economic Sciences
Attn: Division of International Programs
4201 Wilson Boulevard
Arlington, VA 22230
(703) 292-8710 (800) 437-7408
TDD: (703) 292-5090
Web site: www.nsf.gov/sbe/int/start.htm

Purpose To support the work of U.S. scientists and engineers cooperating on research and related activities with engineers in other countries

Eligibility Researchers in fields supported by the National Science Foundation (NSF) may apply for support for international collaborations, carried out either in the United States or abroad. The proposed project should initiate international collaboration with foreign counterparts or promote new types of activities with established international partners. Applicants are encouraged to include students and junior researchers as participants in the project. Recent Ph.D., junior faculty, women, minority, and disabled scientists and engineers are especially encouraged to apply. Selection is based on research objectives and methodology; description of cooperative arrangement/division of labor/complementary expertise; scientific significance of the host country/counterpart institution; expertise of the foreign partner; history of collaborative efforts with the foreign counterpart (if any); and expected scientific, engineering, and mutual international benefits to be derived from the project.

Financial data Support is provided for the international travel and associated living and research costs for the U.S. participant at the foreign site. Publication and communication charges and minor pieces of equipment may also be provided. If students and junior researchers are included in the project, the program provides additional support for their international travel and associated living and research costs. For projects with developing countries or with countries whose currency is not convertible, support may sometimes be provided for the travel and living costs for the foreign collaborator to visit the United States.

Duration 2 or 3 years.

Limitations Activities typically require approval of both NSF and the counterpart agency in the participating country before funding is made by either country. For a list of counterpart agencies in various other countries, write to the address above.

Deadline Applications may be submitted at any time, but they must be received at least 10 months prior to the proposed beginning of the cooperative research.

[151]
NATIONAL SCIENCE FOUNDATION DISSERTATION ENHANCEMENT AWARDS

National Science Foundation
Directorate for Social, Behavioral, and Economic Sciences
Attn: Division of International Programs
4201 Wilson Boulevard
Arlington, VA 22230
(703) 292-8710 TDD: (703) 292-5090
Web site: www.nsf.gov/sbe/int/start.htm

Purpose To provide support to U.S. doctoral students in science and engineering who wish to conduct research abroad in collaboration with host country institutions.

Eligibility This program is open to U.S. citizens and permanent residents enrolled in science and engineering Ph.D. programs at U.S. institutions. Students from developing countries who are enrolled in Ph.D. programs at U.S. institutions may also apply, but preference is given to U.S. citizens and permanent residents. Proposals must be submitted through regular university channels by the dissertation advisor on behalf of the graduate student. A proposal may be submitted while the student is completing other requirements for the doctorate. Applicants must be proposing to work in close cooperation with a host country institution and investigator. Selection is based on research objectives and methodology; description of cooperative arrangement/division of labor/complementary expertise; scientific significance of the host country/counterpart institution; a description of the role of the foreign institution/country in the applicant's career objectives and tentative schedule of activities during the stay abroad; and expected scientific, engineering, and mutual international benefits to be derived from the project.

Financial data Grants cover international travel and associated living costs. Support may also be provided for materials and supplies, survey fees, field assistants, specialized research equipment, and other expenses when justified as necessary for the conduct of the dissertation research.

Duration Varies, depending upon the scope of the funded project.

Limitations No support is provided for teaching, writing textbooks, preparation of prior research results for publication, or similar activities.

Deadline Applications may be submitted at any time, but they must be received at least 6 months prior to the proposed date of departure.

[152]
NATIONAL SCIENCE FOUNDATION INTERNATIONAL PLANNING VISITS

National Science Foundation
Directorate for Social, Behavioral, and Economic Sciences
Attn: Division of International Programs
4201 Wilson Boulevard
Arlington, VA 22230
(703) 292-8710 (800) 437-7408
TDD: (703) 292-5090
Web site: www.nsf.gov/sbe/int/start.htm

Purpose To provide funding to American scholars who are interested in consulting with prospective foreign partners to finalize plans for a cooperative activity eligible for support from the National Science Foundation (NSF).

Eligibility This program is open to science and engineering researchers interested in consulting with prospective foreign partners. Applicants must submit 1) a description of the proposed research project and progress to date in planning the joint activity; 2) actions needed to finalize the project plan that cannot be accomplished through communications at a distance; and 3) tentative schedule of activities. Evidence of substantive prior communication and preparation is required.

Financial data Grants provide round-trip international economy airfare on U.S. flag carriers, associated living costs, and incidental expenses at the foreign site.

Duration From 1 to 2 weeks.

Limitations Applicants should consult with the appropriate NSF program officer before submitting a proposal.

Number awarded Varies each year.

Deadline Applications may be submitted at any time, but they must be received at least 4 months prior to the proposed visit.

[153]
NATIONAL SCIENCE FOUNDATION JOINT SEMINARS AND WORKSHOPS

National Science Foundation
Directorate for Social, Behavioral, and Economic Sciences
Attn: Division of International Programs
4201 Wilson Boulevard
Arlington, VA 22230
(703) 292-8710   (800) 437-7408
TDD: (703) 292-5090
Web site: www.nsf.gov/sbe/int/start.htm

Purpose To allow U.S. and foreign counterpart investigators to identify common priorities in specific science and engineering research areas and to begin preparation of cooperative research proposals.

Eligibility U.S. scientists and engineers may organize a seminar or workshop in cooperation with a foreign scholar, to be held either in the United States or overseas. Applications for funding should describe the seminar or workshop topic and explain its importance for the respective field of science or engineering, for science and engineering education, or for international science policy-relevant research. Workshops and seminars normally involve a total of 25 to 35 participants. The program supports 10 to 15 U.S. participants, with no more than 2 from the same U.S. institution. Foreign participants may come from more than 1 country. The pool of U.S. participants should include junior researchers, women and members of underrepresented groups, and/or graduate and undergraduate students. Participant diversity is considered in the selection process.

Financial data In general, grants provide support for the airfare (domestic or international depending on site) for the U.S. participants. As justified in the proposal, U.S. co-organizers may also request organizational fees and publication charges.

Deadline Proposals may be submitted at any time, but they must be received at least 10 months prior to the scheduled workshop or seminar.

[154]
NEDO INTERNATIONAL JOINT RESEARCH PROGRAM

New Energy and Industrial Technology Development Organization
Industrial Technology Department
Attn: International Joint Research Program
Sunshine 60 Building, 29F
3-1-1, Higashi-Ikebukuro, Toshima-ku
Tokyo 170-6028
Japan
81 3 3987 9357   Fax: 81 3 5952 0082
E-mail: nedogrant@nedo.go.jp
Web site: www.nedo.go.jp

Purpose To promote research in any country on materials sciences and topics related to energy and the environment.

Eligibility Applications are accepted from research teams, whose members select 1 of their group to serve as research coordinator (to take the central role in planning and conducting the research). Each team must consist of at least 4 researchers, each of whom is well qualified, actively engaged in scientific research, and associated with a research organization; the researchers must include 2 or more different nationalities, and their research organizations must be located in 2 or more countries. Research may be conducted anywhere, but 1 member of the team must be designated as the administrative coordinator, and that member must be affiliated with a research organization in Japan. Specific research areas have changed slightly from year to year but have generally focused on the areas of materials, energy, international standard development, and global environment.

Financial data The maximum annual grants are 24 million yen for research related to materials, 30 million yen for energy, 20 million for international standard development, and 30 million for global environment. Funds are provided for facilities and equipment expenses, travel expenses, remuneration for services provided by persons other than members of the team, materials and supplies, conferences, and certain miscellaneous expenses related to preparing the results of the research for publication. No funds are available to pay the wages of members of the team.

Duration 1 year; may be renewed for up to 2 additional years.

Special features The New Energy and Industrial Technology Development Organization (NEDO) is a semi-governmental agency established in October 1980 and supervised by the Japanese Ministry of International Trade and Industry. The global environment awards are sponsored jointly with the Research Institute of Innovative Technology for the Earth (RITE).

Limitations Proposals for research to develop military technology or on topics unrelated to industrial technology are not accepted.

Number awarded Varies each year; recently, 7 teams received support: 5 to conduct research on materials, 1 on international standard development, and 1 on global environment. No awards in the field of energy were made in the most recent round of grants.

Deadline March of each year.

[155]
NEOTROPICAL BIRD CLUB CONSERVATION AWARDS

Neotropical Bird Club
c/o The Lodge
Sandy
Bedsfordshire SG19 2DL
United Kingdom
E-mail: awards@neotropicalbirdclub.org
Web site: www.neotropicalbirdclub.org/club/awrdform.html

Purpose To provide funding to scholars interested in conducting ornithological research related to birds in tropical areas.

Eligibility This program is open to scholars interested in engaging in tropical bird conservation work or research that may be of conservation benefit. Applicants must provide a 100-word description of the objectives of the proposal; a 250-word abstract on habitats and threatened, near-threatened, and endemic species involved; the names, ages, and relevant experience of project team members; a budget; the expected output; and additional funding sources. Priority is given to projects carried out by nationals from within the region.

Financial data Grants range from $500 to $1,000.

Limitations Recipients must agree not to collect any bird specimens.

Number awarded Varies each year.

[156]
NEPORANY RESEARCH AND TEACHING FELLOWSHIP

Canadian Institute of Ukrainian Studies
c/o University of Alberta
Athabasca Hall, Room 352
Edmonton, Alberta T6G 2E8
Canada
(780) 492-2972   Fax: (780) 492-4967
E-mail: cius@ualberta.ca
Web site: www.ualberta.ca/~cius/cius-grants.htm

Purpose To provide funding to scholars from any country who are interested in teaching and conducting research in Ukrainian studies.

Eligibility This program is open to scholars from any country who hold a doctorate or have equivalent professional experience in Ukrainian studies. Applicants must submit a 3- to 5-page research proposal, 2 letters of recommendation, information on the course to be taught at the host institution, and a letter of support from the host institution indicating how the scholar's stay and teaching will benefit the development of Ukrainian studies.

Financial data The maximum stipend is $C20,000.

Duration 1 academic term (i.e., half of the academic year); may be extended if the fellow is successful in receiving supplemental funding from other sources.

Special features Funds for this program are supplied by the Osyp and Josaphat Neporany Educational Fund. The fellowship is tenable at any university in the world with research facilities at which the fellow's academic Ukrainian studies specialty may be pursued and the fellow enabled to teach a course related to the specialty.

Number awarded 1 each year.

Deadline February of each year.

[157]
NEW CENTURY SCHOLARS PROGRAM

Council for International Exchange of Scholars
3007 Tilden Street, N.W., Suite 5L
Washington, DC 20008-3009
(202) 686-6252   Fax: (202) 362-3442
E-mail: NCS@cies.iie.org
Web site: www.iie.org/cies

Purpose To provide funding to American and foreign scholars and professionals interested in conducting collaborative research in other countries.

Eligibility This program is open to both professional and academic candidates. For academic applicants, a Ph.D. or equivalent terminal degree in a relevant field is required. For applicants in the professional fields, the appropriate terminal degree in a relevant field is required. U.S. applicants must have U.S. citizenship and be residing in the United States. Non-U.S. applicants must be citizens of the country from which they are applying and residing in that country. Relevant disciplines include, but are not limited to, history, law, philosophy, sociology, political science, anthropology, religious studies, psychology, economics, and geography. Applicants must be interested in participating in a program that includes a period of research in the United States or abroad; continued interaction and networking focusing, not only on individual research projects, but on mutually agreed upon group objectives as well; an in-person orientation at the program's beginning; an electronic seminar at midpoint; and a plenary seminar in the Washington, D.C. area at the end of the program year. Selection is based on activity in the academic, public, or private sector; demonstrated outstanding qualifications; and a distinguished record of experience, research, and accomplishment in an area clearly related to the annual theme.

Financial data The stipend is $40,000. Travel and per diem for the final plenary seminar and program orientation are also provided.

Duration 1 year, including 2 to 6 months devoted to furthering research and investigating comparative approaches by interacting with colleagues abroad or in the United States. The concluding plenary session lasts 2 weeks.

Special features This program was first offered for 2002. Each year, a theme is established, around which all research should revolve. A recent theme was "Addressing Sectarian, Ethnic and Cultural Conflict within and across National Borders." Participants have an opportunity to maintain contact and exchange ideas throughout the program year.

Number awarded Approximately 25 to 30 each year. Approximately one-third of the participants are U.S. scholars and the remaining two-thirds are visiting scholars from outside the United States.

Deadline November of each year.

[158]
NORWICH JUBILEE ESPERANTO FOUNDATION AWARDS

Norwich Jubilee Esperanto Foundation
c/o Secretary
37 Granville Court
Cheney Lane
Oxford OX3 0HS
England
44 1865 245509

Purpose To promote international understanding by awarding travelships to students of Esperanto.
Eligibility Applicants must be traveling to meet Esperantists in other countries or on an approved individual journey abroad. They must be under 25 years of age, in need of financial aid, and fluent in Esperanto. Proof of competence may be required (in the form of a tape recording or an oral test).
Financial data The value of these awards varies, up to 1,000 pounds, depending on the length of time abroad and the needs of the candidates. Organizers of parties traveling to take part in an Esperanto activity (e.g., a children's congress or a students' conference) can apply for per capita aid.
Duration Varies, depending upon the travel plans of the recipient.
Limitations Part of the monetary award is withheld until the recipient submits a report of the travel results (this should be within 1 month of returning home). Funds can be used to cover travel expenses within a country but cannot be used to travel to a country. American recipients must use their grants to come to the British Isles.
Number awarded Varies each year.
Deadline Travel requests may be submitted at any time.

[159]
NOVARTIS FOUNDATION SYMPOSIUM BURSARIES

Novartis Foundation
Attn: Bursary Scheme Administrator
41 Portland Place
London W1N 4BN
England
44 20 7636 9456   Fax: 44 20 7436 2840
E-mail: bursary@novartisfound.org.uk
Web site: www.novartisfound.org.uk

Purpose To provide financial assistance to scientists from any country who are interested in attending symposia in England and then conducting research anywhere in the world.
Eligibility Scientists between the ages of 23 and 35 from any country are eligible to apply if they are interested in conducting medical, chemical, or biological research and attending related international symposia at the Novartis Foundation in London. Applicants must be actively engaged in research on the specific topic of the symposium they propose to attend.
Financial data The bursary covers all travel expenses incurred in attending the symposium and visiting the host laboratory afterwards; bed and breakfast accommodations and an additional allowance for meals during the meeting itself; and board and lodging during the visit to the host laboratory.

Duration Up to 3 months, including travel, attendance at a Novartis Foundation symposium in London, and 4 to 12 weeks in the laboratory of 1 of the participants in any country.
Special features Advertisements appear every 3 to 6 months in *Nature* and other scientific journals and announce the specific topics of projected symposia. The sponsor of this program was formerly the Ciba Foundation.
Number awarded Up to 8 each year.
Deadline June or November of each year.

[160]
NOVARTIS TRANSLATIONAL CANCER RESEARCH FELLOWSHIPS

International Union against Cancer
3 rue du Conseil-Général
CH-1205 Geneva
Switzerland
41 22 809 1840   Fax: 41 22 809 1810
E-mail: fellows@uicc.org
Web site: www.uicc.org

Purpose To fund cancer investigators from any country who are interested in conducting research that bridges from basic, experimental, and applied research into clinical applications.
Eligibility Eligible to apply are appropriately qualified investigators from any country who are actively engaged in cancer research on the staff of a research laboratory, institution, teaching hospital, university, or similar establishment. Applicants must be interested in translating basic, experimental, and applied research insights into their clinical applications in the form of new drugs and treatments, and of vaccines and other effective prevention or intervention strategies. Their proposed research must be conducted in another country. Selection is based on the innovativeness of the approach; the project's scientific excellence; the professional background, experience, and potential of the candidate; and the commitment of an enduring collaboration between the home and host institutes.
Financial data The stipend is $55,000.
Duration 12 months.
Special features This program, funded by Novartis (Switzerland), began in 1998.
Number awarded 1 each year.
Deadline November of each year.

[161]
NZFGW DAPHNE PURVES GRANTS

International Federation of University Women
8 rue de l'Ancien-Port
CH-1201 Geneva
Switzerland
41 22 731 2380   Fax: 41 22 738 0440
E-mail: info@ifuw.org
Web site: www.ifuw.org

Purpose To enable university women to undertake a program of study or original research in another country.
Eligibility An applicant must be a member of 1 of the 67 national federations or associations affiliated with the International Federation of University Women (IFUW) or, if she resides in a country that does not yet have an IFUW affiliate, an inde-

pendent member of the IFUW. She must have completed at least 1 year of graduate study and should propose to continue her study or research in a country other than where she received her education or in which she habitually resides.

Financial data The stipend ranges from 3,000 to 6,000 Swiss francs.

Duration Stipends are intended to cover at least 8 months of work and should be used within 9 months from the date of the award.

Special features This program is sponsored by the New Zealand Federation of Graduate Women (NZFGW). American applicants should submit their applications to the American Association of University Women (AAUW), 1111 16th Street, N.W., Washington, DC 20036-4873, (202) 785-7700, (800) 821-4364.

Limitations Fellowships are not awarded for the first year of a doctoral program.

Number awarded 1 each even-numbered year.

Deadline Applications, whether submitted through a national affiliate (such as the AAUW) or by an independent member, must reach IFUW headquarters before the end of October in odd-numbered years. National affiliates set earlier deadlines; for the AAUW, this is the end of September.

[162]
OCLC/ALISE LIBRARY AND INFORMATION SCIENCE RESEARCH GRANTS

Association for Library and Information Science Education
11250 Roger Bacon Drive, Suite 8
Reston, VA 20190-5202
(703) 234-4146   Fax: (703) 435-4390
Web site: www.alise.org

Purpose To provide funding for research to faculty at schools of library and information science.

Eligibility This program is open to faculty at schools of library and information science who are interested in conducting a research project. The sponsors encourage international proposals and collaborative projects. Priority is given to junior faculty and applicants who have not previously received funds from the program. Selection is based on the clarity of the project and its research objectives, the review of the literature, the appropriateness of the methodology, the significance of the research, and the availability of resources.

Financial data Grants up to $10,000 are available. Funds may be applied to the costs of release time from teaching for the principal investigator, research assistants, project-related travel, equipment necessary for the research, and other research expenses. Staff training, general operating or overhead expenses, and other indirect costs are not funded.

Duration The project should be completed within 1 year, beginning in January.

Special features This program is administered by the Association for Library and Information Science Education (ALISE) and funded by Online Computer Library Center (OCLC), Office of Research, 6565 Frantz Road, Dublin, OH 43017-3395, (614) 764-6000, ext. 6487.

Number awarded 1 or more each year.

Deadline August of each year.

[163]
O'HARA-JOHNSON NP INTERNATIONAL PROJECT GRANT

American Academy of Nurse Practitioners
Attn: AANP Foundation
P.O. Box 10729
Glendale, AZ 85318-0729
(623) 376-9467   Fax: (623) 376-0369
E-mail: foundation@aanp.org
Web site: www.aanp.org

Purpose To provide funding to members of the American Academy of Nurse Practitioners (AANP) who wish to develop a community-based health care project in a foreign country.

Eligibility This program is open to members of the academy who are currently licensed, practicing nurse practitioners (NPs) in the United States. Applicants must be interested in funding an international project designed and administered by NPs providing 1) NP-related health care in a specified community located outside the United States, and/or 2) health care education to a specified community/population located outside the United States. Health care or health care education must be administered by the NPs named in the grant proposal.

Financial data The grant is $1,350.

Duration 1 year.

Limitations There is a $10 application fee.

Number awarded 1 each year.

Deadline October of each year.

[164]
OTIS AND VELMA DAVIS DOZIER ARTIST TRAVEL GRANTS

Dallas Museum of Art
Attn: Awards to Artists
1717 North Harwood
Dallas, TX 75201
(214) 922-1334   Fax: (214) 720-0862

Purpose To support the foreign and domestic travel of artists in Texas.

Eligibility To be eligible, artists must be at least 30 years of age, have lived in Texas for at least the last 3 years, be practicing professionals, be current Texas residents, and be interested in pursuing travel in the United States or abroad to expand their artistic horizons. Applicants must submit 6 examples of recent work on 35mm slides.

Financial data Up to $6,000; the exact amount will depend upon the scope of the proposed travel and the financial needs of the recipient.

Duration The grants are awarded annually.

Number awarded 1 or more each year.

Deadline February of each year.

[165]
PAUL MELLON FELLOWSHIP

National Gallery of Art
Attn: Center for Advanced Study in the Visual Arts
Sixth Street and Constitution Avenue, N.W.
Washington, DC 20565
(202) 842-6482 Fax: (202) 842-6733
TDD: (202) 842-6176 E-mail: advstudy@nga.gov
Web site: www.nga.gov/resources/casvapre.htm

Purpose To provide financial assistance to doctoral candidates interested in conducting research here and abroad on the history, theory, and criticism of Western art, architecture, and urbanism.

Eligibility Applicants must be interested in conducting research on the history, theory, and criticism of Western art, architecture, and urbanism. They must have completed their residence requirements and course work for the Ph.D. as well as general or preliminary examinations before the date of application. In addition, they must know 2 foreign languages related to the topic of the dissertation and be U.S. citizens or enrolled in an American university. Application for this fellowship must be made through the chair of the student's graduate department of art history or other appropriate department; the chair should act as a sponsor for the applicant. Departments must limit their nominations to 1 candidate. Nominees should be interested in conducting research abroad and then working in Washington, D.C. Finalists are invited to Washington during February for interviews.

Financial data The stipend is $16,000 per year.

Duration 3 years: 2 years abroad conducting research and 1 year in residence at the National Gallery of Art's Center for Advanced Study in the Visual Arts in Washington, D.C. to complete the dissertation. The fellowship begins in September and is not renewable.

Special features The fellowship is intended to allow a candidate of exceptional promise to develop expertise in a specific city, region, or locality abroad.

Number awarded 1 each year.

Deadline November of each year.

[166]
PEACE CORPS PROGRAM

Peace Corps
1111 20th Street, N.W.
Washington, DC 20526
(800) 424-8580 E-mail: dpinfo@peacecorps.gov
Web site: www.peacecorps.gov

Purpose To provide an opportunity for Americans to make a difference worldwide.

Eligibility Americans who are 18 years of age or older, are interested in working in a Peace Corps program in 1 of 90 countries worldwide, and are prepared to meet the demands of living abroad (primarily in underdeveloped or developing countries) are eligible to apply. Most assignments require a baccalaureate degree and some also require 3 to 5 years of related work experience. The most requested specialties from foreign countries are for agriculturalists; educators; health professionals; skilled trades professionals; environmental workers; businesspeople; and math, science, and engineering majors; college graduates with general liberal arts degrees experience the most competition, and they generally need to have some other work experience in order to be accepted.

Financial data During their term of service, volunteers receive a stipend (that varies by country) to cover the basic necessities of food, housing, and local transportation. Round-trip international transportation and medical and dental care are also provided. At the conclusion of their service, volunteers receive a "readjustment allowance" of $225 per month of service, up to a total of $6,075.

Duration 2 years; may be renewed.

Special features Academic credit programs are available.

Number awarded Varies each year.

Deadline Applications may be submitted at any time.

[167]
POPULATION COUNCIL POSTDOCTORAL TRAINING FELLOWSHIPS

Population Council
Attn: Fellowship Coordinator
One Dag Hammarskjold Plaza
New York, NY 10017
(212) 339-0671 Fax: (212) 755-6052
E-mail: ssfellowship@popcouncil.org
Web site: www.popcouncil.org/opportunities/socscifellowships.html

Purpose To provide funding for postdoctoral training or research in population studies (including demography and biostatistics).

Eligibility Awards are open to candidates who have a Ph.D. or equivalent degree and who wish to undertake postdoctoral training or research at an institution (anywhere in the world) other than where they received their Ph.D. degree. The field of study must be population studies or population in combination with a social science discipline, such as economics, sociology, anthropology, geography, or public health. Grants are made only to applicants whose proposals deal with the developing world. Awards are contingent upon admission to a training or research institution with a strong program in population studies, regardless of geographic location. Selection is based on academic excellence and prospective contribution to the population field. Awards are open to all qualified persons, but strong preference is given to applicants from developing countries who have a firm commitment to return home upon completion of their training programs.

Financial data Awards consist of a monthly stipend (based on type of fellowship and place of study), transportation expenses (for fellow only), and health insurance.

Duration Up to 1 year; nonrenewable.

Number awarded 3 or 4 each year.

Deadline December of each year.

[168]
POPULATION COUNCIL PREDOCTORAL TRAINING FELLOWSHIPS

Population Council
Attn: Fellowship Coordinator
One Dag Hammarskjold Plaza
New York, NY 10017
(212) 339-0671   Fax: (212) 755-6052
E-mail: ssfellowship@popcouncil.org
Web site:
www.popcouncil.org/opportunities/socscifellowships.html

Purpose To provide funding for doctoral research in population studies (including demography and biostatistics).

Eligibility Awards are open to candidates who have completed all course work requirements for the Ph.D. or an equivalent degree in 1 of the social sciences. Applicants may request support for either the dissertation field work or the dissertation writing period. The field of study must be population studies or population in combination with a social science discipline, such as economics, sociology, anthropology, geography, or public health. Grants are made only to applicants whose proposals deal with the developing world. Awards are contingent upon admission to a training or research institution with a strong program in population studies, regardless of geographic location. Selection is based on academic excellence and prospective contribution to the population field. Awards are open to all qualified persons, but strong preference is given to applicants from developing countries who have a firm commitment to return home upon completion of their research.

Financial data Awards consist of a monthly stipend (based on type of fellowship and place of research), tuition payments and related fees, transportation expenses (for fellow only), and health insurance.

Duration Up to 1 year; nonrenewable.

Number awarded Approximately 15 each year.

Deadline December of each year.

[169]
POSTDOCTORAL FELLOWSHIPS IN EAST EUROPEAN STUDIES

American Council of Learned Societies
Attn: Office of Fellowships and Grants
228 East 45th Street
New York, NY 10017-3398
(212) 697-1505   Fax: (212) 949-8058
E-mail: grants@acls.org
Web site: www.acls.org/eeguide.htm

Purpose To provide funding to postdoctorates interested in conducting original research, anywhere in the world (except eastern Europe), in the social sciences and humanities relating to eastern Europe.

Eligibility Applicants must be U.S. citizens or permanent residents who hold a Ph.D. degree or equivalent as demonstrated by professional experience and publications. Their field of study must be in the social sciences or humanities relating to Albania, Bulgaria, the Czech Republic, Estonia, Hungary, Latvia, Lithuania, Poland, Romania, Slovakia, or the successor states of Yugoslavia. Proposals dealing with Albania, Bulgaria, Romania, or the former Yugoslavia are especially encouraged. Comparative work considering more than 1 country of east Europe or relating east European societies to those of other parts of the world are also supported. All proposals should be for scholarly work, the product of which is to be disseminated in English. The fellowships are to be used for work outside east Europe, although short visits to the area may be proposed as part of a coherent program primarily based elsewhere. Selection is based on the scholarly merit of the proposal, its importance to the development of eastern European studies, and the scholarly potential, accomplishments, and financial need of the applicant. Applications are particularly invited from women and members of minority groups.

Financial data Up to $25,000 is provided as a stipend. Funds are intended primarily as salary replacement, but they may be used to supplement sabbatical salaries or awards from other sources.

Duration 6 to 12 consecutive months.

Special features This program is sponsored jointly by the American Council of Learned Societies, (ACLS) and the Social Science Research Council, funded by the U.S. Department of State under the Research and Training for Eastern Europe and the Independent States of the Former Soviet Union Act of 1983 (Title VIII) but administered by ACLS.

Number awarded Approximately 5 to 7 each year.

Deadline October of each year.

[170]
POSTDOCTORAL FELLOWSHIPS ON CONFLICT, PEACE AND SOCIAL TRANSFORMATIONS

Social Science Research Council
810 Seventh Avenue
New York, NY 10019
(212) 377-2700   Fax: (212) 377-2727
E-mail: gsc@ssrc.org
Web site: www.ssrc.org

Purpose To provide financial assistance to postdoctoral scholars interested in conducting research anywhere in the world on the causes and conditions of international conflict and insecurity.

Eligibility Applicants must 1) hold a Ph.D. degree or have equivalent research and teaching experience and 2) speak, read, and write English at a level that allows for intellectual exchange between fellows. The first half of the fellowship must be spent gaining work experience in a non-governmental, international, or multilateral organization directly involved in peace, international cooperation, or security issues. Applicants are encouraged to select a hosting organization that is based outside their country of residence but are not required to do so. The other half of the fellowship must be spent doing research on a topic directly related to or informed by that experience. Field research is encouraged and may be done anywhere that is appropriate to the research design. Topics of interest include, but are not limited to, the human security implications of human rights; inequality; religious, national, and ethnic revivalism; military affairs; weapons proliferation and arms control; peace-keeping and peace-building; the spread of disease; ecosystem degradation; international migration; international crime; trafficking in humans; food supplies; and global finance and trade. There are no citizenship, nationality, or residence requirements for this program. Women and residents of developing countries are encouraged to apply.

Financial data The amount of the grant depends on need, to a maximum of $38,000 per year. In addition, each fellow has a budget for research and institutional expenses.
Duration 12 to 18 months.
Number awarded Varies each year.
Deadline November of each year.

[171]
POSTDOCTORAL RESEARCH FELLOWSHIPS IN BIOLOGICAL INFORMATICS

National Science Foundation
Directorate for Biological Sciences
Attn: Division of Biological Infrastructure
4201 Wilson Boulevard, Room 615
Arlington, VA 22230
(703) 292-8470   TDD: (703) 292-5090
E-mail: ckimsey@nsf.gov
Web site: www.nsf.gov/bio

Purpose To provide opportunities for junior doctoral-level scientists to conduct research and acquire training either in the United States or abroad in biological fields that overlap with the informational, computational, mathematical, and statistical sciences.
Eligibility This program is open to persons who are citizens, nationals, or permanent residents of the United States at the time of application. Applicants must have earned a Ph.D. no earlier than 2 years preceding the deadline date and have not been a principal investigator or co-principal investigator on a federal research grant of more than $20,000. Applicants must be proposing a research and training plan in biological informatics at an appropriate nonprofit U.S. or foreign host institution (colleges and universities, government and national laboratories and facilities, and privately-sponsored nonprofit institutes and museums). Preference is given to applicants who choose foreign locations or those moving to new institutions and research environments with which they have not had prior affiliation. The fellowship may not be held at the same institution as where the doctorate was earned. Applications are strongly encouraged from women, minorities, and persons with disabilities.
Financial data The grant is $50,000 per year; that includes an annual stipend of $36,000; a research allowance of $9,000 per year paid to the fellow for materials and supplies, subscription fees, and recovery costs for databases, travel, and publication expenses; and an institutional allowance of $5,000 per year for fringe benefits and expenses incurred in support of the fellow.
Duration 2 years; may be renewed for 1 additional year at a U.S. institution if the first 2 years are at a foreign institution.
Number awarded Approximately 20 each year.
Deadline November of each year.

[172]
POSTDOCTORAL RESEARCH FELLOWSHIPS IN MICROBIAL BIOLOGY

National Science Foundation
Directorate for Biological Sciences
Attn: Division of Biological Infrastructure
4201 Wilson Boulevard, Room 615
Arlington, VA 22230
(703) 292-8470   TDD: (703) 292-5090
E-mail: ckimsey@nsf.gov
Web site: www.nsf.gov/bio

Purpose To provide opportunities for junior doctoral-level scientists to conduct research and acquire training either in the United States or abroad in microbial biology.
Eligibility This program is open to persons who are citizens, nationals, or permanent residents of the United States at the time of application. Applicants must have earned a Ph.D. no earlier than 18 months preceding the deadline date and have not received a federal research grant previously. They must be proposing a research and training plan in microbial biology (including systematics, ecology, physiology, biochemistry, and genetics) at an appropriate nonprofit U.S. or foreign host institution (colleges and universities, government and national laboratories and facilities, and privately-sponsored nonprofit institutes and museums). Preference is given to applicants who choose foreign locations or those moving to new institutions and research environments with which they have not had prior affiliation. The fellowship may not be held at the same institution as where the doctorate was earned. Applications are strongly encouraged from women, minorities, and persons with disabilities.
Financial data The grant is $50,000 per year; that includes an annual stipend of $36,000; a research allowance of $9,000 per year paid to the fellow for materials and supplies, subscription fees, and recovery costs for databases, travel, and publication expenses; and an institutional allowance of $5,000 per year for fringe benefits and expenses incurred in support of the fellow.
Duration 2 or 3 years. Fellows are encouraged to spend at least part of that time at a foreign host institution.
Number awarded 20 each year. Approximately $2 million is available for this program each year.
Deadline September of each year.

[173]
RALPH I. GOLDMAN FELLOWSHIP IN INTERNATIONAL JEWISH COMMUNAL SERVICE

American Jewish Joint Distribution Committee, Inc.
711 Third Avenue
New York, NY 10017-4014
(212) 687-6200   Fax: (212) 370-5467
E-mail: service@jdcny.org
Web site: www.jdc.org/help/volunteer.htm

Purpose To provide funding for a year of work-study in an overseas field office of the American Jewish Joint Distribution Committee.
Eligibility This fellowship is intended for individuals in the early stages of their career who have demonstrated a strong interest in international Jewish communal affairs and a talent for leadership in communal services. Candidates should have

at least a master's degree or its equivalent and should be interested in working in an overseas field office of the Joint Distribution Committee. Applicants should send a letter expressing their interest; the letter should include details of their educational background and work experience, their plans for the future, their reasons for interest in the fellowship, and a list of references. Knowledge of a foreign language is a plus but not a requirement.
Financial data The stipend is $25,000.
Duration 1 year, beginning in September.
Special features This program was established in 1985.
Limitations The fellow must submit a work report at the end of the fellowship year.
Number awarded 1 each year.
Deadline October of each year.

[174]
RALPH W. STONE AWARD
National Speleological Society
2813 Cave Avenue
Huntsville, AL 35810-4413
(256) 852-1300   Fax: (256) 851-9241
E-mail: nss@caves.org
Web site: www.caves.org

Purpose To provide funding for cave-related thesis research to members of the National Speleological Society (NSS).
Eligibility To qualify, candidates must be graduate students, working on a cave-related thesis in the biological, social, or earth sciences, and members of the society. The proposed research may involve hydrology, geology, bats and other cave inhabitants, or related topics. It may be conducted anywhere in the world. The proposal package should include a project description, a personal resume, a detailed academic record, and 2 letters of recommendation.
Financial data The award is $1,700.
Duration 1 academic year.
Special features NSS members currently pursuing thesis work anywhere in the world are eligible to apply.
Number awarded 1 each year.
Deadline March of each year.

[175]
RESEARCH FELLOWSHIPS FOR PROFESSIONALS WORKING IN INTERNATIONAL AFFAIRS
Social Science Research Council
810 Seventh Avenue
New York, NY 10019
(212) 377-2700   Fax: (212) 377-2727
E-mail: gsc@ssrc.org
Web site: www.ssrc.org

Purpose To provide financial assistance to professionals interested in conducting research anywhere in the world on the causes and conditions of international conflict and insecurity.
Eligibility This program is open to non-governmental organization professionals, activists, government and multilateral organization officials, journalists, doctors, lawyers, and others. Applicants must 1) have 5 to 15 years of experience working at a local, national, or international level on issues related to global security and cooperation, and 2) speak, read, and write English at a level that allows for intellectual exchange between fellows. They must be proposing to conduct a research project under the supervision of an academic mentor at a university or research institute. The host institution may be anywhere in the world; applicants are encouraged to spend their fellowship period outside their country of residence but are not required to do so. Significant intellectual products that address the causes and consequences of violent conflict and war and create new frameworks for building cooperation and peace are expected as a result. Products may include books or series of articles; films, or educational web sites. Topics of interest include, but are not limited to, the human security implications of human rights; inequality; religious, national, and ethnic revivalism; military affairs; weapons proliferation and arms control; peace-keeping and peace-building; the spread of disease; ecosystem degradation; international migration; international crime; trafficking in humans; food supplies; and global finance and trade. There are no citizenship, nationality, or residence requirements for this program. Women and residents of developing countries are encouraged to apply.
Financial data The amount of the grant depends on need, to a maximum of $38,000 per year. In addition, each fellow has a budget for research and institutional expenses.
Duration 8 to 18 months.
Number awarded Varies each year.
Deadline November of each year.

[176]
ROBERT COCHRANE FUND FOR LEPROSY
Royal Society of Tropical Medicine and Hygiene
Manson House
26 Portland Place
London W1B 1EY
England
44 20 7580 2127   Fax: 44 20 7436 1389
E-mail: mail@rstmh.org
Web site: www.rstmh.org

Purpose To provide travel funds for research or training related to leprosy anywhere in the world.
Eligibility There are no restrictions on country of origin or destination. Funds are available to 1) leprosy workers who are interested in pursuing practical training in field work or research, and 2) experienced leprologists who are interested in pursuing practical clinical training in a developing country.
Financial data The fund provides 1,000 English pounds to cover international travel expenses.
Number awarded Up to 3 each year.
Deadline Applications are accepted at any time but must be received at least 6 months before the proposed trip.

[177]
ROBERT F. GOHEEN PRIZE IN CLASSICAL STUDIES

Woodrow Wilson National Fellowship Foundation
Attn: Director
5 Vaughn Drive, Suite 300
CN 5329
Princeton, NJ 08543-5329
(609) 452-7007   Fax: (609) 452-0066
E-mail: mellon@woodrow.org
Web site: www.woodrow.org

Purpose To provide funding for travel and study to Andrew W. Mellon Fellows in Humanistic Studies who are specializing in a field related to classics.

Eligibility This program is open to past and present holders of Andrew W. Mellon Fellowships in Humanistic Studies in classics, classical studies, history related to the ancient world, or literary studies outside the United States. Applicants must be interested in travel and study at a classical site or center for studies. This is explicitly a graduate prize and is not intended for faculty holding the doctorate. It is intended to be a travel and study support grant, not strictly a research grant for work in the home library.

Financial data The award is $3,000.

Duration This is a nonrenewable 1-time grant.

Special features This program is funded by the Andrew W. Mellon Foundation and administered by the Woodrow Wilson National Fellowship Foundation.

Number awarded 1 each year.

Deadline March of each year.

[178]
ROBERT H. AND CLARICE SMITH FELLOWSHIP

National Gallery of Art
Attn: Center for Advanced Study in the Visual Arts
Sixth Street and Constitution Avenue, N.W.
Washington, DC 20565
(202) 842-6482   Fax: (202) 842-6733
TDD: (202) 842-6176   E-mail: advstudy@nga.gov
Web site: www.nga.gov/resources/casvapre.htm

Purpose To provide financial assistance to doctoral candidates for the advancement or completion, in the United States or abroad, of either a dissertation or a resulting publication on Dutch or Flemish art history.

Eligibility Applicants must have completed their residence requirements and course work for the Ph.D. as well as general or preliminary examinations before the date of application. They must be interested in working (in the United States or abroad) on a dissertation on Dutch or Flemish art history. In addition, they must know 2 foreign languages related to the topic of the dissertation and be U.S. citizens or enrolled in an American university. Application for this fellowship must be made through the chair of the student's graduate department of art history or other appropriate department; the chair should act as a sponsor for the applicant. Departments must limit their nominations to 1 candidate. Finalists are invited to Washington during February for interviews.

Financial data The stipend is $16,000 per year.

Duration 1 year. The fellowship begins in September and is not renewable.

Special features There are no residency requirements at the National Gallery of Art, although the fellow may be based at the center if desired.

Number awarded 1 each year.

Deadline November of each year.

[179]
ROCKEFELLER FOUNDATION AGRICULTURAL SCIENCES PROGRAM GRANTS

Rockefeller Foundation
420 Fifth Avenue
New York, NY 10018-2702
(212) 869-8500   Fax: (212) 852-8436
Web site: www.rockfound.org

Purpose To support research and other activities related to agricultural sciences in the developing world.

Eligibility Scientists from any country who are agricultural specialists are eligible to submit proposals for research designed to increase crop yields of smallholder farmers in developing countries profitably and without degrading natural resources. The foundation is especially interested in research on biotechnology and smallholder crop management.

Financial data Awards vary, depending upon the needs and nature of the request. Recently, more than $17 million was provided through this program, including more than $8.3 million for biotechnology research and more than $8.6 million for research on smallholder crop management.

Duration 1 year; may be renewed.

Number awarded Varies each year.

Deadline Applications may be submitted any time.

[180]
ROCKEFELLER FOUNDATION GLOBAL ENVIRONMENT PROGRAM GRANTS

Rockefeller Foundation
420 Fifth Avenue
New York, NY 10018-2702
(212) 869-8500   Fax: (212) 852-8436
Web site: www.rockfound.org

Purpose To support activities in the United States and other countries that are related to improvement of the global environment.

Eligibility Scientists from any country who are environmental specialists are eligible to submit proposals for research on topics of current interest to the foundation: 1) building international leadership capable of initiating and carrying out innovative approaches to sustainable development; and 2) facilitating the transition to environmentally sound and economically viable energy systems. The proposed research may be conducted in any developing country.

Financial data Awards vary, depending upon the needs and nature of the request. Recently, more than $13 million was provided through this program, including $6.4 million for developing leadership, $6.3 million for advanced energy transition, and $500,000 for other activities.

Duration 1 year; may be renewed.

Number awarded Varies each year.
Deadline Applications may be submitted at any time.

[181]
ROCKEFELLER FOUNDATION HEALTH SCIENCES PROGRAM GRANTS

Rockefeller Foundation
420 Fifth Avenue
New York, NY 10018-2702
(212) 869-8500   Fax: (212) 852-8436
Web site: www.rockfound.org

Purpose To support research and other activities related to health sciences in the developing world.
Eligibility Scientists from any country who are health specialists are eligible to submit proposals for research on topics of current interest to the foundation, which has recently redesigned this program to stress 1) advancing understanding of health equity; 2) promoting equity-oriented health research and development; and 3) strengthening the capacity of health systems to reduce inequities in health. The proposed research may be conducted in any developing country.
Financial data Awards vary, depending upon the needs and nature of the request. Recently, more than $11.6 million was provided through this program, including more than $8.9 million for population-based health care and $2.7 million for research to improve reproductive health.
Duration 1 year; may be renewed.
Number awarded Varies each year.
Deadline Applications may be submitted any time.

[182]
ROCKEFELLER FOUNDATION POPULATION SCIENCES PROGRAM GRANTS

Rockefeller Foundation
420 Fifth Avenue
New York, NY 10018-2702
(212) 869-8500   Fax: (212) 852-8436
Web site: www.rockfound.org

Purpose To support research and other activities related to population sciences in the developing world.
Eligibility Scientists from any country who are population specialists are eligible to submit proposals for activities on topics of current interest to the foundation: 1) support of policy dialogue and policy research among developing country government officials, scientists, and donors who are leading efforts to improve population policies and increase the range of available reproductive health and family planning services; 2) support of research on innovative contraceptive technologies that are focused on methods that women say they want, including new approaches to male contraception; and 3) support of research to improve the quality and coverage of reproductive health and family planning services. The proposed research may be conducted in any developing country.
Financial data Awards vary, depending upon the needs and nature of the request. Recently, more than $16.8 million was provided through this program, including more than $9.1 million for policy dialogue and research, $5.1 million for research on contraceptives, and $2.6 million for research to improve reproductive health.

Duration 1 year; may be renewed.
Number awarded Varies each year.
Deadline Applications may be submitted any time.

[183]
ROTARY GRANTS FOR UNIVERSITY TEACHERS TO SERVE IN DEVELOPING COUNTRIES

Rotary Foundation
Attn: Scholarship Program Supervisor
One Rotary Center
1560 Sherman Avenue
Evanston, IL 60201-3698
(847) 866-3000   Fax: (847) 328-8554
Web site: www.rotary.org

Purpose To provide funding to academic faculty from any country who are interested in teaching in developing countries.
Eligibility Eligible to apply are academic faculty from any country with a Rotary Club who wish to teach in developing countries (defined as those with a per capita GNP of $6,375 or less). Candidates must hold (or if retired, have held) a college or university teaching or research position for at least 3 years, at any academic rank. They must be proficient in the language of the host country. Priority is given to applicants with demonstrated excellence in teaching and/or research in international relations or in fields of particular importance to the host country. Both Rotary members and non-Rotarians are eligible to apply. Awards are not restricted by gender, age, or marital status.
Financial data These grants are $12,500 for 3 to 5 months of service or $22,500 for 6 to 10 months of service.
Duration 2 types of awards are available: either 3 to 5 months or 6 to 10 months.
Special features Examples of teaching fields that are particularly needed in low-income countries include agriculture, business and economics, computer science and technology, education and literacy, engineering, and health care and medicine.
Limitations Although recipients may engage in research, at least half of their working time at the host institution must be devoted to teaching. Applications must be submitted to a local Rotary Club, not the Rotary Foundation.
Number awarded Varies each year.
Deadline Individual Rotary clubs and districts set their own deadlines, which may be as early as March or as late as July of each year. District-endorsed applications must be received by the Rotary Foundation before the end of September of each year.

[184]
ROTCH TRAVELLING SCHOLARSHIP PROGRAM

Boston Society of Architects
Attn: Secretary
52 Broad Street
Boston, MA 02109-4301
(617) 951-1433, ext. 221   Fax: (617) 951-0845
Web site: www.rotchscholarship.org

Purpose To provide financial assistance to architects for 8 months of travel throughout the world.

Eligibility Applicants must be U.S. citizens under 35 years of age who are interested in traveling abroad and meet 1 of the following requirements: 1) a degree from an accredited school of architecture plus 1 year in a Massachusetts architectural firm; or 2) a degree from an accredited Massachusetts school of architecture plus 1 year in any U.S. architectural firm. Selection is based on a 2-stage design competition.

Financial data The first-place winner receives $35,000 and the second-place winner $15,000. Funds must be used for travel abroad.

Duration 8 months of travel throughout the world.

Special features This program, the oldest architectural competition in the United States, was established in 1883.

Number awarded 2 each year.

Deadline December of each year.

[185]
RSNA INTERNATIONAL VISITING PROFESSOR PROGRAM

Radiological Society of North America
Attn: Committee on International Relations and Education
820 Jorie Boulevard
Oak Brook, IL 60523-2251
(630) 571-7741   Fax: (630) 571-7837
E-mail: cire@rsna.org
Web site: www.rsna.org/international/CIRE/ivpp.html

Purpose To provide funding to 3-member teams of radiologists from North America who are interested in lecturing in emerging nations.

Eligibility This program is open to teams of 3 experienced radiology teachers who currently hold an academic appointment in North America. Applicants must be interested in traveling to an emerging nation in order to lecture at a national radiology society meeting or at host institutions with radiology residency training programs. Each year, a geographic region of the world is selected and national radiological societies in that region are invited to apply to host visiting professors to attend their annual meeting. That society selects and organizes visits to educational institutions that have active radiology training programs with the need and potential for educational enrichment from a visiting professor team. Applications must be filed jointly by the national radiology society and the host institutions. Each application must specify the names of institution staff fluent in English, the number of residents in each year of training, and the percentage of those residents who are capable of understanding teaching presentations delivered in English. The host country whose application is approved is then matched with an appropriate visiting professor team from North America.

Financial data Grants provide each member of the team with funding that includes an allowance for travel expenses.

Duration Up to 2 weeks, including time spent at the national society meeting and travel to 2 or 3 host institutions.

Special features This program began in 1986.

Number awarded 1 team is supported each year.

Deadline August of each year.

[186]
RUTH SATTER MEMORIAL AWARD

Association for Women in Science
1200 New York Avenue, N.W., Suite 650
Washington, DC 20005
(202) 326-8940   (800) 886-AWIS
Fax: (202) 326-8960   E-mail: awis@awis.org
Web site: www.awis.org

Purpose To provide financial assistance to reentry women interested in working on a doctoral degree in the sciences.

Eligibility Female students enrolled in any life science, physical science, social science, or engineering program leading to a Ph.D. degree are eligible to apply if they have had to interrupt their education for 3 or more years to raise a family. Winners traditionally have been at the dissertation level of their graduate work. Foreign students must be enrolled in a U.S. institution of higher education, but U.S. citizens may study or conduct research in the United States or abroad.

Financial data The stipend is $1,000. Funds may be used for tuition, books, housing, research, equipment, etc.

Duration 1 year.

Number awarded 1 each year.

Deadline January of each year.

[187]
SAMUEL H. KRESS FELLOWSHIP

National Gallery of Art
Attn: Center for Advanced Study in the Visual Arts
Sixth Street and Constitution Avenue, N.W.
Washington, DC 20565
(202) 842-6482   Fax: (202) 842-6733
TDD: (202) 842-6176   E-mail: advstudy@nga.gov
Web site: www.nga.gov/resources/casvapre.htm

Purpose To provide financial assistance to doctoral candidates interested in conducting research here and abroad on the history, theory, and criticism of Western art, architecture, and urbanism.

Eligibility Applicants must have completed their residence requirements and course work for the Ph.D. as well as general or preliminary examinations before the date of application. They must be interested in conducting their research in Washington, D.C. and abroad. In addition, they must know 2 foreign languages related to the topic of the dissertation and be U.S. citizens or enrolled in an American university. Application for this fellowship must be made through the chair of the student's graduate department of art history or other appropriate department; the chair should act as a sponsor for the applicant. Departments must limit their nominations to 1 candidate. Finalists are invited to Washington during February for interviews.

Financial data The stipend is $16,000 per year.

Duration 2 years: 1 year abroad conducting research for the dissertation and 1 year in residence at the National Gallery of Art's Center for Advanced Study in the Visual Arts in Washington, D.C. The fellowship begins in September and is not renewable.

Special features Fellows spend 1 year in residence at the National Gallery of Art, completing the dissertation and devoting half time to gallery research projects designed to complement the subject of the dissertation and to provide curatorial

experience. Fellows may apply for a postdoctoral curatorial fellowship if the dissertation has been accepted by June of the second fellowship year.
Number awarded 1 each year.
Deadline November of each year.

[188]
SCHLANGER OCEAN DRILLING PROGRAM FELLOWSHIPS

Joint Oceanographic Institutions Incorporated
Attn: Fellowship Coordinator
1755 Massachusetts Avenue, N.W., Suite 700
Washington, DC 20036-2102
(202) 939-1623   Fax: (202) 462-8754
E-mail: joi@brook.edu
Web site: www.joi-odp.org/usssp

Purpose To provide financial assistance to outstanding doctoral students who are interested in conducting research compatible with the goals of the Ocean Drilling Program (ODP).
Eligibility Fellowship opportunities are open to all graduate students who are enrolled in a full-time Ph.D. program at a U.S. university. The research proposed by the student must be approved by the faculty advisor before the application process. Proposed research should relate directly to ODP interests and may involve either shipboard (conducted at sites around the world) or shorebased (studies of previously collected ODP cores and downhole logs) research. Selection is based on research potential and quality.
Financial data The award is $23,000 per year, payable through the candidate's home institution. The entire amount is intended to be applied directly to the research project, student stipend, tuition, benefits, and related travel. Travel to and from the drillship and to the pre- and post-cruise meetings is paid separately. No part of the award may be used to cover institutional overhead, administrative costs, or permanent equipment.
Duration Both 1-year and 2-year fellowships are available.
Special features This program is supported by the Joint Oceanographic Institutions/U.S. Science Advisory Committee (JOI/USSAC); the fellowships were designated the JOI/USSAC Ocean Drilling Program Fellowships until 1999, when the current name was adopted. Funding is provided through a contract with the National Science Foundation. Research is conducted aboard the *JOIDES Resolution,* a vessel originally constructed in 1978. Current research cruises include periods from 1 to 2 months in the Pacific and Atlantic, with port stops in San Juan (Puerto Rico), Panama, Acapulco (Mexico), San Francisco, Victoria (British Columbia, Canada), San Diego, Barbados, Charleston (South Carolina), Lisbon (Portugal), Halifax (Nova Scotia, Canada), New York City, Las Palmas (Spain), and Cape Town (South Africa).
Number awarded Approximately 5 each year.
Deadline Proposals are accepted twice each year: April for shipboard or shorebased proposals, November for shorebased proposals.

[189]
SEARCH ASSOCIATES INTERNATIONAL SCHOOL INTERN PROGRAM

Search Associates
P.O. Box 636
Dallas, PA 18612
(570) 696-4600   Fax: (570) 696-9500
Web site: www.search-associates.com

Purpose To offer recent college graduates the opportunity to serve as teaching interns in overseas international schools.
Eligibility Candidates must have earned either a bachelor's or master's degree. Although teacher certification is not required, it is preferred. Applicants should have a willingness to consider serving in several regions of the world, extraordinary flexibility and adaptability, exceptional academic achievement (3.5 or higher grade point average), emotional maturity, personal commitment, resourcefulness and creativity, intercultural living or working experience, and a sense of humor.
Financial data Interns receive round-trip transportation, health insurance, and a monthly stipend.
Duration 1 year, beginning in August.
Special features This program began in 1991. In 1994, Search Associates acquired the International School Internship Program from the Overseas School Assistance Corporation (OSAC). As a result, Search associates is now the only organization that actively seeks placement in international schools for large numbers of intern candidates from colleges and universities in the United States. Some of the countries where interns have been placed include: Abu Dhabi, Argentina, Australia, Belgium, Bolivia, Brazil, Bulgaria, Costa Rica, Ecuador, Germany, Guatemala, Hong Kong, Indonesia, Israel, Italy, Japan, Jordan, Korea, Kuwait, Malaysia, Morocco, Netherlands, Norway, Pakistan, Panama, Peru, Philippines, Poland, Singapore, Spain, Switzerland, Taiwan, Tunisia, Turkey, and Venezuela. Most of the overseas schools where interns are placed are private-tuition American and international schools with a curriculum similar to U.S. schools. English is the language of instruction.
Limitations There is a registration fee of $100 and a $200 fee if the candidate accepts a position through the direct or indirect assistance of Search Associates.

[190]
SECOND PROFESSIONAL DEGREE MASTER OF ARCHITECTURE TRAVELING FELLOWSHIP

Skidmore, Owings & Merrill Foundation
224 South Michigan Avenue, Suite 1000
Chicago, IL 60604
(312) 427-4202   Fax: (312) 360-4548
E-mail: somfoundation@som.com
Web site: www.som.com/html/som_foundation.html

Purpose To provide financial assistance to architecture students who wish to travel in the United States or abroad.
Eligibility Applicants may be citizens of any country but must be completing their master of architecture degree from an accredited (1 to 2 year) graduate professional degree program in the United States. Candidates must be chosen by the school they attend and submit a portfolio of their work. A jury consisting of educators, professional architects, architecture critics, and other professionals selects 2 finalists and conducts interviews to choose the recipient. Selection is based on the

evaluation of the portfolios and the candidates' proposed travel/study plans.
Financial data The stipend is $10,000.
Special features This award is offered through the Skidmore, Owings & Merrill (SOM) Architecture Traveling Fellowship Program. Recipients may travel to any country.
Limitations In the event the candidate does not complete his/her studies and graduate with a degree, the fellowship is forfeited back to the SOM Foundation.
Number awarded 1 each year.

[191]
SENATOR JOHN HEINZ FELLOWSHIP IN ENVIRONMENTAL REPORTING

International Center for Journalists
1616 H Street, N.W., Third Floor
Washington, DC 20006
(202) 737-3700   Fax: (202) 737-0530
E-mail: heinz@icfj.org
Web site: www.icfj.org

Purpose To enable educators and news media professionals from the United States to travel abroad to write about international environmental issues.
Eligibility This program is open to working journalists from the print and broadcast media and to journalism educators. Applicants must be interested in working with a host organization abroad (either a media association or a university) where they divide their time between training local journalists and reporting and writing about the environment. Selection is based on experience in environmental journalism, overseas experience, demonstrated ability to work in difficult conditions, training experience, spirit of adventure, and willingness to share expertise with others. Preference is given to applications for assignments in countries or regions in the developing world or in new democracies.
Financial data Fellows receive travel, hotel, health insurance, and other benefits while on assignment. Costs of a traveling companion or spouse are not covered.
Duration Up to 3 months.
Special features This program, established in 1997, is funded by the Teresa and H. John Heinz III Foundation.
Limitations Upon returning to the United States, fellows are expected to share their experiences with others through lectures and seminars.
Number awarded 1 each year.
Deadline November of each year.

[192]
SIGMA THETA TAU INTERNATIONAL SMALL RESEARCH GRANT

Sigma Theta Tau International
Attn: Research Department
550 West North Street
Indianapolis, IN 46202-3191
(317) 634-8171   (888) 634-7575
Fax: (317) 634-8188   E-mail: research@stti.iupui.edu
Web site: www.nursingsociety.org/small_grant.html

Purpose To provide funding to nurses interested in conducting research.
Eligibility Proposals for pilot and/or developmental research may be submitted. Multidisciplinary and international research is encouraged. Applicants must be registered nurses with a current license, be U.S. citizens, and have earned at least a master's degree. Applications from novice researchers who have received no other national research funds are encouraged and will receive special consideration. All other qualifications being equal, preference is given to Sigma Theta Tau members. Selection is based on the quality of the proposed research, the future promise of the applicant, and the applicant's research budget.
Financial data The maximum grant is $5,000.
Duration 1 year.
Number awarded 10 to 15 each year.
Deadline November of each year.

[193]
SOCIETY OF ANTIQUARIES MINOR GRANTS

Society of Antiquaries of London
Attn: General Secretary
Burlington House
Piccadilly
London W1J 0BE
England
44 20 7734 0193   Fax: 44 20 7287 6967
E-mail: admin@sal.org.uk
Web site: www.sal.org.uk

Purpose To provide financial assistance to scholars and others interested in conducting archaeological or other research involving antiquities.
Eligibility This program is normally open to fellows of the Society of Antiquarians of London and U.K. citizens who are not fellows, although consideration is also given to non-fellows from abroad who are working in cooperation with people from the United Kingdom and whose research is directly related to the United Kingdom. Applicants must be proposing to conduct archaeological, documentary, or antiquarian research; there are no geographical or chronological limitations. Awards are not made for research related to an undergraduate or graduate degree unless the project, although related to the applicant's academic work, has an independent research status. In no circumstances will the cost of dissertation or thesis preparation be considered.
Financial data Grants up to 2,000 pounds are available.
Duration 1 year; may be renewed for up to 2 additional years.

Special features This program includes 2 specialized funds: the Joan Pye Awards for research in prehistoric and Roman archaeology of the United Kingdom and the Hugh Chapman Memorial Research Fund for research projects involving the western Roman empire and antiquarian matters in London and its environs.

Limitations Recipients are required to submit, by the end of February of the year following that in which a grant is made, a report of 500 to 5,000 words on how the research objectives were met.

Number awarded Varies each year; recently, 18 of these grants with a total value of 29,680 pounds were awarded.

Deadline January of each year.

[194]
SOCIETY OF ECONOMIC GEOLOGISTS STUDENT RESEARCH GRANTS

Society of Economic Geologists Foundation
Attn: SEG Grants Program
7811 Schaffer Parkway
Littleton, CO 80127
(720) 981-7882   Fax: (720) 981-7874
E-mail: seg@segweb.org
Web site: www.segweb.org

Purpose To provide funding to graduate students from any country who wish to conduct geological research anywhere in the world.

Eligibility This program is open to graduate students from any country who are interested in conducting master's or doctoral thesis research. Applicants should be proposing projects involving geologic mapping or field studies (anywhere in the world) designed to increase knowledge and documentation of inadequately described ore deposits, mining districts, and ore fields. Proposals for laboratory work or laboratory-oriented studies are also considered.

Financial data Stipends range from $500 to $1,000. Funds may be used for travel expenses, living costs in the field, expendable supplies, field expenses, and other expenses directly necessary for the research; they are not intended for the purchase of ordinary field equipment, living costs of assistants or families of the grantees, attendance at professional meetings, preparation of theses, or reimbursement for work already accomplished.

Number awarded Varies each year; recently, 11 of these grants were awarded.

Deadline January of each year.

[195]
SOROS SENIOR JUSTICE FELLOWSHIPS

Open Society Institute
Attn: Center on Crime, Communities and Culture
400 West 59th Street, Third Floor
New York, NY 10019
(212) 548-0135   Fax: (212) 548-4677
E-mail: mporter@sorosny.org
Web site: www.soros.org/crime

Purpose To provide funding to experienced professionals in the field of criminal justice who are interested in working on independent projects in the United States or overseas.

Eligibility Applicants must be able to demonstrate expertise or scholarship in criminal justice or a related field. They must be proposing to work independently on research, writing, program design, community development, or other appropriate projects in the United States or overseas. Doctoral candidates are not eligible. Applicants who propose projects overseas should explain their proposal's relevance to cross-border information exchange in the field of criminal justice. Selection is based on the project's potential to enhance public discourse on criminal justice and public safety, the need for the proposed project, and the capacity of the applicant to implement it.

Financial data Support for the fellowships varies according to the scope of the project, ranging from $40,000 to $70,000. Finalists are asked to provide additional budget information.

Duration 1 year; may be renewed for an additional year.

Number awarded Up to 5 each year.

Deadline September of each year.

[196]
SPALDING TRUST GRANTS

Spalding Trust
Attn: Secretary
P.O. Box 85
Stowmarket IP14 3NY
England
Fax: 44 1359 240739

Purpose To provide funding for the study of or research on religion anywhere in the world.

Eligibility Applicants may be from any country. They must have earned at least a bachelor's degree, be studying a religion other than their own, and not have access to other sources of funding. Proposed research may be conducted in any country. Special consideration is given to research projects that are backed by a professional ability to raise the standard of knowledge of religious principles and practices, and to interpret their relation to contemporary society. Applicants may propose projects that deal with their own religion only if the study or project will significantly improve inter-religious understanding. Consideration is given to applications that are not academically oriented, but only if they will have a practical and beneficial effect on inter-religious understanding.

Financial data Grants are usually less than 1,500 pounds.

Duration Varies, depending upon the scope of the funded project.

Special features Awards are tenable worldwide.

Number awarded Varies each year.

Deadline Applications may be submitted at any time.

[197]
SPENCER POSTDOCTORAL FELLOWSHIP PROGRAM

National Academy of Education
c/o New York University
School of Education
726 Broadway, Room 509
New York, NY 10003-9580
(212) 998-9035   Fax: (212) 995-4435
Web site: www.nae.nyu.edu

Purpose To encourage young researchers to pursue studies in the field of education.

Eligibility Applicants should have earned a doctorate no more than 5 years prior to applying for this program. Candidates may be from the fields of education, the behavioral sciences, the humanities, or the social sciences, as long as they propose research relevant to the field of education; it may be conducted in the United States or abroad. Selection is based on the applicant's past research record, the promise of early work, and the quality of the project described in the application.

Financial data Fellows receive $50,000 for 1 academic year of research or $25,000 for each of 2 contiguous years, working half time. The funds are to be used to cover travel expenses, research costs, secretarial assistance, computer costs, and other expenses incurred in professional activities. The funds are administered by the fellow's home institution, but no institutional overhead may be charged against the grant.

Duration Up to 2 years.

Special features Funding for this program is provided by the Spencer Foundation.

Number awarded Up to 30 each year.

Deadline November of each year.

[198]
STELLA BLUM RESEARCH GRANT

Costume Society of America
55 Edgewater Drive
P.O. Box 73
Earleville, MD 21919
(410) 275-1619   (800) CSA-9447
Fax: (410) 275-8936
E-mail: national.office@costumesocietyamerica.com
Web site: www.costumesocietyamerica.com

Purpose To provide funding to members of the Costume Society of America interested in conducting research in the United States or abroad on North American costumes.

Eligibility Applicants must be working on a degree in costume and be a member of the society. Their proposed research must deal with North American costumes. Selection is based on the applicant's academic record, experience, references, significance of research subject, project goals, methodology, proposed tangible results, and feasibility of project's time, budget, and resources.

Financial data Grants up to $3,000 are provided. Funds must be used for research-related expenses (such as transportation and living at the research site, photographic reproductions and film, postage, telephone, typing, computer searches, and graphics); funding is not provided for tuition, materials for course work, or salaries.

Duration 1 year.

Special features Research may be conducted in the United States or selected other countries. This program was established in 1986.

Number awarded 1 each year.

Deadline April of each year.

[199]
STEWARDSON KEEFE LEBRUN TRAVEL GRANTS

American Institute of Architects-New York Chapter
Attn: New York Foundation for Architecture
200 Lexington Avenue, Sixth Floor
New York, NY 10016
(212) 683-0023, ext. 14   E-mail: pwest@aiany.org
Web site: www.aiany.org/nyfoundation

Purpose To provide funding for travel both within North America and overseas to practitioners interested in architecture.

Eligibility To qualify for a grant, applicants must be U.S. citizens, full-time practitioners, and either registered or nonregistered with a professional architecture degree. They must have a travel program planned that would further their professional self education. At least 2 of the grants are awarded to architects who received their first professional degree 5 or more years ago. To apply, practitioners must submit a resume, a 500-word statement of purpose regarding travel plans, and 3 letters of recommendation.

Financial data Stipends average $3,000.

Duration The grants are offered annually.

Special features These chapter travel grants are funded from the consolidation of the Stewardson, Keefe, and LeBrun bequests.

Limitations Recipients must write a brief report upon completion of their travel.

Number awarded Up to 5 each year.

Deadline April of each year.

[200]
STUDY OF THE PROBLEMS OF NUTRITION IN THE WORLD GRANTS

Nestlé Foundation
4 place de la Gare
P.O. Box 581
CH-1001 Lausanne
Switzerland
41 21 320 3351   Fax: 41 21 320 3392

Purpose To provide funding for research on human nutrition, especially in developing countries.

Eligibility Scientists from industrialized countries are eligible to apply if they are interested in conducting research on human nutrition in developing countries. Research may deal with 1) energy and macronutrient metabolism and requirements; 2) micronutrients; 3) interactions among nutrition, immune defense, and infection; 4) infant feeding; or 5) effects of fetal and infant nutrition on risk factors and disease in later life. Studies in other areas of human nutrition research might also be considered as long as they are related to the problems of malnutrition in developing countries. Projects that will not be

considered for funding include: 1) experiments *in vitro* and on animals; 2) research on food policy, production, and food technology; or 3) nutrition surveys. Applications from candidates for academic degrees are not accepted.
Financial data The amount awarded varies, depending upon the scope of the proposed research.
Duration From 2 months to 2 or more years.
Special features Recipients must work in close collaboration with local scientists in the host country, which must be part of the developing world.
Number awarded Varies each year.
Deadline February or June of each year.

[201]
SUPPLEMENTS TO AWARDS FROM NSF DISCIPLINARY PROGRAMS
National Science Foundation
Directorate for Social, Behavioral, and Economic Sciences
Attn: Division of International Programs
4201 Wilson Boulevard
Arlington, VA 22230
(703) 292-8710   (800) 437-7408
TDD: (703) 292-5090
Web site: www.nsf.gov/sbe/int/start.htm

Purpose To provide funding to principal investigators on projects supported by the National Science Foundation (NSF) who wish to include an international dimension to their project.
Eligibility The principal investigator of any NSF program that provides support for scientific and engineering research and education may apply for this supplementary funding to add an international dimension to an existing research grant or agreement. Applicants should describe the benefit of the proposed collaboration, the plan of work, the responsibilities of the U.S. and foreign partners, the foreign colleague's area of expertise, and the anticipated contribution from his or her role in the project.
Financial data Funding depends on the nature of the proposal but is intended to cover incremental costs that are incurred directly as a result of the international collaboration (transportation and subsistence of U.S. participants, expendable materials and supplies, and publication charges).
Limitations This program does not provide core support for research (salaries, stipends, major equipment, and major supplies); that must come from other sources.
Deadline Applications may be submitted at any time, but they must be received at least 6 months in advance of the project's proposed start date.

[202]
SYLVIA LANE MENTOR RESEARCH FELLOWSHIP
Committee on Women in Agricultural Economics
c/o Cheryl Doss
YCIAS
P.O. Box 208206
New Haven, CT 06520-8206
(203) 432-9395   E-mail: Charyl.Doss@yale.edu
Web site: www.aaea.org/cwae/lane.htm

Purpose To provide funding to young female scholars who are working on food, agricultural, or resource issues and interested in relocating in order to conduct research with an established expert at another university, institution, or firm.
Eligibility These fellowships are awarded to mentee/mentor pairs of individuals. Mentees must have completed at least 1 year in residence in an accredited American graduate degree program in agricultural economics or a closely-related discipline; women with Ph.D. degrees and advanced graduate students are encouraged to apply. Mentors must have a Ph.D. and established expertise in an area of food, agriculture, or natural resources. The goal is to enable scholars, particularly women, to relocate in order to conduct research with an established expert at another university, institution, or firm, even though they may reside in different parts of the country or the world. Selection is based on the relevance of the research problem, potential for generating output, synergy of the mentor/mentee pairing, and opportunity for advancing the mentee's research skills beyond her graduate studies and current position.
Financial data Awards range from $1,000 to $4,500. Funds may be used to cover direct research costs, travel, and temporary relocation expenses for the mentee.
Duration Several weeks.
Special features This program is sponsored by the American Agricultural Economics Association Foundation and by academic, foundation, and industry donors; it is administered by the Committee on Women in Agricultural Economics.
Number awarded Varies each year; recently, 3 of these fellowships were available.
Deadline June of each year.

[203]
THRASHER RESEARCH FUND GRANTS
Thrasher Research Fund
50 East South Temple Street, 3W
Salt Lake City, UT 84150-6910
(801) 240-4753   Fax: (801) 240-1625
Web site: www.thrasherresearch.org

Purpose To provide funding for applied pediatric health research projects in any country.
Eligibility Applicants may be from any country and must be interested in conducting basic or applied research into pediatric health issues. Proposed research may be conducted in any country. Preference is given to applied research projects in the following areas: 1) prevention of significant diseases, injuries, and disabilities; 2) promotion of child health and healthy families; 3) nutrition; and 4) sanitation and safe water. The proposed project should be culturally appropriate, involve local people, and be transferable to other sites and cultures; document methods and practices at the local level that have long-term application; be effectively integrated into sustainable develop-

ment efforts; have specific aims and a well-designed methodology; and evaluate the significance of the project for child health and well-being. Projects initiated in developing countries are encouraged.

Financial data The amount of the awards depends on the nature of the proposed research; up to 7 percent of the yearly grant budget may be awarded to the sponsoring institution for indirect costs. Funds are not provided for general operations, construction or renovation of buildings or facilities, loans, or scholarships.

Duration Up to 3 years.

Special features Research may be conducted at a research institution in any country.

Deadline Applications may be submitted at any time.

[204]
TOSHIO NAKAO FELLOWSHIP AWARD

International Association for Dental Research
Attn: Administrative Coordinator
1619 Duke Street
Alexandria, VA 22314-3406
(703) 548-0066   Fax: (703) 548-1883
E-mail: research@iadr.com
Web site: www.iadr.com

Purpose To provide funding to members of the International Association for Dental Research (IADR) for projects on dental materials science to be conducted at an institution and/or country other than their own.

Eligibility This program is open to members of the association who wish to conduct research at a facility outside their institution and/or country. The subject of the proposed research must be dental materials science. Applicants must hold a degree in dentistry or in a scientific discipline (dental, master's, or Ph.D.) and have held the degree for less than 5 years. The fellowship rotates among divisions/sections of the IADR so that no division/section may have more than 1 recipient in any 6-year period. Preference is given to applicants from regions with less developed research programs in the field of materials science.

Financial data Grants up to $15,000 are available.

Duration Up to 6 months.

Special features Funding for this program is provided by GC Corporation.

Number awarded 1 every other year.

Deadline October of each odd-numbered year.

[205]
TWIN CITIES JOURNALISTS' FUND

Minnesota Newspaper Foundation
12 South Sixth Street, Suite 1116
Minneapolis, MN 55402
(612) 672-0948   Fax: (612) 342-2958
E-mail: mnf@mna.org
Web site: www.mnnewspapernet.org/mnf.htm

Purpose To provide financial assistance to college students in Minnesota who are preparing for a career in journalism and are interested in living and studying abroad.

Eligibility This program is open to students enrolled in a college or university in Minnesota who have completed their freshmen year and are committed to a career in public affairs journalism. Applicants must be interested in studying or conducting a reporting project abroad. They are not required to major in journalism or to speak a foreign language. Preference is given to applicants who are the least able to pay to go abroad.

Financial data Stipends range up to $4,000.

Duration Up to 1 academic year.

Special features This fund was created in 1998. Though it is expected that most recipients will spend a full academic year abroad, the fund directors will consider proposals for short-term projects.

Deadline February of each year.

[206]
UNESCO-ASM TRAVEL AWARDS

American Society for Microbiology
Attn: Minority and International Activities
1752 N Street, N.W.
Washington, DC 20036-2904
(202) 942-9368   Fax: (202) 942-9328
E-mail: international@asmusa.org
Web site: www.asmusa.org/international/international-unesco.htm

Purpose To provide funding to young microbiologists throughout the world who are interested in traveling to another country or a distant site to obtain additional training.

Eligibility This program is open to students and fellows at the predoctoral or postdoctoral level and to young scientists who have completed postdoctoral training within the past 5 years in any of the microbiological sciences. Candidates must be nominated (in English) by their predoctoral and postdoctoral supervisor or mentor. Nominees must be interested in traveling to another country or a distant site to obtain expertise in a method, procedure, or specific topic. Such knowledge should not be available in their own laboratories and should be needed by the applicants to work in their own laboratories and countries. Preference is given to nominees from developing countries traveling to visit a MIRCEN (Microbiology Resource Center) laboratory. Both the home country and the host country must be a member of the United Nations.

Financial data The maximum award is $4,000. Funds may be used for travel and subsistence (room and board), but not for salary or medical insurance.

Duration Up to 3 months.

Number awarded Up to 8 each year.

Deadline February of each year.

[207]
URBAN DESIGN TRAVELING FELLOWSHIP PROGRAM

Skidmore, Owings & Merrill Foundation
224 South Michigan Avenue, Suite 1000
Chicago, IL 60604
(312) 427-4202   Fax: (312) 360-4548
E-mail: somfoundation@som.com
Web site: www.som.com/html/som_foundation.html

Purpose To provide financial assistance to students or recent graduates in urban design who wish to travel in the United States or abroad.

Eligibility Applicants may be citizens of any country who hold or are completing a master's degree in architecture, landscape architecture, or planning (with a concentration in urban design) from an accredited program in the United States. Candidates must be chosen by the school they attend and submit a portfolio of their work. A jury consisting of educators, professional architects/urban designers, architecture/urban design critics, and other professionals selects 2 finalists and conducts interviews to choose the recipient. Selection is based on the evaluation of the portfolios and the candidates' proposed travel/study plans.

Financial data The stipend is $7,500. Funds are to be used for travel abroad.

Special features This award is offered through the Skidmore, Owings & Merrill (SOM) Urban Design Traveling Fellowship Program. Recipients may travel to any country.

Limitations In the event the candidate does not complete his/her studies and graduate with a degree, the fellowship is forfeited back to the SOM Foundation.

Number awarded 1 each year.

[208]
UREP GRANTS FOR FIELD RESEARCH

University of California
Attn: University Research Expeditions Program
One Shields Avenue
Davis, CA 95616
(530) 752-0692   Fax: (530) 752-0681
E-mail: urep@ucdavis.edu
Web site: urep.ucdavis.edu

Purpose To provide financial assistance to University of California faculty/staff/graduate students (from any of the 9 campuses) who are interested in conducting a field research project through the University Research Expeditions Program (UREP).

Eligibility Faculty members or staff researchers from any of the University of California campuses are eligible to apply for partial or full funding through UREP. Principal investigator status is not required for consideration. Graduate students may apply as independent field directors with the sponsorship of a faculty advisor or receive partial or full funding under the program by assisting members of a faculty member's staff. Selection is based on the scientific merits of the proposal and the feasibility of including donor-participants.

Financial data Funding can be used for short- or long-term field research, as seed money for new research, to continue ongoing projects, to supplement other grants, to support graduate students, or to provide full funding for new or ongoing studies. Funds can be also be used for field and/or travel costs.

Special features Since its inception, UREP has sponsored hundreds of field teams in more than 50 countries worldwide. These grants support investigations into issues of importance in animal behavior, archaeology/paleontology, the arts and humanities, environmental studies, and marine studies. Some of the recent projects funded include: folk medicine in Russia, erosion of the Himalayas in Nepal, and Pampas parasitoids in Argentina.

Deadline April for projects between November and May; October for projects between June and October.

[209]
UREP STUDENT RESEARCH SCHOLARSHIP PROGRAM

University of California
Attn: University Research Expeditions Program
One Shields Avenue
Davis, CA 95616
(530) 752-0692   Fax: (530) 752-0681
E-mail: urep@ucdavis.edu
Web site: urep.ucdavis.edu

Purpose To provide funding to undergraduate and graduate students from any school who are interested in participating in the University of California's University Research Expeditions Program (UREP).

Eligibility Undergraduate and graduate students from any academic institution in the United States are eligible to apply to participate in UREP; enrollment in the University of California is not a requirement.

Financial data Partial and full funding is available (without funding, students generally pay about $1,000 to participate in the program).

Duration Varies; generally, from 2 to 4 weeks.

Special features Since its inception, UREP has sponsored hundreds of field teams in more than 50 countries worldwide. These grants support investigations into issues of importance in animal behavior, archaeology/paleontology, the arts and humanities, environmental studies, and marine studies. Some of the recent projects funded include: geology of Zanskar in India, Tetons on the move in Wyoming, and grass eaters of the east African plains in Kenya.

Limitations Travel costs are not covered by these scholarships.

Number awarded Up to 50 each year.

Deadline March of each year.

[210]
W. STULL HOLT DISSERTATION FELLOWSHIP

Society for Historians of American Foreign Relations
National Office
c/o Department of History
Wright State University
Dayton, OH 45435
(937) 873-3110
Web site: www.ohiou.edu/~shafr/shafr.htm

Purpose To provide funding for doctoral research on American foreign relations.

Eligibility Eligible to apply are U.S. doctoral candidates who are working on a dissertation on a topic related to the history of American foreign relations. They must have completed all degree requirements except the dissertation. Applicants must submit a prospectus of the dissertation (indicating work already completed as well as contemplated research), an academic transcript, 3 letters of recommendation, and their travel needs.

Financial data Awards are $2,000 for first place, $1,500 for second place, and $1,000 for third place. The funds are to be used to pay for the costs of travel associated with the dissertation research, particularly foreign travel.

Duration Up to 1 year.

Special features Research may be conducted abroad (preferred) or in the United States. Further information is available from Elizabeth McKillen, University of Maine, History Department, 5774 Stevens Hall, Orono, ME 04469-5774.

Number awarded 3 each year.

Deadline April of each year.

[211]
WALTER READ HOVEY FELLOWSHIP

Pittsburgh Foundation
Attn: Grants Coordinator
One PPG Place, 30th Floor
Pittsburgh, PA 15222-5401
(412) 394-2649   Fax: (412) 391-7259
E-mail: email@pghfdn.org
Web site: www.pittsburghfoundation.org

Purpose To provide financial assistance to graduate students who wish to study or conduct research in art history or a related field.

Eligibility Master's and doctoral students working on a degree in art history or related fields (museum work, conservation, restoration) at an American school are eligible to apply if they have completed at least 1 year of study and need to conduct research for their thesis/dissertation. Applicants must submit a 1,000-word statement on why art history or conservation/museumship is their chosen field and what they hope to accomplish with this award. The recipient may continue their studies or research at the school in which they are currently enrolled or at any other qualified institution in the world. U.S. citizenship is required.

Financial data The stipend is approximately $3,000; funds may be used to cover travel, books, living costs, and research expenses. No funds are available to pay the recipient's tuition.

Duration Varies, depending upon the nature of the proposed research project.

Number awarded 1 or more each year.

Deadline January of each year.

[212]
WELCH FOUNDATION SCHOLARSHIP

International Union for Vacuum Science, Technique and Applications
c/o Dr. Frank R. Shepherd
Nortel Networks
Department C115, 3500 Carling Avenue
Nepean, Ontario K2H 8E9
Canada
(613) 763-3285   Fax: (613) 763-2404
E-mail: frsims@nortelnetworks.com
Web site: www.vacuum.org/iuvsta

Purpose To provide financial assistance to young scholars of any nationality who wish to conduct research in vacuum science techniques or their application in any field.

Eligibility Candidates should have at least a bachelor's degree in a field related to the study of vacuum science techniques or their application, although a doctoral degree is preferred. The laboratory where they propose to conduct research may be in any country other than their own. Applicants must produce satisfactory evidence of reasonable fluency either in the language of the country where the proposed research is to be conducted or in English.

Financial data The grant is $15,000, payable in 3 installments of $7,500 at the beginning of the research, $7,000 after 6 months, and $500 upon delivery of a final report after completion of the funded work.

Duration 1 year; may not be renewed.

Special features This scholarship, funded by the Welch Foundation, was established in 1967.

Number awarded 1 each year.

Deadline April of each year.

[213]
WENNER-GREN FOUNDATION DISSERTATION FIELDWORK GRANTS

Wenner-Gren Foundation for Anthropological Research, Inc.
220 Fifth Avenue, 16th Floor
New York, NY 10001-7708
(212) 683-5000   Fax: (212) 683-9151
E-mail: info@wennergren.org
Web site: www.wennergren.org

Purpose To aid individuals from any country who are conducting doctoral dissertation or thesis research in anthropology.

Eligibility This program is open to doctoral candidates from any country who wish to conduct research in any appropriate country. Application must be made jointly with a senior scholar who will undertake responsibility for supervising the project. The field of research may be any branch of anthropology, including cultural/social anthropology, ethnology, biological/physical anthropology, archaeology, and anthropological linguistics.

Financial data Up to $20,000; funds may be used to cover research expenses directly related and essential to the project (e.g., travel, living expenses during field work, equipment, supplies).

Special features Field research may be conducted in any country appropriate to the study.

Limitations Awards are contingent upon the applicant's successful completion of all requirements for the degree other than the dissertation/thesis. Funds may not be used to cover salary or fringe benefits for the applicant, tuition, travel to meetings, or institutional support.

Deadline April or October of each year.

[214]
WENNER-GREN FOUNDATION POST-PH.D. GRANTS

Wenner-Gren Foundation for Anthropological Research, Inc.
220 Fifth Avenue, 16th Floor
New York, NY 10001-7708
(212) 683-5000 Fax: (212) 683-9151
E-mail: info@wennergren.org
Web site: www.wennergren.org

Purpose To provide funding for postdoctoral research projects in anthropology.

Eligibility Scholars from any country in the world are eligible to submit a proposal if they hold the doctorate (or its equivalent) in any branch of anthropology (including cultural/social anthropology, ethnology, biological/physical anthropology, archaeology, and anthropological linguistics). Proposed research may be conducted in any appropriate country. Grants are made to seed innovative approaches and ideas, to cover specific expenses or phases of a project, and/or to encourage aid from other funding agencies. The foundation particularly invites projects employing comparative perspectives or integrating 2 or more subfields of anthropology. A small number of awards is available for projects designed to develop resources for anthropological research and scholarly exchange.

Financial data Up to $20,000; funds may be used to cover research expenses directly related and essential to the project (e.g., travel, living expenses during field work, equipment, supplies, research assistance).

Duration Varies, depending upon the scope of the project.

Special features Field research may take place in any country of the world.

Limitations Low priority is given to dissertation write-up or revision, publication subvention, and filmmaking. Aid is not provided for expenses incurred prior to the effective date of the award, salary or fringe benefits for the applicant, tuition, nonproject personnel, travel to meetings, institutional overhead, or institutional support.

Deadline April or October of each year.

[215]
WENNER-GREN INTERNATIONAL COLLABORATIVE RESEARCH GRANTS

Wenner-Gren Foundation for Anthropological Research, Inc.
220 Fifth Avenue, 16th Floor
New York, NY 10001-7708
(212) 683-5000 Fax: (212) 683-9151
E-mail: info@wennergren.org
Web site: www.wennergren.org

Purpose To provide funding for collaborative research on anthropology.

Eligibility Scholars from any country may apply for funding to assist anthropological research projects undertaken jointly by 2 or more investigators from different countries. Priority is given to those projects involving at least 1 principal investigator from outside North America and western Europe, but other international collaborations are considered. Both investigators must hold a doctorate or equivalent in a branch of anthropology (including cultural/social anthropology, ethnology, biological/physical anthropology, archaeology, and anthropological linguistics). Projects primarily for purposes other than research, such as training, education, or writing, are not eligible for this program.

Financial data Up to $30,000; funds may be used to cover research expenses directly related and essential to the project (e.g., travel, living expenses during field work, equipment, supplies, research assistance). Aid is not provided for expenses incurred prior to the effective date of the award, salary or fringe benefits for the applicant, tuition, nonproject personnel, travel to meetings, institutional overhead, or institutional support.

Duration Varies, depending upon the scope of the project.

Special features Field research may take place in any country of the world.

Deadline May or November of each year.

[216]
WINIFRED CULLIS GRANTS

International Federation of University Women
8 rue de l'Ancien-Port
CH-1201 Geneva
Switzerland
41 22 731 2380 Fax: 41 22 738 0440
E-mail: info@ifuw.org
Web site: www.ifuw.org

Purpose To assist women graduates who are interested in pursuing a program of additional study or research in another country.

Eligibility Applicants must be members of 1 of the 67 national federations or associations affiliated with the International Federation of University Women (IFUW) or, if a resident of a country that does not yet have an IFUW affiliate, independent members of the IFUW. They must intend to obtain specialized training essential to their research and further study or to carry out independent research (including ongoing projects). Preference is given to candidates whose research, study, or training is to be undertaken in a country other than that in which she received her education or in which she usually resides.

Financial data The stipend is 3,000 to 6,000 Swiss francs, depending on the recipient's need.
Duration At least 2 to 3 months.
Special features In the United States, the IFUW affiliate is the American Association of University Women (AAUW), 1111 16th Street, N.W., Washington, DC 20036-4873, (202) 785-7700, (800) 821-4364.
Number awarded Varies each year; recently, the IFUW awarded a total of 18 grants through this program and the Dorothy Leet Grants program.
Deadline Applications, whether submitted through a national affiliate (such as the AAUW) or by an independent member, must reach IFUW headquarters before the end of October in odd-numbered years. National affiliates set earlier deadlines; for the AAUW, this is the end of September.

[217]
WOOD-WHELAN RESEARCH FELLOWSHIPS

International Union of Biochemistry and Molecular Biology
c/o Dr. Yasuhiro Anraku, Professor of Biochemistry
Teikyo University of Science and Technology
Department of Biosciences
Uenohara 2525, Kitatsuru-gun
Yamanashi 409-0193
Japan
81 554 63 6832   Fax: 81 554 63 4431
E-mail: anraku@ntu.ac.jp
Web site: iubmb.unibe.ch

Purpose To support young researchers from member countries of the International Union of Biochemistry and Molecular Biology (IUBMB) who need funding to travel to scientific laboratories worldwide.
Eligibility This program is open to residents of IUBMB member countries who are graduate students or researchers in biochemistry or molecular biology younger than 35 years of age. Applicants must be interested in traveling to other laboratories in the IUBMB or International Council of Scientific Unions (ICSU) region for the purpose of carrying out experiments that require special techniques or for other forms of scientific collaboration or advanced training. They must submit a complete description of the proposed research, a short curriculum vitae, a letter of acceptance from the receiving institute, and a letter of recommendation from the head of the department of their institution indicating why the fellowship will be beneficial. Support is not provided to supplement scientific visits otherwise fully covered or to attend courses, symposia, meetings, or congresses.
Financial data The fellowship is intended to cover travel costs, to a maximum of $2,000, and incidental expenses.
Duration From 1 to 4 months.
Special features Funds for these fellowships come from an endowment fund of the IUBMB to honor Professors Harlan Wood and William J. Whelan, and from grants by the ICSU to the IUBMB.
Number awarded Varies; generally, at least 10 each year.
Deadline Applications may be submitted at any time.

[218]
WORLD NATURE ASSOCIATION RESEARCH GRANTS

World Nature Association, Inc.
P.O. Box 673
Silver Spring, MD 20918-0673
Fax: (301) 593-2522

Purpose To provide funding to individuals interested in conducting research outside the United States on the conservation of fauna, flora, and habitats.
Eligibility This programs is open to affiliated and nonaffiliated researchers (although applied research will be given preference over basic research). The proposed study site must be outside the United States and the project must have educational and conservation components; local people must be involved. Funds are given only for the conservation of fauna, flora, and habitats, and for related environmental education. Recent projects have included the reestablishment of natural habitats in Lake Titicaca, Peru and various environmental education projects for children in Latin America.
Financial data Grants range up to $2,000 (although $750 is the average amount).
Deadline Applications are due in February or September.

[219]
WYETH FELLOWSHIP

National Gallery of Art
Attn: Center for Advanced Study in the Visual Arts
Sixth Street and Constitution Avenue, N.W.
Washington, DC 20565
(202) 842-6482   Fax: (202) 842-6733
TDD: (202) 842-6176   E-mail: advstudy@nga.gov
Web site: www.nga.gov/resources/casvapre.htm

Purpose To provide financial assistance to doctoral candidates interested in conducting research in the United States or abroad on the history, theory, and criticism of the visual arts of the United States before 1945.
Eligibility Applicants must have completed their residence requirements and course work for the Ph.D. as well as general or preliminary examinations before the date of application. They should be interested in conducting research, here or abroad, on art before 1945. In addition, they must know 2 foreign languages related to the topic of the dissertation and be U.S. citizens or enrolled in an American university. Application for this fellowship must be made through the chair of the student's graduate department of art history or other appropriate department; the chair should act as a sponsor for the applicant. Departments must limit their nominations to 1 candidate. Finalists are invited to Washington during February for interviews.
Financial data The stipend is $16,000 per year.
Duration 2 years: 1 year of research in the United States or abroad on a dissertation topic and 1 year in residence at the National Gallery of Art's Center for Advanced Study in the Visual Arts in Washington, D.C. The fellowship begins in September and is not renewable.
Special features Fellows spend 1 year in residence at the National Gallery of Art to complete the dissertation.
Number awarded 1 each year.
Deadline November of each year.

[220]
YAMAGIWA-YOSHIDA MEMORIAL INTERNATIONAL CANCER STUDY GRANTS

International Union against Cancer
3 rue du Conseil-Général
CH-1205 Geneva
Switzerland
41 22 809 1840   Fax: 41 22 809 1810
E-mail: fellows@uicc.org
Web site: www.uicc.org

Purpose To provide travel funding to cancer investigators from any country who are interested in undertaking joint research abroad or establishing bilateral research projects.

Eligibility Eligible to apply are appropriately qualified investigators from any country who are actively engaged in cancer research on the staff of a research laboratory, institution, teaching hospital, university, or similar establishment. Applicants must have adequate language fluency so they can communicate effectively at their host institution, which may be in any country.

Financial data The average stipend is $9,000, plus airfare; no allowances are provided for dependents.

Duration 3 to 6 months.

Special features These grants are funded by the Japanese National Committee of the International Union against Cancer and receive strong support from the Kyowa Hakko Kogyo Company Ltd. and Toray Industries Incorporated.

Limitations These fellowships may not be granted to prolong or run consecutively with other fellowships, even those administered by other agencies, nor can they be granted to applicants already at the specified host institution. They cannot be used for the purpose of just visiting institutions, for participating in congresses or conferences, for attending meetings or lectures, or for purely clinical training.

Number awarded Approximately 15 each year.

Deadline June or December of each year.

[221]
YOUTH ACTIVITY FUND GRANTS

Explorers Club
46 East 70th Street
New York, NY 10021
(212) 628-8383   Fax: (212) 288-4449
E-mail: youth@explorers.org
Web site: www.explorers.org

Purpose To provide funding to high school and college students who are interested in participating in field research in the natural sciences under the supervision of a qualified scientist.

Eligibility This program is open to high school and college undergraduate students. Grants may be requested to cover investigations anywhere in the world. Awards are to support field work or closely-related endeavors.

Financial data Grants range from $500 to $1,500.

Duration Varies, up to 1 year.

Limitations Only a limited number of applicants from a single institution can expect to be funded in any year. Recipients must submit a report/essay with an itemized statement of expenses at the end of the project. Publications based on work supported entirely or in part by the Explorers Club must credit the Explorers Club Youth Activity Fund.

Deadline January of each year.

[222]
YVAR MIKHASHOFF YOUNG PROFESSIONAL AWARDS

Yvar Mikhashoff Trust for New Music
P.O. Box 8
Forestville, NY 14062-0008
(716) 965-2128   Fax: (716) 965-9726
E-mail: YMTrust@aol.com
Web site: www.emf.org/organizations/mikhashofftrust

Purpose To provide financial assistance to musicians who are interested in engaging in professional development activities in the United States or abroad.

Eligibility This program is open to professional musicians who are younger than 30 years of age. Applicants must be proposing to conduct a project for career-advancing research or documentation, such as seminar or workshop study, travel, or recording. All applicants must include a short biography, 2 letters of recommendation, and a detailed proposal that includes a budget. Performers must submit a cassette tape (up to 20 minutes in length) from the representative 20th-century solo repertoire; composers must submit representative compositions. Proposals may be for work in the United States or abroad.

Financial data Awards range from $1,000 to $5,000.

Duration 1 year.

Number awarded Varies each year.

Deadline November of each year.

Asia

Described here are 151 scholarships, fellowships, loans, grants, and/or internships open to American students (high school through doctoral), professionals, and postdoctorates that support research or creative activities in Asia, including Bangladesh, Cambodia, India, Japan, Mongolia, Myanmar, Nepal, People's Republic of China, Singapore, South Korea, Thailand, and many other countries in that region of the world. If you haven't already checked the "Any Foreign Country" chapter, be sure to do that next; identified there are 222 more sources of funding that can be used to support activities in Asia (as well as other regions).

ASIA

[223]
AAS/CIAC SMALL GRANTS
Association for Asian Studies
Attn: China and Inner Asia Council
1021 East Huron Street
Ann Arbor, MI 48104
(734) 665-2490   Fax: (734) 665-3801
E-mail: postmaster@aasianst.org
Web site: www.aasianst.org

Purpose To provide financial assistance to North American graduate students and scholars who wish to complete projects related to China or inner Asia in Taiwan, Canada, or the United States.

Eligibility Applications are accepted for the following types of projects related to China or inner Asia: 1) curriculum development at the college or secondary level; 2) organization of small conferences and seminars away from major centers of Chinese studies; 3) travel expenses for scholars from isolated institutions to speak at major centers; 4) travel expenses for junior faculty from isolated institutions to attend seminars at major centers; 5) funding for dissertation-level graduate students to attend colloquia, workshops, and seminars related to their fields; 6) short research trips for dissertation-level graduate students, and for scholars at non-research institutions, to travel to major libraries and collections in North America and Taiwan; 7) translations of scholarly books and articles; 8) specialist or regional newsletters disseminating important information in their respective fields; and 9) collaborative projects to facilitate communication and limited travel by scholars working on a common project in Taiwan and North America. Membership in the Association for Asian Studies is required. Junior and independent scholars, adjunct faculty, and dissertation-level graduate students are especially encouraged to apply.

Financial data Up to $1,500.

Special features Funding for this program is provided by the Chiang Ching-kuo Foundation for International Scholarly Exchange. Information is also available from Jean C. Oi, Stanford University, Department of Political Science, Encina Hall West, 616 Serra Street, Stanford, CA 94305, E-mail: joi@leland.stanford.edu.

Deadline January of each year.

[224]
ABE FELLOWSHIP PROGRAM
Social Science Research Council
810 Seventh Avenue
New York, NY 10019
(212) 377-2700   Fax: (212) 377-2727
E-mail: abe@ssrc.org
Web site: www.ssrc.org

Purpose To support postdoctoral research on contemporary policy-relevant affairs in Japan.

Eligibility This program is open to American and Japanese research professionals who have doctorate-equivalent or professional experience (other nationals affiliated with an American or Japanese institution are also eligible to apply). Applicants should be interested in policy-relevant topics of long-range importance; they must be willing and able to become key members of a bilateral and global research network built around such topics. Previous language training is not a prerequisite for this fellowship. Minorities and women are particularly encouraged to apply.

Financial data The terms of the fellowship include a base award and funds to pay supplementary research and travel expenses as necessary for completion of the research project.

Duration 3 to 12 months (although fellowship tenure need not be continuous).

Special features Fellows are expected to affiliate with an American or Japanese institution appropriate to their research aims. In addition to receiving fellowship awards, fellows attend annual Abe Fellows Conferences, which promote the development of an international network of scholars concerned with research on contemporary policy issues. Funds are provided by the Japan Foundation's Center for Global Partnership.

Limitations Fellows should plan to spend at least one third of their tenure abroad in Japan or the United States.

Deadline August of each year.

[225]
ABMAC VISITING SCIENTIST PROGRAM
American Bureau for Medical Advancement in China
Attn: Executive Director
45 John Street, Suite 1100
New York, NY 10038
(212) 233-0608   Fax: (212) 233-0614
E-mail: phyllis@abmac.org
Web site: www.abmac.org

Purpose To provide funding to scientists interested in teaching at medical schools and hospitals in Taiwan.

Eligibility This program is open to medical professors and specialists interested in working in Taiwan. Selection is based on professional credentials, interest to colleagues in Taiwan, potential to contribute needed and requested expertise, and willingness to carry out specific projects.

Financial data Funding is shared by the American Bureau for Medical Advancement in China (ABMAC) and the host institution in Taiwan.

Number awarded Varies each year.

[226]
ACLS/SSRC/NEH INTERNATIONAL AND AREA STUDIES FELLOWSHIPS
American Council of Learned Societies
Attn: Office of Fellowships and Grants
228 East 45th Street
New York, NY 10017-3398
(212) 697-1505   Fax: (212) 949-8058
E-mail: grants@acls.org
Web site: www.acls.org/felguide.htm

Purpose To provide funding to postdoctoral scholars for research on the societies and cultures of Asia, Africa, the Near and Middle East, Latin America, eastern Europe, and the former Soviet Union.

Eligibility This program is open to U.S. citizens and residents who have lived in the United States for at least 3 years. Applicants must have a Ph.D. degree and not have received supported research leave time for at least 3 years prior to the start of the proposed research. They must be interested in conducting humanities and humanities-related social science research on the societies and cultures of Asia, Africa, the Near and Middle East, Latin America, east Europe, or the former Soviet Union. Selection is based on the intellectual merit of the proposed research and the likelihood that it will produce significant and innovative scholarship. Applications are particularly invited from women and members of minority groups.

Financial data The maximum grant is $50,000 for full professors and equivalent, $40,000 for associate professors and equivalent, and $30,000 for assistant professors and equivalent. These fellowships may not be held concurrently with another major fellowship.

Duration 6 to 12 months.

Special features This program is jointly supported by the American Council of Learned Societies (ACLS) and the Social Science Research Council (SSRC), with funding provided by the National Endowment for the Humanities (NEH).

Number awarded Approximately 10 each year.

Deadline September of each year.

[227]
ACTR/ACCELS COMBINED RESEARCH AND LANGUAGE TRAINING PROGRAM

American Councils for International Education
Attn: Program Officer, Russian and Eurasian Programs
1776 Massachusetts Avenue, N.W., Suite 700
Washington, DC 20036
(202) 833-7522   Fax: (202) 833-7523
E-mail: outbound@actr.org
Web site: www.actr.org

Purpose To provide funding to U.S. graduate students and faculty interested in combining research with language training in the non-Russian languages of the former Soviet Union.

Eligibility This program is open to graduate students, Ph.D. candidates, faculty, and scholars at different professional levels. Applicants must be U.S. citizens and proposing a program of research combined with supplemental language instruction in participating nations: Armenia, Azerbaijan, Belarus, Georgia, Kazakhstan, Kyrgyzstan, Moldova, Russia, Turkmenistan, Ukraine, and Uzbekistan. They must have attained at least an intermediate level of proficiency to conduct research while receiving language training. In addition to the support for that training, funding is available for research in the humanities, social sciences, literatures, linguistics, and area studies of the region.

Financial data The amount of the award depends on the nature of the proposal.

Duration At least 3 months.

Special features This program, initiated in 1986, is funded by the Bureau of Educational and Cultural Affairs of the Department of State and administered by the American Councils for International Education, the American Council of Teachers of Russian (ACTR) and the American Council for Collaboration and Education in Language Study (ACCELS).

Number awarded Approximately 25 each year.

Deadline January of each year for summer, fall, and academic year programs; September of each year for spring programs.

[228]
ACTR/ACCELS RESEARCH SCHOLAR PROGRAM

American Councils for International Education
Attn: Program Officer, Russian and Eurasian Programs
1776 Massachusetts Avenue, N.W., Suite 700
Washington, DC 20036
(202) 833-7522   Fax: (202) 833-7523
E-mail: outbound@actr.org
Web site: www.actr.org

Purpose To provide funding to U.S. graduate students and faculty interested in studying or conducting research in the Newly Independent States (NIS) of the former Soviet Union.

Eligibility This program is open to graduate students, Ph.D. candidates, faculty, and scholars at different professional levels. Applicants must be U.S. citizens and proposing a program of study or research at key academic centers in participating nations: Armenia, Azerbaijan, Belarus, Georgia, Kazakhstan, Kyrgyzstan, Moldova, Russia, Turkmenistan, Ukraine, and Uzbekistan. Funding is available for research or study in the humanities, social sciences, literatures, linguistics, and area studies of the region.

Financial data The amount of the award depends on the nature of the proposal.

Duration At least 3 months.

Special features This program, initiated in 1986, is funded by the Bureau of Educational and Cultural Affairs of the Department of State and administered by the American Councils for International Education, the American Council of Teachers of Russian (ACTR) and the American Council for Collaboration and Education in Language Study (ACCELS).

Number awarded Approximately 20 each year.

Deadline January of each year for work during the summer or fall; September of each year for work during the spring.

[229]
AMERICAN INSTITUTE FOR SRI LANKAN STUDIES POSTDOCTORAL FELLOWSHIPS

American Institute for Sri Lankan Studies
c/o Chair, Selection Committee, John Rogers
Tufts University
Department of History
Medford, MA 02155
E-mail: jrogers1@tufts.edu
Web site:
www.geocities.com/Tokyo/Harbor/6196/fellowship.html

Purpose To provide funding for scholars interested in conducting research in Sri Lanka.

Eligibility This program is open to U.S. citizens who hold a Ph.D. in a humanities or social sciences field and are interested in conducting research in Sri Lanka. Applications are accepted from 3 categories of scholars: 1) those with an established interest in Sri Lanka who can show that their research will contribute to the understanding of historical or contemporary connections between the island and the outside world; 2) those whose primary interest is not in Sri Lanka but who wish to include Sri Lanka as part of a broader project; and 3) those whose primary interest has not been in Sri Lanka but who wish to undertake, or examine the feasibility of undertaking, a major research project there.

Financial data Fellows receive a grant of $1,800 per month, round-trip airfare, and a limited budget for research expenses.
Duration 2 to 4 months.
Special features The American Institute for Sri Lankan Studies was established in 1996.
Number awarded 1 or more each year.
Deadline December of each year.

[230]
AMERICAN INSTITUTE OF INDIAN STUDIES JUNIOR RESEARCH FELLOWSHIPS

American Institute of Indian Studies
1130 East 59th Street
Chicago, IL 60637
(773) 702-8638 E-mail: aiis@uchicago.edu
Web site: www.indiastudies.org/fellow.htm

Purpose To provide financial assistance to American graduate students who need to conduct their dissertation research in India.
Eligibility Applicants must be U.S. citizens or resident aliens affiliated with American colleges or universities. Their dissertation research must deal with some aspect of India and have the approval of the Indian government. A formal affiliation with Indian universities and Indian research supervisors is also required.
Financial data Fellows receive a maintenance stipend of 25,875 rupees per month, a research and travel allowance of Rs 11,250 per month, a dollar supplement of $58 per month, and a dependent allowance of Rs 6,750 per dependent per month. Fellows based in Bangalore, Calcutta, Chennai (Madras), Mumbai (Bombay), or New Delhi receive an additional 15 percent cost of living supplement for the maintenance stipend, dollar supplement, and dependent allowance.
Duration 9 to 11 months.
Special features Funding for these fellowships is provided by the Smithsonian Institution, the National Science Foundation, the Bureau of Educational and Cultural Affairs of the United States Department of State, the National Endowment for the Humanities, and the Council of American Overseas Research Centers. The program is administered by the American Institute of Indian Studies (AIIS).
Number awarded Varies each year.
Deadline June of each year.

[231]
AMERICAN INSTITUTE OF INDIAN STUDIES SENIOR RESEARCH FELLOWSHIPS

American Institute of Indian Studies
1130 East 59th Street
Chicago, IL 60637
(773) 702-8638 E-mail: aiis@uchicago.edu
Web site: www.indiastudies.org/fellow.htm

Purpose To provide funding to established American scholars who wish to conduct research on Indian studies in India.
Eligibility Applicants must be U.S. citizens or resident aliens engaged in full-time research or teaching at American colleges or universities. They must be academic specialists in south Asian studies who possess the Ph.D. or equivalent. Their proposed research must have the approval of the Indian government and a formal affiliation with an Indian university.
Financial data Fellows receive a maintenance stipend of 45,000 rupees per month, a research and travel allowance of Rs 18,000 per month, and a dollar supplement of $100 per month. Short-term awards include a short-term supplement of Rs 4,500 per month. Long-term awards include a dependent allowance of Rs 6,750 per dependent per month. Fellows based in Bangalore, Calcutta, Chennai (Madras), Mumbai (Bombay), or New Delhi receive an additional 15 percent cost of living supplement for the maintenance stipend, dollar supplement, and dependent allowance.
Duration Short-term awards are up to 4 months; long-term awards are for 6 to 10 months.
Special features Funding for these fellowships is provided by the Smithsonian Institution, the National Science Foundation, the Bureau of Educational and Cultural Affairs of the United States Department of State, the National Endowment for the Humanities, and the Council of American Overseas Research Centers. The program is administered by the American Institute of Indian Studies (AIIS).
Limitations Recipients must pay an administrative overhead charge of $250 for short-term awards or $500 for long-term awards.
Number awarded Varies each year.
Deadline June of each year.

[232]
AMERICAN INSTITUTE OF INDIAN STUDIES SENIOR SCHOLARLY DEVELOPMENT FELLOWSHIPS

American Institute of Indian Studies
1130 East 59th Street
Chicago, IL 60637
(773) 702-8638 E-mail: aiis@uchicago.edu
Web site: www.indiastudies.org/fellow.htm

Purpose To provide funding to conduct research in India to American scholars who have not previously specialized in Indian studies and established American professionals who have not previously worked or studied in India.
Eligibility Applicants must be U.S. citizens or resident aliens engaged in research or teaching at American colleges or universities in fields other than Indian studies, or professionals who have not previously worked or studied in India. Their proposed research must have the approval of the Indian government, a formal affiliation with an Indian university, a substantial research or project component, and clearly-defined anticipated results.
Financial data Fellows receive a maintenance stipend of 45,000 rupees per month, a research and travel allowance of Rs 18,000 per month, a dollar supplement of $100 per month, and a dependent allowance of Rs 6,750 per dependent per month. Fellows based in Bangalore, Calcutta, Chennai (Madras), Mumbai (Bombay), or New Delhi receive an additional 15 percent cost of living supplement for the maintenance stipend, dollar supplement, and dependent allowance.
Duration 6 to 9 months.
Special features Funding for these fellowships is provided by the Smithsonian Institution, the National Science Foundation, the Bureau of Educational and Cultural Affairs of the

United States Department of State, the National Endowment for the Humanities, and the Council of American Overseas Research Centers. The program is administered by the American Institute of Indian Studies (AIIS).
Limitations Recipients must pay an administrative overhead charge of $500.
Number awarded Varies each year.
Deadline June of each year.

[233]
AMERICAN INSTITUTE OF PAKISTAN STUDIES POSTDOCTORAL FELLOWSHIPS
American Institute of Pakistan Studies
c/o Dr. Brian Spooner, President
University of Pennsylvania Museum
3260 South Street
Philadelphia, PA 19104-6398
(215) 898-5207   Fax: (215) 898-7462
E-mail: spooner@sas.upenn.edu
Web site: jsis.artsci.washington.edu/programs

Purpose To provide funding to scholars interested in conducting postdoctoral research on Pakistan.
Eligibility This program is open to scholars who are U.S. citizens interested in conducting research in Pakistan on ancient, medieval, or modern times there (in any field of the humanities or social sciences). Topics by specialists in other countries or areas that include research on Pakistan in a comparative perspective are also accepted. Applications for summer awards from faculty members are encouraged.
Financial data Grants provide a stipend of $3,550 per month and travel expenses up to $2,500.
Duration 2 to 9 months.
Number awarded 2 or more each year.
Deadline January of each year.

[234]
AMERICAN INSTITUTE OF PAKISTAN STUDIES PREDOCTORAL FELLOWSHIPS
American Institute of Pakistan Studies
c/o Dr. Brian Spooner, President
University of Pennsylvania Museum
3260 South Street
Philadelphia, PA 19104-6398
(215) 898-5207   Fax: (215) 898-7462
E-mail: spooner@sas.upenn.edu
Web site: jsis.artsci.washington.edu/programs/soasia/AIPS/aipshome.htm

Purpose To provide funding to doctoral candidates interested in conducting research in Pakistan.
Eligibility This program is open to graduate students who have fulfilled all residence, language, and preliminary examination requirements for the doctorate. Their dissertation proposals must have the approval of their faculty. Applicants must be U.S. citizens who are interested in engaging in research in Pakistan on ancient, medieval, or modern times there (in any field of the humanities or social sciences).
Financial data Grants provide a stipend of $2,750 per month and travel expenses up to $2,500.

Duration 4 to 9 months.
Number awarded 4 or more each year.
Deadline January of each year.

[235]
AMERICAN RESEARCH IN THE HUMANITIES IN THE PEOPLE'S REPUBLIC OF CHINA
American Council of Learned Societies
Attn: Office of Fellowships and Grants
228 East 45th Street
New York, NY 10017-3398
(212) 697-1505   Fax: (212) 949-8058
E-mail: grants@acls.org
Web site: www.acls.org/csccguid.htm

Purpose To provide financial support for research in China by American scholars in the humanities.
Eligibility Eligible to apply are U.S. citizens or permanent residents who have a doctoral degree or equivalent in the humanities at the time of application. The research proposal must reflect an understanding of the present Chinese academic and research environment and should include a persuasive statement of the need to conduct the research in China. Projects may include in-depth research on China or the Chinese portion of a comparative study. Applicants should demonstrate that they have fully utilized the available resources in the United States and are prepared by virtue of study, training, and planning to take full advantage of an opportunity to do research in China.
Financial data Grants provide a monthly stipend and a travel allowance.
Duration 4 to 12 months.
Special features This program was formerly administered by the Committee on Scholarly Communication with China. It is funded by the National Endowment for the Humanities.
Number awarded Approximately 5 each year.
Deadline November of each year.

[236]
APEC POSTDOCTORAL FELLOWSHIPS IN SCIENCE AND ENGINEERING
Korea Science and Engineering Foundation
180-1 Kajung-dong, Yusung-gu
Taejon 305-350
Korea
82 42 869 6423   Fax: 82 42 869 6613
E-mail: tsmin@kosef.re.kr
Web site: www.kosef.re.kr/english

Purpose To provide funding to scientists from designated countries in the APEC region who are interested in conducting science and technology research at a Korean university or research laboratory.
Eligibility This program is open to young scientists from the following countries: Australia, Brunei, Canada, Chile, China, Hong Kong, Indonesia, Japan, Malaysia, Mexico, New Zealand, Papua New Guinea, Peru, Philippines, Russia, Singapore, Taiwan, Thailand, Vietnam, and the United States. Applicants must have received a Ph.D. within the past 10 years, have a good command of spoken and written English (or Korean), be

in good health, and be recommended by a nominating authority in their home country. Before applying, they must make contact with a Korean sponsoring scientist at a Korean university, government-supported research institution, private industry-affiliated research institution, or university-affiliated research institution. Eligible fields include the basic sciences (biology, chemistry, earth science, mathematics, ocean science, and physics) and applied sciences (agricultural technology, chemical engineering, civil and architectural engineering, electrical engineering and electronics, energy and resources engineering, food engineering, and textile engineering).

Financial data Fellows receive a living allowance of 1,300,000 won per month, round-trip airfare, overseas travel accident insurance, and an industry tour arranged by the sponsor.

Duration 6 to 12 months, beginning between January and April.

Special features In the United States, the nominating agencies are the Department of State, Office of East Asia and Policy Affairs, 2201 C Street, N.W., Room 7821, Washington, DC 20520, (202) 647-4835, Fax: (202) 647-0136 or the Department of Commerce, Division of Asia Pacific Technology Programs, Office of Technology Policy, Room 4226, Washington, DC 20230, (202) 482-1287, Fax: (202) 219-3310.

Number awarded Varies each year.

Deadline September of each year.

[237]
ARTISTS FELLOWSHIP PROGRAM

Japan Foundation
152 West 57th Street, 39th Floor
New York, NY 10019
(212) 489-0299   Fax: (212) 489-0409
E-mail: info@jfny.org
Web site: www.jfny.org

Purpose To provide American artists and specialists in the arts with the opportunity to pursue creative projects in Japan and to meet and consult with their Japanese counterparts.

Eligibility This program is open to American artists (e.g., writers, musicians, painters, sculptors, stage artists, movie directors) and specialists in the arts (e.g., scenario writers, curators). Applicants must be accredited professional artists or specialists. Affiliation with a Japanese artist or institution is required. Artists who have been in Japan more than 2 months for research or other creative activities during the preceding year or who have lived in Japan for more than 1 year are not eligible.

Financial data Fellows receive round-trip airfare, traveler's insurance, 239,000 yen settling-in allowance, 64,000 yen departure allowance, 370,000 to 430,000 yen monthly allowance (depending on professional status), 50,000 yen monthly dependent allowance (if appropriate), and 40,000 yen monthly cultural activities allowance.

Duration From 2 to 6 months.

Special features The address for the foundation in Japan is: ARK Mori Building, 20-21F, 1-12-32 Akasaka, Minato-ku, Tokyo 107-6021, Japan. In addition to the New York address listed above, there is also a west coast address: 2425 West Olympic Boulevard, Suite 650E, Santa Monica, CA 90404-4034, (310) 449-0027, (888) 667-0880, Fax: (310) 449-1127.

Applications from the western United States should be sent to that address.

Number awarded Varies each year; recently, 4 of these grants were awarded.

Deadline November of each year.

[238]
ARTSLINK PROJECTS

CEC International Partners
12 West 31st Street, Suite 400
New York, NY 10001-4415
(212) 643-1985, ext. 22   Fax: (212) 643-1996
E-mail: artslink@cecip.org
Web site: www.cecip.org

Purpose To provide funding to U.S. artists who wish to work collaboratively with colleagues in central Europe, eastern Europe, and Eurasia.

Eligibility This program is open to U.S. artists, curators, and nonprofit organizations in the arts. Individuals must be U.S. citizens or permanent residents. Scholars, administrators, critics, students, and amateur groups are not eligible. Applicants must be interested in working with counterparts in 27 designated countries in central Europe, eastern Europe, the Newly Independent States of the former Soviet Union, and the Baltics to pursue artistic collaborations that will enrich creative or professional development; create new work that draws inspiration from interaction with artists and the community in the country visited; and establish a mutually beneficial exchange of ideas and expertise between artists, arts organizations or audiences, and the local community. Projects focused solely on research or film/video post-production are not eligible. Artists must submit a set of work samples with descriptions (not original artwork). Curators must submit 2 examples of published professional writing or documentation of past curatorial projects. Organizations must submit evidence of nonprofit status. All applicants must submit a project description that includes resumes of all U.S. participants and international colleagues. Selection is based on the artistic excellence and merit of the applicant's work, quality and feasibility of the project plan, potential for interactive dialogue and benefit of proposed project to both U.S. applicant and overseas participants, and the project's potential to bring the benefit of cross-cultural exchange to other artists or audiences in both the United States and the international participant's country. The areas of specialization alternate between visual, design, and media arts in odd-numbered years and theater, dance, music, and literature in even-numbered years.

Financial data Grants range from $2,500 to $10,000.

Duration 1 year, beginning in May.

Special features ArtsLink is a partnership of CEC International Partners (formerly the Citizen Exchange Council) with the U.S. National Endowment for the Arts, Ohio Arts Council, the Kettering Fund, and the Trust for Mutual Understanding. The eligible countries are Albania, Armenia, Azerbaijan, Belarus, Bosnia and Herzegovina, Bulgaria, Croatia, Czech Republic, Estonia, Georgia, Hungary, Kazakhstan, Kyrgyzstan, Latvia, Lithuania, Macedonia, Moldova, Mongolia, Poland, Romania, Russia, Slovakia, Slovenia, Tajikistan, Ukraine, Uzbekistan, and Yugoslavia (including Serbia, Kosovo, and Montenegro).

Number awarded Varies each year.

Deadline January of each year.

[239]
ASIAN ART AND RELIGION FELLOWSHIPS
Asian Cultural Council
437 Madison Avenue, 37th Floor
New York, NY 10022-7001
(212) 812-4300　　　　　　　Fax: (212) 812-4299
E-mail: acc@accny.org
Web site: www.asianculturalcouncil.org

Purpose To enable American scholars and artists to conduct research and undertake projects in Asia involving the interdisciplinary analysis of Asian arts and religious systems.

Eligibility Eligible to apply are American postdoctorates, scholars, specialists, and artists interested in conducting relevant projects in south, southeast, and east Asia.

Financial data The amount awarded varies, depending upon the scope of the funded projects.

Duration 1 to 6 months.

Special features These fellowships can be used to conduct research, underwrite the expenses of visiting professorships, and cover travel costs in Asia.

Number awarded Up to 5 each year.

Deadline January or July of each year.

[240]
ASIAN CULTURAL COUNCIL HUMANITIES FELLOWSHIPS
Asian Cultural Council
437 Madison Avenue, 37th Floor
New York, NY 10022-7001
(212) 812-4300　　　　　　　Fax: (212) 812-4299
E-mail: acc@accny.org
Web site: www.asianculturalcouncil.org

Purpose To provide funding to scholars, graduate students, and specialists who are interested in undertaking research or study of the performing or visual arts in Asia.

Eligibility Eligible to apply are U.S. citizens who are scholars, doctoral students, or specialists in the humanities. They must be interested in pursuing training or conducting research in south, southeast, or east Asia in the following subject fields: archaeology; conservation; museum studies; and the theory, history, and criticism of architecture, art, dance, design, film, music, photography, and theater. The program also supports American and Asian scholars participating in conferences, exhibitions, visiting professorships, and similar projects.

Financial data Fellows receive travel and living allowances.

Duration 1 to 9 months.

Limitations The program is tenable in Asia only.

Number awarded 12 each year.

Deadline January or July of each year.

[241]
ASIAN CULTURAL COUNCIL RESIDENCY PROGRAM IN ASIA
Asian Cultural Council
437 Madison Avenue, 37th Floor
New York, NY 10022-7001
(212) 812-4300　　　　　　　Fax: (212) 812-4299
E-mail: acc@accny.org
Web site: www.asianculturalcouncil.org

Purpose To provide financial assistance to Americans who are interested in undertaking research, teaching, or creative work in Asia.

Eligibility Eligible to apply are scholars, artists, and professionals in both the traditional and contemporary arts, including archaeology, architecture (design, history, and theory), art history, conservation, crafts, dance, film, museology, music, painting, photography, printmaking, sculpture, theater, and video. Applications are not accepted for work in arts education, commercial design, mass communications, landscape architecture, or urban planning. Applicants must be interested in conducting research, teaching, or participating in creative activities in east and southeast Asia.

Financial data Fellows receive travel and living allowances.

Duration 1 to 3 months.

Special features This program was established in 1995.

Limitations Awards may not be used for personal exhibitions, individual performance tours, undergraduate study, or film and video production.

Number awarded Varies; approximately 9 each year.

Deadline January of each year.

[242]
ATSUMI INTERNATIONAL SCHOLARSHIPS
Atsumi International Scholarship Foundation
3-5-8 Sekiguchi, Bunkyo-ku
Tokyo 112-0014
Japan
81 3 3943 7612　　　　　　　Fax: 81 3 3943 1512
E-mail: aisf@sh0.po.iijnet.or.jp
Web site: www.aisf.or.jp/index.html

Purpose To provide financial assistance for doctoral study or research in Japan.

Eligibility This program is open to Ph.D. candidates from any country who are in the final year of their studies. Applicants must be fluent in Japanese and must be attending 1 of 14 designated universities in the Kanto area (Tokyo, Kanagawa, Saitama, Chiba, Ibaraki, Tochigi, and Gunma prefectures). They must be interested in continuing their doctoral studies or conducting research in Japan.

Financial data The stipend is 200,000 yen per month.

Duration 1 year.

Special features The Atsumi International Scholarship Foundation was founded in 1995.

Limitations Applications are submitted through the university.

Number awarded Approximately 12 each year.

Deadline September of each year.

ASIA

[243]
BANGLADESH PREDISSERTATION FELLOWSHIPS
Social Science Research Council
810 Seventh Avenue
New York, NY 10019
(212) 377-2700   Fax: (212) 377-2727
E-mail: s-asia@ssrc.org
Web site: www.ssrc.org

Purpose To support short-term field trips to Bangladesh for graduate students who will be working on a dissertation related to the country.
Eligibility This program is open to students who have completed at least 1 year of graduate study in a program leading to a Ph.D. in the social sciences or humanities with an emphasis on Bangladesh or Bengal-related studies. Applicants must be enrolled at a North American university and interested in taking short-term field trips to Bangladesh to conduct preliminary dissertation field activities, such as investigating potential research sites and research materials, developing language skills, and establishing local research contacts. There are no citizenship requirements. Minorities and women are encouraged to apply.
Financial data The maximum award is $5,200.
Duration 3 to 4 months.
Special features Funding for this program is provided by the Ford Foundation.
Number awarded Varies each year.
Deadline November of each year.

[244]
BIJUTSU KOGEI SHINKO SATO KIKIN FELLOWSHIPS
Bijutsu Kogei Shinko Sato Kikin
5-9-39 Jomyoji, Kamakura-shi
Kanagawa 248-0003
Japan
81 3 3881 1590   Fax: 81 3 3881 1409

Purpose To provide financial assistance to scholars and students from outside of Japan who wish to visit Japan to research or study Japanese culture, arts, and crafts.
Eligibility Applicants may be from any country. They must be interested in researching or studying such crafts as pottery, glasswork, metalwork, stonework, lacquerwork, dyeing, and weaving in Japan. Admission to a leading Japanese school of crafts near Kamakura City is required prior to applying for a scholarship or fellowship.
Financial data The stipend is 80,000 yen per month. Housing is also provided.
Duration Up to 3 years.
Special features The English name of this foundation is the Satoh Artcraft Research and Scholarship Foundation.
Number awarded Up to 2 each year.
Deadline December of each year.

[245]
BIODIVERSITY SURVEYS AND INVENTORIES PROGRAM (BSI) GRANTS
National Museum of Natural History
Attn: Biodiversity Programs Office
10th Street and Constitution Avenue N.W.
Washington, DC 20560-0180
(202) 357-3313   Fax: (202) 786-2563
E-mail: parentil@nmnh.si.edu
Web site: www.mnh.si.edu/biodiversity

Purpose To support descriptive studies of taxa that are central to research efforts of the National Museum of Natural History (NMNH), especially in Burma, the Caribbean, and China.
Eligibility This program is open to research scientists and curators currently receiving funding from the museum. Applicants must be proposing to conduct field studies primarily aimed at the discovery and enumeration of taxa and for projects that make use of the archival collections at the museum and other institutions. Research in any taxonomic group and geographical area is considered, but the program has identified biodiversity research in Burma (Myanmar), the Insular Caribbean (particularly Cuba and Hispaniola), and China for special emphasis. Proposals may include non-museum colleagues as participants. Applications must include a scientific justification for the project, statement of materials and methods, expected scientific product, detailed budget, and curriculum vitae for non-museum participants. Selection is based on scientific merit, suitability for support by the museum biodiversity programs, ability to enhance museum research collections, collaboration with host country scientists, feasibility of the project, and expected final result.
Financial data The amount awarded varies, depending upon the scope of the project. Recently, the average award was $11,670.
Duration Varies, depending upon the scope of the project.
Special features This project, operating since 1995, is part of the Biodiversity Program of NMNH.
Limitations Recipients are expected to share their data with the host country's sponsoring institutions. Participants must work within conventions and other agreements between the host countries and the NMNH. They are also expected to develop collegial relationships with their counterparts in the host country.
Number awarded Varies each year.
Deadline September of each year.

[246]
CAORC FELLOWSHIPS FOR ADVANCED MULTI-COUNTRY RESEARCH
Council of American Overseas Research Centers
c/o Smithsonian Institution
10th and Constitution Streets, N.W.
CE-123, MRC 178
Washington, DC 20560-0178
(202) 842-8636   Fax: (202) 786-2430
E-mail: caorc@caorc.org
Web site: www.caorc.org

Purpose To provide financial assistance to pre- and post-doctoral scholars who wish to conduct research in the humanities, social sciences, or allied natural sciences at a participating member of the Council of American Overseas Research Centers (CAORC).

Eligibility This program is open to doctoral candidates and established scholars with U.S. citizenship who wish to carry out research on broad questions of multi-country significance in the fields of humanities, social sciences, and related natural sciences. Applicants must be proposing to conduct field research in at least 2 countries, 1 of which must host a constituent member of the Council: the American Academy in Rome, the American School of Classical Studies at Athens, the American Institute of Iranian Studies, the American Institute for Maghrib Studies (Tunisia and Morocco), the American Research Center in Egypt, the W.F. Albright Institute of Archaeological Research in Jerusalem, the American Center of Oriental Research in Amman, the American Research Institute in Turkey, the American Institute for Yemeni Studies, the American Institute of Indian Studies, the American Institute of Pakistan Studies, the American Institute of Bangladesh Studies, the American Institute for Sri Lankan Studies, the Cyprus American Archaeological Research Institute, or the West African Research Association. Selection is based on 1) the scholar's intellectual capacity, maturity, and fitness for field work; and 2) the proposal's significance, relevance, and potential contribution to regional and/or trans-regional scholarly research.

Financial data Fellowships are intended as small grants, with a maximum of $3,000 for travel and $6,000 for stipend. No dependent allowance is available.

Duration At least 3 months.

Special features Fellows are granted all privileges normally accorded other fellows at the center with which they affiliate. In addition to the countries that host overseas research centers (Bangladesh, Cyprus, Egypt, Greece, India, Iran, Israel, Italy, Jordan, Morocco, Pakistan, Senegal, Sri Lanka, Tunisia, Turkey, and Yemen), research may be conducted in other countries in North Africa, the Middle East, and South Asia, subject to official security and/or travel restrictions or warnings. Funding for this program is provided by a grant from the Bureau of Educational and Cultural Affairs of the U.S. Department of State.

Limitations Fellowships are authorized only after the center with which the fellow intends to affiliate has given approval and a security clearance has been granted.

Number awarded 8 each year.

Deadline December of each year.

[247]
CCI GRADUATE FELLOWSHIPS PROGRAM

Kobe College Corporation
Attn: Cross Cultural Institute
2201 North Dodge Street
P.O. Box 4030
Iowa City, IA 52243-4030
(319) 337-1204   Fax: (319) 337-1650
E-mail: ccigfp@act.org
Web site: www.crossculturalinstitute.org

Purpose To provide financial assistance to American graduate students who wish to study or conduct research in Japan.

Eligibility This program is open to graduate students who have a record of teaching effectively about Japan or who show promise to do so in the future. Applicants must be planning to conduct research or study in Japan, with no restrictions on the location in Japan. There are also no restrictions on the field of study or research, but preference is given to applicants who have documented interest in Japanese studies, including the arts, culture, education, language, history, journalism, or business. Preference is also given to applicants who have not previously lived or studied in Japan and to applicants who provide written confirmation of the research or study site in Japan. U.S. citizenship is required. Some fellowships may be specifically set aside for women. Selection is based on the scholarly excellence of the applicant, the quality of the proposal, the quality of preparation to undertake the proposed fellowship plan, the plan for teaching upon completion of the degree, documented interest in women's education, and feasibility of the project and proposed schedule.

Financial data The stipend is $24,000. Funding is intended to cover living and academic expenses for the recipient for full-time study or research during the fellowship year. No funding is available for family members.

Duration 1 year; nonrenewable.

Special features The Kobe College Corporation (KCC) was founded in 1920 by American women members of the Congregational Church in Illinois. Its original purpose was to raise money for new buildings at Kobe College, founded in 1875 by U.S. Congregational missionaries to provide college education to Japanese women. The Cross Cultural Institute (CCI) Graduate Fellowships Program was established in 1997. This program includes the following named fellowships: the Beulah B. Scott Fellowship, the Mary Longbrake Fellowship, the Harold Finley Fellowship, and the Mildred J. Follett Fellowship.

Number awarded Up to 3 each year; 1 or more of those may be restricted to women.

Deadline November of each year.

[248]
CCK FELLOWSHIPS FOR PH.D. DISSERTATIONS AND POSTDOCTORAL GRANTS

Chiang Ching-kuo Foundation for International Scholarly Exchange
8361 B Greensboro Drive
McLean, VA 22102
(703) 903-7460   Fax: (703) 903-7462
E-mail: CCKFNAO@aol.com
Web site: www.cckf.org/amprogram/cckfphd.html

Purpose To provide financial assistance to pre- and post-doctoral candidates who are interested in conducting research in Chinese studies in the United States or in Taiwan.

Eligibility This program is open to 1) doctoral candidates who have completed all other requirements for their Ph.D. degree except the dissertation, and 2) postdoctoral scholars who completed their degree within the past 2 years and are pursuing a scholarly project with the sponsorship of an academic institution. Applicants must be U.S. citizens or permanent residents interested in conducting research on Chinese studies in the United States or in Taiwan. Proposed research should relate to the following areas: Chinese cultural heritage; classical studies (especially literary and historical works); the Republic of China (including any subject related to the Republic of China, its development and transformation since its establishment, through the Nanking Period, and up to the present);

Taiwan area studies (including history, archaeology, culture, politics, and socioeconomic aspects); and China-related comparative studies. Selection is based on the significance of the contribution that the proposed project will make to the advancement of research and knowledge in the field of Chinese studies; the quality or the promise of quality of the applicant's work as a creative interpreter of Chinese studies; the quality of the conception, organization, research strategy, and source material of the proposed project; and the feasibility that the applicant can complete the entire project.

Financial data The maximum grant is $15,000 for predoctoral candidates or $30,000 for postdoctoral candidates. Funds must be used to subsidize living and travel expenses.

Duration Up to 1 year.

Special features The Chiang Ching-kuo Foundation for International Scholarly Exchange (the CCK Foundation) was established in 1989 in memory of the late president of the Republic of China. Its headquarters are at 13B, 65 Tun-hwa South Road, Section II, Taipei, Taiwan, 886 2 2704 5333, Fax: 886 2 2701 6762, E-mail: CCKF@ms1.hinet.net.

Number awarded Varies each year.

Deadline October of each year.

[249]
CCK FOUNDATION GRANTS FOR ASSISTANT, ASSOCIATE AND FULL PROFESSORS

Chiang Ching-kuo Foundation for International Scholarly Exchange
8361 B Greensboro Drive
McLean, VA 22102
(703) 903-7460   Fax: (703) 903-7462
E-mail: CCKFNAO@aol.com
Web site: www.cckf.org/amprogram/gaafp.html

Purpose To provide funding to faculty members from the United States interested in conducting research on Chinese studies in the United States or in Taiwan.

Eligibility This program is open to assistant, associate, and full professors in the field of Chinese studies who are interested in a period of sabbatical research and writing in the United States or in Taiwan. Proposed research should relate to the following areas: Chinese cultural heritage; classical studies (especially literary and historical works); the Republic of China (including any subject related to the Republic of China, its development and transformation since its establishment, through the Nanking Period, and up to the present); Taiwan area studies (including history, archaeology, culture, politics, and socioeconomic aspects); and China-related comparative studies.

Financial data The maximum grant is $45,000 per year to replace half of the salary of faculty on sabbatical or for time off for research and writing.

Duration 1 year; nonrenewable.

Special features The Chiang Ching-kuo Foundation for International Scholarly Exchange (the CCK Foundation) was established in 1989 in memory of the late president of the Republic of China. Its headquarters are at 13B, 65 Tun-hwa South Road, Section II, Taipei, Taiwan, 886 2 2704 5333, Fax: 886 2 2701 6762, E-mail: CCKF@ms1.hinet.net.

Number awarded A limited number are available each year.

Deadline October of each year.

[250]
CCK FOUNDATION RESEARCH GRANTS

Chiang Ching-kuo Foundation for International Scholarly Exchange
8361 B Greensboro Drive
McLean, VA 22102
(703) 903-7460   Fax: (703) 903-7462
E-mail: CCKFNAO@aol.com
Web site: www.cckf.org/amprogram/rg.html

Purpose To provide funding to scholars interested in conducting research on Chinese studies in the United States or in Taiwan.

Eligibility This program is open to scholars at academic institutions who are interested in conducting research on the political, social, economic, and cultural development of Taiwan over the past few decades. Priority is given to projects that involve collaboration with scholars in Taiwan.

Financial data The maximum grant is $50,000 per year; recently, grants have averaged $24,000 per year. As a budgetary guideline, the foundation recommends living costs abroad of $120 per day for the first month and $60 per day thereafter. Round-trip costs from the East coast of North America to Taiwan are approximately $1,500. Salary for the researcher is not included except for summer, calculated at one-ninth of the scholar's annual salary plus fringe benefits.

Duration 2 years.

Special features The Chiang Ching-kuo Foundation for International Scholarly Exchange (the CCK Foundation) was established in 1989 in memory of the late president of the Republic of China. Its headquarters are at 13B, 65 Tun-hwa South Road, Section II, Taipei, Taiwan, 886 2 2704 5333, Fax: 886 2 2701 6762, E-mail: CCKF@ms1.hinet.net.

Number awarded Varies each year.

Deadline October of each year.

[251]
CCK FOUNDATION VISITING FELLOWSHIPS

Chiang Ching-kuo Foundation for International Scholarly Exchange
8361 B Greensboro Drive
McLean, VA 22102
(703) 903-7460   Fax: (703) 903-7462
E-mail: CCKFNAO@aol.com
Web site: www.cckf.org/amprogram/vf.html

Purpose To provide funding to faculty members from the United States interested in visiting Taiwan to become acquainted with research facilities there.

Eligibility This program is open to assistant and associate professors who have not conducted research in Taiwan. Applicants must be interested in visiting Taiwan to become acquainted with such research facilities as the Academia Sinica, the Palace Museum, and leading universities. Applications must be accompanied by a letter of acceptance from a host institute in Taiwan.

Financial data The maximum grant is $10,000.

Duration Up to 3 months.

Special features The Chiang Ching-kuo Foundation for International Scholarly Exchange (the CCK Foundation) was established in 1989 in memory of the late president of the Republic of China. Its headquarters are at 13B, 65 Tun-hwa South Road, Section II, Taipei, Taiwan, 886 2 2704 5333, Fax: 886 2 2701 6762, E-mail: CCKF@ms1.hinet.net.

Number awarded Varies each year.

Deadline October of each year.

[252]
CIVIC EDUCATION PROJECT VISITING LECTURESHIPS

Civic Education Project
1717 Massachusetts Avenue, N.W., Suite 506
Washington, DC 20036-2001
(202) 663-7793   Fax: (202) 663-7799
E-mail: cepdc@jhu.edu
Web site: www.cep.org.hu

Purpose To provide an opportunity for American scholars to teach at universities in central and eastern Europe, the former Soviet Union, and Eurasia.

Eligibility This program is open to U.S. scholars (including faculty, advanced graduate students, and professionals) in economics, education, environmental policy, European studies, history (including art history), international relations, journalism, law, library science, philosophy, political science, psychology, public administration and policy studies, social work, and sociology. Applicants must be interested in teaching their specialty at selected universities in Albania, Armenia, Belarus, Bulgaria, Czech Republic, Estonia, Georgia, Hungary, Kazakstan, Kyrgyzstan, Latvia, Lithuania, Moldova, Poland, Romania, Russia, Slovakia, Ukraine, or Uzbekistan.

Financial data The host university provides a salary in the local currency equal to the salary paid to a lecturer or professor of the same academic rank at that university, paid living accommodations, office space, and reasonable access to available office equipment (photocopy machine, telephone, e-mail, fax). This program provides a supplemental living stipend of $5,500 per year, round-trip airfare, health insurance, teaching materials for the lecturer's courses, and access to academic events and program funding.

Duration 1 year.

Special features Visiting lecturers teach up to 4 courses a year in their academic discipline and may teach more if requested by their university. Instruction is in the language of the lecturer, usually English. Participants also develop a variety of projects loosely termed "outreach activities," including revising curriculum, building departmental and university libraries, developing teaching materials in local languages, organizing faculty training seminars, sponsoring academic conferences on topical issues, creating networks through which scholars and other professionals can interact and exchange ideas, and developing Internet-based research and curriculum development projects. This program is sponsored by the Higher Education Support Program of the Open Society Institute, the Eurasia Foundation, the Andrew W. Mellon Foundation, Ford Foundation, Starr Foundation, Robert Bosch Foundation, Citicorp Foundation, John D. and Catherine T. MacArthur Foundation, and other donors. The European office is located at Nador u. 9, Budapest 1051, Hungary, 36 1 327 3219, Fax: 36 1 327 3221, E-mail: cep@osi.hu.

Number awarded Approximately 100 each year.

Deadline February of each year.

[253]
COLLABORATION IN BASIC SCIENCE AND ENGINEERING (COBASE) PROJECT DEVELOPMENT AND INITIATION GRANTS

National Research Council
Attn: Office of International Affairs
2101 Constitution Avenue, N.W., FO 2060
Washington, DC 20418
(202) 334-2644   Fax: (202) 334-2614
E-mail: ocee@nas.edu
Web site: www.nationalacademies.org/oia

Purpose To support American specialists who wish to visit colleagues in Eurasia, central/eastern Europe (CEE) or the Newly Independent States (NIS) of the former Soviet Union to prepare a collaborative research proposal in the basic sciences and engineering for submission to the National Science Foundation (NSF) or other funding organizations.

Eligibility Applications may be submitted by American specialists who possess or will possess a Ph.D. or equivalent research experience. They must be U.S. citizens or permanent residents affiliated with a U.S. university or other nonprofit research institution. Specialists who have received their doctoral degree within the past 6 years are especially encouraged to apply, as are applicants wishing to work with colleagues in less frequently represented countries and regions. Requests to develop research proposals are limited to the following fields funded by the NSF: archaeology and anthropology; astronomy; biochemistry, biophysics, and genetics; biological sciences; chemistry; computer science; earth sciences; economics; engineering; environmental sciences; geography; history and philosophy of science; mathematics; physics; psychology; science and technology policy; and social sciences. No proposals involving agricultural production; drug testing or development; research on the diagnosis, etiology, or treatment of physical or mental diseases or disorders; or the use of animal models of human diseases or conditions are accepted. Proposals must involve collaboration with scientists in the following CEE and NIS countries: Armenia, Azerbaijan (traveling only), Belarus (no hosting of Belarusian government employees), Bosnia (hosting in the United States only), Bulgaria, Croatia, Czech Republic, Estonia, Georgia, Hungary, Kazakhstan, Kyrgyzstan, Latvia, Lithuania, Former Yugoslav Republic of Macedonia, Moldova, Poland, Romania, Russia (designated institutes are excluded), Slovakia, Slovenia, Tajikistan, Turkmenistan, Ukraine, or Uzbekistan. Selection is based on applicant's technical abilities; quality of the proposed project; feasibility of carrying out the proposed project; and prospects for long-term collaboration following the completion of the current project.

Financial data Grants provide up to $2,500 per visit in round-trip airfare between the United States and CEE/NIS; living expenses for foreign visitors to the United States of up to $1,750 for 2 weeks, up to $2,500 for 4 weeks, or up to $5,000 for 8 weeks; living expenses for U.S. visitors to the CEE/NIS of up to $1,500 for 2 weeks, up to $2,000 for 4 weeks, or up to $4,000 for 8 weeks; and up to $100 per visit-week for expendable supplies for the research projects. Living expenses for visits of other durations are calculated proportionately. The total amount of the grant ranges from $2,500 to $10,000.

Duration Each grant may support up to 2 visits in either or both directions (i.e., either traveling to CEE/NIS or hosting a colleague from the region here in the U.S.) with the total combined duration of the visit(s) not to exceed 8 weeks. Each proposed individual visit must be at least 2 weeks in length.

Special features American recipients may travel to the participating countries to prepare collaborative research proposals. A parallel program allows American scholars to host scientists from CEE or NIS countries. Funding for this program comes from NSF; it is administered by the National Research Council, the operating arm of the National Academy of Sciences, National Academy of Engineering, and Institute of Medicine.

Limitations Visits developed primarily to present lectures or to organize or attend conferences are ineligible.

Deadline April, August, or January of each year.

[254]
COUNCIL OF INTERNATIONAL PROGRAMS EXCHANGE INTERNSHIPS

Council of International Programs
1700 East 13th Street, Suite 4ME
Cleveland, OH 44114-3214
(216) 566-1088   Fax: (216) 566-1490
E-mail: cipusa@compuserve.com
Web site: www.cipusa.org

Purpose To allow U.S. professionals in the fields of education, health, and social work to participate in a summer internship program in designated foreign countries.

Eligibility Applicants must be U.S. citizens engaged, as professionals or volunteers, in social work, associated health work, or education. They must be interested in participating in a summer internship program abroad. Most programs operate in English, although German is desirable in Austria and required in Germany, French is required in France, Greek is desirable in Greece, and Italian is desirable in Italy.

Financial data Sponsoring organizations in the foreign countries pay for living expenses, usually through host families, and travel within their respective countries. Recipients must pay for their own international airfare.

Duration 4 to 8 weeks.

Special features Countries currently participating in this program are Austria, Finland, France, Germany, Greece, Hungary, India, Israel, Italy, the Netherlands, Norway, Scotland, Slovenia, Sweden, and Turkey.

Limitations Program fees are required for some countries: $120 for Austria and Hungary, $1,000 for France, $200 for Greece, $600 for India, $250 for Israel, $200 for Italy and Slovenia, $75 for the Netherlands, or $300 for Turkey. No program fees are required for the other countries.

Number awarded Varies each year; recently, the number of available positions was 3 to 6 in Austria and Hungary, 8 to 10 in Finland, 12 to 15 in France, 12 to 15 in Germany, 8 in Greece, 10 to 15 in India, 2 in Israel, 4 in Italy and Slovenia, 8 in the Netherlands, 8 in Norway, 6 to 8 in Scotland, 8 to 12 in Sweden, and 4 to 6 in Turkey.

Deadline February of each year for France, Germany, India, Italy, and Slovenia; November of each year for Austria, Finland, Greece, Hungary, Israel, the Netherlands, Norway, Scotland, Sweden, and Turkey.

[255]
CULTURAL PROPERTIES SPECIALISTS FELLOWSHIP

Japan Foundation
152 West 57th Street, 39th Floor
New York, NY 10019
(212) 489-0299   Fax: (212) 489-0409
E-mail: info@jfny.org
Web site: www.jfny.org

Purpose To provide American specialists in the conservation and restoration of cultural properties with the opportunity to conduct joint research with Japanese specialists and/or to develop their professional skills.

Eligibility This program is open to Americans who specialize in the conservation and restoration of cultural properties, such as remains, artistic objects, handicrafts, old documents, films, and records. They must be interested in going to Japan to conduct research or develop their professional skills. Specialists who have been in Japan more than 2 months for research or other creative activities during the preceding year or who have lived in Japan for more than 1 year are not eligible.

Financial data Fellows receive round-trip airfare, traveler's insurance, 239,000 yen settling-in allowance, 64,000 yen departure allowance, 370,000 to 430,000 yen monthly allowance (depending on professional status), 50,000 yen monthly dependent allowance (if appropriate), and 40,000 yen monthly cultural activities allowance.

Duration From 2 to 6 months.

Special features The address for the foundation in Japan is: ARK Mori Building, 20-21F, 1-12-32 Akasaka, Minato-ku, Tokyo 107-6021, Japan. In addition to the New York address listed above, there is also a west coast address: 2425 West Olympic Boulevard, Suite 650E, Santa Monica, CA 90404-4034, (310) 449-0027, (888) 667-0880, Fax: (310) 449-1127. Applications from the western United States should be sent to that address.

Number awarded Varies each year.

Deadline November of each year.

[256]
ED A. HEWETT POLICY FELLOWSHIP PROGRAM

National Council for Eurasian and East European Research
910 17th Street, N.W., Suite 300
Washington, DC 20006
(202) 822-6950   Fax: (202) 822-6955
E-mail: nceeerdc@aol.com
Web site: www.nceeer.gov

Purpose To provide funding to scholars who are interested in conducting research at U.S. government agencies that relates to the Newly Independent States (NIS) of the former Soviet Union, Eurasia, and central and eastern Europe (CEE).

Eligibility This program is open to U.S.-based scholars who hold a Ph.D. in the humanities or social sciences, with a concentration and considerable background in some aspect of the history, culture, politics, and economics of the countries of the NIS and CEE. Applicants must be interested in conducting research under the auspices of and with placement at a U.S. government agency with responsibility for the administration of some aspect of U.S. foreign policy toward the NIS and CEE. As part of the application process, candidates must submit 1) a description of the proposed research, including its direct relevance to contemporary concerns of U.S. policy makers responsible for the formulation or implementation of U.S. foreign policy toward 1 or more countries of the region; and 2) a written agreement with a U.S. government agency that the agency is willing to provide placement and suitable office space and related equipment for the scholar or researcher.

Financial data Grants up to $40,000 are available. Funds may be used for salary support, benefits, and travel to the region (if such travel is consistent with the needs and interests of the sponsoring U.S. government agency).

Duration Up to 1 year.

Special features Funding for this program is provided by the U.S. Department of State under the Research and Training for Eastern Europe and the Independent States of the Former Soviet Union Act of 1983 (Title VIII).

Number awarded 1 each year.

Deadline March of each year.

[257]
EDILIA AND FRANCOIS-AUGUSTE DE MONTEQUIN FELLOWSHIP

Society of Architectural Historians
1365 North Astor Street
Chicago, IL 60610-2144
(312) 573-1365   Fax: (312) 573-1141
E-mail: info@sah.org
Web site: www.sah.org

Purpose To fund travel for research on Spanish, Portuguese, or Ibero-American architecture.

Eligibility This fellowship is aimed primarily at junior scholars (including graduate students) and senior scholars. Proposed research must focus on Spanish, Portuguese, or Ibero-American architecture, including colonial architecture produced by the Spaniards in the Philippines and in the Americas. Applicants must have been members of the Society of Architectural Historians for at least 1 year.

Financial data Awards are $2,000 for junior scholars and $6,000 for senior scholars.

Duration 1 year.

Number awarded 1 each year to a junior scholar; 1 each odd-numbered year to a senior scholar.

Deadline November of each year for junior scholars; November of even-numbered years for senior scholars.

[258]
EURASIA POSTDOCTORAL FELLOWSHIPS

Social Science Research Council
810 Seventh Avenue
New York, NY 10019
(212) 377-2700   Fax: (212) 377-2727
E-mail: eurasia@ssrc.org
Web site: www.ssrc.org

Purpose To improve the academic employment and tenure opportunities of scholars who recently received a Ph.D. in the study of Eurasia.

Eligibility This program is open to U.S. citizens and permanent residents who have received a Ph.D. within the last 6 years but who are still untenured. Applicants may propose research in any discipline of the social sciences and humanities as long as it relates to the Soviet Union and its successor states. They must indicate the anticipated location of their research. Women and members of minority groups are especially encouraged to apply.

Financial data The maximum grant is $24,000.

Duration The grant may be spent flexibly over a 2-year period.

Special features Funding for this program is provided by the U.S. Department of State under the Program for Research and Training on Eastern Europe and the Independent States of the Former Soviet Union (Title VIII).

Number awarded Varies each year; recently, 3 of these fellowships were awarded.

Deadline October of each year.

[259]
FELLOWSHIPS IN INTERNATIONAL HUMAN RIGHTS

Human Rights Watch
Attn: Fellowship Committee
350 Fifth Avenue, 34th Floor
New York, NY 10118-3299
(212) 290-4700, ext. 312   Fax: (212) 736-1300
E-mail: hrwnyc@hrw.org
Web site: www.hrw.org

Purpose To provide an opportunity for recent recipients of law or graduate degrees to engage in human rights monitoring and advocacy while working for Human Rights Watch.

Eligibility These fellowships are available to recent graduates of law schools or graduate programs in journalism, international relations, or area studies from any university worldwide. Applicants must be interested in working with a division of Human Rights Watch, based in Washington, D.C. or New York. Their assignment involves monitoring human rights developments in various countries, conducting on-site investigations, drafting reports on human rights conditions, and engaging in advocacy efforts aimed at publicizing and curtailing human rights violations. Applicants must demonstrate analytic skills, an ability to write and speak clearly, and a commitment to work in the human rights field in the future on a paid or volunteer basis. Proficiency in a language in addition to English is strongly recommended. Familiarity with countries or regions where serious human rights violations occur is also valued.

Financial data The stipend is $35,000. Fringe benefits are also provided.

Duration 1 year.

Special features This program includes 2 named fellowships open to applicants from any law or graduate school: the Schell Fellowship and the Finberg Fellowship. In addition, 3 fellowships are restricted to graduates of specific schools: the Sandler Fellowship for recent graduates of Columbia Law School, the Furman Fellowship for recent graduates of New York University School of Law, and the Bloomberg Fellowship for recent graduates of graduate programs at Johns Hopkins University. Past fellows have conducted fact-finding missions to Albania, Azerbaijan, Bangladesh, Bolivia, Brazil, Burma, Cambodia, Colombia, Cuba, the Dominican Republic, Egypt, El Salvador, Ethiopia, Guatemala, Haiti, Honduras, Hong Kong, India (including Kashmir and Punjab), Iran, Kenya, Moldova, Namibia, Nigeria, Pakistan, the Philippines, Russia, Rwanda, South Africa, Sudan, Syria, Tajikistan, Uganda, the U.S.-Mexican border, and Venezuela.

Number awarded 5 each year.

Deadline October of each year.

[260]
FOGARTY INTERNATIONAL RESEARCH COLLABORATION AWARD (FIRCA)

Fogarty International Center
Attn: Division of International Training and Research
31 Center Drive, Room B2C39
Bethesda, MD 20892-2220
(301) 496-1653   Fax: (301) 402-0779
E-mail: FIRCA@nih.gov
Web site: www.nih.gov/fic/programs/firca.html

Purpose To encourage collaboration among scientists in the United States and developing countries in areas of research supported by the National Institutes of Health (NIH).

Eligibility Proposals may be submitted by American scientists who are already principal investigators of grants funded by the institutes and who are interested in working collaboratively with scientists in Africa, Asia (except Japan, Singapore, South Korea, and Taiwan), central and eastern Europe, Russia and the Newly Independent States of the former Soviet Union, Latin America and the non-U.S. Caribbean, the Middle East, and the Pacific Ocean Islands (except Australia and New Zealand). All biomedical and behavioral research topics supported by the institutes are eligible for inclusion in this program. Racial/ethnic minority individuals, women, and persons with disabilities are encouraged to apply as principal investigators.

Financial data Grants provide up to $32,000 per year in direct costs. Funds may be used to pay for materials, supplies, equipment, and travel. Up to 20 percent of the total direct costs may be requested for the U.S. principal investigator, the foreign collaborator, and/or their colleagues or students for visits to each other's laboratory or research site. Up to $5,000 of the total grant may be allocated as a stipend for the foreign collaborator(s). Up to $2,000 of the total grant may be allocated for the foreign collaborator(s) to attend a scientific conference.

Duration Up to 3 years.

Limitations Research related to HIV and AIDS is not eligible for support through this program. A separate companion program, HIV–AIDS and Related Illnesses Collaboration Award, provides funding for research on AIDS.

Number awarded Varies; generally, at least 40 each year.

Deadline Applications may be submitted in November, March, or July of each year.

[261]
FOREIGN RESEARCHER INVITATION PROGRAM FOR THE AGENCY OF INDUSTRIAL SCIENCE AND TECHNOLOGY

New Energy and Industrial Technology Development Organization
Attn: Foreign Researcher Invitation Program
Sunshine 60 Building, 29F
3-1-1, Higashi-Ikebukuro, Toshima-ku
Tokyo 170-6028
Japan
81 3 3987 9403   Fax: 81 3 3981 1536
E-mail: nedogrant@nedo.go.jp
Web site: www.nedo.go.jp

Purpose To enable researchers from outside Japan to work directly with staff researchers at institutes that are part of Japan's Agency of Industrial Science and Technology (AIST).

Eligibility This program is open to non-Japanese nationals pursuing research in the field of industrial science and technology as a member of the permanent staff or faculty at an overseas university or research institute. Applicants must hold a doctoral degree in science or engineering, be under the age of 35, and have an adequate command of English or Japanese to be able to conduct research in Japan. They must be recommended by 1 of the 15 laboratories of AIST where they propose to conduct research. Most recipients work at public research institutes in developing countries, although researchers from other countries are also considered if their research accomplishments demonstrate excellent promise.

Financial data Researchers receive a living expense allowance (9,450 yen per day for long-term grants, 15,750 yen per day for short-term grants) and round-trip airfare. In addition, long-term researchers receive a housing allowance of up to 100,000 yen per month, a family allowance of 52,500 yen per month (for researchers accompanied by their families), and a relocation allowance of 210,000 yen.

Duration Short-term grants are up to 90 days. Long-term grants are up to 1 year.

Special features Funding for this program is provided by the New Energy and Industrial Technology Development Organization (NEDO), a semi-governmental agency established in October 1980 and supervised by the Japanese Ministry of International Trade and Industry.

Number awarded Varies each year.

Deadline April of each year.

[262]
FREEMAN FOUNDATION STUDENT-FACULTY FELLOWS PROGRAM

ASIANetwork
Attn: Freeman Programs Director
Kalamazoo College
Chinese Language and Literature
1200 Academy Street
Kalamazoo, MI 49006
(616) 337-7325   Fax: (616) 337-7251
E-mail: chu@kzoo.edu
Web site: www.asianetwork.org

Purpose To provide funding to student-faculty teams that wish to conduct collaborative research in Asia.

Eligibility This program is open to teams consisting of a faculty member at an ASIANetwork-member institution and up to 5 undergraduate students from the same institution. The team must propose to conduct research in Asia. Preference is given to proposals in which a faculty mentor is willing to work with more than 1 student, but the selection committee recognizes that in certain cases 1-on-1 faculty-to-student collaboration is most appropriate. Faculty members must describe the significance of the project, their qualifications, the importance of the project for professional development, and their ability to supervise student research. Students must identify their backgrounds, their abilities to pursue the project, and the importance of the proposed project for career preparation. Proposals must also indicate why travel to Asia is important in conducting the research and how the research will contribute to a better understanding of Asia (including a reference to the desired end product). Although proposed research may be in any field, it should provide a positive impact on Asian studies and general education programs at the participating colleges.

Financial data Each of the 2 team members receives a grant of $5,000 to be used for transportation, lodging, meals, and incidental expenses. An additional $3,000 is available to the faculty member to acquire books and other teaching materials. A $1,000 stipend is paid to the faculty member upon submission of a project report, including detailed financial expenses of both the faculty member and the student.

Duration At least 3 weeks, during the summer.

Special features This program began in 1998. Funding is provided by the Freeman Foundation. Information is also available from Theodora O. Amoloza, Illinois Wesleyan University, International Studies, Bloomington, IL 61702-2900, (309) 556-3405, Fax: (309) 556-3719, E-mail: tamoloza@titan.iwu.edu.

Number awarded At least 30 students with their faculty members are supported each year.

Deadline December of each year.

[263]
FUJI BANK INTERNATIONAL FOUNDATION SCHOLARSHIPS

Fuji Bank International Foundation
Otemachi Financial Center Building
1-5-4 Otemachi, Chiyoda-ku
Tokyo 100-0004
Japan
81 3 3201 7718   Fax: 81 3 3216 2895
E-mail: fbifyume@mb.infoweb.ne.jp

Purpose To provide financial assistance to undergraduate or graduate students who are studying or conducting research at a college or university in Japan.

Eligibility This program is open to students from countries outside Japan who are already enrolled as undergraduates or graduate students majoring in the humanities, sciences, or social sciences. Applicants must be interested in studying or conducting research in Japan. They must not be receiving other scholarship assistance and must be recommended by their universities.

Financial data The stipend is 120,000 yen per month.

Duration 2 years.

Number awarded Up to 10 each year.

Deadline January of each year.

[264]
FULBRIGHT TRAVEL GRANTS

Institute of International Education
Attn: Student Programs Division
809 United Nations Plaza
New York, NY 10017-3580
(212) 984-5330   Fax: (212) 984-5325
Web site: www.iie.org/fulbright

Purpose To provide travel grants as a supplement to funds received from other sources by American graduate students for study or research abroad in specified countries.

Eligibility Applicants for these grants must meet the eligibility requirements for Fulbright Full Grants administered by the Institute of International Education (IIE). If they do not receive any of those grants to 4 specified countries, (Germany, Hungary, Italy, and Korea), they may be considered for a Travel Grant. Students may also apply for these Travel Grants to the 4 specified countries to supplement their own funds or financial aid from other non-IIE services. Applicants may be required to provide statements of their ability to support themselves while overseas.

Financial data Travel Grants provide round-trip transportation to the country where the recipient will be studying, limited health and accident insurance, and the cost of an orientation course abroad, if applicable.

Duration 1 academic year.

Special features This program, created in 1946 and funded by the U.S. Department of State, is administered by the Institute of International Education (IIE). Students who are currently enrolled in the United States are to apply through the Fulbright program adviser on their campus; at-large applicants (those not currently enrolled) may obtain applications and information directly from the IIE.

Number awarded Varies each year; recently, 10 of these grants were offered for travel to Germany, 2 to Hungary, 2 to Italy, and 2 to Korea.

Deadline October of each year.

[265]
GEN FOUNDATION GRANTS

Gen Foundation
45 Old Bond Street
London W1X 2AQ
England
44 20 7495 5564   Fax: 44 20 7495 4450
E-mail: info@genfoundation.org.uk
Web site: www.genfoundation.org.uk

Purpose To provide funding to students and scholars who are interested in conducting research in Japan in specified disciplines of the humanities and natural sciences.

Eligibility This program is open to students and scholars who are interested in conducting research in Japan in art, modern languages, music, and natural science. Preference is given to candidates from the United Kingdom and Japan, although applicants of all nationalities are considered. Applications must be accompanied by an up-to-date curriculum vitae, a recent passport photograph, 2 letters of reference, a 1,000-word essay on the reasons for applying and details of the proposed research project, a 200-word abstract of that essay, and details of the research project and the educational institution where it will take place.

Financial data The average grant is 3,000 British pounds.

Duration 1 year; nonrenewable.

Special features The Gen Foundation was registered in the United Kingdom in 1998.

Number awarded Varies each year; recently, 5 of these grants, with a total value of 19,000 British pounds, were awarded.

Deadline February of each year.

[266]
GOVERNANCE IN POST-COMMUNIST SOCIETIES TRAVEL GRANTS

National Research Council
Attn: Office of International Affairs
2101 Constitution Avenue, N.W., FO 2060
Washington, DC 20418
(202) 334-2658   Fax: (202) 334-2614
E-mail: ocee@nas.edu
Web site: www.nationalacademies.org/oia

Purpose To provide funding to American pre- and postdoctoral scholars who are interested in traveling to central and eastern Europe, Eurasia, and the former Soviet Union to conduct research related to governance in post-Communist societies.

Eligibility This program is open to scholars at the postdoctoral level and to advanced graduate students (if the travel and research are directly relevant to their dissertation topic) who are affiliated with a U.S. university or research institution. Applicants must be interested in traveling to central or eastern Europe or the former Soviet Union to conduct research related to 1 of the subthemes of the subject of governance in post-Communist societies: 1) science and democratization—the role of scientists, engineers, and health professionals in the transition and the impact of the transition on the scientific community; 2) organized crime, terrorism, and proliferation of weapons of mass destruction—the causes of criminal activity (including counterfeiting, extortion, money-laundering, narcotics, arms trafficking, diversion of natural resources, terrorism, and proliferation), their impacts, and efforts to combat them; 3) technology and industrial economics—problems and potential technology commercialization and industrial development. Preference is given to applicants who possess relevant language capabilities and who propose to collaborate closely with a scholar from the region.

Financial data Grant amounts depend on the length of the visit and the destination of the scholar but generally range from $2,500 to $4,000. Funding covers travel costs, including international airfare and travel expenses while abroad. No provision is made for stipends, salary replacement, or indirect costs.

Duration 2 to 6 weeks.

Number awarded Varies each year.

Deadline May or December of each year.

Special features Support for this program is provided by the U.S. Department of State through its Research and Training Program for Eastern Europe and the Newly Independent States of the Former Soviet Union (Title VIII).

[267]
H. WILLIAM HARRIS VISITING PROFESSORSHIP

American Bureau for Medical Advancement in China
Attn: Executive Director
45 John Street, Suite 1100
New York, NY 10038
(212) 233-0608   Fax: (212) 233-0614
E-mail: phyllis@abmac.org
Web site: www.abmac.org

Purpose To enable selected American physicians to visit and lecture in medical schools in Taiwan.

Eligibility Outstanding medical professionals interested in visiting or lecturing in medical school in Taiwan are nominated or invited to apply for this support. Priority areas are determined annually by a committee of medical professionals in Taiwan.

Financial data The funding provides comfortable living quarters and a stipend comparable to the U.S. standard of a visiting professorship. Accommodations for spouses are also provided.

Duration 1 or more months.

Number awarded 6 each year.

[268]
HAYASHIBARA INTERNATIONAL CANCER RESEARCH FELLOWSHIP

Fujisaki Cell Center
675-1 Fujisaki
Okayama 702-8006
Japan
81 86 276 8621   Fax: 81 86 274 2150
E-mail: fcch@hayashibara.co.jp
Web site: www.hayashibara.co.jp

Purpose To provide financial support for cancer research at the Fujisaki Cell Center in Japan.

Eligibility Applicants must be interested in conducting research at the Fujisaki Cell Center. They must possess a Ph.D., M.D., or equivalent degree and be qualified to engage in fundamental leukemia-lymphoma research, cytokine-lymphokine research, or hematopoietic cell lines.

Financial data The stipend is 4.5 to 5.0 million yen per year, depending on qualifications and family considerations. Round-trip travel is also provided for the fellow. Housing within the Hayashibara Group in the city of Okoyama may be supplied, or the sponsors will assist in locating suitable accommodations within the city; in either case, the fellowship includes partial financial assistance for housing.

Duration 1 year; may be renewed for up to 4 additional years.

Special features Hayashibara Biochemical Laboratories, Inc. established the Fujisaki Cell Center in 1985 as a facility for basic research. The Hayashibara Mutual Aid Fund, a nonprofit organization within the Hayashibara Group, began offering these fellowships in 1986.

Number awarded 2 each year.

Deadline Applications may be submitted at any time.

[269]
HIV–AIDS AND RELATED ILLNESSES RESEARCH COLLABORATION AWARD

Fogarty International Center
Attn: Division of International Training and Research
31 Center Drive, Room B2C39
Bethesda, MD 20892-2220
(301) 496-1653   Fax: (301) 402-0779
E-mail: FIRCA@nih.gov
Web site: www.nih.gov/fic/programs/aidsfirc.html

Purpose To provide assistance for U.S. investigators with current funding from the National Institutes of Health (NIH) to conduct research related to AIDS at foreign sites in collaboration with foreign scientists.

Eligibility Applications may be submitted by U.S. nonprofit organizations, public and private, such as universities, colleges, hospitals, laboratories, units of state and local governments, and eligible agencies of the federal government on behalf of principal investigators. The proposed U.S. principal investigator must be the principal investigator of an AIDS or AIDS-related research grant project funded by the institutes. Racial/ethnic minority individuals, women, and persons with disabilities are encouraged to apply as principal investigators. The foreign collaborator must hold a position at an institution in a foreign country that will allow him or her adequate time and provide appropriate facilities to conduct the proposed research. Most countries are eligible for participation in this program; applications for purchase of equipment as part of the grant are limited to research in the developing countries of Africa, Asia, (except Japan, Singapore, South Korea, and Taiwan), central and eastern Europe, Russia and the Independent States of the former Soviet Union, Latin America and the non-U.S. Caribbean, the Middle East, and the Pacific Ocean Islands (except Australia and New Zealand). The application must demonstrate that the award will enhance the scientific contributions of both the U.S. and foreign scientist and will enhance or expand the contribution of the institutes-sponsored research project.

Financial data Grants up to $32,000 per year are available. Funds may be used for supplies at the foreign institution, expenses incurred at the U.S. institution to support the collaboration, and research-related travel and subsistence expenses for both the U.S. and foreign investigators. For collaborations in developing countries as defined above, requests for purchase of equipment (including computers and fax machines) are considered; up to $5,000 may be allocated as a stipend for the foreign collaborator and up to $2,000 may be allocated for the foreign collaborator to attend an AIDS-related scientific conference. Travel funds may be requested up to 20 percent of the total direct costs (up to $6,400) for the U.S. principal investigator, the foreign collaborator, and/or their colleagues or students for visits to each other's laboratory or research site, if such visits are directly related to the subject of the collaborative research.

Duration Up to 3 years.

Special features This program is the counterpart to the Fogarty International Research Collaboration Award (FIRCA) program for non-AIDS related research. It is also designated as AIDS-FIRCA.

Deadline April, August, or December of each year.

[270]
HONG KONG–AMERICA CENTER DIRECTOR OF RESEARCH AND DEVELOPMENT

Council for International Exchange of Scholars
3007 Tilden Street, N.W., Suite 5L
Washington, DC 20008-3009
(202) 686-4021   Fax: (202) 362-3442
E-mail: scholars@cies.iie.org
Web site: www.iie.org/cies

Purpose To provide funding to American administrators interested in an assignment as director of research and development at the Hong Kong–America Center.

Eligibility Applicants for this assignment as director of research and development at the center should have strong administrative skills; experience in fund-raising, philanthropy, and organizing conferences and symposia; interest and experience in program and institutional development, especially higher education initiatives; a Ph.D.; and university teaching, research, and administrative experience. They must be interested in working at the Hong Kong–America Center in developing programs; working with academic units at member universities on center-sponsored projects; assisting the director; engaging in fund-raising; designing and implementing conferences, seminars, and workshops; and expanding linkages between higher education institutions in the United States and Hong Kong. Academic backgrounds of particular interest include American studies, U.S.-China relations, higher education in Asia, environmental policy studies, and philanthropy and "Third Sector" development in Asia. Associate or full professors are preferred. Professionals will be considered if they have indicated credentials and experience. U.S. citizenship is required.

Financial data The base stipend ranges from $2,400 to $3,500 per month; other benefits include a subsistence allowance of $1,900 to $2,150 per month (depending on the number of accompanying dependents), a travel and relocation allowance of $3,550 to $7,350 (depending on the number of accompanying dependents), an apartment (for which some rent is charged), and a utilities stipend of $400 per month.

Duration Up to 2 academic years.

Special features This is a Fulbright scholar program, sponsored by the Bureau of Educational and Cultural Affairs of the U.S. Department of State and administered by the Council for International Exchange of Scholars. Teaching responsibilities on an adjunct basis may be negotiated with appropriate departments in the social sciences, humanities, or business at the Chinese University of Hong Kong.

Number awarded 1 each year.

Deadline July of each year.

[271]
HOSEI INTERNATIONAL FUND FOREIGN SCHOLARS FELLOWSHIPS

Hosei University
International Center
2-17-1 Fujimi, Chiyoda-ku
Tokyo 102-8160
Japan
81 3 3264 9315   Fax: 81 3 3238 9873
E-mail: ic@i.hosei.ac.jp
Web site: www.hosei.ac.jp/ic

Purpose To provide funding to scholars from any country who are interested in conducting research in Japan.

Eligibility Eligible to apply are individuals from any country who are interested in conducting research in Japan, have earned a master's degree (or the equivalent), are under 35 years of age, and are fluent in either Japanese or English. They must propose a program of non-degree research in the humanities, social sciences, engineering, or natural sciences. Funding is not provided for research in medical or veterinary sciences, pharmacology, nursing, agriculture, marine sciences, home economics, fine arts, or crafts.

Financial data The program provides a monthly maintenance fee of 210,000 yen, 150,000 yen for transportation to Japan, another 150,000 yen for travel to the home country if the travel takes place within 30 days after completion of the research program, and a 1-time grant of 46,000 yen for research travel within Japan.

Duration From 6 to 12 months.

Number awarded 3 each year.

Deadline July of each year.

[272]
HUBERT H. HUMPHREY JUNIOR FELLOWSHIP PROGRAM

American Institute of Bangladesh Studies
c/o Syedur Rahman
111 Sowers Street, Suite 501
State College, PA 16801-5681
(814) 865-0436   Fax: (814) 865-8299
E-mail: sxr17@psu.edu
Web site: www.aibs.net

Purpose To provide funding to doctoral students interested in conducting research in Bangladesh.

Eligibility This program is open to U.S. citizens or permanent residents whose usual residence is in the United States, who wish to conduct research in Bangladesh, and who have completed all requirements for the doctorate except the dissertation. Applicants must be affiliated with an institution that belongs to the American Institute of Bangladesh Studies (AIBS), or they must pay an application fee of $250. Proposals are evaluated on the basis of their potential contribution to the scholarly understanding of Bangladeshi society and culture.

Financial data Awards provide a stipend in Bangladeshi currency, transportation to and from Bangladesh, and a small dollar supplement.

Duration From 6 to 12 months.

Special features The Centre for Development Research in Bangladesh is responsible for the management of fellowships and acts as the counterpart organization to AIBS.

Number awarded Several each year.

Deadline January of each year.

[273]
HUBERT H. HUMPHREY SENIOR FELLOWSHIP PROGRAM

American Institute of Bangladesh Studies
c/o Syedur Rahman
111 Sowers Street, Suite 501
State College, PA 16801-5681
(814) 865-0436   Fax: (814) 865-8299
E-mail: sxr17@psu.edu
Web site: www.aibs.net

Purpose To provide funding to postdoctorates interested in conducting research in Bangladesh.

Eligibility This program is open to U.S. citizens or permanent residents whose usual residence is in the United States, who hold the Ph.D. or its recognized disciplinary equivalent, and who wish to conduct research in Bangladesh. Applicants must be affiliated with an institution that belongs to the American Institute of Bangladesh Studies (AIBS), or they must pay an application fee of $250. Proposals are evaluated on the basis of their potential contribution to the scholarly understanding of Bangladeshi society and culture.

Financial data Awards provide a stipend in Bangladeshi currency, transportation to and from Bangladesh, and a small dollar supplement. For grants longer than 4 months, transportation and a stipend supplement are also provided for 1 dependent.

Duration From 3 to 12 months.

Special features The Centre for Development Research in Bangladesh is responsible for the management of fellowships and acts as the counterpart organization to AIBS.
Number awarded Several each year.
Deadline January of each year.

[274] HUMAN FRONTIER SCIENCE PROGRAM LONG-TERM FELLOWSHIPS

Human Frontier Science Program Organization
Bureaux Europe
20, place des Halles
67080 Strasbourg
France
33 3 88 21 51 21   Fax: 33 3 88 32 88 97
E-mail: fellow@hfsp.org
Web site: www.hfsp.org

Purpose To provide financial support for postdoctoral research in biology to junior scholars who wish to go abroad.
Eligibility This program is open to researchers who have held a Ph.D. degree for less than 5 years. Applicants must wish to conduct basic research for the elucidation of brain functions and biological functions through molecular level approaches. They may be citizens of Austria, Belgium, Canada, Denmark, Finland, France, Germany, Greece, Ireland, Italy, Japan, Luxembourg, the Netherlands, Portugal, Spain, Sweden, Switzerland, the United Kingdom, or the United States, and must be seeking to conduct their research in any of those countries for which they have adequate language skills. Candidates may not conduct research in their own country nor at the institution where they obtained their Ph.D. Researchers from outside those countries are also eligible if they wish to conduct research within those countries.
Financial data Grants provide approximately $45,000 per year to cover relocation costs, living expenses and family support, a research allowance (which may be used for laboratory support or health insurance premiums), and travel to scientific meetings.
Duration 1 to 3 years; nonrenewable.
Special features The first awards under this program were presented in 1990.
Number awarded Varies each year.
Deadline August of each year.

[275] HUMAN FRONTIER SCIENCE PROGRAM RESEARCH GRANTS

Human Frontier Science Program Organization
Bureaux Europe
20 place des Halles
67080 Strasbourg
France
33 3 88 21 51 21   Fax: 33 3 88 32 88 97
E-mail: grant@hfsp.org
Web site: www.hfsp.org

Purpose To provide funding for basic research on cell biology and neurobiology to teams of researchers from member nations of the Human Frontier Science Program (HFSP).
Eligibility Scientists who are from Austria, Belgium, Canada, Denmark, Finland, France, Germany, Greece, Ireland, Italy, Japan, Luxembourg, the Netherlands, Portugal, Spain, Sweden, Switzerland, the United Kingdom, or the United States may apply for these grants to conduct basic research for the elucidation of brain functions. The proposed research must be carried out jointly by research teams, preferably of 2 to 4 members. All members of the team must have a doctoral degree or equivalent research experience, an independent laboratory, and an established record for independent research. Young Investigator Grants are for teams of researchers within the first 5 years of establishing an independent laboratory; Program Grants are for teams of researchers at any stage of their careers. The team must designate 1 of its members as the principal applicant, and that member must be a national (not just a resident) of 1 of the participating countries; other team members may be from any country. At least 1 member of the team must be of a nationality different from that of the principal applicant and at least 1 member must be affiliated with an institution located in a country other than that in which the principal applicant's institution is located. Teams should only have 1 member from any 1 country. Applications for Young Investigator Grants and Program Grants are reviewed together; the proportion of grants awarded to the 2 categories depends on the quality of applications received. Research carried out within only 1 country is not eligible.
Financial data The average grant is approximately $250,000 per year.
Duration 1 year; may be renewed up to 2 additional years.
Number awarded Varies each year; recently, 54 research grants (including both Young Investigator and Program Grants) were awarded.
Deadline August of each year.

[276] HUMAN FRONTIER SCIENCE PROGRAM SHORT-TERM FELLOWSHIPS

Human Frontier Science Program Organization
Bureaux Europe
20 place des Halles
67080 Strasbourg
France
33 3 88 21 51 21   Fax: 33 3 88 32 88 97
E-mail: fellow@hfsp.org
Web site: www.hfsp.org

Purpose To provide funding for basic research on cell biology and neurobiology to scientists from member nations of the Human Frontier Science Program (HFSP).
Eligibility Researchers who are from Austria, Belgium, Canada, Denmark, Finland, France, Germany, Greece, Ireland, Italy, Japan, Luxembourg, the Netherlands, Portugal, Spain, Sweden, Switzerland, the United Kingdom, or the United States and have a Ph.D. degree or equivalent research experience are eligible to apply. Preference is given to young investigators at an early stage of their careers. Applicants must be proposing to work in a laboratory in 1 of the other countries to learn new techniques or develop collaborations in the areas supported by the program: brain functions and biological functions at the molecular level. Scientists from non-member countries may participate if they are associated with a scientist from a mem-

ber country. All applicants must have adequate language skills to carry out the proposed project at a host institution.

Financial data Fellowships cover round-trip travel expenses to the host institution and living expenses; the exact amount depends on the country where the research is conducted.

Duration 2 weeks to 3 months.

Limitations These fellowships are not intended to enable researchers to attend workshops, courses, or symposia; to provide support during periods of sabbatical leave; to plan future work; or to write papers, books, or reviews.

Number awarded Varies; generally, 70 or more each year.

Deadline Applications may be submitted at any time.

[277]
ICFJ-KKC FELLOWSHIP IN JAPAN

International Center for Journalists
1616 H Street, N.W., Third Floor
Washington, DC 20006
(202) 737-3700   Fax: (202) 737-0530
E-mail: editor@icfj.org
Web site: www.icfj.org

Purpose To provide support to American journalists who wish to travel to Japan.

Eligibility Applicants must be U.S. citizens between the ages of 25 and 50 who have at least 5 years of experience as reporters or editors at newspapers, magazines, or news agencies. They must be interested in pursuing an individual reporting or research project in Japan. This should be their first visit to the country.

Financial data All travel, living, and program-related costs, including the advance orientation, are provided.

Duration 2 weeks.

Special features Participants are given the opportunity to work with news organizations in Japan. Funding for this program, established in 1991, is provided by the Keizai Koho Center (KKC), affiliated with the Japan Institute for Social and Economic Affairs. It is administered by the International Center for Journalists (ICFJ). Since the program began in 1991, 58 American journalists from 23 different states have participated.

Number awarded Up to 5 each year.

Deadline July of each year.

[278]
ICHIRO KANEHARA FOUNDATION SCHOLARSHIP FOR FOREIGN STUDENTS

Ichiro Kanehara Foundation
Akamon Royal Heights 1003
5-29-12 Hongo, Bunkyo-ku
Tokyo 113-0033
Japan
81 3 3815 7801

Purpose To provide financial assistance to graduate students and postdoctorates from other countries who are interested in obtaining training or conducting medical research in Japan.

Eligibility Eligible to apply are graduate students or postdoctorates from other countries who wish to conduct basic medical research or learn about surgical techniques at research facilities in Japan. Applications are sent to deans of medical colleges and directors of research institutions in Japan who distribute them to qualified students. Most recipients are from developing nations.

Financial data Fellows receive 100,000 yen per month.

Duration 1 year.

Number awarded 2 to 4 each year.

Deadline December of each year.

[279]
ICRISAT RESEARCH SCHOLARSHIPS

International Crops Research Institute for the Semi-Arid Tropics
Patancheru 502 324
Andhra Pradesh
India
91 40 329 6161   Fax: 91 40 324 1239
E-mail: icrisat@cgiar.org
Web site: www.icrisat.org

Purpose To provide financial assistance to graduate students from the semi-arid tropics or those interested in gaining experience in tropical agriculture.

Eligibility Applicants must be candidates for M.Sc. or Ph.D. degrees in agricultural or related sciences whose universities will accept thesis research conducted at facilities of the International Crops Research Institute for the Semi-Arid Tropics (ICRISAT) in India, Kenya, Malawi, Mali, Niger, Nigeria, or Zimbabwe. Normally they are nominated by their national agricultural agency, most often in a developing country. The nominating agency usually provides or arranges funding, although it may apply directly to ICRISAT (which has limited funding for these scholarships). The proposed research must relate to agronomy, plant breeding, genetics, biotechnology (applied genomics and genetic transformation), genetic resources, physiology, entomology, pathology, microbiology, cytogenetics, soil physics, socio-economics, virology, land and water management, agriclimatology, or statistical techniques related to sorghum, pearl millet, groundnuts, pigeonpea, chickpea, and rainfed semi-arid tropical resource management.

Financial data Scholarships provide transportation, a maintenance allowance for personal expenses, and a living allowance to cover room, food, medical insurance, research, and other expenses.

Duration 1 to 3 years.

Number awarded Varies each year.

Deadline March of each year.

[280]
ICRISAT VISITING SCHOLARSHIPS

International Crops Research Institute for the Semi-Arid Tropics
Patancheru 502 324
Andhra Pradesh
India
91 40 329 6161   Fax: 91 40 324 1239
E-mail: icrisat@cgiar.org
Web site: www.icrisat.org

Purpose To provide financial assistance to scholars who are interested in pursuing additional research training on subjects supported by the International Crops Research Institute for the Semi-Arid Tropics (ICRISAT).

Eligibility Applicants must have received a Ph.D. or M.Sc. degree in agricultural or related sciences. They must be nominated by their national agricultural agency, usually in a developing country. Normally the nominating agency provides or arranges funding, although ICRISAT has limited funding for which the nominating agency may apply on behalf of the candidate. The proposed research must relate to agronomy, plant breeding, genetics, biotechnology (applied genomics and genetic transformation), genetic resources, physiology, entomology, pathology, microbiology, cytogenetics, soil physics, socio-economics, virology, land and water management, agriclimatology, or statistical techniques related to sorghum, pearl millet, groundnuts, pigeonpea, chickpea, and rainfed semi-arid tropical resource management.

Financial data Fellowships provide transportation, a maintenance allowance for personal expenses, and a living allowance to cover room, food, medical insurance, research, and other expenses.

Duration 1 year, with a potential 1-year extension.

Special features The supervised training program may be conducted at ICRISAT locations in India, Kenya, Malawi, Kenya, Niger, Nigeria, or Zimbabwe.

Number awarded Varies each year.

[281]
INDIVIDUAL ADVANCED RESEARCH OPPORTUNITIES IN CENTRAL AND EASTERN EUROPE AND EURASIA

International Research & Exchanges Board
1616 H Street, N.W.
Washington, DC 20006
(202) 628-8188   Fax: (202) 628-8189
E-mail: irex@irex.org
Web site: www.irex.org

Purpose To provide research opportunities for predoctoral and postdoctoral scholars at institutions in central Europe, eastern Europe, and Eurasia.

Eligibility Eligibility requirements include: U.S. citizenship or permanent residency for 3 years prior to applying; command of host-country language sufficient for research; and affiliation with a university as a faculty member or advanced doctoral candidate. Applications are accepted in all disciplines, but policy research and development, the humanities and social sciences, and cross-disciplinary studies are emphasized. Limited assistance is available for cross-regional research in Turkey and Iran for postdoctoral humanities scholars.

Financial data The grant provides round-trip airfare and visa fees, a stipend (in the form of a monthly allowance for graduate students or a stipend in lieu of salary for faculty members), host-country room and board, a local research allowance, and excess baggage allowance; support for accompanying family members may be available.

Duration From 2 to 9 months.

Special features The International Research & Exchanges Board (IREX) was established in 1968 at the request of U.S. universities by the American Council of Learned Societies (ACLS) and the Social Science Research Council (SSRC) to administer research exchange programs with the socialist countries of eastern Europe and the former Soviet Republics. Funding for this program is provided by the U.S. Department of State as a Title VIII program and the National Endowment for the Humanities

Limitations Exchange applicants in modern foreign languages and area studies must apply simultaneously for Department of Education Fulbright-Hays grants.

Number awarded Approximately 37 each year; recently, 12 grants were for central and eastern Europe and 25 for Eurasia.

Deadline October of each year.

[282]
INTERNATIONAL AFFAIRS FELLOWSHIP IN JAPAN

Council on Foreign Relations
Attn: Membership and Fellowship Affairs
58 East 68th Street
New York, NY 10021
(212) 434-9489   Fax: (212) 434-9801
E-mail: fellowships@cfr.org
Web site: www.cfr.org/public/fp.html

Purpose To enable outstanding young American leaders and thinkers to expand their intellectual and professional horizons by working and living in Japan.

Eligibility Application for these fellowships is primarily by invitation, on the recommendation of a national panel of individuals in academic, government, and other institutions who have had the opportunity to identify persons well suited for the experience the program provides. Others who inquire directly and who meet preliminary requirements may also be invited to apply without formal nomination. Eligible for this program are American citizens between 27 and 45 years of age who have not had prior substantial experience in Japan. Applicants may come from academia (including think tanks), government (including executive and legislative branches at both the federal and state level), business, and the media. They must be interested in living and working in Japan. Knowledge of the Japanese language is not a requirement. Selection is based on academic and professional accomplishments, as well as on the merits of the specific research or action projects proposed by the applicants.

Financial data The fellowship covers living expenses in Japan, plus international transportation, health and travel insurance, and necessary research expenses.

Duration Fellows spend from 3 to 12 months in Japan.

Special features Funds for this program, established in 1997, are provided by Hitachi, Ltd. Participants can conduct policy-oriented research or engage in related professional activities. The council will assist in arranging affiliation with academic, governmental, or private sector institutions in Japan. Hitachi, Ltd. will assist in locating housing and getting the participants settled in the Japanese environment.

Limitations The program does not fund pre- or postdoctoral research, work toward a degree, or the completion of projects on which substantial progress has already been made.

Number awarded Varies each year; recently, 2 of these fellowships were awarded.

Deadline September of each year.

[283]
INTERNATIONAL RESEARCH EXCHANGE FOUNDATION FOR JAPANESE STUDIES FELLOWSHIPS

International Research Exchange Foundation for Japanese Studies
c/o International Research Center for Japanese Studies
3-2 Oeyama-cho, Goryo, Nishikyo-ku, Kyoto-shi
Kyoto 610-1192
Japan
81 75 332 1868   Fax: 81 75 333 1565

Purpose To provide financial assistance to scholars from any country who are interested in conducting doctoral research in selected subjects in Japan.

Eligibility Eligible to apply are students from countries other than Japan who are interested in conducting dissertation research as doctoral students in Japan at any of 16 public or 19 private colleges and universities. The research may be in anthropology, economics, psychology, geography, sociology, political science, humanities, history of scientific technology, philosophy, history, or literature, but must have a focus on Japanese studies. Applicants must demonstrate financial need and not be receiving scholarship assistance from any other source.

Financial data The stipend is 150,000 yen per month.

Duration 2 years.

Number awarded 2 each year.

Deadline April of each year.

[284]
INTERNATIONAL RESEARCH SCIENTIST DEVELOPMENT AWARD

Fogarty International Center
Attn: Division of International Training and Research
31 Center Drive, Room B2C39
Bethesda, MD 20892-2220
(301) 496-1653   Fax: (301) 402-0779
E-mail: IRSDA@nih.gov
Web site: www.nih.gov/fic

Purpose To provide funding to U.S. biomedical scientists interested in continuing research in, or extending their research into, developing countries.

Eligibility Applicants must have received a doctoral, dental, or medical degree within the past 7 years in a basic biomedical, behavioral, or epidemiological/clinical field. They must have established a relationship with 2 prospective mentors, 1 in the United States and 1 in a developing country, who have ongoing, funded, international collaborative research. The U.S. mentor should be at a U.S. institution of higher learning or nonprofit research institution. The developing country mentor should be in an internationally developing country research institution addressing some of that country's major health problems. Eligible countries include those in the following regions: Africa, Asia (except Japan, Singapore, South Korea, and Taiwan), central and eastern Europe, Russia and the Newly Independent States of the former Soviet Union, Latin America and the non-U.S. Caribbean, the Middle East (except Israel), and the Pacific Ocean Islands (except Australia and New Zealand). Applications to work in institutions in sub-Saharan Africa are especially encouraged. Racial/ethnic minority individuals, women, and persons with disabilities are encouraged to apply as principal investigators. Applications must be submitted on behalf of the candidate by the U.S. mentor's institution. The applicant need not already be at that institution at the time of application, but it is expected that the U.S. component of the project will be carried out by the fellow at the U.S. mentor's institution.

Financial data Grants provide up to $300,000 for the complete project, prorated at a rate of $8,333 per month (including $6,250 per month direct costs for salary and fringe benefits and $2,083 per month for all other allowable costs). Other allowable costs include travel (round-trip airfare and necessary ground transportation for the candidate to the foreign site up to 5 times over the duration of the project, round-trip airfare for each dependent accompanying the awardee for 6 months or more abroad, excess baggage allowance), health insurance up to $50 per month for the candidate and each dependent during the time abroad, a supplemental living allowance of $150 per month for each dependent accompanying the awardee for 6 months or more, and research development support. An administrative supplement, up to $20,000, may be provided during the third year of the award to fellows who obtain a tenure-track faculty position upon return to the United States.

Duration Support is provided for 36 months, which may be spread over a period of 5 years. A total of at least 24 months should be at the foreign site under the joint supervision of the U.S. and foreign mentors. A period of work in the foreign country should be at least 3 months in length. A total of up to 12 months will be funded for work at the U.S. institution under the U.S. mentor's supervision.

Number awarded Varies each year.

Deadline February of each year.

[285]
INVITATION PROGRAM OF FOREIGN RESEARCHERS TO JAPANESE INSTITUTES

Foundation for Promotion of Cancer Research
c/o National Cancer Center
5-1-1 Tsukiji, Chuo-ku
Tokyo 104-0045
Japan
81 3 3543 0332   Fax: 81 3 3546 7826
E-mail: tkoseki@info.ncc.go.jp
Web site: www.ncc.go.jp

Purpose To promote international scientific cooperation in the field of cancer research.

Eligibility Applications are accepted from scientists at 3 different levels: 1) distinguished scientists who have made major contributions to the field of cancer research or who currently hold important positions in cancer research institutions; 2) professors or senior scientists who carry out independent research and manage their own research group; and 3) assistant professors, postdoctoral researchers, or junior scientists with professional experience equivalent to assistant professors. Citizenship is unrestricted. Applications are submitted through a Japanese host scientist, who usually is affiliated with either the National Cancer Center, the National Institute of Health (Shinagawa-ku, Tokyo 141), or the National Institute of Hygienic Sciences (Setagaya-ku, Tokyo 158).

Financial data The program provides a monthly stipend that depends on the qualifications and research experience of the grantee and round-trip airfare. Fellows staying more than 3 months receive round-trip airfare for their spouse and children, an allowance for educational costs for the children, and an allowance for apartment accommodations or a hotel. Commuter costs and limited insurance expenses are also covered.

Duration 1 to 2 years; applications for stays of a few weeks are also considered.

Special features The Foundation for Promotion of Cancer Research was established in September 1968 by Japan's Ministry of Health and Welfare to support various activities for cancer research. In March 1984, it reorganized as a nongovernmental collaborative organization, including the National Cancer Center and the Japanese government, and began inviting eminent scientists from abroad to Japan for promotion of cancer research.

Number awarded Approximately 20 each year.

Deadline Applications are accepted at any time.

[286]
ISEAS RESEARCH FELLOWSHIPS

Institute of Southeast Asian Studies
Attn: Head of Administration
30 Heng Mui Keng Terrace
Pasir Panjang Road
Singapore 119614
Republic of Singapore
65 778 0955   Fax: 65 778 1735
E-mail: admin@iseas.edu.sg
Web site: www.iseas.edu.sg

Purpose To enable established scholars and other well-qualified individuals to conduct research at the Institute of Southeast Asian Studies (ISEAS) on topics related to southeast Asian studies.

Eligibility This program is open to senior scholars who wish to conduct research at the institute in Singapore. Their proposed research may involve any discipline with a focus on southeast Asia, but the institute emphasizes economics, anthropology, political science, and international relations. Preference is given to applicants who specialize in Indonesia and Malaysia, particularly in the field of politics, and have the requisite knowledge of those countries' national languages.

Financial data The gross monthly stipend ranges from $S5,488 to $S12,641, depending on the fellow's qualifications and experience. Fellows from overseas also receive a housing subsidy, passage assistance, and a baggage allowance.

Duration Up to 1 year.

Special features ISEAS is funded by grants from major foundations and by an operating subsidy from the Singapore Government.

Number awarded Varies each year.

Deadline August of each year.

[287]
JAPAN ADVANCED RESEARCH GRANTS

Social Science Research Council
810 Seventh Avenue
New York, NY 10019
(212) 377-2700   Fax: (212) 377-2727
E-mail: japan@ssrc.org
Web site: www.ssrc.org

Purpose To provide financial assistance for advanced research, in any country, on Japan in all areas of the social sciences and humanities.

Eligibility Eligible to apply are scholars who are U.S. citizens (or have been resident in the United States for at least 3 consecutive years) and have either a Ph.D. or equivalent research or analytical experience. The program encourages innovative research in the social sciences that is comparative and contemporary in nature, and has long-range applied policy implications, or that engages Japan in wide regional and global debates. Special attention is given to Japan specialists who are interested in broadening their skills and expertise through additional training or comparative work in an additional geographic area. Minorities and women are particularly encouraged to apply.

Financial data The maximum award is $25,000.

Duration 2 months to 1 year.

Special features Depending on the nature of the proposed project, the research may be carried out in Japan, the United States, and/or other countries. Scholars may apply for support to conduct research in collaboration with Japanese scholars who have other support. Funding for this program is provided by the Japan-United States Friendship Commission.

Limitations These grants are not for training and candidates for academic degrees are not eligible. If travel is planned, applicants must try to arrange for affiliation with an American or foreign university or research institute.

Number awarded Varies each year.

Deadline November of each year.

[288]
JAPAN FOUNDATION DOCTORAL FELLOWSHIPS

Japan Foundation
152 West 57th Street, 39th Floor
New York, NY 10019
(212) 489-0299   Fax: (212) 489-0409
E-mail: info@jfny.org
Web site: www.jfny.org

Purpose To provide financial assistance to American doctoral candidates who are interested in conducting research in Japan.

Eligibility Doctoral candidates in the arts, social sciences, and humanities are eligible to apply if they are American citizens or permanent residents and wish to conduct research in Japan. Applicants must have completed all requirements except the dissertation when they begin the fellowship. They are expected to be proficient enough in the Japanese language to pursue their research in Japan.

Financial data Doctoral fellowships carry a monthly stipend of 310,000 yen, insurance, economy-class round-trip transportation, a dependent allowance of 50,000 yen per month, a settling-in allowance of 239,000 yen, a research/cultural activities allowance of 40,000 yen per month, a departure allowance of 64,000 yen, and the actual amount of enrollment fees up to 50,000 yen per month.

Duration From 4 to 14 months.

Special features The address for the foundation in Japan is: ARK Mori Building, 20-21F, 1-12-32 Akasaka, Minato-ku, Tokyo 107-6021, Japan. In addition to the New York address listed above, there is also a west coast address: 2425 West Olympic Boulevard, Suite 650E, Santa Monica, CA 90404-4034, (310) 449-0027, (888) 667-0880, Fax: (310) 449-1127. Applications from the western United States should be sent to that address.

Limitations Fellowships are tenable only in Japan. Fellows are expected to devote full time to their proposed research and may not accept employment in Japan during the term of the award. Applicants whose research projects require the cooperation of Japanese professionals or institutions are expected to make the necessary arrangements themselves. Fellows are expected to submit a report of their research (or other activities) at the end of the program. They may not hold another major grant concurrently with the Japan Foundation fellowship.

Number awarded Approximately 11 each year.

Deadline October of each year.

[289]
JAPAN FOUNDATION RESEARCH FELLOWSHIPS

Japan Foundation
152 West 57th Street, 39th Floor
New York, NY 10019
(212) 489-0299   Fax: (212) 489-0409
E-mail: info@jfny.org
Web site: www.jfny.org

Purpose To provide financial assistance to American scholars who wish to conduct research in Japan.

Eligibility Candidates for these fellowships should be American citizens or permanent residents of the United States. American citizens residing abroad are also eligible to apply. They must have completed their Ph.D. degree or successfully defended their dissertation prior to the date applications are due. Further, they should have an academic position in a research institution as well as substantial experience in research, teaching, and writing in their field of study. All research topics are eligible for support, if they relate in substantial part to Japan in the humanities and social sciences. Former fellowship holders are requested to refrain from reapplying for at least 3 years after the completion of their fellowships.

Financial data These fellowships carry monthly stipends of 370,000 to 430,000 yen (depending upon the recipient's professional career position). In addition, fellows receive insurance, business-class round-trip travel, a dependent allowance (50,000 yen per month), a settling-in allowance (239,000 yen), a research/cultural activities allowance (40,000 yen per month), a departure allowance (64,000 yen), and an allowance for enrollment fees (actual amount up to 50,000 yen per month).

Duration 2 to 12 months.

Special features The address for the foundation in Japan is: ARK Mori Building, 20-21F, 1-12-32 Akasaka, Minato-ku, Tokyo 107-6021, Japan. In addition to the New York address listed above, there is also a west coast address: 2425 West Olympic Boulevard, Suite 650E, Santa Monica, CA 90404-4034, (310) 449-0027, (888) 667-0880, Fax: (310) 449-1127. Applications from the western United States should be sent to that address.

Limitations Fellowships are tenable in Japan, although fellows may request to spend part of their term in the United States if the proposed research is indispensable to the project and the fellow will still spend more than two-thirds of the research time in Japan on a project at least 4 months in duration. Fellows are expected to devote full time to their proposed research and may not accept employment in Japan during the term of the award. Proficiency in Japanese is desirable but is not required, except in those cases where it is necessary to complete the research project. Applicants whose research projects require the cooperation of Japanese professionals or institutions are expected to make the necessary arrangements themselves. Fellows are expected to submit a report of their research (or other activities) at the end of the program. They may not hold another major grant concurrently with the Japan Foundation fellowship.

Number awarded Approximately 11 each year.

Deadline October of each year.

[290]
JAPAN FULBRIGHT FELLOWSHIPS FOR GRADUATING SENIORS

Institute of International Education
Attn: Student Programs Division
809 United Nations Plaza
New York, NY 10017-3580
(212) 984-5330   Fax: (212) 984-5325
Web site: www.iie.org/fulbright

Purpose To provide an opportunity for recent American college graduates to conduct independent study or research in Japan.

Eligibility Applicants must be U.S. citizens who will graduate with a bachelor's degree in any field of study (including the creative and performing arts and natural sciences) between January and August of the year following application. Some Japanese language study and course work is preferred. Recipients are placed in institutions outside Tokyo, but they do not enroll as degree students. They structure their own programs, combining language study, selected course study according to their language proficiency, and individual research under the guidance of an assigned professor. All applicants for the Fulbright Full Grants in Japan are automatically considered for these awards.

Financial data The grant provides a monthly stipend and allowances for settling-in, baggage, housing, dependents, and research. Also, fees for university affiliation and Japanese language study, as necessary, are covered.

Duration 1 year; nonrenewable.

Special features Some awards are funded by the private sector through contributions to the Japanese alumni's Fulbright Foundation. Others are funded through the Fulbright program, administered in the United States by the Institute of International Education (IIE). Students who are currently enrolled in the United States are to apply through the Fulbright program adviser on their campus; at-large applicants (those not cur-

FINANCIAL AID PROGRAMS

rently enrolled) may obtain applications and information directly from the IIE.

Limitations Recipients must arrive in Japan in time to participate in an orientation program in September and must also participate in a mid-year conference.

Number awarded Approximately 10 each year, of which 1, sponsored by the American Chamber of Commerce in Japan, is designated for a student in business and includes an internship.

Deadline October of each year.

[291]
JAPAN TRAVEL GRANTS FOR ACM FACULTY

Associated Colleges of the Midwest
Attn: Program Officer
205 West Wacker Drive, Suite 1300
Chicago, IL 60606
(312) 263-5000   Fax: (312) 263-5879
E-mail: acm@acm.edu
Web site: www.acm.edu/faculty/travel.htm

Purpose To provide funding to faculty members at schools belonging to the Associated Colleges of the Midwest (ACM) who wish to visit Japan.

Eligibility This program is open to faculty from ACM colleges who wish to visit Japan for research or course development. The proposed projects should impact the Japan-related curriculum or the co-curricular life of the applicant's home campus.

Financial data Grants cover round-trip airfare between the recipient's college and Japan.

Special features The ACM colleges are Beloit College, Carleton College, University of Chicago, Coe College, Cornell College, Colorado College, Grinnell College, Knox College, Lake Forest College, Lawrence University, Macalester College, Monmouth College, Ripon College, and St. Olaf College. Information is also available from Kevin Morrison, Earlham College, Japan Study Program, Richmond, IN 47374, (765) 983-1224, E-mail: japanstu@earlham.edu.

Number awarded 4 to 6 each year.

Deadline November of each year.

[292]
JAPAN-U.S. JOURNALISTS' EXCHANGE

International Center for Journalists
1616 H Street, N.W., Third Floor
Washington, DC 20006
(202) 737-3700   Fax: (202) 737-0530
E-mail: maia@icfj.org
Web site: www.icfj.org

Purpose To provide support to U.S. and Japanese journalists who wish to participate in an exchange program.

Eligibility This program is open to Japanese and U.S. editors and journalists who wish to learn more about Japan-U.S. relations. Applicants must be interested in a program that includes visits with news media, business leaders, and government officials in the country other than their own.

Financial data All international airfare, hotel, meal, and local transportation costs are covered.

Duration U.S. journalists spend 12 days in Japan, while Japanese journalists are visiting the United States. At the end of that time, both groups meet at the East-West Center in Honolulu for 2 days of conferences.

Special features Funding for this program, established in 1972, is provided by the United States-Japan Foundation. It is administered by the International Center for Journalists (ICFJ). During the trip, ample time is provided to participants to pursue their own story ideas.

Number awarded 12 each year: 6 from Japan and 6 from the United States.

Deadline June of each year.

[293]
JAPANESE-LANGUAGE EDUCATION FELLOWSHIP PROGRAM

Japan Foundation
Attn: Los Angeles Language Center
The Water Garden
2425 West Olympic Boulevard, Suite 650E
Santa Monica, CA 90404-4034
(310) 449-0027, ext. 104   (888) 667-0880, ext. 104
Fax: (310) 449-1127   E-mail: jfla@jflalc.org
Web site: www.jflalc.org

Purpose To provide an opportunity for teachers of Japanese from other countries to develop teaching resources and methodology in cooperation with education specialists in Japan.

Eligibility Any university, college, or nonprofit educational institution is eligible to apply for funding for professionals involved in Japanese language instruction. The proposal must be for travel to Japan to participate in cooperation with, or under the guidance of, Japanese professionals in 1) the development of Japanese language teaching resources that meet the needs of their own countries; 2) the development or study of Japanese language teaching methods and curriculum based on concrete teaching resources and themes that meet the needs of their own countries; or 3) research in a field that is relevant to Japanese language education. Applications must be submitted through Japanese language educational institutions that develop teaching resources or methods; direct applications from individuals are not accepted.

Financial data The program provides round-trip airfare, a stipend of 210,000 or 270,000 yen per month (depending on the fellow's professional status), a materials allowance of 30,000 yen per month, an arrival allowance of 65,000 yen, a research allowance of 80,000 yen, and a departure allowance of 64,000 yen. If relevant, advisors receive an honorarium of 40,000 yen per month. Fellows are also provided with housing at the institute; if they prefer not to live there, they receive a housing allowance of 100,000 yen per month plus a gift-money allowance of 110,000 yen, if necessary, upon renting a house. Fellows accompanied by dependents receive a family allowance of 50,000 yen per month (regardless of the number of dependents).

Duration Grants are made either for short-term fellowships (1 to 3 months) or for long-term fellowships (3 to 8 months).

Special features The address for the foundation in Japan is: ARK Mori Building, 20-21F, 1-12-32 Akasaka, Minato-ku, Tokyo 107-6021, Japan.

Number awarded In recent years, 1 grant has been awarded each year in the United States; if the grant has been for short-term fellowships, up to 2 people per project may visit Japan; if the grant has been for long-term fellowships, 1 person per project may visit Japan. The total number of fellows from all countries ranges from 12 to 14 each year.

Deadline November of each year.

[294]
JAPAN–UNITED STATES ARTS PROGRAM FELLOWSHIPS

Asian Cultural Council
437 Madison Avenue, 37th Floor
New York, NY 10022-7001
(212) 812-4300   Fax: (212) 812-4299
E-mail: acc@accny.org
Web site: www.asianculturalcouncil.org

Purpose To provide funding for a cultural exchange between humanists in the United States and Japan.

Eligibility Eligible to apply are artists, art specialists, or art scholars in the United States or Japan who are interested in undertaking research, study, travel, or creative projects in the other country. Their specialties must include: archaeology, architecture (design, history, or theory), art history, conservation, crafts, dance, film, literature, museum studies, music, painting, photography, printmaking, sculpture, theater, or video. Applications are not accepted for lecture programs, personal exhibitions, individual performance tours, undergraduate study, or activities conducted by individuals in their home countries.

Financial data Fellows receive international and domestic travel allowances, a living allowance, and an allocation for miscellaneous expenses (including books and supplies). Partial fellowships are available for fellows with supplementary assistance from other sources.

Duration 1 to 6 months.

Special features This program also provides grants to institutions in Japan and the United States that wish to sponsor cultural activities by artists from the other country.

Number awarded Varies each year; recently, 11 individuals (8 from Japan and 3 from the United States) and 13 institutions received support from this program.

Deadline January of each year.

[295]
JAUW INTERNATIONAL FELLOWSHIP

Japanese Association of University Women
Attn: Fellowship Chair
11-6-101 Samon-cho, Shinjuku-ku
Tokyo 160-0017
Japan
81 3 3358 2882   Fax: 81 3 3358 2889
E-mail: jauw@tky2.3web.ne.jp
Web site: www3.tky.3web.net.jp/~jauw

Purpose To encourage university-educated women to undertake advanced study or original research in Japan.

Eligibility An applicant must be a member of a national federation or association affiliated with the International Federation of University Women (IFUW) and must wish to carry out independent research or advanced study on the postgraduate level in Japan. The applicant must have earned at least the equivalent of a bachelor's degree and must have been accepted by a Japanese institution.

Financial data The stipend ranges from 1,000,000 to 1,500,000 yen.

Duration 3 to 6 months.

Special features This program includes the Holmes Fellowship, the Yasui Fellowship for Medical Students, and the Morita Fellowship Award (established in 1998) for scientific research by young women. In the United States, the IFUW affiliate is the American Association of University Women (AAUW), 1111 16th Street, N.W., Washington, DC 20036-4873, (202) 785-7700, (800) 821-4364.

Limitations A final report must be submitted within 1 year of the completion of the program.

Number awarded 2 each year.

Deadline May of each year.

[296]
JAZZ AMBASSADORS PROGRAM

John F. Kennedy Center for the Performing Arts
Education Department
Attn: Jazz Ambassadors Program
2700 F Street, N.W.
Washington, DC 20566
(202) 416-8869   Fax: (202) 416-8802
E-mail: artsabroad@kennedy-center.org
Web site: www.kennedy-center.org/programs/jazz/ambassadors

Purpose To enable American jazz musicians to perform in foreign countries.

Eligibility Jazz musicians from the United States who are U.S. citizens at least 21 years of age may audition to participate in this program. Successful applicants must demonstrate artistic and musical ability, be conversant with broader aspects of contemporary American culture, and be adaptable to rigorous traveling through countries in Africa, Latin America, the Near East, and south Asia that are less frequently visited by other American artists. While abroad, they present concerts and conduct master classes and lecture-recitals for musicians.

Financial data Each Jazz Ambassador is compensated for all travel, living, and program expenses and receives a modest honorarium of $200 per day.

Duration Tours last 4 to 6 weeks.

Special features This program is sponsored jointly by the John F. Kennedy Center for the Performing Arts and the U.S. Department of State's Bureau of Educational and Cultural Affairs. The program began in 1997 with the Artistic Ambassadors Program that presented classical musicians. The program switched to jazz for 1998.

Number awarded 7 trios are selected each year.

Deadline May of each year.

[297]
JEAN AND KATSUMA DAN FELLOWSHIP FUND
Woods Hole Marine Biological Laboratory
Attn: Fellowship Coordinator
7 MBL Street
Woods Hole, MA 02543-1015
(508) 289-7441   Fax: (508) 457-1924
E-mail: skaufman@mbl.edu
Web site: www.mbl.edu

Purpose To support an exchange between Japanese and American marine biologists.

Eligibility Eligible to be nominated are American junior investigators who are qualified to work at marine biology laboratories in Japan. Nominations for this fellowship should be submitted directly to the Director's Office of the Woods Hole Marine Biological Laboratory (MBL).

Financial data Funds are available from the MBL to support the costs associated with this exchange.

Number awarded Varies each year.

Deadline January of each year.

[298]
JET PROGRAM ASSISTANT LANGUAGE TEACHER
Embassy of Japan
Attn: Office of the JET Program
2520 Massachusetts Avenue, N.W.
Washington, DC 20008
(202) 939-6772   (800) INFO-JET
E-mail: eojjet@erols.com
Web site: www.mofa.go.jp/j_info/visit/jet/position.html

Purpose To offer participants from selected countries the opportunity to work as teachers of foreign languages in Japan.

Eligibility This program is open to citizens of 37 countries outside Japan, including the United States. Applicants from this country must be U.S. citizens, be under the age of 35, have earned at least a bachelor's degree (or its equivalent), and have an interest and experience in the teaching of English in Japan.

Financial data Participants receive approximately 3.6 million yen per year, as well as round-trip transportation and a travel allowance inside of Japan.

Duration 1 year.

Special features Participants are placed in public or private schools or local boards of education. They engage in language instruction under the guidance of teachers' consultants or Japanese teachers of the foreign language. The Japan Exchange and Teaching (JET) program was started in 1987. It is sponsored by the Japan Ministry of Foreign Affairs, the Japan Ministry of Education, Culture, Sports, Science and Technology, the Japan Ministry of Home Affairs, and local governments in Japan.

Number awarded Varies each year; recently, more than 4,500 people participated in this program, of whom 2,432 were Americans.

Deadline November of each year.

[299]
JET PROGRAM COORDINATOR FOR INTERNATIONAL RELATIONS
Embassy of Japan
Attn: Office of the JET Program
2520 Massachusetts Avenue, N.W.
Washington, DC 20008
(202) 939-6772   (800) INFO-JET
E-mail: eojjet@erols.com
Web site: www.mofa.go.jp/j_info/visit/jet/position.html

Purpose To offer participants from foreign countries the opportunity to serve in local governments in Japan.

Eligibility This program is open to citizens of 37 countries outside Japan, including the United States. Applicants from this country must be U.S. citizens, be under the age of 35, have earned at least a bachelor's degree (or its equivalent), have functional command of the Japanese language, and be interested in serving in local government in Japan.

Financial data Participants receive approximately 3.6 million yen per year, as well as round-trip transportation and a travel allowance inside of Japan.

Duration 1 year.

Special features Participants are placed in offices of prefectures or designated local governments. Their responsibilities include: assistance with projects related to international activities carried out by local governments; assistance with the language instruction of government employees and local residents; assistance with and participation in activities of local private groups or organizations engaging in international exchange; assistance with exchange activities related to local residents' cross-cultural understanding; and other duties as specified by division management in offices of prefectures, cities, towns, or villages. The Japan Exchange and Teaching (JET) program was started in 1987. It is sponsored by the Japan Ministry of Foreign Affairs, the Japan Ministry of Education, Culture, Sports, Science and Technology, the Japan Ministry of Home Affairs, and local governments in Japan.

Number awarded Varies each year; recently, approximately 450 people participated in this program, of whom 126 were Americans.

Deadline November of each year.

[300]
JET PROGRAM SPORTS EXCHANGE ADVISOR
Embassy of Japan
Attn: Office of the JET Program
2520 Massachusetts Avenue, N.W.
Washington, DC 20008
(202) 939-6772   (800) INFO-JET
E-mail: eojjet@erols.com
Web site: www.mofa.go.jp/j_info/visit/jet/position.html

Purpose To offer participants from foreign countries the opportunity to participate in sports exchange with local governments in Japan.

Eligibility This program is open to citizens of 37 countries outside Japan, including the United States. Applicants from this country must be U.S. citizens, be under the age of 35, have earned at least a bachelor's degree (or its equivalent), and be interested in engaging in an international sports exchange under the guidance of the division management in offices in prefectures or designated cities in Japan. This program does not accept unsolicited applications; a Japanese sports organization contacts its American counterpart to find someone to fill a position. Persons in this country who are interested should contact a relevant sports organization here.

Financial data Participants receive approximately 3.6 million yen per year, as well as round-trip transportation and a travel allowance inside of Japan.

Duration 1 year.

Special features Responsibilities include: assistance with sports training programs carried out by local governments (including cooperating and advising on planning, designing, and implementing sports projects); assistance with sports training of local talented athletes; assistance with sports training of local government employees and residents; advising on the planning of sports projects organized by local private groups or organizations engaging in international exchange; and other duties as specified by the host institution. The Japan Exchange and Teaching (JET) program was started in 1987. It is sponsored by the Japan Ministry of Foreign Affairs, the Japan Ministry of Education, Culture, Sports, Science and Technology, the Japan Ministry of Home Affairs, and local governments in Japan. The sports component began in the 1994-95 year.

Number awarded Varies each year; recently, 44 advisors participated in this program, including 4 from the United States.

Deadline November of each year.

[301]
JEWISH SERVICE CORPS
American Jewish Joint Distribution Committee, Inc.
711 Third Avenue
New York, NY 10017-4014
(212) 687-6200 Fax: (212) 370-5467
E-mail: service@jdcny.org
Web site: www.jdc.org/help/volunteer.htm

Purpose To provide service to Jewish communities in selected countries abroad.

Eligibility This program is open to Jewish volunteers who are interested in providing service to the Jewish communities in selected foreign countries. Applicants should have a strong Jewish background, formal or informal teaching experience (such as being a camp counselor, youth group leader, or teacher), proficiency in Hebrew, cultural tolerance, and at least a bachelor's degree. They should be flexible, creative, resourceful, and able to function independently. Teenagers are not eligible; adult applicants, from recent college graduates to retirees, are welcomed.

Financial data The program provides round-trip travel, housing, health care, and a monthly stipend for basic living expenses.

Duration 1 year, generally beginning in the summer.

Special features Currently, openings are available in India, Poland, Romania, Turkey, and the former Soviet Union.

Number awarded Varies each year.

Deadline Applications are accepted at any time.

[302]
JOHN D. ROCKEFELLER 3RD AWARD
Asian Cultural Council
437 Madison Avenue, 37th Floor
New York, NY 10022-7001
(212) 812-4300 Fax: (212) 812-4299
E-mail: acc@accny.org
Web site: www.asianculturalcouncil.org

Purpose To enable individuals who have made outstanding contributions to the visual or performing arts of Asia to engage in international travel or research.

Eligibility Individuals from the United States or Asia who have made significant contributions to the understanding, practice, or study of the visual or performing arts of Asia can be nominated for this award, which provides international travel. They may be affiliated with an institution or working independently. Nominations may be submitted by artists, scholars, and other professionals involved in Asian art or culture.

Financial data The award is $25,000. The funds are to be used for international travel or research.

Duration The award is presented annually.

Number awarded 1 each year.

[303]
JSPS LONG-TERM INVITATION FELLOWSHIPS FOR BIOMEDICAL AND BEHAVIORAL RESEARCH AT NATIONAL LABORATORIES AND SIMILAR INSTITUTIONS
Fogarty International Center
Attn: Division of International Training and Research
31 Center Drive, Room B2C39
Bethesda, MD 20892-2220
(301) 496-1653 Fax: (301) 402-0779
E-mail: jsps@nih.gov
Web site: www.nih.gov/fic/programs/jspsinvite.html

Purpose To provide funding to U.S. scientists who have been invited to conduct long-term collaborative research at Japanese national laboratories and other eligible institutions and laboratories.

Eligibility This program is open to U.S. citizens and permanent residents who either 1) have held a doctoral degree in the behavioral or biomedical sciences for more than 6 years; or 2) are university professors, associate/assistant professors, research associates, or other persons who do not hold a doctoral degree (nor will receive 1 during the applicable fiscal year) but have substantial professional experience. Applicants must have been invited by Japanese scientists to conduct research at Japanese national laboratories, public corporations, nonprofit organizations, or prefectural research institutes. The proposed research may be in the behavioral or biomedical sciences.

Financial data The program provides a monthly maintenance allowance of 297,000 yen; round-trip economy airfare for fellows only; research expenses of 40,000 yen; a domestic research travel allowance of 100,000 yen; overseas travel accident and sickness insurance coverage while in Japan for fellows only; and housing accommodations arranged by the host institute and the Japan International Science and Technology Exchange Center (JISTEC).

Duration From 6 to 10 months.

Special features The Japan Society for the Promotion of Science (JSPS or Gakushin) operates under the auspices of the Japanese Ministry of Education, Culture, Sports, Science and Technology (Monbukagakusho). Further information is available from the JSPS Foreign Fellowship Office, Jochi-Kioizaka Building, 6-26-3 Kioicho, Chiyoda-ku, Tokyo 102-0094, Japan, 81 3 3263 1721, Fax: 81 3 3262 1854.

Number awarded Varies each year.

Deadline September of each year.

[304]
JSPS LONG-TERM POSTDOCTORAL FELLOWSHIPS FOR BIOMEDICAL AND BEHAVIORAL RESEARCH AT NATIONAL LABORATORIES AND SIMILAR INSTITUTIONS

Fogarty International Center
Attn: Division of International Training and Research
31 Center Drive, Room B2C39
Bethesda, MD 20892-2220
(301) 496-1653   Fax: (301) 402-0779
E-mail: jsps@nih.gov
Web site: www.nih.gov/fic/programs/jspspostdoclong.html

Purpose To provide opportunities for U.S. scientists to conduct long-term collaborative research at Japanese national laboratories and other eligible institutions and laboratories.

Eligibility Applicants must be U.S. citizens or permanent residents who have received a doctoral or equivalent degree in the behavioral or biomedical sciences within the past 6 years. Research must be conducted at Japanese national laboratories, public corporations, nonprofit organizations, or prefectural research institutes. The proposed research may be in the behavioral or biomedical sciences. Applicants must have arranged in advance a research plan for their stay in Japan with their prospective host researcher. U.S. citizenship or permanent resident status is required.

Financial data The program provides a monthly stipend of 320,000 yen; round-trip economy airfare for fellows only; a settling-in allowance of 200,000 yen; an annual domestic research travel allowance of up to 115,000 yen; overseas travel accident and sickness insurance coverage while in Japan for fellows only; and housing accommodations arranged by the host institute and the Japan International Science and Technology Exchange Center (JISTEC). A research grant of up to 1,500,000 yen per year is also available to cover cooperative research-related expenses; application for this grant must be made by the host researcher.

Duration From 12 to 24 months.

Special features The Japan Society for the Promotion of Science (JSPS or Gakushin) operates under the auspices of the Japanese Ministry of Education, Culture, Sports, Science and Technology (Monbukagakusho). Further information is available from the JSPS Foreign Fellowship Office, Jochi-Kioizaka Building, 6-26-3 Kioicho, Chiyoda-ku, Tokyo 102-0094, Japan, 81 3 3263 1721, Fax: 81 3 3262 1854.

Number awarded Varies each year.

Deadline September of each year.

[305]
JSPS LONG-TERM POSTDOCTORAL FELLOWSHIPS FOR BIOMEDICAL AND BEHAVIORAL RESEARCH AT UNIVERSITIES AND SIMILAR INSTITUTIONS

Fogarty International Center
Attn: Division of International Training and Research
31 Center Drive, Room B2C39
Bethesda, MD 20892-2220
(301) 496-1653   Fax: (301) 402-0779
E-mail: jsps@nih.gov
Web site: www.nih.gov/fic/programs/jspspostdoclong.html

Purpose To provide opportunities for U.S. scientists to conduct long-term collaborative research at Japanese universities and other eligible institutions and laboratories.

Eligibility Applicants must be U.S. citizens or permanent residents who have received a doctoral or equivalent degree in the behavioral or biomedical sciences within the past 6 years. Research must be conducted at Japanese universities, inter-university research institutes, or research institutes and scientific research corporations under the jurisdiction of the Japanese Ministry of Education, Culture, Sports, Science and Technology (Monbukagakusho). The proposed research may be in the behavioral or biomedical sciences. Applicants must have arranged in advance a research plan for their stay in Japan with their prospective host researcher. U.S. citizenship or permanent resident status is required.

Financial data The program provides a monthly stipend of 392,000 yen; round-trip economy airfare for fellows only; a settling-in allowance of 200,000 yen; an annual domestic research travel allowance of 58,500 yen; and overseas travel accident and sickness insurance coverage while in Japan for fellows only. A research grant of up to 1,500,000 yen per year is also available to cover cooperative research-related expenses; application for this grant must be made by the host researcher.

Duration From 12 to 24 months.

Special features The Japan Society for the Promotion of Science (JSPS or Gakushin) operates under the auspices of Monbukagakusho. Further information is available from the JSPS Foreign Fellowship Office, Jochi-Kioizaka Building, 6-26-3 Kioicho, Chiyoda-ku, Tokyo 102-0094, Japan, 81 3 3263 1721, Fax: 81 3 3262 1854.

Number awarded Varies each year.

Deadline May of each year.

[306]
JSPS POSTDOCTORAL FELLOWSHIP FOR FOREIGN RESEARCHERS

Japan Society for the Promotion of Science
Attn: Washington Liaison Office
1800 K Street, N.W., Suite 920
Washington, DC 20006
(202) 659-8190   Fax: (202) 659-8199
E-mail: webmaster@jspsusa.org
Web site: www.jspsusa.org

Purpose To provide financial assistance to postdoctoral researchers from the United States or other countries who wish to conduct research in Japan.

Eligibility The fellows are selected in 2 different ways: through the recommendations of relevant academic organizations from the home countries (in the United States, the National Science Foundation (NSF), the National Institutes of Health (NIH), and the Social Science Research Council (SSRC) perform that function), together with prior consent of Japanese host scientists; or through applications submitted directly from Japanese researchers who wish to host foreign research fellows in Japan. Recipients must have received a doctorate within the past 6 years. For applications submitted through NSF, NIH, or SSRC, the nominating organization specifies the fields of research; for applications submitted by Japanese host researchers, all fields within the humanities, social sciences, natural sciences, engineering, and medicine are included.

Financial data The fellowship includes round-trip airfare for the fellow only, a monthly stipend of 270,000 yen, an allowance of 200,000 yen for settling-in, a family allowance of 50,000 yen per month if accompanied by dependents, a housing subsidy of 72,000 yen per month, a domestic research travel allowance of 58,500 yen per year, and accident and sickness insurance for the fellow only.

Duration 12 to 24 months.

Special features This program began in 1988. The Japan Society for the Promotion of Science (JSPS) is a quasi-governmental organization that operates under the auspices of Japan's Ministry of Education, Culture, Sports, Science and Technology (Monbukagakusho). Recipients of these fellowships may apply to Monbukagakusho for a "Grant-in-Aid for JSPS Fellows" of up to 1,500,000 yen.

Number awarded Approximately 300 each year; in past years, approximately 40 have been from the United States.

Deadline Applications from Japanese researchers must by submitted by September or November of each year.

[307]
JSPS SHORT-TERM FELLOWSHIPS FOR BIOMEDICAL AND BEHAVIORAL RESEARCH AT UNIVERSITIES AND SIMILAR INSTITUTIONS

Fogarty International Center
Attn: Division of International Training and Research
31 Center Drive, Room B2C39
Bethesda, MD 20892-2220
(301) 496-1653   Fax: (301) 402-0779
E-mail: jsps@nih.gov
Web site: www.nih.gov/fic/programs/jspsshort.html

Purpose To provide opportunities for U.S. scientists and doctoral students to conduct short-term collaborative research at Japanese universities and other eligible institutions and laboratories.

Eligibility This program is open to scientists (holding a Ph.D., M.D., or other doctoral degree) engaged in biomedical or behavioral science research. Applicants must have arranged in advance to conduct research in Japanese universities, inter-university research institutes, or research institutes and scientific research corporations under the jurisdiction of the Japanese Ministry of Education, Culture, Sports, Science and Technology (Monbukagakusho). Doctoral (Ph.D. and M.D.) candidates and postdoctoral researchers may also apply if they can demonstrate that their collaboration with Japanese colleagues holds exceptional professional promise. U.S. citizenship or permanent resident status is required.

Financial data The program provides a daily stipend of 18,000 yen for senior researchers (6 years or more past receipt of a Ph.D.) or 16,000 yen for others; round-trip economy airfare for fellows only (business class for senior researchers); a domestic research-related travel allowance of 150,000 yen; and accident and sickness insurance coverage while in Japan.

Duration From 7 to 60 days.

Special features The Japan Society for the Promotion of Science (JSPS or Gakushin) operates under the auspices of Monbukagakusho. Further information is available from the JSPS Foreign Fellowship Office, Jochi-Kioizaka Building, 6-26-3 Kioicho, Chiyoda-ku, Tokyo 102-0094, Japan, 81 3 3263 1721, Fax: 81 3 3262 1854.

Number awarded Up to 20 each year.

Deadline April or October of each year.

[308]
JSPS SHORT-TERM INVITATION FELLOWSHIPS FOR BIOMEDICAL AND BEHAVIORAL RESEARCH AT NATIONAL LABORATORIES AND SIMILAR INSTITUTIONS

Fogarty International Center
Attn: Division of International Training and Research
31 Center Drive, Room B2C39
Bethesda, MD 20892-2220
(301) 496-1653   Fax: (301) 402-0779
E-mail: jsps@nih.gov
Web site: www.nih.gov/fic/programs/jspsinvite.html

Purpose To provide funding to U.S. scientists who have been invited to participate in scholarly activities on a short-term basis at Japanese national laboratories and other eligible institutions and laboratories.

Eligibility This program is open to U.S. citizens and permanent residents who are senior scientists, university professors, and other persons who have substantial professional experience. Applicants must have been invited by Japanese scientists to participate in discussions, attend seminars, give lectures, or perform similar duties at Japanese national laboratories, public corporations, nonprofit organizations, or prefectural research institutes. The proposed activities may be in the behavioral or biomedical sciences.

Financial data The program provides round-trip airfare, a daily maintenance allowance of 15,000 yen, and overseas travel accident and sickness insurance coverage while in Japan.

Duration From 14 to 90 days.

Special features The Japan Society for the Promotion of Science (JSPS or Gakushin) operates under the auspices of the Japanese Ministry of Education, Culture, Sports, Science and Technology (Monbukagakusho). Further information is available from the JSPS Foreign Fellowship Office, Jochi-Kioizaka Building, 6-26-3 Kioicho, Chiyoda-ku, Tokyo 102-0094, Japan, 81 3 3263 1721, Fax: 81 3 3262 1854.

Number awarded Varies each year.

Deadline September of each year.

[309]
JSPS SHORT-TERM POSTDOCTORAL FELLOWSHIPS FOR BIOMEDICAL AND BEHAVIORAL RESEARCH AT UNIVERSITIES AND SIMILAR INSTITUTIONS
Fogarty International Center
Attn: Division of International Training and Research
31 Center Drive, Room B2C39
Bethesda, MD 20892-2220
(301) 496-1653   Fax: (301) 402-0779
E-mail: jsps@nih.gov
Web site: www.nih.gov/fic/programs/jspspostdoc.html

Purpose To provide opportunities for U.S. scientists to conduct short-term collaborative research at Japanese universities and other eligible institutions and laboratories.

Eligibility Applicants must be U.S. citizens or permanent residents who have received a doctoral or equivalent degree in the behavioral or biomedical sciences within the past 10 years. Research must be conducted at Japanese universities, inter-university research institutes, or research institutes and scientific research corporations under the jurisdiction of the Japanese Ministry of Education, Culture, Sports, Science and Technology (Monbukagakusho). U.S. citizenship or permanent resident status is required.

Financial data The program provides a monthly stipend of 270,000 yen; round-trip economy airfare for fellows only; a settling-in allowance of 200,000 yen; a monthly housing allowance up to 100,000 yen; a monthly family allowance of 50,000 yen if accompanied by dependents; a domestic research-related travel allowance of 150,000 yen; and accident and sickness insurance coverage while in Japan for fellows only.

Duration From 3 to 11 months.

Special features The Japan Society for the Promotion of Science (JSPS or Gakushin) operates under the auspices of Monbukagakusho. Further information is available from the JSPS Foreign Fellowship Office, Jochi-Kioizaka Building, 6-26-3 Kioicho, Chiyoda-ku, Tokyo 102-0094, Japan, 81 3 3263 1721, Fax: 81 3 3262 1854.

Number awarded Varies each year.

Deadline April or October of each year.

[310]
JSPS SHORT-TERM POSTDOCTORAL FELLOWSHIPS FOR U.S. RESEARCHERS
Japan Society for the Promotion of Science
Attn: Washington Liaison Office
1800 K Street, N.W., Suite 920
Washington, DC 20006
(202) 659-8190   Fax: (202) 659-8199
E-mail: webmaster@jspsusa.org
Web site: www.jspsusa.org

Purpose To provide financial assistance to U.S. scholars who wish to conduct research in Japan.

Eligibility This program is open to U.S. citizens and permanent residents who hold a doctoral degree that was received less than 10 years from the proposed commencement date of the fellowship. Candidates must be proposing to conduct research in any field (natural sciences, engineering, medical sciences, social sciences, or humanities) at Japanese universities and university-related research institutions. Applications may be submitted through either of 2 procedures: 1) Japanese researchers may apply for the fellowship on behalf of an American counterpart, or 2) the candidate may apply through a U.S. nominating authority (the National Science Foundation, the Fogarty International Center of the National Institutes of Health, or the Social Science Research Council).

Financial data The fellowship includes round-trip airfare (for the fellow only), a maintenance allowance of 270,000 yen per month, a settling-in allowance of 200,000 yen, a monthly housing subsidy of up to 72,000 yen, a monthly family allowance of 50,000 yen (if accompanied by dependents), and accident and sickness insurance coverage (for the fellow only).

Duration 3 to 11 months.

Special features This program began in 1997. The Japan Society for the Promotion of Science (JSPS) is a quasi-governmental organization that operates under the auspices of Japan's Ministry of Education, Culture, Sports, Science and Technology (Monbukagakusho).

Number awarded Approximately 45 each year.

Deadline Applications from Japanese researchers must by submitted by September or November of each year.

[311]
KOSEF INTERNSHIPS
Korean-American Scientists and Engineers Association
Attn: KOSEF Summer Internship Program
1952 Gallows Drive, Suite 300
Vienna, VA 22182
(703) 748-1221   Fax: (703) 748-1331
E-mail: sejong@ksea.org
Web site: www.ksea.org/activity/scholarships.html

Purpose To provide an opportunity for Korean American students to participate in a summer research program at research institutes and industrial organizations in Korea.

Eligibility This program is open to Korean American juniors, seniors, and graduate students who graduated from a high school in the United States, have a good comprehension of the Korean language, and are majoring in science, engineering, or a related field. Applicants must be interested in participating in research at a university, government-supported research institute, or industry-affiliated research institute in Korea. They must be recommended by a current or present officer of the Korean-American Scientists and Engineers Association (KSEA).

Financial data The Korea Science and Engineering Foundation (KOSEF) provides $750 for airfare to Korea and pays all expenses for a 5-day industrial tour that is part of the program. The stipends, paid by the host institution, vary.

Duration At least 2 months, beginning in June.

Special features This program is sponsored by KOSEF, which selects the participants on the recommendation of KSEA.

Number awarded Varies each year.

Deadline January of each year.

[312]
KUMAHIRA SCHOLARSHIP

Kumahira Scholarship Foundation
c/o Kumahira Safe Company, Inc.
2-4-34 Ujina-higashi, Minani-ku, Hiroshima-shi
Hiroshima 734-8567
Japan
81 82 251 2111   Fax: 81 82 254 3750

Purpose To provide financial assistance for postsecondary study or research in Japan.

Eligibility This program is open to foreign students who are enrolled in universities, graduate schools, or research institutes located in Hiroshima prefecture for the purposes of study or research. Applications must be submitted through the institution. Students receiving assistance from the Ministry of Education of Japan are not eligible.

Financial data The stipend is 70,000 yen per month.

Duration 1 year; may be renewed.

Number awarded 50 each year.

Deadline March of each year.

[313]
LONG-TERM INVITATION FELLOWSHIP PROGRAMS FOR RESEARCH IN JAPAN

Japan Society for the Promotion of Science
Attn: Washington Liaison Office
1800 K Street, N.W., Suite 920
Washington, DC 20006
(202) 659-8190   Fax: (202) 659-8199
E-mail: webmaster@jspsusa.org
Web site: www.jspsusa.org

Purpose To invite scholars for cooperative research work with counterparts at Japanese universities or research institutes.

Eligibility University professors, associate professors, assistant professors, research associates, and other persons with substantial professional experience from any country that has diplomatic relations with Japan are eligible for this program. Applicants must either 1) be professionals who do not hold a doctorate and will not receive such a degree during the term of the award, or 2) have held a doctoral degree for more than 6 years. Applications must be submitted by Japanese researchers at universities or research institutes; foreign scholars may not apply directly. Scholars who wish to participate in this program are advised to establish contact with Japanese researchers in the same field. All areas of the humanities, social sciences, and natural sciences are included.

Financial data The fellowship includes round-trip airfare for the fellow only, a monthly maintenance allowance of 270,000 to 300,000 yen depending on the professional status of the fellow, research expenses of 40,000 yen, a monthly housing allowance up to 72,000 yen, a domestic research travel allowance of 100,000 yen, and accident and sickness insurance coverage for the fellow only.

Duration 6 to 10 months.

Special features This program began in 1959. The Japan Society for the Promotion of Science (JSPS) is a quasi-governmental organization that operates under the auspices of Japan's Ministry of Education, Culture, Sports, Science and Technology (Monbukagakusho).

Number awarded Approximately 58 each year; generally, 2 or 3 are from the United States.

Deadline September of each year.

[314]
LOUIS DUPREE PRIZE FOR RESEARCH ON CENTRAL ASIA

Social Science Research Council
810 Seventh Avenue
New York, NY 10019
(212) 377-2700   Fax: (212) 377-2727
E-mail: eurasia@ssrc.org
Web site: www.ssrc.org

Purpose To provide funding for extended dissertation travel in eastern Europe and central Asia.

Eligibility Only candidates who receive a dissertation research fellowship from a program administered by the Social Science Research Council (SSRC) or American Council of Learned Societies (ACLS) are eligible to apply for this program. Candidates who wish to be considered for this prize should so indicate on the applications for those fellowships. The prize is awarded for the most promising dissertation proposal involving field research in Central Asia, including Afghanistan, Azerbaijan, Kirghizia, Mongolia, Turkmenistan, Tajikistan, Uzbekistan and culturally-related contiguous areas of Iran, Pakistan, Kazakhstan, and China. Minorities and women are particularly encouraged to apply.

Financial data The prize is $2,500.

Duration The prize is intended to enrich the recipient's field experience by making possible a longer stay or more extensive travel within the region.

Number awarded 1 each year.

[315]
LOUISE WALLACE HACKNEY FELLOWSHIP FOR THE STUDY OF CHINESE ART

American Oriental Society
Attn: Secretary-Treasurer
University of Michigan
Hatcher Graduate Library, Room 110D
Ann Arbor, MI 48109-1205
(734) 764-7555   Fax: (734) 763-6743
E-mail: jrodgers@umich.edu
Web site: www.umich.edu/~aos/hackney.htm

Purpose To provide financial assistance for travel or for the translation into English of works on the subject of Chinese art.

Eligibility Applicants must be postdoctoral or doctoral students, be U.S. citizens, and have completed 3 years of study of the Chinese language or its equivalent. In no case shall a fellowship be awarded to scholars of well-recognized standing, but only to people who show aptitude or promise in the field. They must be interested in 1) studying Chinese art, with special relation to painting and its reflection of Chinese culture, or 2) translating into English works on the subject of Chinese painting.

Financial data The award is $8,000 per year. Funds are intended to be used for travel, if such travel is possible.

Duration 1 year, extending from July 1 of the year of the award until June 30 of the following year; may be renewed but not in consecutive years.
Number awarded 1 each year.
Deadline February of each year.

[316]
MAMIE KWOH WANG NURSE–VISITING SCHOLAR FUND

American Bureau for Medical Advancement in China
Attn: Executive Director
45 John Street, Suite 1100
New York, NY 10038
(212) 233-0608   Fax: (212) 233-0614
E-mail: phyllis@abmac.org
Web site: www.abmac.org

Purpose To enable American expert nurses to teach and lecture in hospitals and/or nursing schools in Taiwan.
Eligibility Outstanding nursing experts in the United States may be nominated or invited to apply for this support. Applicants must be interested in conducting workshops and bedside teaching in Taiwan. Selection is based on academic and specialized practice qualifications.
Financial data The award covers travel expenses, a stipend, and housing.
Duration Up to 3 months.
Special features Visiting professors are expected to visit hospitals and schools of nursing in Taiwan. This program was established in 1989, as a counterpart to the H. William Harris Visiting Professorship.
Number awarded 1 to 3 each year.

[317]
MATSUMAE INTERNATIONAL FOUNDATION FELLOWSHIPS

Matsumae International Foundation
New Marunouchi Building, Room 6-002
1-5-1 Marunouchi, Chiyoda-ku
Tokyo 100-0005
Japan
81 3 3214 7611   Fax: 81 3 3214 7613
E-mail: contact@matsumae-if.org
Web site: www.matsumae-if.org

Purpose To support research in Japan that will contribute to a greater understanding of Japan and a lasting world peace.
Eligibility Applicants must be non-Japanese nationals who meet all of the following general eligibility requirements: 1) hold a degree equivalent to a Japanese doctoral degree, or have a minimum of 2 years of research experience after receipt of a master's degree, or be recognized by the foundation as possessing equivalent academic qualifications; 2) be 40 years of age or younger; 3) have sufficient conversational ability in Japanese or English to prevent difficulties in conducting research in Japan; 4) not have been in Japan previously; 5) submit applications from their home country (applicants may not presently be in Japan); 6) have firm positions and professions in their home nations to which they will return upon completion of the fellowship. While it is the policy of the foundation to accept researchers from as many nations as possible, applicants from developing nations specializing in such fields as natural science, engineering, and medicine receive preferential consideration. Disciplines in the social sciences, humanities, and arts are given lower priority.
Financial data Fellows receive 1) economy-class round-trip airfare; 2) 300,000 Japanese yen upon arrival, to assist with the cost of accommodations, local travel expenses, etc.; 3) a stipend of 200,000 yen monthly, to pay for tuition, research, meals, transportation, etc.; 4) a subsidy for housing of up to 50,000 yen per month; and 5) insurance for personal accidents and illness (both with medical treatment and death benefit). No support to family members is available.
Duration 3 to 12 months; no extension is permitted.
Special features Applicants may select a host institution (university research laboratory, national research institution, corresponding private facility) in which to carry out their research, but they must obtain acceptance from the host institutions prior to submitting their applications. To promote a deeper understanding of Japan, the foundation organizes a study tour during the fellows' tenure in Japan.
Number awarded 20 each year: 2 for 3 to 5 months, 16 for 6 months, and 2 for 7 to 12 months.
Deadline July of each year. Delayed applications will be treated as submissions for the following year.

[318]
MICKEY LELAND–BILL EMERSON INTERNATIONAL HUNGER FELLOWS PROGRAM

Congressional Hunger Center
229 1/2 Pennsylvania Avenue, S.E.
Washington, DC 20003
(202) 547-7022   Fax: (202) 547-7575
E-mail: fellows@hungercenter.org
Web site: www.hungercenter.org/international/int.htm

Purpose To provide emerging leaders in the fight against hunger with an opportunity to participate in field projects at sites in developing countries.
Eligibility This program is open to U.S. citizens who have a bachelor's degree, either a graduate degree or significant experience working to fight hunger, at least 6 months of continuous anti-poverty or sustainable development work in a developing country, written and spoken proficiency in a language appropriate to a field placement, demonstrated leadership qualities and abilities, creativity and initiative in problem solving, and a strong commitment to alleviating hunger and poverty with an enthusiasm for day-to-day work. Applicants must be interested in participating in a program that includes 1) work at field sites in sub-Saharan Africa, south Asia, Central America, and the Caribbean where they work in anti-hunger and development activities and 2) a policy placement in Rome (where they work with U.N. food institutions such as UNFAO, UNWFP, or IFAD) or in Washington, D.C., Baltimore, or Boston (where they work at the U.S. headquarters of the organizations at which they were placed during their field experience). Selection is based on the applicants' commitment to social change, diversity of experience and perspective, vision for the future, demonstrated leadership potential, and willingness to learn and have their lives changed by the experience.
Financial data Fellows receive a stipend of $1,000 per month. During their policy placement, they also receive a hous-

ing allowance. The program also pays for medical insurance and travel to and from field placements. Upon completion of the program, fellows receive an end-of-service award to help them make the transition to the next phase of their career.

Duration 3 years, including a 2-year placement in the field in sub-Saharan Africa, south Asia, Central America, or the Caribbean and a 1-year policy placement in Rome or the United States.

Number awarded 10 each year. Field assignments are provided for 4 fellows in sub-Saharan Africa, 3 in south Asia, and 3 in Central America or the Caribbean. Alternatively, 1 fellow may be placed in North Korea. For their policy assignments, 3 fellows are placed in Rome and the remaining fellows in Washington, D.C., Baltimore, or Boston.

Deadline January of each year.

[319]
MIDDLE EAST, NORTH AFRICA, SOUTH ASIA REGIONAL RESEARCH PROGRAM

Council for International Exchange of Scholars
3007 Tilden Street, N.W., Suite 5L
Washington, DC 20008-3009
(202) 686-4019   Fax: (202) 362-3442
E-mail: scholars@cies.iie.org
Web site: www.iie.org/cies

Purpose To provide financial assistance to American scholars for research in any academic or professional field in the Middle East, north Africa, or south Asia.

Eligibility Applicants must be U.S. citizens who are area specialists or who have had limited experience in the countries of the region. Possible fields of research include, but are not limited to, architecture, area studies, biological sciences, communications, education, environmental sciences, humanities, law, medical sciences, physical sciences, and social sciences. Field work must be conducted in 2 or more countries of the region. Projects that involve collaboration with colleagues and institutions in the host country and that contribute to cooperation within the region are especially encouraged. Appropriate language proficiency to complete the research is required. The following countries participate in this program: Bahrain, Bangladesh, Egypt, India, Israel, Jordan, Kuwait, Lebanon, Morocco, Nepal, Oman, Pakistan, Palestinian National Authority (Gaza or West Bank), Qatar, Saudi Arabia, Sri Lanka, Syria, Tunisia, United Arab Emirates, and Yemen.

Financial data In most countries, the monthly base stipend is $1,700; special base stipends are provided in Egypt, India, Israel, Jordan, Morocco, Nepal, Pakistan, and Sri Lanka. In all countries, awards also include a monthly maintenance allowance of $1,700 to $3,000 (depending on country and number of accompanying dependents) to cover local costs of living, a research allowance of $3,000, and an allowance to cover international travel for grantee and up to 2 accompanying dependents for grants of 4 months or more.

Duration 3 to 9 months.

Special features This is a Fulbright scholar program, sponsored by the Bureau of Educational and Cultural Affairs of the U.S. Department of State and administered by the Council for International Exchange of Scholars.

Number awarded Up to 10 each year.

Deadline July of each year.

[320]
MIKE MANSFIELD FELLOWSHIP PROGRAM

Mansfield Center for Pacific Affairs
601 13th Street, N.W., Suite 400 South
Washington, DC 20005
(202) 347-1994   Fax: (202) 347-3941
Web site: www.mcpa.org/manabout.html

Purpose To provide an opportunity for U.S. federal government employees to develop an indepth understanding of Japan and establish relationships with their counterparts in Japan's government and business sectors.

Eligibility To be eligible for participation in this program, applicants must be U.S. citizens and current federal government employees with at least 2 consecutive years of service immediately preceding the application deadline. Applicants must be able to demonstrate the following: a strong career interest in areas of importance to the U.S.-Japan relations; the ability to articulate in a project plan clear goals and objectives and placement preferences for the year in Japan; their agency's interest in U.S.-Japan issues and how participation in the fellowship will contribute to their agency's mission; service in U.S. agencies with jurisdiction over issues of importance to U.S.-Japan relations; a willingness and openness to learn about Japan; and an interest in living and working in the Japanese cultural context. In addition, they must be willing to serve in the federal government a minimum of 2 years after returning from Japan and they must demonstrate the following personal qualities: self discipline; a willingness to work long hours under stress where Japanese is the only language used; the capacity to deal with ambiguity; the ability to work successfully as a student and as a member of a team; a willingness to meet new people and build professional relationships; moral integrity; and sociability, curiosity, tact, and adaptability, patience, flexibility, resourcefulness, independence, and self reliance. Preference is given to applicants with at least 3 years of government service and to candidates whose agencies are involved in timely issues affecting U.S.-Japan relations. In addition, preference is given to applicants whose positions are not time limited, who are neither Schedule C employees nor presidential appointees, and whose official responsibilities do not include intelligence gathering or other intelligence-related activities.

Financial data Fellows who are "detailees" (agency funded) receive salary and benefits through the sponsoring federal agency. "Non-detailees" receive their salary and benefits (but not retirement benefits) from this program. During the first year, all fellows receive a $300 monthly stipend if they must relocate to Washington, D.C. to take part in the language training sessions. During the year in Japan, fellows receive a living quarters allowance, a post allowance (to cover Japan's high cost of living), an education allowance for dependents, a shipping of excess baggage allowance of up to $1,000, and round-trip economy airfare for the fellow and immediate family members.

Duration 2 years.

Special features This program was created in 1994. It is named after a former U.S. ambassador to Japan and Senate majority leader from Montana. Fellows spend a year working full time in Japanese government offices, preceded by a year of full-time language and area studies in the United States. Through the program, fellows develop networks of contacts in Japan and an understanding of the political, economic, and strategic dimensions of the U.S.-Japan relations. The program is administered by the Mansfield Center for Pacific Affairs, with the Bureau of Educational and Cultural Affairs of the U.S. Department of State as grantor.

Limitations After the year in Japan, fellows must serve at least 2 additional years in the federal government (generally, on projects dealing with Japan issues or on cooperative programs with Japan).

Number awarded 10 each year: at least 7 detailed employees (who continue to receive their salaries and benefits from the sponsoring agency) and a maximum of 3 non-detailees (whose salaries and benefits are funded through the fellowship program).

Deadline March of each year.

[321]
MONBUKAGAKUSHO SUMMER PROGRAM IN JAPAN

National Science Foundation
Directorate for Social, Behavioral, and Economic Sciences
Attn: Division of International Programs
4201 Wilson Boulevard
Arlington, VA 22230
(703) 292-8710   TDD: (703) 292-5090
E-mail: EAPinfo@nsf.gov
Web site: www.nsf.gov/sbe/int/start.htm

Purpose To provide science and engineering graduate students from selected countries with an opportunity to conduct research in Japan.

Eligibility This program is open to engineering and science graduate students at universities in France, Germany, the United Kingdom, and the United States. Applicants must be interested in a program in Japan that includes a 1-week introduction to Japanese language and culture upon arrival followed by an internship or cooperative research program at a national university or inter-university research institute. In the United States, women, minorities, and persons with disabilities are strongly encouraged to apply.

Financial data The National Science Foundation (NSF) provides a stipend of $2,500. The Japanese government provides round-trip airfare and allowances for accommodations, food, and professional travel within Japan. The Graduate University of Advanced Studies (Soken-dai) provides logistical support for the program. Participants are responsible for their own insurance and any additional expenditures.

Duration 8 weeks, beginning in late June.

Special features This program began in 1993 when the NSF and counterpart organizations in Germany and the United Kingdom joined the predecessor of the Japanese Ministry of Education, Culture, Sports, Science and Technology (Monbukagakusho) in a trial program. Monbukagakusho formally established it in 1995. Unlike the Summer Institute in Japan for U.S. Graduate Students in Science and Engineering which it resembles, this program does not provide intensive language instruction.

Limitations Due to the intensive nature of the program, dependents are not allowed to accompany participants.

Number awarded Varies each year; recently, 50 participants were selected from the United States.

Deadline November of each year.

[322]
MONGOLIA RESEARCH FELLOWSHIP PROGRAM

International Research & Exchanges Board
1616 H Street, N.W.
Washington, DC 20006
(202) 628-8188   Fax: (202) 628-8189
E-mail: mrf@irex.org
Web site: www.irex.org

Purpose To provide funding to Ph.D. candidates and postdoctoral scholars who wish to conduct field research in Mongolia.

Eligibility Applicants must have been U.S. citizens or permanent residents for at least 3 years prior to applying and are normally required to have a full-time affiliation with a higher education university as either a doctoral candidate or faculty member. Applicants must be interested in conducting field research in Mongolia. They should already have language capability sufficient for advanced research; they may be required to take a written and/or oral test of Mongolian language.

Financial data Grants provide round-trip airfare and visa fees, a living allowance, health insurance, and a research materials allowance. No support for dependents is provided.

Duration 1 to 4 months.

Special features The International Research & Exchanges Board (IREX) was established in 1968 at the request of U.S. universities by the American Council of Learned Societies (ACLS) and the Social Science Research Council (SSRC) to administer research exchange programs with the socialist countries of eastern Europe and the former Soviet republics. As part of this program, Mongolian scholars also visit the United States. Funding for this program is provided by the Henry Luce Foundation.

Number awarded Varies each year; recently, 7 of these fellowships were offered, including 4 for Mongolian scholars to visit the United States and 3 (2 doctoral candidates and 1 faculty member) for U.S. scholars to visit Mongolia.

Deadline January of each year.

[323]
NATIONAL COUNCIL FOR EURASIAN AND EAST EUROPEAN RESEARCH COMPETITION

National Council for Eurasian and East European Research
910 17th Street, N.W., Suite 300
Washington, DC 20006
(202) 822-6950   Fax: (202) 822-6955
E-mail: nceeerdc@aol.com
Web site: www.nceeer.gov

Purpose To encourage and sustain high-quality collaborative research projects dealing with current developments in the former Soviet republics, eastern Europe, and Eurasia.

Eligibility This program is open to collaborative projects involving 2 or more U.S.-based postdoctoral scholars who are U.S. citizens or permanent residents. Although foreign scholars may participate in the collaboration, the 2 or more U.S.-based scholars' roles in the project must be principal and substantive. The field of study may be in the social sciences or humanities, including history, geography, demography, and environmental studies. Proposals for research may include such activities as research-specific training, especially involving graduate students in research projects; contact among scholars and specialists in government and private enterprise; development of data banks and other research aids; and dissemination of research data, methodology, and findings from Council-sponsored research. The proposals must involve research, to be conducted in the United States or abroad, on the following countries: Albania, Armenia, Belarus, Bosnia and Herzegovina, Bulgaria, Croatia, Czech Republic, Estonia, Georgia, Hungary, Kazakstan, Kyrgyzstan, Latvia, Lithuania, Moldova, Poland, Romania, Russia, Serbia (including Kosovo and Montenegro), Slovakia, Slovenia, Tajikistan, Turkmenistan, Ukraine, Uzbekistan, and the former Yugoslav Republic of Macedonia. Research related to the former German Democratic Republic or the natural sciences is not eligible.

Financial data The budget covers salaries and wages for the principal investigator and assistants, fringe benefits, foreign and domestic travel, supplies, materials, services, and institutional overhead. The maximum award is $70,000. At least 20 percent of the project cost must be provided by an institutional sponsor with nonfederal funds.

Duration Up to 2 years; shorter projects are encouraged.

Special features Funding for this program is provided by the U.S. Department of State under the Research and Training for Eastern Europe and the Independent States of the Former Soviet Union Act of 1983 (Title VIII).

Deadline February of each year.

[324]
NATIONAL COUNCIL FOR EURASIAN AND EAST EUROPEAN RESEARCH GRANTS

National Council for Eurasian and East European
  Research
910 17th Street, N.W., Suite 300
Washington, DC 20006
(202) 822-6950   Fax: (202) 822-6955
E-mail: nceeerdc@aol.com
Web site: www.nceeer.gov

Purpose To encourage and sustain high-quality individual research projects dealing with current developments in the former Soviet republics, eastern Europe, and Eurasia.

Eligibility This program is open to individual scholars who are U.S. citizens or permanent residents 1) at the postdoctoral level for academic participants or 2) with equivalent maturity and relevant professional employment for those from other fields. The field of study may be in the social sciences or humanities, including history, geography, demography, and environmental studies. Proposals for research may include such activities as research-specific training, especially involving graduate students in research projects; contact among scholars and specialists in government and private enterprise; development of data banks and other research aids; and dissemination of research data, methodology, and findings from Council-sponsored research. The proposals must involve research, to be conducted in the United States or abroad, on the following countries: Albania, Armenia, Belarus, Bosnia and Herzegovina, Bulgaria, Croatia, Czech Republic, Estonia, Georgia, Hungary, Kazakstan, Kyrgyzstan, Latvia, Lithuania, Moldova, Poland, Romania, Russia, Serbia (including Kosovo and Montenegro), Slovakia, Slovenia, Tajikistan, Turkmenistan, Ukraine, Uzbekistan, and the former Yugoslav Republic of Macedonia. Research related to the former German Democratic Republic or the natural sciences is not eligible.

Financial data The maximum award is $40,000.

Duration Up to 2 years; shorter projects are encouraged.

Special features Funding for this program is provided by the U.S. Department of State under the Research and Training for Eastern Europe and the Independent States of the Former Soviet Union Act of 1983 (Title VIII).

Deadline February of each year.

[325]
NATO COLLABORATIVE LINKAGE GRANTS

North Atlantic Treaty Organization
Attn: Scientific Affairs Division
Boulevard Leopold III
B-1110 Brussels
Belgium
32 2 707 4111   Fax: 32 2 707 4232
Web site: www.nato.int/science

Purpose To support collaborative scientific research by providing travel funding to teams in different member countries of the North Atlantic Treaty Organization (NATO) and those in Euro-Atlantic Partnership Council (EAPC) countries (including Eurasia).

Eligibility This program is open to collaborations between scientists in NATO countries (the United States, Canada, 14 countries in western Europe, and 3 countries in eastern Europe and Eurasia) and NATO's partner countries of the EAPC (15 former Soviet republics and 7 other nations in eastern Europe). Scientists of the Mediterranean Dialogue countries (Algeria, Egypt, Israel, Jordan, Mauritania, Morocco, and Tunisia) may also apply for a grant in cooperation with scientists from NATO countries. All applicant teams must be interested in conducting research in 1 of the 4 priority areas currently selected by NATO: physical and engineering science and technology (PST), life science and technology (LST), environmental and earth science and technology (EST), and security-related civil science and technology (SST).

Financial data Funding is provided to cover the costs incurred by investigators to visit the collaborating teams abroad. Amounts awarded are normally between $5,000 (for 1 year of collaboration by 2 or 3 scientists) to a maximum of $25,000 (for 2 years' collaboration by 5 research teams). Basic costs (salaries, equipment, consumables, page charges) should already be covered from other national sources. Support is not provided for 1) institutional overhead expenses; 2) scientists while on sabbatical or other extended leave abroad; 3) travel that is not related to the research project; 4) purely domestic travel; 5) visits for 1 researcher or 1 research group only; or 6) long study periods abroad.

Duration The grants may be used over a period of 1 to 2 years. During the time period of a grant, research visits are expected to be of short duration and should not exceed 2 months.

Number awarded Since 1960, support has been given to more than 6,000 joint projects. At present, about 600 grants are awarded each year (of which an average of 450 are for new projects).

Deadline Deadlines for PST grants are February, July, or October of each year; deadlines for LST and EST grants are

March, August, or November of each year; deadlines for SST grants are January, April, or September of each year.

[326]
NATO EXPERT VISITS

North Atlantic Treaty Organization
Attn: Scientific Affairs Division
Boulevard Leopold III
B-1110 Brussels
Belgium
32 2 707 4111   Fax: 32 2 707 4232
Web site: www.nato.int/science

Purpose To provide financial assistance to scientists from member nations of the North Atlantic Treaty Organization (NATO) for visits to research laboratories in Euro-Atlantic Partnership Council (EAPC) countries (including Eurasia), and vice versa.

Eligibility Experts from NATO countries (the United States, Canada, 14 countries in western Europe, and 3 countries in eastern Europe) may visit research laboratories in an EAPC country (15 former Soviet republics and 7 countries in eastern Europe) to consult on current research projects. EAPC scientists may also visit a NATO country. Scientists in the 7 Mediterranean Dialogue countries (Algeria, Egypt, Israel, Jordan, Mauritania, Morocco, and Tunisia) are also eligible if they draw up applications in cooperation with a scientist from a NATO country. This program is available primarily, but not exclusively, for research in 1 of the 4 priority areas currently selected by NATO: physical and engineering science and technology (PST), life science and technology (LST), environmental and earth science and technology (EST), and security-related civil science and technology (SST). Applications must be submitted by the project director at the institute to be visited and signed by both the host institute project director and the visiting expert.

Financial data Fellows receive research, travel, and living (up to $100 per day) allowances. Support is not provided for 1) long study periods abroad, 2) salaries, stipends, or institutional overhead; 3) scientists on sabbatical or other extended leave abroad; or 4) attendance at conferences, symposia, workshops, etc.

Duration From a few days to 1 month.

Number awarded Varies each year.

Deadline Deadlines for PST grants are February, July, or October of each year; deadlines for LST and EST grants are March, August, or November of each year; deadlines for SST grants are January, April, or September of each year.

[327]
NCAER GRANTS

Institute of International Education
Attn: Student Programs Division
809 United Nations Plaza
New York, NY 10017-3580
(212) 984-5330   Fax: (212) 984-5325
Web site: www.iie.org/fulbright

Purpose To provide funding to American graduate students interested in conducting research on the Indian economy at the National Council of Applied Economics Research (NCAER) in New Delhi.

Eligibility This program is open to graduate students who are registered for their doctoral programs, with emphasis on the Indian economy. Applicants must be interested in conducting research at NCAER.

Financial data The stipend is 17,000 rupees per month to cover maintenance, housing, and an incidental and internal transportation allowance. No allowance is provided for research-related expenses. For high cost cities, however, an extra housing allowance may be reimbursed up to a maximum of 3,000 rupees per month upon application. International air travel is provided for the grantee only.

Duration 12 months.

Special features This program is jointly funded by the Fulbright Foundation in India and the NCAER. It is administered in the United States by the Institute of International Education (IIE) as part of the Fulbright program. Students who are currently enrolled in the United States are to apply through the Fulbright program adviser on their campus; at-large applicants (those not currently enrolled) may obtain applications and information directly from the IIE.

Number awarded 1 each year.

Deadline October of each year.

[328]
NEDO INDUSTRIAL TECHNOLOGY FELLOWSHIPS

New Energy and Industrial Technology Development
   Organization
Industrial Technology Department
Attn: Research and Coordination Division
Sunshine 60 Building, 29F
3-1-1, Higashi-Ikebukuro, Toshima-ku
Tokyo 170-6028
Japan
81 3 3987 9354   Fax: 81 3 3981 1536
E-mail: matsuists@nedo.go.jp
Web site: www.nedo.go.jp

Purpose To provide an opportunity for scientists to work in Japan in laboratories funded by the New Energy and Industrial Technology Development Organization (NEDO).

Eligibility Applicants for this program must hold a doctorate degree (or will receive it before beginning work) and have Japanese or English language skills sufficient to work with other researchers and live everyday life in Japan. They must be interested in working at Japanese research associations, foundations, universities, and private corporations that are conducting research for NEDO as part of its ongoing technology research and development projects. Candidates are recruited from Japanese universities, Japanese enterprises, and overseas. Currently, NEDO funds research on 28 industrial technology topics at institutions throughout Japan.

Financial data The stipend is 630,000 yen per month. The actual transportation expenses for researchers to move from their home or place of residence to their place of work in Japan are also reimbursed.

Duration 1 year, beginning in April; may be renewed for up to 2 additional years.

Special features NEDO is a semi-governmental agency established in October 1980 and supervised by the Japanese Ministry of International Trade and Industry.

Number awarded 30 each year.

Deadline November of each year.

[329]
NIDDK AND NIAID INTERNATIONAL COLLABORATION AWARDS

National Institute of Diabetes and Digestive and Kidney Diseases
Attn: Division of Digestive Diseases and Nutrition
45 Center Drive, Room 6AN-12A
Bethesda, MD 20892-6600
(301) 594-8871   Fax: (301) 480-8300
E-mail: tk13v@nih.gov
Web site: www.niddk.nih.gov

Purpose To provide support for research relevant to the mission of the National Institute of Diabetes and Digestive and Kidney Diseases (NIDDK) to be conducted at international centers supported by the National Institute of Allergy and Infectious Diseases (NIAID).

Eligibility This program is open to investigators at domestic and foreign, for-profit and nonprofit, public and private organizations, such as universities, colleges, hospitals, laboratories, units of state and local governments, and eligible agencies of the federal government. Applicants must be proposing to conduct research on the following topics of interest to the NIDDK: autoimmune liver diseases and hepatitis, gastric ulcer disease and Helicobacter pylori, parasitic diseases that have an impact on liver, mucosal immunity, pediatric liver disease, influence of altered nutritional status on health and disease, parasitic diseases with kidney/urinary tract sequelae, hemolytic uremic syndrome, infectious diseases of the kidney, benign prostatic hypertrophy in minority populations, therapies for hematologic disorders such as iron chelating agents, diabetic kidney disease, and hypertensive kidney disease. Research should be conducted in collaboration with an NIAID international center.

Financial data Grants up to $50,000 per year for direct costs are available through this program.

Duration Up to 2 years; nonrenewable.

Special features Current NIAID international centers, and their major research interests, are located in: Brazil (leishmaniasis, malaria, schistosomiasis, Chagas' Disease, immunoparasitology, diarrheal diseases, and hydatid diseases), Cameroon (malaria), Chile (cholera and enteric diseases), Egypt (lymphatic filariasis), Israel (diarrheal diseases, leishmaniasis, hydatid diseases), Jordan (leishmaniasis), Kenya (schistosomiasis, filariasis, hydatid diseases), Lebanon (leishmaniasis), Mexico (tuberculosis), Morocco (leishmaniasis), Nepal (geohelminths), Peru (enteric pathogens, neurocysticercosis), South Africa (amoebiasis), Thailand (malaria), Tunisia (hydatid diseases), and Uganda (tuberculosis). Information on the NIAID international centers is available from the Parasitology and International Programs Branch, Solar Building, Room 3A12, 6003 Executive Boulevard MSC 7630, Bethesda, MD 20892-7630, (301) 496-7115, Fax: (301) 402-0659, E-mail: mg35s@nih.gov.

Number awarded Varies, depending on the availability of funds.

Deadline Applications may be submitted at any time.

[330]
NISSHO IWAI FOUNDATION SCHOLARSHIP

Nissho Iwai Foundation
2-4-5 Akasaka, Minato-ku
Tokyo 107-8655
Japan
81 3 3588 2115   Fax: 81 3 3588 4832
E-mail: zaidan@nisshoiwai.co.jp
Web site: www.nisshoiwai.co.jp

Purpose To provide financial assistance to postsecondary students from other countries who are interested in studying or conducting research in Japan.

Eligibility Eligible to apply are undergraduates (under 30 years of age) in their third or fourth year of study and graduate students (under 35 years of age) from countries outside of Japan who wish to attend 1 of 15 designated universities in Japan. Applicants may not be receiving other scholarship assistance.

Financial data The stipend is 70,000 yen per month for undergraduates or 100,000 yen per month for graduate students.

Duration Up to 2 years.

Number awarded 10 each year.

Deadline May of each year.

[331]
NSF/JSPS LONG-TERM INVITATION FELLOWSHIPS AT NATIONAL LABORATORIES AND SIMILAR INSTITUTIONS

National Science Foundation
Directorate for Social, Behavioral, and Economic Sciences
Attn: Division of International Programs
East Asia and Pacific Program
4201 Wilson Boulevard, Room 935
Arlington, VA 22230
(703) 292-8704   Fax: (703) 292-9175
E-mail: eapinfo@nsf.gov
Web site: www.twics.com/~nsftokyo/JSPS01.html

Purpose To offer promising young researchers from the United States the opportunity to engage in long-term research at national laboratories in Japan.

Eligibility These awards are available for research in any field of science or engineering supported by the National Science Foundation (NSF). Applicants must be U.S. citizens who received their Ph.D. degree more than 6 years previously. They must propose to conduct research at a Japanese national laboratory, public corporation, nonprofit research organization, or prefectural research institution.

Financial data The Japan Society for the Promotion of Science (JSPS) provides round-trip airfare for the fellow, a monthly maintenance allowance of 297,000 yen, a research travel allowance in Japan of 100,000 yen, research expenses of 40,000 yen, housing, and overseas travel accident and sickness insurance coverage. Applicants who plan to stay in Japan for 6 months or more and will be accompanied by dependents may be eligible to apply to NSF for dependent support. That support includes round-trip economy-class airfare, up to $300 in excess baggage per dependent, a relocation allowance of up to $500 per dependent, an allowance of $50 per month per dependent towards the cost of health insurance, and a schooling allowance for children in grades K-12 of up to $1,000 per child per year in public schools or up to $12,000 per child per year in private schools.

Duration 6 to 10 months.

Special features Information is also available from the NSF Tokyo Office, U.S. Embassy Japan, Unit 45004, Box 236, APO AP 96337-5004. NSF selects the recipients for this program, but administration and most of the funding is provided by the JSPS. For further information, contact its Washington Liaison Office, 1800 K Street, N.W., Suite 920, Washington, DC 20006, (202) 659-8190, Fax: (202) 659-8199, E-mail: webmaster@jspsusa.org.

Number awarded Varies each year.

Deadline Applications may be submitted at any time, but they must be received at least 5 months prior to the proposed date of the fellowship.

[332]
NSF/JSPS POSTDOCTORAL FELLOWSHIPS AT NATIONAL LABORATORIES AND SIMILAR INSTITUTIONS

National Science Foundation
Directorate for Social, Behavioral, and Economic Sciences
Attn: Division of International Programs
East Asia and Pacific Program
4201 Wilson Boulevard, Room 935
Arlington, VA 22230
(703) 292-8704   Fax: (703) 292-9175
E-mail: eapinfo@nsf.gov
Web site: www.twics.com/~nsftokyo/JSPS01.html

Purpose To offer promising young researchers from the United States the opportunity to engage in long-term research at national laboratories in Japan.

Eligibility These awards are available for research in any field of science or engineering supported by the National Science Foundation (NSF). Applicants must be U.S. citizens who have earned a doctoral degree within 6 years before the date of application, or have equivalent experience beyond the master's degree, or expect to receive the doctoral degree by the award date. They must propose to conduct research in a Japanese national laboratory, public corporation, nonprofit research organization, or prefectural research institution.

Financial data The Japan Society for the Promotion of Science (JSPS) provides round-trip economy-class airfare for the fellow, a monthly maintenance allowance of 320,000 yen, a relocation allowance of 200,000 yen, an annual research travel allowance in Japan of up to 115,000 yen, overseas travel accident and sickness insurance coverage, housing, tuition reimbursement of up to 200,000 yen for Japanese language training in Japan, and up to 1,500,000 yen per year to cover expenses related to equipment, materials, supplies, and research-related travel. Applicants who plan to stay in Japan for 6 months or more and will be accompanied by dependents may be eligible to apply to NSF for dependent support. That support includes round-trip economy-class airfare, up to $300 in excess baggage per dependent, a relocation allowance of up to $500 per dependent, an allowance of $50 per month per dependent towards the cost of health insurance, and a schooling allowance for children in grades K-12 of up to $1,000 per child per year in public schools or up to $12,000 per child per year in private schools.

Duration 12 to 24 months.

Special features Information is also available from the NSF Tokyo Office, U.S. Embassy Japan, Unit 45004, Box 236, APO AP 96337-5004. NSF selects the recipients for this program, but administration and most of the funding is provided by the JSPS. For further information, contact its Washington Liaison Office, 1800 K Street, N.W., Suite 920, Washington, DC 20006, (202) 659-8190, Fax: (202) 659-8199, E-mail: webmaster@jspsusa.org.

Number awarded Varies each year.

Deadline Applications may be submitted at any time, but they must be received at least 5 months prior to the proposed date of the fellowship.

[333]
NSF/JSPS POSTDOCTORAL FELLOWSHIPS AT UNIVERSITIES AND SIMILAR INSTITUTIONS

National Science Foundation
Directorate for Social, Behavioral, and Economic Sciences
Attn: Division of International Programs
East Asia and Pacific Program
4201 Wilson Boulevard, Room 935
Arlington, VA 22230
(703) 292-8704   Fax: (703) 292-9175
E-mail: eapinfo@nsf.gov
Web site: www.twics.com/~nsftokyo/JSPS01.html

Purpose To offer promising young researchers from the United States the opportunity to engage in long-term research at university laboratories in Japan.

Eligibility These awards are available for research in any field of science or engineering supported by the National Science Foundation (NSF). Applicants must be U.S. citizens who have earned a doctoral degree within 6 years before the date of application, or have equivalent experience beyond the master's degree, or expect to receive the doctoral degree by the award date. They must propose to conduct research in a Japanese university, inter-university research institute, or other research facility affiliated with the Japanese Ministry of Education, Culture, Sports, Science and Technology (MEXT).

Financial data The Japan Society for the Promotion of Science (JSPS) provides round-trip economy-class airfare for the fellow, a monthly maintenance allowance of 392,000 yen, a relocation allowance of 200,000 yen, overseas travel accident and sickness insurance coverage, tuition reimbursement of up to 200,000 yen for Japanese language training in Japan, and up to 1,500,000 yen per year to cover expenses related to equipment, materials, supplies, and research-related travel. Applicants who plan to stay in Japan for 6 months or more and will be accompanied by dependents may be eligible to apply to NSF for dependent support. That support includes round-trip economy-class airfare, up to $300 in excess baggage per dependent, a relocation allowance of up to $500 per dependent, an allowance of $50 per month per dependent towards the cost of health insurance, and a schooling allowance for children in grades K-12 of up to $1,000 per child per year in public schools or up to $12,000 per child per year in private schools.

Duration 12 to 24 months.

Special features Information is also available from the NSF Tokyo Office, U.S. Embassy Japan, Unit 45004, Box 236, APO AP 96337-5004. NSF selects the recipients for this program, but administration and most of the funding is provided by the JSPS. For further information, contact its Washington Liaison Office, 1800 K Street, N.W., Suite 920, Washington, DC 20006, (202) 659-8190, Fax: (202) 659-8199, E-mail: webmaster@jspsusa.org.

Number awarded Varies each year.

Deadline Applications may be submitted at any time, but they must be received at least 5 months prior to the proposed date of the fellowship.

[334]
NSF/JSPS SHORT-TERM INVITATION FELLOWSHIPS AT NATIONAL LABORATORIES AND SIMILAR INSTITUTIONS

National Science Foundation
Directorate for Social, Behavioral, and Economic Sciences
Attn: Division of International Programs
East Asia and Pacific Program
4201 Wilson Boulevard, Room 935
Arlington, VA 22230
(703) 292-8704   Fax: (703) 292-9175
E-mail: eapinfo@nsf.gov
Web site: www.twics.com/~nsftokyo/JSPS01.html

Purpose To offer promising young researchers from the United States the opportunity to engage in short-term research at national laboratories in Japan.

Eligibility These awards are available for research in any field of science or engineering supported by the National Science Foundation (NSF). Applicants must be U.S. citizens who have earned a doctoral degree or expect to receive the doctoral degree by the award date. They must propose to conduct research at a Japanese national laboratory, public corporation, nonprofit research organization, or prefectural research institution.

Financial data The Japan Society for the Promotion of Science (JSPS) provides round-trip economy-class airfare (business-class for senior researchers), a maintenance allowance of 15,000 yen per day, and overseas travel accident and sickness insurance coverage.

Duration 14 to 90 days.

Special features Information is also available from the NSF Tokyo Office, U.S. Embassy Japan, Unit 45004, Box 236, APO AP 96337-5004. NSF selects the recipients for this program, but administration and most of the funding is provided by the JSPS. For further information, contact its Washington Liaison Office, 1800 K Street, N.W., Suite 920, Washington, DC 20006, (202) 659-8190, Fax: (202) 659-8199, E-mail: webmaster@jspsusa.org.

Number awarded Varies each year.

Deadline Applications may be submitted at any time, but they must be received at least 4 months prior to the proposed date of the fellowship.

[335]
NSF/JSPS SHORT-TERM INVITATION FELLOWSHIPS AT UNIVERSITIES AND SIMILAR INSTITUTIONS

National Science Foundation
Directorate for Social, Behavioral, and Economic Sciences
Attn: Division of International Programs
East Asia and Pacific Program
4201 Wilson Boulevard, Room 935
Arlington, VA 22230
(703) 292-8704   Fax: (703) 292-9175
E-mail: eapinfo@nsf.gov
Web site: www.twics.com/~nsftokyo/JSPS01.html

Purpose To offer promising young researchers from the United States the opportunity to engage in short-term research at university laboratories in Japan.

Eligibility These awards are available for research in any field of science or engineering supported by the National Science Foundation (NSF). Applicants must be U.S. citizens who have earned a doctoral degree or expect to receive the doctoral degree by the award date. They must propose to conduct research at a Japanese university, inter-university research institute, or other research facility affiliated with the Japanese Ministry of Education, Culture, Sports, Science and Technology (MEXT).

Financial data The Japan Society for the Promotion of Science (JSPS) provides round-trip economy-class airfare (business-class for senior researchers), a maintenance allowance of 16,000 yen per day (18,000 yen for senior researchers), overseas travel accident and sickness insurance coverage, and a research travel allowance in Japan of 150,000 yen.

Duration 7 to 60 days.

Special features Information is also available from the NSF Tokyo Office, U.S. Embassy Japan, Unit 45004, Box 236, APO AP 96337-5004. NSF selects the recipients for this program, but administration and most of the funding is provided by the JSPS. For further information, contact its Washington Liaison Office, 1800 K Street, N.W., Suite 920, Washington, DC 20006, (202) 659-8190, Fax: (202) 659-8199, E-mail: webmaster@jspsusa.org.

Number awarded Varies each year.

Deadline Applications may be submitted at any time, but they must be received at least 4 months prior to the proposed date of the fellowship.

[336]
NSF/JSPS SHORT-TERM POSTDOCTORAL FELLOWSHIPS AT UNIVERSITIES AND SIMILAR INSTITUTIONS

National Science Foundation
Directorate for Social, Behavioral, and Economic Sciences
Attn: Division of International Programs
East Asia and Pacific Program
4201 Wilson Boulevard, Room 935
Arlington, VA 22230
(703) 292-8704   Fax: (703) 292-9175
E-mail: eapinfo@nsf.gov
Web site: www.twics.com/~nsftokyo/JSPS01.html

Purpose To offer promising young researchers from the

United States the opportunity to engage in short-term research at university laboratories in Japan.

Eligibility These awards are available for research in any field of science or engineering supported by the National Science Foundation (NSF). Applicants must be U.S. citizens who have earned a doctoral degree within 10 years before the date of application, or have equivalent experience beyond the master's degree, or expect to receive the doctoral degree by the award date. They must propose to conduct research in a Japanese university, inter-university research institute, or other research facility affiliated with the Japanese Ministry of Education, Culture, Sports, Science and Technology (MEXT).

Financial data The Japan Society for the Promotion of Science (JSPS) provides round-trip economy-class airfare for the fellow, a monthly maintenance allowance of 392,000 yen, a relocation allowance of 200,000 yen, overseas travel accident and sickness insurance coverage, and a research travel allowance in Japan of 150,000 yen. Applicants who plan to stay in Japan for 6 months or more and will be accompanied by dependents may be eligible to apply to NSF for dependent support. That support includes round-trip economy-class airfare, up to $300 in excess baggage per dependent, a relocation allowance of up to $500 per dependent, an allowance of $50 per month per dependent towards the cost of health insurance, and a schooling allowance for children in grades K-12 of up to $1,000 per child per year in public schools or up to $12,000 per child per year in private schools.

Duration 3 to 11 months.

Special features Information is also available from the NSF Tokyo Office, U.S. Embassy Japan, Unit 45004, Box 236, APO AP 96337-5004. NSF selects the recipients for this program, but administration and most of the funding is provided by the JSPS. For further information, contact its Washington Liaison Office, 1800 K Street, N.W., Suite 920, Washington, DC 20006, (202) 659-8190, Fax: (202) 659-8199, E-mail: webmaster@jspsusa.org.

Number awarded Varies each year.

Deadline Applications may be submitted at any time, but they must be received at least 5 months prior to the proposed date of the fellowship.

[337]
NSF–NATO POSTDOCTORAL FELLOWSHIPS IN SCIENCE AND ENGINEERING

National Science Foundation
Directorate for Education and Human Resources
Attn: Division of Graduate Education
4201 Wilson Boulevard, Room 907N
Arlington, VA 22230
(703) 292-8697   TDD: (703) 292-5090
E-mail: nsf-nato@nsf.gov
Web site: www.ehr.nsf.gov

Purpose To enable young scientists and engineers from the United States to conduct research in the 18 member countries of the North Atlantic Treaty Organization (NATO) or the 18 NATO Partner countries.

Eligibility Eligible to apply for this support are U.S. citizens, nationals, or permanent residents who have received their doctorates within the past 5 years or who will have done so by the start of their tenure. They must be planning to pursue a program of research at an appropriate government or nonprofit scientific institution located in a NATO member or a NATO Partner country other than the United States. Eligible fields of study and research include mathematics; engineering; computer and information science; geosciences; the physical, biological, social, behavioral, and economic sciences; the history and philosophy of science; and interdisciplinary areas comprised of 2 or more of those fields. Research in the teaching and learning of science, mathematics, technology, and engineering is also eligible. Women, underrepresented minorities, and persons with disabilities are particularly encouraged to apply.

Financial data The program provides a monthly stipend of $2,750; dependency allowances of $200 per month for a spouse and each of not more than 2 children; and travel allowances of $2,500 for the fellow ($1,000 to Canada), $2,500 for an accompanying spouse ($1,000 to Canada), and $1,000 for 1 accompanying dependent child ($600 to Canada). In addition, the fellow is provided with $100 per month to aid in defraying costs of research and special travel.

Duration 12 months.

Special features The National Science Foundation manages these fellowships at the request of the U.S. Department of State. Members of NATO are Belgium, Canada, Czech Republic, Denmark, France, Germany, Greece, Hungary, Iceland, Italy, Luxembourg, the Netherlands, Norway, Poland, Portugal, Spain, Turkey, and the United Kingdom. The NATO Partner countries include the 15 republics of the former Soviet Union and 6 countries in eastern Europe (Albania, Bulgaria, Romania, Slovak Republic, Slovenia, and the former Yugoslav Republic of Macedonia).

Number awarded Approximately 5 each year.

Deadline November of each year.

[338]
OCK RANG CULTURAL FOUNDATION FELLOWSHIP PROGRAM OF THE ASIAN CULTURAL COUNCIL

Asian Cultural Council
437 Madison Avenue, 37th Floor
New York, NY 10022-7001
(212) 812-4300   Fax: (212) 812-4299
E-mail: acc@accny.org
Web site: www.asianculturalcouncil.org

Purpose To provide funding for a cultural exchange between humanists in the United States and Korea.

Eligibility Eligible to apply are artists and specialists from Korea pursuing research, study, and creative work in the United States, primarily in the technical theater arts. The program also funds American specialists traveling to Korea and Asian artists presenting workshops and surveying arts activities in Korea. Applications are not accepted for lecture programs, personal exhibitions, individual performance tours, undergraduate study, or activities conducted by individuals in their home countries.

Financial data Fellows receive international and domestic travel allowances, a living allowance, and an allocation for miscellaneous expenses (including books and supplies). Partial fellowships are available for fellows with supplementary assistance from other sources.

Duration 1 to 6 months.

Special features Support for this program, established in 1995, is also provided by the Ock Rang Cultural Foundation.

Number awarded 1 to 4 each year.

Deadline January of each year.

[339]
OLIVIA JAMES TRAVELING FELLOWSHIP

Archaeological Institute of America
656 Beacon Street, Fourth Floor
Boston, MA 02215-2010
(617) 353-9361   Fax: (617) 353-6550
E-mail: aia@bu.edu
Web site: www.archaeological.org

Purpose To provide financial assistance to American graduate students and scholars who wish to conduct research in Greece, the Aegean Islands, Sicily, southern Italy, Asia Minor, or Mesopotamia.

Eligibility Although applicants are not required to be registered in academic institutions, preference is given to individuals engaged in dissertation research or to recent (within 5 years) recipients of the Ph.D. They must be U.S. citizens or permanent residents and interested in conducting research on the classics, sculpture, architecture, archaeology, or history in Greece, the Aegean Islands, Sicily, southern Italy, Asia Minor, or Mesopotamia.

Financial data The amount of the award is $22,000.

Duration Preference is given to work of at least half a year's duration.

Number awarded 1 each year.

Deadline October of each year.

[340]
PEOPLE'S REPUBLIC OF CHINA DISTINGUISHED LECTURESHIPS

Council for International Exchange of Scholars
3007 Tilden Street, N.W., Suite 5L
Washington, DC 20008-3009
(202) 686-4021   Fax: (202) 362-3442
E-mail: scholars@cies.iie.org
Web site: www.iie.org/cies

Purpose To provide funding to American scholars to present lectures, seminars, and workshops in the People's Republic of China (PRC).

Eligibility Applicants must be U.S. citizens who possess a Ph.D. and a distinguished record of scholarship and publication; preference is given to full professors. Positions in the PRC are available in American foreign policy, economics or business administration (international economics and trade, international finance, and money and banking), and law.

Financial data The award provides a monthly stipend of $2,400 to $4,000; a maintenance allowance of $2,100 to $2,700 per month (depending on the number of accompanying dependents and the city of placement); a travel/relocation allowance of $3,150 for the grantee, $2,000 for 1 dependent, and $3,500 for 2 dependents; a book allowance of $2,000 per semester; and up to $500 for language study upon submission of receipts. Host institutions provide housing. If the combined benefit package and other income the grantee will receive during the grant period is less than a grantee's normal salary, the grantee receives a supplemental payment to bring the grant package to the same level as their salary for a comparable period, to a maximum of $100,000.

Duration 5 or 10 months.

Special features This is a Fulbright scholar program, sponsored by the Bureau of Educational and Cultural Affairs of the U.S. Department of State and administered by the Council for International Exchange of Scholars. In addition to teaching undergraduate and graduate courses, grantees are expected to consult on curriculum and program development, advise graduate students on theses, and give seminars, workshops, and public lectures. The assignment in American foreign policy is at the People's (Renmin) University of China (Beijing), in economics or business administration at Xiamen University, and in law at Tsinghua University (Beijing).

Number awarded 3 each year: 1 in each field.

Deadline July of each year.

[341]
POLICY RESEARCH FELLOWSHIP PROGRAM OF THE NATIONAL COUNCIL FOR EURASIAN AND EAST EUROPEAN RESEARCH

National Council for Eurasian and East European
  Research
910 17th Street, N.W., Suite 300
Washington, DC 20006
(202) 822-6950   Fax: (202) 822-6955
E-mail: nceeerdc@aol.com
Web site: www.nceeer.gov

Purpose To provide funding to junior scholars who are interested in conducting research on politics and society in the former Soviet republics and eastern Europe (including Eurasia).

Eligibility This program is open to U.S.-based scholars who have obtained a Ph.D. within the past 10 years. Applicants must be interested in conducting field research that will contribute to the general understanding of politics and society in the region of the former Soviet Union and eastern Europe (including Eurasia). Affiliation with a U.S. college or university is required, except in the case of independent scholars. Applicants must be U.S. citizens or permanent residents and sufficiently proficient in the host country language to meet the demands of their research.

Financial data The grant is $40,000.

Duration Up to 1 year.

Special features Funding for this program is provided by the U.S. Department of State under the Research and Training for Eastern Europe and the Independent States of the Former Soviet Union Act of 1983 (Title VIII).

Deadline January of each year.

[342]
PROFESSIONAL DEVELOPMENT FELLOWSHIPS
Institute of International Education
Attn: Student Programs Division
809 United Nations Plaza
New York, NY 10017-3580
(212) 984-5330   Fax: (212) 984-5325
E-mail: pdfnis@iie.org
Web site: www.iie.org/pgms/pdfnis

Purpose To provide financial assistance to American graduate students and postgraduates who wish to carry out a program of research, study, or internship in eastern Europe, central Europe, or Eurasia.

Eligibility This program is open to U.S. citizens who either 1) are at least in the second (or terminal) year of a graduate or professional degree program, or 2) have graduated within 5 years from a graduate or professional degree program. Applicants must propose a feasible research, study, or internship plan for the period of the fellowship and indicate a desired institutional affiliation in the host country; applications solely in support of dissertation research or language research are not accepted. Host countries include Albania, Armenia, Azerbaijan, Belarus, Bulgaria, Croatia, Estonia, Georgia, Kazakhstan, Kyrgyzstan, Latvia, Lithuania, Macedonia, Moldova, Romania, Russia, Slovak Republic, Tajikistan, Turkmenistan, Ukraine, and Uzbekistan. Fields of study include business, economics, education reform, environmental and conservation policy, international relations, journalism, law, public administration, and public health. Applicants must have language ability sufficient to carry out the proposed project by the time of departure from the United States. They must indicate how the proposed study, research, or internship will benefit their future plans and professional careers.

Financial data Fellowships provide payment of round-trip international airfare, a monthly living stipend, insurance, and allowances for books and travel in the host country. No provision is made for dependents.

Duration 3 to 7 months.

Special features Funding for this program is provided by the U.S. Department of State through Title VIII (the Research and Training for Eastern Europe and the Independent States of the Former Soviet Union Act of 1983).

Deadline January of each year.

[343]
PROGRAM TO ASSIST FOREIGN SCHOLARS IN CHINESE STUDIES
Center for Chinese Studies
20 Chungshan South Road
Taipei 10001
Taiwan
886 2 2314 7321   Fax: 886 2 2371 2126
E-mail: ccsgrant@msg.ncl.edu.tw

Purpose To provide financial aid to foreign graduate students and scholars who wish to conduct research in Chinese studies in Taiwan.

Eligibility Eligible are faculty members, Ph.D. candidates, and researchers in Chinese studies at universities or institutes outside of Taiwan who are interested in conducting research in Taiwan.

Financial data The monthly stipend is $NT50,000 for full professors, $NT40,000 for associate professors, $NT30,000 for assistant professors, or $NT20,000 for doctoral candidates; researchers at research institutes receive comparable grants. Round-trip economy-class airfare is also provided.

Duration 3 to 12 months.

Number awarded 5 each year.

Deadline April of each year.

[344]
RESEARCH STUDENT SCHOLARSHIPS OF THE JAPANESE GOVERNMENT (MONBUKAGAKUSHO)
Japan Ministry of Education, Culture, Sports, Science and Technology
c/o Embassy of Japan
2520 Massachusetts Avenue, N.W.
Washington, DC 20008
(202) 238-6700   Fax: (202) 328-2187
Web site: www.embjapan.org

Purpose To provide financial assistance to college graduates from outside of Japan who wish to pursue graduate studies (as nondegree students) or conduct research in selected fields at a Japanese university.

Eligibility This program is open to citizens of countries other than Japan who are college graduates under 35 years of age. Previous Japanese language study in not required, but applicants must be willing to study Japanese after arrival in Japan. They must be interested in studying (as nondegree research students) the same field as their undergraduate major, provided it is offered by Japanese universities. Fields of study include agriculture, dentistry, engineering, fisheries, home science, the humanities, medicine, the natural sciences, pharmacology, and the social sciences.

Financial data Scholarship benefits include: a monthly allowance of 185,500 yen; round-trip air transportation; an arrival allowance of 25,000 yen; remission of entrance, examination, and tuition fees; an annual research allowance; and reimbursement of 80 percent of medical fees.

Duration 2 years, including 6 months of Japanese language training for students who require it.

Special features All instruction is given in Japanese. Applications are available from the Japanese embassy in Washington, any Japanese consulate in the United States, or universities in Japan for students who are already enrolled.

Limitations Recipients who are not fluent in Japanese must study the language for 6 months as part of their tenure in Japan before they are permitted to attend a university. The Japanese Ministry of Education, Culture, Sports, Science and Technology (Monbukagakusho) decides which university each recipient may attend.

Number awarded 3,730 of these scholarships are awarded to students from around the world each year.

Deadline Each consulate in the United States sets its own deadline; most are in August of each year. Check with the consulate for your area for more information.

[345]
SAROJINI NAIDU MEMORIAL SCHOLARSHIP

University Women's Association of Delhi
Attn: Scholarships Convenor
6 Bhagwandas Road
New Delhi 110 001
India

Purpose To provide funding to women from any country who are interested in pursuing graduate study or research in India.

Eligibility This program is open to women college graduates from any country who qualify for study or research at the graduate level in Delhi, India. Applicants must be interested in studying the humanities or social sciences, with special reference to India.

Financial data The stipend is 600 rupees per month.

Duration Up to 1 year.

Special features The University Women's Association of Delhi is 1 of the components of the Indian Federation of University Women's Associations.

Limitations The recipient must be in residence in Delhi for the duration of the award.

Number awarded 1 each year.

Deadline December of each year.

[346]
SCMRE GRADUATE ARCHAEOLOGICAL INTERNSHIP

Smithsonian Center for Materials Research and Education
Attn: Coordinator of Education and Training
Museum Support Center, Room D2002
4210 Silver Hill Road
Suitland, MD 20746-2863
(301) 238-3700, ext. 153   Fax: (301) 238-3709
Web site: www.si.edu/scmre/arcintern.html

Purpose To provide training at the Smithsonian Center for Materials Research and Education (SCMRE) and affiliated overseas facilities to graduate students interested in archaeological conservation.

Eligibility This program is open to graduate students entering the internship year in a conservation training program or the equivalent. Recipients spend approximately half the year at archaeological sites with which SCMRE is associated; in the past, SCMRE conservators have worked with excavation teams at Harappa (Pakistan), Cerén (El Salvador), and Copán (Honduras). For the remainder of the time, interns work in the Objects Conservation Laboratory at SCMRE, where they treat archaeological artifacts or carry out research. Minorities are particularly encouraged to apply.

Financial data Travel costs and living expenses at the archaeological site are provided; supplemental funding up to $14,000 and an additional $2,000 for travel and research may also be available.

Duration 1 year.

Number awarded 1 each year.

Deadline February of each year.

[347]
SCMRE POSTGRADUATE ARCHAEOLOGICAL FELLOWSHIP

Smithsonian Center for Materials Research and Education
Attn: Coordinator of Education and Training
Museum Support Center, Room D2002
4210 Silver Hill Road
Suitland, MD 20746-2863
(301) 238-3700, ext. 153   Fax: (301) 238-3709
Web site: www.si.edu/scmre/arcintern.html

Purpose To provide postgraduate fellows with an opportunity to conduct research at the Smithsonian Center for Materials Research and Education (SCMRE) and affiliated overseas facilities.

Eligibility This program is open to recent graduates of recognized conservation training programs and persons with comparable training and experience. Recipients spend approximately half the year at archaeological sites with which SCMRE is associated; in the past, SCMRE conservators have worked with excavation teams at Harappa (Pakistan), Cerén (El Salvador), and Copán (Honduras). For the remainder of the time, interns work in the Objects Conservation Laboratory at SCMRE, where they treat archaeological artifacts or carry out research. Minorities are particularly encouraged to apply.

Financial data Travel and living expenses at the archaeological site are covered; supplemental funding up to $22,000 and an additional $2,000 for travel and research may also be available.

Duration 1 year.

Number awarded 1 each year.

Deadline February of each year.

[348]
SHORT-TERM INVITATION FELLOWSHIP PROGRAMS FOR RESEARCH IN JAPAN

Japan Society for the Promotion of Science
Attn: Washington Liaison Office
1800 K Street, N.W., Suite 920
Washington, DC 20006
(202) 659-8190   Fax: (202) 659-8199
E-mail: webmaster@jspsusa.org
Web site: www.jspsusa.org

Purpose To invite senior scholars to participate in discussions, attend seminars, give lectures, or perform similar duties at Japanese universities or research institutes.

Eligibility Senior scientists, university professors, and other persons with substantial professional experience from any country that has diplomatic relations with Japan are eligible for this program. Applications must be submitted by Japanese researchers at universities or research institutes; foreign scholars may not apply directly. Scholars who wish to participate in this program are advised to establish contact with Japanese researchers in the same field. All fields of the humanities, social sciences, and natural sciences are included.

Financial data The fellowship includes round-trip airfare for the fellow only, a daily maintenance allowance of 18,000 yen, a domestic research travel allowance of 150,000 yen, and accident and sickness insurance coverage for the fellow only.

Duration 14 to 60 days.

Special features This program began in 1959. The Japan Society for the Promotion of Science (JSPS) is a quasi-governmental organization that operates under the auspices of Japan's Ministry of Education, Culture, Sports, Science and Technology (Monbukagakusho).
Number awarded Approximately 195 each year; in recent years, 75 to 80 have been from the United States.
Deadline May or September of each year.

[349]
SHORT-TERM RESEARCH TRAVEL TO KOREA
Association for Asian Studies
Attn: Northeast Asia Council
1021 East Huron Street
Ann Arbor, MI 48104
(734) 665-2490   Fax: (734) 665-3801
E-mail: postmaster@aasianst.org
Web site: www.aasianst.org

Purpose To provide financial assistance to American scholars who wish to travel to Korea to conduct a specific project explicitly related to Korean studies.
Eligibility American citizens and permanent U.S. residents are eligible to apply if they are engaged in scholarly research on Korea and wish to travel to Korea to conduct a research study. These grants are intended for short-term trips by scholars who are already familiar with Korea and with their topic but now need time in Korea in order to complete their work.
Financial data Up to $2,500, to be used to cover basic transportation costs or to be applied to per diem costs for travel to Korea to conduct the research project.
Duration Up to 1 month.
Special features This program is supported by the Northeast Asia Council of the Association for Asian Studies, in conjunction with the Korea Foundation.
Limitations Dissertation research cannot be supported under this program. All travel costs paid by the grant must be on American carriers.
Deadline January or September of each year.

[350]
SHORT-TERM RESIDENCIES FOR U.S. HISTORIANS IN JAPANESE UNIVERSITIES
Organization of American Historians
Attn: Selection Coordinator, International Residencies
112 North Bryan Street
Bloomington, IN 47408-4199
(812) 855-7311   Fax: (812) 855-0696
E-mail: japan@oah.org
Web site: www.oah.org

Purpose To provide an opportunity for U.S. historians to visit Japan to offer lectures and seminars on the subject of their specialty.
Eligibility This program is open to historians, especially those in mid-career, at universities in the United States. Applicants should be interested in visiting Japan, generally for the first time, to offer lectures and seminars as part of the collegial life of a host university.
Financial data The award covers round-trip airfare to Japan, housing, and modest daily expenses.
Duration 2 weeks.
Special features This program, established in 1997, is jointly administered by the Organization of American Historians and the Japanese Association for American Studies, with support from the Japan-U.S. Friendship Commission.
Number awarded 3 each year.
Deadline December of each year.

[351]
SHORT-TERM TRAVEL GRANTS FOR CENTRAL AND EASTERN EUROPE AND EURASIA
International Research & Exchanges Board
1616 H Street, N.W.
Washington, DC 20006
(202) 628-8188   Fax: (202) 628-8189
E-mail: irex@irex.org
Web site: www.irex.org

Purpose To allow U.S. scholars to pursue their individual research or other activities in the social sciences or humanities in central Europe, eastern Europe, or Eurasia.
Eligibility Applicants must be U.S. citizens who have the Ph.D. or an equivalent professional doctoral degree and need support for humanities or social sciences projects. Proposals may include library or archival research, carrying out interviews, presentations at scholarly conferences, invited lectures or consultations, or collaborative projects (such as joint publications or comparative surveys). The project must involve central Europe, eastern Europe, or Eurasia, including, in special circumstances, Iran or Turkey.
Financial data Grants up to a maximum of $3,000 may be awarded; funds may be used for round-trip airfare on a U.S. flag carrier, per diem up to $100 per day for food and lodging, conference registration fees, and visa fees.
Duration Up to 60 days; a per diem will be allowed only up to 14 days.
Special features The International Research & Exchanges Board (IREX) was established in 1968 at the request of U.S. universities by the American Council of Learned Societies (ACLS) and the Social Science Research Council (SSRC) to administer research exchange programs with the socialist countries of eastern Europe and the former Soviet republics. This program is funded by the U.S. Department of State as a Title VIII program and the National Endowment for the Humanities (NEH).
Number awarded Varies each year; in a recent round, 32 of these grants were awarded, including 4 funded by NEH and 28 by the Department of State.
Deadline January or May of each year.

[352]
SHORT-TERM TRAVEL TO JAPAN FOR PROFESSIONAL PURPOSES

Association for Asian Studies
Attn: Northeast Asia Council
1021 East Huron Street
Ann Arbor, MI 48104
(734) 665-2490   Fax: (734) 665-3801
E-mail: postmaster@aasianst.org
Web site: www.aasianst.org

Purpose To provide financial assistance to American scholars who wish to travel to Japan to conduct a specific project explicitly related to Japan.

Eligibility American citizens and permanent U.S. residents are eligible to apply if they are engaged in scholarly research on Japan and wish to travel to Japan to conduct a research study. These grants are intended for short-term trips by scholars who are already familiar with Japan and with their topic but now need time in Japan in order to complete their work. Applicants must hold a Ph.D. or comparable professional qualification; Ph.D. candidates are not eligible.

Financial data Up to 200,000 yen, to be used to cover expenses in Japan; funds may not be used for reimbursement of international transportation.

Duration Up to 1 month.

Special features This program is supported by the Northeast Asia Council of the Association for Asian Studies, in conjunction with the Japan-United States Friendship Commission.

Deadline January or September of each year.

[353]
SMITHSONIAN INSTITUTION FOREIGN CURRENCY GRANT PROGRAM

Smithsonian Institution
Attn: Office of International Relations
S. Dillon Ripley Center, Room 3123
Washington, DC 20560-0705
(202) 357-4795   Fax: (202) 275-0489

Purpose To provide financial aid to American scholars interested in conducting research in countries where the United States holds excess foreign currencies.

Eligibility The program welcomes proposals from senior scholars at American institutions of higher learning (including the Smithsonian Institution) in the fields of anthropology and archaeology, cultural history, evolutionary and conservation biology, astrophysics and earth sciences, and museum programs. Applicants must be interested in conducting research in "excess currency countries." Proposals should provide a summary and description of the research, including methodology, bibliography, biographical information on major participants, and a detailed budget.

Financial data The awards are in local currency and cover international and local travel, living allowance, and research expenses.

Duration 1 year; renewable is possible.

Special features For the purposes of this program, "excess currency countries" are defined as those in which the U.S. government owns local currencies derived from sales of agricultural commodities under Public Law 480. Most recently, the excess currency countries were Croatia, Czech Republic, Hungary, India, Poland, Slovak Republic, and Slovenia.

Limitations Host government approval for the conduct of research funded through this program is required in all excess currency countries. In some cases, local and state authorities must also approve projects. In addition, U.S. embassy concurrence is required. Funds cannot be authorized until all necessary governmental clearances have been obtained.

Deadline October of each year.

[354]
SSRC/JSPS POSTDOCTORAL FELLOWSHIPS

Social Science Research Council
810 Seventh Avenue
New York, NY 10019
(212) 377-2700   Fax: (212) 377-2727
E-mail: japan@ssrc.org
Web site: www.ssrc.org

Purpose To provide financial assistance to scholars interested in conducting postdoctoral research in Japan in all areas of the social sciences and humanities.

Eligibility This program is open to U.S. citizens or permanent residents who received a doctoral degree recently; long-term fellowships are available to scholars who received the Ph.D. within the preceding 6 years and short-term fellowships to those who received the Ph.D. within the preceding 10 years. All applicants must have arranged an affiliation with an eligible host research institution in Japan to conduct research in the social sciences or humanities. Projects need not be explicitly related to the study of Japan, but they must propose work with colleagues and resources in Japan. Proposals are especially encouraged that involve cooperative research with colleagues in Japan under the guidance of a senior host sponsor. All accredited universities and research institutions in Japan under the jurisdiction of the Ministry of Education, Culture, Sports, Science and Technology (Monbukagakusho) are eligible host institutions. Minorities and women are particularly encouraged to apply.

Financial data The program provides round-trip airfare, a stipend of 392,000 yen per month, insurance coverage for accidents and illness, a settling-in allowance of 200,000 yen, eligibility for up to an additional 1,500,000 yen annually for research expenses for stays of 12 to 24 months, and a research and domestic travel allowance of 150,000 yen for stays of 3 to 11 months.

Duration Long-term fellowships may extend from 12 to 24 months; short-term fellowships are 3 to 11 months.

Special features Funding for this program is provided by the Japan Society for the Promotion of Science (JSPS). For further information, contact its Washington Liaison Office, 1800 K Street, N.W., Suite 920, Washington, DC 20006, (202) 659-8190, Fax: (202) 659-8199, E-mail: webmaster@jspsusa.org.

Number awarded Up to 20 each year.

Deadline December of each year.

[355]
SUITCASE FUND

Dance Theater Workshop
Attn: Director and Producer of Inter/National Programs
219 West 19th Street
New York, NY 10011-4079
(212) 691-6500   Fax: (212) 633-1974
E-mail: cathy@dtw.org
Web site: www.dtw.org

Purpose To promote the performing arts through an international exchange.

Eligibility To promote cultural equity in a pluralistic America, the fund helps artists of all backgrounds and origins to maintain access to the contemporary arts of their homelands. Applicants should be independent professional artists working without the support of major institutions. They must be seeking to study, teach, collaborate, or perform in another part of the world.

Financial data The amount awarded varies, depending upon the needs of the recipient.

Special features Participating artists and producers are placed in Africa, Asia, Latin America, and the Caribbean, as well as Europe. Funding for this program is provided by the Rockefeller Foundation, the Trust for Mutual Understanding, and the Asian Cultural Council.

Limitations The Fund does not function as an all-purpose emergency travel fund, nor will it duplicate the well-established initiatives of other producers or funders.

Deadline Applications may be submitted at any time.

[356]
SUMMER INSTITUTE IN JAPAN FOR U.S. GRADUATE STUDENTS IN SCIENCE AND ENGINEERING

National Science Foundation
Directorate for Social, Behavioral, and Economic Sciences
Attn: Division of International Programs
4201 Wilson Boulevard
Arlington, VA 22230
(703) 292-8701   Fax: (703) 292-9176
TDD: (703) 292-5090   E-mail: eapinfo@nsf.gov
Web site: www.nsf.gov/sbe/int/start.htm

Purpose To provide U.S. science and engineering graduate students with an opportunity to participate in a study and research institute in Japan.

Eligibility Applicants must be enrolled at a U.S. institution in a Ph.D. program or enrolled in an engineering graduate program, must have completed at least 1 year of graduate study, and must be pursuing studies in the sciences (including agricultural, biomedical, and health sciences) or engineering. Selection is based on the applicant's competence in science or engineering, potential for continued professional growth as a research scientist or engineer, relevant professional interests, potential to benefit from a trip to Japan, and willingness and preparation to live in and adapt to the Japanese culture (relevant factors include language aptitude or achievement, previous study abroad, membership in intercultural organizations, and research collaboration with foreign scientists). Women, minorities, and persons with disabilities are strongly encouraged to apply.

Financial data This program pays travel costs to and from Japan and an allowance of $2,500. The Japanese government provides accommodations as well as allowances for food and professional travel within Japan. The Japan International Science and Technology Exchange Center (JISTEC) provides logistical support. Participants must pay for their own insurance and any additional expenditures.

Duration 8 weeks, beginning in June.

Special features The institute is held in Tokyo and in Tsukuba City, Ibaraki Prefecture (about 60 km northeast of Tokyo). The program provides an internship at a Japanese government or corporate laboratory in Tsukuba, intensive language training, lectures and discussion on U.S.-Japan comparative science policy and history, presentations by Japanese and U.S. scientists resident in Japan on the current status of science and engineering in Japan, and group visits to facilities in Tsukuba and elsewhere in Japan. On the Japanese side, this program is sponsored by the Science and Technology Agency of Japan and the Japan Science and Technology Corporation. On the U.S. side, it is cosponsored by the Agricultural Research Service of the Department of Agriculture (which supports research related to agriculture), the Fogarty International Center of the National Institutes of Health (which supports research in the biomedical and health sciences), and the National Science Foundation (which supports engineering and science research).

Limitations Due to the intensive nature of the program, dependents are not allowed to accompany participants.

Number awarded 60 each year.

Deadline November of each year.

[357]
SUMMER INSTITUTE IN KOREA FOR U.S. GRADUATE STUDENTS IN SCIENCE AND ENGINEERING

National Science Foundation
Directorate for Social, Behavioral, and Economic Sciences
Attn: Division of International Programs
4201 Wilson Boulevard
Arlington, VA 22230
(703) 292-8701   Fax: (703) 292-9176
TDD: (703) 292-5090   E-mail: eapinfo@nsf.gov
Web site: www.nsf.gov/sbe/int/start.htm

Purpose To provide U.S. science and engineering graduate students with an opportunity to participate in a study and research institute in Korea.

Eligibility Applicants must be U.S. citizens or permanent residents enrolled at a U.S. institution in a science or engineering Ph.D. program or enrolled in an engineering master's program of which at least 1 year has been completed. Selection is based on the applicant's competence in science or engineering, potential for continued professional growth as a research scientist or engineer, relevant professional interests, potential to benefit from a trip to Korea, and willingness and preparation to live in and adapt to the Korean culture (relevant factors include language aptitude or achievement, previous study abroad, membership in intercultural organizations, and research collaboration with foreign scientists). Women, minorities, and persons with disabilities are encouraged to apply.

Financial data This program pays travel costs to and from Korea and an allowance of $2,500. The Korea Science and

Engineering Foundation provides living accommodations, food, professional travel within Korea, and logistical support. Participants must pay for their own insurance and any additional costs.

Duration 8 weeks, beginning in June.

Special features This program began in 1995; it is jointly administered by the National Science Foundation (NSF) and the Korea Science and Engineering Foundation, P.O. Box 11, Daeduk Science Town, Taejon 305-306, Korea. Participants intern at a research laboratory in Seoul, Daeduk Science Town, or Pohang. They also participate in language training and practice with Korean instructors and site visits to Korean centers of scientific and cultural interest.

Limitations Due to the intensive nature of the program, dependents are not allowed to accompany participants.

Number awarded 20 each year.

Deadline November of each year.

[358]
SUMMER INSTITUTE IN TAIWAN FOR U.S. GRADUATE STUDENTS IN SCIENCE AND ENGINEERING

National Science Foundation
Directorate for Social, Behavioral, and Economic Sciences
Attn: Division of International Programs
4201 Wilson Boulevard
Arlington, VA 22230
(703) 292-8701   Fax: (703) 292-9176
TDD: (703) 292-5090   E-mail: eapinfo@nsf.gov
Web site: www.nsf.gov/sbe/int/start.htm

Purpose To provide U.S. science and engineering graduate students with an opportunity to participate in a study and research institute in Taiwan.

Eligibility Applicants must be U.S. citizens or permanent residents enrolled at a U.S. institution in a science or engineering Ph.D. program, an M.D. program with an interest in biomedical research, or a science or engineering master's program of which at least 1 year has been completed. Selection is based on the applicant's competence in science or engineering, potential for continued professional growth as a research scientist or engineer, relevant professional interests, potential to benefit from a trip to Taiwan, and willingness and preparation to live in and adapt to the Taiwanese culture (relevant factors include language aptitude or achievement, previous study abroad, membership in intercultural organizations, and research collaboration with foreign scientists). Women, minorities, and persons with disabilities are encouraged to apply.

Financial data This program pays travel costs to and from Taiwan and an allowance of $2,500. The Taiwan National Science Council provides living accommodations, food, professional travel within Taiwan, and logistical support. Participants must pay for their own insurance and any additional costs.

Duration 8 weeks, beginning in June.

Special features This program began in 2000; it is jointly administered by the National Science Foundation (NSF) and the Taiwan National Science Council. Participants intern at several national laboratories, central science and technology units and research institutes, universities, and private sector research centers in Taipei and Hsinchu Science-Based Industrial Park (approximately 100 km south of Taipei). They also participate in a 1-week introduction to Chinese language and culture at Tsing Hua University in Taiwan.

Limitations Due to the intensive nature of the program, dependents are not allowed to accompany participants.

Number awarded 10 each year.

Deadline November of each year.

[359]
SYCIP DISTINGUISHED LECTURING AWARDS

Council for International Exchange of Scholars
3007 Tilden Street, N.W., Suite 5L
Washington, DC 20008-3009
(202) 686-4024   Fax: (202) 362-3442
E-mail: scholars@cies.iie.org
Web site: www.iie.org/cies

Purpose To allow distinguished American scholars to lecture on American studies at universities in the Philippines.

Eligibility This program is open to scholars who have a distinguished scholarly or professional record and a national reputation in the field of American foreign policy, American economic policy, or American business practices. Applicants must be interested in giving lectures and presenting workshops at major universities in the Manila metropolitan area and possibly addressing professional organizations. U.S. citizenship is required.

Financial data The grant provides a monthly stipend of up to $6,000 plus funds for travel within the Philippines.

Duration 2 weeks to 2 months.

Special features This is a Fulbright scholar program, sponsored by the Bureau of Educational and Cultural Affairs of the U.S. Department of State and administered by the Council for International Exchange of Scholars. It is funded by a grant from the SyCip Family Foundation.

Number awarded 2 each year.

Deadline July of each year.

[360]
TAIWAN FELLOWSHIP PROGRAM OF THE ASIAN CULTURAL COUNCIL

Asian Cultural Council
437 Madison Avenue, 37th Floor
New York, NY 10022-7001
(212) 812-4300   Fax: (212) 812-4299
E-mail: acc@accny.org
Web site: www.asianculturalcouncil.org

Purpose To provide funding for a cultural exchange between humanists in the United States and Taiwan.

Eligibility Eligible to apply are artists, art specialists, or art scholars in the United States or Taiwan who are interested in undertaking research, study, travel, or creative projects in the other country. Their specialties must include: archaeology, architecture (design, history, or theory), art history, conservation, crafts, dance, film, literature, museum studies, music, painting, photography, printmaking, sculpture, theater, or video. Applications are not accepted for lecture programs, personal exhibitions, individual performance tours, undergraduate study, or activities conducted by individuals in their home countries.

Financial data Fellows receive international and domestic travel allowances, a living allowance, and an allocation for miscellaneous expenses (including books and supplies). Partial fellowships are available for fellows with supplementary assistance from other sources.
Duration 1 to 6 months.
Special features Support for this program, established in 1995, is also provided by the Sino-American Cultural Foundation.
Deadline January of each year.

[361]
TAIWAN INTERNSHIPS
Institute of International Education
Attn: Student Programs Division
809 United Nations Plaza
New York, NY 10017-3580
(212) 984-5330   Fax: (212) 984-5325
Web site: www.iie.org/fulbright

Purpose To provide work experience in Taiwan for U.S. college graduates who need to fulfill an internship requirement related to their field of study or who wish to broaden their experience.
Eligibility This program is open to U.S. citizens who are articulate native English speakers with superior writing ability. Applicants must hold a master's degree or be currently enrolled in a graduate program and be interested in 1) every aspect of the media, including mass media and multimedia, or 2) international education, cross-cultural counseling, or teaching English as a second language. They must be interested in working in Taiwan in a program that includes up to 20 hours per week of work at a nonprofit or governmental organization and another 20 hours per week devoted to language study or an independent study/research project. Applications should include a description of study or career interests and well-thought-out plans for projects.
Financial data The amount awarded varies.
Duration 6 to 10 months.
Special features This program is administered in the United States by the Institute of International Education (IIE) as part of the Fulbright program. Students who are currently enrolled in the United States are to apply through the Fulbright program adviser on their campus; at-large applicants (those not currently enrolled) may obtain applications and information directly from the IIE.
Limitations Interns are not permitted to assume any other employment, since the purpose of the internship is to provide a learning experience.
Number awarded 4 each year.
Deadline October of each year.

[362]
TAKASE SCHOLARSHIP
Takase Scholarship Foundation
Takase Building
1-10-9 Shinbashi, Minato-ku
Tokyo 105-0004
Japan
81 3 3571 9401   Fax: 81 3 3571 4622

Purpose To provide financial assistance for study or research to undergraduate and graduate students from other countries who are in Japan.
Eligibility Applicants must be 1) short-term students from other countries who have come to Japan under an inter-university exchange agreement; 2) enrolled in a special course taught in English at a designated graduate school; or 3) graduate students doing research related to international development assistance or international cooperation. The schools participating in this program include: University of Tsukuba, Saitama University, University of Tokyo, Tokyo Medical and Dental University, Tokyo University of Foreign Studies, Tokyo Institute of Technology, Hitotsubashi University, Yokohama National University, Hiroshima University, Kyushu University, Keio University, International Christian University, Sophia University Chiba University, Tokyo University of Agriculture, Japan Women's University, and Waseda University. Generally, applicants should be under the age of 30.
Financial data The stipend is 100,000 yen per month.
Duration 1 year.
Number awarded Varies; up to 30 each year.
Deadline February for the spring semester; September for the fall semester.

[363]
TARGET OF OPPORTUNITY FELLOWSHIPS
Institute of Current World Affairs, Inc.
Attn: Program Administrator
Wheelock House
4 West Wheelock Street
Hanover, NH 03755
(603) 643-5548   Fax: (603) 643-9599
E-mail: icwa@valley.net
Web site: www.icwa.org

Purpose To provide opportunities for independent research in selected foreign countries or on designated topics.
Eligibility Individuals who have completed their formal education are eligible to apply if they are interested in conducting research in either an area of their own choice or in selected areas (Burma, Korea, Japan, Iran, southeast Asia, south Asia, Siberia, Poland, north Africa, or the former East Germany) or on designated topics (the seas, fresh water). Generally, applicants must be under the age of 36 and have good command of written and spoken English.
Financial data The institute provides full support for the fellows and their families.
Duration At least 2 years.
Limitations Fellowships are not awarded to support work toward academic degrees, to write books, or to undertake specific studies or research projects. Fellows are required to submit monthly reports.

Number awarded 1 or more each year.
Deadline March or August of each year.

[364]
THAILAND DISTINGUISHED LECTURESHIP IN MICROELECTRONICS

Council for International Exchange of Scholars
3007 Tilden Street, N.W., Suite 5L
Washington, DC 20008-3009
(202) 686-4021   Fax: (202) 362-3442
E-mail: scholars@cies.iie.org
Web site: www.iie.org/cies

Purpose To enable American scholars to teach courses on microelectronics in Thailand.

Eligibility Applicants must hold a Ph.D. in a major area of microelectronics and should be an assistant, associate, or full professor with at least 5 years of recent university teaching experience. They must be able to teach graduate courses in microelectronic circuit design and its applications at the School of Advanced Technologies, Asian Institute of Technology, Bangkok. U.S. citizenship is required.

Financial data The stipend is 105,000 baht per month. Other benefits include free housing on campus or a housing allowance of 15,000 to 30,000 baht per month, depending on the location and number of accompanying dependents; a monthly subsistence allowance of 6,000 to 17,000 baht per month, depending on the location and number of accompanying dependents; international travel for grantee and 1 dependent; a settling-in allowance of 22,500 baht; an in-transit allowance of 4,500 baht; up to 15,000 baht for excess-baggage charges; reimbursement of up to 14,000 baht for purchase of books, supplies, and services essential to the project; reimbursement of up to 20,000 baht for Thai language study; and 63,000 to 165,000 baht in actual tuition costs for accompanying school-age children.

Duration 4 to 12 months, beginning in January, May, or September.

Special features This is a Fulbright scholar program, sponsored by the Bureau of Educational and Cultural Affairs of the U.S. Department of State and administered by the Council for International Exchange of Scholars. Recipients also consult on program and curriculum development, supervise theses, conduct seminars, and engage in collaborative research.

Number awarded 1 each year.
Deadline July of each year.

[365]
TOYOBO BIOTECHNOLOGY FOUNDATION LONG-TERM RESEARCH GRANTS

Toyobo Biotechnology Foundation
2-2-8 Dojimahama, Kita-ku
Osaka 530-8230
Japan
81 6 6348 4111   Fax: 81 6 6348 3331
E-mail: biofund@toyobo.co.jp

Purpose To provide financial assistance for postdoctoral research in Japan.

Eligibility This program is open to candidates who have a doctoral degree, less than 5 years of postdoctoral experience, and an interest in conducting research in Japan. The proposed research must deal with biotechnology and its related research fields. Applicants must not be more than 40 years of age and should not already hold a permanent research position. Both Japanese and foreign researchers are considered for these grants.

Financial data Grants range from 900,000 to 3,600,000 yen.
Duration Up to 1 year.
Number awarded Varies; generally, up to 5 each year.
Deadline August of each year.

[366]
UNITED STATES/JAPAN CREATIVE ARTISTS' PROGRAM

Japan-U.S. Friendship Commission
1110 Vermont Avenue, N.W., Suite 800
Washington, DC 20005
(202) 418-9800   Fax: (202) 418-9802
E-mail: jusfc@jusfc.gov
Web site: www.jusfc.gov

Purpose To enable American artists to enrich their art by living and working in Japan.

Eligibility Candidates for the U.S. part of the program must be citizens or permanent residents of the United States. They must be professional creative artists (contemporary or traditional) working as architects, choreographers, composers, creative writers (of poetry, fiction, and creative nonfiction), designers, media artists, playwrights, solo theater artists (including puppeteers, storytellers, and performance artists) who work with original material, or visual artists. Students, scholars, or critics of the arts are not eligible. Generally, candidates who have spent more than a total of 3 months within the last 10 years in Japan are not eligible because this program is directed at artists who have little or no experience in Japan. Candidates must be able to spend 6 consecutive months in Japan. Those who cannot make this commitment should not apply. Proficiency in the Japanese language is not required. Selection is based on the artistic excellence of the applicant's work and the artistic merit of the proposed residency, the extent to which working in Japan is consistent with the applicant's artistic vision and would contribute to his or her artistry, the applicant's ability to meet cross-cultural challenges successfully, and the availability of resources in Japan that are necessary to the artist's proposed residency.

Financial data Fellows receive monthly stipends of 400,000 yen for living expenses, 100,000 yen as a housing supplement, and up to 100,000 yen for professional support services. In addition, each artist receives $6,000 for round-trip transportation (for the artist, domestic partner, and/or unmarried children up to the age of 18) and a baggage/storage allowance. If needed, a stipend for pre-departure Japanese language study in the United States is provided.

Duration 6 months.

Special features A similar program is available for Japanese artists who wish to visit the United States. This program operates under an agreement between the National Endowment for the Arts (NEA) and the Agency for Cultural Affairs of Japan. Funding for the fellowships for American artists is provided by NEA and the Japan-U.S. Friendship Commission.

Limitations Finalists should be prepared to go to Japan within 1 year of notification that they have been selected. During the period they are participating in the fellowship in Japan, artists are not allowed to earn additional income for performances, lectures, or demonstrations of their work.
Number awarded Up to 5 each year.
Deadline June of each year.

[367]
UNITED STATES–NIS AWARDS FOR EXCELLENCE IN TEACHING

American Councils for International Education
Attn: Office of Faculty Exchanges
1776 Massachusetts Avenue, N.W., Suite 700
Washington, DC 20036
(202) 833-7522 Fax: (202) 833-7523
E-mail: hollis@actr.org
Web site: www.actr.org

Purpose To enable outstanding secondary school teachers in the United States to visit schools and communities in the Newly Independent States (NIS) of the former Soviet Union (including Eurasia).
Eligibility As part of this program, 75 teachers from Kazakhstan, Kyrgyzstan, Russia, Turkmenistan, Ukraine, and Uzbekistan visit the United States for a 7-week professional development seminar. In return, U.S. secondary school teachers of the humanities, social sciences, or language arts visit the schools and communities of those NIS participants. Applicants must have been recognized for excellence in teaching at the national, state, or local level in the past 8 years. Selection is based on ability to teach and innovation in teaching, interest in NIS teaching methodology in foreign languages and area studies, desire and ability to share experience and knowledge with colleagues from the NIS, and ability to develop partnerships with NIS participants and their schools beyond completion of the program.
Financial data All travel expenses are paid by the program; funding for salaries and/or substitute teachers is not provided.
Duration 2 weeks, in October.
Special features This program is funded by the Bureau of Educational and Cultural Affairs of the Department of State and administered by the American Councils for International Education, the American Council of Teachers of Russian (ACTR), and the American Council for Collaboration and Education in Language Study (ACCELS). It was established in 1996. Activities in the NIS may include discussions on English and American studies programs, introduction of American studies into foreign language curricula, and (if appropriate) lecturing.
Number awarded Up to 24 each year.
Deadline January of each year.

[368]
U.S. NAVY COMMANDER FLEET ACTIVITY POSTGRADUATE RESEARCH PARTICIPATION PROGRAM

Oak Ridge Institute for Science and Education
Attn: Education and Training Division
P.O. Box 117
Oak Ridge, TN 37831-0117
(865) 576-8503 Fax: (865) 241-5220
E-mail: bowlingb@orau.gov
Web site: www.orau.gov/orise.htm

Purpose To provide an opportunity for recent postgraduates to participate in environmental research and training activities of the U.S. Navy in Okinawa, Japan.
Eligibility Applicants should have completed a bachelor's, master's, or doctoral degree within the past 3 years; others are considered on a case-by-case basis. Their field of study should have been a scientific or engineering discipline related to the military environmental research and training activities of the U.S. Navy Commander Fleet Activity in Okinawa (where they will conduct the research). U.S. citizenship is required.
Financial data The stipend is based on research area and degree; a limited reimbursement for inbound travel and moving is also provided.
Duration 1 year; renewable.
Special features This program is funded by the U.S. Navy through an interagency agreement with the U.S. Department of Energy and administered by the Education and Training Division (ETD) of Oak Ridge Institute for Science and Education (ORISE).
Number awarded Varies each year.
Deadline Applications may be submitted at any time.

[369]
U.S.–JAPAN INTERNATIONAL EDUCATION ADMINISTRATORS PROGRAM

Council for International Exchange of Scholars
3007 Tilden Street, N.W., Suite 5L
Washington, DC 20008-3009
(202) 686-4021 Fax: (202) 362-3442
E-mail: scholars@cies.iie.org
Web site: www.iie.org/cies

Purpose To acquaint U.S. administrators with various aspects of Japanese higher education, society, and culture by allowing them to participate in a group program in Japan.
Eligibility This program is open to international education administrators (e.g., foreign student advisors, study abroad advisors, foreign student admissions) or senior-level university administrators (deans, vice presidents, provosts, presidents) with substantial (at least 25 percent) responsibility for enhancing the international dimension of their institutions. Applicants must be affiliated with a 4-year college or university or a nonprofit international education exchange organization and have at least 3 years of full-time work experience. They must be interested in participating in a group program in Japan. Directors of English language programs and instructors in such programs are not eligible. Preference is given to candidates who have not had significant professional visits to Japan in the last 5 years. U.S. citizenship is required.

Financial data The grant provides round-trip international travel and a per diem allowance sufficient to cover all in-country expenses (lodging, meals, and local transportation). No provisions are made for accompanying spouses.

Duration 3 weeks.

Special features This is a Fulbright scholar program, sponsored by the Bureau of Educational and Cultural Affairs of the U.S. Department of State and administered by the Council for International Exchange of Scholars. This program consists of briefings, campus visits, selected government appointments, attendance at the meeting of the Japan Association for Foreign Student Affairs, homestays, and cultural activities.

Limitations This program is not intended to be a vehicle for initiating or implementing an American institution's linkage programs, student recruitment, or establishment of branch campuses.

Number awarded 5 each year.

Deadline October of each year.

[370]
U.S.–KOREA INTERNATIONAL EDUCATION ADMINISTRATORS PROGRAM

Council for International Exchange of Scholars
3007 Tilden Street, N.W., Suite 5L
Washington, DC 20008-3009
(202) 686-4021   Fax: (202) 362-3442
E-mail: scholars@cies.iie.org
Web site: www.iie.org/cies

Purpose To acquaint U.S. administrators with various aspects of Korean higher education, society, and culture by allowing them to participate in a group program in Korea.

Eligibility This program is open to international education administrators (e.g., foreign student advisors, study abroad advisors, foreign student admissions) or senior-level university administrators (deans, vice presidents, provosts, presidents) with substantial (at least 25 percent) responsibility for enhancing the international dimension of their institutions. Applicants must be affiliated with a 2- or 4-year college or university or a nonprofit international education exchange organization and have at least 3 years of full-time work experience. They must be interested in participating in a group program in Korea. Directors of English language programs and instructors in such programs are not eligible. Preference is given to candidates who have not had significant professional visits to Korea in the last 5 years. U.S. citizenship is required.

Financial data The grant provides round-trip international travel, lodging, and a per diem that includes a meal allowance for those meals not provided. No provisions are made for accompanying spouses.

Duration 2 weeks.

Special features This is a Fulbright scholar program, sponsored by the Bureau of Educational and Cultural Affairs of the U.S. Department of State and administered by the Council for International Exchange of Scholars. The program consists of information sessions; visits to campuses, private sector agencies or organizations, and selected government agencies; and presentations by participants to small groups of Korean academics and professionals.

Limitations This program is not intended to be a vehicle for initiating or implementing an American institution's linkage programs, student recruitment, or establishment of branch campuses.

Number awarded 4 each year.

Deadline October of each year.

[371]
WALTER JUDD FELLOWSHIP

Chiang Ching-kuo Foundation for International Scholarly Exchange
8361 B Greensboro Drive
McLean, VA 22102
(703) 903-7460   Fax: (703) 903-7462
E-mail: CCKFNAO@aol.com
Web site: www.cckf.org/amprogram/wjrf.html

Purpose To provide funding to scholars interested in conducting research on Chinese studies in the United States or Taiwan.

Eligibility This program is open to scholars in the field of Chinese studies who are seeking support for a period of research and writing. Proposed research should relate to the following areas: Chinese cultural heritage; classical studies (especially literary and historical works); the Republic of China (including any subject related to the Republic of China, its development and transformation since its establishment, through the Nanking Period, and up to the present); Taiwan area studies (including history, archaeology, culture, politics, and socioeconomic aspects); and China-related comparative studies. Priority is given to research focusing on contemporary Chinese studies. Selection is based on the significance of the contribution that the proposed project will make to the advancement of research and knowledge in the field of Chinese studies; the quality or the promise of quality of the applicant's work as a creative interpreter of Chinese studies; the quality of the conception, organization, research strategy, and source material of the proposed project; and the feasibility that the applicant can complete the entire project.

Financial data The grant is $15,000 per year.

Duration 1 year; nonrenewable.

Special features The Chiang Ching-kuo Foundation for International Scholarly Exchange (the CCK Foundation) was established in 1989 in memory of the late president of the Republic of China. Its headquarters are at 13B, 65 Tun-hwa South Road, Section II, Taipei, Taiwan, 886 2 2704 5333, Fax: 886 2 2701 6762, E-mail: CCKF@ms1.hinet.net.

Number awarded 1 each year.

Deadline October of each year.

FINANCIAL AID PROGRAMS

[372]
WOMEN'S INTERNATIONAL SCIENCE COLLABORATION PROGRAM

American Association for the Advancement of Science
Attn: International Directorate
Program on Europe and Central Asia
1200 New York Avenue, N.W., Seventh Floor
Washington, DC 20005
(202) 326-7027   Fax: (202) 289-4958
E-mail: kgrill@aaas.org
Web site: www.aaas.org/international/eca/wisc.shtml

Purpose To provide funding to women scientists interested in establishing new research partnerships with colleagues in central/eastern Europe (CEE), the Newly Independent States of the former Soviet Union (NIS), and Eurasia.

Eligibility This program is open to men and women scientists who have a Ph.D. or equivalent research experience, although applications from male co-principal investigators must be accompanied by an application from a female co-principal investigator as part of a research team. Male and female Ph.D. candidates are also eligible to apply if they will be conducting research in an established Ph.D. program in the United States and will be traveling with their Ph.D. advisor and will serve as a co-principal investigator on future proposals. All applicants must be U.S. citizens or permanent residents. Only fields of study funded by the National Science Foundation (NSF) are eligible; that includes archaeology and anthropology; astronomy; biochemistry, biophysics, and genetics; biological sciences; chemistry; computer science; earth sciences; economics; engineering; environmental sciences; geography; history and philosophy of science; linguistics; mathematics; physics; political science; non-clinically oriented psychology; science and technology policy; and sociology. No proposals involving agricultural production; drug testing or diagnosis; research on the diagnosis, etiology, or treatment of physical or mental diseases or disorders; or the use of animal models of human diseases or conditions are accepted. Specialists who have completed their doctoral degrees within the past 6 years receive special consideration, as do scientists applying to work with colleagues in less frequently represented countries and regions. All proposals must involve travel to a CEE or NIS nation to develop a research program and design. Scientists and engineers who have an existing NSF grant and are eligible for an NSF international supplement should not apply to this program. Selection is based on the applicant's technical abilities, quality of the proposed project, feasibility of carrying out the proposed project, and prospects for long-term collaboration following the completion of the current project.

Financial data Grants up to $4,000 provide travel and living support for the U.S. women scientist and, when appropriate, an additional grant of $4,000 to her American male or female co-principal investigator. Funds may not be used for the sole purpose of teaching, training, or attending conferences or workshops. Grants are administered by and disbursed through the recipient's institution, but no overhead or other indirect charges may be assessed.

Duration Up to 4 weeks.

Special features This program is funded by NSF. Eligible countries include Albania, Armenia, Bosnia, Bulgaria, Croatia, Czech Republic, Estonia, Georgia, Hungary, Kazakhstan, Kyrgyzstan, Latvia, Lithuania, Macedonia, Moldova, Poland, Romania, Russia, Slovak Republic, Slovenia, Tajikistan, Turkmenistan, Ukraine, and Uzbekistan.

Number awarded Varies each year.

Deadline January, March, or July of each year.

[373]
YING-CHIEN CHANG SCIENCE AWARD

Society of Vertebrate Paleontology
60 Revere Drive, Suite 500
Northbrook, IL 60062
(847) 480-9080   Fax: (847) 480-9282
E-mail: svp@vertpaleo.org
Web site: www.vertpaleo.org/awards/chang.html

Purpose To provide funding to teams of U.S.-China students and professionals interested in conducting research in vertebrate paleontology in China.

Eligibility This program is open to teams of professionals and students from the United States and China who are interested in conducting vertebrate paleontology field work in China. Applicants must be members of the Society of Vertebrate Paleontology. The funding is intended to provide such opportunities as adding a participant to an existing, funded project; lengthening a field season (e.g., to undertake exploratory research); or enabling a student to undertake a pilot study or join an expedition.

Financial data The maximum grant is $2,000.

Duration 1 year.

Special features Information is also available from Dr. R. Ewan Fordyce, University of Otago, Department of Geology, P.O. Box 56, Dunedin, New Zealand, 64-3-479-7510, Fax: 64-3-479-7527, E-mail: ewan.fordyce@stonebow.otago.ac.nz.

Number awarded 1 each year.

Deadline April of each year.

Canada/Arctic Region

Described here are 75 scholarships, fellowships, loans, grants, and/or internships open to American students (high school through doctoral), professionals, and postdoctorates that support research or creative activities in Canada, Greenland, and the Arctic Region. If you haven't already checked the "Any Foreign Country" chapter, be sure to do that next; identified there are 222 more sources of funding that can be used in Canada and the Arctic Region (as well as other areas).

[374]
AAS/CIAC SMALL GRANTS
Association for Asian Studies
Attn: China and Inner Asia Council
1021 East Huron Street
Ann Arbor, MI 48104
(734) 665-2490   Fax: (734) 665-3801
E-mail: postmaster@aasianst.org
Web site: www.aasianst.org

Purpose To provide financial assistance to North American graduate students and scholars who wish to complete projects related to China or inner Asia in Taiwan, Canada, or the United States.

Eligibility Applications are accepted for the following types of projects related to China or inner Asia: 1) curriculum development at the college or secondary level; 2) organization of small conferences and seminars away from major centers of Chinese studies; 3) travel expenses for scholars from isolated institutions to speak at major centers; 4) travel expenses for junior faculty from isolated institutions to attend seminars at major centers; 5) funding for dissertation-level graduate students to attend colloquia, workshops, and seminars related to their fields; 6) short research trips for dissertation-level graduate students, and for scholars at non-research institutions, to travel to major libraries and collections in North America and Taiwan; 7) translations of scholarly books and articles; 8) specialist or regional newsletters disseminating important information in their respective fields; and 9) collaborative projects to facilitate communication and limited travel by scholars working on a common project in Taiwan and North America. Membership in the Association for Asian Studies is required. Junior and independent scholars, adjunct faculty, and dissertation-level graduate students are especially encouraged to apply.

Financial data Up to $1,500.

Special features Funding for this program is provided by the Chiang Ching-kuo Foundation for International Scholarly Exchange. Information is also available from Jean C. Oi, Stanford University, Department of Political Science, Encina Hall West, 616 Serra Street, Stanford, CA 94305, E-mail: joi@leland.stanford.edu.

Deadline January of each year.

[375]
ALBERTA HERITAGE FOUNDATION FOR MEDICAL RESEARCH SUMMER STUDENTSHIPS
Alberta Heritage Foundation for Medical Research
3125 ManuLife Place
10180 - 101 Street
Edmonton, Alberta T5J 3S4
Canada
(780) 423-5727   Fax: (780) 429-3509
E-mail: postmaster@ahfmr.ab.ca
Web site: www.ahfmr.ab.ca

Purpose To provide financial assistance to undergraduate and medical students who wish to continue research training on a full-time basis during the summer at a university in Alberta.

Eligibility This program is open to students who meet 1 of the following criteria: 1) registered in an Alberta undergraduate degree program in a medical or health-related field; 2) registered in an undergraduate degree program outside Alberta, interested in undertaking research training at an Alberta institution; 3) registered in an M.D. program, and who may already hold an undergraduate or graduate degree; 4) exceptional high school students with records of participation in the health care system and clear interest in a health research career; and 5) currently in the last term of an undergraduate program, and who have applied to medical school or to a graduate program that will start in the following fall. Applicants must arrange to work with a supervisor at an Alberta university; no more than 2 candidates may be sponsored by a supervisor in any given year, and a separate project should be described for each.

Financial data The stipend is $C1,300 per month.

Duration From 2 to 4 months, although 3 months is preferable.

Number awarded Varies each year.

Deadline February of each year.

[376]
ARCTIC RESEARCH OPPORTUNITIES
National Science Foundation
Attn: Office of Polar Programs
4201 Wilson Boulevard
Arlington, VA 22230
(703) 292-8030   TDD: (703) 292-5090
Web site: www.nsf.gov/od/opp

Purpose To provide funding for research related to the Arctic.

Eligibility This program is open to investigators affiliated with U.S. universities, research institutions, or other organizations, including local or state governments. Applicants must be proposing to conduct research in the 3 program areas of Arctic Natural Sciences (including atmospheric sciences, biological sciences, earth sciences, glaciology, and ocean sciences); Arctic Social Sciences (including anthropology, archaeology, economics, geography, linguistics, political science, psychology, and sociology); and Arctic System Science (encompassing 5 components: 1) how will the Arctic climate change over the next 50 to 100 years? 2) how will human activities interact with future global change to affect the sustainability of natural ecosystems and human societies? 3) how will changes in Arctic biogeochemical cycles and feedbacks affect Arctic and global systems? 4) how will changes in Arctic hydrologic cycles and feedbacks affect Arctic and global systems; and 5) are predicted changes in the Arctic system detectable?). Proposals should involve field studies in the Arctic, although projects outside the Arctic but directly related to Arctic science and engineering are also considered, as are related laboratory and theoretical studies. The program particularly encourages proposals from women, minorities, and persons with disabilities.

Financial data The amounts of the awards depend on the nature of the proposal and the availability of funds.

Number awarded Varies each year. Recently, this program planned to make from 130 to 160 awards with total funding of $20 to $25 million.

Deadline August or February of each year.

FINANCIAL AID PROGRAMS

[377]
BOMBARDIER SCHOLARSHIP

Institute of International Education
Attn: Student Programs Division
809 United Nations Plaza
New York, NY 10017-3580
(212) 984-5330   Fax: (212) 984-5325
Web site: www.iie.org/fulbright

Purpose To provide financial assistance to American graduate students engaged in aerospace study or research in Canada.

Eligibility Applicants must be U.S. citizens who hold a B.A. degree or equivalent before the beginning date of the grant and plan to study or conduct research in aerospace in Canada. At most universities, English is the language of instruction, but proficient written and spoken French is needed for study at the 21 francophone universities; at the 6 bilingual universities, students may choose French or English as the language of instruction. Candidates must have been accepted by a Canadian university and a Canadian faculty adviser.

Financial data The stipend is $15,000.

Duration 1 academic year.

Special features These grants are offered as part of the Fulbright program, administered by the Institute of International Education (IIE). Students who are currently enrolled in the United States are to apply through the Fulbright program adviser on their campus; at-large applicants (those not currently enrolled) may obtain applications and information directly from the IIE.

Number awarded 1 each year.

Deadline October of each year.

[378]
CANADIAN INSTITUTE OF UKRAINIAN STUDIES RESEARCH GRANTS

Canadian Institute of Ukrainian Studies
c/o University of Alberta
Athabasca Hall, Room 352
Edmonton, Alberta T6G 2E8
Canada
(780) 492-2972   Fax: (780) 492-4967
E-mail: cius@ualberta.ca
Web site: www.ualberta.ca/~cius/cius-grants.htm

Purpose To provide funding to scholars from any country who are interested in conducting research in Ukrainian or Ukrainian Canadian studies.

Eligibility This program is open to scholars on the faculty of a university or other postsecondary institution, in Canada or elsewhere, and to private scholars. Applicants must be interested in conducting research in Ukrainian and Ukrainian Canadian studies in history, literature, language, education, social sciences, and library sciences.

Financial data Grants are provided only to defray actual direct costs attributable to the project, not for overhead costs or personal income.

Duration 1 year.

Number awarded Varies each year.

Deadline February of each year.

[379]
CANADIAN STUDIES INTERNSHIPS

International Council for Canadian Studies
Attn: Director of Administration and Programs
75 Albert Street, Suite 908
Ottawa, Ontario K1P 5E7
Canada
(613) 789-7828   Fax: (613) 789-7830
E-mail: gvallieres@iccs-ciec.ca
Web site: www.iccs-ciec.ca

Purpose To provide funding to recent postdoctorates in Canadian studies who are interested in a teaching or research internship in Canada or another country.

Eligibility This program is open to Canadian or foreign scholars who recently completed a doctoral degree on a topic primarily related to Canada and who are not employed in a full-time university teaching position. Applicants must have obtained a formal commitment from a foreign or Canadian university to host a research or teaching internship there.

Financial data Up to $C2,500 per month. A return airline ticket is also provided.

Duration 1 to 3 months.

Special features Assistance in locating a university that might be willing to collaborate with a recent postdoctorate in this program is available from the International Council for Canadian Studies (ICCS) at the address above or from the national Canadian studies association in the applicant's home country. In the United States, this is the Association for Canadian Studies in the United States, 1317 F Street, N.W., Suite 920, Washington, DC 20004-1151, (202) 393-2580, Fax: (202) 393-2582, E-mail: info@acsus.org, Web site: www.acsus.org. This program is administered by the ICCS with funding from the Canadian Department of Foreign Affairs and International Trade.

Number awarded Varies each year; recently, 2 of these internships were awarded.

Deadline December of each year.

[380]
CANADIAN STUDIES SENIOR FELLOWSHIP PROGRAM

Canadian Embassy
Attn: Academic Relations
501 Pennsylvania Avenue, N.W.
Washington, DC 20001
(202) 682-1740   Fax: (202) 682-7791
E-mail: daniel.abele@dfait-maeci.gc.ca
Web site: www.canadianembassy.org

Purpose To provide senior scholars in the United States with an opportunity to complete and publish a major study that will significantly benefit the development of Canadian studies in the United States.

Eligibility This program is open to full-time tenured faculty members at accredited 4-year colleges or universities in the United States who are fully involved in Canadian studies. These "Canadianists" should be in the process of completing research for a book or major monograph on a subject of widespread interest to the Canadian studies community in the United States as well as in Canada. An individual may not receive 2 individual Canadian Studies grants during the same grant period. Priority is given to applicants who have a book project in which a publisher is interested.

Financial data Up to $3,000 per month. Funds are available for research conducted in Canada (or the United States).

Duration Up to 6 months.

Special features Recipients may travel in Canada to pursue their research studies. This program is funded by the Canadian Department of Foreign Affairs and International Trade.

Limitations Recipients should be granted a sabbatical or leave of absence during the award period.

Number awarded A limited number of these fellowships are awarded every other year.

Deadline June of odd-numbered years.

[381]
CAREER AWARDS IN THE BIOMEDICAL SCIENCES

Burroughs Wellcome Fund
21 T.W. Alexander Drive, Suite 100
P.O. Box 13901
Research Triangle Park, NC 27709-3901
(919) 991-5100　　　　Fax: (919) 991-5160
E-mail: info@bwfund.org
Web site: www.bwfund.org

Purpose To provide funding to biomedical scientists in the United States and Canada who require assistance to make the transition from postdoctoral training to faculty appointment.

Eligibility This program is open to U.S. and Canadian researchers in the biomedical sciences who have completed at least 1 but not more than 4 years of postdoctoral training and require support for bridging research to faculty status. Individuals who hold a tenure-track faculty appointment are not eligible. The biomedical sciences are defined to include reproductive science. Applicants must be U.S. or Canadian citizens pursuing postdoctoral training at an accredited degree-granting institution in the United States, Canada, or the United Kingdom. Each U.S. and Canadian institution may nominate up to 6 candidates; institutions that nominate at least 1 candidate in the reproductive sciences may nominate a total of 7 candidates; institutions that nominate at least 1 candidate from an underrepresented minority group (African American, Hispanic, or Native American) may nominate an additional candidate. A U.K. institution, including its medical school, graduate schools, and all affiliated hospitals and research institutes, may nominate up to 2 candidates. Following their postdoctoral training, awardees may accept a faculty position at a U.S. or Canadian institution. The sponsor encourages applications from women and members of underrepresented minority groups.

Financial data In the first year of postdoctoral support, the stipend is $38,000, the research allowance is $15,360, and the administrative fee is $4,640; in the second year of postdoctoral support, the stipend is $41,000, the research allowance is $12,360, and the administrative fee is $4,640; in the first year of faculty support, the stipend is $54,000, the research allowance is $63,600, and the administrative fee is $10,400; in the second year of faculty support, the stipend is $59,000, the research allowance is $58,600, and the administrative fee is $10,400; in the third year of faculty support, the stipend is $65,000, the research allowance is $52,600, and the administrative fee is $10,400. The maximum portion of the award that can be used during the postdoctoral period is $116,000 or $58,000 per year. The faculty portion of the award is $500,000 minus the portion used during the postdoctoral years. The maximum support per year in the faculty portion of the award is $128,000.

Duration The awards provide 1 to 2 years of postdoctoral support and up to 3 years of support during the faculty appointment.

Special features Since this program began in 1995, more than $70 million in support has been provided to 149 U.S. and Canadian scientists.

Limitations Awardees are required to devote at least 80 percent of their time to research-related activities.

Number awarded At least 21 each year: approximately half of the awards go to researchers with a Ph.D. degree in a biomedical science and half go to researchers with an M.D. or M.D./Ph.D. degree.

Deadline September of each year.

[382]
CENTRE FOR CHEMICAL PHYSICS SENIOR VISITING FELLOWSHIPS

University of Western Ontario
Centre for Interdisciplinary Studies in Chemical Physics
Attn: Visiting Fellows Committee
Physics and Astronomy Building, Room 102
London, Ontario N6A 3K7
Canada
(519) 661-4088　　　　Fax: (519) 661-3032
E-mail: ccp@julian.uwo.ca
Web site: www.uwo.ca/ccp

Purpose To provide funding to senior scientists who are interested in conducting research on chemical physics at the Centre for Interdisciplinary Studies in Chemical Physics in London, Ontario.

Eligibility Eligible to apply are senior scientists from any country who are interested in conducting research in the following areas at the Centre for Interdisciplinary Studies in Chemical Physics: applied mathematics, chemistry, geology, materials engineering, or physics.

Financial data Fellows receive travel and living allowances, to a maximum of $C2,000 per month.

Duration From 2 to 12 months.

Special features This fellowship may be held concurrently with other awards.

Number awarded Varies; up to 4 each year.

Deadline October of each year.

[383]
CIHR INVESTIGATORS PROGRAM
Canadian Institutes of Health Research
Attn: Programs Branch
410 Laurier Avenue West, Ninth Floor
Address Locator 4209A
Ottawa, Ontario K1A 0W9
Canada
(613) 954-1961   Fax: (613) 954-1800
E-mail: ajackson@cihr.ca
Web site: www.cihr.ca

Purpose To provide funding for research in Canada to independent investigators of outstanding ability who have shown promise of becoming leaders in their respective research fields.

Eligibility While the program is designed primarily for applicants who are citizens or permanent residents of Canada, awards may also be made to foreign candidates who wish to undertake research in Canada. Candidates must hold a degree in medicine, dentistry, pharmacy, optometry, or veterinary medicine, or a Ph.D. degree (or the equivalent) and have at least 5 but no more than 10 years of experience as an independent investigator in a university position or its equivalent.

Financial data The Canadian Institutes of Health Research (CIHR) provides a contribution to the researcher's salary of $C70,000 per year and also provides for fringe benefits.

Duration 5 years; nonrenewable.

Special features The CIHR was formerly the Medical Research Council (MRC) of Canada. This program was formerly the MRC Scientists Program.

Limitations The awards are tenable in Canada only. Recipients from outside of Canada are personally responsible for obtaining an entry visa into Canada from a Canadian embassy. Appointees are expected to devote at least 75 percent of their time to research. They may engage in teaching and consultation to a limited extent.

Number awarded Varies each year.

Deadline September of each year.

[384]
CIHR NEW INVESTIGATORS PROGRAM
Canadian Institutes of Health Research
Attn: Programs Branch
410 Laurier Avenue West, Ninth Floor
Address Locator 4209A
Ottawa, Ontario K1A 0W9
Canada
(613) 954-1961   Fax: (613) 954-1800
E-mail: ajackson@cihr.ca
Web site: www.cihr.ca

Purpose To fund independent research in the health sciences in Canada.

Eligibility While the program is designed primarily for applicants who are citizens or permanent residents of Canada, awards may also be made to foreign candidates who wish to undertake research in Canada. Candidates must hold a degree in medicine, dentistry, pharmacy, optometry, or veterinary medicine, or a Ph.D. degree (or the equivalent) and show promise of attaining competence as an independent investigator. They should not be registered for a higher degree at the time of application or undertake such studies during the period of appointment. A candidate who has held research funding, as a principal grantee, for more than 5 years is not eligible for an award.

Financial data The Canadian Institutes of Health Research (CIHR) provides a contribution to the researcher's salary of $C50,000 per year and also provides for fringe benefits.

Duration Up to 5 years.

Special features The CIHR was formerly the Medical Research Council (MRC) of Canada. This program was formerly the MRC Scholarships Program.

Limitations The awards are tenable in Canada only. Recipients from outside of Canada are personally responsible for obtaining an entry visa into Canada from a Canadian embassy. Appointees are expected to devote at least 75 percent of their time to research. They may engage in teaching and consultation to a limited extent.

Number awarded Varies each year.

Deadline September of each year.

[385]
CIHR SENIOR INVESTIGATOR PROGRAM
Canadian Institutes of Health Research
Attn: Programs Branch
410 Laurier Avenue West, Ninth Floor
Address Locator 4209A
Ottawa, Ontario K1A 0W9
Canada
(613) 954-1961   Fax: (613) 954-1800
E-mail: ajackson@cihr.ca
Web site: www.cihr.ca

Purpose To provide funding to highly renowned scientists who are at the forefront of health research and are interested in conducting research in Canada.

Eligibility While the program is designed primarily for applicants who are citizens or permanent residents of Canada, awards may also be made to foreign candidates who wish to undertake research in Canada. Candidates must hold a degree in medicine, dentistry, pharmacy, optometry, or veterinary medicine, or a Ph.D. degree (or the equivalent) and have at least 10 years of experience as an independent investigator in a university position or its equivalent.

Financial data The Canadian Institutes of Health Research (CIHR) provides a contribution to the researcher's salary of $C70,000 per year.

Duration 5 years; nonrenewable.

Special features The CIHR was formerly the Medical Research Council (MRC) of Canada. This program combines 2 former programs, the MRC Senior Scientist Program and the MRC Distinguished Scientist Program.

Limitations The awards are tenable in Canada only. Recipients from outside of Canada are personally responsible for obtaining an entry visa into Canada from a Canadian embassy. Appointees are expected to devote at least 75 percent of their time to research. They may engage in teaching and consultation to a limited extent.

Number awarded Varies each year.

Deadline September of each year.

[386]
CLINICIAN SCIENTIST AWARDS OF THE CANADIAN INSTITUTES OF HEALTH RESEARCH

Canadian Institutes of Health Research
Attn: Programs Branch
410 Laurier Avenue West, Ninth Floor
Address Locator 4209A
Ottawa, Ontario K1A 0W9
Canada
(613) 957-8671   Fax: (613) 954-1800
E-mail: srobertson@cihr.ca
Web site: www.cihr.ca

Purpose To encourage the development of medical clinician-scientists in Canada.

Eligibility This program is open to highly qualified and motivated clinicians who are nominated by a Canadian medical school. Nominees must have the potential to become outstanding clinician-scientists. At the time of nomination, the candidate must hold a professional degree in medicine and have completed at least 2 years of specialty or sub-specialty clinical training in an area accredited with or without certification by the Royal College of Physicians and Surgeons of Canada. At the time of taking up the award, the successful candidate must have completed clinical training and be ready to engage in full-time research training and, subsequently, independent research. Nominees need not be Canadian citizens or permanent residents.

Financial data During the first phase, the stipend is $C47,586 per year. A research allowance is provided for each year of the training phase of the award; $C3,850 in the first year and $C3,350 thereafter. This sum is made available to supervisors, through the institution concerned, to be used at their discretion for the purchase of materials and supplies, for travel to scientific meetings, for the relocation of the trainee to/from the laboratory, or to meet other research costs incurred by awardees. During the second phase, the maximum salary of the investigator is $C50,000 per year. For the first 3 years of the second phase, the council provides a research allowance of $C40,000 per year.

Duration The program has 2 phases. Phase 1 provides stipend support for up to 6 years of research training. Phase 2 provides a contribution to the salary of the recipient for up to 6 years.

Special features The Canadian Institutes of Health Research (CIHR) was formerly the Medical Research Council (MRC) of Canada.

Limitations While Canadians can use the award outside of Canada, recipients from other countries may use the award only in Canada.

Deadline September of each year.

[387]
DANISH POLAR CENTER RESEARCH GRANTS

Danish Polar Center
Attn: Commission for Scientific Research in Greenland
Strandgade 100 H
DK-1401 Copenhagen K
Denmark
45 32 88 01 00   Fax: 45 32 88 01 01
E-mail: dpc@dpc.dk
Web site: www.dpc.dk

Purpose To provide funding for scientific research in Greenland.

Eligibility Applicants must be scientific investigators who are interested in conducting polar research, especially on 3 subjects: global environment, Arctic natural resources, and Arctic social development (including health). Funding is primarily given to Danish researchers, but other nationalities may also be eligible.

Financial data The amount awarded varies, depending upon the scope of the funded proposal.

Duration Varies, up to 1 year.

Limitations Research projects must be conducted at field stations in Greenland.

Number awarded Varies; generally, at least 30 each year.

Deadline September of each year.

[388]
EARTHWATCH STUDENT CHALLENGE AWARDS PROGRAM

Earthwatch
Attn: Student Challenge Awards Program
3 Clock Tower Place, Suite 100
P.O. Box 75
Maynard, MA 01754-0075
(978) 461-0081   (800) 776-0188
Fax: (978) 461-2332   E-mail: drobbins@earthwatch.org
Web site: www.earthwatch.org

Purpose To provide funding to scientists who wish to utilize high school students as assistants on laboratory or field research projects.

Eligibility This program is open to principal investigators in the physical sciences who are interested in utilizing high school students as part of a research project conducted at a research center, laboratory, observatory, or field station. Most research sites are in the United States, although proposals are also welcomed for projects in Canada, the Caribbean, Mexico, and Costa Rica. In addition to the principal investigator, each team is accompanied by a graduate student to oversee the students' work, provide additional adult supervision, and act as a career counselor and team facilitator. Graduate student mentors are expected to have significant understanding of the research being conducted by the principal investigator. They should also be capable of handling the complex social, emotional, and intellectual needs of high school students. Selection of the high school students is based on their creativity and scholarship; they should be gifted in the arts and humanities but have sufficient interest and training in science to handle the challenges of the experience. Students are assigned to sites very different from their home environment, usually in rural locations. The program is committed to bringing together students from different backgrounds and regions of the United States, to attracting a diversity of students, and to providing this experience to students with disabilities.

Financial data The budget may include, for the high school students, grants from $1,600 to $1,800 per student. Allowable expenses include food and accommodations for students and staff; principal investigator and graduate student mentor transportation to the field; team transportation; equipment and supplies; administrative costs (telephone costs, mail, copying, report preparation); enrichment activities (e.g., museum entrance fees, theater tickets); and staff stipends. The staff stipend line item may include a $500 honorarium for the principal investigator, but the grants do not cover salary for principal investigators, institutional overhead, capital equipment, or publication costs. The complete grant may range from $6,000 to $14,000.

Duration 12 to 18 days, in July or August.

Special features This program began in 1990. It is currently funded by the Durfee Foundation.

Limitations Principal investigators are expected to stay in the same accommodations as the students and graduate student mentors; they need to be available to support the students 24 hours a day.

Number awarded Each year, 10 to 12 research projects are funded, each utilizing from 6 to 8 high school students.

Deadline Principal investigators must submit proposals by September of each year.

[389]
EASTERN BIRD BANDING ASSOCIATION MEMORIAL RESEARCH GRANTS

Eastern Bird Banding Association
c/o Richard N. Roberts, Memorial Grants Chairperson
7212 Fiddler Bay Lane
Chincoteague, VA 23336-2017
E-mail: nroberts@shore.intercom.net
Web site: www.pronetisp.net/~bpbird/eb00006.htm

Purpose To provide funding to researchers interested in projects using bird banding data or banding techniques.

Eligibility Applicants must be interested in conducting research projects that use bird banding data or banding techniques. They should submit a resume of their banding and ornithological background, the project plan, including the significance of the study site, and a budget. Preference is given to research in the eastern United States or with species that spend part of their life there, but projects in other portions of the United States, North America, or the western hemisphere are also eligible. Research studies with conservation or management implications are particularly encouraged.

Financial data The amount of the grant depends on the nature of the proposal and the availability of funds. Travel grants are also available.

Duration 1 year.

Limitations Grantees are required to submit a summary of their work at the end of the year or present at least part of their study at the annual meeting of the sponsoring organization.

Number awarded 1 or more each year.

Deadline March of each year.

[390]
FACULTY ENRICHMENT PROGRAM IN CANADIAN STUDIES

Canadian Embassy
Attn: Academic Relations
501 Pennsylvania Avenue, N.W.
Washington, DC 20001
(202) 682-1740   Fax: (202) 682-7791
E-mail: daniel.abele@dfait-maeci.gc.ca
Web site: www.canadianembassy.org

Purpose To provide U.S. college and university faculty with an opportunity to develop courses that contain content related to Canada.

Eligibility This program is intended for full-time faculty members at accredited U.S. 4-year colleges and universities. Applicants must be able to demonstrate that they are already teaching or will be authorized to teach courses with a substantial (at least 33 percent) Canadian content. Team teaching applications are welcome. Proposals must be for the purpose of developing a new course on Canada, enhancing on existing course on Canada, or modifying an existing course with little or no Canadian content. The new or modified course must have at least 33 percent Canadian content to be eligible. Priority topics include bilateral trade and economics; Canada-U.S. border issues; cultural policy and values; environmental, natural resources, and energy issues; and security cooperation. Projects that examine Canadian politics, economics, culture, and society as well as Canada's role in international affairs are also welcome. Applicants are ineligible to receive the same grant in 2 consecutive years or to receive 2 different Canadian Studies grants in the same grant period.

Financial data Faculty may request funding up to $4,500. Grants are intended to help defray only direct costs related to the project, such as research, travel primarily within Canada and the United States as necessary, lodging, materials, and course preparation; no provision is made for released-time stipends or for overhead costs to the institution.

Duration Up to 3 months.

Special features This program is funded by the Canadian Department of Foreign Affairs and International Trade.

Limitations Recipients are expected to conduct research in Canada for at least 3 weeks during the award period.

Number awarded Varies each year; recently, 14 of these grants were awarded.

Deadline October of each year.

[391]
FIGHT FOR SIGHT GRANTS-IN-AID

Fight for Sight, Inc.
381 Park Avenue South, Suite 809
New York, NY 10016
(212) 679-6060   Fax: (212) 679-4466
Web site: www.fightforsight.com

Purpose To assist young professionals who have limited funding for research in ophthalmology, vision, and related sciences.

Eligibility Eligible are young professionals in ophthalmology, vision, or related sciences who wish to conduct pilot research projects but have limited research funding. Applications from U.S. or Canadian citizens for research in foreign countries will be considered if the proposed investigation cannot be carried out as effectively in the United States or Canada.

Financial data Grants range from $1,000 to $12,000 and are intended to cover the costs of personnel (excluding the applicant), equipment, and supplies for a specific research project.

Duration 1 year; may be renewed.

Special features Fight for Sight is the research division of Prevent Blindness America, formerly the National Society to Prevent Blindness.

Limitations Applications are generally not considered from residents, postdoctoral fellows, or senior investigators with significant research support.

Number awarded Approximately 15 each year.

Deadline February of each year.

[392]
FULBRIGHT FELLOWSHIP ON THE INFORMATION REVOLUTION AND INTERNATIONAL SECURITY

Council for International Exchange of Scholars
3007 Tilden Street, N.W., Suite 5L
Washington, DC 20008-3009
(202) 686-6238   Fax: (202) 362-3442
E-mail: scholars@cies.iie.org
Web site: www.iie.org/cies

Purpose To provide funding to scholars interested in conducting research on the information revolution and international security at institutions in Canada.

Eligibility This program is open to junior and senior scholars who hold a doctoral degree, preferably in international relations although specialists in political science, strategic studies, and information technology are also eligible. Applicants must be interested in conducting research at the University of Quebec on the impact of the new technologies of information and communications on international relations and security problems. The proposed research may also focus on how that revolution could accelerate economic, political, and social processes in the developing world to improve economic well-being and undermine the legitimacy of violence as a tool of policy. Although not a priority, research pertaining to military aspects of new information technologies may also be explored. U.S. citizenship and an ability to work in a French-speaking environment are required.

Financial data The stipend is $15,000 per academic year.

Duration 4 and a half or 9 months.

Special features This is a Fulbright scholar program, sponsored by the Bureau of Educational and Cultural Affairs of the U.S. Department of State and administered by the Council for International Exchange of Scholars.

Number awarded 1 each year.

Deadline July of each year.

[393]
FULBRIGHT/NATIVE NORTH AMERICAN SCHOLARSHIPS

Institute of International Education
Attn: Student Programs Division
809 United Nations Plaza
New York, NY 10017-3580
(212) 984-5330   Fax: (212) 984-5325
Web site: www.iie.org/fulbright

Purpose To provide financial assistance to American graduate students of Native North American origin for study or research in Canada.

Eligibility Applicants must be U.S. citizens who hold a B.A. degree or equivalent before the beginning date of the grant and plan to study or conduct research in Canada. At most universities, English is the language of instruction, but proficient written and spoken French is needed for study at the 21 francophone universities; at the 6 bilingual universities, students may choose French or English as the language of instruction. Candidates must have been accepted by a Canadian university and a Canadian faculty adviser. This program is limited to students of Native North American origin.

Financial data This program provides round-trip transportation, tuition, book and research allowances, a monthly maintenance allowance based on living costs, and supplemental health and accident insurance.

Duration 1 academic year.

Special features These grants are offered as part of the Fulbright program, administered by the Institute of International Education (IIE). Students who are currently enrolled in the United States are to apply through the Fulbright program adviser on their campus; at-large applicants (those not currently enrolled) may obtain applications and information directly from the IIE.

Number awarded 2 each year.

Deadline October of each year.

[394]
GERMAN STUDIES RESEARCH GRANTS

German Academic Exchange Service (DAAD)
950 Third Avenue, 19th Floor
New York, NY 10022
(212) 758-3223   Fax: (212) 755-5780
E-mail: daadny@daad.org
Web site: www.daad.org

Purpose To finance undergraduate or graduate research on the cultural, political, historical, economic, and social aspects of modern and contemporary German affairs.

Eligibility This program is open to undergraduates with at least junior standing pursuing a German studies track or minor, master's degree students and Ph.D. candidates working on a certificate in German studies, and Ph.D. candidates doing preliminary dissertation research. Students whose dissertation proposals have been formally accepted are not eligible. Candidates must be nominated by a department and/or program chair at a U.S. or Canadian institution of higher education. They must have completed 2 years of college-level German and a minimum of 3 German studies courses by the deadline. Grants are restricted to U.S. or Canadian citizens who are enrolled full

time at the university that nominates them. Research may be conducted in either North America or Germany.
Financial data Grant support, ranging from $1,500 to $3,000, is intended to offset possible living and travel costs during the research phase.
Duration 1 academic year, 1 summer term, or both.
Deadline April or October of each year.

[395]
GRADUATE STUDENT FELLOWSHIP PROGRAM IN CANADIAN STUDIES
Canadian Embassy
Attn: Academic Relations
501 Pennsylvania Avenue, N.W.
Washington, DC 20001
(202) 682-1740   Fax: (202) 682-7791
E-mail: daniel.abele@dfait-maeci.gc.ca
Web site: www.canadianembassy.org

Purpose To provide American graduate students with the opportunity to conduct part of their doctoral research in Canada.
Eligibility This program is aimed at full-time doctoral students at accredited U.S. or Canadian colleges and universities whose dissertations are related in substantial part to the study of Canada. Priority topics include bilateral trade and economics; Canada-U.S. border issues; cultural policy and values; environmental, natural resources, and energy issues; and security cooperation. Projects that examine Canadian politics, economics, culture, and society as well as Canada's role in international affairs are also welcome. Candidates must be citizens or permanent residents of the United States and should have completed all doctoral requirements except the dissertation. They must be interested in conducting at least part of their doctoral research in Canada.
Financial data The fellowship provides $850 per month to help pay direct costs (travel, lodging, meals, photocopying, etc.) resulting from the time spent in Canada to do research.
Duration Up to 9 months.
Special features This program is funded by the Canadian Department of Foreign Affairs and International Trade.
Number awarded Varies each year; recently, 6 of these grants were awarded.
Deadline October of each year.

[396]
GRADUATE STUDENT SCHOLARSHIPS OF THE INTERNATIONAL COUNCIL FOR CANADIAN STUDIES
International Council for Canadian Studies
Attn: Director of Administration and Programs
75 Albert Street, Suite 908
Ottawa, Ontario K1P 5E7
Canada
(613) 789-7828   Fax: (613) 789-7830
E-mail: gvallieres@iccs-ciec.ca
Web site: www.iccs-ciec.ca

Purpose To provide funding to graduate students in other countries who are majoring in Canadian studies and are interested in visiting Canada to conduct research.
Eligibility This program is open to graduate students outside of Canada who have already begun work on a thesis or dissertation on Canada. Candidates must be interested in visiting a Canadian university or research site other than their own to conduct research. The program is not intended to initiate a thesis or dissertation but to provide access to crucial scholarly information and resources in Canada in support of a thesis or dissertation that is close to or at the point of writing.
Financial data Grants provide up to $C3,500 for all expenses. An additional grant of $C1,500 is available from selected Canadian universities that offer Canadian Studies Institutional Support Awards.
Duration 4 to 6 weeks.
Special features Candidates must be nominated by their national Canadian studies association. In the United States, this is the Association for Canadian Studies in the United States, 1317 F Street, N.W., Suite 920, Washington, DC 20004-1151, (202) 393-2580, Fax: (202) 393-2582, E-mail: info@acsus.org, Web site: www.acsus.org. This program was formerly known as the International Council for Canadian Studies Scholarship for a Graduate Student Thesis/Dissertation. The universities that offer the Canadian Studies Institutional Support Award include Acadia University, University of Alberta, University of Manitoba, Université de Montréal, Memorial University of Newfoundland, University of Ottawa/Université d'Ottawa, and Simon Fraser University.
Number awarded 10 each year.
Deadline December of each year.

[397]
GRANT NOTLEY MEMORIAL POSTDOCTORAL FELLOWSHIP
University of Alberta
Faculty of Graduate Studies and Research
Attn: Graduate Awards Coordinator
105 Administration Building
Edmonton, Alberta T6G 2M7
Canada
(780) 492-3499   (800) 758-7136
Fax: (780) 492-0692   Fax: (800) 803-4132
E-mail: grad.mail@ualberta.ca
Web site: www.ualberta.ca/gradstudies

Purpose To enable nationals of any country to conduct research in selected fields at the University of Alberta.
Eligibility Applicants may be nationals of any country, but they must be able to satisfy Canadian immigration requirements, be proficient in English, have completed a Ph.D. degree at a recognized university within the last 3 years or expect to obtain the degree before taking up the award, and wish to conduct research at the University in the history, economy, politics, or society of western Canada. Students who received their doctoral degree from the University of Alberta are normally not eligible to apply.
Financial data The stipend is $C35,000 per year; round-trip airfare and a 1-time research grant of $C3,000 are also provided.
Duration 2 years.
Special features Fellows may teach 1 course each year.

Number awarded 1 every other year.
Deadline December of even-numbered years.

[398] HAROLD HIBBERT MEMORIAL FELLOWSHIP

McGill University
Attn: Chair, Department of Chemistry
Maass Chemistry Building, Room 322
801 Sherbrooke Street West
Montreal, Quebec H3A 2K6
Canada
E-mail: BUTLER@OMC.Lan.McGill.CA

Purpose To provide financial assistance to scholars from any country who wish to conduct research in Canada on issues related to the pulp and paper industry.

Eligibility Applicants must have a Ph.D. or equivalent degree in chemistry or physics and be interested in engaging in full-time research in the department of chemistry at McGill University and in the Pulp and Paper Research Institute of Canada in chemistry, chemical engineering, or mechanical engineering in relation to the pulp and paper industry. Nationals of all countries are eligible.

Financial data The stipend is $C25,000 per year.
Duration 1 year; may be renewed.
Number awarded 1 each year.
Deadline January of each year.

[399] HEART AND STROKE FOUNDATION OF CANADA VISITING SCIENTIST PROGRAM

Heart and Stroke Foundation of Canada
222 Queen Street, Suite 1402
Ottawa, Ontario K1P 5V9
Canada
(613) 569-4361   Fax: (613) 569-3278
E-mail: mtaylor@hsf.ca
Web site: www.hsf.ca

Purpose To allow Canadian heart researchers to study abroad or at another Canadian institution, and to allow foreign visitors to conduct heart research at Canadian institutions.

Eligibility Eligible are senior researchers in fields related to heart and stroke whose contribution and visit will be mutually rewarding to the host institution and the recipient. Applications must be accompanied by a letter from the home institution (stating that the scientist intends to return) and a letter of invitation from the proposed host institution. Canadians may work abroad or at another Canadian institution, but foreign visitors must work at a Canadian institution.

Financial data The maximum stipend is $C1,000 per month, intended to supplement the visiting scientist's salary. Round-trip travel costs are also provided for successful applicants and their immediate families.

Duration 3 to 12 months.
Number awarded Varies each year.
Deadline December of each year.

[400] HICKOK-RADFORD FUND GRANTS

Society of Economic Geologists Foundation
Attn: SEG Grants Program
7811 Schaffer Parkway
Littleton, CO 80127
(720) 981-7882   Fax: (720) 981-7874
E-mail: seg@segweb.org
Web site: www.segweb.org

Purpose To provide funding to graduate students and recent graduates in geology who wish to conduct research in Alaska, British Columbia, or other northern regions.

Eligibility This program is open to 1) graduate students conducting master's or doctoral thesis research and 2) postgraduates who have completed either a bachelor's or advanced degree in geology or a related earth science within 2 years prior to applying. Applicants must be proposing to conduct field research in economic geology, especially its application in the exploration for metallic mineral deposits. The research may be conducted anywhere in the world with challenging terrain, but preference is given to projects in Alaska, British Columbia, or other regions located north of latitude 60 degrees north. Preference is also given to projects that can demonstrate an affiliation with private industry, either through direct co-sponsorship or other indications of interest or support. Applicants may be from any country.

Financial data Stipends range from $500 to $3,000. Funds may be used for travel expenses, living costs in the field, expendable supplies, field expenses, and other expenses directly necessary for the research; they are not intended for purchase of ordinary field equipment, living costs of assistants or families of the grantees, attendance at professional meetings, preparation of theses, or reimbursement for work already accomplished.

Number awarded Varies each year; recently, 3 of these grants were awarded.
Deadline January of each year.

[401] HILLEL'S STEINHARDT JEWISH CAMPUS SERVICE CORPS FELLOWSHIP

Hillel: The Foundation for Jewish Campus Life
Attn: Steinhardt Scholars Program
1640 Rhode Island Avenue, N.W.
Washington, DC 20036-3279
(202) 857-6558   Fax: (202) 857-6693
E-mail: info@hillel.org
Web site: www.hillel.org

Purpose To provide funding to Jewish college graduates who are interested in providing 1 year of service to Jewish campus communities.

Eligibility This program is open to Jewish college graduates; they must have graduated within the past 2 years. Candidates must posses: a commitment to service; a willingness to use their time, abilities, and talents to enhance the lives of others; and a dedication to strengthening Jewish identity among the students with whom they would be working (in the United States or abroad). Finalists are interviewed. Fellows are selected on the basis of leadership skills and ability to create dynamic and innovative engagement strategies designed to reach Jewish college students.

Financial data The stipend is $19,000. Health and dental insurance are also provided.

Duration 11 months, beginning in August of each year.

Special features Fellows are assigned to a campus community either in North America or in Israel. They work with students, members of the university community, and Jewish communal professionals. As part of their professional training, fellows attend international conferences.

Deadline February of each year.

[402]
HUMAN FRONTIER SCIENCE PROGRAM LONG-TERM FELLOWSHIPS

Human Frontier Science Program Organization
Bureaux Europe
20, place des Halles
67080 Strasbourg
France
33 3 88 21 51 21   Fax: 33 3 88 32 88 97
E-mail: fellow@hfsp.org
Web site: www.hfsp.org

Purpose To provide financial support for postdoctoral research in biology to junior scholars who wish to go abroad.

Eligibility This program is open to researchers who have held a Ph.D. degree for less than 5 years. Applicants must wish to conduct basic research for the elucidation of brain functions and biological functions through molecular level approaches. They may be citizens of Austria, Belgium, Canada, Denmark, Finland, France, Germany, Greece, Ireland, Italy, Japan, Luxembourg, the Netherlands, Portugal, Spain, Sweden, Switzerland, the United Kingdom, or the United States, and must be seeking to conduct their research in any of those countries for which they have adequate language skills. Candidates may not conduct research in their own country nor at the institution where they obtained their Ph.D. Researchers from outside those countries are also eligible if they wish to conduct research within those countries.

Financial data Grants provide approximately $45,000 per year to cover relocation costs, living expenses and family support, a research allowance (which may be used for laboratory support or health insurance premiums), and travel to scientific meetings.

Duration 1 to 3 years; nonrenewable.

Special features The first awards under this program were presented in 1990.

Number awarded Varies each year.

Deadline August of each year.

[403]
HUMAN FRONTIER SCIENCE PROGRAM RESEARCH GRANTS

Human Frontier Science Program Organization
Bureaux Europe
20 place des Halles
67080 Strasbourg
France
33 3 88 21 51 21   Fax: 33 3 88 32 88 97
E-mail: grant@hfsp.org
Web site: www.hfsp.org

Purpose To provide funding for basic research on cell biology and neurobiology to teams of researchers from member nations of the Human Frontier Science Program (HFSP).

Eligibility Scientists who are from Austria, Belgium, Canada, Denmark, Finland, France, Germany, Greece, Ireland, Italy, Japan, Luxembourg, the Netherlands, Portugal, Spain, Sweden, Switzerland, the United Kingdom, or the United States may apply for these grants to conduct basic research for the elucidation of brain functions. The proposed research must be carried out jointly by research teams, preferably of 2 to 4 members. All members of the team must have a doctoral degree or equivalent research experience, an independent laboratory, and an established record for independent research. Young Investigator Grants are for teams of researchers within the first 5 years of establishing an independent laboratory; Program Grants are for teams of researchers at any stage of their careers. The team must designate 1 of its members as the principal applicant, and that member must be a national (not just a resident) of 1 of the participating countries; other team members may be from any country. At least 1 member of the team must be of a nationality different from that of the principal applicant and at least 1 member must be affiliated with an institution located in a country other than that in which the principal applicant's institution is located. Teams should only have 1 member from any 1 country. Applications for Young Investigator Grants and Program Grants are reviewed together; the proportion of grants awarded to the 2 categories depends on the quality of applications received. Research carried out within only 1 country is not eligible.

Financial data The average grant is approximately $250,000 per year.

Duration 1 year; may be renewed up to 2 additional years.

Number awarded Varies each year; recently, 54 research grants (including both Young Investigator and Program Grants) were awarded.

Deadline August of each year.

[404]
HUMAN FRONTIER SCIENCE PROGRAM SHORT-TERM FELLOWSHIPS

Human Frontier Science Program Organization
Bureaux Europe
20 place des Halles
67080 Strasbourg
France
33 3 88 21 51 21   Fax: 33 3 88 32 88 97
E-mail: fellow@hfsp.org
Web site: www.hfsp.org

Purpose To provide funding for basic research on cell biology and neurobiology to scientists from member nations of the Human Frontier Science Program (HFSP).

Eligibility Researchers who are from Austria, Belgium, Canada, Denmark, Finland, France, Germany, Greece, Ireland, Italy, Japan, Luxembourg, the Netherlands, Portugal, Spain, Sweden, Switzerland, the United Kingdom, or the United States and have a Ph.D. degree or equivalent research experience are eligible to apply. Preference is given to young investigators at an early stage of their careers. Applicants must be proposing to work in a laboratory in 1 of the other countries to learn new techniques or develop collaborations in the areas supported by the program: brain functions and biological functions at the molecular level. Scientists from non-member countries may participate if they are associated with a scientist from a member country. All applicants must have adequate language skills to carry out the proposed project at a host institution.

Financial data Fellowships cover round-trip travel expenses to the host institution and living expenses; the exact amount depends on the country where the research is conducted.

Duration 2 weeks to 3 months.

Limitations These fellowships are not intended to enable researchers to attend workshops, courses, or symposia; to provide support during periods of sabbatical leave; to plan future work; or to write papers, books, or reviews.

Number awarded Varies; generally, 70 or more each year.

Deadline Applications may be submitted at any time.

[405]
INTER AMERICAN PRESS ASSOCIATION SCHOLARSHIP FUND

Inter American Press Association
1801 S.W. Third Avenue
Miami, FL 33129
(305) 634-2465   Fax: (305) 635-2272
E-mail: info@sipiapa.org
Web site: www.sipiapa.org

Purpose To provide financial assistance to young journalists and journalism school graduates from the United States or Canada for study, work, and research in Latin America.

Eligibility Eligible to apply are print journalists with at least 5 years of professional experience and journalism school seniors/graduates. Applicants must be between the ages of 21 and 35 and demonstrate proficiency in the language of the country where they plan to be placed. Latin American and Caribbean applicants must attend an American or Canadian university with a recognized school of journalism for a full school year. American and Canadian applicants must submit a proposed study and work plan that includes 1) a minimum of 3 university courses in any country in Latin America or the Caribbean; 2) a major research project; and 3) participation in the fund's reporting program.

Financial data American and Canadian recipients are given $13,000 and health insurance for the duration of their stay abroad; Latin American and Caribbean scholars receive the same and also round-trip airfare.

Duration 1 year, to begin within the calendar year following the award.

Special features The Inter American Press Association was established in 1942 to defend and promote the right of the peoples of the Americas to be fully and freely informed through an independent press. It established the Scholarship Fund in 1954.

Number awarded At least 10 each year.

Deadline December of each year.

[406]
INTERNATIONAL RESEARCH LINKAGES IN CANADIAN STUDIES

International Council for Canadian Studies
Attn: Director of Administration and Programs
75 Albert Street, Suite 908
Ottawa, Ontario K1P 5E7
Canada
(613) 789-7828   Fax: (613) 789-7830
E-mail: gvallieres@iccs-ciec.ca
Web site: www.iccs-ciec.ca

Purpose To provide funding to teams of scholars from Canada and other countries interested in conducting research on Canadian studies.

Eligibility This program is open to research teams, each consisting of at least 2 scholars who have completed their Ph.D. in Canadian studies. Proposals must be submitted by at least 2 teams, 1 of which is based at a Canadian university. Each team must be engaged in a program of research and must show how it intends to pursue linkages after the initial activity. Applications must be submitted in 1 of Canada's official languages.

Financial data Up to $C8,000.

Special features Funding for this program is provided by the Canadian Department of Foreign Affairs and International Trade.

Number awarded Varies each year.

Deadline December of each year.

[407]
IZAAK WALTON KILLAM MEMORIAL POSTDOCTORAL FELLOWSHIP

University of Alberta
Faculty of Graduate Studies and Research
Attn: Graduate Awards Coordinator
105 Administration Building
Edmonton, Alberta T6G 2M7
Canada
(780) 492-3499　　　　　　　　(800) 758-7136
Fax: (780) 492-0692　　　　　Fax: (800) 803-4132
E-mail: grad.mail@ualberta.ca
Web site: www.ualberta.ca/gradstudies

Purpose To provide funding to postdoctorates from any country who are interested in conducting research at the University of Alberta.

Eligibility This program is open to nationals of any country. They must have completed their Ph.D. degree within the past 3 years, be proficient in English, and wish to conduct research in any field at the University of Alberta. Individuals who received their degree from the University of Alberta and those on sabbatical or study leave are not eligible to apply.

Financial data The stipend is $C35,000 per year; round-trip airfare and a 1-time research grant of $C3,000 are also provided.

Duration 2 years.

Number awarded 5 each year.

Deadline December of each year.

[408]
IZAAK WALTON KILLAM MEMORIAL POSTDOCTORAL FELLOWSHIPS

University of British Columbia
Attn: Faculty of Graduate Studies
180-6371 Crescent Road
Vancouver, British Columbia V6T 1Z2
Canada
(604) 822-2933　　　　　　　Fax: (604) 822-5802
E-mail: killam@mercury.ubc.ca
Web site: www.grad.ubc.ca/prostudents

Purpose To provide funding to scholars from any country who are interested in conducting research at the University of British Columbia.

Eligibility This program is open to nationals of any country who have completed a Ph.D. degree at a recognized university within the preceding 2 years and are interested in conducting research at the University of British Columbia. Preference may be given to Canadian citizens or permanent residents. Individuals who received their degree from the University of British Columbia or who hold faculty positions at universities or colleges are generally not eligible. Preference is given to applicants who have not yet held a postdoctoral award.

Financial data The stipend is $C36,000 per year. An additional $C3,000 over the term of the award is available as a travel allowance.

Duration 2 years.

Number awarded 10 to 15 each year.

Deadline November of each year.

[409]
IZAAK WALTON KILLAM POSTDOCTORAL FELLOWSHIP PROGRAM

Dalhousie University
Attn: Dean, Faculty of Graduate Studies
Arts and Administration Building, Room 314
Halifax, Nova Scotia B3H 4H6
Canada
(902) 494-6727　　　　　　　Fax: (902) 494-8797
E-mail: Killam.Trust@dal.ca
Web site: www.dal.ca/~ktrust

Purpose To enable nationals of any country to conduct research at Dalhousie University in Halifax, Nova Scotia.

Eligibility This program is open to nationals of any country who can satisfy Canadian immigration requirements, are proficient in English, have completed a Ph.D. degree at a recognized university within the previous 2 years or expect to obtain the degree before taking up the award, and wish to conduct research in any field at Dalhousie University. Candidates cannot have a current connection with Dalhousie University.

Financial data The stipend is $C33,000 per year. Other provisions include a travel allowance for transportation to Halifax, a research allowance, and a conference travel grant.

Duration 1 year.

Number awarded 4 each year.

Deadline October of each year.

[410]
JACOBS RESEARCH FUNDS SMALL GRANTS PROGRAM

Whatcom Museum
Attn: Jacobs Research Funds
121 Prospect Street
Bellingham, WA 98225
(360) 676-6981　　　　　　　Fax: (360) 738-7409
E-mail: jacobs@cob.org
Web site: www.cob.org/cobweb/museum/jacobs.htm

Purpose To provide funds for research in the field of social and cultural anthropology among living American native peoples.

Eligibility Research projects in the field of social and cultural anthropology among living American native peoples are eligible. Preference is given to the Pacific Northwest as an area of investigation, but other regions of North America (including Mexico) are eligible for consideration. Grants are given for work that addresses cultural expressive systems, such as music, language, dance, mythology, world view, plastic and graphic arts, intellectual life, and religion (including comparative psychological analysis). Projects in archaeology, physical anthropology, applied linguistics, and applied anthropology are not eligible; archival research is not supported. The program also does not support proprietary research to provide information for the exclusive use of any entity, public or private (national, state, provincial, local governments, public or private charities, churches or foundations, tribes or bands, or community groups).

Financial data Grant amounts vary; generally, up to $1,200 is awarded. Funds may cover fees for consultants, supplies, transportation to and from the field, and lodging in the field.

Funds are not supplied for salaries, ordinary living expenses, or major equipment.

Duration 1 year; renewable.

Special features This program was formerly known as the Melville and Elizabeth Jacobs Research Fund.

Number awarded Varies each year; recently, 11 grants were awarded.

Deadline February of each year.

[411]
JEANNE TIMMINS COSTELLO FELLOWSHIPS

Montreal Neurological Institute and Hospital
Attn: Liaison Officer
3801 University Street, Room 636
Montreal, Quebec H3A 2B4
Canada
(514) 398-1902   Fax: (514) 398-8248
E-mail: director@mni.lan.mcgill.ca
Web site: www.mcgill.ca/mni

Purpose To provide funding for study and research in neurology at the Montreal Neurological Institute and Hospital.

Eligibility Applicants may be from any country. They must hold an M.D. degree and have completed specialty training in neurosurgery or neurology, or have earned a Ph.D. degree in neuroscience. They must be interested in pursuing studies or research in clinical and basic neurology at the Institute and Hospital.

Financial data Up to $C25,000 per year.

Duration 1 year.

Deadline October of each year.

[412]
JENNIFER ROBINSON MEMORIAL SCHOLARSHIP

Arctic Institute of North America
c/o University of Calgary
2500 University Drive N.W.
Calgary, Alberta T2N 1N4
Canada
(403) 220-7515   Fax: (403) 282-4609
E-mail: mdickers@ucalgary.ca
Web site: www.ucalgary.ca/aina/scholar/scholar.html

Purpose To provide financial assistance to graduate students engaged in research on the biology of the Arctic regions.

Eligibility Eligible to apply are graduate students in biology whose proposed project requires field research in the Arctic regions.

Financial data This fellowship is $C5,000.

Special features The Arctic Institute of North America was founded in 1945 and became an institute of the University of Calgary in 1979. An American corporation is headquartered at the University of Alaska, Fairbanks. The Jennifer Robinson Memorial Scholarship was first awarded in 1987.

Number awarded 1 each year.

Deadline January of each year.

[413]
KILLAM POSTDOCTORAL FELLOWSHIPS

University of Calgary
Attn: Research Services
602 Earth Sciences Building
Calgary, Alberta T2N 1N4
Canada
(403) 220-3380, ext. 2461   Fax: (403) 289-0693
E-mail: mflynn@ucalgary.ca
Web site: www.ucalgary.ca

Purpose To provide funding to postdoctorates from any country who are interested in conducting research at the University of Calgary.

Eligibility This program is open to nationals of any country who completed a Ph.D. degree within the past 2 years. Applicants must be proficient in English and wish to conduct research in any field at the University of Calgary. They must be nominated by the head of the department in which they intend to conduct research; individuals may not apply on their own behalf.

Financial data The stipend of $C35,000 includes a relocation and research allowance of $2,600. If the fellow engages in teaching, extra compensation may be provided.

Duration 12 months; nonrenewable.

Limitations Fellows are expected to carry out a program of independent research, present 1 or more departmental seminars for students and faculty, and contribute on an informal basis to other departmental activities. By arrangement with the department, they may also teach up to the equivalent of 1 full course.

Number awarded 1 each year.

Deadline October of each year.

[414]
KILLAM VISITING SCHOLAR AWARDS

University of Calgary
Attn: Research Services
602 Earth Sciences Building
Calgary, Alberta T2N 1N4
Canada
(403) 220-3380, ext. 2461   Fax: (403) 289-0693
E-mail: mflynn@ucalgary.ca
Web site: www.ucalgary.ca

Purpose To provide funding to postdoctorates from any country who are interested in teaching and conducting research at the University of Calgary.

Eligibility This program is open to nationals of any country who have a distinguished record of research and teaching. Applicants must be interested in participating in the research and teaching programs of the host department at the university as well as engaging in their own research. They must be nominated by the head of the department in which they intend to conduct research; individuals may not apply on their own behalf.

Financial data The award consists of an honorarium of $C20,000 plus a research and travel allowance of $3,000.

Duration 1 academic term (either fall or spring).

Number awarded 1 or more each year.

Deadline October of each year.

[415]
LAIDLAW INC. SCHOLARSHIP

Institute of International Education
Attn: Student Programs Division
809 United Nations Plaza
New York, NY 10017-3580
(212) 984-5330   Fax: (212) 984-5325
Web site: www.iie.org/fulbright

Purpose To provide financial assistance to American graduate students for study or research in Canada.

Eligibility Applicants must be U.S. citizens who hold a B.A. degree or equivalent before the beginning date of the grant and plan to study or conduct research in Canada. Candidates must have been accepted by a Canadian university and a Canadian faculty adviser. Preference is given to students who study or do their research at McMaster University.

Financial data This program provides round-trip transportation, tuition, book and research allowances, a monthly maintenance allowance based on living costs, and supplemental health and accident insurance.

Duration 1 academic year.

Special features These grants are offered as part of the Fulbright program, administered by the Institute of International Education (IIE). Students who are currently enrolled in the United States are to apply through the Fulbright program adviser on their campus; at-large applicants (those not currently enrolled) may obtain applications and information directly from the IIE.

Number awarded 1 each year.

Deadline October of each year.

[416]
MARUSIA AND MICHAEL DOROSH MASTER'S FELLOWSHIPS

Canadian Institute of Ukrainian Studies
c/o University of Alberta
Athabasca Hall, Room 352
Edmonton, Alberta T6G 2E8
Canada
(780) 492-2972   Fax: (780) 492-4967
E-mail: cius@ualberta.ca
Web site: www.ualberta.ca/~cius/cius-grants.htm

Purpose To provide funding to graduate students from any country who are interested in conducting master's degree-related research in Canada on a Ukrainian or Ukrainian Canadian issue.

Eligibility Eligible to apply are students from any country who have completed all other requirements for a master's degree and are ready to begin working on a thesis on a Ukrainian or Ukrainian Canadian topic. They must be working on a degree in 1 of the following disciplines: education, history, arts, humanities, law, library science, social sciences, or women's studies. Preference is given to Canadian citizens and residents (who may hold the fellowship at any institution of higher learning) and to foreign students who are currently enrolled at the University of Alberta. Research must be conducted in Canada.

Financial data The maximum stipend is $C10,000.

Duration 1 year; nonrenewable.

Number awarded 1 each year.

Deadline February of each year.

[417]
MAXWELL BOULTON JUNIOR FELLOWSHIP

McGill University
Attn: Faculty of Law
3644 Peel Street
Montreal, Quebec H3A 1W9
Canada
(514) 398-6604   Fax: (514) 398-4659

Purpose To provide funding to junior scholars from any country who are interested in conducting legal research in Canada.

Eligibility This program is open to junior legal scholars from any country who wish to conduct a major research project at McGill University. Fellows may be working to fulfill the requirements of a higher degree. Preference is given to proposed research that deals with the Canadian legal system or legal community.

Financial data Up to $C35,000 per year.

Duration 1 academic year.

Limitations Fellows may be given a teaching assignment.

Number awarded 2 each year.

Deadline January of each year.

[418]
MAXWELL BOULTON SENIOR FELLOWSHIP

McGill University
Attn: Faculty of Law
3644 Peel Street
Montreal, Quebec H3A 1W9
Canada
(514) 398-6604   Fax: (514) 398-4659

Purpose To provide funding to established scholars from any country who are interested in conducting legal research in Canada.

Eligibility This program is open to senior legal scholars from any country who wish to conduct a major research project at McGill University. Preference is given to proposed research that deals with the Canadian legal system or legal community.

Financial data Up to $C35,000 per year.

Duration 1 academic year.

Limitations Fellows may be given a teaching assignment.

Number awarded 1 each year.

Deadline January of each year.

[419]
MELLON POSTDOCTORAL FELLOWSHIPS AT THE PONTIFICAL INSTITUTE OF MEDIAEVAL STUDIES

Pontifical Institute of Mediaeval Studies
59 Queen's Park Crescent East
Toronto, Ontario M5S 2C4
Canada
(416) 926-7142　　　　Fax: (416) 926-7292
E-mail: pontifex@epas.utoronto.ca
Web site: www.pims.ca/mellons.html

Purpose To provide funding to young scholars interested in conducting research at the Pontifical Institute of Mediaeval Studies Library in Canada.

Eligibility This program is open to scholars who received their Ph.D or equivalent degree within the previous 5 years and are starting their professional academic career at the assistant professor level. They must be interested in conducting a research project in medieval studies that requires use of the resources of the Pontifical Institute's library.

Financial data Fellows receive a stipend of $30,000 (or approximately $C45,000).

Duration 1 year; may be renewed 1 additional year.

Special features This program, which began in 2001, is funded by the Andrew W. Mellon Foundation

Limitations Fellows are required to participate in an interdisciplinary research seminar along with fellows of the institute and other interested scholars, including those from the graduate faculty of the University of Toronto. English is the language of instruction and discussion.

Number awarded Up to 4 each year.

Deadline February of each year.

[420]
MICHAEL AND DARIA KOWALSKY RESEARCH GRANTS

Canadian Institute of Ukrainian Studies
c/o University of Alberta
Athabasca Hall, Room 352
Edmonton, Alberta T6G 2E8
Canada
(780) 492-2972　　　　Fax: (780) 492-4967
E-mail: cius@ualberta.ca
Web site: www.ualberta.ca/~cius/cius-grants.htm

Purpose To provide funding to scholars from any country who are interested in conducting research in Canada on Ukrainian studies.

Eligibility This program is open to scholars on the faculty of a university or other postsecondary institution, in Canada or elsewhere, and to private scholars. Applicants must be interested in conducting research in Canada on Ukrainian history, literature, language, education, society, law, or ethnography. Preference is given to topics dealing with eastern and southern Ukraine, especially on questions pertaining to the national revival in those regions. Support may be provided for research proposals whose primary focus is the development or preparation of specialized material for teaching at the postsecondary level, or for the publication of scholarly works (including textbooks, anthologies, readers, bibliographies, and collections of documentary or primary source materials). Grants are not provided to support research for a degree or course requirements, or for work intended primarily for use in public schools.

Financial data Grants are provided only to defray actual direct costs attributable to the project, not for overhead costs or personal income.

Duration 1 year.

Number awarded Varies each year.

Deadline February of each year.

[421]
MITT, RED RIVER TRADE CORRIDOR, IISD SCHOLARSHIP

Institute of International Education
Attn: Student Programs Division
809 United Nations Plaza
New York, NY 10017-3580
(212) 984-5330　　　　Fax: (212) 984-5325
Web site: www.iie.org/fulbright

Purpose To provide financial assistance to American graduate students for study or research in Canada.

Eligibility Applicants must be U.S. citizens who hold a B.A. degree or equivalent before the beginning date of the grant and plan to study or conduct research in Canada. Candidates must have been accepted by a Canadian university and a Canadian faculty adviser. Preference is given to students in sustainable economic and social development of the Red River region of the great northern plains, and those who study or do their research at an institution in Winnipeg.

Financial data This program provides round-trip transportation, tuition, book and research allowances, a monthly maintenance allowance based on living costs, and supplemental health and accident insurance.

Duration 1 academic year.

Special features These grants are offered as part of the Fulbright program, administered by the Institute of International Education (IIE). Students who are currently enrolled in the United States are to apply through the Fulbright program adviser on their campus; at-large applicants (those not currently enrolled) may obtain applications and information directly from the IIE.

Number awarded 1 each year.

Deadline October of each year.

[422]
NATIONAL CAPITAL RESEARCH SCHOLARSHIP

International Council for Canadian Studies
Attn: Director of Administration and Programs
75 Albert Street, Suite 908
Ottawa, Ontario K1P 5E7
Canada
(613) 789-7828　　　　Fax: (613) 789-7830
E-mail: gvallieres@iccs-ciec.ca
Web site: www.iccs-ciec.ca

Purpose To provide funding to scholars interested in conducting research related to Canada's national capital.

Eligibility This program is open to researchers and teams of researchers interested in conducting a project on the enhancement and development of capital cities, particularly the relation between capital city and city functions, the international and symbolic role of capital cities in a rapidly changing world, the leading role of capital cities in the tourism industry in general or the regional economy in particular, and the administration of capital cities. Applicants must be committed to spending at least 3 weeks in Canada. The main thrust of their research must be Canada's capital, although a comparative approach is not precluded. Applications must be submitted in either of Canada's official languages.

Financial data The grant is $C5,000.

Special features Applications may be submitted through a national Canadian studies association. In the United States, this is the Association for Canadian Studies in the United States, 1317 F Street, N.W., Suite 920, Washington, DC 20004-1151, (202) 393-2580, Fax: (202) 393-2582, E-mail: info@acsus.org, Web site: www.acsus.org. Funding for this program is provided by the National Capital Commission (NCC), a crown corporation mandated to make Canada's capital a meeting place for all Canadians and to ensure that it reflects Canada to Canadians.

Number awarded 1 each year.

Deadline December of each year.

[423]
NATIONAL RESEARCH COUNCIL RESEARCH ASSOCIATESHIPS

National Research Council
Attn: RA Program Coordinator
Ottawa, Ontario K1A 0R6
Canada
(613) 998-4126   Fax: (613) 990-7669
E-mail: RA.Coordinator@nrc.ca

Purpose To offer researchers from any country the opportunity to work at National Research Council (NRC) laboratories in Canada.

Eligibility This program is open to researchers from any country (although preference is given to Canadians) who have earned a master's degree in engineering or a Ph.D. in engineering or the natural sciences during the past 5 years. They must have demonstrated an ability to perform original scientific or engineering research of a high quality.

Financial data Salaries are commensurate with experience; at the Ph.D. level, the base rate is $C39,366 per year.

Duration 2 years; may be renewed.

Special features Associates are assigned to work on challenging research problems at the National Research Council laboratories. For a complete list of NRC laboratories and facilities, write to the address above.

[424]
NATO COLLABORATIVE LINKAGE GRANTS

North Atlantic Treaty Organization
Attn: Scientific Affairs Division
Boulevard Leopold III
B-1110 Brussels
Belgium
32 2 707 4111   Fax: 32 2 707 4232
Web site: www.nato.int/science

Purpose To support collaborative scientific research by providing travel funding to teams in different member countries of the North Atlantic Treaty Organization (NATO) and those in Euro-Atlantic Partnership Council (EAPC) countries (including Eurasia).

Eligibility This program is open to collaborations between scientists in NATO countries (the United States, Canada, 14 countries in western Europe, and 3 countries in eastern Europe and Eurasia) and NATO's partner countries of the EAPC (15 former Soviet republics and 7 other nations in eastern Europe). Scientists of the Mediterranean Dialogue countries (Algeria, Egypt, Israel, Jordan, Mauritania, Morocco, and Tunisia) may also apply for a grant in cooperation with scientists from NATO countries. All applicant teams must be interested in conducting research in 1 of the 4 priority areas currently selected by NATO: physical and engineering science and technology (PST), life science and technology (LST), environmental and earth science and technology (EST), and security-related civil science and technology (SST).

Financial data Funding is provided to cover the costs incurred by investigators to visit the collaborating teams abroad. Amounts awarded are normally between $5,000 (for 1 year of collaboration by 2 or 3 scientists) to a maximum of $25,000 (for 2 years' collaboration by 5 research teams). Basic costs (salaries, equipment, consumables, page charges) should already be covered from other national sources. Support is not provided for 1) institutional overhead expenses; 2) scientists while on sabbatical or other extended leave abroad; 3) travel that is not related to the research project; 4) purely domestic travel; 5) visits for 1 researcher or 1 research group only; or 6) long study periods abroad.

Duration The grants may be used over a period of 1 to 2 years. During the time period of a grant, research visits are expected to be of short duration and should not exceed 2 months.

Number awarded Since 1960, support has been given to more than 6,000 joint projects. At present, about 600 grants are awarded each year (of which an average of 450 are for new projects).

Deadline Deadlines for PST grants are February, July, or October of each year; deadlines for LST and EST grants are March, August, or November of each year; deadlines for SST grants are January, April, or September of each year.

[425]
NATO EXPERT VISITS

North Atlantic Treaty Organization
Attn: Scientific Affairs Division
Boulevard Leopold III
B-1110 Brussels
Belgium
32 2 707 4111   Fax: 32 2 707 4232
Web site: www.nato.int/science

Purpose To provide financial assistance to scientists from member nations of the North Atlantic Treaty Organization (NATO) for visits to research laboratories in Euro-Atlantic Partnership Council (EAPC) countries (including Eurasia), and vice versa.

Eligibility Experts from NATO countries (the United States, Canada, 14 countries in western Europe, and 3 countries in eastern Europe) may visit research laboratories in an EAPC country (15 former Soviet republics and 7 countries in eastern Europe) to consult on current research projects. EAPC scientists may also visit a NATO country. Scientists in the 7 Mediterranean Dialogue countries (Algeria, Egypt, Israel, Jordan, Mauritania, Morocco, and Tunisia) are also eligible if they draw up applications in cooperation with a scientist from a NATO country. This program is available primarily, but not exclusively, for research in 1 of the 4 priority areas currently selected by NATO: physical and engineering science and technology (PST), life science and technology (LST), environmental and earth science and technology (EST), and security-related civil science and technology (SST). Applications must be submitted by the project director at the institute to be visited and signed by both the host institute project director and the visiting expert.

Financial data Fellows receive research, travel, and living (up to $100 per day) allowances. Support is not provided for 1) long study periods abroad, 2) salaries, stipends, or institutional overhead; 3) scientists on sabbatical or other extended leave abroad; or 4) attendance at conferences, symposia, workshops, etc.

Duration From a few days to 1 month.

Number awarded Varies each year.

Deadline Deadlines for PST grants are February, July, or October of each year; deadlines for LST and EST grants are March, August, or November of each year; deadlines for SST grants are January, April, or September of each year.

[426]
NEPORANY RESEARCH AND TEACHING FELLOWSHIP

Canadian Institute of Ukrainian Studies
c/o University of Alberta
Athabasca Hall, Room 352
Edmonton, Alberta T6G 2E8
Canada
(780) 492-2972   Fax: (780) 492-4967
E-mail: cius@ualberta.ca
Web site: www.ualberta.ca/~cius/cius-grants.htm

Purpose To provide funding to scholars from any country who are interested in teaching and conducting research in Ukrainian studies.

Eligibility This program is open to scholars from any country who hold a doctorate or have equivalent professional experience in Ukrainian studies. Applicants must submit a 3- to 5-page research proposal, 2 letters of recommendation, information on the course to be taught at the host institution, and a letter of support from the host institution indicating how the scholar's stay and teaching will benefit the development of Ukrainian studies.

Financial data The maximum stipend is $C20,000.

Duration 1 academic term (i.e., half of the academic year); may be extended if the fellow is successful in receiving supplemental funding from other sources.

Special features Funds for this program are supplied by the Osyp and Josaphat Neporany Educational Fund. The fellowship is tenable at any university in the world with research facilities at which the fellow's academic Ukrainian studies specialty may be pursued and the fellow enabled to teach a course related to the specialty.

Number awarded 1 each year.

Deadline February of each year.

[427]
NORTH AMERICAN JOURNALIST EXCHANGE

Institute of International Education
Attn: North American Journalist Exchange
809 United Nations Plaza
New York, NY 10017-3580
(212) 984-5390   Fax: (212) 984-5393
E-mail: plink@iie.org
Web site: www.iie.org

Purpose To provide an opportunity for journalists from the United States, Mexico, and Canada to participate in an international exchange program.

Eligibility This program is open to print journalists (newspaper or periodical) who have at least 3 years of professional experience. Applicants must be employed by or (for freelance journalists) affiliated with an independent media organization in the United States, Canada, or Mexico. They must be interested in visiting a host media organization in 1 of the other 2 countries. Applications must be accompanied by 1) a brief autobiography (in English, French, or Spanish) identifying a significant advance and a troubling setback in personal or professional life and the way the applicant dealt with both success and disappointment; 2) a statement of personal reasons for wanting to participate in the program, what they hope to gain from the program, and what they consider to be key issues in North American international relations, for possible articles; 3) copies of 4 published articles; and 4) a letter from their immediate supervisor indicating that the publication supports their participation in the program, that the publication will guarantee to pay their salary while they are participating in the program; and that the publication guarantees continued employment upon their return. Documents in French or Spanish should be accompanied by an English translation.

Financial data This program provides payment of all travel and living expenses plus a stipend for participants.

Duration 3 month, from April through June.

Special features This program, established in 1994, is sponsored by the Freedom Forum. Journalists applying from Canada or the United States should write to the Institute of International Education (IIE) in New York. Journalists applying from Mexico should write to the Intercambio Académico, Instituto Internacional de Educación, Londres 16-2 piso, Colonia Juárez, 06600, Mexico, D.F., Mexico, 52 5 703 1067, Fax: 52 5 535 5597, E-mail: tsanroman@solar.sar.net.

Limitations Fellows are expected to send articles about the host country to their publications at home. At the midpoint of the program, fellows are also expected to submit to IIE a short article suitable for publication, evaluating their experiences during the stay and discussing the relevance of the fellowship to their career goals and professional development.

Number awarded Varies each year.

Deadline November of each year.

[428]
NSF–NATO POSTDOCTORAL FELLOWSHIPS IN SCIENCE AND ENGINEERING

National Science Foundation
Directorate for Education and Human Resources
Attn: Division of Graduate Education
4201 Wilson Boulevard, Room 907N
Arlington, VA 22230
(703) 292-8697   TDD: (703) 292-5090
E-mail: nsf-nato@nsf.gov
Web site: www.ehr.nsf.gov

Purpose To enable young scientists and engineers from the United States to conduct research in the 18 member countries of the North Atlantic Treaty Organization (NATO) or the 18 NATO Partner countries.

Eligibility Eligible to apply for this support are U.S. citizens, nationals, or permanent residents who have received their doctorates within the past 5 years or who will have done so by the start of their tenure. They must be planning to pursue a program of research at an appropriate government or nonprofit scientific institution located in a NATO member or a NATO Partner country other than the United States. Eligible fields of study and research include mathematics; engineering; computer and information science; geosciences; the physical, biological, social, behavioral, and economic sciences; the history and philosophy of science; and interdisciplinary areas comprised of 2 or more of those fields. Research in the teaching and learning of science, mathematics, technology, and engineering is also eligible. Women, underrepresented minorities, and persons with disabilities are particularly encouraged to apply.

Financial data The program provides a monthly stipend of $2,750; dependency allowances of $200 per month for a spouse and each of not more than 2 children; and travel allowances of $2,500 for the fellow ($1,000 to Canada), $2,500 for an accompanying spouse ($1,000 to Canada), and $1,000 for 1 accompanying dependent child ($600 to Canada). In addition, the fellow is provided with $100 per month to aid in defraying costs of research and special travel.

Duration 12 months.

Special features The National Science Foundation manages these fellowships at the request of the U.S. Department of State. Members of NATO are Belgium, Canada, Czech Republic, Denmark, France, Germany, Greece, Hungary, Iceland, Italy, Luxembourg, the Netherlands, Norway, Poland, Portugal, Spain, Turkey, and the United Kingdom. The NATO Partner countries include the 15 republics of the former Soviet Union and 6 countries in eastern Europe (Albania, Bulgaria, Romania, Slovak Republic, Slovenia, and the former Yugoslav Republic of Macedonia).

Number awarded Approximately 5 each year.

Deadline November of each year.

[429]
ORGANIZATION OF AMERICAN STATES REGULAR TRAINING PROGRAM (PRA)

Organization of American States
Inter-American Agency for Cooperation and Development
Attn: Division of Cooperation for Development of Human Resources
1889 F Street, N.W., 2nd Floor
Washington, DC 20006-4499
(202) 458-3792   Fax: (202) 458-3878
E-mail: Fellowships_Department@oas.org
Web site: www.oas.org

Purpose To provide financial assistance to residents of Organization of American States (OAS) member countries who are interested in advanced study or research in another member country.

Eligibility Eligible to apply are citizens or permanent residents of an OAS member country: United States, Antigua and Barbuda, Argentina, Bahamas, Barbados, Belize, Bolivia, Brazil, Canada, Chile, Colombia, Costa Rica, Dominica, Dominican Republic, Ecuador, El Salvador, Grenada, Guatemala, Guyana, Haiti, Honduras, Jamaica, Mexico, Nicaragua, Panama, Paraguay, Peru, Saint Kitts and Nevis, Saint Lucia, Saint Vincent and the Grenadines, Suriname, Trinidad and Tobago, Uruguay, and Venezuela. They must have at least a bachelor's degree and have demonstrated the ability to pursue advanced studies. There is no subject limitation (except for the medical sciences and language training). Candidates must know the language of the study country and make the necessary contacts to secure acceptance or show evidence that the facilities needed to complete a research project will be provided.

Financial data Fellowships provide funds sufficient to cover travel expenses, tuition fees, books and study materials, health insurance, and a subsistence allowance (the amount varies from country to county). No benefits are provided to the family of fellowship holders.

Duration Up to 12 months; may be renewed for 1 additional year.

Special features There are 2 kinds of fellowships: those for advanced study at the graduate level and those for research. U.S. citizens submit their applications directly to OAS headquarters at the address above; citizens of other member countries submit their applications to the National Liaison Office (ONE) of their country of origin.

Limitations Funds cannot be used for undergraduate-level studies or for introductory language training. Fellows cannot study or conduct research in their own country.

Deadline February of each year.

[430]
POSTDOCTORAL FELLOWSHIPS OF THE CANADIAN INSTITUTES OF HEALTH RESEARCH

Canadian Institutes of Health Research
Attn: Programs Branch
410 Laurier Avenue West, Ninth Floor
Address Locator 4209A
Ottawa, Ontario K1A 0W9
Canada
(613) 954-1964   Fax: (613) 954-1800
E-mail: smichaud@cihr.ca
Web site: www.cihr.ca

Purpose To provide financial assistance for research training in Canada to postdoctorates who are interested in the health sciences.

Eligibility While the program is designed primarily for applicants who are Canadian citizens or permanent residents of Canada, awards may also be made to foreign candidates who wish to undertake postdoctoral training in Canada. They must hold a professional degree in medicine, dentistry, nursing, rehabilitative science, pharmacy, optometry, or veterinary medicine, or a Ph.D. degree (or its equivalent). Applicants with a health professional degree may apply for awards to undertake graduate studies leading to a master's or Ph.D. degree, although registration in a graduate degree program is not required. Individuals who wish to undertake postdoctoral training in the same research environment in which they received their predoctoral training are not eligible to apply. Also ineligible are candidates beyond their fifth year of postdoctoral experience.

Financial data The value of each fellowship relates to the recipient's educational attainment and professional experience. The annual stipend for holders of degrees in medicine, dentistry, optometry, or veterinary medicine is $C35,000 for those with 2 or fewer years of experience or $C45,000 for those with more than 2 years of experience. The stipend for Ph.D. recipients is $C35,000 per year. The stipend for fellows with an undergraduate professional degree in pharmacy, nursing, or rehabilitative science is $C19,030 per year; for fellows with a graduate professional degree in those fields, the annual stipend is $C35,000 with 2 or fewer years of experience or $C45,000 with more than 2 years of experience. In addition, all fellows receive a yearly research allowance of $C3,500.

Duration The duration of support depends on the degrees held by the recipient: up to 4 years for those with a health professional degree who do not intend to proceed to a Ph.D. degree; up to 5 years for those with a health professional degree who intend to proceed to a Ph.D. degree; up to 3 years for those with a Ph.D. degree or a health professional degree and a Ph.D. degree.

Special features The Canadian Institutes of Health Research (CIHR) was formerly the Medical Research Council (MRC) of Canada. This program was formerly the MRC Fellowships Program.

Limitations This award is tenable in Canada only for applicants who are neither citizens nor permanent residents of Canada. Canadian citizens and permanent residents may use it anywhere in the world if the desired nature and caliber of training is not available in Canada.

Deadline March or October of each year.

[431]
QUEBEC STUDIES PROGRAM GRANTS FOR PROFESSORS AND RESEARCHERS

Ministère des Relations Internationales
Direction générale des affaires publiques
Attn: Quebec Studies Officer
525, boulevard René-Lévesque Est
Québec, Québec, G1R 5R9
Canada
(418) 649-2333   Fax: (418) 649-2656
Web site: www.mri.gouv.qc.ca

Purpose To provide financial assistance to professors and doctoral candidates from U.S. colleges and universities who are interested in conducting research in Quebec.

Eligibility This program is open to 1) full-time professors at accredited U.S. universities and 4-year colleges and 2) doctoral students at the dissertation writing stage. Applicants must be interested in conducting research in Quebec on subjects with a specific relevance to Quebec or its relationship with the United States. Topics must deal with important social or cultural issues in the social sciences, humanities, literature, or business (broadly defined). The research should lead to 1) writing an article-length manuscript to be published as an article in a scholarly periodical or as part of a book or dissertation; 2) the creation of a new course on Quebec; or 3) the addition of a new and substantial unit on Quebec to an already established course.

Financial data The grant is $5,000. Funds must be used to help pay expenses directly related to projects carried out in Quebec. Payment of two-thirds of the grant is made upon arrival in Quebec. The remainder is released upon receipt of a research report and a completed manuscript or a syllabus of the new course.

Duration Research trips must last at least 3 weeks.

Number awarded 1 or more each year.

Deadline February of each year.

[432]
R. HOWARD WEBSTER FELLOWSHIPS

Delta Waterfowl and Wetlands Research Station
Attn: Student Programs
Rural Route 1
Portage La Prairie
Manitoba R1N 3A1
Canada
(204) 239-1900   Fax: (204) 239-5950
E-mail: dw4ducks@portage.com

Purpose To support students interested in conducting research in Canada on waterfowl and wetland ecology.

Eligibility Undergraduate and graduate students in ecology from the United States or Canada are eligible to apply if they are interested in conducting research at the Delta Waterfowl and Wetlands Research Station in Manitoba. Preference is given to students who have or will have a baccalaureate degree and are applying to do graduate work on waterfowl.

Financial data The stipend is $C1,500 per month.

Duration From 3 to 5 months, beginning in April.

Special features Most of the graduate students whose research is funded by this program previously worked in the program as undergraduate field assistants.
Number awarded Varies; generally, 5 or more each year.
Deadline January of each year.

[433]
RAY D. WOLFE PRE-DOCTORAL AND POST-DOCTORAL FELLOWSHIPS FOR ADVANCED RESEARCH IN JEWISH STUDIES

University of Toronto
Faculty of Arts and Science
Attn: Jewish Studies Program
University College, Room 314
15 King's College Circle
Toronto, M5S 3H7
Canada
(416) 946-3229   Fax: (416) 971-2027

Purpose To provide an opportunity for doctoral students and young postdoctoral scholars who are interested in pursuing an academic career in Jewish studies to conduct research using the facilities of the University of Toronto.
Eligibility This program is open to graduate students working on their doctorate and postdoctoral applicants who completed their degree no more than 3 years earlier. They may be residents of Canada or from other countries. Applicants must be engaged in research related to the history, culture, literature, religion, or thought of the Jewish people. They must be interested in spending a year at the University of Toronto working on their doctoral dissertation or preparing their dissertation for publication.
Financial data The stipend is $C40,000.
Duration 1 year; renewable only in exceptional circumstances.
Special features Fellows spend the academic year at the University of Toronto. They have access to the library and other university facilities. Funds for this program come from the Canadian Jewish News.
Limitations Fellows are expected to teach 1 course each term. Graduate students working on their doctorate are expected to complete their thesis by the end of their fellowship term. All fellows must submit a brief report of their accomplishments at the end of their term.
Number awarded 2 or more each year.
Deadline February of each year; while late applications may be considered, they would be evaluated only after decisions are made on the applicants who meet the deadline.

[434]
RESEARCH GRANT PROGRAM IN CANADIAN STUDIES

Canadian Embassy
Attn: Academic Relations
501 Pennsylvania Avenue, N.W.
Washington, DC 20001
(202) 682-1740   Fax: (202) 682-7791
E-mail: daniel.abele@dfait-maeci.gc.ca
Web site: www.canadianembassy.org

Purpose To assist American scholars in writing article-length manuscripts of publishable quality about Canada.
Eligibility This program is open to full-time faculty members at accredited 4-year colleges or universities in the United States as well as scholars at American research and policy-planning institutes who are undertaking significant Canadian, Canada-U.S., or Canada-North America research projects. Recent Ph.D. recipients who are citizens or permanent residents of the United States are also eligible. Applicants are ineligible to receive the same grant in 2 consecutive years or to receive 2 different Canadian Studies grants in the same grant period. Priority topics include bilateral trade and economics; Canada-U.S. border issues; cultural policy and values; environmental, natural resources, and energy issues; and security cooperation. Projects that examine Canadian politics, economics, culture, and society as well as Canada's role in international affairs are also welcome.
Financial data Awards range up to $10,000 for individuals. Principal investigators applying on behalf of a group may request up to $15,000. Funds are provided to help pay only direct costs related to a project, including travel primarily within Canada and the United States as necessary, books, and possible publishing fees. No provision is made for released time stipends, conference travel, or overhead costs to the institution.
Duration 1 year.
Special features This program is funded by the Canadian Department of Foreign Affairs and International Trade.
Number awarded Varies each year; recently, 30 of these grants were awarded.
Deadline September of each year.

[435]
RESEARCH TRAINING CENTRE POSTDOCTORAL FELLOWSHIPS

Hospital for Sick Children
Attn: Coordinator, Faculty Development
555 University Avenue
Toronto, Ontario M5G 1X8
Canada
(416) 813-8545   Fax: (416) 813-5085
E-mail: patricia.cayetano@sickkids.on.ca
Web site: www.sickkids.on.ca

Purpose To provide an opportunity for postdoctorates to pursue a program of research training in pediatrics at the Hospital for Sick Children in Canada.
Eligibility Applicants may be citizens of any country who hold a Ph.D. or medical degree and are interested in a program of research training at the hospital in Toronto. They must first select a supervisor who is a scientist or associate scientist at the hospital and jointly agree on the project or training program.

Financial data Annual stipends range from $C17,000 to $C30,000, depending on the number of years of academic training completed by the recipient.
Duration 2 years.
Number awarded Varies each year.
Deadline April or October of each year.

[436]
RESEARCH TRAINING CENTRE VISITING SCIENTIST PROGRAM
Hospital for Sick Children
Attn: Coordinator, Faculty Development
555 University Avenue
Toronto, Ontario M5G 1X8
Canada
(416) 813-8545   Fax: (416) 813-5085
E-mail: patricia.cayetano@sickkids.on.ca
Web site: www.sickkids.on.ca

Purpose To allow visiting scientists to conduct research in pediatrics at the Hospital for Sick Children in Canada.
Eligibility Eligible to apply are citizens of any country who are interested in conducting research at the hospital in Toronto. They must be senior scientists or academicians who hold appointments at other institutions anywhere in the world. Applications must originate from investigators at the hospital who propose to have a visiting scientist working in their laboratory.
Financial data Awards up to $C20,000 are available; the stipend is intended to serve as a supplement to the recipient's sabbatical stipend from the home institution.
Duration Up to 1 year.
Limitations Foreign visiting scientists must present the official letter of invitation for processing at the Canadian Consulate in their home country, along with a letter from their home institution indicating that they are still being paid by that institution and that their position will be available upon return.
Number awarded Up to 4 each year.
Deadline Applications may be submitted at any time.

[437]
SAMUEL LUNENFELD RESEARCH SUMMER STUDENT PROGRAM
Hospital for Sick Children
Attn: Coordinator, Faculty Development
555 University Avenue
Toronto, Ontario M5G 1X8
Canada
(416) 813-8545   Fax: (416) 813-5085
E-mail: patricia.cayetano@sickkids.on.ca
Web site: www.sickkids.on.ca

Purpose To provide an opportunity for students to conduct a summer research project in pediatrics at the Hospital for Sick Children in Canada.
Eligibility This program is open to university students who are interested in conducting a research project at the hospital in Toronto. Applicants must have completed at least 1 year of university study in a basic science or medicine program and have achieved high academic marks. Students enrolled in a M.Sc. or Ph.D. program are not eligible. The program also supports 1 foreign exchange student.
Financial data The stipend is $C4,000.
Duration 12 weeks, in the summer.
Number awarded Approximately 100 each year.
Deadline January of each year.

[438]
SAVOY FOUNDATION POSTDOCTORAL AND CLINICAL RESEARCH FELLOWSHIPS
Savoy Foundation
230 rue Foch
C.P. 69
Saint-Jean-sur-Richelieu, Québec J3B 6Z1
Canada
(450) 358-9779   Fax: (450) 346-1045
E-mail: epilepsy@savoy-foundation.ca
Web site: www.savoy-foundation.ca

Purpose To provide funding to postdoctoral researchers from any country who are interested in conducting research on epilepsy in Canada.
Eligibility Applicants must be established scientists (Ph.D.s or M.D.s) who are interested in conducting research into the biological, behavioral, or social science aspects of epilepsy. Fellowships are available to Canadian citizens or for projects conducted in Canada.
Financial data Grants up to $C25,000 are available.
Duration Up to 1 year; may be renewed 1 additional year and, in exceptional cases, for a third year.
Deadline January of each year.

[439]
SAVOY FOUNDATION RESEARCH GRANTS
Savoy Foundation
230 rue Foch
C.P. 69
Saint-Jean-sur-Richelieu, Québec J3B 6Z1
Canada
(450) 358-9779   Fax: (450) 346-1045
E-mail: epilepsy@savoy-foundation.ca
Web site: www.savoy-foundation.ca

Purpose To provide funding to clinicians and/or established scientists from any country who are interested in conducting research on epilepsy in Canada.
Eligibility Applicants must be clinicians or scientists who are interested in conducting research into the biological, behavioral, or social science aspects of epilepsy. Grants may be used for launching of a project, preliminary studies in preparation of a more substantial request to another agency, pursuit or completion of a project, contribution to the funding of a research project of particular interest in the field of epilepsy, or contribution to the funding of a scientific activity (e.g., publication, meeting) related to the field of epilepsy. Grants are available to Canadian citizens or for projects conducted in Canada.
Financial data Grants up to $C25,000 are available.
Duration Up to 1 year; nonrenewable.
Deadline January of each year.

[440]
SAVOY FOUNDATION STUDENTSHIPS

Savoy Foundation
230 rue Foch
C.P. 69
Saint-Jean-sur-Richelieu, Québec J3B 6Z1
Canada
(450) 358-9779 Fax: (450) 346-1045
E-mail: epilepsy@savoy-foundation.ca
Web site: www.savoy-foundation.ca

Purpose To provide funding to graduate students from any country who are interested in acquiring training or conducting research on epilepsy in Canada.

Eligibility Applicants must be graduate students who are interested in acquiring training or pursuing research in a biomedical discipline, the health sciences, or social sciences related to epilepsy. They must have a good undergraduate record and have arranged that a qualified researcher affiliated with a university and/or hospital will supervise their work. Coinciding registration in an M.Sc. or Ph.D. program is encouraged. Studentships are available to Canadian citizens or for projects/studies conducted in Canada.

Financial data The studentship is $C12,000 for the first year, with an increase of $C1,000 for each year of renewal. An annual grant of $C1,000 is awarded to the sponsoring laboratory or institution.

Duration 1 year; may be renewed for up to 3 additional years.

Deadline January of each year.

[441]
SOCIETY FOR THE ADVANCEMENT OF SCANDINAVIAN STUDIES TRAVEL GRANTS

Swedish Information Service
One Dag Hammarskjold Plaza, 45th Floor
New York, NY 10017-2201
(212) 751-5900 Fax: (212) 752-4789
E-mail: requests@swedeninfo.com
Web site: www.swedeninfo.com

Purpose To provide funding for travel associated with the study of or research on Swedish studies to members of the Society for the Advancement of Scandinavian Studies.

Eligibility This program is open to members of the society, preferably graduate students or untenured faculty members. Applicants must be interested in studying or conducting research in the following areas: Swedish language, linguistics, or literature. They may conduct this research in Sweden or in North America. Graduate students in the social sciences may use the grants for intensive Swedish language study in Sweden.

Financial data The amount awarded varies, depending upon the needs of the recipient.

Duration Up to 1 year.

Number awarded Varies; generally, up to 5 each year.

Deadline March of each year.

[442]
THEODORE ROOSEVELT MEMORIAL GRANTS

American Museum of Natural History
Attn: Office of Grants and Fellowships
Central Park West at 79th Street
New York, NY 10024-5192
(212) 769-5495 E-mail: bynum@amnh.org
Web site: www.amnh.org

Purpose To provide financial support for research on North American fauna.

Eligibility Although no formal educational restrictions for application exist, grants are principally intended to cover research expenses of advanced predoctoral candidates and postdoctoral researchers for projects to be conducted in North America. The proposed research must deal with North American fauna, except birds.

Financial data Awards range from $200 to $2,000 and average $1,400.

Duration Grants are intended for short-term research only.

Special features The Theodore Roosevelt Memorial Fund was established in 1960 to perpetuate the spirit of Roosevelt's lifelong concern with wildlife conservation in North America. It supports research projects anywhere in North America.

Number awarded Approximately 200 grants from this and other funds are awarded by the museum each year.

Deadline February of each year.

[443]
THOMAS O. ENDERS FELLOWSHIP

Association for Canadian Studies in the United States
1317 F Street, N.W., Suite 920
Washington, DC 20004-1151
(202) 393-2580 Fax: (202) 393-2582
E-mail: info@acsus.org
Web site: www.acsus.org

Purpose To provide funding to scholars who wish to conduct research in Canada on Canada and U.S.-Canadian relations.

Eligibility This program is open to 1) senior scholars; 2) postdoctoral candidates; 3) professionals in government or the diplomatic service; and 4) scholars at research institutions. All applicants must be proposing to conduct research in Canada on Canadian studies or U.S.-Canadian relations. Preference is given to bilingual (French and English) candidates who have not had the opportunity to be affiliated with a Canadian university during the previous 12 months. U.S. citizenship or permanent resident status is required.

Financial data Awards up to $30,000 are available. The host universities provide the fellow access to an office, library privileges, and an e-mail account during the tenure of the fellowship.

Duration Up to 9 months.

Special features The site of the fellowship varies; recently it was shared by McGill University and the Université de Montréal.

Number awarded 1 or more each year.

Deadline September of each year.

[444]
UNIVERSITY OF CALGARY CHAIR IN NORTH AMERICAN STUDIES

Council for International Exchange of Scholars
3007 Tilden Street, N.W., Suite 5L
Washington, DC 20008-3009
(202) 686-6245   Fax: (202) 362-3442
E-mail: scholars@cies.iie.org
Web site: www.iie.org/cies

Purpose To provide funding for senior scholars to teach Canadian–American relations in Canada.

Eligibility Applicants must have a record of academic and scholarly prominence in North American studies. They must be interested in teaching Canadian–American relations at a university in Canada. Fields may include anthropology, archaeology, economics, geography, history, linguistics, political science, psychology, or sociology, as long as they are approached in a North American context. U.S. citizenship is required.

Financial data The stipend is approximately $C15,000 plus $C20,000.

Duration 4 to 5 months.

Special features This is a Fulbright scholar program, sponsored by the Bureau of Educational and Cultural Affairs of the U.S. Department of State and administered by the Council for International Exchange of Scholars. The recipient teaches undergraduate and graduate courses as part of the Faculty of Social Sciences at the University of Calgary.

Number awarded 1 each year.

Deadline April of each year.

[445]
UNIVERSITY OF NEW BRUNSWICK CHAIR IN PROPERTY STUDIES

Council for International Exchange of Scholars
3007 Tilden Street, N.W., Suite 5L
Washington, DC 20008-3009
(202) 686-6245   Fax: (202) 362-3442
E-mail: scholars@cies.iie.org
Web site: www.iie.org/cies

Purpose To provide funding to senior scholars interested in teaching property studies at the University of New Brunswick in Canada.

Eligibility Applicants must have a record of academic and scholarly prominence in property studies. They must be interested in teaching property studies at the University of New Brunswick. Fields may include agriculture, anthropology, economics, environmental studies, geography, history, law, or public administration, as long as they relate to property systems. U.S. citizenship is required.

Financial data The stipend is approximately $25,000 per academic term.

Duration 4 to 5 months.

Special features This is a Fulbright scholar program, sponsored by the Bureau of Educational and Cultural Affairs of the U.S. Department of State and administered by the Council for International Exchange of Scholars. The recipient teaches undergraduate and graduate courses at the Centre for Property Studies at the University of New Brunswick.

Number awarded Approximately 1 each year.

Deadline April of each year.

[446]
UPPER ATMOSPHERIC FACILITIES PROGRAM

National Science Foundation
Directorate for Geosciences
Attn: Division of Atmospheric Sciences
4201 Wilson Boulevard, Room 775
Arlington, VA 22230
(703) 292-8531   TDD: (703) 292-5090
Web site: www.geo.nsf.gov/start.htm

Purpose To promote basic research on the structure and dynamics of the earth's upper atmosphere at facilities supported by the National Science Foundation (NSF).

Eligibility The facilities of the NSF Upper Atmospheric Facilities (UAF) program in Greenland, Peru, Puerto Rico, and Boston are available on a competitive basis to all qualified scientists. Research may be directed toward 1) supporting the operation and scientific research on the incoherent-scatter radars that comprise the longitudinal chain of NSF atmospheric facilities; and 2) ensuring that these radars are maintained as state-of-the-art research tools available to all interested and qualified scientists. Selection is based on scientific merit of the proposed research, capabilities of the radars to carry out the proposed observations, and availability of the requested time.

Financial data The amount of the award depends on the nature of the proposal.

Duration Varies, depending upon the nature of the proposed research.

Special features The UAF program supports the following 4 facilities: Sondrestrom Radar Facility at Sondre Stromfjord, Greenland (which is operated by SRI International under an NSF cooperative agreement); Millstone Hill Radar, near Boston, Massachusetts (which is operated by MIT under an NSF cooperative agreement); Arecibo Observatory at Arecibo, Puerto Rico (which is operated under contract to the NSF by the National Astronomy and Ionosphere Center of Cornell University); Jicamarca Radio Observatory, at the magnetic equator in Jicamarca, Peru (which is operated under an NSF cooperative agreement with Cornell University).

Deadline Applications may be submitted at any time.

[447]
VISITING FELLOWSHIPS IN CANADIAN GOVERNMENT LABORATORIES

Natural Science and Engineering Research Council of
  Canada
Attn: Visiting Fellowships Office
200 Kent Street
Ottawa, Ontario K1A 1H5
Canada
(613) 992-9169   E-mail: schol@nserc.ca
Web site: www.nserc.ca

Purpose To provide promising young scientists and engineers with an opportunity to work with well-established research groups or leaders in their fields and to foster close relationships among Canadian government laboratories, universities, and research institutions.

Eligibility Applicants should hold, or expect to receive, a doctorate from a recognized university prior to taking up the fellowship. They should not have received their doctorate more than 5 years prior to the date of application. In addition, they must be interested in conducting research at a participating institution in Canada. At least two-thirds of the awards must be made to Canadian citizens or permanent residents.

Financial data The award is $C35,184 per year; additionally, fellows and their families are provided with an allowance towards the cost of travel between the place of residence at the time the award is made and the laboratory at which the award is to be held. Both the stipend and the travel allowance are subject to Canadian income tax.

Duration 1 year; may be renewed 1 additional year.

Special features Laboratories that participate in this program include those of Agriculture and Agri-Food Canada; Canadian Museum of Nature; Canadian Space Agency; Environment Canada; Fisheries and Oceans Canada; Health Canada; Industry Canada; National Defence; National Research Council Canada; and Natural Resources Canada. The Natural Sciences and Engineering Research Council of Canada administers this program on behalf of the agencies involved.

Limitations Only applications received from Canadian citizens can be considered by the 6 laboratories of the Department of National Defence, although the 3 military colleges are prepared to consider applications from citizens of NATO countries as well as citizens of Canada.

Number awarded Varies each year.

Deadline March, July, and November of each year.

[448]
YORK UNIVERSITY DISTINGUISHED CHAIR

Council for International Exchange of Scholars
3007 Tilden Street, N.W., Suite 5L
Washington, DC 20008-3009
(202) 686-6245 Fax: (202) 362-3442
E-mail: scholars@cies.iie.org
Web site: www.iie.org/cies

Purpose To provide funding to senior scholars interested in teaching at York University in Canada.

Eligibility Applicants must have a record of academic and scholarly prominence in their field. They must be interested in lecturing at the graduate and undergraduate levels in a field that fits the programs at York University in North York, Ontario. U.S. citizenship is required.

Financial data The stipend is approximately $C20,000 per academic term.

Duration 4 and a half months.

Special features This is a Fulbright scholar program, sponsored by the Bureau of Educational and Cultural Affairs of the U.S. Department of State and administered by the Council for International Exchange of Scholars.

Number awarded Approximately 1 each year.

Deadline April of each year.

Europe/Scandinavia/British Isles

Described in this section are 493 scholarships, fellowships, grants, loans, and/or internships open to American students (high school through doctoral), professionals, and postdoctorates that support research or creative activities in eastern and western Europe, Scandinavia, and the British Isles. If you haven't already checked the "Any Foreign Country" chapter, be sure to do that next; identified there are 222 more sources of funding that can be used to support activities in these specific regions (as well as other areas of the world).

[449]
ACADEMY CENTRE FOR STUDIES AND RESEARCH IN INTERNATIONAL LAW AND INTERNATIONAL RELATIONS

Hague Academy of International Law
Attn: Secretariat
Peace Palace
Carnegieplein 2
2517 KJ The Hague
Netherlands
31 70 302 4242 Fax: 31 70 302 4153
E-mail: interlaw@planet.nl
Web site: www.hagueacademy.nl

Purpose To provide financial assistance to those interested in conducting research at the Centre for Studies and Research in International Law and International Relations at the Hague Academy of International Law.

Eligibility Applicants must hold an advanced university degree or have at least 3 years' practical experience in international affairs. They must be interested in conducting research at the Hague Academy and must demonstrate their capacity for research and their ability to contribute to group work. The maximum age is 40 years. Candidates must describe their interest in the subject chosen for the year's study (recently: Water Resources and International Law) and their qualifications to conduct research on it.

Financial data Participants receive an allowance of the Euro equivalent of 75 Dutch guilders per day and half of their traveling expenses, to the EUR equivalent of a maximum of Dfl 2,000.

Duration 3 weeks in the summer.

Special features Participants carry out their work in the Peace Palace in The Hague and use its library to conduct their research on the subject for that year.

Limitations Participants must submit a report on the subject of the program by November following the summer in which they attend the Centre.

Number awarded 24 participants are selected annually, 12 for the French-speaking section and 12 for the English-speaking section.

Deadline March of each year.

[450]
ACI BOOK AND DISSERTATION PRIZES

University of Minnesota
Attn: Center for Austrian Studies
314 Social Sciences Building
267 19th Avenue South
Minneapolis, MN 55455
(612) 624-9811 Fax: (612) 626-9004
E-mail: casahy@tc.umn.edu
Web site: www.cas.umn.edu

Purpose To provide funding for research in Austria to the authors of the best books and Ph.D. dissertations in Austrian studies.

Eligibility Eligible to be considered for this award are books and Ph.D. dissertations in Austrian studies completed within the past 2 years. The prizes are awarded in alternate years in 2 broad categories: "Historical and Contemporary Studies" (in even-numbered years) and "Cultural Studies" (in odd-numbered years). Nominations may be submitted by the author, publisher, or any other individual. Authors must be residents of North America, must hold U.S., Canadian, or Austrian citizenship, and must be interested in conducting additional research in Austria. Dissertations must have been completed at a university in North America.

Financial data The prize is a travel grant for the purpose of carrying out research in Austria.

Duration The prize is awarded annually.

Special features The Austrian Cultural Institute (ACI) in New York funds the prizes.

Number awarded 2 each year: 1 for a book and 1 for a Ph.D. dissertation.

Deadline January of each year.

[451]
ACLS/SSRC/NEH INTERNATIONAL AND AREA STUDIES FELLOWSHIPS

American Council of Learned Societies
Attn: Office of Fellowships and Grants
228 East 45th Street
New York, NY 10017-3398
(212) 697-1505 Fax: (212) 949-8058
E-mail: grants@acls.org
Web site: www.acls.org/felguide.htm

Purpose To provide funding to postdoctoral scholars for research on the societies and cultures of Asia, Africa, the Near and Middle East, Latin America, eastern Europe, and the former Soviet Union.

Eligibility This program is open to U.S. citizens and residents who have lived in the United States for at least 3 years. Applicants must have a Ph.D. degree and not have received supported research leave time for at least 3 years prior to the start of the proposed research. They must be interested in conducting humanities and humanities-related social science research on the societies and cultures of Asia, Africa, the Near and Middle East, Latin America, east Europe, or the former Soviet Union. Selection is based on the intellectual merit of the proposed research and the likelihood that it will produce significant and innovative scholarship. Applications are particularly invited from women and members of minority groups.

Financial data The maximum grant is $50,000 for full professors and equivalent, $40,000 for associate professors and equivalent, and $30,000 for assistant professors and equivalent. These fellowships may not be held concurrently with another major fellowship.

Duration 6 to 12 months.

Special features This program is jointly supported by the American Council of Learned Societies (ACLS) and the Social Science Research Council (SSRC), with funding provided by the National Endowment for the Humanities (NEH).

Number awarded Approximately 10 each year.

Deadline September of each year.

[452]
ACTR/ACCELS COMBINED RESEARCH AND LANGUAGE TRAINING PROGRAM

American Councils for International Education
Attn: Program Officer, Russian and Eurasian Programs
1776 Massachusetts Avenue, N.W., Suite 700
Washington, DC 20036
(202) 833-7522				Fax: (202) 833-7523
E-mail: outbound@actr.org
Web site: www.actr.org

Purpose To provide funding to U.S. graduate students and faculty interested in combining research with language training in the non-Russian languages of the former Soviet Union.

Eligibility This program is open to graduate students, Ph.D. candidates, faculty, and scholars at different professional levels. Applicants must be U.S. citizens and proposing a program of research combined with supplemental language instruction in participating nations: Armenia, Azerbaijan, Belarus, Georgia, Kazakhstan, Kyrgyzstan, Moldova, Russia, Turkmenistan, Ukraine, and Uzbekistan. They must have attained at least an intermediate level of proficiency to conduct research while receiving language training. In addition to the support for that training, funding is available for research in the humanities, social sciences, literatures, linguistics, and area studies of the region.

Financial data The amount of the award depends on the nature of the proposal.

Duration At least 3 months.

Special features This program, initiated in 1986, is funded by the Bureau of Educational and Cultural Affairs of the Department of State and administered by the American Councils for International Education, the American Council of Teachers of Russian (ACTR) and the American Council for Collaboration and Education in Language Study (ACCELS).

Number awarded Approximately 25 each year.

Deadline January of each year for summer, fall, and academic year programs; September of each year for spring programs.

[453]
ACTR/ACCELS RESEARCH SCHOLAR PROGRAM

American Councils for International Education
Attn: Program Officer, Russian and Eurasian Programs
1776 Massachusetts Avenue, N.W., Suite 700
Washington, DC 20036
(202) 833-7522				Fax: (202) 833-7523
E-mail: outbound@actr.org
Web site: www.actr.org

Purpose To provide funding to U.S. graduate students and faculty interested in studying or conducting research in the Newly Independent States (NIS) of the former Soviet Union.

Eligibility This program is open to graduate students, Ph.D. candidates, faculty, and scholars at different professional levels. Applicants must be U.S. citizens and proposing a program of study or research at key academic centers in participating nations: Armenia, Azerbaijan, Belarus, Georgia, Kazakhstan, Kyrgyzstan, Moldova, Russia, Turkmenistan, Ukraine, and Uzbekistan. Funding is available for research or study in the humanities, social sciences, literatures, linguistics, and area studies of the region.

Financial data The amount of the award depends on the nature of the proposal.

Duration At least 3 months.

Special features This program, initiated in 1986, is funded by the Bureau of Educational and Cultural Affairs of the Department of State and administered by the American Councils for International Education, the American Council of Teachers of Russian (ACTR) and the American Council for Collaboration and Education in Language Study (ACCELS).

Number awarded Approximately 20 each year.

Deadline January of each year for work during the summer or fall; September of each year for work during the spring.

[454]
A.D. TRENDALL FELLOWSHIP

University of London
Attn: Institute of Classical Studies
Senate House
Malet Street
London WC1E 7HU
England
44 20 7862 8700				Fax: 44 20 7862 8722
Web site: www.sas.ac.uk/icls/institute/aboutin.htm

Purpose To provide an opportunity for classical scholars from universities outside the United Kingdom to conduct research at the University of London.

Eligibility This program is open to scholars of the classics from universities outside the United Kingdom. Applicants must be interested in working as a visiting fellow at the University of London's Institute of Classical Studies. Preference is given to scholars whose research interests are in south Italian archaeology, history, or art history.

Financial data A grant of 1,500 pounds is provided to help pay travel, accommodation, and research expenses. Fellows also receive use of office and computer facilities.

Duration Fellows are expected to spend at least 6 weeks at the institute.

Number awarded 1 every other year.

Deadline January of the year of the award.

[455]
ADDISON WHEELER FELLOWSHIPS

University of Durham
Attn: Personnel Office
Old Shire Hall
Durham DH1 3HP
England
44 191 374 3660				Fax: 44 191 374 3740
E-mail: Philippa.Hardy@durham.ac.uk
Web site: www.dur.ac.uk

Purpose To support beginning scholars who wish to conduct research in the sciences at the University of Durham in England.

Eligibility Applications are invited from researchers who recently earned their Ph.D. They may be from any country, must be under the age of 28, and must be interested in conducting research in the life sciences (or related fields) while affiliated with the University of Durham.

Financial data The amount of the stipend varies, from 15,159 to 22,785 pounds per year.
Duration From 3 to 5 years.
Limitations The fellowship is awarded every 2 or 3 years when vacancies occur.
Deadline June in the years when an award is to be made.

[456]
ADOLFO OMODEO SCHOLARSHIP
Italian Institute of Historical Studies
Palazzo Filomarino
via Benedetto Croce 12
I-80134 Naples
Italy
39 81 551 7159   Fax: 39 81 551 2390

Purpose To provide financial assistance to college graduates for historical research in Naples, Italy.
Eligibility Applicants may be citizens of any country who have at least a bachelor's degree from an accredited college or university and who desire to conduct research at the Italian Institute of Historical Studies (Istituto Italiano per gli Studi Storici) in Naples.
Financial data The award is the Euro equivalent of 12,000,000 Italian lire.
Duration 8 months.
Special features Recipients must reside in Naples and attend weekly seminars.
Number awarded 1 each year.
Deadline October of each year.

[457]
ADRIAN RESEARCH FELLOWSHIP
University of Cambridge
Darwin College
Attn: Master
Silver Street
Cambridge CB3 9EU
England
44 1223 335660   Fax: 44 1223 335667
E-mail: deanery@dar.cam.ac.uk
Web site: www.dar.cam.ac.uk

Purpose To provide funding to postdoctoral scholars interested in conducting research in the field of continental European studies at Darwin College of the University of Cambridge in England.
Eligibility This program is open to scholars from any country who are interested in conducting research at Darwin College in the field of continental European studies, including historical, literary, linguistic, political, economic, or social aspects. Work that principally or exclusively focuses on British materials is not eligible. Applicants must be younger than 35 years of age and either 1) hold a Ph.D. or equivalent degree or 2) be able to present substantial amounts of written work, published or unpublished.
Financial data The annual stipend is 13,050 or 13,930 pounds, depending on age and experience. Other benefits include limited free meals in college, a travel and research allowance of up to 1,000 pounds per year, and a conference subsidy of 500 pounds per year.
Duration 3 years; may be renewed for 1 additional year.
Special features This fellowship is funded by a donation from Trinity College, Cambridge. Along with their research, fellows may engage in undergraduate teaching up to 6 hours per week at Trinity College or another college at Cambridge for the standard rate of pay.
Number awarded This fellowship is offered periodically.
Deadline October in the years it is available.

[458]
AEGEAN INITIATIVE IN GREECE AND TURKEY
Council for International Exchange of Scholars
3007 Tilden Street, N.W., Suite 5L
Washington, DC 20008-3009
(202) 686-6246   Fax: (202) 362-3442
E-mail: scholars@cies.iie.org
Web site: www.iie.org/cies

Purpose To provide funding to American scholars interested in conducting seminars or lecturing in Greece and Turkey.
Eligibility This program is open to U.S. citizens who possess a doctorate in an area other than the hard sciences. Areas of potential interest include, but are not limited to, regional economic development, disaster management and emergency preparedness, environmental protection and advocacy, ecotourism, and tourism development and management. Applicants must be interested in dividing their time equally between Greece and Turkey, lecturing and/or conducting seminars in an area of specialization of relevance to both countries. English is sufficient for lecturing.
Financial data During stays in Greece, the monthly maintenance allowance is the Euro equivalent of 450,000 to 540,000 Greek drachmas, depending on the number of accompanying dependents. During stays in Turkey, scholars receive a base stipend of $1,500 to $2,000 per month and a maintenance allowance of $500 per month. Allowances to cover international and intercountry travel, as well as related miscellaneous expenses, are also provided.
Duration 3 to 4 months.
Special features This is a Fulbright scholar program, sponsored by the Bureau of Educational and Cultural Affairs of the U.S. Department of State and administered by the Council for International Exchange of Scholars. It was established in 1999.
Number awarded Up to 2 each year.
Deadline July of each year.

[459]
ALBERT GALLATIN FELLOWSHIP IN INTERNATIONAL AFFAIRS

University of Virginia
Attn: International Studies Office
208 Minor Hall
Charlottesville, VA 22903
(804) 982-3013   Fax: (804) 982-3011
E-mail: rgd@virginia.edu
Web site: virginia.edu/~intstu

Purpose To provide an opportunity for American Ph.D. candidates in international studies to conduct research at the Graduate Institute of International Studies in Geneva.

Eligibility This program is open to U.S. citizens who are actively engaged in doctoral research in some aspect of international studies. Applicants must possess a speaking and reading knowledge of French adequate for research as well as for participation in technically-oriented discussions and lectures. They must be interested in conducting their research in Geneva.

Financial data The fellowship provides a stipend of $11,250 and round-trip transportation between New York to Geneva.

Duration 9 months, from October through July of each year.

Special features The Graduate Institute of International Studies in Geneva was founded in 1927 as a center for the study of international relations; it provides doctoral instruction in international law and politics, international economics, international institutions, and international development. The Feris Foundation of America was established in 1972 to promote study and research in international affairs and to foster cultural understanding between the United States and other countries. From 1976 through 1994, it financed the Albert Gallatin Fellowships. In 1994, it transferred its assets to the University of Virginia, which currently administers this program.

Number awarded Varies each year.

Deadline February of each year.

[460]
ALEXANDER S. ONASSIS PUBLIC BENEFIT FOUNDATION SHORT-TERM RESEARCH GRANTS

Alexander S. Onassis Public Benefit Foundation
Attn: Public Relations
7 Eschinou Street
GR-105 58 Athens
Greece
30 1 331 0902, ext. 140   Fax: 30 1 323 6044
E-mail: pubrel@onassis.gr
Web site: www.onassis.gr

Purpose To provide funding for research to professionals and scholars from countries other than Greece who are interested in coming to Greece for a short period of time to conduct research in the humanistic or political sciences at an educational or research institute.

Eligibility This program is open to researchers from outside of Greece who are interested in visiting the country to conduct research or to collaborate with an educational or research institute/organization. Applicants must be academicians or university professors whose scholarly or artistic work in the humanistic or political sciences has been highly acclaimed. While, in principal, this program is aimed at persons of other than Greek nationality, persons of Greek descent (second generation only) are also eligible, provided they are permanently residing and working outside of Greece and have studied or are currently studying at universities outside of Greece. In addition, scholars of Greek descent or citizenship may apply if they have worked for at least 10 years at a university or research institute outside of Greece. Also eligible for the program are teachers of the Greek language who are of Greek descent or citizenship, if they work at an elementary or secondary school outside of Greece. Knowledge of the Greek language is not required; however, preference is given to applicants with an elementary knowledge of Greek.

Financial data The grant provides a monthly allowance (Euro equivalent of 350,000 Greek drachmas) plus room and board (EUR equivalent of 500,000 drhs if the grantee is accompanied by his/her spouse). The foundation also covers travel expenses from and to the country of origin.

Duration 1 month.

Limitations During their stay in Greece, recipients may be asked to deliver a lecture or seminar at either the Onassis Cultural Centre of Athens or at a university or other scholarly center in Greece.

Number awarded Up to 10 each year.

Deadline January of each year.

[461]
ALEXANDER S. ONASSIS PUBLIC BENEFIT FOUNDATION SIX-MONTH RESEARCH GRANTS

Alexander S. Onassis Public Benefit Foundation
Attn: Public Relations
7 Eschinou Street
GR-105 58 Athens
Greece
30 1 331 0902, ext. 140   Fax: 30 1 323 6044
E-mail: pubrel@onassis.gr
Web site: www.onassis.gr

Purpose To provide funding for research to academicians from countries other than Greece who are interested in coming to Greece to conduct research in the humanistic or political sciences at an educational or research institute.

Eligibility This program is open to faculty members from outside of Greece who are interested in visiting the country to conduct research or to collaborate with an educational or research institute/organization. Applicants must be no more than 55 years of age and their work in the humanistic or political sciences must have been highly acclaimed. While, in principal, this program is aimed at persons of other than Greek nationality, persons of Greek descent (second generation only) are also eligible, provided they are permanently residing and working outside of Greece and have studied or are currently studying at universities outside of Greece. In addition, scholars of Greek descent or citizenship may apply if they have worked for at least 10 years at a university or research institute outside of Greece. Also eligible for the program are teachers of the Greek language who are of Greek descent or citizenship, if they work at an elementary or secondary school outside of Greece. Knowledge of the Greek language is not required; however, preference is given to applicants with an elementary knowledge of Greek.

Financial data The grant provides a monthly allowance (Euro equivalent of 300,000 Greek drachmas) plus accommodations in a furnished apartment in central Athens. The foundation also covers travel expenses from and to the country of origin.
Duration Up to 6 months.
Limitations During their stay in Greece, recipients may be asked to deliver a lecture or seminar at either the Onassis Cultural Centre of Athens or at a university or other scholarly center in Greece.
Number awarded Up to 15 each year.
Deadline January of each year.

[462]
ALICE TONG SZE RESEARCH FELLOWSHIP

University of Cambridge
Lucy Cavendish College
Attn: President's Secretary
Lady Margaret Road
Cambridge CB3 0BU
England
44 1223 332196   Fax: 44 1223 332178
E-mail: bjy21@cam.ac.uk
Web site: www.lucy-cav.cam.ac.uk

Purpose To provide funding to women postdoctoral scholars interested in conducting research in the arts at Lucy Cavendish College of the University of Cambridge in England.
Eligibility This program is open to women from any country who hold a doctorate or whose dissertation is under examination. Applicants must be interested in conducting research at Lucy Cavendish College in the arts, especially languages, that relates scholarship to current issues facing the world.
Financial data The stipend is approximately 11,000 pounds per year. Other allowances may be available for accommodations, child care, and/or research expenses.
Duration 1 year; may be renewed for up to 2 additional years, subject to satisfactory progress and annual reports.
Number awarded This fellowship is offered from time to time.
Deadline January in the years it is available.

[463]
ALL SOULS COLLEGE POSTDOCTORAL RESEARCH FELLOWSHIPS

University of Oxford
All Souls College
Attn: Warden's Secretary
High Street
Oxford OX1 4AL
England
44 1865 279315
Web site: www.all-souls.ox.ac.uk

Purpose To provide financial assistance to beginning researchers who wish to conduct social science research while affiliated with All Souls College of the University of Oxford in England.
Eligibility Applicants must have completed a doctoral degree, be younger than 30 years of age, and be interested in conducting research at All Souls College. Selection is based on submitted original research, a proposal for future research, a curriculum vitae, academic references, and an interview.
Financial data Fellows receive an annual salary that ranges from 14,800 to 23,322 pounds; rooms, dinners, and lunches without charge; and a housing allowance for those living out of college.
Duration Up to 5 years.
Number awarded 2 each even-numbered year.
Deadline September of each odd-numbered year.

[464]
AMBASSADOR AND MRS. DAY OLIN MOUNT SCHOLARSHIP

Institute of International Education
Attn: Student Programs Division
809 United Nations Plaza
New York, NY 10017-3580
(212) 984-5330   Fax: (212) 984-5325
Web site: www.iie.org/fulbright

Purpose To provide funding to American graduate students interested in conducting research at the Vestmannaeyjar Research Center in Iceland on the relationship between humans and the ocean.
Eligibility This program is open to advanced graduate students at universities in the United States in fields (such as anthropology, social sciences, environmental sciences, ocean sciences, and marine biology) that involve the relationship between humans and the oceans. Applicants must be interested in conducting research in Iceland at the center.
Financial data The Icelandic government provides a monthly maintenance stipend. Allowances for international travel, baggage, and books are also included.
Duration 4 months, beginning in June.
Special features The Vestmannaeyjar Research Center, affiliated with the University of Iceland, is located in the Westman Islands of the North Atlantic. It has 5 laboratories, a library, an aquarium, 2 research boats, and an adjacent folk museum. This program is administered in the United States by the Institute of International Education (IIE) as part of the Fulbright program. Students who are currently enrolled in the United States are to apply through the Fulbright program adviser on their campus; at-large applicants (those not currently enrolled) may obtain applications and information directly from the IIE.
Number awarded 1 each year.
Deadline October of each year.

[465]
AMERICA-NORWAY HERITAGE FUND

Norsemen's Federation
Attn: Executive Secretary
Raadhusgata 23 B
N-0158 Oslo 1
Norway
47 2 335 7170   Fax: 47 2 335 7175
E-mail: norseman@online.no

Purpose To award grants to selected Americans for travel to Norway.

Eligibility Americans of Norwegian descent who have made significant contributions to American culture and are interested in traveling in Norway are eligible to apply. They must submit a curriculum vitae, a concrete proposal, an estimated budget, and 3 letters of recommendation.

Financial data Travel expenses and an honorarium are provided.

Duration 1 to 2 weeks, between October and April.

Special features The American-Norway Heritage Fund was established in 1985 by a grant from the Lutheran Brotherhood Insurance Society to the Norsemen's Federation and the Norway-America Association (Drammensveien 20 C, N-0255 Oslo 2, Norway). Applications may be sent to either organization. Recipients share the result of their work with the people of Norway through lectures, exhibitions, and/or performances at 2 to 4 different geographic locations in Norway. With these, it is hoped that Norwegians will become better acquainted with the cultural, economic, political, and religious contributions made by Norwegian Americans in the building of America.

Deadline February of each year.

[466]
AMERICAN HUNGARIAN FOUNDATION FELLOWSHIPS AND SCHOLARSHIPS

American Hungarian Foundation
Attn: President
300 Somerset Street
P.O. Box 1084
New Brunswick, NJ 08903-1084
(732) 846-5777   Fax: (732) 249-7033
E-mail: info@ahfoundation.org
Web site: www.ahfoundation.org

Purpose To support the training or research of students, professionals, and postdoctorates who are interested in careers in Hungarian studies.

Eligibility Fellowship applicants must be either 1) currently-enrolled full-time undergraduate or graduate students at academic institutions in the United States or Canada or 2) individuals who are well established in an academic or professional position. They must be interested in conducting scientific research that increases the existing stock of knowledge about Hungary and the Hungarian people; in pursuing advanced studies about the Hungarian culture; or in publishing works that describe the results of existing research studies. No age limit is set for applicants, but fellowships are generally not offered to persons under 18 years of age. The funded project may take place in Hungary, the United States, or any other appropriate location.

Financial data Fellowship awards vary in amount, according to demonstrated need and availability of funds.

Duration Up to 1 year.

Number awarded 1 or more each year.

[467]
AMERICAN SCHOOL OF CLASSICAL STUDIES ADVANCED FELLOWSHIPS

American School of Classical Studies at Athens
Attn: Committee on Admissions and Fellowships
6-8 Charlton Street
Princeton, NJ 08540-5232
(609) 683-0800   Fax: (609) 924-0578
E-mail: ascsa@ascsa.org
Web site: www.ascsa.org

Purpose To provide financial support to American or Canadian graduate students who are interested in researching archaeology or history at the American School of Classical Studies at Athens.

Eligibility Applicants must be regular members of the American School of Classical Studies at Athens who have already completed the regular term or 1 year as an associate member. Regular membership is open to graduate students in classical studies (literature, archaeology, history) in the United States or Canada who have finished at least 1 year of graduate work but who have not yet completed the Ph.D. degree. Associate membership is open to 1) graduate students in classics who have passed the Ph.D. qualifying exams but do not intend to follow the regular program of research in literature, archaeology, or history, and 2) similarly advanced graduate students who are working outside the area of classics but studying history of art, anthropology, prehistory, studies in post-classical Greece, or related fields. Selection is based on recommendations from the applicants' advisors and the record of their previous work at the school.

Financial data The stipend is $8,840 in cash plus fees, room, and board.

Duration 1 academic year.

Special features This program includes the following named fellowships: the Samuel H. Kress Fellowship in Art History, the Gorham Phillips Stevens Fellowship in the History of Architecture, the Homer A. and Dorothy B. Thompson Fellowship in the Study of Pottery, and 3 unrestricted fellowships: the Edward Capps Fellowship, the Doreen Canaday Spitzer Fellowship, and the Eugene Vanderpool Fellowship.

Number awarded Several each year.

Deadline February of each year.

[468]
AMERICAN SCHOOL OF CLASSICAL STUDIES SENIOR ASSOCIATE MEMBERSHIP FELLOWSHIPS

American School of Classical Studies at Athens
Attn: Committee on Admissions and Fellowships
6-8 Charlton Street
Princeton, NJ 08540-5232
(609) 683-0800   Fax: (609) 924-0578
E-mail: ascsa@ascsa.org
Web site: www.ascsa.org

Purpose To provide financial support to American or Canadian postdoctoral scholars who are interested in conducting research at the American School of Classical Studies at Athens.

Eligibility This program is open to independent and postdoctoral scholars who are interested in becoming senior associate members of the school. Applicants must be interested in conducting research that is appropriate to the activities of the school. That includes postdoctoral scholarship in classical studies (literature, archaeology, and history) but also in such related fields as history of art, anthropology, prehistory, and studies in post-classical Greece.

Financial data The stipend depends on the nature of the proposed research project.

Duration Up to 1 academic year.

Number awarded Varies each year.

Deadline Applications may be submitted at any time.

[469]
AMERICAN SCHOOL OF CLASSICAL STUDIES STUDENT ASSOCIATE MEMBERSHIP FELLOWSHIPS

American School of Classical Studies at Athens
Attn: Committee on Admissions and Fellowships
6-8 Charlton Street
Princeton, NJ 08540-5232
(609) 683-0800   Fax: (609) 924-0578
E-mail: ascsa@ascsa.org
Web site: www.ascsa.org

Purpose To provide financial support to American or Canadian graduate students who are interested in researching archaeology or history at the American School of Classical Studies at Athens.

Eligibility This program is open to student associate members of the American School of Classical Studies at Athens; that status includes 1) graduate students in classics who have passed the Ph.D. qualifying exams but do not intend to follow the regular program of research in literature, archaeology, or history, and 2) similarly advanced graduate students who are working outside the area of classics but studying history of art, anthropology, prehistory, studies in post-classical Greece, or related fields. Applicants must be students at institutions in Canada or the United States who are proposing a program of research at the school in Athens.

Financial data The stipend is $8,840 in cash plus fees, room, and board.

Duration 1 academic year.

Number awarded Several each year.

Deadline January of each year.

[470]
AMERICAN WOMEN'S CLUB IN SWEDEN TRAVEL GRANTS

American Women's Club in Sweden
Attn: Scholarship Foundation
P.O. Box 12054
S-102 22 Stockholm
Sweden
Web site: www.awc.nu

Purpose To provide travel assistance to American women who wish to study or conduct research in Sweden.

Eligibility This program is open to American women citizens, aged 18 to 25, who have been accepted for a period of study or research at a Swedish educational institution or agency. Applicants must write a letter describing themselves and their anticipated study and stating why they should be chosen for the scholarship.

Financial data The program pays for a round-trip ticket between New York City to Sweden.

Number awarded 1 or more each year.

Deadline March of each year.

[471]
AMERICAN-ITALIAN CANCER FOUNDATION REGULAR FELLOWSHIPS

American-Italian Cancer Foundation
112 East 71st Street
New York, NY 10021
(212) 628-9090   Fax: (212) 517-6089
E-mail: aicf@aicfonline.org
Web site: www.aicfonline.org

Purpose To provide funding to young scientists in Italy and the United States who are interested in pursuing cancer research training in the United States and Italy, respectively.

Eligibility Applicants must have obtained a Ph.D., M.D., D.Sc., or D.V.M. degree not more than 3 years prior to the date of application. They must be Italians interested in working in the United States or Americans interested in working in Italy. The proposed activity must be a program of research and advanced training in pre-clinical or clinical research in cancer. Selection is based on the qualifications, experience, and productivity of the candidate and the host sponsor; merit of the research proposal; and training and research environment available to the candidate.

Financial data The stipend is $30,000 per year.

Duration 1 year; may be renewed 1 additional year.

Special features The American-Italian Cancer Foundation serves as the U.S. representative of the European School of Oncology.

Number awarded Varies each year.

Deadline February of each year.

[472]
AMERICAN-ITALIAN CANCER FOUNDATION SPECIAL FELLOWSHIPS

American-Italian Cancer Foundation
112 East 71st Street
New York, NY 10021
(212) 628-9090   Fax: (212) 517-6089
E-mail: aicf@aicfonline.org
Web site: www.aicfonline.org

Purpose To provide funding to young scientists in Italy and the United States who are interested in pursuing cancer research training in the United States and Italy, respectively.

Eligibility Applicants must have obtained a Ph.D., M.D., D.Sc., or D.V.M. degree prior to the date of application. They must be Italians interested in working in the United States or Americans interested in working in Italy. The proposed activity must be a program of research and advanced training in pre-clinical or clinical research in cancer. Selection is based on the qualifications, experience, and productivity of the candidate and the host sponsor; merit of the research proposal; and training and research environment available to the candidate.

Financial data The stipend is $2,000 per month.

Duration 3 to 6 months.

Special features The American-Italian Cancer Foundation serves as the U.S. representative of the European School of Oncology.

Number awarded Varies each year.

Deadline February of each year.

[473]
AMERICAN-SCANDINAVIAN FOUNDATION FELLOWSHIPS

American-Scandinavian Foundation
58 Park Avenue
New York, NY 10016-3007
(212) 879-9779   Fax: (212) 249-3444
E-mail: asf@amscan.org
Web site: www.amscan.org

Purpose To encourage longer-term (1 year) advanced study or research activities in the Scandinavian countries.

Eligibility Awards are open to U.S. citizens and permanent residents who will have completed their undergraduate education at the time their overseas program begins. They must be interested in a program of study or research that will last 1 year. Preference is given to graduate students at the dissertation level and to applicants who have not previously had a foundation award. Team projects are eligible, but each member must submit a fully-documented application. Selection is based on the significance and feasibility of the proposal for study or research, the qualifications of the applicant to pursue the program, and the special merit of pursuing the program in Scandinavia. Language competence and prior arrangements for affiliation at a host institution in Scandinavia are also taken into consideration.

Financial data The stipend is $18,000.

Duration 1 year.

Special features This study/research program is supported by a number of named funds: for Denmark: Henrik Kauffmann Fund, Helen Lee and Emil Lassen Fund, Amanda E. Roleson Fund, and Hans K. Lorentzen Fund; for Denmark or Norway: Carol and Hans Christian Sonne Fund; for Finland: Carl G. and Rikke Fredriksen Barth Fund, Martha and Jack McFall Fund, Finnish Fund, and Thor and Saimie Soderholm Fund; for Iceland: Thor Thors Memorial Fund; for Norway: Crown Princess Märtha Friendship Fund, King Olav V Fund, Norwegian Thanksgiving Fund, Haakon Styri Fund, and Alice and Corrin Strong Fund; for Sweden: John G. Bergquist Fund, Selma C. Swanson Fund, and Thord-Gray Memorial Fund; for Scandinavia in general: Sven Bernhard Fund and Former Fellows Fund.

Limitations There is a non-refundable $10 application fee. Recipients may reapply for support, but not for 2 consecutive grants. Applicants are expected to arrange their academic or professional affiliation in Scandinavia as far in advance as possible. The foundation does not provide funds for acquisition of language skills, research assistants, loan obligations, publication costs, retroactive program support, equipment purchases, institutional overhead, study at English-language institutions, beginning studies of any subject matter, support for dependents, performances or exhibitions, repayment of loans or other personal obligations, conference attendance, foregone salary, or supplementation of substantial sabbatical support. Applications may not be submitted by fax.

Number awarded Varies each year; recently, 10 of these fellowships were awarded.

Deadline October of each year.

[474]
AMERICAN-SCANDINAVIAN FOUNDATION GRANTS

American-Scandinavian Foundation
58 Park Avenue
New York, NY 10016-3007
(212) 879-9779   Fax: (212) 249-3444
E-mail: asf@amscan.org
Web site: www.amscan.org

Purpose To encourage short-term advanced study or research activities in the Scandinavian countries.

Eligibility Awards are open to U.S. citizens and permanent residents who will have completed their undergraduate education at the time their overseas program begins. Preference is given to scholars and professionals (senior or junior) who are planning a research or study program in Scandinavia that will last only a few weeks or months. Team projects are eligible, but each member must submit a fully-documented application. Selection is based on the significance and feasibility of the proposal for study or research, the qualifications of the applicant to pursue the program, and the special merit of pursuing the program in Scandinavia. Language competence and prior arrangements for affiliation at a host institution in Scandinavia are also taken into consideration.

Financial data The award is $3,000.

Duration From 1 to 3 months.

Special features This study/research program is made up of a number of named funds: for Denmark: Henrik Kauffmann Fund, Helen Lee and Emil Lassen Fund, Amanda E. Roleson Fund, and Hans K. Lorentzen Fund; for Denmark or Norway: Carol and Hans Christian Sonne Fund; for Finland: Carl G. and Rikke Fredriksen Barth Fund, Martha and Jack McFall Fund, Finnish Fund, and Thor and Saimie Soderholm Fund; for Iceland: Thor Thors Memorial Fund; for Norway: Crown Princess Märtha Friendship Fund, King Olav V Fund, Norwegian Thanksgiving Fund, Haakon Styri Fund, and Alice and Corrin Strong Fund; for Sweden: John G. Bergquist Fund, Selma C. Swanson Fund, and Thord-Gray Memorial Fund; for Scandinavia in general: Sven Bernhard Fund and Former Fellows Fund.

Limitations There is a non-refundable $10 application fee. Recipients may reapply for support, but not for 2 consecutive grants. Applicants are expected to arrange their academic or professional affiliation in Scandinavia as far in advance as possible. The foundation does not provide funds for acquisition of language skills, research assistants, loan obligations, publication costs, retroactive program support, equipment purchases, institutional overhead, study at English-language institutions, beginning studies of any subject matter, support for dependents, performances or exhibitions, repayment of loans or other personal obligations, conference attendance, foregone salary, or supplementation of substantial sabbatical support. Applications may not be submitted by fax.

Number awarded Varies each year; recently, 15 of these grants were awarded.
Deadline October of each year.

[475]
ANDREW W. MELLON POSTDOCTORAL RESEARCH FELLOWSHIPS AT THE AMERICAN ACADEMY IN ROME

American Academy in Rome
Attn: Fellowship Coordinator
7 East 60th Street
New York, NY 10022-1001
(212) 751-7200   Fax: (212) 751-7220
E-mail: info@aarome.org
Web site: www.aarome.org

Purpose To provide an opportunity for American postdoctoral scholars in art history, classical studies and archaeology, and post-classical humanistic/modern Italian studies to engage in research at the American Academy in Rome.

Eligibility This program is open to U.S. citizens or permanent residents who have a Ph.D. in 1 of the fields of the awards. Applicants must be an assistant professor, have been appointed associate professor within the previous 2 years, or be independent scholars who have received the Ph.D. within the prior 6 or 7 years. Their field of study may be 1) classical studies and archaeology; 2) history of art, or 3) post-classical humanistic studies (political, economic, cultural, and church history, or history of literature and musicology, all since 300 A.D.) and modern Italian studies. They must be interested in conducting their research at the American Academy in Rome.

Financial data The fellowship provides a stipend of up to $20,000, meals, a bedroom with private bath, and a study or studio. Fellows with children under 18 are housed outside the McKim, Mead & White building and are provided with an allowance that helps cover the cost of off-campus housing.

Duration 10 months, from mid-September through mid-July.

Special features The American Academy in Rome, founded in 1894 by the American architect Charles F. McKim, is a center for independent study and advanced research in the fine arts and humanities. It consists of a School of Fine Arts (including architecture, landscape architecture, design arts, painting and sculpture, musical composition, and literature) and a School of Classical Studies (including classical studies and archaeology, history of art, and post-classical humanistic/modern Italian studies). This program is funded by the Andrew W. Mellon Foundation.

Number awarded 3 each year, including 1 each in classical studies and archaeology, history of art, and post-classical humanistic/modern Italian studies.

Deadline November of each year.

[476]
ANIMAL HEALTH TRUST RESEARCH GRANTS

Animal Health Trust
Lanwades Park
Kentford, Newmarket
Suffolk CB8 7UU
England
44 1638 751000   Fax: 44 1638 750410
E-mail: info@aht.org.uk
Web site: www.aht.org.uk

Purpose To provide funding for veterinarians or scientists to conduct research on farm animal diseases at approved institutions in the United Kingdom.

Eligibility This program is open to veterinarians or scientists from any country who have postdoctoral research experience. Applicants must be interested in conducting research at approved institutions in the United Kingdom. Proposed research must deal with the diagnosis, cure, and/or prevention of farm animal diseases. Finalists must be interviewed in the United Kingdom.

Financial data Grants range up to 30,000 pounds per year.

Duration From 1 to 3 years.

Special features This program includes 2 named funds, the A.D. and P.A. Allen Memorial Fund and the Livesey Memorial Fund.

Number awarded Up to 6 each year.

Deadline March of each year.

[477]
ANITA CECIL O'DONOVAN FELLOWSHIP

American Schools of Oriental Research
Attn: Administrative Director
656 Beacon Street, Fifth Floor
Boston, MA 02215-2010
(617) 353-6570   Fax: (617) 353-6575
E-mail: asor@bu.edu
Web site: www.asor.org

Purpose To provide funding to students who are interested in a period of residence at the Cyprus American Archaeological Research Institute (CAARI) in Nicosia, Cyprus.

Eligibility Eligible to apply are undergraduate and graduate students from any country who wish to conduct research in the social sciences or humanities at CAARI in Cyprus.

Financial data The stipend is $1,000.

Duration 1 to 3 months.

Limitations Recipients are expected to reside at CAARI and participate actively in its work.

Number awarded 1 each year.

Deadline January of each year.

[478]
ANNA BIEGUN WARBURG JUNIOR RESEARCH FELLOWSHIP

University of Oxford
St. Anne's College
Attn: Senior Tutor's Secretary
Oxford OX2 6HS
England
44 1865 274800   Fax: 44 1865 274899
Web site: www.stannes.ox.ac.uk

Purpose To provide funding to doctoral candidates from any university who wish to conduct research in the human and social sciences at St. Anne's College of the University of Oxford in England.

Eligibility Applicants should be graduates in the second or subsequent year of study for a higher degree, should have completed a significant amount of research, and must have completed the residence requirements at their home institution. Their field of study must be the human and social sciences. They must be interested in conducting research at St. Anne's College.

Financial data The stipend is 10,120 pounds per year. Fellows also receive free accommodation or a living-out allowance and are members of the senior common room.

Duration 1 year; may be renewed for 1 additional year.

Limitations The fellow must live in Oxford and take part in college life.

Number awarded This fellowship is offered periodically.

Deadline October of the year prior to the award.

[479]
ANNA C. AND OLIVER C. COLBURN FELLOWSHIP

Archaeological Institute of America
656 Beacon Street, Fourth Floor
Boston, MA 02215-2006
(617) 353-9361   Fax: (617) 353-6550
E-mail: aia@bu.edu
Web site: www.archaeological.org

Purpose To provide financial assistance to American and Canadian graduate students and scholars who wish to conduct research at the American School of Classical Studies at Athens.

Eligibility Eligible to apply are predoctoral students and recent (within 5 years) Ph.D. recipients. Applicants must have been accepted as an incoming associate member or student associate member of the American School of Classical Studies at Athens. They must be citizens or permanent residents of the United States or Canada. Applicants may not be members of the American School during the year of application.

Financial data The stipend is $14,000.

Duration Up to 1 year.

Limitations No other fellowship may be held concurrently by the recipient.

Number awarded 1 each year.

Deadline January of each year.

[480]
ANNETTE KADE FELLOWSHIP IN FRENCH OR GERMAN STUDIES IN THE MIDDLE AGES OR RENAISSANCE

Newberry Library
Attn: Committee on Awards
60 West Walton Street
Chicago, IL 60610-3305
(312) 255-3666   Fax: (312) 255-3513
E-mail: research@newberry.org
Web site: www.newberry.org

Purpose To provide funding to American doctoral candidates interested in conducting research in medieval or early modern French or German studies at the Newberry Library and at an institution in Germany or France.

Eligibility This program is open to Ph.D. candidates at the dissertation stage enrolled at a university that is a member of the Newberry Library's Center for Renaissance Studies consortium. Applicants must be interested in conducting research in medieval or early modern French or German studies, spending part of their time at the Newberry and part at a library or other archival institution in Germany or France.

Financial data The stipend is $30,000.

Duration 1 year: 6 months at the Newberry followed by 6 months in Germany or France.

Special features This program is offered by the Newberry Library in cooperation with the Annette Kade Charitable Trust.

Number awarded 1 each year.

Deadline January of each year.

[481]
ARCHITECTURE ROME PRIZE FELLOWSHIP

American Academy in Rome
Attn: Fellowship Coordinator
7 East 60th Street
New York, NY 10022-1001
(212) 751-7200   Fax: (212) 751-7220
E-mail: info@aarome.org
Web site: www.aarome.org

Purpose To provide financial support to American artists interested in conducting research in architecture at the School of Fine Arts of the American Academy in Rome.

Eligibility This program is open to U.S. citizens who hold an accredited degree in architecture. Applications must include a 1-page statement describing how an experience in Rome would be beneficial professionally and identifying any special resources in Italy that are important to the work, a portfolio with at least 6 examples of design work, up to 18 slides of design work, and letters of recommendation from 3 professionals. Full-time students are not eligible.

Financial data The fellowship provides a stipend of up to $20,000, meals, a bedroom with private bath, and a study or studio. Fellows with children under 18 are housed outside the McKim, Mead & White building and are provided with an allowance that helps cover the cost of off-campus housing.

Duration 1 year, beginning in September.

Special features The American Academy in Rome, founded in 1894 by the American architect Charles F. McKim, is a center for independent study and advanced research in the fine arts and humanities. It consists of a School of Fine Arts (including architecture, landscape architecture, design arts, painting and sculpture, musical composition, and literature) and a School of Classical Studies (including classical studies and archaeology, history of art, and post-classical humanistic/modern Italian studies).

Limitations There is a $40 application fee. Prize winners may not hold full-time jobs while at the Academy.

Number awarded 2 each year.

Deadline November of each year.

[482]
ARIT FELLOWSHIP PROGRAM

American Research Institute in Turkey
c/o University of Pennsylvania Museum
33rd and Spruce Streets
Philadelphia, PA 19104-6324
(215) 898-3474   Fax: (215) 898-0657
E-mail: leinwand@sas.upenn.edu
Web site: mec.sas.upenn/edu/ARIT

Purpose To provide financial aid to American and Canadian students and scholars for research in Turkey.

Eligibility Scholars and advanced graduate students (those who have fulfilled all preliminary requirements for the doctorate) interested in conducting research in Turkey in any field of the humanities or social sciences are eligible to apply if they are members in good standing of educational institutions in the United States or Canada.

Financial data Stipends are provided, based on the proposed expenses of the research project.

Duration Up to 1 year, but preference is given to projects of shorter duration (generally no less than 2 months).

Special features Hostel, research, and study facilities of the American Research Institute in Turkey (ARIT) are available in Istanbul and Ankara. This fellowship program is supported in part by a grant from the U.S. Department of State.

Number awarded Varies each year.

Deadline November of each year.

[483]
ARTHUR F. BURNS FELLOWSHIP PROGRAM

International Center for Journalists
1616 H Street, N.W., Third Floor
Washington, DC 20006
(202) 737-3700   Fax: (202) 737-0530
E-mail: burns@icfj.org
Web site: www.icfj.org

Purpose To provide young journalists from the United States and Germany with the opportunity to work and report from abroad.

Eligibility This is a highly competitive program. Applicants must be interested in working and reporting from abroad. The general qualifications for U.S. participants are 1) working journalists in any news media under 35 years of age; 2) demonstrated journalistic talent; and 3) interest in U.S.-European affairs. Proficiency in the German language is not required but does receive favorable consideration in the selection process.

Financial data Participants receive a $4,000 stipend to cover basic travel and living costs.

Duration 2 months during the summer, beginning in July.

Special features Initially, this program provided an opportunity for young German journalists to work in the United States, but since 1990 enough funding has been raised to make this a 2-way exchange. The Burns fellows are based in cities and at host news organizations in each of the respective countries. Participants spend approximately half of the program covering news for their home organizations (in effect, serving as foreign correspondents). For the second half of the program, participants are expected to work at their host organizations. In most cases, American participants are given the opportunity to stay at least part of the time with German families and to travel within the country.

Limitations Participants must write a summary report of their experiences at the end of the program; excerpts will be published in an alumni newsletter.

Number awarded 10 journalists from the United States (and an equal number from Germany).

Deadline February of each year.

[484]
ARTIST RESIDENCY AT GIVERNY PROGRAM

Arts International
251 Park Avenue South
New York, NY 10010-7302
(212) 674-9744   Fax: (212) 674-9092
E-mail: giverny@artsinternational.org
Web site: www.artsinternational.org

Purpose To enable American artists to spend a residency in Giverny, France.

Eligibility Applicants must be 1) U.S. citizens or permanent residents; 2) visual artists working in the disciplines of painting, works on paper, photography, sculpture, crafts, or other arts-based genre; and 3) recipients during the previous 2 years of a national or regional arts fellowship from the National Endowment for the Arts or 1 of the 6 regional art organizations. This program is open by invitation only. Invitees must be interested in a residency in Giverny, France.

Financial data The award includes round-trip transportation to Giverny for the recipient, a furnished studio apartment at Giverny, a working studio shared with the other recipients, a grant of $2,000 before departure to France, a monthly stipend of $1,600 payable in Euros during the residency, use of a car while in residence in Giverny, and a grant of $1,900 upon return to the United States.

Duration 3 months.

Special features Following Claude Monet's death in 1926, the gardens at Giverny deteriorated. His son bequeathed the property to the Academie des Beaux-Arts of the Institut de France, which in 1977 asked Gerald van der Kemp to undertake the restoration of the house and gardens. Currently, residencies there are managed by Arts International, which was founded in 1981 by Nancy Hanks, former chair of the National Endowment for the Arts. In 1987 it became part of the Institute of International Education but in 1999 it became an independent organization with funding from the Ford and Rockefeller Foundations.

Limitations Recipients may not hold other fellowships concurrently and may not hold a regular job in France during their residency. Accommodations at Giverny are not suitable for children, so artists with children must make living and child-care arrangements at their own expense.
Number awarded Up to 3 each year.

[485]
ARTSLINK PROJECTS
CEC International Partners
12 West 31st Street, Suite 400
New York, NY 10001-4415
(212) 643-1985, ext. 22   Fax: (212) 643-1996
E-mail: artslink@cecip.org
Web site: www.cecip.org

Purpose To provide funding to U.S. artists who wish to work collaboratively with colleagues in central Europe, eastern Europe, and Eurasia.

Eligibility This program is open to U.S. artists, curators, and nonprofit organizations in the arts. Individuals must be U.S. citizens or permanent residents. Scholars, administrators, critics, students, and amateur groups are not eligible. Applicants must be interested in working with counterparts in 27 designated countries in central Europe, eastern Europe, the Newly Independent States of the former Soviet Union, and the Baltics to pursue artistic collaborations that will enrich creative or professional development; create new work that draws inspiration from interaction with artists and the community in the country visited; and establish a mutually beneficial exchange of ideas and expertise between artists, arts organizations or audiences, and the local community. Projects focused solely on research or film/video post-production are not eligible. Artists must submit a set of work samples with descriptions (not original artwork). Curators must submit 2 examples of published professional writing or documentation of past curatorial projects. Organizations must submit evidence of nonprofit status. All applicants must submit a project description that includes resumes of all U.S. participants and international colleagues. Selection is based on the artistic excellence and merit of the applicant's work, quality and feasibility of the project plan, potential for interactive dialogue and benefit of proposed project to both U.S. applicant and overseas participants, and the project's potential to bring the benefit of cross-cultural exchange to other artists or audiences in both the United States and the international participant's country. The areas of specialization alternate between visual, design, and media arts in odd-numbered years and theater, dance, music, and literature in even-numbered years.

Financial data Grants range from $2,500 to $10,000.
Duration 1 year, beginning in May.
Special features ArtsLink is a partnership of CEC International Partners (formerly the Citizen Exchange Council) with the U.S. National Endowment for the Arts, Ohio Arts Council, the Kettering Fund, and the Trust for Mutual Understanding. The eligible countries are Albania, Armenia, Azerbaijan, Belarus, Bosnia and Herzegovina, Bulgaria, Croatia, Czech Republic, Estonia, Georgia, Hungary, Kazakhstan, Kyrgyzstan, Latvia, Lithuania, Macedonia, Moldova, Mongolia, Poland, Romania, Russia, Slovakia, Slovenia, Tajikistan, Ukraine, Uzbekistan, and Yugoslavia (including Serbia, Kosovo, and Montenegro).

Number awarded Varies each year.
Deadline January of each year.

[486]
ASCSA FELLOWSHIPS FOR REGULAR STUDENTS
American School of Classical Studies at Athens
Attn: Committee on Admissions and Fellowships
6-8 Charlton Street
Princeton, NJ 08540-5232
(609) 683-0800   Fax: (609) 924-0578
E-mail: ascsa@ascsa.org
Web site: www.ascsa.org

Purpose To provide financial support to American or Canadian graduate students who are interested in researching archaeology or history at the American School of Classical Studies at Athens.

Eligibility Applicants must be regular members of the American School of Classical Studies at Athens; admission to regular membership is granted annually to graduate students in classical studies (literature, archaeology, history) in the United States or Canada who have finished at least 1 year of graduate work but who have not yet completed the Ph.D. degree. Transcripts, recommendations, and examinations in Greek language, history, and archaeology are required.

Financial data The stipend is $8,840 in cash plus fees, room, and board.
Duration 1 academic year.
Special features This program consists of the following named fellowships: the John Williams White Fellowship in Archaeology, the Heinrich Schliemann Fellowship in Archaeology, the Thomas Day Seymour Fellowship in History and Literature, the James Rignall Wheeler Fellowship (unrestricted), the Virginia Grace Fellowship (unrestricted), the Lucy Shoe Meritt Fellowship (unrestricted), 2 Brunilde Ridgway Fellowships in Art History, the Michael Jameson Fellowship (unrestricted), the Philip Lockhart Fellowship (unrestricted), the Martin Ostwald Fellowship (unrestricted), the James and Mary Ottaway, Jr. Fellowship, and the Bert Hodge Hill Fellowship (unrestricted but with preference for a student in art history).

Number awarded 13 each year.
Deadline January of each year.

[487]
AUSTRIA SCHOLARSHIP
Austrian Cultural Institute
950 Third Avenue, 20th Floor
New York, NY 10022
(212) 759-5165   Fax: (212) 319-9636
E-mail: desk@aci.org
Web site: www.austriaculture.net

Purpose To provide financial assistance to graduate students or young scholars who are interested in conducting research or study projects on Austrian topics at Austrian universities or other institutions.

Eligibility This program is open to doctoral or advanced graduate students as well as young postdoctorates. Applicants must be between 20 and 35 years of age, be from countries other than Austria, have a working knowledge of German, and wish to carry out research or study projects in Austria. They may be working on any topic, but preference is given to proposals on Austria-related subjects, such as Austrian economics and political and legal systems (after World War II), contemporary Austrian history, or contemporary Austrian literature.

Financial data The award is the Euro equivalents of 7,800 Austrian schillings per month for scholars who do not have a master's degree, ATS 8,500 per month for Ph.D. candidates who already have a master's degree, or ATS 10,000 per month for postdoctorates who are older than 30 years of age. A 1-time starting allowance of the Euro equivalent of ATS 2,500 is also provided to scholars who will be in Austria for more than 4 months.

Duration 2 to 9 months for Ph.D. candidates and postdoctorates; 1 to 4 months for other graduate students.

Special features Funding for this program is provided by the Austrian Federal Ministry of Science and Transport. It is also identified by its German title, *Osterreich Stipendium*.

Number awarded Varies each year.

Deadline February of each year.

[488]
AUSTRIAN RESEARCH INSTITUTE ON MOLECULAR PATHOLOGY THESIS SCHOLARSHIP

Austrian Cultural Institute
950 Third Avenue, 20th Floor
New York, NY 10022
(212) 759-5165   Fax: (212) 319-9636
E-mail: desk@aci.org
Web site: www.austriaculture.net

Purpose To enable doctoral students in biochemistry, genetics, or microbiology to write their dissertation in Austria.

Eligibility This program is offered by the Austrian Research Institute on Molecular Pathology and the University Institutes in the Vienna Biocenter. It is open to doctoral students in biochemistry, genetics, or microbiology who intend to write their dissertation on the subjects of cancer, cell cycle, cell biology, evolutionary biology, gene expression, gene therapy, or microbiological genetics.

Financial data The stipend is the Euro equivalent of 260,000 Austrian schillings per year.

Duration 3 years.

Special features Applications are also available from Forschungsinstitut für Molekulare Pathologie GesmbH, Dr. Bohr-Gasse 7, A-1030 Vienna, Austria, or Universitätinstitute im Vienna Biocenter, Dr. Bohr-Gasse 9, A-1030 Vienna, Austria.

Number awarded Varies each year.

Deadline Applications may be submitted at any time.

[489]
AUSTRIAN-HUNGARIAN JOINT RESEARCH AWARD

Council for International Exchange of Scholars
3007 Tilden Street, N.W., Suite 5L
Washington, DC 20008-3009
(202) 686-6240   Fax: (202) 362-3442
E-mail: scholars@cies.iie.org
Web site: www.iie.org/cies

Purpose To provide funding to U.S. scholars who wish to conduct research in the humanities or social sciences on the relationship between Austria and Hungary in collaboration with Austrian and Hungarian specialists.

Eligibility This program is open to all fields and topics, provided that proposals have a strong bilateral Austrian-Hungarian or regional emphasis, including (but not limited to) the arts, economics, ecology, European integration, European Union expansion, geography, history (1526 to the present), and political science. Research may be in English, German, and/or Hungarian, depending on the project. Applicants must have arranged an affiliation with institutions in Austria and Hungary and include letters of invitation. U.S. citizenship is required.

Financial data The maintenance allowance during the Austrian portion is 2,100 Euros per month. During the Hungarian portion, allowances are $1,700 per month for maintenance, 45,000 forints per month for housing, and 20,000 forints per month for living expenses. A travel allowance of $1,000 is also provided. No dependent allowance is provided.

Duration 4 months: 2 months in residence in Austria and 2 months in residence in Hungary.

Special features This is a Fulbright scholar program, sponsored by the Bureau of Educational and Cultural Affairs of the U.S. Department of State and administered by the Council for International Exchange of Scholars.

Number awarded 1 each year.

Deadline July of each year.

[490]
BALLIOL COLLEGE JUNIOR RESEARCH FELLOWSHIPS

University of Oxford
Balliol College
Attn: College Secretary
Oxford OX1 3BJ
England
44 1865 277777   Fax: 44 1865 277803
E-mail: college.secretary@balliol.ox.ac.uk
Web site: www.balliol.ox.ac.uk

Purpose To provide funding to postdoctoral scholars from any country who wish to conduct research in designated areas at Balliol College of the University of Oxford in England.

Eligibility This program is open to residents of any country who are interested in conducting postdoctoral research while in residence at Balliol College. Each year, the fields are announced and advertised in Michaelmas Term.

Financial data The stipend is 14,079 pounds for the first year. Fellows also receive free meals and rooms (or, for married fellows, a housing allowance).

Duration 3 years.

Special features Recently, the fields were engineering or psychology for 1 fellowship and politics, law, or Oriental studies for the other fellowship.
Number awarded 2 fellowships are offered each year.
Deadline December of each year.

[491]
BANK OF SWEDEN TERCENTENARY FOUNDATION GRANTS

Bank of Sweden Tercentenary Foundation
Box 5675
S-114 86 Stockholm
Sweden
46 8 50 62 6400   Fax: 46 8 50 62 6430
E-mail: rj@rj.se
Web site: www.rj.se

Purpose To provide financial assistance for research related to Sweden and aimed at expanding knowledge about the impact of technical, economic, and social changes on the society and on individual citizens.
Eligibility Applications are accepted from qualified scholars of any nationality who wish to conduct advanced research in Sweden. Most support is in the form of project grants to individual researchers or groups of researchers in the humanities and social sciences, including theology and law. For the Bank of Sweden Donation, research should shed light on how social, cultural, political, economic, and technical changes have affected the development of society and its impact on the individual. Priority is given to fields of research whose funding requirements are not adequately met in other ways. For the Humanities and Social Sciences Donation, support is provided for 1) projects and programs involving a multidisciplinary or interdisciplinary approach; 2) the establishment of networks or more permanent forms of cooperation, nationally and internationally; 3) the promotion of postgraduate education and researcher recruitment; 4) the promotion of mobility among researchers internationally and between universities/university colleges and other activities; and 5) the promotion of advanced studies in the humanities and social sciences. That donation emphasizes "the fundamentals of the humanities and social sciences" and "social changes in time and space." All applicants should write a short description of their projects; non-Swedish applicants must describe prospective cooperation with Swedish scholars or research institutes.
Financial data The average size of annual grants recently has been about 650,000 Swedish krona for the Bank of Sweden Donation or SEK 2.4 million for the Humanities and Social Sciences Donation.
Duration The average duration of projects is 3 to 4 years.
Special features The Swedish Riksdag established the Bank of Sweden Tercentenary Foundation in 1962 to highlight the Bank's tricentennial in 1968. Effective January 1, 1988, the foundation became independent of the Bank of Sweden, with a board of directors appointed by Riksdagen. In 1993 the Swedish government presented the foundation with an additional donation for research in the humanities and social sciences.
Number awarded Varies each year; recently, just over SEK 423 million was available for research purposes, including about SEK 173 million from the Bank of Sweden Donation and SEK 250 million from the Humanities and Social Sciences Donation.
Deadline February of each year.

[492]
BARCLAYS SCHOLARSHIP

Oxford Centre for Islamic Studies
Attn: Awards Secretary
George Street
Oxford OX1 2AR
England
44 1865 278730   Fax: 44 1865 248942
E-mail: islamic.studies@oxcis.ac.uk
Web site: www.oxcis.ac.uk

Purpose To provide funding to graduate students from any country who are interested in conducting research on topics related to the Muslim world at the Oxford Centre for Islamic Studies in England.
Eligibility This program is open to graduate students who are proposing to conduct research at the Oxford Centre in any area of the arts, humanities, or social sciences (especially anthropology, economics, geography, history, international relations, law, literature, philosophy, politics, religion, or sociology) that has relevance to the study of Islam or the Muslim world. Preference is given to applicants whose circumstances would otherwise prevent them from coming to England.
Financial data A stipend is provided (amount not specified).
Duration 9 months (although shorter periods are considered), beginning in October.
Special features The Oxford Centre for Islamic Studies is an associated institution of the University of Oxford and has links with universities and research centers throughout the Muslim world.
Limitations Scholars are expected to devote most of their time to research and writing on their own projects at the center. They are encouraged to participate in the center's activities and seminars.
Number awarded 1 or more each year.
Deadline November of each year.

[493]
BARNS JUNIOR RESEARCH FELLOWSHIP IN EGYPTOLOGY

University of Oxford
Queen's College
Attn: College Secretary
Oxford OX1 4AW
England
44 1865 279167   Fax: 44 1865 790819
E-mail: college.secretary@queens.ox.ac.uk
Web site: www.queens.ox.ac.uk

Purpose To provide funding to postdoctoral scholars from any country who wish to conduct research in Egyptology science at Queen's College of the University of Oxford in England.
Eligibility This program is open to residents of any country who are interested in conducting postdoctoral research in Egyptology while in residence at Queen's College. Applicants

may not have accumulated more than 10 years of full-time postdoctoral study or research.
Financial data The stipend is 12,994 pounds per year. Fellows also receive free meals and various other allowances.
Duration 3 years.
Number awarded This fellowship is offered periodically; it is not likely to be offered prior to 2003.

[494]
BARNUM FESTIVAL FOUNDATION/JENNY LIND COMPETITION FOR SOPRANOS
Barnum Festival Foundation
Attn: Director
1070 Main Street
Bridgeport, CT 06604
(203) 367-8495

Purpose To recognize and reward outstanding young female singers who have not yet reached professional status.
Eligibility Applicants must be sopranos between the ages of 20 and 27 who have not yet attained professional status and who are residents and citizens of the United States. Past finalists may reapply, but former first-place winners and mezzo-sopranos are not eligible. The preliminary audition for 16 contestants chosen on the basis of audio tapes is held at the Barnum Festival in Bridgeport, Conncecticut every April. From this audition, 6 finalists are chosen. Final selection of the winner is based on technique, musicianship, diction, interpretation, and stage presence.
Financial data The winner of the competition is presented with a $2,000 scholarship award to further her musical education at a recognized voice training school, academy, or college or with a recognized voice teacher or coach, is featured in a concert in June with the Swedish Jenny Lind at a locale in Connecticut, and is sent to Sweden with her Swedish counterpart to perform in concerts for 2 weeks in August. Other scholarship awards are $1,000 for second place and $500 for third place.
Duration The competition is held annually.
Special features The winner of this competition serves as the American Jenny Lind, a 20th-century counterpart of the Swedish Nightingale brought to the United States for a successful concert tour in 1850 by P.T. Barnum.
Number awarded 3 each year: 1 each of first, second, and third place.
Deadline February of each year.

[495]
BERLIN PROGRAM FOR ADVANCED GERMAN AND EUROPEAN STUDIES
Social Science Research Council
810 Seventh Avenue
New York, NY 10019
(212) 377-2700   Fax: (212) 377-2727
E-mail: berlin@ssrc.org
Web site: www.ssrc.org

Purpose To encourage pre- and postdoctoral scholars to conduct research on the economic, political, and social aspects of modern and contemporary German and European affairs at the Free University of Berlin.
Eligibility The program is open to full-time graduate students enrolled in doctoral programs in the United States and Canada and Ph.D.s who have received the doctorate with the past 2 calendar years. Support is provided to anthropologists, economists, political scientists, sociologists, and all scholars in germane social science and cultural studies fields, including historians working on the period since the mid-19th century. Applicants must be citizens or permanent residents of the United States and Canada interested in conducting research at the Free University of Berlin. They should show an appropriate level of training and skill to undertake the proposed field research, including evidence of language fluency adequate to complete the project and participate in the seminar. Minorities and women are particularly encouraged to apply.
Financial data The monthly stipend is the Euro equivalents of 2,000 Deutsche marks for individuals, DM 2,250 for fellows accompanied by a spouse who is not working or on scholarship, and DM 2,500 if the couple is accompanied by a child. Other benefits include round-trip airfare for the fellow and spouse (but not children) and funds for intra-European travel to research sites between the semesters when the program is in session (to a maximum of the EUR equivalent of DM 7,000).
Duration 9 to 12 months.
Special features Fellows participate in the program's seminars twice monthly and present their work alongside senior scholars. The program, established in 1986, is based at the Free University of Berlin. It is funded by the Federal State of Berlin with administrative costs provided by the German Marshall Fund of the United States.
Limitations Fellows are expected to produce a research monograph (doctoral dissertation, book manuscript, etc.) dealing with some aspect of German or European affairs, including U.S.-European relations.
Number awarded Varies each year.
Deadline November of each year.

[496]
BERTHA VON SUTTNER SCHOLARSHIP
Austrian Cultural Institute
950 Third Avenue, 20th Floor
New York, NY 10022
(212) 759-5165   Fax: (212) 319-9636
E-mail: desk@aci.org
Web site: www.austriaculture.net

Purpose To provide financial assistance to doctoral students in the sciences who are interested in writing their dissertation in Austria.
Eligibility This program is open to students between 20 and 27 years of age, from countries other than Austria, who have a working knowledge of German and are completing a dissertation in a field of science other than medicine. They must be interested in writing their dissertations in Austria. Applications should be submitted by an Austrian doctoral supervisor.
Financial data The stipend is the Euro equivalent of 8,500 Austrian schillings per month; a 1-time book allowance of the EUR equivalent of ATS 2,500 is also provided.
Duration 1 year; may be extended to a maximum of 27 months.
Special features Funding for this program is provided by the Austrian Federal Ministry of Science and Transport.

Number awarded Varies each year.
Deadline May of each year.

[497]
BERYL MAVIS GREEN SCHOLARSHIP

British Federation of Women Graduates
Attn: The Secretary
4 Mandeville Courtyard
142 Battersea Park Road
London SW11 4NB
England
44 20 7498 8037 Fax: 44 20 7498 8037
E-mail: bfwg@bfwg.demon.co.uk
Web site: homepages.wyenet.co.uk/bfwg

Purpose To provide financial assistance for graduate or postdoctoral research to women from the United Kingdom or for research in the United Kingdom.

Eligibility Women who have already completed at least 1 year of graduate study may apply; they may be of any age and may be studying at the master's, doctoral, or postdoctoral level. Candidates from the United Kingdom may be studying overseas or within the United Kingdom; candidates of other nationalities who wish to conduct research in the United Kingdom are also eligible, although they may not plan to study outside the United Kingdom.

Financial data Scholarships are at least 1,000 pounds.

Duration 1 year.

Limitations Awards are only for postgraduate research, not courses. Requests for applications must be accompanied by a self-addressed stamped envelope. There is a 12 pound application fee.

Number awarded 1 or more each year.

Deadline April of each year.

[498]
BFWG CHARITABLE FOUNDATION MAIN GRANTS

British Federation of Women Graduates Charitable Foundation
Attn: Grants Administrator
28 Great James Street
London WC1N 3ES
England
44 20 7404 6447 Fax: 44 20 7404 6505
E-mail: bfwg.charity@btinternet.com
Web site: www.bcfgrants.org.uk

Purpose To provide financial aid to women from any country who wish to study or conduct research in Great Britain.

Eligibility Women graduate students from any country who are registered for study or research at an approved institution of higher education in Great Britain may apply for these grants. Applicants must have completed at least 1 year of study or research. Funding is not provided for 1-year courses or the first year of a course, a second first degree, field work outside of Great Britain, travel cost outside of Great Britain, or conferences, exhibitions, or seminars either overseas or within Great Britain. Selection is based on the needs of the applicant and academic caliber.

Financial data Grants up to 2,500 pounds are available; funds are intended to assist with living expenses, not fees.

Special features The sponsoring organization for these grants is the charity of the British Federation of Women Graduates (BFWG).

Number awarded Varies each year.

Deadline March of each year.

[499]
BFWG SCHOLARSHIPS

British Federation of Women Graduates
Attn: The Secretary
4 Mandeville Courtyard
142 Battersea Park Road
London SW11 4NB
England
44 20 7498 8037 Fax: 44 20 7498 8037
E-mail: bfwg@bfwg.demon.co.uk
Web site: homepages.wyenet.co.uk/bfwg

Purpose To provide financial assistance for graduate or postdoctoral research in the United Kingdom.

Eligibility Women who have already completed at least 1 year of graduate study may apply; they may be of any age and may be studying at the master's, doctoral, or postdoctoral level. United Kingdom nationals may study overseas or within the United Kingdom; candidates from other countries whose studies take place in the United Kingdom are also eligible, although they are not eligible if they plan to conduct research outside the United Kingdom.

Financial data Up to 1,000 pounds in scholarships and up to 750 pounds in grants.

Duration 1 year.

Special features Included in the grants are the Caroline Spurgeon, Muriel L. Lloyd, Lumsden Nichol, Jane Finlay, Eila Campbell, Christine Fell, and Elsie Conway Memorial Awards.

Limitations Awards are only for postgraduate research, not individual courses. Requests for applications must be accompanied by a self-addressed stamped envelope. There is a 12 pound application fee.

Number awarded Varies each year; normally, 1 or 2 scholarships and several grants are awarded.

Deadline April of each year.

[500]
BICENTENNIAL CHAIR IN AMERICAN STUDIES

Council for International Exchange of Scholars
3007 Tilden Street, N.W., Suite 5L
Washington, DC 20008-3009
(202) 686-6245 Fax: (202) 362-3442
E-mail: scholars@cies.iie.org
Web site: www.iie.org/cies

Purpose To allow a distinguished American scholar to lecture in American studies at the University of Helsinki.

Eligibility Applicants must have the rank of associate or full professor in American studies, including American history, American literature, political science, cultural studies (such as art history, music history, film history), sociology, or international relations. They must be interested in lecturing at the University of Helsinki. U.S. citizenship is required.

Financial data The stipend is $5,555 per month paid in local currency; also provided are a travel allowance for the grantee and 1 dependent, an excess baggage allowance, and housing (utilities not included).

Duration 1 academic year.

Special features This is a Fulbright scholar program, sponsored by the Bureau of Educational and Cultural Affairs of the U.S. Department of State and administered by the Council for International Exchange of Scholars. The scholar teaches 1 survey course and a seminar in area of expertise, supervises graduate theses, conducts research-sharing groups, assists in curriculum development, and gives occasional guest lectures at the other 4 universities in Finland with American studies programs (Tampere, Turku, Oulu, and Jyvaskyla).

Number awarded 1 each year.

Deadline April of each year.

[501]
BIOMEDICAL RESEARCH COLLABORATION GRANTS

Wellcome Trust
Attn: Grants Section (International)
183 Euston Road
London NW1 2BE
England
44 20 7611 8428   Fax: 44 20 7611 8373
E-mail: international@wellcome.ac.uk
Web site: www.wellcome.ac.uk

Purpose To provide funding to scientists in fields related to animal or human health for collaborations between research groups in 1) the United Kingdom and Ireland and 2) any other country in the world.

Eligibility This program is open to scientists in any branch of the natural and clinical sciences that has a bearing on human or animal health, with the exception of cancer research. Applicants must be seeking to promote new or existing collaborations between 2 research groups to enable members of the teams to meet regularly, to work in each other's laboratories for short periods, and to exchange experimental materials. Applications must be submitted jointly by the collaborating groups, of which 1 must be located in the United Kingdom or Ireland and the other may be in any other country in the world.

Financial data Grants up to 6,000 pounds per year are available. These funds are not intended to cover the costs of the research programs in the collaborating laboratories. Awards are administered by the U.K. or Irish institution.

Duration Up to 3 years.

Number awarded Varies each year.

Deadline February or August of each year.

[502]
BOEHRINGER INGELHEIM FONDS SCHOLARSHIPS FOR PH.D. STUDENTS

Boehringer Ingelheim Fonds
Attn: Secretariat
Schlossmuhle, Grabenstrasse 46
55262 Heidesheim
Germany
49 6132 89 85 0   E-mail: secretariat@bifonds.de
Web site: www.bifonds.de

Purpose To provide financial support for dissertation and other advanced research in medical and natural sciences by young scholars in Europe.

Eligibility This program is open to Ph.D. candidates from any country. Natural scientists may apply after having completed a master's thesis or equivalent work; physicians, veterinary surgeons, and pharmacists should have passed the state examinations. European citizens are supported in Europe and abroad; non-European citizens are only supported in Europe. Except in special circumstances, applicants must be under 28 years of age and may not have a permanent job. Applications must be accompanied by a confirmation from the head of the institute or clinic where the research is to be conducted and, if the project is for research outside the applicant's own country, evidence that such foreign research is necessary. Selection is based on the personal qualities the applicant has demonstrated to date, the originality of the proposed Ph.D. project, and the scientific quality of the laboratories where the research is to be conducted.

Financial data The basic grant is the Euro equivalent of 1,800 Deutsche marks per month, plus the EUR equivalent of DM 200 per month to cover minor project-related costs (books, travel expenses) and premiums for personal insurance. A supplement for the respective country and/or a spouse allowance (but no child allowance) may be added.

Duration 2 years; may be extended up to 12 additional months.

Number awarded Approximately 45 each year.

Deadline March, July, or November of each year.

[503]
BOEHRINGER INGELHEIM FONDS TRAVEL AWARDS

Boehringer Ingelheim Fonds
Attn: Secretariat
Schlossmuhle, Grabenstrasse 46
55262 Heidesheim
Germany
49 6132 89 85 0   E-mail: secretariat@bifonds.de
Web site: www.bifonds.de

Purpose To provide funding to pre- and postdoctoral natural scientists from any country who are interested in a program of research and/or study in Europe.

Eligibility This program is open to Ph.D. students and postdoctoral scientists who wish to visit laboratories to study clearly-defined techniques useful for their ongoing research and the work of their research group at home. Support is also provided for participation in research-oriented courses and summer or winter schools where a selected number of participants learn clearly-defined techniques in practical settings as well as lectures and discussions. Vocational training and attendance at conferences, symposia, and workshops are not supported. European citizens are supported in Europe and abroad; non-European citizens are only supported in Europe. Except in special circumstances, predoctoral applicants must be under 30 years of age and postdoctoral applicants under 32 years of age. Selection is based on the applicant's achievements to date, the originality of the research project, and the scientific quality of the laboratories involved.

Financial data Grants provide a flat-rate contribution that may cover the expenses for travel, lodging, and/or course fees. The sponsoring organization expects the home institution to continue to pay the applicant's salary and the host institute to cover research-related costs.

Duration Up to 3 months; nonrenewable.

Number awarded Varies each year.

Deadline Applications may be submitted at any time, but they must be received at least 6 weeks prior to the proposed activity.

[504]
BOLOGNA CHAIR IN AMERICAN HISTORY AND POLITICAL SCIENCE

Council for International Exchange of Scholars
3007 Tilden Street, N.W., Suite 5L
Washington, DC 20008-3009
(202) 686-6245   Fax: (202) 362-3442
E-mail: scholars@cies.iie.org
Web site: www.iie.org/cies

Purpose To allow a distinguished American scholar to lecture to advanced undergraduates at the University of Bologna in Italy.

Eligibility Applicants must be full professors with at least 10 years of experience and a distinguished record of research and teaching in American political history in the 20th century, history of political ideas and culture, political parties, presidential politics, and comparative politics. They must be interested in lecturing at the University of Bologna. U.S. citizenship is required. Some knowledge of Italian is useful but not required.

Financial data The stipend is the Euro equivalent of 16,800,000 Italian lire plus a settling-in allowance of 1,500,000 lire. The grant also provides international travel (for the grantee only) plus the EUR equivalent of 200,000 lire per month for each accompanying dependent.

Duration 3 months.

Special features This is a Fulbright scholar program, sponsored by the Bureau of Educational and Cultural Affairs of the U.S. Department of State and administered by the Council for International Exchange of Scholars.

Number awarded 1 each year.

Deadline April of each year.

[505]
BOURSE DOROTHY LEET

French Association of University Women
4 rue de Chevreuse
75006 Paris
France
33 1 43 20 01 32   Fax: 33 1 45 25 95 53
Fax: affdu@club-internet.fr
Web site: www.ifuw.org/france

Purpose To provide financial assistance to women for research in France or the United States.

Eligibility This program is open to women who are finishing their doctoral studies or have already received a doctorate. They must be French citizens planning to conduct research in the United States or U.S. citizens planning to conduct research in France. The research may be in any field.

Financial data The amount awarded depends on the nature of the proposed research and the availability of funds, but ranges from the Euro equivalent of 2,000 to 10,000 French francs.

Duration Up to 1 year.

Special features In the United States, further information on this scholarship is available from the American Association of University Women (AAUW), 1111 16th Street, N.W., Washington, DC 20036-4873, (202) 785-7700, (800) 821-4364.

Number awarded 2 or 3 each year.

Deadline March of each year.

[506]
BRASENOSE COLLEGE JUNIOR RESEARCH FELLOWSHIPS

University of Oxford
Brasenose College
Attn: Senior Tutor
Oxford OX1 4AJ
England
44 1865 277823   Fax: 44 1865 277822
E-mail: college.office@bnc.ox.ac.uk
Web site: www.bnc.ox.ac.uk

Purpose To provide funding to postdoctoral scholars from any country who wish to conduct research at Brasenose College of the University of Oxford in England.

Eligibility This program is open to residents of any country who are interested in conducting research while in residence at Brasenose College. In odd-numbered years, fellowships are offered in science, engineering, and mathematics. In even-numbered years, fields in the humanities and social sciences are selected. Applicants may not have spent more than 7 years in full-time education or research since they qualified for their first degree.

Financial data Fellows receive free lunches and dinners, a research allowance, and either free rooms in college or a housing allowance. No stipend is provided; it is expected that fellows will hold a grant from the British Academy or other salaried support.

Duration 3 years.

Number awarded 1 each year.

Deadline February of each year.

[507]
BRISTOL-MYERS SQUIBB RESEARCH FELLOWSHIP IN PHARMACO-ECONOMICS

University of Cambridge
Pembroke College
Attn: Dr. Wendy Fernie
Trumpington Street
Cambridge CB2 1RF
England
44 1223 338100   Fax: 44 1223 338163
E-mail: wendy.fernie@pem.cam.ac.uk
Web site: www.pem.cam.ac.uk

Purpose To provide funding to postdoctoral scholars interested in conducting research in pharmaco-economics at the University of Cambridge in England.

Eligibility This program is open to scholars from any country who have a strong research record in the fields of health and pharmaco-economics. Applicants must be interested in conducting research jointly at Pembroke College and The Judge Institute of Management (the University of Cambridge's business school).

Financial data The stipend is negotiable, depending on experience.

Duration 3 years; may be renewed.

Special features Funding for this program is provided by Bristol-Myers Squibb Company.

Number awarded This fellowship is offered from time to time.

Deadline January in the years it is available.

[508]
BRITISH ACADEMY VISITING LECTURESHIPS

British Academy
10 Carlton House Terrace
London SW1Y 5AH
England
44 20 7969 5200   Fax: 44 20 7969 5300
E-mail: secretary@britac.ac.uk
Web site: www.britac.ac.uk

Purpose To provide funding to distinguished scholars from other countries who have been invited to deliver a lecture in the United Kingdom.

Eligibility This program is open to distinguished scholars from overseas who have been invited to deliver a lecture or series of lectures at centers within the United Kingdom. The visitor is normally based at 1 center with shorter visits to up to 3 other sites, but other arrangements are possible. The program may involve a combination of formal lectures and less formal seminars. This program is not intended to provide support for research or conference attendance.

Financial data The program provides travel expenses to the United Kingdom, accommodation costs at the rate of 100 pounds per night, and a maintenance allowance at the rate of 30 pounds per day (up to a total of 1,000 pounds per week).

Duration From 10 days to 2 weeks.

Number awarded 4 each year.

Deadline December of each year.

[509]
BRITISH ACADEMY VISITING PROFESSORSHIPS/FELLOWSHIPS FOR OVERSEAS SCHOLARS

British Academy
10 Carlton House Terrace
London SW1Y 5AH
England
44 20 7969 5200   Fax: 44 20 7969 5300
E-mail: secretary@britac.ac.uk
Web site: www.britac.ac.uk

Purpose To provide funding to scholars from other countries who are interested in conducting research in the United Kingdom.

Eligibility Eligible are both young and established scholars from countries other than the United Kingdom who are interested in conducting social science or humanities research in the United Kingdom. They must have a doctorate and be sponsored by an academic or research institution in the United Kingdom. Applications must be submitted by a sponsoring agency that wishes to invite the candidate to the United Kingdom; direct applications from foreign scholars are not accepted.

Financial data The program provides travel expenses to the United Kingdom and subsistence to a maximum of 700 pounds a week.

Duration The normal maximum visit is 1 month, although applications for longer periods may be considered.

Special features Senior scholars are designated Visiting Professors and junior scholars are designated Visiting Fellows, but all conditions for either designation (including the compensation) are the same.

Deadline December of each year.

[510]
BRITISH FEDERATION CROSBY HALL FELLOWSHIP

International Federation of University Women
8 rue de l'Ancien-Port
CH-1201 Geneva
Switzerland
41 22 731 2380   Fax: 41 22 738 0440
E-mail: info@ifuw.org
Web site: www.ifuw.org

Purpose To provide assistance to women from any country who wish to conduct research or to study in Great Britain and reside at Crosby Hall.

Eligibility Members of any national federation or association of the International Federation of University Women are eligible to apply if they are interested in conducting doctoral or postdoctoral research or pursuing studies at an approved institution of higher education in Great Britain. Applicants must have started their research program; awards are not made for the first year of a Ph.D. program.

Financial data The stipend is 2,500 pounds, of which 1,000 pounds is paid at the beginning of the academic year on proof of registration.

Duration Stipends are intended to cover at least 8 months of work and should be used within 9 months from the date of the award.
Special features Funding for these fellowships is provided by the British Federation of Women Graduates Charitable Foundation. Americans should submit their applications through the American Association of University Women (AAUW), 1111 16th Street, N.W., Washington, DC 20036-4873, (202) 785-7700, (800) 821-4364.
Number awarded 1 each even-numbered year.
Deadline Applications, whether submitted through a national affiliate (such as the AAUW) or by an independent member, must reach IFUW headquarters before the end of October of odd-numbered years. National affiliates set earlier deadlines; for the AAUW, this is the end of September.

[511]
BRITISH HEART FOUNDATION OVERSEAS VISITING FELLOWSHIPS

British Heart Foundation
Attn: Research Funds Department
14 Fitzhardinge Street
London W1H 4DH
England
44 20 7487 9408   Fax: 44 20 7486 1273
E-mail: research@bhf.org.uk
Web site: www.bhf.org.uk

Purpose To provide funding for cardiologists from other countries who are interested in conducting research in the United Kingdom.
Eligibility Eligible are cardiologists from countries outside of the United Kingdom who are recognized as established researchers and are interested in conducting basic or applied research on cardiology at an academic or research institution in the United Kingdom. Applications must be made by the head of the department at the U.K. institution on behalf of the fellow.
Financial data Fellows receive a salary plus travel and living allowances for 1 dependent if accompanying the fellow to the United Kingdom for 1 year or more. The U.K. institution may receive up to 5,000 pounds per year as a contribution toward research expenses.
Duration Up to 2 years.
Deadline February, May, August, or November of each year.

[512]
BRITISH HEART FOUNDATION TRAVELLING FELLOWSHIPS

British Heart Foundation
Attn: Research Funds Department
14 Fitzhardinge Street
London W1H 4DH
England
44 20 7487 9408   Fax: 44 20 7486 1273
E-mail: research@bhf.org.uk
Web site: www.bhf.org.uk

Purpose To provide funding for researchers from overseas to come to train laboratory staff members in the United Kingdom.

Eligibility The foundation will consider requests from the heads of departments in the United Kingdom who wish to invite named researchers from overseas to train members in British laboratories in new research techniques.
Financial data The head of a department may request funds to cover the cost of economy return travel and a reasonable subsistence allowance for the fellow. Applications may also be made for up to 3,000 pounds to cover research expenses. It is expected that the fellow's salary will continue to be paid by the home institution.
Duration From a few days to a maximum of 6 months.
Deadline February, May, August, or November of each year.
Number awarded Varies each year.

[513]
BROODBANK FELLOWSHIPS

University of Cambridge
Attn: Registry Division
The Old Schools
Trinity Lane
Cambridge CB2 1TN
England
44 1223 332317   Fax: 44 1223 332332
E-mail: mrf25@admin.cam.ac.uk
Web site: www.cam.ac.uk

Purpose To provide financial assistance to scholars who want to conduct scientific research at the University of Cambridge in England.
Eligibility Nationals from any country are eligible to apply if they are interested in conducting biochemical or biophysical research (with special reference to the practice and principles of food preservation) at the University of Cambridge. The academic level of candidates is open, but preference is given to postdoctoral applicants.
Financial data The amount awarded is determined on an individual basis by the university managers according to the age-related scale for research associates at the university. The current scale ranges from 15,735 to 23,651 pounds per year.
Duration Up to 3 years.
Deadline Applications are accepted only irregularly, when the position becomes available.

[514]
BROWNE RESEARCH FELLOWSHIP

University of Oxford
Queen's College
Attn: College Secretary
Oxford OX1 4AW
England
44 1865 279167   Fax: 44 1865 790819
E-mail: college.secretary@queens.ox.ac.uk
Web site: www.queens.ox.ac.uk

Purpose To provide funding to postdoctoral scholars from any country who wish to conduct research in animal or plant science at Queen's College of the University of Oxford in England.
Eligibility This program is open to residents of any country who are interested in conducting postdoctoral research while in residence at Queen's College. Applicants may not have

accumulated more than 6 years of full-time postdoctoral study or research. The field of research may be animal or plant sciences (excluding medical sciences).
Financial data The stipend is 15,159 pounds per year. Fellows also receive free accommodation and meals and an annual research grant of 4,000 pounds.
Duration 3 years.
Number awarded This fellowship is offered periodically.

[515]
BULGARIA DISTINGUISHED CHAIR IN THE HUMANITIES AND SOCIAL SCIENCES
Council for International Exchange of Scholars
3007 Tilden Street, N.W., Suite 5L
Washington, DC 20008-3009
(202) 686-6246   Fax: (202) 362-3442
E-mail: scholars@cies.iie.org
Web site: www.iie.org/cies

Purpose To provide funding for scholars to teach designated fields in the humanities and social sciences at the University of Sofia in Bulgaria.
Eligibility This program is open to established scholars with a prominent record of accomplishment, rank of associate or full professor, and at least 5 years of teaching experience, preferably at the graduate level. Their field of study may be anthropology, business, cultural studies, economics, history, law, literature, philosophy, political science, sociology, or other areas of the humanities or social sciences. They must be interested in teaching at the University of Sofia. English is sufficient for lecturing.
Financial data The program provides a stipend of $3,500 per month, a subsistence allowance of $200 to $300 per month, a housing allowance of $250 to $450 per month, and a travel allowance of $1,700 for the grantee only.
Duration 2 or 3 months.
Special features This is a Fulbright scholar program, sponsored by the Bureau of Educational and Cultural Affairs of the U.S. Department of State and administered by the Council for International Exchange of Scholars. The recipient lectures and gives seminars in the area of specialization at the graduate and faculty levels. Other responsibilities include consulting on thesis writing and curricular and program development.
Number awarded 1 each year.
Deadline July of each year.

[516]
BULGARIA FULBRIGHT EXCHANGE OF ADMINISTRATORS
U.S. Department of State
c/o Graduate School, USDA
600 Maryland Avenue, S.W., Room 320
Washington, DC 20024-2520
(202) 314-3520   Fax: (202) 479-6806
E-mail: fulbright@grad.usda.gov
Web site: www.grad.usda.gov/International/ftep.html

Purpose To promote mutual understanding between the people of the United States and the people of Bulgaria through an educational administrator exchange program.
Eligibility This program is open to administrators from elementary schools, secondary schools, and 2-year colleges who are interested in working with administrators in Bulgaria (and vice versa). The assignment may be in the areas of personnel administration, student affairs, or educational policy. Applicants must 1) be U.S. citizens; 2) hold at least a bachelor's degree; 3) be fluent in English; 4) have a current full-time administrative assignment in the U.S. or a territory; 5) have the approval of their school administration; 6) have at least 3 years of full-time experience; and 7) not have participated in a Fulbright Teacher Exchange longer than 8 weeks during the last 2 years. Preference is given to applicants who have not participated previously in the program and may be given to applicants who have not previously lived in Bulgaria. Geographic distribution of awards within the United States is also a factor in selection. This program does not discriminate on the basis of race, color, religion, age, sex, or national origin and encourages the applications of members of minority communities. Other considerations being equal, veterans are given preference.
Financial data Round-trip economy airfare and a $3,000 cost of living stipend are provided. Participants must obtain a leave of absence with or without pay from their jobs in the United States.
Duration 6 weeks, twice during the year.
Special features This program is sponsored by the Bureau of Educational and Cultural Affairs of the U.S. Department of State and administered by the Graduate School, USDA.
Limitations Dependents are not permitted in this program. Applicants selected for exchange must attend orientation programs of the sponsoring agencies in the United States or abroad.
Number awarded Varies each year.
Deadline October of each year.

[517]
BULGARIA FULBRIGHT TEACHER EXCHANGE
U.S. Department of State
c/o Graduate School, USDA
600 Maryland Avenue, S.W., Room 320
Washington, DC 20024-2520
(202) 314-3520   Fax: (202) 479-6806
E-mail: fulbright@grad.usda.gov
Web site: www.grad.usda.gov/International/ftep.html

Purpose To promote mutual understanding between the people of the United States and the people of Bulgaria through a teacher exchange program.
Eligibility This program is open to teachers (grades 9 through 12) and 2-year college instructors of English as a second language, biology, chemistry, history, English and American literature, physics, and social studies who are interested in teaching in Bulgaria. Applicants must 1) be U.S. citizens; 2) hold at least a bachelor's degree; 3) be fluent in English; 4) have a current full-time teaching assignment in the U.S. or a territory; 5) have the approval of their school administration; 6) have at least 3 years of full-time experience; and 7) not have participated in a Fulbright Teacher Exchange longer than 8 weeks during the last 2 years. Fluency in Bulgarian is not required, although knowledge of Bulgarian or Russian is helpful. Teaching couples may apply. However, because of the limited num-

ber of positions available and, often, the lack of foreign candidate pairs with similar qualifications for interchanges, it may not be possible to arrange suitable assignments in the same locality or to place both teachers. Preference is given to applicants who have not participated previously in the program and may be given to applicants who have not previously lived in Bulgaria. Geographic distribution of awards within the United States is also a factor in selection. This program does not discriminate on the basis of race, color, religion, age, sex, or national origin and encourages the applications of members of minority communities. Other considerations being equal, veterans are given preference.

Financial data Round-trip transportation for the exchange teacher only is provided. Participants must obtain a leave of absence with pay from their jobs in the United States. The U.S. school must agree to accept a teacher from Bulgaria who must secure a leave of absence with pay; the Bulgarian teacher receives a stipend, but no additional cost accrues to the U.S. school.

Duration 9 months, beginning in September.

Special features This program is sponsored by the Bureau of Educational and Cultural Affairs of the U.S. Department of State and administered by the Graduate School, USDA.

Limitations This program provides for the direct exchange of teaching assignments between Bulgaria and the United States. Applicants selected for exchange must attend orientation programs of the sponsoring agencies in the United States or abroad.

Number awarded 2 each year.

Deadline October of each year.

[518]
CAIRD SENIOR RESEARCH FELLOWSHIPS
National Maritime Museum
Centre for Maritime Research
Attn: Research Administrator
Greenwich
London SE10 9NF
England
44 20 8312 6716   Fax: 44 20 8312 6722
E-mail: research@nmm.ac.uk
Web site: www.nmm.ac.uk

Purpose To provide funding to recent Ph.D.s from any country who are interested in conducting research at the National Maritime Museum in Greenwich, England.

Eligibility This program is open to scholars of any nationality who have recently completed a Ph.D. or expect to do so before the commencement of the fellowship. Applicants must be interested in conducting research using the museum's collections in any field of British naval and maritime history. Proposals from maritime historians and from scholars from other disciplines who are interested in broader cultural, social, and political aspects of maritime history are especially encouraged.

Financial data The stipend is 13,500 pounds per year.

Duration 1 year; may be renewed for 1 additional year in exceptional cases.

Number awarded Up to 2 each year.

[519]
CAIRD SHORT-TERM RESEARCH FELLOWSHIPS
National Maritime Museum
Centre for Maritime Research
Attn: Research Administrator
Greenwich
London SE10 9NF
England
44 20 8312 6716   Fax: 44 20 8312 6722
E-mail: research@nmm.ac.uk
Web site: www.nmm.ac.uk

Purpose To provide funding to scholars from any country who are interested in conducting short-term research at the National Maritime Museum in Greenwich, England.

Eligibility This program is open to scholars of any nationality who are interested in conducting research using the museum's collections in any field of British naval and maritime history. The fellowships are specifically intended for scholars and museum professionals who live abroad or at a distance from London.

Financial data The stipend is 1,500 pounds per month.

Duration Up to 3 months.

Number awarded Varies each year.

[520]
CALOUSTE GULBENKIAN FOUNDATION RESEARCH OR SPECIALIZATION FELLOWSHIPS
Calouste Gulbenkian Foundation
Serviço Internacional
Avenida de Berna, 45-A
1067-001 Lisbon
Portugal
351 21 782 3000   Fax: 351 21 782 3021
E-mail: inter@gulbenkian.pt
Web site: www.gulbenkian.pt

Purpose To provide funding to graduate students from outside of Portugal who are interested in conducting research on themes relating to Portuguese culture.

Eligibility Applicants must be advanced postgraduates of non-Portuguese nationality who intend to conduct research in Portugal on themes relating to Portuguese culture, primarily in the humanities. In exceptional cases, fellowships may be awarded for research outside Portugal when the proposed programs relate to Portuguese cultural themes. Candidates must arrange to conduct research through a Portuguese institution and obtain its approval of the program.

Financial data The program provides a complementary supplement to the salaries or normal incomes that the grantees may continue to receive from their countries of origin. In some cases, the grant may include economy-class air transportation for a direct return trip to the country of residence.

Duration Up to 12 months.

Limitations Fellowships are not awarded to beginners in any branch of knowledge, and they may not be used solely to attend courses at teaching establishments in Portugal.

Number awarded Varies each year.

Deadline October of each year.

[521]
CAORC FELLOWSHIPS FOR ADVANCED MULTI-COUNTRY RESEARCH

Council of American Overseas Research Centers
c/o Smithsonian Institution
10th and Constitution Streets, N.W.
CE-123, MRC 178
Washington, DC 20560-0178
(202) 842-8636 Fax: (202) 786-2430
E-mail: caorc@caorc.org
Web site: www.caorc.org

Purpose To provide financial assistance to pre- and post-doctoral scholars who wish to conduct research in the humanities, social sciences, or allied natural sciences at a participating member of the Council of American Overseas Research Centers (CAORC).

Eligibility This program is open to doctoral candidates and established scholars with U.S. citizenship who wish to carry out research on broad questions of multi-country significance in the fields of humanities, social sciences, and related natural sciences. Applicants must be proposing to conduct field research in at least 2 countries, 1 of which must host a constituent member of the Council: the American Academy in Rome, the American School of Classical Studies at Athens, the American Institute of Iranian Studies, the American Institute for Maghrib Studies (Tunisia and Morocco), the American Research Center in Egypt, the W.F. Albright Institute of Archaeological Research in Jerusalem, the American Center of Oriental Research in Amman, the American Research Institute in Turkey, the American Institute for Yemeni Studies, the American Institute of Indian Studies, the American Institute of Pakistan Studies, the American Institute of Bangladesh Studies, the American Institute for Sri Lankan Studies, the Cyprus American Archaeological Research Institute, or the West African Research Association. Selection is based on 1) the scholar's intellectual capacity, maturity, and fitness for field work; and 2) the proposal's significance, relevance, and potential contribution to regional and/or trans-regional scholarly research.

Financial data Fellowships are intended as small grants, with a maximum of $3,000 for travel and $6,000 for stipend. No dependent allowance is available.

Duration At least 3 months.

Special features Fellows are granted all privileges normally accorded other fellows at the center with which they affiliate. In addition to the countries that host overseas research centers (Bangladesh, Cyprus, Egypt, Greece, India, Iran, Israel, Italy, Jordan, Morocco, Pakistan, Senegal, Sri Lanka, Tunisia, Turkey, and Yemen), research may be conducted in other countries in North Africa, the Middle East, and South Asia, subject to official security and/or travel restrictions or warnings. Funding for this program is provided by a grant from the Bureau of Educational and Cultural Affairs of the U.S. Department of State.

Limitations Fellowships are authorized only after the center with which the fellow intends to affiliate has given approval and a security clearance has been granted.

Number awarded 8 each year.

Deadline December of each year.

[522]
CAREER AWARDS IN THE BIOMEDICAL SCIENCES

Burroughs Wellcome Fund
21 T.W. Alexander Drive, Suite 100
P.O. Box 13901
Research Triangle Park, NC 27709-3901
(919) 991-5100 Fax: (919) 991-5160
E-mail: info@bwfund.org
Web site: www.bwfund.org

Purpose To provide funding to biomedical scientists in the United States and Canada who require assistance to make the transition from postdoctoral training to faculty appointment.

Eligibility This program is open to U.S. and Canadian researchers in the biomedical sciences who have completed at least 1 but not more than 4 years of postdoctoral training and require support for bridging research to faculty status. Individuals who hold a tenure-track faculty appointment are not eligible. The biomedical sciences are defined to include reproductive science. Applicants must be U.S. or Canadian citizens pursuing postdoctoral training at an accredited degree-granting institution in the United States, Canada, or the United Kingdom. Each U.S. and Canadian institution may nominate up to 6 candidates; institutions that nominate at least 1 candidate in the reproductive sciences may nominate a total of 7 candidates; institutions that nominate at least 1 candidate from an underrepresented minority group (African American, Hispanic, or Native American) may nominate an additional candidate. A U.K. institution, including its medical school, graduate schools, and all affiliated hospitals and research institutes, may nominate up to 2 candidates. Following their postdoctoral training, awardees may accept a faculty position at a U.S. or Canadian institution. The sponsor encourages applications from women and members of underrepresented minority groups.

Financial data In the first year of postdoctoral support, the stipend is $38,000, the research allowance is $15,360, and the administrative fee is $4,640; in the second year of postdoctoral support, the stipend is $41,000, the research allowance is $12,360, and the administrative fee is $4,640; in the first year of faculty support, the stipend is $54,000, the research allowance is $63,600, and the administrative fee is $10,400; in the second year of faculty support, the stipend is $59,000, the research allowance is $58,600, and the administrative fee is $10,400; in the third year of faculty support, the stipend is $65,000, the research allowance is $52,600, and the administrative fee is $10,400. The maximum portion of the award that can be used during the postdoctoral period is $116,000 or $58,000 per year. The faculty portion of the award is $500,000 minus the portion used during the postdoctoral years. The maximum support per year in the faculty portion of the award is $128,000.

Duration The awards provide 1 to 2 years of postdoctoral support and up to 3 years of support during the faculty appointment.

Special features Since this program began in 1995, more than $70 million in support has been provided to 149 U.S. and Canadian scientists.

Limitations Awardees are required to devote at least 80 percent of their time to research-related activities.

Number awarded At least 21 each year: approximately half of the awards go to researchers with a Ph.D. degree in a

biomedical science and half go to researchers with an M.D. or M.D./Ph.D. degree.
Deadline September of each year.

[523]
CENTER FOR AUSTRIAN STUDIES TRAVEL GRANTS

University of Minnesota
Attn: Center for Austrian Studies
314 Social Sciences Building
267 19th Avenue South
Minneapolis, MN 55455
(612) 624-9811 Fax: (612) 626-9004
E-mail: casahy@tc.umn.edu
Web site: www.cas.umn.edu

Purpose To provide funding to U.S. students interested in traveling to Austria for language study or research projects.
Eligibility This program is open to 3 categories of students: 1) undergraduate students at the University of Minnesota; 2) graduate students at the University of Minnesota; and 3) students at other U.S. colleges and universities. Applicants must be interested in traveling to Austria for language study or research in the social sciences, humanities, or business administration. U.S. citizenship is required.
Financial data Grants are intended to cover travel expenses, to a maximum of $1,000.
Duration These are 1-time grants.
Number awarded Varies each year; recently, 2 Minnesota undergraduates, 2 Minnesota graduate students, and 1 student at another university received grants.
Deadline March of each year.

[524]
CENTRE FOR EUROPEAN POLICY STUDIES GRANT

Institute of International Education
Attn: Student Programs Division
809 United Nations Plaza
New York, NY 10017-3580
(212) 984-5330 Fax: (212) 984-5325
Web site: www.iie.org/fulbright

Purpose To provide financial assistance to American graduate students who wish to conduct research at the Centre for European Policy Studies (CEPS) in Brussels, Belgium.
Eligibility Applicants must be U.S. citizens who hold a B.A. degree or equivalent before the beginning date of the grant and plan to conduct research at the CEPS. Their research interests should fit into 1 of the 2 principal research programs at the center: European economic policy (including macroeconomic and monetary policies within the framework of EMU, the external implications of EMU, trade and investment, economic and social cohesion, regulatory policy, environmental policy, and transport and other infrastructures) and politics, institutions, and society in the EU and Europe (including EU politics and institutions, EU enlargement, EU policy towards southeastern Europe, EU Mediterranean policy, the emerging pan-European security structure, and relations between the EU, Russia, Ukraine, and other successor states of the former Soviet Union). Applicants must expect to take an active part in the life of the center, including, as appropriate, the organization of seminar series and/or workshops, bringing together not only academic experts but politicians and officials active in the EU institutions and the member states.
Financial data Fellows receive a maintenance allowance based on the cost of living, round-trip international travel, and health and accident insurance. The CEPS provides supplemental funding of the Euro equivalent of 40,000 Belgian francs per month.
Duration 1 academic year.
Special features This is a Fulbright program, funded by the U.S. Department of State and administered by the Institute of International Education (IIE). Students who are currently enrolled in the United States are to apply through the Fulbright program adviser on their campus; at-large applicants (those not currently enrolled) may obtain applications and information directly from the IIE.
Number awarded 1 each year.
Deadline October of each year

[525]
CENTRE FOR EUROPEAN POLICY STUDIES RESEARCH PROGRAM

Council for International Exchange of Scholars
3007 Tilden Street, N.W., Suite 5L
Washington, DC 20008-3009
(202) 686-6247 Fax: (202) 362-3442
E-mail: scholars@cies.iie.org
Web site: www.iie.org/cies

Purpose To enable American scholars to conduct research at the Centre for European Policy Studies in Belgium.
Eligibility This program is open to scholars who wish to conduct research that is compatible with the program units at the Centre: European economic policy, European policies and business strategy, European Union (EU) enlargement to the east and south, European security, and EU politics and institutions. Applicants must have foreign language competence as required for the project. U.S. citizenship is required.
Financial data The stipend is the Euro equivalent of 64,000 to 80,000 Belgian francs per month, depending on the number of accompanying dependents. Also provided are round-trip travel for the grantee only and a research supplement of the EUR equivalent of BF 50,000 per month.
Duration 10 months.
Special features This is a Fulbright scholar program, sponsored by the Bureau of Educational and Cultural Affairs of the U.S. Department of State and administered by the Council for International Exchange of Scholars. The scholar is also expected to take an active part in the Centre's academic life, helping to organize seminars and workshops and bringing together academic experts, politicians, and officials active in EU institutions and member states.
Number awarded 1 each year.
Deadline July of each year.

[526]
CERN SCIENTIFIC ASSOCIATESHIPS
Centre Européen de la Recherche Nucléaire
Attn: Recruitment Service, Human Resources Division
CH-1211 Geneva 23
Switzerland
Fax: 41 22 767 2750
E-mail: recruitment.service@cern.ch
Web site: www.cern.ch/jobs

Purpose To provide nuclear physicists an opportunity to use the research facilities of the Centre Européen de la Recherche Nucléaire (CERN).

Eligibility Applicants must be young postdoctoral scholars engaged in research in experimental and theoretical particle physics, as well as related activities in applied physics, electronics, computing, and engineering. Most associateships are reserved for nationals of member states of CERN, but a few are provided to scientists who are not of member state nationality. Priority is given to applicants who can make a definite contribution to the work of CERN and to those who cannot obtain adequate scientific facilities in their own countries.

Financial data Most associates from nonmember states come to CERN with independent support, such as from their home institutes, or with fellowships awarded by external organizations, or under exchange programs with other laboratories, but CERN has a limited amount of money available for the assistance of those who cannot obtain adequate support from other sources.

Duration Up to 1 year; may be extended an additional year in exceptional cases.

Special features The member states of CERN are Austria, Belgium, Bulgaria, Czech Republic, Denmark, Finland, France, Germany, Greece, Hungary, Italy, Netherlands, Norway, Poland, Portugal, Slovak Republic, Spain, Sweden, Switzerland, and United Kingdom.

Number awarded Varies each year.

Deadline April, September, or December of each year.

[527]
CHATEAUBRIAND FELLOWSHIPS IN SCIENCE AND TECHNOLOGY
Embassy of France
Attn: Office of Science and Technology
4101 Reservoir Road, N.W.
Washington, DC 20007-2176
(202) 944-6253   Fax: (202) 944-6244
E-mail: chateaubriand@amb-wash.fr
Web site: www.chateaubriand.amb-wash.fr

Purpose To provide financial assistance to American citizens who are doctoral candidates or recent Ph.D.s interested in conducting research at a French university, school of engineering, or state-funded laboratory.

Eligibility Applicants must be U.S. citizens, be registered in a U.S. university or national laboratory, and be working on their Ph.D. in science or engineering (including biomedical and agricultural sciences) or have completed it within the last 3 years. They must be proposing to conduct research in France at a university, a school of engineering, or a public or private laboratory. Before applying, they must have been accepted by the laboratory; applicants who do not have contacts with a research institution in France may register with the embassy in order to have their file circulated to various French laboratories that may contact them directly.

Financial data The monthly stipend is $1,528 for doctoral fellows or $1,800 for postdoctoral fellows; health insurance and a round-trip ticket are also provided.

Duration 6 to 12 months, beginning in September.

Number awarded At least 25 each year.

Deadline November of each year.

[528]
CHATEAUBRIAND SCHOLARSHIPS FOR HUMANITIES
French Cultural Services
972 Fifth Avenue
New York, NY 10021-0144
(212) 439-1433   Fax: (212) 439-1455
E-mail: new-york.culture@diplomatie.fr
Web site: www.frenchculture.org

Purpose To provide financial support for research in France to American doctoral candidates in the social sciences or humanities.

Eligibility Applicants must be U.S. citizens currently working on a Ph.D. at an American university; the research should pertain to French literature, cinema, the humanities, the arts, history, philosophy, political science, or related disciplines. Sufficient proficiency in written and spoken French to carry out the proposed research must be demonstrated.

Financial data The stipend is the Euro equivalent of 8,700 French francs per month; health insurance and round-trip airfare are also provided.

Duration 9 months.

Number awarded Varies each year.

Deadline January of each year.

[529]
CHRIST CHURCH JUNIOR RESEARCH FELLOWSHIPS
University of Oxford
Christ Church
Attn: Censors' Office
Oxford OX1 1DP
England
44 1865 286574   Fax: 44 1865 276488
E-mail: vichy.rolls@chch.ox.ac.uk
Web site: www.chch.ox.ac.uk

Purpose To provide funding to junior investigators interested in conducting research at Christ Church of the University of Oxford in England.

Eligibility This program is open to scholars in designated fields of the arts and sciences who are nearing completion of their doctoral research or have begun postdoctoral study. Researchers who have held a comparable appointment at a college in the Universities of Cambridge or Oxford or have completed more than 6 years of postgraduate study or research are not eligible. Applicants must be interested in undertaking a specific research project at Oxford.

Financial data The fellow receives a stipend of 14,851 pounds per year, subsidized lunches and free dinners at High Table, and free accommodation in college or an annual housing allowance of 2,082 pounds.

Duration 3 years; may be renewed for 1 additional year.

Special features In the most recent offering of these fellowships, the fields were anthropology, archaeology, biology, chemistry, engineering, geography, modern history, and music.

Number awarded 4 (2 in the arts and 2 in the sciences) on a triennial schedule: 2004-05, 2007-8.

Deadline December of the year prior to the fellowship's availability.

[530]
CIMO BILATERAL SCHOLARSHIPS

Center for International Mobility
Attn: Information Services
P.O. Box 343
Hakaniemenkatu 2
FIN-00531 Helsinki
Finland
358 9 7747 7033 Fax: 358 9 7747 7064
E-mail: cimoinfo@cimo.fi
Web site: www.cimo.fi

Purpose To provide funding for study or research in Finland to doctoral candidates and university faculty from designated countries.

Eligibility This program is open to nationals of countries that have a bilateral cultural agreement with Finland. Applicants may be either 1) doctoral candidates under the age of 35 who wish to study or conduct research at a university in Finland, or 2) university teaching or research staff members and cultural experts in various fields who wish to strengthen cooperation between their institution and a Finnish counterpart. All applicants must establish contact with the receiving institute in Finland prior to applying.

Financial data For doctoral students, the monthly allowance is the Euro equivalent of 4,100 Finnish marks. University faculty and staff receive a daily allowance of the EUR equivalent of FIM 157; living accommodations are also provided.

Duration From 3 to 9 months for doctoral candidates; from 1 to 2 weeks for faculty and staff.

Special features The Center for International Mobility (CIMO) is an agency of the Finnish Ministry of Education. The countries that currently have a bilateral cultural agreement with Finland are Australia, Austria, Belgium, Bulgaria, Canada, China, Cuba, Czech Republic, Denmark, Egypt, France, Germany, Great Britain, Greece, Hungary, Iceland, India, Ireland, Israel, Italy, Japan, Luxembourg, Mexico, Mongolia, the Netherlands, Norway, Poland, Portugal, Republic of Korea, Romania, Slovakia, Spain, Sweden, Switzerland, Turkey, and the United States.

Limitations Applications must first be submitted to the appropriate authority in the candidate's country, who proposes the applicants to CIMO. In the United States, this is the Institute of International Education, U.S. Student Programs, 809 United Nations Plaza, New York, NY 10017, (212) 883-8200, Fax: (212) 984-5325.

Deadline Applications must be submitted to CIMO by February of each year.

[531]
CIVIC EDUCATION PROJECT VISITING LECTURESHIPS

Civic Education Project
1717 Massachusetts Avenue, N.W., Suite 506
Washington, DC 20036-2001
(202) 663-7793 Fax: (202) 663-7799
E-mail: cepdc@jhu.edu
Web site: www.cep.org.hu

Purpose To provide an opportunity for American scholars to teach at universities in central and eastern Europe, the former Soviet Union, and Eurasia.

Eligibility This program is open to U.S. scholars (including faculty, advanced graduate students, and professionals) in economics, education, environmental policy, European studies, history (including art history), international relations, journalism, law, library science, philosophy, political science, psychology, public administration and policy studies, social work, and sociology. Applicants must be interested in teaching their specialty at selected universities in Albania, Armenia, Belarus, Bulgaria, Czech Republic, Estonia, Georgia, Hungary, Kazakstan, Kyrgyzstan, Latvia, Lithuania, Moldova, Poland, Romania, Russia, Slovakia, Ukraine, or Uzbekistan.

Financial data The host university provides a salary in the local currency equal to the salary paid to a lecturer or professor of the same academic rank at that university, paid living accommodations, office space, and reasonable access to available office equipment (photocopy machine, telephone, e-mail, fax). This program provides a supplemental living stipend of $5,500 per year, round-trip airfare, health insurance, teaching materials for the lecturer's courses, and access to academic events and program funding.

Duration 1 year.

Special features Visiting lecturers teach up to 4 courses a year in their academic discipline and may teach more if requested by their university. Instruction is in the language of the lecturer, usually English. Participants also develop a variety of projects loosely termed "outreach activities," including revising curriculum, building departmental and university libraries, developing teaching materials in local languages, organizing faculty training seminars, sponsoring academic conferences on topical issues, creating networks through which scholars and other professionals can interact and exchange ideas, and developing Internet-based research and curriculum development projects. This program is sponsored by the Higher Education Support Program of the Open Society Institute, the Eurasia Foundation, the Andrew W. Mellon Foundation, Ford Foundation, Starr Foundation, Robert Bosch Foundation, Citicorp Foundation, John D. and Catherine T. MacArthur Foundation, and other donors. The European office is located at Nador u. 9, Budapest 1051, Hungary, 36 1 327 3219, Fax: 36 1 327 3221, E-mail: cep@osi.hu.

Number awarded Approximately 100 each year.

Deadline February of each year.

[532]
CLARE HALL RESEARCH FELLOWSHIPS
University of Cambridge
Clare Hall
Attn: Tutorial Secretary
Herschel Road
Cambridge CB3 9AL
England
44 1223 332360   Fax: 44 1223 332335
E-mail: tutorial.secretary@clarehall.cam.ac.uk
Web site: www.clarehall.cam.ac.uk

Purpose To provide funding to postdoctoral scholars interested in conducting research in the arts or social sciences at Clare Hall of the University of Cambridge in England.

Eligibility This program is open to scholars from any country who are interested in conducting research at Clare Hall in the arts or social sciences. There are no restrictions on age, sex, or previous standing, but former college research fellows at Cambridge or Oxford are not eligible.

Financial data The annual stipend is comparable to those for research fellowships at other colleges at Cambridge.

Duration Normally 3 years.

Number awarded 1 each year.

Deadline November of each year.

[533]
CLAUDE BERNARD SCHOLARSHIPS
Association Claude Bernard
13 rue Scipion
75005 Paris
France
33 1 40 27 42 79   Fax: 33 1 40 27 52 61

Purpose To provide funding to scientists interested in conducting research in France.

Eligibility Eligible to apply for funding from this source are high-level physicians and biologists from other countries who are interested in conducting scientific research in France.

Financial data The stipend is the Euro equivalent of 9,000 French francs per month; no travel expenses are covered.

Duration Up to 1 year.

Number awarded 5 each year.

Deadline March of each year.

[534]
CNES DOCTORAL GRANTS
Centre National d'Etudes Spatiales
18 avenue Edouard-Belin
31401 Toulouse
France
33 5 61 27 31 31   Fax: 33 5 61 27 31 79
Web site: www.cnes.fr

Purpose To provide funding to doctoral candidates interested in conducting scientific or technological research in France.

Eligibility This program is open to young university or engineering school graduates from any country who are working on a doctoral dissertation. Applicants must be interested in working in a government research laboratory in France, except those of the Centre National d'Etudes Spatiales (CNES). The proposed research must fall into 1 of the following topics: life sciences in space, physical sciences in microgravity, teledetection application, orbital systems technologies, or space transport systems technologies.

Financial data The stipend is the Euro equivalent of 10,000 French francs per month.

Duration 1 year; may be renewed for 2 additional years.

Number awarded Varies each year.

Deadline March of each year.

[535]
CNES POSTDOCTORAL GRANTS
Centre National d'Etudes Spatiales
18 avenue Edouard-Belin
31401 Toulouse
France
33 5 61 27 31 31   Fax: 33 5 61 27 31 79
Web site: www.cnes.fr

Purpose To provide funding to postdoctorates interested in conducting scientific or technological research in France.

Eligibility This program is open to scientists from any country who have a doctorate, have a good grasp of both English and French, and are interested in working in any government research laboratory in France except the Centre National d'Etudes Spatiales (CNES). The proposed research must fall into 1 of the following areas: sciences of the universe, sciences of planet Earth, life sciences in space, physical sciences in microgravity, orbital systems technologies, or space transport systems technologies.

Financial data The stipend is the Euro equivalent of 12,700 French francs per month.

Duration 1 year; may be renewed for 1 additional year.

Number awarded Up to 40 each year.

Deadline March of each year.

[536]
COLLABORATION IN BASIC SCIENCE AND ENGINEERING (COBASE) PROJECT DEVELOPMENT AND INITIATION GRANTS
National Research Council
Attn: Office of International Affairs
2101 Constitution Avenue, N.W., FO 2060
Washington, DC 20418
(202) 334-2644   Fax: (202) 334-2614
E-mail: ocee@nas.edu
Web site: www.nationalacademies.org/oia

Purpose To support American specialists who wish to visit colleagues in Eurasia, central/eastern Europe (CEE) or the Newly Independent States (NIS) of the former Soviet Union to prepare a collaborative research proposal in the basic sciences and engineering for submission to the National Science Foundation (NSF) or other funding organizations.

Eligibility Applications may be submitted by American specialists who possess or will possess a Ph.D. or equivalent research experience. They must be U.S. citizens or permanent residents affiliated with a U.S. university or other nonprofit research institution. Specialists who have received their doctoral degree within the past 6 years are especially encouraged to apply, as are applicants wishing to work with colleagues in less frequently represented countries and regions. Requests to develop research proposals are limited to the following fields funded by the NSF: archaeology and anthropology; astronomy; biochemistry, biophysics, and genetics; biological sciences; chemistry; computer science; earth sciences; economics; engineering; environmental sciences; geography; history and philosophy of science; mathematics; physics; psychology; science and technology policy; and social sciences. No proposals involving agricultural production; drug testing or development; research on the diagnosis, etiology, or treatment of physical or mental diseases or disorders; or the use of animal models of human diseases or conditions are accepted. Proposals must involve collaboration with scientists in the following CEE and NIS countries: Armenia, Azerbaijan (traveling only), Belarus (no hosting of Belarusian government employees), Bosnia (hosting in the United States only), Bulgaria, Croatia, Czech Republic, Estonia, Georgia, Hungary, Kazakhstan, Kyrgyzstan, Latvia, Lithuania, Former Yugoslav Republic of Macedonia, Moldova, Poland, Romania, Russia (designated institutes are excluded), Slovakia, Slovenia, Tajikistan, Turkmenistan, Ukraine, or Uzbekistan. Selection is based on applicant's technical abilities; quality of the proposed project; feasibility of carrying out the proposed project; and prospects for long-term collaboration following the completion of the current project.

Financial data Grants provide up to $2,500 per visit in round-trip airfare between the United States and CEE/NIS; living expenses for foreign visitors to the United States of up to $1,750 for 2 weeks, up to $2,500 for 4 weeks, or up to $5,000 for 8 weeks; living expenses for U.S. visitors to the CEE/NIS of up to $1,500 for 2 weeks, up to $2,000 for 4 weeks, or up to $4,000 for 8 weeks; and up to $100 per visit-week for expendable supplies for the research projects. Living expenses for visits of other durations are calculated proportionately. The total amount of the grant ranges from $2,500 to $10,000.

Duration Each grant may support up to 2 visits in either or both directions (i.e., either traveling to CEE/NIS or hosting a colleague from the region here in the U.S.) with the total combined duration of the visit(s) not to exceed 8 weeks. Each proposed individual visit must be at least 2 weeks in length.

Special features American recipients may travel to the participating countries to prepare collaborative research proposals. A parallel program allows American scholars to host scientists from CEE or NIS countries. Funding for this program comes from NSF; it is administered by the National Research Council, the operating arm of the National Academy of Sciences, National Academy of Engineering, and Institute of Medicine.

Limitations Visits developed primarily to present lectures or to organize or attend conferences are ineligible.

Deadline April, August, or January of each year.

[537]
CORPUS CHRISTI RESEARCH FELLOWSHIPS

University of Cambridge
Corpus Christi College
Attn: Admissions Secretary
Trumpington Street
Cambridge CB2 1RH
England
44 1223 338056   Fax: 44 1223 338057
E-mail: admissions@corpus.cam.ac.uk
Web site: www.corpus.cam.ac.uk

Purpose To provide funding to postdoctoral scholars who wish to conduct research in designated fields at Corpus Christi College of the University of Cambridge in England.

Eligibility This program is open to graduates of any university who completed a doctoral degree within the preceding 5 years and are engaged in research in specified disciplines that change annually. Recently, the fields were electronic engineering, philosophy, psychology, or theology. Applicants must be interested in affiliating with Corpus Christi College of the University of Cambridge.

Financial data The stipend is 14,398 pounds in the first year, rising to 17,102 in the third year. Fellows also receive free accommodation in the college or a living-out allowance. An annual allowance for research expenditures is also available.

Duration 3 years.

Special features Fellows are allowed to teach up to 6 hours per week for additional remuneration.

Limitations Fellows are expected to participate in the intellectual life of Leckhampton, the college's graduate center.

Number awarded 2 or more each year.

Deadline January of each year.

[538]
COUNCIL OF INTERNATIONAL PROGRAMS EXCHANGE INTERNSHIPS

Council of International Programs
1700 East 13th Street, Suite 4ME
Cleveland, OH 44114-3214
(216) 566-1088   Fax: (216) 566-1490
E-mail: cipusa@compuserve.com
Web site: www.cipusa.org

Purpose To allow U.S. professionals in the fields of education, health, and social work to participate in a summer internship program in designated foreign countries.

Eligibility Applicants must be U.S. citizens engaged, as professionals or volunteers, in social work, associated health work, or education. They must be interested in participating in a summer internship program abroad. Most programs operate in English, although German is desirable in Austria and required in Germany, French is required in France, Greek is desirable in Greece, and Italian is desirable in Italy.

Financial data Sponsoring organizations in the foreign countries pay for living expenses, usually through host families, and travel within their respective countries. Recipients must pay for their own international airfare.

Duration 4 to 8 weeks.

Special features Countries currently participating in this program are Austria, Finland, France, Germany, Greece, Hungary, India, Israel, Italy, the Netherlands, Norway, Scotland, Slovenia, Sweden, and Turkey.

Limitations Program fees are required for some countries: $120 for Austria and Hungary, $1,000 for France, $200 for Greece, $600 for India, $250 for Israel, $200 for Italy and Slovenia, $75 for the Netherlands, or $300 for Turkey. No program fees are required for the other countries.

Number awarded Varies each year; recently, the number of available positions was 3 to 6 in Austria and Hungary, 8 to 10 in Finland, 12 to 15 in France, 12 to 15 in Germany, 8 in Greece, 10 to 15 in India, 2 in Israel, 4 in Italy and Slovenia, 8 in the Netherlands, 8 in Norway, 6 to 8 in Scotland, 8 to 12 in Sweden, and 4 to 6 in Turkey.

Deadline February of each year for France, Germany, India, Italy, and Slovenia; November of each year for Austria, Finland, Greece, Hungary, Israel, the Netherlands, Norway, Scotland, Sweden, and Turkey.

[539]
CRAY-PAS WONDERFUL COLORFUL WORLD CONTEST

Sakura of America
30780 San Clemente Street
Hayward, CA 94544
(510) 475-8800   Fax: (510) 475-0973
E-mail: express@sakuraofamerica.com
Web site: www.gellyroll.com

Purpose To recognize and reward 1) outstanding paintings done in oil pastels by elementary school students and 2) their teachers (who win a trip to France).

Eligibility Students attending public or private schools in the United States, its territories, and Canada are eligible to enter this content if they are in grades K-8. They are invited to submit a piece of original art, the majority of which is done in oil pastels. The painting can be no larger than 12 x 18 inches (with or without matte); the artwork must be flat (2 dimensional). Teachers may submit color copies, but the original work of art must be available if 1 of the students wins. The subject of the artwork may be individually determined or may be a class project. Each entry must be the work of 1 student only, and 1 student can enter only 1 piece of art. Submissions are judged on the basis of originality, Cray-Pas oil pastel art techniques, and visual impact. Prizes are awarded to the winning students and to their teachers.

Financial data First-place student winners (3) receive $300 savings bonds, national media recognition, placement in the online Wonderful Colorful Word Gallery, and a supply of Cray-Pas (for a total value of approximately $600). The teachers of the winning students receive a trip to France, a digital camera, national media recognition, placement in the online Wonderful Colorful World Gallery, and a supply of Cray-Pas (for a total of approximately $4,500). In addition, 3 second-place winners and their teachers receive a digital camera, national media recognition, placement in the online Wonderful Colorful World Gallery, and a supply of Cray-Pas (for a total of $500) and 3 other second-place students receive a $200 U.S. savings bond, national media attention, placement in the online Wonderful Colorful World Gallery, and a supply of Cray-Pas (approximate value of $400); 3 third-place winners receive a $100 savings bond; and 9 placing schools receive a supply of art materials (valued at approximately $1,000).

Duration The competition is held annually.

Limitations The sponsor manufactures Cray-Pas oil pastels and recommends using Cray-Pas products in producing the submitted artwork.

Number awarded 12 students, 3 teachers, and 9 placing schools.

Deadline December of each year.

[540]
CZECH REPUBLIC FULBRIGHT TEACHER EXCHANGE

U.S. Department of State
c/o Graduate School, USDA
600 Maryland Avenue, S.W., Room 320
Washington, DC 20024-2520
(202) 314-3520   Fax: (202) 479-6806
E-mail: fulbright@grad.usda.gov
Web site: www.grad.usda.gov/International/ftep.html

Purpose To promote mutual understanding between the people of the United States and the people of the Czech Republic through a teacher exchange program.

Eligibility This program is open to secondary school teachers (grades 7 through 12) and 2-year college instructors of English as a second language, English literature, social studies, education, arts, or science who are interested in teaching in the Czech Republic. Applicants must 1) be U.S. citizens; 2) hold at least a bachelor's degree; 3) be fluent in English; 4) have a current full-time teaching assignment in the U.S. or a territory; 5) have the approval of their school administration; 6) have at least 3 years of full-time experience; and 7) not have participated in a Fulbright Teacher Exchange longer than 8 weeks during the last 2 years. Fluency in Czech is not required although some ability is useful. The language of instruction is English. Teaching couples may apply. However, because of the limited number of positions available and, often, the lack of foreign candidate pairs with similar qualifications for interchanges, it may not be possible to arrange suitable assignments in the same locality or to place both teachers. Preference is given to applicants who have not participated previously in the program and may be given to applicants who have not previously lived in the Czech Republic. Geographic distribution of awards within the United States is also a factor in selection. This program does not discriminate on the basis of race, color, religion, age, sex, or national origin and encourages the applications of members of minority communities. Other considerations being equal, veterans are given preference.

Financial data Round-trip transportation for the exchange teacher only is provided. Participants must obtain a leave of absence with pay from their jobs in the United States. The U.S. school must agree to accept a teacher from the Czech Republic who must secure a leave of absence with pay; the Czech teacher receives a stipend, but no additional cost accrues to the U.S. school.

Duration 9 months, beginning in September.

Special features This program is sponsored by the Bureau of Educational and Cultural Affairs of the U.S. Department of State and administered by the Graduate School, USDA.

Limitations This program provides for the direct exchange of teaching assignments between the Czech Republic and the United States. Applicants selected for exchange must attend orientation programs of the sponsoring agencies in the United States or abroad.

Number awarded 4 each year.

Deadline October of each year.

[541]
DAAD RESEARCH GRANTS FOR RECENT PH.D.S AND PH.D. CANDIDATES

German Academic Exchange Service (DAAD)
950 Third Avenue, 19th Floor
New York, NY 10022
(212) 758-3223   Fax: (212) 755-5780
E-mail: daadny@daad.org
Web site: www.daad.org

Purpose To provide financial assistance for research in Germany to Ph.D candidates and recent Ph.D.s.

Eligibility Applicants must be Ph.D. candidates or recent Ph.D.s who have completed their degree within the previous 2 years; preference is given to applicants who are younger than 35 years of age. They must wish to carry out dissertation or postdoctoral research at libraries, archives, institutes, or laboratories in Germany. Applicants must be U.S. or Canadian citizens enrolled at U.S. or Canadian universities; foreign nationals may be eligible if they have been full-time students at a U.S. or Canadian university for at least 1 year. Adequate knowledge of the German language, to carry out the proposed research, is required (except in the natural sciences and engineering).

Financial data The grant provides a monthly maintenance allowance of 1,700 Deutsche marks (869.19 Euros), an international travel subsidy of DM 1,000 (EUR 511.29), and health insurance. Additional support for family members is not available.

Duration 1 to 6 months.

Number awarded Varies each year.

Deadline January of each year for research to begin during the months from July through December; July of each year for research to begin during the months from January through June.

[542]
DAAD STUDY VISIT RESEARCH GRANTS FOR FACULTY

German Academic Exchange Service (DAAD)
950 Third Avenue, 19th Floor
New York, NY 10022
(212) 758-3223   Fax: (212) 755-5780
E-mail: daadny@daad.org
Web site: www.daad.org

Purpose To provide funding to faculty members interested in conducting research in Germany.

Eligibility Applicants must have at least 2 years of teaching and/or research experience at a U.S. or Canadian university or research institution after receipt of the Ph.D. or equivalent degree. They must be able to demonstrate a previous research record in the proposed field and adequate knowledge of the German language to carry out the proposed research (except in the natural sciences or engineering). The program is open to U.S. or Canadian citizens or to permanent residents of the United States or Canada who have been affiliated with a U.S. or Canadian institution in full-time employment for at least 2 consecutive years (6 years for German nationals) and who wish to conduct research in Germany.

Financial data The grant provides a monthly maintenance allowance that ranges from 3,400 to 3,700 Deutsche marks (1,738.39 to 1,891.77 Euros). An additional stipend of DM 300 (EUR 153.3) for travel within Germany may be awarded. Additional support for family members is not available.

Duration 1 to 3 months.

Limitations Grants may not be used for travel only, attendance at conferences or conventions, editorial meetings, lecture tours, or extended guest-professorships.

Number awarded Varies each year.

Deadline January of each year for research to begin during the months from July through December; July of each year for research to begin during the months from January through June.

[543]
DAAD-LEO BAECK INSTITUTE GRANTS

Leo Baeck Institute
15 West 16th Street
New York, NY 10011-6301
(212) 744-6400   Fax: (212) 988-1305
E-mail: emusso@lbi.cjh.org
Web site: www.lbi.org/grants/daad.html

Purpose To provide financial assistance to doctoral students working on their dissertations and recent Ph.D.s preparing a scholarly essay or book on the history of German-speaking Jewry.

Eligibility Eligible to apply are Ph.D. candidates or recent Ph.D.s currently enrolled at or affiliated with a U.S. university or college; all applicants must be U.S. citizens interested in conducting research on the social, communal, or intellectual history of German-speaking Jewry.

Financial data If the fellow utilizes the facilities of the Leo Baeck Institute in New York, the stipend is $2,000; grants for research in Germany consist of a monthly maintenance allowance of the Euro equivalent of 1,700 Deutsche marks and an international travel subsidy of the EUR equivalent of DM 1,000. Support for family members is not available.

Duration Fellowships for research at the Leo Baeck Institute are tenable for a period of 6 weeks; grants for research in Germany cover up to 6 months in 1 calendar year.

Number awarded Varies each year.

Deadline October of each year.

[544]
DAAD–NSF COLLABORATIVE RESEARCH GRANTS

German Academic Exchange Service (DAAD)
950 Third Avenue, 19th Floor
New York, NY 10022
(212) 758-3223   Fax: (212) 755-5780
E-mail: daadny@daad.org
Web site: www.daad.org

Purpose To provide funding to U.S. scholars and scientists who wish to conduct research in natural sciences, engineering, and social sciences in Germany.

Eligibility Applicants must be scholars or scientists at U.S. universities or research institutes who wish to carry out joint research projects in the natural, engineering, or social sciences with colleagues at German universities and Fachhochschulen. Projects should foster the advancement and specialization of young scientists within the framework of the proposed collaboration.

Financial data This program covers travel and living expenses.

Special features The German Academic Exchange Service (Deutscher Akademischer Austauschdienst) administers this program jointly with the National Science Foundation (NSF); further information is also available from NSF, Directorate for Social, Behavioral, and Economic Sciences, Division of International Programs, 4201 Wilson Boulevard, Arlington, Virginia, 22230, (703) 306-1702, Fax: (703) 306-0476, E-mail: msuskin@nsf.gov.

Number awarded Varies each year.

Deadline June of each year.

[545]
DAVID E. FINLEY FELLOWSHIP

National Gallery of Art
Attn: Center for Advanced Study in the Visual Arts
Sixth Street and Constitution Avenue, N.W.
Washington, DC 20565
(202) 842-6482   Fax: (202) 842-6733
TDD: (202) 842-6176   E-mail: advstudy@nga.gov
Web site: www.nga.gov/resources/casvapre.htm

Purpose To provide financial assistance to doctoral candidates interested in conducting research in Europe on the history, theory, and criticism of Western art, architecture, and urbanism.

Eligibility Applicants must have completed their residence requirements and course work for the Ph.D. and general or preliminary examinations before the date of application. In addition, they must know 2 foreign languages related to the topic of the dissertation, be U.S. citizens or enrolled in an American university, be interested in museum work (although there is no requirement as to the candidate's subsequent choice of a career), and be interested in conducting research in Europe on the history, theory, and criticism of Western art, architecture, and urbanism. Application for this fellowship must be made through the chair of the student's graduate department of art history or other appropriate department; the chair should act as a sponsor for the applicant. Departments must limit their nominations to 1 candidate. Finalists are invited to Washington during February for interviews.

Financial data The stipend is $16,000 per year.

Duration 3 years: 2 years in Europe conducting research and 1 year in residence at the National Gallery of Art's Center for Advanced Study in the Visual Arts in Washington, D.C. to complete the dissertation. The fellowship begins in September and is not renewable.

Special features Half of the residency at the gallery is devoted to research projects designed to complement the topic of the fellow's dissertation.

Number awarded 1 each year.

Deadline November of each year.

[546]
DAVID PHILLIPS FELLOWSHIPS

Biotechnology and Biological Sciences Research Council
Attn: Secretariat and Liaison Branch
Polaris House
North Star Avenue
Swindon SN2 1UH
United Kingdom
44 1793 413348   Fax: 44 1793 413382
E-mail: postdoc.fellowships@bbsrc.ac.uk
Web site: www.bbsrc.ac.uk

Purpose To provide funding to scientists from any country who are interested in conducting biological research in the United Kingdom.

Eligibility This program is open to postdoctoral scientists with no more than 5 and a half years of active postdoctoral research experience. Candidates from outside the European Economic Area must hold a valid U.K. work permit and comply with Department for Education and Employment requirements. All applicants must be interested in conducting research at an institute sponsored by the Biotechnology and Biological Sciences Research Council (BBSRC) or at an appropriate U.K. university. They are responsible for making the necessary arrangements with the institution before submitting an application and for ensuring that the facilities available for the proposed research are appropriate and accessible.

Financial data The starting salary is set at point 13 of the RAII scale.

Duration Up to 5 years.

Special features The BBSRC was established by Royal Charter to promote and support basic, strategic, and applied research relating to the understanding and exploitation of biological systems.

Number awarded Varies each year.

Deadline November of each year.

[547]
DAVID T.K. WONG FELLOWSHIP
University of East Anglia
Attn: School of English and American Studies
Norwich NR4 7TJ
England
44 1603 592810 Fax: 44 1603 507728
E-mail: v.striker@uea.ac.uk
Web site: www.uea.ac.uk/eas/intro/prizes/wong/intro.htm

Purpose To provide funding to fiction writers who are interested in writing about the Far East while in residence at the University of East Anglia in Norwich, England.

Eligibility Applicants must be interested in writing a work of fiction (in English) that deals seriously with an aspect of life in the Far East. Along with their application, they must submit an original piece of fiction, up to 5,000 words in length. They may be from any country and of any age and must be willing to reside at the University of East Anglia during the fellowship period.

Financial data The stipend is 25,000 pounds.

Duration 1 year.

Special features This program was established in 1997 and the first fellow appointed in 1998.

Limitations The application fee is 5 pounds.

Number awarded 1 each year.

Deadline October of each year.

[548]
DE MONTFORT UNIVERSITY POSTDOCTORAL RESEARCH AWARD
Council for International Exchange of Scholars
3007 Tilden Street, N.W., Suite 5L
Washington, DC 20008-3009
(202) 686-6245 Fax: (202) 362-3442
E-mail: scholars@cies.iie.org
Web site: www.iie.org/cies

Purpose To provide financial assistance to American scholars who wish to conduct research in England.

Eligibility Applicants must be U.S. citizens who possess a Ph.D. degree or the equivalent. They must be interested in conducting postdoctoral research at De Montfort University in Leicester, England.

Financial data The stipend is 5,000 pounds and round-trip travel.

Duration 12 months.

Special features This is a Fulbright scholar program, sponsored by the Bureau of Educational and Cultural Affairs of the U.S. Department of State and administered by the Council for International Exchange of Scholars. Information on research opportunities at De Montfort University are available from Professor Graham Chapman, De Montfort University, The Gateway, Leicester LE1 9BH, Fax: 44 116 255 0307, E-mail: gmc@dmu.ac.uk.

Number awarded 1 each year.

Deadline July of each year.

[549]
DELFT UNIVERSITY OF TECHNOLOGY RESEARCH FELLOWSHIPS
Delft University of Technology
Attn: Secretary to the Research Fellowship Committee
Julianalaan 134
2628 BL Delft
Netherlands
31 15 278 1685 Fax: 31 15 278 7749
E-mail: m.w.m.waanders@stafcvb.tudelft.nl

Purpose To provide financial assistance to young scientists and graduate students who are interested in conducting research at Delft University of Technology in the Netherlands.

Eligibility Applicants must have completed work on a Ph.D. or possess a master's degree with at least 1 additional year of experience in research. They must be proposing to conduct research in applied earth sciences, applied physics, architecture, chemical technology, engineering (aerospace, civil, electrical, geodetic, industrial, mechanical, or systems), marine technology, materials sciences, policy analysis and management, technical mathematics, technical informatics, or technology and society at Delft University. Knowledge of the Dutch language is not required, but proficiency in English, French, or German is necessary. Applicants must be younger than 36 years of age.

Financial data The monthly stipend is the Euro equivalents of 6,433.65 Dutch florins for senior fellows or Dfl 4,110.00 for junior fellows.

Duration 6 to 12 months.

Number awarded A limited number are awarded each year.

Deadline March or September of each year.

[550]
DESIGN ARTS ROME PRIZE FELLOWSHIPS
American Academy in Rome
Attn: Fellowship Coordinator
7 East 60th Street
New York, NY 10022-1001
(212) 751-7200 Fax: (212) 751-7220
E-mail: info@aarome.org
Web site: www.aarome.org

Purpose To provide financial support to American professionals interested in conducting research in design arts at the School of Fine Arts of the American Academy in Rome.

Eligibility Applicants must have had at least 7 years of professional experience and be currently engaged in practice in the field of the award, which includes graphic design, industrial design, interior design, set design, or urban design and planning. A baccalaureate degree or its equivalent and a license to practice, if appropriate, are also required. All applicants must be U.S. citizens. They must be interested in conducting research in design arts at the American Academy in Rome. Full-time students are not eligible.

Financial data The fellowship provides a stipend of up to $10,000, meals, a bedroom with private bath, and a study or studio. Fellows with children under 18 are housed outside the McKim, Mead & White building and are provided with an allowance that helps cover the cost of off-campus housing.

Duration 6 months, beginning in September.

Special features The American Academy in Rome, founded in 1894 by the American architect Charles F. McKim, is a center for independent study and advanced research in the fine arts and humanities. It consists of a School of Fine Arts (including architecture, landscape architecture, design arts, painting and sculpture, musical composition, and literature) and a School of Classical Studies (including classical studies and archaeology, history of art, and post-classical humanistic/modern Italian studies).

Limitations There is a $40 application fee. Prize winners may not hold full-time jobs while at the Academy.

Number awarded 2 each year.

Deadline November of each year.

---

[551]
DEUTSCHER AKADEMISCHER AUSTAUSCHDIENST (GERMAN ACADEMIC EXCHANGE SERVICE) GRANTS

Institute of International Education
Attn: Student Programs Division
809 United Nations Plaza
New York, NY 10017-3580
(212) 984-5330 Fax: (212) 984-5325
Web site: www.iie.org/fulbright

Purpose To provide funding to American graduate students for doctoral research at a German university.

Eligibility This program is open to U.S. citizens who have a good knowledge of German and wish to conduct research in Germany. Preference is given to Ph.D. candidates pursuing doctoral research. Candidates may not be younger than 18 or older than 32.

Financial data The stipend is the Euro equivalent of 1,185 to 2,070 Deutsche marks a month, depending upon the recipient's level of academic training and marital status. Other benefits include round-trip travel between the grantee's home town and the place of study in Germany, an excess baggage allowance, a start-up allowance, a book allowance, a health and accident insurance allowance, and a spouse allowance, if appropriate.

Duration 10 months, beginning in October.

Special features This program is funded by the German Academic Exchange Service, which is a private, self-governing organization of universities in Germany founded in 1925 and re-established in 1950 to promote international relations between institutions of higher education; further information is also available from the German Academic Exchange Service (950 Third Avenue, 19th Floor, New York, NY 10022). The program is administered in the United States by the Institute of International Education (IIE) as part of the Fulbright program. Students who are currently enrolled in the United States are to apply through the Fulbright program adviser on their campus; at-large applicants (those not currently enrolled) may obtain applications and information directly from the IIE.

Limitations Recipients may not use these grants to finance U.S. college-sponsored programs in Germany.

Number awarded 30 each year.

Deadline October of each year.

---

[552]
DIPLOMATIC ACADEMY VISITING PROFESSOR OF INTERNATIONAL RELATIONS

Council for International Exchange of Scholars
3007 Tilden Street, N.W., Suite 5L
Washington, DC 20008-3009
(202) 686-6240 Fax: (202) 362-3442
E-mail: scholars@cies.iie.org
Web site: www.iie.org/cies

Purpose To provide funding to scholars who are interested in teaching at the Diplomatic Academy in Vienna.

Eligibility This program is open to scholars of international relations who have some experience as practitioners. Applicants must be interested in teaching at the Diplomatic Academy. Instruction is in English, but some proficiency in German in desirable. U.S. citizenship is required.

Financial data The maintenance allowance is 3,300 Euros per month. Also provided are a travel award of EUR 770 for the grantee only and an allowance for legal accompanying dependents of EUR 145 per month per dependent (up to 3 accompanying dependents). Housing is provided by the institution.

Duration 4 months.

Special features This is a Fulbright scholar program, sponsored by the Bureau of Educational and Cultural Affairs of the U.S. Department of State and administered by the Council for International Exchange of Scholars. The recipient teaches 3 courses at the graduate level.

Number awarded 1 each year.

Deadline July of each year.

---

[553]
DOCTORAL RESEARCH IN ITALY FELLOWSHIP

National Italian American Foundation
Attn: Education Director
1860 19th Street, N.W.
Washington, DC 20009
(202) 387-0600 Fax: (202) 387-0800
E-mail: maria@niaf.org
Web site: www.niaf.org

Purpose To provide financial assistance to Italian American doctoral students who are interested in conducting research in Italy.

Eligibility This program is open to Italian American Ph.D. candidates in modern history, politics, and economics. Applicants must be interested in conducting research in Italy. They must provide an extensive abstract of work to be conducted and their advisor must provide a letter of support. Selection is based on academic merit, financial need, and community service.

Financial data The stipend is $5,000.

Duration 1 year.

Limitations There is a $10 registration fee.

Number awarded 1 each year.

Deadline May of each year.

[554]
DOROTHY HODGKIN FELLOWSHIPS
Royal Society
Attn: Executive Secretary
6 Carlton House Terrace
London SW1Y 5AG
England
44 20 7451 2542　　　　　Fax: 44 20 7451 2692
E-mail: UKResearch.Appointments@royalsoc.ac.uk
Web site: www.royalsoc.ac.uk

Purpose To provide financial assistance to junior scholars interested in conducting scientific research in the United Kingdom.

Eligibility This program is open to postdoctoral scientists of any nationality who are normally resident in the United Kingdom (either be currently employed there or have at some time been resident for a continuous period of 3 years other than for the sole purpose of receiving full-time education). Applicants must be interested in conducting research in the natural sciences (including mathematics and engineering but excluding the social sciences) at a university or research institution in the United Kingdom. They should be under the age of 35 and have no more than 4 years' postdoctoral research experience. Women are especially encouraged to apply.

Financial data The stipend is equivalent to salaries at research staff IIA/II scales.

Duration At least 4 years.

Special features These fellowships were first offered in 1995.

Number awarded Varies each year; recently, 12 of these fellowships were offered.

Deadline February of each year.

[555]
DOWNING COLLEGE RESEARCH FELLOWSHIP
University of Cambridge
Downing College
Attn: Senior Tutor
Regent Street
Cambridge CB2 1DQ
England
44 1223 334800　　　　　Fax: 44 1223 467934
E-mail: Senior-tutor@dow.cam.ac.uk
Web site: www.dow.cam.ac.uk

Purpose To provide funding to postdoctoral scholars interested in conducting research in designated fields at Downing College of the University of Cambridge in England.

Eligibility This program is open to scholars from any country who are interested in conducting research at Downing College in fields that change annually (recently: chemical engineering, chemistry, computer sciences, earth sciences, engineering, materials science and metallurgy, mathematics, physical geography, and physics). Applicants must be either under 30 years of age or have completed no more than 12 terms as registered research students. They should have completed or be near completion of a Ph.D. degree.

Financial data The annual stipend is 13,912 pounds for predoctoral fellows or 14,851 pounds for postdoctoral fellows. Unmarried fellows are provided with free accommodations in the college. Fellows who reside outside the college receive an additional living-out allowance.

Duration Up to 3 years.

Number awarded 1 each year.

Deadline December of each year.

[556]
DR. HEINRICH JORG VISITING SCHOLARSHIP
Austrian Cultural Institute
950 Third Avenue, 20th Floor
New York, NY 10022
(212) 759-5165　　　　　Fax: (212) 319-9636
E-mail: desk@aci.org
Web site: www.austriaculture.net

Purpose To provide funding to scholars interested in conducting research in the Department of Science at the Karl-Franzens-Universität in Graz, Austria.

Eligibility This program is open to scientists from any country who are interested in conducting research at the university in Austria. Applicants must be willing to participate in a joint project.

Financial data The amount of the grant depends on the nature of the project and the qualifications of the scholar.

Duration Varies.

Special features Information is also available from the Dr.-Heinrich-Jörg-Stiftung, Universität Graz, Dekanat der Naturwissenschaftlichen Facultät der, Universitätsplatz 3, A-8010 Graz, Austria.

Number awarded Varies each year.

[557]
DR. WERNER KUBSCH AWARD FOR ACHIEVEMENT IN INTERNATIONAL EDUCATION
Community Colleges for International Development
c/o Kirkwood Community College
6301 Kirkwood Boulevard, S.W.
Cedar Rapids, IA 52406
(319) 398-1257　　　　　Fax: (319) 392-1255
E-mail: tmikula@kirkwood.cc.ia.us
Web site: www.ccid.kirkwood.cc.ia.us/werner.htm

Purpose To honor community college educators who have demonstrated outstanding achievement in international education related to community colleges.

Eligibility Nominees may be faculty, administrators, or non-instructional staff members of community colleges who have demonstrated outstanding achievement in international education. Selection is based on the nominees' contribution to community college students' ability to understand the impact of other countries and cultures on their daily lives; expansion of opportunities for international students to study in the United States and Canada or for community college students to study abroad; development or implementation of opportunities for faculty exchanges and study abroad; development of linkages with educational systems or institutions in other countries; and development or participation in educational projects overseas that benefit educational systems, institutions, or people in other countries.

Financial data The award provides a 1-week all expense paid trip to Germany, a complimentary registration at the Community Colleges for International Development (CCID) annual conference on international education, and a stipend of $500.
Special features The CCID was founded in 1976 as a consortium of 40 U.S. and Canadian community colleges that sponsors international programs and projects to benefit other countries as well as its own member institutions and other community colleges.
Number awarded 1 each year.
Deadline Nominations must be submitted by early December of each year.

[558]
DRAPERS' COMPANY JUNIOR RESEARCH FELLOWSHIP

University of Oxford
St. Anne's College
Attn: Senior Tutor's Secretary
Oxford OX2 6HS
England
44 1865 274800   Fax: 44 1865 274899
Web site: www.stannes.ox.ac.uk

Purpose To provide funding to doctoral candidates from any university who wish to conduct research in the sciences or mathematics at St. Anne's College of the University of Oxford in England.
Eligibility Applicants should be graduates in the second or subsequent year of study for a higher degree, should already have completed a significant amount of research, and must have completed the residence requirements at their home institution. Their field of study must be the sciences or mathematics. They must be interested in conducting research at St. Anne's College.
Financial data The stipend is 10,120 pounds per year. Fellows also receive free accommodation or a living-out allowance and are members of the senior common room.
Duration 1 year; may be renewed for 1 additional year.
Limitations The fellow must live in Oxford and take part in college life.
Number awarded This fellowship is offered periodically; it was most recently offered for 2001 for engineering, materials science, or earth science.
Deadline October of the year prior to the award.

[559]
DUBLIN INSTITUTE RESEARCH SCHOLARSHIPS

Dublin Institute for Advanced Studies
Attn: Registrar
10 Burlington Road
Dublin 4
Ireland
353 1 614 0100   Fax: 353 1 668 0561

Purpose To provide financial assistance for research in Celtic studies, theoretical physics, or cosmic physics at the Dublin Institute for Advanced Studies.
Eligibility Applicants may be citizens of any country who hold a college degree or higher in an appropriate and relevant subject. The 3 schools that comprise the institute deal with Celtic studies, theoretical physics, and cosmic physics (astronomy, astrophysics, and geophysics). Fellows must pursue a definite line of research under the direction of a senior professor at the institute. Candidates should have a reasonable fluency in English, and those for the school of Celtic studies should also demonstrate knowledge of Celtic.
Financial data The award is the Euro equivalents of 5,500 to 5,720 Irish pounds for primary degree holders, 6,050 to 6,490 Irish pounds per year for master's degree holders, and 8,470 to 9,020 Irish pounds for doctoral degree holders; in exceptional cases the annual stipend may be as high as 10,780 Irish pounds. Separate rates apply to the School of Theoretical Physics, where stipends range from the Euro equivalent of 14,000 to 15,000 Irish pounds. In addition, grants up to 900 Irish pounds may be available for general moving expenses.
Duration 1 year; may be renewed for 1 additional year.
Special features The institute was founded by Parliament in 1940 with the School of Celtic Studies and the School of Theoretical Physics; the School of Cosmic Physics was added in 1947.
Limitations Scholars are required to be in full-time residence at the schools and may not study elsewhere. The institute is not a degree-granting institution.
Number awarded 18 each year: 6 in each of the schools.
Deadline March of each year.

[560]
E. DE ROTHSCHILD AND Y. MAYENT FELLOWSHIPS

Institut Curie
Attn: Research Division
26, rue d'Ulm
75248 Paris 05
France
E-mail: cdrom@curie.fr
Web site: www.curie.fr

Purpose To provide financial assistance to prominent scientists from any country interested in pursuing research training in the laboratories of the Institut Curie in France.
Eligibility This program is open to established scientists from any country. Applicants must be interested in pursuing a research project in a laboratory of the Institut Curie in 1 of the following areas: cell and developmental biology, molecular biophysics, human genetics and cancer, genotoxicology, pharmacochemistry, physical chemistry of the living cell, technology transfer, or cell signaling. They must submit a full curriculum vitae, a letter of support from a group head of the Institut research division indicating a willingness to host the applicant in the laboratory, a letter describing the possible scientific interactions with Institut scientists, and confirmation that 3 to 5 conferences will be delivered at the Institut on a topic of the applicant's choice.
Financial data Stipends range from 3,150 to 3,500 Euros per month, plus round-trip airfare.
Duration 4 to 9 months, usually during a sabbatical from the home institution.
Special features This program was established in 1994.

Number awarded Varies each year; recently, 12 of these fellowships were awarded.
Deadline October of each year.

[561]
EASA SALEH AL-GURG SCHOLARSHIP

Oxford Centre for Islamic Studies
Attn: Awards Secretary
George Street
Oxford OX1 2AR
England
44 1865 278730   Fax: 44 1865 248942
E-mail: islamic.studies@oxcis.ac.uk
Web site: www.oxcis.ac.uk

Purpose To provide funding to graduate students from any country who are interested in conducting research on topics related to the Muslim world at the Oxford Centre for Islamic Studies in England.
Eligibility This program is open to graduate students who are proposing to conduct independent research at the Oxford Centre for Islamic Studies in any area of the arts, humanities, or social sciences (especially anthropology, economics, geography, history, international relations, law, literature, philosophy, politics, religion, or sociology) that has relevance to the study of Islam or the Muslim world. Applicants should include a brief description of their research interests and letters of recommendation from 2 referees familiar with their work. Selection is based on the merit and significance of the applicant's proposed or current research.
Financial data A stipend is provided (amount not specified).
Duration 9 months (although shorter periods are considered), beginning in October.
Special features The Oxford Centre for Islamic Studies is an associated institution of the University of Oxford and has links with universities and research centers throughout the Muslim world. This scholarship is also open to candidates for a research degree at the University of Oxford.
Limitations Scholars are expected to devote most of their time to research and writing on their own projects at the center. They are encouraged to participate in the center's activities and seminars.
Number awarded 1 or more each year.
Deadline November of each year.

[562]
ED A. HEWETT POLICY FELLOWSHIP PROGRAM

National Council for Eurasian and East European
  Research
910 17th Street, N.W., Suite 300
Washington, DC 20006
(202) 822-6950   Fax: (202) 822-6955
E-mail: nceeerdc@aol.com
Web site: www.nceeer.gov

Purpose To provide funding to scholars who are interested in conducting research at U.S. government agencies that relates to the Newly Independent States (NIS) of the former Soviet Union, Eurasia, and central and eastern Europe (CEE).
Eligibility This program is open to U.S.-based scholars who hold a Ph.D. in the humanities or social sciences, with a concentration and considerable background in some aspect of the history, culture, politics, and economics of the countries of the NIS and CEE. Applicants must be interested in conducting research under the auspices of and with placement at a U.S. government agency with responsibility for the administration of some aspect of U.S. foreign policy toward the NIS and CEE. As part of the application process, candidates must submit 1) a description of the proposed research, including its direct relevance to contemporary concerns of U.S. policy makers responsible for the formulation or implementation of U.S. foreign policy toward 1 or more countries of the region; and 2) a written agreement with a U.S. government agency that the agency is willing to provide placement and suitable office space and related equipment for the scholar or researcher.
Financial data Grants up to $40,000 are available. Funds may be used for salary support, benefits, and travel to the region (if such travel is consistent with the needs and interests of the sponsoring U.S. government agency).
Duration Up to 1 year.
Special features Funding for this program is provided by the U.S. Department of State under the Research and Training for Eastern Europe and the Independent States of the Former Soviet Union Act of 1983 (Title VIII).
Number awarded 1 each year.
Deadline March of each year.

[563]
EDILIA AND FRANCOIS-AUGUSTE DE MONTEQUIN FELLOWSHIP

Society of Architectural Historians
1365 North Astor Street
Chicago, IL 60610-2144
(312) 573-1365   Fax: (312) 573-1141
E-mail: info@sah.org
Web site: www.sah.org

Purpose To fund travel for research on Spanish, Portuguese, or Ibero-American architecture.
Eligibility This fellowship is aimed primarily at junior scholars (including graduate students) and senior scholars. Proposed research must focus on Spanish, Portuguese, or Ibero-American architecture, including colonial architecture produced by the Spaniards in the Philippines and in the Americas. Applicants must have been members of the Society of Architectural Historians for at least 1 year.
Financial data Awards are $2,000 for junior scholars and $6,000 for senior scholars.
Duration 1 year.
Number awarded 1 each year to a junior scholar; 1 each odd-numbered year to a senior scholar.
Deadline November of each year for junior scholars; November of even-numbered years for senior scholars.

[564]
ELIZABETH A. WHITEHEAD VISITING PROFESSORSHIPS
American School of Classical Studies at Athens
Attn: Committee on Personnel
6-8 Charlton Street
Princeton, NJ 08540-5232
(609) 683-0800   Fax: (609) 924-0578
E-mail: ascsa@ascsa.org
Web site: www.ascsa.org

Purpose To provide funding to American scholars who are interested in conducting research at the American School of Classical Studies at Athens.

Eligibility Eligible to apply are faculty members at the 137 institutions that cooperate with the American School of Classical Studies or members of the school's Managing Committee. They must be interested in conducting a research project that utilizes the facilities of the school and enriches the educational research life of the school.

Financial data The stipend is $18,000 plus round-trip airfare, housing, and board.

Duration 1 academic year.

Limitations In addition to research activities, fellows traditionally conduct at least 1 seminar at the American School of Classical Studies at Athens and participate in some of the school's trips.

Number awarded 2 each year.

Deadline January of each year.

[565]
ELLEN GLEDITSCH STIPENDIEFOND
Norwegian Federation of University Women
c/o Sunni Ese
P.O. Box 251
N-5000 Bergen
Norway
47 67 53 50 49   Fax: 47 67 53 50 49
Web site: www.fou.uib.no/nka

Purpose To provide financial assistance to women interested in conducting research or pursuing graduate study in Norway.

Eligibility This program is open to women who hold an academic degree equivalent to at least a bachelor's at an approved tertiary institute in Norway. Applicants must be interested in pursuing independent research or advanced studies at the graduate level in Norway. Norwegians interested in studying or conducting research abroad are also eligible.

Financial data The stipend is 50,000 Norwegian kroner.

Duration 1 year.

Number awarded 1 each year.

Deadline July of each year.

[566]
EMBO LONG-TERM FELLOWSHIPS
European Molecular Biology Organization
Meyerhofstrasse 1
Postfach 1022.40
D-69012 Heidelberg
Germany
49 62 21 383031   Fax: 49 62 21 384879
E-mail: EMBO@EMBL-Heidelberg.de

Purpose To provide funding to molecular biologists from any country who are seeking advanced training through research in member countries of the European Molecular Biology Organization (EMBO).

Eligibility Eligible to apply are doctoral recipients from any country under the age of 35 who have at least 1 first author publication in press or have published in an international peer reviewed journal. If the applicants are from member nations of the Organization, they may apply to conduct research in any country other than their own (although preference is given to applicants interested in going to another member nation). Applicants from non-member countries (such as the United States) must apply to conduct research in a member nation and such applications are subject to more stringent criteria than those from European candidates. Interviews may be required. Selection is based on the perceived benefits of the proposed research to the host laboratory as distinct from the benefits and training the candidate will receive.

Financial data For fellows from the United States, the stipend is $26,720 for fellows under 30 or $31,717 for fellows over 30; an additional payment of $3,073 is provided for each dependent.

Duration 4 months to 2 years; may be renewed.

Special features EMBO currently receives its budget from the following member countries: Austria, Belgium, Croatia, Czech Republic, Denmark, Finland, France, Germany, Greece, Hungary, Iceland, Ireland, Israel, Italy, Netherlands, Norway, Poland, Portugal, Slovenia, Spain, Sweden, Switzerland, Turkey, and the United Kingdom.

Number awarded Varies; generally, at least 100 per year.

Deadline February or August of each year.

[567]
EMMANUEL COLLEGE RESEARCH FELLOWSHIP
University of Cambridge
Emmanuel College
Attn: Research Fellowships' Secretary
St. Andrew's Street
Cambridge CB2 3AP
England
44 1223 334200   Fax: 44 1223 334426
E-mail: res-fell-info-package@emma.cam.ac.uk
Web site: www.emma.cam.ac.uk

Purpose To provide funding to postdoctoral scholars interested in conducting research at Emmanuel College of the University of Cambridge in England.

Eligibility This program is open to scholars from any country who are interested in conducting research at Emmanuel College. Applicants must be either under 30 years of age and have completed or be near completion of a Ph.D. degree.

Financial data The annual stipend for fellows who have not yet completed the Ph.D. is 14,418 pounds if they are resident in college or 15,918 pounds if they are living out. For fellows who have completed the Ph.D., the annual stipend is 15,361 if they are resident in college or 16,861 pounds if they are living out. Other benefits include grants for research expenses and academic travel, a book allowance, and assistance with computing facilities.
Duration Up to 3 years.
Number awarded 1 or more each year.
Deadline October of each year.

[568]
ENGINEERING AND PHYSICAL SCIENCES RESEARCH COUNCIL VISITING FELLOWSHIPS
Engineering and Physical Sciences Research Council
Attn: Programme Manager
Polaris House
North Star Avenue
Swindon SN2 1ET
44 1793 444100   Fax: 44 1793 444456
Web site: www.epsrc.ac.uk

Purpose To provide funding to scientists or engineers from within the United Kingdom or abroad who are interested in visiting a U.K. institution to give advice and assistance on a research project.
Eligibility Applications for these grants must be submitted by a researcher working in the United Kingdom on a project supported by the Engineering and Physical Sciences Research Council (EPSRC). The proposal must involve inviting a scientist or engineer of acknowledged standing to visit the proposer's institution to 1) give advice and assistance in research fields in which the visitor is eminent, and 2) introduce new techniques and developments that may advance research work in the United Kingdom in connection with specific research projects supported by the EPSRC.
Financial data Grants provide funds for salary (including indirect costs), travel, and subsistence.
Duration Up to 12 months.
Special features The EPSRC was established by Royal Charter to promote and support basic, strategic, and applied research in engineering and the physical sciences.
Number awarded Varies each year.

[569]
E.P. ABRAHAM CEPHALOSPORIN JUNIOR RESEARCH FELLOWSHIP
University of Oxford
Lincoln College
Attn: Senior Tutor
Turl Street
Oxford OX1 3DR
England
44 1865 279836   Fax: 44 1865 279802
Web site: www.linc.ox.ac.uk

Purpose To provide funding to postdoctorates from any country who are interested in conducting scientific research at Lincoln College of the University of Oxford in England.
Eligibility This program is open to graduates of any university who are interested in conducting postdoctoral research at Lincoln College in the medical, biological, or chemical sciences. Applicants must be assured of adequate funding from other sources for the duration of the fellowship.
Financial data The stipend is 14,812 pounds in the first year, rising to 16,775 in the third year. Fellows also receive a book allowance and meals at the college.
Duration 3 years.
Number awarded This fellowship is offered periodically. It was last scheduled for 2002.

[570]
E.P. ABRAHAM JUNIOR RESEARCH FELLOWSHIP AT ST. CROSS COLLEGE
University of Oxford
St. Cross College
Attn: Master
St. Giles
Oxford OX1 3LZ
England
44 1865 278458   Fax: 44 1865 278484
Web site: www.stx.ox.ac.uk

Purpose To provide funding to postdoctorates from any country who are interested in conducting scientific research at St. Cross College of the University of Oxford in England.
Eligibility This program is open to graduates of any university who are interested in conducting postdoctoral research at St. Cross College in the medical, biological, or chemical sciences.
Financial data The stipend is 16,286 pounds. Recipients are also entitled to meals at the college.
Duration 2 years; may be renewed for 1 additional year.
Number awarded This fellowship is offered periodically. It is next scheduled for 2003.

[571]
E.P. ABRAHAM JUNIOR RESEARCH FELLOWSHIP AT ST. HILDA'S COLLEGE
University of Oxford
St. Hilda's College
Attn: Academic Office
Oxford OX4 1DY
England
44 1865 276815   Fax: 44 1865 276816
E-mail: college.office@st-hildas.ox.ac.uk
Web site: www.st-hildas.ox.ac.uk

Purpose To provide funding to women from any country who are interested in conducting scientific research at St. Hilda's College of the University of Oxford in England.
Eligibility This program is open to women graduates from any country who are interested in conducting postdoctoral research at St. Hilda's College in the medical, biological, or chemical sciences.
Financial data The stipend is 10,790 pounds. Recipients are also entitled to a 1,000 pound research allowance and free room and board.
Duration 2 years; may be renewed for 1 additional year.

Number awarded This fellowship is offered periodically. It was last scheduled for 2002.

[572]
E.P.A. CEPHALOSPORIN JUNIOR RESEARCH FELLOWSHIP

University of Oxford
Linacre College
Attn: Principal's Secretary
St. Cross Road
Oxford OX1 3JA
England
44 1865 271650   Fax: 44 1865 271668
Web site: www.linacre.ox.ac.uk

Purpose To provide funding to postdoctorates from any country who are interested in conducting scientific research at Linacre College of the University of Oxford in England.

Eligibility This program is open to graduates of any university who are interested in conducting postdoctoral research at Linacre College in the medical, biological, or chemical sciences. Applicants must be assured of adequate funding from other sources for the duration of the fellowship.

Financial data Fellows receive a book allowance of 250 pounds. These funds are expected to supplement other awards. Dining rights are provided.

Duration 1 year; may be renewed for 1 additional year.

Number awarded 3 each year.

Deadline January of each year.

[573]
EPA CEPHALOSPORIN RESEARCH FELLOWSHIP

University of Oxford
Lady Margaret Hall
Attn: Principal's Secretary
Norham Gardens
Oxford OX2 6QA
England
44 1865 274302   Fax: 44 1865 511069
Web site: www.lmh.ox.ac.uk

Purpose To provide funding to college graduates from any country who are interested in conducting scientific research at Lady Margaret Hall of the University of Oxford in England.

Eligibility This program is open to graduates of any university who are interested in conducting research at the University of Oxford in the medical, biological, or chemical sciences.

Financial data The stipend is at least 3,000 pounds. These funds are expected to supplement other awards. Dining rights are provided.

Duration 2 years; nonrenewable.

Number awarded Varies each year.

[574]
ERCIM FELLOWSHIP PROGRAM

European Research Consortium for Informatics and Mathematics
Attn: Aurelie Richard
2004 route des Lucioles
BP 93
F-06902 Sophia-Antipolis
France
33 4 92 38 50 11   Fax: 33 1 92 38 50 11
E-mail: aurelie.richard@ercim.org
Web site: www.ercim.org

Purpose To provide funding to scientists from any country interested in conducting research at the institutes that comprise the European Research Consortium for Informatics and Mathematics (ERCIM).

Eligibility This program is open to scientists from any country interested in conducting research at 1 of the 14 institutes that comprise ERCIM. Scientists from both industry and academic institutions are encouraged to apply. Applicants must have a Ph.D. degree or equivalent, be fluent in English, and be discharged or deferred from military service. They must be interested in conducting research in the following areas: multimedia systems, database research, programming language technologies, constraints technology and applications, control and systems theory, formal methods, electronic commerce, user interfaces, environmental modeling, health and information technology, digital libraries, e-learning, software systems validation, computer graphics, mathematics in computer science, robotics, or networking. Selection is based on the quality of the applicant, the overlap of interest between applicant and the hosting institution, and the availability of funding.

Financial data Stipends vary from country to country. Travel costs are also paid.

Duration 18 months.

Special features The component institutions are the Czech Research Consortium for Informatics and Mathematics (CRCIM), the Danish Consortium for Information Technology (DANIT), the Technical Research Center of Finland (VKK), the French National Institute for Research in Computer Science and Control (INRIA), the National Research Center for Information Technology (GMD) of Germany, the Institute of Computer Science (ICS) of Greece, the Computer and Automation Research Institute of the Hungarian Academy of Sciences (MTA SZATAKI), the National Research Council (CNR) of Italy, the National Research Institute for Mathematics and Computer Science in the Netherlands (CWI), the Norwegian SINTEF Group, the Slovak Research Consortium for Informatics and Mathematics (SRCIM), the Swedish Institute of Computer Science (SICS), the Swiss Association for Research in Information Technology (SARIT), and the Council for the Central Laboratory of the Research Councils (CLRC) of the United Kingdom.

Limitations Each laboratory may host only 1 fellow of the same nationality at a time.

Number awarded Varies each year.

Deadline April or October of each year.

[575]
ERICSSON CHAIR IN INFORMATION TECHNOLOGY AT LINKOPING UNIVERSITY
Council for International Exchange of Scholars
3007 Tilden Street, N.W., Suite 5L
Washington, DC 20008-3009
(202) 686-6245   Fax: (202) 362-3442
E-mail: scholars@cies.iie.org
Web site: www.iie.org/cies

Purpose To provide funding for American scholars to teach information technology in Sweden.

Eligibility Applicants must hold the rank of full professor in communication electronics, communication software, real-time systems, or protocols. U.S. citizenship is required.

Financial data The award provides a stipend of $100,000 plus an allowance for travel. Housing is provided.

Duration 9 months.

Special features This is a Fulbright scholar program, sponsored by the Bureau of Educational and Cultural Affairs of the U.S. Department of State and administered by the Council for International Exchange of Scholars. The recipients teach 2 seminar series at Linkoping University and 1 seminar series at Ericsson Telecommunications. They also assist in supervising graduate students and must be available for discussions at Ericsson 1 day every second week.

Number awarded 1 each year.

Deadline April of each year.

[576]
ERNEST COOK JUNIOR RESEARCH FELLOWSHIP
University of Oxford
Somerville College
Attn: College Secretary
Woodstock Road
Oxford OX2 6HD
England
44 1865 270600   Fax: 44 1865 270620
E-mail: secretariat@somerville.ox.ac.uk
Web site: www.some.ox.ac.uk

Purpose To provide financial support to postgraduate students interested in pursuing research in environmental studies at Somerville College of the University of Oxford in England.

Eligibility Candidates for the award must be postgraduate students interested in using the facilities of Somerville College to pursue a research project in environmental studies

Financial data The annual stipend is approximately 15,000 pounds. Free room and board at the college is also offered, with a housing allowance for non-residential fellows.

Duration 3 years; nonrenewable.

Special features This fellowship will next be offered in 2003.

Number awarded 1 every 3 years.

Deadline January of the competition year.

[577]
ERNST MACH SCHOLARSHIP
Austrian Cultural Institute
950 Third Avenue, 20th Floor
New York, NY 10022
(212) 759-5165   Fax: (212) 319-9636
E-mail: desk@aci.org
Web site: www.austriaculture.net

Purpose To provide financial assistance to graduate students or young scholars who are interested in conducting research or study projects at Austrian universities or other institutions.

Eligibility This program is open to doctoral or advanced graduate students as well as young postdoctorates. Applicants must be between 20 and 35 years of age, be from countries other than Austria, have a working knowledge of German, and wish to carry out research or study projects in Austria. They may be working on any topic.

Financial data The award is the Euro equivalents of 7,800 Austrian schillings per month for scholars who do not have a master's degree, ATS 8,500 per month for Ph.D. candidates who already have a master's degree, or ATS 10,000 per month for postdoctorates who are older than 30 years of age. A 1-time starting allowance of the EUR equivalent of ATS 2,500 is also provided to scholars who will be in Austria for more than 4 months.

Duration 2 to 9 months for Ph.D. candidates and postdoctorates; 1 to 4 months for other graduate students.

Special features Funding for this program is provided by the Austrian Federal Ministry of Science and Transport.

Number awarded Varies each year.

Deadline February of each year.

[578]
ESA RECOGNITION AWARD IN ENTOMOLOGY
Entomological Society of America
Attn: Executive Director
9301 Annapolis Road
Lanham, MD 20706-3115
(301) 731-4535   Fax: (301) 731-4538
E-mail: esa@entsoc.org
Web site: www.entsoc.org

Purpose To recognize and reward entomologists who have made or are making significant contributions to agriculture.

Eligibility A nominee must have contributed significantly to agricultural advancement through work in the field of entomology and must be a member of the Entomological Society of America (ESA). A recipient of a widely-recognized scientific award is not eligible unless the accomplishment cited as the basis for nomination represents new work. Previous recipients of the award are not eligible. Renomination of unsuccessful candidates is encouraged.

Financial data The winners is awarded an 8-day, all expenses-paid trip to Europe to visit agricultural research facilities and commercial farming operations. The recipient also receives an inscribed plaque or certificate.

Duration The award is presented annually.

Special features This award is sponsored by Novartis Crop Protection, Inc. which sponsors similar awards for 6 other agriculturally-related associations. The other 6 recipients accompany the Entomological Society of America winner.

Limitations Recipients are expected to be present at the association's annual meeting, to receive the award.

Number awarded 1 each year.

Deadline Nominations must be submitted by the end of June of each year.

[579]
ESTONIA FULBRIGHT TEACHER EXCHANGE
U.S. Department of State
c/o Graduate School, USDA
600 Maryland Avenue, S.W., Room 320
Washington, DC 20024-2520
(202) 314-3520   Fax: (202) 479-6806
E-mail: fulbright@grad.usda.gov
Web site: www.grad.usda.gov/International/ftep.html

Purpose To promote mutual understanding between the people of the United States and the people of Estonia through a teacher exchange program.

Eligibility This program is open to secondary school teachers (grades 7 through 12) of English as a second language, American studies and literature, social studies, art, music, or other subjects who are interested in teaching in Estonia. Applicants must 1) be U.S. citizens; 2) hold at least a bachelor's degree; 3) be fluent in English; 4) have a current full-time teaching assignment in the U.S. or a territory; 5) have the approval of their school administration; 6) have at least 3 years of full-time experience; and 7) not have participated in a Fulbright Teacher Exchange longer than 8 weeks during the last 2 years. Fluency in Estonian is not required although some ability is useful. Teaching couples may apply. However, because of the limited number of positions available and, often, the lack of foreign candidate pairs with similar qualifications for interchanges, it may not be possible to arrange suitable assignments in the same locality or to place both teachers. Preference is given to applicants who have not participated previously in the program and may be given to applicants who have not previously lived in Estonia. Geographic distribution of awards within the United States is also a factor in selection. This program does not discriminate on the basis of race, color, religion, age, sex, or national origin and encourages the applications of members of minority communities. Other considerations being equal, veterans are given preference.

Financial data Round-trip transportation for the exchange teacher only and an educational materials allowance are provided. Participants must obtain a leave of absence with pay from their jobs in the United States. The U.S. school must agree to accept a teacher from Estonia who must secure a leave of absence with pay; the Estonian teacher receives a stipend, but no additional cost accrues to the U.S. school.

Duration 9 months, beginning in September.

Special features This program is sponsored by the Bureau of Educational and Cultural Affairs of the U.S. Department of State and administered by the Graduate School, USDA.

Limitations This program provides for the direct exchange of teaching assignments between Estonia and the United States. Applicants selected for exchange must attend orientation programs of the sponsoring agencies in the United States or abroad.

Number awarded 2 each year.

Deadline October of each year.

[580]
ETHEL CRUICKSHANK RESEARCH FELLOWSHIP
University of Cambridge
Lucy Cavendish College
Attn: President's Secretary
Lady Margaret Road
Cambridge CB3 0BU
England
44 1223 332196   Fax: 44 1223 332178
E-mail: bjy21@cam.ac.uk
Web site: www.lucy-cav.cam.ac.uk

Purpose To provide funding to women postdoctoral scholars interested in conducting scientific research at Lucy Cavendish College of the University of Cambridge in England.

Eligibility This program is open to women from any country who hold a doctorate in a scientific subject. Applicants must be seeking supplemental funding to undertake or continue a research project at Lucy Cavendish College

Financial data The stipend, up to 3,000 pounds per year, is intended to supplement other funding.

Duration 1 year; may be renewed for up to 2 additional years, subject to satisfactory progress and annual reports.

Number awarded This fellowship is offered from time to time.

Deadline December in the years it is available.

[581]
ETRUSCAN FOUNDATION FIELDWORK FELLOWSHIP
Etruscan Foundation
Attn: Graduate Scholarship Committee
Fisher Mews, Suite D-2
377 Fisher Road
Grosse Pointe, MI 48230
(313) 882-2462   Fax: (313) 882-6036
Web site: www.etruscanfoundation.org

Purpose To provide funding to undergraduate and graduate students who are interested in going to a field school or doing field work in Italy.

Eligibility This program is open to advanced undergraduates (including seniors) and graduate students at accredited institutions. They must be interested in attending a field school or participating in field work in Italy. These fellowships are not limited to work on Etruscan sites; applications for archaeological work at any ancient site in Italy are welcome.

Financial data The maximum fellowship is $2,000. Funds may be used for travel, room, board, and/or fees connected with the excavation.

Duration 2 weeks or longer.

Special features This fellowship was established in 2002.

Number awarded Up to 4 each year.

Deadline March of each year.

[582]
EURASIA POSTDOCTORAL FELLOWSHIPS
Social Science Research Council
810 Seventh Avenue
New York, NY 10019
(212) 377-2700   Fax: (212) 377-2727
E-mail: eurasia@ssrc.org
Web site: www.ssrc.org

Purpose To improve the academic employment and tenure opportunities of scholars who recently received a Ph.D. in the study of Eurasia.

Eligibility This program is open to U.S. citizens and permanent residents who have received a Ph.D. within the last 6 years but who are still untenured. Applicants may propose research in any discipline of the social sciences and humanities as long as it relates to the Soviet Union and its successor states. They must indicate the anticipated location of their research. Women and members of minority groups are especially encouraged to apply.

Financial data The maximum grant is $24,000.

Duration The grant may be spent flexibly over a 2-year period.

Special features Funding for this program is provided by the U.S. Department of State under the Program for Research and Training on Eastern Europe and the Independent States of the Former Soviet Union (Title VIII).

Number awarded Varies each year; recently, 3 of these fellowships were awarded.

Deadline October of each year.

[583]
EUROPEAN FORUM FELLOWSHIPS
European University Institute
Attn: Publications and Information Offices
Convento
Via dei Roccettini 9
I-50016 San Domenico di Fiesole
Italy
39 55 4685 731   Fax: 39 55 4685 775
E-mail: forinfo@datacomm.iue.it
Web site: www.iue.it

Purpose To allow scholars to engage in comparative and interdisciplinary research on a chosen topic at the European University Institute in Florence, Italy.

Eligibility This program is open to candidates holding a doctoral degree or having equivalent research experience. Applicants must be interested in conducting research at the European University Institute. They should have a good knowledge of the languages most relevant to their proposed research; academic activities at the institute are usually held in English or French, and occasionally in Italian. Most fellows are nationals of European Union member states, although applications from nationals of other countries (such as the United States) may be considered. Fellowships are open to academics on leave, but fellows may not engage in teaching or research activities at another institution.

Financial data For junior fellows without salary, the fellowships vary from 1,200 to 2,000 Euros per month, plus family allowances. For senior fellows on paid leave, the fellowship is the Euro equivalent of 3,500,000 Italian lire per month; if senior fellows are not on paid leave, the salary may be adjusted.

Duration 1 academic year.

Special features The European Forum brings together experts on a chosen subject, emphasizing its international, comparative, and interdisciplinary aspects; it coordinates and compares their research in seminars that also include invited experts and research members of the European University Institute. A recent forum topic was "Europe in the World: The External Dimensions of the Europeanization Process."

Limitations Fellowships are full-time, and fellows are expected to be in residence in Florence for the duration of the program; fellows should not participate in academic activities in another university or research center during their stay.

Number awarded 12 to 15 each year; several visiting grants of short duration are also awarded.

Deadline October of each year.

[584]
EUROPEAN UNION AFFAIRS RESEARCH PROGRAM
Council for International Exchange of Scholars
3007 Tilden Street, N.W., Suite 5L
Washington, DC 20008-3009
(202) 686-6247   Fax: (202) 362-3442
E-mail: scholars@cies.iie.org
Web site: www.iie.org/cies

Purpose To provide financial assistance to American scholars for research on European Union affairs.

Eligibility Applicants must be U.S. citizens who possess a Ph.D. degree or the equivalent. Preference is given to projects focusing on the organizations of the European Union (EU), particularly on the process of institution building within the EU. Appropriate foreign language competence is expected. Interdisciplinary proposals are welcomed. Projects may be based at EU headquarters in Brussels or at an academic institution within the EU.

Financial data Stipends are the Euro equivalent of 64,000 to 80,000 Belgian francs per month, depending upon the number of accompanying dependents. Round-trip transportation is provided for the grantee only.

Duration 5 months.

Special features This is a Fulbright scholar program, sponsored by the Bureau of Educational and Cultural Affairs of the U.S. Department of State and administered by the Council for International Exchange of Scholars. Collaboration with EU institutions is welcomed.

Number awarded Generally 1 each year.

Deadline July of each year.

[585]
EUROPEAN UNION FULBRIGHT GRANTS
Institute of International Education
Attn: Student Programs Division
809 United Nations Plaza
New York, NY 10017-3580
(212) 984-5330   Fax: (212) 984-5325
Web site: www.iie.org/fulbright

Purpose To provide funding to doctoral candidates in the United States who are working on projects focusing on the European Union (EU).

Eligibility Eligible to apply are American citizens who are at the advanced stages of a doctoral degree that focuses on the new mechanisms for supranational governance emerging within the administrative framework of the EU. Preference is given to proposals that require the applicant to go to the EU headquarters in Brussels, in addition to any other mutually agreed upon location. English-language facility is generally sufficient. Proficiency in other languages may be necessary or useful, depending upon the project or location.

Financial data This grant provides round-trip transportation, tuition (when appropriate), books, maintenance allowance, and health/accident insurance.

Duration 1 year, beginning in September.

Special features Academic course work may be incorporated into the project, but it is not a requirement. Depending on the project, grantees may follow courses on EU topics at EU-related institutions.

Special features This is a Fulbright program, funded by the U.S. Department of State and administered by the Institute of International Education (IIE). Students who are currently enrolled in the United States are to apply through the Fulbright program adviser on their campus; at-large applicants (those not currently enrolled) may obtain applications and information directly from the IIE.

Limitations Grants are not provided for participation in an internship program at EU.

Number awarded 3 each year.

Deadline October of each year.

[586]
FALCONER MADAN AWARD
Bibliographical Society
c/o The Honorary Secretary, David Pearson
The Wellcome Library
183 Euston Road
London NW1 2BE
England
Web site: www.users.zetnet.co.uk/djshaw/bibsoc/grants.htm

Purpose To provide funding to scholars from any country interested in conducting bibliographical research at the University of Oxford in England.

Eligibility This program is open to scholars interested in conducting research at Oxford on such topics as book history, textual transmission, publishing, printing, book ownership, and book collecting. Applicants may be of any age or nationality and need not be members of the Bibliographical Society.

Financial data The grant is 500 pounds.

Duration This is a 1-time grant.

Special features Further information is also available from Dr. Maureen Bell, Birmingham University, School of English, Edgbaston, Birmingham B15 2TT, England, E-mail: M.Bell@bham.ac.uk. Support for this program is provided by the Oxford Bibliographical Society.

Number awarded 1 each year.

Deadline November of each year.

[587]
FEDERICO CHABOD SCHOLARSHIP
Italian Institute of Historical Studies
Palazzo Filomarino
via Benedetto Croce 12
I-80134 Naples
Italy
39 81 551 7159   Fax: 39 81 551 2390

Purpose To provide financial assistance to college graduates for historical research in Naples, Italy.

Eligibility Applicants may be citizens of any country who have a bachelor's degree from an accredited college or university and who desire to conduct research at the Italian Institute of Historical Studies (Istituto Italiano per gli Studi Storici) in Naples.

Financial data The award is 12,000,000 Italian lire.

Duration 8 months.

Special features Recipients must reside in Naples and attend weekly seminars.

Number awarded 1 each year.

Deadline October of each year.

[588]
FELLOWSHIP IN LANDSCAPE ARCHITECTURE
Garden Club of America
Attn: Scholarship Committee
14 East 60th Street
New York, NY 10022-1006
(212) 753-8287   Fax: (212) 753-0134
E-mail: scholarship@gcamerica.org
Web site: www.gcamerica.org

Purpose To provide American landscape architects with an opportunity for advanced work at the American Academy in Rome.

Eligibility Eligible to apply are certified landscape architects who wish to engage in an independent research program at the American Academy in Rome.

Financial data The award covers all expenses at the American Academy in Rome.

Duration 1 year.

Special features This program was established in 1928. Further information is available from the American Academy in Rome, 7 East 60th Street, New York, NY 10022-1001, (212) 751-7200, Fax: (212) 751-7220.

Limitations Requests for applications must be accompanied by a self-addressed stamped envelope.

Number awarded 1 each year.

Deadline November of each year.

[589]
FELLOWSHIP PROGRAM OF THE NETHERLANDS MINISTRY OF AGRICULTURE, NATURE MANAGEMENT AND FISHERIES

International Agricultural Centre
P.O. Box 88
6700 AB Wageningen
Netherlands
31 31 749 5495   Fax: 31 31 749 5395
E-mail: iac@iac.agro.nl
Web site: www.iac.agro.nl

Purpose To provide financial assistance for postgraduate study and/or research in the field of agriculture.

Eligibility Applicants must be citizens of a European country (except member states of the European Union and the former Yugoslavian republics), the United States, Canada, Australia, New Zealand, Israel, South Africa, or Japan and should be the holder of at least an M.Sc.-level degree and an employee of an official government institution. Fellowships are available for individual research at an institution in the Netherlands or in connection with participation in a course organized by the International Agricultural Centre (IAC). Applicants should have several years of experience in the particular subject on which they wish to focus.

Financial data For study or research in Wageningen, fellows receive free board and lodging in the IAC hostel plus a daily allowance of the Euro equivalent of 33 Netherlands guilders; for study or research elsewhere in the Netherlands, the daily allowance is NLG 54. Also included are a book allowance ranging of the EUR equivalent of 165 to NLG 610, free medical and third-party liability insurance, and contributions toward travel expenses within the Netherlands or surrounding countries (but not to and from the institution where the study or research takes place). Accommodations are also available for spouses and children.

Duration 3 to 6 months.

Special features The fellowships are provided by the Netherlands Ministry of Agriculture, Nature Management and Fisheries and managed by the IAC.

Number awarded Varies each year.

Deadline July of each year.

[590]
FELLOWSHIPS IN INTERNATIONAL HUMAN RIGHTS

Human Rights Watch
Attn: Fellowship Committee
350 Fifth Avenue, 34th Floor
New York, NY 10118-3299
(212) 290-4700, ext. 312   Fax: (212) 736-1300
E-mail: hrwnyc@hrw.org
Web site: www.hrw.org

Purpose To provide an opportunity for recent recipients of law or graduate degrees to engage in human rights monitoring and advocacy while working for Human Rights Watch.

Eligibility These fellowships are available to recent graduates of law schools or graduate programs in journalism, international relations, or area studies from any university worldwide. Applicants must be interested in working with a division of Human Rights Watch, based in Washington, D.C. or New York. Their assignment involves monitoring human rights developments in various countries, conducting on-site investigations, drafting reports on human rights conditions, and engaging in advocacy efforts aimed at publicizing and curtailing human rights violations. Applicants must demonstrate analytic skills, an ability to write and speak clearly, and a commitment to work in the human rights field in the future on a paid or volunteer basis. Proficiency in a language in addition to English is strongly recommended. Familiarity with countries or regions where serious human rights violations occur is also valued.

Financial data The stipend is $35,000. Fringe benefits are also provided.

Duration 1 year.

Special features This program includes 2 named fellowships open to applicants from any law or graduate school: the Schell Fellowship and the Finberg Fellowship. In addition, 3 fellowships are restricted to graduates of specific schools: the Sandler Fellowship for recent graduates of Columbia Law School, the Furman Fellowship for recent graduates of New York University School of Law, and the Bloomberg Fellowship for recent graduates of graduate programs at Johns Hopkins University. Past fellows have conducted fact-finding missions to Albania, Azerbaijan, Bangladesh, Bolivia, Brazil, Burma, Cambodia, Colombia, Cuba, the Dominican Republic, Egypt, El Salvador, Ethiopia, Guatemala, Haiti, Honduras, Hong Kong, India (including Kashmir and Punjab), Iran, Kenya, Moldova, Namibia, Nigeria, Pakistan, the Philippines, Russia, Rwanda, South Africa, Sudan, Syria, Tajikistan, Uganda, the U.S.-Mexican border, and Venezuela.

Number awarded 5 each year.

Deadline October of each year.

[591]
FINLAND FULBRIGHT TEACHER EXCHANGE

U.S. Department of State
c/o Graduate School, USDA
600 Maryland Avenue, S.W., Room 320
Washington, DC 20024-2520
(202) 314-3520   Fax: (202) 479-6806
E-mail: fulbright@grad.usda.gov
Web site: www.grad.usda.gov/International/ftep.html

Purpose To promote mutual understanding between the people of the United States and the people of Finland through a teacher exchange program.

Eligibility This program is open to teachers of any subject at the level of elementary school through 2-year college who are interested in teaching in Finland. The subject field is determined by the availability of comparable candidates in both the United States and Finland. Vocational subjects include natural resources, business, hotel and restaurant management, recreation, and health care. Applicants must 1) be U.S. citizens; 2) hold at least a bachelor's degree; 3) be fluent in English; 4) have a current full-time teaching assignment in the U.S. or a territory; 5) have the approval of their school administration; 6) have at least 3 years of full-time experience; and 7) not have participated in a Fulbright Teacher Exchange longer than 8 weeks during the last 2 years. Fluency in Finnish is not required; the language of instruction is English. Teaching couples may apply. However, because of the limited number of positions available and, often, the lack of foreign candidate pairs with similar qualifications for interchanges, it may not be possible to arrange suitable assignments in the same locality or to place both teachers. Preference is given to applicants who have not participated previously in the program and may be given to applicants who have not previously lived in Finland. Geographic distribution of awards within the United States is also a factor in selection. This program does not discriminate on the basis of race, color, religion, age, sex, or national origin and encourages the applications of members of minority communities. Other considerations being equal, veterans are given preference.

Financial data Only round-trip transportation is provided. Participants must obtain a leave of absence with pay from their jobs in the United States. The U.S. school must agree to accept a teacher from Finland who must secure a leave of absence with pay.

Duration 9 months, beginning in August.

Special features This program is sponsored by the Bureau of Educational and Cultural Affairs of the U.S. Department of State and administered by the Graduate School, USDA.

Limitations This program provides for the direct exchange of teaching assignments between Finland and the United States. Applicants selected for exchange must attend orientation programs of the sponsoring agencies in the United States or abroad.

Number awarded 8 each year.

Deadline October of each year.

[592]
FINNISH UNIVERSITY SCHOLARSHIPS FOR POSTGRADUATE FINNISH STUDIES AND RESEARCH

Center for International Mobility
Attn: Information Services
P.O. Box 343
Hakaniemenkatu 2
FIN-00531 Helsinki
Finland
358 9 7747 7033   Fax: 358 9 7747 7064
E-mail: cimoinfo@cimo.fi
Web site: www.cimo.fi

Purpose To provide financial support for advanced study or research in Finnish language, literature, and other related areas at a Finnish university.

Eligibility This program is open to nationals of countries other than Finland who are graduate students and researchers under the age of 35, fluent in Finnish, and interested in studying or conducting research in Finland in any of the following areas: Finnish language, Finnish literature, Finno-Ugric linguistics, ethnology, or folklore. Applicants should have already completed a master's degree in those subjects and established contact with staff members at Finnish universities who will agree to act as the scholarship recipient's host. The Finnish hosts apply for the grant. No scholarship can be granted without invitation/admission of the candidate by the receiving host institute.

Financial data A monthly allowance of the Euro equivalent of at least 4,100 Finnish marks is provided. No travel grants are available to or from Finland.

Duration From 4 to 9 months (1 to 2 semesters).

Special features The Center for International Mobility (CIMO) is an agency of the Finnish Ministry of Education.

Limitations Recipients must study at Finnish universities or institutions of higher education.

Deadline Applications may be submitted at any time.

[593]
FLAD CHAIRS AT THE ISCTE OR INDEG

Council for International Exchange of Scholars
3007 Tilden Street, N.W., Suite 5L
Washington, DC 20008-3009
(202) 686-6245   Fax: (202) 362-3442
E-mail: scholars@cies.iie.org
Web site: www.iie.org/cies

Purpose To provide funding to American scholars who are interested in lecturing at the Higher Institute of Labor and Business Studies (ISCTE) or the Institute for Business Administration Development (INDEG) in Lisbon, Portugal.

Eligibility This program is open to scholars who have a doctorate and, preferably, 10 years of teaching experience (5 years for the chair in marketing). Applicants must be interested in lecturing at the ISCTE or INDEG in 1) banking, 2) marketing, or 3) strategic management. U.S. citizenship is required.

Financial data The stipend is $3,500 per month, paid in local currency. Round-trip airfare for the grantee and 1 legal accompanying dependent is also provided. The host institution provides housing or a housing allowance.

Duration 3 months.

Special features This is a Fulbright scholar program, sponsored by the Bureau of Educational and Cultural Affairs of the U.S. Department of State and administered by the Council for International Exchange of Scholars. Additional support is provided by the Luso-American Development Foundation (FLAD). Other responsibilities of the scholars may include providing research leadership, assisting with special programs for professionals, curriculum development, advising students, and assisting with tutorials.

Number awarded 3 each year: 1 in each of the 3 areas of specialization.

Deadline April of each year.

[594]
FLAD CHAIRS AT THE TECHNICAL UNIVERSITY OF LISBON

Council for International Exchange of Scholars
3007 Tilden Street, N.W., Suite 5L
Washington, DC 20008-3009
(202) 686-6245   Fax: (202) 362-3442
E-mail: scholars@cies.iie.org
Web site: www.iie.org/cies

Purpose To provide funding to American scholars who are interested in lecturing and conducting research at the School of Business and Economics of the Technical University of Lisbon in Portugal.

Eligibility This program is open to scholars who have a Ph.D., at least 5 years of teaching experience, and a rank of associate or full professor. Applicants must be interested in lecturing at the Technical University of Lisbon in doctoral and master's programs, assisting with curriculum development, participating in seminars and collaborative research, and advising doctoral students. Their areas of specialization may be: 1) management information systems, 2) finance, or 3) marketing. U.S. citizenship is required.

Financial data The stipend is $3,500 per month, paid in local currency. Round-trip airfare for the grantee and 1 legal accompanying dependent is also provided. The host institution provides housing or a housing allowance.

Duration 3 months.

Special features This is a Fulbright scholar program, sponsored by the Bureau of Educational and Cultural Affairs of the U.S. Department of State and administered by the Council for International Exchange of Scholars. Additional support is provided by the Luso-American Development Foundation (FLAD).

Number awarded 3 each year: 1 in each of the 3 areas of specialization.

Deadline April of each year.

[595]
FLORENCE DISTINGUISHED CHAIR

Council for International Exchange of Scholars
3007 Tilden Street, N.W., Suite 5L
Washington, DC 20008-3009
(202) 686-6245   Fax: (202) 362-3442
E-mail: scholars@cies.iie.org
Web site: www.iie.org/cies

Purpose To provide funding for scholars to lecture in history and civilization at the European University Institute in Florence, Italy.

Eligibility This program is open to full professors with at least 10 years' teaching experience and a prominent record of accomplishments in history and civilization. Scholars must be interested in lecturing at the doctoral level at the European University Institute of Florence on a topic that changes periodically. Recent topics have included 1) cultural history between the 17th and 20th centuries from a transatlantic perspective and 2) international law, comparative law, and legal theory. U.S. citizenship is required. Some knowledge of Italian and another European language is desirable but not required.

Financial data The stipend is the Euro equivalent of 16,800,000 Italian lire plus the settling-in allowance of 1,500,000 lire. The grant also provides international travel (for the grantee only) plus the EUR equivalent of 200,000 lire per month for each accompanying dependent.

Duration 3 months.

Special features This is a Fulbright scholar program, sponsored by the Bureau of Educational and Cultural Affairs of the U.S. Department of State and administered by the Council for International Exchange of Scholars.

Number awarded 1 each year.

Deadline April of each year.

[596]
FLORENCE GOULD FOUNDATION PRE-DISSERTATION FELLOWSHIPS FOR RESEARCH IN FRANCE

Council for European Studies
c/o Columbia University
1203 International Affairs Building, MC3310
420 West 118th Street
New York, NY 10027
(212) 854-4172   Fax: (212) 854-8808
E-mail: ces@columbia.edu
Web site: www.europanet.org

Purpose To enable graduate students in the social sciences to pursue short-term exploratory research in France, in order to determine the viability and to refine the scope of their proposed dissertation.

Eligibility Applicants must be enrolled in a doctoral program at a U.S. university and must have completed the equivalent of at least 2 but less than 3 years of full-time graduate study prior to the beginning date of their proposed research. They must be interested in conducting short-term exploratory research in France. Fellowships are restricted to citizens or permanent residents of the United States. Students are ineligible if they are beyond the third year of graduate study, are in France at the time of the competition, have a fellowship for research in France from another organization with a stipend of $3,000 or more, or have undertaken exploratory research in France during the current year. Eligible fields of study include cultural anthropology, geography, history (post-1750 only), political science, sociology, and urban and regional planning. The topic must focus on France, including cross-national projects that encompass France as a major focus and studies of France in relation to her former colonies.

Financial data Fellowships provide $4,000 for travel and living expenses.

Duration 3 months, during the summer or autumn.

Special features The first awards for this program were offered in 2000.

Number awarded 6 each year.

Deadline January of each year.

[597]
FLOREY RESEARCH FELLOWSHIP

University of Oxford
Lady Margaret Hall
Attn: Principal's Secretary
Norham Gardens
Oxford OX2 6QA
England
44 1865 274302   Fax: 44 1865 511069
Web site: www.lmh.ox.ac.uk

Purpose To provide funding to college graduates from any country who are interested in conducting scientific research at Lady Margaret Hall of the University of Oxford in England.

Eligibility This program is open to graduates of any university who are interested in conducting research at the University of Oxford in pathology, bacteriology, physiology, biochemistry, pharmacology, anatomy, or another science related to medicine.

Financial data The stipend is at least 3,000 pounds. These funds are expected to supplement other awards. Dining rights are provided.
Duration 2 years; nonrenewable.
Number awarded Varies each year.

[598]
FOGARTY INTERNATIONAL RESEARCH COLLABORATION AWARD (FIRCA)
Fogarty International Center
Attn: Division of International Training and Research
31 Center Drive, Room B2C39
Bethesda, MD 20892-2220
(301) 496-1653   Fax: (301) 402-0779
E-mail: FIRCA@nih.gov
Web site: www.nih.gov/fic/programs/firca.html

Purpose To encourage collaboration among scientists in the United States and developing countries in areas of research supported by the National Institutes of Health (NIH).
Eligibility Proposals may be submitted by American scientists who are already principal investigators of grants funded by the institutes and who are interested in working collaboratively with scientists in Africa, Asia (except Japan, Singapore, South Korea, and Taiwan), central and eastern Europe, Russia and the Newly Independent States of the former Soviet Union, Latin America and the non-U.S. Caribbean, the Middle East, and the Pacific Ocean Islands (except Australia and New Zealand). All biomedical and behavioral research topics supported by the institutes are eligible for inclusion in this program. Racial/ethnic minority individuals, women, and persons with disabilities are encouraged to apply as principal investigators.
Financial data Grants provide up to $32,000 per year in direct costs. Funds may be used to pay for materials, supplies, equipment, and travel. Up to 20 percent of the total direct costs may be requested for the U.S. principal investigator, the foreign collaborator, and/or their colleagues or students for visits to each other's laboratory or research site. Up to $5,000 of the total grant may be allocated as a stipend for the foreign collaborator(s). Up to $2,000 of the total grant may be allocated for the foreign collaborator(s) to attend a scientific conference.
Duration Up to 3 years.
Limitations Research related to HIV and AIDS is not eligible for support through this program. A separate companion program, HIV–AIDS and Related Illnesses Collaboration Award, provides funding for research on AIDS.
Number awarded Varies; generally, at least 40 each year.
Deadline Applications may be submitted in November, March, or July of each year.

[599]
FOULERTON RESEARCH PROFESSORSHIP
Royal Society
Attn: Executive Secretary
6 Carlton House Terrace
London SW1Y 5AG
England
44 20 7451 2542   Fax: 44 20 7451 2692
E-mail: UKResearch.Appointments@royalsoc.ac.uk
Web site: www.royalsoc.ac.uk

Purpose To provide funding to established scholars interested in conducting medical research in the United Kingdom.
Eligibility This program is open to internationally respected scientists of any nationality who are interested in a professorship at an appropriate university or research institute in the United Kingdom. Applicants must be interested in conducting research in medicine or other sciences that are connected with the discovery of the causes of disease and the relief of human suffering. Scientists who are currently employed outside the United Kingdom and wish to return are particularly encouraged to apply.
Financial data The salary provided by the Royal Society is the national professorial minimum plus 40 percent (currently 50,961 pounds). The host university or institute may supplement that salary if it so wishes. Professors receive a start-up grant when they begin their assignment and they may apply for research expenses up to 16,000 pounds per year. Successful applicants from overseas receive some assistance with moving expenses.
Duration These professorships are intended to extend until normal retirement age, but funding from the Royal Society extends for 15 years for professors under 40 years of age or 10 years for those over 40 years of age (or until they reach 55 years of age, whichever is longer). After expiration of Royal Society funding, the university or research institute is solely responsible for the professorship.
Number awarded 1 each year.
Deadline August of each year.

[600]
FOWLER HAMILTON VISITING RESEARCH FELLOWSHIP
University of Oxford
Christ Church
Attn: The Very Reverend the Dean
Oxford OX1 1DP
England
44 1865 276161   Fax: 44 1865 276238
Web site: www.chch.ox.ac.uk

Purpose To allow distinguished senior scholars in the humanities or the social sciences to conduct research at Christ Church of the University of Oxford in England.
Eligibility Eligible for this fellowship are distinguished senior scholars in the humanities or social sciences from outside Great Britain. They must be interested in conducting research at Christ Church.
Financial data The fellow is entitled to free family accommodations, use of a study room in the college, and free lunches and dinners. Return economy fares from the country of origin

are paid for each fellow and family. Limited stipends may also be offered, depending on individual circumstances.
Duration Up to 11 months.
Number awarded 1 or more each year.
Deadline February of each year.

[601]
FRANCE FULBRIGHT TEACHER EXCHANGE
U.S. Department of State
c/o Graduate School, USDA
600 Maryland Avenue, S.W., Room 320
Washington, DC 20024-2520
(202) 314-3520   Fax: (202) 479-6806
E-mail: fulbright@grad.usda.gov
Web site: www.grad.usda.gov/International/ftep.html

Purpose To promote mutual understanding between the people of the United States and the people of France (and the French Antilles) through a teacher exchange program.
Eligibility This program is open to secondary school (grades 7 through 12) and 2-year college instructors of French language, literature, and civilization who are interested in teaching English language or American literature and civilization in France. Exchanges are also possible with the islands of Guadeloupe and Martinique in the French Antilles and with the island of Reunion in the Indian Ocean. Applicants must 1) be U.S. citizens; 2) hold at least a bachelor's degree; 3) be fluent in English; 4) have a current full-time teaching assignment in the U.S. or a territory; 5) have the approval of their school administration; 6) have at least 3 years of full-time experience; and 7) not have participated in a Fulbright Teacher Exchange longer than 8 weeks during the last 2 years. Fluency in French is required. Teaching couples may apply. However, because of the limited number of positions available and, often, the lack of foreign candidate pairs with similar qualifications for interchanges, it may not be possible to arrange suitable assignments in the same locality or to place both teachers. Preference is given to applicants who have not participated previously in the program and may be given to applicants who have not previously lived in France. Geographic distribution of awards within the United States is also a factor in selection. This program does not discriminate on the basis of race, color, religion, age, sex, or national origin and encourages the applications of members of minority communities. Other considerations being equal, veterans are given preference.
Financial data Only partial round-trip transportation is provided. Participants must obtain a leave of absence with pay from their jobs in the United States. The U.S. school must agree to accept a French teacher who must secure a leave of absence with pay. The cost of housing and the salary levels of French and U.S. teachers make an exchange of accommodations a virtual necessity.
Duration 9 months, beginning in September.
Special features This program is sponsored by the Bureau of Educational and Cultural Affairs of the U.S. Department of State and administered by the Graduate School, USDA.
Limitations This program provides for the direct exchange of teaching assignments between France and the United States. Applicants selected for exchange must attend orientation programs of the sponsoring agencies in the United States or abroad.

Number awarded 20 each year.
Deadline October of each year.

[602]
FRANZ WERFEL SCHOLARSHIP
Austrian Cultural Institute
950 Third Avenue, 20th Floor
New York, NY 10022
(212) 759-5165   Fax: (212) 319-9636
E-mail: desk@aci.org
Web site: www.austriaculture.net

Purpose To provide financial assistance to American professors of Austrian literature who wish to conduct research in Austria.
Eligibility This program is open to faculty members teaching Austrian literature at U.S. colleges and universities who are younger than 35 years of age. Applicants must be interested in conducting research at Austrian archives, libraries, and other research institutions. An excellent knowledge of German is required.
Financial data The stipend is the Euro equivalent of 10,000 Austrian schillings per month; also provided are the EUR equivalents of a 1-time starting allowance of ATS 2,500, a 1-time book gift of up to ATS 5,000, and a monthly book budget of ATS 1,000. Tuition and health insurance are covered. In exceptional cases, housing benefits can be obtained.
Duration 4 to 9 months; may be extended to a maximum of 18 months.
Special features Funding for this program is provided by the Austrian Federal Ministry of Science and Transport. After completing the grant, scholars receive 1 invitation per year to attend a literacy symposium, a 1-month research grant every 3 years, yearly book donations, a subscription to an Austrian newspaper, and regular information on scientific cooperation regarding advanced and graduate students as well as young scholars.
Number awarded Varies each year.
Deadline February of each year.

[603]
FREDERICK BURKHARDT RESIDENTIAL FELLOWSHIPS FOR RECENTLY TENURED SCHOLARS
American Council of Learned Societies
Attn: Office of Fellowships and Grants
228 East 45th Street
New York, NY 10017-3398
(212) 697-1505   Fax: (212) 949-8058
E-mail: grants@acls.org
Web site: www.acls.org/burkguid.htm

Purpose To provide funding to scholars in all disciplines of the humanities and the humanities-related social sciences who are interested in conducting research at designated residential centers.
Eligibility This program is open to citizens and permanent residents of the United States and Canada who achieved tenure in a humanities or humanities-related social science discipline at a U.S. or Canadian institution within the past 4 years. Applicants must be interested in conducting research at 1 of

9 participating residential centers in the United States or abroad. Appropriate fields of specialization include, but are not limited to, anthropology, archaeology, art history, economics, geography, history, languages and literatures, law, linguistics, musicology, philosophy, political science, psychology, religion, and sociology. Proposals in those fields of the social sciences are eligible only if they employ predominantly humanistic approaches (e.g., economic history, law and literature, political philosophy). Proposals in interdisciplinary and cross-disciplinary studies are welcome, as are proposals focused on any geographic region or on any cultural or linguistic group. Applications are particularly invited from women and members of minority groups.

Financial data The stipend is $65,000. If that stipend exceeds the fellow's normal academic year salary, the excess is available for research and travel expenses.

Duration 1 academic year.

Special features This program, which began in 1999, is supported by funding from the Andrew W. Mellon Foundation with additional support from the Rockefeller Foundation. The participating residential research centers are the National Humanities Center (Research Triangle Park, North Carolina), the Center for Advanced Study in the Behavioral Sciences (Stanford, California), the Institute for Advanced Study, Schools of Historical Studies and Social Science (Princeton, New Jersey), the American Antiquarian Society (Worcester, Massachusetts), the Folger Shakespeare Library (Washington, D.C.), the Newberry Library (Chicago, Illinois), the Huntington Library, Art Collections, and Botanical Gardens (San Marino, California), the American Academy in Rome, and Villa I Tatti (Florence, Italy).

Number awarded Up to 11 each year.

Deadline September of each year.

[604]
FRENCH INSTITUTE OF WASHINGTON FELLOWSHIPS

Institut Français de Washington
c/o University of North Carolina at Chapel Hill
Department of Romance Languages
234 Dey Hall, CB#3170
Chapel Hill, NC 27599-3170
(919) 962-0154   Fax: (919) 962-5457
E-mail: cmaley@email.unc.edu
Web site: www.unc.edu/depts/institut

Purpose To provide funding to Ph.D. candidates or recent recipients who are interested in conducting research on French studies in France.

Eligibility Applicants must be either Ph.D. candidates in the final stage of their dissertation or recent graduates who have held their Ph.D. degree no longer than 6 years before the application deadline. They must write a 2-page statement describing their proposed research project and their planned trip. Ph.D. candidates must also include a curriculum vitae and letter of recommendation from their dissertation director. Research may be conducted in French studies in the areas of art, economics, history, history of science, linguistics, literature, or social sciences.

Financial data The award is $1,000. Funds are provided for maintenance, not travel.

Duration Research must be conducted for at least 2 months in France.

Special features This program includes the following named fellowships: the Gilbert Chinard Research Fellowships, the Edouard Morot-Sir Fellowship in Literature, and the Harmon Chadbourn Rorison Fellowship.

Limitations Awards are for maintenance only, not travel.

Number awarded 4 each year.

Deadline January of each year.

[605]
FRENCH-AMERICAN FOUNDATION CHAIR IN AMERICAN CIVILIZATION

French-American Foundation
Attn: Director, Professional Exchanges
509 Madison Avenue, Suite 310
New York, NY 10022
(212) 829-8800   Fax: (212) 829-8810
E-mail: vlenoir@frenchamerican.org
Web site: www.frenchamerican.org

Purpose To fund a chair in American Civilization at the Ecole des Hautes Etudes en Sciences Sociales in Paris.

Eligibility Each year, a distinguished U.S. scholar is appointed to this chair in American Civilization.

Financial data The yearly stipend is $55,000.

Duration From November to June of each year.

Special features This program was established in 1980.

Number awarded 1 each year.

[606]
FRIEDRICH EBERT FOUNDATION DOCTORAL RESEARCH FELLOWSHIPS

Friedrich Ebert Foundation
342 Madison Avenue, Suite 1912
New York, NY 10173
(212) 687-0208   Fax: (212) 687-0261
E-mail: fesny@igc.apc.org
Web site: www.fesdc.org

Purpose To provide doctoral candidates with an opportunity to conduct research for their dissertation in Germany with the assistance of a German university professor.

Eligibility Applicants must be U.S. citizens who are qualified Ph.D. candidates at an American university, have completed all of the prerequisites for a doctorate except for the dissertation, and can provide evidence that their knowledge of the German language is adequate for their research purposes. They must be interested in conducting their dissertation research in Germany. Applicable disciplines are political science, sociology, history, and economics; special consideration is given to socio-historical studies, contemporary history, and studies on current political problems (including comparative studies).

Financial data The monthly maintenance allowance is the Euro equivalent of 1,390 Deutsche marks; other expenses covered are airfare between the United States and Germany plus domestic travel expenses; an allowance for luggage costs, health insurance, and book expenses; and tuition and fees if applicable.

Duration From 5 to 12 months.

Special features Further information is available from the Friedrich Ebert Foundation at 1155 15th Street, N.W., Suite 1100, Washington, DC 20005, (202) 331-1819, Fax: (202) 331-1837. Information may also be obtained from Friedrich-Ebert-Stiftung, Abteilung Studienförderung, Referat für ausländisch Stipendiaten, Godesberger Allee 149, D-53170 Bonn 2, Germany, 49 228 883 634, Fax: 49 228 883 697.

Number awarded 15 fellowships are awarded by the Friedrich Ebert Foundation each year.

Deadline February of each year.

[607]
FRIEDRICH EBERT FOUNDATION POSTDOCTORAL/YOUNG SCHOLAR FELLOWSHIPS

Friedrich Ebert Foundation
342 Madison Avenue, Suite 1912
New York, NY 10173
(212) 687-0208 Fax: (212) 687-0261
E-mail: fesny@igc.apc.org
Web site: www.fesdc.org

Purpose To provide young scholars who have already accumulated a certain amount of experience in teaching and/or research an opportunity to conduct independent study or research in Germany.

Eligibility Applicants must have a Ph.D. or equivalent university degree and at least 2 years of subsequent experience in research and/or teaching at universities or in related research institutions, must indicate a German counterpart who would be available for cooperation and assistance during their stay in Germany, must have an appropriate knowledge of German, and must be U.S. citizens. Applicable disciplines are political science, sociology, history, and economics, with preference given to applicants who wish to carry out studies on politically relevant subjects, particularly those involving a comparative approach. Considerable importance is attached to the establishment of contacts and cooperative relationships with competent German counterparts in the same field.

Financial data The monthly maintenance allowance is 1,700 Deutsche marks; other expenses covered are airfare between the United States and Germany plus domestic travel expenses; an allowance for luggage costs, health insurance, and book expenses; and tuition and fees if applicable.

Duration From 5 to 12 months.

Special features Further information is available from the Friedrich Ebert Foundation at 1155 15th Street, N.W., Suite 1100, Washington, DC 20005, (202) 331-1819, Fax: (202) 331-1837. Information may also be obtained from Friedrich-Ebert-Stiftung, Abteilung Studienförderung, Referat für ausländisch Stipendiaten, Godesberger Allee 149, D-53170 Bonn 2, Germany, 49 228 883 634, Fax: 49 228 883 697.

Number awarded 15 fellowships are awarded by the Friedrich Ebert Foundation each year.

Deadline February of each year.

[608]
FRIEDRICH EBERT FOUNDATION PRE-DISSERTATION/ADVANCED GRADUATE FELLOWSHIPS

Friedrich Ebert Foundation
342 Madison Avenue, Suite 1912
New York, NY 10173
(212) 687-0208 Fax: (212) 687-0261
E-mail: fesny@igc.apc.org
Web site: www.fesdc.org

Purpose To provide advanced graduate students with an opportunity for study and research at a university in Germany under the guidance of a German university professor in order to develop a dissertation proposal or complete a specific research project.

Eligibility Eligible to apply are U.S. citizens who are qualified graduate students intending to pursue a doctoral degree and/or participating within a special research project in political science, sociology, history, or economics; they must have completed at least 2 years of graduate study at an American university, submit a description of their study and/or research objective, and provide proof that they have sufficient knowledge of German to study or conduct research at a university in Germany.

Financial data The monthly maintenance allowance is the Euro equivalent of 1,250 Deutsche marks; other expenses covered are airfare between the United States and Germany plus domestic travel expenses; an allowance for luggage costs, health insurance, and book expenses; and tuition and fees if applicable.

Duration From 5 to 12 months.

Special features Further information is available from the Friedrich Ebert Foundation at 1155 15th Street, N.W., Suite 1100, Washington, DC 20005, (202) 331-1819, Fax: (202) 331-1837. Information may also be obtained from Friedrich-Ebert-Stiftung, Abteilung Studienförderung, Referat für ausländisch Stipendiaten, Godesberger Allee 149, D-53170 Bonn 2, Germany, 49 228 883 634, Fax: 49 228 883 697.

Number awarded 15 fellowships are awarded by the Friedrich Ebert Foundation each year.

Deadline February of each year.

[609]
FULBRIGHT LECTURESHIP IN U.S.-E.U. RELATIONS

Council for International Exchange of Scholars
3007 Tilden Street, N.W., Suite 5L
Washington, DC 20008-3009
(202) 686-6247 Fax: (202) 362-3442
E-mail: scholars@cies.iie.org
Web site: www.iie.org/cies

Purpose To provide funding for senior scholars to lecture on transatlantic relations in Belgium.

Eligibility This program is open to senior scholars who wish to teach a course on transatlantic relations and a seminar on a more specialized aspect of relations between the United States and the European Union at the College of Europe in Bruges, Belgium. Courses are taught in the framework of a master's program to a select group of graduates from all European countries and North America. Fluency in French is desirable but not required. U.S. citizenship is required.

Financial data Stipends are the Euro equivalent of 79,000 to 93,000 Belgian francs per month, depending upon the number of accompanying dependents. Round-trip transportation is provided for the grantee only.

Duration 6 months, beginning in January.

Special features This is a Fulbright scholar program, sponsored by the Bureau of Educational and Cultural Affairs of the U.S. Department of State and administered by the Council for International Exchange of Scholars.

Number awarded 1 each year.

Deadline July of each year.

[610]
FULBRIGHT TRAVEL GRANTS

Institute of International Education
Attn: Student Programs Division
809 United Nations Plaza
New York, NY 10017-3580
(212) 984-5330   Fax: (212) 984-5325
Web site: www.iie.org/fulbright

Purpose To provide travel grants as a supplement to funds received from other sources by American graduate students for study or research abroad in specified countries.

Eligibility Applicants for these grants must meet the eligibility requirements for Fulbright Full Grants administered by the Institute of International Education (IIE). If they do not receive any of those grants to 4 specified countries, (Germany, Hungary, Italy, and Korea), they may be considered for a Travel Grant. Students may also apply for these Travel Grants to the 4 specified countries to supplement their own funds or financial aid from other non-IIE services. Applicants may be required to provide statements of their ability to support themselves while overseas.

Financial data Travel Grants provide round-trip transportation to the country where the recipient will be studying, limited health and accident insurance, and the cost of an orientation course abroad, if applicable.

Duration 1 academic year.

Special features This program, created in 1946 and funded by the U.S. Department of State, is administered by the Institute of International Education (IIE). Students who are currently enrolled in the United States are to apply through the Fulbright program adviser on their campus; at-large applicants (those not currently enrolled) may obtain applications and information directly from the IIE.

Number awarded Varies each year; recently, 10 of these grants were offered for travel to Germany, 2 to Hungary, 2 to Italy, and 2 to Korea.

Deadline October of each year.

[611]
FULFORD JUNIOR RESEARCH FELLOWSHIP

University of Oxford
St. Anne's College
Attn: Senior Tutor's Secretary
Oxford OX2 6HS
England
44 1865 274800   Fax: 44 1865 274899
Web site: www.stannes.ox.ac.uk

Purpose To provide funding to doctoral candidates from any university who wish to conduct research in the arts at St. Anne's College of the University of Oxford in England.

Eligibility Applicants should be graduates in the second or subsequent year of study for a higher degree, should already have completed a significant amount of research, and must have completed the residence requirements at their home institution. They must be interested in conducting research in the arts at St. Anne's College.

Financial data The stipend is 10,120 pounds per year. Fellows also receive free accommodation or a living-out allowance and are members of the senior common room.

Duration 1 year; may be renewed for 1 additional year.

Limitations The fellow must live in Oxford and take part in college life.

Number awarded This fellowship is offered periodically; it was most recently offered for 2002 for English literature (medieval and modern), European and Oriental literature, modern languages, and cultural studies.

Deadline October of the year prior to the award.

[612]
FYSSEN FOUNDATION POSTDOCTORAL RESEARCH GRANTS

Fyssen Foundation
Attn: Executive Secretary
194 rue de Rivoli
75001 Paris
France
33 1 42 97 53 16   Fax: 33 1 42 60 17 95
E-mail: secretariat@fondation-fyssen.org
Web site: www.fondation-fyssen.org

Purpose To provide funding for training and research in France and other countries on topics related to cognitive mechanisms, including thought and reasoning.

Eligibility This program is open to scholars in anthropology and ethnology, neurobiology, ethnology and psychology, and human paleontology and archaeology. Applicants may be French scientists wishing to work abroad or foreign scientists wishing to work in French laboratories. They must have earned a Ph.D. degree, but scholars in biological sciences cannot be more than 35 years of age and those in human sciences must be younger than 40 years of age.

Financial data Grants range from 100,000 to 200,000 French francs (15,000 to 30,000 Euros).

Duration 1 year; nonrenewable.

Limitations Grants awarded to French citizens are tenable worldwide. Grants awarded to researchers from other countries must be used in France.

Deadline October of each year.

[613]
GEORGE PEPLER INTERNATIONAL AWARD

Royal Town Planning Institute
Attn: Awards and Events Assistant
26 Portland Place
London W1N 4BE
England
44 20 7636 9107   Fax: 44 20 7323 1582
E-mail: georgepepler@rtpi.org.uk
Web site: www.rtpi.org.uk

Purpose To provide financial assistance for international travel to learn about town and country planning.

Eligibility This program is open to people younger than 30 years of age who are interested in visiting Britain or (if residents of Britain) traveling to another country. Candidates need not be members or students of the Royal Town Planning Institute. However, they must have a plan for investigating the theory or practice of town and country planning or a particular aspect of planning. They must submit a proposal that specifies the aims and objectives of the study, the specific subject matter of the study, how the work is to be done, and the final form of the results.

Financial data The stipend is 1,500 pounds, with the majority paid before the visit and the balance after the final report is submitted.

Duration 3 to 4 weeks.

Special features This award was offered for the first time in 1963. It was established to recognize George Pepler, who was 1 of the founders of the Town Planning Institute in 1913.

Limitations At the conclusion of the visit, the recipient must submit a full report to the institute. This award is not intended to provide basic support for students or to finance postgraduate or doctoral studies.

Number awarded 1 every other year.

Deadline March of even-numbered years.

[614]
GERMAN CHANCELLOR SCHOLARSHIP PROGRAM

Alexander von Humboldt Foundation
Attn: U.S. Liaison Office
1012 14th Street, N.W., Suite 301
Washington, DC 20005
(202) 783-1907   Fax: (202) 783-1908
E-mail: avh@bellatlantic.net
Web site: www.humboldt-foundation.de

Purpose To provide an opportunity for future American leaders to come to Germany to study or to conduct research.

Eligibility Applicants can apply or be nominated. They must be individuals under 35 years of age who, in the future, could play a pivotal role in shaping the relationship between Germany and the United States. They must be U.S. citizens, college graduates, and proposing a program of study or research in Germany in fields that, in the past, have included social and policy sciences, government, law, journalism, communications, management, finance, economics, architecture, arts, performing arts, humanities, public service, and environmental affairs. Command of German is not required.

Financial data The stipend is the Euro equivalent of 3,500 to 5,000 Deutsche marks per month. In addition, travel expenses, a special allowance for spouses and children, a study tour, an introductory seminar, costs for language learning, and a final meeting in Bonn are included in the award.

Duration 1 year, beginning in September.

Special features Recipients spend a year in Germany, in academic or other public institutions. An extensive German language course precedes the program. Then, there is a 4-week introductory seminar in Bonn or Cologne (where representatives from scientific, industrial, social, and political sectors are present), a study tour of Germany, and a meeting in Bonn to conclude the program. In between, fellows are given the opportunity to continue or follow up their studies/research at a German university and/or research institute. All Bundeskanzler Scholars are assisted by academic advisers and mentors during their stay in Germany. Former scholarship holders are given the opportunity to visit Germany again, 3 years after their return to the United States. Originally founded in 1860, the Alexander von Humboldt Foundation was re-established in 1953 by the German government, which provides the major portion (94 percent) of its funds. This program is under the patronage of Germany's Federal Chancellor (Bundeskanzler) and the President of the United States.

Number awarded Up to 10 each year.

Deadline October of each year.

[615]
GERMAN DISTINGUISHED CHAIR IN AMERICAN STUDIES

Council for International Exchange of Scholars
3007 Tilden Street, N.W., Suite 5L
Washington, DC 20008-3009
(202) 686-6245   Fax: (202) 362-3442
E-mail: scholars@cies.iie.org
Web site: www.iie.org/cies

Purpose To provide funding for scholars to teach American studies at Humboldt University in Berlin.

Eligibility Scholars at the rank of full or associate professor in American studies, with an emphasis on American history, law, political science, or American social sciences may apply for this position if they are interested in teaching American studies at Humboldt University. German proficiency is helpful but not required. Preference is given to applicants who have had little or no prior experience with Germany. Scholars who have had a grant to Germany during the past 5 years are not eligible.

Financial data The stipend is approximately 50,000 Euros for maintenance and all other benefits. The exact amount depends on the actual duration of the grant, number of dependents, and other factors.

Duration 5 to 10 months.

Special features This is a Fulbright scholar program, sponsored by the Bureau of Educational and Cultural Affairs of the U.S. Department of State and administered by the Council for International Exchange of Scholars. The recipient teaches graduate seminars and 1 lecture course, and participates in research. occasional lectures outside the host institution and engage in other activities involving American studies outreach in Germany.

Number awarded 1 each year.
Deadline April of each year.

[616]
GERMAN HISTORICAL INSTITUTE SUMMER SEMINAR IN PALEOGRAPHY AND ARCHIVAL STUDIES

German Historical Institute
Attn: Deputy Director
1607 New Hampshire Avenue, N.W.
Washington, DC 20009-2562
(202) 387-3355　　　　Fax: (202) 483-3430
E-mail: T.Goebel@ghi-dc.org
Web site: www.ghi-dc.org/scholarship.html

Purpose To provide an opportunity for North American Ph.D. candidates to visit Germany to prepare for writing their dissertation.

Eligibility Candidates must be enrolled in a Ph.D. program in the United States or Canada. They must be fluent in German. Applicants must be interested in participating in a program that introduces them to German handwriting styles, familiarizes them with German archives and libraries, and helps them plan their dissertation research. Preference is given to those who have already chosen a dissertation topic that makes the consultation of German archives necessary. Fields of study include art history, history, linguistics, literature and musicology.

Financial data The program provides round-trip airfare (economy class) to Germany; rail transportation to the handwriting and archives course in Koblenz and the tour of archives in Bonn, Heidelberg, and Köln; and accommodations. Students already in Europe are reimbursed for rail travel to and from Koblenz (the starting point of the program).

Duration 2 weeks during the summer.

Special features One of the main purposes of the program is to assist participants in planning the course of their future dissertation research in Germany. Participants attend courses in German handwriting of various periods and in archival science at the federal and state archives in Koblenz, Germany. They also visit a wide variety of archives, including business, media, church, city, and university archives. This program is co-organized by the German Historical Institute and the University of Wisconsin's German Department.

Number awarded 10 each year.
Deadline December of each year.

[617]
GERMAN MARSHALL FUND RESEARCH FELLOWSHIP PROGRAM

German Marshall Fund of the United States
11 Dupont Circle, N.W., Suite 750
Washington, DC 20036
(202) 745-3950　　　　Fax: (202) 265-1662
E-mail: info@gmfus.org
Web site: www.gmfus.org

Purpose To provide funding to American pre- and postdoctoral scholars to conduct research on contemporary economic, political, and social developments relating to Europe, European integration, and relations between Europe and the United States.

Eligibility This program is open to graduate students, recent Ph.D. recipients, and more senior scholars. Graduate students must be enrolled in a doctoral program at a U.S. institution and have completed the equivalent of at least 2 years of full-time graduate study; postdoctoral and advanced candidates must have a Ph.D. or LL.M. degree and not have received support from this fund for at least 5 years. Special consideration is given to applicants seeking support for dissertation field work in 1 or more European countries and to projects involving parallel or collaborative research by both established and younger scholars, including projects designed on a transatlantic basis. Applicants seeking predissertation grants for a project related to Europe are also eligible if they can demonstrate special need for such support. Selection is based on scholarly qualifications, promise, and (for applicants who have completed the Ph.D. or LL.M.) achievements; quality, originality, and importance of the proposed research; disciplinary and/or policy relevance of the project and its expected results; demonstrable need for support that is unavailable from other sources; and the likelihood of completing the proposed research or field work during the support period.

Financial data For predissertation research, the maximum award is $3,000; for dissertation field work, the maximum grant is $20,000, with an additional $2,000 to cover travel costs; for advanced research, the maximum award is $40,000 (not to exceed the recipient's current income), with an additional $2,000 to cover travel costs. All recipients are responsible for arranging their own housing, insurance, benefits, and travel.

Duration Predissertation research: from 6 weeks to 2 months; dissertation field work: up to 1 academic year; advanced research: 1 academic term to 1 academic year.

Special features The German Marshall Fund of the United States is an independent American organization established in 1972 by a gift from the government of Germany as a memorial to the Marshall Plan.

Number awarded Varies each year.
Deadline November of each year.

[618]
GERMAN STUDIES RESEARCH GRANTS

German Academic Exchange Service (DAAD)
950 Third Avenue, 19th Floor
New York, NY 10022
(212) 758-3223　　　　Fax: (212) 755-5780
E-mail: daadny@daad.org
Web site: www.daad.org

Purpose To finance undergraduate or graduate research on the cultural, political, historical, economic, and social aspects of modern and contemporary German affairs.

Eligibility This program is open to undergraduates with at least junior standing pursuing a German studies track or minor, master's degree students and Ph.D. candidates working on a certificate in German studies, and Ph.D. candidates doing preliminary dissertation research. Students whose dissertation proposals have been formally accepted are not eligible. Candidates must be nominated by a department and/or program chair at a U.S. or Canadian institution of higher education. They must have completed 2 years of college-level German and a minimum of 3 German studies courses by the deadline. Grants are restricted to U.S. or Canadian citizens who are enrolled full

time at the university that nominates them. Research may be conducted in either North America or Germany.
Financial data Grant support, ranging from $1,500 to $3,000, is intended to offset possible living and travel costs during the research phase.
Duration 1 academic year, 1 summer term, or both.
Deadline April or October of each year.

[619]
GERMAN/AMERICAN JOURNALIST EXCHANGE PROGRAM

Radio and Television News Directors Foundation
Attn: German/American Journalist Exchange Program
1000 Connecticut Avenue, N.W., Suite 615
Washington, DC 20036-5302
(202) 467-5215   Fax: (202) 223-4007
E-mail: Margarete@rtndf.org
Web site: www.rtnda.org/asfi/fellowships/gax.html

Purpose To provide funding to U.S. radio and television journalists who are interested in a story program in Germany.
Eligibility This program is open to U.S. radio and television journalists who are working full time in news, foreign affairs, politics, economics, or culture. Knowledge of German is preferred but not required. Applicants must be interested in visiting Germany as part of a structured study tour and then possibly pursuing individual research projects, filing stories for their station, or participating in an internship at a German radio or television station. There is no application form; candidates must submit a resume and current job description; a 1-page essay on why they want to participate in the program, what they hope to get out of it, and their long-term career goals; a 1-page description of 2 recent stories they have done that are relevant to the program; a 1-page description of 2 stories they would like to produce as a result of participating in this program; and a letter of reference from their news director.
Financial data The program provides payment of round-trip airfare from home city to Germany, transfers during the program, hotel, and per diem for meals equivalent to approximately $35 per day. No payments are made for passport and visa fees, telephone, laundry, airport parking and transfers from home to airport in the United States, meal expenses in excess of the provided per diem, or other personal expenses.
Duration The structured study tour lasts 2 weeks; participants may remain for an additional 1 to 14 days to engage in an individual project. Each summer, there are 2 programs, 1 beginning in June and the other in September.
Special features This program, which began in 1994, is jointly sponsored by the Radio and Television News Directors Foundation and the RIAS (Radio in the American Sector) Berlin Commission.
Number awarded 12 to 20 participants in each program each year.
Deadline March of each year for the first program; June of each year for the second program.

[620]
GERMANY FULBRIGHT TEACHER EXCHANGE

U.S. Department of State
c/o Graduate School, USDA
600 Maryland Avenue, S.W., Room 320
Washington, DC 20024-2520
(202) 314-3520   Fax: (202) 479-6806
E-mail: fulbright@grad.usda.gov
Web site: www.grad.usda.gov/International/ftep.html

Purpose To promote mutual understanding between the people of the United States and the people of Germany through a teacher exchange program.
Eligibility This program is open to teachers (grades 7 through 12) and 2-year or 4-year college faculty members who are teaching German, English, or other subjects and are interested in teaching English language and literature in Germany. Applicants must 1) be U.S. citizens; 2) hold at least a bachelor's degree; 3) be fluent in English; 4) have a current full-time teaching assignment in the U.S. or a territory; 5) have the approval of their school administration; 6) have at least 3 years of full-time experience; and 7) not have participated in a Fulbright Teacher Exchange longer than 8 weeks during the last 2 years. Fluency in German is desirable; some familiarity is required. Preference is given to applicants with German speaking ability. Non-speakers of German are considered for placement in select schools. Teaching couples may apply. However, because of the limited number of positions available and, often, the lack of foreign candidate pairs with similar qualifications for interchanges, it may not be possible to arrange suitable assignments in the same locality or to place both teachers. Preference is given to applicants who have not participated previously in the program and may be given to applicants who have not previously lived in Germany. Geographic distribution of awards within the United States is also a factor in selection. This program does not discriminate on the basis of race, color, religion, age, sex, or national origin and encourages the applications of members of minority communities. Other considerations being equal, veterans are given preference.
Financial data Participants receive round-trip transportation and, at the discretion of the Fulbright Commission in Germany, a cost of living supplement of the Euro equivalent of 900 Deutsche marks per month. The U.S. school must agree to accept a German teacher who must secure a leave of absence with pay.
Duration 10 months, beginning in August.
Special features This program is sponsored by the Bureau of Educational and Cultural Affairs of the U.S. Department of State and administered by the Graduate School, USDA.
Limitations This program provides for the direct exchange of teaching assignments between Germany and the United States. Applicants selected for exchange must attend orientation programs of the sponsoring agencies in the United States or abroad.
Number awarded 20 each year.
Deadline October of each year.

[621]
GERTRUDE SMITH PROFESSORSHIPS
American School of Classical Studies at Athens
Attn: Committee on Personnel
6-8 Charlton Street
Princeton, NJ 08540-5232
(609) 683-0800　　　　　　　　Fax: (609) 924-0578
E-mail: ascsa@ascsa.org
Web site: www.ascsa.org

Purpose To provide funding to American scholars who are interested in administering the academic program of the American School of Classical Studies at Athens.

Eligibility This program is open to scholars who are former members of the school and have at least 2 years' teaching experience in a postsecondary educational institution. Applicants must have full training in classics with some knowledge of classical archaeology and modern Greek. They must be interested in planning, organizing, and conducting the academic program of the school under the supervision of the director.

Financial data The salary is commensurate with rank and experience but ranges from $4,500 to $6,000 plus travel and expenses.

Duration Summer months.

Special features Information is also available from Michael Hoff, University of Nebraska, Department of Art and Art History, Nelle Cochrane Woods Hall, Lincoln, NE 68588-0114.

Number awarded 2 each year.

Deadline January of each year.

[622]
THE GILLIAN AWARD
Studio Art Centers International
c/o Institute of International Education
Attn: SACI Coordinator
809 United Nations Plaza
New York, NY 10017-3580
(212) 984-5548　　　　　　　　E-mail: saci@iie.org
Web site: www.saci-florence.org

Purpose To provide women artists with an opportunity to live and work at the Studio Art Centers International (SACI) in Florence, Italy.

Eligibility This program is open to female artists with demonstrated artistic achievement and a bachelor's degree. Applicants must have a history of exhibiting in galleries and other venues. They must be interested in living and working in Florence, Italy and utilizing the resources of SACI.

Financial data Participants receive housing and full tuition from September to April. The estimated value of the award is $22,500.

Duration 8 months, beginning in September.

Special features SACI is a U.S. college-affiliated studio art school in Florence, Italy that was founded in 1975.

Number awarded 1 each year.

Deadline March of each year.

[623]
GIRTON COLLEGE RESEARCH FELLOWSHIPS
University of Cambridge
Girton College
Attn: Secretary to the Research Fellowship Committee
Huntingdon Road
Cambridge CB3 0JG
England
44 1223 338999　　　　　　　　Fax: 44 1223 338896
E-mail: ff204@cam.ac.uk
Web site: www.girton.cam.ac.uk

Purpose To provide funding to postdoctoral scholars interested in conducting research at Girton College of the University of Cambridge in England.

Eligibility This program is open to graduates of any university who are interested in conducting research at Cambridge's Girton College in the arts or sciences. There are no age limits, but applicants should be in the early stage of their career and have recently completed their Ph.D. or be close to completion.

Financial data In the first year, the stipend is 10,619 pounds per year for fellows who have not yet completed their Ph.D. or 13,328 for fellows who have completed the degree. In the final year, the stipend is 14,678 for postdoctoral fellows. Other benefits include residence in the college at a moderate charge or a living-out allowance of 2,000 pounds per year and reimbursement of research expenses up to 1,500 pounds over the term of the fellowship.

Duration Normally 3 years.

Number awarded 2 each year: 1 in the arts and 1 in the sciences.

Deadline September of each year.

[624]
GLADYS KRIEBLE DELMAS FOUNDATION GRANTS FOR INDEPENDENT RESEARCH IN VENICE AND THE VENETO
Gladys Krieble Delmas Foundation
521 Fifth Avenue, Suite 1612
New York, NY 10175-1699
(212) 687-0011　　　　　　　　Fax: (212) 687-8877
E-mail: info@delmas.org
Web site: www.delmas.org

Purpose To provide financial support to predoctoral and postdoctoral scholars interested in conducting research in Venice and the Veneto.

Eligibility Applicants must be citizens or permanent residents of the United States, have some experience in advanced research, be interested in conducting research in Venice and the Veneto, and, if graduate students, have fulfilled all doctoral requirements except for completion of the dissertation at the time of application. The proposed research must deal with the history of Venice and the former Venetian empire in the humanities and social sciences, including but not limited to archaeology, architecture, art, bibliography, economics, history, history of science, law, literature, music, political science, religion, and theater. Additional support may be available to conduct research in European libraries and archives outside Venice and for publication of research results.

Financial data The maximum grant is $16,500. Recipients may apply for additional funding up to $3,000 to conduct research in European libraries and archives outside Venice. Publishers may apply for up to $4,000 for publication of studies resulting from research made possible by these grants.

Duration 1 academic year. Supplemental grants for research outside Venice are limited to 1 month.

Number awarded Varies each year; recently, 20 of these grants were awarded.

Deadline December of each year.

[625]
GLENN T. SEABORG NOBEL TRAVEL AWARD

Swedish Council of America
2600 Park Avenue
Minneapolis, MN 55407
(612) 871-0593

Purpose To recognize and reward outstanding students majoring in science or mathematics in college with a trip to Sweden.

Eligibility Candidates for this award must be enrolled full time and majoring in mathematics or science at 1 of the 6 American colleges founded by Swedish immigrants: Augustana College, Bethany College, Bethel College, Gustavus Adolphus College, North Park College, or Upsala College. Each institution may nominate 1 student to be considered for the award. Generally, nominees should be in their senior year. Selection is based on academic achievement, creative potential, and ability to represent effectively the 6 Swedish American colleges and the Swedish Council of America at the Nobel Awards in Sweden.

Financial data The award consists of round-trip airfare to Stockholm, hostel accommodations, and some living expenses for the week of the Nobel Awards (generally in December).

Duration The competition is held annually.

Special features This award was established in 1979 in honor of Dr. Glenn T. Seaborg, chemist and Nobel laureate who discovered or co-discovered numerous atomic elements, including element number 106, officially named Seaborgium in honor of Dr. Seaborg in 1994.

Number awarded 1 each year.

Deadline Nominations must be submitted by the end of March of each year.

[626]
GOLESTAN FELLOWSHIP

Netherlands Institute for Advanced Study in the
  Humanities and Social Sciences
Meijboomlaan 1
2242 PR Wassenaar
Netherlands
31 70 512 2700   Fax: 31 70 511 7162
E-mail: nias@nias.knaw.nl

Purpose To provide financial assistance to scholars who wish to conduct research on the relationship between the social sciences and medical science at the Netherlands Institute for Advanced Study (NIAS).

Eligibility Eligible are scholars from countries other than the Netherlands who wish to conduct research at the Institute on the relationship between the social sciences and medical science. Selection is based on scholarly achievements, reputation, and publications.

Financial data The stipend is no more than 45 percent of the gross annual salary of a university professor of equal rank and seniority in the Netherlands. In practice, financial stipends range from the Euro equivalent of 3,000 to 6,000 Dutch guilders per month, depending on the amount of support the fellows receive from their own institutions as well as on their academic standing. In addition to the monthly stipend, the government of the Netherlands pays the fellows' travel costs to and from the institute. However, each fellow is responsible for the travel costs of family members and for additional baggage or shipping expenses.

Duration 10 months, from September to July.

Special features Funding for this fellowship is provided by the Golestan Foundation. Fellows are chosen by the Scholarship Committee of NIAS, the Royal Netherlands Academy of Arts and Sciences, and the Swiss Academy of Medical Science.

Number awarded 1 each year.

Deadline Applications may be submitted at any time, but they must arrive at least 18 months before the date the applicant wishes to begin residency.

[627]
GOTTLIEB DAIMLER-UND-KARL BENZ-STIFTUNG GRANTS

Gottlieb Daimler-und-Karl Benz-Stiftung
Dr. Carl Benz Platz 2
D-68526 Ladenburg
Germany
49 0 6203 15924   Fax: 49 0 6203 16624
E-mail: GD-KB-Stiftung@t-online.de

Purpose To provide research funding to young Germans doing research in foreign countries and to foreigners doing research in German institutions.

Eligibility This program is open to young researchers (30 years and under) in any discipline. Applicants may be Germans interested in conducting research in other countries or foreigners interested in conducting research in Germany. Applicants must have a clearly-defined research project of their own and work in cooperation with a host institution. To apply, researchers must submit a brief description of their proposed research (up to 3 pages), a letter of invitation from a host institution, estimated costs and financial plans for the entire stay, a curriculum vitae, a letter of reference, and academic certificates (transcripts, diploma, etc.).

Financial data Competitive grants are offered (amount not specified).

Duration 1 year.

Limitations Study visits and practical training are not supported under this program.

Number awarded Approximately 45 each year.

Deadline Applications may be submitted in January, May, or September.

[628]
GOVERNANCE IN POST-COMMUNIST SOCIETIES TRAVEL GRANTS

National Research Council
Attn: Office of International Affairs
2101 Constitution Avenue, N.W., FO 2060
Washington, DC 20418
(202) 334-2658   Fax: (202) 334-2614
E-mail: ocee@nas.edu
Web site: www.nationalacademies.org/oia

Purpose To provide funding to American pre- and postdoctoral scholars who are interested in traveling to central and eastern Europe, Eurasia, and the former Soviet Union to conduct research related to governance in post-Communist societies.

Eligibility This program is open to scholars at the postdoctoral level and to advanced graduate students (if the travel and research are directly relevant to their dissertation topic) who are affiliated with a U.S. university or research institution. Applicants must be interested in traveling to central or eastern Europe or the former Soviet Union to conduct research related to 1 of the subthemes of the subject of governance in post-Communist societies: 1) science and democratization—the role of scientists, engineers, and health professionals in the transition and the impact of the transition on the scientific community; 2) organized crime, terrorism, and proliferation of weapons of mass destruction—the causes of criminal activity (including counterfeiting, extortion, money-laundering, narcotics, arms trafficking, diversion of natural resources, terrorism, and proliferation), their impacts, and efforts to combat them; 3) technology and industrial economics—problems and potential technology commercialization and industrial development. Preference is given to applicants who possess relevant language capabilities and who propose to collaborate closely with a scholar from the region.

Financial data Grant amounts depend on the length of the visit and the destination of the scholar but generally range from $2,500 to $4,000. Funding covers travel costs, including international airfare and travel expenses while abroad. No provision is made for stipends, salary replacement, or indirect costs.

Duration 2 to 6 weeks.

Number awarded Varies each year.

Deadline May or December of each year.

Special features Support for this program is provided by the U.S. Department of State through its Research and Training Program for Eastern Europe and the Newly Independent States of the Former Soviet Union (Title VIII).

[629]
GOVERNMENT OF IRELAND RESEARCH FELLOWSHIPS IN THE HUMANITIES AND SOCIAL SCIENCES

Irish Research Council for the Humanities and Social Sciences
Attn: Academic Secretary
Higher Education Authority
Marine House
Clanwilliam Court
Dublin 2
Ireland
353 1 661 2748   Fax: 353 1 661 0492
E-mail: info@hea.ie
Web site: www.hea.ie

Purpose To provide funding to scholars in the humanities and social sciences (including law and business) interested in conducting research in Ireland.

Eligibility This program is open to scholars from any country who have received a doctoral degree in the humanities or social sciences within the preceding 5-year period. Applicants must include a formal invitation from the head of a humanities, social sciences, law, or business department at a third-level institution in Ireland, and they must identify a departmental mentor within the host institution.

Financial data Fellows receive a stipend of the Euro equivalent of up to 20,000 Irish pounds per year and an archival/field work bursary of the EUR equivalent of up to 2,000 Irish pounds.

Duration 1 year; may be renewed for 1 additional year.

Special features The Irish Research Council for the Humanities and Social Sciences was established in 2000.

Limitations During the first year, fellows must devote all their time to their proposed research project. During the second year, if a renewal is granted, they may teach 1 full academic course on the departmental syllabus and/or coordinate a departmental research seminar for graduate students and postdoctoral scholars within the host department.

Number awarded Varies each year.

Deadline May of each year.

[630]
GRADUATE AND POSTGRADUATE STUDY AND RESEARCH IN POLAND PROGRAM

Kosciuszko Foundation
Attn: Grants Office
15 East 65th Street
New York, NY 10021-6595
(212) 734-2130   Fax: (212) 628-4552
E-mail: Thekfschol@aol.com
Web site: www.kosciuszkofoundation.org/grants/GRADRES.shtml

Purpose To provide financial assistance to graduate students and faculty members who wish to conduct research in Poland.

Eligibility This program is open to graduate students and faculty members who wish to conduct research at a university in Poland. Applicants must be U.S. citizens or permanent residents who possess Polish language proficiency sufficient to conduct the proposed research project. The proposed host institution must fall under the jurisdiction of the Polish Ministry of National Education. Selection is based on academic excellence and motivation for pursuing research in Poland.

Financial data Grantees receive a stipend for dormitory housing and living expenses. Funding is not provided for travel to or from Poland or for tuition expenses for American students who wish to attend classes at Polish universities.

Duration 1 academic year or semester.

Special features Funding for this program is provided by the Polish Ministry of National Education.

Limitations There is a $50 application fee. Graduate students interested in studying at a Polish university should apply for the Kosciuszko Foundation Tuition Scholarships for Study in Poland.

Number awarded Several each year.

Deadline January of each year.

[631]
GRANTS IN DEAFNESS, BILINGUAL EDUCATION, AND COMMUNICATION

Institute of International Education
Attn: Student Programs Division
809 United Nations Plaza
New York, NY 10017-3580
(212) 984-5330   Fax: (212) 984-5325
Web site: www.iie.org/fulbright

Purpose To provide financial assistance to graduate students interested in conducting research in Italy related to deafness.

Eligibility This program is open to graduate students, both deaf and hearing, who have experiences in the area of the proposed project that go beyond university studies. Applicants must be interested in conducting cross-cultural research in Italy and/or collaborating on projects aimed at improving education for deaf children and developing tools that will contribute to the creation of an environment in which deaf people can enjoy full expression and access to curriculum and information. They must be fluent in American Sign Language and have a working knowledge of Italian Sign Language, a working knowledge of written Italian, and (for hearing candidates) a working knowledge of spoken Italian. Examples of project areas include parent-infant programs, sign language teaching and linguistic research, bilingual preschool education, language assessment, production of multimedia tools for education and training, interpreter training, tactile sign research and the use of tactile signs in deaf-blind education and interpreting, and training deaf people as professionals with deaf and deaf-blind children.

Financial data The grant provides a maintenance allowance based on the cost of living, round-trip international travel, and health and accident insurance. Candidates selected for these awards are considered for Fulbright Travel Grants.

Duration 4 months.

Special features These grants are offered as part of the Fulbright program, administered in the United States by the Institute of International Education (IIE). Students who are currently enrolled in the United States are to apply through the Fulbright program adviser on their campus; at-large applicants (those not currently enrolled) may obtain applications and information directly from the IIE.

Number awarded 3 each year.

Deadline October of each year

[632]
GREENWOOD BIDDER RESEARCH FELLOWSHIP

University of Cambridge
Lucy Cavendish College
Attn: President's Secretary
Lady Margaret Road
Cambridge CB3 0BU
England
44 1223 332196   Fax: 44 1223 332178
E-mail: bjy21@cam.ac.uk
Web site: www.lucy-cav.cam.ac.uk

Purpose To provide funding to women postdoctoral scholars interested in conducting research at Lucy Cavendish College of the University of Cambridge in England.

Eligibility This program is open to women from any country who hold a doctorate or whose dissertation is under examination. Applicants must be seeking supplemental funding to undertake or continue a research project at Lucy Cavendish College.

Financial data The stipend, up to 3,000 pounds per year, is intended to supplement other funding.

Duration 1 year; may be renewed for up to 2 additional years, subject to satisfactory progress and annual reports.

Number awarded This fellowship is offered from time to time.

Deadline January in the years it is available.

[633]
HARRIET AND LEON POMERANCE FELLOWSHIP

Archaeological Institute of America
656 Beacon Street, Fourth Floor
Boston, MA 02215-2006
(617) 353-9361   Fax: (617) 353-6550
E-mail: aia@bu.edu
Web site: www.archaeological.org

Purpose To provide financial support to American and Canadian graduate students or scholars for individual research on a project relating to Aegean Bronze Age archaeology.

Eligibility Although applicants need not be registered in academic institutions, preference is given to individuals engaged in dissertation research related to Aegean Bronze Age archaeology or to recent recipients of the Ph.D. Applicants must be residents of the United States or Canada. Projects requiring travel to the Mediterranean area are given priority.

Financial data The stipend is $4,000.

Duration 1 academic year.

Number awarded 1 each year.

Deadline October of each year.

[634]
HARRY BIKAKIS FELLOWSHIP
American School of Classical Studies at Athens
Attn: Director
54 Souidias Street
GR-106 76 Athens
Greece
30 1 723 6313   Fax: 30 1 725 0584
Web site: www.ascsa.org

Purpose To provide financial support for research on ancient Greek law at the American School of Classical Studies at Athens.

Eligibility This program is open to graduate students who are attending a North American institution and to Greek graduate students who are working on an excavation at the school or its Blegen or Gennadius Libraries. Applicants must be interested in conducting research on ancient Greek law in Athens.

Financial data The stipend is $1,500.

Duration Up to 1 year.

Number awarded Awards are presented periodically, but not more than once a year.

Deadline January of each year.

[635]
HAYWARD JUNIOR RESEARCH FELLOWSHIP
University of Oxford
Oriel College
Attn: College Secretary
Oxford OX1 4EW
England
44 1865 276555
Web site: www.oriel.ox.ac.uk

Purpose To provide funding to postdoctorates from any country who are interested in conducting research in the medical or life sciences at Oriel College of the University of Oxford in England.

Eligibility This program is open to graduates of any university who are interested in conducting postdoctoral research at Oriel College in the medical or life sciences. Applicants normally should be younger than 30 years of age.

Financial data Fellows receive meals at the common table and free rooms in college or a housing allowance. Other financial arrangements depend on the circumstances of the fellow.

Duration 3 years.

Number awarded This fellowship is normally offered triennially: 2003, 2006, etc.

Deadline February of the years when offered.

[636]
HEDLEY BULL AND TALBOT JUNIOR RESEARCH FELLOWSHIP
University of Oxford
Lady Margaret Hall
Attn: Principal's Secretary
Norham Gardens
Oxford OX2 6QA
England
44 1865 274302   Fax: 44 1865 511069
Web site: www.lmh.ox.ac.uk

Purpose To provide financial assistance to pre- and postdoctorates who wish to conduct research on international relations while affiliated with Lady Margaret Hall of the University of Oxford in England.

Eligibility This program is open to graduates of any university who are engaged in, or have recently completed, doctoral research in the field of international relations. Applicants must be interested in conducting research while affiliated with Lady Margaret Hall.

Financial data The stipend is approximately 10,000 pounds per year; also included are a living-out allowance, dining rights, and a research allowance.

Duration 3 years; nonrenewable.

Number awarded 1 every 3 years (2003, 2006, etc.)

Deadline July of the year the award is to be made.

[637]
HEINRICH HERTZ FOUNDATION GRANTS
Heinrich Hertz Foundation
c/o Ministerium für Wissenschaft und Forschung des
  Landes Nordrhein-Westfalen
Völklingerstrasse 49
D-40221 Düsseldorf
Germany
49 211 896 4266   Fax: 49 211 896 4407
Web site: www.mwf.nrw.de

Purpose To provide funding to scientists who are interested in conducting research in Germany.

Eligibility Eligible to apply are scientists, professors, and (on occasion) exceptional graduate students from any country who are interested in conducting scientific research at academic institutions or research institutes in North-Rhine-Westphalia. Applicants must be proficient in German. Applications must be submitted by a sponsoring professor at an institute of higher education in the state of North-Rhine-Westphalia, not directly by the candidate.

Financial data The amount awarded depends upon the needs of the recipient.

Duration Up to 1 year; may be renewed.

Deadline Applications may be submitted at any time.

[638]
HELEN WADDELL VISITING PROFESSORSHIP
Queen's University of Belfast
Attn: Academic Council Office
Administration Building
Belfast BT7 1NN
Northern Ireland
44 28 9027 3006   Fax: 44 28 9031 3537
E-mail: academic.council@qub.ac.uk
Web site: www.qub.ac.uk

Purpose To offer women a visiting professorship at Queen's University of Belfast in Northern Ireland.

Eligibility Candidates may be women who have either a proven academic standing and appropriate achievement in research and scholarship, or who have attained professional eminence in industry, business, government service, the professions, the arts, medicine, engineering, or the sciences. They may be from any country and must desire a short-term assignment in Northern Ireland. The assignment may be in the field of women's studies. Normally, candidates should be on paid leave of absence from their employment.

Financial data The stipend is 1,600 pounds; funds are to be used to cover travel and living expenses.

Duration 1 month.

Number awarded 1 each year.

Deadline October of each year.

[639]
HERTFORD COLLEGE JUNIOR RESEARCH FELLOWSHIPS
University of Oxford
Hertford College
Attn: Principal's Secretary
Oxford OX1 3BW
England
44 1865 279405   Fax: 44 1865 279437
E-mail: lihua.li@hertford.ox.ac.uk
Web site: www.hertford.ox.ac.uk

Purpose To provide funding to postdoctoral scholars from any country who wish to conduct research in the arts or sciences at Hertford College of the University of Oxford in England.

Eligibility This program is open to graduates of any university under the age of 30 who hold a doctoral degree and are already engaged in independent research in the arts or sciences. They must be seeking to conduct research at Hertford College.

Financial data The stipend is 12,534 pounds per year, rising annually by increments of 500 pounds. Fellows also receive free meals and free accommodations (or a housing allowance of 2,738 pounds) and computer and research allowances.

Duration 3 years.

Number awarded 2 fellowships (1 in the arts and 1 in science) are offered from time to time.

Deadline January of the years when offered.

[640]
HERZOG AUGUST BIBLIOTHEK WOLFENBUTTEL FELLOWSHIP
Newberry Library
Attn: Committee on Awards
60 West Walton Street
Chicago, IL 60610-3305
(312) 255-3666   Fax: (312) 255-3513
E-mail: research@newberry.org
Web site: www.newberry.org

Purpose To provide financial support to pre- and postdoctoral scholars who wish to conduct joint research at the Newberry Library and at the Herzog August Bibliothek in Wolfenbüttel, Germany.

Eligibility This program is open to doctoral candidates and postdoctoral scholars who intend to conduct related research at the 2 libraries, the Newberry in Chicago and the Herzog August in Wolfenbüttel. The proposed project must link the collections of both libraries. Applicants should also hold a Newberry fellowship.

Financial data For the German portion of the research, the award provides a stipend of the Euro equivalents of 2,000 Deutsche marks per month and up to DM 1,200 in travel expenses.

Duration Both short-term (2 weeks to 6 months) and long-term (up to 11 months) awards are available.

Special features Nearly all of the Newberry's 1 million volumes and 5 million manuscripts relate to the history of western Europe and the Americas.

Number awarded 1 or more each year.

Deadline January of each year for long-term awards; February of each year for short-term awards.

[641]
HISTORIC PRESERVATION/CONSERVATION ROME PRIZE FELLOWSHIP
American Academy in Rome
Attn: Fellowship Coordinator
7 East 60th Street
New York, NY 10022-1001
(212) 751-7200   Fax (212) 751-7220
E-mail: info@aarome.org
Web site: www.aarome.org

Purpose To provide financial support to American artists interested in conducting research in conservation and historic preservation at the School of Fine Arts of the American Academy in Rome.

Eligibility Applicants must be U.S. citizens who hold a baccalaureate degree or equivalent in conservation or historic preservation. They must have at least 7 years of professional experience and currently be practicing in the field. Applications must include a 1-page statement describing how the Rome experience will be beneficial professionally and identifying any special resources in Italy that are important to the work, a portfolio with at least 6 examples of design work, and up to 18 slides of design work. Full-time students are not eligible.

Financial data The fellowship provides a stipend of up to $10,000, meals, a bedroom with private bath, and a study or studio. Fellows with children under 18 are housed outside the

McKim, Mead & White building and are provided with an allowance that helps cover the cost of off-campus housing.

Duration 6 months, beginning in September.

Special features The American Academy in Rome, founded in 1894 by the American architect Charles F. McKim, is a center for independent study and advanced research in the fine arts and humanities. It consists of a School of Fine Arts (including architecture, landscape architecture, design arts, painting and sculpture, musical composition, and literature) and a School of Classical Studies (including classical studies and archaeology, history of art, and post-classical humanistic/modern Italian studies).

Limitations There is a $40 application fee. Prize winners may not hold full-time jobs while at the Academy.

Number awarded 2 each year.

Deadline November of each year.

[642]
HISTORICAL RESEARCH TRUST AWARDS

Royal Institute of British Architects
Attn: Centre for Architectural Education
66 Portland Place
London W1N 4AD
England
44 20 7580 5533 Fax: 44 20 7255 1541
E-mail: admin@inst.riba.org
Web site: www.architecture.com

Purpose To provide financial assistance to individuals who wish to pursue a program of education or research in the United Kingdom related to architectural history.

Eligibility Eligible to apply are young people, whether or not they are graduates or have completed a normal course of architectural studies, who are interested in pursuing a program of education or research in the United Kingdom on architecture, other than contemporary and recent architecture, including the decoration and furnishing of buildings in any part of the world. Teachers and practicing architects may also apply. Applications are accepted from outside the United Kingdom, but the work must be conducted under the supervision of a scholar within the U.K.

Financial data Grants are either 10,000 or 6,000 pounds. Funds may be used to cover stipends, travel expenses, staff expenses, publication costs, and other research-related expenses, but not course fees or subsistence costs.

Duration Up to 2 years.

Number awarded 5 every other year: 1 at 10,000 pounds and 4 at 6,000 pounds.

Deadline April of odd-numbered years.

[643]
HIV–AIDS AND RELATED ILLNESSES RESEARCH COLLABORATION AWARD

Fogarty International Center
Attn: Division of International Training and Research
31 Center Drive, Room B2C39
Bethesda, MD 20892-2220
(301) 496-1653 Fax: (301) 402-0779
E-mail: FIRCA@nih.gov
Web site: www.nih.gov/fic/programs/aidsfirc.html

Purpose To provide assistance for U.S. investigators with current funding from the National Institutes of Health (NIH) to conduct research related to AIDS at foreign sites in collaboration with foreign scientists.

Eligibility Applications may be submitted by U.S. nonprofit organizations, public and private, such as universities, colleges, hospitals, laboratories, units of state and local governments, and eligible agencies of the federal government on behalf of principal investigators. The proposed U.S. principal investigator must be the principal investigator of an AIDS or AIDS-related research grant project funded by the institutes. Racial/ethnic minority individuals, women, and persons with disabilities are encouraged to apply as principal investigators. The foreign collaborator must hold a position at an institution in a foreign country that will allow him or her adequate time and provide appropriate facilities to conduct the proposed research. Most countries are eligible for participation in this program; applications for purchase of equipment as part of the grant are limited to research in the developing countries of Africa, Asia, (except Japan, Singapore, South Korea, and Taiwan), central and eastern Europe, Russia and the Independent States of the former Soviet Union, Latin America and the non-U.S. Caribbean, the Middle East, and the Pacific Ocean Islands (except Australia and New Zealand). The application must demonstrate that the award will enhance the scientific contributions of both the U.S. and foreign scientist and will enhance or expand the contribution of the institutes-sponsored research project.

Financial data Grants up to $32,000 per year are available. Funds may be used for supplies at the foreign institution, expenses incurred at the U.S. institution to support the collaboration, and research-related travel and subsistence expenses for both the U.S. and foreign investigators. For collaborations in developing countries as defined above, requests for purchase of equipment (including computers and fax machines) are considered; up to $5,000 may be allocated as a stipend for the foreign collaborator and up to $2,000 may be allocated for the foreign collaborator to attend an AIDS-related scientific conference. Travel funds may be requested up to 20 percent of the total direct costs (up to $6,400) for the U.S. principal investigator, the foreign collaborator, and/or their colleagues or students for visits to each other's laboratory or research site, if such visits are directly related to the subject of the collaborative research.

Duration Up to 3 years.

Special features This program is the counterpart to the Fogarty International Research Collaboration Award (FIRCA) program for non-AIDS related research. It is also designated as AIDS-FIRCA.

Deadline April, August, or December of each year.

[644]
HORNIK MEMORIAL FELLOWSHIP IN INTELLECTUAL HISTORY

University of Oxford
Wolfson College
Attn: President's Secretary
Linton Road
Oxford OX2 6UD
England
44 1865 274100   Fax: 44 1865 274125
E-mail: sue.hales@wolfson.ox.ac.uk
Web site: www.wolfson.ox.ac.uk

Purpose To provide funding to postdoctoral scholars from any country who wish to conduct research in intellectual history at Wolfson College of the University of Oxford in England.

Eligibility This program is open to residents of any country who are interested in conducting postdoctoral research while in residence at Wolfson College. Applicants should normally be younger than 30 years of age and should have at least 2 years of research experience in the subject. Their field of research must be intellectual history. Selection is based on a sample of the applicant's written work, up to 10,000 words.

Financial data The stipend is 11,478 pounds per year. Fellows also receive room and board. Fellows who are married or who require family accommodations may live at the college and pay the difference in rent or live outside the college and receive a housing allowance equivalent to the cost of single accommodation in the college.

Duration 3 years.

Special features Fellows are permitted to undertake up to 6 hours of teaching per week.

Number awarded The fellowship is offered whenever funds permit. It is next scheduled for 2006.

Deadline March of the years the fellowship is offered.

[645]
HUMAN FRONTIER SCIENCE PROGRAM LONG-TERM FELLOWSHIPS

Human Frontier Science Program Organization
Bureaux Europe
20, place des Halles
67080 Strasbourg
France
33 3 88 21 51 21   Fax: 33 3 88 32 88 97
E-mail: fellow@hfsp.org
Web site: www.hfsp.org

Purpose To provide financial support for postdoctoral research in biology to junior scholars who wish to go abroad.

Eligibility This program is open to researchers who have held a Ph.D. degree for less than 5 years. Applicants must wish to conduct basic research for the elucidation of brain functions and biological functions through molecular level approaches. They may be citizens of Austria, Belgium, Canada, Denmark, Finland, France, Germany, Greece, Ireland, Italy, Japan, Luxembourg, the Netherlands, Portugal, Spain, Sweden, Switzerland, the United Kingdom, or the United States, and must be seeking to conduct their research in any of those countries for which they have adequate language skills. Candidates may not conduct research in their own country nor at the institution where they obtained their Ph.D. Researchers from outside those countries are also eligible if they wish to conduct research within those countries.

Financial data Grants provide approximately $45,000 per year to cover relocation costs, living expenses and family support, a research allowance (which may be used for laboratory support or health insurance premiums), and travel to scientific meetings.

Duration 1 to 3 years; nonrenewable.

Special features The first awards under this program were presented in 1990.

Number awarded Varies each year.

Deadline August of each year.

[646]
HUMAN FRONTIER SCIENCE PROGRAM RESEARCH GRANTS

Human Frontier Science Program Organization
Bureaux Europe
20 place des Halles
67080 Strasbourg
France
33 3 88 21 51 21   Fax: 33 3 88 32 88 97
E-mail: grant@hfsp.org
Web site: www.hfsp.org

Purpose To provide funding for basic research on cell biology and neurobiology to teams of researchers from member nations of the Human Frontier Science Program (HFSP).

Eligibility Scientists who are from Austria, Belgium, Canada, Denmark, Finland, France, Germany, Greece, Ireland, Italy, Japan, Luxembourg, the Netherlands, Portugal, Spain, Sweden, Switzerland, the United Kingdom, or the United States may apply for these grants to conduct basic research for the elucidation of brain functions. The proposed research must be carried out jointly by research teams, preferably of 2 to 4 members. All members of the team must have a doctoral degree or equivalent research experience, an independent laboratory, and an established record for independent research. Young Investigator Grants are for teams of researchers within the first 5 years of establishing an independent laboratory; Program Grants are for teams of researchers at any stage of their careers. The team must designate 1 of its members as the principal applicant, and that member must be a national (not just a resident) of 1 of the participating countries; other team members may be from any country. At least 1 member of the team must be of a nationality different from that of the principal applicant and at least 1 member must be affiliated with an institution located in a country other than that in which the principal applicant's institution is located. Teams should only have 1 member from any 1 country. Applications for Young Investigator Grants and Program Grants are reviewed together; the proportion of grants awarded to the 2 categories depends on the quality of applications received. Research carried out within only 1 country is not eligible.

Financial data The average grant is approximately $250,000 per year.

Duration 1 year; may be renewed up to 2 additional years.

Number awarded Varies each year; recently, 54 research grants (including both Young Investigator and Program Grants) were awarded.

Deadline August of each year.

[647]
HUMAN FRONTIER SCIENCE PROGRAM SHORT-TERM FELLOWSHIPS

Human Frontier Science Program Organization
Bureaux Europe
20 place des Halles
67080 Strasbourg
France
33 3 88 21 51 21   Fax: 33 3 88 32 88 97
E-mail: fellow@hfsp.org
Web site: www.hfsp.org

Purpose To provide funding for basic research on cell biology and neurobiology to scientists from member nations of the Human Frontier Science Program (HFSP).

Eligibility Researchers who are from Austria, Belgium, Canada, Denmark, Finland, France, Germany, Greece, Ireland, Italy, Japan, Luxembourg, the Netherlands, Portugal, Spain, Sweden, Switzerland, the United Kingdom, or the United States and have a Ph.D. degree or equivalent research experience are eligible to apply. Preference is given to young investigators at an early stage of their careers. Applicants must be proposing to work in a laboratory in 1 of the other countries to learn new techniques or develop collaborations in the areas supported by the program: brain functions and biological functions at the molecular level. Scientists from non-member countries may participate if they are associated with a scientist from a member country. All applicants must have adequate language skills to carry out the proposed project at a host institution.

Financial data Fellowships cover round-trip travel expenses to the host institution and living expenses; the exact amount depends on the country where the research is conducted.

Duration 2 weeks to 3 months.

Limitations These fellowships are not intended to enable researchers to attend workshops, courses, or symposia; to provide support during periods of sabbatical leave; to plan future work; or to write papers, books, or reviews.

Number awarded Varies; generally, 70 or more each year.

Deadline Applications may be submitted at any time.

[648]
HUMBOLDT RESEARCH FELLOWSHIPS FOR FOREIGN SCHOLARS

Alexander von Humboldt Foundation
Attn: U.S. Liaison Office
1012 14th Street, N.W., Suite 301
Washington, DC 20005
(202) 783-1907   Fax: (202) 783-1908
E-mail: avh@bellatlantic.net
Web site: www.humboldt-foundation.de

Purpose To provide financial support to foreign scholars interested in carrying out research projects in Germany.

Eligibility Scholars (under 40 years of age) from all disciplines and all nations may apply, if they have a doctoral degree or equivalent, high academic qualifications, academic publications, and a detailed research plan for scientific cooperation with German colleagues. Applicants in the humanities and social sciences must demonstrate sound German language abilities; applicants in the physical, life, and engineering sciences must have good command of English or German. Research fellows whose knowledge of German is insufficient are granted a fellowship to attend a German language course at a recognized language school in Germany prior to the commencement of the actual research fellowship.

Financial data Research fellowship rates are the Euro equivalent of 3,600 to 4,400 Deutsche marks monthly; other covered expenses include travel expenses and grants for married accompanying partners. Fellows who participate in language training prior to their research program receive payment of tuition fees, the cost of bed and breakfast, and a supplementary allowance of the EUR equivalent of DM 1,200 per month for additional meals and expenses. Language fellowships or language courses may also be granted to spouses of research fellows.

Duration 6 to 12 months; as much as 4 months of that time may be spent at research institutions in other European countries, or up to 6 months in German research institutions located elsewhere in Europe. Language fellowships are an additional 4 months.

Special features Originally founded in 1860, the Alexander von Humboldt Foundation was re-established in 1953 by the German government, which provides the major portion (94 percent) of its funds.

Limitations Funds are not available for training purposes, short-term study tours, or participation in conferences.

Number awarded Up to 500 each year.

Deadline Applications may be submitted at any time.

[649]
HUMBOLDT RESEARCH PRIZES FOR FOREIGN SCHOLARS

Alexander von Humboldt Foundation
Attn: U.S. Liaison Office
1012 14th Street, N.W., Suite 301
Washington, DC 20005
(202) 783-1907   Fax: (202) 783-1908
E-mail: avh@bellatlantic.net
Web site: www.humboldt-foundation.de

Purpose To allow internationally-renowned foreign scholars in any field to engage in long-term research projects of their own choice at a German research institute.

Eligibility Scholars from any nation in any field, who hold a full or associate professorship or equivalent position and whose research work has received international recognition, may be nominated for these awards by German scholars; no foreign scholars may apply themselves.

Financial data The value of the award is the Euro equivalent of 20,000 to 150,000 Deutsche marks net, along with travel expenses. Scholars and/or their spouses are also eligible to receive funding for the costs of language study during their research stay in Germany.

Duration From 4 to 12 months.

Special features Originally founded in 1860, the Alexander von Humboldt Foundation was re-established in 1953 by the German government, which provides the major portion (94 percent) of its funds.

Number awarded Up to 150 each year.

Deadline Nominations may be submitted at any time, but they must be received at least 4 months prior to selection meetings that are held in March and October of each year.

[650]
HUNGARIAN GOVERNMENT GRANTS

Institute of International Education
Attn: Student Programs Division
809 United Nations Plaza
New York, NY 10017-3580
(212) 984-5330   Fax: (212) 984-5325
Web site: www.iie.org/fulbright

Purpose To provide financial assistance to American graduate students for study or research in Hungary.

Eligibility Applicants must be U.S. citizens who hold a B.A. degree or equivalent before the beginning date of the grant and plan a program of research or study in Hungary. U.S. citizens holding dual Hungarian citizenship are not eligible. Candidates may propose to work in any field of study, but preference is given to subjects in arts and humanities (history, literature, music, folklore, and film), social sciences as they relate to recent social and economic changes in Hungary (political science and comparative politics), history and culture of east central Europe, and the sciences (e.g., mathematics). Master's and Ph.D. candidates are preferred, but graduating seniors are considered. A working knowledge of Hungarian is recommended, but only if necessary for the successful completion of the projected research.

Financial data The Hungarian government provides a monthly stipend and a housing allowance. A Fulbright grant provides a fixed sum payment equal to at least the cost of round-trip transportation for the grantee plus a monthly stipend. The basic amount of the Fulbright grant is increased for grantees with dependents by $100 per month for 1 dependent and by $200 per month for 2 or more dependents.

Duration 1 academic year.

Special features These grants are awarded under the exchange program between the governments of Hungary and the United States and administered as part of the Fulbright program by the Institute of International Education (IIE). Students who are currently enrolled in the United States are to apply through the Fulbright program adviser on their campus; at-large applicants (those not currently enrolled) may obtain applications and information directly from the IIE.

Number awarded Approximately 8 each year.

Deadline October of each year.

[651]
HUNGARY FULBRIGHT TEACHER EXCHANGE

U.S. Department of State
c/o Graduate School, USDA
600 Maryland Avenue, S.W., Room 320
Washington, DC 20024-2520
(202) 314-3520   Fax: (202) 479-6806
E-mail: fulbright@grad.usda.gov
Web site: www.grad.usda.gov/International/ftep.html

Purpose To promote mutual understanding between the people of the United States and the people of Hungary through a teacher exchange program.

Eligibility This program is open to senior high school teachers (grades 9 through 12) and 2-year college instructors of art, music, mathematics, English, science, English as a second language, foreign languages, history, education, or geography who are interested in teaching at a secondary or postsecondary institution in Hungary. Applicants must 1) be U.S. citizens; 2) hold at least a bachelor's degree; 3) be fluent in English; 4) have a current full-time teaching assignment in the U.S. or a territory; 5) have the approval of their school administration; 6) have at least 3 years of full-time experience; and 7) not have participated in a Fulbright Teacher Exchange longer than 8 weeks during the last 2 years. Fluency in Hungarian is not required; some ability is useful. The language of instruction is English. Teaching couples may apply. However, because of the limited number of positions available and, often, the lack of foreign candidate pairs with similar qualifications for interchanges, it may not be possible to arrange suitable assignments in the same locality or to place both teachers. Preference is given to applicants who have not participated previously in the program and may be given to applicants who have not previously lived in Hungary. Geographic distribution of awards within the United States is also a factor in selection. This program does not discriminate on the basis of race, color, religion, age, sex, or national origin and encourages the applications of members of minority communities. Other considerations being equal, veterans are given preference.

Financial data Round-trip transportation for the exchange teacher only is provided. Participants must obtain a leave of absence with pay from their jobs in the United States. The U.S. school must agree to accept a Hungarian teacher who must secure a leave of absence with pay; the Hungarian teacher receives a stipend, but no additional cost accrues to the U.S. school.

Duration 9 months, beginning in September.

Special features This program is sponsored by the Bureau of Educational and Cultural Affairs of the U.S. Department of State and administered by the Graduate School, USDA.

Limitations This program provides for the direct exchange of teaching assignments between Hungary and the United States. Applicants selected for exchange must attend orientation programs of the sponsoring agencies in the United States or abroad.

Number awarded 3 each year.

Deadline October of each year.

[652]
HUNTINGTON–BRITISH ACADEMY FELLOWSHIPS FOR STUDY IN GREAT BRITAIN

Huntington Library, Art Collections, and Botanical Gardens
Attn: Committee on Fellowships
1151 Oxford Road
San Marino, CA 91108
(626) 405-2194   Fax: (626) 449-5703
E-mail: cpowell@huntington.org
Web site: www.huntington.org

Purpose To provide funding to young scholars in the fields of British and American history, literature, and art who are interested in conducting research at the British Academy.

Eligibility This program is open to scholars who hold a Ph.D. or the equivalent. Applicants must be interested in an exchange fellowship at the British Academy in any of the fields in which the Huntington library is strong (British and American history, literature, and art).

Financial data A stipend is provided (amount not specified).

Duration 1 month.

Number awarded Several each year.
Deadline December of each year.

[653]
IACI VISITING FELLOWSHIP IN IRISH STUDIES

Irish American Cultural Institute
One Lackawanna Place
Morristown, NJ 07960
(973) 605-1991   Fax: (973) 605-8875
E-mail: irishwaynj@aol.com
Web site: www.irishaci.org/ucg.htm

Purpose To enable scholars from the United States to conduct research in Irish studies at University College Galway in Ireland.
Eligibility Scholars normally resident in the United States who wish to spend a semester at University College Galway and whose work relates to any aspect of Irish studies may apply for these grants.
Financial data The stipend is $13,000; transatlantic air transportation is also provided for the recipient.
Duration 1 semester (not less than 4 months).
Special features University College Galway provides the fellow with office accommodations and a number of privileges appropriate to the status of a visiting faculty member.
Limitations The fellow is expected to give a faculty seminar on the subject of his or her research, to be available for limited consultation with postgraduates in the appropriate discipline, to provide a brief written report to the board of directors of the Irish American Cultural Institute (IACI), to submit some part of fellowship-funded research and writing for consideration by the editors of *EIRE-IRELAND*, and to prepare and deliver a lecture based on his or her research for an audience to be selected by the IACI.
Number awarded 1 each year.
Deadline December of each year.

[654]
IARC POSTDOCTORAL POSITIONS

International Agency for Research on Cancer
150 cours Albert-Thomas
69372 Lyon 08
France
33 472 73 84 48   Fax: 33 472 73 83 22
E-mail: sta@iarc.fr
Web site: www.iarc.fr

Purpose To provide opportunities for postdoctoral scholars to conduct research at the International Agency for Research on Cancer (IARC) in Lyons, France.
Eligibility These awards are offered by different units of the agency, and each sets its own specialized requirements. Generally, the positions require a doctoral degree in medicine, epidemiology, biostatistics, or molecular biology, with an emphasis on cancer biology. Applicants may be from any country, but they must be fluent in English or French. They should be younger than 35 years of age with no more than 3 years of postdoctoral research experience.
Financial data The salary is the Euro equivalent of 12,000 French francs per month.

Duration Most positions are for 1 year. They may be renewed for up to 2 additional years.
Special features The International Agency for Research on Cancer is an agency of the World Health Organization.
Number awarded 5 each year.
Deadline December of each year.

[655]
IARC VISITING SCIENTIST AWARD

International Agency for Research on Cancer
150 cours Albert-Thomas
69372 Lyon 08
France
33 472 73 84 48   Fax: 33 472 73 83 22
E-mail: vsa@iarc.fr
Web site: www.iarc.fr

Purpose To provide funding to senior scientists interested in conducting research at the International Agency for Research on Cancer (IARC) in Lyons, France.
Eligibility This program is open to experienced investigators who are on the staff of a university or research institution in any country and who are interested in conducting research at IARC. Applicants must be interested in working on a collaborative research project in a research area related to the agency's own programs: epidemiology, biostatistics, nutrition and cancer, environmental and viral carcinogenesis, cell and molecular biology, cancer genetics, and mechanisms of carcinogenesis.
Financial data The salary depends on the recipient's regular salary, to a maximum of $70,00 per year.
Duration 1 year.
Special features The International Agency for Research on Cancer is an agency of the World Health Organization.
Number awarded 1 each year.
Deadline January of each year.

[656]
ICELANDIC GOVERNMENT GRANTS

Institute of International Education
Attn: Student Programs Division
809 United Nations Plaza
New York, NY 10017-3580
(212) 984-5330   Fax: (212) 984-5325
Web site: www.iie.org/fulbright

Purpose To provide financial assistance to American graduate students for study or research in Iceland.
Eligibility Applicants must be U.S. citizens who hold a B.A. degree or the equivalent before the beginning date of the grant and wish to conduct research or study in Icelandic language, history, or literature. A knowledge of Icelandic, Old Norse, or other Scandinavian language is required at the time of application. Advanced graduate students, capable of working independently, are preferred.
Financial data The Icelandic government provides a monthly maintenance stipend. Allowances for international travel, baggage, and books are also included.
Duration 1 academic year.
Special features Funds for these fellowships are provided by the Icelandic government through its Ministry of Culture and

Education, but the program is administered in the United States by the Institute of International Education (IIE) as part of the Fulbright program. Students who are currently enrolled in the United States are to apply through the Fulbright program adviser on their campus; at-large applicants (those not currently enrolled) may obtain applications and information directly from the IIE.
Number awarded 1 each year.
Deadline October of each year.

[657]
ICP POSTDOCTORAL FELLOWSHIPS

Christian de Duve Institute of Cellular Pathology
Attn: Central Administration
75 avenue Hippocrate - Box 75.50
B-1200 Brussels
Belgium
32 2 764 7588   Fax: 32 2 764 7573
E-mail: vandemaele@icp.ucl.ac.be
Web site: www.icp.ucl.ac.be

Purpose To provide financial aid for research and training at the Christian de Duve Institute of Cellular Pathology (ICP) laboratory in Brussels.
Eligibility Applicants must possess a doctoral degree (M.D. or Ph.D.) in biomedical sciences. They must be interested in conducting research or pursuing training at the ICP. Normally, scientists must be younger than 33 years of age (30 years for fellows from non-EU countries). Eligible fields of study include biochemistry, cell biology, molecular biology, immunology, microbiology, and parasitology.
Financial data The fellowship provides a tax-free net monthly allowance of the Euro equivalent of 57,300 Belgian francs.
Duration 1 year; may be renewed for 1 additional year.
Special features A special fund supports a related program, the Michel de Visscher Fellowship, created in memory of a former head of the General Pathology unit. The ICP is an international institute of biomedical research created for a dual purpose: to contribute to the advancement of knowledge in basic biology and to exploit those advances for the benefit of human health and welfare. It is part of the Faculty of Medicine complex at the Université Catholique de Louvain in Brussels.
Number awarded 6 each year, 1 designated as the Michel de Visscher Fellowship and 5 others supported by the ICP's own funds.
Deadline February or September of each year.

[658]
ICTP POSTDOCTORAL RESEARCH FELLOWSHIPS

Abdus Salam International Centre for Theoretical Physics
Strada Costiera, 11
I-34014 Trieste
Italy
39 040 224 0111   Fax: 39 040 224 163
E-mail: sci_info@ictp.trieste.it
Web site: www.ictp.trieste.it

Purpose To provide funding to postdoctoral scholars from any country who wish to conduct research at the Abdus Salam International Centre for Theoretical Physics (ICTP) in Italy.
Eligibility This program is open to scientists in mathematics or high energy and condensed matter physics who are younger than 35 years of age and obtained their Ph.D. within the past 5 years. They may be of any nationality as long as they plan to conduct research at the center in Trieste, Italy. Fluency in English, the working language of the center, is required.
Financial data The net salary is the Euro equivalent of 2,260,000 Italian lire per month or higher, depending on seniority. A small allowance for travel and moving expenses is also provided.
Duration 1 year; may be renewed 1 additional year.
Special features The ICTP is jointly sponsored by the International Atomic Energy Agency (IAEA), the United Nations Educational, Scientific and Cultural Organization (UNESCO), and the government of Italy.
Limitations The majority of the fellows are from Africa, Asia, and Europe.
Number awarded Approximately 20 each year.
Deadline December of each year.

[659]
IFK GRANTS

Institute of International Education
Attn: Student Programs Division
809 United Nations Plaza
New York, NY 10017-3580
(212) 984-5330   Fax: (212) 984-5325
Web site: www.iie.org/fulbright

Purpose To provide American graduate students with an opportunity to conduct research at the Internationales Forschungszentrum Kulturwissenschaften (IFK) in Vienna.
Eligibility This program is open to U.S. citizens who are Ph.D. candidates in cultural studies with fields of specialization thematically related to Austrian and Central European traditions and IFK's interest in the comparative dimensions of cultural studies. Applicants must be interested in conducting research at IFK, where they will have access to a work station and are expected to participate in seminars, workshops, and symposia. Proficiency in spoken and written German is required.
Financial data The stipend is the Euro equivalents of approximately 15,000 Austrian schillings per month plus a grant of approximately AS 11,000 (800 Euros) for round-trip travel.
Duration 9 months, beginning in October.
Special features This program is administered in the United States by the Institute of International Education (IIE) as part of the Fulbright program. Students who are currently enrolled in the United States are to apply through the Fulbright program adviser on their campus; at-large applicants (those not currently enrolled) may obtain applications and information directly from the IIE.
Number awarded 2 each year.
Deadline October of each year.

[660]
IFK VISITING SCHOLAR IN CULTURAL STUDIES

Council for International Exchange of Scholars
3007 Tilden Street, N.W., Suite 5L
Washington, DC 20008-3009
(202) 686-6240   Fax: (202) 362-3442
E-mail: scholars@cies.iie.org
Web site: www.iie.org/cies

Purpose To provide funding to scholars who wish to conduct research in cultural studies at the Internationales Forschungszentrum Kulturwissenschaften (IFK) in Vienna.

Eligibility Applicants must have several years of teaching/research experience in fields related to the IFK's overall research program, with a specialization in interdisciplinary and comparative research in cultural studies on Viennese, Austrian, and central European traditions. In addition to their research, they must be willing to offer occasional lectures and participate in seminars, workshops, and symposia. U.S. citizenship and proficiency in German are required.

Financial data The maintenance allowance is 3,300 Euros per month for the grantee only; no dependent allowance is provided. Grantees also receive a travel grant of EUR 770. The institution provides housing and office space with library, computer, Internet, and E-mail facilities.

Duration 4 months.

Special features This is a Fulbright scholar program, sponsored by the Bureau of Educational and Cultural Affairs of the U.S. Department of State and administered by the Council for International Exchange of Scholars.

Number awarded 1 each year.

Deadline July of each year.

[661]
IMPERIAL CANCER RESEARCH FUND POSTDOCTORAL FELLOWSHIPS

Imperial Cancer Research Fund
Attn: Personnel Department
44 Lincoln's Inn Fields
P.O. Box 123
London WC2A 3PX
England
44 20 7242 0200   Fax: 44 20 7269 0010
E-mail: personnel@icrf.icnet.uk
Web site: www.icnet.uk

Purpose To provide financial support to postdoctoral scholars of any nationality for cancer research at the Imperial Cancer Research Fund in England.

Eligibility Applicants must be postdoctoral scholars from any country, up to 30 years of age, who wish to conduct research at facilities of the Imperial Cancer Research Fund in England.

Financial data The stipends cover travel and living expenses and depend on age and experience; for assignments in central London, the stipends range from 22,275 to 26,198 pounds per year; in outer London from 21,225 to 25,868 pounds annually. Stipends at other research sites are comparably based on the cost of living.

Duration Normally, 3 years; visiting fellowships for 1 or 2 years are also offered.

Number awarded Approximately 30 each year.

Deadline December, April, or August of each year.

[662]
INDIVIDUAL ADVANCED RESEARCH OPPORTUNITIES IN CENTRAL AND EASTERN EUROPE AND EURASIA

International Research & Exchanges Board
1616 H Street, N.W.
Washington, DC 20006
(202) 628-8188   Fax: (202) 628-8189
E-mail: irex@irex.org
Web site: www.irex.org

Purpose To provide research opportunities for predoctoral and postdoctoral scholars at institutions in central Europe, eastern Europe, and Eurasia.

Eligibility Eligibility requirements include: U.S. citizenship or permanent residency for 3 years prior to applying; command of host-country language sufficient for research; and affiliation with a university as a faculty member or advanced doctoral candidate. Applications are accepted in all disciplines, but policy research and development, the humanities and social sciences, and cross-disciplinary studies are emphasized. Limited assistance is available for cross-regional research in Turkey and Iran for postdoctoral humanities scholars.

Financial data The grant provides round-trip airfare and visa fees, a stipend (in the form of a monthly allowance for graduate students or a stipend in lieu of salary for faculty members), host-country room and board, a local research allowance, and excess baggage allowance; support for accompanying family members may be available.

Duration From 2 to 9 months.

Special features The International Research & Exchanges Board (IREX) was established in 1968 at the request of U.S. universities by the American Council of Learned Societies (ACLS) and the Social Science Research Council (SSRC) to administer research exchange programs with the socialist countries of eastern Europe and the former Soviet Republics. Funding for this program is provided by the U.S. Department of State as a Title VIII program and the National Endowment for the Humanities

Limitations Exchange applicants in modern foreign languages and area studies must apply simultaneously for Department of Education Fulbright-Hays grants.

Number awarded Approximately 37 each year; recently, 12 grants were for central and eastern Europe and 25 for Eurasia.

Deadline October of each year.

[663]
INSERM POSTDOCTORAL FELLOWSHIPS FOR YOUNG FOREIGN RESEARCHERS

Institut National de la Santé et de la Recherche Médicale
Attn: Département des Relations Internationales
101 rue de Tolbiac
75654 Paris 13
France
33 1 44 23 61 81   Fax: 33 1 45 85 14 87
E-mail: novaki@tolbiac.inserm.fr
Web site: www.inserm.fr

Purpose To provide opportunities for junior foreign scientists to engage in biomedical research at the French Institut National de la Santé et de la Recherche Médicale (INSERM).

Eligibility Eligible are postdoctoral scientists under 40 years of age from outside France whose prior research has been at the level performed by adjunct researchers in an INSERM laboratory. Preference is given to applicants for exchanges who are working on a problem that is similar to that of an existing INSERM laboratory researcher. This program is not open to foreigners who already reside in France or who have already received more than 1 year of temporary funding. Current priorities are 1) emerging experimental and technological models in physiology and physiopathology, study of the postgenome; 2) mental health and psychiatric pathologies: biological mechanisms, clinical approaches, vulnerability and protection factors; 3) drugs: innovation, therapeutic strategy, and assessment methodology; 4) cellular therapy, gene therapy, transplants, and vaccines: innovation and assessment methodology; 5) biomaterials, biomechanics, microinvasive and robotic surgery: innovation and assessment methodology; and 6) information science and clinical epidemiology, research on the health care system.

Financial data The stipend is equivalent to the salary received by INSERM researchers with comparable qualifications and experience.

Duration 6 to 12 months; may be renewed once.

Special features These fellowships are also designated as INSERM Green Programs.

Number awarded Varies each year.

Deadline Applications may be submitted at any time, but they must be received at least 2 months prior to beginning work for candidates from the European Economic Area or 4 months for candidates from outside the European Economic Area.

[664]
INSERM SENIOR FELLOWSHIPS FOR FOREIGN RESEARCHERS

Institut National de la Santé et de la Recherche Médicale
Attn: Département des Relations Internationales
101 rue de Tolbiac
75654 Paris 13
France
33 1 44 23 61 81   Fax: 33 1 45 85 14 87
E-mail: novaki@tolbiac.inserm.fr
Web site: www.inserm.fr

Purpose To provide opportunities for senior foreign scientists to engage in biomedical research at the French Institut National de la Santé et de la Recherche Médical (INSERM).

Eligibility Applicants must be senior researchers from any country, under the age of 60, who can spend long periods of research in INSERM laboratories. This program is not open to foreigners who already reside in France or who have already received more than 1 year of temporary funding. Current research priorities are: 1) emerging experimental and technological models in physiology and physiopathology, study of the postgenome; 2) mental health and psychiatric pathologies: biological mechanisms, clinical approaches, vulnerability and protection factors; 3) drugs: innovation, therapeutic strategy, and assessment methodology; 4) cellular therapy, gene therapy, transplants, and vaccines: innovation and assessment methodology; 5) biomaterials, biomechanics, microinvasive and robotic surgery: innovation and assessment methodology; and 6) information science and clinical epidemiology, research on the health care system.

Financial data The stipend should on the same level as received by directors of research at INSERM, generally ranging from the Euro equivalent of 14,000 to 18,000 French francs per month. Travel expenses are not covered.

Duration 6 to 12 months; nonrenewable.

Number awarded Varies each year.

Deadline Applications may be submitted at any time, but they must be received at least 2 months prior to beginning work for candidates from the European Economic Area or 4 months for candidates from outside the European Economic Area.

[665]
INSERM/IBRO RESEARCH FELLOWSHIP

International Brain Research Organization
51 Blvd de Montmorency
75016 Paris
France
33 1 46 47 92 92   Fax: 33 1 45 20 60 06
E-mail: ibro@wanadoo.fr
Web site: www.ibro.org

Purpose To provide funding to junior neuroscientists who are interested in conducting research in France at a laboratory sponsored by the Institut National de la Santé et de la Recherche Médicale (INSERM).

Eligibility This program is open to neuroscientists from any country who are under the age of 45. Applicants should submit a short curriculum vitae, a short research synopsis, a list of their 5 most important publications, and a letter of acceptance from the receiving INSERM laboratory.

Financial data The amount of the grant depends on the nature of the proposal and the availability of funds.

Duration 1 year.

Number awarded 1 each year.

Deadline March of each year.

[666]
INSTITUT CURIE POSTDOCTORAL FELLOWSHIPS

Institut Curie
Attn: Research Division
26, rue d'Ulm
75248 Paris 05
France
E-mail: cdrom@curie.fr
Web site: www.curie.fr

Purpose To provide financial assistance to recent postdoctorates from any country interested in pursuing research training in the laboratories of the Institut Curie in France.

Eligibility This program is open to recent postdoctorates from any country. Applicants must be interested in pursuing research training in a laboratory of the Institut Curie in 1 of the following areas: cell and developmental biology, molecular biophysics, human genetics and cancer, genotoxicology, pharmacochemistry, physical chemistry of the living cell, technology transfer, or cell signaling. They must submit a full curriculum vitae, a letter of recommendation, a letter of acceptance from the host laboratory, and a brief description of their proposed research project. Selection is based on the quality of the CV, previous achievements, and the importance of the project for the research teams of the Institut.

Financial data Stipends range from 1,900 to 2,300 Euros per month, depending on the age and experience of the fellow.

Duration 1 year; may be renewed for 1 additional year.

Special features This program was established in 1997.

Number awarded Varies each year.

[667]
INSTITUT FRANCAIS DU PETROLE GRANT

American Association of Petroleum Geologists Foundation
Attn: Chair, AAPG Grants-in-Aid Committee
1444 South Boulder Avenue
P.O. Box 979
Tulsa, OK 74101-0979
(918) 560-2664   Fax: (918) 560-2642
E-mail: shyer@aapg.org
Web site: www.aapg.org/foundation

Purpose To enable French graduate students or students studying at a school in France to conduct research related to earth science aspects of the petroleum industry.

Eligibility Applicants must be French students or students from another country studying in France. They must be interested in conducting research on earth science aspects of the petroleum industry. Selection is based on merit and, in part, on financial need. Factors weighed in selecting the successful applicants include: past performance, originality and imagination of the proposed project, departmental support, and perceived significance of the project to petroleum, energy-minerals, and related environmental geology. The project must relate to the search for and development of petroleum and energy-minerals resources, and to related environmental geology issues. Both master's degree and doctoral students may apply.

Financial data The maximum award is $2,000. Funds are to be applied to research-related expenses (e.g., a summer of field work). They may not be used to purchase capital equipment or to pay salaries, tuition, room or board.

Duration 1 year. Doctoral candidates may receive a 1-year renewal.

Special features This award is funded by the Institut Français du Pétrole.

Number awarded 1 each year.

Deadline January of each year.

[668]
INSTITUT NATIONAL DE RECHERCHE EN INFORMATIQUE ET EN AUTOMATIQUE–NATIONAL SCIENCE FOUNDATION COLLABORATIVE RESEARCH

National Science Foundation
Directorate for Social, Behavioral, and Economic Sciences
Attn: Division of International Programs
4201 Wilson Boulevard
Arlington, VA 22230
(703) 292-8702   Fax: (703) 292-9177
TDD: (703) 292-5090   E-mail: rgombay@nsf.gov
Web site: www.nsf.gov/sbe/int/w_europe/inria.htm

Purpose To provide funding to American scientists interested in conducting collaborative computer-related research in France.

Eligibility Eligible to apply are scientists, engineers, and mathematicians in related areas from universities and other nonprofit research institutions in the United States. Applicants must be interested in conducting research in France on a topic designed to maximize potential benefits of complementary U.S. and French strengths in the areas of software, networking, computational and applied mathematics, and systems control. Proposals should provide a rationale for the international-team-research mode in the context of a given theme and identify the role of the U.S. and French participants.

Financial data Grants cover the following costs: international airfare of principal investigators, advanced graduates, and/or postdoctoral researchers, including participation in workshops and their organizational costs; per diem living allowance for lodging, meals, and miscellaneous expenses; and limited amounts for materials, supplies, publications costs, and computer equipment to facilitate access to electronic networks. Most awards range from $10,000 to $50,000.

Duration Up to 15 months.

Special features This program, which began in 1987, is a collaborative effort between the National Science Foundation and the French National Institute for Computer Science and Applied Mathematics, the Institut National de Recherche en Informatique et en Automatique (INRIA). Information is also available from INRIA at Domaine de Voluceau, Rocquencourt, BP 105, 78153 Le Chesney, France, 33-39-63-56-46, E-mail: nissen@nuri.inria.fr.

Number awarded Varies each year.

Deadline Applications may be submitted at any time.

[669]
INSTITUTE FOR EUROPEAN HISTORY FELLOWSHIPS

Institute for European History
Alte Universitätsstrasse 19
D-55116 Mainz
Germany
49 6131 399360　　　　　　　Fax: 49 6131 237988
E-mail: ieg2@inst-euro-history.uni-mainz.de
Web site: www.inst-euro-history.uni-mainz.de

Purpose To provide financial assistance to pre- and postdoctoral scholars interested in conducting research in Mainz, Germany at the Institute for European History.

Eligibility Candidates for a fellowship must have a thorough command of German and be either at the advanced stages of their dissertation or already in possession of their doctorate. They must be interested in conducting research at the institute, particularly in the history of occidental religion or the history of Europe from the 16th to the 20th centuries.

Financial data Fellows with a bachelor's degree receive a monthly stipend of the Euro equivalent of 1,500 Deutsche marks; for fellows in the advanced stages of graduate work, the monthly stipend is the EUR equivalent of DM 1,800. The institute also contributes the EUR equivalent of DM 95 monthly toward each fellow's health insurance and provides funds for travel expenses directly related to academic pursuits. Married fellows whose spouses come to Germany and have personal incomes of the EUR equivalent of less than DM 610 per month receive an additional monthly allowance of the EUR equivalent of DM 380.

Duration 6 to 12 months.

Special features The Institute for European History (Institut für Europäische Geschichte) was founded in 1950 to promote historical research. Fellows live and work in the "domus universitatis," formerly the seat of the university but currently the home of the Institute. Rooms in the residence sections are rented for DM 250 per month.

Number awarded 20 each year.

Deadline February, June, and October of each year.

[670]
INSTITUTO CAMOES RESEARCH SPONSORSHIP PROGRAM FOR FOREIGNERS

Instituto Camoes
Campo Grande, 56-7
1700-078 Lisbon
Portugal
351 21 795 5470　　　　　　Fax: 351 21 795 6113
E-mail: dslpic.icamoes@mail.telepac.pt
Web site: www.instituto-camoes.pt

Purpose To provide funding to scholars who wish to conduct research in Portugal.

Eligibility This program is open to college graduates, university teachers, and artists who wish to carry out research in Portugal on Portuguese culture and/or language. Applicants must submit a curriculum vitae, a copy of their academic qualifications, an acceptance document from the Portuguese institution where they propose to conduct their research, and a statement that they are not receiving support from any other Portuguese institution.

Financial data The stipend is the Euro equivalent of 100,000 escudos per month.

Duration From 1 to 12 months.

Number awarded Varies each year; recently, 84 of these scholarships were awarded.

Deadline April of each year.

[671]
INTEL INTERNATIONAL SCIENCE AND ENGINEERING FAIR

Science Service
Attn: Director of Youth Programs
1719 N Street, N.W.
Washington, DC 20036
(202) 785-2255　　　　　　Fax: (202) 785-1243
E-mail: sciedu@sciserv.org
Web site: www.sciserv.org

Purpose To recognize and reward outstanding high school students interested in engineering or the sciences.

Eligibility The International Science and Engineering Fair (ISEF), known as the "World Series" of science fairs, involves students from the 9th through 12th grades who first compete in approximately 500 affiliated fairs around the world. Each fair then sends 2 individuals and 1 team (up to 3 members) to compete in the ISEF in 1 of 15 categories: behavioral and social sciences, biochemistry, botany, chemistry, computer science, earth and space sciences, engineering, environmental science, gerontology, mathematics, medicine and health, microbiology, physics, team projects, and zoology. Each entry consists of a science project and a 250-word abstract that summarizes the project. Judging of individual projects is based on creative ability (30 percent), scientific thought and engineering goals (30 percent), thoroughness (15 percent), skill (15 percent), and clarity (10 percent).

Financial data The Intel Young Scientist Scholarships, granted to the presenters of the most outstanding research, are $50,000. In each of the categories, the first-place winner receives a $3,000 scholarship, second place $1,500, third place $1,000, and fourth place $500. Winners also qualify for all-expense paid trips to attend the Nobel Prize Ceremony in Stockholm, Sweden (the Glenn T. Seaborg Nobel Prize Visit Award) and the European Union Contest for Young Scientists. The Intel Best of Category Awards, for the project that exemplifies the best in each scientific category that has also won a first-place in the category, are $5,000 to the students, $1,000 to their schools, and $1,000 to their science fair. The Intel Achievement Awards are $5,000 each for outstanding work in any field. The Intel Excellence in Teaching Awards are $10,000 and $5,000. Other prizes, worth more than $1.5 million, include scholarships from individual colleges and universities, expense-paid trips to scientific and engineering installations or national conventions, summer jobs at research institutes, and laboratory equipment provided by Intel.

Duration The fair is held annually. The Intel Young Scientist Scholarships are paid in 8 equal installments. Most other awards are for 1 year.

Special features Costs for the entry fee, as well as those for transportation, meals, and housing of the finalists, are borne by the affiliated fairs. The ISEF, currently sponsored by Intel and other major corporations, was first held in 1950.

Number awarded 3 Pinnacle Awards are presented each year. In addition, 60 other scholarships are awarded: 4 in each of the 15 categories. Other awards include 8 Intel Achievement Awards and 7 Intel Excellence in Teaching Awards (1 at $10,000 and 6 at $5,000). Many other special awards, regional awards, and scholarships from individual colleges are also presented.

Deadline The fair is always held in May.

[672] INTERNATIONAL RESEARCH SCIENTIST DEVELOPMENT AWARD

Fogarty International Center
Attn: Division of International Training and Research
31 Center Drive, Room B2C39
Bethesda, MD 20892-2220
(301) 496-1653   Fax: (301) 402-0779
E-mail: IRSDA@nih.gov
Web site: www.nih.gov/fic

Purpose To provide funding to U.S. biomedical scientists interested in continuing research in, or extending their research into, developing countries.

Eligibility Applicants must have received a doctoral, dental, or medical degree within the past 7 years in a basic biomedical, behavioral, or epidemiological/clinical field. They must have established a relationship with 2 prospective mentors, 1 in the United States and 1 in a developing country, who have ongoing, funded, international collaborative research. The U.S. mentor should be at a U.S. institution of higher learning or nonprofit research institution. The developing country mentor should be in an internationally developing country research institution addressing some of that country's major health problems. Eligible countries include those in the following regions: Africa, Asia (except Japan, Singapore, South Korea, and Taiwan), central and eastern Europe, Russia and the Newly Independent States of the former Soviet Union, Latin America and the non-U.S. Caribbean, the Middle East (except Israel), and the Pacific Ocean Islands (except Australia and New Zealand). Applications to work in institutions in sub-Saharan Africa are especially encouraged. Racial/ethnic minority individuals, women, and persons with disabilities are encouraged to apply as principal investigators. Applications must be submitted on behalf of the candidate by the U.S. mentor's institution. The applicant need not already be at that institution at the time of application, but it is expected that the U.S. component of the project will be carried out by the fellow at the U.S. mentor's institution.

Financial data Grants provide up to $300,000 for the complete project, prorated at a rate of $8,333 per month (including $6,250 per month direct costs for salary and fringe benefits and $2,083 per month for all other allowable costs). Other allowable costs include travel (round-trip airfare and necessary ground transportation for the candidate to the foreign site up to 5 times over the duration of the project, round-trip airfare for each dependent accompanying the awardee for 6 months or more abroad, excess baggage allowance), health insurance up to $50 per month for the candidate and each dependent during the time abroad, a supplemental living allowance of $150 per month for each dependent accompanying the awardee for 6 months or more, and research development support. An administrative supplement, up to $20,000, may be provided during the third year of the award to fellows who obtain a tenure-track faculty position upon return to the United States.

Duration Support is provided for 36 months, which may be spread over a period of 5 years. A total of at least 24 months should be at the foreign site under the joint supervision of the U.S. and foreign mentors. A period of work in the foreign country should be at least 3 months in length. A total of up to 12 months will be funded for work at the U.S. institution under the U.S. mentor's supervision.

Number awarded Varies each year.

Deadline February of each year.

[673] IOMA EVANS-PRITCHARD JUNIOR RESEARCH FELLOWSHIP

University of Oxford
St. Anne's College
Attn: Senior Tutor's Secretary
Oxford OX2 6HS
England
44 1865 274800   Fax: 44 1865 274899
Web site: www.stannes.ox.ac.uk

Purpose To provide funding to doctoral candidates from any university who wish to conduct research in social anthropology at St. Anne's College of the University of Oxford in England.

Eligibility Applicants should be graduates in the second or subsequent year of study for a higher degree, should already have completed a significant amount of research, and must have completed the residence requirements at their home institution. They must be interested in conducting research at St. Anne's College in the field of social anthropology.

Financial data The stipend is 10,120 pounds per year. Fellows also receive free accommodations or a living-out allowance and are members of the senior common room.

Duration 1 year; may be renewed for 1 additional year.

Limitations The fellow must live in Oxford and take part in college life.

Number awarded This fellowship is offered periodically; it was most recently offered for 2002.

Deadline October of the year prior to the award.

[674] IRISH RESEARCH FUND

Irish American Cultural Institute
One Lackawanna Place
Morristown, NJ 07960
(973) 605-1991   Fax: (973) 605-8875
E-mail: irishwaynj@aol.com
Web site: www.irishaci.org

Purpose To provide funding to scholars (including predoctoral students) who are interested in conducting research on the Irish in America.

Eligibility Scholars interested in conducting research on the Irish experience in America are eligible to apply. Proposals that deal solely with the Irish in Ireland are generally not approved. Research may be conducted in the United States or in Ireland, depending upon the needs of the researcher. Travel to collec-

tions in Ireland will be supported, if the resources there are not available in the United States.
Financial data Grants range from $1,000 to $4,000.
Duration Varies, depending upon the scope of the funded research.
Limitations Predoctoral and independent scholars may receive grants, but not for tuition or matriculation fees and only if the proposed research is separate from attainment of a degree.
Number awarded 4 to 10 each year.
Deadline September of each year.

[675]
IRISH-AMERICAN RESEARCH TRAVEL FELLOWSHIP
American Society for Eighteenth-Century Studies
c/o Wake Forest University
P.O. Box 7867
Winston-Salem, NC 27109
(336) 727-4694   Fax: (336) 727-4697
E-mail: asecs@wfu.edu
Web site: www.press.jhu.edu/associations/asecs

Purpose To provide travel assistance to members of the American Society for Eighteenth-Century Studies who wish to travel to conduct research in Ireland.
Eligibility This program is open to members of the society who are seeking to travel to research collections in Ireland (either the Republic or the North). Applicants must be scholars from North America planning to use primary sources for research on Ireland during the period between the Treaty of Limerick (1691) and the Act of Union (1800).
Financial data The grant is $1,500. Funds are to be used for research-related travel.
Special features In alternate years, this program provides funding to Irish scholars who wish to travel to North America. Information is also available from Dr. A.C. Elias, Jr., 318 West Highland Avenue, Philadelphia, PA 19118-3731.
Number awarded 1 each odd-numbered year.
Deadline October of even-numbered years.

[676]
ISAIAH BERLIN JUNIOR RESEARCH FELLOWSHIP IN THE HISTORY OF IDEAS
University of Oxford
Wolfson College
Attn: President's Secretary
Linton Road
Oxford OX2 6UD
England
44 1865 274100   Fax: 44 1865 274125
E-mail: sue.hales@wolfson.ox.ac.uk
Web site: www.wolfson.ox.ac.uk

Purpose To provide funding to postdoctoral scholars from any country who wish to conduct research in intellectual history at Wolfson College of the University of Oxford in England.
Eligibility This program is open to residents of any country who are interested in conducting postdoctoral research while in residence at Wolfson College. Applicants should normally be younger than 30 years of age and should have at least 2 years of research experience in the subject. Selection is based on a sample of the applicant's written work, up to 10,000 words. Their field of research must be intellectual history.
Financial data The stipend is 11,478 pounds per year. Fellows also receive room and board at the college. Fellows who are married or who require family accommodations may live at the college and pay the difference in rent or live outside the college and receive a housing allowance equivalent to the cost of single accommodations at the college.
Duration 3 years.
Special features Fellows are permitted to undertake up to 6 hours of teaching per week.
Number awarded This fellowship was first offered in 2000. It will be offered again whenever funds permit.
Deadline March of the years the fellowship is offered.

[677]
ITALIAN NATIONAL INSTITUTE OF HEALTH FELLOWSHIPS
Istituto Superiore di Sanità
Viale Regina Elena 299
I-00161 Rome
Italy
Fax: 39 64 938 7118
Web site: www.iss.it

Purpose To allow junior foreign scholars to conduct research in laboratories of the Italian Istituto Superiore di Sanità.
Eligibility Eligible are researchers under the age of 36 who are citizens of countries other than Italy. They must wish to conduct research in the fields of pharmaceutical science, medical biology, or health technology in laboratories of the Istituto Superiore di Sanità. Applicants must be fluent in Italian.
Financial data The stipend depends on the qualifications of the recipient.
Duration 8 months.
Special features Founded in 1934, the Instituto Superiore di Sanità became the technical and scientific body of the Italian National Health Service in 1978. Its role within the Italian health system is to promote public health through scientific research, surveys, controls, and analytical tests in the different fields of health sciences.
Number awarded 3 each year: 1 in pharmaceutical science, 1 in medical biology, and 1 in health technology.

[678]
IWM JUNIOR VISITING FELLOWSHIPS
Institut für die Wissenschaften vom Menschen
Attn: Fellows Coordinator
Spittelauer Lände 3
A-1090 Vienna
Austria
43 1 313 58 335   Fax: 43 1 313 58 30
E-mail: iwm@iwm.at
Web site: www.univie.ac.at/iwm

Purpose To provide funding to doctoral candidates and recent doctorates who wish to conduct research in the humanities or social sciences at the Institute for Human Sciences (IWM) in Vienna.

Eligibility This program is open to doctoral candidates who are in the concluding stages of their dissertations or postdoctorates who have very recently received their doctorates in economics, international relations, modern history, philosophy, or political science. Preference is given to applicants who propose research projects in fields of special interest to the institute, including political philosophy of the 19th and 20th centuries, gender studies, political and social transformation in central and eastern Europe, reform of the welfare state, and reform of higher education and research. Applicants should be younger than 35 years of age and have a good working knowledge of German and/or English.

Financial data The stipend is the Euro equivalent of 108,000 Austrian schillings is to cover transportation, rent, and living expenses. Fellows also receive office space and access to in-house and Viennese research facilities.

Duration 6 months.

Number awarded Approximately 40 each year.

Deadline August of each year for the January to June term; February of each year for the July to December term.

[679]
J. LAWRENCE ANGEL FELLOWSHIP IN HUMAN SKELETAL STUDIES

American School of Classical Studies at Athens
Attn: Chair, Committee on the Wiener Laboratory
6-8 Charlton Street
Princeton, NJ 08540-5232
(609) 683-0800   Fax: (609) 924-0578
E-mail: ascsa@ascsa.org
Web site: www.ascsa.org

Purpose To provide financial support to pre- or postdoctoral scholars who wish to study human skeletal remains from archaeological contexts in Greece.

Eligibility This program is open to scholars with a Ph.D. and those working on a doctoral dissertation who wish to conduct research on human skeletal remains from archaeological contexts at the Wiener Laboratory of the American School of Classical Studies at Athens. Applicants must have a well-defined project that can be undertaken within the given time in the laboratory or in collaboration with local research institutions.

Financial data The stipend ranges from $15,500 to $25,000, depending on seniority and experience.

Duration 1 academic year, beginning in September.

Special features Information is also available from Sherry C. Fox, Director, Wiener Laboratory, 54 Souidias Street, GR-106 76, Athens, Greece, Fax: 30 1 725 0854, E-mail: sfox@ascsa.edu.gr.

Limitations In addition to the proposed research, the fellow is expected to contribute to the development of the laboratory, assist with queries from excavators, offer a lecture on the work undertaken while at the laboratory, participate in a regular member school trip, and contribute to seminars on aspects of archaeological science as part of the school's annual curriculum.

Number awarded 1 each year.

Deadline January of each year.

[680]
JACOB HIRSCH FELLOWSHIP

American School of Classical Studies at Athens
Attn: Committee on Admissions and Fellowships
6-8 Charlton Street
Princeton, NJ 08540-5232
(609) 683-0800   Fax: (609) 924-0578
E-mail: ascsa@ascsa.org
Web site: www.ascsa.org

Purpose To provide financial assistance to American or Israeli graduate students or postdoctorates who are interested in conducting research on archaeology at the American School of Classical Studies at Athens.

Eligibility Applicants must be graduate students writing a dissertation in archaeology or recent Ph.D.s completing a project, such as a dissertation for publication. The project must require substantial residence in Greece. Applicants must be Student Associate Members of the school who are, or have been, students in the United States or Israel.

Financial data The stipend is $8,840 in cash plus fees, room, and board.

Duration 1 academic year.

Number awarded 1 each year.

Deadline January of each year.

[681]
JACOBSEN FELLOWSHIP IN PHILOSOPHY

University of London
Academic Office
Attn: Mrs. R.J.M. Davey
Senate House, Room 233
Malet Street
London WC1E 7HU
England
44 20 7862 8038   Fax: 44 20 7862 8042
E-mail: r.davey@academic.lon.ac.uk

Purpose To provide financial assistance for research in philosophy at the University of London in England.

Eligibility This program is open to scholars from any country who wish to conduct research related to philosophy at the University of London. The term "philosophy" is interpreted broadly, and in the past has included metaphysics, interpretation, and philosophical issues in psychology and psychiatry. Applicants must hold a doctorate or have effectively completed their doctoral thesis at the start of tenure of a fellowship.

Financial data The stipend is 15,873 pounds per year, including a London allowance of 2,134 pounds.

Duration Up to 2 years.

Limitations Fellows are expected to be in residence in London for the duration of the fellowship.

Number awarded 1 every other year.

Deadline February of odd-numbered years.

[682]
JAN PATOCKA JUNIOR VISITING FELLOWSHIPS
Institut für die Wissenschaften vom Menschen
Attn: Fellows Coordinator
Spittelauer Lände 3
A-1090 Vienna
Austria
43 1 313 58 335   Fax: 43 1 313 58 30
E-mail: iwm@iwm.univie.ac.at
Web site: www.univie.ac.at/iwm

Purpose To provide funding to doctoral candidates and recent doctorates who wish to conduct research in the humanities or social sciences at the Institute for Human Sciences (IWM) in Vienna.

Eligibility This program is open to doctoral candidates who are in the concluding stages of their dissertations or postdoctorates who have very recently received their doctorates in economics, international relations, modern history, philosophy, or political science. Preference is given to applicants who propose research projects in fields of special interest to the Czech philosopher Jan Patocka (1907-1977), including political philosophy, phenomenology, philosophy of history, and Czech history and culture. Applicants should be younger than 35 years of age and have a good working knowledge of German and/or English. They must be interested in conducting their research at IWM in Vienna.

Financial data The stipend is the Euro equivalent of 108,000 Austrian schillings is to cover transportation, rent, and living expenses. Fellows also receive office space and access to in-house and Viennese research facilities.

Duration 6 months.

Number awarded 2 each year.

Deadline August of each year for the January to June term; February of each year for the July to December term.

[683]
JEAN MONNET FELLOWSHIPS
European University Institute
Attn: Adviser for Academic Affairs
Badia Fiesolana
Via dei Roccettini 9
I-50016 San Domenico di Fiesole
Italy
39 55 4685 635   Fax: 39 55 4685 444
E-mail: applyjmf@datacomm.iue.it
Web site: www.iue.it

Purpose To allow postdoctoral scholars to engage in research at the European University Institute in Florence, Italy on topics related to Europe.

Eligibility This program is open to candidates holding a doctoral degree or having equivalent research experience. Applicants should have a good knowledge of the languages most relevant to their proposed research; academic activities at the institute are usually held in English or French, and occasionally in Italian. Most fellows are nationals of European Union member states, although applications from nationals of other countries (such as the United States) may be considered. Fellowships are open to academics on leave, but fellows may not engage in teaching or research activities at another institution. Research must be conducted in 1 of 3 areas: 1) comparative research in a European perspective; 2) research on the European Union (EU) or on a topic of interest for the development of Europe; or 3) fundamental research related to an innovative subject of importance in a discipline contributing to the development of Europe's cultural and academic heritage.

Financial data The basic stipend ranges from 1,200 to 2,000 Euros per month. For fellows already occupying a stable post in a university or research center, the stipend offered takes account of any continuation of their salary by their home university. Medical insurance (for fellows and their families) and limited reimbursement of travel expenses (for fellows only) are also provided.

Duration 1 academic year.

Special features The European University Institute was founded in 1976 by the European Community member countries to provide advanced academic and cultural training on a European basis. It supports research in a European perspective in 4 departments: history and civilization, law, economics, and political science and social sciences. Fellows are invited to participate in the teaching and research activities of the Institute, including the supervision of doctoral or master's theses.

Limitations Fellows are required to reside in Florence for the duration of their fellowship.

Number awarded 10 to 12 each year.

Deadline October of each year.

[684]
JEANNE CHATON AWARD
French Association of University Women
4 rue de Chevreuse
75006 Paris
France
33 1 43 20 01 32   Fax: 33 1 45 25 95 53
Fax: affdu@club-internet.fr
Web site: www.ifuw.org/france

Purpose To provide financial assistance to members of the International Federation of University Women (IFUW) interested in conducting research in France.

Eligibility This program is open to members of the IFUW or 1 of its national affiliates at the doctoral or postdoctoral level. Applicants must be interested in conducting research on the status of women, human rights, or international contacts for the establishment of peace. French women may conduct research in France or abroad; women from other countries must carry out research in France.

Financial data The stipend is the Euro equivalent of 40,000 French francs.

Duration Up to 1 year.

Special features In the United States, the IFUW affiliate is the American Association of University Women (AAUW), 1111 16th Street, N.W., Washington, DC 20036-4873, (202) 785-7700, (800) 821-4364.

Number awarded 1 each year.

Deadline March of each year.

[685]
JESUS COLLEGE JUNIOR RESEARCH FELLOWSHIPS

University of Oxford
Jesus College
Attn: Principal's Secretary
Oxford OX1 3DW
England
44 1865 279718   Fax: 44 1865 279696
E-mail: gpeissel@jesus.ox.ac.uk
Web site: www.jesus.ox.ac.uk

Purpose To provide funding to postdoctoral scholars from any country who wish to conduct research in chemistry or philosophy at Jesus College of the University of Oxford in England.

Eligibility This program is open to residents of any country who are interested in conducting research while in residence at Jesus College. Applicants must hold (or be nearing completion of) a doctoral degree in chemistry or philosophy.

Financial data The stipend ranges from 16,286 to 18,185 pounds per year. Fellows also receive a housing allowance of 2,800 pounds per year.

Duration 2 or 3 years.

Number awarded 2 each year: 1 in chemistry and 1 in philosophy.

Deadline November of each year.

[686]
JEWISH SERVICE CORPS

American Jewish Joint Distribution Committee, Inc.
711 Third Avenue
New York, NY 10017-4014
(212) 687-6200   Fax: (212) 370-5467
E-mail: service@jdcny.org
Web site: www.jdc.org/help/volunteer.htm

Purpose To provide service to Jewish communities in selected countries abroad.

Eligibility This program is open to Jewish volunteers who are interested in providing service to the Jewish communities in selected foreign countries. Applicants should have a strong Jewish background, formal or informal teaching experience (such as being a camp counselor, youth group leader, or teacher), proficiency in Hebrew, cultural tolerance, and at least a bachelor's degree. They should be flexible, creative, resourceful, and able to function independently. Teenagers are not eligible; adult applicants, from recent college graduates to retirees, are welcomed.

Financial data The program provides round-trip travel, housing, health care, and a monthly stipend for basic living expenses.

Duration 1 year, generally beginning in the summer.

Special features Currently, openings are available in India, Poland, Romania, Turkey, and the former Soviet Union.

Number awarded Varies each year.

Deadline Applications are accepted at any time.

[687]
JOAN DAWKINS AWARD FOR HEPATITIS C

British Medical Association
Attn: Executive Officer, Board of Science and Education
Tavistock Square
London WC1H 9JP
England
44 20 7383 6351   Fax: 44 20 7383 6399
E-mail: info.scienceawards@bma.org.uk
Web site: www.bma.org.uk

Purpose To provide funding to specialists interested in conducting research in the United Kingdom on hepatitis C.

Eligibility This program is open to registered medical practitioners and non-medical scientists. Applicants must be interested in conducting research that relates to the prevention of hepatitis C infection of health care staff in the course of their work or for the development of protocols for post-exposure prophylaxis following needlestick injury. The proposed research must be relevant to the United Kingdom and conducted there, but no citizenship requirements are specified.

Financial data The grant is 15,000 pounds.

Duration 1 year.

Limitations Recipients must submit a progress report of 500 words not later than 6 months after receipt of the award and a final report of at least 1,500 words on completion of the work.

Number awarded 1 each year.

Deadline March of each year.

[688]
JOAN DAWKINS AWARD FOR HOUSING AND HEALTH

British Medical Association
Attn: Executive Officer, Board of Science and Education
Tavistock Square
London WC1H 9JP
England
44 20 7383 6351   Fax: 44 20 7383 6399
E-mail: info.scienceawards@bma.org.uk
Web site: www.bma.org.uk

Purpose To provide funding to specialists interested in conducting research in the United Kingdom on housing and health.

Eligibility This program is open to registered medical practitioners and non-medical scientists. Applicants must be interested in conducting research that relates to housing and health. The proposed research must be relevant to the United Kingdom and conducted there, but no citizenship requirements are specified.

Financial data The grant is 14,000 pounds.

Duration 1 year.

Limitations Recipients must submit a progress report of 500 words not later than 6 months after receipt of the award and a final report of at least 1,500 words on completion of the work.

Number awarded 1 each year.

Deadline March of each year.

[689]
JOANNA RANDALL-MACIVER JUNIOR RESEARCH FELLOWSHIP

University of Oxford
Lady Margaret Hall
Attn: Senior Tutor's Secretary
Norham Gardens
Oxford OX2 6QA
England
44 1865 274321
E-mail: senior.tutor.secretary@lmn.ox.ac.uk
Web site: www.lmh.ox.ac.uk/joanna_randall.htm

Purpose To provide funding to women college graduates from any country who are interested in conducting research in the humanities at the University of Oxford in England.

Eligibility This program is open to women who are graduates of any university and are interested in conducting research at the University of Oxford in painting, sculpture, music, or literature of any nation in any period. Applicants should be completing, or have completed, a doctoral thesis.

Financial data The annual stipend is approximately 12,000 pounds, plus free room and board (for a single person).

Duration 2 years; nonrenewable.

Special features This fellowship is tenable, in rotation, at different colleges at Oxford: St. Hilda's (2003), St. Anne's (2004), Somerville (2005), Lady Margaret Hall (2006), and St. Hugh's (2007).

Number awarded 1 each year.

Deadline December of each year.

[690]
JOHANNES KEPLER UNIVERSITY OF LINZ DISTINGUISHED CHAIR IN INTERNATIONAL BUSINESS

Council for International Exchange of Scholars
3007 Tilden Street, N.W., Suite 5L
Washington, DC 20008-3009
(202) 686-6245   Fax: (202) 362-3442
E-mail: scholars@cies.iie.org
Web site: www.iie.org/cies

Purpose To provide funding to scholars who are interested in teaching international business at the University of Linz in Austria.

Eligibility This program is open to scholar/teachers with interdisciplinary interests in fields associated with international business who are involved in theoretical, methodological, and practical issues. Applicants must be interested in working in the field of international business with 1 or more of the 26 departments in the Faculty of Social Sciences, Economics, and Business at the University of Linz. U.S. citizenship is required. Fluency in German is desirable but not a prerequisite; some conversational German is a pragmatic necessity.

Financial data The stipend is 4,360 Euros per month. Also provided are a travel award of EUR 800 for the grantee only and an allowance for legal accompanying dependents of EUR 145 per month.

Duration 4 months.

Special features This is a Fulbright scholar program, sponsored by the Bureau of Educational and Cultural Affairs of the U.S. Department of State and administered by the Council for International Exchange of Scholars. The recipient teaches 3 courses at the advanced undergraduate and graduate level.

Number awarded 1 each year.

Deadline April of each year.

[691]
JOHN ADAMS CHAIR IN AMERICAN HISTORY

Council for International Exchange of Scholars
3007 Tilden Street, N.W., Suite 5L
Washington, DC 20008-3009
(202) 686-6245   Fax: (202) 362-3442
E-mail: scholars@cies.iie.org
Web site: www.iie.org/cies

Purpose To allow distinguished American scholars to lecture in American history at a university in the Netherlands.

Eligibility The lecturer is selected from among applicants whose credentials include distinguished research and teaching in American history. The grantee is placed at 1 of 5 participating Netherlands universities (Amsterdam, Groningen, Leiden, Nijmegen, or Utrecht). U.S. citizenship is required.

Financial data The award includes a stipend of 20,000 Euros for senior scholars or EUR 16,000 for junior scholars, as well as an international travel allowance up to EUR 1,000 for the grantee only.

Duration 4 months.

Special features This is a Fulbright scholar program, sponsored by the Bureau of Educational and Cultural Affairs of the U.S. Department of State and administered by the Council for International Exchange of Scholars. The recipient teaches undergraduate and graduate seminars in American history, offers general lectures, provides limited supervision of graduate theses, and provides consultation on curriculum.

Number awarded 1 each year.

Deadline April of each year.

[692]
JOHN DINKELOO FELLOWSHIP COMPETITION

Van Alen Institute
30 West 22nd Street
New York, NY 10010
(212) 924-7000   Fax: (212) 366-5836
E-mail: vanalen@vanalen.org
Web site: www.vanalen.org

Purpose To provide financial assistance to architectural students and architects who wish to study and/or travel abroad, in Italy and in other countries.

Eligibility The competition is open to U.S. citizens who received their first professional degree in architecture during the preceding 4 and a half years. An application must be accompanied by a portfolio illustrating the candidate's work and a brief description of the proposed project, which must involve travel and a stay in Rome. Any submission not conforming with the presentation requirements listed on the application form will not be considered for the award.

Financial data Each fellowship is $5,000, of which $3,500 is for 4 months of travel and $1,500 is applied to 2 months'

room and board at the American Academy in Rome. Any additional expenses must be covered by the recipient.
Duration 6 months: 4 months of travel and 2 months at the American Academy in Rome.
Special features This award is jointly sponsored by the Van Alen Institute (formerly the National Institute for Architectural Education), the John Dinkeloo Bequests, and the American Academy in Rome.
Number awarded The competition is held only in certain years; in those years, 1 fellow is selected.
Deadline February of the years in which the competition is held.

[693]
JOHN MARSHALL CHAIR IN POLITICAL SCIENCE
Council for International Exchange of Scholars
3007 Tilden Street, N.W., Suite 5L
Washington, DC 20008-3009
(202) 686-6245   Fax: (202) 362-3442
E-mail: scholars@cies.iie.org
Web site: www.iie.org/cies

Purpose To enable senior scholars to teach U.S. government, politics, and political institutions in Hungary.
Eligibility Applicants should be senior scholars with outstanding records of teaching and writing on U.S. political institutions. A background in comparative political systems or parliamentary systems is desirable. U.S. citizenship is required.
Financial data The base stipend is $3,500 per month. Other benefits include a monthly maintenance allowance of $100 to $200 per month based on the number of accompanying dependents; a housing allowance of up to 45,000 forints per month; a living allowance of up to 20,000 forints per month; reimbursement of round-trip airfare for grantee up to $2,000; dependent travel of $500 for 1 dependent or $1,000 for 2 or more dependents; and a settling-in allowance of $300.
Duration 5 to 9 months.
Special features This is a Fulbright scholar program, sponsored by the Bureau of Educational and Cultural Affairs of the U.S. Department of State and administered by the Council for International Exchange of Scholars. Recipients teach at the Budapest University of Economic Sciences or at another Hungarian higher educational institution; assignments include a course on U.S. government, politics, and political institutions for upper-division students; 1 or more advanced courses or faculty seminars in their specialty; and consultation on the development of the political science curriculum.
Number awarded 1 each year.
Deadline April of each year.

[694]
JOHN O. CRANE MEMORIAL FELLOWSHIPS
Institute of Current World Affairs, Inc.
Attn: Program Administrator
Wheelock House
4 West Wheelock Street
Hanover, NH 03755
(603) 643-5548   Fax: (603) 643-9599
E-mail: icwa@valley.net
Web site: www.icwa.org

Purpose To provide opportunities for independent research in eastern Europe or the Middle East.
Eligibility Individuals who have completed their formal education are eligible to apply if they are interested in conducting research in either eastern Europe or the Middle East. Generally, applicants must be under the age of 36 and have good command of written and spoken English.
Financial data The institute provides full support for the fellows and their families.
Duration At least 2 years.
Limitations Fellowships are not awarded to support work toward academic degrees, to write books, or to undertake specific studies or research projects. Fellows are required to submit monthly reports.
Number awarded 1 or more each year.
Deadline March or August of each year.

[695]
JOHNSTONE AND FLORENCE STONEY STUDENTSHIP FUND
British Federation of Women Graduates
Attn: The Secretary
4 Mandeville Courtyard
142 Battersea Park Road
London SW11 4NB
England
44 20 7498 8037   Fax: 44 20 7498 8037
E-mail: bfwg@bfwg.demon.co.uk
Web site: homepages.wyenet.co.uk/bfwg

Purpose To provide financial assistance for graduate or postdoctoral research in biological, geological, meteorological, or radiological science to women of any nationality.
Eligibility Women who have already completed at least 1 year of graduate study may apply; they may be of any age and may be studying at the master's, doctoral, or postdoctoral level. They must propose a plan of research in biological, geological, meteorological, or radiological science, preferably in Australia, New Zealand, or South Africa, although applications are also accepted from candidates not of U.K. nationality whose research would take place in the United Kingdom.
Financial data Up to 1,000 pounds is awarded.
Duration 1 year.
Limitations Awards are only for postgraduate research, not for courses. Requests for applications must be accompanied by a self-addressed stamped envelope. There is a 12 pound application fee.
Number awarded 1 each year.
Deadline April of each year.

[696]
JOURNALS OF REPRODUCTION AND FERTILITY VACATION SCHOLARSHIPS

Journals of Reproduction and Fertility Ltd.
Attn: Company Secretary
22 Newmarket Road
Cambridge CB5 8DT
England
44 1223 351809   Fax: 44 1223 359754
E-mail: cosec@jrfadmin.demon.co.uk

Purpose To provide funding to undergraduate students from any country who are interested in conducting research related to reproduction in the United Kingdom or Ireland.

Eligibility This program is open to undergraduate students who are in the middle years of their degree studies and considering research as a career. Applicants must be interested in working in universities or research institutes in the United Kingdom or Irish Republic on research projects related to reproduction, fertility, and lactation in humans and animals.

Financial data Funding is provided to cover basic living expenses.

Duration 8 weeks, during vacation periods.

Number awarded Varies each year.

Deadline March of each year for summer vacation projects; November of each year for Easter and/or summer vacation projects.

[697]
JULIA CHILD HONORARIUM AWARD

International Association of Culinary Professionals
  Foundation
Attn: Program Coordinator
304 West Liberty Street, Suite 201
Louisville, KY 40202
(502) 581-9786, ext. 237   (800) 928-4227
Fax: (502) 589-3602   E-mail: iacp@hqtrs.com
Web site: www.iacpfoundation.org

Purpose To provide funding to women culinary professionals interested in conducting independent study and research in France.

Eligibility This program is open to women teachers and writers interested in furthering their studies and research in subjects related to French food, wine, and the culinary disciplines. Applicants must be proposing a program of independent study or research in France.

Financial data The award is $10,000.

Duration 1 year.

Limitations There is a $25 application fee.

Number awarded 1 each year.

Deadline November of each year.

[698]
JULIA CHILD SCHOLARSHIP AWARD

International Association of Culinary Professionals
  Foundation
Attn: Program Coordinator
304 West Liberty Street, Suite 201
Louisville, KY 40202
(502) 581-9786, ext. 237   (800) 928-4227
Fax: (502) 589-3602   E-mail: iacp@hqtrs.com
Web site: www.iacpfoundation.org

Purpose To provide funding to culinary professionals interested in conducting research or other activities in France.

Eligibility This program is open to culinary professionals interested in a program of research, writing, and/or teaching related to French food, wine, and the culinary disciplines. Applicants must be proposing to work independently in France.

Financial data The award is $10,000.

Duration 1 year.

Limitations There is a $25 application fee.

Number awarded 1 each year.

Deadline November of each year.

[699]
JULIA MANN JUNIOR RESEARCH FELLOWSHIP

University of Oxford
St. Hilda's College
Attn: Academic Office
Oxford OX4 1DY
England
44 1865 276815   Fax: 44 1865 276816
E-mail: college.office@st-hildas.ox.ac.uk
Web site: www.st-hildas.ox.ac.uk

Purpose To provide funding to women from any country who are interested in conducting postdoctoral research at St. Hilda's College of the University of Oxford in England.

Eligibility This program is open to women graduates from any country who are interested in conducting postdoctoral research at St. Hilda's College. The field of study is announced whenever the fellowship is available.

Financial data The stipend is 10,790 pounds. Recipients are also entitled to a 1,000 pound research allowance and free board and accommodations.

Duration 2 years; may be renewed for 1 additional year.

Number awarded This fellowship is offered periodically. It was last offered for 2001.

[700]
JURGEN HEIDEKING FELLOWSHIP

German Historical Institute
Attn: Deputy Director
1607 New Hampshire Avenue, N.W.
Washington, DC 20009-2562
(202) 387-3355   Fax: (202) 483-3430
E-mail: C.Brown@ghi-dc.org
Web site: www.ghi-dc.org/heideking.html

Purpose To provide an opportunity for postdoctoral scholars in designated disciplines to conduct research in residence at the University of Cologne in Germany.

Eligibility This program is open to postdoctoral scholars from the United States who are working in 1 of the following areas: 1) American history and German-American relations from the early modern period to the present; 2) international history of the 19th and 20th centuries, including the history of international relations and the comparative history of colonial systems and societies; or 3) German history of the 20th century, with special emphasis on America's influence on German society between 1918 and 1949. Applicants must be interested in conducting research at the University of Cologne. Preference is given to applicants in the final stages of their research projects.
Financial data The stipend is the Euro equivalent of 41,500 Deutsche marks. A family allowance is also provided, if applicable.
Duration 1 academic year.
Special features Support for this program is provided by the Fritz Thyssen Foundation.
Limitations Fellows are expected to be in residence at the University of Cologne, participate in the university's academic activities, and give a public lecture on their research.
Number awarded 1 each year.
Deadline August of each year.

[701]
KARL FRANZENS UNIVERSITY DISTINGUISHED CHAIR IN CULTURAL STUDIES
Council for International Exchange of Scholars
3007 Tilden Street, N.W., Suite 5L
Washington, DC 20008-3009
(202) 686-6245   Fax: (202) 362-3442
E-mail: scholars@cies.iie.org
Web site: www.iie.org/cies

Purpose To provide funding to scholars who are interested in teaching cultural studies at Karl Franzens University in Austria.
Eligibility This program is open to scholar/teachers with interests in fields centrally associated with cultural studies who are interested in teaching in the Faculty of the Humanities at Karl Franzens University in Graz. Preference is given to applicants involved in theoretical and methodological issues and who can utilize interdisciplinary approaches with 1 or more of the faculty's 18 departments in the fields of American studies, ancient and modern history, archaeology, art history, classical and modern languages and literature, education, ethnology, linguistics, musicology, and philosophy. U.S. citizenship is required. Fluency in German is desirable but not a prerequisite; some conversational German is a pragmatic necessity.
Financial data The stipend is 4,360 Euros per month. Also provided are a travel award of EUR 800 for the grantee only and an allowance for legal accompanying dependents of EUR 145 per month.
Duration 4 months.
Special features This is a Fulbright scholar program, sponsored by the Bureau of Educational and Cultural Affairs of the U.S. Department of State and administered by the Council for International Exchange of Scholars. The recipient teaches 3 courses at the advanced undergraduate and graduate level.
Number awarded 1 each year.

Deadline April of each year.

[702]
KATHLEEN HALL MEMORIAL FELLOWSHIP FUND
British Federation of Women Graduates
Attn: The Secretary
4 Mandeville Courtyard
142 Battersea Park Road
London SW11 4NB
England
44 20 7498 8037   Fax: 44 20 7498 8037
E-mail: bfwg@bfwg.demon.co.uk
Web site: homepages.wyenet.co.uk/bfwg

Purpose To provide financial assistance to women from any country who wish to conduct research in the United Kingdom.
Eligibility This program is open to women from any country who are currently enrolled in graduate school in the United Kingdom, and to women of U.K. nationality who are studying overseas. Normally, an award is not made for the first year's work toward a doctorate, a 2-year master's degree, or individual courses. Also eligible to apply are women already holding a doctoral degree. Preference is given to applicants from countries with a low per capita income.
Financial data The stipend is at least 1,000 pounds.
Duration 1 academic year.
Limitations Within 6 months of completing the program, recipients must submit a written report on the work undertaken. Requests for applications must be accompanied by a self-addressed stamped envelope. There is a 12 pound application fee.
Number awarded 1 or more each year.
Deadline April of each year.

[703]
KENAN T. ERIM AWARD
Archaeological Institute of America
656 Beacon Street, Fourth Floor
Boston, MA 02215-2006
(617) 353-9361   Fax: (617) 353-6550
E-mail: aia@bu.edu
Web site: www.archaeological.org

Purpose To provide financial assistance to researchers or scholars interested in conducting research on Aphrodisias material.
Eligibility This program is open to American or foreign researchers or excavating scholars interested in working on Aphrodisias material. Current officers and members of the governing board of the Archaeological Institute of America are not eligible to apply. If the project involves work at Aphrodisias, candidates must submit written approval from the field director with their applications.
Financial data The award is $4,000.
Duration 1 year.
Special features This award was established in 1992 by the American Friends of Aphrodisias.
Limitations Recipients must submit a final report to both the Archaeological Institute of America and the American Friends

of Aphrodisias (Box 989, Lenox Hill Station, New York, NY 10021).

Number awarded 1 each year.
Deadline October of each year.

[704]
KING'S COLLEGE JUNIOR RESEARCH FELLOWSHIP

University of Cambridge
King's College
Attn: Provost
King's Parade
Cambridge CB2 1ST
England
44 1223 331332   Fax: 44 1223 331315
E-mail: provost@kings.cam.ac.uk
Web site: www.kings.cam.ac.uk

Purpose To provide funding to postdoctoral scholars interested in conducting research in the arts, humanities, or social sciences at King's College of the University of Cambridge in England.
Eligibility This program is open to scholars from any country who are interested in conducting research at King's College in the arts, humanities, or social sciences. Applicants must have completed, or expect to complete, a Ph.D. or equivalent degree. They must submit a 1,000-word statement describing their proposed research.
Financial data The stipend ranges from 14,259 to 18,200 pounds per year. Other benefits include free lunch or dinner, limited financial support for research expenses, a study room, and single accommodation in college. Fellows from outside the United Kingdom may claim limited travel and moving expenses.
Duration Up to 4 years.
Number awarded 1 each year.
Deadline October of each year.

[705]
KIRK-GREENE JUNIOR RESEARCH FELLOWSHIP IN TROPICAL AFRICAN STUDIES

University of Oxford
St. Antony's College
Attn: Bursar
62 Woodstock Road
Oxford OX2 6JF
England
44 1865 284724   Fax: 44 1865 310518
E-mail: bursar.sec@sant.ox.ac.uk
Web site: www.sant.ox.ac.uk

Purpose To provide funding to postdoctoral scholars from any university who wish to conduct research in African studies at St. Antony's College of the University of Oxford in England.
Eligibility This program is open to scholars from any country who are interested in conducting postdoctoral research in the field of 20th-century history, politics, or international relations of 1 of the following countries in tropical Africa while in residence at St. Antony's College: Nigeria, Ghana, Sierra Leone, Francophone West Africa (excluding Mauritania but including Cameroon), Kenya, Tanzania, or Uganda. They must have successfully completed a doctoral thesis at the time of accepting the fellowship and may not have accumulated more than 6 years of full-time postdoctoral study or research. Normally, fellows should be able to write up their doctoral thesis for publication.
Financial data The stipend is 8,000 pounds. Fellows also are entitled to free lunches at the college and selected meals during the term. A research grant of up to 300 pounds is also provided.
Duration 2 terms (Hilary and Trinity); nonrenewable.
Number awarded 1 each year.
Deadline September of each year.

[706]
KRESS AGORA PUBLICATION FELLOWSHIP

American School of Classical Studies at Athens
Attn: Committee on Personnel
6-8 Charlton Street
Princeton, NJ 08540-5232
(609) 683-0800   Fax: (609) 924-0578
E-mail: ascsa@ascsa.org
Web site: www.ascsa.org

Purpose To provide funding to scholars who are interested in working on an Agora publication assignment at the American School of Classical Studies at Athens.
Eligibility This program is open to scholars who are working on an Agora publication assignment and are interested in continuing their work at the school in Athens. Preference is given to those working on an Agora volume. Applicants should submit a curriculum vitae, project outline, and account of the present state of the project.
Financial data The stipend is $18,000.
Duration The minimum stay is 6 to 8 months.
Number awarded 1 each year.
Deadline January of each year.

[707]
KRESS FELLOWSHIPS IN ART HISTORY

Samuel H. Kress Foundation
174 East 80th Street
New York, NY 10021
(212) 861-4993   Fax: (212) 628-3146
Web site: www.shkf.org

Purpose To provide financial assistance to American graduate students who are completing their doctoral research on the history of art.
Eligibility Candidates must be nominated by their department. Their doctoral dissertation research must relate to art history and they must need to complete their research at a cooperating foreign institute of art history. Candidates must be U.S. citizens or students at U.S. institutions.
Financial data The annual stipend is $18,000. The foreign institution chosen by the fellow receives a sustaining grant.
Duration 2 years.
Special features The cooperating institutes are: Kunsthistorisches Institut, Florence; Nelson Glueck School of Biblical Archaeology, Hebrew Union College, Jerusalem; Prentenkabinet/Kunsthistorisch Instituut der Rijks Universiteit, Leiden; Courtauld Institute of Art and Warburg Institute, University of

London; Zentralinstitut für Kunstgeschichte, Munich; Cyprus American Archaeological Research Institute, Nicosia; American University of Paris; Bibliotheca Hertziana, Rome; and Swiss Institute for Art Research, Zurich.

Number awarded Varies; generally, 4 each year.

Deadline November of each year.

[708]
KRESS/ARIT PRE-DOCTORAL FELLOWSHIP IN THE HISTORY OF ART AND ARCHAEOLOGY

American Research Institute in Turkey
c/o University of Pennsylvania Museum
33rd and Spruce Streets
Philadelphia, PA 19104-6324
(215) 898-3474 Fax: (215) 898-0657
E-mail: leinwand@sas.upenn.edu
Web site: mec.sas.upenn.edu/ARIT

Purpose To provide financial aid for advanced dissertation research in Turkey in archaeology or the history of art.

Eligibility This program is open to students engaged in advanced dissertation research that requires a period of study in Turkey. Eligible fields include archaeology and the history of art and architecture from antiquity to the present. Applicants must be U.S. citizens enrolled at a university in the United States.

Financial data The maximum award is $15,000.

Duration Up to 1 year, but projects of shorter duration (generally no less than 2 months) are also possible.

Special features Hostel, research, and study facilities of the American Research Institute in Turkey (ARIT) are available in Istanbul and Ankara. This fellowship program is supported by a grant from the Samuel H. Kress Foundation.

Number awarded 1 or more each year.

Deadline November of each year.

[709]
LANDSCAPE ARCHITECTURE ROME PRIZE FELLOWSHIP

American Academy in Rome
Attn: Fellowship Coordinator
7 East 60th Street
New York, NY 10022-1001
(212) 751-7200 Fax: (212) 751-7220
E-mail: info@aarome.org
Web site: www.aarome.org

Purpose To provide financial support to American artists interested in conducting research in landscape architecture at the School of Fine Arts of the American Academy in Rome.

Eligibility Eligible are U.S. citizens who hold an accredited degree in landscape architecture. Applications must include a 1-page statement describing how the Rome experience will be beneficial professionally and identifying any special resources in Italy that are important to the work, a portfolio with at least 6 examples of design work, and up to 18 slides of design work. Full-time students are not eligible.

Financial data The fellowship provides a stipend of up to $20,000, meals, a bedroom with private bath, and a study or studio. Fellows with children under 18 are housed outside the McKim, Mead & White building and are provided with an allowance that helps cover the cost of off-campus housing.

Duration 1 year, beginning in September.

Special features The American Academy in Rome, founded in 1894 by the American architect Charles F. McKim, is a center for independent study and advanced research in the fine arts and humanities. It consists of a School of Fine Arts (including architecture, landscape architecture, design arts, painting and sculpture, musical composition, and literature) and a School of Classical Studies (including classical studies and archaeology, history of art, and post-classical humanistic/modern Italian studies).

Limitations There is a $40 application fee. Prize winners may not hold full-time jobs while at the Academy.

Number awarded 2 each year.

Deadline November of each year.

[710]
LASZLO ORSZAGH CHAIR IN AMERICAN STUDIES

Council for International Exchange of Scholars
3007 Tilden Street, N.W., Suite 5L
Washington, DC 20008-3009
(202) 686-6245 Fax: (202) 362-3442
E-mail: scholars@cies.iie.org
Web site: www.iie.org/cies

Purpose To enable senior scholars to teach American studies in Hungary.

Eligibility Applicants should be established scholars at the associate or full professor level; experience in teaching graduate students and supervising Ph.D. theses is desirable. Their field of study may be any of the disciplines comprising American studies, including, but not limited to, art history, African American culture and literature, history, literature, philosophy, political science, religion, or sociology. Priority is given to specialists in 19th- and 20th-century U.S. history, society, or political life. They must be interested in teaching American studies in Hungary. U.S. citizenship is required.

Financial data The base stipend is $3,500 per month. Other benefits include a monthly maintenance allowance of $100 to $200 per month based on the number of accompanying dependents; a housing allowance of up to 45,000 forints per month; a living allowance of up to 20,000 forints per month; reimbursement of round-trip airfare for grantee up to $2,000; and dependent travel of $500 for 1 dependent or $1,000 for 2 or more dependents; and a settling-in allowance of $300.

Duration 5 to 9 months.

Special features This is a Fulbright scholar program, sponsored by the Bureau of Educational and Cultural Affairs of the U.S. Department of State and administered by the Council for International Exchange of Scholars. Recipients teach courses, direct research, and offer lectures or seminars at the undergraduate and graduate levels; assist in curriculum development; and offer short-term courses for Hungarian faculty as requested.

Number awarded 1 each year.

Deadline April of each year.

[711]
LATVIA FULBRIGHT TEACHER EXCHANGE
U.S. Department of State
c/o Graduate School, USDA
600 Maryland Avenue, S.W., Room 320
Washington, DC 20024-2520
(202) 314-3520   Fax: (202) 479-6806
E-mail: fulbright@grad.usda.gov
Web site: www.grad.usda.gov/International/ftep.html

Purpose To promote mutual understanding between the people of the United States and the people of Latvia through a teacher exchange program.

Eligibility This program is open to teachers (grades 5 through 12) and 2-year college instructors of English as a second language, English literature, foreign language, social studies, mathematics, science, or education who are interested in teaching in Latvia. Applicants must 1) be U.S. citizens; 2) hold at least a bachelor's degree; 3) be fluent in English; 4) have a current full-time teaching assignment in the U.S. or a territory; 5) have the approval of their school administration; 6) have at least 3 years of full-time experience; and 7) not have participated in a Fulbright Teacher Exchange longer than 8 weeks during the last 2 years. The language of instruction is English. Fluency in Latvian is not required although some ability is useful. Teaching couples may apply. However, because of the limited number of positions available and, often, the lack of foreign candidate pairs with similar qualifications for interchanges, it may not be possible to arrange suitable assignments in the same locality or to place both teachers. Preference is given to applicants who have not participated previously in the program and may be given to applicants who have not previously lived in Latvia. Geographic distribution of awards within the United States is also a factor in selection. This program does not discriminate on the basis of race, color, religion, age, sex, or national origin and encourages the applications of members of minority communities. Other considerations being equal, veterans are given preference.

Financial data Round-trip economy airfare for the exchange teacher only is provided. Participants must obtain a leave of absence with pay from their jobs in the United States. The U.S. school must agree to accept a teacher from Latvia who must secure a leave of absence with pay; the Latvian teacher receives a stipend, but no additional cost accrues to the U.S. school.

Duration 9 months, beginning in September.

Special features This program is sponsored by the Bureau of Educational and Cultural Affairs of the U.S. Department of State and administered by the Graduate School, USDA.

Limitations This program provides for the direct exchange of teaching assignments between Latvia and the United States. Applicants selected for exchange must attend orientation programs of the sponsoring agencies in the United States or abroad.

Number awarded 2 each year.

Deadline October of each year.

[712]
LEE-GARROD MEDICAL RESEARCH FELLOWSHIP
University of Oxford
Christ Church
Attn: Censors' Office
Oxford OX1 1DP
England
44 1865 286574   Fax: 44 1865 276488
E-mail: vichy.rolls@chch.ox.ac.uk
Web site: www.chch.ox.ac.uk

Purpose To provide funding to investigators interested in conducting a medical research project at Christ Church of the University of Oxford in England.

Eligibility This program is open to medical researchers who are younger than 33 years of age. Applicants must be interested in undertaking a specific research project at Oxford.

Financial data The fellow receives a stipend ranging from 15,095 to 19,155 pounds per year, meals at High Table, and other benefits depending on circumstances.

Duration 3 years; may be renewed for 1 additional year.

Number awarded The fellowship is offered when available, most recently in 2001-02.

Deadline December of the year prior to the fellowship's availability.

[713]
LEMMERMANN FOUNDATION SCHOLARSHIP AWARDS
Lemmermann Foundation
c/o Studio Associato Romanelli
via Cosseria, 5
I-00192 Rome
Italy
39 6 324 3023   Fax: 39 6 322 1788
E-mail: lemmermann@mail.nexus.it
Web site: lemmermann.nexus.it

Purpose To provide funding to university students from any country who wish to carry out research in Rome.

Eligibility This program is open to university students from any country who need to carry out thesis research in Rome. Their thesis must deal with Rome and Roman culture from the pre-Roman period to the present day in the subject areas of literature, archaeology, or history of art. Applicants must not be older than 30 years of age, must be attending a recognized university, and must have a basic knowledge of the Italian language.

Financial data The stipend is the Euro equivalent of 1,500,000 Italian lire per month.

Duration Depends on the proposed research.

Number awarded Varies each year.

Deadline March or September of each year.

[714]
LH SYSTEMS INTERNSHIP

American Society for Photogrammetry and Remote Sensing
Attn: ASPRS Awards Program
5410 Grosvenor Lane, Suite 210
Bethesda, MD 20814-2160
(301) 493-0290, ext. 101   Fax: (301) 493-0208
E-mail: scholarships@asprs.org
Web site: www.asprs.org

Purpose To provide a research experience at facilities of LH Systems to graduate student members of the American Society for Photogrammetry and Remote Sensing (ASPRS).

Eligibility This program is open to graduate students in photogrammetry and remote sensing who are members of the society. Applicants must be interested in an internship at LH Systems in the United States or Switzerland that provides an opportunity to carry out a small research project of their own choice or to work on an existing project as part of a team. They must submit a 1,000-word statement describing the research project they wish to conduct, including its significance, proposed methodology, expected results, and a schedule. Topics in areas in which LH Systems has a commercial interest receive special consideration.

Financial data The internship provides a stipend of $2,500 plus an allowance for travel and living expenses.

Duration 8 weeks.

Special features This program is administered by ASPRS and funded by LH Systems, LLC. Interns work with LH Systems personnel in facilities in San Diego, Denver, and Heerbrugg, Switzerland

Number awarded 1 each year.

Deadline November of each year.

[715]
LITERATURE ROME PRIZE FELLOWSHIP

American Academy in Rome
Attn: Fellowship Coordinator
7 East 60th Street
New York, NY 10022-1001
(212) 751-7200   Fax: (212) 751-7220
E-mail: info@aarome.org
Web site: www.aarome.org

Purpose To provide distinguished writers with the opportunity to engage in research at the American Academy in Rome.

Eligibility No applications for this fellowship are accepted. Nominations are submitted by members of the American Academy of Arts and Letters (AAAL), a committee of which selects the fellow. Nominees must be interested in conducting research at the academy in Rome.

Financial data The fellowship provides a stipend of up to $20,000, meals, a bedroom with private bath, and a study or studio. Fellows with children under 18 are housed outside the McKim, Mead & White building and are provided with an allowance that helps cover the cost of off-campus housing.

Duration 1 year.

Special features The American Academy in Rome, founded in 1894 by the American architect Charles F. McKim, is a center for independent study and advanced research in the fine arts and humanities. It consists of a School of Fine Arts (including architecture, landscape architecture, design arts, painting and sculpture, musical composition, and literature) and a School of Classical Studies (including classical studies and archaeology, history of art, and post-classical humanistic/modern Italian studies). This is 1 of the Rome Prize Fellowships offered by the Academy. Information is also available from the AAAL, 633 West 155th Street, New York, NY 10032-7599, (212) 368-5900.

Number awarded 1 each year, beginning in September.

Deadline November of each year.

[716]
LONG-TERM POSTGRADUATE TRAINING COURSE ON MODERN PROBLEMS IN BIOLOGY AND MICROBIAL TECHNOLOGY

Academy of Sciences of the Czech Republic
Attn: Institute of Microbiology
Vídeňská 1083
142 20 Prague 4
Czech Republic
420 2 475 2379   Fax: 420 2 475 2384
E-mail: nerud@biomed.cas.cz
Web site: www.biomed.cas.cz/mbu/unesco_course/info.htm

Purpose To provide financial assistance for recent doctoral recipients who are interested in training in the Czech Republic for a research career in microbiology.

Eligibility Applicants must have received a Ph.D. or equivalent degree and have been practicing in their field for 2 or 3 years. They must be interested in pursuing research training in the Czech Republic. Most participants are from central and eastern European countries, but a limited number of students from other regions are accepted. Proficiency in English, the language of the program, is also required.

Financial data Participants receive tuition, use of research facilities, and medical care free of charge. Foreign scholars are awarded a stipend of 5,000 Czech netto per month. The organizing committee provides accommodations for unmarried scholars in a students' hostel.

Duration 11 months, beginning in October.

Special features The first 2 months consist of practical training in radioisotope techniques, biosynthesis of proteins and nucleic acids, biochemical fractioning of the cell, and application of nuclear magnetic resonance, mass spectrometry, and computing methods in biology. The remaining period is spent on a research project in 1 of the institutes or laboratories of the Academy of Sciences of the Czech Republic. The program is jointly sponsored by the United Nations Educational, Scientific, and Cultural Organization (UNESCO).

Number awarded 15 each year.

Deadline March of each year.

[717]
LOUIS DUPREE PRIZE FOR RESEARCH ON CENTRAL ASIA

Social Science Research Council
810 Seventh Avenue
New York, NY 10019
(212) 377-2700   Fax: (212) 377-2727
E-mail: eurasia@ssrc.org
Web site: www.ssrc.org

Purpose To provide funding for extended dissertation travel in eastern Europe and central Asia.

Eligibility Only candidates who receive a dissertation research fellowship from a program administered by the Social Science Research Council (SSRC) or American Council of Learned Societies (ACLS) are eligible to apply for this program. Candidates who wish to be considered for this prize should so indicate on the applications for those fellowships. The prize is awarded for the most promising dissertation proposal involving field research in Central Asia, including Afghanistan, Azerbaijan, Kirghizia, Mongolia, Turkmenistan, Tajikistan, Uzbekistan and culturally-related contiguous areas of Iran, Pakistan, Kazakhstan, and China. Minorities and women are particularly encouraged to apply.

Financial data The prize is $2,500.

Duration The prize is intended to enrich the recipient's field experience by making possible a longer stay or more extensive travel within the region.

Number awarded 1 each year.

[718]
LU GWEI-DJEN RESEARCH FELLOWSHIP

University of Cambridge
Lucy Cavendish College
Attn: President's Secretary
Lady Margaret Road
Cambridge CB3 0BU
England
44 1223 332196   Fax: 44 1223 332178
E-mail: bjy21@cam.ac.uk
Web site: www.lucy-cav.cam.ac.uk

Purpose To provide funding to women postdoctoral scholars interested in conducting research in the sciences at Lucy Cavendish College of the University of Cambridge in England.

Eligibility This program is open to women from any country who hold a doctorate or whose dissertation is under examination. Applicants must be interested in conducting research at Lucy Cavendish College in a scientific subject, preferably applied medicine or biology, that relates scholarship to current issues facing the world.

Financial data The stipend is approximately 11,000 pounds per year. Other allowances may be available for accommodations, child care, and/or research expenses.

Duration 1 year; may be renewed for up to 2 additional years, subject to satisfactory progress and annual reports.

Number awarded This fellowship is offered from time to time.

Deadline January in the years it is available.

[719]
LUSO-AMERICAN FOUNDATION PRE-DISSERTATION FELLOWSHIPS FOR RESEARCH IN PORTUGAL

Council for European Studies
c/o Columbia University
1203 International Affairs Building, MC3310
420 West 118th Street
New York, NY 10027
(212) 854-4172   Fax: (212) 854-8808
E-mail: ces@columbia.edu
Web site: www.europanet.org

Purpose To enable graduate students in the social sciences to pursue short-term exploratory research in Portugal, in order to determine the viability and to refine the scope of their proposed dissertation.

Eligibility Applicants must be enrolled in a doctoral program at a U.S. university and must have completed the equivalent of at least 2 but less than 3 years of full-time graduate study prior to the beginning date of their proposed research. Fellowships are restricted to citizens or permanent residents of the United States. Eligible fields of study include cultural anthropology, geography, history (post-1750 only), political science, sociology, and urban and regional planning. The topic must focus on Portugal and the research must be conducted there. Students seeking support for language training or tuition for courses at a Portuguese university are not eligible.

Financial data Fellowships provide $4,000 for travel and living expenses.

Duration 3 months, during the summer or autumn.

Special features The first awards for this program, sponsored by the Luso-American Foundation, were offered in 2000.

Number awarded 2 each year.

Deadline January of each year.

[720]
LYDIA CABRERA AWARDS FOR CUBAN HISTORICAL STUDIES

Conference on Latin American History
c/o University of South Florida
Soc 107
4202 East Fowler Avenue
Tampa, FL 33620
(813) 974-8132   Fax: (813) 974-6228
E-mail: clah@chuma.cas.usf.edu
Web site: www.emory.edu/HISTORY/LatAm/clah

Purpose To provide financial support to graduate students and scholars interested in conducting research or publishing on Cuba between 1492 and 1868.

Eligibility Applicants for these awards must be trained in Latin American history and fluent in Spanish. They may be currently enrolled in graduate studies at a U.S. institution or affiliated with a college/university faculty or accredited historical association in the United States. Proposals may be submitted for 1) original research on Cuban history conducted in Spanish, Mexican, or U.S. archives; 2) the publication of meritorious books on Cuba currently out of print; or 3) the publication of historical statistics, historical documents, or guides to Spanish archives relating to Cuban history between 1492 and 1868.

Financial data Awards up to $5,000 are available.
Special features Recipients are expected to disseminate the results of their research in scholarly publications and/or professional papers delivered at scholarly conferences and public lectures at educational institutions.
Number awarded 1 or more each year.
Deadline May of each year.

[721]
M. ALISON FRANTZ FELLOWSHIP IN POST-CLASSICAL STUDIES AT THE GENNADIUS LIBRARY

American School of Classical Studies at Athens
Attn: Committee on the Gennadius Library
6-8 Charlton Street
Princeton, NJ 08540-5232
(609) 683-0800   Fax: (609) 924-0578
E-mail: ascsa@ascsa.org
Web site: www.ascsa.org

Purpose To provide financial support to young American or Canadian scholars who need to use the Gennadius Library in Greece for their research.
Eligibility Applicants must be graduate students writing a dissertation on some aspect of post-classical Greece (late antiquity, Byzantine studies, or modern Greek studies, including the period of the Turkokratia) or recent Ph.D.s in that field who are completing a project (such as the revision of a dissertation for publication). Students must be enrolled in or have recently graduated from a university in the United States or Canada, and their proposed research project must demonstrate the need for using the Gennadius Library in Athens.
Financial data The grant provides $8,840 in cash, plus room, board, and waiver of fees at the American School of Classical Studies at Athens.
Duration 1 year.
Special features This fellowship was formerly known as the Gennadeion Fellowship in Post-Classical Studies.
Number awarded 1 each year.
Deadline January of each year.

[722]
MANSFIELD COLLEGE JUNIOR RESEARCH FELLOWSHIP IN HUMANITIES

University of Oxford
Mansfield College
Attn: College Secretary
Oxford OX1 3TF
England
44 1865 270999   Fax: 44 1865 270970
E-mail: info@sea.mansfield.ox.ac.uk
Web site: www.mansfield.ox.ac.uk

Purpose To provide funding to postdoctorates from any country who are interested in conducting research in the humanities at Mansfield College of the University of Oxford in England.
Eligibility This program is open to graduates of any university who are interested in conducting postdoctoral research at Mansfield College in the humanities.

Financial data The stipend is 15,320 pounds per year. A housing allowance is also provided.
Duration 2 years; may be renewed for 1 additional year.
Number awarded This fellowship is offered periodically. It was last awarded in 2002.

[723]
MARGARET K.B. DAY MEMORIAL SCHOLARSHIPS

British Federation of Women Graduates
Attn: The Secretary
4 Mandeville Courtyard
142 Battersea Park Road
London SW11 4NB
England
44 20 7498 8037   Fax: 44 20 7498 8037
E-mail: bfwg@bfwg.demon.co.uk
Web site: homepages.wyenet.co.uk/bfwg

Purpose To provide financial assistance for graduate or postdoctoral research to women of United Kingdom nationality or for research in the United Kingdom.
Eligibility Women who have already completed at least 1 year of graduate study may apply; they may be of any age and may be studying at the master's, doctoral, or postdoctoral level. Candidates of United Kingdom nationality may be studying overseas or within the United Kingdom; candidates not of U.K. nationality but whose studies take place in the United Kingdom are also eligible, although they may not plan to study outside the United Kingdom.
Financial data Scholarships are at least 1,000 pounds.
Duration 1 year.
Limitations Awards are only for postgraduate research, not courses. Requests for applications must be accompanied by a self-addressed stamped envelope. There is a 12 pound application fee.
Number awarded 1 or more each year.
Deadline April of each year.

[724]
MARGARET SMITH RESEARCH FELLOWSHIP

University of Cambridge
Girton College
Attn: Secretary to the Research Fellowship Committee
Huntingdon Road
Cambridge CB3 0JG
England
44 1223 338999   Fax: 44 1223 338896
E-mail: ff204@cam.ac.uk
Web site: www.girton.cam.ac.uk

Purpose To provide funding to postdoctoral scholars interested in conducting research on religion or literature at Girton College of the University of Cambridge in England.
Eligibility This program is open to graduates of any university who are interested in conducting research at Girton College in 1) eastern or western religions (including comparative religion and mysticism) or 2) Arabic or Persian literature (or both). There are no age limits, but applicants should be in the early stage

of their career and have recently completed their Ph.D. or be close to completion.

Financial data In the first year, the stipend is 10,619 pounds per year for fellows who have not yet completed their Ph.D. or 13,328 for fellows who have completed the degree. In the final year, the stipend is 14,678 for postdoctoral fellows. Other benefits include residence in the college at a moderate charge or a living-out allowance of 2,000 pounds per year and reimbursement of research expenses up to 1,500 pounds over the term of the fellowship.

Duration Normally 3 years.

Number awarded 1 in the years it is offered (the last award was in 2002).

Deadline September of years offered.

[725]
MARINE BIOLOGICAL ASSOCIATION RESEARCH BURSARIES

Marine Biological Association of the United Kingdom
Attn: Director
Laboratory
Citadel Hill
Plymouth PL1 2PB
England
44 1752 633331   Fax: 44 1752 669762
E-mail: sjha@mba.ac.uk
Web site: www1.npm.ac.uk/mba

Purpose To provide funding to scientific investigators from any country who are interested in conducting research in the marine sciences at the Marine Biological Association of the United Kingdom's laboratory in Plymouth.

Eligibility Postgraduate and postdoctoral researchers from any country are eligible to apply for this program, if they are interested in conducting research on marine biology or physiology in collaboration with resident scientists at the laboratory in Plymouth. Applicants need not be members of the association, but they are expected to become members if they receive a bursary.

Financial data Awards up to 1,500 pounds are available.

Number awarded 3 to 6 each year.

Deadline Applications may be submitted at any time, but available funds for any given year are usually committed by the end of March.

[726]
MARINE BIOLOGICAL ASSOCIATION RESEARCH FELLOWSHIPS

Marine Biological Association of the United Kingdom
Attn: Director
Laboratory
Citadel Hill
Plymouth PL1 2PB
England
44 1752 633331   Fax: 44 1752 669762
E-mail: sjha@mba.ac.uk
Web site: www1.npm.ac.uk/mba

Purpose To provide funding to scientific investigators from any country who are interested in conducting research in the marine sciences at the Marine Biological Association of the United Kingdom's laboratory in Plymouth.

Eligibility Junior and senior researchers from any country are eligible to apply for this program, if they are interested in conducting research on marine biology or physiology at the laboratory in Plymouth. Applicants need not be members of the association, but they are expected to become members if they receive a fellowship.

Financial data Fellowships provide a salary, laboratory facilities, and a grant for recurrent expenditures.

Duration Up to 5 years.

Number awarded Varies each year.

Deadline Applications may be submitted at any time, but they must be received by the association at least 1 year before the anticipated visit.

[727]
MARINE BIOLOGICAL ASSOCIATION STUDENT BURSARIES

Marine Biological Association of the United Kingdom
Attn: Director
Laboratory
Citadel Hill
Plymouth PL1 2PB
England
44 1752 633331   Fax: 44 1752 669762
E-mail: sjha@mba.ac.uk
Web site: www1.npm.ac.uk/mba

Purpose To provide funding to undergraduate students from any country who are interested in gaining research experience in the marine sciences at the Marine Biological Association of the United Kingdom's laboratory in Plymouth.

Eligibility Undergraduate students from any country are eligible to apply for this program, if they are interested in gaining experience in research on marine biology or physiology in collaboration with resident scientists at the laboratory in Plymouth. Applicants need not be members of the association, but they are expected to become members if they receive a bursary.

Financial data Awards up to 1,000 pounds are available.

Special features Awards are funded from the Spooner Fund or, for botanists, from the Mary Parke Fund.

Number awarded Varies each year.

Deadline Applications may be submitted at any time, but students wishing to be considered for summer vacation should apply before the end of March.

[728]
MARTINUS NIJHOFF INTERNATIONAL WEST EUROPEAN SPECIALIST STUDY GRANT

American Library Association
Attn: Association of College and Research Libraries
50 East Huron Street
Chicago, IL 60611-2795
(312) 280-2516 (800) 545-2433, ext. 2516
Fax: (312) 280-2520 TDD: (312) 944-7298
E-mail: acrl@ala.org
Web site: www.ala.org/acrl

Purpose To provide financial support for travel and research pertaining to west European studies, librarianship, or the book trade.

Eligibility Applicants must be personal members of the American Library Association (ALA) who can document their ability to complete a study of the acquisition, organization, or use of library materials from or relating to western Europe.

Financial data The award covers air travel to and from Europe, transportation in Europe, and lodging and board, to a maximum of 4,500 Euros or U.S. dollar equivalent.

Duration No more than 14 consecutive days.

Special features Established in 1985, this grant is funded by Swets Blackwell and administered by the Western European Specialists Section of ALA's Association of College and Research Libraries.

Limitations Funds may not be used for salaries, research-related supplies, publication costs, conference fees, or equipment purchases.

Number awarded 1 each year.

Deadline November of each year.

[729]
MARY BALL WASHINGTON CHAIR IN AMERICAN HISTORY

Council for International Exchange of Scholars
3007 Tilden Street, N.W., Suite 5L
Washington, DC 20008-3009
(202) 686-6245 Fax: (202) 362-3442
E-mail: scholars@cies.iie.org
Web site: www.iie.org/cies

Purpose To allow distinguished American scholars to lecture on American history at University College in Dublin, Ireland.

Eligibility The chair will be filled from among applicants whose credentials demonstrate distinguished research and teaching in an area of specialization in American history. Preference is given to 20th-century historians who specialize in the American presidency or American diplomatic history, but other specialties are considered. Both junior and senior scholars may apply. Applicants must be U.S. citizens.

Financial data The stipend is the Euro equivalent of approximately 46,000 Irish punts; a supplemental allowance of $5,000 is also provided to cover travel and incidentals.

Duration 9 months.

Special features This is a Fulbright scholar program, sponsored by the Bureau of Educational and Cultural Affairs of the U.S. Department of State and administered by the Council for International Exchange of Scholars. This appointment is the only permanently endowed chair in American studies at an Irish university. The scholar must teach 3 courses at the advanced undergraduate level and assist with tutorials; 1 course is broadly based and the other 2 are more specialized.

Number awarded 1 each year.

Deadline April of each year.

[730]
MARY EWART JUNIOR RESEARCH FELLOWSHIP

University of Oxford
Somerville College
Attn: College Secretary
Woodstock Road
Oxford OX2 6HD
England
44 1865 270600 Fax: 44 1865 270620
E-mail: secretariat@somerville.ox.ac.uk
Web site: www.some.ox.ac.uk

Purpose To provide financial support to postgraduate students interested in pursuing research at Somerville College of the University of Oxford in England.

Eligibility Candidates for the award must be interested in using the facilities of Somerville College to pursue a research project in a field that is announced when the fellowship is offered. The fellowship is intended for a relatively junior scholar, but that may be a person of any age.

Financial data The annual stipend is approximately 12,520 pounds. Free room and board at the college are also offered, except during the brief periods when the school is closed. Married recipients cannot be housed on campus; for them and other non-residential fellows, a housing allowance of 750 pounds per year is available.

Duration 3 years; nonrenewable.

Limitations Semifinalists will be interviewed at Somerville College. While overnight accommodations will be provided free of charge, applicants must pay their own traveling expenses. Recipients are expected to pursue a line of study approved by the governing body, to present an annual report on their work to the governing body, and to reside in Oxford during the fellowship period, unless the circumstances of their work require other arrangements. Permission to reside outside of Oxford for any part of the tenure of the fellowship must be obtained from the governing board and will be granted only when there are valid academic reasons. The fellow is not expected to hold another appointment but, with the permission of the governing body, may undertake university or college teaching up to 6 hours per week.

Number awarded 1 every 3 years (2004, 2007).

Deadline January of the competition year.

[731]
MARY ISABEL SIBLEY FELLOWSHIP FOR FRENCH STUDIES

Phi Beta Kappa Society
1785 Massachusetts Avenue, N.W., Fourth Floor
Washington, DC 20036
(202) 265-3808   Fax: (202) 986-1601
E-mail: lsurles@pbk.org
Web site: www.pbk.org

Purpose To support women involved in advanced research or writing projects dealing with French language or literature.

Eligibility Candidates must be unmarried women between 25 and 35 years of age who have demonstrated their ability to carry on original research. They must hold the doctorate or have fulfilled all the requirements for the doctorate except the dissertation, and they must be planning to devote full time to their research during the fellowship year. Eligibility is not restricted to members of Phi Beta Kappa or to U.S. citizens.

Financial data The award carries a stipend of $20,000, one half of which will be paid after June 1 following the award and the balance 6 months later.

Duration 1 year (the fellowship is offered in even-numbered years only).

Limitations Periodic progress reports are not required, but they are welcomed. It is the hope of the committee that the results of the year of research will be made available in some form, although no pressure for publication will be put on the recipient.

Number awarded 1 every other year.

Deadline January of even-numbered years.

[732]
MARY ISABEL SIBLEY FELLOWSHIP FOR GREEK STUDIES

Phi Beta Kappa Society
1785 Massachusetts Avenue, N.W., Fourth Floor
Washington, DC 20036
(202) 265-3808   Fax: (202) 986-1601
E-mail: lsurles@pbk.org
Web site: www.pbk.org

Purpose To support women involved in advanced research or writing projects dealing with Greek language, literature, history, or archaeology.

Eligibility Candidates must be unmarried women between 25 and 35 years of age who have demonstrated their ability to carry on original research. They must hold the doctorate or have fulfilled all the requirements for the doctorate except the dissertation, and they must be planning to devote full time to their research during the fellowship year. Eligibility is not restricted to members of Phi Beta Kappa or to U.S. citizens.

Financial data The award carries a stipend of $20,000, one half of which will be paid after June 1 following the award and the balance 6 months later.

Duration 1 year (the fellowship is offered in odd-numbered years only).

Limitations Periodic progress reports are not required, but they are welcomed. It is the hope of the committee that the results of the year of research will be made available in some form, although no pressure for publication will be put on the recipient.

Number awarded 1 every other year.

Deadline January of odd-numbered years.

[733]
MARY SOMERVILLE JUNIOR RESEARCH FELLOWSHIP

University of Oxford
Somerville College
Attn: College Secretary
Woodstock Road
Oxford OX2 6HD
England
44 1865 270600   Fax: 44 1865 270620
E-mail: secretariat@somerville.ox.ac.uk
Web site: www.some.ox.ac.uk

Purpose To provide financial support to postgraduate students interested in conducting research at Somerville College of the University of Oxford in England.

Eligibility Candidates for the fellowship must be interested in using the facilities of Somerville College to pursue a research project in a field that is announced when the fellowship is offered. The fellowship is intended for a relatively junior scholar, but that may be a person of any age.

Financial data The annual stipend is approximately 12,520 pounds. Free room and board at the college is also offered, except during the brief periods when the school is closed. Married recipients cannot be housed on campus; for them and other non-residential fellows, a housing allowance of 750 pounds per year is available.

Duration 3 years; nonrenewable.

Limitations Semifinalists are interviewed at Somerville College. While overnight accommodations are provided free of charge, applicants must pay their own traveling expenses. Recipients are expected to pursue a line of study approved by the governing body, to present an annual report on their work to the governing body, and to reside in Oxford during the fellowship period, unless the circumstances of their work require other arrangements. Permission to reside outside of Oxford for any part of the tenure of the fellowship must be obtained from the governing board and will be granted only when there are valid academic reasons. The fellow is not expected to hold another appointment but, with the permission of the governing body, may undertake university or college teaching up to 6 hours per week.

Number awarded 1 every 3 years (2003, 2006).

Deadline January of years in which the fellowship is awarded.

[734]
MASARYK AWARD
Council for International Exchange of Scholars
3007 Tilden Street, N.W., Suite 5L
Washington, DC 20008-3009
(202) 686-6249   Fax: (202) 362-3442
E-mail: scholars@cies.iie.org
Web site: www.iie.org/cies

Purpose To provide funding to American scholars interested in teaching and conducting research on nongovernment (NGO) management and development in the Czech Republic.

Eligibility This program is open to established scholars and those early in their career with a specialization in NGO management and development. Professionals with equivalent experience are also eligible. Applicants must be interested in teaching undergraduate and graduate courses and conducting research in their area of specialization at an institution in the Czech Republic. U.S. citizenship is required.

Financial data The stipend is $2,000 per month for researchers, $2,700 per month for lecturers at the rank of assistant professor or below, or $2,900 per month for lecturers at the rank of associate or full professor. Also provided is a dependent allowance of $200 per month for 1 dependent or $350 per month for 2 or more dependents. Reimbursement for housing costs is provided up to 10,000 Czech crowns for a single grantee, 11,500 crowns for grantees with 1 dependent, or 13,000 crowns for grantees with 2 or more dependents. The travel and relocation allowance is $2,000 for the grantee, $500 for 1 dependent, or $1,000 for 2 or more dependents. A research allowance of $750 is provided for research grants of up to 4 months or $1,500 for research grants of 5 months or more.

Duration 4 to 9 months for lecturing awards, beginning in February or September. Research grants are 3 to 9 months.

Special features This is a Fulbright scholar program, sponsored by the Bureau of Educational and Cultural Affairs of the U.S. Department of State and administered by the Council for International Exchange of Scholars. Grantees may also assist with curriculum and program development, as requested.

Number awarded 1 each year.
Deadline July of each year.

[735]
MAUDE CLARKE VISITING PROFESSORSHIP
Queen's University of Belfast
Attn: Academic Council Office
Administration Building
Belfast BT7 1NN
Northern Ireland
44 28 9027 3006   Fax: 44 28 9031 3537
E-mail: academic.council@qub.ac.uk
Web site: www.qub.ac.uk

Purpose To offer women a visiting professorship at Queen's University of Belfast in Northern Ireland.

Eligibility Candidates may be women who have either a proven academic standing and appropriate achievement in research and scholarship, or who have attained professional eminence in industry, business, government service, the professions, the arts, medicine, engineering, or the sciences. They may be from any country and must be interested in a short-term assignment in Northern Ireland. The assignment may be in the field of women's studies. Normally, candidates should be on paid leave of absence from their employment.

Financial data The stipend is 1,600 pounds; funds are to be used to cover travel and living expenses.

Duration 1 month.
Number awarded 1 each year.
Deadline October of each year.

[736]
MAX HAYWARD FELLOWSHIP IN RUSSIAN LITERATURE
University of Oxford
St. Antony's College
Attn: Secretary, Russian and East European Center
62 Woodstock Road
Oxford OX2 6JF
England
44 1865 284724   Fax: 44 1865 310518
E-mail: study.enquiries@sant.ox.ac.uk
Web site: www.sant.ox.ac.uk

Purpose To provide funding to postdoctoral scholars from any country who are interested in working in Russian literature at St. Antony's College of the University of Oxford in England.

Eligibility This program is open to postdoctoral scholars from any country who are interested in working in the field of Russian literature while in residence at St. Antony's. Applicants may engage in research, criticism, editing, translation, preparation of a thesis for publication, or other forms of literary scholarship, broadly defined, that may embrace themes on literature and society.

Financial data The stipend is 10,000 pounds with accommodations for a single person at the college or 15,500 without accommodations. Free lunches and special dinners are also provided.

Duration 1 academic year.
Number awarded This fellowship is offered periodically.
Deadline February of the years in which the fellowship is offered.

[737]
MAX PLANCK INSTITUTE FOR THE HISTORY OF SCIENCE DOCTORAL FELLOWSHIPS
Max Planck Institute for the History of Science
Wilhelmstrasse 44
D-10117 Berlin
Germany
49 30 226 67210   Fax: 49 30 226 67299
E-mail: jsr@mpiwg-berlin.mpg.de
Web site: www.mpiwg-berlin.mpg.de

Purpose To provide financial support to doctoral students from any country interested in conducting research on the history of science in Germany.

Eligibility This program is open to doctoral candidates of all nationalities who have a background in history of science, cultural studies, or media history. Applicants must be interested in conducting research in Germany on such topics as the relations between experimental phonetics and communication

technology, the experimentalization of life, and the evolution of forms for expressing and transmitting experiments in science and art. Other proposals around the theme of experimentation in science, art, literature, and technology are especially welcomed. Women are encouraged to apply. Other qualifications being equal, preference is given to candidates with disabilities.
Financial data The monthly stipend for applicants from abroad is the Euro equivalent of 1,800 to 2,100 Deutsche marks.
Duration 2 and a half years.
Limitations Fellows are required to be in residence in Berlin at the Max-Planck-Institut für Wissenschaftsgeschichte (Max Planck Institute for the History of Science).
Number awarded 1 each year.
Deadline October of each year.

[738]
MAX PLANCK INSTITUTE FOR THE HISTORY OF SCIENCE POSTDOCTORAL FELLOWSHIPS

Max Planck Institute for the History of Science
Wilhelmstrasse 44
D-10117 Berlin
Germany
49 30 226 67210   Fax: 49 30 226 67299
E-mail: jsr@mpiwg-berlin.mpg.de
Web site: www.mpiwg-berlin.mpg.de

Purpose To support research in Germany that combines elements from the history of science with the philosophy of science and/or the history of philosophy.
Eligibility This program is open to scholars of all nationalities who completed their doctorate in the history of science within the past 5 years. Projects on the following topics are especially welcomed: digital image processing and computer modeling, modes of classification in the 18th and 19th centuries, and relations between academic chemistry and chemical workshops or industry in the 18th and 19th centuries. Research must be conducted in Berlin at the Max-Planck-Institut für Wissenschaftsgeschichte (Max Planck Institute for the History of Science). Women are encouraged to apply. Other qualifications being equal, preference is given to candidates with disabilities.
Financial data The monthly stipend for applicants from abroad is the Euro equivalent of 3,400 Deutsche marks.
Duration Up to 2 years, beginning in spring.
Number awarded 1 each year.
Deadline December of each year.

[739]
MAX PLANCK RESEARCH AWARDS FOR INTERNATIONAL COOPERATION

Alexander von Humboldt Foundation
Attn: U.S. Liaison Office
1012 14th Street, N.W., Suite 301
Washington, DC 20005
(202) 783-1907   Fax: (202) 783-1908
E-mail: avh@bellatlantic.net
Web site: www.humboldt-foundation.de

Purpose To provide funding for long-term cooperative research projects between German and non-German scholars.
Eligibility Eligible to be nominated for this program are internationally recognized non-German and German scholars who are interested in conducting long-term, project-oriented cooperative research. The foreign award winners, who may be from any discipline and country, cooperate with German scholars in Germany while German award winners cooperate with foreign scholars in their countries. Nominations may only be submitted by presidents of German universities, academies of sciences, the Max Planck Society for the Advancement of Science, the Hermann von Helmholtz Association of German Research Centres, the Fraunhofer Society, or the German Research Association; by former Max Planck Research Award winners; and by former members of the selection committee.
Financial data The total value of the award is the Euro equivalent of up to 250,000 Deutsche marks to be used for travel, research stays at partner institutions, joint academic conferences, workshops, supplies, and research support personnel. Funds are not available to cover the personal salaries of award winners or their partners.
Duration 3 years; may be extended for 2 additional years.
Special features These awards are jointly sponsored by the Alexander von Humboldt Foundation and the Max Planck Society for the Advancement of Science.
Number awarded 12 each year: 6 pairs of German and non-German scholars.
Deadline March of each year.

[740]
MAX RHEINSTEIN SENIOR FELLOWSHIPS FOR THE STUDY OF LAW IN THE FEDERAL REPUBLIC OF GERMANY

Alexander von Humboldt Foundation
Attn: U.S. Liaison Office
1012 14th Street, N.W., Suite 301
Washington, DC 20005
(202) 783-1907   Fax: (202) 783-1908
E-mail: avh@bellatlantic.net
Web site: www.humboldtfoundation.org

Purpose To enable established American legal scholars to conduct research in Germany.
Eligibility Applicants must have been active in teaching and/or research at an American university for at least 5 years and have already distinguished themselves through legal publications. Candidates must be interested in conducting research in Germany, able to demonstrate proficiency in German, and no more then 40 years of age.
Financial data The fellowships provide a stipend of the Euro equivalent of 3,000 to 3,300 Deutsche marks per month, round-trip airfare for recipient only, an allowance of the Euro equivalent of DM 380 per month for spouses accompanying the recipient for at least 3 months, and the full cost of language training for 2 to 4 months preceding the fellowship term.
Duration From 6 to 12 months; may be extended in exceptional cases.
Special features Originally founded in 1860, the Alexander von Humboldt Foundation was re-established in 1953 by the German government, which provides the major portion (94 percent) of its funds.
Number awarded 1 or 2 each year.

[741]
MBL SCIENCE WRITING FELLOWSHIPS PROGRAM

Woods Hole Marine Biological Laboratory
Attn: Communications Office
7 MBL Street
Woods Hole, MA 02543-1015
(508) 289-7423   Fax: (508) 457-1924
E-mail: pclapp@mbl.edu
Web site: www.mbl.edu

Purpose To provide research experience or professional development opportunities at the Marine Biology Laboratory (MBL) and selected countries for science reporters and editors.

Eligibility Science editors and reporters who have at least 2 years of experience are eligible to apply for fellowships at MBL. Some fellowship opportunities are also available abroad. Preference is given to print and broadcast journalists with staff positions. Freelancers may also be considered. Members of minority groups and women are strongly encouraged to apply.

Financial data Fellowship support covers the cost of the laboratory course, tuition, housing, library fees, and round-trip transportation for the fellow only. Fellows from other countries are expected to pay for their own travel to the United States.

Duration Fellows first participate in either of 2 laboratory courses (molecular and cellular laboratory techniques or environmental science) for 1 week. Some fellows then stay for an additional 3 to 7 weeks to do field research in ecology (in the United States or abroad) or to follow the lectures and laboratory sessions in such disciplines as embryology, microbiology, physiology, parasitology, and neurobiology.

Special features Fellows attend lectures with graduate students on the latest research methods, participate in laboratory assignments with investigators carrying out research, and are often given projects of their own to conduct.

Number awarded Varies each year; at least 1 is awarded to a reporter wishing to participate in Arctic ecosystems research on the North Slope of Alaska's Brooks Range; depending on funding, other fellowships opportunities may be available at field sites in Brazil and Sweden.

Deadline March of each year.

[742]
MELLON RESEARCH FELLOWSHIP IN AMERICAN HISTORY

University of Cambridge
Faculty of History
Attn: Secretary, Managers to the Mellon Fellowship Fund
West Road
Cambridge CB3 9EF
England
44 1223 335317   Fax: 44 1223 335968
E-mail: agh21@cus.cam.ac.uk
Web site: www.hist.cam.ac.uk

Purpose To provide financial assistance to scholars from other countries who want to conduct research on American history at the University of Cambridge in England.

Eligibility Postdoctoral candidates from any country (outside of England) are eligible to apply if they have already earned their doctoral degree, wish to be affiliated with the University of Cambridge, and are interested in conducting American history research (from the colonial period) during the fellowship period. Applicants must be proficient in English.

Financial data The stipend ranges from 16,286 to 24,479 pounds.

Duration 1 year; may be renewed for up to 3 additional years.

Number awarded 1, when a vacancy occurs.

Deadline January in the years when a vacancy is available.

[743]
MERES SENIOR STUDENTSHIPS FOR MEDICAL RESEARCH

University of Cambridge
St. John's College
Attn: The Master
St. John's Street
Cambridge CB2 1TP
England
44 1223 338635   Fax: 44 1223 338707
E-mail: Enquiries@joh.cam.ac.uk
Web site: www.joh.cam.ac.uk

Purpose To bring outstanding medical researchers from around the world to St. John's College of the University of Cambridge in England.

Eligibility Candidates may be from any country. They should hold a Ph.D. degree or have other substantial research experience and be interested in conducting medical research either at the University of Cambridge or in the Cambridge area. A degree in medicine or surgery is not a requirement.

Financial data The maximum stipend is 29,048 pounds per year.

Duration From 1 to 3 years.

Number awarded 1 or more on an irregular basis. This program was last offered in 1999.

Deadline May in the years when offered.

[744]
MERTON COLLEGE JUNIOR RESEARCH FELLOWSHIPS

University of Oxford
Merton College
Attn: The Warden's Secretary
Oxford OX1 4JD
England
44 1865 276352   Fax: 44 1865 276282
Web site: www.ox.ac.uk

Purpose To provide funding to junior investigators interested in conducting research at Merton College of the University of Oxford in England.

Eligibility This program is open to scholars in designated fields of the arts and sciences who are nearing completion of their doctoral research or have begun postdoctoral study.

Researchers who have held a comparable appointment at a college in the Universities of Cambridge or Oxford or have completed more than 6 years of postgraduate study or research are not eligible. Applicants must be interested in undertaking a specific research project at Oxford.

Financial data The fellow receives a stipend of 14,851 pounds per year, free meals at High Table, and free accommodations at the college or an annual housing allowance of 2,082 pounds.

Duration 3 years.

Special features In the most recent offering of these fellowships, the fields were biochemistry, computer science, economics, geology, metallurgy, Oriental studies, philosophy, physics, politics, and theology.

Number awarded 4 (2 in the arts and 2 in the sciences) on a triennial schedule: 2004-05, 2007-08.

Deadline December of the year prior to the fellowship's availability.

[745]
MICKEY LELAND–BILL EMERSON INTERNATIONAL HUNGER FELLOWS PROGRAM

Congressional Hunger Center
229 1/2 Pennsylvania Avenue, S.E.
Washington, DC 20003
(202) 547-7022   Fax: (202) 547-7575
E-mail: fellows@hungercenter.org
Web site: www.hungercenter.org/international/int.htm

Purpose To provide emerging leaders in the fight against hunger with an opportunity to participate in field projects at sites in developing countries.

Eligibility This program is open to U.S. citizens who have a bachelor's degree, either a graduate degree or significant experience working to fight hunger, at least 6 months of continuous anti-poverty or sustainable development work in a developing country, written and spoken proficiency in a language appropriate to a field placement, demonstrated leadership qualities and abilities, creativity and initiative in problem solving, and a strong commitment to alleviating hunger and poverty with an enthusiasm for day-to-day work. Applicants must be interested in participating in a program that includes 1) work at field sites in sub-Saharan Africa, south Asia, Central America, and the Caribbean where they work in anti-hunger and development activities and 2) a policy placement in Rome (where they work with U.N. food institutions such as UNFAO, UNWFP, or IFAD) or in Washington, D.C., Baltimore, or Boston (where they work at the U.S. headquarters of the organizations at which they were placed during their field experience). Selection is based on the applicants' commitment to social change, diversity of experience and perspective, vision for the future, demonstrated leadership potential, and willingness to learn and have their lives changed by the experience.

Financial data Fellows receive a stipend of $1,000 per month. During their policy placement, they also receive a housing allowance. The program also pays for medical insurance and travel to and from field placements. Upon completion of the program, fellows receive an end-of-service award to help them make the transition to the next phase of their career.

Duration 3 years, including a 2-year placement in the field in sub-Saharan Africa, south Asia, Central America, or the Caribbean and a 1-year policy placement in Rome or the United States.

Number awarded 10 each year. Field assignments are provided for 4 fellows in sub-Saharan Africa, 3 in south Asia, and 3 in Central America or the Caribbean. Alternatively, 1 fellow may be placed in North Korea. For their policy assignments, 3 fellows are placed in Rome and the remaining fellows in Washington, D.C., Baltimore, or Boston.

Deadline January of each year.

[746]
MICROSOFT RESEARCH FELLOWSHIP

University of Cambridge
Darwin College
Attn: Master
Silver Street
Cambridge CB3 9EU
England
44 1223 335660   Fax: 44 1223 335667
E-mail: deanery@dar.cam.ac.uk
Web site: www.dar.cam.ac.uk

Purpose To provide funding to postdoctoral scholars interested in conducting research in the field of adaptive computing at Darwin College of the University of Cambridge in England.

Eligibility This program is open to scholars from any country who are interested in conducting research at Darwin College in the field of adaptive computing, including such topics as pattern recognition, probabilistic inference, statistical learning theory, and computer vision. Applicants must have a doctorate or an equivalent qualification, or expect to have submitted their thesis before taking up the fellowship. They may be of any age.

Financial data The stipend depends on age and experience. Other benefits include limited free meals in college, accommodations at the college or an accommodation allowance, and funding for conference participation.

Duration 2 years.

Special features Funding for this fellowship is provided by Microsoft Research Limited.

Number awarded This fellowship is offered whenever it is available; it is next scheduled for 2004.

Deadline October in the years it is available.

[747]
MIDDLEBURY JUNIOR RESEARCH FELLOWSHIP

University of Oxford
Harris Manchester College
Attn: Academic Administrator
Mansfield Road
Oxford OX1 3TD
England
44 1865 271006   Fax: 44 1865 271012
E-mail: hmcinfo@sable.ox.ac.uk
Web site: www.hmc.ox.ac.uk

Purpose To provide funding to postdoctoral scholars from any country who wish to participate in a program that combines research at Harris Manchester College of the University of Oxford in England with teaching at Middlebury College in Vermont.

Eligibility This program is open to residents of any country who are interested in conducting postdoctoral research while in residence at Harris Manchester College. Applicants must also be qualified to teach at Middlebury College. They must be at least 30 years of age.

Financial data The stipend is $12,000 per year. Accommodations and meals are provided at Harris Manchester.

Duration 3 years.

Special features Fellows spend the month of January teaching at Middlebury and the remainder of the year at Oxford.

Number awarded This fellowship is awarded periodically. It was last offered in 2002.

[748]
MILENA JESENSKA FELLOWSHIPS FOR JOURNALISTS

Institut für die Wissenschaften vom Menschen
Attn: Fellows Coordinator
Spittelauer Lände 3
A-1090 Vienna
Austria
43 1 313 58 335   Fax: 43 1 313 58 30
E-mail: iwm@iwm.univie.ac.at
Web site: www.univie.ac.at/iwm

Purpose To provide funding to journalists who wish to work in Vienna on long-term projects of their own choice.

Eligibility This program is open to journalists who wish to conduct writing projects in Vienna. Preference is given to applicants who propose projects in fields of special interest to the institute, including political philosophy of the 19th and 20th centuries, gender studies, political and social transformation in central and eastern Europe, reform of the welfare state, and reform of higher education and research. Applicants should submit a curriculum vitae and a concise project proposal (not more than 3 double-spaced pages) in English or German.

Financial data Fellows receive a stipend of the Euro equivalent of 105,000 Austrian schillings, a personal computer, office space, access to in-house and Viennese research facilities, and a travel grant up to the EUR equivalent of ATS 25,000 for research visits to neighboring countries.

Duration 3 months.

Special features These fellowships are jointly administered by the Institut für die Wissenschaften vom Menschen (Institute for Human Sciences) and the Project Syndicate (an association of 45 newspapers in 34 countries). They are named in honor of Milena Jesenská, a journalist who mediated between the Czech and German cultures in Bohemia until her death in 1944 in a Nazi concentration camp. Funding is provided by the European Cultural Foundation of Amsterdam.

Number awarded 2 each year.

Deadline January of each year.

[749]
MINORITY STUDIES REGIONAL RESEARCH PROGRAM

Council for International Exchange of Scholars
3007 Tilden Street, N.W., Suite 5L
Washington, DC 20008-3009
(202) 686-6249   Fax: (202) 362-3442
E-mail: scholars@cies.iie.org
Web site: www.iie.org/cies

Purpose To provide funding to American scholars interested in conducting research on minority studies in central and eastern Europe.

Eligibility This program is open to U.S. citizens who possess a doctorate in an academic field related to minority studies, including Holocaust studies, Jewish studies, the Roma, ethnic studies, ethnic conflict and resolution, minority rights, and religious issues. Applicants must be interested in conducting research in Belarus, Bosnia and Hercegovina, Bulgaria, Croatia, the Czech Republic, Estonia, Hungary, Latvia, Lithuania, the former Yugoslav Republic of Macedonia, Poland, Romania, the Slovak Republic, Slovenia, or Ukraine. Proposals involving research in more than 1 country are especially welcome. Preference is given to proposals that 1) involve collaboration with scholars from host countries; 2) contribute to development of innovative curriculum and/or new research methodologies; or 3) include plans for informal seminars or potential workshops. The research should result in publications, textbooks, or new academic programs that contribute to greater public understanding of the critical issues affecting minorities. U.S. citizenship and language proficiency appropriate to the research project are required.

Financial data The program provides funds for international and intercountry travel, living and research allowances, and a monthly stipend.

Duration 3 to 10 months.

Special features This is a Fulbright scholar program, sponsored by the Bureau of Educational and Cultural Affairs of the U.S. Department of State and administered by the Council for International Exchange of Scholars.

Number awarded Up to 3 each year.

Deadline July of each year.

[750]
MITTAG-LEFFLER INSTITUTE GRANTS

Mittag-Leffler Institute
Attn: Institute Director
Auravägen 17
S-182 62 Djursholm
Sweden
46 8 622 0560   Fax: 46 8 622 0589
E-mail: widman@ml.kva.se
Web site: www.ml.kva.se

Purpose To provide funding for mathematicians who wish to conduct research at the Mittag-Leffler Institute in Sweden.

Eligibility Recent Ph.D.s or advanced graduate students in mathematics from any country are eligible to apply if their research requires them to use the resources of the Mittag-Leffler Institute. Preference is given to applications for longer stays.

Financial data The stipend is 12,000 Swedish krona per month, plus travel expenses to and from Stockholm.
Duration 10 months, from September through June.
Special features The Mittag-Leffler Institute, founded in 1916 but not activated until 1969, is 1 of 7 scientific institutes within the Royal Swedish Academy of Sciences. Each year it selects a topic and invites experts to work at the Institute for 1 or 2 months, conduct seminars, and interact with the younger scholars resident there. A recent topic was "Probability and Conformal Mappings."
Deadline January of each year.

[751] MODERN ARCHITECTURE AND TOWN PLANNING TRUST AWARDS

Royal Institute of British Architects
Attn: Centre for Architectural Education
66 Portland Place
London W1N 4AD
England
44 20 7580 5533   Fax: 44 20 7255 1541
E-mail: admin@inst.riba.org
Web site: www.architecture.com

Purpose To provide financial assistance to young people who wish to pursue a program of education or research in the United Kingdom related to contemporary and recent architecture.
Eligibility Eligible to apply are young people, whether or not they are graduates or have completed a normal course of architectural studies, who are interested in pursuing a program of education or research in the United Kingdom related to contemporary and recent architecture, including the decoration and furnishing of buildings and the arrangement and landscaping of land adjacent to buildings in any part of the world. Teachers and practicing architects may also apply. Applications are accepted from outside the United Kingdom, but the work must be conducted under the supervision of a scholar within the U.K.
Financial data Grants are either 10,000 or 6,000 pounds. Funds may be used to cover stipends, travel expenses, staff expenses, publication costs, and other research-related expenses, but not course fees or subsistence costs.
Duration Up to 2 years.
Number awarded 5 every other year: 1 at 10,000 pounds and 4 at 6,000 pounds.
Deadline April of even-numbered years.

[752] MONSANTO SENIOR RESEARCH FELLOWSHIP

University of Oxford
Exeter College
Attn: The Rector
Oxford OX1 3DP
England
44 1865 279600   Fax: 44 1865 279645
E-mail: academic.administration@exeter.ox.ac.uk
Web site: www.exeter.ox.ac.uk

Purpose To provide funding to postdoctoral scholars from any country who wish to conduct biological or biochemical research at Exeter College of the University of Oxford in England.
Eligibility This program is open to residents of any country who are interested in conducting postdoctoral research in molecular or cellular biology or in biochemistry while in residence at Exeter College.
Financial data A stipend is provided at the rate of Grade 1A at the University of Oxford.
Duration 3 years; may be renewed for 2 additional years.
Number awarded This fellowship is awarded periodically. It is next scheduled for 2004.

[753] MOSES AND MARY FINLEY RESEARCH FELLOWSHIP

University of Cambridge
Darwin College
Attn: Master
Silver Street
Cambridge CB3 9EU
England
44 1223 335660   Fax: 44 1223 335667
E-mail: deanery@dar.cam.ac.uk
Web site: www.dar.cam.ac.uk

Purpose To provide funding to postdoctoral scholars interested in conducting research in the field of ancient history at Darwin College of the University of Cambridge in England.
Eligibility This program is open to scholars from any country who are interested in conducting research at Darwin College in the field of ancient history of the Mediterranean world and/or the Near East to the end of the 6th century. Applicants must be younger than 35 years of age and either 1) hold a Ph.D. or equivalent degree or 2) be able to present substantial amounts of written work, published or unpublished.
Financial data The annual stipend is 13,050 or 13,930 pounds, depending on age and experience. Other benefits include limited free meals at the college, a travel and research allowance of up to 1,000 pounds per year, and a conference subsidy of 500 pounds per year.
Duration 3 years; may be renewed for 1 additional year.
Number awarded This fellowship is offered whenever it is available; it is next scheduled for 2003.
Deadline October in the years it is available.

[754] MUHAMMAD ALI ZAINAL ALIREZA FELLOWSHIP

Oxford Centre for Islamic Studies
Attn: Awards Secretary
George Street
Oxford OX1 2AR
England
44 1865 278730   Fax: 44 1865 248942
E-mail: islamic.studies@oxcis.ac.uk
Web site: www.oxcis.ac.uk

Purpose To provide funding to scholars interested in conducting research on Islamic art at the Oxford Centre for Islamic Studies in England.

Eligibility This program is open to scholars from any country. Applicants should be interested in promoting the practice and teaching of Islamic art and Arabic calligraphy. The research they propose must be conducted at the Oxford Centre for Islamic Studies.

Financial data A stipend is awarded (amount not specified).

Duration 9 months (although shorter periods are considered), beginning in October.

Special features The Oxford Centre for Islamic Studies is an associated institution of the University of Oxford and has links with universities and research centers throughout the Muslim world.

Number awarded 1 each year.

Deadline November of each year.

[755]
MULTIPLE SCLEROSIS SOCIETY OF GREAT BRITAIN AND NORTHERN IRELAND GRANTS

Multiple Sclerosis Society of Great Britain and Northern Ireland
c/o MS National Centre
372 Edgwave Road
London NW1 6ND
England
44 20 8438 0700   Fax: 44 20 8438 0701
E-mail: info@mssociety.org.uk
Web site; www.mssociety.org.uk

Purpose To provide financial assistance for research to be conducted in the United Kingdom on multiple sclerosis.

Eligibility Applications are accepted from nationals of all countries, normally for research to be conducted in the United Kingdom. The proposed research should attempt to answer a single question or a small group of related questions, and the application should indicate its relevance to multiple sclerosis. Grants are also awarded for Ph.D. studentships and to fund infrastructure.

Financial data Applications may include requests for personal support of the researcher, salary support for scientific and other assistants, other expenses, and apparatus.

Duration Up to 3 years.

Number awarded Varies each year.

Deadline January or July of each year.

[756]
MUNBY FELLOWSHIP IN BIBLIOGRAPHY

University of Cambridge Library
Attn: Deputy Librarian
West Road
Cambridge CB3 9DR
England
44 1223 333000   Fax: 44 1223 333160
E-mail: jh296@cam.ac.uk
Web site: www.cam.ac.uk

Purpose To sponsor bibliographic research based on the collections of the libraries of the University of Cambridge in England.

Eligibility This program is open to university graduates in any discipline, at any university, and of any nationality. Applicants must be interested in conducting bibliographical research on a topic that may be of their own choosing but should be based, at least in part, directly or indirectly on the collections of the university and colleges of Cambridge and be of benefit to scholars using them. Preference is given to younger scholars at postdoctoral or equivalent level.

Financial data The stipend is 17,000 pounds; employee's National Health Insurance contributions are deducted. Munby fellows are also offered a nonmonetary research or visiting fellowship at Darwin College, where they are entitled to take meals without payment; the College provides practical but not financial help in finding accommodations.

Duration 1 academic year.

Special features This fellowship was founded in memory of the late Alan Noel Latimer Munby, a long-time Librarian of King's College and a Syndic of the University Library. Fellows are given work space in the University Library and are permitted access to its collections on the same terms as members of its permanent staff.

Number awarded 1 each year.

Deadline September of each year.

[757]
MUSICAL COMPOSITION ROME PRIZE FELLOWSHIP

American Academy in Rome
Attn: Fellowship Coordinator
7 East 60th Street
New York, NY 10022-1001
(212) 751-7200   Fax: (212) 751-7220
E-mail: info@aarome.org
Web site: www.aarome.org

Purpose To provide financial support to composers who are interested in a residency at the American Academy in Rome.

Eligibility Applicants must hold at least a baccalaureate degree in music, musical composition, or its equivalent from an accredited institution. They must 1) be U.S. citizens; 2) be interested in a residency at the School of Fine Arts at the American Academy in Rome; and 3) submit at least 2 but not more than 3 scores (1 of which should have been written for a large ensemble or orchestra). Cassette tapes of the compositions are not required, but they are strongly recommended. Recordings in other formats are not acceptable. Full-time students are not eligible.

Financial data The fellowship provides a stipend of up to $20,000, meals, a bedroom with private bath, and a study or studio. Fellows with children under 18 are housed outside the McKim, Mead & White building and are provided with an allowance that helps cover the cost of off-campus housing.

Duration 1 year, beginning in September.

Special features The American Academy in Rome, founded in 1894 by the American architect Charles F. McKim, is a center for independent study and advanced research in the fine arts and humanities. It consists of a School of Fine Arts (including architecture, landscape architecture, design arts, painting and sculpture, musical composition, and literature) and a School of Classical Studies (including classical studies and archaeology, history of art, and post-classical humanistic/modern Italian studies).

Limitations There is a $40 application fee. Prize winners may not hold full-time jobs in Rome during their residencies.
Number awarded 2 each year.
Deadline November of each year.

[758]
NACBS DISSERTATION YEAR FELLOWSHIP
North American Conference on British Studies
c/o Brian Levack, Executive Secretary
University of Texas
Department of History
Austin, TX 78712
(512) 475-7204   Fax: (512) 475-7222
E-mail: levack@mail.texas.edu
Web site: www.nacbs.org

Purpose To provide financial assistance for American or Canadian graduate students interested in conducting dissertation research in the United Kingdom.
Eligibility This program is open to doctoral students who are interested in conducting dissertation research in the United Kingdom on any topic or era of British (including Scottish, Irish, and Imperial) history. They must have completed all degree requirements except the dissertation. Candidates must be nominated by their home institution (which must be in the United States or Canada); each institution may nominate 1 candidate.
Financial data The award is $6,000. The runner-up receives a $2,000 travel grant.
Duration At least 6 months.
Special features This program was established in 1988.
Limitations Recipients must conduct full-time research in the United Kingdom. They cannot hold any other major fellowship or assistantship while participating in this program.
Number awarded 1 fellowship and 1 travel grant are awarded each year.
Deadline March of each year.

[759]
NADIA ET LILI BOULANGER INTERNATIONAL FOUNDATION GRANTS
Nadia et Lili Boulanger International Foundation
Attn: Alexandra Laederich
25 avenue des Gobelins
F-75013 Paris
France
33 1 47 07 05 93   Fax: 33 1 45 35 09 43

Purpose To provide funding to nationals from any country for musical research or creative activities in France.
Eligibility Serious musicians from any country may apply for this support in France if they are between 20 and 35 years of age (in some cases, the foundation may waive this requirement). The program is open equally to performers, musicians, and scholars (research topics can be in either music history or theory).
Financial data The amount awarded varies, depending upon the scope of the funded project.
Duration Up to 1 year.

Special features This program is named for "two women musicians whose personalities bore the stamp of genius."
Number awarded 1 or more each year.
Deadline June of each year.

[760]
NAPIER RESEARCH PROFESSORSHIP
Royal Society
Attn: Executive Secretary
6 Carlton House Terrace
London SW1Y 5AG
England
44 20 7451 2542   Fax: 44 20 7451 2692
E-mail: UKResearch.Appointments@royalsoc.ac.uk
Web site: www.royalsoc.ac.uk

Purpose To provide funding to established scholars interested in conducting cancer-related research in the United Kingdom.
Eligibility This program is open to internationally respected scientists of any nationality who are interested in a professorship at an appropriate university or research institute in the United Kingdom. Applicants must be interested in conducting research "with the object of ascertaining the cause of cancer, including any corresponding allied disease and the means of prevention, cure and alleviation." Scientists who are currently employed outside the United Kingdom and wish to return are particularly encouraged to apply.
Financial data The salary provided by the Royal Society is the national professorial minimum plus 40 percent (currently 50,961 pounds). The host university or institute may supplement that salary if it so wishes. Professors receive a start-up grant when they begin their assignment and they may apply for payment of research expenses up to 16,000 pounds per year. Successful applicants from overseas receive some assistance with moving expenses.
Duration These professorships are intended to extend until normal retirement age, but funding from the Royal Society extends for 15 years for professors under 40 years of age or 10 years for those over 40 years of age (or until they reach 55 years of age, whichever is longer). After expiration of Royal Society funding, the university or research institute is solely responsible for the professorship.
Number awarded 1 each year.
Deadline August of each year.

[761]
NAPLES DISTINGUISHED CHAIR
Council for International Exchange of Scholars
3007 Tilden Street, N.W., Suite 5L
Washington, DC 20008-3009
(202) 686-6245   Fax: (202) 362-3442
E-mail: scholars@cies.iie.org
Web site: www.iie.org/cies

Purpose To provide funding for scholars to lecture on literature at the University of Naples in Italy.
Eligibility This program is open to U.S. citizens, preferably with the rank of full professor, who are interested in lecturing at the University of Naples on the introductory level and presenting a seminar for advanced students. The topic changes

periodically; recent topics have included 1) American literature and 2) civil and common law. A knowledge of Italian is useful but not required.

Financial data The stipend is the Euro equivalent of 16,800,000 Italian lire plus a settling-in allowance of the EUR equivalent of 1,500,000 lire. The grant also provides international travel (for the grantee only) plus the EUR equivalent of 200,000 lire per month for each accompanying dependent.

Duration 3 months.

Special features This is a Fulbright scholar program, sponsored by the Bureau of Educational and Cultural Affairs of the U.S. Department of State and administered by the Council for International Exchange of Scholars.

Number awarded 1 each year.

Deadline April of each year.

[762]
NATIONAL COUNCIL FOR EURASIAN AND EAST EUROPEAN RESEARCH COMPETITION

National Council for Eurasian and East European Research
910 17th Street, N.W., Suite 300
Washington, DC 20006
(202) 822-6950   Fax: (202) 822-6955
E-mail: nceeerdc@aol.com
Web site: www.nceeer.gov

Purpose To encourage and sustain high-quality collaborative research projects dealing with current developments in the former Soviet republics, eastern Europe, and Eurasia.

Eligibility This program is open to collaborative projects involving 2 or more U.S.-based postdoctoral scholars who are U.S. citizens or permanent residents. Although foreign scholars may participate in the collaboration, the 2 or more U.S.-based scholars' roles in the project must be principal and substantive. The field of study may be in the social sciences or humanities, including history, geography, demography, and environmental studies. Proposals for research may include such activities as research-specific training, especially involving graduate students in research projects; contact among scholars and specialists in government and private enterprise; development of data banks and other research aids; and dissemination of research data, methodology, and findings from Council-sponsored research. The proposals must involve research, to be conducted in the United States or abroad, on the following countries: Albania, Armenia, Belarus, Bosnia and Herzegovina, Bulgaria, Croatia, Czech Republic, Estonia, Georgia, Hungary, Kazakstan, Kyrgyzstan, Latvia, Lithuania, Moldova, Poland, Romania, Russia, Serbia (including Kosovo and Montenegro), Slovakia, Slovenia, Tajikistan, Turkmenistan, Ukraine, Uzbekistan, and the former Yugoslav Republic of Macedonia. Research related to the former German Democratic Republic or the natural sciences is not eligible.

Financial data The budget covers salaries and wages for the principal investigator and assistants, fringe benefits, foreign and domestic travel, supplies, materials, services, and institutional overhead. The maximum award is $70,000. At least 20 percent of the project cost must be provided by an institutional sponsor with nonfederal funds.

Duration Up to 2 years; shorter projects are encouraged.

Special features Funding for this program is provided by the U.S. Department of State under the Research and Training for Eastern Europe and the Independent States of the Former Soviet Union Act of 1983 (Title VIII).

Deadline February of each year.

[763]
NATIONAL COUNCIL FOR EURASIAN AND EAST EUROPEAN RESEARCH GRANTS

National Council for Eurasian and East European Research
910 17th Street, N.W., Suite 300
Washington, DC 20006
(202) 822-6950   Fax: (202) 822-6955
E-mail: nceeerdc@aol.com
Web site: www.nceeer.gov

Purpose To encourage and sustain high-quality individual research projects dealing with current developments in the former Soviet republics, eastern Europe, and Eurasia.

Eligibility This program is open to individual scholars who are U.S. citizens or permanent residents 1) at the postdoctoral level for academic participants or 2) with equivalent maturity and relevant professional employment for those from other fields. The field of study may be in the social sciences or humanities, including history, geography, demography, and environmental studies. Proposals for research may include such activities as research-specific training, especially involving graduate students in research projects; contact among scholars and specialists in government and private enterprise; development of data banks and other research aids; and dissemination of research data, methodology, and findings from Council-sponsored research. The proposals must involve research, to be conducted in the United States or abroad, on the following countries: Albania, Armenia, Belarus, Bosnia and Herzegovina, Bulgaria, Croatia, Czech Republic, Estonia, Georgia, Hungary, Kazakstan, Kyrgyzstan, Latvia, Lithuania, Moldova, Poland, Romania, Russia, Serbia (including Kosovo and Montenegro), Slovakia, Slovenia, Tajikistan, Turkmenistan, Ukraine, Uzbekistan, and the former Yugoslav Republic of Macedonia. Research related to the former German Democratic Republic or the natural sciences is not eligible.

Financial data The maximum award is $40,000.

Duration Up to 2 years; shorter projects are encouraged.

Special features Funding for this program is provided by the U.S. Department of State under the Research and Training for Eastern Europe and the Independent States of the Former Soviet Union Act of 1983 (Title VIII).

Deadline February of each year.

[764]
NATIONAL ENDOWMENT FOR THE HUMANITIES FELLOWSHIPS FOR RESEARCH IN TURKEY

American Research Institute in Turkey
c/o University of Pennsylvania Museum
33rd and Spruce Streets
Philadelphia, PA 19104-6324
(215) 898-3474　　　　　　Fax: (215) 898-0657
E-mail: leinwand@sas.upenn.edu
Web site: mec.sas.upenn.edu/ARIT

Purpose To provide funding to American scholars who wish to conduct research in Turkey.

Eligibility American postdoctorates are eligible to apply if they wish to conduct research in the humanities (including prehistory, history, art, archaeology, literature, linguistics, and the interdisciplinary aspects of cultural history) at the American Research Institute in Turkey (ARIT) in Istanbul or in Ankara.

Financial data Stipends range from $10,000 to $30,000, depending upon the scope of the funded proposal.

Duration 4 to 12 months.

Special features This program is supported by the National Endowment for the Humanities (NEH). ARIT maintains 2 research institutes in Turkey: ARIT-Istanbul has a research library focused on Byzantine, Ottoman, and modern studies of Turkey. ARIT-Ankara focuses on art, archaeology, and ancient history in its library. Both institutes have residential facilities for fellows and provide general assistance as well as introductions to colleagues, institutions, and authorities in Turkey.

Number awarded 2 to 3 each year.

Deadline November of each year.

[765]
NATIONAL ENDOWMENT FOR THE HUMANITIES POST-DOCTORAL RESEARCH FELLOWSHIPS TO NICOSIA

American Schools of Oriental Research
Attn: Administrative Director
656 Beacon Street, Fifth Floor
Boston, MA 02215-2010
(617) 353-6570　　　　　　Fax: (617) 353-6575
E-mail: asor@bu.edu
Web site: www.asor.org

Purpose To provide funding to postdoctoral scholars who wish to conduct research at the Cyprus American Archaeological Research Institute in Nicosia.

Eligibility Applicants must be U.S. citizens, permanent residents, or foreign nationals who have lived in the United States for the past 3 years, have earned the Ph.D. degree (or are recognized scholars), and are interested in conducting research in any field of the humanities that requires residence in Cyprus.

Financial data Stipends are paid at the rate of $30,000 per year.

Duration From 4 to 12 months.

Special features This program is jointly sponsored by the National Endowment for the Humanities (NEH) and the American Schools of Oriental Research (ASOR). Membership in ASOR is not required.

Number awarded 1 or more each year.

Deadline January of each year.

[766]
NATIONAL RESEARCH COUNCIL TWINNING PROGRAM

National Research Council
Attn: Office of International Affairs
2101 Constitution Avenue, N.W., FO 2060
Washington, DC 20418
(202) 334-2644　　　　　　Fax: (202) 334-2614
E-mail: ocee@nas.edu
Web site: www.nationalacademies.org/oia

Purpose To support American scientists and engineers who wish to participate in collaborative research programs with their counterparts in designated countries of central Europe and Eurasia.

Eligibility This program is open to U.S. citizens, nationals, and permanent residents who hold a Ph.D., are engaged in research careers (or research and teaching careers), are affiliated with an educational or research institution in the United States, and have existing contacts with researchers and/or institutions in the relevant countries. Applicants may be of any age, but preference is given to those who received their doctoral degrees within the past 6 years or who are entering into an international collaboration for the first time. Only proposals for collaborations in fields normally supported by the National Science Foundation (NSF) will be considered. Those include archaeology and anthropology; astronomy; biochemistry, biophysics, and genetics; biological sciences; chemistry; computer science; earth sciences; economics; engineering; environmental sciences; geography; history and philosophy of science; linguistics; mathematics; physics; political science; non-clinically oriented psychology; science and technology policy; and sociology. No proposals involving agricultural production; drug testing or development; research on the diagnosis, etiology, or treatment of physical or mental diseases or disorders; or the use of animal models of human diseases or conditions are accepted. Scientists and engineers who hold a current NSF grant and are eligible for an NSF international supplement are not eligible for this program. Selection is based on the professional accomplishments and qualifications of the U.S. applicants and foreign partners, the scientific merit and feasibility of the proposed research, its potential benefits to the U.S. and foreign partners and their institutions, and potential for the development of follow-on proposals to NSF for longer-term collaboration.

Financial data Grants generally range from $13,000 to $15,000, although higher amounts may be considered in exceptional circumstances. Funding requests must include round-trip travel between the United States and abroad, and may also include living expenses for the U.S. and/or European partner, scientific supplies, computer fees, and publication costs.

Duration Activities normally extend over a period of 2 years.

Special features Funding for this program comes from NSF; it is administered by the National Research Council, the operating arm of the National Academy of Sciences, National Academy of Engineering, and Institute of Medicine. It began in 1999 with grants to Georgia, Romania, and Ukraine; the program for 2000 provided grants to Estonia, Latvia, and Lithuania, and for 2001 to Ukraine.

Deadline September of each year.

[767]
NATIONAL SHAKESPEARE COMPETITION
English-Speaking Union
16 East 69th Street
New York, NY 10021
(212) 879-6800   Fax: (212) 772-2886
E-mail: info@english-speakingunion.org
Web site: www.english-speakingunion.org

Purpose To recognize and reward American high school students who participate in the National Shakespeare Competition.

Eligibility This program is open to students at high schools in the United States. Participants develop their language and public speaking skills through the memorization and interpretation of a monologue and sonnet. Students first compete in their local community and the winners advance to the national finals in New York.

Financial data The national winner receives a 2-week acting course at the Oxford School of Drama in England. The runner-up receives a $1,000 cash award.

Duration The competition is held annually.

Special features The program began in 1983.

Number awarded At the national level, 1 winner and 1 runner-up are selected.

Deadline The national finals are in April.

[768]
NATIONAL VOCAL COMPETITION FOR YOUNG OPERA SINGERS
Loren L. Zachary Society for the Performing Arts
Attn: Director, National Vocal Competition for Young Opera Singers
2250 Gloaming Way
Beverly Hills, CA 90210
(310) 276-2731   Fax: (310) 275-8245

Purpose To provide funding to American opera singers who are interested in traveling to Europe to audition.

Eligibility Female singers (21 to 33 years of age) and male singers (21 to 35 years of age) are eligible to compete if they are interested in singing in operas in Europe. Applicants must have completed full operatic training, be prepared to pursue a professional stage career, and be at all phases of the auditions.

Financial data The first-prize winner receives $10,000, a flight to Vienna, Austria, and cash prizes. Each final contestant receives a minimum of $1,000.

Duration This competition is held annually.

Special features This competition is conducted to identify singers who are qualified to sing in European opera houses. Regional auditions are held in New York in March and Los Angeles in April; the finals are in Los Angeles in June.

Limitations There is a $35 entrance fee.

Deadline January for the New York competition and March for the Los Angeles competition.

[769]
NATO COLLABORATIVE LINKAGE GRANTS
North Atlantic Treaty Organization
Attn: Scientific Affairs Division
Boulevard Leopold III
B-1110 Brussels
Belgium
32 2 707 4111   Fax: 32 2 707 4232
Web site: www.nato.int/science

Purpose To support collaborative scientific research by providing travel funding to teams in different member countries of the North Atlantic Treaty Organization (NATO) and those in Euro-Atlantic Partnership Council (EAPC) countries (including Eurasia).

Eligibility This program is open to collaborations between scientists in NATO countries (the United States, Canada, 14 countries in western Europe, and 3 countries in eastern Europe and Eurasia) and NATO's partner countries of the EAPC (15 former Soviet republics and 7 other nations in eastern Europe). Scientists of the Mediterranean Dialogue countries (Algeria, Egypt, Israel, Jordan, Mauritania, Morocco, and Tunisia) may also apply for a grant in cooperation with scientists from NATO countries. All applicant teams must be interested in conducting research in 1 of the 4 priority areas currently selected by NATO: physical and engineering science and technology (PST), life science and technology (LST), environmental and earth science and technology (EST), and security-related civil science and technology (SST).

Financial data Funding is provided to cover the costs incurred by investigators to visit the collaborating teams abroad. Amounts awarded are normally between $5,000 (for 1 year of collaboration by 2 or 3 scientists) to a maximum of $25,000 (for 2 years' collaboration by 5 research teams). Basic costs (salaries, equipment, consumables, page charges) should already be covered from other national sources. Support is not provided for 1) institutional overhead expenses; 2) scientists while on sabbatical or other extended leave abroad; 3) travel that is not related to the research project; 4) purely domestic travel; 5) visits for 1 researcher or 1 research group only; or 6) long study periods abroad.

Duration The grants may be used over a period of 1 to 2 years. During the time period of a grant, research visits are expected to be of short duration and should not exceed 2 months.

Number awarded Since 1960, support has been given to more than 6,000 joint projects. At present, about 600 grants are awarded each year (of which an average of 450 are for new projects).

Deadline Deadlines for PST grants are February, July, or October of each year; deadlines for LST and EST grants are March, August, or November of each year; deadlines for SST grants are January, April, or September of each year.

[770]
NATO EXPERT VISITS

North Atlantic Treaty Organization
Attn: Scientific Affairs Division
Boulevard Leopold III
B-1110 Brussels
Belgium
32 2 707 4111   Fax: 32 2 707 4232
Web site: www.nato.int/science

Purpose To provide financial assistance to scientists from member nations of the North Atlantic Treaty Organization (NATO) for visits to research laboratories in Euro-Atlantic Partnership Council (EAPC) countries (including Eurasia), and vice versa.

Eligibility Experts from NATO countries (the United States, Canada, 14 countries in western Europe, and 3 countries in eastern Europe) may visit research laboratories in an EAPC country (15 former Soviet republics and 7 countries in eastern Europe) to consult on current research projects. EAPC scientists may also visit a NATO country. Scientists in the 7 Mediterranean Dialogue countries (Algeria, Egypt, Israel, Jordan, Mauritania, Morocco, and Tunisia) are also eligible if they draw up applications in cooperation with a scientist from a NATO country. This program is available primarily, but not exclusively, for research in 1 of the 4 priority areas currently selected by NATO: physical and engineering science and technology (PST), life science and technology (LST), environmental and earth science and technology (EST), and security-related civil science and technology (SST). Applications must be submitted by the project director at the institute to be visited and signed by both the host institute project director and the visiting expert.

Financial data Fellows receive research, travel, and living (up to $100 per day) allowances. Support is not provided for 1) long study periods abroad, 2) salaries, stipends, or institutional overhead; 3) scientists on sabbatical or other extended leave abroad; or 4) attendance at conferences, symposia, workshops, etc.

Duration From a few days to 1 month.

Number awarded Varies each year.

Deadline Deadlines for PST grants are February, July, or October of each year; deadlines for LST and EST grants are March, August, or November of each year; deadlines for SST grants are January, April, or September of each year.

[771]
NEH POSTDOCTORAL FELLOWSHIPS AT THE AMERICAN ACADEMY IN ROME

American Academy in Rome
Attn: Fellowship Coordinator
7 East 60th Street
New York, NY 10022-1001
(212) 751-7200   Fax: (212) 751-7220
E-mail: info@aarome.org
Web site: www.aarome.org

Purpose To provide an opportunity for American postdoctoral scholars in the history of art, classical studies and archaeology, and post-classical humanistic/modern Italian studies to engage in research at the American Academy in Rome.

Eligibility This program is open to U.S. citizens or individuals who have resided in the United States for at least 3 years. Applicants must have a Ph.D. in 1 of the fields of the awards: 1) classical studies and archaeology; 2) history of art, or 3) post-classical humanistic studies (political, economic, cultural, and church history, or history of literature and musicology, all since 300 A.D.) and modern Italian studies.

Financial data The fellowship provides a stipend of up to $20,000, meals, a bedroom with private bath, and a study or studio. Fellows with children under 18 are housed outside the McKim, Mead & White building and are provided with an allowance that helps cover the cost of off-campus housing.

Duration 8 and a half months, from mid-September to the end of May.

Special features The American Academy in Rome, founded in 1894 by the American architect Charles F. McKim, is a center for independent study and advanced research in the fine arts and humanities. It consists of a School of Fine Arts (including architecture, landscape architecture, design arts, painting and sculpture, musical composition, and literature) and a School of Classical Studies (including classical studies and archaeology, history of art, and post-classical humanistic/modern Italian studies). This program is funded by the National Endowment for the Humanities.

Number awarded 3 each year, including 1 each in classical studies and archaeology, history of art, and post-classical humanistic/modern Italian studies.

Deadline November of each year.

[772]
NEH SENIOR RESEARCH FELLOWSHIP AT THE AMERICAN SCHOOL OF CLASSICAL STUDIES AT ATHENS

American School of Classical Studies at Athens
Attn: NEH Fellowship
6-8 Charlton Street
Princeton, NJ 08540-5232
(609) 683-0800   Fax: (609) 924-0578
E-mail: ascsa@ascsa.org
Web site: www.ascsa.org

Purpose To provide financial support to American postdoctoral scholars who are interested in researching any area of classical or Byzantine studies at the American School of Classical Studies at Athens.

Eligibility This program is open to postdoctoral scholars at all levels, from assistant to full professor, who are U.S. citizens or foreign nationals and have lived in the United States for the 3 years immediately preceding the application deadline. Applicants must have completed their professional training, but they do not have to hold a Ph.D. Their field of study may be history, philosophy, language, literature, art, or archaeology of Greece and the Greek world, from pre-Hellenic times to the present. Applications must indicate the need for use of the facilities of the school.

Financial data The maximum stipend is $15,000 for a 5-month project or $30,000 for a 10-month project.

Duration 5 to 10 months.

Special features Funding for these fellowships is provided by the National Endowment for the Humanities (NEH).

Number awarded 2 to 4 each year.

Deadline November of each year.

[773]
NETHERLAND-AMERICA FOUNDATION FELLOWSHIPS

Netherland-America Foundation
500 Park Avenue, Third Floor
New York, NY 10022-1606
(212) 308-2442   Fax: (212) 308-2290
E-mail: wflecknaf@aol.com

Purpose To provide financial assistance for graduate and postgraduate study or research in the Netherlands.

Eligibility Eligible to apply for this program are Americans who are interested in pursuing independent or structured study or research on the graduate/postgraduate level in the Netherlands. Students are selected on the merits of their proposals, which must focus on access to unique Dutch resources.

Financial data The monetary award is the same as the Fulbright Fellowship stipend. In some instances, travel grants are awarded as well.

Duration 1 year.

Special features Applications are processed by the Fulbright program. The foundation also offers several interest-free study loans for Americans interested in studying in the Netherlands.

Number awarded 9 fellowships and up to 6 study loans each year.

[774]
NETHERLAND-AMERICA FOUNDATION GRANTS

Institute of International Education
Attn: Student Programs Division
809 United Nations Plaza
New York, NY 10017-3580
(212) 984-5330   Fax: (212) 984-5325
Web site: www.iie.org/fulbright

Purpose To provide financial assistance to American graduate students who wish to study and conduct research in the Netherlands.

Eligibility Applicants must be U.S. citizens who hold a B.A. degree or equivalent before the beginning date of the grant and plan to study or conduct research in the Netherlands. All academic fields of study (including projects in all disciplines of the creative and performing arts) are eligible as long as the educational and cultural resources for the desired field of study are uniquely available in the Netherlands. A working knowledge of Dutch is useful at the time of arrival, because university lectures are in both English and Dutch.

Financial data Fellows receive a maintenance allowance based on the cost of living, round-trip international travel, and health and accident insurance.

Duration 9 months, beginning in September.

Special features This award is funded by the Netherland–America Foundation, established to maintain and strengthen the ties between the United States and the Netherlands. It is administered in the United States by the Institute of International Education (IIE) as part of the Fulbright program. Students who are currently enrolled in the United States are to apply through the Fulbright program adviser on their campus; at-large applicants (those not currently enrolled) may obtain applications and information directly from the IIE.

Number awarded 9 each year.

Deadline October of each year

[775]
NETHERLANDS FULBRIGHT TEACHER EXCHANGE

U.S. Department of State
c/o Graduate School, USDA
600 Maryland Avenue, S.W., Room 320
Washington, DC 20024-2520
(202) 314-3520   Fax: (202) 479-6806
E-mail: fulbright@grad.usda.gov
Web site: www.grad.usda.gov/International/ftep.html

Purpose To promote mutual understanding between the people of the United States and the people of the Netherlands through a teacher exchange program.

Eligibility This program is open to high school teachers (grades 10 through 12) and 2-year college faculty members who are interested in teaching in the Netherlands. Applicants must 1) be U.S. citizens; 2) hold at least a bachelor's degree; 3) be fluent in English; 4) have a current full-time teaching assignment in the U.S. or a territory; 5) have the approval of their school administration; 6) have at least 3 years of full-time experience; and 7) not have participated in a Fulbright Teacher Exchange longer than 8 weeks during the last 2 years. Fluency in Dutch is not required for U.S. teachers of English language or physical education. U.S. teachers of other subjects must be able to teach from a Dutch text and be fluent in Dutch. Teaching couples may apply. However, because of the limited number of positions available and, often, the lack of foreign candidate pairs with similar qualifications for interchanges, it may not be possible to arrange suitable assignments in the same locality or to place both teachers. Preference is given to applicants who have not participated previously in the program and may be given to applicants who have not previously lived in the Netherlands. Geographic distribution of awards within the United States is also a factor in selection. This program does not discriminate on the basis of race, color, religion, age, sex, or national origin and encourages the applications of members of minority communities. Other considerations being equal, veterans are given preference.

Financial data Only round-trip transportation is provided. Participants must obtain a leave of absence with pay from their jobs in the United States. The U.S. school must agree to accept a Dutch teacher who must secure a leave of absence with pay.

Duration 10 months, beginning in August.

Special features This program is sponsored by the Bureau of Educational and Cultural Affairs of the U.S. Department of State and administered by the Graduate School, USDA.

Limitations This program provides for the direct exchange of teaching assignments between the Netherlands and the United States. Applicants selected for exchange must attend orientation programs of the sponsoring agencies in the United States or abroad.

Number awarded 2 each year.

Deadline October of each year.

[776]
NEW COLLEGE JUNIOR RESEARCH FELLOWSHIPS

University of Oxford
New College
Attn: Senior Tutor
Holywell Street
Oxford OX1 3BN
England
44 1865 279596   Fax: 44 1865 279590
E-mail: tuition@new.ox.ac.uk
Web site: www.new.ox.ac.uk

Purpose To provide funding to postdoctoral scholars from any country who wish to conduct research in designated areas at New College of the University of Oxford in England.

Eligibility This program is open to residents of any country who are interested in conducting postdoctoral research while in residence at New College. There is no age limit, but applicants should have completed their first degree at least 3 years previously and be at an early stage in their career. The fields of study are announced each year.

Financial data The stipend is 12,372 pounds per year. Fellows also receive free meals and rooms (or, for fellows who live out, a housing allowance of 1,250 pounds per year), a book allowance of 300 pounds per year, an entertainment allowance of 125 pounds per year, and a research allowance of 540 pounds per year.

Duration 3 years.

Special features The following named scholarships are included in this program: the Astor Junior Research Fellowship, the Sir Christopher Cox Junior Research Fellowship, the Esmée Fairbairn Fellowship, the G.H. Hardy Junior Research Fellowship, the Julianna Cuyler Matthews Fellowship, the J. Arthur Rank and C.A.W. Manning Junior Research Fellowship, the Harold Salvesen Junior Research Fellowship, the W.W. Spooner Junior Research Fellowship, the Todd-Bird Junior Research Fellowship, and the Weston Junior Research Fellowship.

Number awarded 1 or more each year.

Deadline February of each year.

[777]
NEW HALL RESEARCH FELLOWSHIPS

University of Cambridge
c/o Academic Secretary, Churchill College
Storey's Way
Cambridge CB3 0DS
England
44 1223 336190   Fax: 44 1223 336045
E-mail: jrf@chu.cam.ac.uk
Web site: www.chu.cam.ac.uk

Purpose To provide funding to postdoctoral scholars interested in conducting research in the arts or social sciences at New Hall of the University of Cambridge in England.

Eligibility This program is open to scholars from any country who are interested in conducting research at New Hall in the arts or social sciences. There is no age limit, but applicants should have completed their Ph.D. recently or be close to completion. Candidates who have no previous educational connection with Cambridge or Oxford universities are particularly welcome. Applicants whose academic history has been interrupted should explain any intermissions. Selection is based on a 1,000-word statement on the proposed research.

Financial data The annual stipend for a fellow who has completed the Ph.D. is 12,982 pounds in the first year, rising to 14,851 pounds in the third year. The annual stipend for a fellow still working on a Ph.D. is 12,051 pounds in the first year, rising to 13,912 pounds in the third year. Fellows may be offered subsidized accommodations in college, subject to availability.

Duration Normally 3 years.

Number awarded 1 each year.

Deadline January of each year. E-mailed applications must be received by December.

[778]
NEWBERRY–BRITISH ACADEMY FELLOWSHIP FOR STUDY IN GREAT BRITAIN

Newberry Library
Attn: Committee on Awards
60 West Walton Street
Chicago, IL 60610-3305
(312) 255-3666   Fax: (312) 255-3513
E-mail: research@newberry.org
Web site: www.newberry.org

Purpose To offer American scholars financial assistance for research in Great Britain in any field in the humanities in which the Newberry Library's collections are strong.

Eligibility Applicants must be established scholars at the postdoctoral level (or its equivalent). They must be interested in conducting research in Great Britain in any area in which the Newberry Library is strong. Preference is given to readers and staff of the library and to scholars who have previously used the library.

Financial data The stipend is 1,350 pounds per month while the fellow is in Great Britain.

Duration Up to 3 months.

Special features Nearly all of the Newberry's 1 million volumes and 5 million manuscripts relate to the history of western Europe and the Americas. This program is offered by the Newberry Library in cooperation with the British Academy.

Limitations The home institution is expected to continue to pay a fellow's salary during the tenure of the program.

Number awarded Varies each year.

Deadline January of each year.

[779]
NEWNHAM COLLEGE RESEARCH FELLOWSHIP IN SCIENCE, MATHEMATICS, OR ENGINEERING

University of Cambridge
Newnham College
Attn: Principal's Secretary
Sidgwick Avenue
Cambridge CB3 9DF
England
44 1223 335700 Fax: 44 1223 359155
E-mail: smc26@cam.ac.uk
Web site: www.newn.cam.ac.uk

Purpose To provide financial assistance to women who wish to conduct research in science, mathematics, or engineering at Newnham College of the University of Cambridge in England.

Eligibility This program is open only to women who have recently completed or are nearing completion of a Ph.D. Applicants must be interested in conducting research at Newnham College in science, mathematics, or engineering. They may be from any country and graduates of any university.

Financial data Free meals and accommodations are provided. The stipend for residential fellows is 13,912 pounds per year for postdoctorates or 12,051 pounds per year for fellows still completing their doctorate. Fellows living out of college receive a supplement of approximately 3,000 pounds per year. All fellows may apply for additional support for certain research or conference expenses. They are permitted to teach up to 6 hours per week at the standard college rate of remuneration.

Duration Up to 3 years.

Number awarded 1 each year.

Deadline January of each year.

[780]
NEWNHAM COLLEGE RESEARCH FELLOWSHIP IN THE HUMANITIES OR SOCIAL SCIENCES

University of Cambridge
Newnham College
Attn: Principal's Secretary
Sidgwick Avenue
Cambridge CB3 9DF
England
44 1223 335700 Fax: 44 1223 359155
E-mail: smc26@cam.ac.uk
Web site: www.newn.cam.ac.uk

Purpose To provide financial assistance to women who wish to conduct research in the humanities or social sciences at Newnham College of the University of Cambridge in England.

Eligibility This program is open only to women who have recently completed or are nearing completion of a Ph.D. Applicants must be interested in conducting research at Newnham College in the humanities or social sciences. They may be from any country and graduates of any university.

Financial data Free meals and accommodations are provided. The stipend for residential fellows is 13,912 pounds per year for postdoctorates or 12,051 pounds per year for fellows still completing their doctorate. Fellows living out of college receive a supplement of approximately 3,000 pounds per year. All fellows may apply for additional support for certain research or conference expenses. They are permitted to teach up to 6 hours per week at the standard college rate of remuneration.

Duration Up to 3 years.

Number awarded 1 each year.

Deadline January of each year.

[781]
NIAS FELLOWSHIPS

Netherlands Institute for Advanced Study in the
 Humanities and Social Sciences
Meijboomlaan 1
2242 PR Wassenaar
Netherlands
31 70 512 2700 Fax: 31 70 511 7162
E-mail: nias@nias.knaw.nl

Purpose To provide financial assistance to a carefully chosen group of scholars from the Netherlands and abroad who are interested in continuing their research at the Netherlands Institute for Advanced Study in the Humanities and Social Sciences (NIAS).

Eligibility Fellows are selected on the basis of qualitative criteria, including scholarly achievements, reputation, and publications. Each year, a conscious attempt is made to have a stimulating mixture of disciplines and experience in the social sciences and humanities represented at the institute. Most of the successful candidates are invited to participate in multidisciplinary research theme groups, 3 of which are formed each year and which consist of about 8 fellows whose fields of study coincide with a proposed topic or theme. Other fellows are selected to conduct individual research.

Financial data Fellows who come from universities or institutes outside the Netherlands receive financial stipends on an individual basis, which are set at no more than 45 percent of the gross annual salary of a university professor of equal rank and seniority in the Netherlands. In practice, financial stipends range from the Euro equivalent of 3,000 to 6,000 Dutch florins per month, depending on the amount of support the fellows receive from their own institutions as well as on their academic standing. In addition to the monthly stipend, the government of the Netherlands pays the fellows' travel costs to and from the institute. However, each fellow is responsible for the travel costs of family members and for additional baggage or shipping expenses.

Duration 10 months, from September 1 to June 30.

Special features The NIAS was officially established on November 19, 1970 with the support of all universities in the Netherlands, the Netherlands Science Foundation, and the Royal Netherlands Academy of Arts and Sciences. On January 1, 1988, it became an Institute of the Royal Netherlands Academy of Arts and Sciences. Most of the financing has been provided by the Ministry of Education, Culture and Science.

Number awarded 40 each year (25 to 27 in the multidisciplinary research groups and 13 to 15 individual researchers), about 50 percent of whom come from countries outside of the Netherlands.

Deadline Applications may be submitted at any time, but they must arrive at least 18 months before the date the applicant wishes to begin residency.

[782]
NIKOLAY V. SIVACHEV DISTINGUISHED CHAIR IN AMERICAN HISTORY

Council for International Exchange of Scholars
3007 Tilden Street, N.W., Suite 5L
Washington, DC 20008-3009
(202) 686-6245   Fax: (202) 362-3442
E-mail: scholars@cies.iie.org
Web site: www.iie.org/cies

Purpose To provide funding to senior scholars interested in lecturing on American history at Moscow State University in Russia.

Eligibility Senior scholars in any specialization of American history may apply for this award. Candidates must be U.S. citizens who hold the rank of associate or full professor and are interested in lecturing in Russia.

Financial data The base stipend is $3,500 per month; other benefits include a maintenance allowance of $1,000 to $1,400 per month (depending on the number of accompanying dependents), a travel and relocation allowance of $3,500 to $8,500 (depending on the number of accompanying dependents), and an allowance for tuition assistance for K-12 dependents.

Duration 5 months.

Special features This is a Fulbright scholar program, sponsored by the Bureau of Educational and Cultural Affairs of the U.S. Department of State and administered by the Council for International Exchange of Scholars. The recipient acts as a lecturer for advanced undergraduate and graduate students at Moscow State University.

Number awarded 1 each year.

Deadline April of each year.

[783]
NOKIA FELLOWSHIP

Council for International Exchange of Scholars
3007 Tilden Street, N.W., Suite 5L
Washington, DC 20008-3009
(202) 686-6245   Fax: (202) 362-3442
E-mail: scholars@cies.iie.org
Web site: www.iie.org/cies

Purpose To provide funding to American scholars interested in teaching and conducting research on electronics in Finland.

Eligibility This program is open to scholars with a specialization in electronics or information or telecommunication technology. Applicants must be interested in lecturing and participating in collaborative research at an institution in Finland. They must arrange an institutional affiliation and include with their application a letter of invitation that indicates the teaching and research that is planned. U.S. citizenship is required.

Financial data The stipend is the EUR equivalent of 16,000 Finnish marks per month for scholars without dependents or the EUR equivalent of FIM 17,500 per month for grantees with dependents. International travel is provided for the grantee and 1 dependent. The host institution is expected to provide housing.

Duration 4 to 9 months, beginning in January or September (preferred).

Special features This is a Fulbright scholar program, sponsored by the Bureau of Educational and Cultural Affairs of the U.S. Department of State and administered by the Council for International Exchange of Scholars.

Number awarded 1 each year.

Deadline July of each year.

[784]
NORDDEUTSCHE LANDESBANK RESEARCH FELLOWSHIP AT THE WARBURG INSTITUTE AND HERZOG AUGUST BIBLIOTHEK

University of London
Attn: Warburg Institute
Woburn Square
London WC1H 0AB
England
44 20 7862 8949   Fax: 44 20 7862 8955

Purpose To provide funding to younger scholars interested in conducting research in early modern European history at the University of London's Warburg Institute and the Herzog August Bibliothek in Wolfenbüttel, Germany.

Eligibility This program is open to scholars from any country who are under 35 years of age. Doctoral candidates must have completed at least 1 year's research on their dissertation; applicants employed at assistant professor, lecturer, or equivalent grade in a university or learned institution must take unpaid leave for the entire period of the award. All applicants must be interested in conducting research at the Warburg Institute and the Herzog August Bibliothek on the cultural and intellectual history of early modern Europe.

Financial data The stipend is 5,000 pounds, or the Euro equivalent of approximately 15,500 Deutsche marks. Funds may be used for travel, living, and other incidental expenses.

Duration 4 months: 2 of which must be spent at each institution.

Special features This program, established in 2000, is funded by the Norddeutsche Landesbank.

Limitations Applications must be submitted simultaneously to the Herzog August Bibliothek, Attn: Director, Postfach 1364, D-38299, Wolfenbüttel, Germany.

Number awarded 1 each year.

Deadline December of each year.

[785]
NORMAN CAPENER TRAVELING FELLOWSHIPS

Royal College of Surgeons of England
Attn: Secretary's Office
35/43 Lincoln's Inn Fields
London WC2A 3PN
England
44 20 7405 3474, ext. 4005   Fax: 44 20 7831 9438
E-mail: msorensen@rcseng.ac.uk
Web site: www.rcseng.ac.uk

Purpose To provide funding to surgeons interested in conducting a research project that involves travel to or from the United Kingdom.

Eligibility This program is open to surgeons who are enrolled for advanced training in orthopedic surgery or who have recently completed a course in orthopedic or hand surgery. Applicants need not be fellows of the sponsoring organization.

They must be interested in a research project that involves travel to or from the United Kingdom.

Financial data The amount of the grant depends on the availability of funds and the nature of the project. The proposed budget should list expenses in sterling.

Number awarded 1 every other year.

Deadline June of even-numbered years.

[786]
NORWAY FULBRIGHT TEACHER EXCHANGE

U.S. Department of State
c/o Graduate School, USDA
600 Maryland Avenue, S.W., Room 320
Washington, DC 20024-2520
(202) 314-3520   Fax: (202) 479-6806
E-mail: fulbright@grad.usda.gov
Web site: www.grad.usda.gov/International/ftep.html

Purpose To promote mutual understanding between the people of the United States and the people of Norway through a teacher exchange program.

Eligibility This program is open to high school teachers (grades 10 through 12) and 2-year college faculty members who are interested in teaching in Norway. Applicants must 1) be U.S. citizens; 2) hold at least a bachelor's degree; 3) be fluent in English; 4) have a current full-time teaching assignment in the U.S. or a territory; 5) have the approval of their school administration; 6) have at least 3 years of full-time experience; and 7) not have participated in a Fulbright Teacher Exchange longer than 8 weeks during the last 2 years. Fluency in Norwegian is not required for U.S. teachers of English language or physical education. U.S. teachers of other subjects must be able to teach from a Norwegian text and be fluent in Norwegian. Teaching couples may apply. However, because of the limited number of positions available and, often, the lack of foreign candidate pairs with similar qualifications for interchanges, it may not be possible to arrange suitable assignments in the same locality or to place both teachers. Preference is given to applicants who have not participated previously in the program and may be given to applicants who have not previously lived in Norway. Geographic distribution of awards within the United States is also a factor in selection. This program does not discriminate on the basis of race, color, religion, age, sex, or national origin and encourages the applications of members of minority communities. Other considerations being equal, veterans are given preference.

Financial data Only round-trip transportation is provided. Participants must obtain a leave of absence with pay from their jobs in the United States. The U.S. school must agree to accept a Norwegian teacher who must secure a leave of absence with pay.

Duration 10 months, beginning in August.

Special features This program is sponsored by the Bureau of Educational and Cultural Affairs of the U.S. Department of State and administered by the Graduate School, USDA.

Limitations This program provides for the direct exchange of teaching assignments between Norway and the United States. Applicants selected for exchange must attend orientation programs of the sponsoring agencies in the United States or abroad.

Number awarded 2 to 3 each year.

Deadline October of each year.

[787]
NORWEGIAN INFORMATION SERVICE IN THE UNITED STATES TRAVEL GRANTS

Norwegian Information Service in the United States
825 Third Avenue, 38th Floor
New York, NY 10022-7584
(212) 421-7333   Fax: (212) 754-0583

Purpose To provide financial assistance to students and teachers who wish to travel to Norway for research or study purposes.

Eligibility Citizens and residents of the United States who are members of the Society for the Advancement of Scandinavian Study are eligible to apply. They must be 1) graduate students or college/university teachers of Norwegian language or culture and 2) interested in studying or conducting research in Norway.

Financial data The grants range from $750 to $1,500.

Special features The funds may be used for travel, research, and/or study. The grants are offered jointly by the Norwegian Information Service in the United States and the Norwegian Ministry of Foreign Affairs.

Number awarded Varies each year.

Deadline April of each year.

[788]
NORWEGIAN MARSHALL FUND

Norwegian Information Service in the United States
825 Third Avenue, 38th Floor
New York, NY 10022-7584
(212) 421-7333   Fax: (212) 754-0583

Purpose To provide funding to Americans who wish to come to Norway for postgraduate research in science and the humanities.

Eligibility U.S. citizens who have arranged to do research in Norway are eligible to apply for a grant. The program seeks to support research projects in science and the humanities at Norwegian universities and institutions of higher learning where participation by Americans is desirable. Under special circumstances, the awards can be extended to Norwegians for study or research in the United States.

Financial data The size of the individual grant varies, depending upon the nature of the project and the intended length of stay in Norway. In previous years, the grants have ranged between 10,000 and 30,000 Norwegian kroner (or up to $5,000).

Duration Up to 1 year.

Special features The Norwegian Marshall Fund was established in 1977 as a gesture of gratitude for the fundamental importance of the Marshall Plan for Norway during the reconstruction of Europe after World War II. The fund was made possible through contributions from Norwegian individuals and corporations as an expression of thanks from the Norwegian people to the American people.

Limitations Applications must be accompanied by a letter of support from the project sponsor or affiliated research institution in Norway. Further information and application forms are

available from the Norway-America Association, Drammensveien 20C, N-0255 Oslo 2, Norway, Fax: 47 22 44 76 83.
Deadline March of each year.

[789]
NORWEGIAN SENIOR SCIENTIST VISITING FELLOWSHIPS

Research Council of Norway
Attn: Department for Scientific and Industrial Research
P.O. Box 2700 St. Hanshaugen
N-0131 Oslo
Norway
47 22 03 75 03   Fax: 47 22 03 73 62
E-mail: jhw@forskningsradet.no
Web site: www.forskningsradet.no/english

Purpose To provide funding to scholars from outside of Norway who are interested in pursuing research in Norway in the fields of applied sciences and technology.
Eligibility Well-established, internationally recognized scientists who reside outside of Norway are eligible to apply if they have arranged to conduct research at a Norwegian research institution or university. Preference is given to scientists at the postdoctoral level. The research may be conducted in any 1 of the 6 areas supported by the Research Council of Norway: bioproduction and processing (including agriculture, forestry, fisheries, aquaculture, the food industries, and veterinary science), industry and energy, culture and society (including social sciences and the humanities), medicine and health, environment and development, and science and technology.
Financial data The fellowship provides 37,000 Norwegian kroner per month for each of the first 2 months and NOK 18,000 per month for each succeeding month. Funding is not intended to cover a salary (which is to be paid by the sponsoring Norwegian institution) but only extra expenses connected with the stay in Norway. Additional allowances are available to cover round-trip transportation and expenses for a spouse and minor children.
Duration 1 to 12 months.
Special features The Research Council of Norway was established in January 1993 by a merger of the 5 former research councils: the Royal Norwegian Council for Scientific and Industrial Research, the Norwegian Research Council for Science and the Humanities, the Agricultural Research Council of Norway, the Norwegian Council of Fishery Research, and the Norwegian Research Council for Applied Social Science.
Limitations Applications must be submitted by the sponsoring Norwegian institution on behalf of the scientist. Applications submitted directly to the Research Council are not accepted and the Council does not supply potential candidates with lists or university departments and/or research institutions or help in establishing contact with them.
Deadline The main deadline is June of each year; additional deadlines are September and March for medicine and health.

[790]
NORWICH JUBILEE ESPERANTO FOUNDATION AWARDS

Norwich Jubilee Esperanto Foundation
c/o Secretary
37 Granville Court
Cheney Lane
Oxford OX3 0HS
England
44 1865 245509

Purpose To promote international understanding by awarding travelships to students of Esperanto.
Eligibility Applicants must be traveling to meet Esperantists in other countries or on an approved individual journey abroad. They must be under 25 years of age, in need of financial aid, and fluent in Esperanto. Proof of competence may be required (in the form of a tape recording or an oral test).
Financial data The value of these awards varies, up to 1,000 pounds, depending on the length of time abroad and the needs of the candidates. Organizers of parties traveling to take part in an Esperanto activity (e.g., a children's congress or a students' conference) can apply for per capita aid.
Duration Varies, depending upon the travel plans of the recipient.
Limitations Part of the monetary award is withheld until the recipient submits a report of the travel results (this should be within 1 month of returning home). Funds can be used to cover travel expenses within a country but cannot be used to travel to a country. American recipients must use their grants to come to the British Isles.
Number awarded Varies each year.
Deadline Travel requests may be submitted at any time.

[791]
NOVARTIS FOUNDATION SYMPOSIUM BURSARIES

Novartis Foundation
Attn: Bursary Scheme Administrator
41 Portland Place
London W1N 4BN
England
44 20 7636 9456   Fax: 44 20 7436 2840
E-mail: bursary@novartisfound.org.uk
Web site: www.novartisfound.org.uk

Purpose To provide financial assistance to scientists from any country who are interested in attending symposia in England and then conducting research anywhere in the world.
Eligibility Scientists between the ages of 23 and 35 from any country are eligible to apply if they are interested in conducting medical, chemical, or biological research and attending related international symposia at the Novartis Foundation in London. Applicants must be actively engaged in research on the specific topic of the symposium they propose to attend.
Financial data The bursary covers all travel expenses incurred in attending the symposium and visiting the host laboratory afterwards; bed and breakfast accommodations and an additional allowance for meals during the meeting itself; and board and lodging during the visit to the host laboratory.

Duration Up to 3 months, including travel, attendance at a Novartis Foundation symposium in London, and 4 to 12 weeks in the laboratory of 1 of the participants in any country.

Special features Advertisements appear every 3 to 6 months in *Nature* and other scientific journals and announce the specific topics of projected symposia. The sponsor of this program was formerly the Ciba Foundation.

Number awarded Up to 8 each year.

Deadline June or November of each year.

[792]
NSF-NATO POSTDOCTORAL FELLOWSHIPS IN SCIENCE AND ENGINEERING

National Science Foundation
Directorate for Education and Human Resources
Attn: Division of Graduate Education
4201 Wilson Boulevard, Room 907N
Arlington, VA 22230
(703) 292-8697   TDD: (703) 292-5090
E-mail: nsf-nato@nsf.gov
Web site: www.ehr.nsf.gov

Purpose To enable young scientists and engineers from the United States to conduct research in the 18 member countries of the North Atlantic Treaty Organization (NATO) or the 18 NATO Partner countries.

Eligibility Eligible to apply for this support are U.S. citizens, nationals, or permanent residents who have received their doctorates within the past 5 years or who will have done so by the start of their tenure. They must be planning to pursue a program of research at an appropriate government or nonprofit scientific institution located in a NATO member or a NATO Partner country other than the United States. Eligible fields of study and research include mathematics; engineering; computer and information science; geosciences; the physical, biological, social, behavioral, and economic sciences; the history and philosophy of science; and interdisciplinary areas comprised of 2 or more of those fields. Research in the teaching and learning of science, mathematics, technology, and engineering is also eligible. Women, underrepresented minorities, and persons with disabilities are particularly encouraged to apply.

Financial data The program provides a monthly stipend of $2,750; dependency allowances of $200 per month for a spouse and each of not more than 2 children; and travel allowances of $2,500 for the fellow ($1,000 to Canada), $2,500 for an accompanying spouse ($1,000 to Canada), and $1,000 for 1 accompanying dependent child ($600 to Canada). In addition, the fellow is provided with $100 per month to aid in defraying costs of research and special travel.

Duration 12 months.

Special features The National Science Foundation manages these fellowships at the request of the U.S. Department of State. Members of NATO are Belgium, Canada, Czech Republic, Denmark, France, Germany, Greece, Hungary, Iceland, Italy, Luxembourg, the Netherlands, Norway, Poland, Portugal, Spain, Turkey, and the United Kingdom. The NATO Partner countries include the 15 republics of the former Soviet Union and 6 countries in eastern Europe (Albania, Bulgaria, Romania, Slovak Republic, Slovenia, and the former Yugoslav Republic of Macedonia).

Number awarded Approximately 5 each year.

Deadline November of each year.

[793]
NUFFIELD COLLEGE POSTDOCTORAL PRIZE RESEARCH FELLOWSHIPS

University of Oxford
Nuffield College
Attn: Secretary to the PRF Competition
Oxford OX1 1NF
England
44 1865 278527   Fax: 44 1865 278621
E-mail: ffion.moyle@nuffield.oxford.ac.uk
Web site: www.nuff.ox.ac.uk

Purpose To provide financial assistance to beginning researchers who wish to conduct social science research while affiliated with Nuffield College of the University of Oxford in England.

Eligibility This program is open to nationals of any country (outside of England) who wish to conduct research at Oxford in the areas of economics, politics, and sociology (although those are broadly interpreted to include, for example, recent history, social and medical statistics, international relations, area studies, and social psychology). Applicants must have completed a doctorate no more than 8 years ago (or be at a comparable place in their careers).

Financial data Fellows receive an annual salary of 16,134 pounds and either a housing allowance of 3,946 pounds per year or free single accommodation at the college. A research budget of 2,000 pounds is also provided.

Duration 2 years, beginning in October; may be extended for 1 additional year.

Special features Fellows have no formal commitments other than to be active in research, although they may undertake paid teaching of undergraduates at other colleges. The fellowships are also available to students working on a doctorate at the College.

Number awarded Varies each year; recently, 6 of these fellowships were awarded.

Deadline November of each year.

[794]
ODENSE CHAIR IN AMERICAN STUDIES

Council for International Exchange of Scholars
3007 Tilden Street, N.W., Suite 5L
Washington, DC 20008-3009
(202) 686-6245   Fax: (202) 362-3442
E-mail: scholars@cies.iie.org
Web site: www.iie.org/cies

Purpose To provide funding for scholars to lecture in American studies at a university in Denmark.

Eligibility This assignment is open to established scholars with a prominent record of accomplishments in American studies. Applicants should submit a detailed letter of interest in lecturing at a Danish university, including a statement outlining suitability for the appointment and professional reasons for seeking the position. Areas of interest include American studies (especially with an interdisciplinary focus), American history, American literature, business administration, cultural studies (art history, music history, film history), economics, international relations, political science, and sociology. U.S. citizenship is required.

Financial data The stipend is 315,000 Danish kroner. Grantees are responsible for their own travel expenses, but free medical care is available.

Duration 9 months.

Special features This is a Fulbright scholar program, sponsored by the Bureau of Educational and Cultural Affairs of the U.S. Department of State and administered by the Council for International Exchange of Scholars. Appointees teach graduate and advanced undergraduate courses (approximately 6 hours per week) in their area of specialization at the Center for American Studies, Odense. They are also expected to offer at least 1 seminar on their research and to represent the center through guest lecturing and seminar participation at other Danish universities and in communities.

Number awarded 1 each year.

Deadline April of each year.

[795]
OLIVER GATTY STUDENTSHIP
University of Cambridge
Attn: Registry Division
The Old Schools
Trinity Lane
Cambridge CB2 1TN
England
44 1223 332317   Fax: 44 1223 332332
E-mail: mrf25@admin.cam.ac.uk
Web site: www.cam.ac.uk

Purpose To provide funding to scientists and graduate students interested in conducting research at the University of Cambridge in England.

Eligibility Eligible to apply for this program are graduate students and postdoctorates from any country who are interested in conducting research in the fields of biophysical or colloid science at the University of Cambridge. Preference is given to applicants currently residing outside of Great Britain.

Financial data The amount awarded varies but is in line with the salary of a research assistant at the university (currently 16,286 pounds).

Duration 1 year; may be (and usually is) renewed for up to 2 additional years.

Deadline This scholarship is offered only when available; the next application deadline is scheduled for February 2003.

[796]
OLIVIA JAMES TRAVELING FELLOWSHIP
Archaeological Institute of America
656 Beacon Street, Fourth Floor
Boston, MA 02215-2010
(617) 353-9361   Fax: (617) 353-6550
E-mail: aia@bu.edu
Web site: www.archaeological.org

Purpose To provide financial assistance to American graduate students and scholars who wish to conduct research in Greece, the Aegean Islands, Sicily, southern Italy, Asia Minor, or Mesopotamia.

Eligibility Although applicants are not required to be registered in academic institutions, preference is given to individuals engaged in dissertation research or to recent (within 5 years) recipients of the Ph.D. They must be U.S. citizens or permanent residents and interested in conducting research on the classics, sculpture, architecture, archaeology, or history in Greece, the Aegean Islands, Sicily, southern Italy, Asia Minor, or Mesopotamia.

Financial data The amount of the award is $22,000.

Duration Preference is given to work of at least half a year's duration.

Number awarded 1 each year.

Deadline October of each year.

[797]
OPEN SOCIETY ARCHIVES RESEARCH GRANTS
Open Society Archives
Central European University
Attn: Research Grant Selection Committee
P.O. Box 458
H-1396 Budapest
Hungary
Fax: 36 1 327 3260   E-mail: archives@ceu.hu
Web site: www.osa.ceu.hu/grants/index.htm

Purpose To provide research grants to scholars and journalists from any country interested in using the Open Society Archives (OSA) at Central European University in Hungary.

Eligibility Researchers, journalists, graduate students, academics, and artists from any country who are interested in using OSA's holdings are eligible to apply. Applications are particularly encouraged from citizens of central and eastern Europe and the former Soviet Union. There is no application form. Application are asked to submit a cover letter indicating the dates and length of the research period requested, as well as the following documentation: curriculum vitae, a research proposal (500 to 800 words) emphasizing the relationship of the archives to the project, 2 letters of recommendation, and a list of publications.

Financial data Researchers who live outside Budapest are provided travel to and from Budapest, a stipend, and free accommodations at the university.

Duration Up to 2 months.

Limitations Recipients are expected to make a short presentation on their research to the staff and students of Central European University.

Deadline December for fellowships from February to April; March for fellowship from May to June; June for fellowships from August to October; and September for fellowships from November to January.

[798]
OSCAR BRONEER FELLOWSHIP IN CLASSICAL STUDIES

American Academy in Rome
Attn: Fellowship Coordinator
7 East 60th Street
New York, NY 10022-1001
(212) 751-7200   Fax: (212) 751-7220
E-mail: info@aarome.org
Web site: www.aarome.org

Purpose To allow fellows of the American Academy in Rome to spend a second year engaged in research at the American School of Classical Studies at Athens, and to allow fellows of the American School of Classical Studies at Athens to spend a second year engaged in research at the American Academy in Rome.

Eligibility Applicants must currently be fellows at either the American Academy in Rome or the American School of Classical Studies at Athens. They must be interested in conducting research at the nonfellowship school.

Financial data This fellowship provides for room and partial board at the respective institutions in Athens or in Rome and an annual stipend ($8,840 in Athens, $11,600 in Rome).

Duration 1 year.

Special features Information is also available from the American School of Classical Studies at Athens, 6-8 Charlton Street, Princeton, NJ 08540-5232. Fellows already in Europe may contact the American School of Classical Studies, 54 Souidias Street, GR-106 76 Athens, Greece or the American Academy in Rome, Via Angelo Masina 5, 00153 Rome, Italy.

Number awarded 1 each year.

Deadline January of each year.

[799]
OXFORD CENTRE FOR HEBREW AND JEWISH STUDIES VISITING FELLOWS PROGRAM

Oxford Centre for Hebrew and Jewish Studies
Attn: Fellowships and Visitors Coordinator
Yarnton Manor, Yarnton
Oxford OX5 1PY
England
44 1865 377946   Fax: 44 1865 375079
E-mail: ochjs@sable.ox.ac.uk
Web site: associnst.ox.ac.uk/ochjs

Purpose To provide funding to scholars who wish to conduct research at the Oxford Centre for Hebrew and Jewish Studies in England.

Eligibility This program is open to scholars who wish to conduct research at the Centre in areas of Jewish history, literature, languages, and thought. Applicants must have a good command of the English language. Candidates for academic degrees are not eligible.

Financial data Fellows receive free accommodations at the Yarnton Manor Estate and a stipend of 1,000 pounds per month.

Duration Normally 5 months, covering a full Oxford term. Applications for longer or shorter periods may be considered in exceptional circumstances.

Number awarded Varies each year.

Deadline Applications may be submitted at any time.

[800]
OXFORD CENTRE FOR ISLAMIC STUDIES DISTINGUISHED FELLOWSHIPS

Oxford Centre for Islamic Studies
Attn: Awards Secretary
George Street
Oxford OX1 2AR
England
44 1865 278730   Fax: 44 1865 248942
E-mail: islamic.studies@oxcis.ac.uk
Web site: www.oxcis.ac.uk

Purpose To provide funding to distinguished scholars interested in conducting research at the Oxford Centre for Islamic Studies in England.

Eligibility These awards are offered by invitation only to eminent scholars who have made an outstanding contribution to the knowledge and understanding of Islam and the Islamic world. Fellows are expected to devote most of their time to their own research and writing and to participate in the academic and social activities of the Centre.

Financial data Fellows are provided with an office, some secretarial support, access to academic facilities and libraries, and a research stipend.

Duration 1 term.

Special features The Oxford Centre for Islamic Studies is an associated institution of the University of Oxford and has links with universities and research centers throughout the Muslim world.

Number awarded These fellowships are awarded periodically.

[801]
OXFORD CENTRE FOR ISLAMIC STUDIES VISITING FELLOWSHIPS

Oxford Centre for Islamic Studies
Attn: Awards Secretary
George Street
Oxford OX1 2AR
England
44 1865 278730   Fax: 44 1865 248942
E-mail: islamic.studies@oxcis.ac.uk
Web site: www.oxcis.ac.uk

Purpose To provide funding to scholars interested in conducting independent research at the Oxford Centre for Islamic Studies in England.

Eligibility This program is open to scholars from any country who are interested in conducting independent research at the Centre. Normally Senior Research Fellowships are awarded to those holding senior faculty positions, although appointments are also made to suitably qualified candidates who do not hold full-time academic posts. Junior Research Fellowships are awarded to scholars or writers at the postdoctoral or equivalent level. The proposed research must be in an area of the arts, humanities, or social sciences (especially anthropology, economics, geography, history, international relations, law, literature, philosophy, politics, religion, or sociology) that has relevance to the study of Islam or the Muslim world.

Financial data The stipend of 4,000 pounds is intended as a supplementary award and may be held in conjunction with other research grants, sabbatical salaries, or other research stipends.

Duration Normally 9 months, although shorter periods may be considered.

Special features The Oxford Centre for Islamic Studies is an associated institution of the University of Oxford and has links with universities and research centers throughout the Muslim world. Fellows are provided with office space and access to libraries. This program includes the Abdul Aziz Al-Mutawa Visiting Fellowship and the Muhammad Bin-Ladin Visiting Fellowship.

Limitations Fellows are expected to be in residence at the center for the duration of the program. They are encouraged to participate in the center's activities and seminars.

Number awarded Varies each year.

Deadline November of each year.

[802]
PAUL CELAN FELLOWSHIPS
Institut für die Wissenschaften vom Menschen
Attn: Fellows Coordinator
Spittelauer Lände 3
A-1090 Vienna
Austria
43 1 313 58 335 Fax: 43 1 313 58 30
E-mail: iwm@iwm.univie.ac.at
Web site: www.univie.ac.at/iwm

Purpose To provide funding to translators who wish to work on a project at the Institute for Human Sciences (IWM) in Vienna.

Eligibility This program is open to scholars who wish to translate major works in the humanities or social sciences from western European languages into eastern European languages and vice versa, or from 1 eastern European language into another. Preference is given to works that are thematically related to IWM's fields of research and ongoing projects: political philosophy of the 19th and 20th centuries, gender studies, the philosophy of Jan Patocka, and the history of political and economic ideas in central and eastern Europe. Projects must be conducted at the IWM in Vienna.

Financial data Fellows receive a stipend of 160,000 Austrian schillings (11,627 Euros), a personal computer, office space, and access to in-house and Viennese research facilities.

Duration 6 months.

Special features Funding for this program is provided by the European Cultural Foundation of Amsterdam.

Limitations Fellows are expected to be in residence at the institute.

Number awarded Generally, 4 each year.

Deadline January of each year.

[803]
PAUL MELLON CENTRE JUNIOR FELLOWSHIPS
Paul Mellon Centre for Studies in British Art
Attn: Director of Studies
16 Bedford Square
London WC1B 3JA
England
44 20 7580 0311 Fax: 44 20 7636 6730
E-mail: info@paul-mellon-centre.ac.uk

Purpose To provide funding to doctoral candidates who wish to conduct research on British art at the Paul Mellon Centre for Studies in British Art (in London) or the Yale Center for British Art (in New Haven, Connecticut).

Eligibility This program is open to doctoral candidates who are already engaged in research on a topic related to the history of British art. Candidates may be of any nationality but normally must be enrolled in a graduate program at an American university (for research in England) or at a non-American university (for research in the United States). Applications must indicate the field of study, progress made so far, how the fellowship will aid research, and preferred dates of tenure.

Financial data The monthly stipend is 1,500 pounds or $1,500 and return airfare.

Duration 3 months.

Special features Fellows conduct research on British art at the Paul Mellon Centre for Studies in British Art (in London) or the Yale Center for British Art (in New Haven, Connecticut).

Number awarded Varies each year.

Deadline January of each year.

[804]
PAUL MELLON CENTRE POSTDOCTORAL FELLOWSHIPS
Paul Mellon Centre for Studies in British Art
Attn: Director of Studies
16 Bedford Square
London WC1B 3JA
England
44 20 7580 0311 Fax: 44 20 7636 6730
E-mail: info@paul-mellon-centre.ac.uk

Purpose To provide funding to recent postdoctorates from any country who wish to conduct research on the history of British art or architecture.

Eligibility This program is open to scholars who received a doctorate within the previous 4 years in British art or architecture. Applicants may be seeking either to 1) transform doctoral research into publishable form as a book, series of articles, exhibition catalogue, etc., or 2) support new research arising out of a successfully submitted doctoral dissertation where that research may lead to publication. Fellows may choose, if appropriate, to be affiliated with either the Paul Mellon Centre in London or the Yale Center for British Art in New Haven.

Financial data Grants (up to 6,000 pounds) are made either as a stipend to the fellow or to fund a temporary replacement at the fellow's institution.

Duration 3 to 6 months.

Number awarded Varies each year.

Deadline January of each year.

[805]
PAUL MELLON CENTRE RESEARCH SUPPORT GRANTS

Paul Mellon Centre for Studies in British Art
Attn: Director of Studies
16 Bedford Square
London WC1B 3JA
England
44 20 7580 0311   Fax: 44 20 7636 6730
E-mail: info@paul-mellon-centre.ac.uk

Purpose To provide funding to pre- and postdoctoral scholars from any country who are interested in conducting research on British art or architecture.

Eligibility This program is open to scholars already engaged in graduate or postdoctoral research involving British art or architecture. Applicants, who may be of any nationality, must be interested in visiting collections, libraries, archives, conferences, or historic sites within the United Kingdom or abroad.

Financial data The maximum grant is 2,000 pounds or $3,500. Funds are to be used for travel and subsistence.

Duration 6 months.

Number awarded Varies each year.

Deadline January or September of each year.

[806]
PAUL MELLON CENTRE ROME FELLOWSHIP

Paul Mellon Centre for Studies in British Art
Attn: Director of Studies
16 Bedford Square
London WC1B 3JA
England
44 20 7580 0311   Fax: 44 20 7636 6730
E-mail: info@paul-mellon-centre.ac.uk

Purpose To provide funding to scholars from any country who wish to conduct research at the British School at Rome.

Eligibility This program is open to scholars working on Grand Tour subjects or in the field of Anglo-Italian cultural and artistic relations. Applicants must indicate the field of research and the importance of a residency in Rome to the research. They should be competent in spoken and written Italian.

Financial data The fellowship provides full residential accommodation at the British School at Rome, a stipend of 1,000 pounds per month, and round-trip travel to Rome.

Duration 2 to 6 months.

Number awarded 1 each year.

Deadline January of each year.

[807]
PAUL MELLON CENTRE SENIOR FELLOWSHIPS

Paul Mellon Centre for Studies in British Art
Attn: Director of Studies
16 Bedford Square
London WC1B 3JA
England
44 20 7580 0311   Fax: 44 20 7636 6730
E-mail: info@paul-mellon-centre.ac.uk

Purpose To provide funding to established scholars from any country who wish to complete a manuscript on the history of British art or architecture.

Eligibility This program is open to established scholars in the field of British art or architecture who wish to complete a manuscript or book for immediate publication. Applicants must demonstrate that they can complete their manuscript within the period they specify. Fellows may choose, if appropriate, to be affiliated with either the Paul Mellon Centre in London or the Yale Center for British Art in New Haven.

Financial data Grants (up to 25,000 or 42,000 pounds) are made either as a stipend to the fellow or to fund a temporary replacement at the fellow's institution. A small traveling allowance may also be provided.

Duration Up to 12 months.

Number awarded A limited number are offered each year.

Deadline January of each year.

[808]
PETER BAKER FELLOWSHIP

Marine Biological Association of the United Kingdom
Attn: Director
Laboratory
Citadel Hill
Plymouth PL1 2PB
England
44 1752 633331   Fax: 44 1752 669762
E-mail: sjha@mba.ac.uk
Web site: www1.npm.ac.uk/mba

Purpose To enable postdoctoral scientists to conduct research at the Marine Biological Association of the United Kingdom's laboratory in Plymouth.

Eligibility Established research scientists from any country are eligible to apply for this program, if they are interested in conducting research on marine biology or, preferably, physiology at the Marine Biological Association of the United Kingdom's laboratory in Plymouth, England. Applicants need not be members of the association.

Financial data Awards provide living and travel expenses; bench fees are waived and a small stipend may be available for research expenses.

Duration Approximately 2 months.

Special features This fellowship was established in 1995.

Number awarded 1 each year.

Deadline Applications may be submitted at any time.

[809]
PHILIPPE FOUNDATION GRANT PROGRAM

Philippe Foundation
405 Lexington Avenue, 35th Floor
New York, NY 10174
(212) 687-3290   Fax: (212) 687-3418
E-mail: shapiro@pimny.com

Purpose To facilitate the exchange of French and American doctors engaged in medical research (particularly cancer research).

Eligibility American and French physicians and scientists interested in a research exchange program are eligible to apply. Preference is given to applicants conducting research on cancer. They must have a statement from the head of the host laboratory indicating acceptance from the laboratory and approval of the proposed work. Selection is based on the applicant's record and demonstrated capacity, supporting recommendations, worthiness of the project, renown of the host laboratory, and financial needs of the applicant and spouse or companion (taking into consideration their income, family situation, and place of residence).

Financial data The amount awarded varies, depending upon the nature of the proposed visit. Generally, however, the amount awarded is enough to facilitate but not completely pay for the visit (i.e., $1,000 to $6,000).

Duration 1 year or less; may be renewed.

Number awarded Varies; generally, 70 each year.

Deadline Applications may be submitted at any time; they are reviewed at the end of each calendar quarter.

[810]
PHILOSOPHY OF SCIENCE JUNIOR RESEARCH FELLOWSHIP AT WOLFSON COLLEGE

University of Oxford
Wolfson College
Attn: President's Secretary
Linton Road
Oxford OX2 6UD
England
44 1865 274100   Fax: 44 1865 274125
E-mail: sue.hales@wolfson.ox.ac.uk
Web site: www.wolfson.ox.ac.uk

Purpose To provide funding to postdoctoral scholars from any country who wish to conduct research in the philosophy of science, including mathematics, at Wolfson College of the University of Oxford in England.

Eligibility This program is open to residents of any country who are interested in conducting postdoctoral research while in residence at Wolfson College. Applicants should normally be younger than 30 years of age and should have at least 2 years of research experience in the subject. Selection is based on a sample of the applicant's written work, up to 10,000 words. Proposed research must be on the philosophy of science, including mathematics.

Financial data The stipend is 11,478 pounds per year. Fellows also receive room and board at the college. Fellows who are married or who require family accommodations may live at the college and pay the difference in rent or live outside the college and receive a housing allowance equivalent to the cost of single accommodations at the college.

Duration 3 years.

Special features Fellows are permitted to undertake up to 6 hours of teaching per week.

Number awarded 1 every 3 years; the current schedule is to offer a fellowship in 2003.

Deadline March of the years the fellowship is offered.

[811]
PISA DISTINGUISHED CHAIR

Council for International Exchange of Scholars
3007 Tilden Street, N.W., Suite 5L
Washington, DC 20008-3009
(202) 686-6245   Fax: (202) 362-3442
E-mail: scholars@cies.iie.org
Web site: www.iie.org/cies

Purpose To provide funding for scholars to lecture on engineering at a university in Italy.

Eligibility This program is open to professors of engineering who are interested in lecturing in Italy on a topic that changes periodically. Recent topics have included 1) microengineering (integrated design, microfabrication technologies, robotics, MEMS teleoperation, and mechatronics); and 2) advanced industrial dynamics and applied industrial organization. U.S. citizenship is required. Some knowledge of Italian is useful but not required.

Financial data The stipend is the Euro equivalent of 16,800,000 Italian lire plus a settling-in allowance of the EUR equivalent of 1,500,000 lire. The grant also provides international travel (for the grantee only) plus the EUR equivalent of 200,000 lire per month for each accompanying dependent.

Duration 3 months.

Special features This is a Fulbright scholar program, sponsored by the Bureau of Educational and Cultural Affairs of the U.S. Department of State and administered by the Council for International Exchange of Scholars. The appointee offers 2 advanced courses at Sant'Anna School of University Studies and Doctoral Research, Pisa. Other responsibilities include assisting with graduate thesis advising and participating in collaborative research.

Number awarded 1 each year.

Deadline April of each year.

[812]
POLAND CHAIR IN AMERICAN LITERATURE

Council for International Exchange of Scholars
3007 Tilden Street, N.W., Suite 5L
Washington, DC 20008-3009
(202) 686-6245   Fax: (202) 362-3442
E-mail: scholars@cies.iie.org
Web site: www.iie.org/cies

Purpose To enable distinguished American scholars to lecture on American literature in Poland.

Eligibility Applicants must be established scholars with a minimum rank of associate professor and considerable teaching experience; work with Ph.D. students is highly desirable. They must be interested in teaching courses, directing research, and offering lectures or seminars at the undergraduate and graduate levels in Poland; assisting in curriculum development; and offering short-term courses for Polish faculty as requested. Priority is given to specialists in 19th-century literature (transcendentalists), 20th-century literature (including women's, ethnic, modernist, and postmodern literature), literary theory and criticism, or popular culture and media. U.S. citizenship is required.

Financial data The stipend is $3,600 per month, paid in local currency. Other benefits include travel/relocation allowances of $3,000 for the grantee, $2,000 for 1 dependent, and $4,000 for

2 or more dependents; housing or a housing allowance, paid on a reimbursable basis; and an in-country stipend in zloty of approximately $300 per month.

Duration 5 to 9 months.

Special features This is a Fulbright scholar program, sponsored by the Bureau of Educational and Cultural Affairs of the U.S. Department of State and administered by the Council for International Exchange of Scholars. Grantees work at the University of Lodz, Marie Curie-Sklodowska University in Lublin, the University of Silesia, or the University of Warsaw.

Number awarded 1 each year.

Deadline April of each year.

[813]
POLAND CHAIR IN AMERICAN MEDIA STUDIES

Council for International Exchange of Scholars
3007 Tilden Street, N.W., Suite 5L
Washington, DC 20008-3009
(202) 686-6245   Fax: (202) 362-3442
E-mail: scholars@cies.iie.org
Web site: www.iie.org/cies

Purpose To enable distinguished American scholars to lecture on American media studies in Poland.

Eligibility Applicants must be established scholars with a minimum rank of associate professor and considerable teaching experience; work with Ph.D. students is highly desirable. They must be interested in teaching courses, directing research, and offering lectures or seminars at the undergraduate and graduate levels; assisting in curriculum development; and offering short-term courses for Polish faculty as requested. Priority is given to specialists in American media and society, media and the presidency, history of American film, popular music, media and culture, and history of advertising, television, or print media. U.S. citizenship is required.

Financial data The stipend is $3,600 per month, paid in local currency. Other benefits include travel/relocation allowances of $3,000 for the grantee, $2,000 for 1 dependent, and $4,000 for 2 or more dependents; housing or a housing allowance, paid on a reimbursable basis; and an in-country stipend in zloty of approximately $300 per month.

Duration 5 to 9 months.

Special features This is a Fulbright scholar program, sponsored by the Bureau of Educational and Cultural Affairs of the U.S. Department of State and administered by the Council for International Exchange of Scholars. Grantees work at the University of Lodz or the University of Warsaw.

Number awarded 1 each year.

Deadline April of each year.

[814]
POLAND FULBRIGHT TEACHER EXCHANGE

U.S. Department of State
c/o Graduate School, USDA
600 Maryland Avenue, S.W., Room 320
Washington, DC 20024-2520
(202) 314-3520   Fax: (202) 479-6806
E-mail: fulbright@grad.usda.gov
Web site: www.grad.usda.gov/International/ftep.html

Purpose To promote mutual understanding between the people of the United States and the people of Poland through a teacher exchange program.

Eligibility This program is open to teachers (grades 9 through 12) of English as a second language, foreign languages, English literature, social studies, education, mathematics, or sciences who are interested in teaching in Poland. Applicants must 1) be U.S. citizens; 2) hold at least a bachelor's degree; 3) be fluent in English; 4) have a current full-time teaching assignment in the U.S. or a territory; 5) have the approval of their school administration; 6) have at least 3 years of full-time experience; and 7) not have participated in a Fulbright Teacher Exchange longer than 8 weeks during the last 2 years. Fluency in Polish is not required although some ability is useful; the language of instruction is English. Teaching couples may apply. However, because of the limited number of positions available and, often, the lack of foreign candidate pairs with similar qualifications for interchanges, it may not be possible to arrange suitable assignments in the same locality or to place both teachers. Preference is given to applicants who have not participated previously in the program and may be given to applicants who have not previously lived in Poland. Geographic distribution of awards within the United States is also a factor in selection. This program does not discriminate on the basis of race, color, religion, age, sex, or national origin and encourages the applications of members of minority communities. Other considerations being equal, veterans are given preference.

Financial data Only round-trip transportation is provided. Participants must obtain a leave of absence with pay from their jobs in the United States. The U.S. school must agree to accept a Polish teacher who must secure a leave of absence with pay; the Polish teacher receives a stipend, but no additional cost accrues to the U.S. school.

Duration 9 months, beginning in September.

Special features This program is sponsored by the Bureau of Educational and Cultural Affairs of the U.S. Department of State and administered by the Graduate School, USDA.

Limitations This program provides for the direct exchange of teaching assignments between Poland and the United States. Applicants selected for exchange must attend orientation programs of the sponsoring agencies in the United States or abroad.

Number awarded 3 to 4 each year.

Deadline October of each year.

[815]
POLICE STUDIES FELLOWSHIP
Council for International Exchange of Scholars
3007 Tilden Street, N.W., Suite 5L
Washington, DC 20008-3009
(202) 686-6245   Fax: (202) 362-3442
E-mail: scholars@cies.iie.org
Web site: www.iie.org/cies

Purpose To provide American police professionals with an opportunity to conduct research in the United Kingdom.

Eligibility Police officers and police administrators in the United States are eligible to apply. Candidates should hold a bachelor's degree in criminal justice, police studies, or a related discipline in the social sciences. They must be currently employed by a police department or equivalent organization at the level of sworn sergeant or above and be recommended by supervisory staff within the department. Candidates must develop a substantive research project to be conducted in the United Kingdom and demonstrate that participation in the program will produce benefits of significance to the larger law enforcement community.

Financial data The grant is a fixed sum of 5,000 pounds. Applicants must have full or partial support during their leaves of absence from their home department.

Duration At least 3 months.

Special features This is a Fulbright scholar program, sponsored by the Bureau of Educational and Cultural Affairs of the U.S. Department of State and administered by the Council for International Exchange of Scholars.

Limitations Grantees are expected to arrange an affiliation at a higher education host institution in the United Kingdom appropriate to the research topic.

Number awarded Up to 2 each year.

Deadline July of each year.

[816]
POLICY RESEARCH FELLOWSHIP PROGRAM OF THE NATIONAL COUNCIL FOR EURASIAN AND EAST EUROPEAN RESEARCH
National Council for Eurasian and East European Research
910 17th Street, N.W., Suite 300
Washington, DC 20006
(202) 822-6950   Fax: (202) 822-6955
E-mail: nceeerdc@aol.com
Web site: www.nceeer.gov

Purpose To provide funding to junior scholars who are interested in conducting research on politics and society in the former Soviet republics and eastern Europe (including Eurasia).

Eligibility This program is open to U.S.-based scholars who have obtained a Ph.D. within the past 10 years. Applicants must be interested in conducting field research that will contribute to the general understanding of politics and society in the region of the former Soviet Union and eastern Europe (including Eurasia). Affiliation with a U.S. college or university is required, except in the case of independent scholars. Applicants must be U.S. citizens or permanent residents and sufficiently proficient in the host country language to meet the demands of their research.

Financial data The grant is $40,000.

Duration Up to 1 year.

Special features Funding for this program is provided by the U.S. Department of State under the Research and Training for Eastern Europe and the Independent States of the Former Soviet Union Act of 1983 (Title VIII).

Deadline January of each year.

[817]
POLISH GOVERNMENT GRANTS
Institute of International Education
Attn: Student Programs Division
809 United Nations Plaza
New York, NY 10017-3580
(212) 984-5330   Fax: (212) 984-5325
Web site: www.iie.org/fulbright

Purpose To provide financial assistance to American graduate students for study or research in Poland.

Eligibility Applicants must be U.S. citizens who hold a B.A. degree or equivalent before the beginning date of the grant and plan to conduct research for their Ph.D. dissertation in any field at Polish institutions of higher learning or using Polish archival sources. Excellent Polish is required for students pursuing research in drama or film; for other fields, proficiency in Polish at the level required by the proposed study is necessary by the beginning date of the grant. All students must have a formal institutional affiliation and may be required to attend classes.

Financial data The Polish government provides a monthly stipend of 975 zloty. Grantees may be provided with dormitory housing by Polish universities or may be required to find their own housing. In addition, a Fulbright grant provides grantees with dependents an additional payment of $100 per month for 1 accompanying dependent and of $200 per month for 2 or more dependents.

Duration 1 academic year.

Special features These grants are awarded under the exchange program between the governments of Poland and the United States and administered as part of the Fulbright program by the Institute of International Education (IIE). Students who are currently enrolled in the United States are to apply through the Fulbright program adviser on their campus; at-large applicants (those not currently enrolled) may obtain applications and information directly from the IIE.

Number awarded 12 each year.

Deadline October of each year.

[818]
POSTDOCTORAL GRANTS FOR SUMMER TRAVEL/RESEARCH IN TURKEY

Institute of Turkish Studies
c/o Georgetown University
Intercultural Center
P.O. Box 571033
Washington, DC 20057-1033
(202) 687-0295   Fax: (202) 687-3780
E-mail: sayaris@gunet.georgetown.edu
Web site: www.turkishstudies.org

Purpose To provide funding for travel to Turkey for research purposes.

Eligibility Eligible to apply are U.S. citizens or residents who have earned a Ph.D. degree in a social science or humanities discipline, are recognized scholars, are interested in traveling to Turkey to conduct research on Turkish studies, and are in need of funding to underwrite their travel expenses.

Financial data The amount of the award depends on the nature of the proposal. The maximum award is round-trip airfare. No university overhead costs are paid.

Duration Recipients are expected to spend at least 4 weeks in Turkey.

Deadline April of each year.

[819]
POSTDOCTORAL RESEARCH FELLOWSHIPS IN ATHEROSCLEROSIS

French Atherosclerosis Society
c/o INSERM U 498
Hôpital Du Bocage
BP 1542
21034 Dijon Cedex
France
E-mail: laurent.lagrost@u.bourgogne.fr

Purpose To provide funding to scientists interested in conducting research related to atherosclerosis in France.

Eligibility Applicants must have a doctorate in medicine or science. They must be interested in conducting research related to atherosclerosis and its thromboembolic complications at a laboratory of their choice in France.

Financial data The grant is 120,000 French francs (18,293 Euros).

Duration 1 year.

Special features This program is jointly offered by the Cardiovascular Department of Parke-Davis France and the French Atherosclerosis Society.

Number awarded 1 each year.

Deadline July of each year.

[820]
POSTGRADUATE SCHOLARSHIPS FOR GREEK LANGUAGE TEACHERS

Alexander S. Onassis Public Benefit Foundation
Attn: Public Relations
7 Eschinou Street
GR-105 58 Athens
Greece
30 1 331 0902, ext. 140   Fax: 30 1 323 6044
E-mail: pubrel@onassis.gr
Web site: www.onassis.gr

Purpose To provide funding to teachers of Greek language or Greek studies from countries other than Greece who are interested in coming to Greece to study and share information with their Greek colleagues.

Eligibility This program is open to elementary and high school teachers from outside of Greece who are interested in visiting the country to collaborate, study, and exchange information with their Greek counterparts. They must teach Greek language, literature, history, or civilization in their home country. While, in principal, this program is aimed at persons of other than Greek nationality, persons of Greek descent (second generation only) are also eligible, provided they are permanently residing and working outside of Greece and have studied or are currently studying at universities outside of Greece. Knowledge of the Greek language is not required; however, preference is given to applicants with an elementary knowledge of Greek. A recommendation from the director of the applicant's school is required.

Financial data The grant provides a monthly allowance (the Euro equivalent of 200,000 Greek drachmas) plus hotel accommodations (single room with shower and breakfast). The foundation also covers travel expenses from and to the country of origin.

Duration Up to 2 months.

Limitations It is expected that recipients will continue to offer their services to their home country after they have completed their visit to Greece. During their stay in Greece, recipients may be asked to deliver a lecture or seminar at either the Onassis Cultural Centre of Athens or at a university or other scholarly center in Greece.

Number awarded Up to 5 each year.

Deadline January of each year.

[821]
PRAEGER COMMITTEE GRANTS FOR FIELD WORK IN NATURAL HISTORY

Royal Irish Academy
Attn: Executive Secretary
Academy House
19 Dawson Street
Dublin 2
Ireland
353 1 676 4222   Fax: 353 1 676 2346
E-mail: admin@ria.ie
Web site: www.ria.ie

Purpose To provide funding for field work relevant to the natural history of Ireland.

Eligibility Anyone may apply for these grants, but applications are particularly welcome from amateur natural historians.

Awards are not available for support of undergraduate or graduate student programs or for any part of the applicants' professional work. Applications must be for field work relevant to the natural history of Ireland, but grantees need not be based in Ireland. Preference is given to projects that concern sites of specific scientific interest and/or endangered species.

Financial data The maximum grant is 1,000 Irish pounds.

Duration Up to 1 year.

Number awarded 2 each year.

Deadline February of each year.

[822]
PREDISSERTATION GRADUATE FELLOWSHIPS IN TURKISH STUDIES

Institute of Turkish Studies
c/o Georgetown University
Intercultural Center
P.O. Box 571033
Washington, DC 20057-1033
(202) 687-0295   Fax: (202) 687-3780
E-mail: sayaris@gunet.georgetown.edu
Web site: www.turkishstudies.org

Purpose To provide financial assistance to graduate students in Turkish Studies.

Eligibility This program is open to graduate students in the humanities or social sciences who have completed at least 1 year of modern Turkish. Applicants must be U.S. citizens or permanent residents proposing summer travel to Turkey for language study and/or research. Students currently engaged in dissertation research or writing are not eligible.

Financial data Grants range from $4,000 to $6,000.

Duration Normally 2 months, during the summer.

Number awarded Varies each year.

Deadline April of each year.

[823]
PRINCE RAINIER III OF MONACO BURSARY

Institute of Human Paleontology
Attn: Prince Albert Foundation of Monaco
1 rue René Panhard
75013 Paris
France
33 1 43 31 62 91   Fax: 33 1 43 31 22 79

Purpose To provide funding for research at the Institute of Human Paleontology in Paris.

Eligibility Applicants may be young researchers from any country. They must be interested in conducting research on geology, paleontology, or prehistory at the Institute of Human Paleontology.

Financial data The award is the Euro equivalent of 20,000 French francs.

Duration Varies, depending upon the scope of the funded research project.

Number awarded 1 each odd-numbered year.

Deadline December of each even-numbered year.

[824]
PROFESSIONAL DEVELOPMENT FELLOWSHIPS

Institute of International Education
Attn: Student Programs Division
809 United Nations Plaza
New York, NY 10017-3580
(212) 984-5330   Fax: (212) 984-5325
E-mail: pdfnis@iie.org
Web site: www.iie.org/pgms/pdfnis

Purpose To provide financial assistance to American graduate students and postgraduates who wish to carry out a program of research, study, or internship in eastern Europe, central Europe. or Eurasia.

Eligibility This program is open to U.S. citizens who either 1) are at least in the second (or terminal) year of a graduate or professional degree program, or 2) have graduated within 5 years from a graduate or professional degree program. Applicants must propose a feasible research, study, or internship plan for the period of the fellowship and indicate a desired institutional affiliation in the host country; applications solely in support of dissertation research or language research are not accepted. Host countries include Albania, Armenia, Azerbaijan, Belarus, Bulgaria, Croatia, Estonia, Georgia, Kazakhstan, Kyrgyzstan, Latvia, Lithuania, Macedonia, Moldova, Romania, Russia, Slovak Republic, Tajikistan, Turkmenistan, Ukraine, and Uzbekistan. Fields of study include business, economics, education reform, environmental and conservation policy, international relations, journalism, law, public administration, and public health. Applicants must have language ability sufficient to carry out the proposed project by the time of departure from the United States. They must indicate how the proposed study, research, or internship will benefit their future plans and professional careers.

Financial data Fellowships provide payment of round-trip international airfare, a monthly living stipend, insurance, and allowances for books and travel in the host country. No provision is made for dependents.

Duration 3 to 7 months.

Special features Funding for this program is provided by the U.S. Department of State through Title VIII (the Research and Training for Eastern Europe and the Independent States of the Former Soviet Union Act of 1983).

Deadline January of each year.

[825]
PROFESSIONAL GRANTS IN JOURNALISM

Institute of International Education
Attn: Student Programs Division
809 United Nations Plaza
New York, NY 10017-3580
(212) 984-5330   Fax: (212) 984-5325
Web site: www.iie.org/fulbright

Purpose To provide funding to journalists who are interested in using their skills in Spain.

Eligibility Eligible to apply to go to Spain are junior to mid-career professionals active in the fields of print, broadcast, or business journalism. They must be fluent in written and spoken Spanish.

Financial data The grantee receives round-trip transportation and a monthly stipend of the Euro equivalent of 250,000 pesetas.
Duration 3 months.
Special features Grantees will be affiliated with both professional and academic institutions in Spain. Some projects may include lectures or training seminars. Projects may also emphasize editorial or production aspects of journalism. This program is administered by the Institute of International Education as part of the Fulbright program.
Number awarded 2 each year.
Deadline January of each year.

[826]
PROGRAM FOR CULTURAL COOPERATION RESEARCH GRANTS

University of Minnesota
Attn: The Global Campus
230 Heller Hall
271 19th Avenue South
Minneapolis, MN 55455
(612) 625-9888　　　　　　　Fax: (612) 626-8009
E-mail: zimme001@umn.edu
Web site: www.umabroad.umn.edu/pcc/pcc/pcc.html

Purpose To provide funding to scholars from the United States interested in conducting research in Spain.
Eligibility This program is open to scholars at colleges and universities in the United States interested in undertaking or completing research projects in Spain. Selection is based on scholarly quality of the proposal and its relevance to the dissemination of Spanish culture in the United States.
Financial data Grants cover up to 50 per cent of the cost, to a maximum of $2,000 per month. Only direct costs (travel, room and board, photocopies) are included. The cost of computer equipment is not covered and salaries are not subsidized.
Duration Up to 3 months.
Special features This program was established in 1983 as a result of an agreement between the government of Spain and a group of Hispanicists from the United States. Since its establishment, it has been administered at the University of Minnesota.
Number awarded Varies each year.
Deadline March of each year.

[827]
P.S. ALLEN JUNIOR RESEARCH FELLOWSHIP

University of Oxford
Corpus Christi College
Attn: President's Secretary
Merton Street
Oxford OX1 4JF
England
44 1865 276691　　　　　　Fax: 44 1865 276767
E-mail: college.office@ccc.ox.ac.uk
Web site: www.ccc.ox.ac.uk

Purpose To provide funding to postdoctoral scholars from any country who wish to conduct research in classical studies or modern history in England.
Eligibility This program is open to residents of any country who are interested in conducting research, half the time in residence at Corpus Christi College, Oxford and half the time in residence at Corpus Christi College, Cambridge. The field of specialization alternates between classical studies and modern history.
Financial data The stipend is 13,420 pounds. Also provided are free accommodations (or a housing allowance), an allowance for hospitality, and a small research allowance.
Duration 4 years: 2 years at Oxford and 2 years at Cambridge.
Number awarded 1 each year.

[828]
QUEEN SOFIA RESEARCH FELLOWSHIP IN MODERN AND CONTEMPORARY SPANISH LITERATURE

University of Oxford
Exeter College
Attn: The Rector
Oxford OX1 3DP
England
44 1865 279600　　　　　　Fax: 44 1865 279645
E-mail: academic.administration@exeter.ox.ac.uk
Web site: www.exeter.ox.ac.uk

Purpose To provide funding to postdoctoral scholars from any country who wish to conduct research in Spanish literature at Exeter College of the University of Oxford in England.
Eligibility This program is open to residents of any country who are interested in conducting postdoctoral research in modern and contemporary Spanish literature while in residence at Exeter College.
Financial data The stipend is 9,724 pounds per year. Fellows also receive college housing or a housing allowance.
Duration 2 years; may be renewed for 1 additional year.
Number awarded This fellowship is awarded periodically. It was last offered in 2002.

[829]
QUEEN'S COLLEGE JUNIOR RESEARCH FELLOWSHIP

University of Oxford
Queen's College
Attn: College Secretary
Oxford OX1 4AW
England
44 1865 279167　　　　　　Fax: 44 1865 790819
E-mail: college.secretary@queens.ox.ac.uk
Web site: www.queens.ox.ac.uk

Purpose To provide funding to postdoctoral scholars from any country who wish to conduct research in designated areas at Queen's College of the University of Oxford in England.
Eligibility This program is open to residents of any country who are interested in conducting postdoctoral research while in residence at Queen's College. Applicants may not have accumulated more than 6 years of full-time postdoctoral study or research. The field of research is announced each year; recently, it was law.

Financial data The stipend is 12,994 pounds per year. Fellows also receive free meals and rooms (or, in approved cases, a housing allowance of 2,497 pounds per year).
Duration 3 years.
Number awarded 1 each year.
Deadline October of each year.

[830]
QUEEN'S COLLEGE RESEARCH FELLOWSHIPS

University of Cambridge
Queen's College
Attn: Clerk to the Tutors
Silver Street
Cambridge CB3 9ET
England
44 1223 335511   Fax: 44 1223 335522
E-mail: ph209@cam.ac.uk
Web site: www.quns.cam.ac.uk

Purpose To provide funding to postdoctoral scholars interested in conducting research in designated fields at Queen's College of the University of Cambridge in England.
Eligibility This program is open to graduates of any university who either are already members of Queen's College or are interested in coming to Queen's College to conduct research in the following areas: anthropology, archaeology, engineering, or philosophy. Applicants should be at an early stage in their academic career and, if over 30 years of age, have completed no more than 4 years of research.
Financial data The stipend is 11,645 pounds per year, with annual increments of 645 pounds to 12,935 pounds. A non-resident marriage allowance may be available. Other benefits include free accommodations at the college, dining rights, and small grants for research expenses.
Duration 3 years.
Number awarded 1 or 2 each year.
Deadline October of each year.

[831]
QUEEN'S UNIVERSITY OF BELFAST VISITING PROFESSORSHIPS

Queen's University of Belfast
Attn: Academic Council Office
Administration Building
Belfast BT7 1NN
Northern Ireland
44 28 9027 3006   Fax: 44 28 9031 3537
E-mail: academic.council@qub.ac.uk
Web site: www.qub.ac.uk

Purpose To encourage interchange between business and academic life in Northern Ireland.
Eligibility Senior scholars and professionals successful in business in any country are invited to apply if they are interested in sharing their expertise with the students and faculty of Queen's University of Belfast. Normally they should be on paid leave of absence from their employment.
Financial data The stipend is 1,600 pounds; funds are to be used to cover travel and living expenses.
Duration 1 month.

Number awarded 3 each year.
Deadline October of each year.

[832]
RAIZISS/DE PALCHI TRANSLATION FELLOWSHIP

Academy of American Poets
Attn: Program Director
584 Broadway, Suite 1208
New York, NY 10012-3250
(212) 274-0343   Fax: (212) 274-9427
E-mail: academy@poets.org
Web site: www.poets.org

Purpose To provide funding to Americans in the process of translating Italian poetry into English.
Eligibility This program is open to U.S. citizens who are translating modern or contemporary Italian poetry into English. They must be interested in participating in a residency in Rome.
Financial data The grant is $20,000. The recipient also receives a residency at the American Academy in Rome.
Duration The prize is awarded biennially, in odd-numbered years. The residency in Rome is for 6 weeks.
Special features The award is given in conjunction with the New York Community Trust; it was established in 1995 with a $400,000 bequest from Sonia Raiziss Giop.
Number awarded 1 every other year.
Deadline October of even-numbered years.

[833]
RAY LANKESTER INVESTIGATORSHIPS

Marine Biological Association of the United Kingdom
Attn: Director
Laboratory
Citadel Hill
Plymouth PL1 2PB
England
44 1752 633331   Fax: 44 1752 669762
E-mail: sjha@mba.ac.uk
Web site: www1.npm.ac.uk/mba

Purpose To enable established research scientists to spend time on sabbatical leave at the Marine Biological Association of the United Kingdom's laboratory in Plymouth, England.
Eligibility Established research scientists from any country are eligible to apply for this program, if they are interested in conducting research on marine biology or physiology in Plymouth as part of a sabbatical leave. Applicants need not be members of the association at the time of application, but recipients are expected to become members.
Financial data Awards are 1,500 pounds per month.
Duration 1 to 5 months.
Special features Awards are subject to approval by the Director and Council of the Marine Biological Association, the Linacre Professor of Comparative Anatomy at Oxford University, and the Professor of Zoology at Cambridge University.
Number awarded 1 or 2 each year.
Deadline Applications may be submitted at any time, but available funds for any given year are usually committed by the end of March.

[834]
RENATA POGGIOLI AWARD FOR TRAVEL IN GREECE OR ITALY

Classical Association of New England
c/o John R. McVey, Chair, Committee on Scholarships
The Rivers School
333 Winter Street
Weston, MA 02493-1021
(781) 431-7831 Fax: (781) 239-3916
E-mail: j.mcvey@rivers.org
Web site: www.caneweb.org

Purpose To provide financial assistance to teachers in New England who wish to study and/or conduct research in Italy or Greece.
Eligibility Applicants for this program must be New England residents who are either secondary school teachers with less than 10 years of experience or college instructors with a rank no higher than untenured assistant professor. They must be interested in conducting research in Greece or Italy. Usually they should not have access to major university research or travel grants. Membership in the Classical Association of New England is not required.
Financial data The stipend ranges from $4,000 to $6,000.
Duration Summer months.
Special features This program began in 1991.
Number awarded 1 every other year.
Deadline January of even-numbered years.

[835]
RESEARCH FELLOWSHIP IN FAUNAL STUDIES

American School of Classical Studies at Athens
Attn: Chair, Committee on the Wiener Laboratory
6-8 Charlton Street
Princeton, NJ 08540-5232
(609) 683-0800 Fax: (609) 924-0578
E-mail: ascsa@ascsa.org
Web site: www.ascsa.org

Purpose To provide financial support to pre- or postdoctoral scholars who wish to study faunal remains from archaeological contexts in Greece.
Eligibility This program is open to scholars with a Ph.D. and those working on a doctoral dissertation who wish to conduct research on faunal remains from archaeological contexts at the Wiener Laboratory of the American School of Classical Studies at Athens. Applicants must have a well-defined project that can be undertaken within the given time in the laboratory or in collaboration with local research institutions.
Financial data The stipend ranges from $15,500 to $25,000, depending on seniority and experience.
Duration 1 academic year, beginning in September.
Special features Information is also available from Sherry C. Fox, Director, Wiener Laboratory, 54 Souidias Street, GR-106 76, Athens, Greece, Fax: 30 1 725 0854, E-mail: sfox@ascsa.edu.gr.
Limitations In addition to the proposed research, the fellow is expected to develop and curate the laboratory's comparative collection; contribute to the development of the laboratory; assist with queries from excavators; offer a lecture on the work undertaken while at the laboratory; participate in a regular member school trip; and contribute to seminars on aspects of archaeological science as part of the school's annual curriculum.
Number awarded 1 each year.
Deadline January of each year.

[836]
RESEARCH FELLOWSHIP IN GEOARCHAEOLOGY

American School of Classical Studies at Athens
Attn: Chair, Committee on the Wiener Laboratory
6-8 Charlton Street
Princeton, NJ 08540-5232
(609) 683-0800 Fax: (609) 924-0578
E-mail: ascsa@ascsa.org
Web site: www.ascsa.org

Purpose To provide financial support to pre- or postdoctoral scholars who wish to study geoarchaeology in Greece.
Eligibility This program is open to scholars with a Ph.D. and those working on a doctoral dissertation who wish to conduct research on geoarchaeology at the Wiener Laboratory of the American School of Classical Studies at Athens. Applicants must have a well-defined project that can be undertaken within the given time in the laboratory or in collaboration with local research institutions. The project should address significant archaeological questions in areas of study which may include quarried stone, lithics, building materials, ceramics, and soil and sediment studies.
Financial data The stipend ranges from $15,500 to $25,000, depending on seniority and experience.
Duration 1 academic year, beginning in September.
Special features Information is also available from Sherry C. Fox, Director, Wiener Laboratory, 54 Souidias Street, GR-106 76, Athens, Greece, Fax: 30 1 725 0854, E-mail: sfox@ascsa.edu.gr.
Limitations In addition to the proposed research, the fellow is expected to contribute to the laboratory's permanent collections of lithic, ceramic, and building materials; contribute to the development of the laboratory; assist with queries from excavators; offer a lecture on the work undertaken while at the laboratory; participate in a regular member school trip; and contribute to seminars on aspects of archaeological science as part of the school's annual curriculum.
Number awarded 1 each year.
Deadline January of each year.

[837]
RESEARCH FELLOWSHIP IN REPRODUCTION

Journals of Reproduction and Fertility Ltd.
Attn: Company Secretary
22 Newmarket Road
Cambridge CB5 8DT
England
44 1223 351809 Fax: 44 1223 359754
E-mail: cosec@jrfadmin.demon.co.uk

Purpose To provide funding to postdoctoral scholars from any country who wish to conduct research related to reproduction in the United Kingdom.

Eligibility Applicants must have a Ph.D. or equivalent research experience in a field related to fertility and reproduction. They must be interested in conducting research in the United Kingdom. Newly-qualified postdoctoral scientists and overseas candidates are particularly welcome. Applications must be accompanied by a statement of support from the head of a prospective host university department or research institute in the United Kingdom.

Financial data The stipend depends on the age and experience of the recipient.

Duration 2 years.

Number awarded 1 each year.

Deadline March of each year.

[838]
RESEARCH FELLOWSHIP IN THE HISTORY OF MUSLIMS IN SOUTH ASIA

Oxford Centre for Islamic Studies
Attn: Awards Secretary
George Street
Oxford OX1 2AR
England
44 1865 278730   Fax: 44 1865 248942
E-mail: islamic.studies@oxcis.ac.uk
Web site: www.oxcis.ac.uk

Purpose To provide funding to scholars interested in conducting research on Muslims in south Asia at the Oxford Centre for Islamic Studies in England.

Eligibility This program is open to scholars from any country. Applicants must be interested in conducting their research in England at the Oxford Centre for Islamic Studies. They should have a specialized knowledge of Indo-Muslim history focusing on Muslims in south Asia from the 13th to the 20th centuries. Scholars with an interest in the history of Persian-Central Asian lands may also be considered. Some acquaintance with computer analysis of data is desirable but not essential.

Financial data The stipend ranges from 12,000 to 19,300 pounds, depending on the qualifications and experience of the recipient.

Duration 1 year; may be renewed for 1 additional year.

Special features The Oxford Centre for Islamic Studies is an associated institution of the University of Oxford and has links with universities and research centers throughout the Muslim world.

Number awarded 2 each year.

Deadline December of each year.

[839]
RESEARCH FELLOWSHIPS IN IRISH STUDIES

Queen's University of Belfast
Attn: Institute of Irish Studies
8 Fitzwilliam Street
Belfast BT7 6AW
Northern Ireland
44 1232 273386   Fax: 44 1232 439238
E-mail: iis@qub.ac.uk
Web site: www.qub.ac.uk

Purpose To provide funding to junior scholars who wish to conduct research on Irish studies at Queen's University of Belfast.

Eligibility Junior scholars from any country are eligible to apply if they wish to conduct research in Irish studies at the university's Institute of Irish Studies and need to work on material for publication. Preference is given to postdoctoral students or candidates with evidence of publications in press or in print, but graduate students are also occasionally considered for the program. Preference is also given to candidates under the age of 33 or within 2 years of having completed their Ph.D.

Financial data The stipend is 16,286 pounds per year.

Duration 1 year, beginning in October.

Limitations Fellows are required to be based at the institute for the duration of the fellowship, to attend and present a paper to the institute's seminars, and to contribute fully to the life of the institute.

Number awarded Up to 3 each year.

Deadline January of each year.

[840]
RESEARCH INTO AGEING PRIZE PH.D. STUDENTSHIPS

Research into Ageing
Attn: Research Manager
Baird House
15/17 St. Cross Street
London EC1N 8UW
England
44 20 7404 6878   Fax: 44 20 7404 6816
E-mail: grants@ageing.org
Web site: www.ageing.org/research/grant.html

Purpose To provide financial assistance to Ph.D. candidates interested in conducting research on aging at an institution in the United Kingdom.

Eligibility This program supports basic, clinical, and epidemiological research on all aspects of aging, including the basic biology of aging, stroke and neurodegenerative diseases (including Alzheimer's), sensory loss, and the causes, treatment, or prevention of falls and fractures. Support for cancer research is not provided. Applicants may be of any nationality, but they must be proposing to conduct research at a university in the United Kingdom. They must be nominated by their potential Ph.D. supervisor. Selection is based on the scientific merit of the project, its relevance to the aims of the sponsoring organization, and the supervision record and quality of training offered by the department and proposed supervisor.

Financial data Grants provide a stipend of 12,500 pounds per year, university fees up to 3,000 pounds per year, and an allowance for consumables and travel up to 3,000 pounds per year.

Duration 1 year.

Special features Research into Ageing is a registered U.K. charity that raises money to fund research to improve the quality of life of older people.

Number awarded Varies each year.

Deadline November of each year.

[841]
RESEARCH INTO AGEING RESEARCH FELLOWSHIPS

Research into Ageing
Attn: Research Manager
Baird House
15/17 St. Cross Street
London EC1N 8UW
England
44 20 7404 6878   Fax: 44 20 7404 6816
E-mail: grants@ageing.org
Web site: www.ageing.org/research/grant.html

Purpose To provide financial assistance to postdoctoral scientists interested in conducting research on aging at an institution in the United Kingdom.

Eligibility This program supports basic, clinical, and epidemiological research on all aspects of aging, including the basic biology of aging, stroke and neurodegenerative diseases (including Alzheimer's), sensory loss, and the causes, treatment, or prevention of falls and fractures. Support for cancer research is not provided. Applicants may be of any nationality, but they must be proposing to conduct research at a hospital, university, hospital trust, or recognized research institute in the United Kingdom. They should have no more than 10 years of postdoctoral experience and intend to maintain a long-term interest in aging research. Selection is based on the scientific merit of the proposed research, the potential of the candidate to become an independent and competitive researcher, the quality of the environment in which the award is to be held, and the support provided by the host institution to help develop the candidate's career in research.

Financial data Grants provide personal support at registrar or university pay scales and up to 15,000 pounds per year for research expenses.

Duration Up to 3 years.

Special features Research into Ageing is a registered U.K. charity that raises money to fund research to improve the quality of life of older people.

Number awarded Varies each year.

Deadline January of each year.

[842]
RESIDENTS AT THE AMERICAN ACADEMY IN ROME

American Academy in Rome
Attn: Fellowship Coordinator
7 East 60th Street
New York, NY 10022-1001
(212) 751-7200   Fax: (212) 751-7220
E-mail: info@aarome.org
Web site: www.aarome.org

Purpose To open the facilities of the American Academy in Rome to artists and scholars from any country.

Eligibility This program is open to artists and scholars of any nationality. Residencies are offered in the School of Fine Arts (architecture, landscape architecture, design arts, painting and sculpture, musical composition, and literature) and the School of Classical Studies (classical studies and archaeology, history of art, post-classical humanistic studies, and modern Italian studies) in Rome. Residents in the School of Fine Arts are selected by invitation only; residents in the School of Classical Studies may apply by writing to the Director in Rome.

Financial data Each resident is given an apartment, studio (as appropriate), and meals.

Duration From 2 to 4 months.

Special features Residents sometimes serve as senior advisors to the winners and other members of the academy community. The address in Rome is Via Angelo Masina 5, 00153 Rome, Italy.

Limitations During their stay, residents are expected to offer 1 academy event, such as a concert, an exhibition or studio visit, a lecture or reading, or an instructional walk in Rome.

Number awarded Varies each year.

Deadline Applications may be submitted at any time.

[843]
RHODES VISITING FELLOWSHIP FOR WOMEN

University of Oxford
St. Hilda's College
Attn: Academic Office
Oxford OX4 1DY
England
44 1865 276815   Fax: 44 1865 276816
E-mail: college.office@st-hildas.ox.ac.uk
Web site: www.st-hildas.ox.ac.uk

Purpose To provide funding to women from outside the United Kingdom who are interested in conducting postdoctoral research at St. Hilda's College of the University of Oxford in England.

Eligibility This program is open to women graduates from outside the United Kingdom who are interested in conducting postdoctoral research at St. Hilda's College. The field of study is announced whenever the fellowship is available.

Financial data The stipend is 12,110 pounds. Recipients are also entitled to a 1,000 pound research allowance, travel expenses, and free room and board.

Duration 2 years; may be renewed for 1 additional year.

Special features This fellowship is offered alternately to different area, e.g. Commonwealth countries, South Africa, the United States.

Number awarded This fellowship is offered periodically. It is next scheduled for 2003.

[844]
ROBERT CORMACK UNDERGRADUATE VACATION RESEARCH SCHOLARSHIPS

Royal Society of Edinburgh
Attn: Research Fellowships Secretary
22-24 George Street
Edinburgh EH2 2PQ
Scotland
44 131 240 5000   Fax: 44 131 240 5024
E-mail: rse@rse.org.uk
Web site: www.ma.hw.ac.uk/RSE

Purpose To provide funding to undergraduate students who are interested in conducting research in astronomy in Scotland.

Eligibility This program is open to full-time undergraduate students (normally in their junior year) who are nominated by a department in a Scottish institution of higher education. There is no restriction on home institution or nationality, but the research must be conducted at a Scottish institution and must relate to astronomy.

Financial data The stipend is 600 pounds.

Duration 6 weeks, during the summer.

Number awarded 6 each year.

Deadline March of each year.

[845]
ROBERT SCHUMAN CENTRE FOR ADVANCED STUDIES FELLOWSHIPS

European University Institute
Attn: Robert Schuman Centre for Advanced Studies
Badia Fiesolana
Via dei Roccettini 9
I-50016 San Domenico di Fiesole
Italy
39 55 4685 635   Fax: 39 55 4685 444
E-mail: applyjmf@datacomm.iue.it
Web site: www.iue.it

Purpose To allow postdoctoral scholars to engage in research at the Robert Schuman Centre for Advanced Studies in Florence, Italy on topics related to Europe.

Eligibility This program is open to candidates holding a doctoral degree or having equivalent research experience. Applicants should have a good knowledge of the languages most relevant to their proposed research; academic activities at the center are usually conducted in English or French, and occasionally in Italian. Most fellows are nationals of European Union member states, although applications from nationals of other countries (such as the United States) may be considered. Fellowships are open to academics on leave, but fellows may not engage in teaching or research activities at another institution. Research must be conducted in the following 3 areas: 1) What is Europe? 2) Europe's social and political problems; or 3) Europe and the rest of the world.

Financial data The basic stipend ranges from 1,200 to 2,000 Euros per month. For fellows already occupying a stable post in a university or research center, the stipend offered takes into account any continuation of their salary by their home university. Medical insurance (for fellows and their families) and limited reimbursement of travel expenses (for fellows only) are also provided.

Duration 1 academic year.

Limitations Fellows are required to reside in Florence for the duration of their fellowship.

Number awarded Varies each year.

Deadline October of each year.

[846]
ROCHE RESEARCH FOUNDATION FELLOWSHIPS

Roche Research Foundation
Attn: Professor A. Fischli
Grenzacherstrasse 124
Building 71/502
CH-4070 Basel
Switzerland
41 61 688 5227   Fax: 41 61 688 1460
E-mail: research.foundation@roche.com
Web site: www.research-foundation.org

Purpose To support biomedical research at Swiss universities, institutes, and hospitals.

Eligibility This program is open to undergraduate, doctoral, and postdoctoral students, and to other young researchers. Candidates may be from any country, may not be older than 40 years of age, and should have a record of original and significant research contributions or a special methodological knowledge. Applications must be submitted by the sponsoring Swiss institution. Preference is given to interdisciplinary natural science projects of particular importance for biology and medicine.

Financial data Fellowships provide support for the recipient, and the university receives a grant to support the project. Covered expenses include salaries, equipment, material, and travel expenses for the beneficiary and family (for stays longer than 3 months).

Duration Up to 2 years for Ph.D. students in the natural sciences; up to 1 year for other candidates. Ph.D. students may apply for additional funding for a third and final year.

Number awarded Varies each year.

Deadline January, April, July, or October of each year.

[847]
ROMANIA FULBRIGHT TEACHER EXCHANGE

U.S. Department of State
c/o Graduate School, USDA
600 Maryland Avenue, S.W., Room 320
Washington, DC 20024-2520
(202) 314-3520   Fax: (202) 479-6806
E-mail: fulbright@grad.usda.gov
Web site: www.grad.usda.gov/International/ftep.html

Purpose To promote mutual understanding between the people of the United States and the people of Romania through a teacher exchange program.

Eligibility This program is open to high school teachers (grades 9 through 12) and 2-year college instructors of English as a second language, American studies (American literature, history, geography, or social studies), science, or education who are interested in teaching in Romania. Applicants must 1) be U.S. citizens; 2) hold at least a bachelor's degree; 3) be fluent in English; 4) have a current full-time teaching assignment in the U.S. or a territory; 5) have the approval of their school administration; 6) have at least 3 years of full-time experience; and 7) not have participated in a Fulbright Teacher Exchange longer than 8 weeks during the last 2 years. Fluency in Romanian is not required although some ability is useful; the language of instruction is English. Teaching couples may apply. However, because of the limited number of positions available and, often, the lack of foreign candidate pairs with similar qualifications for interchanges, it may not be possible to arrange suitable assignments in the same locality or to place both teachers. Preference is given to applicants who have not participated previously in the program and may be given to applicants who have not previously lived in Romania. Geographic distribution of awards within the United States is also a factor in selection. This program does not discriminate on the basis of race, color, religion, age, sex, or national origin and encourages the applications of members of minority communities. Other considerations being equal, veterans are given preference.

Financial data Round-trip economy airfare for the exchange teacher only and a monthly stipend in local currency are provided. Participants must obtain a leave of absence with pay from their jobs in the United States. The U.S. school must agree to accept a Romanian teacher who must secure a leave of absence with pay; the Romanian teacher receives a stipend, but no additional cost accrues to the U.S. school.

Duration 9 months, beginning in September.

Special features This program is sponsored by the Bureau of Educational and Cultural Affairs of the U.S. Department of State and administered by the Graduate School, USDA.

Limitations This program provides for the direct exchange of teaching assignments between Romania and the United States. Applicants selected for exchange must attend orientation programs of the sponsoring agencies in the United States or abroad.

Number awarded 2 each year.

Deadline October of each year.

[848]
ROMANIAN GOVERNMENT GRANTS

Institute of International Education
Attn: Student Programs Division
809 United Nations Plaza
New York, NY 10017-3580
(212) 984-5330   Fax: (212) 984-5325
Web site: www.iie.org/fulbright

Purpose To provide financial assistance to American graduate students for study or research in Romania.

Eligibility Applicants must be U.S. citizens who hold a B.A. degree or equivalent before the beginning date of the grant and plan to study or conduct research in Romania for a Ph.D. dissertation in any field. A knowledge of spoken and written Romanian is needed by the beginning date of the grant. English and French are useful second languages throughout Romania. German and Hungarian are useful in Transylvania and Banat, especially at the Universities of Cluj-Napoca and Timisoara. Applicants who have begun intensive language study at the time of application will be considered. Advanced graduate students with appropriate preparation for individual research and study are preferred.

Financial data The Romanian government provides a monthly stipend of 1,500,000 lei and housing in university apartments. In addition, a Fulbright grant provides grantees with dependents an additional payment of $100 per month for 1 accompanying dependent and $200 per month for 2 or more accompanying dependents.

Duration 1 academic year.

Special features These grants are awarded under the exchange program between the governments of Romania and the United States and administered as part of the Fulbright program by the Institute of International Education (IIE). Students who are currently enrolled in the United States are to apply through the Fulbright program adviser on their campus; at-large applicants (those not currently enrolled) may obtain applications and information directly from the IIE.

Limitations Grantees, particularly those who wish to do field work, often encounter difficulties and delays in getting the necessary approvals for access to research sources and should be prepared for this. Grantees will encounter much less difficulty if they submit in their application a detailed, specific, focused proposal for research and do not deviate from it after they reach Romania.

Number awarded Approximately 7 each year.

Deadline October of each year.

[849]
ROYAL COLLEGE OF VETERINARY SURGEONS FELLOWSHIP

Council for International Exchange of Scholars
3007 Tilden Street, N.W., Suite 5L
Washington, DC 20008-3009
(202) 686-6245   Fax: (202) 362-3442
E-mail: scholars@cies.iie.org
Web site: www.iie.org/cies

Purpose To provide financial assistance to American veterinarians who wish to conduct research in the United Kingdom.

Eligibility This program is open to veterinarians or senior academics with teaching and/or research experience in veterinary medicine. Applicants must be interested in conducting research at the Royal College of Veterinary Surgeons on a topic in veterinary medicine and science of mutual interest and concern in both the United States and the United Kingdom. U.S. citizenship is required.

Financial data The stipend is 7,500 pounds and round-trip travel.

Duration 4 to 5 months.

Special features This is a Fulbright scholar program, sponsored by the Bureau of Educational and Cultural Affairs of the U.S. Department of State and administered by the Council for International Exchange of Scholars.

Number awarded 1 each year.

Deadline July of each year.

[850]
ROYAL IRISH ACADEMY SENIOR VISITING FELLOWSHIPS

Royal Irish Academy
Attn: Executive Secretary
Academy House
19 Dawson Street
Dublin 2
Ireland
353 1 676 4222   Fax: 353 1 676 2346
E-mail: admin@ria.ie
Web site: www.ria.ie

Purpose To permit senior scientists working in Ireland to engage in short study visits to relevant institutions abroad and to sponsor specialists from other countries who wish to visit Ireland to advise on specific techniques and developments.

Eligibility Applicants must have full professional standing and the backing of their institutions. They must be interested in visiting Ireland to advise on scientific activities. Applications are considered from all scientific disciplines except the social sciences (including economics), theoretical and clinical medicine (including pharmacy), and dentistry. The program does not support research projects as such or study leading to higher degrees.

Financial data Awards are typically in the range of the Euro equivalent of 1,500 Irish pounds. If additional funding is needed, applicants must apply to other sources.

Duration 2 to 6 weeks.

Special features Visits need not be restricted to 1 institution.

Number awarded Up to 15 each year.

Deadline October of each year.

[851]
ROYAL SOCIETY/GLAXOWELLCOME RESEARCH PROFESSORSHIP

Royal Society
Attn: Executive Secretary
6 Carlton House Terrace
London SW1Y 5AG
England
44 20 7451 2542   Fax: 44 20 7451 2692
E-mail: UKResearch.Appointments@royalsoc.ac.uk
Web site: www.royalsoc.ac.uk

Purpose To provide funding to established scholars interested in conducting medical research in the United Kingdom.

Eligibility This program is open to internationally respected scientists of any nationality who are interested in a professorship at an appropriate university or research institute in the United Kingdom. Applicants must be interested in conducting research into molecular aspects of medicine. Scientists who are currently employed outside the United Kingdom and wish to return are particularly encouraged to apply.

Financial data The salary provided by the Royal Society is the national professorial minimum plus 40 percent (currently 50,961 pounds). The host university or institute may supplement that salary if it so wishes. Professors receive a start-up grant when they begin their assignment and they may apply for research expenses up to 16,000 pounds per year. Successful applicants from overseas receive some assistance with moving expenses.

Duration These professorships are intended to extend until normal retirement age, but funding from the Royal Society extends for 15 years for professors under 40 years of age or 10 years for those over 40 years of age (or until they reach 55 years of age, whichever is longer). After expiration of Royal Society funding, the university or research institute is solely responsible for the professorship.

Special features Recipients are encouraged to maintain close links with the Royal Society and the research and development departments of GlaxoWellcome throughout the duration of the appointment.

Number awarded 1 each year.

Deadline August of each year.

[852]
RSA–ISTITUTO NAZIONALE GRANT

Renaissance Society of America
Attn: Editor, Renaissance Quarterly
24 West 12th Street
New York, NY 10011
(212) 998-3797   Fax: (212) 995-4205
E-mail: rsa@is.nyu.edu
Web site: www.r-s-a.org

Purpose To provide funding to younger scholars interested in conducting art history research in Florence, Italy.

Eligibility This program is open to younger scholars (including assistant professors; associate professors in the first 2 years of appointment at that rank; temporary, adjunct, and/or part-time professors; and independent scholars holding the Ph.D.). Applicants must be interested in using the archival, manuscript, and printed book collections of Florence and/or study the works of art of Florence and the surrounding area.

Financial data Under the terms of the grant, the Renaissance Society of America (RSA) awards the recipient $2,000 toward travel and other costs. The Istituto Nazionale di Studi sul Rinascimento provides lodging in Florence for up to 4 weeks and access to its collections.

Duration Up to 4 weeks.

Special features This program began in 2000.

Number awarded 1 each year.

Deadline October of each year.

[853]
SACKLER RESEARCH FELLOWSHIPS IN THE HISTORY OF ASTRONOMY AND NAVIGATIONAL SCIENCES

National Maritime Museum
Centre for Maritime Research
Attn: Research Administrator
Greenwich
London SE10 9NF
England
44 20 8312 6716   Fax: 44 20 8312 6722
E-mail: research@nmm.ac.uk
Web site: www.nmm.ac.uk

Purpose To provide funding to junior scholars from any country who are interested in conducting research in the history of science and scientific instruments at the Royal Observatory in Greenwich, England.

Eligibility This program is open to young postgraduate and postdoctoral scholars of any nationality, but individuals who have demonstrated equivalent commitment to advanced research in the field may also be eligible. Applicants must be interested in using the Observatory's collections of scientific instruments in the categories of astronomy, horology, hydrography, and navigation. They must have completed advanced research in 1 or more of the types of instruments represented by the collection, into the work of a particular individual or group of instrument makers related to the collection, or into some aspect of the history of the navigational sciences or the Observatory.

Financial data The stipend is 12,500 pounds per year.

Duration 1 year.

Number awarded Varies each year.

[854]
SAMUEL H. KRESS JOINT ATHENS–JERUSALEM FELLOWSHIP

American Schools of Oriental Research
Attn: Administrative Director
656 Beacon Street, Fifth Floor
Boston, MA 02215-2010
(617) 353-6570   Fax: (617) 353-6575
E-mail: asor@bu.edu
Web site: www.asor.org

Purpose To provide financial support to graduate students in selected areas of the arts or humanities who are interested in conducting dissertation research at the Albright Institute of Archaeological Research (AIAR) in Jerusalem and the American School of Classical Studies at Athens (ASCSA).

Eligibility Doctoral students in art history, architecture, archaeology or classical studies are eligible to apply for this award if they would benefit from conducting dissertation-related research at the AIAR and the ASCSA. Applicants must be U.S. citizens or North American citizens studying at U.S. institutions.

Financial data The award is $15,000, of which $8,300 is paid to the recipient as a stipend, $3,350 is paid to AIAR for room and half-board, and $3,350 is paid to ASCSA for room and board.

Duration 10 months: 5 months in Athens and 5 months in Jerusalem.

Special features Funding for this fellowship is provided by the Samuel H. Kress Foundation. Information is also available from ASCSA at 6-8 Charlton Street, Princeton, NJ 08540-5232, (609) 683-0800, Fax: (609) 924-0578.

Limitations Fellows must reside at the AIAR in Jerusalem for 5 months and the ASCSA (in Athens) for 5 months. The fellowship period should be continuous, without frequent trips outside Greece and Israel. The award may not be used in the summer. Recipients must submit a written report within 2 months of completing the program; a portion of the stipend is withheld until the report is received. An acknowledgement of support must be included in published reports of the project.

Number awarded 1 each year.

Deadline October of each year.

[855]
SCHOLARSHIP IN FRENCH CINEMA STUDIES

Society for French American Cultural Services and Educational Aid
c/o French Cultural Services
972 Fifth Avenue
New York, NY 10021
(212) 439-1433   Fax: (212) 439-1455
E-mail: info@facsea.org
Web site: www.facsea.org

Purpose To provide financial assistance to U.S. graduate students interested in conducting research on French cinema in France.

Eligibility This program is open to master's and Ph.D. candidates engaged in studying French cinema. Applicants must be U.S. citizens enrolled at a U.S. university and interested in conducting a project that involves research in France with an accredited French institution. They must have a working knowledge of French.

Financial data The program provides a monthly stipend of approximately 9,000 French francs (1,372 Euros), health insurance while in France, and round-trip air transportation.

Duration 9 months, beginning in September.

Number awarded 1 each year.

Deadline January of each year.

[856]
SCHOLARSHIPS FOR POSTDOCTORAL RESEARCH STUDIES IN GREECE

State Scholarships Foundation
Attn: Section Chief
14 Lyssicratous Street
GR-105 58 Athens
Greece
30 1 325 4385   Fax: 30 1 322 1863

Purpose To provide financial assistance for postdoctoral research studies in Greece to nationals of the United States and other countries.

Eligibility Applicants must be nationals of the United States, Canada, Australia, Japan, or western Europe who hold a doctoral degree from a university in their country. They must have an excellent knowledge of English or French; be younger than 45 years of age; and have an agreement with a professor at a Greek university to cooperate with them during their postdoctoral research studies.

Financial data The scholarship provides a monthly allowance of the Euro equivalent of 200,000 Greek drachmas for living expenses, an allowance of the EUR equivalent of 150,000 drhs for initial expenses, free medical care and medication, exemption from any tuition or registration fees, and a stay of residence permit dues. No funding is provided for a spouse or other dependents.

Duration 6 months to 1 year.

Special features Applications may be obtained from the address above or from Greek diplomatic authorities (embassy or consulate) in the applicant's country, but all applications must be submitted to the latter.

Limitations Support is not provided for conferences, seminars, symposia, or research activities. The recipient is not permitted to undertake paid employment of any kind or any other laboratory or seminar courses.

Number awarded 15 each year.

Deadline February of each year.

[857]
SCHOLARSHIPS FOR YOUNG RESEARCHERS AND UNIVERSITY TEACHING STAFF

Center for International Mobility
Attn: Information Services
P.O. Box 343
Hakaniemenkatu 2
FIN-00531 Helsinki
Finland
358 9 7747 7033   Fax: 358 9 7747 7064
E-mail: cimoinfo@cimo.fi
Web site: www.cimo.fi

Purpose To encourage young researchers from other countries who are interested in conducting research or teaching at a university in Finland.

Eligibility This program is open to nationals of countries other than Finland who are under the age of 35, are fluent in Finnish, and are interested in teaching or conducting a joint research project in Finland. Applicants may be either at the postgraduate (master's degree required) or postdoctoral level. The staff of the Finnish receiving university department must submit the application.

Financial data The award consists of a monthly allowance of the Euro equivalent of 4,000 to 6,000 Finnish marks (depending on academic qualifications of the recipient and support from the receiving institution).

Duration From 3 to 12 months.

Special features The Center for International Mobility (CIMO) is an agency of the Finnish Ministry of Education.

Deadline Applications may be submitted at any time, but they must be received at least 3 months prior to the beginning of the scholarship.

[858]
SCHOOL OF CLASSICAL STUDIES PREDOCTORAL FELLOWSHIPS AT THE AMERICAN ACADEMY IN ROME

American Academy in Rome
Attn: Fellowship Coordinator
7 East 60th Street
New York, NY 10022-1001
(212) 751-7200   Fax: (212) 751-7220
E-mail: info@aarome.org
Web site: www.aarome.org

Purpose To provide an opportunity for American doctoral candidates in history of art, classical studies and archaeology, or post-classical humanistic/modern Italian studies to engage in research at the American Academy in Rome.

Eligibility This program is open to U.S. citizens who have completed all Ph.D. course work in 1) classical studies and archaeology, 2) history of art, or 3) post-classical humanistic studies (political, economic, cultural, and church history, or history of literature and musicology, all since 300 A.D.) and modern Italian studies. They must be interested in conducting their research at the American Academy in Rome. Applicants for 1-year fellowships must have completed approximately 1 year of work on their dissertation.

Financial data The fellowship provides a stipend of up to $15,000 per year, meals, a bedroom with private bath, and a study or studio. Fellows with children under 18 are housed outside the McKim, Mead & White building and are provided with an allowance that helps cover the cost of off-campus housing.

Duration 1 or 2 years.

Special features The American Academy in Rome, founded in 1894 by the American architect Charles F. McKim, is a center for independent study and advanced research in the fine arts and humanities. It consists of a School of Fine Arts (including architecture, landscape architecture, design arts, painting and sculpture, musical composition, and literature) and a School of Classical Studies (including classical studies and archaeology, history of art, and post-classical humanistic/modern Italian studies).

Number awarded 6 each year: 2 for 1 year in classical studies and archaeology, 1 for 2 years in classical studies and archaeology, 1 for 2 years in history of art, and 2 for 1 year in post-classical humanistic/modern Italian studies.

Deadline November of each year.

[859]
SECOND AIR DIVISION USAAF ARCHIVIST/LIBRARIAN

Council for International Exchange of Scholars
3007 Tilden Street, N.W., Suite 5L
Washington, DC 20008-3009
(202) 686-6245   Fax: (202) 362-3442
E-mail: scholars@cies.iie.org
Web site: www.iie.org/cies

Purpose To enable an American librarian to work on the staff of the Second Air Division Memorial Library in the United Kingdom.

Eligibility This program is open to U.S. citizens who hold a 1) master's of library science or master's of information science degree with archives, records, and management specialization, or 2) higher degree in history with archival management experience. Applicants must have experience in inquiry service (especially in a public library), archival cataloging and international standards for archival description, public speaking, information technology, and Web site development. They must be interested in working at the library in Norwich.

Financial data The stipend is approximately 22,000 pounds, plus round-trip travel for the grantee and 1 dependent.

Duration 12 months; may be renewed by mutual agreement.

Special features This is a Fulbright scholar program, sponsored by the Bureau of Educational and Cultural Affairs of the U.S. Department of State and administered by the Council for International Exchange of Scholars. The recipient provides inquiry answering service, maintains the Web site, catalogs material from the archive of the trust, develops and maintains links with schools, serves as a public speaker, and advises the trust staff regarding Memorial Trust materials.

Number awarded 1 each year.

Deadline July of each year.

[860]
SENIOR VISITING RESEARCH FELLOWSHIPS IN IRISH STUDIES

Queen's University of Belfast
Attn: Institute of Irish Studies
8 Fitzwilliam Street
Belfast BT7 6AW
Northern Ireland
44 1232 273386   Fax: 44 1232 439238
E-mail: iis@qub.ac.uk
Web site: www.qub.ac.uk

Purpose To provide support to established scholars who wish to conduct research in Irish studies at the Queen's University of Belfast.

Eligibility Established scholars are eligible to apply if they have a strong publication record and are interested in preparing work for publication in any field of Irish studies at the university's Institute of Irish Studies. Preference is given to candidates based outside Northern Ireland who are on leave from their home institution.

Financial data The stipend is 16,286 pounds per year.

Duration 1 year, beginning in October.

Limitations Fellows are required to be based at the institute during the academic year, to attend and present a paper to the institute's seminars, and to contribute fully to the life of the institute.

Number awarded Up to 2 each year.

Deadline January of each year.

[861]
SHEELAGH MURNAGHAN VISITING PROFESSORSHIP

Queen's University of Belfast
Attn: Academic Council Office
Administration Building
Belfast BT7 1NN
Northern Ireland
44 28 9027 3006   Fax: 44 28 9031 3537
E-mail: academic.council@qub.ac.uk
Web site: www.qub.ac.uk

Purpose To encourage the participation of women in their chosen field of study by providing them with a visiting professorship at Queen's University of Belfast.

Eligibility Candidates may be women who have either a proven academic standing and appropriate achievement in research and scholarship, or who have attained professional eminence in industry, business, government service, the professions, the arts, medicine, engineering, or the sciences. They may be from any country and must be seeking a short-term assignment at the University of Belfast in Northern Ireland. The assignment may be in the field of women's studies. Normally, candidates should be on paid leave of absence from their employment.

Financial data The stipend is 1,600 pounds; funds are to be used to cover travel and living expenses.

Duration 1 month.

Number awarded 1 each year.

Deadline October of each year.

[862]
SHORT-TERM TRAVEL GRANTS FOR CENTRAL AND EASTERN EUROPE AND EURASIA

International Research & Exchanges Board
1616 H Street, N.W.
Washington, DC 20006
(202) 628-8188   Fax: (202) 628-8189
E-mail: irex@irex.org
Web site: www.irex.org

Purpose To allow U.S. scholars to pursue their individual research or other activities in the social sciences or humanities in central Europe, eastern Europe, or Eurasia.

Eligibility Applicants must be U.S. citizens who have the Ph.D. or an equivalent professional doctoral degree and need support for humanities or social sciences projects. Proposals may include library or archival research, carrying out interviews, presentations at scholarly conferences, invited lectures or consultations, or collaborative projects (such as joint publications or comparative surveys). The project must involve central Europe, eastern Europe, or Eurasia, including, in special circumstances, Iran or Turkey.

Financial data Grants up to a maximum of $3,000 may be awarded; funds may be used for round-trip airfare on a U.S. flag carrier, per diem up to $100 per day for food and lodging, conference registration fees, and visa fees.

Duration Up to 60 days; a per diem will be allowed only up to 14 days.

Special features The International Research & Exchanges Board (IREX) was established in 1968 at the request of U.S.

universities by the American Council of Learned Societies (ACLS) and the Social Science Research Council (SSRC) to administer research exchange programs with the socialist countries of eastern Europe and the former Soviet republics. This program is funded by the U.S. Department of State as a Title VIII program and the National Endowment for the Humanities (NEH).

Number awarded Varies each year; in a recent round, 32 of these grants were awarded, including 4 funded by NEH and 28 by the Department of State.

Deadline January or May of each year.

[863]
SIDNEY SUSSEX COLLEGE RESEARCH FELLOWSHIPS

University of Cambridge
Sidney Sussex College
Attn: Master's Secretary
Sidney Street
Cambridge CB2 3HU
England
44 1223 338800   Fax: 44 1223 338884
Web site: www.sid.cam.ac.uk

Purpose To provide funding to postdoctoral scholars interested in conducting research at Sidney Sussex College at the University of Cambridge in England.

Eligibility This program is open to scholars from any country who are interested in conducting research at Sidney Sussex College. Applicants should be close to completing their Ph.D. or have received that degree within the last 3 years.

Financial data The annual stipend is 10,792 pounds, or 12,282 pounds if the fellow already holds the Ph.D. degree. An additional allowance of 2,275 pounds per year is provided to fellows not resident in college. Increments of 450 pounds are payable in successive years of tenure. Fellows are also entitled to a room at the college and to dining and other rights.

Duration 3 years.

Special features Each year the college designates a field or fields for these fellowships (recently, mathematics, the sciences, engineering, medicine, or veterinary medicine). Also available in some years is the Knox-Shaw Research Fellowship in Mathematics.

Number awarded 1 or 2 each year.

Deadline September of each year.

[864]
SIENA CHAIR IN ECONOMICS

Council for International Exchange of Scholars
3007 Tilden Street, N.W., Suite 5L
Washington, DC 20008-3009
(202) 686-6245   Fax: (202) 362-3442
E-mail: scholars@cies.iie.org
Web site: www.iie.org/cies

Purpose To allow distinguished American scholars to lecture on economics at the University of Siena in Italy.

Eligibility Applicants should hold the rank of full professor with a specialization in comparative economic policy, fiscal and monetary policy, international economics (micro and macro), economic theory (including mathematical economics and game theory), international transportation economics, or public economics. They must be interested in lecturing at the University of Siena. U.S. citizenship is required. Some knowledge of Italian is useful but not required.

Financial data The stipend is the Euro equivalent of 16,800,000 Italian lire plus a settling-in allowance of the EUR equivalent of 1,500,000 lire. The grant also provides international travel (for the grantee only) plus the EUR equivalent of 200,000 lire per month for each accompanying dependent.

Duration 3 months.

Special features This is a Fulbright scholar program, sponsored by the Bureau of Educational and Cultural Affairs of the U.S. Department of State and administered by the Council for International Exchange of Scholars. In addition to lecturing at the graduate level at the University of Siena, grantees participate in research collaboration and provide a series of specialized seminars for advanced graduate students and faculty.

Number awarded 1 each year.

Deadline April of each year.

[865]
SIGMUND FREUD SOCIETY VISITING SCHOLAR IN PSYCHOANALYSIS

Council for International Exchange of Scholars
3007 Tilden Street, N.W., Suite 5L
Washington, DC 20008-3009
(202) 686-6240   Fax: (202) 362-3442
E-mail: scholars@cies.iie.org
Web site: www.iie.org/cies

Purpose To provide funding to psychoanalysts who wish to teach a course in Austria and conduct research at the Sigmund Freud Museum in Vienna.

Eligibility Applicants must have several years of teaching/lecturing or professional experience in relevant fields: history, theory, application, and/or practice of psychoanalysis. They must be interested in conducting research at the Sigmund Freud Museum in Vienna and teaching at least 1 lecture course or seminar on a topic related to their research project at a Viennese host institution. Applicants must solicit a letter of invitation from the Sigmund Freud Society by submitting a curriculum vitae and research/lecturing proposal. Some German proficiency is recommended; lecturing is in English. U.S. citizenship is required.

Financial data Grantees receive a maintenance allowance of 3,300 Euros per month and a travel grant of EUR 770). Housing is provided by the institution. No dependent allowances are provided.

Duration 4 months.

Special features This is a Fulbright scholar program, sponsored by the Bureau of Educational and Cultural Affairs of the U.S. Department of State and administered by the Council for International Exchange of Scholars.

Number awarded 1 each year.

Deadline July of each year.

[866]
SIGRID JUSELIUS MEDICAL RESEARCH GRANTS

Sigrid Juselius Foundation
Aleksanterinkatu 48 B
FIN-00100 Helsinki
Finland
358 9 634 461   Fax: 358 9 634 502

Purpose To provide funding for medical research in Finland.

Eligibility Senior scientists from any country are eligible to apply, although preference is given to Finnish investigators. Applicants must be interested in conducting medical research, either clinical or non-clinical, in Finland. Non-Finnish applicants must collaborate on a research project with a Finnish scientist.

Financial data The amount awarded averages $45,000 per year. A total of $3.5 million is distributed annually. Funds may be used for equipment, materials, travel, etc.

Duration Most grants are for a few months, but they may extend as long as 2 years.

Limitations The sponsoring Finnish scientist must administer the grant and act as an employer of the visiting investigator. Applications are not accepted directly from non-Finnish scientists.

Number awarded Varies each year; recently, 84 Finnish and 13 non-Finnish researchers received grants.

Deadline April and September of each year.

[867]
SIMON INDUSTRIAL AND PROFESSIONAL FELLOWSHIPS

University of Manchester
Attn: Director of Personnel
Oxford Road
Manchester M13 9PL
England
44 161 275 2068   Fax: 44 161 275 2445
E-mail: nick.church@man.ac.uk
Web site: www.man.ac.uk

Purpose To provide financial assistance to established professionals who wish to conduct research or participate in other activities while affiliated with the University of Manchester in England.

Eligibility Nationals of any country may apply if they are self employed or employed in industry, commerce, public service, or the professions. They must be proposing to conduct research or to develop a program of teaching or continuing education in any academic department at the University of Manchester. Applicants should have a first degree in a relevant subject or equivalent qualification. A record of research and publications or demonstrated potential for research is essential, and teaching experience is desirable. Candidates from universities and other institutions of higher education in the United Kingdom are not normally accepted.

Financial data The amount awarded depends on the experience and qualifications of the fellow.

Duration 6 weeks.

Special features This program was established in 1990, to complement the Simon Research Fellowships.

Limitations Fellowships are not awarded for postgraduate study.

Number awarded At least 1 each year.

Deadline September of each year.

[868]
SIMON RESEARCH FELLOWSHIPS

University of Manchester
Attn: Director of Personnel
Oxford Road
Manchester M13 9PL
England
44 161 275 2068   Fax: 44 161 275 2445
E-mail: nick.church@man.ac.uk
Web site: www.man.ac.uk

Purpose To provide financial assistance to established scholars who wish to conduct social science research while affiliated with the University of Manchester in England.

Eligibility Nationals of any country may apply if they have earned an advanced degree and have a record of research and publications or demonstrated potential for research in a relevant subject area of the social sciences, defined broadly. They must propose a program of research at the University of Manchester. Preference is given to outstanding researchers who are near the beginning of their academic careers.

Financial data The amount awarded depends on the qualifications and experience of the fellow; the range is from 16,775 to 30,967 pounds per year.

Duration 3 years.

Special features These fellowships were established as the result of a gift in 1944 from the Rt. Hon. Lord Simon of Wythenshawe, of Didsbury.

Number awarded 1 or more each year.

Deadline September of each year.

[869]
SIMON VISITING PROFESSORSHIPS

University of Manchester
Attn: Director of Personnel
Oxford Road
Manchester M13 9PL
England
44 161 275 2068   Fax: 44 161 275 2445
E-mail: nick.church@man.ac.uk
Web site: www.man.ac.uk

Purpose To provide financial assistance to established scholars who are invited to teach and conduct social science research at the University of Manchester in England.

Eligibility This program is open to distinguished scholars in the social sciences, defined to include economic history, education, history, law, philosophy, and social psychology. Candidates must be nominated by the appropriate department at the university to come to lecture and conduct research; direct applications are not accepted.

Financial data Awards provide for payment of travel and subsistence expenses.

Duration Up to 5 weeks.

Special features These professorships were established as the result of a gift in 1944 from the Rt. Hon. Lord Simon of Wythenshawe, of Didsbury.

Limitations Visiting professors are expected to remain in Manchester during the tenure of their professorship and provide lectures and seminars, advise research students, and participate in 1 or more research programs.
Number awarded 1 or more each year.
Deadline September of each year.

[870]
SIMONE AND CINO DEL DUCA FOUNDATION LITERARY SCHOLARSHIPS

Simone and Cino del Duca Foundation
10 rue Alfred de Vigny
75008 Paris
France
33 1 47 66 01 21   Fax: 33 1 47 22 45 02

Purpose To enable young writers of literature in the French language to pursue their work under more favorable conditions.
Eligibility This program is open to authors under the age of 45 who write in the French language in any literary genre (novels, essays, short stories) except poetry. Applicants may be from any country and may conduct their work anywhere in the world.
Financial data The stipends are the Euro equivalent of 50,000 French francs for an author whose work has already been published and the EUR equivalent of FF 20,000 for an unpublished writer.
Duration The scholarships are awarded annually.
Deadline May of each year.

[871]
SIMONE AND CINO DEL DUCA FOUNDATION MAINTENANCE AND TRAVELING GRANTS

Simone and Cino del Duca Foundation
10 rue Alfred de Vigny
75008 Paris
France
33 1 47 66 01 21   Fax: 33 1 47 22 45 02

Purpose To provide financial assistance to biomedical scientists in France who wish to go abroad or to researchers from other countries who wish to conduct research in a French laboratory.
Eligibility This program is open to researchers who specialize in the cardiovascular system (molecular and cellular biology, pathology, pharmacology, epidemiology) or the nervous system (including mental health and behavior). They must be interested in conducting research in a French laboratory. There are no age limits, but applicants must have completed their Ph.D. degree before they apply for the grant.
Financial data Stipends cover all "maintenance" expenses. The exact amount is determined according to the scale of salaries of the research workers in France and to the applicant's current salary, age, and personal needs. Grants are also available to cover round-trip travel expenses between the applicant's laboratory and the host laboratory in France. Funds may not be used to cover conference costs.
Duration From 8 days to 1 year.
Special features This program also enables French research workers to go abroad.

Limitations Recipients must supply their own insurance coverage. They may not hold other grants while participating in this program.
Deadline March of each year.

[872]
SIR ALAN WILSON RESEARCH FELLOWSHIP

University of Cambridge
Emmanuel College
Attn: Research Fellowships' Secretary
St. Andrew's Street
Cambridge CB2 3AP
England
44 1223 334200   Fax: 44 1223 334426
E-mail: res-fell-info-package@emma.cam.ac.uk
Web site: www.emma.cam.ac.uk

Purpose To provide funding to postdoctoral scholars interested in conducting research in the medical or biological sciences at Emmanuel College of the University of Cambridge in England.
Eligibility This program is open to scholars from any country who are interested in conducting research at Emmanuel College in the medical or biological sciences. Applicants must be under 30 years of age and have completed or be near completion of a doctoral degree.
Financial data The annual stipend for fellows who have not yet completed the Ph.D. is 14,418 pounds if they are resident in college or 15,918 pounds if they are living out. For fellows who have completed the Ph.D., the annual stipend is 15,361 if they are resident in college or 16,861 pounds if they are living out. Other benefits include grants for research expenses and academic travel, a book allowance, and assistance with computing facilities.
Duration Up to 3 years.
Special features This fellowship has been endowed by Glaxo Wellcome PLC.
Number awarded 1 or more each year.
Deadline October of each year.

[873]
SIR JAMES KNOTT FELLOWSHIPS

University of Newcastle upon Tyne
Attn: Enquiries and Scholarships Officer
10 Kensington Terrace
Newcastle upon Tyne NE1 7RU
England
44 191 222 5742   Fax: 44 191 222 6139
E-mail: fellowships@ncl.ac.uk
Web site: www.ncl.ac.uk

Purpose To provide financial assistance to established scholars who wish to conduct research while affiliated with the University of Newcastle upon Tyne in England.
Eligibility Nationals of any country (outside of England) may apply if they have earned an advanced degree (normally within the past 10 years), are likely to make a noteworthy contribution to knowledge, and are interested in conducting research while visiting the University of Newcastle upon Tyne. There are no restrictions on the subject of the proposed research.

Financial data The stipend is 17,238 pounds for the first year and 18,185 pounds for the second year.
Duration 2 years.
Number awarded 2 each year.
Deadline November of each year.

[874] SMITHSONIAN INSTITUTION FOREIGN CURRENCY GRANT PROGRAM

Smithsonian Institution
Attn: Office of International Relations
S. Dillon Ripley Center, Room 3123
Washington, DC 20560-0705
(202) 357-4795   Fax: (202) 275-0489

Purpose To provide financial aid to American scholars interested in conducting research in countries where the United States holds excess foreign currencies.
Eligibility The program welcomes proposals from senior scholars at American institutions of higher learning (including the Smithsonian Institution) in the fields of anthropology and archaeology, cultural history, evolutionary and conservation biology, astrophysics and earth sciences, and museum programs. Applicants must be interested in conducting research in "excess currency countries." Proposals should provide a summary and description of the research, including methodology, bibliography, biographical information on major participants, and a detailed budget.
Financial data The awards are in local currency and cover international and local travel, living allowance, and research expenses.
Duration 1 year; renewable is possible.
Special features For the purposes of this program, "excess currency countries" are defined as those in which the U.S. government owns local currencies derived from sales of agricultural commodities under Public Law 480. Most recently, the excess currency countries were Croatia, Czech Republic, Hungary, India, Poland, Slovak Republic, and Slovenia.
Limitations Host government approval for the conduct of research funded through this program is required in all excess currency countries. In some cases, local and state authorities must also approve projects. In addition, U.S. embassy concurrence is required. Funds cannot be authorized until all necessary governmental clearances have been obtained.
Deadline October of each year.

[875] SNORRI STURLUSON ICELANDIC FELLOWSHIPS

Sigurdur Nordal Institute
Pingholtsstraeti 29
P.O. Box 1220
121 Reykjavik
Iceland
354 562 6050   Fax: 354 562 6263
Web site: www.nordals.hi.is

Purpose To provide financial assistance to humanities scholars from outside Iceland who are interested in visiting Iceland to improve their knowledge of Icelandic language, culture, and society.
Eligibility Eligible to apply are writers, translators, and other scholars in the field of humanities who live outside of Iceland and are interested in visiting Iceland to improve their knowledge of Icelandic language, culture, and society. University students are excluded. Preference is given to candidates from eastern or southern Europe, Asia, Africa, Latin America, and Oceania. There is no special application form; applicants should submit a brief but thorough description of the purpose of their proposed visit, as well as details about their education and publications.
Financial data The fellowship covers travel expenses to and from Iceland, plus living expenses while in the country.
Duration At least 3 months.
Special features Sturluson, a famous Icelandic author, completed his written works prior to 1220 A.D.
Limitations At the conclusion of their stay, fellows are expected to submit a report on how the grant was spent.
Number awarded 1 or more each year.
Deadline October of each year.

[876] SOCIAL ANTHROPOLOGY/INDOLOGY JUNIOR RESEARCH FELLOWSHIP AT WOLFSON COLLEGE

University of Oxford
Wolfson College
Attn: President's Secretary
Linton Road
Oxford OX2 6UD
England
44 1865 274100   Fax: 44 1865 274125
E-mail: sue.hales@wolfson.ox.ac.uk
Web site: www.wolfson.ox.ac.uk

Purpose To provide funding to postdoctoral scholars from any country who wish to conduct research in social anthropology or Indology at Wolfson College of the University of Oxford in England.
Eligibility This program is open to residents of any country who are interested in conducting postdoctoral research while in residence at Wolfson College. Applicants should normally be younger than 30 years of age and should have at least 2 years of research experience in the subject. Selection is based on a sample of the applicant's written work, up to 10,000 words. The fields of research alternate between social anthropology and Indology.
Financial data The stipend is 11,478 pounds per year. Fellows also receive room and board at the college. Fellows who are married or who require family accommodations may live in college and pay the difference in rent or live outside the college and receive a housing allowance equivalent to the cost of single accommodations at the college.
Duration 3 years.
Special features Fellows are permitted to undertake up to 6 hours of teaching per week.
Number awarded 1 every 3 years; the current schedule is to offer a fellowship in Indology in 2003 and social anthropology in 2006.
Deadline March of the years the fellowship is offered.

[877]
SOCIETE GENERALE SCHOLARSHIP FOR MUSIC
French Cultural Services
972 Fifth Avenue
New York, NY 10021-0144
(212) 439-1438   Fax: (212) 439-1455
E-mail: emmanuel.morlet@diplomatie.fr
Web site: www.frenchculture.org

Purpose To provide financial assistance to U.S. graduate students interested in conducting research related to music in France.

Eligibility This program is open to U.S. citizens enrolled in a graduate program at a U.S. university or conservatory. Eligible fields of specialization include conducting, performing, composition, and musicology. Applicants must be proposing to conduct research related to French culture and must indicate a need for their research to be conducted in France.

Financial data The stipend is the Euro equivalent of approximately 8,000 French francs per month. Other benefits include round-trip airfare and health insurance.

Duration 9 months.

Special features This program, established in 1998, is financed by the Société Générale, a French banking and finance company.

Number awarded 1 each year.

Deadline May of each year.

[878]
SOCIETY FOR THE ADVANCEMENT OF SCANDINAVIAN STUDIES TRAVEL GRANTS
Swedish Information Service
One Dag Hammarskjold Plaza, 45th Floor
New York, NY 10017-2201
(212) 751-5900   Fax: (212) 752-4789
E-mail: requests@swedeninfo.com
Web site: www.swedeninfo.com

Purpose To provide funding for travel associated with the study of or research on Swedish studies to members of the Society for the Advancement of Scandinavian Studies.

Eligibility This program is open to members of the society, preferably graduate students or untenured faculty members. Applicants must be interested in studying or conducting research in the following areas: Swedish language, linguistics, or literature. They may conduct this research in Sweden or in North America. Graduate students in the social sciences may use the grants for intensive Swedish language study in Sweden.

Financial data The amount awarded varies, depending upon the needs of the recipient.

Duration Up to 1 year.

Number awarded Varies; generally, up to 5 each year.

Deadline March of each year.

[879]
SOCIETY FOR THE ANTHROPOLOGY OF EUROPE PRE-DISSERTATION FELLOWSHIPS FOR RESEARCH IN ANTHROPOLOGY
Council for European Studies
c/o Columbia University
1203 International Affairs Building, MC 3310
420 West 118th Street
New York, NY 10027
(212) 854-4172   Fax: (212) 854-8808
E-mail: ces@columbia.edu
Web site: www.europanet.org

Purpose To enable graduate students in anthropology to pursue short-term exploratory research in Europe, in order to determine the viability and to refine the scope of their proposed dissertation.

Eligibility This program is open to anthropology graduate students at U.S. and Canadian universities who are in the second or third year of a program and have completed, or are close to completing, course work and/or Ph.D. qualifying examinations. Applicants should be interested in working on a dissertation topic in the social and cultural anthropology of contemporary Europe, but should have neither fully formulated nor defended a dissertation prospectus. Students should be seeking to test the feasibility and research design of a projected dissertation in Europe; they may not be pursuing language courses or instruction at a European university nor supplementing a comparable or larger fellowship for research in Europe.

Financial data Fellowships provide $4,000 for travel and living expenses.

Duration 2 to 3 months, during the summer or autumn.

Special features The first awards for this program were offered in 2000.

Number awarded 1 each year.

Deadline January of each year.

[880]
SOCIETY OF ANTIQUARIES MINOR GRANTS
Society of Antiquaries of London
Attn: General Secretary
Burlington House
Piccadilly
London W1J 0BE
England
44 20 7734 0193   Fax: 44 20 7287 6967
E-mail: admin@sal.org.uk
Web site: www.sal.org.uk

Purpose To provide financial assistance to scholars and others interested in conducting archaeological or other research involving antiquities.

Eligibility This program is normally open to fellows of the Society of Antiquarians of London and U.K. citizens who are not fellows, although consideration is also given to non-fellows from abroad who are working in cooperation with people from the United Kingdom and whose research is directly related to the United Kingdom. Applicants must be proposing to conduct archaeological, documentary, or antiquarian research; there are no geographical or chronological limitations. Awards are not made for research related to an undergraduate or graduate degree unless the project, although related to the applicant's academic work, has an independent research status. In no circumstances will the cost of dissertation or thesis preparation be considered.

Financial data Grants up to 2,000 pounds are available.

Duration 1 year; may be renewed for up to 2 additional years.

Special features This program includes 2 specialized funds: the Joan Pye Awards for research in prehistoric and Roman archaeology of the United Kingdom and the Hugh Chapman Memorial Research Fund for research projects involving the western Roman empire and antiquarian matters in London and its environs.

Limitations Recipients are required to submit, by the end of February of the year following that in which a grant is made, a report of 500 to 5,000 words on how the research objectives were met.

Number awarded Varies each year; recently, 18 of these grants with a total value of 29,680 pounds were awarded.

Deadline January of each year.

[881]
SOLOW SUMMER RESEARCH FELLOWSHIPS
American School of Classical Studies at Athens
Attn: Director
54 Souidias Street
GR-106 76 Athens
Greece
30 1 723 6313   Fax: 30 1 725 0584
Web site: www.ascsa.org

Purpose To provide financial support to postdoctoral scholars working on the archaeological excavations of the American School of Classical Studies at Athens.

Eligibility This program is open to postdoctoral scholars working towards publication of material from the school's excavations at the Athenian Agora or Ancient Corinth. Preference is given to those who plan to be in residence for a minimum of 2 months.

Financial data Fellowships provide airfare and a stipend of $1,500 per month.

Duration Up to 3 months.

Special features This program began in summer of 1998. It is sponsored by the American School of Classical Studies at Athens and the Solow Art and Architecture Foundation, 9 West 57th Street, Suite 4500, New York, NY 10019.

Number awarded Several each year.

Deadline January of each year.

[882]
SPAIN FULBRIGHT TEACHER EXCHANGE
U.S. Department of State
c/o Graduate School, USDA
600 Maryland Avenue, S.W., Room 320
Washington, DC 20024-2520
(202) 314-3520   Fax: (202) 479-6806
E-mail: fulbright@grad.usda.gov
Web site: www.grad.usda.gov/International/ftep.html

Purpose To promote mutual understanding between the people of the United States and the people of Spain through a teacher exchange program.

Eligibility This program is open to teachers of any subject in grades 9 through 12 who are interested in teaching English as a foreign language in Spain. Applicants must 1) be U.S. citizens; 2) hold at least a bachelor's degree; 3) be fluent in English; 4) have a current full-time teaching assignment in the U.S. or a territory; 5) have the approval of their school administration; 6) have at least 3 years of full-time experience; and 7) not have participated in a Fulbright Teacher Exchange longer than 8 weeks during the last 2 years. Fluency in Spanish is preferred but not required. Teaching couples may apply. However, because of the limited number of positions available and, often, the lack of foreign candidate pairs with similar qualifications for interchanges, it may not be possible to arrange suitable assignments in the same locality or to place both teachers. Preference is given to applicants who have not participated previously in the program and may be given to applicants who have not previously lived in Spain. Geographic distribution of awards within the United States is also a factor in selection. This program does not discriminate on the basis of race, color, religion, age, sex, or national origin and encourages the applications of members of minority communities. Other considerations being equal, veterans are given preference.

Financial data Only round-trip transportation is provided. Participants must obtain a leave of absence with pay from their jobs in the United States. The U.S. school must agree to accept a Spanish teacher who must secure a leave of absence with pay.

Duration 10 months, beginning in September.

Special features This program is sponsored by the Bureau of Educational and Cultural Affairs of the U.S. Department of State and administered by the Graduate School, USDA.

Limitations This program provides for the direct exchange of teaching assignments between Spain and the United States. Applicants selected for exchange must attend orientation programs of the sponsoring agencies in the United States or abroad.

Number awarded 5 each year.

Deadline October of each year.

[883]
ST. CATHARINE'S COLLEGE RESEARCH FELLOWSHIPS

University of Cambridge
St. Catharine's College
Attn: Secretary for the Research Fellowships Competition
Trumpington Street
Cambridge CB2 1RL
England
44 1223 338300   Fax: 44 1223 338340
Web site: www.caths.cam.ac.uk

Purpose To provide funding to postdoctoral scholars interested in conducting research in the sciences at St. Catharine's College of the University of Cambridge in England.

Eligibility This program is open to graduates of any university who either are members of St. Catharine's College or are engaged in research in the sciences and wish to conduct research at the college. Applicants should be at an early stage in their academic career and should have recently completed (or be close to completing) their Ph.D. research. They should not have been engaged in full-time postgraduate research for longer than 4 years and should not have held a research fellowship elsewhere.

Financial data The stipend is negotiable, depending on experience.

Duration 3 years.

Number awarded 2 each year.

Deadline November of each year.

[884]
ST. JOHN'S COLLEGE JUNIOR RESEARCH FELLOWSHIPS

University of Oxford
St. John's College
Attn: Academic Administrator
St. Giles
Oxford OX1 3JP
England
44 1865 277495   Fax: 44 1865 277435
E-mail: college.office@sjc.ox.ac.uk
Web site: www.sjc.ox.ac.uk

Purpose To provide funding to junior investigators interested in conducting research at St. John's College of the University of Oxford in England.

Eligibility This program is open to scholars in designated fields of the arts and sciences who are nearing completion of their doctoral research or have begun postdoctoral study. Researchers who have held a comparable appointment at a college in the Universities of Cambridge or Oxford or have completed more than 6 years of postgraduate study or research are not eligible. Applicants must be interested in undertaking a specific research project at Oxford.

Financial data The fellow receives a stipend of 14,851 pounds per year, free meals, and free accommodations at the college or an annual housing allowance of 2,082 pounds.

Duration 3 years; may be renewed for 1 additional year.

Special features In the most recent offering of these fellowships, the fields were art history, law, mathematics, medicine, modern languages, physiology, psychology, and sociology.

Number awarded 4 (2 in the arts and 2 in the sciences) on a triennial schedule: 2004-05, 2007-8, etc.

Deadline December of the year prior to the fellowship's availability.

[885]
STAINES MEDICAL RESEARCH FELLOWSHIP

University of Oxford
Exeter College
Attn: The Rector
Oxford OX1 3DP
England
44 1865 279600   Fax: 44 1865 279645
E-mail: academic.administration@exeter.ox.ac.uk
Web site: www.exeter.ox.ac.uk

Purpose To provide funding to postdoctoral scholars from any country who wish to conduct medical research at Exeter College of the University of Oxford in England.

Eligibility This program is open to residents of any country who are interested in conducting postdoctoral research in the medical sciences while in residence at Exeter College.

Financial data The stipend is 10,240 pounds per year. Fellows also receive rooms at the college or a housing allowance.

Duration 2 years; may be renewed for 1 additional year.

Number awarded This fellowship is awarded periodically. It was last awarded in 2002.

[886]
STINT FELLOWSHIPS PROGRAM

Swedish Foundation for International Cooperation in Research and Higher Education
Skeppargatan 8
S-114 52 Stockholm
Sweden
46 8 662 7690   Fax: 46 8 661 9210
E-mail: info@stint.se
Web site: www.stint.se

Purpose To provide funding to establish exchanges between scholars in Sweden and other countries.

Eligibility Applications may be submitted by a university department or research group in Sweden that has established contacts with a foreign partner and wishes to develop an exchange program for researchers and university teachers. Participation in the program is open to all areas of the natural sciences, social sciences, and humanities. The exchange should benefit research as well as postgraduate and undergraduate education. Participation is open to universities in countries outside the European Union (EU). In the humanities and the social sciences, the program will also support exchanges with partner universities within the EU.

Financial data Grants cover costs related to the exchange of faculty, postdoctoral researchers, and postgraduate students of the partner universities. They are not intended for salaries at the home university.

Duration Up to 4 years.

Special features The Swedish Foundation for International Cooperation in Research and Higher Education (STINT) was established in 1994 to administer the visiting programs of all Swedish research councils.

Number awarded Varies each year.
Deadline December of each year.

[887]
STINT VISITING SCIENTISTS/SCHOLARS

Swedish Foundation for International Cooperation in
  Research and Higher Education
Skeppargatan 8
S-114 52 Stockholm
Sweden
46 8 662 7690 Fax: 46 8 661 9210
E-mail: info@stint.se
Web site: www.stint.se

Purpose To provide funding to bring eminent foreign scientists and scholars to Sweden.
Eligibility Applications may be submitted by a university department or research group in Sweden that wishes to invite a foreign scholar to visit. Positions are available in all fields of science and the humanities and may be for any type of scholarly work. Applications must be submitted by the Swedish host, not the foreign scholar.
Financial data The stipend depends on the nature of the proposal.
Duration 6 to 12 months.
Special features Recipients are encouraged to hold lectures and/or seminars for students/colleagues during their stay. The Swedish Foundation for International Cooperation in Research and Higher Education (STINT) was established in 1994 to administer the visiting programs of all Swedish research councils.
Number awarded Varies each year.
Deadline December of each year.

[888]
STOCKHOLM INFORMATION TECHNOLOGY CHAIR IN WIRELESS E-COMMERCE

Council for International Exchange of Scholars
3007 Tilden Street, N.W., Suite 5L
Washington, DC 20008-3009
(202) 686-6245 Fax: (202) 362-3442
E-mail: scholars@cies.iie.org
Web site: www.iie.org/cies

Purpose To provide funding for American scholars to teach information technology in Sweden.
Eligibility Applicants must be able to teach wireless e-commerce in Sweden, especially in the field of Internet-based applications that target business-to-consumer or consumer-to-business applications. They must be able to communicate effectively with graduate students and senior management. Full professors are preferred, but all highly qualified candidates are considered. U.S. citizenship is required.
Financial data The award provides a stipend of $100,000 plus an allowance for travel. Housing is provided.
Duration 9 months.
Special features This is a Fulbright scholar program, sponsored by the Bureau of Educational and Cultural Affairs of the U.S. Department of State and administered by the Council for International Exchange of Scholars. The recipient teaches at the graduate level and provides leadership for accelerating 2-way interaction between the academic and business communities in Sweden and the United States. Research in collaboration with colleagues in both countries and frequent interaction with the information technology business community in Sweden is part of the assignment. Locations are the Center for Information and Communication Research at the Stockholm School of Economics and the School of Information Technology, Royal Institute of Technology, Kista.
Number awarded 1 each year.
Deadline April of each year.

[889]
STUART SWINY FELLOWSHIP

American Schools of Oriental Research
Attn: Administrative Director
656 Beacon Street, Fifth Floor
Boston, MA 02215-2010
(617) 353-6570 Fax: (617) 353-6575
E-mail: asor@bu.edu
Web site: www.asor.org

Purpose To provide funding to scholars who are interested in a period of residence at the Cyprus American Archaeological Research Institute (CAARI) in Nicosia, Cyprus.
Eligibility This program is open to scholars from any country who wish to conduct research at CAARI. They may participate in any phase or aspect of a project that has been approved by the Committee on Archaeological Policy.
Financial data The award is $1,000, to help cover room and board.
Number awarded 1 each year.
Deadline January of each year.

[890]
SUITCASE FUND

Dance Theater Workshop
Attn: Director and Producer of Inter/National Programs
219 West 19th Street
New York, NY 10011-4079
(212) 691-6500 Fax: (212) 633-1974
E-mail: cathy@dtw.org
Web site: www.dtw.org

Purpose To promote the performing arts through an international exchange.
Eligibility To promote cultural equity in a pluralistic America, the fund helps artists of all backgrounds and origins to maintain access to the contemporary arts of their homelands. Applicants should be independent professional artists working without the support of major institutions. They must be seeking to study, teach, collaborate, or perform in another part of the world.
Financial data The amount awarded varies, depending upon the needs of the recipient.
Special features Participating artists and producers are placed in Africa, Asia, Latin America, and the Caribbean, as well as Europe. Funding for this program is provided by the Rockefeller Foundation, the Trust for Mutual Understanding, and the Asian Cultural Council.

Limitations The Fund does not function as an all-purpose emergency travel fund, nor will it duplicate the well-established initiatives of other producers or funders.
Deadline Applications may be submitted at any time.

[891]
SWEA INTERNATIONAL SCHOLARSHIPS

Swedish Women's Educational Association International, Inc.
Attn: Administrator
P.O. Box 30190
Las Vegas, NV 89173-0190
(702) 873-7399   Fax: (702) 873-0492
E-mail: office@swea.org
Web site: www.swea.org

Purpose To provide financial assistance to graduate students who are interested in conducting research in Sweden.
Eligibility This program is open to doctoral candidates who are studying at a non-Swedish university and who reside permanently outside of Sweden. Applicants must be studying either 1) intercultural relations or 2) Swedish language, literature, or linguistics. They should be well into the process of writing their dissertation and should be interested in conducting research at a university in Sweden. Good knowledge of the Swedish language, both written and spoken, is required.
Financial data The stipend is $7,000 per year.
Duration 1 year.
Special features The Swedish Women's Educational Association (SWEA) is a worldwide organization made up of women of Swedish heritage. Information is also available from the International Scholarship Committee, Ia Dubois, 19831 15th Avenue, N.W., Seattle, WA 98177, (206) 546-8207, Fax: (206) 546-3740, E-mail: idubois@u.washington.edu.
Number awarded 2 each year: 1 to a student of Swedish language, literature, or linguistics and 1 to a student of intercultural relations.
Deadline February of each year.

[892]
SWEDISH CANCER SOCIETY VISITING SCIENTIST FELLOWSHIP

Swedish Cancer Society
Attn: Secretary, Scientific Committee
Gamla Brogatan 13
S-101 55 Stockholm
Sweden
46 8 677 1000   E-mail: info@cancerfonden.se
Web site: www.cancerfonden.se

Purpose To support cancer research conducted in Sweden by scientists of any nationality.
Eligibility Candidates from any country may apply, provided they have earned a doctorate (or its equivalent), are interested in conducting cancer research in Sweden, and have a strong research background in at least 1 of the following areas: biochemistry, virology, immunology, cell biology, pathology. They must have made arrangements with a Swedish host institution to conduct the research there.

Financial data The fellowships provide a salary and cover travel costs and living expenses.
Duration 1 year; may be renewed 1 additional year.
Special features Grants are also available to improve the methods of examination and treatment (for surgery, radiotherapy, radiophysics, endocrinology, chemotherapy, and interferon research).
Limitations Applications must be submitted by the Swedish host scientific group rather than by the foreign researcher directly.
Deadline January of each year.

[893]
SWEDISH INSTITUTE GUEST SCHOLARSHIPS

Swedish Institute
Attn: Scholarship Section
Hamngatan 27/Kungsträdgarden
P.O. Box 7434
S-103 91 Stockholm
Sweden
46 8 789 2000   Fax: 46 8 20 72 48
E-mail: grantinfo@si.se
Web site: www.si.se

Purpose To provide financial assistance to non-Swedish students or researchers who wish to continue their work in Sweden.
Eligibility This program is open to students and researchers who wish to come to Sweden from any part of the world except the Nordic countries (for which there is a separate program). Applicants must intend to be guests who do not intend to settle permanently in Sweden. They must be students at an advanced university level or researchers. Assistance is granted for study in all subjects, but only where Sweden can offer special scientific or academic advantages not available in other countries. There are no national quotas.
Financial data Up to 7,060 Swedish krona per month is awarded. The rate is the same for senior scholars as for students. The funds may be used to cover living expenses for 1 person only. There are no grants for family members or for travel.
Duration The scholarships are usually granted for 9 months (1 academic year); they may be renewed for a total of 3 academic years.
Limitations Prior to application, contact must be made with a Swedish university/institution willing to accept the applicant for the proposed studies. This contact should be made through a professor or academic adviser at the applicant's home institution and a copy of the letter from a Swedish university/institute accepting the applicant must accompany the request sent to the Swedish Institute. Scholarships are tenable only in Sweden, at a university or educational institution or for independent research. They cannot be used for elementary courses in Swedish only.
Number awarded Varies each year.
Deadline January of each year.

[894]
SWEDISH NATURAL SCIENCE RESEARCH COUNCIL POSTDOCTORAL EXCHANGE FELLOWSHIPS

Swedish Natural Science Research Council
Regeringsgatan 56
Box 7142
S-103 87 Stockholm
Sweden
46 8 454 4200   Fax: 46 8 454 4250
E-mail: nfr@nfr.se
Web site: www.nfr.se

Purpose To provide funding to scientists from other countries who are interested in conducting research in Sweden.

Eligibility This program is open to young postdoctoral scientists in the fields of biology, chemistry, earth sciences, mathematics, and physics. Applicants must be interested in conducting research in Sweden and must work at the Swedish university or research institute that actually submits the application.

Financial data The salary is 310,000 Swedish kroner.

Duration 1 year.

Number awarded Varies each year

Deadline May of each year.

[895]
SWISS NATIONAL SCIENCE FOUNDATION GRANTS FOR INDIVIDUAL SCIENTIFIC STAYS

Swiss National Science Foundation
Wildhainweg 20
Case postale 8232
CH-3001 Berne
Switzerland
41 31 308 2222   Fax: 41 31 305 2978
E-mail: fellowships@snf.ch
Web site: www.snf.ch

Purpose To provide funding to scholars who are interested in conducting research in Switzerland.

Eligibility Applications for these grants must be submitted by the director of a Swiss research institute who wishes to invite a foreign researcher for continuing collaboration. The stay must not be in the interest of the host laboratory exclusively. Research is supported in the humanities and social sciences; mathematics, natural, and engineering sciences; and biology and medicine.

Financial data Grants provide support for travel expenses and subsistence.

Duration 7 days to 3 months.

Number awarded Varies each year.

Deadline February or September of each year.

[896]
TARGET OF OPPORTUNITY FELLOWSHIPS

Institute of Current World Affairs, Inc.
Attn: Program Administrator
Wheelock House
4 West Wheelock Street
Hanover, NH 03755
(603) 643-5548   Fax: (603) 643-9599
E-mail: icwa@valley.net
Web site: www.icwa.org

Purpose To provide opportunities for independent research in selected foreign countries or on designated topics.

Eligibility Individuals who have completed their formal education are eligible to apply if they are interested in conducting research in either an area of their own choice or in selected areas (Burma, Korea, Japan, Iran, southeast Asia, south Asia, Siberia, Poland, north Africa, or the former East Germany) or on designated topics (the seas, fresh water). Generally, applicants must be under the age of 36 and have good command of written and spoken English.

Financial data The institute provides full support for the fellows and their families.

Duration At least 2 years.

Limitations Fellowships are not awarded to support work toward academic degrees, to write books, or to undertake specific studies or research projects. Fellows are required to submit monthly reports.

Number awarded 1 or more each year.

Deadline March or August of each year.

[897]
T.B.L. WEBSTER FELLOWSHIP

University of London
Attn: Institute of Classical Studies
Senate House
Malet Street
London WC1E 7HU
England
44 20 7862 8700   Fax: 44 20 7862 8722
Web site: www.sas.ac.uk/icls/institute/aboutin.htm

Purpose To provide an opportunity for classical scholars from universities outside the United Kingdom to conduct research at the University of London.

Eligibility This program is open to scholars of the classics from universities outside the United Kingdom. Applicants must be interested in working as a visiting fellow at the University of London's Institute of Classical Studies. Preference is given to scholars whose research interests are in classical art and archaeology or in the ancient theater.

Financial data A grant of 1,500 pounds is provided to help pay travel, accommodation, and research expenses. Fellows also receive use of office and computer facilities.

Duration Fellows are expected to spend at least 6 weeks at the institute.

Number awarded 1 each year.

Deadline January of each year.

[898]
TEACHING ASSISTANTSHIPS/INTERNSHIPS IN HUNGARY

Institute of International Education
Attn: Student Programs Division
809 United Nations Plaza
New York, NY 10017-3580
(212) 984-5330   Fax: (212) 984-5325
Web site: www.iie.org/fulbright

Purpose To enable American graduate students to work while engaged in study or research in Hungary.

Eligibility This program is open to graduate students enrolled in degree programs in the following fields: teaching English as a foreign language, applied linguistics, American literature, American studies, folklore, political science, international education, and educational advising. Applicants must be interested in a position in Hungary that combines 12 hours per week of teaching and other related activities, 12 hours per week of educational advising, and another 12 hours per week reserved for independent study or research projects. Knowledge of Hungarian is an advantage, but applicants must be articulate native-English speakers.

Financial data The program provides round-trip transportation, tuition, book and research allowances, a monthly maintenance allowance based on living costs, and supplemental health and accident insurance.

Duration 1 academic year.

Special features These grants are awarded under the exchange program between the governments of Hungary and the United States and administered as part of the Fulbright program by the Institute of International Education (IIE). Students who are currently enrolled in the United States are to apply through the Fulbright program adviser on their campus; at-large applicants (those not currently enrolled) may obtain applications and information directly from the IIE.

Number awarded 2 each year: 1 in Budapest at Eotvos Lorand University and 1 outside Budapest.

Deadline October of each year.

[899]
TEACHING ENGLISH IN POLAND PROGRAM

Kosciuszko Foundation
Attn: Grants Office
15 East 65th Street
New York, NY 10021-6595
(212) 734-2130   Fax: (212) 628-4552
E-mail: Thekfschol@aol.com
Web site: www.kosciuszkofoundation.org/summer/English.shtml

Purpose To enable American teachers and students to participate in an English language and cultural exchange program in Poland.

Eligibility This program is open to American certified teachers of all subject areas; administrators and those engaged in student services (school nurse, social worker, guidance counselor, school psychologist, etc.) are also eligible. Educators who are actively involved in teaching are given priority, but beginning teachers, retirees, and those on leave are also considered. U.S. college, university, and high school students who are at least 18 years of age may apply as teaching assistants and tutors. Teachers participating in the elementary school and junior high campuses may bring their own younger children who are at least 13 years of age; those younger Americans serve as peer tutors. Applicants must possess excellent communication and interpersonal skills and must adapt readily to cultural differences, but knowledge of the Polish language is not required.

Financial data Awards provide for room, board, and medical insurance; participants are responsible for their own airfare.

Duration 4 weeks, during the summer.

Special features This program is sponsored by the Kosciuszko Foundation in conjunction with the Polish Ministry of National Education and UNESCO of Poland. Approximately 800 Polish high school students and 200 Polish elementary and junior high school students are invited to study and practice conversational English within an American cultural context. The American teachers are responsible for conducting a homeroom period and 3 50-minute classes each weekday morning for small groups of Polish students who are generally at the intermediate level of English proficiency. They organize and lead popular American extracurricular activities or clubs during afternoon and evening recreational periods. They are also required to accompany the students on field trips scheduled during weekdays and on weekends and to maintain the use of English in all contacts with students. Teaching assistants and tutors work with the teachers in preparing classroom materials and assist during classes and extracurricular activities. Various aspects of American life and culture are integrated throughout the program, which operates at 6 sites throughout Poland.

Number awarded The American staff at each of the 6 sites includes 1 group leader, 10 teachers, and several American students as teaching assistants.

Deadline February of each year.

[900]
THEODORA BOSANQUET BURSARY FUND

British Federation of Women Graduates Charitable Foundation
Attn: Grants Administrator
28 Great James Street
London WC1N 3ES
England
44 20 7404 6447   Fax: 44 20 7404 6505
E-mail: bfwg.charity@btinternet.com
Web site: www.bcfgrants.org.uk

Purpose To provide accommodations for women who want to come to London to do research in English literature or history.

Eligibility Women scholars or postgraduate students from any country who wish to use reference libraries or other resources in London to do research in English literature or history are eligible to apply.

Financial data The bursary provides accommodations at a hall of residence in London.

Duration 4 weeks, from July to September.

Special features The bursary was established in memory of Theodora Bosanquet, a writer, administrator, and member of the British Federation and International Federation of University Women.

Limitations Requests for applications must be accompanied by a self-addressed stamped envelope.
Number awarded 1 or 2 each year.
Deadline November of each year.

[901]
THESAURUS LINGUAE LATINAE FELLOWSHIP

American Philological Association
Attn: Executive Director
University of Pennsylvania
291 Logan Hall
249 South 36th Street
Philadelphia, PA 19104-6304
(215) 898-4975   Fax: (215) 573-7874
E-mail: apaclassics@sas.upenn.edu
Web site: www.apaclassics.org

Purpose To provide funding to American scholars interested in conducting research on Latin lexicography at the Thesaurus Linguae Latinae in Germany.
Eligibility Eligible to apply are U.S. citizens or permanent residents who have recently earned a Ph.D. or the equivalent, have a familiarity with and/or special interest in the Latin language, are no higher than the assistant professor level, and are able to read and speak German. The proposed research must be conducted at the Thesaurus Linguae Latinae and may deal with Latin language and literature, Roman law, Roman history, the literature of early Christianity, or other related topics.
Financial data The award is $31,500.
Duration 1 year, beginning in July.
Special features Funding for this program is provided in part through a grant from the National Endowment for the Humanities. Further information is available from Patrick Sinclair, University of California at Irvine, Department of Classics, 121-HOB2, Irvine, CA 92697-2000, (949) 824-5831, E-mail: pjsincla@uci.edu.
Limitations Fellows must be resident at the Thesaurus Linguae Latinae in Munich, Germany for the duration of the program.
Number awarded 1 each year.
Deadline November of each year.

[902]
THOMAS JEFFERSON CHAIR IN AMERICAN SOCIAL STUDIES

Council for International Exchange of Scholars
3007 Tilden Street, N.W., Suite 5L
Washington, DC 20008-3009
(202) 686-6245   Fax: (202) 362-3442
E-mail: scholars@cies.iie.org
Web site: www.iie.org/cies

Purpose To allow scholars to lecture in any field of social science within American studies at a university in the Netherlands.
Eligibility Candidates must present strong credentials in a social science field of American studies (law, economics, political science). Both junior and senior scholars are eligible to apply for this award if they are interested in lecturing at a university in the Netherlands. U.S. citizenship is required.

Financial data The award includes a stipend of 20,000 Euros for senior scholars or EUR 16,000 for junior scholars, as well as an international travel allowance up to EUR 1,000 for the grantee only.
Duration 4 months.
Special features This is a Fulbright scholar program, sponsored by the Bureau of Educational and Cultural Affairs of the U.S. Department of State and administered by the Council for International Exchange of Scholars. The grantee teaches undergraduate and graduate courses in an aspect of American studies and is actively engaged in promoting and expanding the study of American society and culture in the Netherlands by giving guest lectures at various Dutch universities. Lecturing is in English.
Number awarded 1 each year.
Deadline April of each year.

[903]
T.P. GUNTON AWARD

British Medical Association
Attn: Executive Officer, Board of Science and Education
Tavistock Square
London WC1H 9JP
England
44 20 7383 6351   Fax: 44 20 7383 6399
E-mail: info.scienceawards@bma.org.uk
Web site: www.bma.org.uk

Purpose To provide funding to cancer specialists interested in conducting research in the United Kingdom.
Eligibility This program is open to registered medical practitioners and non-medical scientists. Applicants must be interested in conducting research into health education with special regard to cancer. The proposed research must be relevant to the United Kingdom, but no citizenship requirements are specified.
Financial data The grant is 17,250 pounds.
Duration 1 year.
Limitations Recipients must submit a progress report of 500 words not later than 6 months after receipt of the award and a final report of at least 1,500 words on completion of the work.
Number awarded 1 each year.
Deadline March of each year.

[904]
TRANSATLANTIC PROGRAM FELLOWSHIPS

European University Institute
Attn: Robert Schuman Centre for Advanced Studies
Badia Fiesolana
Via dei Roccettini 9
I-50016 San Domenico di Fiesole
Italy
39 55 4685 635   Fax: 39 55 4685 444
E-mail: applyjmf@datacomm.iue.it
Web site: www.iue.it

Purpose To allow postdoctoral scholars to engage in research at the Robert Schuman Centre for Advanced Studies in Florence, Italy on topics related to transatlantic relations.

Eligibility This program is open to candidates holding a doctoral degree or having equivalent research experience. Applicants must be interested in conducting research at the Schuman Centre and should have a good knowledge of the languages most relevant to their proposed research; academic activities at the institute are usually held in English or French, and occasionally in Italian. Most fellows are nationals of European Union member states, although applications from nationals of other countries (such as the United States) may be considered. Fellowships are open to academics on leave, but fellows may not engage in teaching or research activities at another institution. Research must be conducted in 1 of 2 areas: 1) governance of the transatlantic relationship, especially in the area of trade and investment; this includes analyzing the institutional structures for decision making on both sides of the Atlantic; or 2) the international role of Europe, the United States, and the transatlantic relationship in global governance.

Financial data The basic stipend ranges from 1,200 to 2,000 Euros per month. For fellows already occupying a stable post in a university or research center, the stipend offered takes into account any continuation of their salary by their home university. Medical insurance (for fellows and their families) and limited reimbursement of travel expenses (for fellows only) are also provided.

Duration 1 academic year.

Special features This program, established in 2000, is funded by BP-Amoco, the Euro-American oil company.

Limitations Fellows are required to reside in Florence for the duration of their fellowship.

Number awarded 5 each year.

Deadline October of each year.

[905]
TRENTO CHAIR IN COMPARATIVE LAW

Council for International Exchange of Scholars
3007 Tilden Street, N.W., Suite 5L
Washington, DC 20008-3009
(202) 686-6245   Fax: (202) 362-3442
E-mail: scholars@cies.iie.org
Web site: www.iie.org/cies

Purpose To provide funding for scholars to lecture on comparative law at the University of Trento in Italy.

Eligibility This program is open to U.S citizens with a degree in law or, for areas such as constitutional law, law and economics, or law and society, in other relevant fields. Applicants should have some knowledge of European legal systems that makes possible a comparative approach in teaching. They must be interested in lecturing at the University of Trento. Full professors are preferred but applications from associate professors are accepted. Some knowledge of Italian is useful but not required.

Financial data The stipend is the Euro equivalent of 16,800,000 Italian lire plus a settling-in allowance of the EUR equivalent of 1,500,000 lire. The grant also provides international travel (for the grantee only) plus the EUR equivalent of 200,000 lire per month for each accompanying dependent.

Duration 3 months.

Special features This is a Fulbright scholar program, sponsored by the Bureau of Educational and Cultural Affairs of the U.S. Department of State and administered by the Council for International Exchange of Scholars. The appointee teaches a course at the University of Trento and also offers lectures and seminars to graduate students and participates in tutorials and thesis advising.

Number awarded 1 each year.

Deadline April of each year.

[906]
TRIESTE DISTINGUISHED CHAIR

Council for International Exchange of Scholars
3007 Tilden Street, N.W., Suite 5L
Washington, DC 20008-3009
(202) 686-6245   Fax: (202) 362-3442
E-mail: scholars@cies.iie.org
Web site: www.iie.org/cies

Purpose To provide funding for scholars to teach on linguistics at the University of Trieste in Italy.

Eligibility Applicants must be full or associate professors who are interested in teaching at the University of Trieste. The topic alternates between linguistics in even-numbered years and geography (political, economic, and cultural) in odd-numbered years. Some knowledge of Italian is useful but not required. U.S. citizenship is required.

Financial data The stipend is the Euro equivalent of 16,800,000 Italian lire plus a settling-in allowance of the EUR equivalent of 1,500,000 lire. The grant also provides international travel (for the grantee only) plus the EUR equivalent of 200,000 lire per month for each accompanying dependent.

Duration 3 months.

Special features This is a Fulbright scholar program, sponsored by the Bureau of Educational and Cultural Affairs of the U.S. Department of State and administered by the Council for International Exchange of Scholars.

Number awarded 1 each year.

Deadline April of each year.

[907]
TRINITY COLLEGE BARBIERI GRANT IN ITALIAN HISTORY

Society for Italian Historical Studies
Attn: Executive Secretary
Boston College
Department of History
Chestnut Hill, MA 02467-3806
(617) 552-3814   E-mail: alan.reinerman@bc.edu

Purpose To provide funding to American scholars who are interested in conducting research in Italy on approved historical topics.

Eligibility Applicants must be American citizens and residents. They may be either doctoral candidates or postdoctoral scholars. Their proposed research must deal with a period of Italian history from the 18th century to the present. It must be conducted in Italy. To apply, candidates must submit a description of the proposed study, including a budget (not to exceed 5 pages).

Financial data The award ranges between $3,500 and $5,000.

Duration Up to 1 year, beginning in June.

Special features This program is sponsored by the Cesare Barbieri Endowment for Italian Culture at Trinity College and the Society for Italian Historical Studies. Recipients must visit Trinity College and make a public presentation of the results of their funded research; all expenses for this trip will be paid by the sponsor.
Number awarded 1 or more each year.
Deadline January of each year.

[908]
TRINITY COLLEGE JUNIOR RESEARCH FELLOWSHIP
University of Oxford
Trinity College
Attn: Academic Administrator
Broad Street
Oxford OX1 3BH
England
44 1865 279900   Fax: 44 1865 279902
E-mail: katie.andrews@trinity.ox.ac.uk
Web site: www.trinity.ox.ac.uk

Purpose To provide funding to postdoctoral scholars from any country who wish to conduct research in designated areas at Trinity College of the University of Oxford in England.
Eligibility This program is open to residents of any country who are interested in conducting postdoctoral research while in residence at Trinity College. There is no age limit, but applicants should be researchers at the start of an academic career. Scholars whose career is already well established are unlikely to be appointed, and recent graduates seeking to obtain a higher degree are not eligible. Applicants should be engaged in a specific research project that should be outlined in the application.
Financial data The stipend is 14,429 pounds per year. Fellows also receive free meals and rooms (or, for fellows who live out, a housing allowance of 2,790 pounds per year) and a research allowance of 382 pounds per year.
Duration 3 years.
Special features The fields of study rotate every year. For 2003: economics, geography, law, philosophy, politics, or sociology. For 2004: chemistry, earth sciences, engineering, materials, mathematics, or physics. For 2005: classics, English language and literature, modern languages, or philology and linguistics. For 2006: biochemistry, biological sciences, or biomedical sciences. For 2007: ancient history, anthropology, archaeology, history of art, history, or theology.
Number awarded 1 each year.
Deadline October of each year.

[909]
TRINITY HALL RESEARCH FELLOWSHIPS
University of Cambridge
c/o Academic Secretary, Churchill College
Storey's Way
Cambridge CB3 0DS
England
44 1223 336190   Fax: 44 1223 336045
E-mail: jrf@chu.cam.ac.uk
Web site: www.chu.cam.ac.uk

Purpose To provide funding to postdoctoral scholars interested in conducting research in the arts, social sciences, and sciences at Trinity Hall of the University of Cambridge in England.
Eligibility This program is open to scholars from any country who are interested in conducting research at Trinity Hall in the arts, social sciences, or sciences (including mathematics, medicine, and engineering). There is no age limit, but applicants should have completed their Ph.D. recently or be close to completion. Candidates who have no previous educational connection with Cambridge or Oxford universities are particularly welcome. Applicants whose academic history has been interrupted should explain any intermissions. Selection is based on a 1,000-word statement on the proposed research.
Financial data The annual first-year stipend is 11,912 pounds if resident in college or 14,124 if living out. The stipend increases by annual supplements of approximately 500 pounds.
Duration Normally 3 years.
Number awarded 2 each year: 1 in the arts or social sciences and 1 in the sciences.
Deadline January of each year. E-mailed applications must be received by December.

[910]
TURIN CHAIR IN ENVIRONMENTAL STUDIES
Council for International Exchange of Scholars
3007 Tilden Street, N.W., Suite 5L
Washington, DC 20008-3009
(202) 686-6245   Fax: (202) 362-3442
E-mail: scholars@cies.iie.org
Web site: www.iie.org/cies

Purpose To provide funding to scholars interested in lecturing on environmental studies at the University of Turin in Italy.
Eligibility This program is open to professors with experience in teaching environmental studies. Applicants must be interested in lecturing at the University of Turin. U.S. citizenship is required. Some knowledge of Italian is useful but not required.
Financial data The stipend is the Euro equivalent of 16,800,000 Italian lire plus a settling-in allowance of the EUR equivalent of 1,500,000 lire. The grant also provides international travel (for the grantee only) plus the EUR equivalent of 200,000 lire per month for each accompanying dependent.
Duration 3 months.
Special features This is a Fulbright scholar program, sponsored by the Bureau of Educational and Cultural Affairs of the U.S. Department of State and administered by the Council for International Exchange of Scholars. It was first offered for the

2002-03 academic year. The appointee lectures at the advanced undergraduate level at the University of Turin and participates in collaborative research.

Number awarded 1 each year.

Deadline April of each year.

[911]
TURKEY FULBRIGHT EXCHANGE OF ADMINISTRATORS

U.S. Department of State
c/o Graduate School, USDA
600 Maryland Avenue, S.W., Room 320
Washington, DC 20024-2520
(202) 314-3520   Fax: (202) 479-6806
E-mail: fulbright@grad.usda.gov
Web site: www.grad.usda.gov/International/ftep.html

Purpose To promote mutual understanding between the people of the United States and the people of Turkey through an educational administrator exchange program.

Eligibility This program is open to administrators from elementary schools, secondary schools, and 2-year colleges who are interested in working with administrators in Turkey (and vice versa). The assignment may be in the areas of personnel administration, student affairs, or educational policy. Applicants must 1) be U.S. citizens; 2) hold at least a bachelor's degree; 3) be fluent in English; 4) have a current full-time administrative assignment in the U.S. or a territory; 5) have the approval of their school administration; 6) have at least 3 years of full-time experience; and 7) not have participated in a Fulbright Teacher Exchange longer than 8 weeks during the last 2 years. Preference is given to applicants who have not participated previously in the program and may be given to applicants who have not previously lived in Turkey. Geographic distribution of awards within the United States is also a factor in selection. This program does not discriminate on the basis of race, color, religion, age, sex, or national origin and encourages the applications of members of minority communities. Other considerations being equal, veterans are given preference.

Financial data Round-trip economy airfare and a $3,000 cost of living stipend are provided. Participants must obtain a leave of absence with or without pay from their jobs in the United States.

Duration 6 weeks, twice during the year.

Special features This program is sponsored by the Bureau of Educational and Cultural Affairs of the U.S. Department of State and administered by the Graduate School, USDA.

Limitations Dependents are not permitted in this program. Applicants selected for exchange must attend orientation programs of the sponsoring agencies in the United States or abroad.

Number awarded Varies each year.

Deadline October of each year.

[912]
TURKEY FULBRIGHT TEACHER EXCHANGE

U.S. Department of State
c/o Graduate School, USDA
600 Maryland Avenue, S.W., Room 320
Washington, DC 20024-2520
(202) 314-3520   Fax: (202) 479-6806
E-mail: fulbright@grad.usda.gov
Web site: www.grad.usda.gov/International/ftep.html

Purpose To promote mutual understanding between the people of the United States and the people of Turkey through a teacher exchange program.

Eligibility This program is open to teachers (grades 7 through 12) of English as a second language, mathematics, English, or science who are interested in teaching in Turkey. Applicants must 1) be U.S. citizens; 2) hold at least a bachelor's degree; 3) be fluent in English; 4) have a current full-time teaching assignment in the U.S. or a territory; 5) have the approval of their school administration; 6) have at least 3 years of full-time experience; and 7) not have participated in a Fulbright Teacher Exchange longer than 8 weeks during the last 2 years. Fluency in Turkish is not required although some ability is useful; the language of instruction is English. Teaching couples may apply. However, because of the limited number of positions available and, often, the lack of foreign candidate pairs with similar qualifications for interchanges, it may not be possible to arrange suitable assignments in the same locality or to place both teachers. Preference is given to applicants who have not participated previously in the program and may be given to applicants who have not previously lived in Turkey. Geographic distribution of awards within the United States is also a factor in selection. This program does not discriminate on the basis of race, color, religion, age, sex, or national origin and encourages the applications of members of minority communities. Other considerations being equal, veterans are given preference.

Financial data Round-trip transportation for the exchange teacher only and housing are provided. Participants must obtain a leave of absence with pay from their jobs in the United States. The U.S. school must agree to accept a teacher from Turkey who must secure a leave of absence with pay; the Turkish teacher receives a stipend, but no additional cost accrues to the U.S. school.

Duration 9 months, beginning in September.

Special features This program is sponsored by the Bureau of Educational and Cultural Affairs of the U.S. Department of State and administered by the Graduate School, USDA.

Limitations This program provides for the direct exchange of teaching assignments between Turkey and the United States. Applicants selected for exchange must attend orientation programs of the sponsoring agencies in the United States or abroad.

Number awarded 5 each year.

Deadline October of each year.

[913]
TURKEY M.A. TEFL DIRECTOR

Council for International Exchange of Scholars
3007 Tilden Street, N.W., Suite 5L
Washington, DC 20008-3009
(202) 686-6246   Fax: (202) 362-3442
E-mail: scholars@cies.iie.org
Web site: www.iie.org/cies

Purpose To provide funding to American scholars interested in administering the master's degree program in Teaching English as a Foreign Language (TEFL) in Turkey.

Eligibility This program is open to U.S. citizens who have a Ph.D. and at least 5 years of teaching experience in applied linguistics, research methodology, or ESL methodology (quantitative and qualitative). Applicants must be interested in administering a master's degree program in TEFL at Bilkent University in Ankara, Turkey. English is sufficient for lecturing.

Financial data The program provides a base stipend of $1,500 to $2,000 per month, a maintenance allowance of $500 per month, housing or a housing allowance, airfare from hometown to Ankara for grantee and 1 dependent, a $250 excess baggage allowance, a $500 relocation allowance, tuition reimbursement for 1 K-12 dependent, and a 1-time incidentals allowance of $200.

Duration 11 months.

Special features This is a Fulbright scholar program, sponsored by the Bureau of Educational and Cultural Affairs of the U.S. Department of State and administered by the Council for International Exchange of Scholars. The recipient administers the master's program in TEFL, teaches 2 courses in requested areas of specialization, advises thesis students, and assists with curriculum planning and program development.

Number awarded 1 each year.

Deadline July of each year.

[914]
UNDERWOOD FUND

Biotechnology and Biological Sciences Research Council
Attn: Secretariat and Liaison Branch
Polaris House
North Star Avenue
Swindon SN2 1UH
United Kingdom
44 1793 413265   Fax: 44 1793 413382
E-mail: cath.atkinson@bbsrc.ac.uk
Web site: www.bbsrc.ac.uk/international/bbsrc/underwood.html

Purpose To provide funding to scientists from other countries who are interested in visiting the United Kingdom to work with grantees of the Biotechnology and Biological Sciences Research Council (BBSRC).

Eligibility This program is open to senior overseas scientists. Applicants must be interested in visiting the United Kingdom to work with current BBSRC grantholders in U.K. universities and BBSRC-sponsored institutes. Support is not provided for visits to conferences or to make a tour of U.K. research establishments.

Financial data Grants cover travel and living expenses.

Duration 3 to 12 months.

Special features The BBSRC was established by Royal Charter to promote and support basic, strategic, and applied research relating to the understanding and exploitation of biological systems.

Number awarded Varies each year.

[915]
UNITED STATES–NIS AWARDS FOR EXCELLENCE IN TEACHING

American Councils for International Education
Attn: Office of Faculty Exchanges
1776 Massachusetts Avenue, N.W., Suite 700
Washington, DC 20036
(202) 833-7522   Fax: (202) 833-7523
E-mail: hollis@actr.org
Web site: www.actr.org

Purpose To enable outstanding secondary school teachers in the United States to visit schools and communities in the Newly Independent States (NIS) of the former Soviet Union (including Eurasia).

Eligibility As part of this program, 75 teachers from Kazakhstan, Kyrgyzstan, Russia, Turkmenistan, Ukraine, and Uzbekistan visit the United States for a 7-week professional development seminar. In return, U.S. secondary school teachers of the humanities, social sciences, or language arts visit the schools and communities of those NIS participants. Applicants must have been recognized for excellence in teaching at the national, state, or local level in the past 8 years. Selection is based on ability to teach and innovation in teaching, interest in NIS teaching methodology in foreign languages and area studies, desire and ability to share experience and knowledge with colleagues from the NIS, and ability to develop partnerships with NIS participants and their schools beyond completion of the program.

Financial data All travel expenses are paid by the program; funding for salaries and/or substitute teachers is not provided.

Duration 2 weeks, in October.

Special features This program is funded by the Bureau of Educational and Cultural Affairs of the Department of State and administered by the American Councils for International Education, the American Council of Teachers of Russian (ACTR), and the American Council for Collaboration and Education in Language Study (ACCELS). It was established in 1996. Activities in the NIS may include discussions on English and American studies programs, introduction of American studies into foreign language curricula, and (if appropriate) lecturing.

Number awarded Up to 24 each year.

Deadline January of each year.

[916]
UNIVERSITY COLLEGE ARTS JUNIOR RESEARCH FELLOWSHIP

University of Oxford
University College
Attn: College Secretary
Oxford OX1 4BH
England
44 1865 276600 Fax: 44 1865 276985
E-mail: jane.vicat@univ.ox.ac.uk
Web site: www.univ.ox.ac.uk

Purpose To provide funding to postdoctoral scholars from any country who wish to conduct research in designated areas of the humanities at University College of the University of Oxford in England.

Eligibility This program is open to residents of any country who are interested in conducting postdoctoral research while in residence at University College. The terms of the fellowship allow applications from persons up to 35 years of age, but it is normally expected that the successful candidate will be under 30 years of age. The fields of study are designated from the humanities on a rotating basis; recently, they were English, modern languages, and music.

Financial data The stipend is 13,650 pounds per year. Fellows also receive room (or a housing allowance) and board.

Duration 3 years.

Special features Fellows may be asked to do a limited amount of teaching, for which payment is made at the established rate. In some years, the award is designated as the Stevenson Junior Research Fellowship in the Arts.

Number awarded 1 each year.

Deadline October of each year.

[917]
UNIVERSITY COLLEGE SCIENCE JUNIOR RESEARCH FELLOWSHIP

University of Oxford
University College
Attn: College Secretary
Oxford OX1 4BH
England
44 1865 276600 Fax: 44 1865 276985
E-mail: jane.vicat@univ.ox.ac.uk
Web site: www.univ.ox.ac.uk

Purpose To provide funding to postdoctoral scholars from any country who wish to conduct research in science and mathematics at University College of the University of Oxford in England.

Eligibility This program is open to residents of any country who are interested in conducting postdoctoral research while in residence at University College. The terms of the fellowship allow applications from persons up to 35 years of age, but it is normally expected that the successful candidate will be under 30 years of age. Applicants must be interested in conducting research in science (including psychology) or mathematics.

Financial data The stipend is 13,650 pounds per year. Fellows also receive room (or a housing allowance) and board.

Duration 3 years.

Special features Fellows may be asked to do a limited amount of teaching, for which payment is made at the established rate. In some years, the award is designated as the Weir Junior Research Fellowship.

Number awarded 1 each year.

Deadline October of each year.

[918]
UNIVERSITY OF INNSBRUCK DISTINGUISHED CHAIR IN SOCIAL AND ECONOMIC SCIENCES

Council for International Exchange of Scholars
3007 Tilden Street, N.W., Suite 5L
Washington, DC 20008-3009
(202) 686-6245 Fax: (202) 362-3442
E-mail: scholars@cies.iie.org
Web site: www.iie.org/cies

Purpose To provide funding to scholars who are interested in lecturing on globalization at the University of Innsbruck in Austria.

Eligibility This program is open to scholar/teachers with interests in fields centrally related to globalization (economics, management, political science, sociology, and related fields) and who are interested in teaching in the Faculty of Humanities at the University of Innsbruck. Preference is given to applicants with interdisciplinary approaches who are interested in working with more than 1 of the faculty's 17 departments on the ethical, social, political, and economic implications of globalization. U.S. citizenship is required. Fluency in German is desirable but not a prerequisite; some conversational German is a pragmatic necessity.

Financial data The stipend is 4,360 Euros per month. Also provided are a travel award of EUR 800 for the grantee only and an allowance for legal accompanying dependents of EUR 145 per month.

Duration 4 months.

Special features This is a Fulbright scholar program, sponsored by the Bureau of Educational and Cultural Affairs of the U.S. Department of State and administered by the Council for International Exchange of Scholars. The recipient teaches 3 courses at the advanced undergraduate and graduate level.

Number awarded 1 each year.

Deadline April of each year.

[919]
UNIVERSITY OF KLAGENFURT DISTINGUISHED CHAIR IN GENDER STUDIES

Council for International Exchange of Scholars
3007 Tilden Street, N.W., Suite 5L
Washington, DC 20008-3009
(202) 686-6245 Fax: (202) 362-3442
E-mail: scholars@cies.iie.org
Web site: www.iie.org/cies

Purpose To provide funding to scholars who are interested in lecturing on gender studies at the University of Klagenfurt in Austria.

Eligibility This program is open to scholar/teachers who are interested in fields centrally associated with gender studies and are interested in teaching in the Faculty of Humanities at the

University of Klagenfurt. Preference is given to applicants involved in theoretical and methodological issues and interdisciplinary approaches who are interested in working with more than 1 of the faculty's 12 departments in the fields of communication and cultural studies, education, English and American studies, German studies, history, literature, philosophy, and sociology. U.S. citizenship is required. Fluency in German is desirable but not a prerequisite; some conversational German is a pragmatic necessity.

Financial data The stipend is 4,360 Euros per month. Also provided are a travel award of EUR 800 for the grantee only and an allowance for legal accompanying dependents of EUR 145 per month.

Duration 4 months.

Special features This is a Fulbright scholar program, sponsored by the Bureau of Educational and Cultural Affairs of the U.S. Department of State and administered by the Council for International Exchange of Scholars. The recipient teaches 3 courses at the advanced undergraduate and graduate level.

Number awarded 1 each year.

Deadline April of each year.

[920]
UNIVERSITY OF SALZBURG DISTINGUISHED CHAIR

Council for International Exchange of Scholars
3007 Tilden Street, N.W., Suite 5L
Washington, DC 20008-3009
(202) 686-6245   Fax: (202) 362-3442
E-mail: scholars@cies.iie.org
Web site: www.iie.org/cies

Purpose To provide funding to scholars who are interested in teaching at the University of Salzburg in Austria.

Eligibility This program is open to scholar/teachers, on a rotating basis, in natural sciences, law, social sciences, theology, and humanities. Applicants must be interested in teaching in the appropriate faculty at the University of Salzburg. U.S. citizenship is required. Fluency in German is desirable but not a prerequisite; some conversational German is a pragmatic necessity.

Financial data The stipend is 4,360 Euros per month. Also provided are a travel award of EUR 800 for the grantee only and an allowance for legal accompanying dependents of EUR 145 per month.

Duration 4 months.

Special features This is a Fulbright scholar program, sponsored by the Bureau of Educational and Cultural Affairs of the U.S. Department of State and administered by the Council for International Exchange of Scholars. The recipient teaches 3 courses at the advanced undergraduate and graduate level.

Number awarded 1 each year.

Deadline April of each year.

[921]
UNIVERSITY OF VIENNA DISTINGUISHED CHAIR IN THE HUMANITIES OR SOCIAL SCIENCES

Council for International Exchange of Scholars
3007 Tilden Street, N.W., Suite 5L
Washington, DC 20008-3009
(202) 686-6245   Fax: (202) 362-3442
E-mail: scholars@cies.iie.org
Web site: www.iie.org/cies

Purpose To provide funding to scholars who are interested in teaching the humanities or social sciences at the University of Vienna in Austria.

Eligibility This program is open to scholar/teachers in the humanities. Applicants must be interested in teaching either in the Faculty of Humanities (which covers area studies for Africa, America, Asia, Egypt, Japan, east and southeastern Europe, Buddhism, Byzantine, and Judaism as well as the conventional humanities departments in classical and modern languages and literature, comparative literature, linguistics and translating, all fields of history from ancient to contemporary, archaeology, art history, ethnology, and musicology) or the Faculty of Human and Social Sciences (which has departments of education, ethnology, geography, journalism and communications, philosophy, political science, psychology, sports and physical education, sociology, theater, and the theory of science) at the University of Vienna. U.S. citizenship is required. Fluency in German is desirable but not a prerequisite; some conversational German is a pragmatic necessity.

Financial data The stipend is 4,360 Euros per month. Also provided are a travel award of EUR 800 for the grantee only and an allowance for legal accompanying dependents of EUR 145 per month.

Duration 4 months.

Special features This is a Fulbright scholar program, sponsored by the Bureau of Educational and Cultural Affairs of the U.S. Department of State and administered by the Council for International Exchange of Scholars. The recipient teaches 3 courses at the advanced undergraduate and graduate level.

Number awarded 1 each year.

Deadline April of each year.

[922]
UPPSALA CHAIR IN AMERICAN STUDIES

Council for International Exchange of Scholars
3007 Tilden Street, N.W., Suite 5L
Washington, DC 20008-3009
(202) 686-6245   Fax: (202) 362-3442
E-mail: scholars@cies.iie.org
Web site: www.iie.org/cies

Purpose To provide funding to American scholars interested in teaching American studies at Uppsala University in Sweden.

Eligibility Applicants must hold the rank of full professor and have several years of undergraduate and graduate teaching as well as a scholarly publication record. They must be interested in teaching American studies at Uppsala University. Preference is given to scholars with a comparative approach to political science, American history, and American literature. U.S. citizenship is required.

Financial data The award provides a monthly stipend of approximately 350,000 Swedish krona, round-trip travel for the grantee, and a small baggage allowance.
Duration 9 months.
Special features This is a Fulbright scholar program, sponsored by the Bureau of Educational and Cultural Affairs of the U.S. Department of State and administered by the Council for International Exchange of Scholars. The recipient teaches undergraduate and graduate courses at the Swedish Institute for North American Studies at Uppsala University. Other assignments include supervision of student research, delivering an inaugural lecture, and representing the institute through guest lecturing and seminar participation at other Swedish universities.
Number awarded 1 each year.
Deadline April of each year.

[923]
USA/BRITISH ISLES VISITING FELLOWSHIP
Royal College of Obstetricians and Gynaecologists
Attn: Awards Secretary
27 Sussex Place
Regent's Park
London NW1 4RG
England
44 20 7772 6263   Fax: 44 20 7772 6359
E-mail: rdeshmukh@rcog.org.uk
Web site: www.rcog.org.uk

Purpose To enable gynecologists from the United States to visit the British Isles and vice versa.
Eligibility This program is open to junior fellows of the American Gynecological and Obstetrical Society who wish to visit the United Kingdom or Ireland, and to registrars and senior registrars in the British Isles, including medical graduates of not less than 2 years' standing from any approved British or Commonwealth university, who wish to visit the United States. British applicants need not be members of the Royal College of Obstetricians and Gynaecologists. All applicants must be proposing to visit, make contact with, and gain knowledge from a specified center offering new techniques or methods of clinical management within the specialty of obstetrics and gynecology.
Financial data Up to 1,000 pounds, to be used for travel costs and incidental expenses.
Duration The award is granted annually.
Special features This program began in 1990 with initial funding from the American Gynecological and Obstetrical Society and the Gynaecological Visiting Society of Great Britain and Ireland.
Number awarded 1 each year.
Deadline July of each year.

[924]
U.S.–HUNGARIAN SCIENCE AND TECHNOLOGY JOINT FUND
Science and Technology Foundation
Bem József u.2
1027 Budapest
Hungary
36 1 214 7714   Fax: 36 1 214 7712
E-mail: tetalap@elender.hu
Web site: www.elender.hu/~tetalap

Purpose To encourage and support a wide range of scientific and technological cooperation between Hungary and the United States.
Eligibility Scientists from U.S. and Hungarian governmental agencies, scientific institutes, universities, scientific societies, and other national research and development centers are eligible to apply. Individual scientists in either country may initiate research proposals. Support is provided for cooperative research projects, bilateral scientific symposia (workshops), and project development visits. Selection is based on the proposal's intrinsic scientific or technical merit, previous research performance and competence, significance of the research for international cooperation, reasonableness of budget, and proposal relevance within national priorities.
Financial data The following support is offered: round-trip transportation, an allowance for expenses, and per diem. Requests for expenses may include funds in both U.S. dollars and Hungarian forints. No amount is specified, but $10,000 per year for 3 years, matched in forints at the prevailing exchange rate, is considered reasonable.
Duration 1 year or longer.
Special features The Joint Fund was established by an agreement between the United States and Hungary on October 4, 1989. It is managed by the U.S. Department of State and the Hungarian Ministry for Foreign Affairs.
Number awarded Varies each year.
Deadline Proposals may be submitted at any time but should be received at least 6 months prior to the intended start date.

[925]
VENICE CHAIR IN LINGUISTICS AND PHILOSOPHY OF LANGUAGE
Council for International Exchange of Scholars
3007 Tilden Street, N.W., Suite 5L
Washington, DC 20008-3009
(202) 686-6245   Fax: (202) 362-3442
E-mail: scholars@cies.iie.org
Web site: www.iie.org/cies

Purpose To provide funding for scholars to lecture in the philosophy of language or linguistics at the University of Venice in Italy.
Eligibility This program is open to established scholars with a prominent record of accomplishments in the philosophy of language or theoretical linguistics. The rank of full professor is preferred. Applicants must be interested in lecturing in the philosophy of language or linguistics at the University of Venice. Fields of specific interest include syntax and theory of grammar. U.S. citizenship is required. Some knowledge of Italian is useful but not required.

Financial data The stipend is the Euro equivalent of 16,800,000 Italian lire plus a settling-in allowance of the EUR equivalent of 1,500,000 lire. The grant also provides international travel (for the grantee only) plus the EUR equivalent of 200,000 lire per month for each accompanying dependent.

Duration 3 months.

Special features This is a Fulbright scholar program, sponsored by the Bureau of Educational and Cultural Affairs of the U.S. Department of State and administered by the Council for International Exchange of Scholars. The appointee teaches advanced undergraduate or graduate courses and participates in collaborative research at the University of Venice.

Number awarded 1 each year.

Deadline April of each year.

[926]
V.H. GALBRAITH FELLOWSHIP IN MEDIEVAL STUDIES

University of Oxford
St. Hilda's College
Attn: Academic Office
Oxford OX4 1DY
England
44 1865 276815   Fax: 44 1865 276816
E-mail: college.office@st-hildas.ox.ac.uk
Web site: www.st-hildas.ox.ac.uk

Purpose To provide funding to women from any country who are interested in conducting research in medieval studies at St. Hilda's College of the University of Oxford in England.

Eligibility This program is open to women graduates from any country who are interested in conducting postdoctoral research at St. Hilda's College in medieval studies (archaeology, history of art and architecture, history, language and literature, law, music, philosophy, science, or theology).

Financial data The stipend is 12,892 pounds. Recipients are also entitled to a 1,000 pound research allowance and free room and board.

Duration 2 years; nonrenewable.

Number awarded This fellowship is offered periodically. It is next scheduled for 2003.

[927]
VINCENT WRIGHT FELLOWSHIPS

European University Institute
Attn: Robert Schuman Centre for Advanced Studies
Badia Fiesolana
Via dei Roccettini 9
I-50016 San Domenico di Fiesole
Italy
39 55 4685 635   Fax: 39 55 4685 444
E-mail: applyjmf@datacomm.iue.it
Web site: www.iue.it

Purpose To allow postdoctoral scholars and junior academics to engage in research at the Robert Schuman Centre for Advanced Studies in Florence, Italy.

Eligibility This program is open to postdoctoral students and junior academics who are interested in conducting research at the Schuman Centre. Applicants should have a good knowledge of the languages most relevant to their proposed research; academic activities at the institute are usually in English or French, and occasionally in Italian. Most fellows are nationals of European Union member states, although applications from nationals of other countries (such as the United States) may be considered. Research may be conducted in 1 of 2 areas: 1) state formation and the development of administration since the 19th century in Europe; or 2) comparative politics.

Financial data The basic stipend ranges from 1,200 to 2,000 Euros per month. For fellows already occupying a stable post in a university or research center, the stipend offered takes into account any continuation of their salary by their home university. Medical insurance (for fellows and their families) and limited reimbursement of travel expenses (for fellows only) are also provided.

Duration 1 academic year.

Limitations Fellows are required to reside in Florence for the duration of their fellowship.

Number awarded 2 each year: 1 for each of the research areas.

Deadline October of each year.

[928]
VISUAL ARTS ROME PRIZE FELLOWSHIPS

American Academy in Rome
Attn: Fellowship Coordinator
7 East 60th Street
New York, NY 10022-1001
(212) 751-7200   Fax: (212) 751-7220
E-mail: info@aarome.org
Web site: www.aarome.org

Purpose To provide financial support to visual artists who are interested in a residency at the School of Fine Arts at the American Academy in Rome.

Eligibility Applicants must be U.S. citizens, demonstrate at least 3 years of professional commitment, be currently engaged in studio work, and be interested in a residency in Rome. They must submit 20 slides in a standard 8 1/2 by 11 inch slide sleeve, accompanied by a completed slide information sheet, or up to 3 VHS or BETA 1/2 inch or 3/4 inch videotapes, if this is the only way their work can be presented. Full-time students are not eligible.

Financial data The fellowship provides a stipend of up to $20,000, meals, a bedroom with private bath, and a study or studio. Fellows with children under 18 are housed outside the McKim, Mead & White building and are provided with an allowance that helps cover the cost of off-campus housing.

Duration 1 year.

Special features The American Academy in Rome, founded in 1894 by the American architect Charles F. McKim, is a center for independent study and advanced research in the fine arts and humanities. It consists of a School of Fine Arts (including architecture, landscape architecture, design arts, painting and sculpture, musical composition, and literature) and a School of Classical Studies (including classical studies and archaeology, history of art, and post-classical humanistic/modern Italian studies).

Limitations There is a $40 application fee. Prize winners may not hold full-time jobs in Rome during their residencies.

Number awarded 4 each year.
Deadline November of each year.

[929] VITERBO DISTINGUISHED CHAIR

Council for International Exchange of Scholars
3007 Tilden Street, N.W., Suite 5L
Washington, DC 20008-3009
(202) 686-6245   Fax: (202) 362-3442
E-mail: scholars@cies.iie.org
Web site: www.iie.org/cies

Purpose To provide funding to scholars interested in lecturing on management and business policies at the University of Tuscia in Viterbo, Italy.
Eligibility This program is open to full professors with experience in teaching business administration, management, leveraged buy outs (LBOs), and management buy outs (MBOs). Applicants must be interested in lecturing at the University of Tuscia. U.S. citizenship is required. Some knowledge of Italian is useful but not required.
Financial data The stipend is the Euro equivalent of 16,800,000 Italian lire plus a settling-in allowance of the EUR equivalent of 1,500,000 lire. The grant also provides international travel (for the grantee only) plus the EUR equivalent of 200,000 lire per month for each accompanying dependent.
Duration 3 months.
Special features This is a Fulbright scholar program, sponsored by the Bureau of Educational and Cultural Affairs of the U.S. Department of State and administered by the Council for International Exchange of Scholars. The appointee lectures at the advanced undergraduate level at the University of Tuscia in Viterbo and participates in collaborative research.
Number awarded 1 each year.
Deadline April of each year.

[930] WADHAM COLLEGE JUNIOR RESEARCH FELLOWSHIPS

University of Oxford
Wadham College
Attn: Senior Tutor
Parks Road
Oxford OX1 3PN
England
44 1865 277937   Fax: 44 1865 277900
E-mail: admissions@wadham.ox.ac.uk
Web site: www.wadham.ox.ac.uk

Purpose To provide funding to postdoctoral scholars from any country who wish to conduct research at Wadham College of the University of Oxford in England.
Eligibility This program is open to residents of any country who are interested in conducting postdoctoral research while in residence at Wadham College. Some fellowships are linked to a designated trust fund that specifies additional requirements and provisions. Others depend on external funding or special needs.
Financial data Stipends currently range from 15,735 to 23,651 pounds per year. Fellows also receive lunch and dinner free of charge and are entitled to single accommodations at a modest reduction in stipend.
Duration Most fellowships are for 3 years.
Special features The following named fellowships are included: the Bowra Junior Research Fellowship in the Humanities, the Keeley-Rutherford Junior Research Fellowship in Physical Sciences, the Okinaga Junior Research Fellowship in Japanese Studies, the A.F. Thompson Junior Research Fellowship in History, and the R.J.P. Williams Junior Research Fellowship in Chemistry or Biochemistry.
Number awarded Varies each year; approximately 6 fellows are in residence each year.
Deadline Fellowships are advertised when they become available but the college does not have an annual competition open to a wide range of subjects.

[931] WALT WHITMAN CHAIR IN AMERICAN CULTURE STUDIES

Council for International Exchange of Scholars
3007 Tilden Street, N.W., Suite 5L
Washington, DC 20008-3009
(202) 686-6245   Fax: (202) 362-3442
E-mail: scholars@cies.iie.org
Web site: www.iie.org/cies

Purpose To allow distinguished American scholars to lecture in American literature at a university in the Netherlands.
Eligibility This chair is awarded to a promising senior or junior scholar in American literature, communications (such as television studies), music, art history, theater, or related areas of American culture studies. Lectures, presented in English, are rotated every few years among 5 major Dutch universities (Amsterdam, Utrecht, Groningen, Leiden, and Nijmegen).
Financial data The award includes a stipend of 20,000 Euros for senior scholars or EUR 16,000 for junior scholars, as well as an international travel allowance up to EUR 1,000 for the grantee only.
Duration 4 months.
Special features This is a Fulbright scholar program, sponsored by the Bureau of Educational and Cultural Affairs of the U.S. Department of State and administered by the Council for International Exchange of Scholars. The scholar teaches undergraduate courses and graduate seminars, assists in research, and provides consultation on curriculum.
Number awarded 1 each year.
Deadline April of each year.

[932]
WIENER LABORATORY RESEARCH ASSOCIATESHIPS

American School of Classical Studies at Athens
Attn: Chair, Committee on the Wiener Laboratory
6-8 Charlton Street
Princeton, NJ 08540-5232
(609) 683-0800   Fax: (609) 924-0578
E-mail: ascsa@ascsa.org
Web site: www.ascsa.org

Purpose To provide financial support to scholars who are interested in conducting archaeological research in Greece.
Eligibility This program is open to scholars who are interested in conducting limited investigations at the Wiener Laboratory of the American School of Classical Studies at Athens. Applicants must have a well-defined project that can be undertaken within the given time in the laboratory or in collaboration with local research institutions.
Financial data Funding up to $5,000 is available.
Duration The proposed project should be of limited duration.
Special features Information is also available from Sherry C. Fox, Director, Wiener Laboratory, 54 Souidias Street, GR-106 76, Athens, Greece, Fax: 30 1 725 0854, E-mail: sfox@ascsa.edu.gr.
Limitations Research associates are required to pay all fees of the school.
Number awarded Varies each year.
Deadline Applications may be submitted at any time.

[933]
WILFRED HALL FELLOWSHIP

University of Newcastle upon Tyne
Attn: Enquiries and Scholarships Officer
10 Kensington Terrace
Newcastle upon Tyne NE1 7RU
England
44 191 222 5742   Fax: 44 191 222 6139
E-mail: fellowships@ncl.ac.uk
Web site: www.ncl.ac.uk

Purpose To provide financial assistance to established scholars who wish to conduct scientific research while affiliated with the University of Newcastle upon Tyne.
Eligibility Nationals of any country (outside of England) may apply if they have earned an advanced degree (normally within the past 10 years), are likely to make a noteworthy contribution to knowledge, and are interested in conducting scientific research while visiting the University of Newcastle upon Tyne.
Financial data The stipend is 17,238 pounds for the first year and 18,185 pounds for the second year.
Duration 2 years.
Number awarded 1 each year.
Deadline November of each year.

[934]
WILLIAM B. SCHALLEK MEMORIAL GRADUATE FELLOWSHIP AWARDS

Richard III Society, Inc.
c/o Laura Blanchard
2041 Christian Street
Philadelphia, PA 19146
E-mail: lblanch001@aol.com
Web site: www.r3.org/edu.html

Purpose To support graduate research in 15th-century English history.
Eligibility Candidates must be U.S. citizens or have made application for first citizenship papers, be enrolled as a graduate student at a recognized educational institution, and be interested in conducting research on topics in late 15th-century English history or culture. Most recipients are Ph.D. candidates conducting dissertation research. Preference is given to applications for travel funds for dissertation research, to topics most closely related to Yorkist-era England, and to students demonstrating financial need.
Financial data Awards up to $2,000 are available, but they are usually $500 or $1,000.
Duration 1 year; may be renewed.
Special features These awards were first presented in 1980.
Number awarded 3 or 4 each year.
Deadline February of each year.

[935]
WILLIAM R. MILLER JUNIOR RESEARCH FELLOWSHIP IN BIOLOGICAL SCIENCES

University of Oxford
St. Edmund Hall
Attn: Principal
Oxford OX1 4AR
England
44 1865 279000
Web site: www.seh.ox.ac.uk

Purpose To provide funding to postdoctoral scholars from any university who wish to conduct research in biology at St. Edmund Hall of the University of Oxford in England.
Eligibility This program is open to scholars from any country who are interested in conducting postdoctoral research in molecular aspects of biology while in residence at St. Edmund Hall.
Financial data Fellows receive a stipend and dining rights.
Duration 3 years.
Number awarded 1 every 3 years (2003, 2006).
Deadline January of the year of the award.

[936]
WINSTON CHURCHILL FOUNDATION FELLOWSHIPS

Winston Churchill Foundation
P.O. Box 1240, Gracie Station
New York, NY 10028-0048
(212) 879-3480   Fax: (212) 879-3480
E-mail: churchill@aol.com

Purpose To enable outstanding American researchers to pursue their work at Churchill College of the University of Cambridge in England.

Eligibility Distinguished American scholars and researchers are considered for this award if they are interested in working at Churchill College. Preference is given to candidates in engineering, mathematics, and the sciences; some are also awarded to those in the social sciences and humanities.

Financial data The amount awarded varies, depending upon the needs of the fellow and the length of the program.

Duration Varies, depending upon the research needs of the recipient.

Special features 8 Churchill fellows have won Nobel Prizes.

Number awarded Varies each year.

[937]
WOLFSON COLLEGE JUNIOR RESEARCH FELLOWSHIPS IN HUMANITIES

University of Oxford
Wolfson College
Attn: President's Secretary
Linton Road
Oxford OX2 6UD
England
44 1865 274100   Fax: 44 1865 274125
E-mail: sue.hales@wolfson.ox.ac.uk
Web site: www.wolfson.ox.ac.uk

Purpose To provide funding to postdoctoral scholars from any country who wish to conduct research in designated areas of the humanities at Wolfson College of the University of Oxford in England.

Eligibility This program is open to residents of any country who are interested in conducting postdoctoral research in the humanities while in residence at Wolfson College. Applicants should normally be younger than 30 years of age and should have at least 2 years of research experience in the subject. Selection is based on a sample of the applicant's written work, up to 10,000 words. The fields of research rotate according to the following schedule: 2003, European civilization of the medieval and modern periods; 2005, medieval and modern history; 2006, Oriental and African studies; 2008, law, politics, economics, and other social studies (except social anthropology); 2009, philosophy (other than philosophy of science or mathematics), general linguistics, and theology; 2010, the ancient Near East and the Greco-Roman world.

Financial data The stipend is 11,478 pounds per year. Fellows also receive room and board at the in college. Fellows who are married or who require family accommodations may live at the college and pay the difference in rent or live outside the college and receive a housing allowance equivalent to the cost of single accommodations at the college.

Duration 3 years.

Special features Fellows are permitted to undertake up to 6 hours of teaching per week.

Number awarded 2 in each of the years the fellowship is offered.

Deadline March of the years the fellowship is offered.

[938]
WOMEN'S INTERNATIONAL SCIENCE COLLABORATION PROGRAM

American Association for the Advancement of Science
Attn: International Directorate
Program on Europe and Central Asia
1200 New York Avenue, N.W., Seventh Floor
Washington, DC 20005
(202) 326-7027   Fax: (202) 289-4958
E-mail: kgrill@aaas.org
Web site: www.aaas.org/international/eca/wisc.shtml

Purpose To provide funding to women scientists interested in establishing new research partnerships with colleagues in central/eastern Europe (CEE), the Newly Independent States of the former Soviet Union (NIS), and Eurasia.

Eligibility This program is open to men and women scientists who have a Ph.D. or equivalent research experience, although applications from male co-principal investigators must be accompanied by an application from a female co-principal investigator as part of a research team. Male and female Ph.D. candidates are also eligible to apply if they will be conducting research in an established Ph.D. program in the United States and will be traveling with their Ph.D. advisor and will serve as a co-principal investigator on future proposals. All applicants must be U.S. citizens or permanent residents. Only fields of study funded by the National Science Foundation (NSF) are eligible; that includes archaeology and anthropology; astronomy; biochemistry, biophysics, and genetics; biological sciences; chemistry; computer science; earth sciences; economics; engineering; environmental sciences; geography; history and philosophy of science; linguistics; mathematics; physics; political science; non-clinically oriented psychology; science and technology policy; and sociology. No proposals involving agricultural production; drug testing or diagnosis; research on the diagnosis, etiology, or treatment of physical or mental diseases or disorders; or the use of animal models of human diseases or conditions are accepted. Specialists who have completed their doctoral degrees within the past 6 years receive special consideration, as do scientists applying to work with colleagues in less frequently represented countries and regions. All proposals must involve travel to a CEE or NIS nation to develop a research program and design. Scientists and engineers who have an existing NSF grant and are eligible for an NSF international supplement should not apply to this program. Selection is based on the applicant's technical abilities, quality of the proposed project, feasibility of carrying out the proposed project, and prospects for long-term collaboration following the completion of the current project.

Financial data Grants up to $4,000 provide travel and living support for the U.S. women scientist and, when appropriate, an additional grant of $4,000 to her American male or female co-principal investigator. Funds may not be used for the sole purpose of teaching, training, or attending conferences or workshops. Grants are administered by and disbursed through the recipient's institution, but no overhead or other indirect charges may be assessed.

Duration Up to 4 weeks.

Special features This program is funded by NSF. Eligible countries include Albania, Armenia, Bosnia, Bulgaria, Croatia, Czech Republic, Estonia, Georgia, Hungary, Kazakhstan, Kyrgyzstan, Latvia, Lithuania, Macedonia, Moldova, Poland, Romania, Russia, Slovak Republic, Slovenia, Tajikistan, Turkmenistan, Ukraine, and Uzbekistan.

Number awarded Varies each year.

Deadline January, March, or July of each year.

[939]
WOODRUFF TRAVELING FELLOWSHIP

Archaeological Institute of America
656 Beacon Street, Fourth Floor
Boston, MA 02215-2010
(617) 353-9361　　　　Fax: (617) 353-6550
E-mail: aia@bu.edu
Web site: www.archaeological.org

Purpose To provide financial assistance to doctoral candidates who wish to conduct archaeological research in Italy and the western Mediterranean.

Eligibility This program is open to candidates who have completed all requirements for the Ph.D. except the dissertation. Applicants must be seeking to conduct archaeological research on any time period in Italy (outside of Sicily and Magna Graecia) or the western Mediterranean. Preference is given to field-oriented projects.

Financial data The stipend is $6,000. Funds may be used for travel, room and board, and other legitimate research expenses.

Duration Up to 1 year.

Number awarded 1 each year.

Deadline October of each year.

[940]
WORCESTER COLLEGE JUNIOR RESEARCH FELLOWSHIPS

University of Oxford
Worcester College
Attn: College Secretary
Beaumont Road
Oxford OX1 2HB
England
44 1865 278342　　　　Fax: 44 1865 278303
E-mail: janet.redfern@worc.ox.ac.uk
Web site: www.worcester.ox.ac.uk

Purpose To provide funding to postdoctoral scholars from any country who wish to conduct research at Worcester College of the University of Oxford in England.

Eligibility This program is open to residents of any country who are interested in conducting postdoctoral research while in residence at Worcester College. Applicants must have a high standard of research ability in their field, which alternates between the humanities in odd-numbered years and the sciences in even-numbered years. The specific field is identified each year.

Financial data The stipend ranges from 7,897 to 9,741 pounds per year. Fellows also receive free dinners and lunches and an allowance of 330 pounds per year for the purchase of books or other research items for their own use.

Duration 3 years.

Limitations Fellows are required to undertake up to 6 hours of teaching per week, to teach undergraduates in tutorials and small classes, and to take part in the annual admissions procedures for the selection of undergraduates.

Number awarded 1 or more each year.

Deadline March of each year.

[941]
ZENECA TRAVELING LECTURESHIP AWARD

Society of Toxicology
Attn: Education Committee
1767 Business Center Drive, Suite 302
Reston, VA 20190-5332
(703) 438-3115　　　　Fax: (703) 438-3113
E-mail: sothq@toxicology.org
Web site: www.toxicology.org

Purpose To provide funding to members of the Society of Toxicology from North America who wish to undertake a lecture tour of Europe.

Eligibility This program is open to established mid-career North American scientists who are members of the society and demonstrate the ability to develop collaborative relationships with European colleagues. Applications must include a statement of experience and expertise, a proposed European lecture itinerary, the rationale for the itinerary, and a statement of benefits to the applicant.

Financial data Awards provide payment of reasonable travel and accommodation costs.

Duration 3 to 4 weeks.

Special features This program is funded by Zeneca, Ltd.

Limitations The itinerary must include a visit and lecture at Zeneca's Alderley Park Facility in Cheshire, England.

Number awarded 2 each year.

Deadline September of each year.

Latin America/Caribbean

Described in this section are 79 scholarships, fellowships, grants, loans, and/or internships open to American students (high school through doctoral), professionals, and postdoctorates that support research or creative activities in Central America, South America, and the Caribbean. If you haven't already checked the "Any Foreign Country" chapter, be sure to do that next; identified there are 222 more sources of funding that can be used to support activities in Latin America and the Caribbean (as well as other areas of the world).

[942]
ABC SMALL GRANTS PROGRAM

American Bird Conservancy
Attn: Director of International Programs
P.O. Box 249
The Plains, VA 20198
(540) 253-5780　　　　　　　　Fax: (540) 253-5782
E-mail: lnaranjo@abcbirds.org
Web site:
www.abcbirds.org/international/intl_funding.htm

Purpose To provide funding for projects benefiting avian conservation in Latin America and the Caribbean.

Eligibility Applicants must be seeking support for projects that benefit avian conservation in Latin America and the Caribbean. Priorities include conservation actions for threatened species, research on threatened species, research on threatened habitats, and training and environmental education for Latin American and Caribbean conservationists.

Financial data The amount of the grant depends on the nature of the proposal and the availability of funds.

Special features This program works in partnership with the U.S. Fish and Wildlife Service, which matches the funds provided by the American Bird Conservancy (ABC).

Number awarded Varies each year.

Deadline October of each year.

[943]
ACLS/SSRC/NEH INTERNATIONAL AND AREA STUDIES FELLOWSHIPS

American Council of Learned Societies
Attn: Office of Fellowships and Grants
228 East 45th Street
New York, NY 10017-3398
(212) 697-1505　　　　　　　　Fax: (212) 949-8058
E-mail: grants@acls.org
Web site: www.acls.org/felguide.htm

Purpose To provide funding to postdoctoral scholars for research on the societies and cultures of Asia, Africa, the Near and Middle East, Latin America, eastern Europe, and the former Soviet Union.

Eligibility This program is open to U.S. citizens and residents who have lived in the United States for at least 3 years. Applicants must have a Ph.D. degree and not have received supported research leave time for at least 3 years prior to the start of the proposed research. They must be interested in conducting humanities and humanities-related social science research on the societies and cultures of Asia, Africa, the Near and Middle East, Latin America, east Europe, or the former Soviet Union. Selection is based on the intellectual merit of the proposed research and the likelihood that it will produce significant and innovative scholarship. Applications are particularly invited from women and members of minority groups.

Financial data The maximum grant is $50,000 for full professors and equivalent, $40,000 for associate professors and equivalent, and $30,000 for assistant professors and equivalent. These fellowships may not be held concurrently with another major fellowship.

Duration 6 to 12 months.

Special features This program is jointly supported by the American Council of Learned Societies (ACLS) and the Social Science Research Council (SSRC), with funding provided by the National Endowment for the Humanities (NEH).

Number awarded Approximately 10 each year.

Deadline September of each year.

[944]
ALEXANDER SISSON AWARD

Geological Society of America
Attn: Research Grants and Awards Administrator
3300 Penrose Place
P.O. Box 9140
Boulder, CO 80301-9140
(303) 447-2020, ext. 137　　　　Fax: (303) 447-1133
E-mail: lcarter@geosociety.org
Web site: www.geosociety.org

Purpose To provide support to graduate student members of the Geological Society of America (GSA) interested in conducting research in Alaska and the Caribbean.

Eligibility This program is open to GSA members pursuing research for a master's or doctoral degree at a university in the United States, Canada, Mexico, or Central America. Students must be interested in conducting research in Alaska or the Caribbean. Applications from women, minorities, and persons with disabilities are strongly encouraged.

Financial data Although there is no predetermined maximum amount for this and other GSA awards, the largest grant recently was $3,175 and the average was $1,622.

Duration 1 year.

Number awarded 1 or more each year.

Deadline January of each year.

[945]
AMERICAN SOCIETY FOR MICROBIOLOGY INTERNATIONAL PROFESSORSHIP FOR LATIN AMERICA

American Society for Microbiology
Attn: Minority and International Activities
1752 N Street, N.W.
Washington, DC 20036-2904
(202) 942-9368　　　　　　　　Fax: (202) 942-9328
E-mail: international@asmusa.org
Web site: www.asmusa.org/international/international-Professorship.htm

Purpose To provide funding to members of the American Society for Microbiology (ASM) interested in teaching a short course at an institution in Latin America.

Eligibility This program is open to ASM members affiliated with an institution of higher learning in the United States or Canada who are actively involved in teaching at the postsecondary level and nationally recognized for their microbiological expertise. Applicants must be interested in teaching at an institution in Latin America that has 1) graduate students enrolled in a master's, doctoral, or equivalent program, postdoctoral fellows or residents, and teaching faculty; 2) at least 12 students enrolled full time in a short course that the North American applicant proposes to teach; 3) a commitment to maximizing use of the course, as demonstrated by the applicability of the course's contents to existing programs at the institution; 4) a commitment to international collaborations and partnerships; and 5) a commitment to advancing the microbiological sciences through interactions with professional organizations. The applicant must be familiar with the host country culture and language and committed to international collaborations and partnerships.

Financial data The stipend is $4,000. Up to 65 percent of the funding may be utilized to help pay travel expenses for the recipient and up to 35 percent may be for supplies and equipment that are not available at the host institution. An allowance of up to $300 per visit may be used by the visiting professor to defray expenses incurred in reciprocating hospitality or for other contingencies. No portion of the award may be used for housing and board for the visiting professor, but the host institution must match the funds provided by this program and those matching funds may be used for housing and board for the visiting professor.

Duration From 1 to 4 weeks.

Number awarded 1 or more each year.

Deadline April of each year for a course during the July-September quarter; October of each year for a course in the January-March quarter.

[946]
ARGENTINA FULBRIGHT EXCHANGE OF ADMINISTRATORS

U.S. Department of State
c/o Graduate School, USDA
600 Maryland Avenue, S.W., Room 320
Washington, DC 20024-2520
(202) 314-3520   Fax: (202) 479-6806
E-mail: fulbright@grad.usda.gov
Web site: www.grad.usda.gov/International/ftep.html

Purpose To promote mutual understanding between the people of the United States and the people of Argentina through an educational administrator exchange program.

Eligibility This program is open to administrators from elementary schools, secondary schools, and 2-year colleges who are interested in working with administrators in Argentina (and vice versa). The assignment may be in the areas of personnel administration, student affairs, or educational policy. Applicants must 1) be U.S. citizens; 2) hold at least a bachelor's degree; 3) be fluent in English; 4) have a current full-time administrative assignment in the United States or a territory; 5) have the approval of their school administration; 6) have at least 3 years of full-time experience; and 7) not have participated in a Fulbright Teacher Exchange longer than 8 weeks during the last 2 years. Fluency in Spanish is recommended. Preference is given to applicants who have not participated previously in the program and may be given to applicants who have not previously lived in Argentina. Geographic distribution of awards within the United States is also a factor in selection. This program does not discriminate on the basis of race, color, religion, age, sex, or national origin and encourages the applications of members of minority communities. Other considerations being equal, veterans are given preference.

Financial data Round-trip economy airfare and a $3,000 cost of living stipend are provided. Participants must obtain a leave of absence with or without pay from their jobs in the United States.

Duration 6 weeks, twice during the year.

Special features This program is sponsored by the Bureau of Educational and Cultural Affairs of the U.S. Department of State and administered by the Graduate School, USDA.

Limitations Dependents are not permitted in this program. Applicants selected for exchange must attend orientation programs of the sponsoring agencies in the United States or abroad.

Number awarded Varies each year.

Deadline October of each year.

[947]
ARGENTINA FULBRIGHT TEACHER EXCHANGE

U.S. Department of State
c/o Graduate School, USDA
600 Maryland Avenue, S.W., Room 320
Washington, DC 20024-2520
(202) 314-3520   Fax: (202) 479-6806
E-mail: fulbright@grad.usda.gov
Web site: www.grad.usda.gov/International/ftep.html

Purpose To promote mutual understanding between the people of the United States and the people of Argentina through a teacher exchange program.

Eligibility This program is open to teachers in grades 9 through 12 and in 2-year and 4-year colleges of Spanish language, literature, history, geography, or English as a second language. Applicants must 1) be U.S. citizens; 2) hold at least a bachelor's degree; 3) be fluent in English; 4) have a current full-time teaching assignment in the United States or a territory; 5) have the approval of their school administration; 6) have at least 3 years of full-time experience; and 7) not have participated in a Fulbright Teacher Exchange longer than 8 weeks during the last 2 years. Fluency or near-fluency in Spanish is required. Teaching couples may apply. However, because of the limited number of positions available and, often, the lack of foreign candidate pairs with similar qualifications for interchanges, it may not be possible to arrange suitable assignments in the same locality or to place both teachers. Preference is given to applicants who have not participated previously in the program and may be given to applicants who have not previously lived in Argentina. Geographic distribution of awards within the United States is also a factor in selection. This program does not discriminate on the basis of race, color, religion, age, sex, or national origin and encourages the applications of members of minority communities. Other considerations being equal, veterans are given preference.

Financial data Round-trip transportation and a housing allowance are provided. The U.S. teacher must obtain a leave of absence with pay. The U.S. school agrees to accept an Argentine teacher who also secures a leave of absence with pay and receives a stipend, but no additional cost accrues to the U.S. school.

Duration 1 semester, beginning in July.

Special features This program is sponsored by the Bureau of Educational and Cultural Affairs of the U.S. Department of State and administered by the Graduate School, USDA.

Limitations This program provides for the direct exchange of teaching assignments between Argentina and the United

States. Applicants selected for exchange must attend orientation programs of the sponsoring agencies in the United States or abroad.

Number awarded 5 each year.

Deadline October of each year.

[948]
ARGENTINA/BRAZIL/URUGUAY JOINT AWARD IN TRADE INTEGRATION

Council for International Exchange of Scholars
3007 Tilden Street, N.W., Suite 5L
Washington, DC 20008-3009
(202) 686-6238   Fax: (202) 362-3442
E-mail: scholars@cies.iie.org
Web site: www.iie.org/cies

Purpose To provide funding to American scholars interested in lecturing on regional trade integration at universities in Argentina, Brazil, and Uruguay.

Eligibility Applicants must have a Ph.D., at least 4 years of teaching experience, and good to fluent Spanish; a working knowledge of Portuguese is desirable. They must be interested in teaching graduate courses and/or special seminars, engaging in collaborative or independent research, or combining both activities in an area with relevance to regional trade integration and the MERCOSUR and NAFTA trade agreements. The affiliations at the universities where they teach are coordinated by the Fulbright commissions in Argentina, Brazil, and Uruguay, but applicants may express their preferences. U.S. citizenship is required.

Financial data The stipend is $2,000 per month for junior scholars or $2,600 per month for senior scholars. Other benefits include a monthly housing allowance of $700, monthly subsistence allowance of $1,300, tuition reimbursement for accompanying K-12 children to a maximum of $4,000 per family, and up to $1,200 for books and educational materials.

Duration 4 months, to be divided among the 3 countries.

Special features This is a Fulbright scholar program, sponsored by the Bureau of Educational and Cultural Affairs of the U.S. Department of State and administered by the Council for International Exchange of Scholars.

Number awarded 1 each year.

Deadline July of each year.

[949]
ARGENTINA/URUGUAY JOINT AWARD IN ENVIRONMENTAL SCIENCES

Council for International Exchange of Scholars
3007 Tilden Street, N.W., Suite 5L
Washington, DC 20008-3009
(202) 686-6238   Fax: (202) 362-3442
E-mail: scholars@cies.iie.org
Web site: www.iie.org/cies

Purpose To provide funding to American scholars interested in lecturing on environmental sciences at universities in Argentina and Uruguay.

Eligibility Applicants must have a Ph.D., at least 4 years of teaching experience, and good to fluent Spanish. They must be interested in teaching graduate or faculty seminars on an aspect of environmental studies with relevance to both Argentina and Uruguay, consult with faculty at universities in those countries on ongoing research projects, and conduct their own research. U.S. citizenship is required.

Financial data The stipend is approximately $2,000 per month. Other benefits include a monthly housing and subsistence allowance of $900 to $1,850 depending on the number of accompanying dependents, airfare up to $2,400 to cover international travel for grantee and dependents, a relocation allowance of $750, an educational allowance of $250 to $750 depending on the number of accompanying dependents, and an allowance of $500 for educational materials to be donated to host institutions upon grantee's departure.

Duration 4 months, to be divided between the 2 countries.

Special features This is a Fulbright scholar program, sponsored by the Bureau of Educational and Cultural Affairs of the U.S. Department of State and administered by the Council for International Exchange of Scholars.

Number awarded 1 each year.

Deadline July of each year.

[950]
ARIZONA INTERNATIONAL ARTS EXCHANGE

Arizona Commission on the Arts
Attn: Public Information Office
417 West Roosevelt Street
Phoenix, AZ 85003
(602) 255-5882   Fax: (602) 256-0282
E-mail: general@ArizonaArts.com
Web site: az.arts.asu.edu/artscomm

Purpose To provide an opportunity for Arizona artists to tour Mexico.

Eligibility Eligible to apply for this program are artists who reside in Arizona and have been selected to appear on the Roster of the Arizona Commission on the Arts. They must be interested in touring Mexico.

Financial data Sponsors in Mexico provide housing, food, local transportation, and an interpreter (if necessary); the commission provides an honorarium.

Duration Varies.

Special features This program involves federal and state agencies on both sides of the U.S. and Mexican border.

Number awarded Varies each year, depending upon the number of requests from Mexico and the available funding.

Deadline Applications may be submitted at any time.

[951]
A.W. MELLON RESEARCH EXPLORATION AWARDS IN TROPICAL BIOLOGY

Organization for Tropical Studies
Attn: Academic Director
410 Swift Avenue
P.O. Box 90630
Durham, NC 27708-0630
(919) 684-5774   Fax: (919) 684-5661
E-mail: nao@duke.edu
Web site: www.ots.duke.edu

Purpose To provide support to graduate students and senior investigators interested in conducting comparative research at facilities of the Organization for Tropical Studies (OTS) in Costa Rica and the Smithsonian Tropical Research Institute (STRI) in Panama.

Eligibility This program is open to graduate students and senior investigators interested in conducting exploratory research in tropical biology. Applicants who 1) have worked previously at OTS sites and wish to work at an STRI site, and/or 2) are from OTS member institutions should send their proposals to OTS. Applicants who have worked previously at STRI sites and wish to work at an OTS site should send their proposals to Smithsonian Tropical Research Institute, Attn: Office of Education, Unit 0948, APO AA 34002-0948, (507) 212-8031, Fax: (507) 212-8148, E-mail: fellows@tivoli.si.edu. Applicants who 1) wish to work at both sites as part of a single project, and/or 2) have not previously worked at either an OTS or STRI site may send their application materials to either institution (but not both). Proposals may be submitted in either English or Spanish and must include an introduction, specific objectives, methods, anticipated results, budget, literature cited, curriculum vitae, and (for graduate students) a letter of support from the applicant's thesis/research advisor.

Financial data The maximum grant is $3,000 for graduate students or $6,000 for senior investigators. Funding may be provided for travel to and from either/both site(s), station fees at either/both site(s), and minor equipment needs to carry out projects. Proposals to fund travel to 1 or both sites for the purpose of meeting with collaborators will be considered.

Duration Up to 12 months.

Special features Funding for this program is provided by the Andrew W. Mellon Foundation.

Deadline Applications may be submitted at any time.

[952]
BERMUDA BIOLOGICAL STATION GRADUATE INTERNSHIPS

Bermuda Biological Station for Research
Attn: Education Department
17 Biological Station Lane
Ferry Reach
St. George's, GE 01
Bermuda
(441) 297-1880   Fax: (441) 297-8143
E-mail: education@bbsr.edu
Web site: www.bbsr.edu

Purpose To provide an opportunity for graduate students to conduct research at the Bermuda Biological Station for Research (BBSR).

Eligibility This program is open to students in M.S. or Ph.D. programs in marine biology, marine chemistry, carbonate geology, and oceanography at accredited universities who are interested in conducting research at the BBSR. The thesis topic must be approved by the applicant's major advisor and department, and each intern must be accepted by a BBSR faculty member willing to serve as a local faculty advisor.

Financial data Interns are required to provide at least 20 hours per month of service working as teaching assistants in semester and summer courses, conducting laboratory exercises or field trips, or delivering lectures; that service covers the facilities fees. In addition, they may provide research assistance to their local faculty advisor in exchange for a stipend of up to $300 per month and partial payment of room and board.

Duration 6 to 12 months; may be renewed for 1 additional year.

Special features The BBS was established in 1903 by scientists from Harvard University, New York University, and the Bermuda Natural History Society. It moved to its current location in 1932 with funding from the Bermuda government and the Rockefeller Foundation. Since 1969, it has operated year-round, offering a variety of programs and research facilities related largely to marine biology, oceanography, and environmental quality.

Number awarded Varies each year.

[953]
BERMUDA BIOLOGICAL STATION GRANTS-IN-AID

Bermuda Biological Station for Research
Attn: Gillian Spowart
17 Biological Station Lane
Ferry Reach
St. George's, GE 01
Bermuda
(441) 297-1880   Fax: (441) 297-8143
E-mail: gillian@bbsr.edu
Web site: www.bbsr.edu

Purpose To provide financial assistance to students and researchers from any country who wish to conduct research at the Bermuda Biological Station for Research (BBSR).

Eligibility Applicants may be from any country and must be interested in coming to the BBSR. They may be principal investigators and associates doing field or laboratory work for research projects, graduate students and postdoctoral fellows completing field and laboratory work, or undergraduate and secondary school student groups completing the field-work portions of courses.

Financial data Grants range from $500 to $3,000 each and are available to help defray the costs of BBSR in-house charges, including housing, lab fees, and boat rental.

Special features The BBSR was established in 1903 by scientists from Harvard University, New York University, and the Bermuda Natural History Society. It moved to its current location in 1932 with funding from the Bermuda government and the Rockefeller Foundation. Since 1969, it has operated year-round, offering a variety of programs and research facilities related largely to marine biology, oceanography, and environmental quality.

Limitations Grants may not be used for salary, personal expenses, supplies, or airfare.

Number awarded Varies each year.

Deadline Applications for summer projects must be submitted by the end of February; for winter projects, applications are due by the end of September.

[954]
BIODIVERSITY SURVEYS AND INVENTORIES PROGRAM (BSI) GRANTS

National Museum of Natural History
Attn: Biodiversity Programs Office
10th Street and Constitution Avenue N.W.
Washington, DC 20560-0180
(202) 357-3313   Fax: (202) 786-2563
E-mail: parentil@nmnh.si.edu
Web site: www.mnh.si.edu/biodiversity

Purpose To support descriptive studies of taxa that are central to research efforts of the National Museum of Natural History (NMNH), especially in Burma, the Caribbean, and China.

Eligibility This program is open to research scientists and curators currently receiving funding from the museum. Applicants must be proposing to conduct field studies primarily aimed at the discovery and enumeration of taxa and for projects that make use of the archival collections at the museum and other institutions. Research in any taxonomic group and geographical area is considered, but the program has identified biodiversity research in Burma (Myanmar), the Insular Caribbean (particularly Cuba and Hispaniola), and China for special emphasis. Proposals may include non-museum colleagues as participants. Applications must include a scientific justification for the project, statement of materials and methods, expected scientific product, detailed budget, and curriculum vitae for non-museum participants. Selection is based on scientific merit, suitability for support by the museum biodiversity programs, ability to enhance museum research collections, collaboration with host country scientists, feasibility of the project, and expected final result.

Financial data The amount awarded varies, depending upon the scope of the project. Recently, the average award was $11,670.

Duration Varies, depending upon the scope of the project.

Special features This project, operating since 1995, is part of the Biodiversity Program of NMNH.

Limitations Recipients are expected to share their data with the host country's sponsoring institutions. Participants must work within conventions and other agreements between the host countries and the NMNH. They are also expected to develop collegial relationships with their counterparts in the host country.

Number awarded Varies each year.

Deadline September of each year.

[955]
BIOLOGICAL DIVERSITY OF THE GUIANAS (BDG) PROGRAM RESEARCH GRANTS

National Museum of Natural History
Attn: Biodiversity Programs Office
10th Street and Constitution Avenue N.W.
Washington, DC 20560-0180
(202) 786-2518   Fax: (202) 786-2563
E-mail: funkv@nmnh.si.edu
Web site: www.mnh.si.edu/biodiversity

Purpose To support research on topics dealing with biological diversity in the Guianas.

Eligibility All members of the National Museum of Natural History (NMNH) scientific staff, their assistants and colleagues, and graduate students collaborating directly with NMNH scientists are eligible to apply for support if they are interested in conducting research on biological diversity in Guyana, Suriname, or French Guiana. Topics cover botany, entomology, and zoology. The field station for research is in Georgetown, Guyana. Multidisciplinary projects are particularly encouraged. Selection is based on the scientific merit of the proposal.

Financial data The amount awarded varies, depending upon the scope of the project. Recently, the average award was $11,670.

Duration Varies, depending upon the scope of the project.

Special features This project, operating since 1983, is part of the Biodiversity Program of NMNH.

Limitations Recipients are expected to share their data with the host country's sponsoring institutions. Participants must work within conventions and other agreements between the host countries and the NMNH. They are also expected to develop collegial relationships with their counterparts in the host country.

Number awarded Varies each year.

Deadline For most projects, the deadline is September of each year. However, proposals for urgent projects—arising unexpectedly during the year—may be submitted at any time.

[956]
BIOLOGICAL DYNAMICS OF FOREST FRAGMENT PROJECT (BDFFP) RESEARCH GRANTS

National Museum of Natural History
Attn: Biodiversity Programs Office
10th Street and Constitution Avenue N.W.
Washington, DC 20560-0180
(202) 786-2821   Fax: (202) 786-2934
E-mail: roman.argelis@nmnh.si.edu
Web site: www.mnh.si.edu/biodiversity

Purpose To support research on topics dealing with tropical rain forests in Brazil.

Eligibility Research supported by this program may be conducted at 11 forest fragments near Manaus, Brazil and deal with 1 of the following topics: 1) studies of the effects of forest fragmentation on specific taxa, communities, ecological processes, species interactions, physical parameters, and resource distribution, and the genetic structure of selected taxa; 2) studies investigating the process of forest regeneration; 3) basic tropical ecology that can serve as the basis for future investigations of fragmentation effects; 4) studies on the recuperation of degraded areas; or 5) taxonomic and systematic studies of poorly-known or highly diverse taxa. Applicants seeking to serve as a principal investigator must hold a Ph.D. or equivalent degree; collaborators may include graduate students or other qualified researchers. Non-Brazilian researchers should plan to establish a collaborative project with a Brazilian counterpart; that implies involving Brazilian graduate students if necessary. Brazilian researchers and graduate students and Smithsonian Institution researchers receive preference.

Financial data The amount awarded varies, depending upon the scope of the project. Recently, the average award was $11,670.

Duration Varies, depending upon the scope of the project.

Special features This project, which began in 1979, is part of the Biodiversity Program of NMNH and is jointly sponsored by Brazil's National Institute for Amazonian Research. Information is also available from Associacao de Levantamento da Amazonas, c/o INPA-Ecologia, C.P. 478, 69011-970 Manaus, AM, Brazil, 55-92-642-1148, Fax: 55-92-642-2050, E-mail: pdbff@inpa.gov.br.

Limitations Recipients are expected to share their data with the host country's sponsoring institutions. Participants must work within conventions and other agreements between the host countries and the NMNH. They are also expected to develop collegial relationships with their counterparts in the host country.

Number awarded Varies each year.

Deadline May of each year.

[957]
BRAZIL FULBRIGHT TEACHER EXCHANGE

U.S. Department of State
c/o Graduate School, USDA
600 Maryland Avenue, S.W., Room 320
Washington, DC 20024-2520
(202) 314-3520   Fax: (202) 479-6806
E-mail: fulbright@grad.usda.gov
Web site: www.grad.usda.gov/International/ftep.html

Purpose To promote mutual understanding between the people of the United States and the people of Brazil through a teacher exchange program.

Eligibility This program is open to elementary, secondary, and 2- or 4-year college teachers of mathematics, science, or English as a second language (ESL) who are interested in teaching in Brazil. Applicants must 1) be U.S. citizens; 2) hold at least a bachelor's degree; 3) be fluent in English; 4) have a current full-time teaching assignment in the U.S. or a territory; 5) have the approval of their school administration; 6) have at least 3 years of full-time experience; and 7) not have participated in a Fulbright Teacher Exchange longer than 8 weeks during the last 2 years. Portuguese fluency is not required, but preference is given to those with Portuguese speaking ability. Teaching couples may apply. However, because of the limited number of positions available and, often, the lack of foreign candidate pairs with similar qualifications for interchanges, it may not be possible to arrange suitable assignments in the same locality or to place both teachers. Preference is given to applicants who have not participated previously in the program and may be given to applicants who have not previously lived in Brazil. Geographic distribution of awards within the United States is also a factor in selection. This program does not discriminate on the basis of race, color, religion, age, sex, or national origin and encourages the applications of members of minority communities. Other considerations being equal, veterans are given preference.

Financial data Round-trip economy airfare for the exchange teacher only and a $3,000 cost of living stipend are provided. Participants must obtain a leave of absence with or without pay from their jobs in the United States. The U.S. school must agree to accept a teacher from Brazil who must secure a leave of absence with or without pay.

Duration 2 periods of 6 to 8 weeks each during an academic year, with dates to be determined by mutual agreement of the participating institutions.

Special features This program is sponsored by the Bureau of Educational and Cultural Affairs of the U.S. Department of State and administered by the Graduate School, USDA. It is a special initiative in which U.S. and Brazilian educators work in teams across primary, secondary, and tertiary levels on topics of ESL methodology, science, or mathematics.

Limitations Applicants selected for exchange must attend orientation programs of the sponsoring agencies in the United States or abroad.

Number awarded 9 each year.

Deadline October of each year.

[958]
CARIBBEAN CORAL REEF ECOSYSTEMS (CCRE) PROGRAM RESEARCH GRANTS

National Museum of Natural History
Attn: Biodiversity Programs Office
10th Street and Constitution Avenue N.W.
Washington, DC 20560-0180
(202) 786-2130   Fax: (202) 786-2934
E-mail: sitnik.marsha@nmnh.si.edu
Web site: www.mnh.si.edu/biodiversity

Purpose To support research on topics dealing with the Caribbean coral reefs.

Eligibility All members of the National Museum of Natural History (NMNH) scientific staff, their assistants and colleagues, and graduate students collaborating directly with NMNH scientists are eligible to apply for support if they are interested in conducting research on the zoology, botany, carbonate geology, or paleobiology of Caribbean coral reefs. The field station for research is in southern Belize. Multidisciplinary projects are particularly encouraged. Selection is based on the scientific merit of the proposal.

Financial data The amount awarded varies, depending upon the scope of the project. Recently, the average annual award was $11,670.

Duration Varies, depending upon the scope of the project.

Special features This project has been part of the Biodiversity Program of NMNH since 1985.

Limitations Recipients are expected to share their data with the host country's sponsoring institutions. Participants must work within conventions and other agreements between the host countries and the NMNH. They are also expected to develop collegial relationships with their counterparts in the host country.

Number awarded Varies each year.

Deadline For most projects, the deadline is September of each year. However, proposals for urgent projects—arising unexpectedly during the year—may be submitted at any time.

[959]
CARNEGIE OBSERVATORIES POSTDOCTORAL RESEARCH FELLOWSHIP

Carnegie Institution of Washington
Attn: Chair, Fellowship Committee
813 Santa Barbara Street
Pasadena, CA 91101-1292
(626) 577-1122　　　　　Fax: (626) 795-8136
E-mail: cfellow@ociw.edu
Web site: www.ciw.edu

Purpose To provide financial support for astronomers who are interested in conducting astronomical research at Cerro Las Campanas, Chile or other facilities.

Eligibility Applicants must have completed the requirements for a Ph.D. in astronomy prior to assuming the fellowship, preferably within the past 3 years. Proposals are accepted for long-term observational research in optical or infra-red astronomy, to be conducted at the facilities in Pasadena or the observatories of the Carnegie Institution of Washington on Cerro Las Campanas, Chile or on Palomar Mountain.

Financial data The stipend is $39,000.

Duration 1 year; may be renewed for 2 additional years.

Special features Use of the Palomar Observatory is provided by arrangement between the Carnegie Institution of Washington and the California Institute of Technology.

Number awarded 1 each year.

Deadline December of each year.

[960]
CHILE FULBRIGHT TEACHER EXCHANGE

U.S. Department of State
c/o Graduate School, USDA
600 Maryland Avenue, S.W., Room 320
Washington, DC 20024-2520
(202) 314-3520　　　　　Fax: (202) 479-6806
E-mail: fulbright@grad.usda.gov
Web site: www.grad.usda.gov/International/ftep.html

Purpose To promote mutual understanding between the people of the United States and the people of Chile through a teacher exchange program.

Eligibility This program is open to senior high school (grades 9 through 12) and 2-year college teachers of English, Spanish, or social studies who wish to teach English as a foreign language, history, or literature in Chile. Applicants must 1) be U.S. citizens; 2) hold at least a bachelor's degree; 3) be fluent in English; 4) have a current full-time teaching assignment in the U.S. or a territory; 5) have the approval of their school administration; 6) have at least 3 years of full-time experience; and 7) not have participated in a Fulbright Teacher Exchange longer than 8 weeks during the last 2 years. Fluency in Spanish is required. Teaching couples may apply. However, because of the limited number of positions available and, often, the lack of foreign candidate pairs with similar qualifications for interchanges, it may not be possible to arrange suitable assignments in the same locality or to place both teachers. Preference is given to applicants who have not participated previously in the program and may be given to applicants who have not previously lived in Chile. Geographic distribution of awards within the United States is also a factor in selection. This program does not discriminate on the basis of race, color, religion, age, sex, or national origin and encourages the applications of members of minority communities. Other considerations being equal, veterans are given preference.

Financial data Only round-trip transportation is provided. Participants must obtain a leave of absence with pay from their jobs in the United States. The U.S. school must agree to accept a Chilean teacher who must secure a leave of absence with pay; the Chilean teacher receives a stipend, but no additional cost accrues to the U.S. school.

Duration 1 year, beginning in July.

Special features This program is sponsored by the Bureau of Educational and Cultural Affairs of the U.S. Department of State and administered by the Graduate School, USDA.

Limitations This program provides for the direct exchange of teaching assignments between Chile and the United States. Applicants selected for exchange must attend orientation programs of the sponsoring agencies in the United States or abroad.

Number awarded 4 each year.

Deadline October of each year.

[961]
COLOMBIA FULBRIGHT EXCHANGE OF ADMINISTRATORS

U.S. Department of State
c/o Graduate School, USDA
600 Maryland Avenue, S.W., Room 320
Washington, DC 20024-2520
(202) 314-3520　　　　　Fax: (202) 479-6806
E-mail: fulbright@grad.usda.gov
Web site: www.grad.usda.gov/International/ftep.html

Purpose To promote mutual understanding between the people of the United States and the people of Colombia through an educational administrator exchange program.

Eligibility This program is open to administrators from elementary schools, secondary schools, and 2-year colleges who are interested in working with administrators in Colombia (and vice versa). The assignment may be in the areas of personnel administration, student affairs, or educational policy. Applicants must 1) be U.S. citizens; 2) hold at least a bachelor's degree; 3) be fluent in English; 4) have a current full-time administrative assignment in the U.S. or a territory; 5) have the approval of their school administration; 6) have at least 3 years of full-time experience; and 7) not have participated in a Fulbright Teacher Exchange longer than 8 weeks during the last 2 years. Fluency in Spanish is recommended. Preference is given to applicants who have not participated previously in the program and may be given to applicants who have not previously lived in Colombia. Geographic distribution of awards within the United States is also a factor in selection. This program does not discriminate on the basis of race, color, religion, age, sex, or national origin and encourages the applications of members of minority communities. Other considerations being equal, veterans are given preference.

Financial data Round-trip economy airfare and a $3,000 cost of living stipend are provided. Participants must obtain a leave of absence with or without pay from their jobs in the United States.
Duration 6 weeks, twice during the year.
Special features This program is sponsored by the Bureau of Educational and Cultural Affairs of the U.S. Department of State and administered by the Graduate School, USDA.
Limitations Dependents are not permitted in this program. Applicants selected for exchange must attend orientation programs of the sponsoring agencies in the United States or abroad.
Number awarded Varies each year.
Deadline October of each year.

[962]
COLOMBIA FULBRIGHT TEACHER EXCHANGE
U.S. Department of State
c/o Graduate School, USDA
600 Maryland Avenue, S.W., Room 320
Washington, DC 20024-2520
(202) 314-3520   Fax: (202) 479-6806
E-mail: fulbright@grad.usda.gov
Web site: www.grad.usda.gov/International/ftep.html

Purpose To promote mutual understanding between the people of the United States and the people of Colombia through a teacher exchange program.
Eligibility This program is open to elementary and secondary school teachers of Spanish, English, literature, English as a second language, or history who wish to teach English as a foreign language in Colombia. Applicants must 1) be U.S. citizens; 2) hold at least a bachelor's degree; 3) be fluent in English; 4) have a current full-time teaching assignment in the U.S. or a territory; 5) have the approval of their school administration; 6) have at least 3 years of full-time experience; and 7) not have participated in a Fulbright Teacher Exchange longer than 8 weeks during the last 2 years. Fluency in Spanish is required. Teaching couples may apply. However, because of the limited number of positions available and, often, the lack of foreign candidate pairs with similar qualifications for interchanges, it may not be possible to arrange suitable assignments in the same locality or to place both teachers. Preference is given to applicants who have not participated previously in the program and may be given to applicants who have not previously lived in Colombia. Geographic distribution of awards within the United States is also a factor in selection. This program does not discriminate on the basis of race, color, religion, age, sex, or national origin and encourages the applications of members of minority communities. Other considerations being equal, veterans are given preference.
Financial data Round-trip transportation and an allowance for excess baggage are provided. Participants must obtain a leave of absence with pay from their jobs in the United States. The U.S. school must agree to accept a Colombian teacher who must secure a leave of absence with pay; the Colombian teacher receives a stipend, but no additional cost accrues to the U.S. school.
Duration 11 months, beginning in July.

Special features This program is sponsored by the Bureau of Educational and Cultural Affairs of the U.S. Department of State and administered by the Graduate School, USDA.
Limitations This program provides for the direct exchange of teaching assignments between Colombia and the United States. Applicants selected for exchange must attend orientation programs of the sponsoring agencies in the United States or abroad.
Number awarded 4 each year.
Deadline October of each year.

[963]
COSTA RICA TRAVEL GRANTS FOR ACM FACULTY
Associated Colleges of the Midwest
Attn: Program Officer
205 West Wacker Drive, Suite 1300
Chicago, IL 60606
(312) 263-5000   Fax: (312) 263-5879
E-mail: acm@acm.edu
Web site: www.acm.edu/faculty/travel.htm

Purpose To provide funding to faculty members at schools belonging to the Associated Colleges of the Midwest (ACM) who wish to visit Costa Rica.
Eligibility This program is open to faculty from ACM colleges who wish to visit Costa Rica to become more familiar with ACM programs there (Studies in Latin American Culture during the fall semester, Tropical Field Research during the spring semester). Applicants may make professional contacts and explore possible research opportunities. Preference is given to faculty who have not previously received a grant and can visit while a program is in session.
Financial data Grants cover round-trip airfare between the recipient's college and San José.
Special features The ACM colleges are Beloit College, Carleton College, University of Chicago, Coe College, Cornell College, Colorado College, Grinnell College, Knox College, Lake Forest College, Lawrence University, Macalester College, Monmouth College, Ripon College, and St. Olaf College.
Number awarded Approximately 6 each year.
Deadline April of each year.

[964]
DONALD AND BEVERLY STONE ENDOWMENT
Organization for Tropical Studies
Attn: Academic Director
410 Swift Avenue
P.O. Box 90630
Durham, NC 27708-0630
(919) 684-5774   Fax: (919) 684-5661
E-mail: nao@duke.edu
Web site: www.ots.duke.edu

Purpose To provide support to graduate students at member institutions of the Organization for Tropical Studies (OTS) who are interested in conducting field work in tropical biology in Costa Rica.
Eligibility Graduate students who have completed courses offered by the organization as well as other graduate students

in degree programs at member institutions may apply for these fellowships. They must be planning to conduct dissertation research in tropical biology or related fields. Preference is given to proposals for research at 1 of the organization's field stations in Costa Rica (La Selva, Palo Verde, and Las Cruces), but proposals for research at other locations are considered.
Financial data The amount of the award depends on the nature of the proposal and the availability of funds.
Duration Up to 12 months.
Special features This program includes a number of named fellowships: the Emily P. Foster Fellowship, the William L. Brown Fellowship, the Rexford Daubenmire Fellowship, and the Dole Food Fellowship.
Number awarded Varies each year.
Deadline January or September of each year.

[965]
DUMBARTON OAKS PROJECT GRANTS
Dumbarton Oaks
Attn: Office of the Director
1703 32nd Street, N.W.
Washington, DC 20007-2961
(202) 339-6410   Fax: (202) 339-6419
E-mail: DumbartonOaks@doaks.org
Web site: www.doaks.org

Purpose To provide funding for scholarly projects in Byzantine studies, pre-Columbian studies, or landscape architecture.
Eligibility Scholars in Byzantine studies (including related aspects of late Roman, early Christian, western medieval, Slavic, and Near Eastern studies), pre-Columbian studies (of Mexico, Central America, and Andean South America), and studies in landscape architecture (including architectural, art historical, botanical, horticultural, cultural, economic, social, and agrarian) may apply for these grants. Support is generally for archaeological research, as well as for the recovery, recording, and analysis of materials that would otherwise be lost. Selection is based on the ability and preparation of the principal project personnel (including knowledge of the requisite languages), and interest and value of the project to the specific field of study.
Financial data Grants normally range from $3,000 to $10,000.
Duration 1 year, beginning in July.
Limitations Project awards are not offered purely for the purpose of travel, nor for work associated with a degree, for library or archive research, for catalogs, or for conservation and restoration *per se*.
Deadline October of each year.

[966]
EARTHWATCH STUDENT CHALLENGE AWARDS PROGRAM
Earthwatch
Attn: Student Challenge Awards Program
3 Clock Tower Place, Suite 100
P.O. Box 75
Maynard, MA 01754-0075
(978) 461-0081   (800) 776-0188
Fax: (978) 461-2332   E-mail: drobbins@earthwatch.org
Web site: www.earthwatch.org

Purpose To provide funding to scientists who wish to utilize high school students as assistants on laboratory or field research projects.
Eligibility This program is open to principal investigators in the physical sciences who are interested in utilizing high school students as part of a research project conducted at a research center, laboratory, observatory, or field station. Most research sites are in the United States, although proposals are also welcomed for projects in Canada, the Caribbean, Mexico, and Costa Rica. In addition to the principal investigator, each team is accompanied by a graduate student to oversee the students' work, provide additional adult supervision, and act as a career counselor and team facilitator. Graduate student mentors are expected to have significant understanding of the research being conducted by the principal investigator. They should also be capable of handling the complex social, emotional, and intellectual needs of high school students. Selection of the high school students is based on their creativity and scholarship; they should be gifted in the arts and humanities but have sufficient interest and training in science to handle the challenges of the experience. Students are assigned to sites very different from their home environment, usually in rural locations. The program is committed to bringing together students from different backgrounds and regions of the United States, to attracting a diversity of students, and to providing this experience to students with disabilities.
Financial data The budget may include, for the high school students, grants from $1,600 to $1,800 per student. Allowable expenses include food and accommodations for students and staff; principal investigator and graduate student mentor transportation to the field; team transportation; equipment and supplies; administrative costs (telephone costs, mail, copying, report preparation); enrichment activities (e.g., museum entrance fees, theater tickets); and staff stipends. The staff stipend line item may include a $500 honorarium for the principal investigator, but the grants do not cover salary for principal investigators, institutional overhead, capital equipment, or publication costs. The complete grant may range from $6,000 to $14,000.
Duration 12 to 18 days, in July or August.
Special features This program began in 1990. It is currently funded by the Durfee Foundation.
Limitations Principal investigators are expected to stay in the same accommodations as the students and graduate student mentors; they need to be available to support the students 24 hours a day.
Number awarded Each year, 10 to 12 research projects are funded, each utilizing from 6 to 8 high school students.
Deadline Principal investigators must submit proposals by September of each year.

[967]
EASTERN BIRD BANDING ASSOCIATION MEMORIAL RESEARCH GRANTS

Eastern Bird Banding Association
c/o Richard N. Roberts, Memorial Grants Chairperson
7212 Fiddler Bay Lane
Chincoteague, VA 23336-2017
E-mail: nroberts@shore.intercom.net
Web site: www.pronetisp.net/~bpbird/eb00006.htm

Purpose To provide funding to researchers interested in projects using bird banding data or banding techniques.

Eligibility Applicants must be interested in conducting research projects that use bird banding data or banding techniques. They should submit a resume of their banding and ornithological background, the project plan, including the significance of the study site, and a budget. Preference is given to research in the eastern United States or with species that spend part of their life there, but projects in other portions of the United States, North America, or the western hemisphere are also eligible. Research studies with conservation or management implications are particularly encouraged.

Financial data The amount of the grant depends on the nature of the proposal and the availability of funds. Travel grants are also available.

Duration 1 year.

Limitations Grantees are required to submit a summary of their work at the end of the year or present at least part of their study at the annual meeting of the sponsoring organization.

Number awarded 1 or more each year.

Deadline March of each year.

[968]
EDILIA AND FRANCOIS-AUGUSTE DE MONTEQUIN FELLOWSHIP

Society of Architectural Historians
1365 North Astor Street
Chicago, IL 60610-2144
(312) 573-1365   Fax: (312) 573-1141
E-mail: info@sah.org
Web site: www.sah.org

Purpose To fund travel for research on Spanish, Portuguese, or Ibero-American architecture.

Eligibility This fellowship is aimed primarily at junior scholars (including graduate students) and senior scholars. Proposed research must focus on Spanish, Portuguese, or Ibero-American architecture, including colonial architecture produced by the Spaniards in the Philippines and in the Americas. Applicants must have been members of the Society of Architectural Historians for at least 1 year.

Financial data Awards are $2,000 for junior scholars and $6,000 for senior scholars.

Duration 1 year.

Number awarded 1 each year to a junior scholar; 1 each odd-numbered year to a senior scholar.

Deadline November of each year for junior scholars; November of even-numbered years for senior scholars.

[969]
ELEANOR ROOSEVELT PROGRAM IN AMERICAN STUDIES AND PUBLIC POLICY

Council for International Exchange of Scholars
3007 Tilden Street, N.W., Suite 5L
Washington, DC 20008-3009
(202) 686-6238   Fax: (202) 362-3442
E-mail: scholars@cies.iie.org
Web site: www.iie.org/cies

Purpose To provide funding to American scholars interested in lecturing on American studies at a university in Brazil.

Eligibility Applicants must have a Ph.D. in history or political science, at least 5 years of teaching experience, and fluent Spanish or a working knowledge of Portuguese. They must be interested in teaching 2 courses at the University of Sao Paulo in Brazil in their area of specialization within the fields of history, political science, or public policy from a U.S. or comparative perspective. They may also assist with program and curriculum development or a new program in American studies, conduct independent or collaborative research, and build linkages between the University of Sao Paulo and U.S. universities. Because of the language requirement for Spanish or Portuguese, Latin Americanists or Brazilianists are also eligible to apply. U.S. citizenship is required.

Financial data The stipend is $2,000 per month for junior scholars or $2,600 per month for senior scholars. Other benefits include a monthly housing allowance of $700, monthly subsistence allowance of $1,300, tuition reimbursement for accompanying K-12 children to a maximum of $4,000 per family, and up to $1,200 for books and educational materials.

Duration 3 to 5 months.

Special features This is a Fulbright scholar program, sponsored by the Bureau of Educational and Cultural Affairs of the U.S. Department of State and administered by the Council for International Exchange of Scholars.

Number awarded 1 each year.

Deadline July of each year.

[970]
FELLOWSHIPS IN INTERNATIONAL HUMAN RIGHTS

Human Rights Watch
Attn: Fellowship Committee
350 Fifth Avenue, 34th Floor
New York, NY 10118-3299
(212) 290-4700, ext. 312   Fax: (212) 736-1300
E-mail: hrwnyc@hrw.org
Web site: www.hrw.org

Purpose To provide an opportunity for recent recipients of law or graduate degrees to engage in human rights monitoring and advocacy while working for Human Rights Watch.

Eligibility These fellowships are available to recent graduates of law schools or graduate programs in journalism, international relations, or area studies from any university worldwide. Applicants must be interested in working with a division of Human Rights Watch, based in Washington, D.C. or New York. Their assignment involves monitoring human rights developments in various countries, conducting on-site investigations, drafting reports on human rights conditions, and engaging in advocacy efforts aimed at publicizing and curtailing human rights violations. Applicants must demonstrate analytic skills, an ability to write and speak clearly, and a commitment to work in the human rights field in the future on a paid or volunteer basis. Proficiency in a language in addition to English is strongly recommended. Familiarity with countries or regions where serious human rights violations occur is also valued.

Financial data The stipend is $35,000. Fringe benefits are also provided.

Duration 1 year.

Special features This program includes 2 named fellowships open to applicants from any law or graduate school: the Schell Fellowship and the Finberg Fellowship. In addition, 3 fellowships are restricted to graduates of specific schools: the Sandler Fellowship for recent graduates of Columbia Law School, the Furman Fellowship for recent graduates of New York University School of Law, and the Bloomberg Fellowship for recent graduates of graduate programs at Johns Hopkins University. Past fellows have conducted fact-finding missions to Albania, Azerbaijan, Bangladesh, Bolivia, Brazil, Burma, Cambodia, Colombia, Cuba, the Dominican Republic, Egypt, El Salvador, Ethiopia, Guatemala, Haiti, Honduras, Hong Kong, India (including Kashmir and Punjab), Iran, Kenya, Moldova, Namibia, Nigeria, Pakistan, the Philippines, Russia, Rwanda, South Africa, Sudan, Syria, Tajikistan, Uganda, the U.S.-Mexican border, and Venezuela.

Number awarded 5 each year.

Deadline October of each year.

[971]
FLORENCE TERRY GRISWOLD SCHOLARSHIP II

Pan American Round Table of Texas
c/o Geraldine Rice, Scholarship Chair
617 Driftwood Place
Corpus Christi, TX 78411-2223

Purpose To provide financial assistance to women students from Texas who are interested in pursuing research or study in a Pan American country.

Eligibility Applicants must be women who are U.S. citizens and residents of Texas. They may be graduate students, high school teachers, or college professors engaged in specialized study of the Spanish language or Pan American cultures. They must demonstrate their ability to put the results of their study in a Pan American country to use upon their return to Texas.

Financial data The stipend is $2,000; funds are paid directly to the recipient and may be used to support study or research.

Duration 1 year.

Limitations The award is to be used during the same year it is granted. Recipients must report the results of their study to the Pan American Round Table of Texas upon their return.

Number awarded 1 each year.

Deadline January of each year.

[972]
FOGARTY INTERNATIONAL RESEARCH COLLABORATION AWARD (FIRCA)

Fogarty International Center
Attn: Division of International Training and Research
31 Center Drive, Room B2C39
Bethesda, MD 20892-2220
(301) 496-1653   Fax: (301) 402-0779
E-mail: FIRCA@nih.gov
Web site: www.nih.gov/fic/programs/firca.html

Purpose To encourage collaboration among scientists in the United States and developing countries in areas of research supported by the National Institutes of Health (NIH).

Eligibility Proposals may be submitted by American scientists who are already principal investigators of grants funded by the institutes and who are interested in working collaboratively with scientists in Africa, Asia (except Japan, Singapore, South Korea, and Taiwan), central and eastern Europe, Russia and the Newly Independent States of the former Soviet Union, Latin America and the non-U.S. Caribbean, the Middle East, and the Pacific Ocean Islands (except Australia and New Zealand). All biomedical and behavioral research topics supported by the institutes are eligible for inclusion in this program. Racial/ethnic minority individuals, women, and persons with disabilities are encouraged to apply as principal investigators.

Financial data Grants provide up to $32,000 per year in direct costs. Funds may be used to pay for materials, supplies, equipment, and travel. Up to 20 percent of the total direct costs may be requested for the U.S. principal investigator, the foreign collaborator, and/or their colleagues or students for visits to each other's laboratory or research site. Up to $5,000 of the total grant may be allocated as a stipend for the foreign collaborator(s). Up to $2,000 of the total grant may be allocated for the foreign collaborator(s) to attend a scientific conference.

Duration Up to 3 years.

Limitations Research related to HIV and AIDS is not eligible for support through this program. A separate companion program, HIV–AIDS and Related Illnesses Collaboration Award, provides funding for research on AIDS.

Number awarded Varies; generally, at least 40 each year.

Deadline Applications may be submitted in November, March, or July of each year.

[973]
FORREST SHREVE STUDENT RESEARCH AWARD

Ecological Society of America
Attn: Executive Director
1707 H Street, N.W., Suite 400
Washington, DC 20006
(202) 833-8773   Fax: (202) 833-8775
E-mail: esahq@esa.org
Web site: www.sdsc.edu/esa/esa.htm

Purpose To provide funding to graduate students interested in conducting research in the hot deserts of Mexico and the United States.

Eligibility This program is open to graduate students interested in conducting research in the Sonora, Mohave, Chihuahua, or Vizcaino deserts. The proposed research project should be clearly ecological and should increase understanding of the patterns and processes of deserts and/or desert organisms.

Financial data Stipends range from $1,000 to $2,000.
Duration 1 year.
Number awarded 1 or 2 each year.

[974]
FRANCE FULBRIGHT TEACHER EXCHANGE
U.S. Department of State
c/o Graduate School, USDA
600 Maryland Avenue, S.W., Room 320
Washington, DC 20024-2520
(202) 314-3520   Fax: (202) 479-6806
E-mail: fulbright@grad.usda.gov
Web site: www.grad.usda.gov/International/ftep.html

Purpose To promote mutual understanding between the people of the United States and the people of France (and the French Antilles) through a teacher exchange program.

Eligibility This program is open to secondary school (grades 7 through 12) and 2-year college instructors of French language, literature, and civilization who are interested in teaching English language or American literature and civilization in France. Exchanges are also possible with the islands of Guadeloupe and Martinique in the French Antilles and with the island of Reunion in the Indian Ocean. Applicants must 1) be U.S. citizens; 2) hold at least a bachelor's degree; 3) be fluent in English; 4) have a current full-time teaching assignment in the U.S. or a territory; 5) have the approval of their school administration; 6) have at least 3 years of full-time experience; and 7) not have participated in a Fulbright Teacher Exchange longer than 8 weeks during the last 2 years. Fluency in French is required. Teaching couples may apply. However, because of the limited number of positions available and, often, the lack of foreign candidate pairs with similar qualifications for interchanges, it may not be possible to arrange suitable assignments in the same locality or to place both teachers. Preference is given to applicants who have not participated previously in the program and may be given to applicants who have not previously lived in France. Geographic distribution of awards within the United States is also a factor in selection. This program does not discriminate on the basis of race, color, religion, age, sex, or national origin and encourages the applications of members of minority communities. Other considerations being equal, veterans are given preference.

Financial data Only partial round-trip transportation is provided. Participants must obtain a leave of absence with pay from their jobs in the United States. The U.S. school must agree to accept a French teacher who must secure a leave of absence with pay. The cost of housing and the salary levels of French and U.S. teachers make an exchange of accommodations a virtual necessity.

Duration 9 months, beginning in September.

Special features This program is sponsored by the Bureau of Educational and Cultural Affairs of the U.S. Department of State and administered by the Graduate School, USDA.

Limitations This program provides for the direct exchange of teaching assignments between France and the United States. Applicants selected for exchange must attend orientation programs of the sponsoring agencies in the United States or abroad.

Number awarded 20 each year.
Deadline October of each year.

[975]
FULBRIGHT BORDER PROGRAM
Council for International Exchange of Scholars
3007 Tilden Street, N.W., Suite 5L
Washington, DC 20008-3009
(202) 686-6238   Fax: (202) 362-3442
E-mail: scholars@cies.iie.org
Web site: www.iie.org/cies

Purpose To enable faculty at U.S. institutions near the Mexican border to teach or conduct research in Mexico.

Eligibility This program is open to faculty affiliated with an academic institution or research center along the Mexican border. Applicants must be interested in teaching graduate or undergraduate courses and/or conducting research at a Mexican institution in their area of specialization. Eligible fields of specialization include the arts (dance, music, theater, arts education, computer art and graphic design, filmmaking, illustration, painting and drawing, printmaking, photography, and sculpture), arts education, art and architectural restoration, binational business, border studies, crafts, criminology in an international environment, comparative law, demography, education, environmental studies, heritage studies, international relations and trade, migration (international and domestic), public administration, public health, and public policy. Preference is given to candidates with a Ph.D. and at least 3 years of teaching experience. U.S. citizenship and fluent Spanish are required.

Financial data The stipend is approximately $1,000 per month, plus a reimbursable allowance of $500 to $1,000, depending on rank, for books to be donated to the host institution upon the grantee's departure.

Duration 3 to 9 months.

Special features This is a Fulbright scholar program, sponsored by the Bureau of Educational and Cultural Affairs of the U.S. Department of State and administered by the Council for International Exchange of Scholars. U.S. participants live at home but spend 1 or 2 days per week in Mexico on teaching or research assignment.

Number awarded Approximately 2 each year.
Deadline July of each year.

[976]
GARCIA ROBLES GRANTS
Institute of International Education
Attn: Student Programs Division
809 United Nations Plaza
New York, NY 10017-3580
(212) 984-5330   Fax: (212) 984-5325
Web site: www.iie.org/fulbright

Purpose To provide financial assistance to American graduate students and others who are interested in conducting research in Mexico.

Eligibility This program is open to U.S. citizens who are proficient in spoken and written Spanish and wish to conduct a research project in Mexico. Applicants at all degree levels are considered, but preference is given to master's and Ph.D. candidates with at least a 3.5 grade point average and approval of their thesis proposal from their U.S. university. All fields in the humanities and social sciences are eligible, but preference is given to research projects in art and architectural restoration and conservation, arts administration, art education, binational business, border studies, communication, comparative law, computer aided and industrial design, crafts, criminology in an international environment, dance, demography, economics, education, environment, film, graphic design, heritage studies, history of art and the visual arts, international relations, international trade, library science, migration (domestic and international), music, NAFTA, political science, public administration, public health, public policy, television, theater, and urban planning.

Financial data The program provides round-trip transportation, book and research allowances, a monthly maintenance stipend based on living costs, and supplemental health and accident insurance.

Duration Varies; generally, grants last for 10 months and begin early in September.

Special features This is a Fulbright program, funded by the U.S. Department of State and administered by the Institute of International Education (IIE). Students who are currently enrolled in the United States are to apply through the Fulbright program adviser on their campus; at-large applicants (those not currently enrolled) may obtain applications and information directly from the IIE. Further information on this program is also available from the U.S.-Mexico Commission for Educational and Cultural Exchange (COMMEXUS), Fulbright/Garcia Robles Program, P.O. Box 3087, Laredo, TX 78044-3087.

Limitations All recipients need to affiliate with educational and/or research institutions in Mexico.

Number awarded 20 each year.

Deadline October of each year.

[977]
GLADYS W. COLE MEMORIAL RESEARCH AWARDS

Geological Society of America
Attn: Research Grants and Awards Administrator
3300 Penrose Place
P.O. Box 9140
Boulder, CO 80301-9140
(303) 447-2020, ext. 137   Fax: (303) 447-1133
E-mail: lcarter@geosociety.org
Web site: www.geosociety.org

Purpose To provide financial support for research in Mexico and the United States to members of the Geological Society of America.

Eligibility This program is open to members and fellows of the society who hold a doctoral degree and are between 35 and 60 years of age. Applicants must be interested in conducting research on the geomorphology of semiarid and arid terrains in the United States or Mexico.

Financial data Grants are $11,000.

Duration 1 year.

Special features This award was first presented in 1982.

Number awarded 1 each year.

Deadline January of each year.

[978]
GORGAS MEMORIAL INSTITUTE RESEARCH AWARD

American Society of Tropical Medicine and Hygiene
60 Revere Drive, Suite 500
Northbrook, IL 60062
(847) 480-9592   Fax: (847) 480-9282
E-mail: astmh@astmh.org
Web site: www.astmh.org

Purpose To provide funding for short-term travel to young research investigators from Panama, Central and South American countries, the Caribbean Islands, and the United States who are interested in topical diseases.

Eligibility Applicants should be no more than 40 years of age and have a Ph.D. or an M.D. in a relevant field. Exceptions may be made for outstanding candidates with demonstrated equivalent expertise. They should be citizens or permanent residents of Panama, the United States, or 1 of the countries of Central America, South America, or the Caribbean Islands, and they should hold a position at a research, medical, public health, or teaching institution in that country. They must be interested in 1) establishing collaborative biomedical research projects focusing on tropical diseases and 2) learning new techniques and approaches applicable to the study of these diseases. Selection is based on the qualifications of the fellowship applicant and host institution, the relevance of the proposed research plan to health problems of Central America and Panama, and the maintenance of an equitable geographic distribution.

Financial data Fellowships generally do not exceed $25,000; the funds are to be used to cover the total costs of round-trip travel, housing, and supplies required for a project lasting no more than 3 months.

Duration Funding is available for short trips only.

Special features These fellowships support collaborative investigations as well as short-term exchange visits within Mexico, Central American, the Caribbean Islands, the United States, and northern South America (Bolivia, Colombia, Ecuador, Peru, Guyana, Suriname, French Guiana, and Brazil). Funds for this program are provided by the Gorgas Memorial Institute of Tropical and Preventive Medicine.

Limitations Fellows must submit a final report (up to 5 pages) on their accomplishments during the fellowship period.

Number awarded Generally 2 each year; the exact number depends upon the funds available.

Deadline July of each year.

[979]
GRANTS FOR ARCHAEOLOGICAL FIELD RESEARCH IN LATIN AMERICA

Heinz Family Foundation
Attn: H. John Heinz III Fund
CNG Tower
625 Liberty Avenue, Suite 3200
Pittsburgh, PA 15222-5757
(412) 497-5775   Fax: (412) 497-5790

Purpose To provide funding for archaeological field research in Latin America.

Eligibility Applicants should have earned the doctorate (or its equivalent), be affiliated with an academic institution, and be interested in conducting archaeological field research in Latin America. The project may be to determine the feasibility of a full-scale exploration or to carry to completion an important phase of a larger project.
Financial data The maximum grant is $8,000. No university overhead charges are paid.
Limitations No support is offered for dissertation research.
Deadline November of each year.

[980]
HIV–AIDS AND RELATED ILLNESSES RESEARCH COLLABORATION AWARD
Fogarty International Center
Attn: Division of International Training and Research
31 Center Drive, Room B2C39
Bethesda, MD 20892-2220
(301) 496-1653   Fax: (301) 402-0779
E-mail: FIRCA@nih.gov
Web site: www.nih.gov/fic/programs/aidsfirc.html

Purpose To provide assistance for U.S. investigators with current funding from the National Institutes of Health (NIH) to conduct research related to AIDS at foreign sites in collaboration with foreign scientists.
Eligibility Applications may be submitted by U.S. nonprofit organizations, public and private, such as universities, colleges, hospitals, laboratories, units of state and local governments, and eligible agencies of the federal government on behalf of principal investigators. The proposed U.S. principal investigator must be the principal investigator of an AIDS or AIDS-related research grant project funded by the institutes. Racial/ethnic minority individuals, women, and persons with disabilities are encouraged to apply as principal investigators. The foreign collaborator must hold a position at an institution in a foreign country that will allow him or her adequate time and provide appropriate facilities to conduct the proposed research. Most countries are eligible for participation in this program; applications for purchase of equipment as part of the grant are limited to research in the developing countries of Africa, Asia, (except Japan, Singapore, South Korea, and Taiwan), central and eastern Europe, Russia and the Independent States of the former Soviet Union, Latin America and the non-U.S. Caribbean, the Middle East, and the Pacific Ocean Islands (except Australia and New Zealand). The application must demonstrate that the award will enhance the scientific contributions of both the U.S. and foreign scientist and will enhance or expand the contribution of the institutes-sponsored research project.
Financial data Grants up to $32,000 per year are available. Funds may be used for supplies at the foreign institution, expenses incurred at the U.S. institution to support the collaboration, and research-related travel and subsistence expenses for both the U.S. and foreign investigators. For collaborations in developing countries as defined above, requests for purchase of equipment (including computers and fax machines) are considered; up to $5,000 may be allocated as a stipend for the foreign collaborator and up to $2,000 may be allocated for the foreign collaborator to attend an AIDS-related scientific conference. Travel funds may be requested up to 20 percent of the total direct costs (up to $6,400) for the U.S. principal investigator, the foreign collaborator, and/or their colleagues or students for visits to each other's laboratory or research site, if such visits are directly related to the subject of the collaborative research.
Duration Up to 3 years.
Special features This program is the counterpart to the Fogarty International Research Collaboration Award (FIRCA) program for non-AIDS related research. It is also designated as AIDS-FIRCA.
Deadline April, August, or December of each year.

[981]
INTER AMERICAN PRESS ASSOCIATION SCHOLARSHIP FUND
Inter American Press Association
1801 S.W. Third Avenue
Miami, FL 33129
(305) 634-2465   Fax: (305) 635-2272
E-mail: info@sipiapa.org
Web site: www.sipiapa.org

Purpose To provide financial assistance to young journalists and journalism school graduates from the United States or Canada for study, work, and research in Latin America.
Eligibility Eligible to apply are print journalists with at least 5 years of professional experience and journalism school seniors/graduates. Applicants must be between the ages of 21 and 35 and demonstrate proficiency in the language of the country where they plan to be placed. Latin American and Caribbean applicants must attend an American or Canadian university with a recognized school of journalism for a full school year. American and Canadian applicants must submit a proposed study and work plan that includes 1) a minimum of 3 university courses in any country in Latin America or the Caribbean; 2) a major research project; and 3) participation in the fund's reporting program.
Financial data American and Canadian recipients are given $13,000 and health insurance for the duration of their stay abroad; Latin American and Caribbean scholars receive the same and also round-trip airfare.
Duration 1 year, to begin within the calendar year following the award.
Special features The Inter American Press Association was established in 1942 to defend and promote the right of the peoples of the Americas to be fully and freely informed through an independent press. It established the Scholarship Fund in 1954.
Number awarded At least 10 each year.
Deadline December of each year.

[982]
INTERNATIONAL RESEARCH SCIENTIST DEVELOPMENT AWARD

Fogarty International Center
Attn: Division of International Training and Research
31 Center Drive, Room B2C39
Bethesda, MD 20892-2220
(301) 496-1653   Fax: (301) 402-0779
E-mail: IRSDA@nih.gov
Web site: www.nih.gov/fic

Purpose To provide funding to U.S. biomedical scientists interested in continuing research in, or extending their research into, developing countries.

Eligibility Applicants must have received a doctoral, dental, or medical degree within the past 7 years in a basic biomedical, behavioral, or epidemiological/clinical field. They must have established a relationship with 2 prospective mentors, 1 in the United States and 1 in a developing country, who have ongoing, funded, international collaborative research. The U.S. mentor should be at a U.S. institution of higher learning or nonprofit research institution. The developing country mentor should be in an internationally developing country research institution addressing some of that country's major health problems. Eligible countries include those in the following regions: Africa, Asia (except Japan, Singapore, South Korea, and Taiwan), central and eastern Europe, Russia and the Newly Independent States of the former Soviet Union, Latin America and the non-U.S. Caribbean, the Middle East (except Israel), and the Pacific Ocean Islands (except Australia and New Zealand). Applications to work in institutions in sub-Saharan Africa are especially encouraged. Racial/ethnic minority individuals, women, and persons with disabilities are encouraged to apply as principal investigators. Applications must be submitted on behalf of the candidate by the U.S. mentor's institution. The applicant need not already be at that institution at the time of application, but it is expected that the U.S. component of the project will be carried out by the fellow at the U.S. mentor's institution.

Financial data Grants provide up to $300,000 for the complete project, prorated at a rate of $8,333 per month (including $6,250 per month direct costs for salary and fringe benefits and $2,083 per month for all other allowable costs). Other allowable costs include travel (round-trip airfare and necessary ground transportation for the candidate to the foreign site up to 5 times over the duration of the project, round-trip airfare for each dependent accompanying the awardee for 6 months or more abroad, excess baggage allowance), health insurance up to $50 per month for the candidate and each dependent during the time abroad, a supplemental living allowance of $150 per month for each dependent accompanying the awardee for 6 months or more, and research development support. An administrative supplement, up to $20,000, may be provided during the third year of the award to fellows who obtain a tenure-track faculty position upon return to the United States.

Duration Support is provided for 36 months, which may be spread over a period of 5 years. A total of at least 24 months should be at the foreign site under the joint supervision of the U.S. and foreign mentors. A period of work in the foreign country should be at least 3 months in length. A total of up to 12 months will be funded for work at the U.S. institution under the U.S. mentor's supervision.

Number awarded Varies each year.

Deadline February of each year.

[983]
JACOBS RESEARCH FUNDS SMALL GRANTS PROGRAM

Whatcom Museum
Attn: Jacobs Research Funds
121 Prospect Street
Bellingham, WA 98225
(360) 676-6981   Fax: (360) 738-7409
E-mail: jacobs@cob.org
Web site: www.cob.org/cobweb/museum/jacobs.htm

Purpose To provide funds for research in the field of social and cultural anthropology among living American native peoples.

Eligibility Research projects in the field of social and cultural anthropology among living American native peoples are eligible. Preference is given to the Pacific Northwest as an area of investigation, but other regions of North America (including Mexico) are eligible for consideration. Grants are given for work that addresses cultural expressive systems, such as music, language, dance, mythology, world view, plastic and graphic arts, intellectual life, and religion (including comparative psychological analysis). Projects in archaeology, physical anthropology, applied linguistics, and applied anthropology are not eligible; archival research is not supported. The program also does not support proprietary research to provide information for the exclusive use of any entity, public or private (national, state, provincial, local governments, public or private charities, churches or foundations, tribes or bands, or community groups).

Financial data Grant amounts vary; generally, up to $1,200 is awarded. Funds may cover fees for consultants, supplies, transportation to and from the field, and lodging in the field. Funds are not supplied for salaries, ordinary living expenses, or major equipment.

Duration 1 year; renewable.

Special features This program was formerly known as the Melville and Elizabeth Jacobs Research Fund.

Number awarded Varies each year; recently, 11 grants were awarded.

Deadline February of each year.

[984]
JAMAICA DISTINGUISHED CHAIR IN AMERICAN STUDIES

Council for International Exchange of Scholars
3007 Tilden Street, N.W., Suite 5L
Washington, DC 20008-3009
(202) 686-6238   Fax: (202) 362-3442
E-mail: scholars@cies.iie.org
Web site: www.iie.org/cies

Purpose To allow distinguished American scholars to lecture on American politics at the University of the West Indies in Jamaica.

Eligibility Applicants must have a Ph.D., an associate or full professor position, and prior experience with American studies curriculum and programs. They must be interested in lecturing on American electoral politics and/or U.S. constitutional history at the advanced undergraduate level in the department of government at the University of the West Indies, Mona, Jamaica. U.S. citizenship is required.

Financial data The award includes a stipend of $2,400 to $3,500 per month, a maintenance allowance of $1,200 to $1,400 per month depending on the number of accompanying dependents, a travel and relocation allowance of $1,800 to $3,000 depending on the number of accompanying dependents, and an allowance of $1,000 for books and educational materials.

Duration 4 to 9 months.

Special features This is a Fulbright scholar program, sponsored by the Bureau of Educational and Cultural Affairs of the U.S. Department of State and administered by the Council for International Exchange of Scholars. The recipient also supports the development of an interdisciplinary American studies program at the University of the West Indies.

Number awarded 1 each year.

Deadline July of each year.

[985]
JAMES R. SCOBIE MEMORIAL AWARD FOR PRELIMINARY DOCTORAL RESEARCH

Conference on Latin American History
c/o University of South Florida
Soc 107
4202 East Fowler Avenue
Tampa, FL 33620
(813) 974-8132   Fax: (813) 974-6228
E-mail: clah@chuma.cas.usf.edu
Web site: www.emory.edu/HISTORY/LatAm/clah

Purpose To permit Ph.D. candidates in Latin American history to conduct a short exploratory trip abroad to investigate the feasibility of a proposed dissertation topic.

Eligibility Applicants must be Ph.D. candidates in Latin American history who have not yet begun research on their dissertation. They must wish to conduct preliminary research for the purpose of determining the precise outlines of their dissertation topic, and they must submit a research prospectus with a preliminary bibliography and certification of their language competence in either Spanish or Portuguese.

Financial data Up to $1,000.

Duration Grants must be used during the summer following the award.

Limitations Funds received from this program may not be utilized for an extended stay abroad or for actual research on the dissertation itself.

Number awarded 1 or more each year.

Deadline March of each year.

[986]
JAZZ AMBASSADORS PROGRAM

John F. Kennedy Center for the Performing Arts
Education Department
Attn: Jazz Ambassadors Program
2700 F Street, N.W.
Washington, DC 20566
(202) 416-8869   Fax: (202) 416-8802
E-mail: artsabroad@kennedy-center.org
Web site: www.kennedy-center.org/programs/jazz/ambassadors

Purpose To enable American jazz musicians to perform in foreign countries.

Eligibility Jazz musicians from the United States who are U.S. citizens at least 21 years of age may audition to participate in this program. Successful applicants must demonstrate artistic and musical ability, be conversant with broader aspects of contemporary American culture, and be adaptable to rigorous traveling through countries in Africa, Latin America, the Near East, and south Asia that are less frequently visited by other American artists. While abroad, they present concerts and conduct master classes and lecture-recitals for musicians.

Financial data Each Jazz Ambassador is compensated for all travel, living, and program expenses and receives a modest honorarium of $200 per day.

Duration Tours last 4 to 6 weeks.

Special features This program is sponsored jointly by the John F. Kennedy Center for the Performing Arts and the U.S. Department of State's Bureau of Educational and Cultural Affairs. The program began in 1997 with the Artistic Ambassadors Program that presented classical musicians. The program switched to jazz for 1998.

Number awarded 7 trios are selected each year.

Deadline May of each year.

[987]
KATHLEEN S. ANDERSON AWARD FOR PROMISING BIOLOGISTS

Manomet Center for Conservation Sciences
P.O. Box 1770
Manomet, MA 02345
(508) 224-6521   Fax: (508) 224-9220
Web site: www.manomet.org

Purpose To encourage significant avian research in the Americas and to help promising young biologists in their work.

Eligibility Proposals may be submitted by citizens/residents of the United States or countries south of the United States. These proposals should deal with avian research in areas of interest to Kathleen Anderson and the Manomet Observatory. This includes requests for support of ecological and behavioral studies of birds, especially research furthering bird conservation (e.g., endangered or endemic species, population viability, effects of land uses, habitat requirements, migration ecology, feeding ecology, species interactions). Proposed projects must take place in the Americas. Any person, of any age, beginning a career in biology is eligible. Enrollment in an academic program is desirable but not required.

Financial data A total of $1,000 is awarded each year, either to 1 person or divided among 2 or more recipients.

Duration Up to 1 year.

Special features This award was created to honor Kathleen S. Anderson's outstanding contributions to bird conservation. Mrs. Anderson served as Manomet Bird Observatory's executive director from 1969 to 1984.

Number awarded 1 or more each year.

Deadline November of each year.

[988]
KLEINHANS FELLOWSHIP FOR RESEARCH IN TROPICAL NON-TIMBER FOREST PRODUCTS

Rainforest Alliance
65 Bleecker Street
New York, NY 10012
(212) 677-1900   E-mail: canopy@ra.org
Web site: www.rainforest-alliance.org

Purpose To provide funding for research into the practical means of managing and using tropical forest resources in Latin America without destroying the integrity of the forest ecosystem.

Eligibility Although anyone with at least a master's degree in forestry, ecology, environmental science, or related fields may apply for this fellowship, preference is given to doctoral candidates or postdoctoral researchers. Relevant experience may substitute for academic degrees. Applicants must be proposing to conduct research involving tropical forests, either wet or dry, in Latin America. The research should synthesize elements of conservation and business and must lead to the development of a product or marketing technique that can provide incomes for community-based groups living in or near tropical forest areas. In judging the applications, the following questions are asked: Can the research be carried out as proposed? Does the investigator appear to have the necessary skills and experience to bring the research to a fruitful conclusion? Is the proposal practical and does it have commercial potential? Will the research help provide a livelihood for tropical forest inhabitants, without causing the destruction of the forests? If the research is site specific, can the methodology be adapted by people in other countries? Is the project new and entrepreneurial? Will the research be useful to someone with no business experience and with little or no venture capital?

Financial data The grant is $15,000 per year. Funds may not be use for tuition and fees, the purchase of transport vehicles, or unnecessary or unreasonable equipment.

Duration 2 years.

Number awarded 1 or more each year.

Deadline March of each year.

[989]
LYDIA CABRERA AWARDS FOR CUBAN HISTORICAL STUDIES

Conference on Latin American History
c/o University of South Florida
Soc 107
4202 East Fowler Avenue
Tampa, FL 33620
(813) 974-8132   Fax: (813) 974-6228
E-mail: clah@chuma.cas.usf.edu
Web site: www.emory.edu/HISTORY/LatAm/clah

Purpose To provide financial support to graduate students and scholars interested in conducting research or publishing on Cuba between 1492 and 1868.

Eligibility Applicants for these awards must be trained in Latin American history and fluent in Spanish. They may be currently enrolled in graduate studies at a U.S. institution or affiliated with a college/university faculty or accredited historical association in the United States. Proposals may be submitted for 1) original research on Cuban history conducted in Spanish, Mexican, or U.S. archives; 2) the publication of meritorious books on Cuba currently out of print; or 3) the publication of historical statistics, historical documents, or guides to Spanish archives relating to Cuban history between 1492 and 1868.

Financial data Awards up to $5,000 are available.

Special features Recipients are expected to disseminate the results of their research in scholarly publications and/or professional papers delivered at scholarly conferences and public lectures at educational institutions.

Number awarded 1 or more each year.

Deadline May of each year.

[990]
MBL SCIENCE WRITING FELLOWSHIPS PROGRAM

Woods Hole Marine Biological Laboratory
Attn: Communications Office
7 MBL Street
Woods Hole, MA 02543-1015
(508) 289-7423   Fax: (508) 457-1924
E-mail: pclapp@mbl.edu
Web site: www.mbl.edu

Purpose To provide research experience or professional development opportunities at the Marine Biology Laboratory (MBL) and selected countries for science reporters and editors.

Eligibility Science editors and reporters who have at least 2 years of experience are eligible to apply for fellowships at MBL. Some fellowship opportunities are also available abroad. Preference is given to print and broadcast journalists with staff positions. Freelancers may also be considered. Members of minority groups and women are strongly encouraged to apply.

Financial data Fellowship support covers the cost of the laboratory course, tuition, housing, library fees, and round-trip transportation for the fellow only. Fellows from other countries are expected to pay for their own travel to the United States.

Duration Fellows first participate in either of 2 laboratory courses (molecular and cellular laboratory techniques or environmental science) for 1 week. Some fellows then stay for an additional 3 to 7 weeks to do field research in ecology (in the

United States or abroad) or to follow the lectures and laboratory sessions in such disciplines as embryology, microbiology, physiology, parasitology, and neurobiology.

Special features Fellows attend lectures with graduate students on the latest research methods, participate in laboratory assignments with investigators carrying out research, and are often given projects of their own to conduct.

Number awarded Varies each year; at least 1 is awarded to a reporter wishing to participate in Arctic ecosystems research on the North Slope of Alaska's Brooks Range; depending on funding, other fellowships opportunities may be available at field sites in Brazil and Sweden.

Deadline March of each year.

[991]
MELBA DAWSON SCHOLARSHIP

Pan American Round Table of Texas
c/o Geraldine Rice, Scholarship Chair
617 Driftwood Place
Corpus Christi, TX 78411-2223

Purpose To provide financial assistance to women students from Pan American countries who are interested in studying in Texas and to graduate students from Texas who are interested in studying or conducting research in a Pan American country.

Eligibility This program is open to women who are 1) citizens of 1 of the 31 Pan American countries (other than the United States) and interested in studying in a degree program at a Texas state-supported college or university; and 2) women graduate students, high school teachers, and college professors from Texas interested in studying or conducting research on the Spanish language or Pan American cultures in a Pan American country. For applicants from Pan American countries, preference is given to those who plan to return to their home country and put their training to use there after completion of studies in Texas; there are no restrictions on academic field. Applicants from Texas must demonstrate their ability to put the results of their study in a Pan American country to use upon their return to Texas.

Financial data The stipend depends on the availability of funds.

Duration 1 year.

Number awarded This scholarship is awarded whenever funds are available.

Deadline January of each year.

[992]
MEXICO DISTINGUISHED LECTURESHIP ON ENVIRONMENTAL ISSUES

Council for International Exchange of Scholars
3007 Tilden Street, N.W., Suite 5L
Washington, DC 20008-3009
(202) 686-6236   Fax: (202) 362-3442
E-mail: scholars@cies.iie.org
Web site: www.iie.org/cies

Purpose To enable scholars in fields of study related to environmental issues to teach in Mexico.

Eligibility This program is open to scholars, preferably full professors, whose expertise is in an environmental studies field with relevance to U.S.-Mexico relations. Applicants must have a distinguished record of scholarship and publications and be interested in teaching in Mexico. Fluent Spanish is preferred and U.S. citizenship is required.

Financial data The stipend is $3,000 per month. Other benefits include a monthly housing and subsistence allowance up to $1,675 (depending on number of accompanying dependents and location), a settling-in allowance of $1,360, and a reimbursable allowance of $500 to $1,000, depending on rank, for books to be donated to the host institution upon the grantee's departure.

Duration 2 to 4 months.

Special features This is a Fulbright scholar program, sponsored by the Bureau of Educational and Cultural Affairs of the U.S. Department of State and administered by the Council for International Exchange of Scholars. The recipient teaches graduate courses and/or special seminars, engages in collaborative research, or combines both activities at an academic institution or research center in Mexico.

Number awarded 1 each year.

Deadline July of each year.

[993]
MEXICO DISTINGUISHED LECTURESHIP ON NAFTA

Council for International Exchange of Scholars
3007 Tilden Street, N.W., Suite 5L
Washington, DC 20008-3009
(202) 686-6236   Fax: (202) 362-3442
E-mail: scholars@cies.iie.org
Web site: www.iie.org/cies

Purpose To enable scholars in fields of study related to the North American Free Trade Agreement (NAFTA) to teach in Mexico.

Eligibility This program is open to scholars, preferably full professors, whose expertise is in an area with relevance to U.S.-Mexico relations as impacted by NAFTA. Applicants must have a distinguished record of scholarship and publications and be interested in teaching in Mexico. Fluent Spanish is preferred and U.S. citizenship is required.

Financial data The stipend is $3,000 per month. Other benefits include a monthly housing and subsistence allowance up to $1,675 (depending on number of accompanying dependents and location), a settling-in allowance of $1,360, and a reimbursable allowance of $500 to $1,000, depending on rank, for books to be donated to the host institution upon the grantee's departure.

Duration 2 to 4 months.

Special features This is a Fulbright scholar program, sponsored by the Bureau of Educational and Cultural Affairs of the U.S. Department of State and administered by the Council for International Exchange of Scholars. The recipient teaches graduate courses and/or special seminars, engages in collaborative research, or combines both activities at an academic institution or research center in Mexico.

Number awarded 1 each year.

Deadline July of each year.

[994]
MEXICO FULBRIGHT EXCHANGE OF ADMINISTRATORS

U.S. Department of State
c/o Graduate School, USDA
600 Maryland Avenue, S.W., Room 320
Washington, DC 20024-2520
(202) 314-3520   Fax: (202) 479-6806
E-mail: fulbright@grad.usda.gov
Web site: www.grad.usda.gov/International/ftep.html

Purpose To promote mutual understanding between the people of the United States and the people of Mexico through an educational administrator exchange program.

Eligibility This program is open to administrators from elementary schools, secondary schools, and 2-year colleges who are interested in working with administrators in Mexico (and vice versa). The assignment may be in the areas of personnel administration, student affairs, or educational policy. Applicants must 1) be U.S. citizens; 2) hold at least a bachelor's degree; 3) be fluent in English; 4) have a current full-time administrative assignment in the U.S. or a territory; 5) have the approval of their school administration; 6) have at least 3 years of full-time experience; and 7) not have participated in a Fulbright Teacher Exchange longer than 8 weeks during the last 2 years. Fluency in Spanish is required. Preference is given to applicants who have not participated previously in the program and may be given to applicants who have not previously lived in Mexico. Geographic distribution of awards within the United States is also a factor in selection. This program does not discriminate on the basis of race, color, religion, age, sex, or national origin and encourages the applications of members of minority communities. Other considerations being equal, veterans are given preference.

Financial data Round-trip economy airfare and a $3,000 cost of living stipend are provided. Participants must obtain a leave of absence with or without pay from their jobs in the United States.

Duration 6 weeks, twice during the year.

Special features This program is sponsored by the Bureau of Educational and Cultural Affairs of the U.S. Department of State and administered by the Graduate School, USDA.

Limitations Dependents are not permitted in this program. Applicants selected for exchange must attend orientation programs of the sponsoring agencies in the United States or abroad.

Number awarded Varies each year.

Deadline October of each year.

[995]
MEXICO FULBRIGHT TEACHER EXCHANGE

U.S. Department of State
c/o Graduate School, USDA
600 Maryland Avenue, S.W., Room 320
Washington, DC 20024-2520
(202) 314-3520   Fax: (202) 479-6806
E-mail: fulbright@grad.usda.gov
Web site: www.grad.usda.gov/International/ftep.html

Purpose To promote mutual understanding between the people of the United States and the people of Mexico through a teacher exchange program.

Eligibility This program is open to teachers and foreign language coordinators of any subject field in grades 7 through 4-year college who are interested in teaching in Mexico. Priority is given to language teachers. Applicants must 1) be U.S. citizens; 2) hold at least a bachelor's degree; 3) be fluent in English; 4) have a current full-time teaching assignment in the U.S. or a territory; 5) have the approval of their school administration; 6) have at least 3 years of full-time experience; and 7) not have participated in a Fulbright Teacher Exchange longer than 8 weeks during the last 2 years. Fluency in Spanish is required for language teachers. Subject field teachers usually teach in English in bilingual high schools but should have basic knowledge of Spanish. Teaching couples may apply. However, because of the limited number of positions available and, often, the lack of foreign candidate pairs with similar qualifications for interchanges, it may not be possible to arrange suitable assignments in the same locality or to place both teachers. Preference is given to applicants who have not participated previously in the program and may be given to applicants who have not previously lived in Mexico. Geographic distribution of awards within the United States is also a factor in selection. This program does not discriminate on the basis of race, color, religion, age, sex, or national origin and encourages the applications of members of minority communities. Other considerations being equal, veterans are given preference.

Financial data Round-trip transportation for the exchange teacher only is provided. U.S. educators must obtain a 1-semester leave of absence with pay. The U.S. institution must agree to accept a teacher from Mexico who must secure a leave of absence with pay; the Mexican teacher receives a stipend, but no additional cost accrues to the U.S. school.

Duration 1 semester; specific dates to be determined.

Special features This program is sponsored by the Bureau of Educational and Cultural Affairs of the U.S. Department of State and administered by the Graduate School, USDA.

Limitations This program provides for the direct exchange of teaching assignments between Mexico and the United States. Applicants selected for exchange must attend orientation programs of the sponsoring agencies in the United States or abroad.

Number awarded 24 each year.

Deadline October of each year.

[996]
MICKEY LELAND–BILL EMERSON INTERNATIONAL HUNGER FELLOWS PROGRAM

Congressional Hunger Center
229 1/2 Pennsylvania Avenue, S.E.
Washington, DC 20003
(202) 547-7022   Fax: (202) 547-7575
E-mail: fellows@hungercenter.org
Web site: www.hungercenter.org/international/int.htm

Purpose To provide emerging leaders in the fight against hunger with an opportunity to participate in field projects at sites in developing countries.

Eligibility This program is open to U.S. citizens who have a bachelor's degree, either a graduate degree or significant experience working to fight hunger, at least 6 months of continuous anti-poverty or sustainable development work in a developing country, written and spoken proficiency in a language appropriate to a field placement, demonstrated leadership qualities and abilities, creativity and initiative in problem solving, and a strong commitment to alleviating hunger and poverty with an enthusiasm for day-to-day work. Applicants must be interested in participating in a program that includes 1) work at field sites in sub-Saharan Africa, south Asia, Central America, and the Caribbean where they work in anti-hunger and development activities and 2) a policy placement in Rome (where they work with U.N. food institutions such as UNFAO, UNWFP, or IFAD) or in Washington, D.C., Baltimore, or Boston (where they work at the U.S. headquarters of the organizations at which they were placed during their field experience). Selection is based on the applicants' commitment to social change, diversity of experience and perspective, vision for the future, demonstrated leadership potential, and willingness to learn and have their lives changed by the experience.

Financial data Fellows receive a stipend of $1,000 per month. During their policy placement, they also receive a housing allowance. The program also pays for medical insurance and travel to and from field placements. Upon completion of the program, fellows receive an end-of-service award to help them make the transition to the next phase of their career.

Duration 3 years, including a 2-year placement in the field in sub-Saharan Africa, south Asia, Central America, or the Caribbean and a 1-year policy placement in Rome or the United States.

Number awarded 10 each year. Field assignments are provided for 4 fellows in sub-Saharan Africa, 3 in south Asia, and 3 in Central America or the Caribbean. Alternatively, 1 fellow may be placed in North Korea. For their policy assignments, 3 fellows are placed in Rome and the remaining fellows in Washington, D.C., Baltimore, or Boston.

Deadline January of each year.

[997]
MUNSON MARINE SCIENCES GRADUATE FELLOWSHIPS

Bermuda Biological Station for Research
Attn: Education Department
17 Biological Station Lane
Ferry Reach
St. George's, GE 01
Bermuda
(441) 297-1880   Fax: (441) 297-8143
E-mail: education@bbsr.edu
Web site: www.bbsr.edu

Purpose To provide funding to graduate students who wish to conduct research at the Bermuda Biological Station for Research (BBSR).

Eligibility This program is open to students in M.S. or Ph.D. programs in any aspect of coral reef research. Applicants should already have a funded research project that would benefit from working in Bermuda's marine environment and with BBSR faculty.

Financial data This program provides supplemental funding to cover the cost of research equipment and supplies, as well as living costs at BBSR.

Duration Depends on the nature of the research proposal.

Special features The BBS was established in 1903 by scientists from Harvard University, New York University, and the Bermuda Natural History Society. It moved to its current location in 1932 with funding from the Bermuda government and the Rockefeller Foundation. Since 1969, it has operated year-round, offering a variety of programs and research facilities related largely to marine biology, oceanography, and environmental quality.

Number awarded Varies each year.

Deadline February of each year.

[998]
NEOTROPICAL LOWLANDS RESEARCH PROGRAM (NLRP) RESEARCH GRANTS

National Museum of Natural History
Attn: Biodiversity Programs Office
10th Street and Constitution Avenue N.W.
Washington, DC 20560-0180
(202) 357-4027   Fax: (202) 357-2986
E-mail: vari.richard@nmnh.si.edu
Web site: www.mnh.si.edu/biodiversity

Purpose To support research on topics dealing with lowland ecosystems in tropical Latin America.

Eligibility All members of the National Museum of Natural History (NMNH) scientific staff, their assistants and colleagues, and graduate students collaborating directly with NMNH scientists are eligible to apply for support if they are interested in conducting research on the relationships, distributions, and diversities of several types of organisms in order to understand the functioning of lowland ecosystems in tropical Latin America. Multidisciplinary projects are particularly encouraged. Selection is based on the scientific merit of the proposal.

Financial data The amount awarded varies, depending upon the scope of the project. Recently, the average annual award was $11,670.

Duration Varies, depending upon the scope of the project.

Special features This project is part of the Biodiversity Surveys and Inventories Program of NMNH.

Limitations Recipients are expected to share their data with the host country's sponsoring institutions. Participants must work within conventions and other agreements between the host countries and the NMNH. They are also expected to develop collegial relationships with their counterparts in the host country.

Number awarded Varies each year.

Deadline For most projects, the deadline is September of each year. However, proposals for urgent projects—arising unexpectedly during the year—may be submitted at any time.

[999]
NIDDK AND NIAID INTERNATIONAL COLLABORATION AWARDS

National Institute of Diabetes and Digestive and Kidney Diseases
Attn: Division of Digestive Diseases and Nutrition
45 Center Drive, Room 6AN-12A
Bethesda, MD 20892-6600
(301) 594-8871 Fax: (301) 480-8300
E-mail: tk13v@nih.gov
Web site: www.niddk.nih.gov

Purpose To provide support for research relevant to the mission of the National Institute of Diabetes and Digestive and Kidney Diseases (NIDDK) to be conducted at international centers supported by the National Institute of Allergy and Infectious Diseases (NIAID).

Eligibility This program is open to investigators at domestic and foreign, for-profit and nonprofit, public and private organizations, such as universities, colleges, hospitals, laboratories, units of state and local governments, and eligible agencies of the federal government. Applicants must be proposing to conduct research on the following topics of interest to the NIDDK: autoimmune liver diseases and hepatitis, gastric ulcer disease and Helicobacter pylori, parasitic diseases that have an impact on liver, mucosal immunity, pediatric liver disease, influence of altered nutritional status on health and disease, parasitic diseases with kidney/urinary tract sequelae, hemolytic uremic syndrome, infectious diseases of the kidney, benign prostatic hypertrophy in minority populations, therapies for hematologic disorders such as iron chelating agents, diabetic kidney disease, and hypertensive kidney disease. Research should be conducted in collaboration with an NIAID international center.

Financial data Grants up to $50,000 per year for direct costs are available through this program.

Duration Up to 2 years; nonrenewable.

Special features Current NIAID international centers, and their major research interests, are located in: Brazil (leishmaniasis, malaria, schistosomiasis, Chagas' Disease, immunoparasitology, diarrheal diseases, and hydatid diseases), Cameroon (malaria), Chile (cholera and enteric diseases), Egypt (lymphatic filariasis), Israel (diarrheal diseases, leishmaniasis, hydatid diseases), Jordan (leishmaniasis), Kenya (schistosomiasis, filariasis, hydatid diseases), Lebanon (leishmaniasis), Mexico (tuberculosis), Morocco (leishmaniasis), Nepal (geohelminths), Peru (enteric pathogens, neurocysticercosis), South Africa (amoebiasis), Thailand (malaria), Tunisia (hydatid diseases), and Uganda (tuberculosis). Information on the NIAID international centers is available from the Parasitology and International Programs Branch, Solar Building, Room 3A12, 6003 Executive Boulevard MSC 7630, Bethesda, MD 20892-7630, (301) 496-7115, Fax: (301) 402-0659, E-mail: mg35s@nih.gov.

Number awarded Varies, depending on the availability of funds.

Deadline Applications may be submitted at any time.

[1000]
NORTH AMERICAN JOURNALIST EXCHANGE

Institute of International Education
Attn: North American Journalist Exchange
809 United Nations Plaza
New York, NY 10017-3580
(212) 984-5390 Fax: (212) 984-5393
E-mail: plink@iie.org
Web site: www.iie.org

Purpose To provide an opportunity for journalists from the United States, Mexico, and Canada to participate in an international exchange program.

Eligibility This program is open to print journalists (newspaper or periodical) who have at least 3 years of professional experience. Applicants must be employed by or (for freelance journalists) affiliated with an independent media organization in the United States, Canada, or Mexico. They must be interested in visiting a host media organization in 1 of the other 2 countries. Applications must be accompanied by 1) a brief autobiography (in English, French, or Spanish) identifying a significant advance and a troubling setback in personal or professional life and the way the applicant dealt with both success and disappointment; 2) a statement of personal reasons for wanting to participate in the program, what they hope to gain from the program, and what they consider to be key issues in North American international relations, for possible articles; 3) copies of 4 published articles; and 4) a letter from their immediate supervisor indicating that the publication supports their participation in the program, that the publication will guarantee to pay their salary while they are participating in the program; and that the publication guarantees continued employment upon their return. Documents in French or Spanish should be accompanied by an English translation.

Financial data This program provides payment of all travel and living expenses plus a stipend for participants.

Duration 3 month, from April through June.

Special features This program, established in 1994, is sponsored by the Freedom Forum. Journalists applying from Canada or the United States should write to the Institute of International Education (IIE) in New York. Journalists applying from Mexico should write to the Intercambio Académico, Instituto Internacional de Educación, Londres 16-2 piso, Colonia Juárez, 06600, Mexico, D.F., Mexico, 52 5 703 1067, Fax: 52 5 535 5597, E-mail: tsanroman@solar.sar.net.

Limitations Fellows are expected to send articles about the host country to their publications at home. At the midpoint of the program, fellows are also expected to submit to IIE a short article suitable for publication, evaluating their experiences during the stay and discussing the relevance of the fellowship to their career goals and professional development.

Number awarded Varies each year.

Deadline November of each year.

[1001]
NSF-CNPQ COLLABORATIVE RESEARCH OPPORTUNITIES

National Science Foundation
Directorate for Computer and Information Science and Engineering
Attn: Division of Experimental and Integrative Activities
4201 Wilson Boulevard, Room 1160
Arlington, VA 22230
(703) 292-8900   Fax: (703) 292-9074
TDD: (703) 292-5090   E-mail: NSF-braz@nsf.gov
Web site: www.cise.nsf.gov

Purpose To provide funding to U.S. computer scientists and engineers interested in conducting research or other activities in Brazil.

Eligibility This program is open to U.S. and Brazilian scientists and engineers in any field supported by the Directorate for Computer and Information Science and Engineering (CISE) of the National Science Foundation (NSF). U.S. researchers are supported by NSF; Brazilian researchers are supported by the Conselho Nacional de Desenvolvimento Cientifico e Tecnologico (CNPq) of Brazil. Applicants must be interested in international collaborative activity, not individual research efforts. Eligible activities include 1) projects for research collaboration by individuals or research teams in each country, including researchers and graduate students, sharing common research objectives; 2) focused research workshops on topics within the scope both of this program and the guidelines of the 2 supporting organizations; or 3) projects to support cross-national short- and long-term visits by junior (postdoctoral) and senior faculty with the goal of enabling a more in-depth exchange of expertise. Selection of projects is based on mutual scientific benefit: the collaboration should produce scientific results that are unlikely to take place without the interaction.

Financial data Awards up to $200,000 are available.

Duration 1 to 3 years.

Number awarded 6 to 10 each year.

Deadline September of each year.

[1002]
NSF-CONACYT COLLABORATIVE RESEARCH OPPORTUNITIES

National Science Foundation
Directorate for Computer and Information Science and Engineering
Attn: Division of Experimental and Integrative Activities
4201 Wilson Boulevard, Room 1160
Arlington, VA 22230
(703) 292-8900   Fax: (703) 292-9074
TDD: (703) 292-5090   E-mail: NSF-mex@nsf.gov
Web site: www.cise.nsf.gov

Purpose To provide funding to U.S. scientists and engineers interested in conducting research or other activities in Mexico.

Eligibility This program is open to U.S. and Mexican scientists and engineers in areas relating either to the Directorate for Computer and Information Science and Engineering (CISE) or the Directorate for Engineering (ENG) of the National Science Foundation (NSF). U.S. researchers are supported by NSF; Mexican researchers are supported by the Consejo Nacional de Ciencia y Tecnología (CONACyT) of Mexico. Applicants must be interested in international collaborative activity, not individual research efforts. Eligible activities include 1) projects for research collaboration by individuals or research teams in each country, including researchers and graduate students, sharing common research objectives; 2) focused research workshops on topics within the scope both of this program and the guidelines of the 2 supporting organizations; or 3) projects to support cross-national short- and long-term visits by junior (postdoctoral) and senior faculty with the goal of enabling a more in-depth exchange of expertise. Selection of projects is based on mutual scientific benefit: the collaboration should produce scientific results that are unlikely to take place without the interaction.

Financial data Awards up to $100,000 are available.

Duration 1 to 3 years.

Special features This program began as a pilot project in 1991 involving only CISE. It was renewed in 1996 and at that time expanded to include ENG and projects in other areas of engineering research, including biomedical, civil, chemical, electrical, manufacturing, and mechanical systems.

Number awarded Approximately 20 each year by each sponsoring organization.

Deadline January of each year.

[1003]
ORGANIZATION OF AMERICAN STATES REGULAR TRAINING PROGRAM (PRA)

Organization of American States
Inter-American Agency for Cooperation and Development
Attn: Division of Cooperation for Development of Human Resources
1889 F Street, N.W., 2nd Floor
Washington, DC 20006-4499
(202) 458-3792   Fax: (202) 458-3878
E-mail: Fellowships_Department@oas.org
Web site: www.oas.org

Purpose To provide financial assistance to residents of Organization of American States (OAS) member countries who are interested in advanced study or research in another member country.

Eligibility Eligible to apply are citizens or permanent residents of an OAS member country: United States, Antigua and Barbuda, Argentina, Bahamas, Barbados, Belize, Bolivia, Brazil, Canada, Chile, Colombia, Costa Rica, Dominica, Dominican Republic, Ecuador, El Salvador, Grenada, Guatemala, Guyana, Haiti, Honduras, Jamaica, Mexico, Nicaragua, Panama, Paraguay, Peru, Saint Kitts and Nevis, Saint Lucia, Saint Vincent and the Grenadines, Suriname, Trinidad and Tobago, Uruguay, and Venezuela. They must have at least a bachelor's degree and have demonstrated the ability to pursue advanced studies. There is no subject limitation (except for the medical sciences and language training). Candidates must know the language of the study country and make the necessary contacts to secure acceptance or show evidence that the facilities needed to complete a research project will be provided.

Financial data Fellowships provide funds sufficient to cover travel expenses, tuition fees, books and study materials, health insurance, and a subsistence allowance (the amount varies from country to county). No benefits are provided to the family of fellowship holders.

Duration Up to 12 months; may be renewed for 1 additional year.

Special features There are 2 kinds of fellowships: those for advanced study at the graduate level and those for research. U.S. citizens submit their applications directly to OAS headquarters at the address above; citizens of other member countries submit their applications to the National Liaison Office (ONE) of their country of origin.

Limitations Funds cannot be used for undergraduate-level studies or for introductory language training. Fellows cannot study or conduct research in their own country.

Deadline February of each year.

[1004]
OTS FELLOWSHIPS

Organization for Tropical Studies
Attn: Academic Director
410 Swift Avenue
P.O. Box 90630
Durham, NC 27708-0630
(919) 684-5774   Fax: (919) 684-5661
E-mail: nao@duke.edu
Web site: www.ots.duke.edu

Purpose To provide support to graduate students at member institutions of the Organization for Tropical Studies (OTS) who are interested in conducting field work in tropical studies in Costa Rica.

Eligibility Graduate students who have completed courses offered by the organization as well as other graduate students in degree programs at member institutions may apply for these fellowships. They must be planning to conduct dissertation research in tropical biology or related fields. Preference is given to proposals for research at 1 of the organization's field stations in Costa Rica (La Selva, Palo Verde, and Las Cruces), but proposals for research at other locations are considered.

Financial data Research awards up to $3,000 are available; pilot awards for exploratory research may be up to $1,000. Funds are intended to cover such budget items as travel, food, and lodging. Capital expenses, such as equipment, receive lower priority. Salaries or stipends for the investigator are not allowable, but salaries for field assistants are considered.

Duration Varies, depending upon the nature of the project.

Special features Field research may be conducted in tropical biology, ecology, or agroforestry.

Number awarded Varies each year.

Deadline January or September of each year.

[1005]
PERU FULBRIGHT EXCHANGE OF ADMINISTRATORS

U.S. Department of State
c/o Graduate School, USDA
600 Maryland Avenue, S.W., Room 320
Washington, DC 20024-2520
(202) 314-3520   Fax: (202) 479-6806
E-mail: fulbright@grad.usda.gov
Web site: www.grad.usda.gov/International/ftep.html

Purpose To promote mutual understanding between the people of the United States and the people of Peru through an educational administrator exchange program.

Eligibility This program is open to administrators from elementary schools, secondary schools, and 2-year colleges who are interested in working with administrators in Peru (and vice versa). The assignment may be in the areas of personnel administration, student affairs, or educational policy. Applicants must 1) be U.S. citizens; 2) hold at least a bachelor's degree; 3) be fluent in English; 4) have a current full-time administrative assignment in the U.S. or a territory; 5) have the approval of their school administration; 6) have at least 3 years of full-time experience; and 7) not have participated in a Fulbright Teacher Exchange longer than 8 weeks during the last 2 years. Fluency in Spanish is required. Preference is given to applicants who have not participated previously in the program and may be given to applicants who have not previously lived in Peru. Geographic distribution of awards within the United States is also a factor in selection. This program does not discriminate on the basis of race, color, religion, age, sex, or national origin and encourages the applications of members of minority communities. Other considerations being equal, veterans are given preference.

Financial data Round-trip economy airfare and a $3,000 cost of living stipend are provided. Participants must obtain a leave of absence with or without pay from their jobs in the United States.

Duration 6 weeks, twice during the year.

Special features This program is sponsored by the Bureau of Educational and Cultural Affairs of the U.S. Department of State and administered by the Graduate School, USDA.

Limitations Dependents are not permitted in this program. Applicants selected for exchange must attend orientation programs of the sponsoring agencies in the United States or abroad.

Number awarded Varies each year.

Deadline October of each year.

[1006]
PERU FULBRIGHT TEACHER EXCHANGE

U.S. Department of State
c/o Graduate School, USDA
600 Maryland Avenue, S.W., Room 320
Washington, DC 20024-2520
(202) 314-3520   Fax: (202) 479-6806
E-mail: fulbright@grad.usda.gov
Web site: www.grad.usda.gov/International/ftep.html

Purpose To promote mutual understanding between the people of the United States and the people of Peru through a teacher exchange program.

Eligibility This program is open to 2-year college faculty and elementary and secondary school teachers who are interested in teaching in Peru. Subjects include, but are not limited to, Spanish, English, literature, social studies, science, and education. Special consideration is given to computer specialists and computer teachers. Applicants must 1) be U.S. citizens; 2) hold at least a bachelor's degree; 3) be fluent in English; 4) have a current full-time teaching assignment in the U.S. or a territory; 5) have the approval of their school administration; 6) have at least 3 years of full-time experience; and 7) not have participated in a Fulbright Teacher Exchange longer than 8 weeks during the last 2 years. Fluency in Spanish is required for general assignments; for computer teachers and specialists, some Spanish ability but not necessarily fluency is required. Teaching couples may apply. However, because of the limited number of positions available and, often, the lack of foreign candidate pairs with similar qualifications for interchanges, it may not be possible to arrange suitable assignments in the same locality or to place both teachers. Preference is given to applicants who have not participated previously in the program and may be given to applicants who have not previously lived in Peru. Geographic distribution of awards within the United States is also a factor in selection. This program does not discriminate on the basis of race, color, religion, age, sex, or national origin and encourages the applications of members of minority communities. Other considerations being equal, veterans are given preference.
Financial data Only round-trip transportation is provided. Participants must obtain a leave of absence with pay from their jobs in the United States. The U.S. school must agree to accept a teacher from Peru who must secure a leave of absence with pay; the Peruvian teacher receives a stipend, but no additional cost accrues to the U.S. school.
Duration General assignments are for 1 or 2 semesters with a September start date recommended. Assignments for computer teachers and specialists are for 1 semester in Peru, followed by a semester in which the Peruvian teacher "shadows" the U.S. counterpart in the United States.
Special features This program is sponsored by the Bureau of Educational and Cultural Affairs of the U.S. Department of State and administered by the Graduate School, USDA.
Limitations Applicants selected for exchange must attend orientation programs of the sponsoring agencies in the United States or abroad.
Number awarded 2 general assignments and 2 computer assignments each year.
Deadline October of each year.

[1007]
PRINCIPLES OF CONSERVATION BIOLOGY FELLOWSHIPS

Organization for Tropical Studies
Attn: Academic Director
410 Swift Avenue
P.O. Box 90630
Durham, NC 27708-0630
(919) 684-5774   Fax: (919) 684-5661
E-mail: nao@duke.edu
Web site: www.ots.duke.edu

Purpose To provide support to graduate students interested in conducting conservation biology research in Costa Rica.
Eligibility This program is open to graduate students who wish to conduct research on conservation biology in Costa Rica. Applicants must demonstrate the background and independence to carry out the project and a temperament compatible with life and work at a remote field station; Spanish language skills are desirable but not required.
Financial data A stipend is provided (amount not specified).
Duration Up to 12 months.
Special features Funding for this program is provided by proceeds from sales of *Principles of Conservation Biology* by Ron Carroll and Gary Meffe, published by Sinauer Associates.
Deadline January or September of each year.

[1008]
SCMRE GRADUATE ARCHAEOLOGICAL INTERNSHIP

Smithsonian Center for Materials Research and Education
Attn: Coordinator of Education and Training
Museum Support Center, Room D2002
4210 Silver Hill Road
Suitland, MD 20746-2863
(301) 238-3700, ext. 153   Fax: (301) 238-3709
Web site: www.si.edu/scmre/arcintern.html

Purpose To provide training at the Smithsonian Center for Materials Research and Education (SCMRE) and affiliated overseas facilities to graduate students interested in archaeological conservation.
Eligibility This program is open to graduate students entering the internship year in a conservation training program or the equivalent. Recipients spend approximately half the year at archaeological sites with which SCMRE is associated; in the past, SCMRE conservators have worked with excavation teams at Harappa (Pakistan), Cerén (El Salvador), and Copán (Honduras). For the remainder of the time, interns work in the Objects Conservation Laboratory at SCMRE, where they treat archaeological artifacts or carry out research. Minorities are particularly encouraged to apply.
Financial data Travel costs and living expenses at the archaeological site are provided; supplemental funding up to $14,000 and an additional $2,000 for travel and research may also be available.
Duration 1 year.
Number awarded 1 each year.
Deadline February of each year.

[1009]
SCMRE POSTGRADUATE ARCHAEOLOGICAL FELLOWSHIP

Smithsonian Center for Materials Research and Education
Attn: Coordinator of Education and Training
Museum Support Center, Room D2002
4210 Silver Hill Road
Suitland, MD 20746-2863
(301) 238-3700, ext. 153   Fax: (301) 238-3709
Web site: www.si.edu/scmre/arcintern.html

Purpose To provide postgraduate fellows with an opportunity to conduct research at the Smithsonian Center for Materials Research and Education (SCMRE) and affiliated overseas facilities.

Eligibility This program is open to recent graduates of recognized conservation training programs and persons with comparable training and experience. Recipients spend approximately half the year at archaeological sites with which SCMRE is associated; in the past, SCMRE conservators have worked with excavation teams at Harappa (Pakistan), Cerén (El Salvador), and Copán (Honduras). For the remainder of the time, interns work in the Objects Conservation Laboratory at SCMRE, where they treat archaeological artifacts or carry out research. Minorities are particularly encouraged to apply.

Financial data Travel and living expenses at the archaeological site are covered; supplemental funding up to $22,000 and an additional $2,000 for travel and research may also be available.

Duration 1 year.

Number awarded 1 each year.

Deadline February of each year.

[1010]
SMITHSONIAN FELLOWSHIP IN MOLECULAR EVOLUTION

Smithsonian Institution
Attn: Office of Fellowships and Grants
750 Ninth Street, N.W., Suite 9300
Washington, DC 20560-0902
(202) 275-0655   Fax: (202) 275-0489
E-mail: siofg@ofg.si.edu
Web site: www.si.edu/research+study

Purpose To provide opportunities for postdoctoral investigators to conduct research on molecular evolution in association with staff members of the Smithsonian Institution and utilizing the Institution's facilities.

Eligibility Applicants must have completed a Ph.D. degree in a field related to molecular evolution. They must be interested in conducting research at the Smithsonian's facilities in Washington, D.C. or Panama. Selection is based on the proposal's merit, the likelihood that it will be completed in the requested time, the applicant's ability to carry out the proposed research and study, and the extent to which the Smithsonian, through its staff members and resources, can contribute to the research.

Financial data The stipend is $27,000 per year; a travel allowance to the Smithsonian facility is also offered.

Duration 12 to 24 months.

Special features The location of the award rotates annually among 3 Smithsonian facilities: the National Museum of Natural History in Washington, D.C. (in 2003), the Smithsonian Tropical Research Institute in Panama (in 2004), and the National Zoological Park in Washington, D.C. (in 2005)

Deadline January of each year.

[1011]
SMITHSONIAN TROPICAL RESEARCH INSTITUTE SHORT-TERM FELLOWSHIPS IN TROPICAL BIOLOGY

Smithsonian Tropical Research Institute
Attn: Office of Education
Unit 0948
APO AA 34002-0948
(507) 212-8031   Fax: (507) 212-8148
E-mail: fellows@tivoli.si.edu
Web site: www.si.edu/stri/What_we_do/Fellowship_Opportunities.html

Purpose To support researchers who want to work on tropical biology and other related subjects at the Smithsonian Tropical Research Institute (STRI) in Balboa, Panama.

Eligibility Applicants must be interested in conducting research in tropical biology (ecology, human ecology, paleoecology, evolution, behavior, plant physiology, molecular evolution) or archaeology at STRI. Fellowships are primarily for graduate students, although awards are occasionally made to undergraduates or postdoctoral applicants with no previous tropical experience.

Financial data The award provides a stipend of $700 per month, round-trip airfare to Panama, and a research allowance.

Duration Up to 3 months.

Special features This program is funded by the Andrew W. Mellon Foundation and jointly administered by the Organization for Tropical Studies and the Smithsonian Tropical Research Institute.

Limitations These awards are offered only occasionally.

Deadline Applications may be submitted in February, May, August, or November of each year.

[1012]
SOLOMON LEFSCHETZ RESEARCH INSTRUCTORSHIPS IN MATHEMATICS

Mexican Ministry of Education
Attn: Department of Mathematics
Centro de Investigación y de Estudios Avanzados del IPN
Apartado Postal 14-740
07000 Mexico, D.F.
Mexico
52 5 747 3868   Fax: 52 5 747 3876
E-mail: ohernand@math.cinvestav.mx

Purpose To provide work experience in Mexico to young mathematicians from any country who are interested in preparing for an academic career.

Eligibility Academicians of any nationality who have recently earned their doctorate in mathematics and show a marked ability to conduct outstanding research are eligible to apply if they are interested in gaining experience in teaching and research in Mexico. A knowledge of Spanish is desirable but not necessary.

Financial data Recipients are paid the same salary as the academic staff in equivalent positions in Mexican institutions. They also receive an allowance for moving expenses.

Duration 1 year, beginning in September; may be renewed for 1 additional year.

Special features The teaching load is 3 hours per week, at the graduate level.

Deadline December of each year.

[1013]
STANLEY SMITH HORTICULTURAL FELLOWSHIPS

Organization for Tropical Studies
Attn: Academic Director
410 Swift Avenue
P.O. Box 90630
Durham, NC 27708-0630
(919) 684-5774   Fax: (919) 684-5661
E-mail: nao@duke.edu
Web site: www.ots.duke.edu

Purpose To provide support to researchers interested in conducting field work at the Wilson Botanical Garden in Costa Rica.

Eligibility This program is open to scholars who wish to conduct horticultural work and systematics research on tropical plants of interest to the Wilson Botanical Garden in Costa Rica. Applicants must demonstrate the background and independence to carry out the project and a temperament compatible with life and work at a remote field station; Spanish language skills are desirable but not required. Although the program is open to all levels of researchers, curatorial expertise in tropical plant groups is essential.

Financial data The award provides room and board plus access to laboratory, garden, greenhouse, and other facilities. A small stipend and assistance with international travel may be awarded in some cases.

Duration Up to 12 months.

Special features Further information is also available from Luis Diego Gómez, Director of the Las Cruces Biological Station, E-mail: ldgomez@hortus.ots.ac.cr, or Wilson Botanical Garden, (506) 773-4004.

Deadline January or September of each year.

[1014]
SUITCASE FUND

Dance Theater Workshop
Attn: Director and Producer of Inter/National Programs
219 West 19th Street
New York, NY 10011-4079
(212) 691-6500   Fax: (212) 633-1974
E-mail: cathy@dtw.org
Web site: www.dtw.org

Purpose To promote the performing arts through an international exchange.

Eligibility To promote cultural equity in a pluralistic America, the fund helps artists of all backgrounds and origins to maintain access to the contemporary arts of their homelands. Applicants should be independent professional artists working without the support of major institutions. They must be seeking to study, teach, collaborate, or perform in another part of the world.

Financial data The amount awarded varies, depending upon the needs of the recipient.

Special features Participating artists and producers are placed in Africa, Asia, Latin America, and the Caribbean, as well as Europe. Funding for this program is provided by the Rockefeller Foundation, the Trust for Mutual Understanding, and the Asian Cultural Council.

Limitations The Fund does not function as an all-purpose emergency travel fund, nor will it duplicate the well-established initiatives of other producers or funders.

Deadline Applications may be submitted at any time.

[1015]
TUPPER POSTDOCTORAL FELLOWSHIPS IN TROPICAL BIOLOGY

Smithsonian Tropical Research Institute
Attn: Office of Education
Unit 0948
APO AA 34002-0948
(507) 212-8031   Fax: (507) 212-8148
E-mail: fellows@tivoli.si.edu
Web site: www.si.edu/stri/What_we_do/Fellowship_Opportunities.html

Purpose To support scholars who want to work on tropical biology and other related subjects at the Smithsonian Tropical Research Institute (STRI) in Balboa, Panama.

Eligibility This program is open to postdoctoral investigators who are interested in conducting research in tropical biology (ecology, human ecology, paleoecology, evolution, behavior, plant physiology, molecular evolution) or archaeology at STRI. Proposals that include a component to work in other tropical nations are also considered.

Financial data The award provides a stipend, round-trip airfare to Panama, and a research allowance.

Duration 3 years.

Deadline January of each year.

[1016]
UNIVERSITY OF MONTEVIDEO LECTURESHIP

Council for International Exchange of Scholars
3007 Tilden Street, N.W., Suite 5L
Washington, DC 20008-3009
(202) 686-6238   Fax: (202) 362-3442
E-mail: scholars@cies.iie.org
Web site: www.iie.org/cies

Purpose To provide funding to American scholars interested in lecturing on designated fields at the University of Montevideo in Uruguay.

Eligibility This program is open to both professional and academic candidates who have at least 4 years of professional experience. They must be interested in teaching seminars in their area of specialization, collaborating with Uruguayan colleagues on research and program development, and strengthening links between U.S. institutions and the University of Montevideo. The subject areas are law, business administration, education, and engineering. Within the area of law, specialists are sought to lecture on U.S. legal methods, introduction to U.S. law, contracts and torts, trade contracts, international business transactions in Latin America, litigation and ADR, corporations, securities, and capital markets. Within the area of business administration, the eligible specialties include management, arts administration, nonprofit management, organization behavior, and finance. Within the area of education, applicants should be able to lecture on educational administration. Within the area of engineering, the eligible specialty is industrial engineering, with an emphasis on logistics and production. The language of instruction in English, but conversational to fluent Spanish is preferred. U.S. citizenship is required.

Financial data The stipend is approximately $2,000 per month. Other benefits include a monthly housing and subsistence allowance of $900 to $1,850 depending on the number of accompanying dependents, airfare up to $2,400 to cover international travel for grantee and dependents, a relocation allowance of $750, an educational allowance of $250 to $750 depending on the number of accompanying dependents, and an allowance of $500 for educational materials to be donated to host institutions upon grantee's departure.

Duration 3 months.

Special features This is a Fulbright scholar program, sponsored by the Bureau of Educational and Cultural Affairs of the U.S. Department of State and administered by the Council for International Exchange of Scholars.

Number awarded 1 each year.

Deadline July of each year.

[1017]
UPPER ATMOSPHERIC FACILITIES PROGRAM

National Science Foundation
Directorate for Geosciences
Attn: Division of Atmospheric Sciences
4201 Wilson Boulevard, Room 775
Arlington, VA 22230
(703) 292-8531   TDD: (703) 292-5090
Web site: www.geo.nsf.gov/start.htm

Purpose To promote basic research on the structure and dynamics of the earth's upper atmosphere at facilities supported by the National Science Foundation (NSF).

Eligibility The facilities of the NSF Upper Atmospheric Facilities (UAF) program in Greenland, Peru, Puerto Rico, and Boston are available on a competitive basis to all qualified scientists. Research may be directed toward 1) supporting the operation and scientific research on the incoherent-scatter radars that comprise the longitudinal chain of NSF atmospheric facilities; and 2) ensuring that these radars are maintained as state-of-the-art research tools available to all interested and qualified scientists. Selection is based on scientific merit of the proposed research, capabilities of the radars to carry out the proposed observations, and availability of the requested time.

Financial data The amount of the award depends on the nature of the proposal.

Duration Varies, depending upon the nature of the proposed research.

Special features The UAF program supports the following 4 facilities: Sondrestrom Radar Facility at Sondre Stromfjord, Greenland (which is operated by SRI International under an NSF cooperative agreement); Millstone Hill Radar, near Boston, Massachusetts (which is operated by MIT under an NSF cooperative agreement); Arecibo Observatory at Arecibo, Puerto Rico (which is operated under contract to the NSF by the National Astronomy and Ionosphere Center of Cornell University); Jicamarca Radio Observatory, at the magnetic equator in Jicamarca, Peru (which is operated under an NSF cooperative agreement with Cornell University).

Deadline Applications may be submitted at any time.

[1018]
U.S.–MEXICO FUND FOR CULTURE GRANTS

U.S.-Mexico Fund for Culture
Londres 16 P.B.
Colonia Juarez
06600 Mexico, D.F.
Mexico
52 5 592 5386   Fax: 52 5 208 8943
E-mail: usmexcult@fidemexusa.org.mx
Web site: www.fidemexusa.org.mx

Purpose To provide funding to individuals and institutions in the United States and Mexico for exchanges between their countries.

Eligibility This program is open to artists, researchers, independent groups, and related institutions involved in cultural studies, dance, libraries, literature, media arts, music, theater, and visual arts. Applicants must be proposing exchange and collaborative projects that reflect the artistic and cultural diversity of Mexico and the United States and that are capable of leading to long-term relationships. They must demonstrate previous professional experience directly related to the discipline of their project; a familiarity with individuals, groups, audiences, and/or institutions involved in that discipline; and an understanding of the specific issues related to the theme, field, and cultural aspects of their project. Proposals are judged on the viability of their statements about the artistic, cultural, geographic, ethnic, and social realities of both countries, as well as on their capacity to encourage close and lasting relationships among artists, scholars, communities, and cultural institutions in the 2 countries. The potential impact of the project in the cultural spheres of Mexico and the United States is also considered. Support for undergraduate, graduate, or postgraduate work related to obtaining a degree, or for any work or project designed to comply with requirements imposed by an educational institution, is not provided. Also excluded is support for individual artists who seek funding for the acquisition of materials, or for research, creation, or dissemination of their own work.

Financial data Grants range from $2,000 to $25,000.

Duration Projects should be completed within 1 year.

Special features This program was created in 1991 through a joint initiative of Mexico's National Fund for Culture and the Arts (FONCA), the Bancomer Cultural Foundation, and the Rockefeller Foundation.

Number awarded Varies each year.

Deadline April of each year.

[1019]
WATER QUALITY ENVIRONMENTAL OUTREACH PROGRAM

Organization for Tropical Studies
Attn: Academic Director
410 Swift Avenue
P.O. Box 90630
Durham, NC 27708-0630
(919) 684-5774　　　　Fax: (919) 684-5661
E-mail: nao@duke.edu
Web site: www.ots.duke.edu

Purpose To provide support to researchers interested in conducting water quality environmental research in Costa Rica.

Eligibility This program is open to scholars who wish to conduct research on environmental water quality in Costa Rica. Applicants must demonstrate the background and independence to carry out the project and a temperament compatible with life and work at a remote field station; Spanish language skills are desirable but not required. The program is open to all levels of researchers.

Financial data The award provides room and board plus access to laboratory, garden, greenhouse, and other facilities. A small stipend and assistance with international travel may be awarded in some cases.

Duration Up to 12 months.

Special features Further information is also available from Cathy Pringle at the University of Georgia, E-mail: pringle@sparrow.ecology.uga.edu or Claudia Charpentier, Universidad Nacional, Costa Rica, (506) 261-0101, ext. 536, E-mail: ccharpen@una.ac.cr.

Deadline January or September of each year.

[1020]
WORKING GROUP ON CUBA GRANTS

Social Science Research Council
810 Seventh Avenue
New York, NY 10019
(212) 377-2700　　　　Fax: (212) 377-2727
E-mail: cuba@ssrc.org
Web site: www.acls.org

Purpose To provide funding to promote academic collaboration between scholars in Cuba and North America.

Eligibility This program attempts to increase the flow of researchers between Cuba and North America by providing funding for 1) Cuban scholars to participate in international conferences and educational seminars outside of Cuba, 2) North American scholars invited by Cuban institutions to present lectures or participate in workshops in Cuba, and 3) distinguished Cuban scholars to present lectures at North American universities and/or scholarly institutions. In addition, it provides support to libraries, museums, archives, and other repositories of scholarly information by enabling 1) Cuban and North American institutions to acquire, preserve, catalogue, and/or transfer information into more accessible formats (e.g., microfilm, photographs, specimens), and 2) Cuban or North American bibliographers, archivists, and conservation/preservation specialists to share expertise on appropriate professional techniques. It also promotes the dissemination of works by Cuban researchers by providing funds to defray costs associated with publication and/or translation of scholarly volumes. All proposals from North America must include specific documents from Cuban institutions demonstrating that the proposed activities reflect the needs of academic or scientific institutions in Cuba. Preference is given to projects that promise to encourage ongoing institutional cooperation and professional ties among researchers in Cuba and North America.

Financial data The size of each grant depends on project needs. Normally, travel grants do not exceed $2,500 per researcher; grants in support of libraries, museums, and archives are generally limited to $5,000.

Special features This program operates in collaboration with the Academy of Sciences of Cuba and with the Social Science Research Council and the American Council of Learned Societies in North America. Support is provided by the Christopher Reynolds Foundation and the John D. and Catherine T. MacArthur Foundation.

Deadline August of each year.

Middle East/Africa

Described in this section are 107 scholarships, fellowships, grants, loans, and/or internships open to American students (high school through doctoral), professionals, and postdoctorates that support research or creative activities specifically in the Middle East and Africa. If you haven't already checked the "Any Foreign Country" chapter, be sure to do that next; identified there are 222 more sources of funding that can be used to support activities in these regions (as well as other areas of the world).

[1021]
ACLS/SSRC/NEH INTERNATIONAL AND AREA STUDIES FELLOWSHIPS

American Council of Learned Societies
Attn: Office of Fellowships and Grants
228 East 45th Street
New York, NY 10017-3398
(212) 697-1505   Fax: (212) 949-8058
E-mail: grants@acls.org
Web site: www.acls.org/felguide.htm

Purpose To provide funding to postdoctoral scholars for research on the societies and cultures of Asia, Africa, the Near and Middle East, Latin America, eastern Europe, and the former Soviet Union.

Eligibility This program is open to U.S. citizens and residents who have lived in the United States for at least 3 years. Applicants must have a Ph.D. degree and not have received supported research leave time for at least 3 years prior to the start of the proposed research. They must be interested in conducting humanities and humanities-related social science research on the societies and cultures of Asia, Africa, the Near and Middle East, Latin America, east Europe, or the former Soviet Union. Selection is based on the intellectual merit of the proposed research and the likelihood that it will produce significant and innovative scholarship. Applications are particularly invited from women and members of minority groups.

Financial data The maximum grant is $50,000 for full professors and equivalent, $40,000 for associate professors and equivalent, and $30,000 for assistant professors and equivalent. These fellowships may not be held concurrently with another major fellowship.

Duration 6 to 12 months.

Special features This program is jointly supported by the American Council of Learned Societies (ACLS) and the Social Science Research Council (SSRC), with funding provided by the National Endowment for the Humanities (NEH).

Number awarded Approximately 10 each year.

Deadline September of each year.

[1022]
AEGEAN INITIATIVE IN GREECE AND TURKEY

Council for International Exchange of Scholars
3007 Tilden Street, N.W., Suite 5L
Washington, DC 20008-3009
(202) 686-6246   Fax: (202) 362-3442
E-mail: scholars@cies.iie.org
Web site: www.iie.org/cies

Purpose To provide funding to American scholars interested in conducting seminars or lecturing in Greece and Turkey.

Eligibility This program is open to U.S. citizens who possess a doctorate in an area other than the hard sciences. Areas of potential interest include, but are not limited to, regional economic development, disaster management and emergency preparedness, environmental protection and advocacy, ecotourism, and tourism development and management. Applicants must be interested in dividing their time equally between Greece and Turkey, lecturing and/or conducting seminars in an area of specialization of relevance to both countries. English is sufficient for lecturing.

Financial data During stays in Greece, the monthly maintenance allowance is the Euro equivalent of 450,000 to 540,000 Greek drachmas, depending on the number of accompanying dependents. During stays in Turkey, scholars receive a base stipend of $1,500 to $2,000 per month and a maintenance allowance of $500 per month. Allowances to cover international and intercountry travel, as well as related miscellaneous expenses, are also provided.

Duration 3 to 4 months.

Special features This is a Fulbright scholar program, sponsored by the Bureau of Educational and Cultural Affairs of the U.S. Department of State and administered by the Council for International Exchange of Scholars. It was established in 1999.

Number awarded Up to 2 each year.

Deadline July of each year.

[1023]
AFRICAN REGIONAL RESEARCH PROGRAM IN AIDS

Council for International Exchange of Scholars
3007 Tilden Street, N.W., Suite 5L
Washington, DC 20008-3009
(202) 686-6230   Fax: (202) 362-3442
E-mail: scholars@cies.iie.org
Web site: www.iie.org/cies

Purpose To provide funding to American scholars for research that relates to AIDS in sub-Saharan African countries.

Eligibility This program is open to both academic and professional researchers in fields related to AIDS. Preference is given to proposals that focus on AIDS and AIDS-related problems as they impact sub-Saharan Africa, involve collaborations with scholars from host countries, and include plans for seminars, workshops, and research dissemination in the host country or countries. U.S. citizenship is required. Appropriate language facility is needed for research in non-English-speaking areas. Research may not be conducted in Angola, Burundi, Republic of Congo (Brazzaville), Democratic Republic of Congo (Kinshasa), Guinea Bissau, Liberia, Sierra Leone, Somalia, South Africa, Sudan, or any other country with which the United States does not have formal diplomatic relations.

Financial data The awards provide a monthly base stipend of $1,700 per month, a standard maintenance allowance of $350 to $1,500 per month (depending on the cost of living) for recipient and accompanying dependents, a housing allowance, travel/relocation allowances of $5,300 to $10,300 for the grantee and $3,300 to $7,500 per dependent (up to 2), up to $20,000 per family for tuition assistance for 2 or more dependents in grades K-12, and a 1-time research allowance of $3,000.

Duration 3 to 9 months for work in 1 country; 5 to 9 months for work in 2 or 3 countries.

Special features This is a Fulbright scholar program, sponsored by the Bureau of Educational and Cultural Affairs of the U.S. Department of State and administered by the Council for International Exchange of Scholars.

Number awarded Up to 6 each year.

Deadline July of each year.

[1024]
AFRICAN REGIONAL RESEARCH PROGRAM IN ALL FIELDS

Council for International Exchange of Scholars
3007 Tilden Street, N.W., Suite 5L
Washington, DC 20008-3009
(202) 686-6230　　　　　　　Fax: (202) 362-3442
E-mail: scholars@cies.iie.org
Web site: www.iie.org/cies

Purpose To provide funding to American scholars for research in sub-Saharan African countries.

Eligibility Applicants must be U.S. citizens who possess a doctorate in an academic field; African specialists are encouraged to apply, but applications are also welcome from scholars who have limited or no previous experience in Africa. Both Africanists and non-Africanists should include evidence in their proposals of host country support for their research. Multicountry proposals are encouraged. Appropriate language facility is needed for research in non-English-speaking areas. Research may not be conducted in Angola, Burundi, Republic of Congo (Brazzaville), Democratic Republic of Congo (Kinshasa), Guinea Bissau, Liberia, Sierra Leone, Somalia, South Africa, Sudan, or any other country with which the United States does not have formal diplomatic relations.

Financial data The awards provide a monthly base stipend of $1,700 per month, a standard maintenance allowance of $350 to $1,500 per month (depending on the cost of living) for recipient and accompanying dependents, a housing allowance, travel/relocation allowances of $5,300 to $10,300 for the grantee and $3,300 to $7,500 per dependent (up to 2), up to $20,000 per family for tuition assistance for 2 or more dependents in grades K-12, and a 1-time research allowance of $3,000.

Duration 3 to 9 months for work in 1 country; 5 to 9 months for work in 2 or 3 countries.

Special features This is a Fulbright scholar program, sponsored by the Bureau of Educational and Cultural Affairs of the U.S. Department of State and administered by the Council for International Exchange of Scholars. Grantees are expected to give occasional lectures, arranged in consultation with U.S. embassies in host countries.

Number awarded Up to 12 each year.

Deadline July of each year.

[1025]
AFRICAN YOUTH IN A GLOBAL AGE FELLOWSHIPS

Social Science Research Council
810 Seventh Avenue
New York, NY 10019
(212) 377-2700　　　　　　　Fax: (212) 377-2727
E-mail: africa@ssrc.org
Web site: www.ssrc.org

Purpose To provide funding to scholars from Africa and to Ph.D. candidates from the United States who are interested in conducting research on themes related to African youth.

Eligibility This program is open to 1) African scholars (including those based at universities, research institutes, and practitioner organizations) who hold at least a master's degree and are no more than 5 years beyond a Ph.D.; and 2) U.S. based Ph.D. candidates who seek field research funding for their dissertations. All applicants must be interested in conducting research on a theme that changes annually but is related to African youth; a recent theme was "Youth Violence, Activism, and Citizenship." The program includes support for field research and participation in pre- and post-field work workshops. Applications are accepted in English, French, and Portuguese, but workshops are conducted in English so all applicants must be conversational in that language.

Financial data The research grant is $7,500. Support is also provided for participation in the workshops.

Special features This program, established in 2001, is sponsored by the Social Science Research Council (SSRC) and the American Council of Learned Societies (ACLS) in partnership with South Africa's National Research Foundation (NRF) and the Council for the Development of Social Science Research in Africa (CODESRIA).

Number awarded Approximately 8 to 10 each year.

Deadline June of each year.

[1026]
AIMS PRE-DISSERTATION GRANT PROGRAM

American Institute for Maghrib Studies
c/o Becky Schulthies, Executive Director
University of Arizona
Center for Middle Eastern Studies
Franklin Hall, Room 202
P.O. Box 210080
Tucson, AZ 85721
(520) 626-6498　　　　　　　Fax: (520) 621-9257
E-mail: beckys@u.arizona.edu
Web site: www.la.utexas.edu/research/mena/aims

Purpose To provide funding to doctoral student members of the American Institute for Maghrib Studies (AIMS) who wish to conduct research in North Africa while studying Arabic.

Eligibility This program is open to graduate students enrolled in a Ph.D. program in any field or discipline that requires research in North Africa. Applicants must be members of AIMS and U.S. citizens or permanent residents. They must have completed at least 1 year of Modern Standard Arabic and be interested in further Arabic instruction in conjunction with the Tangier Summer Arabic program at the Tangier American Legation Museum (TALM) in Morocco.

Financial data Grants provide funds for travel, per diem, Arabic instruction, and research activities.

Duration These are short-term grants.

Special features Funding for this program, which began in 2001, is provided by the United States Department of State. Grantees are encouraged to use research facilities at TALM. They may conduct research at other sites in the Maghrib, but are responsible for making their own arrangements.

Number awarded Approximately 3 each year.

Deadline March of each year.

[1027]
AIYS GENERAL FELLOWSHIP PROGRAM
American Institute for Yemeni Studies
Attn: Executive Director
P.O. Box 311
Ardmore, PA 19003-0311
(610) 896-5412   Fax: (610) 896-9049
E-mail: ayis@aiys.org
Web site: www.aiys.org

Purpose To provide funding to graduate students and postgraduate scholars who wish to conduct research in Yemen.

Eligibility This program is open to U.S. citizens who are postgraduate scholars or full-time graduate students in recognized degree programs. Applicants must be proposing to conduct feasibility studies or research projects on any subject in the Republic of Yemen. Arabic language study may be included in the project, but only if the study is to be conducted in Yemen as part of a research project in that country.

Financial data The maximum grant is $10,000. Funds may be used only to support research costs incurred in Yemen.

Duration Depends on the nature of the proposal. Language study programs, if included, are for 10 weeks.

Special features Funding for this program is provided by the U.S. Information Agency through the Council of American Overseas Research Centers.

Number awarded Varies each year.

Deadline October of each year.

[1028]
AMERICAN INSTITUTE FOR MAGHRIB STUDIES FULL RESEARCH GRANTS
American Institute for Maghrib Studies
c/o Becky Schulthies, Executive Director
University of Arizona
Center for Middle Eastern Studies
Franklin Hall, Room 202
P.O. Box 210080
Tucson, AZ 85721
(520) 626-6498   Fax: (520) 621-9257
E-mail: beckys@u.arizona.edu
Web site: www.la.utexas.edu/research/mena/aims

Purpose To provide funding to members of the American Institute for Maghrib Studies who wish to conduct long-term research in north Africa.

Eligibility This program is open to graduate students enrolled in Ph.D. programs and faculty in all disciplines who are U.S. citizens or permanent residents. Applicants must be members of the institute interested in conducting research in any of the countries of the Maghrib. The application must include a 1-page summary of the proposed research in either French or Arabic.

Financial data The maximum award is $10,000; funds may be used for travel, a monthly per diem, and a research allowance.

Duration 3 to 9 months.

Special features Funding for this program is provided by the United States Department of State.

Number awarded Approximately 5 each year.

Deadline February of each year.

[1029]
AMERICAN INSTITUTE FOR MAGHRIB STUDIES SHORT-TERM TRAVEL GRANTS
American Institute for Maghrib Studies
c/o Becky Schulthies, Executive Director
University of Arizona
Center for Middle Eastern Studies
Franklin Hall, Room 202
P.O. Box 210080
Tucson, AZ 85721
(520) 626-6498   Fax: (520) 621-9257
E-mail: beckys@u.arizona.edu
Web site: www.la.utexas.edu/research/mena/aims

Purpose To provide funding to members of the American Institute for Maghrib Studies who wish to conduct short-term research in north Africa.

Eligibility This program is open to graduate students enrolled in Ph.D. programs and faculty in all disciplines who are U.S. citizens or permanent residents. Applicants must be members of the institute interested in conducting research in any of the countries of the Maghrib. The application must include a 1-page summary of the proposed research in either French or Arabic.

Financial data The maximum award is $3,000; funds may be used for travel and per diem.

Duration 1 to 6 months.

Special features Funding for this program is provided by the United States Department of State.

Number awarded Approximately 8 each year.

Deadline February of each year.

[1030]
AMERICAN RESEARCH CENTER IN EGYPT FELLOWSHIPS
American Research Center in Egypt
c/o Emory University West Campus
Building A, Suite 423W
1256 Briarcliff Road, N.W.
Atlanta, GA 30306
(404) 712-9854   Fax: (404) 712-9849
E-mail: arce@emory.edu
Web site: www.arce.org

Purpose To provide financial assistance to predoctoral candidates and postdoctoral scholars who wish to conduct research in Egypt in the humanities, fine arts, or social sciences.

Eligibility This program is open to postdoctoral scholars and predoctoral students who have finished all requirements for the doctorate except the dissertation. Applicants must be interested in conducting research in Egypt in the areas of archaeology, architecture, art, economics, Egyptology, history, the humanities, Islamic studies, literature, Near Eastern studies, politics, religious studies, or the humanistic social sciences. Predoctoral applicants must be U.S. citizens; postdoctoral candidates may be either U.S. citizens or foreign-born citizens who have held a teaching position at an American university for at least 3 years.

Financial data Stipends vary according to the academic status and number of dependents of the fellow, ranging from

$1,150 per month for a single student to $3,325 per month for a full professor with spouse and a child. Round-trip transportation between the United States and Cairo is provided for the fellow but not dependents. Predoctoral fellows may receive allowances for up to 3 dependents, postdoctoral fellows for up to 4 dependents. Stipends are paid only for the time the fellow is physically present in Egypt.

Duration 3 to 12 months.

Special features Funding for these fellowships is provided by the Bureau of Educational and Cultural Affairs of the U.S. Department of State.

Limitations Fellows must devote full time to their research and may not accept outside teaching assignments or funds from any other source without written consent of program officers.

Number awarded Varies each year.

Deadline October of each year.

[1031]
AMERICAN RESEARCH CENTER IN EGYPT/NATIONAL ENDOWMENT FOR THE HUMANITIES FELLOWSHIPS

American Research Center in Egypt
c/o Emory University West Campus
Building A, Suite 423W
1256 Briarcliff Road, N.W.
Atlanta, GA 30306
(404) 712-9854   Fax: (404) 712-9849
E-mail: arce@emory.edu
Web site: www.arce.org

Purpose To provide funding to postdoctorates who wish to conduct research in Egypt in the humanities, fine arts, or social sciences.

Eligibility Senior scholars (who have earned a doctoral degree or its equivalent) are eligible to apply if they are interested in conducting research in Egypt in the areas of archaeology, architecture, art, economics, Egyptology, history, the humanities, Islamic studies, literature, Near Eastern studies, politics, religious studies, or the humanistic social sciences. Applicants must be U.S. citizens or foreign nationals who have resided in the United States for at least 3 years.

Financial data Fellows receive a monthly stipend commensurate with academic status and number of accompanying dependents, to a maximum of $30,000 per year. Round-trip transportation is also paid, but for recipients only.

Duration From 4 to 12 months.

Special features Funding for this program is provided by the U.S. National Endowment for the Humanities. A Scholar-in-Residence Fellowship is awarded to 1 of these senior scholars conducting research on a topic in the humanities or humanistic social sciences; that fellowship provides an honorarium of $2,000.

Number awarded 2 or 3 each year.

Deadline October of each year.

[1032]
AMY BIEHL GRANT

Institute of International Education
Attn: Student Programs Division
809 United Nations Plaza
New York, NY 10017-3580
(212) 984-5330   Fax: (212) 984-5325
Web site: www.iie.org/fulbright

Purpose To provide financial assistance to graduate students interested in studying or conducting research in South Africa.

Eligibility This program is open to graduate students at colleges and universities in the United States who are interested in studying or conducting research in South Africa. Most work is in English, but a knowledge of other official South African languages may be helpful to pursue independent research in such fields as history, political science, psychology, and anthropology.

Financial data The grant provides a maintenance allowance based on the cost of living, round-trip international travel, and health and accident insurance.

Duration 1 academic year, beginning in February.

Special features This is a Fulbright program, funded by the U.S. Department of State and administered by the Institute of International Education (IIE). Students who are currently enrolled in the United States are to apply through the Fulbright program adviser on their campus; at-large applicants (those not currently enrolled) may obtain applications and information directly from the IIE. The highest ranked Fulbright applicant for South Africa receives this grant, named to honor a 1993 Fulbright Fellow who was tragically killed while working to promote multiracial democracy in South Africa.

Number awarded 1 each year.

Deadline October of each year

[1033]
ARIT FELLOWSHIP PROGRAM

American Research Institute in Turkey
c/o University of Pennsylvania Museum
33rd and Spruce Streets
Philadelphia, PA 19104-6324
(215) 898-3474   Fax: (215) 898-0657
E-mail: leinwand@sas.upenn.edu
Web site: mec.sas.upenn/edu/ARIT

Purpose To provide financial aid to American and Canadian students and scholars for research in Turkey.

Eligibility Scholars and advanced graduate students (those who have fulfilled all preliminary requirements for the doctorate) interested in conducting research in Turkey in any field of the humanities or social sciences are eligible to apply if they are members in good standing of educational institutions in the United States or Canada.

Financial data Stipends are provided, based on the proposed expenses of the research project.

Duration Up to 1 year, but preference is given to projects of shorter duration (generally no less than 2 months).

Special features Hostel, research, and study facilities of the American Research Institute in Turkey (ARIT) are available in

[1034]
BARD SENIOR RESEARCH FELLOWSHIPS

United States-Israel Binational Agricultural Research and Development Fund
Department of Agriculture
Agricultural Research Service
Attn: Office of International Research Programs
5601 Sunnyside Avenue, Room 4-2104
Beltsville, MD 20705-5134
(301) 504-4584   Fax: (301) 504-4619
E-mail: mlg@ars.usda.gov
Web site: www.bard-isus.com

Purpose To promote cooperative agricultural research between Binational Agricultural Research and Development Fund (BARD) Fellows from the United States and scientists from Israel.

Eligibility This program is open to U.S. citizens who are established research scientists affiliated with U.S. nonprofit research institutions, universities, or federal or state agencies. Applicants must be proposing to conduct research in Israel that is related to agriculture. Selection is based on scientific merit of the proposed research, importance of the research to agriculture, suitability of the candidate, and suitability of the proposed senior scientist in Israel.

Financial data The program provides $3,000 per month and 1 round-trip air ticket.

Duration From 3 to 12 months.

Special features BARD was established in 1977 by the governments of the United States and Israel, for the purpose of promoting and supporting research and development in agriculture for the mutual benefit of both countries. This program was established in 1989. Applications may be submitted in the United States (address above) or in Israel (BARD, P.O. Box 6, Bet Dagan 50250, Israel; telephone: 972 3 965 2244; Fax: 972 3 966 2506, E-mail: bard@bard-isus.com).

Limitations The proposed research program must be implemented within 6 months after receiving the award. A final report, signed by the fellow and the senior scientist, must be submitted not later than 2 months after completion of the fellowship. Acknowledgement of BARD's support must be made in all publications that result from the supported research.

Deadline December of each year.

[1035]
BENIN FULBRIGHT TEACHER EXCHANGE

U.S. Department of State
c/o Graduate School, USDA
600 Maryland Avenue, S.W., Room 320
Washington, DC 20024-2520
(202) 314-3520   Fax: (202) 479-6806
E-mail: fulbright@grad.usda.gov
Web site: www.grad.usda.gov/International/ftep.html

Purpose To promote mutual understanding between the people of the United States and the people of Benin through a teacher exchange program.

Eligibility This program is open to senior high school teachers (grades 9 through 12) of any subject field who wish to teach English as a second language in Benin. Applicants must 1) be U.S. citizens; 2) hold at least a bachelor's degree; 3) be fluent in English; 4) have a current full-time teaching assignment in the U.S. or a territory; 5) have the approval of their school administration; 6) have at least 3 years of full-time experience; and 7) not have participated in a Fulbright Teacher Exchange longer than 8 weeks during the last 2 years. Fluency in French is required. Teaching couples may apply. However, because of the limited number of positions available and, often, the lack of foreign candidate pairs with similar qualifications for interchanges, it may not be possible to arrange suitable assignments in the same locality or to place both teachers. Preference is given to applicants who have not participated previously in the program and may be given to applicants who have not previously lived in Benin. Geographic distribution of awards within the United States is also a factor in selection. This program does not discriminate on the basis of race, color, religion, age, sex, or national origin and encourages the applications of members of minority communities. Other considerations being equal, veterans are given preference.

Financial data The exchange teacher only receives round-trip transportation. Housing is provided by the Beninese Ministry of Education. Participants must obtain a leave of absence with pay from their jobs in the United States. The U.S. school must agree to accept a Beninese teacher who must secure a leave of absence with pay; the Beninese teacher receives a stipend, but no additional cost accrues to the U.S. school.

Duration 11 months, beginning in September.

Special features This program is sponsored by the Bureau of Educational and Cultural Affairs of the U.S. Department of State and administered by the Graduate School, USDA.

Limitations This program provides for the exchange of teaching assignments between Benin and the United States. U.S. teachers are assigned to Beninese lycees selected by the Beninese Ministry of Education, not necessarily the lycees of their exchange partners. Applicants selected for exchange must attend orientation programs of the sponsoring agencies in the United States or abroad.

Number awarded 3 each year.

Deadline October of each year.

[1036]
BRITISH INSTITUTE IN EASTERN AFRICA GRADUATE ATTACHMENTS

British Institute in Eastern Africa
P.O. Box 30710
Nairobi, Kenya
43721   E-mail: pjlane@insightkenya.com

Purpose To provide funding to graduate students interested in conducting research into the history, languages, cultures, and later archaeology of eastern Africa.

Eligibility Graduate students who are interested in familiarizing themselves with current research in the region between the Zambezi and the Middle Nile may apply. Applicants should intend to conduct archaeological or historical research, including archaeological surveys and excavations, oral-historical field work, archival research, or the collection of linguistic and ethnographic data. Preference is normally given to applicants from British and eastern African universities, but qualified graduates from other countries may also apply.

Financial data Awards cover return airfare as well as subsistence in the field and at the Nairobi base of the institute.

Duration 3 to 6 months; may be extended.

Special features Recipients participate in 1 or more of the institute's projects, under the supervision of the director, the assistant director, or a project director. Opportunities may be provided for some independent work to enable students to gain additional experience and to select subjects for subsequent research. Information is also available from the institute's London office, 10 Carlton House Terrace, London SW1Y 5AH, England.

Number awarded Varies each year.

Deadline April of each year.

[1037]
BRITISH INSTITUTE IN EASTERN AFRICA RESEARCH GRANTS

British Institute in Eastern Africa
P.O. Box 30710
Nairobi, Kenya
43721   E-mail: pjlane@insightkenya.com

Purpose To provide funding to scholars from any country interested in conducting research on topics related to eastern Africa.

Eligibility Scholars from any country are eligible to apply if they are interested in conducting research in east Africa in the humanities or social sciences, especially archaeology, African history, anthropology, and related subjects. Currently, funded research focuses on areas bordering Victoria Nyanza and especially projects that cover at least 1 of the following themes: environmental history and management of natural resources; settlement history and the use of space; diet, demography, and nutrition; and technology, style, and exchange.

Financial data Major research grants are those for which funding in excess of 1,000 British pounds is requested. Minor research grants involve less than 1,000 British pounds. Funds may be used only for actual research costs. Grants do not include institutional overhead or stipends for the recipients.

Duration Varies; generally, less than 1 year.

Special features Information is also available from the institute's London office, 10 Carlton House Terrace, London SW1Y 5AH, England.

Number awarded Varies each year.

Deadline June of each year for major research grants; May or November of each year for minor research grants.

[1038]
CAORC FELLOWSHIPS FOR ADVANCED MULTI-COUNTRY RESEARCH

Council of American Overseas Research Centers
c/o Smithsonian Institution
10th and Constitution Streets, N.W.
CE-123, MRC 178
Washington, DC 20560-0178
(202) 842-8636   Fax: (202) 786-2430
E-mail: caorc@caorc.org
Web site: www.caorc.org

Purpose To provide financial assistance to pre- and post-doctoral scholars who wish to conduct research in the humanities, social sciences, or allied natural sciences at a participating member of the Council of American Overseas Research Centers (CAORC).

Eligibility This program is open to doctoral candidates and established scholars with U.S. citizenship who wish to carry out research on broad questions of multi-country significance in the fields of humanities, social sciences, and related natural sciences. Applicants must be proposing to conduct field research in at least 2 countries, 1 of which must host a constituent member of the Council: the American Academy in Rome, the American School of Classical Studies at Athens, the American Institute of Iranian Studies, the American Institute for Maghrib Studies (Tunisia and Morocco), the American Research Center in Egypt, the W.F. Albright Institute of Archaeological Research in Jerusalem, the American Center of Oriental Research in Amman, the American Research Institute in Turkey, the American Institute for Yemeni Studies, the American Institute of Indian Studies, the American Institute of Pakistan Studies, the American Institute of Bangladesh Studies, the American Institute for Sri Lankan Studies, the Cyprus American Archaeological Research Institute, or the West African Research Association. Selection is based on 1) the scholar's intellectual capacity, maturity, and fitness for field work; and 2) the proposal's significance, relevance, and potential contribution to regional and/or trans-regional scholarly research.

Financial data Fellowships are intended as small grants, with a maximum of $3,000 for travel and $6,000 for stipend. No dependent allowance is available.

Duration At least 3 months.

Special features Fellows are granted all privileges normally accorded other fellows at the center with which they affiliate. In addition to the countries that host overseas research centers (Bangladesh, Cyprus, Egypt, Greece, India, Iran, Israel, Italy, Jordan, Morocco, Pakistan, Senegal, Sri Lanka, Tunisia, Turkey, and Yemen), research may be conducted in other countries in North Africa, the Middle East, and South Asia, subject to official security and/or travel restrictions or warnings. Funding for this program is provided by a grant from the Bureau of Educational and Cultural Affairs of the U.S. Department of State.

Limitations Fellowships are authorized only after the center with which the fellow intends to affiliate has given approval and a security clearance has been granted.

Number awarded 8 each year.

Deadline December of each year.

MIDDLE EAST/AFRICA

[1039]
COUNCIL OF INTERNATIONAL PROGRAMS EXCHANGE INTERNSHIPS

Council of International Programs
1700 East 13th Street, Suite 4ME
Cleveland, OH 44114-3214
(216) 566-1088   Fax: (216) 566-1490
E-mail: cipusa@compuserve.com
Web site: www.cipusa.org

Purpose To allow U.S. professionals in the fields of education, health, and social work to participate in a summer internship program in designated foreign countries.

Eligibility Applicants must be U.S. citizens engaged, as professionals or volunteers, in social work, associated health work, or education. They must be interested in participating in a summer internship program abroad. Most programs operate in English, although German is desirable in Austria and required in Germany, French is required in France, Greek is desirable in Greece, and Italian is desirable in Italy.

Financial data Sponsoring organizations in the foreign countries pay for living expenses, usually through host families, and travel within their respective countries. Recipients must pay for their own international airfare.

Duration 4 to 8 weeks.

Special features Countries currently participating in this program are Austria, Finland, France, Germany, Greece, Hungary, India, Israel, Italy, the Netherlands, Norway, Scotland, Slovenia, Sweden, and Turkey.

Limitations Program fees are required for some countries: $120 for Austria and Hungary, $1,000 for France, $200 for Greece, $600 for India, $250 for Israel, $200 for Italy and Slovenia, $75 for the Netherlands, or $300 for Turkey. No program fees are required for the other countries.

Number awarded Varies each year; recently, the number of available positions was 3 to 6 in Austria and Hungary, 8 to 10 in Finland, 12 to 15 in France, 12 to 15 in Germany, 8 in Greece, 10 to 15 in India, 2 in Israel, 4 in Italy and Slovenia, 8 in the Netherlands, 8 in Norway, 6 to 8 in Scotland, 8 to 12 in Sweden, and 4 to 6 in Turkey.

Deadline February of each year for France, Germany, India, Italy, and Slovenia; November of each year for Austria, Finland, Greece, Hungary, Israel, the Netherlands, Norway, Scotland, Sweden, and Turkey.

[1040]
DUMBARTON OAKS PROJECT GRANTS

Dumbarton Oaks
Attn: Office of the Director
1703 32nd Street, N.W.
Washington, DC 20007-2961
(202) 339-6410   Fax: (202) 339-6419
E-mail: DumbartonOaks@doaks.org
Web site: www.doaks.org

Purpose To provide funding for scholarly projects in Byzantine studies, pre-Columbian studies, or landscape architecture.

Eligibility Scholars in Byzantine studies (including related aspects of late Roman, early Christian, western medieval, Slavic, and Near Eastern studies), pre-Columbian studies (of Mexico, Central America, and Andean South America), and studies in landscape architecture (including architectural, art historical, botanical, horticultural, cultural, economic, social, and agrarian) may apply for these grants. Support is generally for archaeological research, as well as for the recovery, recording, and analysis of materials that would otherwise be lost. Selection is based on the ability and preparation of the principal project personnel (including knowledge of the requisite languages), and interest and value of the project to the specific field of study.

Financial data Grants normally range from $3,000 to $10,000.

Duration 1 year, beginning in July.

Limitations Project awards are not offered purely for the purpose of travel, nor for work associated with a degree, for library or archive research, for catalogs, or for conservation and restoration *per se*.

Deadline October of each year.

[1041]
EMBO LONG-TERM FELLOWSHIPS

European Molecular Biology Organization
Meyerhofstrasse 1
Postfach 1022.40
D-69012 Heidelberg
Germany
49 62 21 383031   Fax: 49 62 21 384879
E-mail: EMBO@EMBL-Heidelberg.de

Purpose To provide funding to molecular biologists from any country who are seeking advanced training through research in member countries of the European Molecular Biology Organization (EMBO).

Eligibility Eligible to apply are doctoral recipients from any country under the age of 35 who have at least 1 first author publication in press or have published in an international peer reviewed journal. If the applicants are from member nations of the Organization, they may apply to conduct research in any country other than their own (although preference is given to applicants interested in going to another member nation). Applicants from non-member countries (such as the United States) must apply to conduct research in a member nation and such applications are subject to more stringent criteria than those from European candidates. Interviews may be required. Selection is based on the perceived benefits of the proposed research to the host laboratory as distinct from the benefits and training the candidate will receive.

Financial data For fellows from the United States, the stipend is $26,720 for fellows under 30 or $31,717 for fellows over 30; an additional payment of $3,073 is provided for each dependent.

Duration 4 months to 2 years; may be renewed.

Special features EMBO currently receives its budget from the following member countries: Austria, Belgium, Croatia, Czech Republic, Denmark, Finland, France, Germany, Greece, Hungary, Iceland, Ireland, Israel, Italy, Netherlands, Norway, Poland, Portugal, Slovenia, Spain, Sweden, Switzerland, Turkey, and the United Kingdom.

Number awarded Varies; generally, at least 100 per year.

Deadline February or August of each year.

[1042]
ETHEL PAYNE FELLOWSHIPS

National Association of Black Journalists
Attn: Media Institute Program Associate
8701-A Adelphi Road
Adelphi, MD 20783-1716
(301) 445-7100, ext. 108   Fax: (301) 445-7101
E-mail: warren@nabj.org
Web site: www.nabj.org

Purpose To enable members of the National Association of Black Journalists (NABJ) to obtain reporting experiences in Africa.

Eligibility This program is open to members of the association who have at least 5 years of experience as full-time print or broadcast journalists or freelancers. Applicants must submit an 800-word proposal that covers issues relating to 1 or more African countries, a 300-word essay on their journalistic experiences, 3 samples of work that have been published or aired, and 2 letters of recommendation. Winners must produce news reports for the association from Africa.

Financial data The fellowship is $5,000.

Duration Up to 3 weeks.

Number awarded At least 2 each year.

Deadline April of each year.

[1043]
FELLOWSHIPS IN INTERNATIONAL HUMAN RIGHTS

Human Rights Watch
Attn: Fellowship Committee
350 Fifth Avenue, 34th Floor
New York, NY 10118-3299
(212) 290-4700, ext. 312   Fax: (212) 736-1300
E-mail: hrwnyc@hrw.org
Web site: www.hrw.org

Purpose To provide an opportunity for recent recipients of law or graduate degrees to engage in human rights monitoring and advocacy while working for Human Rights Watch.

Eligibility These fellowships are available to recent graduates of law schools or graduate programs in journalism, international relations, or area studies from any university worldwide. Applicants must be interested in working with a division of Human Rights Watch, based in Washington, D.C. or New York. Their assignment involves monitoring human rights developments in various countries, conducting on-site investigations, drafting reports on human rights conditions, and engaging in advocacy efforts aimed at publicizing and curtailing human rights violations. Applicants must demonstrate analytic skills, an ability to write and speak clearly, and a commitment to work in the human rights field in the future on a paid or volunteer basis. Proficiency in a language in addition to English is strongly recommended. Familiarity with countries or regions where serious human rights violations occur is also valued.

Financial data The stipend is $35,000. Fringe benefits are also provided.

Duration 1 year.

Special features This program includes 2 named fellowships open to applicants from any law or graduate school: the Schell Fellowship and the Finberg Fellowship. In addition, 3 fellowships are restricted to graduates of specific schools: the Sandler Fellowship for recent graduates of Columbia Law School, the Furman Fellowship for recent graduates of New York University School of Law, and the Bloomberg Fellowship for recent graduates of graduate programs at Johns Hopkins University. Past fellows have conducted fact-finding missions to Albania, Azerbaijan, Bangladesh, Bolivia, Brazil, Burma, Cambodia, Colombia, Cuba, the Dominican Republic, Egypt, El Salvador, Ethiopia, Guatemala, Haiti, Honduras, Hong Kong, India (including Kashmir and Punjab), Iran, Kenya, Moldova, Namibia, Nigeria, Pakistan, the Philippines, Russia, Rwanda, South Africa, Sudan, Syria, Tajikistan, Uganda, the U.S.-Mexican border, and Venezuela.

Number awarded 5 each year.

Deadline October of each year.

[1044]
FOGARTY INTERNATIONAL RESEARCH COLLABORATION AWARD (FIRCA)

Fogarty International Center
Attn: Division of International Training and Research
31 Center Drive, Room B2C39
Bethesda, MD 20892-2220
(301) 496-1653   Fax: (301) 402-0779
E-mail: FIRCA@nih.gov
Web site: www.nih.gov/fic/programs/firca.html

Purpose To encourage collaboration among scientists in the United States and developing countries in areas of research supported by the National Institutes of Health (NIH).

Eligibility Proposals may be submitted by American scientists who are already principal investigators of grants funded by the institutes and who are interested in working collaboratively with scientists in Africa, Asia (except Japan, Singapore, South Korea, and Taiwan), central and eastern Europe, Russia and the Newly Independent States of the former Soviet Union, Latin America and the non-U.S. Caribbean, the Middle East, and the Pacific Ocean Islands (except Australia and New Zealand). All biomedical and behavioral research topics supported by the institutes are eligible for inclusion in this program. Racial/ethnic minority individuals, women, and persons with disabilities are encouraged to apply as principal investigators.

Financial data Grants provide up to $32,000 per year in direct costs. Funds may be used to pay for materials, supplies, equipment, and travel. Up to 20 percent of the total direct costs may be requested for the U.S. principal investigator, the foreign collaborator, and/or their colleagues or students for visits to each other's laboratory or research site. Up to $5,000 of the total grant may be allocated as a stipend for the foreign collaborator(s). Up to $2,000 of the total grant may be allocated for the foreign collaborator(s) to attend a scientific conference.

Duration Up to 3 years.

Limitations Research related to HIV and AIDS is not eligible for support through this program. A separate companion program, HIV–AIDS and Related Illnesses Collaboration Award, provides funding for research on AIDS.

Number awarded Varies; generally, at least 40 each year.

Deadline Applications may be submitted in November, March, or July of each year.

MIDDLE EAST/AFRICA

[1045]
GEORGE A. BARTON FELLOWSHIP

American Schools of Oriental Research
Attn: Administrative Director
656 Beacon Street, Fifth Floor
Boston, MA 02215-2010
(617) 353-6570   Fax: (617) 353-6575
E-mail: asor@bu.edu
Web site: www.asor.org

Purpose To allow seminarians, doctoral students, and recent Ph.D. recipients an opportunity to engage in research at the Albright Institute of Archaeological Research (AIAR) in Jerusalem.

Eligibility Eligible to apply are seminarians, doctoral students, and recent (since 1991) Ph.D. recipients who wish to engage in research at AIAR. Applicants must be affiliated with an institution that is a member of the American Schools of Oriental Research (ASOR) or must have been an individual professional member of ASOR for more than 2 years. They must be interested in conducting research on Near Eastern archaeology, geography, history, or biblical studies while residing in Jerusalem.

Financial data The total award is $7,000, including a payment of $3,350 to AIAR for room and half-board for the fellow, and a stipend of $3,650 to the recipient.

Duration 5 months; the award may not be used during the summer.

Limitations Recipients must remain in residency at AIAR for the duration of the program.

Number awarded 1 each year.

Deadline October of each year.

[1046]
HARRELL FAMILY FELLOWSHIP

American Schools of Oriental Research
Attn: Administrative Director
656 Beacon Street, Fifth Floor
Boston, MA 02215-2010
(617) 353-6571   Fax: (617) 353-6575
E-mail: acor@bu.edu
Web site: www.asor.org

Purpose To provide funding to graduate students who wish to participate in an archaeological project supported by the American Center of Oriental Research (ACOR) in Amman, Jordan.

Eligibility This program is open to graduate students of any nationality who wish to participate in an archaeological project supported by ACOR that has passed an academic review process. Applicants may request to participate in an archaeological research project funded by ACOR.

Financial data The stipend is $1,500.

Number awarded 1 each year.

Deadline January of each year.

[1047]
HILLEL'S STEINHARDT JEWISH CAMPUS SERVICE CORPS FELLOWSHIP

Hillel: The Foundation for Jewish Campus Life
Attn: Steinhardt Scholars Program
1640 Rhode Island Avenue, N.W.
Washington, DC 20036-3279
(202) 857-6558   Fax: (202) 857-6693
E-mail: info@hillel.org
Web site: www.hillel.org

Purpose To provide funding to Jewish college graduates who are interested in providing 1 year of service to Jewish campus communities.

Eligibility This program is open to Jewish college graduates; they must have graduated within the past 2 years. Candidates must posses: a commitment to service; a willingness to use their time, abilities, and talents to enhance the lives of others; and a dedication to strengthening Jewish identity among the students with whom they would be working (in the United States or abroad). Finalists are interviewed. Fellows are selected on the basis of leadership skills and ability to create dynamic and innovative engagement strategies designed to reach Jewish college students.

Financial data The stipend is $19,000. Health and dental insurance are also provided.

Duration 11 months, beginning in August of each year.

Special features Fellows are assigned to a campus community either in North America or in Israel. They work with students, members of the university community, and Jewish communal professionals. As part of their professional training, fellows attend international conferences.

Deadline February of each year.

[1048]
HIV–AIDS AND RELATED ILLNESSES RESEARCH COLLABORATION AWARD

Fogarty International Center
Attn: Division of International Training and Research
31 Center Drive, Room B2C39
Bethesda, MD 20892-2220
(301) 496-1653   Fax: (301) 402-0779
E-mail: FIRCA@nih.gov
Web site: www.nih.gov/fic/programs/aidsfirc.html

Purpose To provide assistance for U.S. investigators with current funding from the National Institutes of Health (NIH) to conduct research related to AIDS at foreign sites in collaboration with foreign scientists.

Eligibility Applications may be submitted by U.S. nonprofit organizations, public and private, such as universities, colleges, hospitals, laboratories, units of state and local governments, and eligible agencies of the federal government on behalf of principal investigators. The proposed U.S. principal investigator must be the principal investigator of an AIDS or AIDS-related research grant project funded by the institutes. Racial/ethnic minority individuals, women, and persons with disabilities are encouraged to apply as principal investigators. The foreign collaborator must hold a position at an institution in a foreign country that will allow him or her adequate time and provide appropriate facilities to conduct the proposed research. Most countries are eligible for participation in this program; applications for purchase of equipment as part of the grant are limited to research in the developing countries of Africa, Asia, (except Japan, Singapore, South Korea, and Taiwan), central and eastern Europe, Russia and the Independent States of the former Soviet Union, Latin America and the non-U.S. Caribbean, the Middle East, and the Pacific Ocean Islands (except Australia and New Zealand). The application must demonstrate that the award will enhance the scientific contributions of both the U.S. and foreign scientist and will enhance or expand the contribution of the institutes-sponsored research project.

Financial data Grants up to $32,000 per year are available. Funds may be used for supplies at the foreign institution, expenses incurred at the U.S. institution to support the collaboration, and research-related travel and subsistence expenses for both the U.S. and foreign investigators. For collaborations in developing countries as defined above, requests for purchase of equipment (including computers and fax machines) are considered; up to $5,000 may be allocated as a stipend for the foreign collaborator and up to $2,000 may be allocated for the foreign collaborator to attend an AIDS-related scientific conference. Travel funds may be requested up to 20 percent of the total direct costs (up to $6,400) for the U.S. principal investigator, the foreign collaborator, and/or their colleagues or students for visits to each other's laboratory or research site, if such visits are directly related to the subject of the collaborative research.

Duration Up to 3 years.

Special features This program is the counterpart to the Fogarty International Research Collaboration Award (FIRCA) program for non-AIDS related research. It is also designated as AIDS-FIRCA.

Deadline April, August, or December of each year.

[1049]
HUGH KELLY FELLOWSHIP

Rhodes University
Attn: Dean of Research Division
P.O. Box 94
Grahamstown 6140
South Africa
27 46 603 8179   Fax: 27 46 622 8444
E-mail: pgfinaid-admin@ru.ac.za
Web site: www.rhodes.ac.za/pgfunding

Purpose To provide financial assistance to distinguished scholars who are interested in conducting scientific research at Rhodes University in South Africa.

Eligibility Senior scientists from any country are eligible to apply if they wish to conduct research in South Africa, are interested in being affiliated for the research period with the university, and are pursuing studies in the following areas: biochemistry, botany, chemistry, computer science, electronics, entomology, geography, geology, ichthyology and fisheries science, mathematics, microbiology, pharmaceutical sciences, physics, statistics, water resources, or zoology. Preference is given to applicants who propose to stay at least 4 months.

Financial data Fellows receive 66,000 rand per year plus round-trip airfare. Transportation is also paid for spouses if the recipient stays at the university longer than 4 months.

Duration Up to 1 year.

Number awarded 1 every other year.

Deadline July of even-numbered years.

[1050]
HUGH LE MAY FELLOWSHIP

Rhodes University
Attn: Dean of Research Division
P.O. Box 94
Grahamstown 6140
South Africa
27 46 603 8179   Fax: 27 46 622 8444
E-mail: pgfinaid-admin@ru.ac.za
Web site: www.rhodes.ac.za/pgfunding

Purpose To provide support to distinguished scholars who are interested in conducting research in the humanities at Rhodes University in South Africa.

Eligibility Mature scholars from any country are eligible to apply if they wish to conduct research in the humanities in South Africa, are interested in being affiliated with the university for the research period, and are pursuing studies in 1 of the following fields: philosophy; theology; classics; ancient, medieval, or modern history; classical, Biblical, medieval, or modern languages; political theory; or law.

Financial data Fellows receive return economy airfare, furnished university accommodations, and a small monthly stipend.

Duration From 3 to 4 months.

Number awarded 1 every other year.

Deadline July of odd-numbered years.

[1051]
ICRISAT RESEARCH SCHOLARSHIPS

International Crops Research Institute for the Semi-Arid Tropics
Patancheru 502 324
Andhra Pradesh
India
91 40 329 6161   Fax: 91 40 324 1239
E-mail: icrisat@cgiar.org
Web site: www.icrisat.org

Purpose To provide financial assistance to graduate students from the semi-arid tropics or those interested in gaining experience in tropical agriculture.

Eligibility Applicants must be candidates for M.Sc. or Ph.D. degrees in agricultural or related sciences whose universities will accept thesis research conducted at facilities of the International Crops Research Institute for the Semi-Arid Tropics (ICRISAT) in India, Kenya, Malawi, Mali, Niger, Nigeria, or Zimbabwe. Normally they are nominated by their national agricultural agency, most often in a developing country. The nominating agency usually provides or arranges funding, although it may apply directly to ICRISAT (which has limited funding for these scholarships). The proposed research must relate to agronomy, plant breeding, genetics, biotechnology (applied genomics and genetic transformation), genetic resources, physiology, entomology, pathology, microbiology, cytogenetics, soil physics, socio-economics, virology, land and water management, agriclimatology, or statistical techniques related to sorghum, pearl millet, groundnuts, pigeonpea, chickpea, and rainfed semi-arid tropical resource management.

Financial data Scholarships provide transportation, a maintenance allowance for personal expenses, and a living allowance to cover room, food, medical insurance, research, and other expenses.
Duration 1 to 3 years.
Number awarded Varies each year.
Deadline March of each year.

[1052]
ICRISAT VISITING SCHOLARSHIPS

International Crops Research Institute for the Semi-Arid
  Tropics
Patancheru 502 324
Andhra Pradesh
India
91 40 329 6161   Fax: 91 40 324 1239
E-mail: icrisat@cgiar.org
Web site: www.icrisat.org

Purpose To provide financial assistance to scholars who are interested in pursuing additional research training on subjects supported by the International Crops Research Institute for the Semi-Arid Tropics (ICRISAT).

Eligibility Applicants must have received a Ph.D. or M.Sc. degree in agricultural or related sciences. They must be nominated by their national agricultural agency, usually in a developing country. Normally the nominating agency provides or arranges funding, although ICRISAT has limited funding for which the nominating agency may apply on behalf of the candidate. The proposed research must relate to agronomy, plant breeding, genetics, biotechnology (applied genomics and genetic transformation), genetic resources, physiology, entomology, pathology, microbiology, cytogenetics, soil physics, socio-economics, virology, land and water management, agriclimatology, or statistical techniques related to sorghum, pearl millet, groundnuts, pigeonpea, chickpea, and rainfed semi-arid tropical resource management.

Financial data Fellowships provide transportation, a maintenance allowance for personal expenses, and a living allowance to cover room, food, medical insurance, research, and other expenses.

Duration 1 year, with a potential 1-year extension.

Special features The supervised training program may be conducted at ICRISAT locations in India, Kenya, Malawi, Kenya, Niger, Nigeria, or Zimbabwe.

Number awarded Varies each year.

[1053]
ILRI GRADUATE FELLOWSHIPS

International Livestock Research Institute
Attn: Education Officer
P.O. Box 30709
Nairobi, Kenya
254 2 630743   Fax: 254 2 631499
E-mail: irli@cgiar.org
Web site: www.cgiar.org/ilri

Purpose To provide funding to graduate students who wish to conduct research at facilities of the International Livestock Research Institute (ILRI) in Ethiopia or Kenya.

Eligibility This program is primarily intended for employees of national agricultural research systems (NARS) in developing countries who are enrolled in M.Sc. or Ph.D. studies; in special cases, candidates may be from developed countries or from developing countries but not employed by NARS. Applicants in M.Sc. programs must be registered with an educational institute and have already successfully completed their course work; applicants in Ph.D. programs normally will have registered with a university before joining the institute. All applicants must be interested in working on a project related to existing institute research programs under the supervision of an institute staff member. Their applications must be submitted by their employer, by the educational institute where they are registered, or by both.

Financial data The institute provides financial support, supervision, and research facilities.

Duration 6 months to 3 years.

Deadline Applications may be submitted at any time.

[1054]
ILRI VISITING SCIENTIST PROGRAM

International Livestock Research Institute
Attn: Education Officer
P.O. Box 30709
Nairobi, Kenya
254 2 630743   Fax: 254 1 631499
E-mail: irli@cgiar.org
Web site: www.cgiar.org/ilri

Purpose To allow established investigators in fields related to the work of the International Livestock Research Institute (ILRI) to conduct research in Africa.

Eligibility Eligible are established investigators working in fields related to the institute's research interests: conservation of biodiversity, crop/livestock systems research, utilization of tropical feed resources, animal health improvement, and livestock policy analysis. Applicants should be going on sabbatical leave and seeking to work with institute scientists at Nairobi, Kenya or Addis Ababa, Ethiopia.

Financial data The amount of the grant varies, depending on the salary provided by the grantee's home institution for sabbatical or other leave.

Duration 1 week to 6 months.

Number awarded Varies each year.

Deadline Applications may be submitted at any time.

[1055]
INDIVIDUAL ADVANCED RESEARCH OPPORTUNITIES IN CENTRAL AND EASTERN EUROPE AND EURASIA

International Research & Exchanges Board
1616 H Street, N.W.
Washington, DC 20006
(202) 628-8188   Fax: (202) 628-8189
E-mail: irex@irex.org
Web site: www.irex.org

Purpose To provide research opportunities for predoctoral and postdoctoral scholars at institutions in central Europe, eastern Europe, and Eurasia.

Eligibility Eligibility requirements include: U.S. citizenship or permanent residency for 3 years prior to applying; command of host-country language sufficient for research; and affiliation with a university as a faculty member or advanced doctoral candidate. Applications are accepted in all disciplines, but policy research and development, the humanities and social sciences, and cross-disciplinary studies are emphasized. Limited assistance is available for cross-regional research in Turkey and Iran for postdoctoral humanities scholars.

Financial data The grant provides round-trip airfare and visa fees, a stipend (in the form of a monthly allowance for graduate students or a stipend in lieu of salary for faculty members), host-country room and board, a local research allowance, and excess baggage allowance; support for accompanying family members may be available.

Duration From 2 to 9 months.

Special features The International Research & Exchanges Board (IREX) was established in 1968 at the request of U.S. universities by the American Council of Learned Societies (ACLS) and the Social Science Research Council (SSRC) to administer research exchange programs with the socialist countries of eastern Europe and the former Soviet Republics. Funding for this program is provided by the U.S. Department of State as a Title VIII program and the National Endowment for the Humanities

Limitations Exchange applicants in modern foreign languages and area studies must apply simultaneously for Department of Education Fulbright-Hays grants.

Number awarded Approximately 37 each year; recently, 12 grants were for central and eastern Europe and 25 for Eurasia.

Deadline October of each year.

[1056]
INTERNATIONAL COLLABORATION RESEARCH GRANTS: RECONCEPTUALIZING PUBLIC SPHERES IN THE MIDDLE EAST AND NORTH AFRICA

Social Science Research Council
810 Seventh Avenue
New York, NY 10019
(212) 377-2700   Fax: (212) 377-2727
E-mail: mena@ssrc.org
Web site: www.ssrc.org

Purpose To provide funding to scholars interested in conducting collaborative research in the Middle East and North Africa (MENA) region on the changing role of the public sector.

Eligibility Applicants and all research partners must hold a Ph.D. degree or its equivalent. They can be of any nationality, from any country, and from any discipline as long as the proposed research is well grounded in social science theory and methodology. Research must relate to the changing nature of public spheres in the MENA (defined as Iran to Morocco) region. The term "public spheres" is used in its broadest sense, encompassing the transformation of socio-economic conditions, state and non-state structures, individual and collective identities, and cultural production. Proposals focused on narrowly defined security issues are not eligible. The planned collaboration can involve as many partners in as many locations as desired but must include at least 2 researchers in 2 different countries of the MENA region. The research itself can focus on 1 site or many sites in the MENA region, and intra-regional, cross-regional, and global comparisons are also eligible.

Financial data Grants up to $35,000 are available.

Duration Up to 18 months.

Number awarded Varies each year.

Deadline October of each year.

[1057]
INTERNATIONAL RESEARCH SCIENTIST DEVELOPMENT AWARD

Fogarty International Center
Attn: Division of International Training and Research
31 Center Drive, Room B2C39
Bethesda, MD 20892-2220
(301) 496-1653   Fax: (301) 402-0779
E-mail: IRSDA@nih.gov
Web site: www.nih.gov/fic

Purpose To provide funding to U.S. biomedical scientists interested in continuing research in, or extending their research into, developing countries.

Eligibility Applicants must have received a doctoral, dental, or medical degree within the past 7 years in a basic biomedical, behavioral, or epidemiological/clinical field. They must have established a relationship with 2 prospective mentors, 1 in the United States and 1 in a developing country, who have ongoing, funded, international collaborative research. The U.S. mentor should be at a U.S. institution of higher learning or nonprofit research institution. The developing country mentor should be in an internationally developing country research institution addressing some of that country's major health problems. Eligible countries include those in the following regions: Africa, Asia (except Japan, Singapore, South Korea, and Taiwan), central and eastern Europe, Russia and the Newly Independent States of the former Soviet Union, Latin America and the non-U.S. Caribbean, the Middle East (except Israel), and the Pacific Ocean Islands (except Australia and New Zealand). Applications to work in institutions in sub-Saharan Africa are especially encouraged. Racial/ethnic minority individuals, women, and persons with disabilities are encouraged to apply as principal investigators. Applications must be submitted on behalf of the candidate by the U.S. mentor's institution. The applicant need not already be at that institution at the time of application, but it is expected that the U.S. component of the project will be carried out by the fellow at the U.S. mentor's institution.

Financial data Grants provide up to $300,000 for the complete project, prorated at a rate of $8,333 per month (including $6,250 per month direct costs for salary and fringe benefits and $2,083 per month for all other allowable costs). Other allowable costs include travel (round-trip airfare and necessary ground transportation for the candidate to the foreign site up to 5 times over the duration of the project, round-trip airfare for each dependent accompanying the awardee for 6 months or more abroad, excess baggage allowance), health insurance up to $50 per month for the candidate and each dependent during the time abroad, a supplemental living allowance of $150 per month for each dependent accompanying the awardee for 6 months or more, and research development support. An administrative supplement, up to $20,000, may be provided during the third year of the award to fellows who obtain a tenure-track faculty position upon return to the United States.

Duration Support is provided for 36 months, which may be spread over a period of 5 years. A total of at least 24 months should be at the foreign site under the joint supervision of the U.S. and foreign mentors. A period of work in the foreign country should be at least 3 months in length. A total of up to 12 months will be funded for work at the U.S. institution under the U.S. mentor's supervision.

Number awarded Varies each year.

Deadline February of each year.

[1058]
ISLAMIC STUDIES FELLOWSHIP AT AIAR

American Schools of Oriental Research
Attn: Administrative Director
656 Beacon Street, Fifth Floor
Boston, MA 02215-2010
(617) 353-6570 Fax: (617) 353-6575
E-mail: asor@bu.edu
Web site: www.asor.org

Purpose To provide the opportunity for senior American scholars to engage in teaching and research in Islamic studies at the Albright Institute of Archaeological Research (AIAR) in Jerusalem.

Eligibility U.S. citizens who are senior scholars in the areas of Islamic archaeology, art, and architecture may apply for these fellowships, which are tenable at the Albright Institute.

Financial data The stipend is $20,000, of which $12,200 is paid directly to the appointee and $7,800 is applied toward room and half-board at AIAR.

Duration 10 months.

Special features In addition to pursuing their own research agendas, fellows conduct seminars, direct specialized research, and teach regular courses in the department of archaeology at a local Palestinian university.

Number awarded 1 each year.

Deadline October of each year.

[1059]
ISRAEL FULBRIGHT FELLOWSHIPS

Council for International Exchange of Scholars
3007 Tilden Street, N.W., Suite 5L
Washington, DC 20008-3009
(202) 686-4019 Fax: (202) 362-3442
E-mail: scholars@cies.iie.org
Web site: www.iie.org/cies

Purpose To provide funding to American scholars who are interested in lecturing and conducting research in Israel.

Eligibility Applications are considered from American scholars for 5 programs: 1) the Fulbright–University of Haifa Fellowship for associate or full professors in any field; 2) the Fulbright–Tel Aviv University Fellowship for associate or full professors in any field, with preference for east Asian studies (especially Japanese or Chinese history and politics, modern Japanese studies, religion and philosophy, and Indian religion or philosophy), communications, conflict resolution, studies in government, television, and cinema; 3) the Fulbright–Ben Gurion University Fellowship for associate or full professors in any field, with preference for teaching English as a foreign language; 4) the Fulbright–Technion Fellowship for associate or full professors in architecture and city planning, biology, chemistry, engineering (biomedical, chemical, civil, computer science, food and biotechnology, industrial, materials, mechanical), management, mathematics (pure and applied), medicine, physics, science and technology education, space technology, transportation, and water resources; and 5) the Fulbright–Bar Ilan University Fellowship for associate or full professors in any field, with preference for science teaching, hermeneutics, philosophy of science, and bioethics. U.S. citizenship is required. The program encourages applicants who have had limited (not exceeding 6 months within the past 5 years) or no prior experience in Israel. Knowledge of Hebrew is helpful but not required, except as necessary for research projects.

Financial data The program provides a monthly maintenance allowance ranging from $3,000 to $5,500, depending on the number of accompanying dependents. Other allowances provide for travel, baggage, and settling in.

Duration 4 to 10 months.

Special features This is a Fulbright scholar program, sponsored by the Bureau of Educational and Cultural Affairs of the U.S. Department of State and administered by the Council for International Exchange of Scholars.

Number awarded 5 each year: 1 at each of the participating Israeli universities.

Deadline July of each year.

[1060]
ISRAEL FULBRIGHT TEACHER EXCHANGE

U.S. Department of State
c/o Graduate School, USDA
600 Maryland Avenue, S.W., Room 320
Washington, DC 20024-2520
(202) 314-3520 Fax: (202) 479-6806
E-mail: fulbright@grad.usda.gov
Web site: www.grad.usda.gov/International/ftep.html

Purpose To promote mutual understanding between the people of the United States and the people of Israel through a teacher exchange program.

Eligibility This program is open to senior high school teachers (grades 9 through 12) of general history, English language and literature, or basic science who are interested in teaching in Israel. Applicants must 1) be U.S. citizens; 2) hold at least a bachelor's degree; 3) be fluent in English; 4) have a current full-time teaching assignment in the U.S. or a territory; 5) have the approval of their school administration; 6) have at least 3 years of full-time experience; and 7) not have participated in a Fulbright Teacher Exchange longer than 8 weeks during the last 2 years. The language of instruction is English. Fluency in Hebrew or Arabic is not required. Teaching couples may apply. However, because of the limited number of positions available and, often, the lack of foreign candidate pairs with similar qualifications for interchanges, it may not be possible to arrange suitable assignments in the same locality or to place both teachers. Preference is given to applicants who have not participated previously in the program and may be given to applicants who have not previously lived in Israel. Geographic distribution of awards within the United States is also a factor in selection. This program does not discriminate on the basis of race, color, religion, age, sex, or national origin and encourages the applications of members of minority communities. Other considerations being equal, veterans are given preference.

Financial data Round-trip transportation for the teacher only is provided. Participants must obtain a leave of absence with pay from their jobs in the United States. The U.S. school must agree to accept an Israeli teacher who must secure a leave of absence with pay.

Duration 9 months, beginning in September for academic year exchanges. Also available are 1-semester exchanges that begin in either February or September.

Special features This program is sponsored by the Bureau of Educational and Cultural Affairs of the U.S. Department of State and administered by the Graduate School, USDA.

Limitations This program provides for the direct exchange of teaching assignments between Israel and the United States. Applicants selected for exchange must attend orientation programs of the sponsoring agencies in the United States or abroad.

Number awarded 2 each year.

Deadline October of each year.

[1061]
JAMES A. MONTGOMERY FELLOW/PROGRAM COORDINATOR

American Schools of Oriental Research
Attn: Administrative Director
656 Beacon Street, Fifth Floor
Boston, MA 02215-2010
(617) 353-6570   Fax: (617) 353-6575
E-mail: asor@bu.edu
Web site: www.asor.org

Purpose To provide funding to predoctoral students and postdoctoral scholars who are interested in conducting research at the Albright Institute of Archaeological Research (AIAR) in Jerusalem.

Eligibility This program is open to predoctoral students and postdoctoral scholars specializing in Near Eastern archaeology, geography, history, and biblical studies. Applicants must be interested in conducting research at AIAR and also assisting the Albright Director in planning and implementing the Ernest S. Frerichs Program for Albright Fellows.

Financial data The total award is $14,000, including a payment of $6,700 to AIAR for room and half-board and a stipend of $7,300 to the recipient.

Duration The research period is 10 months.

Limitations Recipients must remain in residency at AIAR for the duration of the program.

Number awarded 1 each year.

Deadline October of each year.

[1062]
JAMES A. SWAN FUND

University of Oxford
Attn: Pitt Rivers Museum
South Parks Road
Oxford OX1 3PP
England
44 1865 270927   Fax: 44 1865 270943
E-mail: kate.white@prm.ox.ac.uk
Web site: www.prm.ox.ac.uk

Purpose To aid research on the archaeological, historical, physical, or cultural nature of the Batwa (the small peoples of Africa, e.g., Bushmen and Pygmies) and their prehistoric antecedents.

Eligibility Applicants must have the academic and experiential background to conduct research on the hunter-gatherer peoples of Africa.

Financial data The amount awarded varies, depending upon the scope of the project and the financial needs of the recipient. Generally, awards range between 1,000 and 2,000 pounds.

Duration Up to 1 year; may be renewable.

Special features Funds are given either for field work or for the publication of field work results.

Limitations Recipients must acknowledge the support received in all appropriate publications.

Number awarded Varies; generally, 10 each year.

Deadline Applications may be submitted at any time. However, the selection committee generally does not meet during the summer.

[1063]
JAZZ AMBASSADORS PROGRAM

John F. Kennedy Center for the Performing Arts
Education Department
Attn: Jazz Ambassadors Program
2700 F Street, N.W.
Washington, DC 20566
(202) 416-8869   Fax: (202) 416-8802
E-mail: artsabroad@kennedy-center.org
Web site: www.kennedy-center.org/programs/jazz/ambassadors

Purpose To enable American jazz musicians to perform in foreign countries.

Eligibility Jazz musicians from the United States who are U.S. citizens at least 21 years of age may audition to participate in this program. Successful applicants must demonstrate artistic and musical ability, be conversant with broader aspects of contemporary American culture, and be adaptable to rigorous traveling through countries in Africa, Latin America, the Near East, and south Asia that are less frequently visited by other American artists. While abroad, they present concerts and conduct master classes and lecture-recitals for musicians.

Financial data Each Jazz Ambassador is compensated for all travel, living, and program expenses and receives a modest honorarium of $200 per day.

Duration Tours last 4 to 6 weeks.

Special features This program is sponsored jointly by the John F. Kennedy Center for the Performing Arts and the U.S. Department of State's Bureau of Educational and Cultural

Affairs. The program began in 1997 with the Artistic Ambassadors Program that presented classical musicians. The program switched to jazz for 1998.
Number awarded 7 trios are selected each year.
Deadline May of each year.

[1064]
JENNIFER C. GROOT FELLOWSHIP
American Schools of Oriental Research
Attn: Administrative Director
656 Beacon Street, Fifth Floor
Boston, MA 02215-2010
(617) 353-6571   Fax: (617) 353-6575
E-mail: acor@bu.edu
Web site: www.asor.org

Purpose To provide financial assistance to undergraduate and graduate students who are interested in participating in archaeological excavations or surveys in Jordan.
Eligibility Eligible to apply are undergraduate or graduate students in any country who have had little or no prior field experience and are interested in participating in excavations or surveys in Jordan. Applicants must be affiliated with an institution that is a member of the American Schools of Oriental Research (ASOR) or must have been an individual professional member of ASOR for more than 2 years. Canadian or U.S. citizenship is required.
Financial data The fellowship provides support in the amount of $1,500.
Duration From 1 to 3 months.
Number awarded 3 each year.
Deadline January of each year.

[1065]
JEWISH SERVICE CORPS
American Jewish Joint Distribution Committee, Inc.
711 Third Avenue
New York, NY 10017-4014
(212) 687-6200   Fax: (212) 370-5467
E-mail: service@jdcny.org
Web site: www.jdc.org/help/volunteer.htm

Purpose To provide service to Jewish communities in selected countries abroad.
Eligibility This program is open to Jewish volunteers who are interested in providing service to the Jewish communities in selected foreign countries. Applicants should have a strong Jewish background, formal or informal teaching experience (such as being a camp counselor, youth group leader, or teacher), proficiency in Hebrew, cultural tolerance, and at least a bachelor's degree. They should be flexible, creative, resourceful, and able to function independently. Teenagers are not eligible; adult applicants, from recent college graduates to retirees, are welcomed.
Financial data The program provides round-trip travel, housing, health care, and a monthly stipend for basic living expenses.
Duration 1 year, generally beginning in the summer.
Special features Currently, openings are available in India, Poland, Romania, Turkey, and the former Soviet Union.

Number awarded Varies each year.
Deadline Applications are accepted at any time.

[1066]
JOHN O. CRANE MEMORIAL FELLOWSHIPS
Institute of Current World Affairs, Inc.
Attn: Program Administrator
Wheelock House
4 West Wheelock Street
Hanover, NH 03755
(603) 643-5548   Fax: (603) 643-9599
E-mail: icwa@valley.net
Web site: www.icwa.org

Purpose To provide opportunities for independent research in eastern Europe or the Middle East.
Eligibility Individuals who have completed their formal education are eligible to apply if they are interested in conducting research in either eastern Europe or the Middle East. Generally, applicants must be under the age of 36 and have good command of written and spoken English.
Financial data The institute provides full support for the fellows and their families.
Duration At least 2 years.
Limitations Fellowships are not awarded to support work toward academic degrees, to write books, or to undertake specific studies or research projects. Fellows are required to submit monthly reports.
Number awarded 1 or more each year.
Deadline March or August of each year.

[1067]
KOSHLAND SCHOLARSHIPS
Weizmann Institute of Science
Feinberg Graduate School
P.O. Box 26
Rehovot 76100
Israel
972 8 934 3834   Fax: 972 8 934 4114
E-mail: nfinfo@weizmann.weizmann.ac.il
Web site: www.weizmann.ac.il

Purpose To provide funding for distinguished scientists who wish to conduct research at the Weizmann Institute in Israel.
Eligibility Citizens of any country who hold the Ph.D. (or its equivalent) in chemistry, life sciences, mathematics, physics, or science teaching are eligible to apply. They must have received their doctoral degree within 3 years of application. Candidates should contact in advance a sponsor in 1 of the research departments at the institute, since applications must be endorsed by the host department.
Financial data Fellows receive 6,958 Israeli shekels per month if single, IS 7,190 per month if married, and IS 7,344 per month if married with a child; $1,335 for participation in scientific meetings abroad; $2,500 per year for professional purposes; $100 to $200 for moving expenses; and reimbursement for at least a 1-way airplane ticket. In addition, they receive a 1-time grant of $5,000 for personal use at the end of the first year of residence.

Duration 2 years; may be renewed for up to 1 additional year.
Number awarded A limited number each year.
Deadline May or December of each year.

[1068]
KRESS FELLOWSHIP IN EGYPTIAN ART AND ARCHITECTURE

American Research Center in Egypt
c/o Emory University West Campus
Building A, Suite 423W
1256 Briarcliff Road, N.W.
Atlanta, GA 30306
(404) 712-9854   Fax: (404) 712-9849
E-mail: arce@emory.edu
Web site: www.arce.org

Purpose To provide financial assistance to predoctoral students who wish to conduct research on Egyptian art in Egypt.
Eligibility Predoctoral students from any accredited university in the United States or Canada are eligible to apply if their doctoral dissertation involves Egyptian art or architecture (from ancient to modern times) and they need to conduct research for the dissertation in Egypt. Applicants may be citizens of any country.
Financial data The stipend is $12,800. Round-trip air transportation is provided for recipients only.
Duration 3 to 12 months.
Special features Funding for these fellowships is provided by the Samuel H. Kress Foundation.
Limitations The funds may not be used for independent research or research at the master's degree level.
Number awarded 1 each year.
Deadline October of each year.

[1069]
KRESS FELLOWSHIP IN THE ART AND ARCHAEOLOGY OF JORDAN

American Schools of Oriental Research
Attn: Administrative Director
656 Beacon Street, Fifth Floor
Boston, MA 02215-2010
(617) 353-6571   Fax: (617) 353-6575
E-mail: acor@bu.edu
Web site: www.asor.org

Purpose To provide funding to graduate students who wish to conduct dissertation research on an art history topic at the American Center of Oriental Research (ACOR) in Amman, Jordan.
Eligibility This program is open to predoctoral students completing dissertation research on an art historical topic, including art history, archaeology, architectural history, and in some cases classical studies. Applicants must be Ph.D. candidates and U.S. citizens or foreign nationals who have enrolled at a U.S. institution. They must plan to be in residence at ACOR.
Financial data The maximum award is $14,000.
Duration 3 to 6 months.
Number awarded 1 or more each year.

Deadline January of each year.

[1070]
KRESS FELLOWSHIPS IN ART HISTORY

Samuel H. Kress Foundation
174 East 80th Street
New York, NY 10021
(212) 861-4993   Fax: (212) 628-3146
Web site: www.shkf.org

Purpose To provide financial assistance to American graduate students who are completing their doctoral research on the history of art.
Eligibility Candidates must be nominated by their department. Their doctoral dissertation research must relate to art history and they must need to complete their research at a cooperating foreign institute of art history. Candidates must be U.S. citizens or students at U.S. institutions.
Financial data The annual stipend is $18,000. The foreign institution chosen by the fellow receives a sustaining grant.
Duration 2 years.
Special features The cooperating institutes are: Kunsthistorisches Institut, Florence; Nelson Glueck School of Biblical Archaeology, Hebrew Union College, Jerusalem; Prentenkabinet/Kunsthistorisch Instituut der Rijks Universiteit, Leiden; Courtauld Institute of Art and Warburg Institute, University of London; Zentralinstitut für Kunstgeschichte, Munich; Cyprus American Archaeological Research Institute, Nicosia; American University of Paris; Bibliotheca Hertziana, Rome; and Swiss Institute for Art Research, Zurich.
Number awarded Varies; generally, 4 each year.
Deadline November of each year.

[1071]
KRESS/ARIT PRE-DOCTORAL FELLOWSHIP IN THE HISTORY OF ART AND ARCHAEOLOGY

American Research Institute in Turkey
c/o University of Pennsylvania Museum
33rd and Spruce Streets
Philadelphia, PA 19104-6324
(215) 898-3474   Fax: (215) 898-0657
E-mail: leinwand@sas.upenn.edu
Web site: mec.sas.upenn.edu/ARIT

Purpose To provide financial aid for advanced dissertation research in Turkey in archaeology or the history of art.
Eligibility This program is open to students engaged in advanced dissertation research that requires a period of study in Turkey. Eligible fields include archaeology and the history of art and architecture from antiquity to the present. Applicants must be U.S. citizens enrolled at a university in the United States.
Financial data The maximum award is $15,000.
Duration Up to 1 year, but projects of shorter duration (generally no less than 2 months) are also possible.
Special features Hostel, research, and study facilities of the American Research Institute in Turkey (ARIT) are available in Istanbul and Ankara. This fellowship program is supported by a grant from the Samuel H. Kress Foundation.
Number awarded 1 or more each year.

MIDDLE EAST/AFRICA

Deadline November of each year.

[1072]
LADY DAVIS POSTDOCTORAL FELLOWSHIPS
Lady Davis Fellowship Trust
c/o Hebrew University
Givat Ram Campus
Jerusalem 91904
Israel
972 2 658 4723   Fax: 972 2 566 3848
E-mail: LDFT@vms.huji.ac.il
Web site: sites.huji.ac.il/LDFT

Purpose To provide funding to postdoctoral candidates interested in conducting research in Israel.

Eligibility These fellowships are open to candidates from any part of the world. Applicants must have completed their doctoral dissertation within the preceding 3 years. They must be interested in conducting research at Hebrew University of Jerusalem or the Technion–Israel Institute of Technology in Haifa. Selection is based on demonstrated excellence in academic work, distinction in the chosen field of specialization, character, and ability to benefit from the opportunity to conduct research in Israel.

Financial data The grant covers the cost of travel, half of the cost of medical insurance if purchased and paid for in Israel, a monthly stipend of 5,075 Israeli shekalim at Hebrew University or $1,250 at the Technion, and a rent allowance approximately equivalent to $100 per month at the Technion or $250 per month at Hebrew University ($150 for single fellows).

Duration 9 to 12 months. Under special circumstances, the fellowship may be extended for a second year.

Special features The Lady Davis Fellowship Trust was established in 1973. Lady Davis was a distinguished philanthropist and benefactor of educational institutions who died in Montreal, Canada in 1963. Information on the program at the Technion is available at 972 4 829 2560, Fax: 972 4 829 4610, E-mail: kayellet@tx.technion.ac.il.

Limitations Fellows must be accepted and approved by the institution with which they wish to affiliate.

Deadline December of each year.

[1073]
LADY DAVIS VISITING PROFESSORSHIPS
Lady Davis Fellowship Trust
c/o Hebrew University
Givat Ram Campus
Jerusalem 91904
Israel
972 2 658 4723   Fax: 972 2 566 3848
E-mail: LDFT@vms.huji.ac.il
Web site: sites.huji.ac.il/LDFT

Purpose To provide funding to faculty members interested in conducting research and teaching in Israel.

Eligibility These professorships are open to candidates from any part of the world. Applicants must be interested in teaching and conducting research at Hebrew University of Jerusalem or the Technion–Israel Institute of Technology in Haifa. They must have the rank of full or associate professor in their home institution. Selection is based on demonstrated excellence in academic work, distinction in the chosen field of specialization, character, and ability to benefit from the opportunity to work in Israel.

Financial data The grant covers the cost of travel, half of the cost of medical insurance if purchased and paid for in Israel, a stipend paid in Israeli shekalim that is based on the cost-of-living index and the exchange rate but is approximately equivalent to $2,000 per month (associate professors) or $2,400 per month (full professors), and a rent allowance approximately equivalent to $100 per month at the Technion or $250 per month at Hebrew University ($150 for single fellows).

Duration 2 to 4 months.

Special features The Lady Davis Fellowship Trust was established in 1973. Lady Davis was a distinguished philanthropist and benefactor of educational institutions who died in Montreal, Canada in 1963. Information on the program at the Technion is available at 972 4 829 2560, Fax: 972 4 829 4610, E-mail: kayellet@tx.technion.ac.il.

Limitations Fellows must be accepted and approved by the institution with which they wish to affiliate.

Deadline November of each year.

[1074]
LESLIE BROWN MEMORIAL GRANT
Raptor Research Foundation
c/o Dr. Jeffrey L. Lincer
9251 Golondrina Drive
La Mesa, CA 91941
E-mail: jllincer@aol.com
Web site: biology.boisestate.edu/raptor/rrfi.htm

Purpose To provide funding to researchers interested in working in areas related to raptors.

Eligibility Applicants must be interested in conducting research and/or disseminating information on raptors. They must send a resume, specific study objectives, an account of how funds will be spent, and a statement indicating how the proposed work relates to other work by the applicant and to other sources of funds. Proposals concerning raptors in Africa receive highest priority.

Financial data Grants up to $1,000 are available.

Number awarded 1 or more each year.

Deadline February of each year.

[1075]
MARYVONNE STEPHAN AWARD
French Association of University Women
4 rue de Chevreuse
75006 Paris
France
33 1 43 20 01 32   Fax: 33 1 45 25 95 53
Fax: affdu@club-internet.fr
Web site: www.ifuw.org/france

Purpose To provide financial assistance to members of the International Federation of University Women (IFUW) interested in conducting research in Senegal.

Eligibility This program is open to members of the IFUW or 1 of its national affiliates. Applicants must be interested in conducting research on agricultural management for women's groups in the river area of Senegal. Fluency in French is required.

Financial data The stipend is the Euro equivalent of 40,000 French francs.

Special features In the United States, the IFUW affiliate is the American Association of University Women (AAUW), 1111 16th Street, N.W., Washington, DC 20036-4873, (202) 785-7700, (800) 821-4364.

Limitations The recipients must agree to undertake research at the project site of the French Association of University Women in Nabadji Civol in Senegal.

Number awarded 1 or more each year.

Deadline March of each year.

[1076]
MESOPOTAMIAN FELLOWSHIP

American Schools of Oriental Research
Attn: Administrative Director
656 Beacon Street, Fifth Floor
Boston, MA 02215-2010
(617) 353-6570   Fax: (617) 353-6575
E-mail: asor@bu.edu
Web site: www.asor.org

Purpose To provide financial support for research about ancient Mesopotamian civilization or culture.

Eligibility Predoctoral students and postdoctoral scholars from any country are invited to apply. Applicants must be affiliated with an institution that is a corporate member of the American Schools of Oriental Research (ASOR) or have been individual professional members for more than 2 years. All applicants must obtain individual membership in ASOR, if they do not already have it. Priority is given to applicants whose projects are affiliated with ASOR. The fellowship is primarily intended to support field research in ancient Mesopotamian civilization carried out in the Middle East, but other research projects (such as museum or archival research related to ancient Mesopotamian studies) may also be considered.

Financial data The grant is $7,000.

Duration 3 to 6 months.

Number awarded 1 each year.

Deadline January of each year.

[1077]
MICKEY LELAND–BILL EMERSON INTERNATIONAL HUNGER FELLOWS PROGRAM

Congressional Hunger Center
229 1/2 Pennsylvania Avenue, S.E.
Washington, DC 20003
(202) 547-7022   Fax: (202) 547-7575
E-mail: fellows@hungercenter.org
Web site: www.hungercenter.org/international/int.htm

Purpose To provide emerging leaders in the fight against hunger with an opportunity to participate in field projects at sites in developing countries.

Eligibility This program is open to U.S. citizens who have a bachelor's degree, either a graduate degree or significant experience working to fight hunger, at least 6 months of continuous anti-poverty or sustainable development work in a developing country, written and spoken proficiency in a language appropriate to a field placement, demonstrated leadership qualities and abilities, creativity and initiative in problem solving, and a strong commitment to alleviating hunger and poverty with an enthusiasm for day-to-day work. Applicants must be interested in participating in a program that includes 1) work at field sites in sub-Saharan Africa, south Asia, Central America, and the Caribbean where they work in anti-hunger and development activities and 2) a policy placement in Rome (where they work with U.N. food institutions such as UNFAO, UNWFP, or IFAD) or in Washington, D.C., Baltimore, or Boston (where they work at the U.S. headquarters of the organizations at which they were placed during their field experience). Selection is based on the applicants' commitment to social change, diversity of experience and perspective, vision for the future, demonstrated leadership potential, and willingness to learn and have their lives changed by the experience.

Financial data Fellows receive a stipend of $1,000 per month. During their policy placement, they also receive a housing allowance. The program also pays for medical insurance and travel to and from field placements. Upon completion of the program, fellows receive an end-of-service award to help them make the transition to the next phase of their career.

Duration 3 years, including a 2-year placement in the field in sub-Saharan Africa, south Asia, Central America, or the Caribbean and a 1-year policy placement in Rome or the United States.

Number awarded 10 each year. Field assignments are provided for 4 fellows in sub-Saharan Africa, 3 in south Asia, and 3 in Central America or the Caribbean. Alternatively, 1 fellow may be placed in North Korea. For their policy assignments, 3 fellows are placed in Rome and the remaining fellows in Washington, D.C., Baltimore, or Boston.

Deadline January of each year.

[1078]
MIDDLE EAST, NORTH AFRICA, SOUTH ASIA REGIONAL RESEARCH PROGRAM

Council for International Exchange of Scholars
3007 Tilden Street, N.W., Suite 5L
Washington, DC 20008-3009
(202) 686-4019   Fax: (202) 362-3442
E-mail: scholars@cies.iie.org
Web site: www.iie.org/cies

Purpose To provide financial assistance to American scholars for research in any academic or professional field in the Middle East, north Africa, or south Asia.

Eligibility Applicants must be U.S. citizens who are area specialists or who have had limited experience in the countries of the region. Possible fields of research include, but are not limited to, architecture, area studies, biological sciences, communications, education, environmental sciences, humanities, law, medical sciences, physical sciences, and social sciences. Field work must be conducted in 2 or more countries of the region. Projects that involve collaboration with colleagues and institutions in the host country and that contribute to cooperation within the region are especially encouraged. Appropriate language proficiency to complete the research is required. The following countries participate in this program: Bahrain, Bangladesh, Egypt, India, Israel, Jordan, Kuwait, Lebanon,

Morocco, Nepal, Oman, Pakistan, Palestinian National Authority (Gaza or West Bank), Qatar, Saudi Arabia, Sri Lanka, Syria, Tunisia, United Arab Emirates, and Yemen.

Financial data In most countries, the monthly base stipend is $1,700; special base stipends are provided in Egypt, India, Israel, Jordan, Morocco, Nepal, Pakistan, and Sri Lanka. In all countries, awards also include a monthly maintenance allowance of $1,700 to $3,000 (depending on country and number of accompanying dependents) to cover local costs of living, a research allowance of $3,000, and an allowance to cover international travel for grantee and up to 2 accompanying dependents for grants of 4 months or more.

Duration 3 to 9 months.

Special features This is a Fulbright scholar program, sponsored by the Bureau of Educational and Cultural Affairs of the U.S. Department of State and administered by the Council for International Exchange of Scholars.

Number awarded Up to 10 each year.

Deadline July of each year.

[1079]
MORITZ AND CHARLOTTE WARBURG RESEARCH FELLOWSHIPS IN JEWISH STUDIES

Hebrew University of Jerusalem
Attn: Institute of Jewish Studies
Joseph and Ceil Mazer Center for Humanities, Room 4110
Jerusalem, Israel

Purpose To provide funding to postdoctorates from any country who wish to conduct research on Jewish studies at the Hebrew University of Jerusalem.

Eligibility Postdoctorates from any country are eligible to apply if they are not more than 30 years of age and are interested in using the facilities of the Institute of Jewish Studies at the Hebrew University of Jerusalem. In exceptional cases, applications of candidates up to age 35 will be considered.

Financial data A generous stipend is provided.

Duration Usually, 1 semester.

Number awarded Varies each year.

Deadline December of each year.

[1080]
MOROCCO FULBRIGHT TEACHER EXCHANGE

U.S. Department of State
c/o Graduate School, USDA
600 Maryland Avenue, S.W., Room 320
Washington, DC 20024-2520
(202) 314-3520   Fax: (202) 479-6806
E-mail: fulbright@grad.usda.gov
Web site: www.grad.usda.gov/International/ftep.html

Purpose To promote mutual understanding between the people of the United States and the people of Morocco through a teacher exchange program.

Eligibility This program is open to teachers (grades 9 through 12) of English as a second language (ESL), French, or Arabic who are interested in teaching in Morocco. Applicants must 1) be U.S. citizens; 2) hold at least a bachelor's degree; 3) be fluent in English; 4) have a current full-time teaching assignment in the U.S. or a territory; 5) have the approval of their school administration; 6) have at least 3 years of full-time experience; and 7) not have participated in a Fulbright Teacher Exchange longer than 8 weeks during the last 2 years. Fluency in French (for ESL teachers) or Arabic (for teachers of Arabic) is desirable but not required. Teaching couples may apply. However, because of the limited number of positions available and, often, the lack of foreign candidate pairs with similar qualifications for interchanges, it may not be possible to arrange suitable assignments in the same locality or to place both teachers. Preference is given to applicants who have not participated previously in the program and may be given to applicants who have not previously lived in Morocco. Geographic distribution of awards within the United States is also a factor in selection. This program does not discriminate on the basis of race, color, religion, age, sex, or national origin and encourages the applications of members of minority communities. Other considerations being equal, veterans are given preference.

Financial data Round-trip airfare for the exchange teacher only and a $3,000 cost of living stipend are provided. Participants must obtain a leave of absence with or without pay from their jobs in the United States. The U.S. school must agree to accept a teacher from Morocco who must secure a leave of absence with pay.

Duration The U.S. teacher visits Morocco for 6 weeks in the fall; the U.S. institution agrees to accept a teacher from Morocco for 6 weeks in the spring.

Special features This program is sponsored by the Bureau of Educational and Cultural Affairs of the U.S. Department of State and administered by the Graduate School, USDA.

Limitations Applicants selected for exchange must attend orientation programs of the sponsoring agencies in the United States or abroad.

Number awarded 3 to 5 each year.

Deadline October of each year.

[1081]
NATIONAL ENDOWMENT FOR THE HUMANITIES FELLOWSHIPS FOR RESEARCH IN TURKEY

American Research Institute in Turkey
c/o University of Pennsylvania Museum
33rd and Spruce Streets
Philadelphia, PA 19104-6324
(215) 898-3474   Fax: (215) 898-0657
E-mail: leinwand@sas.upenn.edu
Web site: mec.sas.upenn.edu/ARIT

Purpose To provide funding to American scholars who wish to conduct research in Turkey.

Eligibility American postdoctorates are eligible to apply if they wish to conduct research in the humanities (including prehistory, history, art, archaeology, literature, linguistics, and the interdisciplinary aspects of cultural history) at the American Research Institute in Turkey (ARIT) in Istanbul or in Ankara.

Financial data Stipends range from $10,000 to $30,000, depending upon the scope of the funded proposal.

Duration 4 to 12 months.

Special features This program is supported by the National Endowment for the Humanities (NEH). ARIT maintains 2 research institutes in Turkey: ARIT-Istanbul has a research library focused on Byzantine, Ottoman, and modern studies of Turkey. ARIT-Ankara focuses on art, archaeology, and ancient history in its library. Both institutes have residential facilities for fellows and provide general assistance as well as introductions to colleagues, institutions, and authorities in Turkey.

Number awarded 2 to 3 each year.

Deadline November of each year.

[1082]
NATIONAL ENDOWMENT FOR THE HUMANITIES POST-DOCTORAL RESEARCH FELLOWSHIPS TO AMMAN

American Schools of Oriental Research
Attn: Administrative Director
656 Beacon Street, Fifth Floor
Boston, MA 02215-2010
(617) 353-6571   Fax: (617) 353-6575
E-mail: acor@bu.edu
Web site: www.asor.org

Purpose To provide funding to postdoctoral scholars who wish to conduct research at the American Center of Oriental Research in Amman, Jordan.

Eligibility Applicants must be U.S. citizens, permanent residents, or foreign nationals who have lived in the United States for the past 3 years, have earned a Ph.D. degree (or are recognized scholars), and are interested in conducting research in Jordan in modern and classical languages, linguistics, literature, history, jurisprudence, philosophy, archaeology, comparative religion, ethics, and the history, criticism, and theory of the arts.

Financial data The stipend is $20,000.

Duration 4 months.

Special features This program is jointly sponsored by the National Endowment for the Humanities (NEH) and the American Schools of Oriental Research (ASOR). Membership in ASOR is not required.

Number awarded 1 or more each year.

Deadline January of each year.

[1083]
NATIONAL ENDOWMENT FOR THE HUMANITIES POST-DOCTORAL RESEARCH FELLOWSHIPS TO JERUSALEM

American Schools of Oriental Research
Attn: Administrative Director
656 Beacon Street, Fifth Floor
Boston, MA 02215-2010
(617) 353-6570   Fax: (617) 353-6575
E-mail: asor@bu.edu
Web site: www.asor.org

Purpose To provide funding to postdoctoral scholars who wish to conduct research at the W.F. Albright Institute of Archaeological Research in Jerusalem.

Eligibility Applicants must be U.S. citizens, permanent residents, or foreign nationals who have lived in the United States for the past 3 years, have earned a Ph.D. degree (or are recognized scholars), and are interested in conducting research in Jerusalem in the humanistically-oriented disciplines that contribute to an understanding of Near East cultures and people: ancient history, anthropology, archaeology, art history, epigraphy, geography, literature, philology, philosophy, biblical studies, Islamic studies, religion, or related disciplines.

Financial data Stipends are paid at the rate of $30,000 per year.

Duration From 4 to 12 months.

Special features This program is jointly sponsored by the National Endowment for the Humanities (NEH) and the American Schools of Oriental Research (ASOR). Membership in ASOR is not required.

Number awarded 2 each year.

Deadline October of each year.

[1084]
NATIONAL RESEARCH FOUNDATION POSTDOCTORAL FELLOWSHIPS FOR RESEARCH IN SOUTH AFRICA

National Research Foundation
Attn: Manager, Bursary and Fellowship Programme
P.O. Box 2600
Pretoria 0001
South Africa
27 12 481 4102   Fax: 27 12 349 1179
E-mail: rose@nrf.ac.za
Web site: www.nrf.ac.za

Purpose To provide funding to recent Ph.D.s from other countries who are interested in conducting research in South Africa.

Eligibility Candidates must have completed their doctoral studies in the natural sciences, social sciences, humanities, engineering, or technology within the preceding 5 years and must have expertise unavailable and needed in South Africa. They may be of any nationality. Direct applications are not accepted; candidates must be nominated by a South African university, technikon, or museum.

Financial data The maximum stipend for research in South Africa is 60,000 rand per year. Other benefits include R10,000 per year for research project expenses and a R5,000 travel grant for fellows who relocate in South Africa.

Duration 1 year; may be renewed for 1 additional year.

Deadline March and September of each year.

[1085]
NATO COLLABORATIVE LINKAGE GRANTS

North Atlantic Treaty Organization
Attn: Scientific Affairs Division
Boulevard Leopold III
B-1110 Brussels
Belgium
32 2 707 4111   Fax: 32 2 707 4232
Web site: www.nato.int/science

Purpose To support collaborative scientific research by providing travel funding to teams in different member countries of the North Atlantic Treaty Organization (NATO) and those in Euro-Atlantic Partnership Council (EAPC) countries (including Eurasia).

Eligibility This program is open to collaborations between scientists in NATO countries (the United States, Canada, 14 countries in western Europe, and 3 countries in eastern Europe and Eurasia) and NATO's partner countries of the EAPC (15 former Soviet republics and 7 other nations in eastern Europe). Scientists of the Mediterranean Dialogue countries (Algeria, Egypt, Israel, Jordan, Mauritania, Morocco, and Tunisia) may also apply for a grant in cooperation with scientists from NATO countries. All applicant teams must be interested in conducting research in 1 of the 4 priority areas currently selected by NATO: physical and engineering science and technology (PST), life science and technology (LST), environmental and earth science and technology (EST), and security-related civil science and technology (SST).

Financial data Funding is provided to cover the costs incurred by investigators to visit the collaborating teams abroad. Amounts awarded are normally between $5,000 (for 1 year of collaboration by 2 or 3 scientists) to a maximum of $25,000 (for 2 years' collaboration by 5 research teams). Basic costs (salaries, equipment, consumables, page charges) should already be covered from other national sources. Support is not provided for 1) institutional overhead expenses; 2) scientists while on sabbatical or other extended leave abroad; 3) travel that is not related to the research project; 4) purely domestic travel; 5) visits for 1 researcher or 1 research group only; or 6) long study periods abroad.

Duration The grants may be used over a period of 1 to 2 years. During the time period of a grant, research visits are expected to be of short duration and should not exceed 2 months.

Number awarded Since 1960, support has been given to more than 6,000 joint projects. At present, about 600 grants are awarded each year (of which an average of 450 are for new projects).

Deadline Deadlines for PST grants are February, July, or October of each year; deadlines for LST and EST grants are March, August, or November of each year; deadlines for SST grants are January, April, or September of each year.

[1086]
NATO EXPERT VISITS

North Atlantic Treaty Organization
Attn: Scientific Affairs Division
Boulevard Leopold III
B-1110 Brussels
Belgium
32 2 707 4111　　　　　　　　　Fax: 32 2 707 4232
Web site: www.nato.int/science

Purpose To provide financial assistance to scientists from member nations of the North Atlantic Treaty Organization (NATO) for visits to research laboratories in Euro-Atlantic Partnership Council (EAPC) countries (including Eurasia), and vice versa.

Eligibility Experts from NATO countries (the United States, Canada, 14 countries in western Europe, and 3 countries in eastern Europe) may visit research laboratories in an EAPC country (15 former Soviet republics and 7 countries in eastern Europe) to consult on current research projects. EAPC scientists may also visit a NATO country. Scientists in the 7 Mediterranean Dialogue countries (Algeria, Egypt, Israel, Jordan, Mauritania, Morocco, and Tunisia) are also eligible if they draw up applications in cooperation with a scientist from a NATO country. This program is available primarily, but not exclusively, for research in 1 of the 4 priority areas currently selected by NATO: physical and engineering science and technology (PST), life science and technology (LST), environmental and earth science and technology (EST), and security-related civil science and technology (SST). Applications must be submitted by the project director at the institute to be visited and signed by both the host institute project director and the visiting expert.

Financial data Fellows receive research, travel, and living (up to $100 per day) allowances. Support is not provided for 1) long study periods abroad, 2) salaries, stipends, or institutional overhead; 3) scientists on sabbatical or other extended leave abroad; or 4) attendance at conferences, symposia, workshops, etc.

Duration From a few days to 1 month.

Number awarded Varies each year.

Deadline Deadlines for PST grants are February, July, or October of each year; deadlines for LST and EST grants are March, August, or November of each year; deadlines for SST grants are January, April, or September of each year.

[1087]
NAVRONGO FELLOWSHIPS

Population Council
Attn: Fellowship Coordinator
One Dag Hammarskjold Plaza
New York, NY 10017
(212) 339-0500　　　　　　　　Fax: (212) 755-6052
E-mail: ssfellowship@popcouncil.org
Web site: www.popcouncil.org

Purpose To provide funding to pre- and postdoctorates interested in conducting research at the Navrongo Health Research Centre (NHRC) in Ghana.

Eligibility This program is open to pre- and postdoctoral scholars from all countries in the fields of public health and demography. Applicants must be interested in conducting research at the center, which functions as an institute within the Ghanaian Ministry of Health, to improve scientific understanding of the causes and consequences of disease and illness in northern Ghana and feasible means of intervention.

Financial data A stipend is provided (amount not specified).

Duration 1 year. Postdoctoral fellowships may be renewed for 1 additional year.

Special features Fellows join the research team of the NHRC in its work on the impact of health technologies, the development of practical means of organizing health and family planning services, and social research on illness and reproductive health.

Number awarded Varies each year.

[1088]
NEAR AND MIDDLE EAST RESEARCH AND TRAINING PROGRAM PRE-DOCTORAL FELLOWSHIPS

American Schools of Oriental Research
Attn: Administrative Director
656 Beacon Street, Fifth Floor
Boston, MA 02215-2010
(617) 353-6571 Fax: (617) 353-6575
E-mail: acor@bu.edu
Web site: www.asor.org

Purpose To provide funding to predoctoral students who are interested in a period of residence at the American Center of Oriental Research (ACOR) in Amman, Jordan.

Eligibility Applicants must be predoctoral students in anthropology, political science, economics, international relations, history, or journalism. Recipients are expected to reside at ACOR in Amman and participate actively in its work. U.S. citizenship is required. Preference is given to students with little or no prior experience in the Middle East.

Financial data Fellowships provide room and board at ACOR, transportation, and a stipend of $750 per month; the maximum award is $9,200.

Duration 2 to 4 months.

Number awarded 2 or more each year.

Deadline January of each year.

[1089]
NELSON MANDELA AWARD FOR HEALTH AND HUMAN RIGHTS

Henry J. Kaiser Family Foundation
1450 G Street, N.W., Suite 250
Washington, DC 20005
(202) 347-5270 Fax: (202) 347-5274
Web site: www.kff.org

Purpose To recognize and reward extraordinary accomplishments in improving the health of disadvantaged people in the United States and South Africa.

Eligibility Individuals in the United States and in South Africa may be nominated for this award if they have contributed to improving the health care of disadvantaged people in the United States and South Africa. Nominees should have demonstrated extraordinary leadership, personal commitment, and accomplishment in the effort to improve the health of underserved populations. Such contributions may include health policy and systems research, public health program development and implementation, leadership in the public health service, political leadership in support of health systems reform, and/or community-based health programs.

Financial data Each recipient is entitled to nominate for a $10,000 grant a nonprofit organization committed to improving health services and health status in the United States or South Africa. In addition, recipients receive funding to spend approximately 1 month in each other's country to investigate health problems and efforts designed to remedy them.

Duration The awards are presented annually.

Special features The first of these awards was presented in 1993. In recent years, the award ceremonies have been held in Cape Town, South Africa, and President Mandela himself has presented the awards.

Number awarded 2 each year: 1 to a citizen of the United States and 1 to a South African.

[1090]
NIDDK AND NIAID INTERNATIONAL COLLABORATION AWARDS

National Institute of Diabetes and Digestive and Kidney Diseases
Attn: Division of Digestive Diseases and Nutrition
45 Center Drive, Room 6AN-12A
Bethesda, MD 20892-6600
(301) 594-8871 Fax: (301) 480-8300
E-mail: tk13v@nih.gov
Web site: www.niddk.nih.gov

Purpose To provide support for research relevant to the mission of the National Institute of Diabetes and Digestive and Kidney Diseases (NIDDK) to be conducted at international centers supported by the National Institute of Allergy and Infectious Diseases (NIAID).

Eligibility This program is open to investigators at domestic and foreign, for-profit and nonprofit, public and private organizations, such as universities, colleges, hospitals, laboratories, units of state and local governments, and eligible agencies of the federal government. Applicants must be proposing to conduct research on the following topics of interest to the NIDDK: autoimmune liver diseases and hepatitis, gastric ulcer disease and Helicobacter pylori, parasitic diseases that have an impact on liver, mucosal immunity, pediatric liver disease, influence of altered nutritional status on health and disease, parasitic diseases with kidney/urinary tract sequelae, hemolytic uremic syndrome, infectious diseases of the kidney, benign prostatic hypertrophy in minority populations, therapies for hematologic disorders such as iron chelating agents, diabetic kidney disease, and hypertensive kidney disease. Research should be conducted in collaboration with an NIAID international center.

Financial data Grants up to $50,000 per year for direct costs are available through this program.

Duration Up to 2 years; nonrenewable.

Special features Current NIAID international centers, and their major research interests, are located in: Brazil (leishmaniasis, malaria, schistosomiasis, Chagas' Disease, immunoparasitology, diarrheal diseases, and hydatid diseases), Cameroon (malaria), Chile (cholera and enteric diseases), Egypt (lymphatic filariasis), Israel (diarrheal diseases, leishmaniasis, hydatid diseases), Jordan (leishmaniasis), Kenya (schistosomiasis, filariasis, hydatid diseases), Lebanon (leishmaniasis), Mexico (tuberculosis), Morocco (leishmaniasis), Nepal (geohelminths), Peru (enteric pathogens, neurocysticercosis), South Africa (amoebiasis), Thailand (malaria), Tunisia (hydatid diseases), and Uganda (tuberculosis). Information on the NIAID international centers is available from the Parasitology and International Programs Branch, Solar Building, Room 3A12, 6003 Executive Boulevard MSC 7630, Bethesda, MD 20892-7630, (301) 496-7115, Fax: (301) 402-0659, E-mail: mg35s@nih.gov.

Number awarded Varies, depending on the availability of funds.

Deadline Applications may be submitted at any time.

MIDDLE EAST/AFRICA

[1091]
OLIVIA JAMES TRAVELING FELLOWSHIP
Archaeological Institute of America
656 Beacon Street, Fourth Floor
Boston, MA 02215-2010
(617) 353-9361   Fax: (617) 353-6550
E-mail: aia@bu.edu
Web site: www.archaeological.org

Purpose To provide financial assistance to American graduate students and scholars who wish to conduct research in Greece, the Aegean Islands, Sicily, southern Italy, Asia Minor, or Mesopotamia.

Eligibility Although applicants are not required to be registered in academic institutions, preference is given to individuals engaged in dissertation research or to recent (within 5 years) recipients of the Ph.D. They must be U.S. citizens or permanent residents and interested in conducting research on the classics, sculpture, architecture, archaeology, or history in Greece, the Aegean Islands, Sicily, southern Italy, Asia Minor, or Mesopotamia.

Financial data The amount of the award is $22,000.

Duration Preference is given to work of at least half a year's duration.

Number awarded 1 each year.

Deadline October of each year.

[1092]
PIERRE AND PATRICIA BIKAI FELLOWSHIPS
American Schools of Oriental Research
Attn: Administrative Director
656 Beacon Street, Fifth Floor
Boston, MA 02215-2010
(617) 353-6571   Fax: (617) 353-6575
E-mail: acor@bu.edu
Web site: www.asor.org

Purpose To provide funding to scholars and students who wish to participate in an archaeological research project while in residency at the American Center of Oriental Research (ACOR) in Amman, Jordan.

Eligibility This program is open to scholars at any level who plan to participate in an archaeological research project operating in Jordan. Applicants must plan to be in residence at ACOR.

Financial data Fellows receive a stipend of $400 per month and room and board at ACOR.

Duration 1 or 2 months.

Number awarded 1 or more each year.

Deadline January of each year.

[1093]
POSTDOCTORAL AWARDS IN ISRAEL
Institute of International Education
Attn: Student Programs Division
809 United Nations Plaza
New York, NY 10017-3580
(212) 984-5330   Fax: (212) 984-5325
Web site: www.iie.org/fulbright

Purpose To provide financial assistance to postdoctorates who are interested in conducting research in Israel.

Eligibility Candidates must meet the general eligibility requirements for Fulbright grants and, in addition, must have received their Ph.D. prior to their arrival in Israel. Preference is given to scholars up to 35 years of age who have not previously studied or conducted research in Israel and who completed their doctorate within the past 2 years.

Financial data This program provides international travel, a settling-in allowance, and a stipend which varies with the duration of the award and the number of dependents. Recently, the stipends for recipients without accompanying dependents were approximately $21,000 for 10 months or $42,400 for 21 months; for recipients with 3 or more dependents, the stipends averaged $36,900 for 10 months or $74,600 for 21 months. The awards for 21 months include an extra round-trip airline ticket.

Duration Up to 21 months.

Special features Recipients are placed in the following Israeli institutions: Tel Aviv University, Weizmann Institute of Science, the Technion, Hebrew University of Jerusalem, Bar Ilan University, Ben Gurion University of the Negev, or University of Haifa.

Limitations Continuation of the award beyond the first academic year is dependent upon evidence of satisfactory progress.

Number awarded 1 or more each year.

Deadline October of each year.

[1094]
POSTDOCTORAL GRANTS FOR SUMMER TRAVEL/RESEARCH IN TURKEY
Institute of Turkish Studies
c/o Georgetown University
Intercultural Center
P.O. Box 571033
Washington, DC 20057-1033
(202) 687-0295   Fax: (202) 687-3780
E-mail: sayaris@gunet.georgetown.edu
Web site: www.turkishstudies.org

Purpose To provide funding for travel to Turkey for research purposes.

Eligibility Eligible to apply are U.S. citizens or residents who have earned a Ph.D. degree in a social science or humanities discipline, are recognized scholars, are interested in traveling to Turkey to conduct research on Turkish studies, and are in need of funding to underwrite their travel expenses.

Financial data The amount of the award depends on the nature of the proposal. The maximum award is round-trip airfare. No university overhead costs are paid.

Duration Recipients are expected to spend at least 4 weeks in Turkey.

Deadline April of each year.

[1095]
PREDISSERTATION GRADUATE FELLOWSHIPS IN TURKISH STUDIES

Institute of Turkish Studies
c/o Georgetown University
Intercultural Center
P.O. Box 571033
Washington, DC 20057-1033
(202) 687-0295 Fax: (202) 687-3780
E-mail: sayaris@gunet.georgetown.edu
Web site: www.turkishstudies.org

Purpose To provide financial assistance to graduate students in Turkish Studies.

Eligibility This program is open to graduate students in the humanities or social sciences who have completed at least 1 year of modern Turkish. Applicants must be U.S. citizens or permanent residents proposing summer travel to Turkey for language study and/or research. Students currently engaged in dissertation research or writing are not eligible.

Financial data Grants range from $4,000 to $6,000.

Duration Normally 2 months, during the summer.

Number awarded Varies each year.

Deadline April of each year.

[1096]
PROFESSOR E.D. BERGMANN MEMORIAL AWARD

United States-Israel Binational Science Foundation
2 Alharizi Street
P.O.B. 7677
Jerusalem 91076
Israel
972 2 561 7314 Fax: 972 2 563 3287
E-mail: bsf@vms.huji.ac.il
Web site: www.bsf.org.il

Purpose To provide a supplemental award to scientists who have received new grants from the United States–Israel Binational Science Foundation (BSF).

Eligibility No separate application is necessary for these grants. All scientists from the United States and Israel who earned their doctoral degrees within the past 5 years, are not more than 35 years old on the date of submission, and are awarded BSF Research Grants automatically become candidates for these grants.

Financial data The stipend, paid in Israeli currency, is equivalent to $5,000.

Duration 1 year.

Special features This program, established in 1976, honors Professor E.D. Bergmann, an organic chemist who played a leading role in initiating the establishment of the BSF.

Limitations In the event that no BSF grantee meets the level of excellence required in this program, none of these grants will be made that year.

Number awarded Varies each year.

[1097]
PROFESSOR HENRY NEUFELD MEMORIAL RESEARCH GRANTS

United States-Israel Binational Science Foundation
2 Alharizi Street
P.O.B. 7677
Jerusalem 91076
Israel
972 2 561 7314 Fax: 972 2 563 3287
E-mail: bsf@vms.huji.ac.il
Web site: www.bsf.org.il

Purpose To provide a supplemental award to scientists who have received new grants in the health or life sciences from the United States–Israel Binational Science Foundation (BSF).

Eligibility No separate application is necessary for these grants. All scientists from the United States and Israel who receive BSF Research Grants in the health or life sciences automatically become candidates for these grants.

Financial data The stipend, paid in Israeli currency, is equivalent to $10,000.

Duration 1 year.

Special features This program, established in 1987, honors Professor Henry Neufeld, an internationally prominent cardiologist who served continuously on the BSF Board of Governors from its charter meeting in 1973 until his death in December, 1986.

Number awarded 1 each year.

[1098]
RHODES UNIVERSITY POSTDOCTORAL FELLOWSHIPS

Rhodes University
Attn: Dean of Research Division
P.O. Box 94
Grahamstown 6140
South Africa
27 46 603 8179 Fax: 27 46 622 8444
E-mail: pgfinaid-admin@ru.ac.za
Web site: www.rhodes.ac.za/pgfunding

Purpose To provide funding to recent postdoctorates who are interested in conducting research at Rhodes University in South Africa.

Eligibility This program is open to postdoctorates in any discipline who are interested in conducting research at Rhodes University. Although there is no age restriction, applicants must hold a recently-awarded doctoral degree from an institution recognized as appropriate to the discipline for which the fellowship is sought. Applicants must demonstrate exceptional merit as evidenced by the quality and extent of publications or other recognized forms of achievement relevant to their discipline. Selection is based strictly on merit, without regard to race, gender, religion, or country of origin.

Financial data Fellows receive 55,000 rand per year plus an allowance of up to 5,000 rand for research and travel expenses.

Duration 1 year; may be renewed for up to 2 additional years.

Number awarded Varies each year.

Deadline July of each year.

[1099]
SAMUEL H. KRESS FOUNDATION FELLOWSHIP

American Schools of Oriental Research
Attn: Administrative Director
656 Beacon Street, Fifth Floor
Boston, MA 02215-2010
(617) 353-6570   Fax: (617) 353-6575
E-mail: asor@bu.edu
Web site: www.asor.org

Purpose To provide financial support to graduate students in selected areas of the arts or humanities who are interested in conducting dissertation research at the Albright Institute of Archaeological Research (AIAR) in Jerusalem.

Eligibility Graduate students in art history, architecture, or archaeology are eligible to apply for this award if they would benefit from conducting dissertation-related research at the AIAR. Applicants must be U.S. citizens or North American citizens studying at U.S. institutions.

Financial data The award is $16,500, of which $9,800 is paid to the recipient as a stipend and $6,700 is paid to the institute (to cover the recipient's room and half of the recipient's board).

Duration 10 months.

Special features Funding for this fellowship is provided by the Samuel H. Kress Foundation.

Limitations Fellows must reside at the AIAR in Jerusalem for the duration of the program. They are expected to conduct a seminar or workshop in their area of specialization and participate in the academic program of the institute. The award may not be used in the summer. Recipients must submit a written report within 2 months of completing the program; a portion of the stipend is withheld until the report is received. An acknowledgement of support must be included in published reports of the project.

Number awarded 1 each year.

Deadline October of each year.

[1100]
SAMUEL H. KRESS JOINT ATHENS–JERUSALEM FELLOWSHIP

American Schools of Oriental Research
Attn: Administrative Director
656 Beacon Street, Fifth Floor
Boston, MA 02215-2010
(617) 353-6570   Fax: (617) 353-6575
E-mail: asor@bu.edu
Web site: www.asor.org

Purpose To provide financial support to graduate students in selected areas of the arts or humanities who are interested in conducting dissertation research at the Albright Institute of Archaeological Research (AIAR) in Jerusalem and the American School of Classical Studies at Athens (ASCSA).

Eligibility Doctoral students in art history, architecture, archaeology or classical studies are eligible to apply for this award if they would benefit from conducting dissertation-related research at the AIAR and the ASCSA. Applicants must be U.S. citizens or North American citizens studying at U.S. institutions.

Financial data The award is $15,000, of which $8,300 is paid to the recipient as a stipend, $3,350 is paid to AIAR for room and half-board, and $3,350 is paid to ASCSA for room and board.

Duration 10 months: 5 months in Athens and 5 months in Jerusalem.

Special features Funding for this fellowship is provided by the Samuel H. Kress Foundation. Information is also available from ASCSA at 6-8 Charlton Street, Princeton, NJ 08540-5232, (609) 683-0800, Fax: (609) 924-0578.

Limitations Fellows must reside at the AIAR in Jerusalem for 5 months and the ASCSA (in Athens) for 5 months. The fellowship period should be continuous, without frequent trips outside Greece and Israel. The award may not be used in the summer. Recipients must submit a written report within 2 months of completing the program; a portion of the stipend is withheld until the report is received. An acknowledgement of support must be included in published reports of the project.

Number awarded 1 each year.

Deadline October of each year.

[1101]
SENEGAL FULBRIGHT TEACHER EXCHANGE

U.S. Department of State
c/o Graduate School, USDA
600 Maryland Avenue, S.W., Room 320
Washington, DC 20024-2520
(202) 314-3520   Fax: (202) 479-6806
E-mail: fulbright@grad.usda.gov
Web site: www.grad.usda.gov/International/ftep.html

Purpose To promote mutual understanding between the people of the United States and the people of Senegal through a teacher exchange program.

Eligibility This program is open to teachers (grades 7 through 12) who can teach English as a foreign language and who are interested in teaching in Senegal. Applicants must 1) be U.S. citizens; 2) hold at least a bachelor's degree; 3) be fluent in English; 4) have a current full-time teaching assignment in the U.S. or a territory; 5) have the approval of their school administration; 6) have at least 3 years of full-time experience; and 7) not have participated in a Fulbright Teacher Exchange longer than 8 weeks during the last 2 years. Fluency in French is required. Teaching couples may apply. However, because of the limited number of positions available and, often, the lack of foreign candidate pairs with similar qualifications for interchanges, it may not be possible to arrange suitable assignments in the same locality or to place both teachers. Preference is given to applicants who have not participated previously in the program and may be given to applicants who have not previously lived in Senegal. Geographic distribution of awards within the United States is also a factor in selection. This program does not discriminate on the basis of race, color, religion, age, sex, or national origin and encourages the applications of members of minority communities. Other considerations being equal, veterans are given preference.

Financial data Participants receive round-trip transportation for the exchange teacher only and housing provided by the Senegalese Ministry of Education or the local institution. They must obtain a leave of absence with pay from their jobs in the United States. The U.S. school must agree to accept a Senegalese teacher who must secure a leave of absence with pay; the Senegalese teacher receives a stipend, but no additional cost accrues to the U.S. school.

Duration 10 months, beginning in September.

Special features This program is sponsored by the Bureau of Educational and Cultural Affairs of the U.S. Department of State and administered by the Graduate School, USDA.

Limitations This program provides for the direct exchange of teaching assignments between Senegal and the United States. Applicants selected for exchange must attend orientation programs of the sponsoring agencies in the United States or abroad.

Number awarded 3 to 4 each year.

Deadline October of each year.

[1102]
SHALEM CENTER GRADUATE FELLOWSHIPS

Shalem Center
Attn: Research Department
22A Hatzfira Street
Jerusalem 93102
Israel
972 2 566 2202   Fax: 972 2 566 1171
E-mail: fellowship@shalem.org.il
Web site: www.shalem.org.il

Purpose To provide funding to graduate students from any country who wish to conduct research in Israel on Jewish national life and culture.

Eligibility Applicants must hold a baccalaureate or higher degree in history, philosophy, law, political science, economics, literature, or other relevant disciplines. They must be interested in conducting research in Israel on a particular problem or set of problems in Jewish public life, such as constitutional reform, economic deregulation, education, government reform, Zionist theory and history, Israeli foreign policy, Jewish social thought, Israeli culture and cultural institutions, or other topics relevant to the public life of the Jewish nation. A working knowledge of Hebrew is required. Selection is based on demonstrated academic ability, intellectual creativity, and research and writing ability.

Financial data The stipend is $15,000 per year.

Duration 1 year, beginning in September.

Special features The Shalem Center was founded in 1994. It may also be contacted at 1140 Connecticut Avenue, N.W., Washington, DC 20036, (202) 887-1270.

Limitations There is a nonrefundable $40 application fee.

Number awarded Approximately 8 each year.

Deadline January of each year.

[1103]
SHALEM CENTER SENIOR FELLOWSHIPS

Shalem Center
Attn: Research Department
22A Hatzfira Street
Jerusalem 93102
Israel
972 2 566 2202   Fax: 972 2 566 1171
E-mail: fellowship@shalem.org.il
Web site: www.shalem.org.il

Purpose To provide funding to established scholars from any country who are interested in writing a book based on research in Israel on Jewish national life and culture.

Eligibility This program is open to scholars who are interested in conducting research in Israel that will lead to a book on a topic in Jewish public life, such as Zionist theory and history, Jewish social thought and religion, Jewish and Israeli literature and culture, legal and constitutional issues, political philosophy, educational policy, economics, foreign policy, and other issues relevant to the public life of the Jewish nation. Books sponsored under this program may be written in either English or Hebrew. Selection is based on the intrinsic interest, value, and relevance of the proposed book; the candidate's demonstrated ability to conduct original research and write compellingly; the candidate's history of completing projects according to agreed schedules; and the candidate's ability to contribute to the intellectual community of the sponsoring organization.

Financial data The stipend is based on the proven capabilities of the applicant and the requirements of the project.

Duration 1 to 2 years.

Special features The Shalem Center was founded in 1994. It may also be contacted at 1140 Connecticut Avenue, N.W., Washington, DC 20036, (202) 887-1270.

Number awarded 1 or more each year.

Deadline April of each year.

[1104]
SHORT-TERM TRAVEL GRANTS FOR CENTRAL AND EASTERN EUROPE AND EURASIA

International Research & Exchanges Board
1616 H Street, N.W.
Washington, DC 20006
(202) 628-8188   Fax: (202) 628-8189
E-mail: irex@irex.org
Web site: www.irex.org

Purpose To allow U.S. scholars to pursue their individual research or other activities in the social sciences or humanities in central Europe, eastern Europe, or Eurasia.

Eligibility Applicants must be U.S. citizens who have the Ph.D. or an equivalent professional doctoral degree and need support for humanities or social sciences projects. Proposals may include library or archival research, carrying out interviews, presentations at scholarly conferences, invited lectures or consultations, or collaborative projects (such as joint publications or comparative surveys). The project must involve central Europe, eastern Europe, or Eurasia, including, in special circumstances, Iran or Turkey.

Financial data Grants up to a maximum of $3,000 may be awarded; funds may be used for round-trip airfare on a U.S.

flag carrier, per diem up to $100 per day for food and lodging, conference registration fees, and visa fees.

Duration Up to 60 days; a per diem will be allowed only up to 14 days.

Special features The International Research & Exchanges Board (IREX) was established in 1968 at the request of U.S. universities by the American Council of Learned Societies (ACLS) and the Social Science Research Council (SSRC) to administer research exchange programs with the socialist countries of eastern Europe and the former Soviet republics. This program is funded by the U.S. Department of State as a Title VIII program and the National Endowment for the Humanities (NEH).

Number awarded Varies each year; in a recent round, 32 of these grants were awarded, including 4 funded by NEH and 28 by the Department of State.

Deadline January or May of each year.

[1105]
SIDNEY M. EDELSTEIN INTERNATIONAL FELLOWSHIP

Chemical Heritage Foundation
Attn: Fellowship Coordinator
315 Chestnut Street
Philadelphia, PA 19106-2702
(215) 925-2222, ext. 232   Fax: (215) 925-1954
E-mail: fellowships@chemheritage.org
Web site: www.chemheritage.org

Purpose To provide funding to scholars conducting research on the history of chemical science and technology.

Eligibility Established scholars who are conducting research in the history of the chemical sciences and technologies and are interested in using the resources at the Chemical Heritage Foundation (CHF) in Philadelphia, Pennsylvania and the Edelstein Center for History and Philosophy of Science, Technology, and Medicine in Jerusalem, Israel are eligible to apply.

Financial data The stipend is at least $36,000. A travel allowance is also available.

Duration 9 months, from September to May.

Special features During the residency in Jerusalem, the recipient has access to the resources of the Edelstein Library, which is especially strong in all aspects of chemical history. During the residency in Philadelphia, the recipient has access to the Othmer Library of Chemical History and the Edgar Fahs Smith Collection. The fellowship may be held in conjunction with other research or sabbatical support.

Number awarded 1 each year.

Deadline November of each year.

[1106]
SIDNEY M. EDELSTEIN INTERNATIONAL STUDENTSHIP

Chemical Heritage Foundation
Attn: Fellowship Coordinator
315 Chestnut Street
Philadelphia, PA 19106-2702
(215) 925-2222, ext. 232   Fax: (215) 925-1954
E-mail: fellowships@chemheritage.org
Web site: www.chemheritage.org

Purpose To provide funding to doctoral students working on their dissertation in the history of chemical science and technology.

Eligibility Doctoral students who are researching and writing their dissertation on the history of the chemical sciences and technologies are eligible to apply. Applicants must have fulfilled all requirements for the Ph.D., except for the dissertation. They must wish to undertake a residency at the Chemical Heritage Foundation (CHF) in Philadelphia, Pennsylvania and a residency at the Hebrew University in Jerusalem, Israel.

Financial data The stipend is at least $16,000. A travel allowance is also available.

Duration 5 to 6 months in Philadelphia and 3 to 4 months in Israel.

Special features During the residency in Jerusalem, the recipient will have access to the resources of the Edelstein Library, which is especially strong in all aspects of chemical history. During the residency in Philadelphia, the recipient will have access to the CHF's Othmer Library of Chemical History and the Edgar Fahs Smith Collection at the University of Pennsylvania.

Number awarded 1 each year.

Deadline November of each year.

[1107]
SOUTH AFRICA FULBRIGHT TEACHER EXCHANGE

U.S. Department of State
c/o Graduate School, USDA
600 Maryland Avenue, S.W., Room 320
Washington, DC 20024-2520
(202) 314-3520   Fax: (202) 479-6806
E-mail: fulbright@grad.usda.gov
Web site: www.grad.usda.gov/International/ftep.html

Purpose To promote mutual understanding between the people of the United States and the people of South Africa through a teacher exchange program.

Eligibility This program is open to elementary, secondary, and 2-year college teachers who are interested in teaching in South Africa. Preference is given to teachers of mathematics, science, English, and social studies. Applicants must 1) be U.S. citizens; 2) hold at least a bachelor's degree; 3) be fluent in English; 4) have a current full-time teaching assignment in the U.S. or a territory; 5) have the approval of their school administration; 6) have at least 3 years of full-time experience; and 7) not have participated in a Fulbright Teacher Exchange longer than 8 weeks during the last 2 years. Teaching couples may apply. However, because of the limited number of positions available and, often, the lack of foreign candidate pairs with similar qualifications for interchanges, it may not be possible to arrange suitable assignments in the same locality or to place both teachers. Preference is given to applicants who have not participated previously in the program and may be given to applicants who have not previously lived in South Africa. Geographic distribution of awards within the United States is also a factor in selection. This program does not discriminate on the basis of race, color, religion, age, sex, or national origin and encourages the applications of members of minority communities. Other considerations being equal, veterans are given preference.

Financial data Only round-trip transportation is provided. Participants must obtain a leave of absence with pay from their jobs in the United States. The U.S. school must agree to accept a South African teacher who must secure a leave of absence with pay; the South African teacher receives a stipend, but no additional cost accrues to the U.S. school.

Duration 11 months, beginning in January.

Special features This program is sponsored by the Bureau of Educational and Cultural Affairs of the U.S. Department of State and administered by the Graduate School, USDA.

Limitations This program provides for the direct exchange of teaching assignments between South Africa and the United States. Applicants selected for exchange must attend orientation programs of the sponsoring agencies in the United States or abroad.

Number awarded 3 to 5 each year.

Deadline October of each year.

[1108]
SUITCASE FUND

Dance Theater Workshop
Attn: Director and Producer of Inter/National Programs
219 West 19th Street
New York, NY 10011-4079
(212) 691-6500   Fax: (212) 633-1974
E-mail: cathy@dtw.org
Web site: www.dtw.org

Purpose To promote the performing arts through an international exchange.

Eligibility To promote cultural equity in a pluralistic America, the fund helps artists of all backgrounds and origins to maintain access to the contemporary arts of their homelands. Applicants should be independent professional artists working without the support of major institutions. They must be seeking to study, teach, collaborate, or perform in another part of the world.

Financial data The amount awarded varies, depending upon the needs of the recipient.

Special features Participating artists and producers are placed in Africa, Asia, Latin America, and the Caribbean, as well as Europe. Funding for this program is provided by the Rockefeller Foundation, the Trust for Mutual Understanding, and the Asian Cultural Council.

Limitations The Fund does not function as an all-purpose emergency travel fund, nor will it duplicate the well-established initiatives of other producers or funders.

Deadline Applications may be submitted at any time.

[1109]
TARGET OF OPPORTUNITY FELLOWSHIPS

Institute of Current World Affairs, Inc.
Attn: Program Administrator
Wheelock House
4 West Wheelock Street
Hanover, NH 03755
(603) 643-5548   Fax: (603) 643-9599
E-mail: icwa@valley.net
Web site: www.icwa.org

Purpose To provide opportunities for independent research in selected foreign countries or on designated topics.

Eligibility Individuals who have completed their formal education are eligible to apply if they are interested in conducting research in either an area of their own choice or in selected areas (Burma, Korea, Japan, Iran, southeast Asia, south Asia, Siberia, Poland, north Africa, or the former East Germany) or on designated topics (the seas, fresh water). Generally, applicants must be under the age of 36 and have good command of written and spoken English.

Financial data The institute provides full support for the fellows and their families.

Duration At least 2 years.

Limitations Fellowships are not awarded to support work toward academic degrees, to write books, or to undertake specific studies or research projects. Fellows are required to submit monthly reports.

Number awarded 1 or more each year.

Deadline March or August of each year.

[1110]
TEL AVIV UNIVERSITY POSTDOCTORAL AWARD

Institute of International Education
Attn: Student Programs Division
809 United Nations Plaza
New York, NY 10017-3580
(212) 984-5330   Fax: (212) 984-5325
Web site: www.iie.org/fulbright

Purpose To provide financial assistance to postdoctorates who are interested in conducting research in designated fields at Tel Aviv University in Israel.

Eligibility Candidates must meet the general eligibility requirements for Fulbright grants and, in addition, must have received their Ph.D. prior to their arrival in Israel. Preference is given to scholars up to 35 years of age who have not previously studied or conducted research in Israel and who completed their doctorate within the past 2 years. The fields of study are cinema, east Asian studies, Indian religion and philosophy, and mass communications.

Financial data This program provides international travel, a settling-in allowance, and a stipend that varies with the duration of the award and the number of dependents. Recently, the stipends for recipients without accompanying dependents were approximately $21,000 for 10 months or $42,400 for 21 months; for recipients with 3 or more dependents, the stipends averaged $36,900 for 10 months or $74,600 for 21 months. The awards for 21 months include an extra round-trip airline ticket.

Duration Up to 21 months.

Limitations Continuation of the award beyond the first academic year is dependent upon evidence of satisfactory progress.

Number awarded 1 each year.

Deadline October of each year.

[1111]
TURKEY FULBRIGHT EXCHANGE OF ADMINISTRATORS

U.S. Department of State
c/o Graduate School, USDA
600 Maryland Avenue, S.W., Room 320
Washington, DC 20024-2520
(202) 314-3520   Fax: (202) 479-6806
E-mail: fulbright@grad.usda.gov
Web site: www.grad.usda.gov/International/ftep.html

Purpose To promote mutual understanding between the people of the United States and the people of Turkey through an educational administrator exchange program.

Eligibility This program is open to administrators from elementary schools, secondary schools, and 2-year colleges who are interested in working with administrators in Turkey (and vice versa). The assignment may be in the areas of personnel administration, student affairs, or educational policy. Applicants must 1) be U.S. citizens; 2) hold at least a bachelor's degree; 3) be fluent in English; 4) have a current full-time administrative assignment in the U.S. or a territory; 5) have the approval of their school administration; 6) have at least 3 years of full-time experience; and 7) not have participated in a Fulbright Teacher Exchange longer than 8 weeks during the last 2 years. Preference is given to applicants who have not participated previously in the program and may be given to applicants who have not previously lived in Turkey. Geographic distribution of awards within the United States is also a factor in selection. This program does not discriminate on the basis of race, color, religion, age, sex, or national origin and encourages the applications of members of minority communities. Other considerations being equal, veterans are given preference.

Financial data Round-trip economy airfare and a $3,000 cost of living stipend are provided. Participants must obtain a leave of absence with or without pay from their jobs in the United States.

Duration 6 weeks, twice during the year.

Special features This program is sponsored by the Bureau of Educational and Cultural Affairs of the U.S. Department of State and administered by the Graduate School, USDA.

Limitations Dependents are not permitted in this program. Applicants selected for exchange must attend orientation programs of the sponsoring agencies in the United States or abroad.

Number awarded Varies each year.

Deadline October of each year.

[1112]
TURKEY FULBRIGHT TEACHER EXCHANGE

U.S. Department of State
c/o Graduate School, USDA
600 Maryland Avenue, S.W., Room 320
Washington, DC 20024-2520
(202) 314-3520   Fax: (202) 479-6806
E-mail: fulbright@grad.usda.gov
Web site: www.grad.usda.gov/International/ftep.html

Purpose To promote mutual understanding between the people of the United States and the people of Turkey through a teacher exchange program.

Eligibility This program is open to teachers (grades 7 through 12) of English as a second language, mathematics, English, or science who are interested in teaching in Turkey. Applicants must 1) be U.S. citizens; 2) hold at least a bachelor's degree; 3) be fluent in English; 4) have a current full-time teaching assignment in the U.S. or a territory; 5) have the approval of their school administration; 6) have at least 3 years of full-time experience; and 7) not have participated in a Fulbright Teacher Exchange longer than 8 weeks during the last 2 years. Fluency in Turkish is not required although some ability is useful; the language of instruction is English. Teaching couples may apply. However, because of the limited number of positions available and, often, the lack of foreign candidate pairs with similar qualifications for interchanges, it may not be possible to arrange suitable assignments in the same locality or to place both teachers. Preference is given to applicants who have not participated previously in the program and may be given to applicants who have not previously lived in Turkey. Geographic distribution of awards within the United States is also a factor in selection. This program does not discriminate on the basis of race, color, religion, age, sex, or national origin and encourages the applications of members of minority communities. Other considerations being equal, veterans are given preference.

Financial data Round-trip transportation for the exchange teacher only and housing are provided. Participants must obtain a leave of absence with pay from their jobs in the United States. The U.S. school must agree to accept a teacher from Turkey who must secure a leave of absence with pay; the Turkish teacher receives a stipend, but no additional cost accrues to the U.S. school.

Duration 9 months, beginning in September.

Special features This program is sponsored by the Bureau of Educational and Cultural Affairs of the U.S. Department of State and administered by the Graduate School, USDA.

Limitations This program provides for the direct exchange of teaching assignments between Turkey and the United States. Applicants selected for exchange must attend orientation programs of the sponsoring agencies in the United States or abroad.

Number awarded 5 each year.

Deadline October of each year.

[1113]
TURKEY M.A. TEFL DIRECTOR

Council for International Exchange of Scholars
3007 Tilden Street, N.W., Suite 5L
Washington, DC 20008-3009
(202) 686-6246   Fax: (202) 362-3442
E-mail: scholars@cies.iie.org
Web site: www.iie.org/cies

Purpose To provide funding to American scholars interested in administering the master's degree program in Teaching English as a Foreign Language (TEFL) in Turkey.

Eligibility This program is open to U.S. citizens who have a Ph.D. and at least 5 years of teaching experience in applied linguistics, research methodology, or ESL methodology (quantitative and qualitative). Applicants must be interested in administering a master's degree program in TEFL at Bilkent University in Ankara, Turkey. English is sufficient for lecturing.

Financial data The program provides a base stipend of $1,500 to $2,000 per month, a maintenance allowance of $500 per month, housing or a housing allowance, airfare from hometown to Ankara for grantee and 1 dependent, a $250 excess baggage allowance, a $500 relocation allowance, tuition reimbursement for 1 K-12 dependent, and a 1-time incidentals allowance of $200.

Duration 11 months.

Special features This is a Fulbright scholar program, sponsored by the Bureau of Educational and Cultural Affairs of the U.S. Department of State and administered by the Council for International Exchange of Scholars. The recipient administers the master's program in TEFL, teaches 2 courses in requested areas of specialization, advises thesis students, and assists with curriculum planning and program development.

Number awarded 1 each year.

Deadline July of each year.

[1114]
UNITED STATES–ISRAEL BINATIONAL SCIENCE FOUNDATION RESEARCH GRANTS

United States-Israel Binational Science Foundation
2 Alharizi Street
P.O.B. 7677
Jerusalem 91076
Israel
972 2 561 7314   Fax: 972 2 563 3287
E-mail: bsf@vms.huji.ac.il
Web site: www.bsf.org.il

Purpose To promote and support cooperative research by members of the U.S. and Israeli scientific communities.

Eligibility Israeli and American principal investigators who hold a doctoral degree or its equivalent may submit applications through an institution of higher learning, government research institution, hospital, or other nonprofit research organization. Proposals cannot be submitted by for-profit or industrial organizations, although the U.S. principal investigator may be affiliated with such an organization. The principal investigator may be either an American or an Israeli, but the research proposal must involve planned, active collaboration between scientists of both nations. Research must be performed in Israel. Areas of research currently emphasized include health and life sciences, natural sciences, energy and the environment, and social and behavioral sciences.

Financial data Budget requests may include the purchase of specific equipment required for the proposed project, supplies, travel both within Israel and between the collaborating laboratories if required for the research, and preparation of reports. Principal investigators of either country are not entitled to receive any part of their salary or supplement to their salary, nor are other scientists on the full-time paid staff of the grantee institution. Part-time scientists and auxiliary personnel may receive salaries based on the proportion of their time devoted to the project. A uniform rate of 25 percent of salaries may be requested for the sponsoring research institution. The average grant is $50,000 per year; proposals requesting a total budget in excess of $230,000 are not accepted.

Duration 1 year; may be renewed for 2 additional years.

Special features The Binational Science Foundation (BSF) was established by the U.S. government and the government of Israel in 1972, to promote and support cooperation between those countries in scientific and technological research. Its annual budget is derived from interest on an endowment fund established by equal contributions of both governments. The base of operations is in Israel, but the Board of Governors consists of 5 Americans and 5 Israelis.

Number awarded Varies each year.

Deadline November of each year.

[1115]
UNIVERSITY OF CAPE TOWN POSTDOCTORAL RESEARCH FELLOWSHIPS

University of Cape Town
Department of Research Development
Attn: Research Information Officer
Private Bag
Rondebosch 7701
South Africa
27 21 650 2892   Fax: 27 21 689 7781
E-mail: reals@bremner.uct.ac.za
Web site: www.uct.ac.za

Purpose To provide financial assistance to scholars interested in conducting research in South Africa.

Eligibility Postdoctorates from any country are eligible to apply if they are interested in conducting research at the University of Cape Town. Preference is given to recently qualified applicants who are not yet in academic or research posts and who have not previously held postdoctoral appointments. There are no restrictions on discipline or field of research, but applications from other African countries and from women are particularly encouraged. The proposed research project must be in an area that has a strong base at the university.

Financial data The stipend for fellows from abroad is 75,000 rands per year; a relocation allowance of R12,000 is also provided. Fellows from within South Africa receive an annual stipend of R54,000.

Duration Up to 12 months.

Number awarded 1 or more each year.

Deadline June of each year.

[1116]
U.S.-EGYPT JOINT SCIENCE AND TECHNOLOGY PROGRAM

National Science Foundation
Directorate for Social, Behavioral, and Economic Sciences
Attn: Division of International Programs
4201 Wilson Boulevard, Room 935
Arlington, VA 22230
(703) 292-8707   Fax: (703) 292-9176
TDD: (703) 292-5090   E-mail: ptsuchit@nsf.gov
Web site: www.usembassy.egnet.net/usegypt/joint-st.htm

Purpose To provide funding to American scientists interested in conducting collaborative research in Egypt.

Eligibility Eligible to apply are scientists from the United States interested in conducting research in collaboration with an Egyptian counterpart. The proposed research must be in the field of biotechnology, energy, environmental technologies, information technology, manufacturing technologies, or standards and metrology. The proposal must describe the nature and degree of cooperation between both partners and clearly define the role of each. It must also clearly demonstrate 1) the significance and mutual benefit of the proposed activity to the United States and Egypt; 2) how the activity will benefit the private sector and, if appropriate, how the technology will be transferred to the private sector; 3) the technical merit and competence of the cooperators; and 4) the feasibility of the project within the proposed time frame and budget.

Financial data The maximum grant is $50,000. Allowable costs include travel and per diem, materials and supplies, equipment, publications, temporary postdoctoral or graduate student assistance, delivery and shipping costs, and other costs associated with the performance of the project. Indirect costs are discouraged, but if necessary, infrastructure costs up to 14 percent of direct costs may be considered.

Duration 2 to 3 years.

Special features Information is also available from Vickie Alaimo Alexander, American Embassy/ECPO, 8 Kamal El Din Salah Street, Garden City, Cairo, Egypt, 20 2 797-2925, Fax: 20 2 797-3150, E-mail: alexanderva@state.gov. This program is funded by the U.S. Agency for International Development, with additional support from the National Institutes of Health, the Department of Agriculture, the Department of Energy, and the Environmental Protection Agency.

Number awarded Varies each year.

Deadline October of each year.

[1117]
USIA ASSOCIATE FELLOWSHIPS AT AIAR

American Schools of Oriental Research
Attn: Administrative Director
656 Beacon Street, Fifth Floor
Boston, MA 02215-2010
(617) 353-6570   Fax: (617) 353-6575
E-mail: asor@bu.edu
Web site: www.asor.org

Purpose To provide the opportunity for American scholars to engage in research in archaeology and Near Eastern history at the Albright Institute of Archaeological Research (AIAR) in Jerusalem, Israel.

Eligibility U.S. citizens who are senior or junior scholars in archaeology or Near Eastern history may apply for these fellowships. They should be interested in conducting research at AIAR.

Financial data The awards provide for payment of administrative fees.

Special features Funding for this program is provided by the United States Information Agency (USIA).

Number awarded These awards are provided to 6 senior and 7 junior fellows each year.

Deadline April of each year.

[1118]
USIA LONG-TERM JUNIOR FELLOWSHIPS AT AIAR

American Schools of Oriental Research
Attn: Administrative Director
656 Beacon Street, Fifth Floor
Boston, MA 02215-2010
(617) 353-6570   Fax: (617) 353-6575
E-mail: asor@bu.edu
Web site: www.asor.org

Purpose To provide the opportunity for American predoctoral students and recent postdoctorates to conduct research on Near Eastern studies at the Albright Institute of Archaeological Research (AIAR) in Jerusalem.

Eligibility Proposals must be for research to be conducted at AIAR. They may deal with any area of Near Eastern studies (from prehistory to modern), including religions and rituals, the economies and demographics of historical Near Eastern societies, Bedouin ethnography, and studies in ancient technologies. In addition, the program may support research in AIAR's more traditional fields of history, language, architecture, art history, and archaeology. Applicants must be U.S. citizens and either doctoral students in ABD status or recent Ph.D. recipients. Membership in the American Schools of Oriental Research (ASOR) is advised but not required.

Financial data The maximum stipend is $16,000, of which $9,300 is paid directly to the appointee and the remainder is applied toward room and half-board at AIAR.

Duration 5 or 10 months.

Special features Funding for this program is provided by the United States Information Agency (USIA).

Limitations Fellows must reside at AIAR for the duration of the program. They are expected to participate in the scholarly and cultural activities of the AIAR community while in residence. If the residency extends past the stipulated term, regular room and board rates will be charged. Recipients must submit a written report within 1 month of completing the program; a portion of the stipend is withheld until the report is received. An acknowledgement of support must be included in published reports of the project.

Number awarded 3 each year.

Deadline October of each year.

[1119]
USIA/CAORC FELLOWSHIPS AT ACOR

American Schools of Oriental Research
Attn: Administrative Director
656 Beacon Street, Fifth Floor
Boston, MA 02215-2010
(617) 353-6571　　　　　　　　Fax: (617) 353-6575
E-mail: acor@bu.edu
Web site: www.asor.org

Purpose To provide funding to predoctoral students and postdoctoral scholars who wish to conduct research in Near Eastern studies at the American Center of Oriental Research (ACOR) in Amman, Jordan.

Eligibility This program is open to U.S. citizens who are predoctoral students and postdoctoral scholars in all fields of the humanities or social sciences that relate to Near Eastern studies. Applicants must be interested in conducting research at ACOR. Membership in the American Schools of Oriental Research (ASOR) is advised but not required.

Financial data The maximum award is $17,000.

Duration From 2 to 6 months.

Special features Funding for this program is provided by the United States Information Agency (USIA) and the Council of American Overseas Research Centers (CAORC).

Limitations Fellows must reside at ACOR for the duration of the program. They are expected to participate in the scholarly and cultural activities of the ACOR community while in residence. If the residency extends past the stipulated term, regular room and board rates will be charged. Recipients must submit a written report within 2 months of completing the program; a portion of the stipend is withheld until the report is received. An acknowledgement of support must be included in published reports of the project.

Number awarded 6 or more each year.

Deadline January of each year.

[1120]
USIA/CAORC SENIOR FELLOWSHIPS AT ACOR

American Schools of Oriental Research
Attn: Administrative Director
656 Beacon Street, Fifth Floor
Boston, MA 02215-2010
(617) 353-6571　　　　　　　　Fax: (617) 353-6575
E-mail: acor@bu.edu
Web site: www.asor.org

Purpose To provide funding to senior postdoctoral scholars who wish to conduct research in Near Eastern studies at the American Center of Oriental Research (ACOR) in Amman, Jordan.

Eligibility This program is open to U.S. citizens who are postdoctoral specialists in all fields of the humanities or social sciences that relate to Near Eastern studies. Applicants must be interested in conducting research at ACOR. Membership in the American Schools of Oriental Research (ASOR) is advised but not required.

Financial data The maximum award is $26,700.

Duration From 2 to 6 months.

Special features Funding for this program is provided by the United States Information Agency (USIA) and the Council of American Overseas Research Centers (CAORC).

Limitations Fellows must reside at ACOR for the duration of the program. They are expected to participate in the scholarly and cultural activities of the ACOR community while in residence. If the residency extends past the stipulated term, regular room and board rates will be charged. Recipients must submit a written report within 2 months of completing the program; a portion of the stipend is withheld until the report is received. An acknowledgement of support must be included in published reports of the project.

Number awarded 1 or more each year.

Deadline January of each year.

[1121]
VAAIDA-BARD POSTDOCTORAL FELLOWSHIPS

United States-Israel Binational Agricultural Research and
　　Development Fund
Department of Agriculture
Agricultural Research Service
Attn: Office of International Research Programs
5601 Sunnyside Avenue, Room 4-2104
Beltsville, MD 20705-5134
(301) 504-4584　　　　　　　　Fax: (301) 504-4619
E-mail: mlg@ars.usda.gov
Web site: www.bard-isus.com

Purpose To promote cooperative agricultural research between postdoctoral fellows from 1 country (United States or Israel) and senior scientists from the other country.

Eligibility Applicants must be American or Israeli citizens. They should have fulfilled the requirements for a Ph.D. degree within the last 3 years. They must be interested in participating in cooperative agricultural research with scientists from the other country. Selection is based on scientific merit of the proposed research, importance of the research to agriculture, suitability of the candidate, and suitability of the proposed senior scientist and laboratory.

Financial data The stipend is $30,000 for modest living expenses plus $2,000 for travel expenses; fellows with children receive an additional stipend of $5,000. The host institution receives a small allowance (up to $3,000) to offset operating expenses of the research.

Duration 1 year, may be renewed if the host institution agrees to pay half the costs on a matching basis.

Special features The United States–Israel Binational Agricultural Research and Development Fund (BARD) was established in 1977 by the governments of the United States and Israel, for the purpose of promoting and supporting research and development in agriculture to mutual benefit both countries. Applications may be submitted to the BARD office in either the United States (address above) or Israel (P.O. Box 6, Bet Dagan 50250, telephone: 972 3 965 2244, Fax: 972 3 966 2506, E-mail: bard@bard-isus.com).

Limitations The research program must be implemented within 6 months after receiving the award. Fellows may not receive funds from other sources that exceed 20 percent of the living expenses awarded by the BARD grant. A final report, signed by the fellow and the senior scientist, must be submitted not later than 2 months after termination of the fellowship.

Acknowledgement of BARD's support must be made in all publications that result from the supported research.
Deadline January of each year.

[1122]
WARA/WARC COLLABORATIVE SCHOLARS-IN-RESIDENCE FELLOWSHIP PROGRAM

West African Research Association
c/o University of Wisconsin
1414 Van Hise Hall
1220 Linden Drive
Madison, WI 53706
(608) 262-2487   Fax: (608) 262-4151
E-mail: emakward@facstaff.wisc.edu
Web site: polyglot.lss.wisc.edu/afrst/wara.html

Purpose To provide funding to faculty at North American institutions who are interested in participating in a collaborative research project at the West African Research Center (WARC) in Senegal with a scholar from that region.

Eligibility This program is open to scholars who have a doctorate or equivalent terminal degree and a permanent faculty or research position at a West African or North American institution of higher education. Applications must be submitted by a pair of researchers (1 from West Africa, 1 from North America) who are interested in conducting a collaborative research project at WARC. Their application must describe the history of their collaboration on the proposed project and summarize the significance of the research, the planned methodology, and the resulting publications. Priority is given to scholars who have already initiated collaborative projects and who require work time together in order to finish a manuscript, such as a book, book chapter, or journal article.

Financial data Each fellowship pays for round-trip transportation from the scholar's home institution to the WARC in Dakar, Senegal and provides a stipend of $5,000. The West African fellow also receives a supplementary stipend of $500 for materials (books, software, photocopies, etc.).

Duration 2 to 3 months.

Special features Information is also available from the West African Research Center, B.P. 5456 (Fann-Residence), Rue Ex Léon G. Damas, Dakar, Senegal, 221 8 24 20 62, Fax: 221 8 24 20 58, E-mail: atoure@mail.ucad.sn.

Limitations Fellows are required to be in residence at the WARC, where they are given office space with adequate research equipment and Internet access.

Number awarded 2 pairs of researchers are funded each year.

Deadline December of each year.

[1123]
WEIZMANN INSTITUTE OF SCIENCE POSTDOCTORAL FELLOWSHIPS

Weizmann Institute of Science
Feinberg Graduate School
P.O. Box 26
Rehovot 76100
Israel
972 8 934 3834   Fax: 972 8 934 4114
E-mail: nfinfo@weizmann.weizmann.ac.il
Web site: www.weizmann.ac.il

Purpose To provide funding to scientists who wish to conduct research at the Weizmann Institute in Israel.

Eligibility Citizens of any country who hold the Ph.D. (or its equivalent) in chemistry, life sciences, mathematics, physics, or science teaching are eligible to apply. They must have received their doctoral degree within 3 years of application. Candidates should contact in advance a sponsor in 1 of the research departments at the Weizmann Institute, since applications must be endorsed by the host department.

Financial data Fellows receive 6,958 Israeli shekels per month if single, IS 7,190 per month if married, and IS 7,344 per month if married with a child; $1,335 for participation in scientific meetings abroad; $100 to $200 for moving expenses; and reimbursement for at least a 1-way airplane ticket.

Duration 1 year; may be renewed for up to 1 additional year.

Number awarded A limited number each year.

Deadline May or December of each year.

[1124]
WEIZMANN INSTITUTE VISITING SCHOLAR PROGRAM

Weizmann Institute of Science
Feinberg Graduate School
P.O. Box 26
Rehovot 76100
Israel
972 8 934 3860   Fax: 972 8 934 1667
E-mail: rsmarjor@weizmann.weizmann.ac.il
Web site: www.weizmann.ac.il

Purpose To provide opportunities for scientists who would like a temporary appointment at the Weizmann Institute in Israel.

Eligibility Applicants may be from any country, but they must have earned a doctoral degree (or its equivalent) in the sciences and hold the rank of full professor at their home institution. They must be interested in lecturing and/or conducting research at the Weizmann Institute.

Financial data Fellows receive a stipend in accordance with the Weizmann Institute salary scale, round-trip airfare for the awardee and spouse, and rent-free housing.

Duration 2 months to 1 year.

Special features This program includes the following named positions: the Weston Visiting Scholar Program, the Erna and Jakob Michael Visiting Professorships, the Joseph Meyerhoff Visiting Professorship, the Rosi and Max Varon Visiting Professorship, and the Morris Belkin Visiting Professorship.

Deadline December of each year.

[1125]
WEST AFRICAN RESEARCH ASSOCIATION FELLOWSHIPS

West African Research Association
c/o University of Wisconsin
1414 Van Hise Hall
1220 Linden Drive
Madison, WI 53706
(608) 262-2487   Fax: (608) 262-4151
E-mail: emakward@facstaff.wisc.edu
Web site: polyglot.lss.wisc.edu/afrst/wara.html

Purpose To provide funding to pre- and postdoctoral scholars who are interested in teaching or conducting research in west Africa.

Eligibility This program is open to pre- and postdoctoral scholars who teach or are enrolled in graduate programs at institutions of higher education in the United States. Applicants must be interested in conducting research in Africa in order to 1) prepare a doctoral research proposal; 2) complete or elaborate upon earlier research; or 3) enhance their understanding of a particular topic to improve teaching effectiveness or broaden course offerings. To apply, they must submit an essay that describes the concept, methodology, and significance of their research project to their academic field or teaching profession.

Financial data Each fellowship pays for round-trip transportation to a west African country and provides a stipend of $5,000.

Duration 10 to 12 weeks.

Special features The West African Research Center in Dakar, Senegal assists in arranging academic contacts and affiliations and provides recommendations for lodging in the country chosen by the fellow. Funding for this program is provided by a grant from the U.S. Department of Education.

Number awarded 2 each year.

Deadline December of each year.

[1126]
ZIMBABWE FULBRIGHT TEACHER EXCHANGE

U.S. Department of State
c/o Graduate School, USDA
600 Maryland Avenue, S.W., Room 320
Washington, DC 20024-2520
(202) 314-3520   Fax: (202) 479-6806
E-mail: fulbright@grad.usda.gov
Web site: www.grad.usda.gov/International/ftep.html

Purpose To promote mutual understanding between the people of the United States and the people of Zimbabwe through a teacher exchange program.

Eligibility This program is open to teachers (grades 9 through 12) and 2-year college instructors of social studies and health/physical education who are interested in teaching in Zimbabwe. Applicants must 1) be U.S. citizens; 2) hold at least a bachelor's degree; 3) be fluent in English; 4) have a current full-time teaching assignment in the U.S. or a territory; 5) have the approval of their school administration; 6) have at least 3 years of full-time experience; and 7) not have participated in a Fulbright Teacher Exchange longer than 8 weeks during the last 2 years. Teaching couples may apply. However, because of the limited number of positions available and, often, the lack of foreign candidate pairs with similar qualifications for interchanges, it may not be possible to arrange suitable assignments in the same locality or to place both teachers. Preference is given to applicants who have not participated previously in the program and may be given to applicants who have not previously lived in Zimbabwe. Geographic distribution of awards within the United States is also a factor in selection. This program does not discriminate on the basis of race, color, religion, age, sex, or national origin and encourages the applications of members of minority communities. Other considerations being equal, veterans are given preference.

Financial data Round-trip transportation for the exchange teacher only and an educational materials allowance are provided. Participants must obtain a leave of absence with pay from their jobs in the United States. The U.S. school must agree to accept a teacher from Zimbabwe who must secure a leave of absence with pay; the Zimbabwean teacher receives a stipend, but no additional cost accrues to the U.S. school.

Duration 10 months, beginning in September.

Special features This program is sponsored by the Bureau of Educational and Cultural Affairs of the U.S. Department of State and administered by the Graduate School, USDA.

Limitations This program provides for the direct exchange of teaching assignments between Zimbabwe and the United States. Applicants selected for exchange must attend orientation programs of the sponsoring agencies in the United States or abroad.

Number awarded 2 each year.

Deadline October of each year.

[1127]
ZIONIST SONG COMPETITION

American Zionist Movement
633 Third Avenue
New York, NY 10017
(212) 318-6100   Fax: (212) 935-3578
E-mail: info@azm.org
Web site: www.azm.org

Purpose To recognize and reward (with a trip to Israel) the composers of outstanding original songs about Israel and the Jewish people.

Eligibility Songwriters may enter either the "amateur" or the "professional" category. A "professional" is anyone who performs regularly for pay and has produced for sale at least 1 audio cassette tape or CD or anyone who is employed full or part time as a cantor, cantorial soloist, or music educator; all other songwriters should enter the "amateur" category. The song submitted to the competition must be original, unpublished, and unrecorded. Lyrics may be original or taken from traditional textual sources; they must be in English and/or Hebrew. All entries must include sheet music for the song, lyrics to the song (typed, with translation, transliteration, and source citation, if applicable), an entry form, and the $18 entry fee. Songs are judged for quality of composition and text; quality of performance on tape is not considered. Finalists are selected from these submissions and invited to perform their songs at Hadassah's national convention.

Financial data Finalists are provided with lodging and meals the night of the concert and the following morning, as well as round-trip transportation. These expenses are covered for only

1 person per song, regardless of how many songwriters or performers there are for an entry. The winner in the "professional" category receives a round-trip ticket to Israel via El Al, plus $500. The winner in the "amateur" category receives a round-trip ticket to Israel via El Al.

Duration The competition is held annually.

Special features The winners' songs may be published and recorded by the American Zionist Movement.

Number awarded 2 each year: 1 professional and 1 amateur winner.

Deadline June of each year.

Oceania

Described in this section are 48 scholarships, fellowships, grants, loans, and/or internships open to American students (high school through doctoral), professionals, and postdoctorates that support research or creative activities in Antarctica, Australia, New Zealand, and the various Pacific Island nations. If you haven't already checked the "Any Foreign Country" chapter, be sure to do that next; identified there are 222 more sources of funding that can be used to support activities in Oceania (as well as other areas of the world).

[1128]
AFUW–WA FOUNDATION BURSARY

Australian Federation of University Women-West Australia
Attn: Bursary Liaison Officer
P.O. Box 48
Nedlands, WA 6909
Australia
Fax: 61 8 9386 3570
E-mail: afuwwa@cygnus.uwa.edu.au
Web site: cygnus.uwa.edu.au/~afuwwa

Purpose To provide funding to women interested in conducting doctoral research in Australia.

Eligibility Applicants may be women from any country who are completing a higher degree by research and who have a degree from a university in West Australia or are enrolled in a university there. Membership in the Australian Federation of University Women or a national federation or association of the International Federation of University Women (IFUW) is required, although nonmembers may apply if they pay a nonrefundable application fee.

Financial data The stipend is $A3,000; travel costs are not paid.

Duration Up to 1 year; nonrenewable.

Special features In the United States, the IFUW affiliate is the American Association of University Women (AAUW), 1111 16th Street, N.W., Washington, DC 20036-4873, (202) 785-7700, (800) 821-4364.

Limitations The application fee for nonmembers is $A20.

Number awarded 1 each year.

Deadline July of each year.

[1129]
ANTARCTIC RESEARCH PROGRAM

National Science Foundation
Attn: Office of Polar Programs
4201 Wilson Boulevard
Arlington, VA 22230
(703) 292-8030   TDD: (703) 292-5090
Web site: www.nsf.gov/od/opp

Purpose To provide funding for research related to Antarctica.

Eligibility This program is open to investigators at U.S. institutions, primarily universities and, to a lesser extent, federal agencies and other organizations. Applicants must be proposing to conduct research in the areas of aeronomy and astrophysics, biology and medicine, geology and geophysics, glaciology, ocean and climate systems, or environmental sciences. Proposals must involve research in Antarctica or related research and data analysis in the United States. The program particularly encourages proposals from women and minorities and welcomes proposals for research projects that include participation by undergraduates and high school students under guidelines established by cross-disciplinary programs of the National Science Foundation (NSF).

Financial data The amounts of the awards depend on the nature of the proposal and the availability of funds.

Special features The NSF operates 3 year-round research stations, additional research facilities and camps, airplanes, helicopters, various types of surface vehicles, and ships.

Number awarded Varies each year; recently, the program planned to make 110 awards with a total budget of $30 million for new and continuing awards.

Deadline May of each year.

[1130]
AUSTRALIAN BUREAU OF STATISTICS RESEARCH FELLOWSHIPS

Australian Bureau of Statistics
Attn: Information Consultancy
Chandler Street
P.O. Box 10
Belconnen, ACT 2616
Australia
61 2 6252 5848   Fax: 61 2 6252 7102
Web site: www.abs.gov.au

Purpose To provide funding to statisticians from any country who are interested in conducting research in Australia.

Eligibility Eligible to apply are statisticians from any country (although preference is given to Australian citizens/residents) who are interested in conducting research in statistical methodology, demography, economics, or technological applications at the Australian Bureau of Statistics in Canberra. Other research sites may also be considered.

Financial data Stipends range from $A28,000 to $A64,000 per year.

Duration Up to 1 year.

Number awarded Fellowships are offered only occasionally.

[1131]
AUSTRALIAN INSTITUTE OF ABORIGINAL AND TORRES STRAIT ISLANDER STUDIES RESEARCH GRANTS

Australian Institute of Aboriginal and Torres Strait Islander Studies
Attn: Research Administration Team
GPO Box 553
Canberra, ACT 2601
Australia
61 2 6246 1157   Fax: 61 2 6249 7714
E-mail: grants@aiatsis.gov.au
Web site: www.aiatsis.gov.au

Purpose To provide funding for research into any aspect of aboriginal Australia.

Eligibility This program is open to postdoctoral fellows, research officers (experienced researchers carrying out work of an independent nature), research assistants, and candidates for a Ph.D. degree. The proposed research may deal with any aspect of Australian indigenous studies, including anthropology, archaeology, arts, education, health, history, linguistics, or politics. Applicants should demonstrate Aboriginal community support for the proposed research (by a permit from the relevant Aboriginal community or land council to enter designated Aboriginal land to carry out the project or by endorsement of appropriate Aboriginal umbrella organizations). Overseas scholars are required to arrange affiliation with an appropriate Australian institution while carrying out research.

Financial data Grants are based on an annual salary rate of $A44,336 for persons holding a doctorate, $A36,633 for research officers, $A30,614 for research assistants, or $A17,071 for Ph.D. candidates. Applicants may also request funding for accommodations and expenses during transit, vehicle rental or private vehicle use, and living expenses. The total value of recent grants ranged from $A1,000 to $A40,000; the mean value was $A14,647 and the median value was $A12,573.

Special features All research projects should attempt to secure short-term and long-term benefit to aboriginal and Torres Strait Islander people. No research should be undertaken if it conflicts with the rights, wishes, beliefs, or freedom of the individual people who are the subjects of the research.

Number awarded Approximately 45 each year.

Deadline January of each year.

[1132]
AUSTRALIAN MUSEUM COLLECTION FELLOWSHIPS

Australian Museum
Attn: Associate Director
6 College Street
Sydney, NSW 2000
Australia
61 2 9320 6230   Fax: 61 2 9320 6015
E-mail: rogerm@austmus.gov.au
Web site: www.austmus.gov.au

Purpose To promote research using significant collections held by the Australian Museum.

Eligibility This program is open to postdoctorates and professionals from any country who are interested in conducting research (including relevant field work) on collections held by the museum for which there is no resident staff specialist. The fields of interest of the museum include natural history, paleontology, mineralogy and petrology, marine ecology, terrestrial ecology, and anthropology of Australia and neighboring regions. Each year collection managers are asked to identify specific fields in which applications for these fellowships might be given preference.

Financial data Awards up to $A400 per week are available to assist in meeting living costs, travel, and related research costs; they may not be used for salary payment.

Duration Up to 1 year.

Number awarded 1 or more each year.

Deadline February of each year.

[1133]
AUSTRALIAN MUSEUM POSTGRADUATE AWARDS

Australian Museum
Attn: Associate Director
6 College Street
Sydney, NSW 2000
Australia
61 2 9320 6230   Fax: 61 2 9320 6015
E-mail: rogerm@austmus.gov.au
Web site: www.austmus.gov.au

Purpose To provide financial assistance to graduate students interested in conducting research at the Australian Museum.

Eligibility This program is open to graduate students from any country who are interested in conducting research under the co-supervision of museum staff. Fields of interest include natural history, paleontology, mineralogy and petrology, marine ecology, terrestrial ecology, and anthropology of Australia and neighboring regions. Selection is based on the relevance of intended outcomes to the aims and objectives of the museum, the significance of the scientific contribution to the field of interest, the quality and clarity of the proposal, the feasibility of the project as a topic and in light of available resources, the adequacy and reasonableness of the proposed budget, the contribution or significance of the intended outcomes to the broader Australian society, the strength of recommendations from supervisors, and the quality of the student's summary academic record.

Financial data Stipends range from $A500 to $A2,500.

Duration The preferred period is about 6 weeks for doctoral candidates or less for those registered for lower degrees.

Number awarded 1 or more each year.

Deadline February of each year.

[1134]
AUSTRALIAN POSTDOCTORAL FELLOWSHIPS

Australian Research Council
Attn: Research Fellowships Scheme
Jerrabomberra Avenue and Hindmarsh Drive
Symonston
GPO Box 9880
Canberra, ACT 2601
Australia
61 2 6284 6600   Fax: 61 2 6284 6601
E-mail: ARC.Publications@detya.gov.au
Web site: www.arc.gov.au/grants/grants_fellow.htm

Purpose To provide opportunities for scholars from any country to undertake research of national significance in Australia.

Eligibility Applicants must have received a Ph.D. degree or the equivalent in any field (except clinical medicine or dentistry), have an excellent academic record, and present a written agreement with an institution in Australia to accommodate the candidate and host the project. No more than 3 years should have elapsed since the award of the Ph.D. Citizens of any nation may apply, although preference is given to Australians. Research may be conducted at any Australian higher education institution, private research institution, or government research organization which has the resources to support the research.

Financial data Stipends range from $A39,868 to $A42,796 per year and average $A41,332. A supplemental research grant of up to $A6,000 is available to cover the costs of equipment, travel, supplies, and assistance. Fellows coming from overseas also receive a relocation allowance, up to $A15,000 for scholars coming from the United States.

Duration 3 years; may not be renewed.

Number awarded 55 each year.

Deadline February of each year.

[1135]
AUSTRALIAN RESEARCH FELLOWSHIPS

Australian Research Council
Attn: Research Fellowships Scheme
Jerrabomberra Avenue and Hindmarsh Drive
Symonston
GPO Box 9880
Canberra, ACT 2601
Australia
61 2 6284 6600   Fax: 61 2 6284 6601
E-mail: ARC.Publications@detya.gov.au
Web site: www.arc.gov.au/grants/grants_fellow.htm

Purpose To provide opportunities for scholars from any country to undertake research of national significance to Australia.

Eligibility Applicants must have a Ph.D. degree or the equivalent in any field (except clinical medicine or dentistry), at least 3 but no more than 8 years of postdoctoral experience at the time of application, an excellent academic record, evidence of innovative research, and an agreement with an institution in Australia to accommodate the candidate and host the project. Citizens of any nation may apply, although preference is given to Australians. Research may be conducted at any Australian higher education institution or private research institution, but not at any research establishment that is substantially funded by the Commonwealth Government.

Financial data Stipends range from $A45,049 to $A53,497 per year and average $A49,273. A supplemental research grant of up to $A7,000 is available to cover the costs of equipment, travel, supplies, and assistance. Fellows coming from overseas also receive a relocation allowance, up to $A15,000 for scholars coming from the United States.

Duration 5 years; may not be renewed.

Number awarded 25 each year.

Deadline February of each year

[1136]
AUSTRALIAN SENIOR RESEARCH FELLOWSHIPS

Australian Research Council
Attn: Research Fellowships Scheme
Jerrabomberra Avenue and Hindmarsh Drive
Symonston
GPO Box 9880
Canberra, ACT 2601
Australia
61 2 6284 6600   Fax: 61 2 6284 6601
E-mail: ARC.Publications@detya.gov.au
Web site: www.arc.gov.au/grants/grants_fellow.htm

Purpose To support outstanding researchers with proven international reputations who are interested in undertaking research that is both of major importance in its field and of significant benefit to Australia.

Eligibility Applicants must possess a Ph.D. degree or the equivalent (in any field except clinical medicine or dentistry), have at least 8 years of research experience since the award of their Ph.D., and have international recognition as a leader in research. Citizens of any nation may apply, although preference is given to Australians. Research may be conducted at any Australian higher education institution or private research institution, but not at any research establishment that is substantially funded by the Commonwealth Government.

Financial data Stipends range from $A55,186 to $A83,593 per year and average $A65,578. Fellows coming from overseas also receive a relocation allowance, up to $A15,000 for scholars coming from the United States.

Duration 5 years; may not be renewed.

Number awarded 15 each year.

Deadline February of each year.

[1137]
DOREEN MCCARTHY BURSARY

Australian Federation of University Women-South Australia Inc. Trust Fund
Attn: Fellowships Trustee
GPO Box 634
Adelaide, SA 5001
Australia
61 8 8401 7124
E-mail: gferrara@scomhbr3.telstra.com.au
Web site: adminwww.flinders.edu.au/WomensInfo/AFUW.htm

Purpose To assist students interested in working on a graduate research degree at a university in South Australia.

Eligibility This program is open to men and women of any nationality studying at a university in South Australia. They should have completed at least 1 year of work on a master's or Ph.D. degree. Students who are in full-time paid employment or on fully-paid study leave are not eligible to apply. Selection is based primarily on academic merit, but financial need, the purpose for which the bursary will be used, and extracurricular activities are also considered.

Financial data The stipend is $A2,500, to be used for equipment, field trips, research expenses, thesis publication costs, and dependent care expenses.

Duration Up to 1 year.

Special features This fellowship may be held concurrently with other awards. Research may be conducted outside Australia as long as it is part of a program for a degree at the university in South Australia where the applicant is enrolled.

Number awarded At least 1 each year.

Deadline February of each year.

[1138]
DOROTHY CAMERON FELLOWSHIP

University of Sydney
Attn: School of Archaeology
Sydney, NSW 2006
Australia
61 2 9351 2364   Fax: 61 2 9351 6392
Web site: www.usyd.edu.au

Purpose To provide financial assistance for research at the University of Sydney on the role of women in prehistoric culture.

Eligibility This program is open to any person who wishes to conduct research at the University of Sydney on the role of women in the culture, rituals, and belief systems in prehistoric societies from the Paleolithic to the Bronze Age. Applicants are not required to be studying for a degree or diploma or to hold academic qualifications. Selection is based on the strength and quality of the proposed research; theoretically innovative and interdisciplinary proposals are especially encouraged. Preference is given to women applicants.

Financial data The grant is $A5,000.

Number awarded 1 each year.

[1139]
FOGARTY INTERNATIONAL RESEARCH COLLABORATION AWARD (FIRCA)

Fogarty International Center
Attn: Division of International Training and Research
31 Center Drive, Room B2C39
Bethesda, MD 20892-2220
(301) 496-1653   Fax: (301) 402-0779
E-mail: FIRCA@nih.gov
Web site: www.nih.gov/fic/programs/firca.html

Purpose To encourage collaboration among scientists in the United States and developing countries in areas of research supported by the National Institutes of Health (NIH).

Eligibility Proposals may be submitted by American scientists who are already principal investigators of grants funded by the institutes and who are interested in working collaboratively with scientists in Africa, Asia (except Japan, Singapore, South Korea, and Taiwan), central and eastern Europe, Russia and the Newly Independent States of the former Soviet Union, Latin America and the non-U.S. Caribbean, the Middle East, and the Pacific Ocean Islands (except Australia and New Zealand). All biomedical and behavioral research topics supported by the institutes are eligible for inclusion in this program. Racial/ethnic minority individuals, women, and persons with disabilities are encouraged to apply as principal investigators.

Financial data Grants provide up to $32,000 per year in direct costs. Funds may be used to pay for materials, supplies, equipment, and travel. Up to 20 percent of the total direct costs may be requested for the U.S. principal investigator, the foreign collaborator, and/or their colleagues or students for visits to each other's laboratory or research site. Up to $5,000 of the total grant may be allocated as a stipend for the foreign collaborator(s). Up to $2,000 of the total grant may be allocated for the foreign collaborator(s) to attend a scientific conference.

Duration Up to 3 years.

Limitations Research related to HIV and AIDS is not eligible for support through this program. A separate companion program, HIV–AIDS and Related Illnesses Collaboration Award, provides funding for research on AIDS.

Number awarded Varies; generally, at least 40 each year.

Deadline Applications may be submitted in November, March, or July of each year.

[1140]
FREDA BAGE FELLOWSHIP

Australian Federation of University Women-Queensland Fellowship Fund Inc.
Attn: The Administrator
217 Hawken Drive
Private Box 8
St. Lucia, QLD 4067
Australia
61 7 3870 5463   E-mail: amm_slss@iname.com
Web site: www.academicdress.com.au/afuwffi/index.html

Purpose To provide financial assistance to women who wish to conduct doctoral research in Australia.

Eligibility All women graduates of universities or recognized advanced institutes in any country are eligible to apply if they wish to conduct research for a Ph.D. degree in Australia. The fellowship is tenable at any Australian university or approved institute and is not restricted to formal university study. Women on full-time salaries or on fully-paid study leave during the fellowship period are not eligible.

Financial data The stipend is $A17,267 per year and is paid in 3 installments: at commencement of the fellowship's tenure, after the first year, and after the second year.

Duration Up to 3 years.

Special features If an Australian receives the fellowship, it may be used at an overseas university but not at the institution through which the applicant received her first degree.

Limitations A written report, including information about any publications resulting from the funded study, is required at completion of the fellowship.

Number awarded 1 each year.

Deadline July of each year.

[1141]
GEORGINA SWEET FELLOWSHIPS

Australian Federation of University Women
Attn: Fellowships Convenor
P.O. Box 14
Bullcreek, WA 6149
Australia
61 8 9360 2646   Fax: 61 8 9310 7495
E-mail: mills@numbat.murdoch.edu.au
Web site: www.adelaide.edu.au/AFUW

Purpose To assist candidates who are working on either a graduate degree or a research project in Australia.

Eligibility Applicants must be women who do not normally live in Australia and who are members of the national federation of university women in their home country. Candidates must hold a degree from a recognized university and must have been formally accepted by the Australian university where they propose to conduct their program of study or research. Applications must be submitted by the national federation to which the applicant belongs, on her behalf.

Financial data The stipend is $A4,500.

Duration 4 to 12 months.

Special features In the United States, the affiliated federation is the American Association of University Women (AAUW),

1111 16th Street, N.W., Washington, DC 20036-4873, (202) 785-7700, (800) 821-4364.
Limitations Applications submitted directly by candidates are not accepted.
Number awarded 1 every other year.
Deadline July of odd-numbered years.

[1142]
GLEDDEN VISITING SENIOR FELLOWSHIPS
University of Western Australia
Attn: Research Administration Unit
Nedlands, WA 6907
Australia
61 8 9380 7299   Fax: 61 8 9380 1919
E-mail: dhockley@admin.uwa.edu.au
Web site: www.acs.uwa.edu.au/research

Purpose To provide financial assistance to scholars from any country who wish to conduct scientific research at the University of Western Australia.
Eligibility Eligible are graduates of any university with a doctoral degree or the equivalent experience in any field of applied science, especially surveying, engineering, or mining. Candidates must be nominated by the appropriate department of the University of Western Australia.
Financial data The award is designed to provide a nominal living allowance and travel expenses; no support is available for dependents or partners.
Duration 3 months to 2 years; most awards are for up to 6 months.
Number awarded Up to 3 each year.
Deadline March of each year.

[1143]
HAROLD T. STEARNS FELLOWSHIP AWARD
Geological Society of America
Attn: Research Grants and Awards Administrator
3300 Penrose Place
P.O. Box 9140
Boulder, CO 80301-9140
(303) 447-2020, ext. 137   Fax: (303) 447-1133
E-mail: lcarter@geosociety.org
Web site: www.geosociety.org

Purpose To provide support to graduate student members of the Geological Society of America (GSA) interested in conducting Pacific Islands geological research.
Eligibility This program is open to GSA members pursuing research for a master's or doctoral degree at a university in the United States, Canada, Mexico, or Central America. Applicants must be interested in conducting research on 1 or more aspects of the geology of the Pacific Islands and of the circum-Pacific region. Applications from minorities, women, and persons with disabilities are strongly encouraged.
Financial data Although there is no predetermined maximum amount for this and other GSA awards, the largest grant recently was $3,175 and the average was $1,622.
Duration 1 year.
Number awarded 1 or more each year.
Deadline January of each year.

[1144]
HAROLD WHITE FELLOWSHIPS
National Library of Australia
Attn: Manuscript Librarian
Canberra, ACT 2600
Australia
61 2 6262 1111   Fax: 61 2 6257 1703
E-mail: g.powell@nla.gov.au
Web site: www.nla.gov.au

Purpose To enable established scholars and writers to conduct research at the National Library of Australia.
Eligibility Fellowships are open to residents of any country, subject to invitation by the library. Funding is available to support publication of original research based on the library's collections; or a description or listing of them; or a study of the methods and techniques used in acquiring, listing, cataloging, arranging, or using them.
Financial data Fellows receive the cost of the cheapest return airfare to Canberra from their homes and, if appropriate, a grant toward living expenses of up to $A500 a week. No travel or grant funds are provided for spouses or children.
Duration 3 to 6 months.
Special features The library instituted these fellowships in 1983 and renamed them in 1985 in honor of Sir Harold White, the first National Librarian, who retired in 1970.
Number awarded 1 each year.
Deadline April of each year.

[1145]
HAROLD WHITE HONORARY FELLOWSHIP
National Library of Australia
Attn: Manuscript Librarian
Canberra, ACT 2600
Australia
61 2 6262 1111   Fax: 61 2 6257 1703
E-mail: g.powell@nla.gov.au
Web site: www.nla.gov.au

Purpose To enable established scholars and writers to conduct research at the National Library of Australia.
Eligibility Fellowships are open to residents of any country, subject to invitation by the library. Candidates must be receiving funding from other sources and need limited assistance from the library.
Financial data The fellowship provides the cost of the cheapest return airfare to Canberra from the recipient's home.
Duration 3 to 6 months.
Special features This fellowship is named for the first National Librarian, who retired in 1970. Fellows are given an office, free photocopying, and library privileges.
Limitations Normally, fellowships are not available to candidates working on a degree. Fellows are expected to spend at least three-quarter time at the library. They are required to give a public lecture and at least 1 seminar to members of the library staff.
Number awarded 1 each year.
Deadline April of each year.

[1146]
HEALTH RESEARCH COUNCIL OF NEW ZEALAND POSTDOCTORAL FELLOWSHIPS

Health Research Council of New Zealand
Attn: Grant Rounds Coordinator
100 Symonds Street, Second Floor
P.O. Box 5541, Wellesley Street
Auckland, Aotearoa
New Zealand
64 9 303 5210   Fax: 64 9 377 9988
E-mail: info@hrc.govt.nz
Web site: www.hrc.govt.nz

Purpose To provide funding to postdoctoral fellows interested in conducting biomedical research in New Zealand.

Eligibility This program is open to residents and citizens of any country who hold a Ph.D. or equivalent degree, have not had more than 3 years of postdoctoral experience, and are interested in conducting research in scientific fields of interest to the Health Research Council (HRC) of New Zealand. The proposed research must be conducted at a university, hospital, or other research institution in New Zealand approved by the HRC.

Financial data Stipends vary from institution to institution but are in the range of New Zealand academic salaries LG1-LG4. An additional annual allowance of up to $NZ1,750 is available to cover limited expenses associated with their research and to allow the fellow to travel to 1 scientific meeting in New Zealand or eastern Australia.

Duration From 2 to 4 years.

Special features The HRC was formerly the Medical Research Council of New Zealand. Its fields of interest include the biomedical sciences relevant to human health and research into the causes, consequences, diagnosis, and treatment of human illness.

Limitations All HRC award recipients are required to submit an annual report to the council.

Number awarded Varies each year.

Deadline August of each year.

[1147]
HIV-AIDS AND RELATED ILLNESSES RESEARCH COLLABORATION AWARD

Fogarty International Center
Attn: Division of International Training and Research
31 Center Drive, Room B2C39
Bethesda, MD 20892-2220
(301) 496-1653   Fax: (301) 402-0779
E-mail: FIRCA@nih.gov
Web site: www.nih.gov/fic/programs/aidsfirc.html

Purpose To provide assistance for U.S. investigators with current funding from the National Institutes of Health (NIH) to conduct research related to AIDS at foreign sites in collaboration with foreign scientists.

Eligibility Applications may be submitted by U.S. nonprofit organizations, public and private, such as universities, colleges, hospitals, laboratories, units of state and local governments, and eligible agencies of the federal government on behalf of principal investigators. The proposed U.S. principal investigator must be the principal investigator of an AIDS or AIDS-related research grant project funded by the institutes. Racial/ethnic minority individuals, women, and persons with disabilities are encouraged to apply as principal investigators. The foreign collaborator must hold a position at an institution in a foreign country that will allow him or her adequate time and provide appropriate facilities to conduct the proposed research. Most countries are eligible for participation in this program; applications for purchase of equipment as part of the grant are limited to research in the developing countries of Africa, Asia, (except Japan, Singapore, South Korea, and Taiwan), central and eastern Europe, Russia and the Independent States of the former Soviet Union, Latin America and the non-U.S. Caribbean, the Middle East, and the Pacific Ocean Islands (except Australia and New Zealand). The application must demonstrate that the award will enhance the scientific contributions of both the U.S. and foreign scientist and will enhance or expand the contribution of the institutes-sponsored research project.

Financial data Grants up to $32,000 per year are available. Funds may be used for supplies at the foreign institution, expenses incurred at the U.S. institution to support the collaboration, and research-related travel and subsistence expenses for both the U.S. and foreign investigators. For collaborations in developing countries as defined above, requests for purchase of equipment (including computers and fax machines) are considered; up to $5,000 may be allocated as a stipend for the foreign collaborator and up to $2,000 may be allocated for the foreign collaborator to attend an AIDS-related scientific conference. Travel funds may be requested up to 20 percent of the total direct costs (up to $6,400) for the U.S. principal investigator, the foreign collaborator, and/or their colleagues or students for visits to each other's laboratory or research site, if such visits are directly related to the subject of the collaborative research.

Duration Up to 3 years.

Special features This program is the counterpart to the Fogarty International Research Collaboration Award (FIRCA) program for non-AIDS related research. It is also designated as AIDS-FIRCA.

Deadline April, August, or December of each year.

[1148]
HUMANITIES RESEARCH CENTRE VISITING FELLOWSHIPS

Australian National University
Attn: Humanities Research Centre
Old Canberra House (Building 73)
Lennox Crossing
Canberra, ACT 0200
Australia
61 2 6125 4357   Fax: 61 2 6248 0054
E-mail: administration.hrc@anu.edu.au
Web site: www.anu.edu.au/HRC

Purpose To encourage humanists from any country to conduct research, especially of an interdisciplinary nature, at the Australian National University's Humanities Research Centre.

Eligibility Both Australian and overseas scholars may apply for these fellowships; each year, the center selects a theme for special study, and most, although not all, of the fellowships are awarded to people with particular interests and skills in areas relevant to the annual nominated theme. A recent theme was

"Culture, Environment, and Human Rights." Applicants must have a doctorate (or equivalent professional experience) and a record of research and publications.

Financial data Grants provide airfare and accommodations at the university. Funds are not intended as salary replacement.

Duration Up to 6 months; most recent fellowships have been for 3 months.

Special features The Humanities Research Centre was established at the Australian National University in 1973 as an international center to stimulate and advance research in the humanities throughout Australia. Fellows meet regularly with other fellows, make public presentations of their research, and avail themselves of other opportunities for interchange.

Limitations Visitors are expected to spend the period of their fellowship in residence in Canberra.

Number awarded Varies each year; recently, 43 of these fellowships were awarded, included 12 to Americans.

Deadline February of each year.

[1149]
INTERNATIONAL RESEARCH SCIENTIST DEVELOPMENT AWARD

Fogarty International Center
Attn: Division of International Training and Research
31 Center Drive, Room B2C39
Bethesda, MD 20892-2220
(301) 496-1653   Fax: (301) 402-0779
E-mail: IRSDA@nih.gov
Web site: www.nih.gov/fic

Purpose To provide funding to U.S. biomedical scientists interested in continuing research in, or extending their research into, developing countries.

Eligibility Applicants must have received a doctoral, dental, or medical degree within the past 7 years in a basic biomedical, behavioral, or epidemiological/clinical field. They must have established a relationship with 2 prospective mentors, 1 in the United States and 1 in a developing country, who have ongoing, funded, international collaborative research. The U.S. mentor should be at a U.S. institution of higher learning or nonprofit research institution. The developing country mentor should be in an internationally developing country research institution addressing some of that country's major health problems. Eligible countries include those in the following regions: Africa, Asia (except Japan, Singapore, South Korea, and Taiwan), central and eastern Europe, Russia and the Newly Independent States of the former Soviet Union, Latin America and the non-U.S. Caribbean, the Middle East (except Israel), and the Pacific Ocean Islands (except Australia and New Zealand). Applications to work in institutions in sub-Saharan Africa are especially encouraged. Racial/ethnic minority individuals, women, and persons with disabilities are encouraged to apply as principal investigators. Applications must be submitted on behalf of the candidate by the U.S. mentor's institution. The applicant need not already be at that institution at the time of application, but it is expected that the U.S. component of the project will be carried out by the fellow at the U.S. mentor's institution.

Financial data Grants provide up to $300,000 for the complete project, prorated at a rate of $8,333 per month (including $6,250 per month direct costs for salary and fringe benefits and $2,083 per month for all other allowable costs). Other allowable costs include travel (round-trip airfare and necessary ground transportation for the candidate to the foreign site up to 5 times over the duration of the project, round-trip airfare for each dependent accompanying the awardee for 6 months or more abroad, excess baggage allowance), health insurance up to $50 per month for the candidate and each dependent during the time abroad, a supplemental living allowance of $150 per month for each dependent accompanying the awardee for 6 months or more, and research development support. An administrative supplement, up to $20,000, may be provided during the third year of the award to fellows who obtain a tenure-track faculty position upon return to the United States.

Duration Support is provided for 36 months, which may be spread over a period of 5 years. A total of at least 24 months should be at the foreign site under the joint supervision of the U.S. and foreign mentors. A period of work in the foreign country should be at least 3 months in length. A total of up to 12 months will be funded for work at the U.S. institution under the U.S. mentor's supervision.

Number awarded Varies each year.

Deadline February of each year.

[1150]
ISH INTERNATIONAL POSTDOCTORAL FELLOWSHIP

Foundation for High Blood Pressure Research
Attn: Honorary Secretary
c/o Monash University
Department of Physiology
Clayton, VIC 3168
Australia
61 3 9905 2555   Fax: 61 3 9905 2566
E-mail: fhbpr@med.monash.edu.au

Purpose To provide funding for research in Australia on blood pressure, hypertension, and associated cardiovascular diseases.

Eligibility Researchers from any country other than Australia are eligible to apply if they have earned their doctorate and are interested in conducting research on hypertension or in areas relevant to the understanding of the causes, prevention, treatment, or effects of hypertension.

Financial data Stipends correspond to those established for postdoctoral researchers at comparable institutions within Australia. Also included are superannuation and laboratory support of $A10,000.

Duration Up to 2 years.

Special features The Foundation for High Blood Pressure Research was founded in 1994 following the 15th Scientific Meeting of the International Society of Hypertension (ISH) in Melbourne.

Limitations Fellowships are tenable only at universities, hospitals, or research institutes in Australia.

Number awarded Varies each year.

Deadline July of each year.

[1151]
JEAN GILMORE BURSARY

Australian Federation of University Women-South Australia Inc. Trust Fund
Attn: Fellowships Trustee
GPO Box 634
Adelaide, SA 5001
Australia
61 8 8401 7124
E-mail: gferrara@scomhbr3.telstra.com.au
Web site: adminwww.flinders.edu.au/WomensInfo/AFUW.htm

Purpose To provide financial assistance to women from any country who are interested in working on a graduate degree by research in Australia.

Eligibility This program is open only to women. Applicants must have completed at least 1 year of graduate school at an Australian university and be working on a master's or doctoral degree by research. Women who are working full time or on fully-paid study leave are not eligible to apply. There is no restriction on field of study. Selection is based primarily on academic merit, although financial need, the purpose for which the bursary will be used, and extracurricular activities are also considered.

Financial data Up to $6,000 is available for equipment, field trips, research, thesis publication, dependent care, or short-term assistance with living expenses.

Duration Up to 1 year.

Special features The recipient may also receive other financial aid. There is no restriction on the field of study/research.

Limitations A fee of $A12 must accompany each application.

Number awarded At least 1 each year.

Deadline February of each year.

[1152]
JILL BRADSHAW BURSARY

Australian Federation of University Women-West Australia
Attn: Bursary Liaison Officer
P.O. Box 48
Nedlands, WA 6909
Australia
Fax: 61 8 9386 3570
E-mail: afuwwa@cygnus.uwa.edu.au
Web site: cygnus.uwa.edu.au/~afuwwa

Purpose To provide funding to women for pre- or postdoctoral research in Australia.

Eligibility Applicants must be women who are completing a higher degree by research or who have completed a higher degree but do not have access to academic support for further research and writing. They must have a degree from a university in West Australia or be enrolled in a university there. Membership in the Australian Federation of University Women or a national federation or association of the International Federation of University Women (IFUW) is required, although nonmembers may apply if they pay a nonrefundable application fee.

Financial data The grant is $A2,250; travel costs are not paid.

Duration Up to 1 year; nonrenewable.

Special features In the United States, the IFUW affiliate is the American Association of University Women (AAUW), 1111 16th Street, N.W., Washington, DC 20036-4873, (202) 785-7700, (800) 821-4364.

Limitations The application fee for nonmembers is $A20.

Number awarded 1 each year.

Deadline July of each year.

[1153]
JOHN DAVID STOUT RESEARCH FELLOWSHIP IN NEW ZEALAND CULTURAL STUDIES

Victoria University of Wellington
Faculty of Arts
Attn: Stout Research Centre
P.O. Box 600
Wellington, New Zealand
64 4 463 5205   Fax: 64 4 463 5239
E-mail: Stout@vuw.ac.nz

Purpose To provide funding to scholars interested in conducting research on the history or culture of New Zealand.

Eligibility Eligible to apply are distinguished scholars from any country whose work relates to New Zealand society, history, and culture. Preference is given to an applicant who proposes a fresh field of research. The fellowship is not generally awarded to anyone whose research is already supported by their regular employment, nor for the writing of a Ph.D. dissertation. Applications are specifically welcomed from women, Pacific Islands peoples, ethnic minorities, and people with disabilities.

Financial data From $NZ43,294 to $NZ65,997 per year, depending on qualifications and experience of the applicant.

Duration 1 year, normally beginning in March.

Special features Research may be conducted anywhere in New Zealand, but the fellows are attached to the Stout Research Centre at Victoria University of Wellington and should plan to spend a major part of their time there.

Limitations This fellowship is not intended to fund the writing of a play, novel, or other similar literary work.

Number awarded 1 each year.

Deadline July of each year.

[1154]
JOYCE RILEY BURSARY

Australian Federation of University Women-West Australia
Attn: Bursary Liaison Officer
P.O. Box 48
Nedlands, WA 6909
Australia
Fax: 61 8 9386 3570
E-mail: afuwwa@cygnus.uwa.edu.au
Web site: cygnus.uwa.edu.au/~afuwwa

Purpose To provide funding to women for doctoral research or study in the humanities or social sciences in Australia.

Eligibility Applicants must be women who are completing a higher degree in the humanities or social sciences by course work or research and who have a degree from a university in West Australia or are enrolled in a university there. Membership in the Australian Federation of University Women or a national federation or association of the International Federation of University Women (IFUW) is required, although nonmembers may apply if they pay a nonrefundable application fee.

Financial data The stipend is $A2,250; travel costs are not paid.

Duration Up to 1 year; nonrenewable.

Special features In the United States, the IFUW affiliate is the American Association of University Women (AAUW), 1111 16th Street, N.W., Washington, DC 20036-4873, (202) 785-7700, (800) 821-4364.

Limitations The application fee for nonmembers is $A20.

Number awarded 1 each year.

Deadline July of each year.

[1155]
LIZARD ISLAND DOCTORAL FELLOWSHIP

Australian Museum
Attn: Lizard Island Research Station
PMB 37
Cairns, QLD 4871
Australia
61 7 4060 3977   Fax: 61 7 4060 3977
E-mail: lizard@austmus.gov.au
Web site: www.austmus.gov.au

Purpose To provide financial assistance to doctoral students who need to conduct field research for their dissertation at the Great Barrier Reef.

Eligibility This program is open to students from any country who are enrolled or about to enroll in a Ph.D. program. Applicants must be interested in conducting field research for their dissertation at the Great Barrier Reef. They must submit a research proposal, curriculum vitae, evidence that they have a stipend from a scholarship or other source for the duration of the fellowship, and supporting letters. Selection is based on significance, quality, and innovation of the proposed research (which must be on an aspect of coral reefs); feasibility of the proposed research within the limitations of budget and safety regulations; significance of usage of the Lizard Island Research Station during each year of funding; evidence that sufficient funding will be available to complete the project as planned, or presentation of a contingency plan for amending the project if additional funding does not become available; evidence of the applicant's research and field work experience; and the applicant's academic and research record.

Financial data The total value of the fellowship is up to $A6,000 per year. That includes bench fees (approximately $A3,200 at the student rate) and cash (up to $A2,800) to be used for additional bench fees, travel, freight, and equipment, but not living expenses or salary.

Duration Up to 3 years.

Special features The Australian Museum established the Research Station at Lizard Island on the northern part of the Great Barrier Reef in 1972 and first awarded this fellowship in 1984. The station supports research into all aspects of the biology, geology, and hydrology of coral reef ecosystems. Air conditioned laboratory space, boats, diving equipment, running sea-water aquaria, and self-contained accommodation units are available at the station.

Number awarded 1 each year.

Deadline September of each year.

[1156]
MARY AND ELSIE STEVENS BURSARY

Australian Federation of University Women-West Australia
Attn: Bursary Liaison Officer
P.O. Box 48
Nedlands, WA 6909
Australia
Fax: 61 8 9386 3570
E-mail: afuwwa@cygnus.uwa.edu.au
Web site: cygnus.uwa.edu.au/~afuwwa

Purpose To provide funding to women for doctoral research in mathematics or the physical sciences in Australia.

Eligibility Applicants must be women who are completing a higher degree in mathematics or the physical sciences by research and who have a degree from a university in West Australia or are enrolled in a university there. Membership in the Australian Federation of University Women or a national federation of association of the International Federation of University Women (IFUW) is required, although nonmembers may apply if they pay a nonrefundable application fee. Research must be conducted in Australia.

Financial data The grant is $A2,250; travel costs are not paid.

Duration Up to 1 year; nonrenewable.

Special features In the United States, the IFUW affiliate is the American Association of University Women (AAUW), 1111 16th Street, N.W., Washington, DC 20036-4873, (202) 785-7700, (800) 821-4364.

Limitations The application fee for nonmembers is $A20.

Number awarded 1 each year.

Deadline July of each year.

[1157]
MARY WALTERS BURSARY

Australian Federation of University Women-West Australia
Attn: Bursary Liaison Officer
P.O. Box 48
Nedlands, WA 6909
Australia
Fax: 61 8 9386 3570
E-mail: afuwwa@cygnus.uwa.edu.au
Web site: cygnus.uwa.edu.au/~afuwwa

Purpose To provide funding to women for doctoral research in Australia.

Eligibility Applicants must be women who are completing a higher degree by research and who have a degree from a university in West Australia or are enrolled in a university there. Membership in the Australian Federation of University Women or a national federation or association of the International Federation of University Women (IFUW) is required, although nonmembers may pay a nonrefundable application fee.

Financial data The stipend is $A2,750; travel costs are not paid.

Duration Up to 1 year; nonrenewable.

Special features In the United States, the IFUW affiliate is the American Association of University Women (AAUW), 1111 16th Street, N.W., Washington, DC 20036-4873, (202) 785-7700, (800) 821-4364.
Limitations The application fee for nonmembers is $A20.
Number awarded 1 each year.
Deadline July of each year.

[1158]
NEW ZEALAND FAMILY PLANNING ASSOCIATION ALICE BUSH SCHOLARSHIP

New Zealand Vice-Chancellors' Committee
94 Dixon Street
P.O. Box 11-915
Wellington 6034
New Zealand
64 4 381 8506   Fax: 64 4 381 8501
E-mail: schols@nzvcc.ac.nz
Web site: www.nzvcc.ac.nz

Purpose To provide funding for graduate study or research in New Zealand on family planning.
Eligibility This program is open to persons who are qualified to register as a candidate for a postgraduate qualification at a New Zealand tertiary institution. Applicants must demonstrate a commitment to and empathy for the issues associated with sexual and reproductive health. The proposal may involve a research project or a program that leads to an advanced degree.
Financial data The stipend is $NZ5,000 per year.
Duration Up to 3 years.
Special features This program is funded by the New Zealand Family Planning Association and administered by the New Zealand Vice-Chancellors' Committee. It honors Dr. Alice Bush, who graduated from the Otago Medical School in 1937, and celebrates 100 years of women's suffrage in New Zealand.
Number awarded 1 each year.
Deadline September of each year.

[1159]
NEW ZEALAND HISTORY RESEARCH TRUST FUND AWARDS IN HISTORY

Department of Internal Affairs
Attn: Historical Branch
P.O. Box 805
Wellington, New Zealand
64 4 495 7200   Fax: 64 4 495 7212

Purpose To provide funding for historians from any country to conduct research in New Zealand.
Eligibility Eligible to apply are scholars from any country who are interested in conducting full-time research in New Zealand. Their proposed research project must relate to New Zealand history.
Financial data Fellows receive travel and research allowances.
Duration From 3 to 6 months.
Limitations The proposed research may not be course related or degree related.
Deadline October of each year.

[1160]
QUEEN ELIZABETH II FELLOWSHIPS

Australian Research Council
Attn: Research Fellowships Scheme
Jerrabomberra Avenue and Hindmarsh Drive
Symonston
GPO Box 9880
Canberra, ACT 2601
Australia
61 2 6284 6600   Fax: 61 2 6284 6601
E-mail: ARC.Publications@detya.gov.au
Web site: www.arc.gov.au/grants/grants_fellow.htm

Purpose To provide funding to distinguished scholars from any country who wish to undertake research of national significance to Australia.
Eligibility Applicants must possess a Ph.D. degree or the equivalent in any field (except clinical medicine or dentistry), at least 3 but no more than 8 years of postdoctoral experience at the time of application, an excellent academic record, evidence of innovative research, and an agreement with an institution in Australia to accommodate the candidate and host the project. Citizens of any nation may apply. Research may be conducted at any Australian higher education institution, private research institution, or government research organization that has the resources to support the research.
Financial data Stipends range from $A48,427 to $A53,497 per year and average $A50,962. A supplemental research grant of up to $A10,500 is available to cover the costs of equipment, travel, supplies, and assistance. Fellows coming from overseas also receive a relocation allowance, up to $A15,000 for scholars coming from the United States.
Duration 5 years; may not be renewed.
Number awarded 5 each year.
Deadline February of each year.

[1161]
QUEENSLAND COMMEMORATIVE FELLOWSHIPS

Australian Federation of University Women-Queensland
   Fellowship Fund Inc.
Attn: The Administrator
217 Hawken Drive
Private Box 8
St. Lucia, QLD 4067
Australia
61 7 3870 5463   E-mail: ann_slss@iname.com
Web site:
www.academicdress.com.au/afuwffi/index.html

Purpose To provide financial assistance to women for postgraduate research or study in Australia.
Eligibility The fellowship is open to women graduates of a university or recognized tertiary institution from any country. Women on full-time salaries or on fully-paid study leave during the fellowship period are not eligible. The fellowship is not restricted to formal university study and is tenable at any university or approved institute in Australia. If an award is made to an Australian citizen, it is also tenable in other countries.
Financial data The stipend is $A17,267, half paid at the beginning of the award and half paid on receipt of a progress report submitted after 6 months.
Duration Up to 1 year; recipients may reapply.

Special features This program includes the following named fellowships: the Molly Budtz-Olsen Fellowship, the Dorothy Davidson Fellowship, the Freda Freeman Fellowship, the Audrey Harrisson Fellowship, the Audrey Jorss Fellowship, the Margaret Mittelheuser Fellowship, the Betty Patterson Fellowship, and the University Women of Queensland Fellowship.

Limitations A written report, including information about any publications resulting from the funded study, is required at completion of the fellowship.

Number awarded Varies each year; recently, 5 of these fellowships were awarded.

Deadline July of each year.

[1162]
RESEARCH CENTRE FELLOWSHIPS AT THE AUSTRALIAN MUSEUM

Australian Museum
Attn: Associate Director
6 College Street
Sydney, NSW 2000
Australia
61 2 9320 6230   Fax: 61 2 9320 6015
E-mail: rogerm@austmus.gov.au
Web site: www.austmus.gov.au

Purpose To promote research in selected fields at the Australian Museum.

Eligibility This program is open to postdoctorates and professionals who are proposing to work as collaborators on specific aspects of projects at the museum's research center. Fields of interest include natural history, paleontology, mineralogy and petrology, marine ecology, terrestrial ecology, and anthropology of Australia and neighboring regions. Fellows are chosen for the skills, knowledge, and/or expertise they might bring to a specific project.

Financial data Awards up to $A400 per week are available to assist in meeting living costs and research expenses (such as travel time, bench fees, and specialist analyses), although awards can also be used for salary replacement.

Duration Up to 1 year.

Special features Awards are held at the museum, although they can be spent partly in the field.

Number awarded 1 or more each year.

Deadline February of each year.

[1163]
RIRDC GRANTS

Rural Industries Research and Development Corporation
Attn: Executive Officer
P.O. Box 4776
Kingston, ACT 2604
Australia
61 2 6272 4819   Fax: 61 2 6272 5877
E-mail: rirdc@rirdc.gov.au
Web site: www.rirdc.gov.au

Purpose To provide funding for researchers and other individuals interested in coming to Australia to conduct research on agriculture.

Eligibility Any individual, company, or organization may apply for support to conduct research in Australia in areas supported by the Rural Industries Research & Development Corporation (RIRDC). Program areas within RIRDC currently include prospective new industries (new plant products and new animal products), emerging new industries (Asian foods, agroforest and farm forestry, deer, essential oils and plant extracts, organic produce, rare natural animal fibers, tea tree oil, wildflowers, and native plants), established rural industries (chicken meat, eggs, honeybees, rice, horses, fodder crops, and pasture seeds), and future agricultural systems. Although applicants may be from any country, selection is based on the potential benefits of the research to the Australian rural sector and its chances of success.

Financial data The amount awarded varies, depending upon the scope of the proposed project. Funds are not available to cover travel costs.

Duration 6 months to 5 years.

Limitations Grants are tenable only in Australia.

Number awarded Varies each year.

Deadline The deadline for preliminary applications is in September of each year; full applications are due in February of each year.

[1164]
ROLF EDGAR LAKE POSTDOCTORAL FELLOWSHIP

University of Sydney
Attn: Faculty of Medicine
Edward Ford Building, Room 231
Sydney, NSW 2006
Australia
61 2 9351 5692   E-mail: kyliep@med.usyd.edu.au
Web site: www.medicine.usyd.edu.au

Purpose To provide funding to postdoctoral scholars who wish to conduct medical research at the University of Sydney in Australia.

Eligibility Applicants for this program must hold a Ph.D. or equivalent and be interested in conducting research in the Faculty of Medicine of the University of Sydney. They may be from any country. Although senior scientists are eligible to apply, preference is given to applicants who have already embarked on a research career but are still at an early stage of that career. Selection is based on academic merit and the appropriateness of the proposed research.

Financial data Fellows receive a stipend at the appropriate level of the university salary scale for research fellows. In addition, they receive grants of up to $A5,000 to cover technical assistance, equipment, and general expenses.

Duration 1 year; may be renewed for up to 2 additional years.

Special features This program was established in 1978.

Number awarded 1 each year.

Deadline October of each year.

[1165]
RUDI LEMBERG TRAVELLING FELLOWSHIP

Australian Academy of Science
GPO Box 783
Canberra, ACT 2601
Australia
61 2 6247 5777   Fax: 61 2 6257 4620
E-mail: ac@science.org.au
Web site: www.science.org.au

Purpose To allow distinguished overseas scientists to visit Australia for public lectures and seminars and to visit scientific centers in Australia.

Eligibility Nominations are accepted for distinguished overseas scientists in any field of biology. Special consideration is given to nominees in the areas of biochemistry, conservation, and the Australian flora.

Financial data The award covers overseas and local airfares.

Duration 2 weeks to 3 months.

Special features This fellowship commemorates the contributions of Professor M.R. Lemberg to science in Australia. Fellowships also are awarded to Australian scientists to spend a similar period within Australia away from their own institutions visiting scientific centers and delivering lectures.

Deadline May of every other year.

[1166]
SELBY FELLOWSHIP

Australian Academy of Science
GPO Box 783
Canberra, ACT 2601
Australia
61 2 6247 5777   Fax: 61 2 6257 4620
E-mail: aas@science.org.au
Web site: www.science.org.au

Purpose To allow distinguished overseas scientists to visit Australia for public lectures and seminars and to visit scientific centers in Australia.

Eligibility Nominations are accepted for fellows who will be expected to visit Australia to increase public awareness of science and scientific issues. They should be outstanding lecturers to the general lay public.

Financial data The award provides overseas and local airfares and a daily allowance.

Duration 2 weeks to 3 months.

Special features This fellowship is financed by the Selby Scientific Foundation.

Deadline August of each year.

[1167]
SIR MARK MITCHELL RESEARCH FOUNDATION GRANTS

Sir Mark Mitchell Research Foundation
c/o Tower Trust Limited
44 Pirie Street
GPO Box 546
Adelaide, SA 5001
Australia
08 8218 4911   Fax: 08 8231 1798
Web site: www.towertrust.com.au

Purpose To provide funding for natural history research in Australia.

Eligibility Eligible to apply are scientists from any country who are interested in conducting research in South Australia. Disciplines that receive the highest priority are zoology and all its branches, earth sciences, and anthropology. The foundation does not support projects related primarily to medical or agricultural sciences. Preference is given to applicants who do not usually have ready access to other research grants.

Financial data The amount awarded varies, depending upon the recipient's qualifications and research needs. Payments are made quarterly.

Duration Awards are made for 1 year only; renewal for a second year is possible.

Special features Research may be conducted at the University of Adelaide, the University of South Australia, or the Royal Society of South Australia Incorporated (the Adelaide Zoo). This program was established in 1965.

Limitations Recipients must submit both a progress and a final report.

Deadline Applications may be submitted at any time.

[1168]
THENIE BADDAMS BURSARY

Australian Federation of University Women-South Australia
   Inc. Trust Fund
Attn: Fellowships Trustee
GPO Box 634
Adelaide, SA 5001
Australia
61 8 8401 7124
E-mail: gferrara@scomhbr3.telstra.com.au
Web site: adminwww.flinders.edu.au/WomensInfo/AFUW.htm

Purpose To provide financial assistance to women from any country who are interested in working on a graduate degree by research in Australia.

Eligibility This program is open only to women. Applicants must have completed at least 1 year of graduate school at an Australian university and be working on a master's or doctoral degree by research. Women who are in full-time paid employment or on fully-paid study leave are not eligible to apply. There is no restriction on field of study. Selection is based primarily on academic merit, although financial need, the purpose for which the bursary will be used, and extracurricular activities are also considered.

Financial data Up to $A6,000 is available for equipment, field trips, research, thesis publication, and dependent care.

Duration Up to 1 year.

Special features The recipient may also receive other financial aid.

Limitations A fee of $A12 must accompany each application.

Number awarded At least 1 each year.

Deadline February of each year.

[1169]
TRAVEL SCHEME FOR INTERNATIONAL COLLABORATIVE RESEARCH

University of Queensland
Attn: Office of Research and Postgraduate Studies
Cumbrae-Stewart Building
Research Road
Brisbane, QLD 4072
Australia
61 7 3365 4582   Fax: 61 7 3365 4455
E-mail: cstratigos@research.uq.edu.au
Web site: www.uq.edu.au/research

Purpose To provide travel assistance to researchers from countries outside of Australia who want to travel to the University of Queensland in Australia to conduct research.

Eligibility Applicants may be from any country. They must have earned a doctorate (or its equivalent), be affiliated with an academic institution in their home country or an internationally-recognized research establishment, and be engaged in academic work that will contribute to the department to which they are attached at the University of Queensland. Individuals already in Australia are not eligible to apply.

Financial data The award covers travel expenses only.

Duration Recipients must stay at the University of Queensland for at least 4 weeks.

Number awarded Up to 5 each year.

Deadline July of each year.

[1170]
UNIVERSITY OF MELBOURNE VISITING RESEARCH SCHOLAR AWARD

University of Melbourne
Attn: Office for the Deputy Vice-Chancellor for Research
Grattan Street
Parkville, VIC 3052
Australia
61 3 8344 7114   Fax: 61 3 9347 6739
E-mail: s.honl@research.unimelb.edu.au
Web site: www.unimelb.edu.au/research/collab/vrs2000.html

Purpose To provide financial assistance to researchers at leading universities and research institutions in any country who wish to visit the University of Melbourne to engage in collaborative research.

Eligibility Senior academics (more than 5 years since receipt of Ph.D. or equivalent) already on full or part salary are eligible to apply if they reside in countries other than Australia. Selection is based on the quality of the research project, the strength of the existing or developing collaboration, the likely impact of the scholar's research on the work of the department, the likelihood that a visit to the University of Melbourne will contribute to further collaboration, and the academic standing of the visiting researcher.

Financial data For researchers from outside Australia, normal grants are $A4,000 for 2 months, $A6,000 for 3 months, $A8,000 for 6 months, $A10,000 for 9 months, or $A12,000 for 12 months; grants are to cover airfare to and from Australia and to supplement other funds for subsistence.

Duration 2 to 12 months.

Special features Applications for second visits may be approved if they include some evidence of the results of the research undertaken during the previous visit, such as joint publications.

Limitations Proposed projects must bring recipients with specific research experience or skills to collaborate with University of Melbourne staff to the benefit of the university.

Number awarded Varies each year.

Deadline March and September of each year.

[1171]
UNIVERSITY OF QUEENSLAND POSTDOCTORAL RESEARCH FELLOWSHIPS

University of Queensland
Attn: Office of Research and Postgraduate Studies
Cumbrae-Stewart Building
Research Road
Brisbane, QLD 4072
Australia
61 7 3365 4582   Fax: 61 7 3365 4455
E-mail: cstratigos@research.uq.edu.au
Web site: www.uq.edu.au/research

Purpose To provide financial assistance to postdoctorates from any country who wish to conduct full-time research (in any subject) at the University of Queensland in Australia.

Eligibility Applicants from any country are eligible if they have completed their Ph.D. degree within the past 5 years (or will have completed the degree by September of the year preceding appointment). They must be interested in conducting research at the University of Queensland. Priority is given to applicants in the early stage of their postdoctoral careers.

Financial data The stipend ranges from $A42,229 to $A47,058 and includes reimbursement for round-trip airfare. No funds are provided for dependents. The host department receives $A3,500 to assist with research expenses.

Duration 2 years.

Limitations Fellows are expected to participate in departmental seminars and research discussions.

Number awarded Varies; generally, 5 each year.

Deadline May of each year.

[1172]
UNIVERSITY OF SYDNEY POSTDOCTORAL RESEARCH FELLOWSHIPS

University of Sydney
Attn: Research and Scholarships Office
Main Quadrangle A14
Sydney, NSW 2006
Australia
61 2 9351 3250   Fax: 61 2 9351 3256
E-mail: scholars@reschols.usyd.edu.au
Web site: www.usyd.edu.au

Purpose To provide financial assistance for postdoctoral research at the University of Sydney in Australia.

Eligibility Applicants from any nation (including Australia) may apply if they have earned a doctorate or its equivalent within the past 5 years. They must be interested in conducting research at the University of Sydney, but they may not be a member of the tenured academic or teaching staff of the university. Overseas applicants must provide details (such as names and ages of children) of any family members who will accompany them to Australia. Before submitting an application, candidates must consult with the head of the school or department at the university where they wish to conduct research; applications must include a statement from the head to support them and their research program.

Financial data The stipends are $A45,475, $A47,145, or $A48,814 per year. For fellows coming from countries other than Australia, there is an additional travel grant to cover economy airfare for themselves (but not family members). An initial setting-up grant of $A25,000 for research purposes is also provided.

Duration 3 years; may be renewed for up to 1 additional year.

Number awarded Up to 15 each year.

Deadline August of each year.

[1173]
UNIVERSITY OF WESTERN AUSTRALIA POSTDOCTORAL RESEARCH FELLOWSHIPS

University of Western Australia
Attn: Research Administration Unit
Nedlands, WA 6907
Australia
61 8 9380 1776   Fax: 61 8 9380 1075
E-mail: tmcglade@acs.uwa.edu.au
Web site: www.acs.uwa.edu.au/research

Purpose To provide financial assistance to junior postdoctoral scholars from any country who are interested in conducting research at the University of Western Australia (UWA).

Eligibility This program is open to residents of any country who have held a Ph.D. or equivalent qualification for not more than 5 years and show evidence of research potential. Candidates must be approved by the Australian Department of Immigration and Ethnic Affairs. They must be nominated by the appropriate UWA department, which must explain the anticipated benefit from having a postdoctoral fellow in the department and the resources available to the fellow.

Financial data Salaries are $A45,034, $A46,688, or $A48,340 per year. Other benefits include a support grant of $A6,000 and a relocation allowance.

Duration 3 years.

Number awarded Up to 4 each year.

Deadline February of each year.

[1174]
VERNON WILLEY AWARDS

Vernon Willey Trust
c/o New Zealand Guardian Trust Company Limited
96 Hereford Street
P.O. Box 9
Christchurch, New Zealand
64 3 379 0644   Fax: 64 3 366 7616
E-mail: fcattermole@nzgt.co.nz

Purpose To provide financial assistance to individuals from other countries who wish to research the wool industry in New Zealand.

Eligibility While most of the awards go to New Zealanders, applications may be submitted by nationals of any country. There are no set educational requirements. Applicants must be interested in researching the production, processing, and marketing of wool and/or the development of the sheep and wool industries in New Zealand.

Financial data Awards range from $NZ1,000 to $NZ10,000.

Duration Up to 1 year; may be renewed.

Limitations Interviews may be required. For overseas recipients, awards are tenable only in New Zealand; recipients from New Zealand may travel to other countries.

Number awarded Varies; generally, up to 8 each year.

Deadline November of each year.

[1175]
WARREN MCDONALD INTERNATIONAL FELLOWSHIP

National Heart Foundation of Australia
Attn: Victorian Division
411 King Street
West Melbourne VIC 3003
Australia
61 3 9329 8511   Fax: 61 3 9321 1574
E-mail: research@heartfoundation.com.au
Web site: www.heartfoundation.com.au

Purpose To provide financial assistance to senior researchers from outside of Australia who are interested in conducting heart research in Australia.

Eligibility Senior researchers interested in cardiovascular disease who wish to conduct research on that topic in Australia are eligible to apply. They must be employed outside of Australia and must be nominated by the host institution. Recipients are selected on the basis of their ability to provide a special perspective or skill unavailable in Australia.

Financial data Stipends at the postdoctoral level range from $A39,886 to $A48,449. A travel grant covers the minimum round-trip airfare for the fellow and family from home to Australia. The host institution receives a grant of up to $A4,000 to cover departmental expenses.

Duration Up to 1 year.

Number awarded 1 each year.

Deadline May of each year.

Annotated Bibliography of Financial Aid Resources

General Directories •
Subject Directories •
Special Groups •
Awards •
Internships •
Nothing over $5.50 •

General Directories

[1176]
Annual Register of Grant Support: A Directory of Funding Sources. Annual.

Nearly 3,000 programs (representing over $100 billion in aid) sponsored by government agencies, private foundations, corporations, unions, church groups, and educational and professional associations are described in the latest edition of this directory. The programs provide grant support in the humanities, international affairs, race and minority concerns, education, environmental and urban affairs, social sciences, physical sciences, life sciences, technology, and other areas. Each entry contains the following information: organization name; address and telephone number; major field(s) of organizational interest; name(s) of grant program(s); purpose; nature of support available; amount of support per award; number of applicants and recipients for the most recent years; legal basis for program; eligibility requirements; application instructions; and deadline. The work is indexed by subject, sponsor, geographic requirements, and personnel.

Price: $225, hardcover.

Available from: R.R. Bowker, 121 Chanlon Road, New Providence, NJ 07974. Telephone: (908) 464-6800. Toll-free: (888) 269-5372.

Web site: www.reedref.com/

[1177]
Catalog of Federal Domestic Assistance. Annual.

This is the "what's what" of government grant programs. It is *the* single source of information on programs administered at the federal level. Over 1,300 domestic assistance programs and activities, administered by at least 60 different federal agencies and departments, are described in this annual publication: grants, loans, loan guarantees and shared revenue; provisions of federal facilities, direct construction of goods and services; donation or provision of surplus property, technical assistance and counseling; statistical and other information services; and service activities and regulatory agencies. These assistance programs are available to state and local governments, public and private organizations and institutions, and individuals. Excluded are automatic payment programs not requiring application; personal recruitment programs of individual federal departments (other than the civil service program); and inactive or unfunded programs. Program entries provide information on purpose, availability, authorizing legislation, administering agency, and sources of additional information. Each annual edition contains more than 1,000 pages of information, making the listing cumbersome to use, even though there is extensive cross indexing. Users may find it easier to access the *Catalog* through the various software programs now available, or through the Federal Assistance Program Retrieval System (FAPRS), the official computerized guide to all federal grants found in the *Catalog*. With FAPRS, and your modem, you can link up with the *Catalog's* database directly.

Price: $87, paper.

Available from: Superintendent of Documents, U.S. Government Printing Office, P.O. Box 371954, Pittsburgh, PA 15250-7954. Telephone: (202) 512-1800, press 1. Toll-free: (800) 669-8331.

Web site: www.access.gpo.gov/su_docs/

[1178]
Corporate Giving Directory: Comprehensive Profiles and Analyses of America's Private Foundations. Annual.

Taft is 1 of the oldest, largest, and best known of the grant information subscription services. This directory, first issued in 1977 and updated annually since then, describes 1,000 of the largest corporate foundations in America. The entries are arranged by program name and present information on sponsoring company, grant distribution, type of grants, areas of interest, contact persons, total assets, sample grants, corporate operating location, and Fortune 500 ranking (profiles average 1 page in length). Multiple indexes are provided (e.g., state, field of interest). Use Taft's monthly *Corporate Updates* and *Corporate Giving Watch* to supplement entries in the annual directory. *Corporate Giving Directory* is available in both print and customized on diskettes and magnetic tapes. For similar information on private foundations, see Taft's *Foundation Reporter: Comprehensive Profiles and Analyses of America's Private Foundation*. The information in both of these directories is also included in *Prospector's Choice,* Taft's CD-ROM product covering 10,000 foundations and corporate giving programs.

Price: $485, hardcover.

Available from: Taft Group, 27500 Drake Road, Farmington Hills, MI 48331-3535. Telephone: (248) 699-4253. Toll free: (800) 877-4253.

Web site: www.galegroup.com/taft/

[1179]
Directory of Research Grants. Annual.

In the latest edition, nearly 6,000 grants, contracts, fellowships, and loan programs for research, training, and innovative effort sponsored by 600 organizations are described. The emphasis is on U.S. programs, although some sponsored by other countries are included. Entries are arranged by program title. Annotations include requirements, restrictions, financial data (but not for all entries), name and addresses, and application procedures. The programs are indexed by subject. The information presented in this publication is also available online (through Dialog) as GRANTS, on CD-ROM with monthly supplements, as an Internet subscription (www.grantselect.com), and in a number of derivative publications, including *Directory of Grants in the Humanities* and *Directory of Biomedical and Health Care Grants*.

Price: $135, paper.

Available from: Oryx Press, 88 Post Road West, Westport, CT 06881. Toll-free: (800) 279-6799.

Web site: www.oryxpress.com/

[1180]
The Foundation Directory. Annual.

The Foundation Center is the only nonprofit organization in the country that focuses on the activities of private foundations. This directory is the standard work on nongovernmental grant-making foundations. It lists nonprofit, nongovernmental organizations with assets in excess of $2 million or which made grants in excess of $200,000 in 1 year. More than 10,000 foundations are identified. These represent only 10 percent of all grantmaking foundations but over 90 percent of all grant money distributed ($8 billion annually). For information on the 10,000 foundations that annually grant between $50,000 and $199,000, see the *Foundation Directory Part II.* Supplements are issued between editions of these directories and list foundations by state for which recent fiscal data are available on microfiche. The directory is also available to be searched online, through Dialog. In addition, the information presented here is included in *FC Search,* the Foundation Center's CD-ROM product that covers more than 40,000 U.S. foundations and corporate givers.

Price: $215, paper.

Available from: Foundation Center, 79 Fifth Avenue, New York, NY 10003-3076. Telephone: (212) 620-4230. Toll-free: (800) 424-9836.

Web site: www.fdncenter.org/

[1181]
Foundation Grants to Individuals. 12th ed.

While most foundation grants are for agencies and institutions, some funding opportunities (including a number of scholarships and loans) have been set up specifically for individual applicants. You can find out about these opportunities in the Foundation Center's *Foundation Grants to Individuals.* The current edition identifies more than 4,300 foundations that annually make grants of at least $2,000 to individuals. The work is organized by type of grant awarded (e.g., scholarships, general welfare, medical assistance) and subdivided by eligibility requirements and means of access (including some "Grants to Foreign Individuals" and "Grants to Employees of Specific Companies"). Collectively, these grants total nearly $100 million each year. However, most of these programs are limited geographically and will relate only to very small segments of the population.

Price: $75, paper.

Available from: Foundation Center, 79 Fifth Avenue, New York, NY 10003-3076. Telephone: (212) 620-4230. Toll-free: (800) 424-9836.

Web site: www.fdncenter.org/

[1182]
Scholarships, Fellowships, and Loans. Annual.

Although this directory will be too expensive for most students (or their parents) to consider buying, it should not be overlooked; many larger libraries have the title in their reference collection. Described here are more than 3,700 scholarships, fellowships, grants, and loans available to undergraduates, graduate students, and postdoctorates in the United States and Canada. Each entry identifies qualifications, funds, purposes, application process, and background. The Vocational Goals Index in the front of the volume summarizes, in chart form, the characteristics of each award (e.g., level of study, subject of study, geographic restrictions, citizenship requirements).

Price: $190, hardcover.

Available from: Gale Group, 27500 Drake Road, Farmington Hills, MI 48331-3535. Telephone: (248) 699-4253. Toll free: (800) 877-4253.

Web site: www.galegroup.com/

Subject Directories

[1183]
Directory of Biomedical and Health Care Grants. Annual.

Use this directory to locate descriptions of nearly 3,000 funding sources in the biomedical and health care areas. The programs described here are sponsored by corporations, foundations, professional organizations, and federal, state, and local governments. Each program profile describes purpose, remuneration, eligibility, renewability, application deadlines, and sources of additional information. The entries are listed by program title and indexed by sponsoring organization, sponsoring organization by type (e.g., business and professional organizations, government agencies), and specific subject terms. The programs listed in the directory are taken from Oryx's GRANTS database, which is also the source for the *Directory of Research Grants;* consequently, many of the programs included in the two publications are duplicates.

Price: $84.50, paper.

Available from: Oryx Press, 88 Post Road West, Westport, CT 06881. Toll-free: (800) 279-6799.

Web site: www.oryxpress.com/

[1184]
Directory of Grants in the Humanities. Annual.

A spinoff from Oryx Press' GRANTS database, this annual directory identifies funding sources in literature, languages, history, anthropology, philosophy, ethics, religion, fine arts, and performing arts (including painting, dance, photography, sculpture, music, drama, crafts, folklore, and mime). The latest edition contains nearly 4,000 entries, each of which includes information on restrictions and requirements, amount of money available, application deadline, renewability, sponsoring organization name and address, and *Catalog of Federal Domestic Assistance* number. More than half of the listing focuses on federal programs; the remainder is devoted to state government programs, university-sponsored programs, and corporate or foundation funding sources. Most of the programs described here are also covered in Oryx Press' more comprehensive *Directory of Research Grants.*

Price: $84.50, paper.

Available from: Oryx Press, 88 Post Road West, Westport, CT 06881. Toll-free: (800) 279-6799.

Web site: www.oryxpress.com/

[1185]
Dramatists Sourcebook: Complete Opportunities for Playwrights, Translators, Composers, Lyricists, and Librettists. Annual.

While one half of this directory focuses on "script opportunities" (theaters willing to review unpublished plays), there are three separate sections that provide funding information: fellowships and grants, colonies and residencies, and emergency funds. The entries in these sections are arranged by sponsoring organization and subdivided by specific programs. The information presented includes eligibility, financial arrangements, purpose, application process, and deadlines. The source book also contains a short bibliography of useful publications, a submission calendar for the programs described, a special interests index, a sponsoring organization index, and several helpful essays in the prologue. Use the Theatre Communications Group's monthly magazine, *American Theatre,* to update the listings in the sourcebook; the "opportunities" column announces new grants and contests as well as revised deadlines.

Price: $19.95, paper.

Available from: Theatre Communications Group, 355 Lexington Avenue, New York, NY 10017-6603. Telephone: (212) 697-5230.

Web site: www.tcg.org/

[1186]

Editor & Publisher Journalism Awards and Fellowships Issue. Annual.

Published as a special pull-out section in the last issue of *Editor & Publisher,* (the "only independent weekly journal of newspapering") each year, this directory describes over 500 scholarships, fellowships, grants, and awards available in the field of journalism. The focus is on programs for reporters, columnists, editors, cartoonists, and photographers. The entries are arranged alphabetically within four main sections: national and international awards; regional awards, honorary awards and citations; and fellowships, grants, and scholarships. The following information is provided for each program: sponsoring organization, address, requirements, and deadlines. Many entries also list the previous year's winners.

Price: $15, paper.

Available from: Editor & Publisher, 770 Broadway, New York, NY 10003-9595. Telephone: (212) 654-5270. Toll-free: (800) 722-6658.

Web site: www.mediainfo.com/

[1187]

Financial Aid for Research and Creative Activities Abroad. Published every odd-numbered year.

This directory will help Americans tap into the millions of dollars available for research, lectureships, exchange programs, work assignments, conference attendance, professional development, and creative projects abroad. The more than 1,000 listings cover every major field of interest, are tenable in practically every country in the world, are sponsored by more than 500 different private and public organizations and agencies, and are open to all segments of the population, from high school students to professionals and postdoctorates. A companion volume (described below) identifies funding opportunities for study and training abroad.

Price: $45, hardcover.

Available from: Reference Service Press, 5000 Windplay Drive, Suite 4, El Dorado Hills, CA 95762. Telephone: (916) 939-9620.

Web site: www.rspfunding.com/

[1188]

Financial Aid for Study and Training Abroad. Published every odd-numbered year.

If you want to go abroad to study and you need money to do so, this is the directory for you. Described here are 1,100 scholarships, fellowships, loans, and grants that Americans can use to support structured or unstructured study abroad, including money for formal academic classes, training courses, degree-granting programs, independent study, seminars, workshops, and student internships. Detailed information is provided for each program: address, telephone number (including fax, toll-free, and e-mail), purpose, eligibility, amount awarded, number awarded, duration, special features, limitations, and deadline date. There's also a currency conversion table and an annotated bibliography of key resources that anyone (interested in study abroad or not) can use to find additional funding opportunities.

Price: $39.50, hardcover.

Available from: Reference Service Press, 5000 Windplay Drive, Suite 4, El Dorado Hills, CA 95762. Telephone: (916) 939-9620.

Web site: www.rspfunding.com/

[1189]

Grants and Awards Available to American Writers. Annual.

Grants and awards in excess of $500, available to American writers for use in the United States and abroad, are described in this directory. According to the editors, this is the only reference work "which combines both domestic and foreign grants for American writers." Additional sections identify grants and awards available to Canadian writers and state arts councils. The listing is wide-ranging but not comprehensive. The 500 entries each year are arranged alphabetically by organization and indexed by award title, type of literature, and sponsoring organization. There is no subject index. Each listing specifies purpose of the award, amount available, eligibility, and application procedures. The programs covered are open to playwrights, poets, journalists, fiction writers, researchers, and scholars. Since many of the awards described here require prior publication or are open only to nominees, this listing will prove most useful to writers with experience and reputation. To update the annual listing, use the *P.E.N. American Center Newsletter.*

Price: $18, paper.

Available from: P.E.N. American Center, 568 Broadway, New York, NY 10012. Telephone: (212) 334-1660.

Web site: www.pen.org/

[1190]

Grants, Fellowships, and Prizes of Interest to Historians. Annual.

Begun as a 46-page pamphlet, this 220+ page annual listing identifies and describes approximately 450 sources of funding for graduate students, postdoctoral researchers, and scholars in the history profession tenable in the United State or abroad. Covered here are fellowships, internships, awards, prizes, and travel grants. The entries are arranged in three sections: support for individual fellowships and grants; support for organizations and groups working in the fields of historical education, study, or preservation; prizes and awards given for books, publications, or manuscripts already completed. A bibliography is also included, which lists books and pamphlets that contain additional information about funding prizes.

Price: $10, members; $12, nonmembers. Paper.

Available from: American Historical Association, 400 A Street, S.E., Washington, DC 20003-3889. Telephone: (202) 544-2422.
Web site: www.theaha.org/

[1191]
Money for Graduate Students in the Biological & Health Sciences.
Money for Graduate Students in the Humanities.
Money for Graduate Students in the Physical & Earth Sciences.
Money for Graduate Students in the Social & Behavioral Sciences. Published every odd-numbered year.

Billions of dollars are available to support graduate study and research each year. These four volumes, issued every odd-numbered year, identify thousands of fellowships, grants, and awards: *Money for Graduate Students in the Biological & Health Sciences:* 1,100 entries; *Money for Graduate Students in the Humanities:* 1,000 entries; *Money for Graduate Students in the Physical & Earth Sciences:* 800 entries; *Money for Graduate Students in the Social & Behavioral Sciences:* 1,100 entries. Full details are given for each program: contact information, purpose, eligibility, money awarded, duration, special features, limitations, number offered, and deadline date. The entries are grouped by purpose (research or study) and indexed by subject, residency, tenability, sponsor, and deadline. These titles can be purchased separately (see pricing below) or at a discounted price as part of the *Graduate Funding Set*.

Price: *Money for Graduate Students in the Biological & Health Sciences,* $42.50. *Money for Graduate Students in the Humanities,* $40. *Money for Graduate Students in the Physical & Earth Sciences,* $35. *Money for Graduate Students in the Social & Behavioral Sciences,* $42.50. Or, all four volumes can be purchased together, as the *Graduate Funding Set,* for the discounted price of $140.

Available from: Reference Service Press, 5000 Windplay Drive, Suite 4, El Dorado Hills, CA 95762. Telephone: (916) 939-9620.
Web site: www.rspfunding.com/

[1192]
RSP Funding for Nursing Students and Nurses. Published every even-numbered year.

The U.S. Department of Labor estimates that nearly 2.5 million nurses will be needed in the early 21st century. Hundreds of financial aid programs, representing millions of dollars, are available to help students prepare for these jobs, as well as to help nurses already in the field fund their professional or research activities. These scholarships, fellowships, loans, and grants are described in detail in this biennial publication. The following information is given for more than 600 funding opportunities: purpose, eligibility, monetary award, duration, special features, limitations, number awarded, and deadline date. Entries are indexed by sponsor, residency, tenability, specialty, and deadline.

Price: $30, spiralbound.
Available from: Reference Service Press, 5000 Windplay Drive, Suite 4, El Dorado Hills, CA 95762. Telephone: (916) 939-9620.
Web site: www.rspfunding.com/

Special Groups

[1193]
Directory of Financial Aids for Women. Published every odd-numbered year.

Are you looking for financial aid for women? Or, do you know women who are? If so, take a look at the *Directory of Financial Aids for Women*. Here, in one place, are descriptions of 1,400 funding programs—representing billions of dollars in financial aid set aside just for women. Each of these programs can be accessed by program title, sponsoring organization, geographic coverage, deadline date, and subject. There's also a list of key sources that identify additional financial aid opportunities.

Price: $45, hardcover.
Available from: Reference Service Press, 5000 Windplay Drive, Suite 4, El Dorado Hills, CA 95762. Telephone: (916) 939-9620.
Web site: www.rspfunding.com/

[1194]
Financial Aid for African Americans.
Financial Aid for Asian Americans.
Financial Aid for Hispanic Americans.
Financial Aid for Hispanic Americans. Published every odd-numbered year.

Despite the recent steps taken to curtail affirmative action and equal opportunity programs, the financial aid picture for minorities has never looked brighter. Find out when, where, and how to get these scholarships, fellowships, grants, loans, awards, and internships in four separate titles, each published in odd-numbered years: *Financial Aid for African Americans* 1,500 funding opportunities; *Financial Aid for Asian Americans,* 1,100 funding opportunities, Financial Aid for Hispanic Americans, 1,400 funding opportunities, and *Financial Aid for Native Americans,* 1,500 funding opportunities. This money can be used to support a whole range of activities, including study, training, research, creative activities, future projects, professional development, and work experience. The listings cover every major subject area and are sponsored by hundreds of private and public agencies and organizations. Full details are given for each program: contact information, purpose, eligibility, money awarded, duration, special features, limitations, number offered, and deadline date. The entries are indexed by subject, residency, tenability, sponsor, and deadline. These titles can be purchased separately (see pricing below) or at a discounted price as part of the *Minority Funding Set*.

Price: *Financial Aid for African Americans,* $37.50; *Financial Aid for Asian Americans,* $35; *Financial Aid for Hispanic Americans,* $37.50; *Financial Aid for Native Americans,* $40. Or, all four volumes can be purchased together, as the *Minority Funding Set,* for the discounted price of $130.

Available from: Reference Service Press, 5000 Windplay Drive, Suite 4, El Dorado Hills, CA 95762. Telephone: (916) 939-9620.
Web site: www.rspfunding.com/

ANNOTATED BIBLIOGRAPHY OF GENERAL FINANCIAL AIDS

[1195]
Financial Aid for the Disabled and Their Families. Published every even-numbered year.

There are more than 1,000 funding opportunities available to meet the individual needs of America's largest minority: 43 million persons with disabilities and their children or parents. To find out about this funding, use *Financial Aid for the Disabled and Their Families.* All disabilities are covered, including visual impairments, hearing impairments, orthopedic disabilities, learning disabilities, and multiple disabilities. The following information is provided for each entry: program title, sponsoring organization address and telephone numbers, purpose, eligibility, financial data, duration, special features, limitations, number awarded, and deadline date. To meet the needs of students with visual impairments, information on programs just for them is also available in a large print report ($30) and on an IBM- or Mac-compatible disk ($50).

Price: $40, hardcover.

Available from: Reference Service Press, 5000 Windplay Drive, Suite 4, El Dorado Hills, CA 95762. Telephone: (916) 939-9620.

Web site: www.rspfunding.com/

[1196]
Financial Aid for Veterans, Military Personnel, and Their Dependents. Published every even-numbered year.

Veterans, military personnel, and their dependents (spouses, children, grandchildren, and dependent parents) make up more than one third of America's population today. Each year, public and private agencies set aside billions of dollars in financial aid for these groups. This directory identifies, in one source, all the federal, state, and privately-funded scholarships, fellowships, loans, grants/grants-in-aid, awards, and internships aimed specifically at individuals with ties to the military. More than 1,100 programs are described in the latest edition. These opportunities are open to applicants at all levels (from high school through postdoctoral) for education, research, travel, training, career development, or emergency situations. The detailed entries are indexed by title, sponsoring organization, geographic coverage, subject, and deadline dates.

Price: $40, hardcover.

Available from: Reference Service Press, 5000 Windplay Drive, Suite 4, El Dorado Hills, CA 95762. Telephone: (916) 939-9620.

Web site: www.rspfunding.com/

Awards

[1197]
Awards, Honors, and Prizes. Annual.

While this massive set is not the kind of publication you're likely to buy for your own financial aid bookshelf, you will definitely want to look at it at a library. It contains the most extensive and up-to-date listing of awards, honors, and prizes available anywhere. It covers all subject areas, all areas of the world, and all types of awards, except scholarships, fellowships, prizes received only as a result of entering contests, and local or regional awards.

Price: Volume 1 (U.S. and Canada): $220; Volume 2 (other countries): $255, hardcover.

Available from: Gale Group, 27500 Drake Road, Farmington Hills, MI 48331-3535. Telephone: (248) 699-4253. Toll free: (800) 877-4253.

Web site: www.galegroup.com/

Internships

[1198]
The Best 106 Internships. Annual.

Unlike Peterson's *Internships* directory (described below), this listing is selective rather than comprehensive. It describes in detail the "top" 100 internships in America, as selected by the Princeton Review and Student Access. Each program entry (generally three pages) provides information on: application process, selection process, compensation, quality of the work experience, locations, duration, prerequisites, and sources of additional information. Previously, this title was issued as *America's Top Internships.*

Price: $21, paper.

Available from: Random House, 400 Hahn Road, Westminster, MD 21157. Telephone: (212) 751-2600. Toll-free: (800) 733-3000.

Web site: www.randomhouse.com/

[1199]
National Directory of Arts Internships. Annual.

If you are interested in finding out about art internships, this is the place to look. More than 5,000 opportunities open to undergraduate and graduate students in the arts are described here. The internships are listed by sponsoring organization in 13 sections, including photography, literacy, film/video, music, dance, and the performing arts. Entries specify purpose, assignment, eligibility requirements, application procedure, and contact person. Both paid and unpaid opportunities are included. In addition to the listings, the directory includes useful sections on how to design an individual internship as well as how to prepare resumes, cover letters, and portfolios.

Price: $75, paper.

Available from: National Network for Artist Placement, 935 West Avenue 37, Los Angeles, CA 90065. Telephone: (323) 222-4305.

Web site: www.artistplacement.com/

[1200]
Peterson's Internships. Annual.

Work experience gained through an internship in a chosen field can provide an advantage in a student's job search. Plus, internships can provided cash for college (in stipends, subsequent scholarships, or both). One of the best ways to find out about internship opportunities is with a copy of the latest edition of this directory, which identifies more than 1,300 organizations offering more than 30,000 on-the-job training opportunities in such fields as architecture, business, communications, and sciences. Program entries describe length and duration of the position, rates of pay, desired qualifications, duties, training involved, availability of college credit, and application contacts, procedures, and deadlines. International internships are also listed, as well as specific information for interns working abroad and non-U.S. citizens applying for U.S. internships.

Price: $24.95, paper.

Available from: Peterson's Guides, Princeton Pike Corporate Center, 2000 Lenox Drive, P.O. Box 67005, Lawrenceville, NJ 08648. Telephone: (609) 896-1800. Toll-free: (800) 338-3282.

Web site: www.petersons.com/

Nothing over $5.50

[1201]

Directory of International Grants and Fellowships in the Health Sciences. 2001.

No activity is more international in scope than the pursuit of scientific knowledge for health. That's because diseases know no national boundaries. This free publication, issued by the Fogarty International Center for Advanced Study in the Health Sciences, lists hundreds of international funding opportunities in biomedical research. Entries are grouped by type (fellowships and grants), are listed be sponsor, and contain information on fields of study supported, number awarded, and deadline dates. This is the Center's most requested publication.

Price: Free, paper.

Available from: John E. Fogarty Center, National Institutes of Health Building 31, Room B2C29, 31 Center Drive, MSC2220, Bethesda, MD 20892-2220. Telephone: (301) 496-2075

Web site: www.nih.gov.fic/

[1202]

Federal Benefits for Veterans and Dependents. Annual.

This is one of the federal government's all-time best-selling publications. The annual pamphlet provides a comprehensive summary of federal government benefits (not all of which are monetary) available to veterans and their dependents. It is updated annually and contains information on alcoholism treatment programs, aid for the blind, burial assistance, clothing allowances, compensation for service-connected disabilities, death payments, dental treatment, dependents' education, education and training loans, etc.

Price: $5.50, paper.

Available from: U.S. Government Printing Office, Washington, DC 20402-9328. Telephone: (202) 512-1800, press 1

Web site: www.access.gpo.gov/su_docs/

[1203]

Financial Assistance for Library and Information Studies. Annual.

This summary of fellowships, scholarships, grants-in-aid, loans, and other funding for library education and research is available from the American Library Association. The booklet is an annually-revised list of awards from state library agencies, national and state library associations, local libraries, and academic institutions offering undergraduate and graduate programs in library education in the United States or Canada. Scholarships of less than $200 are not listed. For each entry, the following information is given: granting body, level of program, type of assistance, number available, academic or other requirements, application deadline, and application address.

Price: Free, paper.

Available from: American Library Association 50 East Huron Street, Chicago, IL 60611. Toll-free: (800) 545-2433.

Web site: www.ala.org/

[1204]

Fulbright and Related Grants for Graduate Study and Research Abroad. Annual.

The Fulbright Student Program is designed to give recent B.S./B.A. graduates, master's degree and doctoral candidates, young professionals, and artists opportunities for personal development and international experience. This annual pamphlet, available without charge from the Institute of International Education (IIE), lists Institute-administered Fulbright fellowships and grants available to U.S. graduate students for study and research abroad. The arrangement is by country in which the recipient will study or conduct research. Entries specify recommended fields of study or investigation, language requirements, duration, selection procedures, financial data, application process, special features, and limitations. A similar publication for more advanced applicants is *Fulbright Scholar Program*, also available without charge from IIE.

Price: Free, paper.

Available from: Institute of International Education, 809 United Nations Plaza, New York, NY 10017-3580. Telephone: (212) 883-8200.

Web site: www.iie.org/

[1205]

Research and Funding: A German-American Guide for Historians and Social Scientists. 1999.

Listed in the current edition are grants and fellowships of interest to graduate students and scholars in the United States and Germany who specialize in history or the social sciences. Focusing on exchanges between the United States and Germany, the guide provides detailed information about institutions that offer financial support and/or affiliations to non-native researchers. It is divided into two sections: funding available for study and research in the United States and funding available for study and research in Germany (funding from German state governments is excluded). Entries are listed by sponsoring organization.

Price: Free, paper.

Available from: German Historical Institute, 1607 New Hampshire Avenue, N.W., Washington, DC 20009. Telephone: (202) 387-3355.

Web site: www.ghi-dc.org/

[1206]

Social Science Research Council Fellowships and Grants for Training and Research. Annual.

The Social Science Research Council is an autonomous, nongovernmental, not-for-profit international association devoted to "the advancement of interdisciplinary research in the social sciences." This annual pamphlet, distributed without charge by the Social Science Research Council, provides a listing and short description of grants that the council sponsors either independently or with the American Council of Learned

Societies. These programs (dissertation fellowships and advanced research grants) apply to the social sciences and humanities in both the United States and, selectively, abroad. They are open to American and foreign citizens on the advanced graduate or postgraduate levels.

Price: Free, paper.

Available from: Social Science Research Council, 810 Seventh Avenue, New York, NY 10019. Telephone: (212) 377-2700.

Web site: www.ssrc.org/

[1207]
The Student Guide: Financial Aid from the U.S. Department of Education. Annual.

Of the more than $80 billion in student aid currently available, one half of it (approximately $40 billion) will be supplied by the federal government. And, most of the federal funds will be channeled through a handful of programs: Pell Grants, Subsidized and Unsubsidized Stafford Loans, PLUS Loans, Federal Supplemental Educational Opportunity Grants, Federal Work-Study, and Federal Perkins Loans. Get information about these programs straight from the source, in this free booklet issued by the U.S. Department of Education. For each program, official information is provided on purpose, financial support offered, application procedures, eligibility, recipient responsibilities, and notification process. The *Guide* is available in print or can be downloaded from the Department of Education's web site.

Price: Free, paper.

Available from: U.S. Department of Education, c/o Federal Student Information Aid Center, P.O. Box 84, Washington, DC 20044. Telephone: (800) 4-FED-AID.

Web site: www.ed.gov/studentaid/

Sponsoring Organization Index

Names of sponsoring organizations are arranged alphabetically here, word by word. To help users select only those programs within their geographic area of interest, each entry number is preceded by an alphabetical code within parentheses: F = Any Foreign Country; A = Asia; C = Canada/Arctic Region; E = Europe, Etc.; L = Latin America/Caribbean; M = Middle East/Africa; and O = Oceania. For example, if the name of a sponsoring organization is followed by (E) 552, a program sponsored by that organization is described in the chapter on Europe, in entry 552. If the same sponsoring organization's name is followed by another entry number—for example, (O) 1150—the user is directed to either a different program sponsored by that organization or to the same program described in the chapter on Oceania, in entry 1150.

Academy of American Poets, (E) 832
Academy of Sciences of Cuba, (L) 1020
Academy of Sciences of the Czech Republic, (E) 716
Agency of Industrial Science and Technology, (A) 261
Alaska State Council on the Arts, (F) 3
Alberta Heritage Foundation for Medical Research, (C) 375
Alexander S. Onassis Public Benefit Foundation, (E) 460–461, 820
Alexander von Humboldt Foundation, (E) 614, 648–649, 739–740
Alicia Patterson Foundation, (F) 4
American Academy in Rome, (F) 106, (E) 475, 481, 550, 588, 603, 641, 692, 709, 715, 757, 771, 798, 842, 858, 928
American Academy of Arts and Letters, (E) 715
American Academy of Nurse Practitioners, (F) 163
American Agricultural Economics Association Foundation, (F) 202
American Alpine Club, (F) 84, 129
American Antiquarian Society, (E) 603
American Association for the Advancement of Science, (A) 372, (E) 938
American Association of Diabetes Educators, (F) 105
American Association of Petroleum Geologists Foundation, (E) 667
American Association of University Women, (F) 5–6, 30, 52, 93, 161, 216, (A) 295, (E) 510, (O) 1128, 1141, 1152, 1154, 1156–1157
American Astronomical Society, (F) 38
American Bird Conservancy, (L) 942
American Bureau for Medical Advancement in China, (A) 225, 267, 316
American Cancer Society, (F) 7–8
American Classical League, (F) 21
American Committee on Clinical Tropical Medicine and Traveler's Health, (F) 25
American Council of Learned Societies, (F) 36, 50, 95, 169, (A) 226, 235, 314, (E) 451, 603, 717, (L) 943, 1020, (M) 1021, 1025
American Councils for International Education, (A) 227–228, 367, (E) 452–453, 915

American Friends of Aphrodisias, (E) 703
American Gynecological and Obstetrical Society, (E) 923
American Heart Association, (F) 9–12
American Hungarian Foundation, (E) 466
American Institute for Maghrib Studies, (M) 1026, 1028–1029
American Institute for Sri Lankan Studies, (A) 229
American Institute for Yemeni Studies, (M) 1027
American Institute of Architects. New York Chapter, (F) 199
American Institute of Bangladesh Studies, (A) 272–273
American Institute of Indian Studies, (A) 230–232
American Institute of Pakistan Studies, (A) 233–234
American Jewish Joint Distribution Committee, Inc., (F) 173, (A) 301, (E) 686, (M) 1065
American Library Association. Association of College and Research Libraries, (E) 728
American Library Association. International Relations Committee, (F) 28
American Museum of Natural History, (F) 62, 124, (C) 442
American Oriental Society, (A) 315
American Philological Association, (E) 901
American Philosophical Society, (F) 13, 63
American Research Center in Egypt, (M) 1030–1031, 1068
American Research Institute in Turkey, (E) 482, 708, 764, (M) 1033, 1071, 1081
American School of Classical Studies at Athens, (E) 467–469, 479, 486, 564, 621, 634, 679–680, 706, 721, 772, 798, 835–836, 854, 881, 932, (M) 1100
American Schools of Oriental Research, (E) 477, 765, 854, 889, (M) 1045–1046, 1058, 1061, 1064, 1069, 1076, 1082–1083, 1088, 1092, 1099–1100, 1117–1120
American Society for Eighteenth-Century Studies, (E) 675
American Society for Microbiology, (F) 206, (L) 945
American Society for Photogrammetry and Remote Sensing, (E) 714
American Society of Tropical Medicine and Hygiene, (F) 25, (L) 978
American Women's Club in Sweden, (E) 470
American Zionist Movement, (M) 1127

F–Any Foreign Country   A–Asia   C–Canada/Arctic Region   E–Europe, Etc.
L–Latin America/Caribbean   M–Middle East/Africa   O–Oceania

SPONSORING ORGANIZATION INDEX

American–Italian Cancer Foundation, (E) 471–472
American–Scandinavian Foundation, (E) 473–474
Amy Lowell Poetry Travelling Scholarship Trust, (F) 14
Andrew W. Mellon Foundation, (F) 36, 95, 177, (A) 252, (C) 419, (E) 475, 531, 603, (L) 951, 1011
Animal Health Trust, (E) 476
Annette Kade Charitable Trust, (E) 480
Antiquarian Bookseller's Association, (F) 27
Aplastic Anemia Foundation of America, Inc., (F) 19
Archaeological Institute of America, (A) 339, (E) 479, 633, 703, 796, 939, (M) 1091
Architectural League of New York, (F) 45
Arizona Commission on the Arts, (L) 950
Arthritis Foundation, (F) 20
Arts International, (F) 73, (E) 484
Asian Cultural Council, (A) 239–241, 294, 302, 338, 355, 360, (E) 890, (L) 1014, (M) 1108
ASIANetwork, (A) 262
Associated Colleges of the Midwest, (A) 291, (L) 963
Association Claude Bernard, (E) 533
Association for Asian Studies, (A) 223, (C) 374
Association for Asian Studies. Northeast Asia Council, (A) 349, 352
Association for Canadian Studies in the United States, (C) 379, 396, 422, 443
Association for Library and Information Science Education, (F) 162
Association for Women in Science, (F) 15, 22, 49, 128, 186
Association of American Geographers, (F) 1, 18
Association to Unite the Democracies, (F) 134
AstraZeneca (UK), (F) 23
Atsumi International Scholarship Foundation, (A) 242
Australia. Rural Industries Research and Development Corporation, (O) 1163
Australian Academy of Science, (O) 1165–1166
Australian Bureau of Statistics, (O) 1130
Australian Federation of University Women, (O) 1141
Australian Federation of University Women. Queensland Fellowship Fund Inc., (O) 1140, 1161
Australian Federation of University Women. South Australia Inc. Trust Fund, (F) 24, 33, (O) 1137, 1151, 1168
Australian Federation of University Women. West Australia, (O) 1128, 1152, 1154, 1156–1157
Australian Institute of Aboriginal and Torres Strait Islander Studies, (O) 1131
Australian Museum, (O) 1132–1133, 1155, 1162
Australian National University. Humanities Research Centre, (O) 1148
Australian Research Council, (O) 1134–1136, 1160
Austria. Federal Ministry of Science and Transport, (E) 487, 496, 577, 602
Austrian Cultural Institute, (E) 450, 487–488, 496, 556, 577, 602
Austrian Research Center on Molecular Pathology, (E) 488

Bancomer Cultural Foundation, (L) 1018
Bank of Sweden Tercentenary Foundation, (E) 491
Barnum Festival Foundation, (E) 494
Bermuda Biological Station for Research, (L) 952–953, 997
Beta Phi Mu, (F) 75
BHP Minerals, (F) 26
Bibliographical Society, (F) 27, 64, (E) 586

Bibliographical Society of America, (F) 64
Bijutsu Kogei Shimbo Sato Kikin, (A) 244
Biotechnology and Biological Sciences Research Council, (E) 546, 914
BirdLife International, (F) 29
Boehringer Ingelheim Fonds, (E) 502–503
Boston Society of Architects, (F) 184
BP Amomo plc, (F) 29
BP–Amoco, (E) 904
Brazil. Conselho Nacional de Desenvolvimento Cientifico e Tecnologico, (L) 1001
Brazil. National Institute for Amazonian Research, (L) 956
Bristol-Myers Squibb Company, (E) 507
British Academy, (E) 508–509, 652, 778
British Federation of Women Graduates, (E) 497, 499, 695, 702, 723
British Federation of Women Graduates Charitable Foundation, (E) 498, 510, 900
British Heart Foundation, (E) 511–512
British Institute in Eastern Africa, (M) 1036–1037
British Medical Association, (E) 687–688, 903
Burroughs Wellcome Fund, (C) 381, (E) 522

Calouste Gulbenkian Foundation, (E) 520
Canada. Department of Foreign Affairs and International Trade, (C) 379–380, 390, 395, 406, 434
Canada. National Capital Commission, (C) 422
Canada. National Research Council, (C) 423
Canadian Embassy, (C) 380, 390, 395, 434
Canadian Federation of University Women, (F) 30
Canadian Institute of Ukrainian Studies, (F) 156, (C) 378, 416, 420, 426
Canadian Institutes of Health Research, (C) 383–386, 430
Canadian Jewish News, (C) 433
Cancer Research Fund of the Damon Runyon–Walter Winchell Foundation, (F) 31
Cancer Research Institute, (F) 98
Carnegie Institution of Washington, (L) 959
CEC International Partners, (A) 238, (E) 485
Center for Chinese Studies, (A) 343
Center for Field Research, (F) 35
Center for International Mobility, (E) 530, 592, 857
Center for the Study of Tropical Birds, Inc., (F) 40
Centre Européen de la Recherche Nucléaire, (E) 526
Centre for Development Research, (A) 272–273
Centre for European Policy Studies, (E) 524–525, (M) 1032
Centre National d'Etudes Spatiales, (E) 534–535
Charles A. and Anne Morrow Lindbergh Foundation, (F) 112, 127
Chemical Heritage Foundation, (M) 1105–1106
Chiang Ching-kuo Foundation for International Scholarly Exchange, (A) 223, 248–251, 371, (C) 374
Christian de Duve Institute of Cellular Pathology, (E) 657
Christopher Reynolds Foundation, (L) 1020
Cintas Foundation, (F) 39
Citicorp Foundation, (A) 252, (E) 531
Civic Education Project, (A) 252, (E) 531
Classical Association of New England, (E) 834
Classical Association of the Empire State, (F) 107
Committee on Women in Agricultural Economics, (F) 202
Community Colleges for International Development, (E) 557
Conference on Latin American History, (E) 720, (L) 985, 989

F–Any Foreign Country   A–Asia   C–Canada/Arctic Region   E–Europe, Etc.
L–Latin America/Caribbean   M–Middle East/Africa   O–Oceania

SPONSORING ORGANIZATION INDEX

Congressional Hunger Center, (A) 318, (E) 745, (L) 996, (M) 1077
Costume Society of America, (F) 44, 198
Council for European Studies, (E) 596, 719, 879
Council for International Exchange of Scholars, (F) 67-70, 157, (A) 270, 319, 340, 359, 364, 369-370, (C) 392, 444-445, 448, (E) 458, 489, 500, 504, 515, 525, 548, 552, 575, 584, 593-595, 609, 615, 660, 690-691, 693, 701, 710, 729, 734, 749, 761, 782-783, 794, 811-813, 815, 849, 859, 864-865, 888, 902, 905-906, 910, 913, 918-922, 925, 929, 931, (L) 948-949, 969, 975, 984, 992-993, 1016, (M) 1022-1024, 1059, 1078, 1113
Council for the Development of Social Science Research in Africa, (M) 1025
Council of American Overseas Research Centers, (A) 230-232, 246, (E) 521, (M) 1038, 1119-1120
Council of International Programs, (A) 254, (E) 538, (M) 1039
Council on Foreign Relations, (A) 282

Dalhousie University, (C) 409
Dallas Museum of Art, (F) 164
Dance Theater Workshop, (A) 355, (E) 890, (L) 1014, (M) 1108
Danish Polar Center, (C) 387
Dayton Hudson Foundation, (F) 104
Delft University of Technology, (E) 549
Delta Waterfowl and Wetlands Research Station, (C) 432
Dr. Heinrich Jörg Foundation, (E) 556
Dublin Institute for Advanced Studies, (E) 559
Dumbarton Oaks, (F) 53, (L) 965, (M) 1040
Durfee Foundation, (C) 388, (L) 966
Dysautonomia Foundation, Inc., (F) 54

Earthwatch, (F) 35, (C) 388, (L) 966
Eastern Bird Banding Association, (C) 389, (L) 967
Ecological Society of America, (L) 973
Elan Pharmaceuticals Corporation, Inc., (F) 65
Eli Lilly and Company, (F) 105
Engineering and Physical Sciences Research Council, (E) 568
English-Speaking Union, (E) 767
English-Speaking Union-Washington Branch, (F) 82
Entomological Society of America, (E) 578
Epilepsy Foundation, (F) 65
Etruscan Foundation, (E) 581
Eurasia Foundation, (A) 252, (E) 531
European Cultural Foundation, (E) 748, 802
European Molecular Biology Organization, (E) 566, (M) 1041
European Research Consortium for Informatics and Mathematics, (E) 574
European University Institute, (E) 583, 683
European University Institute. Robert Schuman Center for Advanced Studies, (E) 845, 904, 927
Explorers Club, (F) 57, 221

Fauna & Flora International, (F) 29
Fight for Sight, Inc., (F) 58, (C) 391
Folger Shakespeare Library, (E) 603
Ford Foundation, (F) 60, 73, (A) 243, 252, (E) 484, 531
Ford Motor Company, (F) 59

Foundation for High Blood Pressure Research, (O) 1150
Foundation for Promotion of Cancer Research, (A) 285
France. Embassy, (E) 527
Frank Huntington Beebe Fund for Musicians, (F) 61
Freedom Forum, (C) 427, (L) 1000
Freeman Foundation, (A) 262
French Association of University Women, (E) 505, 684, (M) 1075
French Atherosclerosis Society, (E) 819
French Cultural Services, (E) 528, 877
French National Institute for Computer Science and Automation, (E) 668
French-American Foundation, (E) 605
Friedrich Ebert Foundation, (E) 606-608
Fritz Thyssen Foundation, (E) 700
Fuji Bank International Foundation, (A) 263
Fujisaki Cell Center, (A) 268
Fyssen Foundation, (E) 612

Garden Club of America, (F) 17, 74, (E) 588
GC Corporation, (F) 204
Gen Foundation, (A) 265
Genentech, Inc., (F) 8
General Mills Foundation, (F) 104
Geological Society of America, (L) 944, 977, (O) 1143
German Academic Exchange Service (DAAD), (C) 394, (E) 541-544, 551, 618
German Historical Institute, (E) 616, 700
German Marshall Fund of the United States, (E) 495, 617
Getty Grant Program, (F) 100-101
Ghana. Ministry of Health, (M) 1087
Gladys Krieble Delmas Foundation, (E) 624
Glaxo Wellcome PLC, (E) 872
GlaxoSmithKline, (F) 42
Gorgas Memorial Institute of Tropical and Preventive Medicine, (L) 978
Gottlieb Daimler-und-Karl Benz-Stiftung, (E) 627
Greece. State Scholarships Foundation, (E) 856
Gynaecological Visiting Society of Great Britain and Ireland, (E) 923

Hague Academy of International Law, (E) 449
Harry Frank Guggenheim Foundation, (F) 77-78
Harvard Travellers Club Permanent Fund, (F) 79
Hayashibara Group, (A) 268
Health Research Council of New Zealand, (O) 1146
Heart and Stroke Foundation of Canada, (C) 399
Hebrew University of Jerusalem, (M) 1079
Heinrich Hertz Foundation, (E) 637
Heinz Family Foundation, (L) 979
Heiser Program for Research in Leprosy and Tuberculosis, (F) 80-81
Helen Hay Whitney Foundation, (F) 83
Henry J. Kaiser Family Foundation, (M) 1089
Henry Luce Foundation, (A) 322
Herzog August Bibliothek, (E) 640, 784
Hillel: The Foundation for Jewish Campus Life, (C) 401, (M) 1047
Hitachi, Ltd., (A) 282
Hosei University, (A) 271
Hospital for Sick Children, (C) 435-437

F-Any Foreign Country   A-Asia   C-Canada/Arctic Region   E-Europe, Etc.
L-Latin America/Caribbean   M-Middle East/Africa   O-Oceania

SPONSORING ORGANIZATION INDEX

Human Frontier Science Program Organization, (A) 274–276, (C) 402–404, (E) 645–647
Human Rights Watch, (A) 259, (E) 590, (L) 970, (M) 1043
Hungary. Ministry for Foreign Affairs, (E) 924
Huntington Library, Art Collections, and Botanical Gardens, (E) 603, 652

Iceland. Ministry of Culture and Education, (E) 656
Ichiro Kanehara Foundation, (A) 278
IDEC Pharmaceuticals Corporation, (F) 8
Imperial Cancer Research Fund, (E) 661
Institut Curie, (E) 560, 666
Institut Français de Washington, (E) 604
Institut Français du Pétrole, (E) 667
Institut für die Wissenschaften vom Menschen, (E) 678, 682, 748, 802
Institut National de la Santé et de la Recherche Médicale, (E) 663–665
Institute for European History, (E) 669
Institute of Current World Affairs, Inc., (F) 109, (A) 363, (E) 694, 896, (M) 1066, 1109
Institute of Human Paleontology, (E) 823
Institute of International Education, (F) 39, 66, (A) 264, 290, 327, 342, 361, (C) 377, 393, 415, 421, 427, (E) 464, 524, 551, 585, 610, 631, 650, 656, 659, 774, 817, 824–825, 848, 898, (L) 976, 1000, (M) 1093, 1110
Institute of Southeast Asian Studies, (A) 286
Institute of Turkish Studies, (E) 818, 822, (M) 1094–1095
Instituto Camoes, (E) 670
Inter American Press Association, (C) 405, (L) 981
International Agency for Research on Cancer, (F) 89, (E) 654–655
International Agricultural Centre, (E) 589
International Association for Dental Research, (F) 108, 204
International Association of Culinary Professionals Foundation, (E) 697–698
International Astronomical Union, (F) 91
International Atherosclerosis Society, (F) 90, 130
International Atomic Energy Agency, (F) 92, (E) 658
International Brain Research Organization, (E) 665
International Center for Journalists, (F) 59, 114, 191, (A) 277, 292, (E) 483
International Center for Theoretical Physics, (F) 92, (E) 658
International Council for Canadian Studies, (C) 379, 396, 406, 422
International Council of Scientific Unions, (F) 217
International Crops Research Institute for the Semi-Arid Tropics, (A) 279–280, (M) 1051–1052
International Federation of University Women, (F) 30, 52, 93, 161, 216, (E) 510
International Livestock Research Institute, (M) 1053–1054
International Mathematical Union, (F) 34
International Reading Association, (F) 43
International Research Exchange Foundation for Japanese Studies, (A) 283
International Research & Exchanges Board, (A) 281, 322, 351, (E) 662, 862, (M) 1055, 1104
International Society of Arboriculture, (F) 88, 111
International Union against Cancer, (F) 7, 23, 94, 160, 220
International Union for Vacuum Science, Technique and Applications, (F) 212

International Union of Biochemistry and Molecular Biology, (F) 217
Internationales Forschungszentrum Kulturwissenchaften, (E) 659–660
Irish American Cultural Institute, (E) 653, 674
Irish Research Council for the Humanities and Social Sciences, (E) 629
Istituto Nazionale di Studi sul Rinascimento, (E) 852
Istituto Superiore di Sanità, (E) 677
Italian Association for Research on Cancer, (F) 89
Italian Institute of Historical Studies, (E) 456, 587

James S. McDonnell Foundation, (F) 135
Jane Coffin Childs Memorial Fund for Medical Research, (F) 102
Japan. Agency for Cultural Affairs, (A) 366
Japan Foundation, (A) 237, 255, 288–289, 293
Japan Foundation. Center for Global Partnership, (A) 224
Japan International Science and Technology Exchange Center, (A) 303–304, 308, 356
Japan. Ministry of Education, Culture, Sports, Science and Technology, (A) 298–300, 303–310, 313, 321, 344, 348
Japan. Ministry of Foreign Affairs, (A) 298–300
Japan. Ministry of Home Affairs, (A) 298–300
Japan. Ministry of International Trade and Industry, (F) 154, (A) 261, 328
Japan Science and Technology Corporation, (A) 356
Japan Society for the Promotion of Science, (A) 303–310, 313, 331–336, 348, 354
Japan–United States Friendship Commission, (F) 103, (A) 287, 350, 352, 366
Japanese Association for American Studies, (A) 350
Japanese Association of University Women, (A) 295
Jerome Foundation, (F) 104
John D. and Catherine T. MacArthur Foundation, (A) 252, (E) 531, (L) 1020
John Dinkeloo Bequests, (F) 106, (E) 692
John F. Kennedy Center for the Performing Arts, (A) 296, (L) 986, (M) 1063
John S. and James L. Knight Foundation, (F) 114
John Simon Guggenheim Memorial Foundation, (F) 110
Joint Oceanographic Institutions Incorporated, (F) 188
Journals of Reproduction and Fertility Ltd., (E) 696, 837

Keizai Koho Center, (A) 277
Kettering Fund, (A) 238, (E) 485
Kobe College Corporation, (A) 247
Korea Foundation, (A) 349
Korea Science and Engineering Foundation, (A) 236, 311, 357
Korean–American Scientists and Engineers Association, (A) 311
Kosciuszko Foundation, (E) 630, 899
Kumahira Scholarship Foundation, (A) 312
Kurt Weill Foundation for Music, Inc., (F) 116–117
Kyowa Hakko Kogyo Company Ltd., (F) 220

Lady Allen of Hurtwood Memorial Trust, (F) 119
Lady Davis Fellowship Trust, (M) 1072–1073
Lady Tata Memorial Trust, (F) 120

F–Any Foreign Country   A–Asia   C–Canada/Arctic Region   E–Europe, Etc.
L–Latin America/Caribbean   M–Middle East/Africa   O–Oceania

Lalor Foundation, (F) 121
Lemmermann Foundation, (E) 713
Leo Baeck Institute, (E) 543
LH Systems, LLC, (E) 714
Life Sciences Research Foundation, (F) 126
Loren L. Zachary Society for the Performing Arts, (E) 768
L.S.B. Leakey Foundation, (F) 122
Luso–American Development Foundation, (E) 593–594
Luso–American Foundation, (E) 719
Lutheran Brotherhood Insurance Society, (E) 465

Manomet Center for Conservation Sciences, (L) 987
Mansfield Center for Pacific Affairs, (A) 320
Marine Biological Association of the United Kingdom, (E) 725–727, 808, 833
Matsumae International Foundation, (A) 317
Max Planck Institute for the History of Science, (E) 737–738
Max Planck Society for the Advancement of Science, (E) 739
McGill University. Department of Chemistry, (C) 398
McGill University. Faculty of Law, (C) 417–418
Mexico. Consejo Nacional de Ciencia y Tecnología, (L) 1002
Mexico. Ministry of Education, (L) 1012
Mexico. National Fund for Culture and the Arts, (L) 1018
Microsoft Research Limited, (E) 746
Minnesota Newspaper Foundation, (F) 205
Missouri Botanical Garden, (F) 17
Mittag–Leffler Institute, (E) 750
Montreal Neurological Institute and Hospital, (C) 411
Multiple Sclerosis Society of Great Britain and Northern Ireland, (E) 755
Music Library Association, (F) 47
Myasthenia Gravis Foundation of America, Inc., (F) 113

Nadia et Lili Boulanger International Foundation, (E) 759
National Academy of Education, (F) 197
National Association of Black Journalists, (M) 1042
National Council for Eurasian and East European Research, (A) 256, 323–324, 341, (E) 562, 762–763, 816
National Council of Applied Economics Research (India), (A) 327
National Foundation for Infectious Diseases, (F) 42
National Gallery of Art, (F) 16, 37, 99, 132, 165, 178, 187, 219, (E) 545
National Geographic Society, (F) 146
National Heart Foundation of Australia, (O) 1175
National Humanities Center, (E) 603
National Italian American Foundation, (E) 553
National Library of Australia, (O) 1144–1145
National Maritime Museum, (E) 518–519, 853
National Research Council, (F) 60, (A) 253, 266, (E) 536, 628, 766
National Science Foundation, (F) 188, (A) 230–232, 253, 372, (E) 536, 766, 938
National Science Foundation. Directorate for Biological Sciences, (F) 55, 141, 171–172
National Science Foundation. Directorate for Computer and Information Science and Engineering, (L) 1001–1002
National Science Foundation. Directorate for Education and Human Resources, (F) 32, (A) 337, (C) 428, (E) 792

National Science Foundation. Directorate for Engineering, (L) 1002
National Science Foundation. Directorate for Geosciences, (C) 446, (L) 1017
National Science Foundation. Directorate for Mathematical and Physical Sciences, (F) 133, 142
National Science Foundation. Directorate for Social, Behavioral, and Economic Sciences, (F) 96, 141, 150–153, 201, (A) 306, 310, 321, 331–336, 356–358, (E) 544, 668, (M) 1116
National Science Foundation. Office of Polar Programs, (C) 376, (O) 1129
National Shellfisheries Association, Inc., (F) 136
National Society for Histotechnology, (F) 123
National Speleological Society, (F) 174
Natural Science and Engineering Research Council of Canada, (C) 447
Neotropical Bird Club, (F) 155
Nestlé Foundation, (F) 200
Netherland–America Foundation, (E) 773–774
Netherlands Institute for Advanced Study, (E) 626, 781
Netherlands Ministry of Agriculture, Nature Management and Fisheries, (E) 589
Netherlands Ministry of Education, Culture and Science, (E) 781
Netherlands Science Foundation, (E) 781
New Energy and Industrial Technology Development Organization, (F) 154, (A) 261, 328
New York Community Trust, (E) 832
New Zealand. Department of Internal Affairs, (O) 1159
New Zealand Federation of University Women, (F) 161
New Zealand Vice–Chancellors' Committee, (O) 1158
Newberry Library, (E) 480, 603, 640, 778
Nissho Iwai Foundation, (A) 330
Norddeutsche Landesbank, (E) 784
Norsemen's Federation, (E) 465
North American Conference on British Studies, (E) 758
North American Serials Interest Group, (F) 131
North Atlantic Treaty Organization, (A) 325–326, (C) 424–425, (E) 769–770, (M) 1085–1086
Norway. Ministry of Foreign Affairs, (E) 787
Norway–America Association, (E) 465, 788
Norwegian Federation of University Women, (E) 565
Norwegian Information Service in the United States, (E) 787–788
Norwich Jubilee Esperanto Foundation, (F) 158, (E) 790
Novartis Crop Protection, Inc., (E) 578
Novartis Foundation, (F) 159, (E) 791
Novartis (Switzerland), (F) 160

Oak Ridge Institute for Science and Education, (A) 368
Ock Rang Cultural Foundation, (A) 338
Ohio Arts Council, (A) 238, (E) 485
Online Computer Library Center, (F) 162
Open Society Archives, (E) 797
Open Society Institute, (F) 195, (A) 252, (E) 531
Organization for Tropical Studies, (L) 951, 964, 1004, 1007, 1011, 1013, 1019
Organization of American Historians, (F) 118, (A) 350
Organization of American States, (C) 429, (L) 1003
Osyp and Josaphat Neporany Educational Fund, (F) 156, (C) 426
Oxford Bibliographical Society, (E) 586

F–Any Foreign Country
L–Latin America/Caribbean
A–Asia
M–Middle East/Africa
C–Canada/Arctic Region
E–Europe, Etc.
O–Oceania

SPONSORING ORGANIZATION INDEX

Pan American Round Table of Texas, (L) 971, 991
Parapsychology Foundation, Inc., (F) 56
Parke–Davis France, (E) 819
Paul Mellon Centre for Studies in British Art, (E) 803–807
Pew Charitable Trusts, (F) 135
Phi Beta Kappa Society, (E) 731–732
Philippe Foundation, (E) 809
Pittsburgh Foundation, (F) 211
Poland. Ministry of Education, (E) 817
Poland. Ministry of National Education, (E) 630, 899
Pontifical Institute of Mediaeval Studies, (C) 419
Population Council, (F) 167–168, (M) 1087
Princeton University. Institute for Advanced Study, (E) 603
Project Syndicate, (E) 748
Pulp and Paper Research Institute of Canada, (C) 398

Québec. Ministère des Relations Internationales, (C) 431
Queen's University of Belfast. Academic Council Office, (E) 638, 735, 831, 861
Queen's University of Belfast. Institute of Irish Studies, (E) 839, 860

Radio and Television News Directors Foundation, (E) 619
Radiological Society of North America, (F) 185
Rainforest Alliance, (L) 988
Raptor Research Foundation, (M) 1074
Renaissance Society of America, (E) 852
Research Council of Norway, (E) 789
Research Institute of Innovative Technology for the Earth, (F) 154
Research into Ageing, (E) 840–841
Rhode Island Foundation, (F) 137
Rhodes University, (M) 1049–1050, 1098
RIAS (Radio in the American Sector) Berlin Commission, (E) 619
Richard III Society, Inc., (E) 934
Robert Bosch Foundation, (A) 252, (E) 531
Roche Research Foundation, (E) 846
Rockefeller Foundation, (F) 73, 179–182, (A) 355, (E) 484, 603, 890, (L) 1014, 1018, (M) 1108
Rotary Foundation, (F) 183
Royal College of Obstetricians and Gynaecologists, (E) 923
Royal College of Surgeons of England, (E) 785
Royal Institute of British Architects, (E) 642, 751
Royal Irish Academy, (E) 821, 850
Royal Netherlands Academy of Arts and Sciences, (E) 626, 781
Royal Society, (E) 554, 599, 760, 851
Royal Society of Edinburgh, (E) 844
Royal Society of Tropical Medicine and Hygiene, (F) 176
Royal Swedish Academy of Sciences, (E) 750
Royal Town Planning Institute, (E) 613

Sakura of America, (E) 539
Samuel H. Kress Foundation, (F) 115, (E) 707–708, 854, (M) 1068, 1070–1071, 1099–1100
Satoh Artcraft Research and Scholarship Foundation, (A) 244
Savoy Foundation, (C) 438–440
Science and Technology Agency of Japan, (A) 356

Science Service, (E) 671
Search Associates, (F) 189
Selby Scientific Foundation, (O) 1166
Shalem Center, (M) 1102–1103
Sigma Theta Tau International, (F) 192
Sigrid Juselius Foundation, (E) 866
Sigurdur Nordal Institute, (E) 875
Simone and Cino del Duca Foundation, (E) 870–871
Sino–American Cultural Foundation, (A) 360
Sir Mark Mitchell Research Foundation, (O) 1167
Skidmore, Owings & Merrill Foundation, (F) 190, 207
Smithsonian Center for Materials Research and Education, (A) 346–347, (L) 1008–1009
Smithsonian Institution, (A) 230–232
Smithsonian Institution. National Museum of Natural History, (A) 245, (L) 954–956, 958, 998, 1010
Smithsonian Institution. National Zoological Park, (L) 1010
Smithsonian Institution. Office of Fellowships and Grants, (L) 1010
Smithsonian Institution. Office of International Relations, (A) 353, (E) 874
Smithsonian Tropical Research Institute, (L) 951, 1010–1011, 1015
Social Science Research Council, (F) 50–51, 95, 103, 169–170, 175, (A) 224, 226, 243, 258, 287, 306, 310, 314, 354, (E) 451, 495, 582, 717, (L) 943, 1020, (M) 1021, 1025, 1056
Society for French American Cultural Services and Educational Aid, (E) 855
Society for Historians of American Foreign Relations, (F) 143, 210
Society for Integrative and Comparative Biology, (F) 125
Society for Italian Historical Studies, (E) 907
Society of Antiquaries of London, (F) 193, (E) 880
Society of Architectural Historians, (A) 257, (E) 563, (L) 968
Society of Economic Geologists Foundation, (F) 26, 85, 87, 194, (C) 400
Society of Toxicology, (E) 941
Society of Vertebrate Paleontology, (A) 373
Solow Art and Architecture Foundation, (E) 881
South Africa. National Research Foundation, (M) 1025, 1084
Spain. Ministry of Education, Culture, and Sports, (E) 826
Spalding Trust, (F) 196
Spencer Foundation, (F) 197
Stanford University. Center for Advanced Study in the Behavioral Sciences, (E) 603
Starr Foundation, (A) 252, (E) 531
Studio Art Centers International, (E) 622
Surgipath Medical Industries, Inc., (F) 123
Swedish Cancer Society, (E) 892
Swedish Council of America, (E) 625
Swedish Foundation for International Cooperation in Research and Higher Education, (E) 886–887
Swedish Information Service, (C) 441, (E) 878
Swedish Institute, (E) 893
Swedish Natural Science Research Council, (E) 894
Swedish Women's Educational Association International, Inc., (E) 891
Swets Blackwell, (E) 728
Swiss Academy of Medical Sciences, (E) 626
Swiss National Science Foundation, (E) 895
SyCip Family Foundation, (A) 359

F–Any Foreign Country
L–Latin America/Caribbean
A–Asia
C–Canada/Arctic Region
M–Middle East/Africa
E–Europe, Etc.
O–Oceania

SPONSORING ORGANIZATION INDEX

Taiwan National Science Council, (A) 358
Takase Scholarship Foundation, (A) 362
Teresa and H. John Heinz III Foundation, (F) 191
Thrasher Research Fund, (F) 203
Toray Industries Incorporated, (F) 220
Toyobo Biotechnology Foundation, (A) 365
Trinity College. Cesare Barbieri Endowment for Italian Culture, (E) 907
Trust for Mutual Understanding, (A) 238, 355, (E) 485, 890, (L) 1014, (M) 1108

U.N. Educational, Scientific, and Cultural Organization, (F) 92, (E) 658, 716
United States–Israel Binational Science Foundation, (M) 1096–1097, 1114
United States–Israel Binational Agricultural Research and Development Fund, (M) 1034, 1121
United States–Japan Foundation, (A) 292
University Institutes in the Vienna Biocenter, (E) 488
University of Alaska at Fairbanks, (C) 412
University of Alberta, (C) 407
University of Alberta. Faculty of Graduate Studies and Research, (C) 397
University of British Columbia, (C) 408
University of Calgary, (C) 413–414
University of Calgary. Arctic Institute of North America, (C) 412
University of California. University Research Expeditions Program, (F) 208–209
University of Cambridge, (E) 513, 795
University of Cambridge. Clare Hall, (E) 532
University of Cambridge. Corpus Christi College, (E) 537, 827
University of Cambridge. Darwin College, (E) 457, 746, 753
University of Cambridge. Downing College, (E) 555
University of Cambridge. Emmanuel College, (E) 567, 872
University of Cambridge. Faculty of History, (E) 742
University of Cambridge. Girton College, (E) 623, 724
University of Cambridge. Judge Institute of Management, (E) 507
University of Cambridge. King's College, (E) 704
University of Cambridge Library, (E) 756
University of Cambridge. Lucy Cavendish College, (E) 462, 580, 632, 718
University of Cambridge. New Hall, (E) 777
University of Cambridge. Newnham College, (E) 779–780
University of Cambridge. Pembroke College, (E) 507
University of Cambridge. Queen's College, (E) 830
University of Cambridge. Sidney Sussex College, (E) 863
University of Cambridge. St. Catherine's College, (E) 883
University of Cambridge. St. John's College, (F) 76, (E) 743
University of Cambridge. Trinity College, (E) 457
University of Cambridge. Trinity Hall, (E) 909
University of Cape Town, (M) 1115
University of Durham, (E) 455
University of East Anglia. School of English and American Studies, (E) 547
University of Iceland. Vestmannaeyjar Research Center, (E) 464
University of London, (E) 681
University of London. Institute of Classical Studies, (F) 138, (E) 454, 897
University of London. Warburg Institute, (E) 784
University of Manchester, (E) 867–869
University of Melbourne, (O) 1170

University of Minnesota. Center for Austrian Studies, (E) 450, 523
University of Minnesota. The Global Campus, (E) 826
University of Newcastle upon Tyne, (E) 873, 933
University of Oxford, (E) 689
University of Oxford. All Souls College, (E) 463
University of Oxford. Balliol College, (E) 490
University of Oxford. Brasenose College, (E) 506
University of Oxford. Christ Church, (E) 529, 600, 712
University of Oxford. Corpus Christi College, (E) 827
University of Oxford. Exeter College, (E) 752, 828, 885
University of Oxford. Harris Manchester College, (E) 747
University of Oxford. Hertford College, (E) 639
University of Oxford. Jesus College, (E) 685
University of Oxford. Lady Margaret Hall, (E) 573, 597, 636
University of Oxford. Linacre College, (E) 572
University of Oxford. Lincoln College, (E) 569
University of Oxford. Mansfield College, (E) 722
University of Oxford. Merton College, (E) 744
University of Oxford. New College, (E) 776
University of Oxford. Nuffield College, (E) 793
University of Oxford. Oriel College, (E) 635
University of Oxford. Oxford Centre for Hebrew and Jewish Studies, (E) 799
University of Oxford. Oxford Centre for Islamic Studies, (E) 492, 561, 754, 800–801, 838
University of Oxford. Pitt Rivers Museum, (M) 1062
University of Oxford. Queen's College, (E) 493, 514, 829
University of Oxford. Somerville College, (E) 576, 730, 733
University of Oxford. St. Anne's College, (E) 478, 558, 611, 673
University of Oxford. St. Antony's College, (E) 705, 736
University of Oxford. St. Cross College, (E) 570
University of Oxford. St. Edmund Hall, (E) 935
University of Oxford. St. Hilda's College, (E) 571, 699, 843, 926
University of Oxford. St. John's College, (E) 884
University of Oxford. Trinity College, (E) 908
University of Oxford. University College, (E) 916–917
University of Oxford. Wadham College, (E) 930
University of Oxford. Wolfson College, (E) 644, 676, 810, 876, 937
University of Oxford. Worcester College, (E) 940
University of Queensland, (O) 1169, 1171
University of Sydney, (O) 1138, 1164, 1172
University of Toronto. Jewish Studies Program, (C) 433
University of Virginia. International Studies Office, (E) 459
University of Western Australia, (O) 1142, 1173
University of Western Ontario. Centre for Interdisciplinary Studies in Chemical Physics, (C) 382
University of Wisconsin at Madison. German Department, (E) 616
University Women's Association of Delhi, (A) 345
U.S. Agency for International Development, (F) 46, (M) 1116
U.S. Department of Agriculture, (M) 1116
U.S. Department of Agriculture. Agricultural Research Service, (A) 356, (M) 1034, 1121
U.S. Department of Agriculture. Graduate School, (E) 516–517, 540, 579, 591, 601, 620, 651, 711, 775, 786, 814, 847, 882, 911–912, (L) 946–947, 957, 960–962, 974, 994–995, 1005–1006, (M) 1035, 1060, 1080, 1101, 1107, 1111–1112, 1126
U.S. Department of Commerce. National Oceanic and Atmospheric Administration, (F) 41
U.S. Department of Education, (M) 1125

F–Any Foreign Country A–Asia C–Canada/Arctic Region E–Europe, Etc.
L–Latin America/Caribbean M–Middle East/Africa O–Oceania

SPONSORING ORGANIZATION INDEX

U.S. Department of Education. Office of Postsecondary Education, (F) 71-72
U.S. Department of Energy, (A) 368, (M) 1116
U.S. Department of State, (F) 50, 66, 169, (A) 227-228, 256, 258, 264, 266, 281, 323-324, 337, 341-342, 351, 367, (C) 428, (E) 452-453, 482, 516-517, 524, 540, 562, 579, 582, 585, 591, 601, 610, 620, 628, 651, 662, 711, 762-763, 775, 786, 792, 814, 816, 824, 847, 862, 882, 911-912, 915, 924, (L) 946-947, 957, 960-962, 974, 976, 994-995, 1005-1006, (M) 1026, 1028-1029, 1032-1033, 1035, 1055, 1060, 1080, 1101, 1104, 1107, 1111-1112, 1126
U.S. Department of State. Bureau of Educational and Cultural Affairs, (F) 67-70, (A) 230-232, 246, 270, 296, 319-320, 340, 359, 364, 369-370, (C) 392, 444-445, 448, (E) 458, 489, 500, 504, 515, 521, 525, 548, 552, 575, 584, 593-595, 609, 615, 660, 690-691, 693, 701, 710, 729, 734, 749, 761, 782-783, 794, 811-813, 815, 849, 859, 864-865, 888, 902, 905-906, 910, 913, 918-922, 925, 929, 931, (L) 948-949, 969, 975, 984, 986, 992-993, 1016, (M) 1022-1024, 1030, 1038, 1059, 1063, 1078, 1113
U.S. Environmental Protection Agency, (F) 139, (M) 1116
U.S. Fish and Wildlife Service, (L) 942
U.S. Geological Survey, (F) 55
U.S. Information Agency, (M) 1027, 1117-1120
U.S. National Aeronautics and Space Administration, (F) 144
U.S. National Endowment for the Arts, (A) 238, 366, (E) 485
U.S. National Endowment for the Humanities, (A) 226, 230-232, 235, 281, 351, (E) 451, 662, 764-765, 771-772, 862, 901, (L) 943, (M) 1021, 1031, 1055, 1081-1083, 1104
U.S. National Institutes of Health, (F) 147, 149
U.S. National Institutes of Health. Fogarty International Center, (F) 2, 55, 86, 97, (A) 260, 269, 284, 303-310, 356, (E) 598, 643, 672, (L) 972, 980, 982, (M) 1044, 1048, 1057, (O) 1139, 1147, 1149
U.S. National Institutes of Health. National Cancer Institute, (F) 94, 97, 145, 148
U.S. National Institutes of Health. National Institute of Allergy and Infectious Diseases, (F) 148, (A) 329, (L) 999, (M) 1090
U.S. National Institutes of Health. National Institute of Arthritis and Musculoskeletal and Skin Diseases, (F) 148
U.S. National Institutes of Health. National Institute of Child Health and Human Development, (F) 97, 148
U.S. National Institutes of Health. National Institute of Dental and Craniofacial Research, (F) 148
U.S. National Institutes of Health. National Institute of Diabetes and Digestive and Kidney Diseases, (A) 329, (L) 999, (M) 1090
U.S. National Institutes of Health. National Institute of Environmental Health Sciences, (F) 55
U.S. National Institutes of Health. National Institute of General Medical Sciences, (F) 55
U.S. National Institutes of Health. National Institute of Mental Health, (F) 97
U.S. National Institutes of Health. National Institute of Nursing Research, (F) 97
U.S. National Institutes of Health. National Institute on Aging, (F) 140, 148
U.S. National Institutes of Health. National Institute on Alcohol Abuse and Alcoholism, (F) 48, 148
U.S. National Institutes of Health. National Institute on Deafness and Other Communication Disorders, (F) 148
U.S. National Institutes of Health. National Institute on Drug Abuse, (F) 97
U.S. Navy, (A) 368

U.S. Peace Corps, (F) 166
U.S. Science Advisory Committee, (F) 188
U.S.-Egypt Joint Board on Scientific and Technological Cooperation, (M) 1116
U.S.-Mexico Fund for Culture, (L) 1018

Van Alen Institute, (F) 106, (E) 692
Vernon Willey Trust, (O) 1174
Victoria University of Wellington, (O) 1153
Villa I Tatti, (E) 603

Weizmann Institute of Science, (M) 1067, 1123-1124
Welch Foundation, (F) 212
Wellcome Trust, (E) 501
Wenner-Gren Foundation for Anthropological Research, Inc., (F) 213-215
West African Research Association, (M) 1122, 1125
West African Research Center, (M) 1122
Whatcom Museum, (C) 410, (L) 983
Winston Churchill Foundation, (E) 936
Woodrow Wilson National Fellowship Foundation, (F) 177
Woods Hole Marine Biological Laboratory, (A) 297, (E) 741, (L) 990
World Health Organization, (F) 89, 97, (E) 654-655
World Learning, (F) 46
World Nature Association, Inc., (F) 218
World Wildlife Fund, (F) 74

Yvar Mikhashoff Trust for New Music, (F) 222

Zeneca, Ltd., (E) 941

F—Any Foreign Country
L—Latin America/Caribbean
A—Asia
M—Middle East/Africa
C—Canada/Arctic Region
E—Europe, Etc.
O—Oceania

Geographic Index

Some of the programs listed in this book can be used only in specific countries. Others may be used anywhere in the world. The Geographic Index identifies funding that is restricted to a specific area as well as funding that has no tenability restrictions (these are listed under the term "Foreign countries"). It is arranged alphabetically (word by word) by geographic area of tenability (country, region, continent). "See" references direct the reader from variant country names to formal index terms. Cross-references provide access to broader or more specific geographic index terms. Remember: in addition to checking the specific areas of interest to you, be sure to check the listings under "Foreign countries," since funding listed there can be used in any area outside the United States.

Aegean Islands, 339, 633, 796, 1091. *See also* Foreign countries; Mediterranean region

Afghanistan, 314, 717. *See also* Asia; Foreign countries

Africa, 86, 226, 260, 269, 284, 296, 318, 355, 363, 451, 598, 643, 672, 745, 890, 896, 943, 972, 980, 982, 986, 996, 1014, 1021, 1023-1026, 1028-1029, 1036-1037, 1042, 1044, 1048, 1056-1057, 1062-1063, 1074, 1077, 1108-1109, 1125, 1139, 1147, 1149. *See also* Foreign countries; names of specific countries

Albania, 238, 252, 259, 281, 323-324, 342, 351, 372, 485, 531, 590, 662, 762-763, 824, 862, 938, 970, 1043, 1055, 1104. *See also* Europe; Foreign countries; Mediterranean region

Algeria, 1026, 1028-1029. *See also* Africa; Foreign countries; Mediterranean region

Antarctica, 1129. *See also* Foreign countries

Antigua and Barbuda, 429, 1003. *See also* Caribbean; Foreign countries

Arctic region, 85, 376, 400, 412, 442. *See also* Foreign countries; names of specific countries

Argentina, 429, 946-949, 1003. *See also* Foreign countries; South America

Armenia, 227-228, 238, 252-253, 281, 323-324, 342, 351, 372, 452-453, 485, 531, 536, 662, 762-763, 824, 862, 938, 1055, 1104. *See also* Europe; Foreign countries; Independent States of the Former Soviet Union

Asia, 86, 226, 239-241, 258, 260, 262, 269, 284, 296, 302, 318, 339, 355, 363, 451, 582, 598, 643, 672, 745, 796, 890, 896, 943, 972, 980, 982, 986, 996, 1014, 1021, 1044, 1048, 1057, 1063, 1077, 1091, 1108-1109, 1139, 1147, 1149. *See also* Foreign countries; names of specific countries

Australia, 1128, 1130-1138, 1140-1142, 1144-1145, 1148, 1150-1152, 1154-1157, 1160-1173, 1175. *See also* Foreign countries

Austria, 254, 274-276, 402-404, 450, 487-489, 496, 523, 538, 552, 556, 566, 577, 602, 645-647, 659-660, 678, 682, 690, 701, 748, 768, 802, 865, 918-921, 1039, 1041. *See also* Europe; Foreign countries

Azerbaijan, 227-228, 238, 253, 259, 281, 314, 323-324, 342, 351, 452-453, 485, 536, 590, 662, 717, 762-763, 824, 862, 970, 1043, 1055, 1104. *See also* Europe; Foreign countries; Independent States of the Former Soviet Union

Bahamas, 429, 1003. *See also* Caribbean; Foreign countries

Bahrain, 319, 1078. *See also* Foreign countries; Middle East

Bangladesh, 243, 246, 259, 272-273, 319, 521, 590, 970, 1038, 1043, 1078. *See also* Asia; Foreign countries

Barbados, 429, 1003. *See also* Caribbean; Foreign countries

Barbuda. *See* Antigua and Barbuda

Belarus, 227-228, 238, 252-253, 281, 323-324, 342, 351, 452-453, 485, 531, 536, 662, 749, 762-763, 824, 862, 1055, 1104. *See also* Europe; Foreign countries; Independent States of the Former Soviet Union

Belgium, 274-276, 402-404, 524-525, 566, 584-585, 609, 645-647, 657, 1041. *See also* Europe; Foreign countries

Belize, 429, 958, 1003. *See also* Central America; Foreign countries

Benin, 1035. *See also* Africa; Foreign countries; Nigeria

Bermuda, 952-953, 997. *See also* Caribbean; Foreign countries

Bolivia, 259, 429, 590, 970, 978, 1003, 1043. *See also* Foreign countries; South America

Brazil, 259, 329, 429, 590, 741, 948, 956-957, 969-970, 978, 990, 999, 1001, 1003, 1043, 1090. *See also* Foreign countries; South America

Britain. *See* United Kingdom

Bulgaria, 238, 252-253, 281, 323-324, 342, 351, 372, 485, 515-517, 531, 536, 662, 749, 762-763, 824, 862, 938, 1055, 1104. *See also* Europe; Foreign countries

Burma. *See* Myanmar

Byelorussia. *See* Belarus

Cambodia, 259, 590, 970, 1043. *See also* Asia; Foreign countries

Cameroon, 329, 999, 1090. *See also* Africa; Foreign countries

411

GEOGRAPHIC INDEX

Canada, 58, 85, 156, 223, 274–276, 325–326, 337, 374–375, 377–386, 388–411, 413–445, 447–448, 522, 618, 645–647, 769–770, 792, 878, 966–967, 981, 983, 1000, 1003, 1047, 1085–1086. *See also* Foreign countries

Caribbean, 86, 226, 257, 260, 269, 284, 318, 355, 388–389, 405, 451, 563, 598, 643, 672, 745, 890, 942–945, 958, 966–968, 971–972, 980–982, 987–988, 991, 996, 998, 1014, 1021, 1044, 1048, 1057, 1077, 1108, 1139, 1147, 1149. *See also* Foreign countries; names of specific countries

Central America, 53, 86, 226, 257, 260, 269, 284, 296, 318, 355, 389, 405, 451, 563, 598, 643, 672, 745, 890, 942–943, 945, 965, 967–968, 971–972, 978–982, 986–988, 991, 996, 998, 1014, 1021, 1040, 1044, 1048, 1057, 1063, 1077, 1108, 1139, 1147, 1149. *See also* Foreign countries; names of specific countries

Chile, 329, 429, 959–960, 999, 1003, 1090. *See also* Foreign countries; South America

China. *See* Hong Kong; People's Republic of China; Taiwan

Colombia, 259, 429, 590, 961–962, 970, 978, 1003, 1043. *See also* Foreign countries; South America

Commonwealth of Independent States. *See* Independent States of the Former Soviet Union

Costa Rica, 388, 429, 951, 963–964, 966, 1003–1004, 1007, 1013, 1019. *See also* Central America; Foreign countries

Croatia, 238, 253, 281, 323–324, 342, 351, 353, 372, 485, 536, 566, 662, 749, 762–763, 824, 862, 874, 938, 1041, 1055, 1104. *See also* Europe; Foreign countries; Mediterranean region

Cuba, 245, 259, 590, 954, 970, 1020, 1043. *See also* Caribbean; Foreign countries

Cyprus, 246, 477, 521, 707, 765, 889, 1038, 1070. *See also* Europe; Foreign countries; Mediterranean region

Czech Republic, 238, 252–253, 281, 323–324, 351, 353, 372, 485, 531, 536, 540, 566, 574, 662, 716, 734, 749, 762–763, 862, 874, 938, 1041, 1055, 1104. *See also* Europe; Foreign countries

Czechoslovakia. *See* Czech Republic

Denmark, 274–276, 402–404, 473–474, 566, 574, 645–647, 794, 1041. *See also* Europe; Foreign countries

Dominica, 429, 1003. *See also* Caribbean; Foreign countries

Dominican Republic, 245, 259, 429, 590, 954, 970, 1003, 1043. *See also* Caribbean; Foreign countries

East Germany. *See* Germany

Ecuador, 429, 978, 1003. *See also* Foreign countries; South America

Egypt, 246, 259, 319, 329, 521, 590, 970, 999, 1030–1031, 1038, 1043, 1068, 1078, 1090, 1116. *See also* Africa; Foreign countries; Mediterranean region; Middle East

El Salvador, 259, 346–347, 429, 590, 970, 1003, 1008–1009, 1043. *See also* Central America; Foreign countries

England, 159, 454–455, 457, 462–463, 478, 490, 492–493, 506–507, 513–514, 518–519, 529, 532, 537, 547–548, 555, 558, 561, 567, 569–573, 576, 580, 586, 597, 600, 611, 623, 632, 635–636, 639, 644, 661, 673, 676, 681, 685, 689, 699, 704–705, 707, 712, 718, 722, 724, 730, 733, 736, 742–744, 746–747, 752–754, 756, 776–777, 779–780, 784, 791, 793, 795, 799–801, 803–804, 807, 810, 827–830, 838, 843, 853, 859, 863, 867–869, 872–873, 876, 883–885, 897, 900, 908–909, 916–917, 926, 930, 933–937, 940, 1070. *See also* Foreign countries; United Kingdom

Estonia, 238, 252–253, 281, 323–324, 342, 351, 372, 485, 531, 536, 579, 662, 749, 762–763, 766, 824, 862, 938, 1055, 1104. *See also* Europe; Foreign countries; Independent States of the Former Soviet Union

Ethiopia, 259, 590, 970, 1043, 1053–1054. *See also* Africa; Foreign countries

Europe, 86, 226, 256, 258, 260, 266, 269, 284, 325–326, 337, 341, 355, 424–425, 428, 451, 502–503, 545, 562, 578, 582, 584–585, 598, 617, 624, 628, 643, 648, 671–672, 694, 728, 769–770, 792, 816, 879, 890, 941, 943, 972, 980, 982, 1014, 1021, 1044, 1048, 1057, 1066, 1085–1086, 1108, 1139, 1147, 1149. *See also* Foreign countries; names of specific countries

Federal Republic of Germany. *See* Germany

Finland, 254, 274–276, 402–404, 473–474, 500, 530, 538, 566, 574, 591–592, 645–647, 783, 857, 866, 1039, 1041. *See also* Europe; Foreign countries

Foreign countries, 1–222, 269, 287, 391, 400, 426, 643, 692, 790–791, 880, 965, 980, 1040, 1048, 1147. *See also* names of specific continents; names of specific countries

Former Soviet Union. *See* Independent States of the Former Soviet Union

France, 254, 274–276, 402–404, 480, 484, 505, 527–528, 533–535, 538–539, 560, 566, 574, 596, 601, 604–605, 612, 645–647, 654–655, 663–668, 684, 697–698, 707, 731, 759, 809, 819, 823, 855, 870–871, 877, 974, 1039, 1041, 1070. *See also* Europe; Foreign countries; Mediterranean region

French Guiana, 955, 978. *See also* Foreign countries; South America

Gaza. *See* West Bank and Gaza

Georgia Republic, 227–228, 238, 252–253, 281, 323–324, 342, 351, 372, 452–453, 485, 531, 536, 662, 762–763, 766, 824, 862, 938, 1055, 1104. *See also* Europe; Foreign countries; Independent States of the Former Soviet Union

German Democratic Republic. *See* Germany

Germany, 254, 264, 274–276, 363, 394, 402–404, 480, 483, 495, 538, 541–544, 551, 557, 566, 574, 606–608, 610, 614–616, 618–620, 627, 637, 640, 645–649, 669, 700, 707, 737–740, 784, 896, 901, 1039, 1041, 1070, 1109. *See also* Europe; Foreign countries

Ghana, 1087. *See also* Africa; Foreign countries

Great Britain. *See* United Kingdom

Greece, 246, 254, 274–276, 339, 402–404, 458, 460–461, 467–469, 479, 486, 521, 538, 564, 566, 574, 621, 633–634, 645–647, 679–680, 703, 706, 721, 732, 772, 796, 798, 820, 834–836, 854, 856, 881, 932, 1022, 1038–1039, 1041, 1091, 1100. *See also* Europe; Foreign countries; Mediterranean region

Greenland, 387, 446, 1017. *See also* Arctic region; Foreign countries

Grenada, 429, 1003. *See also* Caribbean; Foreign countries

Guadeloupe, 601, 974. *See also* Caribbean; Foreign countries

Guatemala, 259, 429, 590, 970, 1003, 1043. *See also* Central America; Foreign countries

Guyana, 429, 955, 978, 1003. *See also* Foreign countries; South America

GEOGRAPHIC INDEX

Haiti, 245, 259, 429, 590, 954, 970, 1003, 1043. *See also* Caribbean; Foreign countries
Holland. *See* Netherlands
Honduras, 259, 346–347, 429, 590, 970, 1003, 1008–1009, 1043. *See also* Central America; Foreign countries
Hong Kong, 259, 270, 590, 970, 1043. *See also* Asia; Foreign countries
Hungary, 238, 252–254, 264, 281, 323–324, 351, 353, 372, 466, 485, 489, 531, 536, 538, 566, 574, 610, 650–651, 662, 693, 710, 749, 762–763, 797, 862, 874, 898, 924, 938, 1039, 1041, 1055, 1104. *See also* Europe; Foreign countries

Iceland, 464, 473–474, 566, 656, 875, 1041. *See also* Europe; Foreign countries
Independent States of the Former Soviet Union, 86, 226, 256, 258, 260, 266, 269, 284, 301, 325–326, 337, 341, 424–425, 428, 451, 562, 582, 598, 628, 643, 672, 686, 769–770, 792, 816, 943, 972, 980, 982, 1021, 1044, 1048, 1057, 1065, 1085–1086, 1139, 1147, 1149. *See also* Asia; Europe; Foreign countries; names of former Soviet republics
India, 230–232, 246, 254, 259, 279–280, 301, 319, 327, 345, 353, 521, 538, 590, 686, 874, 970, 1038–1039, 1043, 1051–1052, 1065, 1078. *See also* Asia; Foreign countries
Iran, 246, 259, 281, 351, 363, 521, 590, 662, 862, 896, 970, 1038, 1043, 1055, 1104, 1109. *See also* Foreign countries; Middle East
Iraq, 339, 796, 1076, 1091. *See also* Foreign countries; Middle East
Ireland, 274–276, 402–404, 501, 559, 566, 629, 645–647, 653, 674–675, 729, 821, 850, 923, 1041. *See also* Europe; Foreign countries
Israel, 246, 254, 319, 329, 401, 521, 538, 566, 707, 854, 999, 1034, 1038–1039, 1041, 1045, 1047, 1058–1061, 1067, 1070, 1072–1073, 1078–1079, 1083, 1090, 1093, 1096–1097, 1099–1100, 1102–1103, 1105–1106, 1110, 1114, 1117–1118, 1121, 1123–1124, 1127. *See also* Foreign countries; Mediterranean region; Middle East
Italy, 106, 246, 254, 264, 274–276, 318, 339, 402–404, 456, 471–472, 475, 481, 504, 521, 538, 550, 553, 566, 574, 581, 583, 587–588, 595, 603, 610, 622, 624, 631, 641, 645–647, 658, 677, 683, 692, 707, 709, 713, 715, 745, 757, 761, 771, 796, 798, 806, 811, 832, 834, 842, 845, 852, 858, 864, 904–907, 910, 925, 927–929, 939, 996, 1038–1039, 1041, 1070, 1077, 1091. *See also* Europe; Foreign countries; Mediterranean region

Jamaica, 429, 984, 1003. *See also* Caribbean; Foreign countries
Japan, 103, 224, 237, 242, 244, 247, 255, 261, 263, 265, 268, 271, 274–278, 282–283, 285, 287–295, 297–300, 303–310, 312–313, 317, 320–321, 328, 330–336, 344, 348, 350, 352, 354, 356, 362–363, 365–366, 368–369, 402–404, 645–647, 896, 1109. *See also* Asia; Foreign countries
Jordan, 246, 319, 329, 521, 999, 1038, 1046, 1064, 1069, 1078, 1082, 1088, 1090, 1092, 1119–1120. *See also* Foreign countries; Middle East

Kampuchea. *See* Cambodia

Kazakhstan, 227–228, 238, 253, 281, 314, 323–324, 342, 351, 367, 372, 452–453, 485, 536, 662, 717, 762–763, 824, 862, 915, 938, 1055, 1104. *See also* Asia; Foreign countries; Independent States of the Former Soviet Union
Kenya, 259, 279–280, 329, 590, 970, 999, 1043, 1051–1054, 1090. *See also* Africa; Foreign countries
Korea. *See* South Korea
Kosovo. *See* Yugoslavia
Kuwait, 319, 1078. *See also* Foreign countries; Middle East
Kyrgyzstan, 227–228, 238, 252–253, 281, 323–324, 342, 351, 367, 372, 452–453, 485, 531, 536, 662, 762–763, 824, 862, 915, 938, 1055, 1104. *See also* Asia; Foreign countries; Independent States of the Former Soviet Union

Latin America. *See* Caribbean; Central America; Mexico; South America
Latvia, 238, 252–253, 281, 323–324, 342, 351, 372, 485, 531, 536, 662, 711, 749, 762–763, 766, 824, 862, 938, 1055, 1104. *See also* Europe; Foreign countries; Independent States of the Former Soviet Union
Lebanon, 319, 329, 999, 1078, 1090. *See also* Foreign countries; Mediterranean region; Middle East
Lithuania, 238, 252–253, 281, 323–324, 342, 351, 372, 485, 531, 536, 662, 749, 762–763, 766, 824, 862, 938, 1055, 1104. *See also* Europe; Foreign countries; Independent States of the Former Soviet Union
Luxembourg, 274–276, 402–404, 645–647. *See also* Europe; Foreign countries

Macedonia, 238, 253, 281, 323–324, 342, 351, 372, 485, 536, 662, 749, 762–763, 824, 862, 938, 1055, 1104. *See also* Europe; Foreign countries
Malawi, 279–280, 1051–1052. *See also* Africa; Foreign countries
Mali, 279–280, 1051–1052. *See also* Africa; Foreign countries
Martinique, 601, 974. *See also* Caribbean; Foreign countries
Mediterranean region, 325–326, 424–425, 769–770, 1085–1086. *See also* Africa; Europe; Foreign countries; Middle East; names of specific countries
Mesopotamia. *See* Iraq
Mexico, 53, 86, 226, 257, 259–260, 269, 284, 296, 329, 355, 388–389, 405, 410, 427, 429, 451, 563, 590, 598, 643, 672, 720, 890, 942–943, 945, 950, 965–968, 970–973, 975–977, 979–983, 986–989, 991–995, 998–1000, 1002–1003, 1012, 1014, 1018, 1021, 1040, 1043–1044, 1048, 1057, 1063, 1090, 1108, 1139, 1147, 1149. *See also* Foreign countries
Middle East, 53, 86, 226, 260, 269, 284, 296, 451, 598, 643, 672, 694, 943, 965, 972, 980, 982, 986, 1021, 1040, 1044, 1048, 1056–1057, 1063, 1066, 1076, 1139, 1147, 1149. *See also* Foreign countries; names of specific countries
Moldova, 227–228, 238, 252–253, 259, 281, 323–324, 342, 351, 372, 452–453, 485, 531, 536, 590, 662, 762–763, 824, 862, 938, 970, 1043, 1055, 1104. *See also* Europe; Foreign countries; Independent States of the Former Soviet Union
Mongolia, 238, 314, 322, 485, 717. *See also* Asia; Foreign countries
Montenegro. *See* Yugoslavia
Morocco, 246, 319, 329, 521, 999, 1026, 1028–1029, 1038, 1078, 1080, 1090. *See also* Africa; Foreign countries; Mediterranean region

GEOGRAPHIC INDEX

Myanmar, 245, 259, 590, 954, 970, 1043. *See also* Asia; Foreign countries

Namibia, 259, 590, 970, 1043. *See also* Africa; Foreign countries
Nepal, 319, 329, 999, 1078, 1090. *See also* Asia; Foreign countries
Netherlands, 254, 274–276, 402–404, 449, 538, 549, 566, 574, 589, 626, 645–647, 691, 707, 773–775, 781, 902, 931, 1039, 1041, 1070. *See also* Europe; Foreign countries
New Zealand, 1146, 1153, 1158–1159, 1174. *See also* Foreign countries
Newly Independent States of the Former Soviet Union. *See* Independent States of the Former Soviet Union
Nicaragua, 429, 1003. *See also* Central America; Foreign countries
Niger, 279–280, 1051–1052. *See also* Africa; Foreign countries
Nigeria, 259, 279–280, 590, 970, 1043, 1051–1052. *See also* Africa; Foreign countries
Northern Ireland, 638, 675, 735, 831, 839, 860–861. *See also* Foreign countries; United Kingdom
Norway, 254, 465, 473–474, 538, 565–566, 574, 786–789, 1039, 1041. *See also* Europe; Foreign countries

Oman, 319, 1078. *See also* Foreign countries; Middle East

Pacific Islands, 86, 260, 269, 284, 598, 643, 672, 972, 980, 982, 1044, 1048, 1057, 1139, 1143, 1147, 1149. *See also* Foreign countries; names of specific islands
Pakistan, 233–234, 246, 259, 314, 319, 346–347, 521, 590, 717, 970, 1008–1009, 1038, 1043, 1078. *See also* Asia; Foreign countries
Panama, 429, 951, 978, 1003, 1010–1011, 1015. *See also* Central America; Foreign countries
Paraguay, 429, 1003. *See also* Foreign countries; South America
People's Republic of China, 235, 245, 314–315, 340, 373, 717, 954. *See also* Asia; Foreign countries
Peru, 329, 429, 446, 978, 999, 1003, 1005–1006, 1017, 1090. *See also* Foreign countries; South America
Philippines, 257, 259, 359, 563, 590, 968, 970, 1043. *See also* Asia; Foreign countries
Poland, 238, 252–253, 281, 301, 323–324, 351, 353, 363, 372, 485, 531, 536, 566, 630, 662, 686, 749, 762–763, 812–814, 817, 862, 874, 896, 899, 938, 1041, 1055, 1065, 1104, 1109. *See also* Europe; Foreign countries
Portugal, 257, 274–276, 402–404, 520, 563, 566, 593–594, 645–647, 670, 719, 968, 1041. *See also* Europe; Foreign countries

Qatar, 319, 1078. *See also* Foreign countries; Middle East

Republic of China. *See* Taiwan
Romania, 238, 252–253, 281, 301, 323–324, 342, 351, 372, 485, 531, 536, 662, 686, 749, 762–763, 766, 824, 847–848, 862, 938, 1055, 1065, 1104. *See also* Europe; Foreign countries

Russia, 86, 227–228, 238, 252–253, 259–260, 269, 281, 284, 323–324, 342, 351, 363, 367, 372, 452–453, 485, 531, 536, 590, 598, 643, 662, 672, 762–763, 782, 824, 862, 896, 915, 938, 970, 972, 980, 982, 1043–1044, 1048, 1055, 1057, 1104, 1109, 1139, 1147, 1149. *See also* Asia; Europe; Foreign countries; Independent States of the Former Soviet Union
Rwanda, 259, 590, 970, 1043. *See also* Africa; Foreign countries

Saudi Arabia, 319, 1078. *See also* Foreign countries; Middle East
Scandinavia, 473–474. *See also* Foreign countries; names of specific countries
Scotland, 254, 538, 844, 1039. *See also* Foreign countries; United Kingdom
Senegal, 246, 521, 1038, 1075, 1101, 1122. *See also* Africa; Foreign countries
Serbia, 323–324, 762–763. *See also* Europe; Foreign countries; Yugoslavia
Singapore, 286. *See also* Asia; Foreign countries
Slovenia, 238, 253–254, 281, 323–324, 351, 353, 372, 485, 536, 538, 566, 662, 749, 762–763, 862, 874, 938, 1039, 1041, 1055, 1104. *See also* Europe; Foreign countries
South Africa, 259, 329, 590, 970, 999, 1032, 1043, 1049–1050, 1084, 1089–1090, 1098, 1107, 1115. *See also* Africa; Foreign countries
South America, 53, 86, 226, 257, 260, 269, 284, 296, 355, 389, 405, 451, 563, 598, 643, 672, 890, 942–943, 945, 965, 967–968, 971–972, 979–982, 985–988, 991, 998, 1014, 1021, 1040, 1044, 1048, 1057, 1063, 1108, 1139, 1147, 1149. *See also* Foreign countries; names of specific countries
South Korea, 236, 264, 311, 338, 349, 357, 363, 370, 610, 896, 1109. *See also* Asia; Foreign countries
Soviet Union. *See* Independent States of the Former Soviet Union
Spain, 257, 274–276, 402–404, 563, 566, 645–647, 720, 825–826, 882, 968, 989, 1041. *See also* Europe; Foreign countries; Mediterranean region
Sri Lanka, 229, 246, 319, 521, 1038, 1078. *See also* Asia; Foreign countries
Sudan, 259, 590, 970, 1043. *See also* Africa; Foreign countries
Suriname, 429, 955, 978, 1003. *See also* Foreign countries; South America
Sweden, 254, 274–276, 402–404, 441, 470, 473–474, 491, 494, 538, 566, 574–575, 625, 645–647, 671, 741, 750, 878, 886–888, 891–894, 922, 990, 1039, 1041. *See also* Europe; Foreign countries
Switzerland, 274–276, 402–404, 459, 526, 566, 574, 645–647, 707, 714, 846, 895, 1041, 1070. *See also* Europe; Foreign countries
Syria, 259, 319, 590, 970, 1043, 1078. *See also* Foreign countries; Mediterranean region; Middle East

Taiwan, 223, 225, 248–251, 267, 316, 343, 358, 360–361, 371, 374. *See also* Asia; Foreign countries
Tajikistan, 238, 253, 259, 281, 314, 323–324, 342, 351, 372, 485, 536, 590, 662, 717, 762–763, 824, 862, 938, 970, 1043, 1055, 1104. *See also* Asia; Foreign countries; Independent States of the Former Soviet Union
Thailand, 329, 364, 999, 1090. *See also* Asia; Foreign countries
Tobago. *See* Trinidad and Tobago

GEOGRAPHIC INDEX

Trinidad and Tobago, 429, 1003. *See also* Caribbean; Foreign countries
Tunisia, 246, 319, 329, 521, 999, 1026, 1028–1029, 1038, 1078, 1090. *See also* Africa; Foreign countries; Mediterranean region
Turkey, 246, 254, 281, 301, 351, 458, 482, 521, 538, 566, 662, 686, 708, 764, 818, 822, 862, 911–913, 1022, 1033, 1038–1039, 1041, 1055, 1065, 1071, 1081, 1094–1095, 1104, 1111–1113. *See also* Europe; Foreign countries; Mediterranean region; Middle East
Turkmenistan, 227–228, 253, 281, 314, 323–324, 342, 351, 367, 372, 452–453, 536, 662, 717, 762–763, 824, 862, 915, 938, 1055, 1104. *See also* Asia; Foreign countries; Independent States of the Former Soviet Union

Uganda, 259, 329, 590, 970, 999, 1043, 1090. *See also* Africa; Foreign countries
Ukraine, 227–228, 238, 252–253, 281, 323–324, 342, 351, 367, 372, 452–453, 485, 531, 536, 662, 749, 762–763, 766, 824, 862, 915, 938, 1055, 1104. *See also* Europe; Foreign countries; Independent States of the Former Soviet Union
United Arab Emirates, 319, 1078. *See also* Foreign countries; Middle East
United Kingdom, 158, 193, 274–276, 381, 402–404, 476, 497–499, 501, 508–512, 522, 546, 554, 566, 568, 574, 599, 613, 642, 645–647, 652, 687–688, 695–696, 702, 723, 725–727, 751, 755, 758, 760, 767, 778, 785, 790, 805, 808, 815, 833, 837, 840–841, 849, 851, 880, 903, 914, 923, 941, 1041. *See also* Europe; Foreign countries; names of specific countries
Uruguay, 429, 948–949, 1003, 1016. *See also* Foreign countries; South America
U.S.S.R. *See* Independent States of the Former Soviet Union
Uzbekistan, 227–228, 238, 252–253, 281, 314, 323–324, 342, 351, 367, 372, 452–453, 485, 531, 536, 662, 717, 762–763, 824, 862, 915, 938, 1055, 1104. *See also* Asia; Foreign countries; Independent States of the Former Soviet Union

Venezuela, 259, 429, 590, 970, 1003, 1043. *See also* Foreign countries; South America

West Bank and Gaza, 319, 1078. *See also* Foreign countries; Mediterranean region; Middle East
West Germany. *See* Germany

Yemen, 246, 319, 521, 1027, 1038, 1078. *See also* Foreign countries; Middle East
Yugoslavia, 238, 281, 351, 485, 662, 862, 1055, 1104. *See also* Europe; Foreign countries; Mediterranean region; names of specific countries

Zimbabwe, 279–280, 1051–1052, 1126. *See also* Africa; Foreign countries

Subject Index

This index is arranged by subject or program emphasis and subdivided by the geographic area where the funding can be used. Subject terms are arranged in alphabetical order, word by word. "See" references direct the reader from variant subject headings to formal index terms. Cross-references provide access to related index terms. Since a large number of programs are not restricted by subject, be sure to check the references listed under the "General programs" heading in the subject index, in addition to the specific terms that directly relate to your interest areas.

Acquired Immunodeficiency Syndrome. *See* AIDS
Acting. *See* Performing arts
Addiction. *See* Alcohol use and abuse
Administration. *See* Business administration; Management; Personnel administration; Public administration
Adolescents: **Middle East/Africa** 1025. *See also* Child development; General programs
Advertising: **Europe Etc.** 813. *See also* Communications; General programs; Marketing
Aerospace engineering. *See* Engineering, aerospace
Aerospace sciences. *See* Space sciences
African American studies: **Europe Etc.** 710. *See also* General programs; Minority studies
African history. *See* History, African
African studies: **Asia** 226; **Europe Etc.** 451, 705, 921; **Latin America/Caribbean** 943; **Middle East/Africa** 1021, 1025, 1036–1037, 1062. *See also* General programs; Humanities
Aged and aging: **Any Foreign Country** 140; **Europe Etc.** 671, 840–841. *See also* General programs; Social sciences
Agribusiness. *See* Agriculture and agricultural sciences; Business administration
Agricultural economics. *See* Economics, agricultural
Agricultural engineering. *See* Engineering, agricultural
Agriculture and agricultural sciences: **Any Foreign Country** 88, 111, 127, 179, 183, 202; **Asia** 279–280, 344, 356; **Canada/Arctic Region** 445, 447; **Europe Etc.** 476, 524, 527, 578, 589, 789; **Latin America/Caribbean** 1004; **Middle East/Africa** 1034, 1051–1052, 1075, 1121; **Oceania** 1163, 1174. *See also* Engineering, agricultural; General programs; Sciences
Agronomy. *See* Agriculture and agricultural sciences
AIDS: **Any Foreign Country** 2, 48, 86; **Asia** 269; **Europe Etc.** 643; **Latin America/Caribbean** 980; **Middle East/Africa** 1023, 1048; **Oceania** 1147. *See also* Disabilities; General programs; Immunology; Medical sciences
Alcohol use and abuse: **Any Foreign Country** 48. *See also* General programs; Health and health care
American history. *See* History, American
American Indian studies. *See* Native American studies
American literature. *See* Literature, American
American studies: **Any Foreign Country** 47; **Asia** 270; **Canada/Arctic Region** 444; **Europe Etc.** 465, 500, 579, 601, 605, 615, 674, 701, 710, 794, 847, 898, 902, 919,
921–922, 931; **Latin America/Caribbean** 969, 974, 984. *See also* General programs; Humanities
Anatomy: **Europe Etc.** 597. *See also* General programs; Medical sciences; Physiology
Ancient history. *See* History, ancient
Anemia: **Any Foreign Country** 19. *See also* General programs; Medical sciences
Anthropology: **Any Foreign Country** 36, 122, 146, 157, 167–168, 213–215; **Asia** 253, 283, 286, 353, 372; **Canada/Arctic Region** 376, 410, 444–445; **Europe Etc.** 464, 467–469, 492, 495, 515, 529, 536, 561, 596, 603, 612, 673, 719, 766, 801, 830, 874, 876, 879, 908, 938; **Latin America/Caribbean** 983; **Middle East/Africa** 1037, 1062, 1083, 1088; **Oceania** 1131–1133, 1162, 1167. *See also* General programs; Social sciences
Applied arts. *See* Arts and crafts
Aquatic sciences. *See* Oceanography
Arabic language. *See* Language, Arabic
Arabic literature. *See* Literature, Arabic
Archaeology: **Any Foreign Country** 36, 53, 122, 138, 146, 193, 208–209, 213–215; **Asia** 240–241, 253, 294, 339, 346–347, 353, 360, 372; **Canada/Arctic Region** 376, 444; **Europe Etc.** 454, 467–468, 475, 486, 529, 536, 564, 581, 603, 612, 621, 624, 633, 679–681, 701, 703, 706, 708, 713, 721, 732, 764, 766, 771–772, 796, 823, 830, 835–836, 842, 854, 858, 874, 880–881, 889, 897, 908, 921, 926, 932, 938–939; **Latin America/Caribbean** 965, 979, 1008–1009, 1011, 1015; **Middle East/Africa** 1030–1031, 1036–1037, 1040, 1045–1046, 1058, 1061–1062, 1064, 1069, 1071, 1076, 1081–1083, 1091–1092, 1099–1100, 1117–1118; **Oceania** 1131, 1138. *See also* General programs; History; Social sciences
Architectural engineering. *See* Engineering, architectural
Architecture: **Any Foreign Country** 16, 37, 39, 45, 53, 99, 106, 132, 138, 165, 184, 187, 190, 199, 207; **Asia** 240–241, 257, 294, 319, 339, 360, 366; **Europe Etc.** 481, 545, 549, 563, 614, 624, 642, 681, 692, 751, 796, 804–805, 807, 842, 854; **Latin America/Caribbean** 965, 968, 976; **Middle East/Africa** 1030–1031, 1040, 1058–1059, 1068–1069, 1078, 1091, 1099–1100, 1118. *See also* Fine arts; General programs; Historical preservation
Archives: **Europe Etc.** 616, 859. *See also* General programs; History; Libraries and librarianship; Museums

417

SUBJECT INDEX

Arithmetic. *See* Mathematics
Armament and disarmament: **Any Foreign Country** 51, 170, 175. *See also* Military affairs; Peace studies
Armed services. *See* Military affairs
Art: **Any Foreign Country** 3, 16, 37, 39, 73, 99, 104, 110, 127, 132, 164–165, 187, 208–209, 219; **Asia** 237–241, 265, 294, 302, 338, 360–361, 366; **Europe Etc.** 484–485, 539, 545, 579, 604, 614, 622, 624, 651, 754, 764, 772, 842, 897, 928; **Latin America/Caribbean** 950, 975, 1018; **Middle East/Africa** 1030–1031, 1068, 1081–1082; **Oceania** 1131. *See also* Education, art; General programs; names of specific art forms
Art conservation: **Any Foreign Country** 211; **Asia** 240–241, 255, 294, 360; **Europe Etc.** 641; **Latin America/Caribbean** 976. *See also* Art; General programs
Art education. *See* Education, art
Art history. *See* History, art
Arthritis: **Any Foreign Country** 20. *See also* Disabilities; General programs; Health and health care; Medical sciences
Arts and crafts: **Asia** 241, 244, 294, 360; **Latin America/Caribbean** 975–976. *See also* Art; General programs; names of specific crafts
Asian history. *See* History, Asian
Asian studies: **Asia** 223, 226, 258, 262; **Canada/Arctic Region** 374; **Europe Etc.** 451, 547, 582, 744, 921; **Latin America/Caribbean** 943; **Middle East/Africa** 1021, 1059, 1110. *See also* General programs; Humanities
Astronomy: **Any Foreign Country** 38, 91, 144, 146; **Asia** 253; **Europe Etc.** 536, 559, 766, 844; **Latin America/Caribbean** 959. *See also* General programs; Physical sciences
Athletics: **Asia** 300. *See also* Education, physical; General programs; names of specific sports
Atmospheric sciences: **Any Foreign Country** 41; **Canada/Arctic Region** 376, 446; **Latin America/Caribbean** 1017; **Oceania** 1129. *See also* General programs; Physical sciences
Attorneys. *See* Legal studies and services
Australian history. *See* History, Australian
Austrian history. *See* History, Austrian
Austrian literature. *See* Literature, Austrian
Austrian studies: **Europe Etc.** 450. *See also* European studies; General programs; Humanities
Automation. *See* Computer sciences; Information science; Technology
Avian science. *See* Ornithology
Aviation: **Any Foreign Country** 127. *See also* General programs; Space sciences; Transportation

Ballet. *See* Dance
Banking: **Europe Etc.** 593. *See also* Finance; General programs
Behavioral sciences: **Any Foreign Country** 22, 48, 60, 140–141, 147–149, 197; **Asia** 260, 284, 303–305, 307–309, 337; **Canada/Arctic Region** 428; **Europe Etc.** 598, 671–672, 792; **Latin America/Caribbean** 972, 982; **Middle East/Africa** 1044, 1057, 1096, 1114; **Oceania** 1139, 1149. *See also* General programs; Social sciences; names of special behavioral sciences
Bengal studies: **Asia** 243. *See also* General programs; Humanities
Biochemistry: **Any Foreign Country** 49, 172; **Asia** 253, 372; **Europe Etc.** 536, 597, 671, 744, 752, 766, 892, 908, 938; **Middle East/Africa** 1049. *See also* Biological sciences; Chemistry; General programs
Biological sciences: **Any Foreign Country** 15, 22, 55, 60, 83, 89, 112, 125–127, 139, 141, 144, 146, 148, 159, 171–172, 174, 186, 206, 208–209, 213–215, 217; **Asia** 236, 245, 253, 260, 274–276, 279–280, 297, 319, 325–326, 337, 353, 365, 372; **Canada/Arctic Region** 376, 402–404, 412, 424–425, 428; **Europe Etc.** 455, 488, 502, 513–514, 517, 527, 529, 533–536, 546, 560, 566, 569–573, 598, 635, 645–647, 654–655, 657, 666, 677, 695, 716, 718, 725–727, 741, 752, 766, 769–770, 791–792, 795, 808, 833, 871–872, 874, 892, 894–895, 908, 914, 935, 938; **Latin America/Caribbean** 945, 951–956, 958, 964, 972, 987, 990, 997–998, 1004, 1007, 1010–1011, 1015; **Middle East/Africa** 1041, 1044, 1049, 1051–1052, 1054, 1059, 1067, 1078, 1085–1086, 1097, 1114, 1116, 1121, 1123; **Oceania** 1129, 1139, 1155, 1165. *See also* General programs; Sciences; names of specific biological sciences
Biomedical engineering. *See* Engineering, biomedical
Biomedical sciences: **Any Foreign Country** 48, 140, 147, 149; **Asia** 284, 303–305, 307–309, 356, 358; **Canada/Arctic Region** 381, 440; **Europe Etc.** 522, 672, 846, 871, 908; **Latin America/Caribbean** 982; **Middle East/Africa** 1057; **Oceania** 1146, 1149. *See also* Biological sciences; General programs; Medical sciences
Birth control. *See* Family planning
Black American studies. *See* African American studies
Blindness. *See* Visual impairments
Botany: **Any Foreign Country** 17, 53, 74, 146; **Asia** 279–280; **Europe Etc.** 514, 671; **Latin America/Caribbean** 955, 958, 965; **Middle East/Africa** 1040, 1049, 1051–1052; **Oceania** 1165. *See also* Biological sciences; General programs
Brain research. *See* Neuroscience
Brazilian language. *See* Language, Portuguese
British studies: **Europe Etc.** 919. *See also* European studies; General programs; Humanities
Broadcast journalism. *See* Journalism, broadcast
Broadcasting. *See* Communications; Radio; Television
Business administration: **Any Foreign Country** 183; **Asia** 290, 342, 359; **Canada/Arctic Region** 390, 395, 431, 434; **Europe Etc.** 515, 523–524, 591, 629, 690, 794, 824, 831, 888, 929; **Latin America/Caribbean** 948, 975–976, 1016. *See also* Entrepreneurship; General programs; Management
Business enterprises. *See* Entrepreneurship
Byzantine studies: **Any Foreign Country** 53; **Europe Etc.** 721, 772, 921; **Latin America/Caribbean** 965; **Middle East/Africa** 1040. *See also* General programs; History; Literature

Canadian history. *See* History, Canadian
Canadian studies: **Canada/Arctic Region** 378–380, 390, 395–396, 406, 422, 431, 434, 443–444. *See also* General programs; Humanities
Cancer: **Any Foreign Country** 7–8, 23, 31, 89, 94, 98, 102, 120, 145, 160, 220; **Asia** 268, 285; **Europe Etc.** 471–472, 488, 560, 654–655, 661, 666, 760, 809, 892, 903. *See also* Disabilities; General programs; Health and health care; Medical sciences
Cardiology: **Any Foreign Country** 9–12; **Canada/Arctic Region** 399; **Europe Etc.** 511–512, 871; **Oceania** 1150, 1175. *See also* General programs; Medical sciences

SUBJECT INDEX

Cartography: **Europe Etc.** 640, 778. *See also* General programs; Geography

Chemical engineering. *See* Engineering, chemical

Chemistry: **Any Foreign Country** 159; **Asia** 236, 253, 279–280, 372; **Canada/Arctic Region** 382, 398; **Europe Etc.** 488, 513, 517, 529, 536, 549, 560, 569–573, 666, 671, 685, 766, 791, 892, 894, 908, 938; **Latin America/Caribbean** 952; **Middle East/Africa** 1049, 1051–1052, 1059, 1067, 1105–1106, 1123; **Oceania** 1129, 1165. *See also* Engineering, chemical; General programs; Physical sciences

Child development: **Any Foreign Country** 119. *See also* Adolescents; General programs

Chinese studies: **Asia** 223, 248–251, 315, 343, 371; **Canada/Arctic Region** 374. *See also* Asian studies; General programs; Humanities

Choreography: **Any Foreign Country** 110; **Asia** 366; **Latin America/Caribbean** 1018. *See also* Dance; General programs; Performing arts

Choruses. *See* Voice

Cinema: **Europe Etc.** 528, 813, 855; **Middle East/Africa** 1110. *See also* Filmmaking; General programs; Literature

City and regional planning: **Any Foreign Country** 16, 37, 99, 132, 165, 187, 207; **Europe Etc.** 545, 550, 596, 613, 719, 751; **Latin America/Caribbean** 976; **Middle East/Africa** 1059. *See also* General programs

Civil engineering. *See* Engineering, civil

Civil rights: **Asia** 259; **Europe Etc.** 590, 684; **Latin America/Caribbean** 970; **Middle East/Africa** 1043. *See also* General programs; Political science and politics

Clairvoyance. *See* Parapsychology

Classical studies: **Any Foreign Country** 21, 53, 107, 177; **Asia** 339; **Europe Etc.** 454, 467–469, 475, 486, 581, 621, 634, 771–772, 796, 798, 827, 834, 842, 854, 858, 897, 908; **Latin America/Caribbean** 965; **Middle East/Africa** 1040, 1050, 1069, 1091, 1100. *See also* General programs; History, ancient; Literature

Climatology: **Any Foreign Country** 41. *See also* Atmospheric sciences; General programs; Physical sciences

Colleges and universities. *See* Education, higher

Commerce. *See* Business administration

Communications: **Asia** 319; **Canada/Arctic Region** 392; **Europe Etc.** 614, 741, 919, 921, 931; **Latin America/Caribbean** 976, 990; **Middle East/Africa** 1059, 1078, 1110. *See also* General programs; Humanities

Community colleges. *See* Education, higher

Community services. *See* Social services

Composers and compositions: **Any Foreign Country** 3, 110, 222; **Asia** 366; **Europe Etc.** 757, 877. *See also* General programs; Music

Computer engineering. *See* Engineering, computer

Computer sciences: **Any Foreign Country** 183; **Asia** 253, 337, 372; **Canada/Arctic Region** 428; **Europe Etc.** 526, 536, 574–575, 668, 671, 744, 746, 766, 792, 938; **Latin America/Caribbean** 1001–1002, 1006; **Middle East/Africa** 1049. *See also* General programs; Information science; Libraries and librarianship; Mathematics; Technology

Computers. *See* Computer sciences

Conservation. *See* Art conservation; Environmental sciences; Preservation

Construction. *See* Housing

Cooking. *See* Culinary arts

Costume: **Any Foreign Country** 44, 198. *See also* Art; General programs

Counseling: **Asia** 361. *See also* Behavioral sciences; General programs; Psychiatry; Psychology

Crafts. *See* Arts and crafts

Criminal justice: **Any Foreign Country** 195; **Asia** 266; **Europe Etc.** 628, 815; **Latin America/Caribbean** 975–976. *See also* General programs; Legal studies and services

Culinary arts: **Europe Etc.** 697–698. *See also* Food service industry; General programs; Home economics

Czech history. *See* History, Czech

Dance: **Any Foreign Country** 3, 73, 104; **Asia** 238, 240–241, 294, 355, 360; **Canada/Arctic Region** 410; **Europe Etc.** 485, 890; **Latin America/Caribbean** 975–976, 983, 1014, 1018; **Middle East/Africa** 1108. *See also* Choreography; General programs; Performing arts

Data entry. *See* Computer sciences

Deafness. *See* Hearing impairments

Defense. *See* Military affairs

Demography. *See* Population studies

Dentistry: **Any Foreign Country** 108, 204; **Asia** 344; **Canada/Arctic Region** 383–385, 430. *See also* General programs; Health and health care; Medical sciences

Design: **Any Foreign Country** 106; **Asia** 238, 240; **Europe Etc.** 485, 550, 692, 842; **Latin America/Caribbean** 976. *See also* Art; General programs

Diabetes: **Any Foreign Country** 105. *See also* Disabilities; General programs; Health and health care; Medical sciences

Dietetics. *See* Nutrition

Disabilities: **Any Foreign Country** 119. *See also* General programs; Rehabilitation; names of specific disabilities

Disabilities, hearing. *See* Hearing impairments

Disabilities, visual. *See* Visual impairments

Disarmament. *See* Armament and disarmament

Documentaries. *See* Filmmaking

Domestic science. *See* Home economics

Drama. *See* Plays

Earth sciences: **Any Foreign Country** 26, 85, 87, 144, 174, 194; **Asia** 236, 253, 325–326, 353, 372; **Canada/Arctic Region** 376, 400, 424–425; **Europe Etc.** 536, 549, 667, 671, 766, 769–770, 874, 894, 908, 938; **Middle East/Africa** 1085–1086; **Oceania** 1129, 1167. *See also* General programs; Natural sciences; names of specific earth sciences

East German history. *See* History, German

East German studies. *See* German studies

Eastern European history. *See* History, European

Eastern European studies. *See* European studies

Ecology. *See* Environmental sciences

Economic development: **Asia** 318; **Canada/Arctic Region** 421; **Europe Etc.** 458, 745; **Latin America/Caribbean** 996; **Middle East/Africa** 1022, 1077. *See also* Economics; General programs

Economic planning. *See* Economics

Economics: **Any Foreign Country** 36, 71–72, 141, 157, 167–168, 183; **Asia** 252–253, 256, 279–280, 283, 286, 327, 337, 340, 342, 359, 372; **Canada/Arctic Region** 376, 390, 394–395, 397, 428, 434, 444–445; **Europe Etc.** 487, 489, 492, 495, 507, 515, 524–525, 531, 536, 553, 561–562, 583, 603–604, 606–608, 614, 617–618, 624, 678, 682–683, 744, 766, 792–794, 801, 824, 864, 869, 902, 904–905, 908, 918,

938; **Latin America/Caribbean** 976, 993; **Middle East/Africa** 1030–1031, 1051–1052, 1088, 1102–1103, 1118; **Oceania** 1130. See also General programs; Social sciences

Economics, agricultural: **Any Foreign Country** 202. See also Agriculture and agricultural sciences; Economics; General programs

Education: **Any Foreign Country** 60, 183, 189, 197; **Asia** 252, 254, 319, 342; **Canada/Arctic Region** 378, 416, 420; **Europe Etc.** 531, 538, 540, 651, 678, 701, 711, 814, 824, 847, 869, 919, 921; **Latin America/Caribbean** 975–976, 1006, 1016; **Middle East/Africa** 1039, 1059, 1078; **Oceania** 1131. See also General programs; specific types and levels of education

Education, art: **Latin America/Caribbean** 975–976. See also Art; Education; General programs

Education, elementary: **Asia** 298; **Europe Etc.** 516, 911; **Latin America/Caribbean** 946, 961, 994, 1005; **Middle East/Africa** 1111. See also Education; General programs

Education, higher: **Asia** 270; **Europe Etc.** 678, 748. See also Education; General programs

Education, international: **Asia** 361, 369–370; **Europe Etc.** 557, 898. See also Education; General programs

Education, physical: **Europe Etc.** 775, 786, 921; **Middle East/Africa** 1126. See also Athletics; Education; General programs

Education, secondary: **Asia** 298, 367; **Europe Etc.** 516, 911, 915; **Latin America/Caribbean** 946, 961, 994, 1005; **Middle East/Africa** 1111. See also Education; General programs

Education, special: **Europe Etc.** 631. See also Disabilities; Education; General programs

Egyptian history. See History, Egyptian

Egyptian studies: **Europe Etc.** 493, 921; **Middle East/Africa** 1030–1031. See also General programs; Humanities; Middle Eastern studies

Electrical engineering. See Engineering, electrical

Electronic engineering. See Engineering, electronic

Electronic journalism. See Journalism, broadcast

Electronics: **Asia** 236, 364; **Europe Etc.** 526, 575, 783, 888; **Middle East/Africa** 1049. See also General programs; Physics

Elementary education. See Education, elementary

Emotional disabilities. See Mental health

Energy: **Any Foreign Country** 154, 180; **Asia** 236; **Canada/Arctic Region** 390, 395, 434; **Europe Etc.** 667, 789; **Middle East/Africa** 1096, 1114, 1116. See also Environmental sciences; General programs; Natural resources

Engineering: **Any Foreign Country** 22, 32, 60, 96, 139, 150–153, 183, 186, 201; **Asia** 253, 271, 306, 310–311, 317, 321, 325–326, 331–337, 344, 356–358, 368, 372; **Canada/Arctic Region** 423–425, 428, 447; **Europe Etc.** 506, 526–527, 529, 536, 544, 554, 568, 671, 766, 769–770, 779, 792, 811, 830, 895, 908–909, 936, 938; **Middle East/Africa** 1059, 1084–1086; **Oceania** 1142. See also General programs; Physical sciences; names of specific types of engineering

Engineering, aerospace: **Canada/Arctic Region** 377; **Europe Etc.** 549. See also Engineering; General programs; Space sciences

Engineering, agricultural: **Asia** 236, 279–280; **Middle East/Africa** 1051–1052. See also Agriculture and agricultural sciences; Engineering; General programs

Engineering, architectural: **Asia** 236. See also Architecture; Engineering; General programs

Engineering, biomedical: **Latin America/Caribbean** 1002; **Middle East/Africa** 1059. See also Biomedical sciences; Engineering; General programs

Engineering, chemical: **Asia** 236; **Canada/Arctic Region** 398; **Latin America/Caribbean** 1002; **Middle East/Africa** 1059. See also Chemistry; Engineering; General programs

Engineering, civil: **Asia** 236; **Europe Etc.** 549; **Latin America/Caribbean** 1002; **Middle East/Africa** 1059. See also Engineering; General programs

Engineering, computer: **Latin America/Caribbean** 1001–1002; **Middle East/Africa** 1059. See also Computer sciences; Engineering; General programs

Engineering, electrical: **Europe Etc.** 549; **Latin America/Caribbean** 1002. See also Engineering; General programs

Engineering, electronic: **Asia** 364. See also Electronics; Engineering; General programs

Engineering, environmental: **Asia** 236; **Latin America/Caribbean** 1002. See also Engineering; Environmental sciences; General programs

Engineering, geological: **Europe Etc.** 549. See also Engineering; General programs; Geology

Engineering, industrial: **Europe Etc.** 549; **Latin America/Caribbean** 1016; **Middle East/Africa** 1059. See also Engineering; General programs

Engineering, manufacturing: **Latin America/Caribbean** 1002; **Middle East/Africa** 1116. See also Engineering; General programs

Engineering, materials: **Middle East/Africa** 1059. See also Engineering; General programs; Materials sciences

Engineering, mechanical: **Asia** 236; **Canada/Arctic Region** 398; **Europe Etc.** 549; **Latin America/Caribbean** 1002; **Middle East/Africa** 1059. See also Engineering; General programs

Engineering, metallurgical: **Asia** 236. See also Engineering; General programs; Metallurgy

Engineering, systems: **Europe Etc.** 549. See also Engineering; General programs

English as a foreign language: **Europe Etc.** 711, 847, 882, 898, 912–913; **Latin America/Caribbean** 957, 960; **Middle East/Africa** 1059, 1080, 1101, 1112–1113. See also English as a second language; General programs; Language and linguistics

English as a second language: **Asia** 361; **Europe Etc.** 517, 540, 579, 651, 814, 847, 912; **Latin America/Caribbean** 947, 957, 962; **Middle East/Africa** 1035, 1112. See also English as a foreign language; General programs; Language and linguistics

English history. See History, English

English language. See Language, English

English literature. See Literature, English

English studies. See British studies

Entomology: **Any Foreign Country** 88, 111; **Asia** 279–280; **Europe Etc.** 578; **Latin America/Caribbean** 955; **Middle East/Africa** 1049, 1051–1052. See also General programs; Zoology

Entrepreneurship: **Asia** 266; **Europe Etc.** 628. See also Business administration; General programs

Environmental engineering. See Engineering, environmental

Environmental sciences: **Any Foreign Country** 29, 55, 59, 74, 124, 127, 139, 146, 154, 180, 191, 208–209, 218; **Asia** 252–253, 270, 279–280, 319, 323–326, 342, 368, 372; **Canada/Arctic Region** 387, 390, 395, 415, 424–425, 432, 434, 442, 445, 447; **Europe Etc.** 458, 464, 489, 524, 531,

536, 576, 614, 667, 671, 741, 762–763, 766, 769–770, 789, 824, 910, 938; **Latin America/Caribbean** 949, 953, 973, 975–976, 987–988, 990, 992, 1004, 1007, 1011, 1015, 1019; **Middle East/Africa** 1022, 1037, 1051–1052, 1078, 1085–1086, 1114, 1116; **Oceania** 1129, 1132–1133, 1162, 1165. See also General programs; Sciences

Epidemiology: **Any Foreign Country** 48, 89; **Asia** 284; **Europe Etc.** 654–655, 663–664, 672; **Latin America/Caribbean** 982; **Middle East/Africa** 1057; **Oceania** 1149. See also General programs; Medical sciences

Epilepsy: **Any Foreign Country** 65; **Canada/Arctic Region** 438–440. See also Disabilities; General programs; Health and health care; Medical sciences

Esperanto. See Language, Esperanto

Ethics: **Middle East/Africa** 1082. See also General programs; Humanities

Ethnic studies. See Minority studies

European history. See History, European

European studies: **Any Foreign Country** 50, 169; **Asia** 226, 252, 258, 323–324; **Europe Etc.** 451, 457, 489, 495, 524–525, 531, 582, 584, 609, 617, 659–660, 678, 728, 748, 762–763, 845, 904, 921, 927; **Latin America/Caribbean** 943; **Middle East/Africa** 1021. See also General programs; Humanities

Evolution: **Any Foreign Country** 122; **Europe Etc.** 488; **Latin America/Caribbean** 1010. See also Biological sciences; General programs; Sciences

Extrasensory perception. See Parapsychology

Eye doctors. See Ophthalmology; Optometry

Eye problems. See Visual impairments

Family planning: **Any Foreign Country** 182; **Europe Etc.** 696, 837; **Oceania** 1158. See also General programs; Population studies; Pregnancy

Farming. See Agriculture and agricultural sciences

Feminist movement. See Women's studies and programs

Fertility. See Family planning; Pregnancy

Fiction: **Any Foreign Country** 110; **Asia** 366; **Europe Etc.** 547. See also General programs; Writers and writing

Film as a literary art. See Cinema

Filmmaking: **Any Foreign Country** 110; **Asia** 237, 294, 360; **Europe Etc.** 650; **Latin America/Caribbean** 975–976; **Middle East/Africa** 1059. See also General programs; Television

Finance: **Europe Etc.** 594, 614; **Latin America/Caribbean** 1016. See also Banking; Economics; General programs

Fine arts: **Any Foreign Country** 16, 37, 73, 99, 110, 132, 164–165, 187, 208–209, 219; **Asia** 237–241, 294, 302, 360, 366; **Europe Etc.** 485, 545, 639, 650, 689, 842, 928; **Latin America/Caribbean** 950; **Middle East/Africa** 1082. See also General programs; Humanities; names of specific fine arts

Finnish language. See Language, Finnish

Finnish literature. See Literature, Finnish

Fishing industry: **Any Foreign Country** 136; **Asia** 344; **Canada/Arctic Region** 447; **Europe Etc.** 789; **Middle East/Africa** 1049. See also General programs

Flight science. See Aviation

Floriculture. See Horticulture

Flying. See Aviation

Folklore: **Europe Etc.** 592, 650, 898. See also General programs; Literature

Food. See Culinary arts; Nutrition

Food service industry: **Europe Etc.** 591, 789. See also General programs

Foreign affairs. See International affairs

Foreign language. See Language and linguistics

Forestry management: **Any Foreign Country** 74, 109; **Europe Etc.** 789; **Latin America/Caribbean** 956, 988, 1004. See also General programs; Management

Fossils. See Paleontology

French history. See History, French

French language. See Language, French

French literature. See Literature, French

French studies: **Europe Etc.** 480, 601, 855; **Latin America/Caribbean** 974. See also European studies; General programs; Humanities

Gardening. See Horticulture

Gender. See Women's studies and programs

General programs: **Any Foreign Country** 5–6, 24, 30, 33, 52, 63, 66–70, 77–78, 82, 93, 110, 137, 161, 166, 183, 216; **Asia** 230–232, 242, 247, 262–264, 272–273, 281, 290–291, 295, 312, 314, 317, 319, 322, 330, 352, 362–363; **Canada/Arctic Region** 393, 407–409, 413–415, 421, 429, 448; **Europe Etc.** 463, 470, 473–474, 487, 490, 497–499, 505, 510, 530, 537, 541–542, 548, 551, 555, 565, 567, 577, 579, 591, 610, 620, 623, 627, 630, 632, 638, 648–650, 662, 694, 699, 702, 717, 723, 730, 733, 735, 739, 747, 773–776, 786, 788, 797, 817, 826, 829–831, 843, 848, 856–857, 861, 863, 867, 873, 882–883, 893, 896, 899, 924, 930; **Latin America/Caribbean** 991, 995, 1003, 1006; **Middle East/Africa** 1024, 1026–1029, 1032, 1035, 1055, 1059, 1066, 1072–1073, 1078, 1093, 1098, 1107, 1109, 1115, 1122; **Oceania** 1128, 1134–1137, 1140–1141, 1144–1145, 1151–1152, 1157, 1160–1161, 1168–1173

Genetics: **Any Foreign Country** 89, 172; **Asia** 253, 279–280; **Europe Etc.** 488, 536, 560, 655, 666, 766; **Middle East/Africa** 1051–1052. See also General programs; Medical sciences

Geography: **Any Foreign Country** 1, 18, 36, 71–72, 146, 157, 167–168; **Asia** 253, 283, 323–324, 372; **Canada/Arctic Region** 376, 444–445; **Europe Etc.** 489, 492, 529, 536, 561, 596, 603, 651, 719, 762–763, 766, 801, 847, 906, 908, 921, 938; **Latin America/Caribbean** 947; **Middle East/Africa** 1045, 1049, 1061, 1083. See also General programs; Social sciences

Geological engineering. See Engineering, geological

Geology: **Any Foreign Country** 26, 85, 87, 146, 174, 194; **Asia** 337; **Canada/Arctic Region** 382, 400, 428; **Europe Etc.** 695, 744, 792, 823, 836; **Latin America/Caribbean** 944, 952, 958, 977; **Middle East/Africa** 1049; **Oceania** 1129, 1143, 1155. See also Earth sciences; General programs; Physical sciences

Geosciences. See Earth sciences

Geriatrics. See Aged and aging

German history. See History, German

German language. See Language, German

German literature. See Literature, German

German studies: **Canada/Arctic Region** 394; **Europe Etc.** 480, 616, 618, 700, 919. See also European studies; General programs; Humanities

Gerontology. See Aged and aging

Government. *See* Political science and politics; Public administration
Grade school. *See* Education, elementary
Graphic arts: **Any Foreign Country** 39, 110; **Asia** 238, 241; **Canada/Arctic Region** 410; **Europe Etc.** 485, 550, 842, 928; **Latin America/Caribbean** 975–976, 983. *See also* Art; Arts and crafts; General programs
Greek history. *See* History, ancient; History, Greek
Greek language. *See* Language, Greek
Greek literature. *See* Literature, Greek
Greek studies: **Europe Etc.** 820. *See also* General programs; Humanities
Guidance. *See* Counseling
Gynecology: **Europe Etc.** 923. *See also* General programs; Medical sciences

Handicapped. *See* Disabilities
Health and health care: **Any Foreign Country** 25, 127, 181, 183, 203; **Asia** 254, 356; **Canada/Arctic Region** 375, 383–385, 430, 440, 447; **Europe Etc.** 507, 538, 591, 671, 677, 688, 789; **Latin America/Caribbean** 976; **Middle East/Africa** 1039, 1089, 1096–1097, 1114; **Oceania** 1131, 1158. *See also* General programs; Medical sciences
Hearing impairments: **Europe Etc.** 631. *See also* Disabilities; General programs; Rehabilitation
Heart disease. *See* Cardiology
Hebrew. *See* Language, Hebrew
High schools. *See* Education, secondary
Higher education. *See* Education, higher
Histology: **Any Foreign Country** 123. *See also* Anatomy; General programs; Biological sciences; Medical sciences
Historical preservation: **Europe Etc.** 641, 842. *See also* General programs; History; Preservation
History: **Any Foreign Country** 36, 71–72, 116, 138, 157; **Asia** 244, 252, 257, 323–324, 339, 353; **Canada/Arctic Region** 376, 416, 442, 445; **Europe Etc.** 456, 475, 479, 492, 515, 517–519, 528–529, 531, 553, 561, 563, 583, 587, 595, 603, 606–608, 640, 644, 650–651, 676, 678, 681–682, 700–701, 756, 762–764, 771, 778, 793, 796, 801, 823, 827, 858–859, 869, 874, 901, 908, 919, 921; **Latin America/Caribbean** 947, 960, 962, 968; **Middle East/Africa** 1050, 1060, 1076, 1081–1083, 1088, 1091, 1102–1103, 1118. *See also* Archaeology; General programs; Humanities; Social sciences; specific types of history
History, African: **Europe Etc.** 705; **Middle East/Africa** 1036–1037, 1062. *See also* African studies; General programs; History
History, American: **Any Foreign Country** 118, 143, 210; **Asia** 350; **Canada/Arctic Region** 444; **Europe Etc.** 465, 500, 504, 615, 640, 652, 691, 700, 710, 729, 742, 778, 782, 794, 813, 847, 922; **Latin America/Caribbean** 969, 984. *See also* American studies; General programs; History
History, ancient: **Any Foreign Country** 177; **Europe Etc.** 581, 701, 753, 908. *See also* Classical studies; General programs; History
History, art: **Any Foreign Country** 16, 36–37, 45, 53, 99–101, 115, 132, 165, 178, 187, 211, 219; **Asia** 240–241, 252, 294, 315, 360; **Europe Etc.** 454, 467–469, 475, 486, 500, 531, 545, 603, 616, 642, 652, 701, 707–708, 710, 713, 771, 794, 803–807, 842, 852, 854, 858, 884, 908, 921, 926, 931; **Latin America/Caribbean** 965, 976; **Middle East/Africa** 1040, 1058, 1068–1071, 1082–1083, 1099–1100, 1118. *See also* Art; General programs; History
History, Asian: **Europe Etc.** 838. *See also* General programs; History
History, Australian: **Oceania** 1131. *See also* General programs; History
History, Austrian: **Europe Etc.** 487, 489. *See also* Austrian studies; General programs; History, European
History, Canadian: **Canada/Arctic Region** 397, 444. *See also* Canadian studies; General programs; History
History, Chinese: **Middle East/Africa** 1059. *See also* Chinese studies; General programs; History, Asian
History, Czech: **Europe Etc.** 682. *See also* European studies; General programs; History, European
History, Egyptian: **Middle East/Africa** 1030–1031. *See also* Egyptian studies; General programs; History, Middle Eastern
History, English: **Europe Etc.** 640, 652, 758, 778, 900, 934. *See also* British studies; General programs; History
History, European: **Asia** 256; **Europe Etc.** 562, 640, 650, 669, 678, 683, 748, 778, 784, 802, 927. *See also* European studies; General programs; History
History, French: **Europe Etc.** 480, 596, 604, 640, 719, 778. *See also* French studies; General programs; History, European
History, German: **Canada/Arctic Region** 394; **Europe Etc.** 480, 495, 543, 616, 618, 700. *See also* General programs; German studies; History, European
History, Greek: **Europe Etc.** 467–469, 486, 564, 706, 721, 732, 772, 820. *See also* Classical studies; General programs; History; History, ancient
History, Hungarian: **Europe Etc.** 489. *See also* General programs; History, European; Hungarian studies
History, Icelandic: **Europe Etc.** 656. *See also* General programs; History
History, Irish: **Europe Etc.** 675, 758. *See also* General programs; History; Irish studies
History, Italian: **Europe Etc.** 454, 624, 907. *See also* General programs; History, European; Italian studies
History, Japanese: **Asia** 247; **Middle East/Africa** 1059. *See also* General programs; History, Asian; Japanese studies
History, Jewish: **Europe Etc.** 799. *See also* General programs; History; Jewish studies
History, Latin American: **Any Foreign Country** 53; **Europe Etc.** 640, 720, 778; **Latin America/Caribbean** 965, 985, 989; **Middle East/Africa** 1040. *See also* General programs; History; Latin American studies
History, medieval: **Any Foreign Country** 53; **Canada/Arctic Region** 419; **Europe Etc.** 480, 926; **Latin America/Caribbean** 965; **Middle East/Africa** 1040, 1050. *See also* General programs; History
History, Middle Eastern: **Middle East/Africa** 1118. *See also* General programs; History; Middle Eastern studies
History, natural: **Europe Etc.** 821; **Oceania** 1132–1133, 1162, 1167. *See also* Sciences; specific aspects of natural history
History, Near Eastern: **Middle East/Africa** 1045, 1058, 1061, 1117. *See also* General programs; History; Near Eastern studies
History, New Zealand: **Oceania** 1153, 1159. *See also* General programs; History
History, Renaissance: **Europe Etc.** 480, 640, 778. *See also* General programs; History; Renaissance studies
History, Russian: **Asia** 256; **Europe Etc.** 562. *See also* General programs; History, European

History, science: **Asia** 283, 372; **Europe Etc.** 604, 624, 737–738, 853, 938; **Middle East/Africa** 1105–1106. See also General programs; History; Sciences
History, Scottish: **Europe Etc.** 758. See also British studies; General programs; History
History, South American. See History, Latin American
History, Ukrainian: **Canada/Arctic Region** 378, 420. See also General programs; History, European; Soviet studies
Home economics: **Asia** 344. See also General programs
Horticulture: **Any Foreign Country** 53, 88, 111; **Latin America/Caribbean** 965, 1013; **Middle East/Africa** 1040. See also Agriculture and agricultural sciences; General programs; Landscape architecture; Sciences
Hospitality industry. See Hotel and motel industry
Hospitals. See Health and health care
Hotel and motel industry: **Europe Etc.** 591. See also General programs
Housing: **Europe Etc.** 688. See also General programs
Human resources. See Personnel administration
Human rights. See Civil rights
Human services. See Social services
Humanities: **Any Foreign Country** 13, 35–36, 50, 60, 77–78, 95, 100–101, 127, 169, 197, 208–209; **Asia** 224, 226–229, 231, 233–235, 243, 246, 258, 271, 281, 283, 288–289, 306, 310, 313, 319, 323–324, 344–345, 348, 351, 354, 367; **Canada/Arctic Region** 416, 431; **Europe Etc.** 451–453, 460–462, 475, 477, 479, 482, 489, 491, 506, 508–509, 515, 520–521, 523, 528, 532, 582, 600, 603, 611, 614, 629, 650, 662, 704, 722, 762–765, 771, 777–778, 780–781, 789, 802, 818, 822, 842, 858, 862, 875, 886–887, 895, 909, 915–916, 920–921, 936–937, 940; **Latin America/Caribbean** 943, 976, 1020; **Middle East/Africa** 1021, 1030–1031, 1033, 1037–1038, 1055, 1078, 1081, 1084, 1094–1095, 1104, 1119–1120, 1125; **Oceania** 1148, 1154. See also General programs; names of specific humanities
Hungarian history. See History, Hungarian
Hungarian studies: **Europe Etc.** 466. See also European studies; General programs; Humanities
Hydrology: **Any Foreign Country** 127, 174; **Oceania** 1155. See also Earth sciences; General programs

Icelandic history. See History, Icelandic
Icelandic language. See Language, Icelandic
Icelandic literature. See Literature, Icelandic
Illustrations and illustrators: **Latin America/Caribbean** 975
Immigration: **Any Foreign Country** 51, 170, 175; **Latin America/Caribbean** 975–976. See also General programs
Immunology: **Any Foreign Country** 98. See also General programs; Medical sciences
Indian studies: **Asia** 230–232, 345; **Europe Etc.** 876, 921. See also General programs; Humanities
Industrial engineering. See Engineering, industrial
Information science: **Any Foreign Country** 162, 171; **Asia** 337; **Canada/Arctic Region** 392, 428; **Europe Etc.** 663–664, 783, 792; **Middle East/Africa** 1059, 1116. See also Computer sciences; General programs; Libraries and librarianship
Interior design: **Europe Etc.** 550. See also Architecture; Design; General programs; Home economics
International affairs: **Any Foreign Country** 46, 71–72, 134, 143, 183, 210; **Asia** 224, 252, 256, 259, 282, 286, 320, 340, 342, 359; **Canada/Arctic Region** 390, 392, 395, 434, 443; **Europe Etc.** 449, 459, 492, 495, 500, 531, 552, 561–562, 590, 617, 636, 678, 682, 700, 705, 793–794, 801, 824; **Latin America/Caribbean** 970, 975–976, 993; **Middle East/Africa** 1043, 1088, 1103. See also General programs; Political science and politics
International education. See Education, international
International relations. See International affairs
Internet design and development: **Europe Etc.** 574, 888. See also General programs; Graphic arts; Technology
Irish history. See History, Irish
Irish studies: **Europe Etc.** 653, 674, 839, 860. See also General programs; Humanities
Islamic studies: **Europe Etc.** 492, 561, 754, 800–801, 838; **Middle East/Africa** 1030–1031, 1058, 1083. See also General programs; Humanities; Middle Eastern studies; Near Eastern studies; Religion and religious activities
Israeli studies: **Middle East/Africa** 1102–1103. See also General programs; Humanities; Jewish studies; Middle Eastern studies; Near Eastern studies
Italian history. See History, Italian
Italian studies: **Europe Etc.** 475, 771, 842, 858. See also European studies; General programs; Humanities

Japanese history. See History, Japanese
Japanese language. See Language, Japanese
Japanese studies: **Any Foreign Country** 103; **Asia** 244, 247, 283, 287, 291; **Europe Etc.** 921; **Middle East/Africa** 1059. See also Asian studies; General programs; Humanities
Jewish affairs: **Any Foreign Country** 173; **Middle East/Africa** 1102–1103, 1127. See also General programs; History, Jewish
Jewish history. See History, Jewish
Jewish studies: **Canada/Arctic Region** 433; **Europe Etc.** 543, 749, 799, 921; **Middle East/Africa** 1079. See also General programs; Israeli studies; Middle Eastern studies; Near Eastern studies; Religion and religious activities
Journalism: **Any Foreign Country** 4, 59, 114, 191, 205; **Asia** 252, 259, 277, 292, 342, 361; **Canada/Arctic Region** 405, 427; **Europe Etc.** 483, 531, 590, 614, 741, 748, 813, 824–825, 921; **Latin America/Caribbean** 970, 981, 990, 1000; **Middle East/Africa** 1042–1043, 1088. See also Communications; General programs; Writers and writing
Journalism, broadcast: **Any Foreign Country** 59, 191; **Europe Etc.** 619, 825. See also Communications; General programs; Radio; Television
Junior colleges. See Education, higher
Jurisprudence. See Legal studies and services

Korean language. See Language, Korean
Korean studies: **Asia** 349. See also Asian studies; General programs; Humanities

Landscape architecture: **Any Foreign Country** 53, 88, 111, 207; **Europe Etc.** 588, 709, 751, 842; **Latin America/Caribbean** 965; **Middle East/Africa** 1040. See also Botany; General programs; Horticulture
Language and linguistics: **Any Foreign Country** 36, 71–72, 213–215; **Asia** 227–228, 265, 367, 372; **Canada/Arctic Region** 376, 410, 444; **Europe Etc.** 452–453, 462, 603, 612,

616, 640, 651, 701, 711, 764, 766, 778, 814, 884, 898, 906, 908, 913, 915, 921, 925–926, 938; **Latin America/Caribbean** 983, 995; **Middle East/Africa** 1036, 1050, 1081–1083, 1113, 1118; **Oceania** 1131. *See also* General programs; Humanities; names of specific languages

Language, Arabic: **Middle East/Africa** 1026–1027, 1080. *See also* General programs; Language and linguistics

Language, Brazilian. *See* Language, Portuguese

Language, English: **Asia** 298; **Europe Etc.** 601, 620, 651, 775, 786, 899, 908, 912; **Latin America/Caribbean** 960, 962, 974, 1006; **Middle East/Africa** 1060, 1107, 1112. *See also* English as a foreign language; English as a second language; General programs; Language and linguistics

Language, Esperanto: **Any Foreign Country** 158; **Europe Etc.** 790. *See also* General Programs; Language and linguistics

Language, Finnish: **Europe Etc.** 592. *See also* General programs; Language and linguistics

Language, French: **Asia** 298; **Europe Etc.** 601, 604, 731; **Latin America/Caribbean** 974; **Middle East/Africa** 1080. *See also* General programs; Language and linguistics

Language, German: **Asia** 298; **Europe Etc.** 523, 620. *See also* General programs; Language and linguistics

Language, Greek: **Any Foreign Country** 107; **Europe Etc.** 460–461, 467, 486, 621, 732, 772, 820; **Middle East/Africa** 1050. *See also* Classical studies; General programs; Language and linguistics

Language, Hebrew: **Europe Etc.** 799. *See also* General programs; Language and linguistics

Language, Icelandic: **Europe Etc.** 656, 875. *See also* General programs; Language and linguistics

Language, Japanese: **Asia** 247, 293. *See also* General programs; Language and linguistics

Language, Korean: **Asia** 357. *See also* General programs; Language and linguistics

Language, Latin: **Any Foreign Country** 107; **Europe Etc.** 901; **Middle East/Africa** 1050. *See also* Classical studies; General programs; Language and linguistics

Language, Norwegian: **Europe Etc.** 787. *See also* General programs; Language and linguistics

Language, Portuguese: **Europe Etc.** 670. *See also* General programs; Language and linguistics

Language, Spanish: **Latin America/Caribbean** 947, 960, 962, 971, 1006. *See also* General programs; Language and linguistics

Language, Swedish: **Canada/Arctic Region** 441; **Europe Etc.** 878, 891. *See also* General programs; Language and linguistics

Language, Turkish: **Europe Etc.** 822; **Middle East/Africa** 1095. *See also* General programs; Language and linguistics

Language, Ukrainian: **Canada/Arctic Region** 378, 420. *See also* General programs; Language and linguistics

Latin. *See* Language, Latin

Latin American history. *See* History, Latin American

Latin American studies: **Asia** 226; **Europe Etc.** 451; **Latin America/Caribbean** 943, 963, 971; **Middle East/Africa** 1021. *See also* General programs; Humanities

Law. *See* Legal studies and services

Law enforcement. *See* Criminal justice

Lawyers. *See* Legal studies and services

Legal studies and services: **Any Foreign Country** 36, 46, 157; **Asia** 252, 319, 340, 342; **Canada/Arctic Region** 376, 416–418, 420, 445; **Europe Etc.** 449, 487, 491–492, 515, 531, 561, 583, 595, 603, 614–615, 624, 629, 634, 683, 740, 761, 801, 824, 869, 884, 902, 905, 908, 920, 926; **Latin America/Caribbean** 975–976, 1016; **Middle East/Africa** 1050, 1078, 1082, 1102–1103. *See also* Criminal justice; General programs; Social sciences

Leprosy: **Any Foreign Country** 80–81, 176. *See also* Disabilities; General programs; Health and health care; Medical sciences

Librarians. *See* Libraries and librarianship

Libraries and librarianship: **Any Foreign Country** 28, 75, 131, 162; **Asia** 252, 255; **Canada/Arctic Region** 378, 416; **Europe Etc.** 531, 728, 756, 859; **Latin America/Caribbean** 976, 1018. *See also* Archives; General programs; Information science; Social sciences

Life sciences. *See* Biological sciences

Linguistics. *See* Language and linguistics

Literacy: **Any Foreign Country** 183. *See also* Education; General programs; Reading

Literature: **Any Foreign Country** 36, 39, 177; **Asia** 227–228, 238, 283, 294, 360; **Canada/Arctic Region** 431; **Europe Etc.** 452–453, 475, 485, 492, 515, 561, 603, 624, 650, 689, 701, 713, 715, 764, 771, 801, 842, 858, 901, 919, 921, 926; **Latin America/Caribbean** 947, 960, 962, 1006, 1018; **Middle East/Africa** 1059, 1081, 1102–1103. *See also* General programs; Humanities; Writers and writing; specific types of literature

Literature, American: **Europe Etc.** 500, 517, 579, 601, 640, 652, 710, 761, 778, 794, 812, 847, 898, 922, 931; **Latin America/Caribbean** 974. *See also* American studies; General programs; Literature

Literature, Arabic: **Europe Etc.** 724. *See also* General programs; Literature, Middle Eastern; Middle Eastern studies

Literature, Austrian: **Europe Etc.** 487, 602. *See also* Austrian studies; General programs; Literature

Literature, English: **Any Foreign Country** 76; **Europe Etc.** 517, 540, 620, 640, 652, 711, 767, 775, 778, 786, 814, 900, 908; **Middle East/Africa** 1060. *See also* British studies; General programs; Literature

Literature, Finnish: **Europe Etc.** 592. *See also* General programs; Literature

Literature, French: **Europe Etc.** 528, 601, 604, 731, 870; **Latin America/Caribbean** 974. *See also* French studies; General programs; Literature

Literature, German: **Europe Etc.** 616. *See also* General programs; German studies; Literature

Literature, Greek: **Europe Etc.** 467–468, 486, 564, 706, 721, 732, 772, 820. *See also* Classical studies; General programs; Literature

Literature, Icelandic: **Europe Etc.** 656, 875. *See also* General programs; Literature

Literature, Middle Eastern: **Middle East/Africa** 1030–1031, 1082–1083. *See also* General programs; Islamic studies; Literature; Middle Eastern studies; Near Eastern studies

Literature, Persian: **Europe Etc.** 724. *See also* General programs; Literature

Literature, Russian: **Europe Etc.** 736. *See also* General programs; Literature

Literature, Spanish: **Europe Etc.** 828. *See also* General programs; Literature; Spanish studies

Literature, Swedish: **Canada/Arctic Region** 441; **Europe Etc.** 878, 891. *See also* General programs; Literature; Scandinavian studies

Literature, Ukrainian: **Canada/Arctic Region** 378, 420. *See also* General programs; Literature; Ukrainian studies

Logistics: **Latin America/Caribbean** 1016. *See also* General programs; Transportation # SUBJECT INDEX

Lung disease: **Any Foreign Country** 80; **Asia** 329; **Latin America/Caribbean** 999; **Middle East/Africa** 1090. See also Disabilities; General programs; Health and health care; Medical sciences

Magazines. See Journalism; Literature
Management: **Europe Etc.** 549, 593-594, 614, 918, 929; **Latin America/Caribbean** 1016; **Middle East/Africa** 1059. See also General programs; Social sciences
Manufacturing engineering. See Engineering, manufacturing
Maps and mapmaking. See Cartography
Marine sciences: **Asia** 297; **Europe Etc.** 464, 549, 725-727, 808, 833; **Oceania** 1129, 1155. See also General programs; Sciences; names of specific marine sciences
Marketing: **Europe Etc.** 593-594. See also Advertising; General programs
Mass communications. See Communications
Materials engineering. See Engineering, materials
Materials sciences: **Any Foreign Country** 154; **Canada/Arctic Region** 382; **Europe Etc.** 549, 908. See also General programs; Physical sciences
Mathematics: **Any Foreign Country** 34, 60, 92, 133, 142, 171; **Asia** 236, 253, 337, 372; **Canada/Arctic Region** 382, 428; **Europe Etc.** 506, 536, 549, 554, 558, 574, 625, 650-651, 658, 671, 711, 750, 766, 779, 792, 810, 814, 884, 894-895, 908-909, 912, 917, 936, 938; **Latin America/Caribbean** 957, 1012; **Middle East/Africa** 1049, 1059, 1067, 1107, 1112, 1123; **Oceania** 1156. See also Computer sciences; General programs; Physical sciences; Statistics
Mechanical engineering. See Engineering, mechanical
Media. See Communications; Radio; Television
Media specialists. See Libraries and librarianship
Medical sciences: **Any Foreign Country** 9-12, 17, 25, 42, 54, 58, 83, 90, 97, 112, 127, 130, 148, 159, 181, 183, 203; **Asia** 225, 260, 267, 278, 295, 306, 310, 317, 319, 329, 344; **Canada/Arctic Region** 375, 383-386, 391, 430; **Europe Etc.** 501-502, 527, 533, 569-573, 597-599, 626, 635, 663-664, 671, 677, 687, 712, 718, 743, 785, 789, 791, 809, 819, 851, 866, 872, 884-885, 895, 909; **Latin America/Caribbean** 972, 978, 999; **Middle East/Africa** 1044, 1059, 1078, 1087, 1089-1090; **Oceania** 1129, 1139, 1164. See also General programs; Health and health care; Sciences; names of specific diseases; names of medical specialties
Medieval history. See History, medieval
Medieval studies: **Any Foreign Country** 53; **Canada/Arctic Region** 419; **Europe Etc.** 926; **Latin America/Caribbean** 965; **Middle East/Africa** 1040. See also General programs; History, medieval; Literature
Mental health: **Europe Etc.** 871. See also General programs; Health and health care; Psychiatry
Metallurgical engineering. See Engineering, metallurgical
Metallurgy: **Europe Etc.** 744. See also Engineering, metallurgical; General programs; Sciences
Meteorology: **Any Foreign Country** 41; **Europe Etc.** 695. See also Atmospheric sciences; General programs
Microcomputers. See Computer sciences
Middle Eastern history. See History, Middle Eastern
Middle Eastern literature. See Literature, Middle Eastern
Middle Eastern studies: **Asia** 226; **Europe Etc.** 451; **Latin America/Caribbean** 943; **Middle East/Africa** 1021. See also General programs; Islamic studies; Humanities

Military affairs: **Any Foreign Country** 51, 143, 170, 175; **Asia** 325-326; **Canada/Arctic Region** 390, 392, 395, 424-425, 434; **Europe Etc.** 524, 769-770; **Middle East/Africa** 1085-1086. See also General programs
Minority studies: **Europe Etc.** 749. See also General programs; names of specific ethnic minority studies
Missionary work. See Religion and religious activities
Motel industry. See Hotel and motel industry
Mountain climbing: **Any Foreign Country** 84, 129. See also Athletics; General programs
Multiple sclerosis: **Europe Etc.** 755. See also Disabilities; General programs; Health and health care; Medical sciences
Museums: **Any Foreign Country** 132, 187, 211; **Asia** 237, 240-241, 255, 294, 353, 360; **Canada/Arctic Region** 447; **Europe Etc.** 545, 874. See also Archives; General programs; Libraries and librarianship
Music: **Any Foreign Country** 3, 39, 47, 61, 73, 104, 116-117, 222; **Asia** 237-238, 240-241, 265, 294, 296, 360; **Canada/Arctic Region** 410; **Europe Etc.** 485, 494, 529, 579, 624, 640, 650-651, 689, 757, 759, 778, 813, 842, 877, 926, 931; **Latin America/Caribbean** 976, 983, 986; **Middle East/Africa** 1063, 1127. See also Fine arts; General programs; Humanities; Performing arts
Musicology: **Any Foreign Country** 36, 116-117; **Europe Etc.** 475, 603, 616, 701, 771, 858, 877, 921. See also General programs; Music
Muslim studies. See Islamic studies
Myasthenia Gravis: **Any Foreign Country** 113. See also Disabilities; General programs; Health and health care; Medical sciences
Mythology: **Canada/Arctic Region** 410; **Latin America/Caribbean** 983. See also Folklore; General programs; Literature

National security. See Military affairs
Native American studies: **Canada/Arctic Region** 410; **Europe Etc.** 640, 778; **Latin America/Caribbean** 983. See also General programs; Minority studies
Natural history. See History, natural
Natural resources: **Any Foreign Country** 179, 202; **Canada/Arctic Region** 390, 395, 434, 447; **Europe Etc.** 591; **Middle East/Africa** 1037. See also General programs; names of specific resources
Natural sciences: **Any Foreign Country** 77-78, 221; **Asia** 246, 265, 271, 306, 310, 313, 317, 344, 348; **Canada/Arctic Region** 423, 447; **Europe Etc.** 501-503, 521, 544, 554, 886, 895, 920; **Middle East/Africa** 1038, 1084, 1096, 1114. See also General programs; Sciences; names of specific sciences
Near Eastern history. See History, Near Eastern
Near Eastern studies: **Any Foreign Country** 53; **Asia** 226; **Europe Etc.** 451, 753; **Latin America/Caribbean** 943, 965; **Middle East/Africa** 1021, 1030-1031, 1040, 1045, 1058, 1061, 1118-1120. See also General programs; Humanities
Neuroscience: **Any Foreign Country** 135; **Asia** 274-276; **Canada/Arctic Region** 402-404, 411; **Europe Etc.** 612, 645-647, 665, 741; **Latin America/Caribbean** 990. See also General programs; Medical sciences
New Zealand history. See History, New Zealand
Newspapers. See Journalism
Nonfiction: **Asia** 366. See also General programs; Writers and writing

Nonprofit sector: **Europe Etc.** 734; **Latin America/Caribbean** 1016. *See also* General programs; Public administration

Norwegian language. *See* Language, Norwegian

Nurses and nursing, general: **Any Foreign Country** 163, 192; **Asia** 316; **Canada/Arctic Region** 383–385, 430. *See also* General programs; Health and health care; Medical sciences; names of specific nursing specialties

Nutrition: **Any Foreign Country** 200, 202–203; **Europe Etc.** 513; **Middle East/Africa** 1037. *See also* General programs; Home economics; Medical sciences

Obstetrics: **Europe Etc.** 923. *See also* General programs; Medical sciences; Pregnancy

Oceanography: **Any Foreign Country** 127, 146, 188; **Asia** 236, 363; **Canada/Arctic Region** 376, 447; **Europe Etc.** 464, 896; **Latin America/Caribbean** 952–953, 997; **Middle East/Africa** 1109; **Oceania** 1129. *See also* General programs; Marine sciences

Oncology. *See* Cancer

Opera. *See* Music; Voice

Ophthalmology: **Any Foreign Country** 58; **Canada/Arctic Region** 391. *See also* General programs; Medical sciences

Optometry: **Canada/Arctic Region** 383–385, 430. *See also* General programs; Medical sciences

Orchestras. *See* Music

Ornithology: **Any Foreign Country** 40, 62, 155; **Canada/Arctic Region** 389, 432; **Latin America/Caribbean** 942, 967, 987; **Middle East/Africa** 1074. *See also* General programs; Zoology

Orthopedics: **Europe Etc.** 785. *See also* General programs; Medical sciences

Painting. *See* Art

Pakistani studies: **Asia** 233–234. *See also* General programs; Humanities

Paleontology: **Any Foreign Country** 122, 124, 146, 208–209; **Asia** 373; **Europe Etc.** 612, 823; **Oceania** 1132–1133, 1162. *See also* Archaeology; General programs; Geology; General programs

Parapsychology: **Any Foreign Country** 56. *See also* General programs; Psychology

Pathology: **Asia** 279–280; **Europe Etc.** 597, 663–664, 892; **Middle East/Africa** 1051–1052. *See also* General programs; Medical sciences

Peace studies: **Any Foreign Country** 51, 143, 170, 175; **Europe Etc.** 684. *See also* General programs; Political science and politics

Pediatrics: **Any Foreign Country** 203; **Canada/Arctic Region** 435–437. *See also* General programs; Medical sciences

Performing arts: **Any Foreign Country** 73, 104, 222; **Asia** 237–238, 240–241, 302, 338, 355, 366; **Europe Etc.** 485, 614, 624, 639, 767, 890; **Latin America/Caribbean** 1014; **Middle East/Africa** 1108. *See also* General programs; names of specific performing arts

Persian literature. *See* Literature, Persian

Personnel administration: **Europe Etc.** 516, 911; **Latin America/Caribbean** 946, 961, 994, 1005; **Middle East/Africa** 1111. *See also* General programs; Management

Pharmaceutical sciences: **Any Foreign Country** 49; **Asia** 344; **Canada/Arctic Region** 383–385, 430; **Europe Etc.** 502, 507, 560, 597, 663–664, 666, 677, 871; **Middle East/Africa** 1049. *See also* General programs; Medical sciences

Philanthropy: **Asia** 270. *See also* General programs

Philology. *See* Language and linguistics

Philosophy: **Any Foreign Country** 36, 157; **Asia** 252, 283; **Canada/Arctic Region** 410; **Europe Etc.** 492, 515, 528, 531, 561, 603, 612, 678, 682, 685, 701, 710, 744, 748, 772, 801–802, 810, 869, 908, 919, 921, 925–926; **Latin America/Caribbean** 983; **Middle East/Africa** 1050, 1059, 1082–1083, 1102–1103, 1110. *See also* General programs; Humanities

Photogrammetry: **Europe Etc.** 714. *See also* Cartography; General programs; Photography

Photography: **Any Foreign Country** 4, 39, 110; **Asia** 240–241, 294, 360; **Latin America/Caribbean** 975. *See also* Fine arts; General programs

Physical education. *See* Education, physical

Physical sciences: **Any Foreign Country** 22, 60, 139, 142, 186, 213–215; **Asia** 319, 325–326, 337; **Canada/Arctic Region** 388, 424–425, 428; **Europe Etc.** 534–535, 568, 769–770, 792; **Latin America/Caribbean** 966; **Middle East/Africa** 1078, 1085–1086; **Oceania** 1156. *See also* General programs; Sciences; names of specific physical sciences

Physics: **Any Foreign Country** 92, 128, 144; **Asia** 236, 253, 353, 372; **Canada/Arctic Region** 382; **Europe Etc.** 513, 517, 526, 536, 549, 559, 658, 671, 744, 766, 795, 874, 894, 908, 938; **Middle East/Africa** 1049, 1059, 1067, 1123; **Oceania** 1129. *See also* General programs; Mathematics; Physical sciences

Physiology: **Any Foreign Country** 121, 126, 172; **Asia** 279–280; **Europe Etc.** 597, 663–664, 725–727, 741, 808, 833, 884; **Latin America/Caribbean** 990; **Middle East/Africa** 1051–1052. *See also* General programs; Medical sciences

Plays: **Any Foreign Country** 110; **Asia** 338, 366; **Europe Etc.** 921, 931; **Latin America/Caribbean** 976, 1018. *See also* General programs; Literature; Performing arts; Writers and writing

Poetry: **Any Foreign Country** 14, 76, 110; **Asia** 366; **Europe Etc.** 832; **Latin America/Caribbean** 1018. *See also* General programs; Literature; Writers and writing

Poisons. *See* Toxicology

Polar studies: **Canada/Arctic Region** 387, 412. *See also* General programs

Police science. *See* Criminal justice

Political science and politics: **Any Foreign Country** 36, 46, 71–72, 134, 157; **Asia** 252, 256, 266, 283, 286, 341, 372; **Canada/Arctic Region** 376, 392, 394, 397, 444; **Europe Etc.** 460–461, 487, 489, 492, 495, 504, 515, 524–525, 528, 531, 553, 561–562, 583–585, 596, 603, 606–608, 614–615, 617–618, 624, 628, 650, 678, 682–683, 693, 705, 710, 719, 744, 748, 766, 793–794, 801–802, 816, 898, 902, 904–905, 908, 918, 921–922, 927, 938; **Latin America/Caribbean** 969, 976, 984; **Middle East/Africa** 1030–1031, 1050, 1059, 1088, 1102–1103; **Oceania** 1131. *See also* General programs; Public administration; Social sciences

Population studies: **Any Foreign Country** 121, 127, 167–168, 182; **Asia** 323–324; **Europe Etc.** 762–763; **Latin America/Caribbean** 975–976; **Middle East/Africa** 1037, 1087, 1118; **Oceania** 1130. *See also* Family planning; General programs; Social sciences

Portuguese language. *See* Language, Portuguese

Portuguese studies: **Europe Etc.** 520, 670. *See also* European studies; General programs; Humanities

SUBJECT INDEX 427

Posters. *See* Graphic arts
Poverty: **Asia** 318; **Europe Etc.** 745; **Latin America/Caribbean** 996; **Middle East/Africa** 1077. *See also* General programs; Social services
Pregnancy: **Any Foreign Country** 121; **Europe Etc.** 696, 837. *See also* Family planning; General programs; Obstetrics
Preservation: **Asia** 255. *See also* General programs; specific types of preservation
Preservation, historical. *See* Historical preservation
Presidents, U.S. *See* History, American
Press. *See* Journalism
Print journalism. *See* Journalism
Prints. *See* Art; Graphic arts
Psychiatry: **Europe Etc.** 663–664, 865. *See also* Behavioral sciences; Counseling; General programs; Medical sciences; Psychology
Psychology: **Any Foreign Country** 36, 157; **Asia** 252–253, 283, 372; **Canada/Arctic Region** 376, 410, 444; **Europe Etc.** 531, 536, 603, 612, 766, 793, 869, 884, 921, 938; **Latin America/Caribbean** 983. *See also* Behavioral sciences; Counseling; General programs; Psychiatry; Social sciences
Public administration: **Any Foreign Country** 205; **Asia** 252, 299, 320, 342; **Canada/Arctic Region** 445; **Europe Etc.** 531, 585, 614, 824, 927; **Latin America/Caribbean** 969, 975–976. *See also* General programs; Management; Political science and politics; Social sciences
Public affairs. *See* Public administration
Public health: **Any Foreign Country** 10, 167–168; **Asia** 342; **Europe Etc.** 824; **Latin America/Caribbean** 975–976, 978; **Middle East/Africa** 1087, 1089. *See also* General programs; Health and health care
Public policy. *See* Public administration
Public sector. *See* Public administration
Publishers and publishing: **Any Foreign Country** 27, 64; **Europe Etc.** 586, 728. *See also* General programs

Radio: **Asia** 361; **Middle East/Africa** 1042. *See also* Communications; General programs
Radiology: **Any Foreign Country** 185; **Europe Etc.** 695. *See also* General programs; Medical sciences
Reading: **Any Foreign Country** 43. *See also* Education; General programs; Literacy
Real estate: **Canada/Arctic Region** 445. *See also* General programs
Recreation: **Europe Etc.** 591. *See also* General programs; names of specific recreational activities
Reentry programs: **Any Foreign Country** 186; **Latin America/Caribbean** 987. *See also* General programs
Regional planning. *See* City and regional planning
Rehabilitation: **Canada/Arctic Region** 430. *See also* General programs; Health and health care; specific types of therapy
Religion and religious activities: **Any Foreign Country** 36, 157, 196; **Asia** 239, 301; **Canada/Arctic Region** 401, 410; **Europe Etc.** 491–492, 561, 603, 624, 669, 686, 710, 724, 744, 801, 908, 920–921, 926; **Latin America/Caribbean** 983; **Middle East/Africa** 1030–1031, 1045, 1047, 1050, 1059, 1061, 1065, 1082–1083, 1110, 1118. *See also* General programs; Humanities; Philosophy
Renaissance history. *See* History, Renaissance
Renaissance studies: **Europe Etc.** 852. *See also* General programs; History, Renaissance; Literature
Reproduction. *See* Family planning; Pregnancy

Restaurants. *See* Food service industry
Risk management: **Canada/Arctic Region** 376. *See also* Business administration; Finance; General programs
Robotics: **Europe Etc.** 574, 811. *See also* General programs; Technology
Roman history. *See* History, ancient
Russian history. *See* History, Russian
Russian literature. *See* Literature, Russian

Scandinavian studies: **Europe Etc.** 787. *See also* General programs; Humanities
Schools. *See* Education
Science, history. *See* History, science
Sciences: **Any Foreign Country** 32, 35, 57, 79, 96, 110, 150–154, 201; **Asia** 261, 266, 295, 311, 321, 328, 331–336, 356–358, 368; **Europe Etc.** 496, 506, 527, 540, 556, 558, 580, 625, 628, 637, 639, 651, 711, 718, 779, 789, 795, 814, 850, 887, 909, 912, 917, 924, 926, 933, 936, 940; **Latin America/Caribbean** 957, 1006; **Middle East/Africa** 1060, 1067, 1107, 1112, 1123–1124; **Oceania** 1142, 1166. *See also* General programs; names of specific sciences
Scottish history. *See* History, Scottish
Sculpture: **Any Foreign Country** 39, 110; **Asia** 237, 241, 294, 339, 360; **Europe Etc.** 689, 796, 928; **Latin America/Caribbean** 975; **Middle East/Africa** 1091. *See also* Fine arts; General programs
Secondary education. *See* Education, secondary
Security, national. *See* Military affairs
Sight impairments. *See* Visual impairments
Singing. *See* Voice
Slavic studies: **Any Foreign Country** 53; **Latin America/Caribbean** 965; **Middle East/Africa** 1040. *See also* European studies; General programs; Humanities
Smoking. *See* Tobacco consumption
Social sciences: **Any Foreign Country** 13, 22, 36, 46, 50, 60, 77–78, 95, 103, 139–141, 169, 174, 186, 197, 208–209; **Asia** 224, 226–229, 233–234, 243, 246, 253, 256, 258, 271, 281, 287–289, 306, 310, 313, 319, 323–324, 327, 337, 341, 344–345, 348, 351, 354, 367; **Canada/Arctic Region** 378, 416, 428, 431, 440; **Europe Etc.** 451–453, 464, 477–478, 482, 489, 491, 495, 506, 508–509, 515, 517, 521, 523, 528, 532, 536, 540, 544, 562, 579, 582–583, 600, 603–604, 614–615, 617, 626, 629, 650, 662, 671, 683, 704, 711, 762–763, 777, 780–781, 789, 792–793, 802, 814, 816, 818, 822, 847, 862, 868–869, 886, 895, 902, 909, 915, 920, 936; **Latin America/Caribbean** 943, 960, 976, 1006, 1020; **Middle East/Africa** 1021, 1030–1031, 1033, 1037–1038, 1055–1056, 1059, 1078, 1084, 1094–1096, 1104, 1107, 1114, 1119–1120, 1125–1126; **Oceania** 1154. *See also* General programs; names of specific social sciences
Social services: **Asia** 301, 318; **Europe Etc.** 686, 745; **Latin America/Caribbean** 996; **Middle East/Africa** 1065, 1077. *See also* General programs; Social work
Social welfare: **Asia** 318; **Europe Etc.** 745; **Latin America/Caribbean** 996; **Middle East/Africa** 1077. *See also* General programs; Social services
Social work: **Asia** 252, 254; **Europe Etc.** 531, 538; **Middle East/Africa** 1039. *See also* General programs; Social sciences
Sociology: **Any Foreign Country** 36, 127, 157, 167–168; **Asia** 252, 283, 372; **Canada/Arctic Region** 376, 397, 444; **Europe Etc.** 492, 495, 500, 515, 531, 561, 596, 603,

606–608, 710, 719, 766, 793–794, 801, 884, 908, 918–919, 921, 938. See also General programs; Social sciences
Soils science: **Any Foreign Country** 88, 111; **Asia** 279–280; **Middle East/Africa** 1051–1052. See also Agriculture and agricultural sciences; General programs; Horticulture
Songs. See Music
South American history. See History, Latin American
South American studies. See Latin American studies
Southeast Asian studies: **Asia** 286. See also Asian studies; General programs; Humanities
Soviet studies: **Asia** 226–228, 256, 258, 323–324, 341; **Europe Etc.** 451–453, 562, 582, 762–763, 816; **Latin America/Caribbean** 943; **Middle East/Africa** 1021. See also European studies; General programs; Humanities
Space sciences: **Any Foreign Country** 127, 144; **Canada/Arctic Region** 377, 447; **Europe Etc.** 534–535, 671; **Middle East/Africa** 1059. See also General programs; Physical sciences
Spanish language. See Language, Spanish
Spanish literature. See Literature, Spanish
Spanish studies: **Europe Etc.** 826. See also European studies; General programs; Humanities
Special education. See Education, special
Sports. See Athletics
Sri Lankan studies: **Asia** 229. See also Asian studies; General programs; Humanities
Stage design. See Performing arts
Statistics: **Any Foreign Country** 89, 171; **Asia** 279–280; **Europe Etc.** 654–655, 793; **Middle East/Africa** 1049, 1051–1052; **Oceania** 1130. See also General programs; Mathematics
Substance abuse. See Alcohol use and abuse
Surgery: **Asia** 278; **Canada/Arctic Region** 411; **Europe Etc.** 663–664, 785. See also General programs; Medical sciences
Surveying: **Europe Etc.** 714. See also General programs
Swedish language. See Language, Swedish
Swedish literature. See Literature, Swedish
Systems engineering. See Engineering, systems

Teaching. See Education
Technology: **Any Foreign Country** 106, 112, 127, 154; **Asia** 253, 261, 266, 283, 325–326, 328, 337, 365, 372; **Canada/Arctic Region** 424–425, 428; **Europe Etc.** 536, 549, 628, 677, 692, 766, 769–770, 789, 792, 850, 924, 938; **Middle East/Africa** 1037, 1059, 1084–1086, 1105–1106, 1116, 1118; **Oceania** 1130. See also Computer sciences; General programs; Sciences
Teenagers. See Adolescents
Telecommunications: **Europe Etc.** 575, 783, 888. See also Communications; General programs; Radio; Television
Telepathy. See Parapsychology
Television: **Asia** 294, 360–361; **Europe Etc.** 813; **Latin America/Caribbean** 976; **Middle East/Africa** 1042, 1059. See also Communications; Filmmaking; General programs
Theater. See Performing arts; Plays
Theology. See Religion and religious activities
Tobacco consumption: **Any Foreign Country** 97. See also General programs; Medical sciences
Tourism: **Europe Etc.** 458; **Middle East/Africa** 1022. See also General programs
Toxicology: **Europe Etc.** 560, 666, 941. See also General programs; Medical sciences

Translators and translations: **Asia** 223; **Canada/Arctic Region** 374; **Europe Etc.** 802, 832, 875, 921; **Latin America/Caribbean** 1018. See also General programs; Language and linguistics; Writers and writing
Transportation: **Middle East/Africa** 1059. See also Aviation; General programs; Space sciences
Travel and tourism. See Tourism
Tropical studies: **Any Foreign Country** 74; **Latin America/Caribbean** 951, 955–956, 958, 963–964, 988, 998, 1004, 1013. See also General programs
Tuberculosis. See Lung disease
Turkish language. See Language, Turkish
Turkish studies: **Europe Etc.** 818, 822; **Middle East/Africa** 1094–1095. See also General programs; Humanities; Near Eastern studies
TV. See Television

Ukrainian history. See History, Ukrainian
Ukrainian language. See Language, Ukrainian
Ukrainian literature. See Literature, Ukrainian
Ukrainian studies: **Any Foreign Country** 156; **Canada/Arctic Region** 378, 416, 420, 426. See also European studies; General programs; Humanities
Universities. See Education, higher
Unrestricted programs. See General programs
Urban planning. See City and regional planning
Urban studies: **Any Foreign Country** 45. See also General programs

Vacuum sciences: **Any Foreign Country** 212. See also General programs; Sciences
Veterans. See Military affairs
Veterinary sciences: **Canada/Arctic Region** 383–385, 430; **Europe Etc.** 476, 502, 514, 789, 849; **Middle East/Africa** 1053–1054; **Oceania** 1155. See also General programs; Sciences
Video. See Filmmaking; Television
Violence: **Any Foreign Country** 77–78. See also General programs
Visual arts. See Art
Visual impairments: **Any Foreign Country** 58; **Canada/Arctic Region** 391. See also Disabilities; General programs; Health and health care
Voice: **Europe Etc.** 768. See also General programs; Music; Performing arts

Water resources: **Asia** 363; **Europe Etc.** 896; **Latin America/Caribbean** 1019; **Middle East/Africa** 1049, 1059, 1109. See also Environmental sciences; General programs; Natural resources
Weather. See Climatology
Web design. See Internet design and development
Welfare. See Social services; Social welfare
West German history. See History, German
West German studies. See German studies
Western European history. See History, European
Western European studies. See European studies

Women's studies and programs: **Canada/Arctic Region** 416; **Europe Etc.** 638, 678, 684, 735, 748, 802, 861; **Middle East/Africa** 1075. *See also* General programs

Wool industry: **Oceania** 1174. *See also* Agriculture and agricultural sciences; General programs

World literature. *See* Literature

Writers and writing: **Any Foreign Country** 3–4, 14, 104, 110; **Asia** 237, 366; **Europe Etc.** 450, 547, 715, 741, 870, 875; **Latin America/Caribbean** 990, 1018; **Oceania** 1144–1145. *See also* General programs; Literature; specific types of writing

Youth. *See* Adolescents; Child development

Yugoslavian studies. *See* Slavic studies

Zoology: **Any Foreign Country** 124, 146; **Europe Etc.** 455, 671; **Latin America/Caribbean** 955, 958, 1011, 1015; **Middle East/Africa** 1049; **Oceania** 1167. *See also* General programs; Sciences; names of specific zoological subfields

Calendar Index

The Calendar Index lists entry numbers for programs with established filing dates. It is divided into seven major sections: Any Foreign Country; Asia; Canada/Arctic Region; Europe, Etc.; Latin America/Caribbean; Middle East/Africa; Oceania. Each of these sections is subdivided by month, beginning with January. Entry numbers follow sequentially. Remember, not all sponsoring organizations supplied deadline information, so not all programs are listed in this index.

Any Foreign Country
January: 15, 17, 21–22, 26, 42, 49, 57, 60, 62, 73, 77, 80–81, 84–85, 87, 102, 108, 114, 119, 121–122, 128, 137, 144, 147, 186, 193–194, 211, 221
February: 24, 33, 58, 98, 106, 120, 129, 135, 138, 156, 164, 200, 205–206, 218
March: 8, 31, 38, 54–55, 75, 79, 82, 104, 107, 124–125, 134, 140, 154, 174, 177, 208–209
April: 25, 39, 45, 73, 86, 88, 131, 148–149, 188, 198–199, 210, 212–214
May: 76, 147, 215
June: 9–12, 41, 112, 127, 159, 200, 202, 220
July: 47, 56, 67–70, 78, 114
August: 20, 31, 44, 73, 83, 86, 122, 148–149, 162, 185
September: 4, 7, 30, 43, 52, 63, 93, 96–97, 105, 110, 113, 126, 134, 136, 147, 161, 172, 195, 208, 216, 218
October: 8, 13–14, 29–30, 36, 50, 52–53, 66, 71–72, 93, 100–101, 111, 116–117, 131, 133, 142, 161, 163, 169, 173, 204, 213–214, 216
November: 5–6, 16, 19, 23, 27, 37, 51, 59, 64, 95, 99, 103, 110, 115, 118, 132, 139–141, 143, 157, 159–160, 165, 170–171, 175, 178, 187–188, 191–192, 197, 215, 219, 222
December: 1, 18, 28, 31, 61, 74, 86, 89–90, 130, 148–149, 167–168, 184, 220
Any time: 3, 34–35, 46, 65, 92, 94, 145–146, 150–153, 158, 166, 176, 179–182, 196, 201, 203, 217

Asia
January: 223, 227–228, 233–234, 238–241, 253, 263, 272–273, 294, 297, 311, 318, 322, 325–326, 338, 341–342, 349, 351–352, 360, 367, 372
February: 252, 254, 265, 284, 315, 323–326, 346–347, 362
March: 256, 260, 279, 312, 320, 325–326, 363, 372
April: 253, 261, 269, 283, 307, 309, 325–326, 343, 373
May: 266, 295–296, 305, 330, 348, 351
June: 230–232, 292, 366
July: 239–240, 260, 270–271, 277, 317, 319, 325–326, 340, 359, 364, 372
August: 224, 253, 269, 274–275, 286, 325–326, 344, 363, 365
September: 226–228, 236, 242, 245, 282, 303–304, 306, 308, 310, 313, 325–326, 348–349, 352, 362
October: 248–251, 258–259, 264, 281, 288–290, 307, 309, 325–327, 339, 353, 361, 369–371

November: 235, 237, 243, 247, 254–255, 257, 260, 287, 291, 293, 299–300, 306, 310, 321, 325–326, 328, 337, 356–358
December: 229, 244, 246, 262, 266, 269, 278, 298, 345, 350, 354
Any time: 268, 276, 285, 301, 329, 331–336, 355, 368

Canada/Arctic Region
January: 374, 398, 400, 412, 417–418, 424–425, 432, 437–440
February: 375–376, 378, 391, 401, 410, 416, 419–420, 424–426, 429, 431, 433, 442
March: 389, 424–425, 430, 441, 447
April: 394, 424–425, 435, 444–445, 448
June: 380
July: 392, 424–425, 447
August: 376, 402–403, 424–425
September: 381, 383–388, 424–425, 434, 443
October: 377, 382, 390, 393–395, 409, 411, 413–415, 421, 424–425, 430, 435
November: 408, 424–425, 427–428, 447
December: 379, 396–397, 399, 405–407, 422
Any time: 404, 436, 446

Europe Etc.
January: 450, 452–454, 460–462, 469, 477, 479–480, 485–486, 507, 528, 536–537, 541–542, 564, 572, 576, 596, 604, 621, 627, 630, 632, 634, 639–640, 655, 667, 679–680, 706, 718–719, 721, 730–733, 742, 745, 748, 750, 755, 765, 768–770, 777–780, 798, 802–807, 816, 820, 824–825, 834–836, 839, 841, 846, 855, 860, 862, 879–881, 889, 892–893, 897, 907, 909, 915, 935, 938
February: 459, 465, 467, 471–472, 483, 487, 491, 494, 501, 506, 511–512, 530–531, 538, 554, 566, 577, 600, 602, 606–608, 635, 640, 657, 669, 672, 678, 681–682, 692, 736, 762–763, 769–770, 776, 795, 821, 856, 891, 895, 899, 934
March: 449, 470, 476, 498, 502, 505, 523, 533–535, 549, 559, 562, 581, 598, 613, 619, 622, 625, 644, 665, 676, 684, 687–688, 694, 696, 713, 716, 727, 739, 741, 758, 768–770, 788–789, 797, 810, 826, 837, 844, 871, 876, 878, 896, 903, 937–938, 940
April: 497, 499–500, 504, 513, 526, 536, 574–575, 593–595, 615, 618, 642–643, 661, 670, 690–691, 693, 695, 701–702, 710, 723, 729, 751, 761, 769–770, 782, 787, 794, 811–813, 818,

822, 846, 864, 866, 888, 902, 905–906, 910, 918–922, 925, 929, 931
May: 496, 511–512, 553, 627–629, 671, 720, 743, 862, 870, 877, 894
June: 455, 544, 578, 619, 669, 759, 785, 789, 791, 797
July: 458, 489, 502, 515, 525, 541–542, 548, 552, 565, 584, 589, 598, 609, 636, 660, 734, 749, 755, 769–770, 783, 815, 819, 846, 849, 859, 865, 913, 923, 938
August: 501, 511–512, 536, 566, 599, 643, 645–646, 661, 678, 682, 694, 700, 760, 769–770, 851, 896
September: 451–453, 463, 510, 522, 526, 549, 603, 623, 627, 657, 674, 705, 713, 724, 756, 766, 769–770, 789, 797, 805, 863, 866–869, 895, 941
October: 456–457, 464, 473–474, 478, 510, 516–517, 520, 524, 540, 543, 547, 551, 558, 560, 567, 574, 579, 582–583, 585, 587, 590–591, 601, 610–612, 614, 618, 620, 631, 633, 638, 650–651, 656, 659, 662, 669, 673, 675, 683, 703–704, 711, 735, 737, 746, 753, 769–770, 774–775, 786, 796, 814, 817, 829–832, 845–848, 850, 852, 854, 861, 872, 874–875, 882, 898, 904, 908, 911–912, 916–917, 927, 939
November: 475, 481–482, 492, 495, 502, 511–512, 527, 532, 538, 545–546, 550, 561, 563, 586, 588, 598, 617, 641, 685, 696–698, 707–709, 714–715, 728, 754, 757, 764, 769–772, 791–793, 801, 840, 858, 873, 883, 900–901, 928, 933
December: 490, 508–509, 521, 526, 529, 539, 555, 557, 580, 616, 624, 628, 643, 652–654, 658, 661, 689, 712, 738, 744, 777, 784, 797, 823, 838, 884, 886–887, 909
Any time: 468, 488, 503, 592, 626, 637, 647–649, 663–664, 668, 686, 725–727, 740, 781, 790, 799, 808–809, 833, 857, 890, 924, 932

Latin America/Caribbean
January: 944, 964, 971, 977, 991, 996, 1002, 1004, 1007, 1010, 1013, 1015, 1019
February: 953, 982–983, 997, 1003, 1008–1009, 1011
March: 967, 972, 985, 988, 990
April: 945, 963, 980, 1018
May: 956, 986, 989, 1011
July: 948–949, 969, 972, 975, 978, 984, 992–993, 1016
August: 980, 1011, 1020
September: 943, 953–955, 958, 964, 966, 998, 1001, 1004, 1007, 1013, 1019
October: 942, 945–947, 957, 960–962, 965, 970, 974, 976, 994–995, 1005–1006
November: 968, 972, 979, 987, 1000, 1011
December: 959, 980–981, 1012
Any time: 950–951, 955, 958, 998–999, 1014, 1017

Middle East/Africa
January: 1046, 1064, 1069, 1076–1077, 1082, 1085–1086, 1088, 1092, 1102, 1104, 1119–1121
February: 1028–1029, 1039, 1041, 1047, 1057, 1074, 1085–1086
March: 1026, 1044, 1051, 1066, 1075, 1084–1086, 1109
April: 1036, 1042, 1048, 1085–1086, 1094–1095, 1103, 1117
May: 1037, 1063, 1067, 1104, 1123
June: 1025, 1037, 1115, 1127
July: 1022–1024, 1044, 1049–1050, 1059, 1078, 1085–1086, 1098, 1113
August: 1041, 1048, 1066, 1085–1086, 1109
September: 1021, 1084–1086
October: 1027, 1030–1032, 1035, 1040, 1043, 1045, 1055–1056, 1058, 1060–1061, 1068, 1080, 1083, 1085–1086, 1091, 1093, 1099–1101, 1107, 1110–1112, 1116, 1118, 1126

November: 1033, 1037, 1039, 1044, 1070–1071, 1073, 1081, 1085–1086, 1105–1106, 1114
December: 1034, 1038, 1048, 1067, 1072, 1079, 1122–1125
Any time: 1053–1054, 1062, 1065, 1090, 1108

Oceania
January: 1131, 1143
February: 1132–1137, 1148–1149, 1151, 1160, 1162, 1168, 1173
March: 1139, 1142, 1170
April: 1144–1145, 1147
May: 1129, 1165, 1171, 1175
July: 1128, 1139–1141, 1150, 1152–1154, 1156–1157, 1161, 1169
August: 1146–1147, 1166, 1172
September: 1155, 1158, 1163, 1170
October: 1159, 1164
November: 1139, 1174
December: 1147
Any time: 1167